Portugal

ry Walker

PARQUE NACIONAL DA PENEDA-GERÊS (p457)
A magnificent national park with fantastic trails surrounded by mountain and forest scenery

PINHÃO (p419)
Gateway to ancient vineyards amid the dramatic beauty of the Douro valley

PARQUE NATURAL DA SERRA DA ESTRELA (p358)
Portugal's highest peak, grand glacial valleys, medieval villages and some of the country's finest cheese

VIANA DO CASTELO (p441)
Vibrant riverside town sprinkled with a fascinating old centre plus gorgeous beaches nearby

BRAGA (p425)
Historic city with looming churches, colourful festivals and a lively student population

PORTO (p383)
Hilly city with an enchanting riverside, historic architecture and an exciting dining and nightlife scene

COIMBRA (p325)
A honeycomb of cobbled streets crowned by Portugal's oldest university, resonating with nightly fado performances

LEGEND

Freeway
Primary Road
Secondary Road
Tertiary Road
Unsealed Road

ELEVATION
1500m
1000m
500m
200m
0

0   40 km
0   20 miles

To La Coruña
To Vigo
To Madrid

SPAIN

Zamora
Salamanca
Plasencia

Orense
Orense

Miranda do Douro
Embalse de Almendra

Bragança
Chaves
Montalegre

Parque Natural de Montesinho

Rio Minho
Valença do Minho
Monção
Ponte de Lima
Viana do Castelo
Barcelos
Braga
Guimarães
Vila do Conde
Porto
Espinho
Ovar
Aveiro
Mira
Figueira da Foz
Leiria
Nazaré
Batalha
Fátima
Pombal

Parque Nacional da Peneda-Gerês

Rio Lima
Rio Cávado
Rio Tâmega

TRÁS-OS-MONTES
MINHO
DOURO

Mirandela
Vila Real
Parque Natural do Alvão
Amarante
Peso da Régua
Lamego
Pinhão
Tua
Vila Nova de Foz Côa
Pocinho
Parque Natural do Douro Internacional
Mogadouro
Barca de Alva
Pinhel
Vilar Formoso
Guarda
Sortelha

BEIRA ALTA

Viseu
Mangualde
São Pedro do Sul
Tondela
Gouveia
Parque Natural da Serra da Estrela
Torre (1993m)
Covilhã
Fundão
Manteigas

BEIRA BAIXA
BEIRA LITORAL

São Pedro do Sul
Luso
Lousã
Coimbra
Serra da Lousã

Castelo Branco
Monsanto
Parque Natural do Tejo Internacional

Rio Douro
Rio Mondego
Rio Zêzere

ATLANTIC OCEAN

S
E N
W

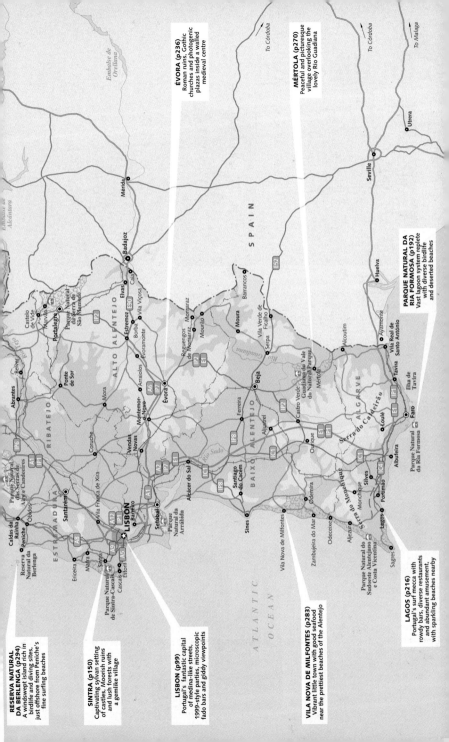

RESERVA NATURAL DA BERLENGA (p294)
A windswept island rich in birdlife and diving sites, just offshore from Peniche's fine surfing beaches

ÉVORA (p236)
Roman ruins, Gothic churches and photogenic plazas inside a walled medieval centre

MÉRTOLA (p270)
Peaceful and picturesque village overlooking the lovely Rio Guadiana

PARQUE NATURAL DA RIA FORMOSA (p192)
Vast lagoon system replete with diverse birdlife and deserted beaches

SINTRA (p150)
Captivating sylvan setting of castles, Moorish ruins and lush forests with a gemlike village

LISBON (p99)
Portugal's fantastic capital of medina-like streets, 1999-style parties, microscopic fado bars and giddy viewpoints

VILA NOVA DE MILFONTES (p283)
Vibrant little town with good seafood near the prettiest beaches of the Alentejo

LAGOS (p216)
Portugal's surf mecca with rowdy bars, diverse restaurants and abundant amusement, with sparkling beaches nearby

On the Road

REGIS ST LOUIS Coordinating Author
Here I am in Valença do Minho (p446), one stop of my journey through *vinho verde* country along the Rio Minho. After snapping this photo, I stumbled upon a medieval fair on the castle grounds: jousting, sword-fighting, damsels, wandering minstrels and a fair bit of ale to keep the crowds content.

GREGOR CLARK Hey, who let the tall guy in? Portugal dos Pequenitos (p333) in Coimbra is a theme park tailor-made for kids, with miniature versions of famous Portuguese monuments. It was a great place for my daughters to work off their jet lag, and kinda fun for Dad too.

KATE ARMSTRONG I returned to Carrapateira (p229) after a 20-year absence in search of a remote seafood shack I'd hiked to (and wobbled back from) late one night. These days, it's a large and thriving restaurant, but the setting hasn't changed – a stunning view of orange cliffs, vast ocean and fresh fish.

KERRY WALKER Lisbon's *sé* (cathedral; (p116) never fails to captivate me. It's Lisbon all over – rich history, rattling vintage trams, light warming its honey bricks in the late afternoon, hidden quirks like the leering gargoyles on its southern flank. It's also the gateway to the labyrinthine Moorish quarter of Alfama, always terrific for an urban treasure hunt.

For full author biographies see p528.

EXPERIENCE PORTUGAL

The once-mighty nation of explorers may be small in size, but it presents a grand array of attractions, from rugged windswept beaches to crisp mountain villages, with jaw-dropping palaces, medieval castles and enchanting city streets all knitted into the landscape. The Portuguese experience is about so many things: you can feast on fresh seafood at a fado-filled tavern, surf big waves off the southern coast, sample award-winning wines at historic vineyards or join the mayhem at a rowdy traditional festival. The only question is where to begin.

Under the Iberian Sun

Portugal's beaches, mountains and rivers set the stage for a multitude of adventures. You can head north for hiking, horse riding and camping amid natural parks or fly south for coastal adventures in the Algarve. In between, there are hundreds of places where you can drink in Portugal's natural beauty.

① Surfing

Blessed with some of the best waves on the southern coast, Carrapateira (p229) is a major surf destination, with gorgeous beaches and a laid-back village. Surf schools offer know-how to those who've always wanted to learn.

② Hiking

Boasting breathtaking scenery, the 703-sq-km Parque Nacional da Peneda-Gerês (p457) is Portugal's wilderness masterpiece. Hiking here means taking in boulder-strewn peaks, idyllic valleys, oak forests and old stone villages slumbering beneath great open skies.

③ Kitesurfing

The wind-buffeted waters off Praia do Cabedelo (p443) harbour handfuls of avid kitesurfers. For the aquatic adrenaline rush par excellence, slide into a wetsuit at this wild Minho beach and join the fray.

④ Beach Combing

Picturesque stretches of Portugal's 800km-long coastline provide a mighty fine backdrop to long beach walks and wave frolicking. Car-free Ilha de Tavira (p198) hides one of Portugal's prettiest beaches.

⑤ Kayaking

For a sunny day's paddle on a scenic river, head to the picturesque town of Ponte de Lima (p450), where you can mingle among other kayakers on the placid Rio Lima.

The Portuguese Table

Classic recipes make fine use of Portugal's bountiful coast-line and fertile countryside. Every region yields its own rewards, from fresh seafood in the Algarve to traditional roast dishes from the Minho. Bread, olives, locally made cheese, seasonal fruits and nicely aged wines are just the beginning…

❶ Fruits of the Sea

Southern Portugal serves up a tempting array of seafood recipes. Perhaps top of the list is delectable *caldeirada,* Portugal's answer to bouillabaisse. Setúbal (p170), just south of Lisbon, is famed for this seafood stew.

❷ The Divine Drop

Portuguese winemakers are garnering more and more international attention each year. For a journey into the most celebrated vineyards, take a trip through the Douro (p420), with its terraced vineyards clinging to steep hillsides along the river.

❸ Sweet Hearts

One of the great wonders of Portugal, the *pastel de nata* (custard tart) can be easily held in one hand and devoured in three – make that two – bites. Some of the world's best are served piping hot in Belém (p136).

❹ Open Markets

No matter where in Portugal you travel, the *mercado* (market) is a great place to take in the local bounty. Porto's 19th-century wrought-iron Mercado do Bolhão (p390) has an enticing array of fruits, smoked meats, cheeses, olives, nuts and so much more.

Festas!

Praying and playing go hand in hand in this traditional Catholic country. Every town and city pays homage to its favourite saint, with colourful processions followed by music, dancing and feasting, with the merrymaking continuing late into the night.

❶ Festa de Santo António

In June, the beloved Santo António, who has a reputation as a matchmaker, is celebrated with particular fervour in Lisbon (p125). Dozens of street parties erupt across town, while Lisboêtas write love poems and hide them in *manjericos* (basil plants).

❷ Festas de São João

In the north, St John the Baptist is the man of the hour. Braga (p429) goes wild with dancing, bonfires, concerts, fireworks and yet more love poems stuffed in basil pots. Squeaky plastic hammers appear, with townsfolk whacking each other merrily/mercilessly.

❸ Romaria de Nossa Senhora d'Agonia

Viana do Castelo throws a spectacular fest in honour of Our Lady of Sorrows (p443). Locals literally paint the streets, and partake in brilliant processions – women in traditional costumes, pounding drum corps and lumbering carnival *gigantones* (giants).

❹ Festa dos Rapazes

Throwing a bit of paganism into the mix, Trás-os-Montes is the setting for the bizarre Festa dos Rapazes (p491). Around Christmas, unmarried young men don robes and wooden masks and make mayhem in village squares.

Remnants of the Past

Portugal has seen the rise and fall of many conquerors and kings over the last few millennia. Previous civilisations left their marks all over the country, from Palaeolithic stone carvings in the northwest to royal palaces outside the capital, with Roman ruins, Visigothic churches and Moorish streetscapes just a few pieces of the Portuguese puzzle.

❶ Megalithic Mysteries

Dating back some 5000 years, the Cromeleque dos Almendres (p247) is one of the great mysteries of Iberia. The circular site of some 95 granite stones – some bearing inscriptions – invites contemplation.

❷ Roman Holiday

Évora is a living museum when it comes to Roman ruins. The photogenic Temple of Diana (p241), with its 14 brilliantly preserved Corinthian columns, is one of the city's great icons.

❸ The Colossus of Mafra

Once a world superpower, Portugal erected astonishing monuments to commemorate its conquests. The Palácio Nacional de Mafra (p167) took 13 years to build with 45,000 artisans working on it at one time.

❹ Castle High

Perched above the peaceful Rio Guadiana, the cobbled streets of Mértola (p270) give a glimpse into medieval Portugal, complete with a 13th-century castle and relics from even earlier civilisations.

❺ Song of Songs

Portugal's native fado emerged in 18th-century Lisbon. Far from being consigned to the history books, this mournful music lives on in the taverns and back lanes of the Alfama (p142).

Contents

Regional Map Contents

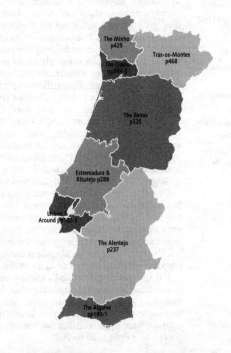

The Minho p425

Trás-os-Montes p468

The Douro pp384-5

The Beiras p325

Estremadura & Ribatejo p288

Lisbon & Around pp162-3

The Alentejo p237

The Algarve pp180-1

Destination Portugal

In a tiny windswept hamlet in northern Portugal, goats still trundle through the dusty streets while elderly widows in black keep watch over the village square against the backdrop of a medieval castle. The hillsides nearby bear the terraced vineyards that were probably planted by the Phoenicians, centuries before the Romans arrived. The latest buzz here revolves around the upcoming Festa de São João, where villagers will decorate statues of Catholic saints with flowers and process alongside the bishop through the streets, followed by much feasting and celebrating at the country fairgrounds.

Meanwhile, a few hundred kilometres away, a group of young friends have gathered at an art opening in the city. Mingling and cocktails are the order of the evening, then a dance party in the bar below the gallery. But after a flurry of text messages, the group heads to the seaside suburbs for a late-night meal in a chrome-and-glass lounge perched above the crashing waves. Later, around 1am, when things begin to pick up, they'll head for the new club that just opened, where a DJ from LA is spinning.

The once-great seafaring empire of Portugal is today a country straddling two very different worlds. In simplest terms, it's the struggle between old and new, long-standing tradition versus widespread modernisation – a conflict that plays out daily in many different ways and in many different settings. And no matter one's age, ideology or socio-economic status, every person in Portugal has a stake in the outcome.

Traditional villages across the country are at the forefront of this clash, as younger generations – seeking educational and job opportunities, or simply a more modern way of life – abandon the small settlements where they grew up and strike out for the city. Yet even the cities face similar demographic shifts. The young and upwardly mobile still largely favour the suburbs, leaving worn and ageing city centres to the elderly – and to tourists. At the same time, other places are undergoing a cultural renaissance, with shops, galleries, restaurants and bars bringing new vitality (and the complicated baggage of gentrification) into some neighbourhoods.

Portugal's economy has confronted similar challenges. Facing ultimatums from the EU to rein in its debt, Portugal had to decide between modernising its economy and keeping the social welfare state intact. In the end it chose modernising, which meant pension reform, higher taxes and other stringent measures that made a few enemies for Prime Minister José Socrates. Although Portugal succeeded in reaching some of its EU-mandated goals ahead of schedule, it's still lumbering under a long spell of stagnant economic growth coupled with rising unemployment.

On other fronts, Portugal is marching head-on into the future. Over the last half decade, Portugal has invested heavily in renewable energy. It has some of the largest solar- and wind-powered plants on the planet and has even opened an experimental wave power plant, which will harness the ocean's power to create energy. More controversial are Portugal's hydroelectric dams, which provide abundant energy but drown much land in their creation – leading back once again to that struggle between old and new.

For the traveller, Portugal's friction between tradition and modernity presents some rewarding opportunities, from visiting old-fashioned wine estates to gallery-hopping in Porto, staying in a medieval stone village to people-watching at a trendy beach resort. Sometimes Portugal is a country happily in conflict with itself, and, while the scales are even, there's no better time to visit.

FAST FACTS

Population: 10.7 million

GDP: €231 billion (world's 46th-largest economy)

GDP per capita: €14,800

GDP growth: 1.9%

Inflation: 2.4%

Unemployment rate: 7.7%

Average life expectancy: 78 years

Annual fish consumption per capita: 76kg

Annual wine consumption per capita: 49L

Getting Started

Although Portugal is small, there are hundreds of ways to partake of the Iberian experience. You can plan a trip around a traditional festival, plot a route through vineyards along the Douro or slip back in time at Celtic monuments in the Alentejo. Vying for attention are beaches, mountainous national parks, hilltop castles and captivating city neighbourhoods. Whatever your itinerary, you can do it cheaper here than just about anywhere else in Western Europe. Portugal has lodging and dining to accommodate every budget.

When planning a trip, keep in mind that from June to September prices rise as the holiday crowds arrive, and you'll need to book accommodation well in advance. Portugal has efficient buses and a decent train system connecting major towns, but if you're heading to out-of-the-way places, renting a car will save you a lot of time.

Other things to keep in mind: most museums close on Monday, and Sundays are awfully quiet (many shops and restaurants close).

See Climate Charts (p495) for more information.

WHEN TO GO

Portugal's high season runs from mid-June to mid-September, when temperatures across the country average around 27°C. In July and August it gets hot, particularly in the Algarve, the Alentejo and the upper Douro valley, where the mercury can climb to over 45°C.

If you'd rather skip the crowds (and the heat), consider a trip in spring, when the countryside is at its most verdant, or in autumn, when it's still warm but the summer crowds have dispersed. During winter (November to March) the rains arrive, falling most heavily in the north and most lightly in the south (the Algarve gets almost year-round sunshine), with a handful of places closing down. Travelling then, however, will net you substantial savings at many hotels, and you'll see the country's most traditional side.

It's worth arriving in time for a Portuguese festival, particularly Carnaval in February or March, and Holy Week (the week before Easter) in March or April.

COSTS & MONEY

Portugal remains excellent value for money, whether you're travelling on the cheap or trying to spend your inheritance. If you're on a shoestring budget, you could get by on around €30 per day, as long as you camp (around €4 per person, plus a charge for your tent and car) or stay in youth hostels (€9 to €16 for a dorm bed), buy your own food and do free stuff such as lying on the beach. Travelling in the low season will help, too.

Many museums are free at certain times (often Sunday mornings). Purchasing family tickets to attractions usually saves a few euros, and student or senior cards often get you discounts. In restaurants you can sometimes share a main course or order a *meia dose* (half-portion). Drink promotions are prevalent in the Algarve, particularly during happy hour, making for a cheap night out. See p66 for more on food and drink.

Midrange travellers can expect to pay around €50 to €70 per person per day, while a cushier holiday with more-stylish digs and fancier meals and cocktails starts at around €100 per person per day.

HOW MUCH?

Lisbon to Porto train ticket €20-40

Bottle of *vinho verde* (young wine) €8-16

uma bica (short black coffee) €0.60

Dinner for two in Lisbon's Alfama district €25-35

Full-day boat ride along the Douro river €55-82

See also the Lonely Planet Index, inside front cover.

TRAVELLING RESPONSIBLY

Every year around six million sun-seeking visitors cram into the over-developed beaches of the Algarve, permanently transforming the coast-line and once-remote habitats. You can't halt the inexorable rise of hotel, villa and apartment-block complexes, but if you want to minimise your impact on the south's delicate landscapes, do beware of supposedly 'ecofriendly' tours such as jeep safaris that damage and disrupt natural habitats.

Instead you could choose organised walks, which are far less de-structive plus you learn first-hand knowledge of environmental issues. Walks organised by the Associação Nacional de Conservação da Natureza (Quercus; p81), the country's leading environmental organisation, are recommended, but we also note other organisations that offer guided walks in local listings in the regional chapters throughout this guide.

Another way to minimise your impact is to visit outside the high season. Spending your money in less-visited areas also helps to even out tourism's financial impact, while simultaneously broadening your experience in the country.

TRAVEL LITERATURE

Living in Portugal (2007), by Anne De Stoop, is a hefty coffee-table book with handsome photographs and accompanying text that explores Portu-gal's villages, its fertile vineyards, architecture and urban scenery.

The Portuguese: The Land and Its People (2006), by Marion Kaplan, is an excellent one-volume introduction to the country, covering history, culture and other facets of Portuguese identity.

Lisbon: A Cultural and Literary Companion (2002), by Paul Buck, takes readers on a journey through some of Lisbon's well-known neighbour-hoods, sharing curious anecdotes spanning the past 500 years or so.

Datus Proper takes readers on a rambling journey in *The Last Old Place: Search through Portugal* (1993). His endearing portrait of the country takes in history, culture, the Portuguese character and a fair bit of trout fishing.

Journey to Portugal: A Pursuit of Portugal's History and Culture (1981) is José Saramago's account of his travels in 1979. Although at times it's slow-going, there are some gems here, as the Nobel Prize winner rumi-nates on Portuguese identity as he wanders his Iberian homeland.

Stepping back in time, Fernando Pessoa's *Lisbon: What the Tourist Should See* (1925) portrays the many faces of the poet's home town, though it too can be a bit of a plod. A more successful work by a great writer is Almeida Garrett's *Travels in my Homeland* (1846), which is

---

DON'T LEAVE HOME WITHOUT...

- a phrasebook
- sunglasses
- a healthy appetite for salted cod
- brushing up a bit on Portugal's latest football news – it's a great way to break the ice
- a waterproof jacket (particularly in the rainy north)
- a compass (useful for getting your bearings even if you're not planning a trek)

For more info on the ins and outs of travel in Portugal, see the Directory (p492), Transport (p504) and Health (p516).

TOP 10

PORTUGAL   Spain

NIGHTSPOTS

1 Pavilhão Chinês (p139) Lisbon's favourite old curiosity shop is packed with arcana and intrigue.

2 A Baîuca (p142) Charmingly intimate fado spot hidden in the narrow streets of the Alfama.

3 Lux (p141) A classic on Lisbon's nightlife circuit, with sunrise views over the Tejo.

4 Catacumbas (p138) Great Bairro Alto spot for catching live jazz.

5 Plano B (p402) Part art gallery, part dance club hidden on a cobbled Porto street.

6 Solar do Vinho do Porto (p403) A touch of sophistication with magnificent views over the Rio Douro and dozens of port wine choices.

7 Maus Habitos (p403) Porto's most bohemian, creatively charged space throws great dance parties.

8 Duna Beach Club (p222) Stylish beach bar on Algarvian sands near Lagos.

9 Á Capella (p337) Coimbra-style fado in a stunning 14th-century setting.

10 Bubble Lounge (p228) Welcoming low-key hangout for surf lovers in Sagres.

FILMS

Portuguese cinema provides a quick entrée into the culture. (These films are covered on p51 unless otherwise noted.)

1 *Fados* (2007; director Carlos Saura)

2 *The Convent* (1995; director Manoel de Oliveira)

3 *Terra Estrangeira* (A Foreign Land; 1996; directors Walter Salles and Daniela Thomas)

4 *Alice* (2005; director Marco Martins)

5 *A Lisbon Story* (1994; director Wim Wenders)

6 *Noite Escura* (In the Darkness of the Night; 2004; director João Canijo)

7 *O Delfim* (The Dauphin; 2002; Fernando Lopes)

8 *Aniki-Bóbó* (1942; director Manoel de Oliveira)

9 *O Milagre Segundo Salomé* (The Miracle According to Salomé; 2004; director Mário Barroso)

10 *Porto da Minha Infância* (Porto of my Childhood; 2002; director Manoel de Oliveira)

BOOKS

Delve into the Lusitanian literary scene by exploring these novels set in Portugal. (See p49 for more on these titles, authors and Portuguese literature in general.)

1 *Manual dos Inquisidores* (The Inquisitors' Manual) by António Lobo Antunes

2 *Balada da Praia dos Cães* (Ballad of Dog's Beach) by José Cardoso Pires

3 *A Caverna* (The Cave) by José Saramago

4 *The Company of Strangers* by Robert Wilson

5 *Over the Edge of the World* by Laurence Bergreen

6 *O Vale da Paixão* (The Painter of Birds) by Lídia Jorge

7 *A Ilustre Casa de Ramires* (The Illustrious House of Ramires) by Eça de Queirós

8 *Night Train to Lisbon* by Pascal Mercier

9 *Contos da Montanha* (Tales from the Mountain) by Miguel Torga

10 *O Livro do Desasossego* (The Book of Disquiet) by Fernando Pessoa

full of wry observations about Portugal but also touches on philosophy, poetry, nature and other Romantic-era topics.

Representing one of the country's many expat admirers is the work by 19th-century Gothic novelist William Beckford. He wrote a rollicking tale of his stay in Sintra and travels around Estremadura in *Recollections of an Excursion to the Monasteries of Alcobaça and Batalha* (1835).

INTERNET RESOURCES

At Tambur (www.attambur.com) A fine introduction to Portuguese music, with info on traditional and folk music, dance and current artists.

Library of Congress Country Studies (http://lcweb2.loc.gov/frd/cs/pttoc.html) Detailed history and socio-economic profile of Portugal.

Lifecooler (www.lifecooler.pt, in Portuguese) Excellent for insider up-to-the-minute reviews, including restaurant, bar, club and hotel listings.

Lonely Planet (www.lonelyplanet.com) Where else would you go for damn fine travel information, links and advice from other travellers?

Portugal Tourism (www.visitportugal.pt) Portugal's official tourism site; includes tips on itineraries and upcoming events.

ViniPortugal (www.viniportugal.pt) Fine overview of Portugal's favourite beverage, covering wine regions, grapes and wine routes.

Events Calendar

Portugal has some thrilling festivals and events, mostly centred on something religious, and which have often grown out of previously pagan events. Here are some of the best.

JANUARY–FEBRUARY

CARNAVAL   4 days before Ash Wednesday
Although small by Brazilian standards, Portugal's Carnaval features much merry-making in the pre-Lenten celebrations. Loulé boasts the best parades, while Lisbon, Nazaré, Ovar and Viana do Castelo all throw a respectable bash.

**FESTIVAL INTERNACIONAL
DO CHOCOLATE**   14-28 Feb
For almost two weeks following Valentine's Day, Óbidos in Estremadura celebrates the sweet temptation of the cacao bean.

FANTASPORTO   late Feb-early Mar
World-renowned two-week international festival (www.fantasporto.com) of fantasy, horror and just plain weird films that takes place in Porto.

MARCH–APRIL

SEMANA SANTA   Mar or Apr
The build-up to Easter is magnificent in saintly Braga, the Minho. During Holy Week, barefoot penitents process through the streets, past rows of makeshift altars, with an explosion of jubilation at the cathedral on the eve of Easter.

**OVIBEJA
AGRICULTURAL FAIR**   last weekend in Apr
This huge nine-day festival in Beja, the Alentejo, features concerts every night, with handicrafts booths and abundant food stalls.

MAY

FEIRA DAS CANTARINHAS   2-4 May
In the far north, this is a huge street fair of traditional handicrafts in Bragança, Trás-os-Montes.

QUEIMA DAS FITAS   1st week in May
Join the mayhem of Burning of the Ribbons at the University of Coimbra (Portugal's Oxford), the Beiras, as students celebrate the end of the academic year with concerts, a parade and copious amounts of drinking.

FESTA DAS CRUZES   1st week in May
Barcelos turns into a fairground of flags, flowers, coloured lights and open-air concerts at the Festival of the Crosses. The biggest days are 1 to 3 May. Monsanto in the Beiras also celebrates, with singing and dancing beside a medieval castle.

FESTA DO MAR   1st weekend in May
This colourful festival features fireworks, a parade with floats dedicated to local fishermen's patron saints and a procession of colourfully decorated boats around Nazaré's harbour, Estremadura.

FÁTIMA ROMARIS   12-13 May
Hundreds of thousands make the pilgrimage to Fátima each year to commemorate the apparitions of the Virgin that occurred in 1917. It also happens in October (12-13).

FEIRA DO ALVARINHO   late May
The self-described cradle of Alvarinho, Monção, the Minho, hosts a five-day fair (www.feiraalvarinho.pt.vu) in honour of its fine-flavoured wine. There's music, folkloric dancing and much eating and drinking.

JUNE

FESTA DO FADO   Jun
Classic and new generation *fadistas* (singers of fado) perform in the atmospheric setting of an illuminated Castelo de São Jorge, Lisbon (www.egeac.pt). Catch free fado on trams every Thursday and Sunday in June.

FESTA DO CORPO DE DEUS   Jun
Celebrated all over the north, this is the biggest party in Monção, the Minho. It's held on Corpus Christi (the ninth Thursday after Easter) and features a religious procession and medieval fair, with a re-enactment of St George battling the dragon.

VACA DAS CORDAS & CORPUS CHRISTI   Jun

Dating back many centuries, this strange event features young men goading a hapless bull through Ponte de Lima, the Minho. It's followed by the more pious Festa do Corpo de Deus, with religious processions and flowers carpeting the streets.

FESTAS DE JUNHO   1st weekend in Jun

Highlights here include an all-night drum competition, a livestock fair, a handicrafts market and fireworks, all rounded off with Sunday's procession in honour of the main man – São Gonçalo, in Amarante, the Douro.

FESTA DE SANTO ANTÓNIO   12-13 Jun

The lively Festival of St Anthony is celebrated with particular fervour in Lisbon's Alfama district, with feasting, drinking and dancing in some 50 *arraiais* (street parties).

FESTA DE SÃO JOÃO   23-24 Jun

St John is the favourite up north, when Porto, Braga and Vila do Conde celebrate with elaborate processions, music and feasting, while folks go around whacking each other with plastic hammers.

FEIRA NACIONAL DA AGRICULTURA   late Jun

The 10-day National Agricultural Fair is famed nationwide for its merriment, horse races, bullfights and night-time bull-running through the streets of Santarém. There are lots of children's events.

FESTAS POPULARES   late Jun

This is one of Évora's biggest, bounciest annual bashes, and one of the Alentejo's best country fairs.

JULY

FESTIVAL INTERNACIONAL DE FOLCLORE   Jul

The week-long International Folk Festival in late July brings in costumed dancers and traditional groups to Porto from across Portugal and beyond.

MERCADO MEDIEVAL   Jul

Don your armour and head to the castle grounds for this lively medieval fair in Óbidos, Estremadura. Attractions include wandering minstrels, jousting matches and plenty of grog. Other medieval fairs are held in Silves, Valença do Minho and other castle towns.

AUGUST

FESTAS DE CIDADE E GUALTERIANAS   1st weekend in Aug

Marked by a free fair, this long-running festival (www.aoficina.pt) in Guimarães, the Minho, has folk dancing, rock concerts, bullfights, fireworks and parades.

FESTIVAL DO SUDOESTE   early August

The Alentejan Glastonbury, in Zambujeira do Mar, attracts a young, surfy crowd with huge parties and big-name bands headlining.

FESTIVAL DO MARISCO   mid-August

This action-packed seafood festival in Olhão features the great Algarvian oceanic dishes, including *caldeirada* (fish stew) and *cataplana* (seafood and meat cooked in a copper dish). Bands add to the fun. For other eating festivals in the Algarve see p212.

ROMARIA DE NOSSA SENHORA D'AGONIA   20 Aug

One of the Minho's most spectacular festivals, in Viana do Castelo, features elaborate street paintings, folk costume parades, drumming, giant puppets and much merry-making (www.festas-agonia.com).

FEIRA DE SÃO MATEUS   mid-Aug–mid-Sep

Folk music, traditional food and fireworks rule the day at the country St Matthew's Fair in Viseu, the Beiras.

FOLKFARO   late Aug

Faro's big folk turns on lots of dance (with local and international folk groups); live music and street fests add to the fun in the Algarve.

NOITES RITUAL ROCK   late Aug

The fine city of Porto hosts a weekend-long rock extravaganza (Festival of Portuguese Rock; www.noitesritual.com) in late August.

FESTA DE NOSSA SENHORA DOS REMÉDIOS   late Aug–early Sep

Lamego's biggest event features rock concerts and late-night revelry, along with a procession on 8 September when ox-drawn carts carry religious *tableaux vivants* (scenes represented by a group of silent, motionless people) through the streets. Hard-core devotees ascend the steep stairway on their knees.

SEPTEMBER–OCTOBER

NOSSA SENHORA DA NAZARÉ   8 Sep
Nazaré's big religious festival features sombre processions, folk dances and bullfights in Estremadura.

FEIRAS NOVAS   3rd week in Sep
One of Portugal's most ancient ongoing events, the New Fairs festival has a massive market and fair, with folk dances, fireworks and brass bands at Ponte de Lima, the Minho.

FEIRA DE SANTA IRIA   late Oct
In the Algarve, Faro's biggest traditional event honours St Irene with fairground rides, stalls and entertainment.

NOVEMBER–DECEMBER

FEIRA DE SÃO MARTINHO   1st half of Nov
In the heart of horse country, this fair has a running of the bulls, bullfights, parades and nightly parties on the town square of Golegã, the Ribatejo.

FESTA DOS RAPAZES   Late Dec
Just after Christmas, the so-called Festival of the Lads is a rollicking time of merry-making by young unmarried men who light bonfires and rampage around in rags and wooden masks. Catch it in Miranda do Douro, Trás-os-Montes.

NEW YEAR'S EVE (LISBON)   31 Dec
Ring in the *Ano Novo* (New Year) with fireworks, free concerts and DJs down by the Tejo.

Itineraries
CLASSIC ROUTES

ALONG THE ATLANTIC COAST
Ten Days/Lisbon to Porto

Start in **Lisbon** (p99), with an exploration of enchanting neighbourhoods, where fado, cafe culture and street parties are all part of the scene. After this urban revelry, head north for a relaxing stay on the hillsides of **Sintra** (p150), then make your way to the lovely hilltop village of **Óbidos** (p295). Next, drink in the heady architecture of **Alcobaça** (p302) and **Batalha** (p304). For a dose of nature, take a stroll along the coastal pinewood of **Pinhal de Leiria** (p309) before dropping in at the colourful university town of **Coimbra** (p325). From here, it's a day trip to Portugal's best-preserved Roman ruins – the mosaics at **Conimbriga** (p339). More sylvan scenery awaits on a walk to the fairy-tale palace (and hotel) at **Mata Nacional do Buçaco** (p339), a prelude to the imposing sight of the castle **Montemor-o-Velho** (p342). Then, go north to **Porto** (p384), Lisbon's rival in beauty. Enjoy a day exploring the Ribeira, then head across the river to **Vila Nova de Gaia** (p393), for an intro to the country's great ports. End with a boat trip or train trip along the **Rio Douro** (p395), taking in the dramatic gorge scenery.

With detours along the way, it's around 355km from Lisbon to Porto. Frequent and inexpensive train connections link the towns, and there is also a decent bus service, which will be your main transport to the suggested stop-offs on the way.

JOURNEY INTO THE PAST   Two Weeks/Lisbon to Lisbon

The Moorish castle ruins atop **Lisbon** (p99) are an excellent starting point
for this journey into Portugal's history. After taking in the capital's fine
panoramas, head northeast to **Monsanto** (p354), a fairy-tale village dating
back to Visigoth times. From there, stop off in neighbouring **Idanha-a-Velha**
(p356), an extraordinary town with Roman and Visigoth roots and, like
Monsanto, a fine castle. Head south to the Alto Alentejo's twin fortress
hilltop towns of **Castelo de Vide** (p265) and **Marvão** (p268), the latter rising
from a craggy peak.

The next stop is **Elvas** (p258), with its extraordinary zigzagging fortifications protecting narrow streets, only 14km from Spain. Its tiny size contrasts nicely with the pristine, walled town of Unesco-listed **Évora** (p236).
Take in the cathedral, Roman ruins, plazas, restaurants and lively student
nightlife. While there, take a day trip out to the impressive Neolithic
ruins, particularly the **Cromeleque dos Almendres** (p247), one of the most
important megalithic sites on the Iberian Peninsula. After a bit of Stone
Age musing, head to the magical hilltop village of **Monsaraz** (p249), overlooking ancient olive groves. From there, dip down to **Beja** (p275), the
sedate, pretty capital of Baixo Alentejo, to access **Mértola** (p270), one of
the Alentejo's most dramatic hilltop villages. An open-air museum with a
Moorish legacy, it's set high above the meandering Rio Guadiana.

This route is
around 850km.
It's possible to
cover it by public
transport, though
you'd spend a lot
of time on buses,
and transport to
some of these
remote towns is
infrequent.

SOUTHERN BEAUTY   Two Weeks/Lisbon to Tavira

This trip will give you a chance to see spectacular contrasts in scenery by following Portugal's southern rivers, beaches and ridges. From **Lisbon** (p99) head to the **Costa da Caparica** (p168), going far south of the tourist hordes to wild, sparsely visited beaches. Next, stop in **Setúbal** (p170) for a seafood feast and a visit to the beautiful protected area of the **Parque Natural da Arrábida** (p174).

From here, it's up to the mountains of **Monchique** (p231), where you'll find densely wooded hills and the Algarve's highest point at 902m. Take advantage of the picturesque walking, biking and pony-trekking opportunities, followed by a spa visit in refreshing **Caldas de Monchique** (p233).

From here you can dive back down to the coast, heading west to the surreal cliffs of **Cabo de São Vicente** (p226), with an overnight in the laid-back town of **Sagres** (p224).

Go straight east along the coast to **Faro** (p181), where you can take in its fine medieval centre before journeying out to the lush **Parque Natural da Ria Formosa** (p192), a lagoon system full of marsh, creeks, dune islands and the wetland birds that live there. From there, head to **Tavira** (p193), set with genteel 18th-century buildings straddling the Rio Gilão. This picturesque river town is a fine base for a boat trip across to the long idyllic beach of **Ilha de Tavira** (p198).

The one-way distance here is around 340km, and can be done largely on public transport, though you'll be able to explore more-remote regions and less-travelled coastline if you hire a car.

ROADS LESS TRAVELLED

BLAZING THE BEIRA BAIXA   Two to Three Weeks/Coimbra to Sortelha

This highly rewarding trip through the Beira Baixa takes you past striking scenery with plenty of opportunity for outdoor adventure; plus, the deeper you delve, the fewer travellers you'll see. Start your foray from **Coimbra** (p325), soaking up the sights before hitting the photographers' paradise and royal retreat and spa of **Luso** and **Buçaco** (both p339).

From here you'll lose the crowds by breaking west to pristine rural idylls such as **Piódão** (p351), or any of the traditional hamlets and villages in the beautiful **Parque Natural da Serra da Estrela** (p358), packed with exquisite scenery, outdoor pursuits and Portugal's highest point – **Torre** (p367), also home to the country's only ski resort. Base yourself bang in the middle at **Manteigas** (p364) to give you the run of the whole mountain range; afterwards, visit beautiful **Belmonte** (p377), a hill town that overlooks the Serra da Estrela and has a fascinating secret history.

You could start the descent from these heady heights via the chilly highland towns of **Covilhã** (p368) or **Guarda** (p374), and then head up north to **Trancoso** (p378), a perfectly preserved medieval walled town.

Other fabulous castles and fortified towns you can visit in the lowland Beiras include northern **Almeida** (p380) and far-flung **Sortelha** (p357), both stunning destinations that see only a fraction of the tourist traffic of coastal Portugal.

This trip has spectacular scenery and sights, but a severe dearth of public transport. With your own wheels you could whiz around this 410km route in two weeks, but relying on buses, you'd have to skip the more remote villages.

MEANDERINGS IN THE MINHO   Two to Three Weeks/Porto to Porto

Portugal's oft-ignored northern region makes a great destination for outdoor adventures, as well as exploring colourful markets or catching a traditional festival. From **Porto** (p384), head up the coast to the beautifully set town of **Viana do Castelo** (p441), which is also just a short ferry ride from the north's best beaches. Continue north to the border fortress of **Valença do Minho** (p446) and **Monção** (p448), both perched scenically over the Minho River.

From here, travel south to the charming town of **Ponte de Lima** (p450), with its garden-lined riverbanks and picture-book Roman bridge. Nearby **Ponte da Barca** (p454) is another handsome riverside town; stock up here before heading to the remote stone village of **Soajo** (p460), a great base for walks amid untouched mountain scenery. For more outdoor adventures inside the **Parque Nacional da Peneda-Gerês** (p457), head to spa town **Vila do Gerês** (p461) and nearby spots for canoeing, mountain biking and hiking.

Next it's on to beautiful **Braga** (p425), a town of magnificent churches and manicured plazas set with fine restaurants and outdoor cafes. For great city views, take in the hilltop sanctuary of **Bom Jesus do Monte** (p431). If you're passing on a Thursday, take a day trip to **Barcelos** (p432) to catch its famous weekly market.

Continuing south, get a dose of early history at the Celtic ruins of **Citânia de Briteiros** (p440), and spend a day (and preferably a night) in **Guimarães** (p436), birthplace of Portugal and home to an immaculately preserved medieval centre.

Leaving the Minho, head to **Amarante** (p409), famous for its monastery, pastries and pretty riverside. For the journey back to Porto, take the narrow-gauge train down to the Douro and transfer to a regular train back to Porto.

Apart from remote corners of the national parks, this route isn't difficult to undertake by public transport. Completing the whole 550km loop will take a long two weeks, or a leisurely three if you want to linger in Peneda-Gerês.

TAILORED TRIPS

A VITICULTURAL VOYAGE

Wine lovers have their work cut out for them on a leisurely journey through the north, Portugal's premier wine-growing region. How quickly you cover this 360km route depends on how much imbibing you plan to do along the way. You can easily cover the distance in under a week, but you may want to linger at some of the delightful guest houses and rural manors along the way.

Any self-respecting port-wine tour will begin in **Porto** (p384), gateway to the world's most famous port-wine region. Hint: don't miss the **Solar do Vinho do Porto** (p403). Across the river from the city is the historic **Vila Nova de Gaia** (p393). Packed with port-wine lodges, this is an excellent place to sample the great fruits of the vine.

After preliminary tastes, it's time to journey up the wine's ancient highway, on a river cruise up the Douro valley to **Peso da Régua** (p417) and beyond to the very heart of vineyard country. The tiny village of **Pinhão** (p419) is ringed with wine estates, many offering splendid overnight stays.

While in the vicinity, take the incredibly scenic drive over the mountains to **Vila Nova de Foz Côa** (p420), famed for the mystifying Palaeolithic stone carvings in the surrounding countryside (don't worry, there are also vineyards nearby). You could also stop in **Vila Real** (p468), erstwhile home of its eponymous rosé wine.

The last stop before returning to Porto is **Lamego** (p413), which is home to one of Portugal's choice sparkling wines.

PORTUGAL FOR KIDS

If you're travelling with children, the Algarve is ideal for long beach days, water parks and abundant youthful amusement. The drive down, however, shouldn't be rushed, as there are some great spots along the way. Start at Lisbon's **Parque das Nações** (p121) with its amazing **Oceanário** (p122). There's also bike rental, air gondola rides along the water and plenty of space for running around. Moseying south, visit the beaches of **Costa da Caparica** (p168) for spade-and-bucket fun. Continue down the beautiful, wild western coast: **Vila Nova de Milfontes** (p283), sleepy **Zambujeira do Mar** (p286) or **Odeceixe** (p230), all with stunning beaches. On the Algarve coast, you are spoilt for choice. Base yourself at vibrant **Lagos** (p216) or **Albufeira** (p205), both of which offer dolphin-spotting boat trips. For a quieter scene, choose **Carvoeiro** (p207) or elegant **Tavira** (p193). Supplement beach days with a day at one of the nearby water parks. Kids may enjoy the castle at **Silves** (p209), or a boat trip from Faro to **Ilha Barreta** (p185), a remote sandy island just off the mainland.

History

EARLY PEOPLES

One of Europe's earliest settlements, the Iberian Peninsula was first inhabited many millennia ago, when hominids wandered across the landscape some time before 200,000 BC. During the Palaeolithic period, early Portuguese ancestors left traces of their time on earth in the fascinating stone carvings in the open air near Vila Nova de Foz Côa in the Alto Douro (p421). These date back some 30,000 years and were only discovered by accident (during a proposed dam building project) in 1992. Other early signs of early human artistry lie hidden in the Alentejo, in the Gruta do Escoural, where cave drawings of animals and humans date back to around 15,000 BC.

Homo sapiens weren't the only bipeds on the scene. Neanderthals co-existed alongside modern humans in a few rare places like Portugal for as long as 10,000 years. In fact, some of the last traces of their existence were found in Iberia prior to their disappearance.

Neanderthals were only the first of a long line of inhabitants to appear (and later disappear) from the Iberian stage. In the 1st millennium BC Celtic people started trickling into the Iberian Peninsula, settling northern and western Portugal around 700 BC. Dozens of *citânias* (fortified villages) popped up, such as the formidable Citânia de Briteiros (p440). Further south, Phoenician traders, followed by Greeks and Carthaginians, founded coastal stations and mined metals inland.

When the Romans swept into southern Portugal in 210 BC, they expected an easy victory. But they hadn't reckoned on the Lusitani, a Celtic warrior tribe settled between the Rio Tejo and Rio Douro that resisted ferociously for half a century. Unable to subjugate the Lusitani, the Romans offered peace instead and began negotiations with Viriato, the Lusitanian leader. Unfortunately for Viriato and his underlings, the peace offer was a ruse, and Roman agents, posing as intermediaries, poisoned him. Resistance collapsed following Viriato's death in 139 BC.

By 19 BC the Romans had eliminated all traces of Lusitanian independence. A capital was established at Olisipo (Lisbon) in 60 BC, and Christianity became firmly rooted in Portugal during the 3rd century AD. For a vivid glimpse into Roman Portugal, you won't see a better site than Conimbriga (p339), near Coimbra, or the monumental remains of the so-called Temple of Diana (p241), in Évora.

By the 5th century, when the Roman Empire had all but collapsed, Portugal's inhabitants had been under Roman rule for 600 years. So what did the Romans ever do for them? Most usefully, they built roads and bridges.

Visits to the Gruta do Escoural can be undertaken by pre-arrangement. Contact the Direção Regional de Cultura de Alentejo on ☎ 266 769 800 or grutadoescoural@cultura-alentejo.pt.

Portugal: A Traveller's History (2004) by Harold Livermore explores some of the richer episodes from the past – taking in cave paintings, vineyards and music, among other topics.

TIMELINE

18,000 BC	5000 BC	700 BC
Ancestors of modern Iberians leave behind a gallery of Palaeolithic art, which features rock carvings in the Alto Douro and cave paintings in the Alentejo.	Little-understood Neolithic peoples build protected hilltop settlements in the lower Tejo valley. They leave behind astounding stone monuments, including megaliths scattered around Évora in present-day Alentejo.	Celtic peoples, migrating across the Pyrenees with their families and flocks, sweep through the Iberian Peninsula. They settle in fortified villages, known as *castros*, and intermarry with local tribes.

THE MYSTERY OF THE NEANDERTHALS

Scientists have never come to agreement about the fate of the Neanderthals – stout and robust beings who used stone tools and fire, buried their dead and had brains larger than those of modern humans. The most common theory was that homo sapiens drove Neanderthals into extinction (perhaps in some sort of genocidal warfare). A less-accepted theory is that Neanderthals and humans bred together and even produced a hybrid species. This idea gained credence when Portuguese archaeologists found a strange skeleton – the first complete Palaeolithic skeleton ever unearthed in Iberia – just north of Lisbon in 1999. In what was clearly a ritual burial, the team led by João Zilhão, director of the Portuguese Institute of Archaeology, discovered the 25,000-year-old remains of a young boy with traits of both early humans (pronounced chin and teeth) and of Neanderthals (broad limbs). Some believe this kind of relationship (love-making rather than war-making) happened over the span of thousands of years, and that some elements of Neanderthals entered the modern human gene pool.

But they also brought wheat, barley, olives and vines; large farming estates called *latifúndios* (still found in the Alentejo); a legal system; and, above all, a Latin-derived language. In fact, no other invader proved so useful.

MOORS & CHRISTIANS

The gap left by the Romans was filled by barbarian invaders from beyond the Pyrenees: Vandals, Alans, Visigoths and Suevi, with Arian Christian Visigoths gaining the upper hand in 469.

Internal Visigothic disputes paved the way for Portugal's next great wave of invaders, the Moors – North African Muslims invited in 711 to help a Visigothic faction. They quickly occupied large chunks of Portugal's southern coast.

Southerners enjoyed peace and productivity under the Moors, who established a capital at Shelb (Silves). The new rulers were tolerant of Jews and Christians. Christian small-holding farmers, called Mozarabs, could keep their land and were encouraged to try new methods and crops, especially citrus and rice. Arabic words filtered into the Portuguese language, such as *alface* (lettuce), *arroz* (rice) and dozens of place names (including Fatima, Silves and Algarve – the latter stemming from the Arabic *'el-gharb'* (the west) – and locals became addicted to Moorish sweets.

Meanwhile in the north, Christian forces were gaining strength and reached as far as Porto in 868. But it was in the 11th century that the Reconquista (Christian reconquest) heated up. In 1064 Coimbra was taken and, in 1085, Alfonso VI thrashed the Moors in their Spanish heartland of Toledo; he is said to have secured Seville by winning a game of chess with its emir. But in the following year, Alfonso's men were driven out by ruthless Moroccan Almoravids who answered the emir's distress call.

The word Portugal comes from Portus Cale, a name the Romans gave to a town near present-day Porto. The word morphed into Portucale under Visigoth rule and expanded significantly in meaning.

197 BC	AD 100	400
After defeating Carthage in the Second Punic Wars, the Romans invade Iberia, expanding their empire west. They face fierce resistance from local tribes, including the Lusitani, but eventually conquer them through treachery.	Romans settle in the area and collect taxes to build roads, bridges and other public works. They cultivate vineyards, teach the natives to preserve fish by salting and drying, and grant local communities much autonomy.	Rome crumbles as German tribes run riot in southern Europe. The Suevi, peasant farmers from the Elbe, settle in present-day Porto. Christian Visigoths follow suit, conquering the land in 469.

UNFORGETTABLE RIVER

When Roman soldiers reached the Rio Lima in 137 BC, they were convinced they had reached the River Lethe, the mythical river of forgetfulness that flowed through Hades and from which no man could return. Unable to persuade his troops to cross the waters leading to certain oblivion, the Roman general Decimus Junius Brutus forged the river alone. Once on the other side he called out to his men, shouting each of their names. Stunned that the general could remember them, they followed after him and continued their campaign. Incidentally, Brutus, who led legions to conquer Iberia after Viriato's death, was later named proconsul of Lusitania.

Alfonso cried for help and European crusaders came running – rallying against the 'infidels'. With the help of Henri of Burgundy, among others, Alfonso made decisive moves towards victory. The struggle continued in successive generations, and by 1139 Afonso Henriques (grandson of Alfonso VI) won such a dramatic victory against the Moors at Ourique (Alentejo) that he named himself Dom – King of Portugal – a title confirmed in 1179 by the pope (after extra tribute was paid, naturally). He also retook Santarém and Lisbon from the Moors.

By the time he died in 1185, the Portuguese frontier was secure to the Rio Tejo, though it would take another century before the south was torn from the Moors.

In 1297 the boundaries of the Portuguese kingdom – much the same then as they are today – were formalised with neighbouring Castile. The kingdom of Portugal had arrived.

Jose Saramago's *History of the Siege of Lisbon* (1998) shuttles between the present and the 12th century, in the story of a proofreader who subverts history by deleting a word.

THE BURGUNDIAN ERA

During the Reconquista, people faced more than just war and turmoil: in the wake of Christian victories came new rulers and settlers.

The Church and its wealthy clergy were the greediest landowners, followed by aristocratic fat cats. Though theoretically free, most common people remained subjects of the landowning class, with few rights. The first hint of democratic rule came with the establishment of the *cortes* (parliament). This assembly of nobles and clergy first met in 1211 at Coimbra, the then capital. Six years later, the capital moved to Lisbon.

The Treaty of Windsor (1386), which established a pact of mutual assistance between Portugal and England, is widely considered to be the oldest-surviving alliance in the world.

Afonso III (r 1248–79) deserves credit for standing up to the Church, but it was his son the 'Poet King' Dinis (r 1279–1325) who really shook Portugal into shape. A far-sighted, cultured man, he took control of the judicial system, started progressive afforestation programmes and encouraged internal trade. He suppressed the dangerously powerful military order of the Knights Templar, refounding them as the Order of Christ (p318). He cultivated music, the arts and education, and founded a university in Lisbon in 1290, which was later transferred to Coimbra (p328).

711	800	1147
The Visigoth King Witiza is assassinated. When Agila, his oldest son, is blocked from the throne he sends for help from North African Berbers. The Muslim force arrives, establishes peace and puts down roots.	The Umayyad dynasty rules the Iberian Peninsula. The region flourishes under the tolerant caliphate. The Arabs introduce irrigation, bring new crops (including oranges and rice) and establish schools.	The Reconquista is underway as Christians, after centuries of trying, attain decisive victories over the Moors. Afonso Henriques leads the attack, laying siege to Lisbon and becoming Portugal's first (self-declared) king.

Dom Dinis' foresight was spot-on when it came to defence: he built or rebuilt some 50 fortresses along the eastern frontier with Castile, and signed a pact of friendship with England in 1308, the basis for a future long-lasting alliance.

It was none too soon. Within 60 years of Dinis' death, Portugal was at war with Castile. Fernando I helped provoke the clash by playing a game of alliances with both Castile and the English. He dangled promises of marriage to his daughter Beatriz in front of both nations, eventually marrying her off to Juan I of Castile, and thus throwing Portugal's future into Castilian hands.

On Fernando's death in 1383, his wife, Leonor Teles, ruled as regent. But she too was entangled with the Spanish, having long had a Galician lover. The merchant classes preferred unsullied Portuguese candidate João, son (albeit illegitimate) of Fernando's father. João assassinated Leonor's lover, Leonor fled to Castile and the Castilians duly invaded.

The showdown came in 1385 when João faced a mighty force of Castilians at Aljubarrota. Even with Nuno Álvares Pereira (the Holy Constable) as his military right-hand man and English archers at the ready, the odds were stacked against him. João vowed to build a monastery if he won – and he did. Nuno Álvares, the brilliant commander-in-chief of the Portuguese troops, deserves much of the credit for the victory. He lured Spanish cavalry into a trap and, with an uphill advantage, his troops decimated the invaders. Within a few hours the Spanish were retreating in disarray and the battle was won.

The victory clinched independence and João made good his vow with Batalha's stunning Mosteiro de Santa Maria da Vitória (aka the Mosteiro da Batalha or Battle Abbey; p304). It also sealed Portugal's alliance with England, and João wed John of Gaunt's daughter. Peace was finally concluded in 1411.

THE AGE OF DISCOVERIES

João's success had whetted his appetite and, spurred on by his sons, he soon turned his military energies abroad. Morocco was the obvious target, and in 1415 Ceuta fell easily to his forces. It was a turning point in Portuguese history, a first step into its golden age.

It was João's third son, Henry, who focused the spirit of the age – a combination of crusading zeal, love of martial glory and lust for gold – into extraordinary explorations across the seas. These explorations were to transform the small kingdom into a great imperial power

The biggest breakthrough came in 1497 during the reign of Manuel I, when Vasco da Gama reached southern India. With gold and slaves from Africa and spices from the East, Portugal was soon rolling in riches. Manuel I was so thrilled by the discoveries (and resultant cash injection) that he ordered a frenzied building spree in celebration. Top of his list was the extravagant

---

It was the Portuguese who started England's obsession with tea: their explorers introduced it to Europe in the mid-17th century and tea enthusiast Catherine of Bragança did the rest.

Some historians believe Portuguese explorers reached Australia in the 1500s, 250 years before its 'official' discoverer, Captain James Cook. For the inside scoop, read Kenneth McIntyre's *The Secret Discovery of Australia* (1982).

King João II financed voyages by Vasco da Gama and others, but he is also known for rejecting Christopher Columbus. The Italian navigator approached Portugal first (in 1485) before turning to Spain.

1242

The last remaining Moors are driven from Portugal in the battle of Tavira in the Algarve. Portugal later establishes its border with Castile (Spain), aided by Dom Dinis: 50 fortresses line the eastern frontier.

1385

Intermarriage between Castilian and Portuguese royal families leads to complications. Juan I of Castile, claiming the Portuguese throne, invades. Although outnumbered, the Portuguese army, with English help, rout the invaders at Aljubarrota.

1411

Newly crowned Dom João commemorates his victory at Aljubarrota by building an elaborate monastery. In need of an ally against Spain, João marries John of Gaunt's daughter, ushering in an alliance with the English that will last centuries.

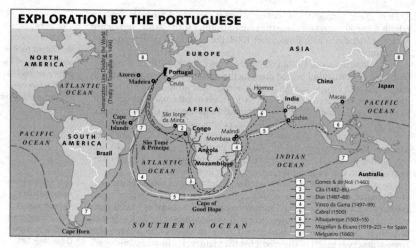

EXPLORATION BY THE PORTUGUESE

1 — Gomes & de Noli (1460)
2 — Cão (1482–85)
3 — Dias (1487–88)
4 — Vasco da Gama (1497–99)
5 — Cabral (1500)
6 — Albuquerque (1503–15)
7 — Magellan & Elcano (1519–22) – for Spain
8 — Melgueiro (1660)

A Nation Upon the Ocean Sea (2007), by Davken Studnicki-Gizbert, is a scholarly look at the remarkable trading empire that Portugal ruled from 1492 to 1640.

Mosteiro dos Jerónimos in Belém (p120), later to become his pantheon. Another brief boost to the Portuguese economy at this time came courtesy of an influx of around 150,000 Jews expelled from Spain in 1492.

Spain, however, had also jumped on the exploration bandwagon and was soon disputing Portuguese claims. Christopher Columbus' 1492 'discovery' of America for Spain led to a fresh outburst of jealous conflict. It was resolved by the pope in the bizarre 1494 Treaty of Tordesillas, by which the world was divided between the two great powers along a line 370 leagues west of the Cape Verde islands. Portugal won the lands to the east of the line, including Brazil, officially claimed in 1500.

The rivalry spurred the first circumnavigation of the world. In 1519 the Portuguese navigator Fernão Magalhães (Ferdinand Magellan), his allegiance transferred to Spain after a tiff with Manuel I, set off in an effort to prove that the Spice Islands (today's Moluccas) lay in Spanish 'territory'. He reached the Philippines in 1521 but was killed in a skirmish there. One of his five ships, under the Basque navigator Juan Sebastián Elcano, reached the Spice Islands and then sailed home via the Cape of Good Hope, proving the earth was round.

The Portuguese were the first Westerners to reach Japan in 1543. They founded Nagasaki, introduced the mosquito net and brought new words to the language, including *pan* (bread) and, possibly, *arrigato* (thank you).

As its explorers reached Timor, China and eventually Japan, Portugal cemented its power with garrison ports and trading posts. The monarchy, taking its 'royal fifth' of profits, became stinking rich – indeed the wealthiest monarchy in Europe, and the lavish Manueline architectural style symbolised the exuberance of the age.

1415	1418	1443
Dom Joã's third son, Prince Henry the Navigator, joins his father in the conquest of Ceuta in North Africa. Thus begins the colonial expansion of Portugal.	Advances in shipbuilding lead to the development of the caravel, a fast and agile ship that changed the face of sailing. Portuguese mariners would put it to brilliant use on long voyages of exploration.	Explorers bring the first African slaves to Portugal; it marks the beginning of a long, dark era of slavery in Europe and later the new world.

THE INQUISITION

'After the earthquake, which had destroyed three-fourths of the city of Lisbon, the sages of that country could think of no means more effectual to preserving the kingdom from utter ruin than to entertain the people with an auto-da-fé, it having been decided by the University of Coimbra that burning a few people alive by a slow fire, and with great ceremony is an infallible secret for preventing earthquakes.' *Candide (Voltaire, 1759)*.

One of the darkest episodes in Portugal's history, the Inquisition was a campaign of church-sanctioned terror and execution that began in 1536. It was initially aimed at Jews who were either expelled from Portugal or forced to renounce their faith. Those who didn't embrace Catholicism risked facing the auto-da-fé (act of faith), a church ceremony consisting of a mass, followed by a procession of the guilty, the reading of their sentences and later their burning at the stake. These trials took place in public squares in Lisbon, Porto, Évora and Coimbra in front of crowds sometimes numbering in the thousands. At the centre atop a large canopied platform sat the Grand Inquisitor, surrounded by his staff of aristocrats, priests, bailiffs, torturers and scribes, who meticulously recorded the proceedings.

The victims usually spent years in prison, often undergoing crippling torture, before seeing the light of day. They stood accused of a wide variety of crimes – such as skipping meals on Jewish fast days (signs of 'unreformed' Jews), leaving pork uneaten on the plate, failing to attend mass or observe the Sabbath, as well as straight-up blasphemy, witchcraft and homosexuality. No matter how flimsy the 'evidence' – often delivered to the tribunal by a grudge-bearing neighbour – very few were found innocent and released. After a decade or so in prison, the condemned were finally brought to their auto-da-fé. Before meeting their judgement, they were dressed in a *san benito* (yellow penitential gown painted with flames) and *coroza* (a high conical cap) and brought before the tribunal.

After the sentence was pronounced, judgement was carried out in a different venue. By dawn the next morning, for instance, executioners would lead the condemned to a killing field outside of town. Those who repented were strangled first before being burned at the stake. The unrepentant were simply burned alive.

During the years of the Inquisition (the last auto-da-fé was held in 1765), the church executed over 2000 victims and tortured or exiled tens of thousands more. The Portuguese even exported the auto-da-fé to the colonies – burning Hindus at the stake in Goa, for instance.

As Voltaire sardonically suggested, superstition played no small part in the auto-da-fé. Some believers thought that the earthquake of 1755 was the wrath of God upon them – and that they were being punished not for their bloody auto-da-fés, but because the Holy Office hadn't done quite enough to punish the heretics.

It couldn't last, of course. By the 1570s the huge cost of expeditions and maintaining an empire was taking its toll. The expulsion of commercially active refugee Spanish Jews in 1496 and the subsequent persecution of converted Jews (*marranos*, or New Christians) during the Inquisition, which began in the 16th century under João III, only worsened the financial situation.

1494	1497	1519
The race for colonial expansion is on: Spain and Portugal carve up the world, with the Treaty of Tordesillas drawing the line 370 leagues west of Cape Verde.	Following Bartolomeu Dias' historic journey around the Cape of Good Hope a few years earlier, Vasco da Gama sails to India and becomes a legend. Trade with the East later brings the crown incredible wealth.	Fernão Magalhães embarks on his journey to circumnavigate the globe. He is killed in the Philippines, but one of his ships returns, completing the epic voyage.

Young, idealistic Sebastião took the throne, and the final straw came in 1578 when, determined to take Christianity to Morocco, he rallied a force of 18,000 and set sail from Lagos, to be disastrously defeated at the Battle of Alcácer-Quibir (also known as the Battle of Three Kings). Sebastião and 8000 others were killed, including much of the Portuguese nobility. His aged successor, Cardinal Henrique, drained the royal coffers ransoming those captured.

On Henrique's death in 1580, Sebastião's uncle, Felipe II of Spain (Felipe I of Portugal), fought for and won the throne. This marked the end of centuries of independence, Portugal's golden age and its glorious moment on the world stage.

SPAIN'S RULE & PORTUGAL'S REVIVAL

Spanish rule began promisingly, with Felipe vowing to preserve Portugal's autonomy and attend the long-ignored parliament. But commoners resented Spanish rule and held on to the dream that Sebastião was still alive (as he was killed abroad in battle in Morocco, some citizens were in denial); pretenders continued to pop up until 1600. Though Felipe was honourable, his successors proved to be considerably less so, using Portugal to raise money and soldiers for Spain's wars overseas, and appointing Spaniards to govern Portugal.

Meanwhile, Portugal's empire was slipping out of Spain's grasp. In 1622 the English seized Hormoz, and by the 1650s the Dutch had taken Malacca, Ceylon (Sri Lanka) and part of Brazil.

An uprising in neighbouring Catalonia gave fuel to Portugal's independence drive (particularly when the Spanish King Felipe III ordered Portuguese troops to quell the uprising), and in 1640 a group of conspirators launched a coup. Nationalists drove the female governor of Portugal and her Spanish garrison from Lisbon. It was then the duke of Bragança reluctantly stepped forward and was crowned João IV.

With a hostile Spain breathing down its neck, Portugal searched for allies. Two swift treaties with England led to Charles II's marriage to João's daughter, Catherine of Bragança, and the ceding of Tangier and Bombay to England.

In return the English promised arms and soldiers: however, a preoccupied Spain made only half-hearted attempts to recapture Portugal, and recognised Portuguese independence in 1668.

Moves towards democracy now stalled under João's successors. The Crown hardly bothered with parliament, and another era of profligate expenditure followed, giving birth to projects like the wildly extravagant monastery-palace in Mafra (see p167).

Into the ensuing economic chaos of the 18th century stepped a man for the moment – the Marquês de Pombal, chief minister to the epicurean Dom

---

CR Boxer's classic text The Portuguese Seaborne Empire *(1969) is still one of the best studies of the explorations by Portuguese mariners and the complex empire that unfolded as a result.*

The Last Kabbalist of Lisbon (2000), by Richard Zimler, is a thriller cast as a long-lost manuscript about the murder of a 16th-century Jewish mystic. It reveals the harrowing life of Jews during Portugal's Inquisition.

1578	**1580**	**1640**
King Sebastião raises an army and invades Morocco. The expedition ends at the disastrous Battle of Alcácer-Quibir. Sebastião and many nobles are killed, and the king leaves no heir, which greatly destabilises the country.	Sebastião's weak successor, the former cardinal Henrique, dies. Seizing the initiative, King Felipe II of Spain invades Portugal and becomes king. Spain will rule for 80 years, draining Portugal's coffers and ending its golden age.	When Catalonia rebels against the oppressive monarchy, Felipe III sends Portuguese troops to quell the uprising. Fuelled by dreams of independence, Portuguese noblemen stage a coup and overthrow Spain. Dom João IV is crowned.

José I (the latter more interested in opera than affairs of state). Described as an enlightened despot, Pombal dragged Portugal into the modern era, crushing opposition with brutal efficiency.

Pombal set up state monopolies, curbed the power of British merchants and boosted agriculture and industry. He abolished slavery and distinctions between traditional and New Christians, and overhauled education.

When Lisbon suffered a devastating earthquake in 1755 (see p100), Pombal swiftly rebuilt the city. He was by then at the height of his power, and succeeded in dispensing with his main enemies by implicating them in an attempt on the king's life.

He might have continued had it not been for the accession of the devout Dona Maria I in 1777. The anticlerical Pombal was promptly sacked, tried and charged with various offences, though never imprisoned. While his religious legislation was repealed, his economic, agricultural and educational policies were largely maintained, helping the country back towards prosperity.

But turmoil was once again on the horizon, as Napoleon swept through Europe.

The Last Day (2008) by Nicholas Shrady paints a harrowing portrait of the Lisbon earthquake of 1755, with drawings and eye-witness accounts from the time.

THE DAWN OF A REPUBLIC

In 1793 Portugal found itself at war again when it joined England in sending naval forces against revolutionary France. Before long, Napoleon threw Portugal an ultimatum: close your ports to British shipping or be invaded.

There was no way Portugal could turn its back on Britain, upon which it depended for half of its trade and protection of its sea routes. In 1807 Portugal's royal family fled to Brazil (where it stayed for 14 years), and Napoleon's forces marched into Lisbon, sweeping Portugal into the Peninsular War (France's invasion of Spain and Portugal, which lasted until 1814).

To the rescue came Sir Arthur Wellesley (later Duke of Wellington), Viscount Beresford and their seasoned British troops, who eventually drove the French back across the Spanish border in 1811.

Free but weakened, Portugal was administered by Beresford while the royals dallied in Brazil. In 1810 Portugal lost a profitable intermediary role by giving Britain the right to trade directly with Brazil. The next humiliation was João's 1815 proclamation of Brazil as a kingdom united with Portugal – he did this to bring more wealth and prestige to Brazil (which he was growing to love) and in turn to him and the rest of the royal family residing there. With soaring debts and dismal trade, Portugal was at one of the lowest points in its history, reduced to a de facto colony of Brazil and a protectorate of Britain.

Meanwhile, resentment simmered in the army. Rebel officers quietly convened parliament and drew up a new liberal constitution. Based on Enlightenment ideals, it abolished many rights of the nobility and clergy, and instituted a single-chamber parliament.

The First Global Village (2002), by Martin Page, is a compact and fascinating survey of Portuguese history from the Romans up to the Revolution of the Carnations.

Brazilian gold made the Braganças enormously wealthy. In 1720 nearly 1 million ounces were being imported annually. King João V's cut gave him an income 30 times greater than that of England's king.

1690	1703	1717
With the economy in tatters and empire fading, the Portuguese pray for a miracle. The prayer is answered when gold is discovered in Brazil; incredible riches soon flow into the royal coffers.	France and England are at war. Facing (disastrous!) wine shortages, the English sign a new treaty with Portugal. England becomes a major player in the Portuguese economy, with port production growing exponentially.	Brazilian gold production nears its peak, with over 600,000oz imported annually. Dom João V becomes Europe's richest monarch, lavishing wealth on ostentatious projects like the Mafra Palace, commissioned that year.

Faced with this fait accompli, João returned and accepted its terms – though his wife and son Miguel were bitterly opposed to it. João's elder son, Pedro, had other ideas: left behind to govern Brazil, he snubbed the constitutionalists by declaring Brazil independent in 1822 and himself its emperor. When João died in 1826, the stage was set for civil war.

Offered the crown, Pedro dashed out a new, less liberal charter and then abdicated in favour of his seven-year-old daughter Maria, provided she marry uncle Miguel and provided uncle Miguel accept the new constitution. Sure enough, Miguel took the oath, but promptly abolished Pedro's charter and proclaimed himself king. A livid Pedro rallied the equally furious liberals and forced Miguel to surrender at Évoramonte in 1834.

After Pedro's death, his daughter Maria, now queen of Portugal at just 15, kept his flame alive with fanatical support of his 1826 charter. The radical supporters of the liberal 1822 constitution grew vociferous over the next two decades, bringing the country to the brink of civil war. The Duke of Saldanha, however, saved the day, negotiating a peace that toned down Pedro's charter, while still radically modernising Portugal's infrastructure.

The latter half of the 19th century was a remarkable period for Portugal, and it became known as one of the most advanced societies in southern Europe. Casual visitors to Lisbon like Hans Christian Andersen were surprised to find tree-lined boulevards with gas street lamps, efficient trams and well-dressed residents. Social advances were less anecdotal. The educational reformer João Arroio dramatically increased the number of schools, doubling the number of boys' schools and quadrupling the number of girls' schools. Women gained the right to own property; slavery was abolished throughout the Portuguese empire, as was the death penalty; and even the prison system received an overhaul – prisoners were taught useful trades while in jail so they could integrate into society upon their release.

Professional organisations, such as the Literary Guild, emerged and became a major impetus to the advancement of ideas in public discourse, inspiring debate in politics, religious life and the art world.

As elsewhere in Europe, this was also a time of great industrial growth, with a dramatic increase in textile production, much of it to be exported. Other major works included the building of bridges and a nationwide network of roads, as well as a flourish of major architectural works like the Pena Palace (p152) above Sintra.

However, by 1900 the tides of discontent among workers began to grow. With increased mechanisation, workers began losing jobs (some factory owners began hiring children to operate the machines), and their demand for fair working conditions went unanswered. Those who went on strike were simply fired and replaced. At the same time, Portugal experienced a dramatic demographic shift: rural areas were increasingly depopulated in favour of cities, and emigration (especially to Brazil) snowballed.

1755	1770	1803
Lisbon suffers beneath Europe's biggest natural disaster in recorded history. On All Saint's Day, three massive earthquakes destroy the city, followed by a tsunami and ravaging fires that kill tens of thousands.	The king's powerful prime minister, the Marquês de Pombal, rebuilds the city following a modern grid. He abolishes slavery, builds schools and develops the economy, crushing those who stand in his way.	England and France are once again at war. Portugal sides with England and refuses Napoleon's call to close its ports to the British. French troops are on the march across Iberia.

Much was changing, and more and more people began to look towards socialism as a cure for the country's inequalities. Nationalist republicanism swept through the lower-middle classes, spurring an attempted coup in 1908. It failed, but the following month King Carlos and Crown Prince Luis Filipe were brutally assassinated in Lisbon.

Carlos' younger son, Manuel II, tried feebly to appease republicans, but it was too little, too late. On 5 October 1910, after an uprising by military officers, a republic was declared. Manuel, dubbed 'the Unfortunate', sailed into exile in Britain where he died in 1932.

THE RISE & FALL OF SALAZAR

After a landslide victory in the 1911 elections, hopes were high among republicans for dramatic changes ahead, but the tides were against them. The economy was in tatters, strained by an economically disastrous decision to join the Allies in WWI. In postwar years the chaos deepened: republican factions squabbled, unions led strikes and were repressed, and the military grew powerful.

The new republic soon had a reputation as Europe's most unstable regime. Between 1910 and 1926 there were an astonishing 45 changes of government, often resulting from military intervention. Another coup in 1926 brought forth new names and faces, most significantly António de Oliveira Salazar, a finance minister who would rise up through the ranks to become prime minister – a post he would hold for the next 36 years.

Salazar hastily enforced his 'New State' – a corporatist republic that was nationalistic, Catholic, authoritarian and essentially repressive. All political parties were banned except for the loyalist National Union, which ran the show, and the National Assembly. Strikes were banned and propaganda, censorship and brute force kept society in order. The sinister new secret police, Polícia Internacional e de Defesa do Estado (PIDE), inspired terror and suppressed opposition by imprisonment and torture. Various attempted coups during Salazar's rule came to nothing. For a chilling taste of life as a political prisoner under Salazar, you could visit the 16th-century Fortaleza at Peniche (p292) – used as a jail by the dictator.

The only good news was a dramatic economic turnaround. Through the 1950s and 1960s Portugal experienced an annual industrial growth rate of 7% to 9%.

Internationally, the wily Salazar played two hands, unofficially supporting Franco's nationalists in the Spanish Civil War, and allowing British use of Azores airfields during WWII despite official neutrality (and illegal sales of tungsten to Germany). It was later discovered that Salazar had also authorised the transfer of Nazi-looted gold to Portugal – 44 tonnes according to Allied records.

The Inquisitor's Manual (2003) by Arnaldo Antunes is a brilliantly written depiction of dark days under Salazar as seen through the eyes of Faulknerian characters like 'the minister' Senhor Francisco.

Officially neutral in WWII, Portugal was a major intersection of both Allied and Nazi spying operations. British secret service agents based there included Graham Greene, Ian Fleming and double agent Kim Philby.

1807	**1822**	**1832**
Napoleon invades Portugal. The Portuguese royal family and several thousand in their retinue pack up their belongings and set sail for Brazil. British warships guard their passage.	In Brazil, Prince Regent Pedro leads a coup d'etat and declares Brazilian independence with himself the new 'emperor'. Dom João VI, his father, returns to Portugal, to reclaim his crown.	Dom Pedro I returns to Portugal where he now must contest his throne with his brother Miguel. Two years of civil war ensue, which end with Miguel's banishment. Dom Pedro's daughter becomes queen.

BEWARE THE ECONOMICS PROFESSOR

When General António Carmona was named Portugal's new president in 1926, he inherited a country in serious debt. Fearing economic catastrophe, Carmona called in an expert, a man by the name of Oliveira Salazar. At the time, Salazar was a 37-year-old bachelor, sharing spartan quarters with a priest (who would later become cardinal of Lisbon). Salazar himself was no stranger to religious life. He spent eight years studying to become a priest, and some residents from his small native village even called him 'father' on his visits. Only a last-minute decision led him to veer into law instead.

Upon graduating, he went into the then fledgling field of economics, becoming one of the country's first economics lecturers, and soon garnered wide respect for his articles on public finance. When General Carmona approached him with the job of finance minister, Salazar accepted on one condition: that the spending of all government ministries fall under his discretion. The general agreed.

Salazar achieved enormous success at firing up the national economy. He severely curtailed government spending, raising taxes and balancing the budget during his first year. Unemployment decreased significantly. Salazar quickly became one of Carmona's star ministers. He also took on adjoining posts as other ministers resigned. In this way he consolidated power until Carmona eventually named him prime minister.

This is when Salazar set the tone for civilian life that would last for many decades to come. He drafted a new constitution around his New State ideals, which were partly modelled on the family as a political idea. Families had no organised internal strife so there was no need for unions or for political parties; a family had a head of household, who would determine where to spend the money. Naturally, Salazar saw himself as the father figure who would be running the family ship; he also saw the church as the 'mother', which would continue to fulfil society's thirst for spiritual values.

Under his authoritarian rule, he did bring stability and prosperity to the country, though at enormous cost: censorship, imprisonment and, in some cases, torture of political opponents. Among his most damning attributes was his attitude towards the working class. He believed in giving them a diet of 'fado, Fátima and football' to keep them happily compliant, but had no intention of bettering their lot; at the end of his rule, Portugal had the highest rate of illiteracy and tuberculosis in Western Europe, and women were still not allowed to vote. Given the socially backward condition of the nation when Salazar relinquished power, the advancements of the last 30 years seem all the more startling.

But it was something else that finally brought the Salazarist era to a close – decolonisation. Refusing to relinquish the colonies, he was faced with ever more costly and unpopular military expeditions. In 1961 Goa was occupied by India, and nationalists rose up in Angola. Guerrilla movements also appeared in Portuguese Guinea and Mozambique.

Salazar, however, didn't have to face the consequences. In 1968 he had a stroke, and died two years later.

1865	**1890**	**1900**
Portugal enjoys a period of peace and prosperity. Railways connect villages with Lisbon and Porto, now modern cities enriched by maritime trade. Significant advancements are made in agriculture, industry, public health and education.	Portugal takes a renewed interest in its African colonies. England, however, aims to control all of sub-Saharan Africa, and threatens Portugal with war. Cowed, Portugal withdraws from Central Africa, causing a crisis at home.	The republican movement gains force. The humiliating Africa issue is one among many grievances against the crown. Other complaints include rising unemployment and growing social inequalities.

His successor, Marcelo Caetano, failed to ease unrest. Military officers sympathetic to African freedom fighters – the officers had seen the horrible living conditions in which the colony lived beneath the Portuguese authorities – grew reluctant to fight colonial wars. Several hundred officers formed the Movimento das Forças Armadas (MFA), which on 25 April 1974 carried out a nearly bloodless coup, later nicknamed the Revolution of the Carnations (after victorious soldiers stuck carnations in their rifle barrels). Carnations are still a national symbol of freedom.

FROM REVOLUTION TO DEMOCRACY

Despite the coup's popularity, the following year saw unprecedented chaos. It began where the revolution had begun – in the African colonies. Independence was granted immediately to Guinea-Bissau, followed by the speedy decolonisation of the Cape Verde islands, São Tomé e Príncipe, Mozambique and Angola.

The transition wasn't smooth: civil war racked Angola, and East Timor, freshly liberated in 1975, was promptly invaded by Indonesia. Within Portugal, too, times were turbulent, with almost a million refugees from African colonies flooding into Portugal.

The country was an economic mess, with widespread strikes and a tangle of political ideas and parties. The communists and a radical wing of the MFA launched a revolutionary movement, nationalising firms and services. Peasant farmers seized land to establish communal farms that failed because of in-fighting and poor management. While revolutionaries held sway in the south, the conservative north was led by Mário Soares and his Partido Socialista (PS; Socialist Party).

It took a more moderate government, formed in 1975, to unite the country after a coup by radical leftists was crushed. At last, the revolution had ended.

THE ROCKY ROAD TO STABILITY

Portugal was soon committed to a blend of socialism and democracy, with a powerful president, an elected assembly and a Council of the Revolution to control the armed forces.

Soares' minority government soon faltered, prompting a series of attempts at government by coalitions and nonparty candidates, including Portugal's first female prime minister, Maria de Lourdes Pintassilgo. In the 1980 parliamentary elections a new political force took the reins – the conservative Aliança Democrática (AD; Democratic Alliance), led by Francisco Sá Carneiro.

After Carneiro's almost immediate (and suspicious) death in a plane crash, Francisco Pinto Balsemão stepped into his shoes. He implemented plans to join the European Community (EC).

The big-budget Portuguese film *Capitães de Abril* (April Captains; 2000), directed by Maria de Medeiros, is a must-see for those interested in the events of 1974's Revolution of the Carnations.

Portugal only narrowly missed claiming Europe's first woman prime minister: in 1979 Margaret Thatcher snatched the honour just three months before Maria de Lourdes Pintassilgo (1930–2004).

1908	**1910**	**1932**
The Braganças try to silence antimonarchist sentiment by shutting down opposition newspapers, exiling dissidents and brutally suppressing demonstrations, but fail. In January, King Carlos and his eldest son, Luís Filipe, are assassinated.	King Carlos' younger son, the 18-year-old Prince Manuel, takes the throne but is soon ousted. Portugal is declared a republic. Chaos rules, however, and the country will see an astounding 45 different governments over the next 16 years.	António de Oliveira Salazar seizes power. Under his government, the Portuguese economy grows but at enormous human cost. Salazar uses censorship, imprisonment and torture to silence his opponents.

The law allowing all Portuguese women to vote was only established in 1975.

It was partly to keep the EC and the International Monetary Fund (IMF) happy that a new coalition government under Soares and Balsemão implemented a strict programme of economic modernisation. Not surprisingly, the belt-tightening wasn't popular. The loudest critics were Soares' right-wing partners in the Partido Social Democrata (PSD; Social Democrat Party), led by the dynamic Aníbal Cavaco Silva. Communist trade unions also organised strikes, and the appearance of urban terrorism by the radical left-wing Forças Populares de 25 Abril (FP-25) deepened unrest.

In 1986, after nine years of negotiations, Portugal joined the EC. Flush with new funds, it raced ahead of its neighbours with unprecedented economic growth. The new cash flow also gave Prime Minister Cavaco Silva the power to push ahead with radical economic reforms. These included labour law reforms that left many disenchanted workers; the 1980s were crippled by strikes – including one involving 1.5 million workers – though all to no avail. The controversial legislation was eventually passed.

The economic growth, however, wouldn't last. In 1992 EC trade barriers fell and Portugal suddenly faced new competition. Fortunes dwindled as recession set in, and disillusionment grew as Europe's single market revealed the backwardness of Portugal's agricultural sector.

Strikes, crippling corruption charges and student demonstrations over rising fees only undermined the PSD further, leading to Cavaco Silva's resignation in 1995.

PORTUGAL TODAY

A Small Death in Lisbon (1999), by Robert Wilson, is an award-winning thriller that moves between 1941 and 1999, showing the impacts of WWII and the Revolution of the Carnations on the Portuguese psyche.

The general elections in 1995 brought new faces to power, with the socialist António Guterres running the show. Despite hopes for a different and less conservative administration, it was business as usual, with Guterres maintaining budgetary rigour that qualified Portugal for the European Economic & Monetary Union (EMU) in 1998. Indeed, for a while Portugal was a star EMU performer with steady economic growth that helped Guterres win a second term. But it couldn't last. Corruption scandals, rising inflation and a faltering economy soon spelt disaster. Portugal slipped into economic stagnation. The result saw a political swing to the centre-right, with Guterres resigning just before his party was squashed in the 2002 general elections by the PSD.

On the international stage, Portugal received some worldwide criticism for hosting the Iraq War Conference in the Azores in 2003 (attended by George W Bush, Tony Blair and Spain's José María Aznar). Initially, Portugal contributed a small force to Iraq (later withdrawn in 2005), which made then Prime Minister Lopes extremely unpopular at home and ultimately contributed to his political downfall.

Meanwhile, 2004 was a time for Portugal's success as host nation in the European Football Championships, and the refocus on sport did wonders for the country's morale, despite its 1-0 loss in the final to Greece.

1943	1961	1974
Portugal, supposedly neutral during WWII, becomes a crossroads for intelligence activities of both Allied and Axis operatives. Salazar works both sides, selling tungsten to Nazi Germany while allowing Britain use of Azorean airfields.	The last vestiges of Portugal's empire begin to crumble as India seizes Goa and other Portuguese possessions. Independence movements are underway in the former African colonies of Angola, Mozambique and Guinea-Bissau.	Army officers overthrow Salazar's successor in the Revolution of the Carnations. Portugal veers to the left, as huge sectors of the economy are nationalised. Communists and moderates struggle for power in the unstable country.

Parliamentary elections in 2005 brought to power socialist José Sócrates, a young, tough-talking legislator who sought to reposition the PS as part of the modern left. His goal upon taking office was to revitalise the economy and tackle unemployment. He cut government spending by slashing pensions, raising the retirement age (from 60 to 65) and privatising public services – all in the effort to reduce one of Europe's biggest budget deficits. The reforms prompted waves of protests by workers claiming Socrates was destroying social security.

Responding to calls from Brussels to rein in the burgeoning government deficit, Sócrates managed to lower it to 2.7% of GDP – achieving its sub-3% goal a year ahead of schedule. Sócrates has been less successful at spurring growth, and the country still limps along under stagnant growth.

In 2007 Sócrates took over the rotating presidency of the EU. In an unusual turn of events, his role brought him face-to-face with his former political opponent José Manuel Barroso, who was now serving as president of the European Commission (Portugal's first appointee to the post). Together, the two brought much attention to Portugal. They championed the rights of smaller states, oversaw the drafting of the Treaty of Lisbon (an agreement designed to bring more unity to the EU) and played a prominent role in discussions about climate change and energy-reduction targets among EU members.

The Political Science Resources website (www .psr.keele.ac.uk/area/por tugal.htm) has good links for politics and current events as well as history.

Sócrates, a former environment minister, set ambitious goals for Portugal in the realm of renewable energy. Under his government, enormous wind farms and solar power plants opened, along with experimental technologies like the wave power plant north of Porto (see p80 for more on these green initiatives). In 2008 Sócrates partnered with Renault and Nissan to sponsor a nationwide network of recharging stations for the electric cars the companies would release worldwide in 2012. Socrates said Portugal was willing to act as 'a laboratory for future electric cars'.

Other big news during Sócrates' term includes major improvements in the education system. In 2008, Portugal purchased 500,000 computers from Intel in a massive boost to its 'e-school' program, signalling Portugal's goals to transform itself into a knowledge-based economy. The same year also marked a ban on smoking in public indoor spaces (including restaurants). On a more contentious topic, Sócrates put the topic of abortion before voters in a referendum. Although 60% voted to legalise abortion, the low voter turnout was not enough to overturn the law outright, and the issue remained in limbo, though Sócrates vowed to convince parliament to change the law.

1986	**1998**	**2007**
In a narrow second-round victory, Mário Soares is elected president of Portugal, becoming its first civilian head of state in 60 years. The same year, Portugal joins the EC along with Spain.	Lisbon hosts Expo 98, a World's Fair that showcases new developments in the capital, including Santiago Calatrava's cutting-edge train station, Europe's largest oceanarium and its longest bridge (the Ponte de Vasco da Gama).	Portugal takes over the rotating EU presidency. The treaty of Lisbon is drafted, an agreement that aims to give new coherence to the EU.

The Culture

THE NATIONAL PSYCHE

Portugal has undergone dramatic changes since the days of Salazar a generation ago, with far greater opportunities, politically and economically, for the majority. The Portuguese identity, however, still has many features reaching back through the years connecting these modern EU citizens with their seafaring past.

In particular, the Portuguese like to indulge in a little *saudade*, the nostalgic, often deeply melancholic longing for better times. The idea is most eloquently expressed in bittersweet fado music – traditional Portuguese singing with yearning laments that express fatalism and exquisite frustration about matters that cannot be changed.

Many parts of Portugal – especially in the north – remain very traditional and conservative. Extremism is definitely not encouraged. While people are friendly, honest, unhurried and gracious, they can also be very formal and polite, and religious festivals and pilgrimages are taken very seriously.

The Salazar years did nothing to wipe out Portugal's fierce sense of national identity, which was forged through a plucky history of expelling numerous invaders and a seafaring tradition in which Portugal once led the world. These days the national pride also finds expression through football, which is avidly followed at both local and national level.

The nation's huge outflow of emigrants and influx of immigrants has inevitably given the national character a certain fluidity, as has its geographic diversity; the colder northern reaches seem to breed a tougher, more reserved character, while the scorching plains in the south encourage an open, sunny outlook. The Portuguese are not averse to mocking their compatriots with blunt stereotypes. For example, the sleeves-up people of Porto recite an old saying about the country's biggest cities: 'Porto works, Coimbra studies, Braga prays and Lisbon plays' – they call their southern counterparts Moors.

However, it is the urban-rural divide that is most dramatic. It's easy to see Portugal as a dynamic, forward-looking nation when you're in one of its cities, but the contrast in the countryside could not be bigger. As their young desert them, many tiny rural communities almost seem to cling all the more fervently to the old ways.

> You won't get a better insider glimpse of the harsh life of 20th-century rural Portugal than in *The Creation of the World* and *Tales from the Mountain* by Miguel Torga, a renowned writer from Trás-os-Montes.

LIFESTYLE

Village life is an integral part of Portuguese society. This holds true in traditional rural settlements in the north, where market day provides the chance to swap gossip, and elderly neighbours mingle on the main squares. In cities, each individual neighbourhood becomes a kind of village – with a web of close-knit communities spread across the urban landscape. Whether inside Lisbon's Alfama district or Porto's Ribeira, lifelong neighbourhood residents stick together – celebrating saint's-day festivals together and commemorating weddings and births – while viewing outsiders with some small degree of suspicion.

Within the larger orbit of community, the family plays an even more essential role, and is often described as the pillar of Portuguese society. Traditionally, the family was patriarchal, with the father making the major decisions for the household. Indeed, during Salazar's days, the head of the household (invariably a man) was the only one allowed to vote, and women remained second-class citizens. In some ways, there have been major advances, with greater opportunities in education and employment for women (see p49), though stereotypes unfortunately persist. The 'conventional' family has also undergone some changes. Couples are marrying later, if at all, as the stigma of living together or having children outside of wedlock has diminished. Women are having fewer children than they did a generation ago. The birth rate in the 1960s was around 3.1 per couple compared to 1.4 today.

The effect of this declining birth rate is obvious to anyone who travels around the country. Some villages seem to be populated with no one under the age of 65. Those who do grow up there don't stick around for long, fleeing to the city in search of better jobs. Partly as a result of this flight Portugal's interior remains staunchly traditional, and pious *romarias* (religious festivals in honour of a patron saint), fairs and markets are a big part of life.

Living standards have risen significantly in the last three decades. There is much more mobility for the working class and the middle class is a heftier demographic – and growing. Despite this, Portugal still lags far behind its neighbours. Worker pensions are low, with a small safety net for those in need of government assistance. Minimum wage is the lowest in Western Europe (at €437 per month in 2006) and the average annual salary (€14,720 in Portugal compared to €20,420 in Spain and the EU average of €22,000 in 2007) doesn't leave much room for unexpected surprises. About 18% of the population lives below the poverty line (compared with 6% of the population in France).

In terms of personal liberty, it's hard to imagine now that only decades ago the Portuguese could not vote freely, or dress or write uninhibitedly, or even own a cigarette lighter without first having a state licence. In light of this, it's extraordinary to consider the government's recent softer drug laws (aimed at rehabilitating rather than criminalising), its pioneering schemes for public access to the internet, and the widespread tolerance shown towards the southern coast's hedonistic resorts. Acceptance of gay and lesbian lifestyles largely depends on your location (see p497).

> The Portuguese are among the world's heaviest drinkers, according to a survey by – we are assured unbiased – French researchers. Apparently the home of port imbibes 11.2L of pure alcohol per person every year.

ECONOMY

While economic growth in Portugal remained above the EU average for much of the 1990s, it hit a speed bump in 2000, and has been in a serious slump ever since. Its GDP shrank in 2003, and recovered slightly in subsequent years, but still only grew an average of 0.7% between 2002 and 2006, making it one of the lowest in the EU (the *Economist* even described Portugal in 2007 as 'the new sick man of Europe'). At present, Portugal's per capita GDP lags behind that of Slovenia, Malta, the Czech Republic and, since 2002, Greece (the latter is a particularly sore point since losing to the Greeks in the 2004 European Football Championship final, which Portugal hosted).

Unemployment has also risen steadily over the last five years, lingering around 7.7% since 2005, although in some areas it remains more than twice that. To add to the country's financial woes, the budget deficit and consumer prices have continued to rise, while wages increased only slightly. All this has made for a rather unhappy population who have all the more reason to give in to a bit of *saudade* (see opposite).

> Despite a high budget deficit in 2005 (6% of GDP), Portugal, through drastic belt-tightening, reined it in to below 3% (the EU requirement) in 2007, one year ahead of schedule.

The government has certainly had its work cut out for it, trying to walk a fine line between keeping the EU happy (ultimatum from Brussels: 'Reign in your budget deficit!') and helping its own citizens. As is often the case, economic priorities trumped social concerns, and the government has adopted austere measures to bring the country economic equanimity. Measures it undertook included raising the value-added tax (VAT) from 19% to 21%, initiating a hiring and promotion freeze on various parts of the public sector and reforming pensions, raising the minimum age for retirement from 60 to 65 – never a pretty topic in a country with 17% of the population over the age of 65.

Meanwhile, Portugal's neighbour and long-time nemesis Spain has continued to outperform Portugal economically over the last two decades. As the Portuguese look eastward, they can't help but ask, with a twinge of envy, 'Why aren't we doing as well as them?'. Portugal still lumbers beneath a significant trade deficit; it imported €25 billion more than it exported in 2007. Portugal's leading market for both imports and exports is (of course) Spain, though Germany, France, Italy and the UK are also players. The Portuguese economy is still based on traditional industries such as textiles, clothing, footwear, cork, paper products, wine and glassware.

Apart from Lisbon, the biggest single community of Portuguese is found in Paris.

Agriculture, once a mainstay of the economy, today accounts for 8% of GDP, and employs 10% of Portugal's workforce. The old-fashioned approach to certain sectors (including agriculture) is one of the reasons why Portugal has difficulty competing with cheaper Eastern European countries that are the popular new kids on the EU block.

The service industry, particularly tourism, is playing an increasingly important role, and certainly more changes are underfoot as Portugal stumbles its way towards the light of economic stability.

POPULATION

Portugal's population breakdown has seen tumultuous changes in the last few decades. The country's emigration rate has long been among Europe's highest, but its immigration rate shot up during the mid-1970s when around 500,000 to 800,000 African *retornados* (refugees) immigrated from former Portuguese colonies.

The nation of explorers is still on the move. An estimated five million Portuguese live abroad; some 100,000 emigrate each year – though many return.

They later came from war-torn Angola and Mozambique, followed by others from Guinea-Bissau and São Tomé e Príncipe. Officially, in 2006, there were just over 400,000 legal immigrants in Portugal – the majority from Africa – plus many illegal immigrants. Africans compose Portugal's largest ethnic group (including 68,000 Cape Verdeans), with especially big communities in Lisbon.

Another influx resulting from Portugal's empire building is of Brazilians, and some have now put down roots here. There's a small resident Roma population and increasing numbers of immigrant workers from Central and Eastern Europe – particularly from Ukraine, with 43,000 Ukrainians living in Portugal. One of the biggest inflows in recent years has been sun-seekers from Western Europe, buying properties and settling in southern regions.

One of the finest all-round books about the Portuguese is Marion Kaplan's perceptive The Portuguese: The Land & Its People (2006). Ranging from literature to emigrants, its female perspective seems appropriate for a country whose men so often seem to be abroad.

Most native Portuguese share typically Mediterranean features, such as brown eyes and dark hair. The majority still live in rural areas, such as in the Minho, one of Portugal's poorest and most densely populated regions, and the ever more crowded Algarve coast. But the urban population has increased dramatically since the 1960s, from 22% of the total to over 50%; smaller villages are fast disappearing as their youth move away and ageing populations fizzle out.

SPORT

Football (soccer) is not a game here: it's a national obsession. Life – male life, at any rate – and often the national economy come to a near standstill during any big match, with bar and restaurant TVs showing nothing else. During big events, like the World Cup and the European Football Championship, many towns put up big-screen TVs on the main plazas so hundreds can gather to watch the games.

Boozy postmatch celebrations are a tradition in themselves, with fans taking to the streets, honking car horns, setting off fireworks and gridlocking entire town centres until the wee hours.

The most recent bout of football hysteria happened in 2008, as Portugal competed in the UEFA European Football Championship. Unlike its successful march in 2004 (when it hosted the event and made it all the way to the finals), 2008 proved challenging. Star players like Ronaldo (one of the luminaries of Manchester United) and Deco couldn't overcome Germany in the quarterfinals. Even before the Euro was finished, however, Portugal's star coach, Brazilian Felipe Scolari, announced he was leaving the team to take over as head coach at Chelsea FC. (Not surprisingly, one of his first signings was Deco – signed from Barcelona.) Succeeding him is Carlos Queiroz, the former assistant coach at Manchester United, who proudly took the reins over his home country's team.

Football madness well and truly took hold in 2004 when Portugal hosted the Euro, the biggest sporting event ever staged there. Sports authorities were counting on the tournament to provide a big shot in the arm for Portuguese football, and they got it. Local clubs, with mounting debts and ageing stadiums, had long watched the country's star players earn a fortune abroad, but sure enough, the authorities set about building and sprucing up Portuguese stadiums and building vital new transport links to the venues.

On a national level, the story of Portuguese football is mainly about Lisbon and Porto. Although 16 teams compete for top honours each year, the big three – Lisbon's Sporting Clube de Portugal and Sport Lisboa e Benfica and Porto's Futebol Clube do Porto – have among them won every national championship but two since the 1920s (Porto's upstart Boavista Futebol Club briefly broke the spell in 2001). Regional titles haven't been

The *jogo do pau* is the old Portuguese martial art of staff fighting, which originated in the north, and is still practised in some parts of Portugal and the Azores.

The website www
.portugoal.net has excellent info on Portugal's football clubs, player stats and team standings as well as in-depth articles on Portuguese players abroad.

BULLFIGHTING

Love it or loathe it, bullfighting is a national institution. First recorded in Portugal a staggering 2000 years ago by a Roman historian, it was honed in the 12th century, when the tourada (bullfight) became a way to maintain military fitness and prepare nobles for battle on horseback. But the gory death of a nobleman in 1799 resulted in a less bloodthirsty version, in which the bull's horns are covered in leather or capped with metal balls and the animal is not killed publicly.

A typical tourada starts with an enraged bull charging into the ring towards a *cavaleiro*, a dashing horseman dressed in 18th-century finery and plumed tricorn hat. The *cavaleiro* sizes up the animal as his team of *peões de brega* (footmen) distract and provoke the bull with capes. Then, with superb horsemanship, he gallops within inches of the bull's horns and plants several barbed *bandarilha* (spears) in the angry creature's neck.

The next phase, the *pega*, features eight brave (read: foolhardy) young *forcados* dressed in breeches, white stockings and short jackets, who face the weakened bull barehanded. The leader swaggers towards the bull, provoking it to charge. Bearing the brunt of the attack, he throws himself onto the animal's head and grabs the horns while his mates rush in to grab the beast, often being tossed in all directions. Their success wraps up the contest and the bull is led out. Though Portuguese bullfighting rules prohibit a public kill, the animals are killed after the show – you just don't witness the final blow.

Bullfighting remains popular here despite opposition from international animal-welfare organisations and Portugal's own anti-bullfighting lobby, the **Liga Portuguesa dos Direitos dos Animais** (LPDA; Portuguese League for Animal Rights; ☎ 214 578 413; www.lpda.pt, in Portuguese).

The season runs from March or late April to October. The most traditional contests take place in bull-breeding Ribatejo province, especially in Santarém (p316) during the June fair, and in the otherwise-unexceptional Vila Franca de Xira during the town's July and October festivals. Frequent touradas in the Algarve and Lisbon are more tourist-oriented. There are also unusual festivals like the Vaca das Cordas (p453), where a bull on a rope runs wild through the streets of Ponte de Lima.

lacking either for the country's top teams, with the Futebol Clube do Porto picking up the 2004 European Champions League title.

The season lasts from September to May, and almost every village and town finds enough players to make up a team. Major teams and their stadiums are noted under bigger towns in this book.

MULTICULTURALISM

Portugal's emigration rate has long been one of Europe's highest, but in the 1970s the tables were turned and the country was flooded with *retornados*. They generally integrated exceptionally well into Portuguese society, with many picking up work in the booming construction industry. Their culture and music has also helped to shape that of the Portuguese, most notably in the kicking African beats still popular in Lisbon clubs. Similarly, the big Brazilian population in Portugal has helped promote its mellow musical tastes here.

However, it's not all jazz and funk in Lisbon's multicultural society. While Portugal has one of the lowest percentages of avowed racists in the EU, at times racism does rear its ugly head in the capital. Gang-related tensions between Angolans and Cape Verdeans have exploded there. Living conditions of many immigrants (who live in *bairros de lata* or 'tin shanty towns' on the edge of the city) are a depressing indication of the lack of government and national attention to the Afro-Portuguese community.

A lower-profile prejudice is sometimes present in rural Portugal and rails against outsiders, especially the Roma population, although some people from small towns can also be wary of tourists. The latest stream of immigrants has been Eastern Europeans, who work in construction jobs and other labour-intensive industries. There's also no slowdown in the flow of expats from Britain and Germany into the southern Algarve; locals often regard them simply as long-stay tourists.

But it's comforting to note that by international standards none of the teething troubles associated with Portuguese immigrant populations are serious. The country seems to take each new wave in its stride.

RELIGION

Christianity has been a pivotal force in shaping Portugal's history, and religion still plays a big part in the lives of its people. The country is famous for its impressive pilgrimages and *romarias,* which continue unabated and are celebrated with a special fervour in the north. One of Europe's most important centres of pilgrimage is in Portugal at Fátima (p310), where up to 300,000 pilgrims congregate every May and October. See p21 for a long list of Portugal's religious celebrations.

However, it's not just through rousing events and festivals that the Portuguese demonstrate their faith. Around half of northern Portugal's population still attends Sunday Mass, as do more than a quarter in Lisbon – though there are noticeably fewer churchgoers on the southern coast.

In the more traditional north, Catholic traditions often mingle with curious folk practices. For example, Trás-os-Montes is renowned for its wild and untamed dancing (p491), while Amarante's patron saint is associated with the swapping of phallic cakes (p411). In Tomar, the singular Festa dos Tabuleiros (p321) also has colourful pagan roots. And on a hill above Ponte de Lima is a chapel (p452) dedicated to Santo Ovídio, patron saint of ears, with walls covered in votive offerings of wax ears. Similar chapels, adorned with wax limbs of all kinds, can be found even inside churches, revealing a pragmatic tolerance by the Catholic Church.

Statistically, around 85% of the population is Roman Catholic, although the number of practising Catholics is steadily dropping. Other Christian

Since traditional bullfighting is outlawed in the US, Portuguese emigrants in central California invented a bloodless bullfight using Velcro-tipped spears. Read more on this bizarre sport at www.ranch cardoso.biz.

One of the more unusual rituals celebrated around Easter is the *enterro do bacalhau* (burying of the codfish), which marks the end of Lent (a time when much fish is eaten).

denominations make up much of the remaining population, along with many Muslims and a small number of Jews.

WOMEN IN PORTUGAL

Women didn't earn full voting rights until 1975, making Portugal one of the last pockets in the northern hemisphere to grant universal suffrage (women in Afghanistan, by comparison, gained the right to vote in 1963). This was one of the many sad legacies of Salazar. In addition to lacking the right to vote, women did not have the authority to administer their own property or to leave the country without a father's or a husband's permission, and if a woman married a foreigner she automatically forfeited her citizenship, along with her inheritance. It wasn't until 1969 that a married woman was allowed to have a passport or leave the country without her husband's consent.

Portugal has come a long ways since the dark days of the dictatorship. Equality is now enshrined in the civil code. Of students enrolled in higher education in 2005, 56% were women, and women make up about 47% of the working population. In total about 70% of working-age women are employed (compared with the EU average of 63%). Although women haven't achieved equality in professional occupations, the gap is narrowing. At last count, 40% of physicians were female, with a similar figure for lawyers.

In politics, 2006 was a watershed year for women. The parliament passed a quota law stipulating that of candidates for the Portuguese parliament, the European parliament and local elections, 33% must be women. Although initially vetoed by President Anibal Cavaco Silva, the bill was later amended and signed into law. Today, women representatives make up about 22% of parliament.

Women enjoy just protection under the legal system, with cases of rape, domestic violence and sexual harassment punishable by imprisonment. Traditional attitudes, however, still discourage abused women from using the legal system, and domestic abuse remains prevalent. Of the more than 13,000 crimes reported annually to the Association for Victim Support, roughly 80% involve domestic violence.

Despite the advancements, gender stereotypes continue to persist, keeping women from playing a more central role in society. Despite being among the first countries in Europe to elect a female prime minister in 1979, women are still seriously underrepresented in senior-management positions in both public and private sectors. Women earn about 30% less than men in both professional and working-class jobs.

One of the more contentious topics in recent years was the abortion debate. The decision to legalise or not was put before the public in a referendum in 2007. Despite a low voter turnout (43.6% of eligible voters), around 60% voted in favour of the proposal, giving women the right to an abortion up to the 10th week of pregnancy. Because the voter turnout was below 50% (the requirement for passing the proposal into law), the issue hung in legal limbo, though Prime Minister José Socrates vowed to get parliament to pass the law. Until then, abortions were illegal and women faced up to three years in prison for having an abortion, while the one providing it faced up to eight years in prison.

ARTS
Literature

Portuguese literature has long been moulded by foreign influences – notably that of Spain – but has retained its individuality throughout. Two major styles dominate: lyric poetry and realistic fiction. The country's most outstanding literary figure is Luís Vaz de Camões (1524–80), a poet who enjoyed little fame or fortune in his lifetime. Only after his death was his genius recognised, thanks largely to an epic poem, *Os Lusiados* (The

---

Maria Velho da Costa is one of the three authors of *Novas Cartas Portuguesas* (The Three Marias: New Portuguese Letters; 1972), whose modern feminist interpretation of the 17th-century *Letters of a Portuguese Nun* so shocked the Salazar regime that its authors were put on trial. The story was made into a film by Jesus Franco in 1977.

With more than 210 million speakers worldwide, Portuguese is among the top 10 of the world's most widely spoken languages – a considerable achievement given the tiny size of Portugal.

TOP FACES IN PORTUGAL

Port and famous navigators may be the country's best-known produce, but there's much more to Portugal than just fortified wines and unpronounceable explorers. Today's stars are making headlines all over the map, in the fields of art, sport, filmmaking, literature and music. Here are a few names to look out for:

Ronaldo: More beloved by Portuguese teenage girls than even Justin Timberlake, the handsome footballer is one of the star players for the national team; he's also a peak performer for Manchester United (though enjoys less than universal love in Britain).

Mariza: The Mozambique-born singer (p92) helped reintroduce the world to fado, by means of an eclectic global sound; the raw power of her voice is undisputed.

Saramago: The prolific and wildly discursive octogenarian writer José Saramago won the Nobel Prize for literature in 1998. An avowed communist and anti-imperialist, his musings sometimes get him in trouble.

Rego: Paula Rego, now in her 70s, is a major presence in the art world. She is considered one of the great early champions of painting from a female perspective, and her work hangs in London's National Portrait Gallery and in Lisbon's Centro de Arte Moderna (p118).

Oliveira: Born in 1908, Manoel de Oliveira still maintains a high profile in the world of cinema. Throughout a very long career, he's made over 40 films, including a handful with Catherine Deneuve and John Malkovich.

Siza: The Pritzker-prize winning architect, Álvaro Siza Vieira is a household name among design followers. Some of his ambitious projects include the wild Museu de Arte Contemporânea (p392) and the handsome Boa Nova Casa-Chá (p401).

Cruz: Marisa Cruz's face is more widely seen (if not always known) than almost any other Portuguese. The model and actress has appeared on the cover of top fashion magazines and is a former Miss Portugal.

Instituto Camões' website (www.instituto-camoes.pt/cvc) presents background information on Portuguese language, literature and theatre, plus potted biographies of the country's most important authors and poets.

The Anarchist Banker (1997), edited by Eugénio Lisboa, is a collection of late-19th- and 20th-century fiction from Portugal. Big names include Eça de Queirós, Antonio Patricio, Irene Lisboa, Fernando Pessoa and José Rodrigues Migueis.

Lusiads; 1572). It tells of Vasco da Gama's 1497 sea voyage to India, but it's also a superbly lyrical paean to the Portuguese spirit, written when Portugal was still one of the most powerful countries in the Western world. Four centuries after its humble publication, it's considered the national epic and the poet a national hero. Indeed, some still make the pilgrimage to see his tomb inside the Mosteiro dos Jerónimos (p120).

In the 19th century a tide of romanticism flooded Portuguese literature. A prominent figure in this movement was poet, playwright and romantic novelist Almeida Garrett (1799–1854), who devoted his life to stimulating political awareness through his writings. Among his works is the novel *Viagens na Minha Terra* (Travels in My Homeland; 1846), an allegory of contemporary political events, presented as a home-grown travelogue. Despite being Portugal's most talented playwright since 16th-century court dramatist Gil Vicente, Garrett was exiled for his political liberalism.

Garrett's contemporary Alexandre Herculano (also exiled) was meanwhile continuing the long Portuguese tradition of historical literature, which flourished most strongly during the Age of Discoveries. Herculano produced a vast body of work, most notably his magnum opus, *História de Portugal* (1846). Towards the end of the 19th century several important writers emerged, among them the ever-popular José Maria Eça de Queirós, who introduced a stark realism to Portuguese literature with his powerful novels and more-entertaining narratives, such as *Os Maias* (The Maya; 1888).

Fernando Pessoa (1888–1935), author of the 1934 *Mensagem* (Message), is posthumously regarded as the most extraordinary poet of his generation. His four different poet-personalities, which he referred to as heteronyms, created four distinct strains of poetry and prose. *A Centenary Pessoa* (1995), published in English, provides a fascinating insight into his work.

However, Portugal's creative energy was soon to be short-circuited. The Salazar dictatorship, spanning much of the early modern era, effectively buried freedom of expression. Several writers suffered during this period, including the poet and storyteller Miguel Torga (1907–95), whose background in Trás-os-Montes brought a radical individualism to his writings, so much so that several of his writings were banned.

One of the most notable writers who survived and often documented this repressive era was José Cardoso Pires (1925–98), a popular novelist and playwright whose finest work, *Balada da Praia dos Cães* (Ballad of Dog's Beach; 1982), is a gripping thriller based on a real political assassination in the Salazar era. Prominent poets of the time were Jorge de Sena (1919–78), a humanist thinker who also wrote much fiction and criticism; and David Mourão-Ferreira (1927–97), whose works include the novel *Un Amor Feliz* (Lucky in Love; 1986). In Portugal's former colonies (particularly Brazil), writers such as Nobel Prize–winner Jorge Amado (1912–2001) have also made their mark on modern Portuguese-language literature.

Today's literary scene is largely dominated by two names: José Saramago (b 1922) and António Lobo Antunes (b 1942). Saramago, who won the Nobel Prize for Literature in 1998, is king of the discursive, brilliantly funny and politically astute novel. Among his best work is *Memorial do Convento* (Baltazar and Blimunda; 1982), an imaginative love story set in the turbulent 18th century. *Cegueira* (Blindness; 1995), a modern-day fable in which everyone in the world goes blind, is an even darker work revealing the human condition in a most wretched and horrific state – themes that recur in his many novels, along with a mild touch of redemption.

Antunes produces magical, fast-paced prose, often with dark undertones and vast historical sweeps. His novel *O Regresso das Caravelas* (The Return of the Caravels; 2002) features a surreal time warp, where 15th-century navigators meet 1970s soldiers and contemporary Lisboêtas. His *Manual dos Inquisidores* (The Inquisitors' Manual; 1996) is a dark look at the run-up to and aftermath of the 1974 revolution.

Hot names on the late-20th-century poetry front included Pedro Tamen and Sophia de Mello Breyner (awarded the Portuguese Camões Prize in 1999), the latter finding fame both as a poet and as a writer of children's stories, using the sea as her central theme. Up-and-coming novelists include Ana Gusmão, whose stories are set in urban landscapes and reflect conflicts in relationships, cultures and traditions; and José Riço Direitinho, whose haunting novel *Breviário das Más Inclinações* (The Book of Bad Habits; 1994) is peopled by folk memories, superstitious peasants and rural traditions. Also consider the work of Mario de Carvalho, who won the Pegasus Prize for Literature with his gripping novel *Deus Passeando Pela Brisa da Tarde* (A God Strolling in the Cool of an Evening; 1996), which is set in Roman Portugal.

Look out for the beautiful novels of Lídia Jorge, whose book *O Vale da Paixao* (The Painter of Birds; 1995), a tale about an Algarve family split by emigration, won her several Portuguese and international awards.

Cinema

Portugal has a distinguished history of film-making, though poor foreign distribution has left the world largely ignorant of it. The only internationally famous director is Manoel de Oliveira, described by the British *Guardian* newspaper as 'the most eccentric and the most inspired of cinema's world masters'. The ex-racing driver has made dozens of films, with all except three made after he turned 60. Despite the flurry of activity in his later years, one of his earliest films still remains one of his best. *Aniki-Bóbó* (1942), set in the director's hometown of Porto, delves into the world of childhood and

One of José Cardoso Pires' novels, *O Delfim* (The Dauphin), set at the end of Salazar's reign, has been made into a great melodramatic film (2002); Fernando Lopez directed.

The Sin of Father Amaro is a powerful 19th-century novel by Eça de Queirós. The book is set in Portugal, though it was relocated for a popular Mexican film, *El Crimen del padre Amaro* (2002).

You can find a wealth of information on Portuguese films, companies, directors and upcoming events on the multilingual website of the Instituto de Cinema Audiovisual e Multimédia: www.icam.pt.

conjures up the magic and folly of the human experience, as seen through the eyes of children.

Half a century later, Oliveira explored quite different themes in *The Convent,* starring Catherine Deneuve and John Malkovich. It's set in a Portuguese convent, follows Malkovich and Deneuve as they travel to Portugal to research the theory that Shakespeare is Spanish-Jewish. Also of gossipy interest, this Portugal connection has led to Malkovich being a player in several Lisbon businesses – namely the Lux nightclub and Bica do Sapato restaurant. Malkovich and Deneuve also appear in the director's French-language *Je Rentre à la Maison* (I'm Going Home; 2002), set in Paris. Oliveira's *Viagem ao Princípio do Mundo* (Voyage to the Beginning of the World; 1997) is a deceptively simple road movie that explores Portugal's rural past. It's a melancholy meditation on ageing and also tells us a great deal about its director. One of his latest films (made when he was 98!), *Belle Toujours,* pays homage to Luís Buñuel's erotic masterpiece *Belle de Jour* (1967), revisiting the characters and their unfulfilled ambitions from the original film.

For a captivating portrait of Lisbon, there's no better film than Wim Wenders' sweet, meandering *A Lisbon Story* (1994). It follows a sound engineer who goes in search of a missing director, discovering the city through the footage his friend left behind. Some of the most memorable scenes take place in the villagelike Alfama, with a lush soundtrack (and supporting roles) by musical group Madredeus.

Although his body of work is small, the director António da Cunha Telles has made some evocative films and documentaries. Once part of the *cinema novo* movement, he abandoned filmmaking in the late '60s, owing to a lack of commercial success. Over the next few decades, he made only a few films, most recently *Kiss Me* (2004), a dark story of small-town life in Salazar's Portugal. It's beautifully photographed in the Algarve, and stars the model-actress Marisa Cruz.

Alongside the older film-makers, a new generation of directors has now emerged, producing works that are often provocative and harrowing, exposing the darker side of Portugal. Ground-breaking films include those by Pedro Costa and Teresa Villaverde, whose 1999 film, *Os Mutantes* (The Mutants), is a disturbing work about unwanted youngsters.

The country's best-known actress is Maria de Medeiros, who turned director with her *Capitães de Abril* (April Captains; 2000), based on the 1974 Revolution of the Carnations. Significantly, this was funded by the Instituto de Cinema Audiovisual e Multimédia (ICAM; Institute for Cinema Audiovisuals & Multimedia), which has grown more daring in its approach. Other up-and-coming female directors include Catarina Ruivo.

Portugal's talent for dark social commentaries continued past the millennium. Another directorial name to emerge in this genre is João Canijo, whose films *Ganhar a Vida* (Get a Life; 2001), about a Portuguese émigré in France, and *Noite Escura* (In the Darkness of the Night; 2003), set around Portugal's seedy rural nightlife, have caused waves internationally. If you can track it down, the hard-hitting film *A Passagem da Noite* (Night Passage; 2003) by Luís Filipe Rocha, about a raped girl who discovers she is pregnant, is also good, if harrowing.

Another film with tragic overtones is *O Milagre Segundo Salomé* (The Miracle According to Salomé; 2004), a film about a gold-hearted prostitute who's swept into a tumultuous world in early 20th-century Portugal. The apparitions at Fátima and political corruption are all part of the backdrop of Mário Barroso's moving tale.

Playing out on a decidedly more modern canvas is the award-winning *Alice* (2005). This affecting if slow-moving film, directed by Marco Martins,

Ossos (Bones; 1998), directed by Pedro Costa, is a dark and disturbing film about life in a creole Lisbon slum. Not for the faint-hearted.

Terra Estrangeira (A Foreign Land; 1995), directed by Walter Salles and Daniela Thomas, is a modern film-noir thriller that jumps between São Paolo and Lisbon at a time when Brazilians were leaving the country in droves.

follows one man's quest to find his missing daughter amid the cacophony of urban life. Lisbon functions as a powerful set piece in Martins' hands, with a wash of blue cinematography and a minimalist score.

Unfortunately, many Portuguese films are hard to find, with extremely limited distribution outside the country. This makes it all the more worthwhile to catch the work of Portugal's home-grown talent while visiting the country. Cinema buffs will find international festivals in Porto in February, the Algarve and Viana do Castelo in May, Tróia in June and Figueira da Foz in September. Lisbon hosts an independent film fest in the spring, along with a festival of gay and lesbian cinema in September.

Music

Fundamental to Portugal's history of musical expression is its foot-tapping folk music, which you can hear at almost every festival. It traces its roots to the medieval troubadour, and is traditionally accompanied by a band of guitars, violins, clarinets, harmonicas and various wooden percussion instruments. In fact, the instruments are often more attractive than the singing, which could be generously described as a high-pitched, repetitive wail.

Fados (2008), by Spanish director Carlos Saura, explores the historical roots of fado against the backdrop of Lisbon. Mariza, Cesária Évora and others star.

Far more enigmatic is Portugal's most famous style of music, fado (Portuguese for 'fate'). These melancholic chants – performed as a set of three songs, each one lasting three minutes – are also said to have their roots in troubadour songs, although African slave songs have had an influence, too. They're traditionally sung by one performer accompanied by a 12-string Portuguese *guitarra* (a pear-shaped guitar). Fado emerged in the 18th century in Lisbon's working-class districts of Alfama and Mouraria and gradually moved upmarket.

There are two styles of fado music, one from Lisbon (still considered the most genuine) and the other from the university town of Coimbra. The latter is traditionally sung by men as it praises the beauty of women. In 1996 *fadista* (fado performer) Manuela Bravo caused an outcry when she recorded a CD of Coimbra fados – the entire issue of CDs mysteriously disappeared almost as soon as it had appeared.

The greatest modern *fadista* was Amália Rodrigues, who brought fado international recognition. She died in 1999 aged 79, after more than 60 years of extraordinary fado performances ('I don't sing fado. It sings me,' she once said). Pick up a copy of her greatest hits to hear what fado should really sound like.

Desgarrada is a style of fado in which two singers play off each other, improvising verses along the way. It can turn into a kind of musical jousting.

However, while fado brings to mind dark bars of the Salazar years, this is not a musical form stuck in time. Top-notch contemporary performers and exponents of a new fado style include the dynamic young *fadista* Mísia, who broke new ground by experimenting with instrumentation and commissioning lyrics by contemporary poets. She has since been followed by several excellent performers.

The current darling of the fado industry is Mariza (p92), whose extraordinary voice and fresh contemporary image has struck a chord both at home and internationally. But the men aren't outdone: one of the great young male voices in traditional fado these days is Camané.

Venues for live fado include Lisbon (p142), Coimbra (p337) and Porto (p403). See p125 for details on an annual fado festival, and p115 for a museum dedicated to its history.

Both fado and traditional folk songs – and, increasingly, musical strains from Europe and Africa – have shaped Portugal's *música popular* (modern folk-music scene). Often censored during the Salazar years, its lyrics became overtly political after 1974, with singers using performances to support various revolutionary factions.

MUSICAL TOP 10

- *Terra* (2008) The latest album by Mariza features the enchanting songstress alongside a talented assembly of musicians from Brazil, Cuba, Spain and the UK.

- *Art of Amália Rodrigues* (1998) Available in two volumes, this album spans the golden years (1952–70) of Portugal's queen of fado.

- *Ulisses* (2005) The angelic voice of *fadista* Cristina Branco continues to captivate audiences across the globe. This is her best-selling album.

- *M'Bem di Fora* (2006) Born in Portugal to Cape Verdean parents, Lura is perhaps heir to Cesária Évora's throne. Her magnificent voice stands out against lush, African-island rhythms.

- *Antologia* (2000) Folk-group Madredeus is known for mesmerising music accompanied by guitar, accordion and cello. This is a good introduction, featuring 17 greatest hits from the '80s and '90s.

- *Para Além da Saudade* (2007) The sultry-voiced Ana Moura is one of the youngest rising stars in the fado world.

- *Afro-Portuguese Odyssey* (2002) Putumayo's wide-ranging look at how the African colonies have musically influenced Portugal, and vice versa.

- *Iniciação a Uma Vida Banal* (2000) Da Weasel's best album is required listening for anyone interested in Portugal's hip-hop scene.

- *Missão Groove & Remixes* (2000) An intriguing blend of jazz, funk and soul by the Lisbon trio Cool Hipnoise.

- *O Primeiro Canto* (2000) A youthful new singer who isn't a *fadista*, Dulce Pontes has a stunning voice, which is nicely matched by the beautiful arrangements. Wayne Shorter and other jazz greats contribute.

The Portuguese guitar, too, took on a new range of expression under masters such as Carlos Paredes and António Chaínho. Well-known folk groups include the venerable Madredeus. At the grass-roots level are student song groups, called *tunas académicas,* who give performances all over the country during March.

Jazz is also hugely popular in Portugal, which hosts several jazz festivals. One of the leading lights of Lisbon's lively African jazz scene is diva Maria João. If you spend time in Lisbon and want a taste of Portuguese jazz, make a beeline for the Hot Clube de Portugal (p144).

On the rock scene, don't miss the old masters Xutos & Pontapés, the quirky Gift and the popular Blind Zero. Or if fresh-faced pop is more your scene, you'll soon discover chart sensation David Fonseca, who sings in English.

African-influenced urban music figures prominently in a number of Lisbon nightclubs. African jazz was at the forefront of this trend, and big names include Cesária Évora from Cape Verde and drum-maestro Guem from Angola.

New styles with African origins have emerged in recent years. Kuduro, described as a kind of house music with coarse break beats with Caribbean undertones, is a current favourite on the club scene. Lisbon groups like Buraka Som Sistema have garnered much attention for their innovative sound.

However, the hottest urban clubs around the country are now dominated by DJ culture. You'll hear lots of hip-hop and funk, made popular by the likes of Hip-Hop Tuga and the hugely popular Da Weasel, and a new wave of Portuguese dance-floor music, increasingly being exported around Europe. Look out for Portugal's top DJs spinning at clubs like Lisbon's Lux (p141) and Porto's Bazaar (p403).

Visual Arts

The earliest visual arts to be found in Portugal were several treasure-troves of 20,000-year-old Palaeolithic carvings. A top place to see some of Iberia's earliest artwork is in Vila Nova de Foz Côa (p420).

The cave-dwellers' modern successors were heavily influenced by French, Italian and Flemish styles. The first major exception was the 15th-century primitive painter Nuno Gonçalves, whose polyptych of the *Panels of São Vicente* is a unique tapestry-style revelation of contemporary Portuguese society.

The 16th-century Manueline school produced some uniquely Portuguese works, remarkable for their incredible delicacy, realism and luminous colours. The big names of this school are Vasco Fernandes (known as Grão Vasco) and Gaspar Vaz, who both worked from Viseu; their best works are in Viseu's first-rate Museu de Grão Vasco (p371). In Lisbon, other outstanding Manueline artists were Jorge Afonso, court painter to Dom Manuel I, and Cristóvão de Figueiredo and Gregório Lopes.

Hot on the heels of the Renaissance, in the 17th century artist Josefa de Óbidos made waves with her rich still lifes. However, the fine arts waned somewhat until the 19th century, when there was an artistic echo of both the naturalist and romantic movements, expressed strongly in the works of Silva Porto and Marquês de Oliveira. Sousa Pinto excelled as a pastel artist in the early 20th century.

Naturalism remained the dominant trend into the 20th century, although Amadeo de Souza-Cardoso struck out on his own path of cubism and expressionism, and Maria Helena Vieria da Silva came to be considered the country's finest abstract painter (although she lived in Paris for most of her life). Some of the best works of Amadeo de Souza-Cardoso hang inside the museum dedicated to him in Amarante (p411).

Other eminent figures in contemporary art include José Sobral de Almada Negreiros, often called the father of Portugal's modern art movement, and Guilherme Santa-Rita, who had a short career in abstract art. Their works and others can be seen in Lisbon's Centro de Arte Moderna (p118) and Porto's Museu Nacional Soares dos Reis (p391).

The conservative Salazar years that followed didn't create the ideal environment to nurture contemporary creativity, and many artists left the country. These include Portugal's best-known modern artist, Paula Rego, who was born in Lisbon in 1935 but has been a resident of the UK since 1951. Rego's signature style developed around fairy-tale paintings given a nightmarish twist. Her works deal in ambiguity and psychological and sexual tension, such as *The Family* (1988), where a seated businessman is either being tortured or smothered with affection by his wife and daughter. Domination, fear, sexuality and grief are all recurring themes in Rego's paintings, and the mysterious and sinister atmosphere, heavy use of chiaroscuro (stark contrasting of light and shade) and strange distortion of scale are reminiscent of surrealists Max Ernst and Giorgio de Chirico.

Rego's contemporary Helena Almeida has had a particularly strong influence on Portugal's younger artists. Her large-scale, often self-reflective, photographic portraits combine drawing, photography and painting, challenging the relationship between illusion and reality.

Among the younger generation, born around the time of the 1974 revolution (an event that inspired a surge of artistic development), Miguel Branco is the link between the new and old eras. His small, evocative paintings bring to mind the Renaissance masters, despite being contemporary in presentation. Eduardo Batarda produces influential works in acrylic, often adapting paintings in comic-strip style. Other late-20th-century stars to

For a peek at some of Paula Rego's work, visit www.saatchi-gallery .co.uk/artists/paula _rego.htm.

keep an eye out for are António Areal, Angelo de Sousa and Nadir Afonso. Graça Morais, a figurative artist from Trás-os-Montes, paints moving scenes from her village life.

However, the biggest trend in Portuguese contemporary art is in innovative video and multimedia projects. Most notably, João Onofre's primitive, grainy creations take a humorous look at social dynamics; Miguel Soares' futuristic, slightly unsettling works reflect Portugal's rapidly changing times; and João Penalva's music and video installations are well worth looking out for. Minimalist painter Julião Sarmento has also dabbled in video and photographic works to explore different ways of seeing.

Other exciting breaks with tradition include the work of young collectives such as the Tone Scientists (Carlos Roque, Rui Valério and Rui Toscano), which blends visual art with classical music, and offbeat events such as the Festival Internacional de Banda Desenhada da Amadora (www.amadorabd .com, in Portuguese), held in late October to early November near Lisbon, showcasing the talents of Portugal's comic-strip artists.

SCULPTURE

Sculptors have excelled throughout Portugal's history. Among the first masterpieces are the carved tombs of the 12th to 14th centuries, including those of Inês de Castro and Dom Pedro in the Mosteiro de Santa Maria de Alcobaça (p302).

In the Manueline era sculptors including Diogo de Boitaca went wild with Portuguese seafaring fantasies and exuberant decoration. At the same time, foreign influences were seeping in, including Flemish, followed in the 16th century by the flamboyant Gothic and plateresque styles of Spanish Galicia and Biscay. During the Renaissance, several French artists settled in Portugal and excelled in architectural sculpting. The ornate pulpit in Coimbra's Igreja de Santa Cruz (p332) is regarded as Nicolas Chanterène's masterpiece.

'In the Manueline era sculptors went wild with Portuguese seafaring fantasies'

Foreign schools continued to influence Portuguese sculptors in the 18th-century baroque era, when Dom João V took advantage of the assembly of foreign artists working on the Convento do Mafra to found an influential school of sculpture. Its most famous Portuguese teacher was Joaquim Machado de Castro.

A century later the work of António Soares dos Reis reflected similar influences. However, Soares also tied himself in knots by attempting to capture in sculpture the melancholic feeling of *saudade*, a uniquely Portuguese and impossibly intangible concept. You can see one of his most famous works, *O Desterrado*, at the museum dedicated to the great sculptor – and other 19th-century artists – in Porto's Museu Nacional Soares dos Reis (p391).

At the turn of the 20th century two names were prominent: Francisco Franco and the prolific sculptor António Teixeira Lopes, whose most famous work is his series of children's heads. These, along with work by Soares, are on display in the Museu Nacional Soares dos Reis in Porto (p391).

Leading lights on the contemporary scene include Noé Sendas, who creates life-size figures in thought-provoking poses and dress; Leonor Antunes, whose sculptural installations invite viewers to explore how they relate to their surroundings; and Lisbon's Pedro-Cabrita Reis, who also creates impressive architectural installations designed to stimulate memories. Also keep an eye out for the dramatic modern sculptures by Rui Chafes, influenced heavily by German Romanticism (late 18th to early 19th century).

HANDICRAFTS & INDIGENOUS ARTS

You only have to visit the big weekly markets in Portugal to see the astounding range of traditional handicrafts available – from myriad forms of ceramics to baskets of rush, willow, cane or rye straw, and from the fabulously painted wooden furniture of the Alentejo to the carved ox yokes of the Minho.

Long traditions of hand-embroidery and weaving are also found throughout Portugal, as is lace-making, which is mainly found along the coast ('where there are nets, there is lace', goes the saying).

For details of where to buy these crafts, see p499.

Theatre & Dance

The theatre scene has finally cast out the demons of the Salazar years. The venerable Teatro Nacional Dona Maria II of Lisbon and Teatro Nacional de São João of Porto have now been joined by numerous private companies, boosted by increased funding from the Ministry of Culture. Portugal's biggest recent theatre success has been the musical *Amália* (about fado's greatest diva), seen by more than a million people. Also keep an eye out for Tomar's innovative theatre company, Fatias de Cá, which tends to perform in amazing venues, such as the Roman ruins of Conímbriga, in a quarry marked by dinosaur footprints near Fátima and in the torchlit halls and courtyards of Tomar's Convento de Cristo.

The Gulbenkian Foundation, one of Portugal's most generous and wide-ranging private arts sponsors, also continues to support new theatre companies and dance. Indeed, Portuguese modern dance is capturing increased international acclaim, and every November contemporary dance fans flock to Lisbon's Festival Internacional de Dança Contemporânea. One of the country's leading choreographers is Vera Mantero, previously a ballerina, now an exponent of cutting-edge experimental dance. Prestigious ballet performances also take place in palatial settings in Sintra during August.

However, it's good old folk dancing that you'll most frequently see in the north. Almost every village has its own dancers, all in flamboyant costumes, with the women draped in jewellery. Their whirling, foot-stomping and finger-waggling routines make for great watching. Some, such as the flowery *pauliteiros* (stick dancers) of Miranda do Douro (see the boxed text, p491), have gone professional, touring the country and abroad.

'Almost every village has its own dancers, all in flamboyant costumes, with the women draped in jewellery'

Architecture

Portugal's varied assortment of cathedrals, castles and *cromeleques* (circles of prehistoric standing stones) are just a few small pieces of the country's great architectural jigsaw puzzle. Travellers with an interest in the past and an eye for the aesthetic have hundreds of sights to satisfy them.

Among the many famous icons here are wildly baroque monasteries, complete with masterfully carved facades, as well as medieval, Renaissance and Gothic churches. Perhaps most fascinating of all are works of the Manueline style, that uniquely Portuguese design of highly imaginative ornamentation in bloom during the Age of Discoveries.

Portuguese Decorative Tiles by Rioletta Sabo (1998) is an all-out wallow in the dazzling colours and diversity of Portugal's favourite wall-covering.

Vestiges of the Roman Empire live on in well-preserved temples and in ruins of former bath houses, villas and even public roads scattered about the countryside. There are also low-rising stone cathedrals left by the Romans' Visigothic successors, and neighbourhoods first laid out during Moorish times – narrow, winding lanes crisscrossing past whitewashed houses whose facades haven't changed much in the last 1000 years.

Medieval castles and walled fortress towns offer a glimpse into Portugal's early nationhood. Visitors to remote outposts are often rewarded with sublime castle-top views over the countryside.

Works from the 19th and 20th centuries show Portugal at its most eclectic, from playful, wrought-iron elevator towers (diminutive cousins of Monsieur Eiffel) to sweeping plazas framed with beaux-arts backdrops. More recent post-millennium works include some truly daring designs, including executions by world-renowned architects like Rem Koolhaas and famed native son Álvaro Siza Vieira.

PALAEOLITHIC PALETTE

A most mysterious group of 95 huge monoliths form a strange circle in an isolated clearing among Alentejan olive groves near Évora. It's one of Europe's most impressive prehistoric sites: the Cromeleque dos Almendres.

All over Portugal, but especially in the Alentejo, you can visit such ancient funerary and religious structures, built during the Neolithic and Megalithic eras about 6000 years ago. Most impressive are the dolmens: funerary chambers – rectangular, polygonal or round – reached by a corridor

---

ARCHITECTURAL TOP 10

- Cromeleque dos Almendres (p247) – a mystical setting of 95 prehistoric big stones.
- Citânia de Briteiros (p440) – a sprawling 2500-year-old site of Portugal's most extensive Celtiberian settlement.
- Mosteiro de Santa Maria de Alcobaça (p302) – lean Gothic at its best.
- Palácio Nacional de Mafra (p167) – jaw-dropping extravagance.
- Convento de Cristo (p319) – mysterious Manueline, Gothic and Renaissance styles.
- Mosteiro de Santa Maria da Vitória (p304) – Gothic grandeur.
- Mosteiro dos Jerónimos (p120) – Manueline masterpiece.
- Casa da Música (p392) – magnificent, hypermodern design.
- Rossio Train Station (p113) – newly restored neo-Maneline masterpiece.
- Boa Nova Casa-Chá (p401) – Alvaro Siza Vieira's modernist-magic ocean-fronting teahouse.

of stone slabs and covered with earth to create an artificial mound. King of these is the Anta Grande do Zambujeiro, also near Évora, and Europe's largest dolmen, with six 6m-high stones forming a huge chamber. Single monoliths, or menhirs, often carved with phallic or religious symbols, also dot the countryside like an army of stone sentinels. Their relationship to promoting fertility seems obvious.

With the arrival of the Celts (800–200 BC) came the first established hilltop settlements, called *castros*. The best-preserved example is the Citânia de Briteiros, in the Minho, where you can literally step into Portugal's past. Stone dwellings were built on a circular or elliptical plan, and the complex was surrounded with a dry-stone defensive wall. In the *citânias* (fortified villages) further south, dwellings tended to be rectangular.

At the well-produced panoramic creation 360°Portugal (www.360portugal.com) you can peer around castles, megaliths, churches, archaeological sites and more.

ROMANS & RUINS

The Romans left their typical architectural and engineering feats – roads, bridges, towns complete with forums (marketplaces), villas, public baths and aqueducts. These have now largely disappeared from the surface, though the majority of Portugal's cities are built on Roman foundations and you can descend into dank foundations under new buildings in Lisbon and Évora, and see Roman fragments around Braga. At Conimbriga, the country's largest Roman site, an entire Roman town is under excavation. Revealed so far are some spectacular mosaics, along with structural or decorative columns, carved entablatures and classical ornamentation, which give a sense of the Roman high life.

Portugal's most famous and complete Roman ruin is the Templo Romano, the so-called Temple of Diana in Évora, with its flouncy-topped Corinthian columns, nowadays echoed by the complementary towers of Évora cathedral. This is the finest temple of its kind on the Iberian Peninsula, its preservation the result of having been walled up in the Middle Ages and later used as a slaughterhouse.

Earth Architecture in Portugal, edited by Felipe Jorge (2005), contains more than 50 essays dealing with the technique, history and anthropology of building with natural materials, aka dirt.

The various Teutonic tribes who invaded after the fall of Rome in the early 5th century left little trace other than a few churches built by the Visigoths, a fierce bunch of Arian Christians. Though heavily restored over the centuries, these ancient churches still reveal a Roman basilica outline, rectangular and divided by columns into a nave and two aisles. Two fine examples are the Capela de São Pedro de Balsemão (outside Lamego, in the Douro) and the Igreja de Santo Amaro in Beja, the Alentejo. Most unusual is the Capela de São Frutuoso (near Braga) – Byzantine (Graeco-Asiatic) in character and laid out in the shape of a Greek cross.

The Visigoths also rebuilt the Roman town of Idanha-a-Velha, now a quiet hamlet near Castelo Branco; you can see their influence in parts of the cathedral here. Many other Visigothic churches were destroyed by the Moors after they kicked out the Visigoths in AD 711.

LESS IS MOOR

Unlike Spain, Portugal has no complete buildings left from the Moorish period. You will find the odd Moorish arch or wall, bits of fortresses, and the atmospheric remains of several *mourarias* (Moorish quarters), notably in the aptly named Moura (in the Alentejo), which retains a well and a Moorish tower as part of its castle. Nearby Mértola retained many of its North African characteristics (nothing like a bit of economic torpor to halt development) and includes a distinctive former mosque converted into a church. Silves was the Moorish capital of the Algarve, and retains an enormous well, now on display as part of the archaeological museum.

The Moors did, however, powerfully influence Portuguese architecture, no matter how hard the Christians tried to stamp out their mark.

Moorish design is particularly noticeable in private homes, and especially in the south: terraces and horseshoe arches, wrought-iron work and whitewash, flat roofs and geometric ornamentation, and the use of water in decoration.

ROBUST & ROMANESQUE

During the Christian recapture of Portugal from the Moors, completed by 1297, most mosques were torn down and replaced by a church or cathedral, often on the same site. These were in the simple, stolid Romanesque style – with rounded arches, thick walls and heavy vaulting – originally introduced to Portugal by Burgundian monks. As in Lisbon and Coimbra, they often resembled fortifications – demonstrating concerns about the Moors wreaking revenge, and anticipating the Castilian threat.

More delicate Romanesque touches can be found in several small, lovely churches, notably the Igreja de São Salvador in Bravães, where portals often display fine animal or plant motifs in their archivolts. Only one complete example of a secular building remains from this time – Bragança's endearing five-sided Domus Municipalis, Portugal's oldest town hall.

Fires of Excellence: Spanish and Portuguese Oriental Architecture by Miles Danby & Matthew Weinreb (1998) is a stunningly photographed exploration of Portugal's Muslim history and aesthetics.

GREAT GOTHIC

Cistercians introduced the Gothic trend, and this reached its pinnacle in Alcobaça, in one of Portugal's most ethereally beautiful buildings. The austere abbey church and cloister of the Mosteiro de Santa Maria de Alcobaça, begun in 1178, has a lightness and simplicity strongly influenced by Clairvaux Abbey in France. Its hauntingly simple Cloisters of Silence were a model for later cathedral cloisters at Coimbra, Lisbon, Évora and many other places. This was the birth of Portuguese Gothic, which flowered and transmuted over the coming years as the country gained more and more experience of the outside world. For centuries Portugal had been culturally dominated and restricted by Spain and the Moors.

By the 14th century, when the Mosteiro de Santa Maria da Vitória (commonly known as Mosteiro da Batalha or Battle Abbey) was constructed, simplicity was a distant, vague memory. Portuguese, Irish and French architects worked on this breathtaking monument for more than two centuries. The combination of their skills and the changing architectural fashions of the times, from Flamboyant (late) Gothic to Gothic Renaissance and then Manueline, turned the abbey into a seething mass of carving, organic decorations, lofty space and slanting stained-glass light. It's a showcase of High Gothic art. It exults in the decorative (especially in its Gothic Royal Cloisters and Chapter House), while the flying buttresses tip their hat to English Perpendicular Gothic.

Secular architecture also enjoyed a Gothic boom, thanks to the need for fortifications against the Moors and to the castle-building fervour of the 13th-century ruler, Dom Dinis. Some of Portugal's most spectacular, huddled, thick-walled castles – for example, Estremoz, Óbidos and Bragança – date from this time, many featuring massive double-perimeter walls and an inner square tower.

In the sleepy Alentejo town of Vila Viçosa lies one of Portugal's largest and least-known palaces, the Paço Ducal.

AMAZING MANUELINE

Manueline is a uniquely Portuguese style, a specific, crazed flavour of late-Gothic architecture. Ferociously decorative, it coincided roughly with the reign of Dom Manuel I (1495–1521) and is interesting not just because of its extraordinarily imaginative designs, burbling with life, but also because this dizzyingly creative architecture skipped hand in hand with the era's booming confidence.

During Dom Manuel's reign, Vasco da Gama and fellow explorers claimed new overseas lands and new wealth for Portugal. The Age of Discoveries was expressed in sculptural creations of eccentric inventiveness, drawing heavily on nautical themes: twisted ropes, coral and anchors in stone, topped by the ubiquitous armillary sphere (a navigational device that became Dom Manuel's personal symbol) and the Cross of the Order of Christ (symbol of the religious military order that largely financed and inspired Portugal's explorations).

Manueline first emerged in Setúbal's Igreja de Jesus, designed in the 1490s by French expatriate Diogo de Boitaca, who gave it columns like trees growing into the ceiling, and ribbed vaulting like twisted ropes. The style quickly caught on, and soon decorative carving was creeping, twisting and crawling over everything (aptly described by 19th-century English novelist William Beckford as 'scollops and twistifications').

Outstanding Manueline masterpieces are Belém's Mosteiro dos Jerónimos, masterminded largely by Diogo de Boitaca and João de Castilho, and Batalha's Mosteiro de Santa Maria da Vitória's otherworldly Capelas Imperfeitas (Unfinished Chapels).

Other famous creations include Belém's Torre de Belém, a Manueline-Moorish cake crossed with a chesspiece by Diogo de Boitaca and his brother Francisco, and Diogo de Arruda's fantastical organic, seemingly barnacle-encrusted window in the Chapter House of Tomar's Convento de Cristo, as well as its fanciful 16-sided Charola – the Templar church, resembling an eerie *Star Wars* set. Many other churches sport a Manueline flourish against a plain facade.

The style was enormously resonant in Portugal, and reappeared in the early 20th century in exercises in mystical Romanticism, such as Sintra's Quinta da Regaleira and Palácio Nacional da Pena, and Luso's over-the-top and extraordinary neo-Manueline Palace Hotel do Buçaco.

RENAISSANCE TOUCHES

After all that froth and fuss, the Portuguese were somewhat slow to take up the Renaissance torch, which signalled a return to Roman classical design and proportion. One of its protagonists, the Italian Andrea Sansovino, is thought to have spent some time in Portugal, though he seems to have made little impression. The Quinta da Bacalhoa, a 15th-century house at Vila Nogueira de Azeitão (near Setúbal) is his only notable contribution. The French sculptor Nicolas Chantorène was the main pioneer of Renaissance ideas here, and from around 1517 onwards, his influence abounds in both sculpture and architectural decoration.

Portugal has few Renaissance buildings, but some examples of the style are the Great Cloisters in Tomar's Convento de Cristo, designed by Spanish Diogo de Torralva in the late 16th century; the nearby Igreja de Nossa Senhora da Conceição; and the Convento de Bom Jesus at Valverde, outside Évora.

MOODY & MANNERIST

Sober and severe, the Mannerist style reflects the spirit of its time, coinciding with the years of Spanish rule (1580–1640) and the heavy influence of the Inquisition and the Jesuits.

This style persisted throughout much of the 17th century. Lisbon's marvellous Igreja de São Vicente de Fora, built between 1582 and 1627 by Felipe Terzi, is a typical example of balanced Mannerist classicism. It served as a model for many other churches.

The Manueline: Portuguese Art and Architecture During the Great Discoveries (2002) provides an in-depth look at the unique and wildly decorative creations from 1469 to 1521.

Portuguese Plain Architecture: Between Spices & Diamonds (1521-1706) by George Kubler (1980) provides a scholarly look at a fascinating period in Portugal's architectural history.

BRAZIL, BAROQUE & BUCKETS OF GOLD

Baroque: Architecture, Sculpture, Painting, edited by Rolf Toman (2008), delves into the ornate interiors that spread across Portugal and Western Europe in the 18th century.

With independence from Spain re-established and the influence of the Inquisition on the wane, Portugal burst out in baroque fever – an architectural style that was exuberant, theatrical and fired straight at the senses. Nothing could rival the Manueline flourish, but the baroque style – named after the Portuguese word for a rough pearl, *barroco* – cornered the market in flamboyance. At its height in the 18th century (almost a century later than in Italy), it was characterised by curvaceous forms, huge monuments, spatially complex schemes and lots and lots and lots of gold.

Financed by the 17th-century gold and diamond discoveries in Brazil, and encouraged by the extravagant Dom João V, local and foreign (particularly Italian) artists created mind-bogglingly opulent masterpieces. You'll see prodigious *talha dourada* (gilded woodwork) in church interiors all over the place, but it reached its most extreme in Aveiro's Convento de Jesus, Lisbon's Igreja de São Roque and Porto's Igreja de São Francisco.

THE ART OF THE TILE

Portugal's favourite decorative art is easy to spot – polished painted tiles called *azulejos* (after the Arabic *al zulaycha,* meaning polished stone). These tiles cover everything from churches to houses to train stations. The Moors introduced the art, having picked it up from the Persians, but the Portuguese liked it so much they tiled anything that stayed still long enough.

Portugal's earliest 16th-century tiles are Moorish, from Seville. These were decorated with interlocking geometric or floral patterns (figurative representations aren't an option for Muslim artists for religious reasons). After the Portuguese captured Ceuta in Morocco in 1415, they began exploring the art themselves. The 16th-century Italian invention of majolica, in which colours are painted directly onto wet clay over a layer of white enamel, gave works a fresco-like brightness and kicked off the Portuguese *azulejo* love affair.

The earliest home-grown examples, polychrome and geometric, date from the 1580s, and may be seen in churches such as Lisbon's Igreja de São Roque, providing an ideal counterbalance to fussy, gold-heavy baroque. Some of Portugal's earliest tiles adorn the Palácio Nacional da Sintra.

The late 17th century saw a fashion for huge panels, depicting everything from cherubs to commerce, saints to seascapes. As demand grew, mass production became necessary and the Netherlands' blue-and-white Delft tiles started to appear all over the walls.

Portuguese tile makers rose to the challenge of this influx, and the splendid work of virtuoso Portuguese masters António de Oliveira Bernardes and his son Policarpo in the 18th century springs from this competitive creativity. You can see their work in Évora, in the impressive Igreja de São João.

By the end of the 1700s, industrial-scale manufacture began to affect quality, coupled with the massive demand for tiles after the 1755 Lisbon earthquake. Tiling answered the need for decoration, but was cheap and practical – a solution for a population that had felt the ground move beneath its feet.

From the late 19th century, the Art Nouveau and Art Deco movements took *azulejos* by storm, providing fantastic facades and interiors for shops, restaurants and residential buildings – notably by Rafael Bordalo Pinheiro (visit Caldas de Rainha, where there is a museum devoted to his work), Jorge Colaço and Jorge Barradas, whose work you can see at the Museu da Cidade in Lisbon.

Azulejos still coat contemporary life, and you can explore the latest in *azulejos* while going places on the Lisbon metro. Maria Keil designed 19 of the stations, from the 1950s onwards – look out for stunning block-type prints at Intendente (considered her masterpiece) and Anjos. Oriente also showcases extraordinary contemporary work. Artists from five continents were invited to contribute, including Austria's Friedensreich Hundertwasser.

For more information on this beautiful art, visit Lisbon's Museu Nacional do Azulejo. There are also many impressive pieces in Lisbon's Museu de Cidade. Lisbon and Porto (p391) have the best on-the-street examples.

The baroque of central and southern Portugal was more restrained. Examples include the chancel of Évora's cathedral and the massive Palácio Nacional de Mafra. Designed by the German architect João Frederico Ludovice to rival the similar palace-monastery of San Lorenzo de El Escorial (near Madrid), the Mafra version is relatively sober, apart from its size – which is such that at one point it had a workforce of 45,000 working on it, looked after by a police force of 7000.

Work on the Palácio Nacional de Mafra was so lavish and expensive it nearly bankrupted the country.

Meanwhile, the Tuscan painter and architect Nicolau Nasoni (who settled in Porto around 1725) introduced a more ornamental baroque style to the north. Nasoni is responsible for Porto's Torre dos Clérigos and Igreja da Misericórdia, and the whimsical Palácio de Mateus near Vila Real (internationally famous as the image on Mateus rosé wine bottles).

In the mid-18th century a school of architecture evolved in Braga. Local artists such as André Soares built churches and palaces in a very decorative style, heavily influenced by Augsburg engravings from southern Germany. Soares' Casa do Raio, in Braga, and much of the monumental staircase of the nearby Bom Jesus do Monte, are typical examples of this period's ornamentation.

Memorial do Convento (Baltazar and Blimunda, 1982) is José Saramago's Nobel prize–winning novel about the Mafra extravaganza – a convent-palace dreamed up by size-junkies and compulsive builders.

Only when the gold ran out did the baroque fad fade. At the end of the 18th century, architects flirted briefly with rococo (best exemplified by Mateus Vicente's Palácio de Queluz, begun in 1747, or the palace at Estói) before embracing neoclassicism.

POST-EARTHQUAKE SOBRIETY

After Lisbon's devastating 1755 earthquake, the autocratic Marquês de Pombal invited architect Eugenio dos Santos to rebuild the Baixa area in a plain style, using classical elements that could be easily built and repeated. This new 'Pombaline' style featured a grid pattern marked by unadorned houses and wide avenues. It had a knock-on effect and led to a reaction against the excesses of the baroque period in other parts of the country. In Porto, for instance, the Hospital de Santo António and the Feitoria Inglesa (Factory House), both designed by Englishmen, show a noticeable return to sober Palladian and classical designs. Lisbon's early-19th-century Palácio Nacional da Ajuda was also designed on neoclassical lines and served as the inspiration for the elegantly restrained Palácio de Brejoeira (near Monção, in the Minho).

Houses were tiled on the outside after the 1755 earthquake as a cheap and more expendable means of decoration.

NEO-EVERYTHING, ART NOUVEAU & THE NEW

In the early 19th century most new building of major monuments came to a halt. This was partly due to the aftereffects of the Peninsular War (1807–14) and partly because a liberal decree in 1834 dissolved the religious orders, allowing their many buildings to be appropriated by the state. Some former monasteries are still used by the government today – notably Lisbon's Benedictine Mosteiro de São Bento, now the seat of parliament.

When new buildings did emerge they tended to draw on all the architectural styles of the past, from Moorish (as in Lisbon's Rossio station) to neoclassical (Porto's stock exchange, the Palácio da Bolsa). A distinctly French influence can be seen in many grand apartment blocks and office buildings built at this time.

Towards the end of the 19th century the increased use of iron and steel reflected Portugal's emergence as an industrial nation. Train stations (eg Lisbon's Alcântara station) and other grand buildings were covered in iron and glass. Gustave Eiffel built iron bridges across the rivers Minho, Lima and Douro, and his followers were responsible for several Gustav Eiffel design-aesthetic (exposed ironwork) lookalikes, including Lisbon's wonderfully eccentric Elevador de Santa Justa (kind of like the Eiffel Tower crossed with a doily).

One of the most delightful movements during this period was Art Nouveau, a burst of carefree, decorative fancy that produced many beautifully decorated cafes and shops – check out Lisbon's Versailles and Pastelaria São Roque, or Porto's Café Majestic.

The Salazar years favoured decidedly severe, Soviet-style, state commissions (eg Coimbra University's dull faculty buildings, which replaced elegant 18th-century neoclassical ones). Ugly buildings and apartment blocks rose on city outskirts. Notable exceptions dating from the 1960s are Lisbon's Palácio da Justiça in the Campolide district, and the gloriously sleek Museu Calouste Gulbenkian. The beautiful wood-panelled Galeto cafe-restaurant is a time capsule from this era.

Álvaro Siza by Brigitte Fleck (2001) is a handy monograph on the great contemporary architect, whose nationwide projects include the clean cubism of Porto's Museu de Arte Contemporânea.

The tendency towards urban mediocrity continued after the 1974 revolution, although architects such as Fernando Távora and Eduardo Souto Moura have produced impressive schemes. Lisbon's postmodern Amoreiras shopping complex, by Tomás Taveira, is another striking contribution.

Portugal's greatest contemporary architect is Álvaro Siza Vieira. A believer in clarity and simplicity, his expressionist approach is reflected in projects such as the Pavilhão de Portugal for Expo 98, Porto's splendid Museu de Arte Contemporânea and the Igreja de Santa Maria at Marco de Canavezes, south of Amarante. He has also restored central Lisbon's historic Chiado shopping district with notable sensitivity, following a major fire in 1988.

Spanish architect Santiago Calatrava designed the lean organic monster Gare do Oriente for the Expo 98, architecture that is complemented by the work of many renowned contemporary artists. The interior is more state-of-the-art spaceship than station. In the same area lies Lisbon's architectural trailblazer the Parque das Nações, with a bevy of unique designs, including a riverfront park and Europe's largest aquarium. The longest bridge in Europe, the Ponte de Vasco da Gama built in 1998, stalks out across the river from nearby.

The Torre Vasco da Gama in Lisbon's Parque das Nações is getting a new lease on life as a lavish 178-room hotel. For more details, visit www.sanahotels.com.

Since the turn of the millennium, Portugal has seen a handful of architecturally ambitious projects come to fruition. One of the grander projects is Rem Koolhaas' Casa da Música in Porto (2005). From a distance, the extremely forward-looking design appears like a solid white block of carefully cut crystal. Both geometric and defiantly asymmetrical, the building mixes elements of tradition (like *azulejos* hidden in one room) with

---

PORTUGAL'S FAVOURITE ARCHITECT

One of Portugal's great contemporary architects, Álvaro Siza Vieira (born 1933) remains fairly unknown outside his home country. This is surprising given his loyal following in the architecture world, his long and distinguished career and his award-winning designs (which garnered him the coveted Pritzker Prize in 1992). Part of the reason for this is perhaps his deceptively minimalist creations.

On the surface, his work may seem less than dazzling. Stucco, stone, tile and glass are his building materials of choice, and his designs might seem to the casual observer like low-rising boxlike structures. Yet, once inside, it's a different story: the whole trumps the parts, and everything – inside and out – morphs into a smoothly integrated work. Place means everything in Siza Vieira's work, with geography and climate carefully considered before any plans are laid.

In recent years, Siza Vieira has begun designing household objects in collaboration with New York–based Ohm Design. This includes a curiously re-imagined port glass. You can see images of his work on www.pritzkerprize.com/siza.htm.

high modernism (enormous curtains of corrugated glass flanking the concert stage).

In 2008 Lisbon regained some bragging rights for architectural glory, with the reopening of the eye-catching Rossio train station. Set in the heart of the city, Rossio has been restored to all its new-Manueline glory, complete with intertwined horseshoe portals at the entrance and an interior lined with columns interconnected by a lacework of cast-iron details.

Projects still in the works include the large-scale Bom Sucesso, a luxury 'design resort' rising up near Obídos. Described as the largest modern architecture project in Europe, some 23 distinguished architects have collaborated on Bom Sucesso, including Álvaro Siza Vieira. Bom Sucesso will contain 600 villas as well as a nature reserve, spa hotel and golf course; among other aesthetic virtues, all roofs and walls will be covered by greenery.

Even more ambitious, however, is the Mata de Sesimbra project south of Lisbon, which will combine a 4800-hectare nature reserve with an ecologically sensitive housing development. For more on that, see p80.

The Lisbon metro is not just about transport – it's an art gallery, showcasing the best of Portuguese contemporary art and architecture, with especially wonderful *azulejos*. Check out Metro Lisboa's website at www.metrolisboa.pt.

Food & Drink

How do the Portuguese eat? With gusto. Food is positively relished and must be shared with family and friends. And, Portuguese cuisine is like the people themselves – proud, generous and well seasoned.

The best of the Portuguese culinary delights are prepared simply, dished up without pretensions and served in massive portions. Distinct and very strong regional differences, rooted in geography and history, form the basis of any food-based experience here. And the Portuguese know their foodstuffs – they willingly travel to a particular village or region to taste say, an *arroz de pato* (duck risotto), prepared as it has been done for centuries, because – no arguments now – it is 'better' there.

On the whole, Portuguese cuisine doesn't 'do' creative preparation and presentation, but it doesn't need to – the fresh and locally produced ingredients are satisfying enough. And while Portugal may not be on the world's gastronomic radar along with (dare we say) nearby France or Spain, it should be, if only for continuing to humbly savour – literally – seasonal produce of the land and the sea. That's not to say that the Portuguese are behind the culinary times; new young Portuguese chefs are embracing – and have been embraced by – the world of gastronomy. Lisbon and the Algarve, in particular, boast fine international restaurants serving innovative (and more costly) dishes. Speaking of creative, vegetarians might need to be just that in requesting their veggie-based dishes – vegetarians are not generally well catered for (see p72). But when it comes to wine, there are plenty of top-dog wine producers using state-of-the-art technology and producing top drops (see p98).

So, how to savour Portugal? It's simple. Eat where the locals do; the Portuguese always follow their judgemental tastebuds. And another thing: think outside the box – the Portuguese pantry will test your concept of what's 'right' and 'wrong'. Mixed textures and tastes. Dry soups. Vegetable jam. Savoury cakes. Pork sweets. Meat with seafood. Strange tablefellows? Maybe. But they all have two great things in common – tradition and flavour.

Final advice to chew over? Loosen your belt a notch, recalibrate your expectations (don't compare to neighbouring countries!), *eat* (or offend your hosts, especially in private home stays), and take your tastebuds on a Portuguese journey…you'll be spending plenty of hours at the table.

Many traditional Portuguese products, such as Serpa cheese and Moscatel de Setúbal, have been accorded a 'protected geographical indication' or 'protected designation of origin' (like the French camembert) that assures quality and status.

STAPLES & SPECIALITIES

Bread, cheese, pork, fish and wine are the standout Portuguese staples. That's not to leave out chicken (especially grilled or with piri-piri), olives and olive oil, and some of Europe's most delectable pastries, especially conventual sweets (pastries and sweets that originated in convents).

THE COST OF COUVERT

There's one essential commandment regarding Portuguese dining etiquette: whatever you eat you must pay for, whether or not you ordered it. Throughout the country, in both dives and flash bistros, waiters bring bread, olives and other goodies (sometimes cheese and fish paste) to your table the moment you sit down. This unordered appetiser is normal practice; it's called 'couvert' and can cost anywhere from €1 per person to over €12 at the priciest places. If you don't want it, you can send it away, no offence taken. There's also no shame in asking the price – 'quanto e isso?' You may also receive extras throughout your meal or a shot of something at dessert. Unless told otherwise, you will have to pay for these.

NO FISH MONDAYS

Because fish markets are closed on Mondays (the fishing fleet takes a rest on Sundays), it's better to start your week off with something nonfishy. Otherwise, you'll be eating leftovers that certainly won't be very fresh.

Bread – *pão* – forms an integral part of every meal. *Pão caseiro* is home-baked, usually crusty bread. Plenty of bread turns up on one-pot dishes, including *açorda* (bread soup), *migas* (breadcrumbs prepared as a side dish) and *ensopados* (stews with toasted or deep-fried bread). Traditionally, meals were served on slabs of bread instead of plates – as well as being practical, this soaked up the delicious juices. As in Greece, Portugal's cheeses are made from ewe's and/or goat's milk. Cheese is common as an appetizer served with a bowl of olives, or as a snack or at the end of a meal. Many regions have their own cheese varieties. You'll definitely pork up (if not out) in Portugal. Pork meat and pork-based products form the basis of many of Portugal's meals. If you're not a great fan, persevere. Portuguese pork (especially *porco preto* – pork from black pigs) will have you oinking happily all the way home. And as for seafood? Even if you *think* you don't like seafood or *bacalhau* (salted cod), two words – learn to. *Bacalhau* is bound up with myth, history and mealtimes, from the everyday dishes to the most important celebrations; fish eaters would be crazy to pass it up. Nowadays, all salted cod is bought from elsewhere, mainly Scandinavian countries. This hasn't stopped the local consumption of massive amounts of the trusty fish. It's well documented that there are more than 365 recipes for cod – one for each day of the year. Finally, good old garlic features in nearly everything.

Cod: A Biography of the Fish That Changed the World (1998) by Mark Kurlansky is a fascinating account of how this simple yet crucial food affected the peoples whose lives it touched and the historic events that ensued.

DRINKS
Wine
When it comes to choosing a wine-producing country, Portugal is an outstanding pick. The country boasts a massive variety of grapes (and even more wines) grown and processed within hundreds of formal wine estates around the country. Portuguese have been growing grapes for at least 2000 years, yet until very recently these were mainly for domestic consumption (port wine aside). The country boasts some unique grape varieties and some of the oldest on the planet. Since joining the European Union in 1986 the country's wine industry has modernised rapidly…and it isn't looking back. Although Portugal was renowned in the past for its port, in recent times the wine world is acknowledging this country's wines, from table wines to superlative fortified drops (for more on Portugal's famous port wine, see p397).

The Portuguese are really pushing their viticulture industry, as well they should. Portugal's wine trade association **ViniPortugal** (www.viniportugal.pt) has organised an excellent range of regional wine routes (complete with maps and details), highlighting *adegas* (wineries) that welcome visitors. *Adega*-hopping is a great way to see the countryside and several have accommodation options and good restaurants attached.

The world's only source of cork for closing wine bottles is Portugal.

Other Drinks
Enthusiastic boozing also extends to beer. While Lisboêtas tend to stick to Sagres (with Branca, the light lager, being the most popular), Super Bock, which is made just outside of Porto, has a more robust, malty flavour, and is extremely popular up north. Beer is strong (5% alcohol) and inexpensive.

FIVE TOP DROPS

There are hundreds of quality Portuguese *vinos*, at good-value prices. The following are five author picks:

Albarinho Not a label *per se*, but a crisp, somewhat fruit-driven *vinho verde* (young wine), from the far north of Minho. Its headquarters are in Monção, just across the border from Spain, which produces its own 'Alvariño'. Of course, both countries think of it as their own.

Esporão's Reserva (see p249) A special selection of two of the best local grape varieties, Trincadeira and Aragonez, aged in oak for elegance and balance. Sublime with local lamb dishes, but you don't need an excuse…

Sogrape's Barca Velha The 'Grange Hermitage' of Portugal, this elegant wine has been produced since 1952 (Sogrape initially hit the world market with its famous Mateus Rosé brand).

Moscatel de Setúbal A popular golden-coloured, velvety fortified *vino*.

Quinta do Barranco Longo's Rosé (see p98) An award-winning rosé by young winemaker Rui Virgínia, this is one to watch out for.

There are also spirited regional *aguardentes* (firewaters), which kick like a mule.

Coffee quality is high, baristas are good and if you're not hooked on coffee culture now, you will be when you leave.

BITE-SIZED REGIONS
Lisbon

Befitting a country's capital, Lisbon is fortunate enough to have some of the best of the country's cuisine. Eateries, from local *tascas* (taverns) to large hotels, serve up traditional dishes as well as more modern international cuisine, or Portuguese takes thereon. That said, Lisbon and surrounds boast their own specialities. You've probably heard of the legendary *pastéis de nata* (custard tarts) from the Antiga Confeitaria de Belém (see p136), and the treats don't stop there.

Leave room for these dishes:

arrábida – spider crab

bacalhau a brás – thin strips of cod with potatoes and eggs

bacalhau espiritual – salt-cod soufflé

caldeirada rica – rich fish stew

choco frito – fried corn

ginjinha – a sweet cherry (and very delicious) liqueur

lulas recheadas – stuffed squid

Moscatel de Setúbal – a velvety muscat (fortified wine)

Queijadas da Sapa – pastry shells filled with cheese and egg

Queijo de Azeitão – ewe's cheese, with a characteristic flavour that owes much to lush
Arrábida pastures and a variety of thistle used in the curdling process

salmonetes – red mullet, speciality of Setúbal

sardinhas assadas – grilled sardines, especially during the Festas dos Santos Populares

travesseiros – light puff pastry, almond-and-egg cream pastries from Sintra (see p150)

Algarve

The Algarve is a culinary conundrum: nowhere else in the country is evidence of the bland internationalisation of local food so tragically apparent, catering to the hordes who visit this heavily touristed region. Conversely, the region boasts more Michelin-star restaurants than anywhere else in the country…so to enjoy some of the world's best cuisine, you are in the right place. To get your teeth into regionally specific dishes, you'll need to head off the beaten track to the inland areas.

MONCHIQUE'S MOONSHINE

You can find commercial brands of *medronho* (a locally made firewater) everywhere in Portugal, but according to those who have suffered enough hangovers to know, the best of all is the Monchique privately made brew (see p231).

The Serra de Monchique is thick with *medronho*'s raw material – the arbutus, or strawberry tree. Its berries are collected in late autumn, fermented and then left for months before being distilled in large copper stills (for sale as souvenirs all over the Algarve).

Homemade *medronho* is usually clear and drunk neat, like schnapps. It's strong, of course, but as long as you don't mix it with other drinks it doesn't give you a hangover (say the connoisseurs). Early spring, when distilling is under way, is the best time to track down some of this brew in Monchique.

This is a bivalve zone, so expect piles of fresh clams, oysters, mussels, cockles and whelks. *Búzio com feijão*, horse mackerel (bonito) or cuttlefish with tomato sauce; seafood *açorda* and rich fish, eel and shellfish soups; squid stuffed with ham and sausage; rice with red wine and octopus; and *xerém*, corn mash made with cockles, and (here it is again), pork.

Before you get too hooked, let's clarify one thing: the tuna is *not* from here (the stocks are depleted and the industry has deteriorated and, as you'll no doubt hear, the Spanish have rights to fish in Portuguese waters) and much of the fish is aquatically farmed (that's *not* to say it's not fresh, however). Price and quality can vary greatly so remember the old adage: follow the locals.

Leave room for these dishes:

amarguinha – almond liqueur

cataplanas – seafood and sausage or meats cooked in a special enclosed copper dish

doces de amêndoa – crafted marzipan sweets

figos cheios – dried figs studded with almonds

medronheira – the region's *aguardente*, a brandy-like spirit made from the fruit of the strawberry tree and sweetened with honey

Alentejo

Alentejo might be the country's poorest region, but it's the richest in culinary traditions; some of the country's best nosh is served up here. Don't hold back here – this region, with its baking plains, covers a third of the country. A quiet whisper to all vegetarians: pork will confront you at every repast. Bread also figures heavily, not just on the table, but also in cooked dishes: in *gaspacho* – a chilled tomato and garlic soup ladled over thick slices of bread, or an *açorda* – bread soup with garlic and herbs (usually coriander) with olive oil, hot water and a poached egg. In hunting season, game features on every menu, especially *perdiz* (partridge), *lebre* (hare) and *javali* (wild boar).

Leave room for these dishes:

açorda de marisco – shellfish and bread stew

carne de porco á Alentejana – a local surf and turf dish of pork and clams, cooked in a *cataplana*

empadas de galinha – small chicken pies

migas – crumbled bread with olive oil, garlic and hot water, served to accompany pork

pastéis de toucinho – a conventual sweet with a smidgeon of pork lard

queijo Serpa – Serpa cheese

regional wines – especially Borba and Esporão

requeijão – fresh ricotta cheese with *bolo podre* (local spiced honey cake), sausage and cheese

wild asparagus – served with scrambled eggs

Greedy gourmands should savour *The Wine & Food Lovers' Guide to Portugal* by Charles Metcalfe & Kathryn McWhirter (Inn House Publishing, 2007). The glossy guide beautifully chronicles Portugal's food and wine scenes.

WE DARE YOU

When the Portuguese slaughter a pig for food then food it shall be – all of it. Not just hams and trotters and shoulders, but brains, organs, guts and all. They will eat everything but the oink. The blood will be made into sausage, rather like an English black pudding. The entrails will be fried or tossed into a stew. The stomach lining will be removed and consigned to soup. Bits of brain and hunks of heart and kilos of kidneys will find their way to market, and to the menu you'll soon be holding in your hand.

While you're at it, don't go past *caracóis* (snails). The summer season has local bars serving tonnes of these little critters, mainly as a *petisco* (snack). Unlike their French cousins, these snails are not baked, but boiled with garlic and herbs and served with bread. You scoop them out of their shells with a toothpick. Matched with an ice-cold beer, we promise you, they slip down a treat.

Estremadura & Ribatejo

Seafood dominates the culinary palate in Estremadura; *cadeiradas de peixe* – fish stews – rule the menus. *Escabeche*, a stew of fish marinated in vinegar, oil and flavourings, comes a close second to *sopas de mariscos* (shellfish soups). Serious carnivores should head further east to the Ribatejo, where meat and tripe abound. *Enguias* (eels), too, slip down a treat. Sweet-toothed souls will simply devour the regions' sinful conventual sweets (all that sugar!).

Leave room for these dishes:

arroz de tomate – tomato risotto

batatas à murro – small, salted potatoes baked in their skins then 'smashed' open with the palm of the hand and seasoned with olive oil and garlic

bolinhose de pinhão – pine nut cakes

Convento das Clarissas of Louriçal – guilt-free olive oil cakes and biscuits

delícia de batata – mashed potato cakes served with almonds and cinnamon

enchidos – sausages and *carnes*, particularly *bucho recheado, choiriço, farinheira, morcelas de arroz, morcelas de sangue, negro* and *presunto (smoked ham)*

meat caldeiradas – made from lamb or kid

melões – sweet and oh-so juicy green-skinned melons (try those from Almaerem)

migas carvoeiras – bread dumplings, seasoned with dripping, and served with thick, juicy roasted ribs

sopa de pedro – a wonderful hearty vegetable and meat and anything-goes soup

tortulhos – sheep's tripe stuffed with more sheep's tripe

Portuguese wild boar are fattened on an exclusive diet of acorns – makes them yummy!

Beiras

Sweet and sour create sensations in the Beiras. There's plenty of salt, salt cod and *ovos moles* (thickened sweet egg yolks) in Aveiro, egg cakes and *chanfana* (goat or lamb stews) in Viseu, and Atlantic seafood from the west coast. Hams, sausages and firmer cheese are found throughout the forests towards Spain and cream and Rabaçal cheese come from Coimbra. The region is renowned for its Serra cheese (Queijo da Serra/Estrela), made from the winter milk of ewes that graze in the Serra de Estrela.

Leave room for these dishes:

cabrito assado no forno – kid

enguias de caldeirada – eel stew

leitão – roast suckling pig

manjar branco – traditional pudding recipe for roast chicken coated in egg and fried, served atop bread dipped in egg and fried, with cinnamon and sugar syrup poured over the top

pão de-ló – the famous collapsed sponge cake (from the town of Ovar), rich with egg yolk and sugar and cinnamon and sometimes left barely cooked in the centre and spooned out like a pudding

pastel de molho da Covilhã – an exceptional dish of thrift of flaky layers of crisp lard pastry, covered in a saffron broth soured with vinegar

torresmos – pork crackling, lush with lard, seasoned with salt, hot or cold

Douro & Trás-os-Montes

This is the perfect place to pig out. Pigs here are often handfed and benefit from potatoes, corn, chestnuts and wheat. Even the sweetest of desserts have a porky punch (don't panic, it's usually a smidgeon of lard; cinnamon is very popular, too). The food is particularly rich with meat, good *presunto* and sausages. Never cross a *tripeiro* (tripe eater) – these are proud locals from Porto for whom nothing beats the rich and gelatinous *tripas á moda do Porto* – a slow-cooked dish of trotters, dried beans, tripe, chicken, sausages, vegetables and cumin.

It's not all so meaty, though. The warm, Mediterranean climate of the Douro valley encourages rich crops of figs, cherries, almonds and oranges, and Trás-os-Montes cheese, Monte, is one of the few cheeses made from the milk of cows and ewes. Still hungry? Dishes enriched with chestnuts such as *sopa de castanhas piladas* (chestnut, bean and rice soup) are a meal in themselves.

Leave room for these dishes:

alheira – sausages with a twist (just try one)

batatas – potatoes

cabrito assado – roast kid

chouriço – small spicy sausages and

cozida á Portuguesa – meats, green vegies, offal and sausages served in their own broth

port wine – of course

presunto – and smoked meats and from Lamego and Amarante

toucinho do-cèu – rich and luscious almond, pumpkin, egg and cinnamon (and maybe bacon) cake

The Portuguese don't drink much port. It's more an English drop.

Minho

This tradition-bound region produces the (in)famous *vinho verde* (green wine). Here, too, you must try *caldo verde* (Galician kale and potato soup), because this is home to the dark and slatternly *couve galega*, the 'correct' cabbage. *Broa de milho* is the golden corn loaf of the region. The winter warm-you-up is the thrifty *sopa seca* (dry soup), shredded cooked poultry or meat, layered in an earthenware dish with slices of cooked carrot and potato, doorstop slices of bread and plenty of mint. Boiling stock is poured over the top and the dish is baked in a hot oven for up to half an hour, where it 'dries', and the result is sublime. Don't go past the seasonal eel-like lamprey, trout and salmon dishes. Trout are often served stuffed with bacon fat, grilled and served with *presunto* on top. The spice of life in the Minho is cumin.

Leave room for these dishes:

açorda de mariscos – shrimp stew in bread bowl

arroz de pato – duck risotto

cabrito assado – roast kid

caldeirada de peixe – fish stew made with conger eel, skate, monkfish and red mullet layered with potatoes, tomatoes and sometimes rice

local trout – from the Minho river

posta de barrosã – an excellent steak from a specialised Minho cattle breed

pudim do Abade de Priscos – from around Braga in Alto Minho, a bacon-flavoured crème caramel spiked with port and spices

WHERE TO EAT & DRINK

Eateries abound in Portugal; there are *restaurantes* or *taberna*s (taverns) in some of the smallest of villages. Many eateries have simply kept their traditional classification in their names – such as Taberna or Restaurante – although in reality, they are often similar. If you're looking for a small, casual neighbourhood tavern, you might end up at a *tasca* or a *casa de pasto*. These often walk a fine line between charming and *azulejo*-clad and dingy.

Meat lovers should seek out *churrasqueiras*, where you can get your chops around chargrilled chicken, sausages, pork and steak. A *marisqueira* (seafood house) serves up a wide variety of fish and crustaceans plus, frequently, *20,000 Leagues Under The Sea*–type decor (fish tanks, shiny blue tiles, fishing nets hung from the rafters). Check the prices – you often pay by the kilo (seasonal prices apply).

Snack and socialise over a cold beer at the *cervejaria* (beer hall). These popular local places are usually colourfully decorated in tiles and rustic decor and they stay open all day and well into the night. Besides cold brew, *cervejarias* serve hearty plates of the usual favourites (seafood, meat) plus *petiscos* (snacks).

Another atmospheric option is the *adega,* which literally means wine cellar, often decked out with antique wine casks. You often find communal wooden tables and a good mix of people there to eat simple, hearty meals (the menus are similar to restaurants') and drink a fair house wine.

Opening hours for most eateries are noon to 3pm and 7pm to 10pm. Cafes that dole out coffee, pastries and sandwiches open by about 8am.

VEGETARIANS & VEGANS

The bad news for nonmeat eaters: Portugal is a disaster zone. Pesco-vegetarians will get by, but serious vegetarians might have more problems. Even vegetable dishes usually include meats or fats. But take heart. Markets contain a good variety of fruits, vegetables and nuts, and the breads are plentiful. Vegetables are rarely served in restaurants, but end up in soups instead (but even these may be cooked with bones to flavour).

HABITS & CUSTOMS

A paper cloth, upturned plate, knife, fork, serviette and glass is the regular Portuguese table decor. These days, new strict nonsmoking laws are in force. It may be out with the butts, but it's in with the TV. Yep, these are everywhere, even in some of the smartest of places.

Meals and snacks seem to roll one into the other. Having said that, the Portuguese don't really 'do' breakfasts. They're usually still so stuffed full from the day before that they don't go there. Snacks are often a roll with butter or ham and cheese. By mid-morning, when peckish, Portuguese nibble on one of a mountain of fresh pastries (including sinful conventual cakes) from one of the many *pastelarias*. But they won't go past a *bica*, an espresso, grabbed standing at a bar.

Lunch is a serious pastime. As the main meal of the day – usually taken between midday and 4pm, lunches are big, hearty and long. Workers

---

GETTING TIPSY

Service is usually not added to the bill. It's fairly customary to leave a few coins or 5% (or even 10%) in smarter places and/or if the service was exceptional. Always ask if they accept credit cards if you're planning to use one.

TOP FIVE RESTAURANTS

There are many atmospheric places to experience Portugal's best dishes. The following are a few of our highly subjective picks.

Douro: O Escondidinho (p400) Traditional cuisine beautifully prepared in a wood-burning oven, amid *azulejos* (hand-painted tiles) and an elegantly set dining room.

Minho: Margarida da Praça (p445) A stylish new restaurant with a Bohemian soul and an eclectic menu featuring the best ingredients from sea and countryside.

Lisbon: Olivier (p134) The first of Lisbon master chef Olivier da Costa's three restaurants, this low-ceilinged Bairro Alto haunt tempts with Med-style specialities rich in texture, colour and seasonal flavour. Signature dishes such as octopus carpaccio and osso bucco pair nicely with Portuguese wines.

Algarve: Vila Joya (p207) A Michelin-star restaurant with a studded setting in a villa by the beach. Impeccable, well, everything, and worthy of all accolades.

Beiras: Palace Hotel do Buçaco (p341) Seven or eight delicious and original courses served in a dining room that is itself a work of art is an experience never to be forgotten.

---

take 90 minutes during the week, but on weekends, this meal can stretch for hours.

As for late afternoon? It's time for a sugar hit – the convential sweets do just the trick for fading energy levels – and tea houses or cafes see another burst of activity.

Increasingly, dinner is on the Portuguese agenda, especially in restaurants, and can be more of the same – large portions of meat-based dishes, but it doesn't cut the same status as the midday meal.

EAT YOUR WORDS

Want to know piri-piri from pimento? Get behind the cuisine scene by getting to know the language. For pronunciation guidelines see p519.

Useful Phrases

Table for ..., please.
Uma mesa para ..., se faz favor.   oo·ma *me·*za *pa·*ra ... se faz fa·*vor*

Can I see the menu, please?
Posso ver o menu, por favor?   po·soo ver o me·*noo*, poor fa·*vor*

Can I see the wine list, please?
Posso ver a lista dos vinhos, por favor?   po·so ver a *leesh·*ta doosh *vee·*nyoosh poor fa·*vor*?

Can you recommend a good local wine?
Pode-me recomendar um bom vinho   po·de me re·ko·meng·*dar* oong bong *vee·*nyoo
da regiao?   da re·*zhowng*?

Do you have a high chair for the baby?
Tem uma cadeira para crianças?   teng oo·ma ka·*day·*ra *pa·*ra kree·ang·*sash*?

I'll have a beer, please.
Vou tomar uma cerveja, se faz favor.   vo to·*mar* oo·ma ser·*ve·*zha se faz fa·*vor*

Can I have the bill/check, please.
A conta, se faz favor.   a *kong·*ta se faz fa·*vor*

I'm vegetarian.
Sou vegetariano/a. (m/f)   so ve·zhe·ta·ree·*a·*noo/a

Food & Drink Glossary

adega	a·de·ga	cellar, usually wine cellar; may also denote a winery; also a traditional bar or bar-restaurant serving wine from the barrel
água-ardente	a·gwar·deng·te	strongly alcoholic 'firewater'

almôndegas	al·*mong*·de·gazh	meatball served in tomato gravy
cachucho	ka·*shoo*·sho	sea bream
camarão	ka·*ma*·rowng	a tinned sausage usually served on a roll
casa de pasto	ka·za de *pash*·to	casual eatery
cervejaria	ser·ve·zha·*ree*·a	beerhouse
chanfana	shang·*fa*·na	mutton or goat stew cooked with red wine
choco	*shoo*·ko	cuttlefish
churrasqueira	shoo·rrash·*kay*·ra	grilled-chicken restaurant
confeitaria	kon·fay·ta·*ree*·a	cake and pastry shop
dose	*do*·ze	serving or portion
empada	eng·*pa*·da	a little pot pie
escabeche	shka·*besh*·she	raw meat or fish marinated in vinegar and oil
espetada	shpe·*ta*·da	kebab
favas	*fa*·vazh	a dish of broad beans
galão	ga·*lowng*	a large glass of hot milk added to an espresso (ask for *galão bem escuro* for a stronger fix)
gambas	*gang*·bas	prawns
gelado	zhe·*la*·doo	ice cream
marisqueira	ma·reesh·*kay*·ra	seafood house
meia dose	*may*·a *do*·ze	half-portion
merenda	me·*reng*·da	light snack
paio	*pai*·oo	smoked pork sausage
pastéis de nata	pash·*taysh* de *na*·ta	custard tarts
pastelaria	pash·te·la·*ree*·a	pastry and cake shop
pequeno almoço	pe·*ke*·noo ow·*mo*·soo	breakfast, traditionally just coffee and a bread roll
pernil no forno	per·*neel* noo *for*·noo	roast leg of pork
pimenta	pee·*meng*·ta	pepper
piri-piri	pee·ree pee·ree	fiery chilli sauce; it is the signature condiment of Portugal
pudim	poo·*deeng*	pudding
queijada	kay·*zha*·da	a cheesecake pastry
rota dos vinhos	*ro*·ta doosh *vee*·nyoosh	wine route
salmão	sal·*mowng*	salmon
sardinhas assadas	sar·*dee*·nyash a·*sa*·dash	grilled sardines
simples	seeng·*plesh*	plain, no filling or icing
tasca	*tash*·ka	tavern
uma bica	*oo*·ma *bee*·ka	a short black
vindima	veeng·*dee*·ma	grape harvest
vinho da casa	*vee*·nyoo da *ka*·za	house wine
vinho maduro	*vee*·nyoo ma·*doo*·ro	wine matured for more than a year
vinho verde	*vee*·nyoo *ver*·de	young (literally, 'green') wine from the Minho region, which can be white, red or rosé.

Environment

The tiny country at the edge of southwestern Europe is a land of rivers, fields and rolling hills, with olive and cork plantations, vineyards and untrammelled forests crisscrossing the land. A wildly varied coastline and a few mountains in the north further diversify the geographic portrait.

The land, its wildlife and the balance between preservation and economic development are the big issues facing the country. Once considered the backwards step-cousin of Europe, Portugal is blazing new trails when it comes to environmental issues, with heavy investment in renewable energy. Unfortunately, the country still faces serious issues like declining numbers of its wildlife, severe forest fires and water pollution in its coastal areas.

THE LAND

Portugal is a small country, even by European standards, covering an area of 92,389 sq km and measuring 560km north to south and 220km east to west. But despite its diminutive size, its land is impressively diverse. A single day's travel could see you pass from dramatic mountain ranges in the north to undulating meadows in the south; meanwhile, the coast switches its mood from wild surf-crashing Atlantic waves to balmy Mediterranean beaches, perfect for paddlers.

In 2005 Portugal experienced one of its worst forest fires in history. Over 300,000 hectares were burned and 18 people were killed.

Together with Ireland and Spain, Portugal dips its toes into the Atlantic at the westernmost extreme of Europe; and it's no accident that, with 830km of Atlantic coastline, Portugal is one of the greatest nations of seafarers and explorers in history. In many ways though, Portugal is at the mercy of its rivers, which bring precious water to its parched southern lands due to the lack of rainfall.

One of Portugal's most important waterways, the Rio Tejo, slices the country almost perfectly in half, flowing northeast to southwest and spilling its contents into the Atlantic at Lisbon, one of Portugal's few natural harbours. The mountains loom mostly north of the Tejo, while vast plains spread to the south.

Topping the country, the heavily populated northwestern Minho is blessed with fertile rolling plateaus and rivers flowing through deep gorges. Step down and neighbouring Beira Alta, Douro and Trás-os-Montes are all carved from high granite, schist and slate plateaus. This region, rising to 800m, is nicknamed the *terra fria* (cold country) for its winter chill.

Meanwhile the southern and eastern Alto Douro (in southern Trás-os-Montes) rightly scores the name *terra quente* (hot country), a scorched landscape of sheltered valleys with dark schists that trap the heat and create the perfect microclimate (described by locals as 'nine months of winter and three months of hell') for pumping out Portugal's famous port wine.

In 1756, the Douro Valley became the first demarcated wine region in the world. Today, the dramatically carved region is a Unesco World Heritage Site.

However, for real mountains you need only look to the Serra da Estrela, which tops out at the 1993m Torre, the highest peak in mainland Portugal and home to a winter ski resort. Rolling down further south, you'll reach the low-lying, often marshy Atlantic coastline of Beira Litoral and Estremadura, sprinkled with river-mouth lagoons and salt marshes.

Inland, between the Rio Tejo and the Rio Guadiana, the Alto Alentejo joins the Spanish tablelands in wide flat plateaus. Further south still, in northern Baixo Alentejo, are ridges of quartz and marble, and a vast undulating landscape of wheat, cork trees and olive trees – a large swath of which is now submerged by the vast Barragem do Alqueva (Alqueva Dam).

Only the eastern Serra do Caldeirão and western Serra de Monchique break the flatness of the south, and are a natural border between the Alentejo and the Algarve. They also act as a climatic buffer for the Algarve, which basks in a Mediterranean glow.

The islands of Madeira and the Azores, originally colonised in the 15th century, are also part of Portugal: Madeira lies 900km to the southwest, off Africa's west coast; the nine-island Azores archipelago sprawls 1440km west of Lisbon.

The 2006 documentary *Ainda Há Pastores?* (Are there Still Any Shepherds?) provides a fascinating glimpse into the lives of Portugal's last true shepherds.

WILDLIFE

While few visitors come to Portugal specifically to track down its wildlife, the country is nonetheless home to some of the rarest and most interesting creatures in Europe. Northern Portugal has forests and hills rich in animal and bird life, while the south's parched plains and coastline also shelter their fair share of fauna.

Animals

The cão d'água, or Portuguese water dog, more than lives up to its name. Capable of diving to depths of 6m, the web-toed canine can even 'herd' fish into nets.

Several of Portugal's rarest creatures are the shaggy-bearded Iberian lynx (see below), teetering on the brink of extinction, and the much-maligned wolf. However, the fauna you're most likely to stumble across are hares and bats. With luck, in more remote areas you might be able to spot foxes, deer, otters or even foraging wild boars.

A few North African species have also sneaked into the picture. The most delightful settler is the Mediterranean chameleon, which was introduced to the eastern coastal Algarve about 70 years ago. Two more such species are the spotted, weasel-like genet, which hides during the day, and the Egyptian mongoose, which you may stumble upon as it trots across quieter Algarve roads.

Bird fanciers will also be kept well occupied. Boasting over 300 species, Portugal has a mixed bag of bird life – from temperate to Mediterranean species, plus migrants too. You have an excellent chance of spying wetland species – including flamingos, egrets, herons, spoonbills and many species of shore birds – in reserves, such as the Reserva Natural do Sapal de Castro Marim e Vila Real de Santo António and the Parque Natural da Ria Formosa.

To read reports and view photos of birdwatchers who have travelled in Portugal, visit www .travellingbirder.com.

You may even score a glimpse of more unusual birds: nimble lesser kestrels and the shy black stork near Mértola and around Castro Verde, vividly coloured purple gallinules in the Parque Natural da Ria Formosa, hefty bustards and sandgrouse on the Alentejo plains, and Iberian species such as the great spotted cuckoo, red-winged nightjar, rufous bushchat and azure-winged magpie.

MISSING LYNX

No endangered animal in Portugal plucks at the heartstrings quite like the tufty-eared Iberian lynx. Though not much bigger than the common house cat, this is the only big cat endemic to Europe and is easily the world's most endangered feline. There are thought to be between 100 and 150 Iberian lynx left in Spain and Portugal, with numbers decimated by disease, poachers, wildfires, dam- and road-building and the scarcity of wild rabbits (its favourite food). It's alarming to think that if the species dies out, it may well be the first feline extinction since prehistoric times.

The last remaining hideouts of the animals in Portugal are mostly in scattered, remote regions of the Algarve – though some conservationists wonder if any lynx remain in Portugal. A network of protected areas, habitat corridors and captive breeding programmes are now being established to save the species. For details of how to help, check the website of **SOS Lynx** (www.soslynx.org).

However, if it's birds of prey that ruffle your feathers, your best bet is in the Parque Natural do Douro Internacional, over which soar various species of eagles, kestrels and vultures.

Portugal's leading ornithological society is the **Sociedade Portuguesa para o Estudo de Aves** (SPEA; ☎ 213 220 430; www.spea.pt, in Portuguese; 2nd fl, Av da Liberdade 105, Lisbon), which runs government-funded projects to map the distribution of Portugal's breeding birds. **Naturetrek** (☎ 01962 733051 in the UK; www.naturetrek.co.uk) runs an eight-day birdwatching excursion around southern Portugal.

ENDANGERED SPECIES

There's not much good news circulating in the animal kingdom. According to a 2008 report by the state **Instituto de Conservação de Natureza** (ICN; http://portal.icnb.pt), 42% of vertebrate species in Portugal are endangered. Perhaps the most high profile of Portugal's endangered animals is the fast-dwindling Iberian lynx (opposite). Other species facing serious decline are several bird species, trout and a number of other freshwater and migratory fish species, of which 69% are reduced to low-lying shoals that may lead to their extinction.

The rusty-coloured Iberian wolf is also in danger. Disturbingly, there are only around 200 left in Portugal (out of an estimated 1500 on the Iberian Peninsula). Most live in the Parque Natural de Montesinho in Trás-os-Montes and adjacent areas of Spain. But despite being protected by law, the wolf is still illegally shot, trapped or poisoned on a regular basis as it is blamed (often mistakenly) for attacking cattle and domestic animals. Those interested in learning more about the wolves might visit the Iberian Wolf Sanctuary (p166) north of Lisbon.

Portugal's protected areas also harbour several endangered birds, including the majestic Spanish imperial eagle, the tawny owl in the Parque Nacional da Peneda-Gerês, and the purple gallinule in the Parque Natural da Ria Formosa.

Outside the parks you can see endangered species in Mértola, which hosts the country's largest nesting colony of lesser kestrels between March and September, or in the Castro Verde region, a haunt of the great bustard, Europe's heaviest bird, and one of the heaviest birds capable of flight, weighing in at a whopping 17kg!

On a brighter note, there are a few species making a comeback, including the mountain goat, now present once again in Portugal's Parque Nacional da Peneda-Gerês. Pronounced extinct in 1990, the hollow-horned ruminant has made a remarkable comeback, owing to efforts by neighbouring Galicia to save the species.

Plants

In spring, Mediterranean flowers set the countryside ablaze in the Algarve and Alentejo; especially enchanting are the white and purple rockroses. The pretty Bermuda buttercup, a South African invader, also paints Algarve fields a brilliant yellow in the winter. Orchid lovers will also have a wild time. They thrive in the Algarve, especially around Faro. Meanwhile, in the rainier northern climes, gorse, heather and broom cloak the hillsides.

Early settlers in the south cultivated vines and citrus trees, while the Moors introduced almonds, carobs, figs, palms and the gorgeous white irises that decorate roadsides. Portuguese explorers and colonists also got in on the act, bringing back various exotics, including South African figs and American prickly-pear cacti.

In Sintra you'll see dozens of exotic species, planted as fashionable novelties in the 18th and 19th centuries. More recently, profitable plantations of

The Mediterranean chameleon, resident of the south coast, has a tongue longer than its body.

Grupo Lobo is a wolf-conservation organisation and runs volunteer programmes. For more information on the disappearing Iberian wolf, see their website (http://lobo.fc.ul.pt).

The Algarve Tiger, by Eduardo Gonçalves et al (2002), is a passionate book about the world's most endangered feline, the Iberian lynx.

Australian eucalyptus have engulfed vast areas with their thirsty monoculture. Eucalyptus trees grow faster than cork (cork takes about 40 years of growing before the tree is commercially viable, versus 12 years for the eucalyptus), and they earn farmers more money – eucalyptus nets about three times as much per hectare as cork. Eucalyptus is used in Portugal to make paper and pulp.

CORK & OTHER ESSENTIAL CROPS

Doggedly battling it out with commercial giants like the eucalyptus are two home-grown trees that have long crafted Portugal's landscape and lifestyle: the olive and the cork oak, the latter now a threatened species. Since Roman times both have been grown and harvested in harmony with the environment, providing not only income but protection for many other species.

The olive tree, in fact, is one of the oldest known cultivated trees in the world, and the Romans considered those who used animal fats instead of olive oil in their diets to be barbarians. Olives have long had a prominent place on the Portuguese table, and the country produces 50,000 tonnes of olive oil annually. Different regions produce different types of olives, and there's much local lore tied up in the rich, oily fruit.

Travel across the vast Alentejo plains and you'll see wild twisted groves of olive trees. Even more predominant, however, are the thousands of cork oak trees: they're the tall, round-topped evergreens with glossy, holly-like leaves and wrinkled bark that's often stripped away, leaving a strangely naked, ochre trunk.

Indeed the cork oak has long been one of the country's prize agricultural performers and Portugal is the biggest cork producer in the world. Treasured for its lightness, admired for its insulating and sealing qualities, and more versatile than any synthetic alternative, cork is used for everything from footwear to floors, gaskets to girders. And, of course, for bottle stoppers. The absence of smell and taste make it the essential 'bung' for quality wines.

Cork is cultivated as carefully as port wine. Trees mature for at least 25 years before their first stripping; indeed, there are laws against debarking too early. After that they may only be shorn every ninth year. Cork cutters slice and snip by hand, as skilfully as barbers. Treated with such respect, a tree can produce cork for up to 200 years: moreover, the largest cork tree in Portugal produced over a tonne of raw cork last time it was harvested.

But this exceptionally sustainable industry is now under threat. There have long been critics of cork stoppers – some 300 million bottles of wine a year do indeed end up 'corked'. Owing to this fungal contamination, many bottlers have decided to replace cork with synthetic (aka plastic) bottle stoppers or even twist-tops, which have become quite prevalent in some countries – particularly Australia.

And much is at stake if cork forests decline. These are areas of exceptional biological diversity on which various threatened species depend, including the Iberian lynx and Bonelli's eagle. An international campaign has been launched to promote 'real cork' and urge producers and retailers to publicise its importance. Check out the website www.corkqc.com for more on the natural cork campaign and the multimillion-euro battle to improve the quality of organic bottle stoppers in the face of their synthetic competition.

NATURAL PARKS & RESERVES

Portugal's myriad natural parks offer vast areas of unspoilt mountains, forests and coastal lagoons. And the reluctance of most Portuguese to go walking anywhere, let alone venture into remote areas, can be a huge bonus for travellers. Step even a short distance off the beaten track and you'll find that you have extraordinary landscapes all to yourself.

Every year around 15 billion natural cork bottle-stoppers are produced in Portugal.

Walking in Portugal, by Bethan Davies and Benjamin Cole (2000), provide details for some 33 country walks in Portugal.

Algarve Landscapes: Car Tours and Walks, by Brian and Eileen Anderson (2007), has lots of useful information for exploring the southern coast.

TOP NATURAL PARKS & RESERVES

Parks & Reserves	Features	Page
Parque Nacional da Peneda-Gerês	lushly forested mountains, rock-strewn plateaus; deer, birds of prey, hot springs, wolves, long-horned cattle	p457
Parque Natural da Arrábida	coastal mountain range, damaged by wildfire; birds of prey, diverse flora	p174
Parque Natural da Ria Formosa	salty coastal lagoons, lakes, marshes & dunes; rich bird life, beaches, Mediterranean chameleons	p192
Parque Natural da Serra da Estrela	pristine mountains – Portugal's highest; rich bird life, rare herbs	p358
Parque Natural das Serras de Aire e Candeeiros	limestone mountains, cave systems; covered in gorse & olive trees	p312
Parque Natural de Montesinho	remote oasis of peaceful grassland & forest; last wild refuge for Iberian wolf	p483
Parque Natural de Sintra-Cascais	rugged coastline & mountains; diverse flora	p151
Parque Natural do Alvão	granite basin, pine forest, waterfalls; rich bird life, deer, boar	p472
Parque Natural do Douro Internacional	canyon country with high cliffs & lakes; home to many endangered birds of prey	p490
Parque Natural do Vale do Guadiana	gentle hills & plains, rivers; rare birds of prey, snakes, toads, prehistoric sites	p273
Parque Natural do Sudoeste Alentejano e Costa Vicentina	coastal cliffs & remote beaches; unique plants, otters, foxes, 200 bird types	p228
Reserva Natural da Berlenga	remote islands in clear seas, rock formations, caves; sea birds	p294
Reserva Natural das Dunas de São Jacinto	thickly wooded coastal park; rich in bird life	p347
Reserva Natural do Estuário do Sado	estuary of mud, marshes, lagoons & dunes; bird life incl flamingos, molluscs, bottlenose dolphins	p175
Reserva Natural do Sapal de Castro Marim e Vila Real de Santo António	marshland & salt pans; flamingos, spoonbills, avocet, caspian terns, white storks	p201

The Parque Nacional da Peneda-Gerês is the only bona fide *parque nacional* (national park) in Portugal, but there are also 24 other *parques naturais* (natural parks), *reservas naturais* (nature reserves) and *paisagens protegidas* (protected landscape areas). These areas total some 6500 sq km – just over 7% of Portugal's land area.

The **Instituto da Conservação da Natureza** (ICN; Map p109; ☎ 213 507 900; www.icn.pt; Rua de Santa Marta 55, Lisbon) is the government agency responsible for the parks. It has general information, but detailed maps and English-language materials are sometimes hard to come by. Standards of maintenance and facilities vary wildly, but there are signs of improvements of trails and resources within the parks. Portugal's mixed bag of natural parks is worth the effort. Browse the table that shows Portugal's parks and nature reserves (above) to get a picture of all the rich wildlife and diverse landscapes on offer.

Every year in late October, the small town of Seia in the Serra da Estrela hosts Cine Eco (www.cineeco.org), an International Environmental Film and Video Festival.

ENVIRONMENTAL ISSUES

Portugal has been slow to address its environmental problems, notably soil erosion, air and water pollution, rubbish disposal and the effects of mass tourism on fragile coastal areas. Of growing concern, too, is the spread of huge, water-thirsty eucalyptus plantations that effectively destroy regional wildlife habitat and aggravate an already serious drought problem brought on by climate change. It's also a highly flammable species, making for some destructive fires. While such intensively cultivated plantations continue to

GREEN PORTUGAL

Compared with other EU members, Portugal typically falls in the middle of the pack regarding energy consumption and renewable initiatives. According to the latest EU report, roughly 20% of Portugal's energy comes from renewable sources (compared with star performer Sweden at 40% and the less inspiring UK at 1.3%). A number of ambitious new projects are in the works or already underway, however, which will push Portugal toward the top of the pack. Portugal's goal is to generate 31% of its energy from renewable resources by 2020. Here are a few of the developments greening the way:

- Mata de Sesimbra (www.bioregional.com/oneplanetliving/portugal) Begun in 2003, this €1 billion project will combine a 5300-hectare nature reserve with a 500-hectare tourist development (with 6000 new dwellings). In addition to massive reforestation plans, the project will create 11,000 new jobs, utilize 50% of food from local sources and create a sustainable transport network, eliminating need for private vehicles. It will be built with a minimum of 50% recycled materials and energy will be generated only by renewable sources.

- In 2008 the world's largest solar farm opened in the Alentejo, near Moura. Taking advantage of Portugal's abundant annual sunshine, the €300 million project features over 2500 giant solar panels (each the size of a tennis court), with enough produced energy to power 30,000 homes.

- Recently, Portugal launched the world's first 'wave farm'. Located 10km off shore, just north of Portugal, the project consists of three 120m-long semisubmersible machines which harvest the ocean's power to the tune of 2.25 MW per year – energy enough for 2000 homes.

- In northern Portugal, one of Europe's largest wind farms was under construction at the time of writing. Portugal has invested heavily in wind energy over the last three years, quadrupling its output from wind energy. Once completed, wind farms across the country will provide enough power for 750,000 homes.

- The more controversial topic of hydroelectric power is still very much in the foreground in Portugal. Four new dams are planned for construction over the next five years (with another six on the table), adding to the already substantial 256 MW capacity of the country's current hydroelectric dams.

- In 2008 Portugal signed an agreement with Renault and Nissan to create a national recharging network to boost the use of electric cars. In so doing, it became one of the world's first countries to offer consumers the possibility of nationwide charging stations. Both carmakers have agreed to mass market their electric cars in Portugal from 2011.

proliferate (now accounting for over one-fifth of the country's forest area), Portugal's traditional, sustainable cork plantations are under serious threat.

Litter is a growing problem, but industrial development is to blame for Portugal's most polluted seasides – you'd be wise to avoid beaches near the industrial centre of Sines. Having said that, in 2008 around 197 Portuguese beaches claimed an international Blue Flag for cleanliness, and some areas have undergone radical clean-ups in recent years.

To keep up to date with water quality, get hold of the free, regularly updated map of coastal water, *Qualidade da Água em Zonas Balneares* from **Instituto da Água** (☎ 218 430 000; www.inag.pt, in Portuguese; inforag@inag.pt).

Fire & Drought

It's water – or rather the lack of it – that has become one of Portugal's worst environmental nightmares. Years of terrible drought in the mid-1990s heralded an alarming trend that continues to grow. Every year around 3% of Portugal's forest goes up in flames, worsening soil erosion and devastating farmland. And matters have only worsened in recent years.

Brush and forest fires in northern and central Portugal on average wipe out 1900 sq km per year, though fires between 2003 and 2006 were particularly bad, burning over 900,000 hectares. Owing to the ongoing dangers, in 2008 Portugal tested a remote monitoring system that could possibly prevent the destruction wrought by fires and even save lives.

Portugal is not alone in its thirst. Squabbles with Spain continue over the two countries' shared water sources. Unfortunately for Portugal, three of its major rivers – the Douro, the Tejo and the Guadiana – originate in Spain. And both countries desperately need this water for agriculture (which accounts for three-quarters of water use in Portugal), hydroelectricity and to counter their dire drought situation in the south. Despite water-sharing agreements with Portugal, Spain is increasing its withdrawals from the Guadiana in order to divert the water to its dry southern lands.

Environmentalists point out the stress that the holiday-making economy places on local infrastructure. One 18-hole golf course, for instance, can use as much water in a year as 10,000 homes, and plans to build some 100,000 holiday homes in the Algarve over the next 10 years are likely to create problems of much greater magnitude.

Meanwhile, Portugal's own answer to this water problem has been to erect large dams – some 100 at last count – to control its precious water supply. Its most recent dam, the Barragem do Alqueva near Beja (p250), is a behemoth, which caused enormous environmental damage during its construction. The huge reservoir (Europe's largest artificial lake) now submerges around 260 sq km of the arid Alentejo. Among its casualties are over a million oak and olive trees and the habitats of several endangered species, including Bonelli's eagle, the otter, black storks, bats and the Iberian lynx. And that's not even mentioning the Stone Age art and Roman fortress now under water. Even the supposed beneficiaries – the farmers themselves – may increasingly find irrigation costs too high.

> For the ultimate story of recycling, pick up *Cork Boat* by John Pollack (2005), about one man's journey along the Douro in a homemade sailboat.

> An excellent general website on Portuguese environmental and nature-related topics is www.naturlink.pt.

Environmental Organisations

Almargem (☎ 289 412 959; www.almargem.org; Alto de São Domingos 14, Loulé) Active in the Algarve.

Associação Nacional de Conservação da Natureza (Quercus; National Association for the Conservation of Nature; ☎ 217 788 474; www.quercus.pt, in Portuguese; Bairro do Calhau, Parque Florestal de Monsanto, Lisbon) Portugal's best and busiest environmental group has branch offices and education centres scattered around Portugal. In addition to churning out studies and publishing environmental guides, Quercus members are Portugal's most active campaigners for environmental causes. Some Quercus branches arrange field trips.

Grupo de Estudos de Ordenamento do Território e Ambiente (Geota; ☎ 213 956 120; www.geota.pt, in Portuguese; Travessa do Moinho de Vento 17, Lisbon) This environment study group is also an activist organisation that arranges weekend trips.

Liga para a Proteção da Natureza (LPN; League for the Protection of Nature; ☎ 217 780 097; www.lpn.pt; Estrela do Calhariz de Benfica 187, Lisbon) This is Portugal's oldest conservation group and often publicises environmental issues.

Portugal Outdoors

With 830km of coastline and beaches for every taste, Portugal naturally attracts its fair share of sun worshippers. Perfect waves and winds make the country a paradise for surfers and windsurfers, and there's a seemingly endless range of other pursuits to enjoy along the country's Atlantic shores: diving, dolphin watching, golfing, kayaking... The list goes on.

But outdoors enthusiasts will find plenty more to appreciate in Portugal beyond sun, surf and sand. Inland, lovely landscapes of cork and olive trees, granite peaks and limestone heights and precipitous river gorges form the backdrop for a whole host of other activities – from birdwatching to horse riding, canoeing to paragliding. As you leave the coast behind, you'll find that the crowds grow thinner, and the prices – already among Europe's lowest – go down as well.

Thanks to Portugal's geographic compactness, there's no reason you can't combine multiple outdoor adventures in a single trip. It's not unreasonable to plan a rock-climbing/surfing vacation or even – in late winter – to trade in your waterskis for a day slaloming down the snowy slopes of Torre, Portugal's highest mountain.

BOATING

Along the coast, especially in the Algarve, pleasure boats predominate, offering everything from barbecue cruises to grotto tours to dolphin-spotting excursions. Inland, Portugal's rivers, lagoons and reservoirs offer a wide variety of boating opportunities, including kayaking, sailing, rafting and canoeing. Rivers popular for boating include the Guadiana (see p201), Mondego, Zêzere, Paiva, Minho and Tâmega.

Companies that rent boats and/or operate boat trips can be found in Lagos (p219), Mértola (p273), Barragem do Alqueva (p250), Tomar (p321), Coimbra (p333), Ponte de Lima (p452), Rio Caldo (p463) and Amarante (p411), just to name a few.

CLIMBING, PARAGLIDING & ADRENALINE SPORTS

In the far north, the granite peaks of Parque Nacional da Peneda-Gerês (p457) are a climber's paradise. Other popular places are the schist cliffs at Nossa Senhora do Salto east of Porto, the rugged 500m-tall granite outcropping of Cántaro Magro (p367) in the Serra da Estrela; the limestone crags of Reguengo

---

FIVE GREAT FAMILY OUTDOOR ADVENTURES

- Learn to surf with the whole family at XXS Surf School in Ericeira (p289).
- Take the invigoratingly bouncy boat ride from Peniche to Berlenga Grande, swim and sunbathe at the island's protected horseshoe-shaped beach and stay overnight in a 17th-century fort converted to a hostel (p294).
- Look for dolphins – and learn about them from an on-board marine biologist – as you ply the Atlantic waters off the Algarve coast (p219).
- Meet sheep, visit shepherds in their old stone houses and dip your toes in the icy river as you hike up the glacial Zêzere Valley in Parque Natural da Serra da Estrela (p365).
- Scan the cliff faces of the Rio Douro gorge for eagles and vultures as you cross the international waters between Spain and Portugal near Miranda do Douro (p490).

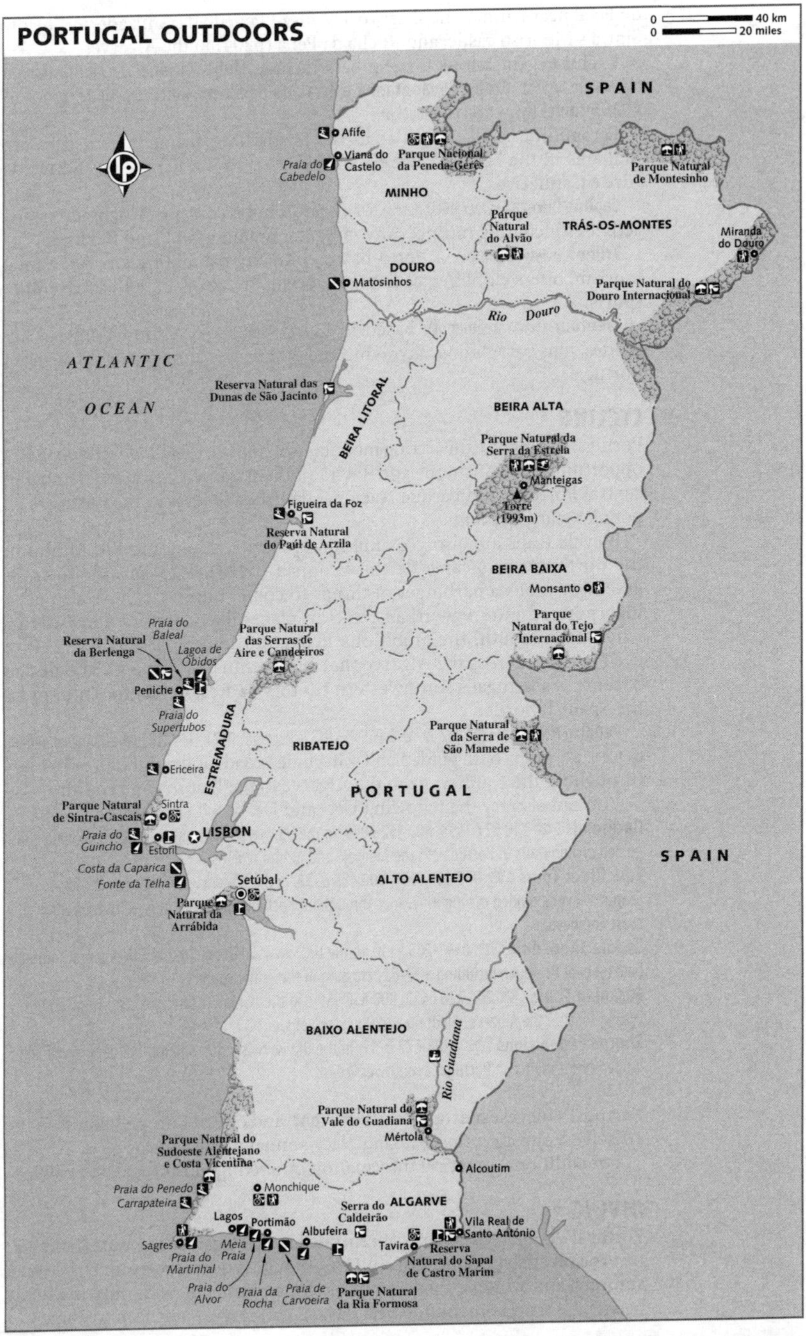
PORTUGAL OUTDOORS
0 40 km
0 20 miles
SPAIN
ATLANTIC
OCEAN
Afife
Viana do Castelo
Praia do Cabedelo
Parque Nacional da Peneda-Gerês
Parque Natural de Montesinho
MINHO
Parque Natural do Alvão
TRÁS-OS-MONTES
Miranda do Douro
DOURO
Matosinhos
Parque Natural do Douro Internacional
Rio Douro
Reserva Natural das Dunas de São Jacinto
BEIRA LITORAL
BEIRA ALTA
Parque Natural da Serra da Estrela
Manteigas
Torre (1993m)
Figueira da Foz
Reserva Natural do Paúl de Arzila
BEIRA BAIXA
Monsanto
Parque Natural do Tejo Internacional
Praia do Baleal
Reserva Natural da Berlenga
Lagoa de Óbidos
Parque Natural das Serras de Aire e Candeeiros
Peniche
Praia do Supertubos
ESTREMADURA
RIBATEJO
Parque Natural da Serra de São Mamede
Ericeira
PORTUGAL
Parque Natural de Sintra-Cascais
Sintra
Praia do Guincho
Estoril
LISBON
Costa da Caparica
Fonte da Telha
SPAIN
Setúbal
Parque Natural da Arrábida
ALTO ALENTEJO
BAIXO ALENTEJO
Rio Guadiana
Parque Natural do Vale do Guadiana
Mértola
Parque Natural do Sudoeste Alentejano e Costa Vicentina
Alcoutim
Praia do Penedo
Carrapateira
Monchique
ALGARVE
Serra do Caldeirão
Lagos
Portimão
Albufeira
Vila Real de Santo António
Sagres
Meia Praia
Tavira
Reserva Natural do Sapal de Castro Marim
Praia do Martinhal
Praia do Alvor
Praia da Rocha
Praia de Carvoeira
Parque Natural da Ria Formosa

do Fetal near Fátima, the sheer rock walls of Penedo da Amizade, just below Sintra's Moorish castle; and Rocha da Pena (p204) in the Algarve.

Useful organisations for climbers include **Clube Nacional de Montanhismo** (www.cnm.org.pt), **Grupo de Montanha e Escalada de Sintra** (http://gmesintra.com) and **ADA/Desnivel** (www.treino.d esnivel.pt).

Paragliding is also popular in the north. Two prime launch sites are Linhares in the Serra da Estrela and Alvados in the Parque das Serras de Aire e Candeeiros.

Capitão Dureza (www.capitaodureza.com), near Coimbra, organises high-adrenaline activities including rafting, canyoning, mountain biking and trekking.

Trilhos (www.trilhos.pt), a Porto-based company promoting environmental tourism, offers climbing, caving, canyoning, trekking and other adventure sports.

Freetour (www.freetour.pt), based in Leiria, sponsors a similar mix of activities, plus paragliding, skydiving and other adrenaline sports throughout Portugal.

CYCLING

Portugal has many exhilarating mountain-biking (*bicicleta todo terreno*; BTT) opportunities. Monchique and Tavira in the Algarve, Sintra and Setúbal in central Portugal and Parque Nacional da Peneda-Gerês in the north are all popular starting points.

Bicycle trails are also growing in popularity. Along the Rio Minho in the north, cyclists can ride the Ecopista (p447), a 13km rails-to-trails greenway that's a harbinger of things to come. Bike trails have also been incorporated into new urban parks in places like Coimbra and Guarda, while down south, the ambitious Ecovia do Litoral (p199) is a 214km cycling route across the Algarve that will eventually connect Cabo de Sao Vicente at Portugal's southwestern tip to Vila Real de Santo António on the Spanish border.

Pedal in Portugal (☎ 282 697 298, 965 753 033 in Portugal, 0871 711 3315 in the UK; www.pedalin portugal.com) offers both guided and self-guided road- and mountain-bike tours throughout the country, from the Algarve to the Douro wine country.

You can also try the following UK- and US-based companies:

Backroads (☎ 510 527 1555, 800 462 2848, in the US; www.backroads.com) Offers a couple of guided cycling tours in Portugal, in the Alentejo and Minho regions.

Easy Rider Tours (☎ 978 463 6955, 800 488 8332, in the US; www.easyridertours.com) Features several guided cycling itineraries throughout Portugal, from the Algarve to the Lisbon coast and beyond.

Saddle Skedaddle (☎ 0191-265 1110, in the UK; www.skedaddle.co.uk) Offers four mountain-bike tours of Portugal, including a 17-day crossing of the entire country.

Saranjan Tours (☎ 206 720 0623, 800 858 9594, in the US; www.saranjan.com) High-end cycling tours in the Algarve, Alentejo and Douro regions.

Sherpa Expeditions (☎ 0208-577 2717, in the UK; www.sherpa-walking-holidays.co.uk) Self-guided cycling tours on Portugal's southwest coast.

Portugal's biggest spectator cycling event, and one of Europe's oldest, is the 10-stage Volta a Portugal, taking place annually in August.

For additional practical information on cycling in Portugal, see p509.

DIVING

Portugal's best dive sites are concentrated in the Algarve. The water temperature is a bit crisp (around 14°C to 16°C, though it doesn't vary much between summer and winter); most divers prefer a 5mm suit. Visibility is usually between 4m and 6m; on the best days, it can range from 15m to 20m.

RESPONSIBLE DIVING

Please consider the following tips when diving and help preserve Portugal's marine ecology:

- Avoid touching or standing on living marine organisms.
- Be conscious of your fins. Even without contact, the surge from fin strokes can damage delicate organisms. Take care not to kick up clouds of sand, which can smother organisms.
- Take great care in underwater caves. Spend as little time within them as possible as your air bubbles may be caught within the roof and thereby leave organisms high and dry. Take turns to inspect the interior of a small cave.
- Resist the temptation to collect or buy shells or to loot marine archaeological sites (mainly shipwrecks).
- Ensure that you take home all your rubbish and any litter you may find as well. Plastics in particular are a serious threat to marine life.
- Do not feed fish.
- Minimise your disturbance of marine animals.

One of the best places for beginners to learn is off Praia do Carvoeiro, with several operators offering PADI-accredited courses in English. **Tivoli Diving** (☎ 282 351 194; www.tivoli-diving.com) offers a range of courses, including a four-dive open-water course (€415). **Divers Cove** (p208; www.diverscove.de) is a reputable, German-run outfit offering a similar range of courses.

PADI-accredited courses are also offered in Sagres (p226), Lagos (p219) and Albufeira (p206).

Up north, more experienced divers can explore the wreck of a German U1277 submarine off Matosinhos. **Mergulho Mania** (☎ 934 837 434; www.mergulho mania.com, in Portuguese) offers dives there as well as PADI-certified courses.

Closer to Lisbon, there are diving outfits at Costa da Caparica (p169) and Reserva Natural da Berlenga (p293).

GOLF

Portugal is a golf mecca, and its championship courses are famous for their rolling greens and ocean vistas. Although many courses are frequented mainly by club members and local property owners, anyone with a handicap certificate can play here. Greens fees usually run from €70 to €100 per round.

Estoril has nearly a dozen spectacular courses. Golf do Estoril, one of Portugal's best-known, has hosted the Portuguese Open Championship 20 times. It's 5262m long and set among eucalyptus, pine and mimosa. Two other Portuguese Open venues lie nearby: Oitavos Dunes, which rolls over windblown dunes and rocky outcrops; and Penha Longa, ranked one of Europe's best courses, with superb views of the Serra de Sintra. See www .estorilsintragolf.net or the Estoril and Cascais *turismos* (tourist offices) for full details of all courses.

Two other well-regarded courses around Lisbon are Troia Golf near Setubal and Praia d'El Rey Golf & Beach Resort near Óbidos.

The Algarve has 36 courses at last count – including the renowned Vilamoura Oceânico Victoria, San Lorenzo, Monte Rei and Vale do Lobo courses.

For golfing packages around Lisbon and in the Algarve, try UK-based **3D Golf** (☎ 0870-122 5050; www.3dgo lf.com).

Bear in mind that golf courses' toll on the environment can be significant, especially in dry and fragile coastal settings like the Algarve (see p205).

HORSE RIDING

Riding is a fantastic way to experience Portugal's countryside. Lusitano thoroughbreds hail from Portugal, and experienced riders can take dressage lessons in Estremadura (below). Otherwise, there are dozens of horse-riding centres – especially in the Alentejo, and in the Algarve at places like Silves, Lagos, Almancil and Portimão. Northern Portugal also offers some pleasant settings for rides, including Ponte de Lima (p453) and the Parque Natural de Montesinho (p484). Rates are usually around €20 to €30 per hour.

The world-renowned school **Escola de Equitação de Alcainça** (☎ 219 662 122; Rua de São Miguel, Alcainça), near Mafra, offers dressage lessons on Lusitano horses.

Switzerland-based **Equitour** (☎ 61 303 31 05; www.equitour.com) offers eight-day riding holidays costing €995 to €1750 per person, including accommodation and some meals. Their signature tour follows the Alentejo Royal Horse Stud Trail, with stays at grand country estates. Other destinations include the southwestern Costa Vicentina.

The Wyoming-based outfit **Equitours** (☎ 307-455 3363, 800-545 0019 from US or Canada; www.ridingtours.com), America's largest and oldest, offers weeklong, intermediate-level rides along the Alentejo coast. Prices range from US$1490 to US$2100, including accommodation and some meals. Equitours also offers a year-round classical dressage programme at the Escola de Equitação de Alcainça (see above), including accommodation plus 90 minutes'/three hours' riding per day for €245/300.

SKIING

Believe it or not, Portugal has a downhill ski run. The country's highest peak, 1993m-high Torre in Parque Natural da Serra da Estrela, offers basic facilities including three lifts and equipment rental (p367). However, for experienced skiers, Torre offers more curiosity value than actual skiing excitement.

SURFING

Portugal has some of Europe's most curvaceous surf, with 30 to 40 major reefs and beaches. It picks up swells from the north, south and west, giving it remarkable consistency. It also has a wide variety of waves and swell size, making it ideal for surfers of all levels. Numerous surf schools in the Algarve and along Portugal's western Atlantic coast offer classes and all-inclusive packages for all skill levels, from beginners to advanced.

When to Surf

The best waves in southern Portugal are generally in the winter from November to March. Further north, spring and autumn tend to be the best seasons. Waves at these times range from 2m to 4.5m high. This is also the low season, meaning you'll pay less for accommodation, and the beaches will be far less crowded. Even during the summer, however, the coast gets good waves (1m to 1.5m on average), and despite the crowds, it's fairly easy to head off and find your own spots (with your own wheels, you can often be on your own just by driving a few minutes up the road).

Surf reports for many Portuguese beaches are available on the international site www.magics eaweed.com.

What to Take

The water temperature here is colder than it is in most other southern European countries, and even in the summer you'll probably want a wetsuit. Board and wetsuit rental are widely available at surf shops and surf camps; you can usually score a discount if you rent long-term – otherwise, you'll be paying around €30 per day for board and wetsuit rental, or €25 per day for the board only.

Prime Spots

One of Portugal's best breaks is around Peniche (p292), where you can count on good waves with just about any wind. An excellent hostel and several residential surf camps make this an affordable base. Supertubos and Baleal are the most popular local beaches.

Other fabled surf spots include Ribeira d'Ilhas (p289) in Ericeira and Praia do Guincho (p161) near Cascais, which often host international championships. Another break that's famous among the global surfing community is Carrapateira (p229) in the western Algarve. Schools and clubs head over this way from Lagos and further afield to take advantage of the crashing waves. Nearby, the area around Praia do Penedo is a good choice for beginners.

In northern Portugal, Figueira da Foz and Afife are two of the best spots.

Information

There are dozens of schools that can help you improve your surfing game. Most offer weekly packages including simple accommodation – dorms, bungalows or camping.

Recommended surf camps north of Lisbon include Ericeira's Ribeira d'Ilhas Surf Camp (p289) and the cluster of camps at Baleal (p292).

In the Algarve, there are many operators, including the popular Algarve Surf Camp (p219), which runs a surf shop in Lagos and surf camps in Sagres and Carrapateira. The English/Aussie-run **Surf Experience** (www.surf-experience.com) in Lagos offers one- to four-week surf packages including accommodation, breakfast and lunch and transport to the beach. Several other outfits are located in Sagres (p226), Carrapateira (p229) and Lagos (p219).

WALKING

Portugal's wonderful walking potential is all the better because few people know about it. Most organised walking clubs are in the Algarve, with marked trails and regular meetings. There is a cluster of organisations around Monchique (p232) but other good bases are Vila Real de Santo António, Sagres and Parque Natural Serra de São Mamede.

When to Walk

Summer temperatures can get stiflingly hot in some regions (particularly the Alentejo and the Algarve). To beat the heat, consider travelling in spring (April to May) or autumn (late September and October).

What to Take

If you're headed to the showery north, be sure to bring reliable rain gear. Otherwise, bring a good compass, maps, a hat and strong sun protection and some type of palliative for aching feet.

Two good companions include *Walking in the Algarve* by Julie Statham, describing 40 coastal and mountain walks, and *Walking in Portugal* by Bethan Davies and Ben Cole, covering walks in the north and as far down as Setúbal.

Prime Spots

Those interested in walking the breadth of the country should consider the Via Algarviana, a 300km route following paved and unpaved roads between Alcoutim and Sagres that takes two to three weeks. For details, see the boxed text, p199.

In the Beiras, the Parque Natural da Serra da Estrela (p359) forms a beautiful backdrop for walking, although trail maintenance and signposting are spotty. In many places you're likely to have the trail to yourself. Especially

RESPONSIBLE WALKING

To help preserve the ecology and beauty of Portugal, consider the following tips when walking.

Rubbish

- Carry out *all* your rubbish. Don't overlook easily forgotten items, such as silver paper, orange peel, cigarette butts and plastic wrappers. Empty packaging should be stored in a dedicated rubbish bag. Make an effort to carry out rubbish left by others.
- Never bury your rubbish: digging disturbs soil and ground cover and encourages erosion. Buried rubbish will likely be dug up by animals, who may be injured or poisoned by it. It may also take years to decompose.
- Minimise waste by taking minimal packaging and no more food than you will need. Take reusable containers or stuff sacks.
- Sanitary napkins, tampons, condoms and toilet paper should be carried out despite the inconvenience. They burn and decompose poorly.

Human Waste Disposal

- Contamination of water sources by human faeces can lead to the transmission of all sorts of nasties. Where there is a toilet, please use it. Where there is none, bury your waste. Dig a small hole 15cm (6in) deep and at least 100m (320ft) from any watercourse. Cover the waste with soil and a rock. In snow, dig down to the soil.

Washing

- Don't use detergents or toothpaste in or near watercourses, even if they are biodegradable.
- For personal washing, use biodegradable soap and a water container (or even a lightweight, portable basin) at least 50m (160ft) away from the watercourse. Disperse the waste water widely to allow the soil to filter it fully.
- Wash cooking utensils 50m (160ft) from watercourses using a scourer, sand or snow instead of detergent.

Erosion

- Hillsides and mountain slopes, especially at high altitudes, are prone to erosion. Stick to existing trails and avoid short cuts.
- If a well-used trail passes through a mud patch, walk through the mud so as not to increase the size of the patch.
- Avoid removing the plant life that keeps topsoils in place.

Fires & Low-Impact Cooking

- Portugal suffers hundreds of devastating fires every year, the majority of them caused by humans. Lighting open fires is prohibited in Portugal. Cook on a light-weight kerosene, alcohol or Shellite (white gas) stove and avoid those stoves powered by disposable butane gas canisters.

Camping & Walking on Private Property

- Always seek permission to camp from landowners.
- Public access to private property without permission is acceptable where public land is otherwise inaccessible, so long as safety and conservation regulations are observed.

beautiful is the Vale do Zêzere, a glacial valley at the foot of Torre, Portugal's highest peak. A good base in this region is the mountain village of Manteigas (p364). Also in the Beiras is the beautiful multiday GR-22 walking route, a 540km circuit of *aldeias históricas* (historic villages) including medieval hill towns such as Sortelha, Linhares and Monsanto.

There's fantastic walking in the far north, where Parque Nacional da Peneda-Gerês (p459) offers gorgeous hikes over mountainous terrain, past very old villages and archaeological sites. A quiet base for adventure is Campo do Gerês, while a busier touristy base (but with lots of services) is Vila do Gerês. In neighbouring Trás-os-Montes, the natural parks of Alvão, Montesinho, and Douro Internacional also have some splendid hiking spots.

Information

Many *turismos* and natural park offices offer free brochures about local walks, although materials frequently go out of print due to insufficient funding. Other organisations that produce free maps of their own trails include Odiana in the Algarve (p201) and the Centro de Interpretaçaõ da Serra da Estrela (CISE) in the Serra da Estrela (p361).

Approximately 10km north of Sagres, walking guide author Julie Statham runs **Portugal Walks** (☎ 282 697 298, 965 753 033 in Portugal, 0871 711 3315 in the UK; www.portugal walks.com), which offers all-inclusive weeklong packages (unguided/guided walks from €545/680) in mainland Portugal as well as Madeira and the Azores.

Try the following UK-based companies for organised walking tours:

ATG Oxford (☎ 0186-531 5678; www.atg-oxford.co.uk) Offers weeklong guided walking holidays around Sintra and the Alentejo.

Headwater (☎ 0160-672 0033 in the UK, 800-567-6286 in the US; www.headwater.com) Weeklong jaunts in the Serra da Estrela region.

Ramblers Holidays (☎ 0170-733 1133; www.ramblersholidays.co.uk) Guided walking holidays in the Algarve.

Sherpa Expeditions (☎ 0208-577 2717; www.sherpa-walking-holidays.co.uk) Self-guided walks in the Alentejo.

Winetrails (☎ 0130-671 2111; www.winetrails.co.uk) Private, tailor-made rambles featuring fine wining and dining, primarily in the Douro.

WILDLIFE WATCHING

Portugal provides excellent opportunities for birdwatching, especially in Atlantic coastal lagoons and in the deep river canyons along the Spanish border. In the south, prime birdwatching spots include the Serra do Caldeirão (p192), Parque Natural da Ria Formosa (p192), Parque Natural do Vale do Guadiana (p273), and the Reserva Natural do Sapal de Castro Marim e Vila Real de Santo Antonio (p201).

North of Lisbon, the Berlenga Islands make a perfect place to observe seabirds (p294). Other good places for birdwatching include Reserva Natural do Paúl de Arzila near Coimbra (p342), Dunas de São Jacinto near Aveiro (p347) and the Tejo and Douro gorges, where vultures and eagles nest in the Parque Natural do Tejo Internacional (p354) and Parque Natural do Douro Internacional (p490).

For guided birdwatching and other nature-oriented trips, contact **Wildaway** (☎ 282 697 298, 965 753 033 in Portugal; 0871 711 3315 in the UK; www.wildaway.com). The company leads tours of the Algarve's lagoons, wetlands, salt marshes and tidal flats. Prices for a guided five-hour day trip start at £70 for one to three people, or £120 for four to six people.

Various companies in the Algarve offer dolphin-spotting trips, including Mar Ilimitado (p226), Algarve Dolphins and Dolphin Seafaris (p219).

WINDSURFING

Praia do Guincho (p161), west of Sintra, and Portimão (p213) in the Algarve are both world championship windsurfing sites. Other prime spots include (from north to south): Viana do Castelo's Praia do Cabedelo; Lagoa de Óbidos, a pretty lagoon that draws both sailors and windsurfers; and (closer to Lisbon) the Costa da Caparica's Fonte da Telha. In the Algarve, Sagres attracts pros (its strong winds and fairly flat seas are ideal for freeriding), while Lagos, Albufeira and Praia da Rocha cater to all.

Windsurf Point (☎ 282 792 315; www.windsurfpoint.com), based at Meia Praia near Lagos, offers classes in windsurfing (€100/180 for five/10 hours) and kitesurfing (€140/250 for four/eight hours).

Other popular venues for windsurfing and kitesurfing lessons include Foz do Arelho (p298) and Peniche (p293).

Meet the Locals

The seafaring country on the edge of the Iberian Peninsula may be small, but it has made significant contributions to human history. Today, with just under 11 million souls, Portugal continues to produce outstanding names – some internationally recognised, others living in obscurity outside their villages – but all making contributions both large and small to the national identity. We've profiled a few Portuguese who are on the cutting edge of their fields: distinguished talents creating soulful fados, award-winning wines, avant-garde designs and environmental conservation. Their Portugal is a place of hope and possibility – a land intimately linked to their life stories.

Connect with a Lisbon designer's unique world view while perusing their wares (p145)

PAUL BERNHARDT

The Queen of Fado

NAME	Mariza
AGE	35
OCCUPATION	Singer
RESIDENCE	Lisbon

'Fado is a really magical genre; it concerns the deepest feelings of the human being. Fado has the power to cross boundaries and touch anyone.'

The neighbourhood where I grew up in Lisbon, Mouraria, had a big role in my life and singing. I lived there since I was three years old, and it was there where I first experienced fado. I started singing at age five at my parents' tavern. It had a magical environment, coloured by the sound of the Portuguese guitar and all those beautiful voices that were my first teachers.

I still live in Lisbon; it will always be home. If you walk around traditional neighbourhoods like the Alfama, Bairro Alto or Mouraria you will breathe fado, as it is part of Lisbon's personality. It is in my city that I learn more about fado, listening to the elders and visiting typical homes.

Fado has the power to cross boundaries and touch anyone inside. That's when nationalities drop frontiers, and there is only emotions and the heart.

Taste fado's melancholy in its heartland at Alfama's Clube de Fado (p142)

GREG ELMS

Resonate with the *guitarra* (pear-shaped guitar) accompanying mournful fado (p53)

PASCALE BEROUJON

GREAT PLACES TO HEAR FADO

'I love going to traditional places where you can listen to *fado vadio* (street fado), such as Tasca do Chico in Bairro Alto, or Mesa de Frades (p143) in Alfama or any other typical restaurant where fado happens.' – Mariza.

Other first-rate spots to hear the soulful music:

Clube de Fado (p142) Hosts the cream of the crop.

Senhor Vinho (p143) Small stylish place owned by *fadista* star Maria da Fé.

A Baiuca (p142) Feels like a family gathering, with fun lively rounds of *fado vadio*.

Á Capella (p337) For a taste of Coimbra-style fado, this converted 14th-century place is pure magic.

Meander past fado memorabilia at the Museu do Fado (p115), Lisbon

GREG ELMS

'Dress' yourself with a la.ga bag (p145)

ANDY CHRISTIANI

ECO-COOL DESIGN HOTSPOTS

Fabrico Infinito (p145) Check out bejewelled toothpick necklaces, Jorge's funky la.ga bags and other recycled-meets-luxury creations at this eco-cool gallery in a former coach house. The ethos? Like nature, no two designs are the same.

Yron (p145) This hip new gallery stages rotating exhibitions that highlight the eco-friendly works of young creatives – from sleek cork stools to born-again Barcelos cockerels.

Articula (p145) Teresa Milheiro's anticonformist workshop raises eyebrows with accessories made from recycled odds and ends, such as a doll's-eye necklace.

Trundle through colourful Lisbon on the arthritic Elevador da Bica funicular (p114)

BRENT WINEBRENNER

A Design For Lisbon

NAME	Jorge Moita
AGE	32
OCCUPATION	Designer and creative director of Krvkurva
RESIDENCE	Lisbon

My big break was la.ga bag winning the national design award in 2002. It's made from recyclable, radioactivity-resistant Tyvek, weighs 40g and supports up to 55kg. The concept is that anything can 'dress' you: furniture, cars, bags... it's all just semiotics. And that style can be sustainable and conscientious.

Today I'm collaborating with Tires women's prison near Cascais to produce la.ga bags. It's the human face of design and I value the inmates' honesty; they'll tell you 'this is shit' or 'it's great, I'm going to fake it when I get out'.

Lisa [Lisbon] is the Havana of Europe with its light, decadence and brightly coloured buildings. You can't dream in a city where everything is overdone. Life here is intuitive and real. Sometimes I become an accidental tourist wandering Alfama, slowing down to notice new details. This is a city for getting lost; I'm still discovering it.

'When I'm in Lisbon, I don't always see the light or river, but it's like love – you miss it when it's not there.'

'Uncertain Regard' – a close-up on a customised la.ga bag by German-born artist Daniela Krstch (p145)

ANDY CHRISTIANI

Preserving Mountain Life

NAME	José Conde
OCCUPATION	Biologist at CISE (Serra da Estrela Interpretive Centre) in Seia
RESIDENCE	São Romão, Beira Alta

'Recreational walking is just starting in Portugal. Things are changing. When people live in cities, they need nature.'

My grandfathers and my uncle were shepherds. I grew up in Lisbon but spent holidays visiting them here in the high country. I always loved animals and wild places. Nowadays very few traditional shepherds remain. The work will end with this generation. It's an extinction process.

Serra da Estrela is one of Portugal's oldest and biggest parks. But conservation is difficult. Sometimes parks exist only on paper; they lack resources, and private owners with historical land rights don't share the parks' priorities.

Development is putting this landscape at risk. People use plastic bags to slide down the mountain in winter, then we find them clogging the waterways in summer. Entrepreneurs want to build more skiing facilities, but the mountain isn't big enough.

Recreational walking is just starting in Portugal. We were poor until recently, so we prefer to drive. But things are changing. When people live in cities, they need nature.

Breathe the mountain air in the Parque Nacional da Peneda-Gerês (p457)

GARETH MCCORMACK

Hike upwards from
Campo do Gerês (p464)
GARETH MCCORMACK

PLACES TO EXPERIENCE MOUNTAIN LIFE

Vale do Zêzere (p365) A mountain-fringed glacial valley in the Serra da Estrela. Shepherds still graze their flocks here, living in stone huts and making cheese.

Linhares (p364) This *aldeia histórica* (historic village) in the Serra da Estrela's north has a medieval fortress with amazing views over the plains.

Monsanto (p354) Dominating the horizon for miles around, Monsanto's stone houses and castle cling to a stony promontory near the Spanish border.

Piódão (p351) This ultra-picturesque schist village has a new museum of traditional rural culture and a network of hiking trails.

Encounter village residents in the Parque Nacional da Peneda-Gerês (p457)

ANDERS BLOMQVIST

A New Vintage

NAME	Rui Virgínia
AGE	40
OCCUPATION	Winemaker, Quinta do Barranco Longo
RESIDENCE	Algoz, the Algarve

PORTUGUESE WINES RUI ADORES

Vintage Quinta do Noval 2000
(www.quintadonoval
.com) Fantastic aromas.

Tributo 2004
(www.ruireguinga
.com) This wine has an outstanding profile.

Monte do Limpo Premium 2005
(www.montedolimpo
.pt) Firm palate of red fruits, compotes and chocolate.

Get familiar with the art and science of Portuguese wine-making (p67)

VASCO CÉLIO

Here at my winery, I have 15 hectares of grapes. I have received several prizes, the most recent one for my rosé. My rosé is fruity like strawberries.

I have a background in management, not wine. I started growing grapes in the Algarve because I saw a good opportunity. The Algarve has no positive references in good wines. When people talk about Algarve wines they talk about bad wines. So why is the venture successful? I am a perfectionist. I say, OK, the Algarve has other vineyards, but *not* like this.

Many people can try [winemaking], if they are wealthy for example, but that doesn't mean the wines are well done. We say, 'The height of the horns makes the cow heavy'.

As for the future? I am building a new *adega* (winery). It will join tradition with modernity. I will use solar power and aim for an omissions-free *adega*. I am the future, not only the past.

Quinta do Barranco Longo (☎ 282 575 253; ☯ 10am-noon & 4-6pm Mon-Fri) is open to visitors.

Lisbon & Around

Imagine you are given a blank canvas to paint a city. First the backdrop: cobalt skies, seven hills (a different view for each day of the week), a blue splash for the river. Hmmm, now for the details: candy-bright houses, twisting alleys, grand plazas where locals relax in the sunshine… It's beautiful, but lacks icons, so you add a likeness of San Francisco's suspension bridge, swirly Manueline turrets, ivory-white domes and - as an afterthought - a Moorish castle on the hillside. Perfect. Now stand back and observe your masterpiece: Lisbon.

Yet Lisa, as locals nickname their city, is no superficial beauty. Step into the painting for exhilarating extremes. Retrospective and innovative, Lisbon is a twilight zone between past and future; dodgem-like trams screech through cobbled streets and Afro-Brazilian beats pulsate in the graffiti-slashed Bairro Alto, Zen-style sushi bars sidle up to one-pan family taverns, and thimble-sized haberdasheries abut eco-cool design stores. Neither time- nor trend-obsessed, Portugal's capital is refreshingly authentic.

This pass-the-parcel of a city rewards those who peel away its layers. Sure, the colonial coffers funded world-class museums, but the real adventure lies in the everyday. Walk medina-like Alfama, where neighbours natter across the laundry; sip *ginjinha* (cherry liqueur) on Largo de São Domingos; or simply appreciate sublime details, from geometric *azulejos* (tiles) to caravels glinting atop wrought-iron lanterns.

Mistress of revels, Lisbon lives for the *noite* (night) and is way up there on Europe's must-party list. Mournful *fadistas* (fado singers) crooning in Alfama's womblike bars, hedonists hitting Bairro Alto for all-night drink-a-thons, clubbers shimmying on the dance floor at Lux at 4am - it's a Cinderella-in-reverse scene where the ball begins at midnight. Da Vinci had Mona, but you can have Lisa - she's brighter, sexier and every bit as enigmatic.

HIGHLIGHTS

- Getting lost in the medina-like **Alfama** (p114) to the backbeat of fado
- Finding pulsating *festas* (parties) on an all-night bar-hop of **Bairro Alto** (p137)
- Taking a rattle-'n'-roll spin of Lisbon's trophy sights on **tram 28** (see boxed text, p112)
- Bidding *bom dia* (good morning) to sharks and sea otters at the mind-blowing **Oceanário** (p122)
- Oohing and aahing at the Manueline fantasy of **Mosteiro dos Jerónimos** (p120)
- Striding through enchanted forests to above-the-clouds palaces and castles in **Sintra** (p150)

★ Sintra

★ Lisbon

■ POPULATION: 580,000 | ■ AREA: 86.5 SQ KM

HISTORY

Imperial riches, fires, plague, Europe's worst recorded earthquake, revolutions, coups and a dictatorship – Lisbon has certainly had its ups and downs.

It's said that Ulysses was here first, but the Phoenicians definitely settled here 3000 years ago, calling the city Alis Ubbo (Delightful Shore). Others soon recognised its qualities: the Greeks, the Carthaginians and then, in 205 BC, the Romans, who stayed until the 5th century AD. After some tribal chaos, the city was taken over by North African Moors in 714. They fortified the city they called Lissabona and fended off the Christians for 400 years.

But in 1147, after a four-month siege, Christian fighters (mainly British crusader hooligan-pillagers) under Dom Afonso Henriques captured the city. In 1255, Afonso III moved his capital here from Coimbra, which proved far more strategic given the city's excellent port and central position.

In the 15th and 16th centuries Lisbon boomed as the opulent centre of a vast empire after Vasco da Gama found a sea route to India. The party raged on into the 1800s, when gold was discovered in Brazil. Merchants flocked to the city, trading in gold, spices, silks and jewels. Frenziedly extravagant architecture held up a mirror to the era, with Manueline works such as Belém's Mosteiro dos Jerónimos.

But at 9.40am on All Saints' Day, 1 November 1755, everything changed. Three major earthquakes hit, as residents celebrated Mass. The tremors brought an even more devastating fire and tsunami. Some estimate that as many as 90,000 of Lisbon's 270,000 inhabitants died. Much of the city was ruined, never to regain its former status. Dom João I's chief minister, the formidable Marquês de Pombal, immediately began rebuilding in a simple, cheap, earthquake-proof style that created today's formal grid.

Two bloodless coups (in 1926 and 1974) rocked the city. In 1974 and 1975 there was a massive influx of refugees from the former African colonies, changing the demographic of the city and adding to its richness culturally, if not financially.

After Portugal joined the European Community (EC) in 1986, massive funding fuelled redevelopment, which was a welcome boost after a 1988 fire in Chiado. Streets became cleaner and investment improved facilities. Lisbon has spent recent years dashing in and out of the limelight as 1994 European City of Culture, and host of Expo 98 and the 2004 European Football Championships. Major development projects throughout the city have continued recently, from the reopening of the restored Campo Pequeno bullring to ongoing work on the metro and, most importantly, much needed building rehab in the Alfama.

ORIENTATION

Lisbon's seven hills – Estrela, Santa Catarina, São Pedro de Alcântara, São Jorge, Graça, Senhora do Monte and Penha de França – sit on the northern side of Portugal's finest natural harbour, the wide mouth of the Rio Tejo. São Jorge is topped by the *castelo* (castle), and each of the others by a church or a stunning *miradouro* (lookout).

At the riverfront is the grand Praça do Comércio. Behind it march the streets of Baixa (lower) district, up to Praça da Figueira and Praça Dom Pedro IV (aka Rossio).

Here the city forks along two arteries. Lisbon's swish, tree-lined boulevard Avenida da Liberdade stretches 1.5km northwest from Rossio and the adjacent Praça dos Restauradores to Praça Marquês de Pombal and the large Parque Eduardo VII. The other fork is the commercial strip of Avenida Almirante Reis, running north for almost 6km from Praça da Figueira (where it's called Rua da Palma) to the airport.

From Baixa it's a steep climb west, through swanky shopping district Chiado, into the narrow streets of nightlife-haven Bairro Alto. Eastwards from the Baixa it's another climb to Castelo de São Jorge and the Moorish, labyrinthine Alfama district around it.

River ferries depart from a pier near Praça do Comércio and from Cais do Sodré to the west. Lisbon's long-haul train stations are Santa Apolónia, Sete Rios, Cais do Sodré, Rossio and Barreiro (across the Tejo). Gare do Oriente is the newest station, combining bus, train and metro stations on the northeastern outskirts of town.

Aside from Gare do Oriente, the main long-distance bus terminal is Sete Rios, near Sete Rios train station and Jardim Zoológico metro station. As well as metro and buses, there are vintage trams and zippy new ones running 6km west from Praça da Figueira to the waterfront suburb of Belém.

Lisbon is connected south across the Tejo to the Costa da Caparica and Setúbal Peninsula by the immense, 70m-high Ponte 25 de Abril, Europe's longest suspension bridge, which also carries trains to the south. Ponte Vasco da Gama – 17.2km long – reaches across the Tejo further north, from Sacavém (near Parque das Nações) to Montijo, speeding up north–south traffic.

Maps

The free, adequate tourist office map of Lisbon has a small metro map and lists major sights, hotels and tourist information points. It also has a blow-up of the central Baixa district. For a street index, Michelin's multilingual 1:11,000 *Lisboa Planta*, which includes metro and pedestrian routes, is available in most bookshops. Free metro maps are available at most stations.

INFORMATION
Bookshops

Secondhand books are sold on Calçada do Carmo, behind Rossio, and from stalls in the arcades of Praça do Comércio at the end of Rua Augusta.

Fnac (Map pp104-5; ☎ 213 221 800; Armazéns do Chiado) One of the city's biggest book and music stores.

Livraria Bertrand Chiado (Map pp104-5; ☎ 213 421 941; Rua Garrett 73); Greater Lisbon (Map pp102-3; Centro Comercial Colombo); Belém (Map p110; Centro Cultural de Belém) Bertrand has excellent selections amid 18th-century charm.

Livraria Buchholz (Map p109; ☎ 213 170 580; Rua Duque de Palmela 4) Huge collection of literature in Portuguese, English, French and German.

Cultural Centres

British Council (Map p108; ☎ 213 214 500; www.british council.org/portugal; Rua Luís Fernandes 1-3) In a palatial building; has a library (open from 2pm to 6pm Monday to Friday), with current English-language newspapers.

Institut Franco-Português (Map p109; ☎ library 213 111 421; www.ifp-lisboa.com; Av Luís Bívar 91) Has regular cultural (including film) events, and a library.

Emergency

Police headquarters (Map pp104-5; ☎ 217 654 242; Rua Capelo 13)

Tourist police post (Map pp104-5; ☎ 213 421 634; Palácio Foz, Praça dos Restauradores; ✆ 24hr)

Internet Access

Many cafes in Lisbon offer free wireless surfing, including Mar Adentro (p133). Cheap internet cafes that double as international call centres huddle around Largo de São Domingos. The places listed here charge around €1.50 to €3 per hour:

@lfa.net (Map pp104-5; Rua dos Remédios 89; ✆ 9am-7.30pm)

Cyber Bica (Map pp104-5; Rua dos Duques de Bragança; per hr €3; ✆ 11am-midnight Mon-Fri) Groovy cafe-bar.

Espaço Ágora (Map p108; ☎ 213 940 170; Armazém 1, Av de Brasília, Santos; ✆ 24hr) Youth centre with free internet.

Internet Café (Map pp104-5; Calçada do Garcia 4; ✆ 10.30am-7.30pm Mon-Fri, 10.30am-3pm Sat) Also offers cheap international calls.

Web Café (Map p107; ☎ 213 421 181; Rua do Diário de Notícias 126; ✆ 7pm-2am)

Internet Resources

http://lisboa.brighterplace.com Fun site with student info on bars and clubs.

http://timeout.sapo.pt Details on upcoming gigs, cultural events and interesting commentary, in Portuguese.

www.askmelisboa.com Multilingual site with info on discount cards.

www.cm-lisboa.pt The groovy municipal site listing upcoming events.

www.golisbon.com Up-to-date info on sightseeing, eating, nightlife and events.

www.visitlisboa.com Lisbon's comprehensive tourism website, with the lowdown on sightseeing, transport and accommodation.

Laundry

Lava Neve (Map pp104-5; Rua da Alegria 37; per 5kg wash/dry €5.50/4.40; ✆ 10am-1pm & 3-7pm Mon-Fri, 9am-1pm Sat) Lisbon's only self-service launderette.

Medical Services

Clínica Médica Internacional (Map p109; ☎ 213 513 310; Av António Augusto de Aguiar 40) A quick (though not cheap), private clinic with English-speaking doctors.

Farmácia Estácio (Map pp104-5; ☎ 213 211 390; Rossio 62) A central pharmacy.

Hospital Británico (British Hospital, Hospital Inglês; Map p108; ☎ 213 943 100, 213 929 360; Rua Saraiva de Carvalho 49) English-speaking staff and doctors.

Hospital de Santa Maria (Map pp102-3; ☎ 217 805 000; Av Professor Egas Moniz)

Money

Multibanco ATMs are widespread throughout the city.

Barclays Bank (Map p109; ☎ 217 911 100; Av da República 50)

Cotacâmbios (Map pp104-5; ☎ 213 220 480; Rossio 41; ✆ 8am-10pm) The best bet for changing cash or travellers cheques is a private-exchange bureau like this one.

(Continued on page 111)

GREATER LISBON

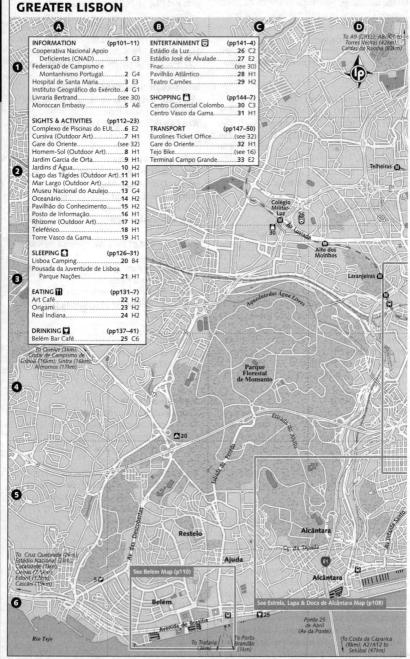

INFORMATION	(pp101–11)
Cooperativa Nacional Apoio Deficientes (CNAD)	**1** G3
Federação de Campismo e Montanhismo Portugal	**2** G4
Hospital de Santa Maria	**3** E3
Instituto Geográfico do Exército	**4** G1
Livraria Bertrand	(see 30)
Moroccan Embassy	**5** A6

SIGHTS & ACTIVITIES	(pp112–23)
Complexo de Piscinas do EUL	**6** E2
Cursiva (Outdoor Art)	**7** H1
Gare do Oriente	(see 32)
Homem-Sol (Outdoor Art)	**8** H1
Jardim Garcia de Orta	**9** H1
Jardins d'Água	**10** H2
Lago das Tágides (Outdoor Art)	**11** H1
Mar Largo (Outdoor Art)	**12** H2
Museu Nacional do Azulejo	**13** G4
Oceanário	**14** H2
Pavilhão do Conhecimento	**15** H2
Posto de Informação	**16** H1
Rhizome (Outdoor Art)	**17** H2
Teleférico	**18** H1
Torre Vasco da Gama	**19** H1

SLEEPING	(pp126–31)
Lisboa Camping	**20** B4
Pousada da Juventude de Lisboa Parque Nações	**21** H1

EATING	(pp131–7)
Art Café	**22** H2
Origami	**23** H2
Real Indiana	**24** H2

DRINKING	(pp137–41)
Belém Bar Café	**25** C6

ENTERTAINMENT	(pp141–4)
Estádio da Luz	**26** C2
Estádio José de Alvalade	**27** E2
Fnac	(see 30)
Pavilhão Atlântico	**28** H2
Teatro Camões	**29** H2

SHOPPING	(pp144–7)
Centro Comercial Colombo	**30** C3
Centro Vasco da Gama	**31** H1

TRANSPORT	(pp147–50)
Eurolines Ticket Office	(see 32)
Gare do Oriente	**32** H1
Tejo Bike	(see 16)
Terminal Campo Grande	**33** E2

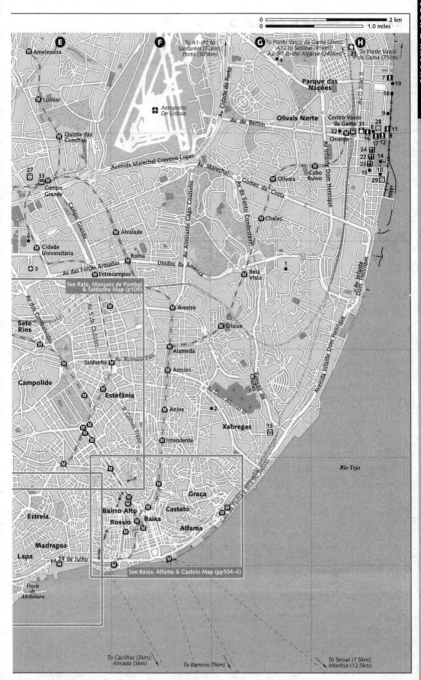

LISBON & AROUND

BAIXA, ALFAMA & CASTELO

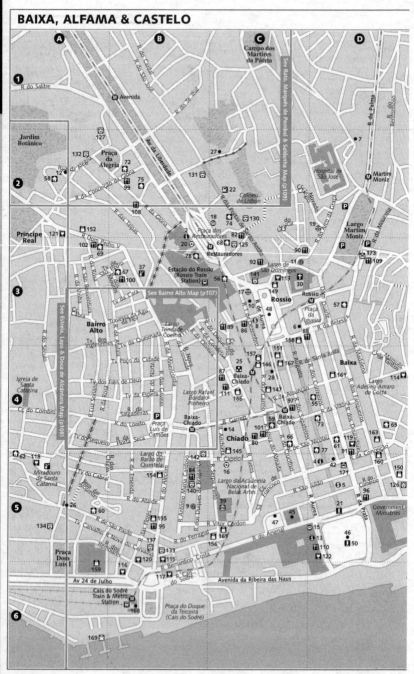

BAIXA, ALFAMA & CASTELO (pp104–5)

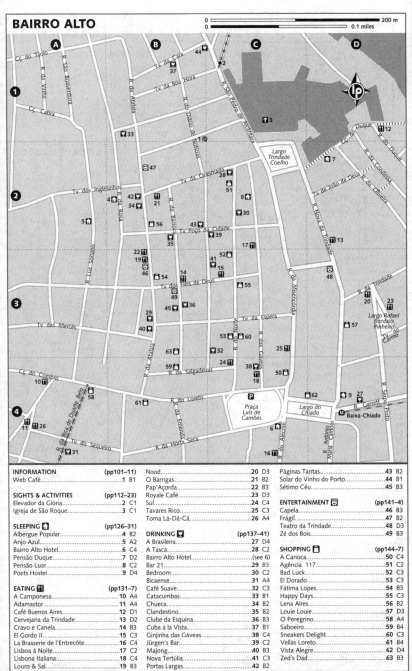

BAIRRO ALTO

ESTRELA, LAPA & DOCA DE ALCÂNTARA

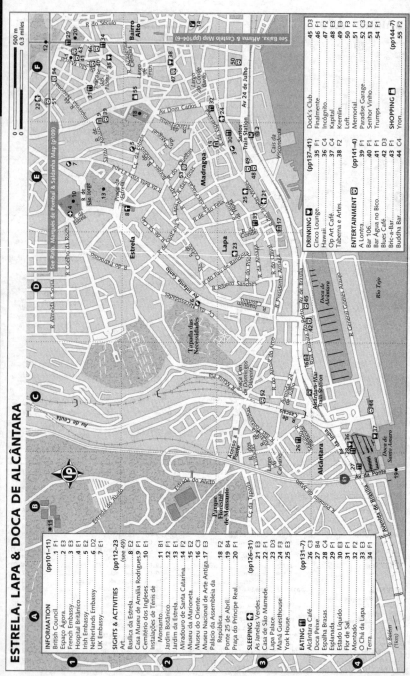

INFORMATION	(pp101–11)
British Council	1 F1
Espaço Ágora	2 E3
French Embassy	3 E3
Hospital Británico	4 E2
Irish Embassy	5 E2
Netherlands Embassy	6 D2
UK Embassy	7 E1

SIGHTS & ACTIVITIES	(pp112–23)
Art	(see 49)
Basílica da Estrela	8 E2
Casa Museu de Amália Rodrigues	9 F1
Cemitério dos Ingleses	10 E1
Instalações de Ténis de Monsanto	11 B1
Jardim Botânico	12 E1
Jardim da Estrela	13 E1
Miradouro de Santa Catarina	14 F2
Museu da Marioneta	15 F2
Museu do Oriente	16 C3
Museu Nacional de Arte Antiga	17 E3
Palácio da Assembleia da República	18 F2
Ponte 25 de Abril	19 B4
Praça do Príncipe Real	20 F1

SLEEPING	(pp126–31)
As Janelas Verdes	21 E3
Casa de São Mamede	22 E1
Lapa Palace	23 D3
Maná Guesthouse	24 E2
York House	25 E3

EATING	(pp131–7)
Alcântara Café	26 C3
Doca Peixe	27 B4
Espalha Brasas	28 C4
Esplanada	29 F1
Estado Líquido	30 F2
Flor de Sal	31 F1
Montado	32 F2
O Chá da Lapa	33 E3
Terra	34 F1

DRINKING	(pp137–41)
Cinco Lounge	35 F1
Hawaii	36 C4
Op Art Café	37 C4
Taberna e Artes	38 F2

ENTERTAINMENT	(pp141–4)
A Lontra	39 F1
Bar 106	40 F1
Bar Água no Bico	41 F1
Blues Café	42 D3
Bric-a-Bar	43 F1
Buddha Bar	44 C4
Dock's Club	45 D3
Finalmente	46 F1
Incógnito	47 F2
Kapital	48 E3
Kremlin	49 F3
Loft	50 F3
Memorial	51 F1
Paradise Garage	52 C3
Senhor Vinho	53 E2
Trumps	54 F1

SHOPPING	(pp144–7)
Yron	55 F2

Bairro Alto

See Baixa, Alfama & Castelo Map (pp104–6)

See Rato, Marquês de Pombal & Saldanha Map (p109)

Estrela

Madragoa

Lapa

Santos
Train Station

Av 24 de Julho

Casa da
Viscondessa

Rio Tejo

Doca de
Alcântara

Alcântara

Alcântara-Mar
Train Station

Doca de
Santo Amaro

Av da Ponte

Parque Florestal
de Monsanto

Tapada das
Necessidades

Av das Necessidades

To Belém
(1km)

0   500 m
0   0.3 miles

RATO, MARQUÊS DE POMBAL & SALDANHA

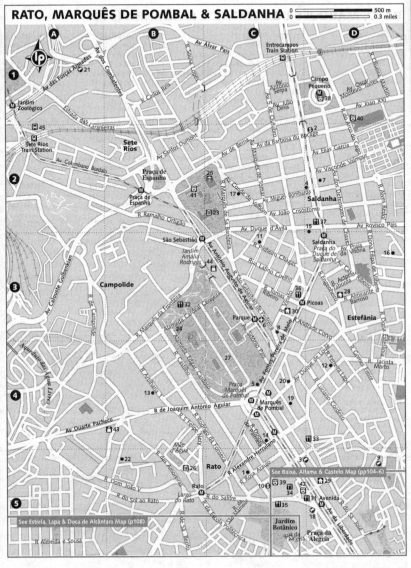

RATO, MARQUÊS DE POMBAL & SALDANHA (p109)

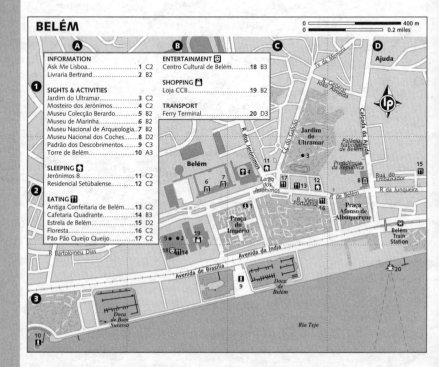

Ajuda

Tr. da Memória
R. General João Almeida
R. dos Jerónimos
Calçada da Ajuda
Jardim do Ultramar
Palácio Nacional de Belém
Presidência da República
Rua do Embaixador
R. da Junqueira
Belém
Largo dos Jerónimos
R. de Belém
R. Vieira Portuense
Praça Afonso de Albuquerque
Belém Train Station
Praça do Império
Avenida da Índia
R. Bartolomeu Dias
Avenida de Brasília
Doca de Belém
Doca de Bom Sucesso
Rio Tejo

(Continued from page 101)

Grupo Deutsche Bank (Map p109; ☎ 210 001 200; Rua Castilho 20)
Top Atlântica (Map p109; ☎ 213 108 800; Av Duque de Loulé 108) Lisbon's American Express representative.

Post
Airport (Map pp102-3; ☒ 9am-8pm Mon-Fri, 9am-1pm & 2-5pm Sat & Sun)
Main post office (Map pp104-5; Praça do Comércio) Has poste restante.
Post office (Map pp104-5; Praça dos Restauradores) Another central post office.

Telephone & Fax
Equipped with a phonecard, including the Portugal Telecom card, you can make international direct-dial (IDD) phone calls from most pay phones. At Portugal Telecom booths in post offices you can pay after you've made the call.
Portugal Telecom (Map pp104-5; Rossio 68; ☒ 8am-11pm) Has rows of booths.
Qamar (Map pp104-5; Rua do Arço da Graça 35; ☒ 10am-10pm) Offers bargain international calls (per minute €0.10/0.35 to USA/Europe).

Tourist Information
Ask Me Lisboa Rua Augusta (Map pp104-5; near Rua Conceição; ☒ 10am-1pm & 2-6pm); Santa Apolónia (Map pp104-5; door 47, inside train station; ☒ 8am-1pm Wed-Sat); Belém (Map p110; Largo dos Jerónimos; ☒ 10am-1pm & 2-6pm Tue-Sat); Palácio Foz (Map pp104-5; near Praça dos Restauradores; ☒ 9am-8pm) Turismo de Lisboa runs several information kiosks; these are the most useful.
Lisboa Welcome Centre (Map pp104-5; ☎ 210 312 810; Praça do Comércio; ☒ 9am-8pm) Main branch of Turismo de Lisboa, providing free city maps, brochures, and hotel and tour booking services. Buy the Lisboa Card (see boxed text, p113) here.
Turismo de Lisboa Airport (☎ 218 450 660; ☒ 7am-midnight) Doles out maps, advises on transport and makes hotel reservations. Also runs Ask Me Lisboa kiosks.

Travel Agencies
Tagus Rato (Map p109; ☎ 213 525 986; www.taguseasy.pt, in Portuguese; Rua Camilo Castelo Branco 20)
Top Atlântica (Map p109; ☎ 213 108 800; Av Duque de Loulé 108)

DANGERS & ANNOYANCES
Lisbon is generally a safe city with a low crime rate, though you'll probably be offered hash and back-of-the-lorry goods in Bairro Alto and Baixa; a firm but polite 'no' keeps hawkers at bay. Mind your wallet at tourist hubs, especially on Rua Augusta and tram 28. Main streets are relatively safe to walk along at night, but be wary around metro stations

---

LISBON IN...

Two Days
Take a rollercoaster ride of Lisbon on **tram 28** (see boxed text, p112), hopping off to scale the vertiginous ramparts of Moorish **Castelo de São Jorge** (p115). Poke around **Alfama**'s (p114) twisting alleys, full of billowing laundry and gabbling locals, pausing for lunch in arty **Pois Café** (p134). Glimpse the fortress-like **sé** (cathedral; p116) en route to **Conserveira de Lisboa** (p147) to buy retro-wrapped tinned fish and **ViniPortugal** (p137) to taste Portuguese wines for free. By night, return to lantern-lit Alfama to hear first-rate fado at **Clube de Fado** (p142).

On day two, wake up over cinnamon-dusted *pastéis de belém* and *bica* (espresso) at the **Antiga Confeitaria** (p136), then explore the fantastical Manueline cloisters of **Mosteiro dos Jerónimos** (p120). Snap the shipshape **Padrão dos Descobrimentos** (p120) and see Picassos and Warhols for free at sleek **Museu Colecção Berardo** (p120). Head back for sundowners and twinkling skylines at **Noobai** (p138), dinner at **Olivier** (p134) and bar-crawling in party-hearty **Bairro Alto** (see boxed text, p138).

Four Days
On your third day, take the metro to **Parque das Nações** (p121) for space-age architecture, riverfront gardens and the head-spinning **Oceanário** (p122). After dark, go sushi at funky **Bica do Sapato** (p135), then pop next door to clubbing temple **Lux** (p141) for superstar DJs spinning house.

Nursing a hangover? What you need is a bracing hike through ferny, boulder-speckled woodlands to fairytale palaces in **Sintra** (p150). Back in Rossio, toast your trip with a shot of *ginjinha* (cherry liqueur) at **A Ginjinha** (p137) and alfresco dining on the cobbled steps of **Calçada do Duque**.

LISBON & AROUND

like Anjos, Martim Moniz and Intendente, where there have been muggings. Take care in the dark alleys of Alfama and Graça.

SIGHTS

Hilltop Moorish ramparts and twirling Manueline turrets, a fortified Romanesque cathedral and Roman theatre ruins – Lisbon's heritage stash would give most cities culture envy. Art fans get their fix with Rodin at Museu do Chiado (p114), Rembrandt at Museu Calouste Gulbenkian (p119) and a free Lichtenstein and Warhol feast at Museu Colecção Berardo (p120).

But Lisbon's rich pickings go beyond the glass and canvas; Graça's giddy *miradouros*, the winding alleys of the maze-like Alfama, serene cloisters bedecked with exquisite *azulejos*, and exotic botanical gardens all invite exploration.

Each neighbourhood packs in a different personality, from nautical adventures catapulting you back to the Age of Discovery in Belém to sci-fi architecture, underwater encounters and outdoor art in Parque das Nações. Bear in mind that many attractions close on Mondays and have free admission on Sunday mornings.

Baixa & Rossio

Starship were bluffing when they sang about building a city on rock and roll; that honour belongs to Marquês de Pombal, who built Baixa and Rossio ruler-straight and rock-solid on the rubble of Lisbon's 1755 earthquake. With grand plazas, dancing fountains and a triumphal arch evoking the heyday of Portuguese royalty, the grid-like district is the architectural antithesis of the higgledy-piggledy Alfama.

The main drag, pedestrianised Rua Augusta, buzzes with bag-toting shoppers, camera-wielding tourists and hawkers trying to flog everything from hash to fake Rolexes and Barcelos cockerel kitsch. For a taste of the trades that once flourished here, mosey down streets named after *sapateiros* (shoemakers), *correeiros* (saddlers), *douradores* (gilders), *fanqueiros* (cutlers) and even *bacalhoeiros* (cod-fishing vessels).

The sights in this section are all on Map pp104–5 unless otherwise noted.

ELEVADOR DE SANTA JUSTA

If the lanky, wrought-iron **Elevador de Santa Justa** (☎ 213 613 054; cnr Rua de Santa Justa & Largo do Carmo; admission €2.70; ☿ 7am-9pm, 7am-11pm summer) seems uncannily familiar, it's probably because the neo-Gothic marvel is the handiwork of Raul Mésnier, Gustave Eiffel's apprentice. It's Lisbon's only vertical street lift. Get there early to beat the crowds and zoom to the top for sweeping views over the city's skyline.

IGREJA DE SÃO DOMINGOS

It's a miracle that the enigmatic **Igreja de São Domingos** (Largo de São Domingos; admission free; ☿ 7.30am-7pm Mon-Fri, noon-6pm Sat) still stands, having barely survived the 1755 earthquake and fire in 1959. A sea of tealights illuminates gashed pillars, battered walls and ethereal sculptures in its musty yet enchanting interior. Note the Star of David outside marking the spot of a bloody anti-Semitic massacre in 1506. The square is a popular hang-out with Lisbon's African community and, at dusk, locals who gather for sundown cherry liqueurs at A Ginjinha (p137).

NÚCLEO ARQUEOLÓGICO

Hidden under Banco Comercial Portuguesa is the **Núcleo Arqueológico** (☎ 213 211 700; Rua dos Correeiros 9; tours free; ☿ 10am-noon & 3-5pm Wed & Sat), a web of tunnels believed to be the remnants of a Roman spa dating from the 1st century AD. You can descend into the depths on a

---

HITCH A RIDE ON TRAM 28

Vintage tram 28 offers the ultimate spin of Lisbon's blockbuster sights – from Basílica da Estrela to the backstreets of Baixa – for the price of a €1.35 ticket. The route from Campo Ourique to Martim Moniz is 45 minutes of astonishing views and absurdly steep climbs. The most exciting bit is when the tram commences its rattling climb to Alfama, where passengers lean perilously out of the window for an in-motion shot of the *sé* or hop out for postcard-perfect views from Miradouro de Santa Luzia. The final stretch negotiates impossibly narrow streets and hairpin bends up to Graça, where most folk get out to explore Igreja de São Vicente de Fora. Keep an eye out for tram-surfers – the fast, fearless and adrenaline-crazed dudes who dodge the fare by clinging to the doors like sticklebricks.

guided tour run by the Museu da Cidade. Phone ahead to book.

PRAÇA DO COMÉRCIO

With its grand 18th-century arcades, lemon-meringue facades and mosaic cobbles, the riverfront **Praça do Comércio** is a square to out-pomp them all. Everyone arriving by boat used to disembark here, and it still feels like the gateway to Lisbon, thronging with activity and rattling trams. At its centre rises the dashing equestrian **statue of Dom José I**, hinting at the square's royal roots as the pre-earthquake site of Palácio da Ribeira. In 1908 the square witnessed the fall of the monarchy, when anarchists assassinated Dom Carlos I and his son. The biggest crowd-puller is Verissimo da Costa's triumphal **Arco da Victória**, crowned with bigwigs such as 15th-century explorer Vasco da Gama; come at dusk to see the arch glow gold. Pop into **ViniPortugal** (p137) to taste Portuguese wines for free.

PRAÇA DO MUNICIPIO

Just northwest of Praça do Comércio, **Praça do Município** is dominated by the former marine arsenal and the neoclassical **Paços do Concelho** (City Hall), where the republic was proclaimed in 1910. The adjacent Rua do Arsenal is lined with hole-in-the-wall grocers selling cheap *vinho* (wine) and *bacalhau* (dried salt-cod).

ROSSIO & PRAÇA DA FIGUEIRA

All roads lead to Praça Dom Pedro IV, which Lisboetas nickname **Rossio**. The square has 24-hour buzz: office workers, hash-peddlers and sightseers drift across its wave-like cobbles, bask in the spray of fountains and gaze up to **Dom Pedro IV** (Brazil's first emperor), perched high on a marble pedestal. Standouts feature the filigree horseshoe-shaped arches of neo-Manueline **Rossio train station**, where trains depart for Sintra (p150), and neoclassical **Teatro Nacional de Dona Maria II** (p143) hiding a dark past as the seat of the Portuguese Inquisition.

Rossio's sidekick is bustling **Praça da Figueira**, flanked by Pombaline town houses and alfresco cafes ideal for sipping a *bica*, admiring the castle on the hillside and watching gravity-defying skateboarders tear past the statue of Dom João I.

Chiado & Bairro Alto

Framed by the ethereal arches of Convento do Carmo, well-heeled Chiado harbours old-world cafes with literary credentials, swish boutiques, grand theatres and elegant 18th-century town houses. Designer divas seeking Portuguese couture, art buffs eager to eyeball Rodin originals and those content to people-watch from a cafe terrace flock here. The chichi district is named after poet António Ribeiro, aka *chiado* (squeak).

Sidling up to Chiado is the party-loving Bairro Alto, whose web of graffiti-slashed streets is sleepy by day. The district comes alive at twilight when hippy chicks hunt for vintage glitz in its retro boutiques and revellers hit its wall-to-wall bars and bistros. For daytime chilling, head to the leafy squares around Príncipe Real.

The following sights are on Map pp104–5 unless otherwise noted.

> **LISBOA CARD**
>
> If you're planning on doing a lot of sightseeing, this discount card represents excellent value. It offers unlimited use of public transport (including trains to Sintra and Cascais), entry to all key museums and attractions, and up to 50% discount on tours, cruises and other admission charges. It's available at Ask Me Lisboa tourist offices (p111), including the one at the airport. The 24-/48-/72-hour versions cost €15/26/32 (children aged five to 11 years €8/13/16). You validate the card when you want to start it.

CONVENTO DO CARMO & MUSEU ARQUEOLÓGICO

Soaring above Lisbon, the skeletal **Convento do Carmo** (☎ 213 478 629; adult/under 14yr €2.50/free, admission free 10am-2pm Sun; 🕑 10am-6pm Apr-Sep, 10am-5pm Oct-Mar) was all but devoured by the 1755 earthquake and precisely that makes it so captivating. Its shattered pillars and wishbone-like arches are completely exposed to the elements. The **Museu Arqueológico** shelters treasures such as 14th-century carved tombs, baroque *azulejos*, Palaeolithic flintstones and a trio of mummies – one battered Egyptian and two gruesome 16th-century Peruvians.

IGREJA DE SÃO ROQUE

The plain facade of 16th-century Jesuit **Igreja de São Roque** (Map p107; ☎ 213 235 381; Largo Trindade Coelho; admission free; 🕑 8.30am-5pm) belies its dazzling interior of gold, marble and Florentine *azulejos* – bankrolled by Brazilian riches. Its star attraction is **Capela de São João Baptista**, to the left of the altar, a lavish confection of amethyst, alabaster, lapis lazuli and Carrara marble. Its four mosaics depicting scenes from the saint's life are as elaborate as oil paintings. Portugal's extravagant king, Dom João V, had the chapel built in Rome in 1742, then shipped it over to Lisbon for a cool UK£225,000.

MIRADOURO DE SANTA CATARINA

Students bashing out rhythms; pot-smoking hippies; stroller-pushing parents; and loved-up couples – all meet at this precipitous **viewpoint** (Map p108) in boho Santa Catarina. The views are fantastic, stretching from the river to the Ponte 25 de Abril and Cristo Rei. If you're coming from Cais do Sodré, it's fun to take the arthritic, 19th-century **Elevador da Bica** funicular up chasm-like Rua da Bica de Duarte Belo to reach the lookout. When Lisbon twinkles, enjoy the same vista over drinks at laid-back **Noobai Café** (p138).

MIRADOURO DE SÃO PEDRO DE ALCÂNTARA

Hitch a ride on vintage **Elevador da Glória** (Map p107) from Praça dos Restauradores, or practise step aerobics climbing the steep Calçada da Glória to this terrific viewpoint atop one of Lisbon's seven hills. Plant yourself next to the fountains and Greek busts for a picnic with castle views. Across the street is **Solar do Vinho do Porto** (p139), where you can taste some of Portugal's finest ports.

MUSEU DO CHIADO

Contemporary art fans flock to **Museu do Chiado** (☎ 213 432 148; www.museudochiado-ipmu seus.pt; Rua Serpa Pinto 4; adult/under 14yr/concession €4/free/2.50, admission free 10am-2pm Sun; ☯ 10am-6pm Tue-Sun), housed in the strikingly converted Convento de São Francisco. Occasionally stowed away for blockbuster exhibitions, such as a recent one on kinetic art, the gallery's permanent collection of 19th- and 20th-century works features pieces by Rodin, Jorge Vieira and José de Almada Negreiros. Revive over coffee in the sculpture garden.

Alfama, Castelo & Graça

Unfurling like a magic carpet at the foot of Castelo de São Jorge, Alfama is Lisbon's Moorish time capsule: a medina-like district of tangled alleys, palm-shaded squares and skinny, terracotta-roofed houses that tumble down to the glittering Tejo. These cobbles have been worn smooth by theatre-going Romans, bath-loving Moors who called it *al-hamma* (Arabic for 'springs'), and stampeding Crusaders.

Here life is literally inside out: women dish the latest *mexericos* (gossip) over strings of freshly washed laundry, men gut sardines on the street then fry them on open grills, plump matrons spontaneously erupt into wailful fado, kids use chapel entrances as football goals, babies cry, budgies twitter, trams rattle and in the midday heat the web of steep lanes falls into its siesta slumber.

Add some altitude to your sightseeing by edging north to Graça, where giddy *miradouros* afford sweeping vistas and the pearly-white Panteão Nacional (p116) and Igreja de São Vicente de Fora (opposite) punctuate the skyline.

The following sights are on Map pp104–5 unless otherwise noted.

GREAT ESCAPES

Tucked away in Príncipe Real district, just north of Bairro Alto, are some of Lisbon's greenest and most peaceful *praças* (town squares), perfect for a crowd-free stroll or picnic. Some of our favourites:

■ **Praça da Alegria** (Map pp104–5) Swooping palms and banyan trees shade tranquil Praça da Alegria, which is actually more round than square. Look out for the bronze bust of 19th-century Portuguese painter and composer Alfredo Keil.

■ **Praça do Príncipe Real** (Map p108) A century-old cedar tree forms a giant natural parasol at the centre of this palm-dotted square, popular among grizzled card players by day and gay cruisers by night. There's a kids playground and a relaxed cafe with alfresco seating. Note the keyhole windows of the neo-Moorish, marshmallow-pink house at No 26.

■ **Praça das Flores** (Map p108) Centred on a fountain, this romantic, leafy square has cobbles, pastel-washed houses and enough doggie-do to make a Parisian proud.

GET LOST IN ALFAMA

There's no place like the labyrinthine Alfama for ditching the map to get lost in sun-dappled alleys and squares full of beauty and banter. Its narrow *becos* (cul de sacs) and *travessas* (alleys) lead you on a spectacular wild goose chase past chalk-white chapels and tiny grocery stores, patios shaded by orange trees, and João's freshly washed underpants. The earthy, working-class residents, *alfacinhas*, fill the lanes with neighbourly chatter, wafts of fried fish and the mournful ballads of fado. Experiencing Alfama is more about luxuriating in the everyday than ticking off the big sights. Take a serendipitous wander through lanes fanning out from Rua de São Miguel, Rua de São João da Praça and Rua dos Remédios.

CASA DOS BICOS

The pincushion facade of **Casa dos Bicos** (House of Points; ☎ 218 810 900; Rua dos Bacalhoeiros 10), the eccentric 16th-century abode of Afonso de Albuquerque, former viceroy to India, grabs your attention on Rua dos Bacalhoeiros. Chequered with 1125 pyramid-shaped stones, it now houses a private organisation, but nip inside if the lobby is open to glimpse remnants of the old Moorish city wall and brick streets.

CASTELO DE SÃO JORGE

Towering dramatically above Lisbon, the hilltop fortifications of **Castelo de São Jorge** (St George's Castle; ☎ 218 800 620; adult/under 10yr/concession €5/free/2.50; 9am-9pm Mar-Oct, 9am-6pm Nov-Feb) sneak into almost every snapshot. These smooth cobbles have seen it all – Visigoths in the 5th century, Moors in the 9th century, Christians in the 12th century, royals from the 14th to 16th centuries, and convicts in every century. Roam its snaking ramparts and pine-shaded courtyards for superlative views over the city's red rooftops to the river.

　　Inside the Ulysses Tower, a camera obscura offers a unique 360-degree angle on Lisbon, with demos every half-hour. Near the castle entrance is **Olisipónia** (9am-5.30pm Nov-Feb, 9am-8pm Mar-Oct), an exhibition with multilingual commentary about Lisbon's history. It uses a video wall to jazz up the already gripping history, but glosses over anything unpalatable (did anyone say slave trade?).

IGREJA DE SÃO VICENTE DE FORA

Graça's serene, gorgeous **Igreja de São Vicente de Fora** (☎ 218 824 400; Largo de São Vicente; adult/concession €4/2; 10am-6pm Tue-Sun) was founded as a monastery in 1147, revamped by Italian architect Felipe Terzi in the late 16th century, and devastated in 1755's earthquake when its dome collapsed on worshippers. Elaborate blue-and-white *azulejos* dance across almost every wall, echoing the curves of the architecture, across the white cloisters and up to the 1st floor. Here you'll find a one-off collection of panels depicting La Fontaine's moral tales of sly foxes and greedy wolves. Under the marble sacristy lie the crusaders' tombs. Seek out the weeping, cloaked woman holding stony vigil in the eerie mausoleum. Have your camera handy for the superb views from the tower.

MUSEU DE ARTES DECORATIVAS

Set in a petite 17th-century palace, the **Museu de Artes Decorativas** (Museum of Decorative Arts; ☎ 218 814 651; www.fress.pt; Largo das Portas do Sol 2; adult/under 14yr/concession €4/free/2; 10am-5pm Tue-Sun) creaks under the weight of treasures including blingy French silverware, priceless Qing vases and Indo-Chinese furniture. It's worth a visit alone to admire the lavish apartments, embellished with baroque *azulejos*, frescos and chandeliers.

MUSEU DO FADO

Fado was born in Alfama. Immerse yourself in its bittersweet symphonies at **Museu do Fado** (☎ 218 823 470; www.museudofado.egeac.pt; Largo do Chafariz de Dentro; adult/concession €2.50/1.25; 10am-6pm Tue-Sun). This engaging museum traces fado's history from its working-class roots to international stardom, taking in discos, recordings, posters, a hall of fame and a re-created guitar workshop. Pick up some fado of your own at the shop.

MUSEU DO TEATRO ROMANO

The light-flooded, ultramodern **Museu do Teatro Romano** (Roman Theatre Museum; ☎ 217 513 200; Pátio do Aljube 5; admission free; 10am-1pm & 2-6pm Tue-Sun) catapults you back to Emperor Augustus' rule in Olisipo (Lisbon). Head upstairs and across the street for the star attraction – a ruined **Roman theatre** extended in AD 57, buried in the 1755 earthquake and finally unearthed in 1964.

MUSEU NACIONAL DO AZULEJO

You haven't really been to Lisbon until you've been on the tiles at the **Museu Nacional**

STAIRWAYS TO HEAVEN

You might curse the cobbles as you're puffing up the steep stairways lacing Alfama and Graça at times, but take heart in the fact that they lead to heavenly *miradouros*. All of the *miradouros* listed here are on Map pp104–5. Have your digicam handy for:

- **Largo das Portas do Sol** This original Moorish gateway affords stunning angles over Alfama's jumble of red rooftops and pastel-coloured houses, underscored by the true blue Tejo.

- **Miradouro de Santa Luzia** A fountain trickles at this lookout shaded by bougainvillea and vines, offering superlative vistas over Alfama's blushing rooftops to the river. At the back, notice the blue-and-white *azulejos* depicting scenes from the Siege of Lisbon in 1147.

- **Miradouro da Graça** Young Lisboetas flock to this pine-fringed square at dusk for sundowners and sweeping vistas over central Lisbon.

- **Miradouro da Senhora do Monte** Lisbon spreads out before you at Graça's highest of the high, Miradouro da Senhora do Monte. Come for the relaxed vibe and the best views of the castle on the hill opposite.

do Azulejo (National Tile Museum; Map pp102-3; ☎ 218 100 340; Rua Madre de Deus 4; adult/concession €4/2, admission free 10am-2pm Sun; ♥ 2-6pm Tue, 10am-6pm Wed-Sun; ⚑). Housed in a sublime 16th-century convent, the museum covers the entire *azulejo* spectrum, from early Ottoman geometry to zinging altars, scenes of lords a-hunting to Goan intricacies. Star exhibits feature a 36m-long panel depicting pre-earthquake Lisbon, a Manueline cloister with weblike vaulting and exquisite blue-and-white *azulejos*, and a gold-smothered baroque chapel. Bedecked with food-inspired *azulejos* – ducks, pigs and the like – the restaurant opens onto a vine-clad courtyard. For more on *azulejos*, see p62.

PANTEÃO NACIONAL

Perched high and mighty above Graça's Campo de Santa Clara, the porcelain-white **Panteão Nacional** (National Pantheon; ☎ 218 854 820; Campo de Santa Clara; adult/concession €2/1, admission free 10am-2pm Sun; ♥ 10am-5pm Tue-Sun; ⚑) is a baroque beauty. Originally intended as a church, it now pays homage to Portugal's heroes and heroines, including 15th-century explorer Vasco da Gama and *fadista* Amália Rodrigues. Lavishly adorned with pink marble and gold swirls, its echoing dome resembles an enormous Fabergé egg. Trudge up to the 4th-floor viewpoint for a sunbake and vertigo-inducing views over Alfama and the river.

SÉ

One of Lisbon's biggest icons is the fortresslike **sé** (cathedral; ☎ 218 866 752; admission free; ♥ 9am-7pm Tue-Sat, 9am-5pm Mon & Sun), built in 1150 on the site of a mosque soon after Christians recaptured

the city from the Moors. It was sensitively restored in the 1930s. Despite the masses outside, the rib-vaulted interior, lit by a rose window, is calm. The **treasury** (admission €2.50; ♥ 10am-5pm Mon-Sat) showcases religious gems, and the **Gothic cloister** (admission €2.50; ♥ 2-6pm Mon-Sat Oct-Apr, to 7pm May-Sep) houses archaeological excavations, including stonework from the 6th century BC, a medieval cistern and the Islamic foundations. Stroll around the cathedral to spy leering gargoyles peeking above the orange trees; the *sé* looks its best when the late-afternoon sun makes its bricks glow honey-gold.

Estrela, Lapa & Doca de Alcântara

Serene and affluent, Estrela and Lapa are the gentrified western neighbours of Bairro Alto. Their tree-fringed lanes, sloping down to the Rio Tejo, are lined with boutique hotels, art galleries, vine-clad courtyards and antique shops. This offbeat corner of Lisbon harbours a handful of must-sees including a neoclassical basilica, exotic gardens, a cavernous ancient art museum, plus the neoclassical Palácio da Assembleia da República (p118), home to Portugal's parliament.

Further south, where suspension bridge Ponte 25 de Abril rumbles, you hit the docks. Here classy becomes cool, with red-brick warehouses getting a new lease of life as ultra-hip clubs, restaurants and galleries such as the shiny new Museu do Oriente (opposite), turning the spotlight on Portugal's links with Asia.

Getting here on westbound tram 28 or 25 is fun. The sights in this section are on Map p108 unless otherwise noted.

BASÍLICA DA ESTRELA

The curvaceous, sugar-white dome and twin belfries of **Basílica da Estrela** (☎ 213 960 915; Praça da Estrela; admission free; ☽ 8am-1pm & 3-8pm) are visible from afar. The neoclassical beauty was completed in 1790 by order of Dona Maria I (whose tomb is here) in gratitude for a male heir. The echoing interior is awash with pink and black marble, which creates a kaleidoscopic effect when you gaze up into the cupola. Climb the dome for far-reaching views over Lisbon.

CASA MUSEU DE AMÁLIA RODRIGUES

A pilgrimage site for fado fans, **Casa Museu de Amália Rodrigues** (☎ 213 971 896; Rua de São Bento 193; admission €5; ☽ 10am-1pm & 2-6pm Tue-Sun) is where the Rainha do Fado (Queen of Fado) Amália Rodrigues lived; note graffiti along the street announcing it as Rua Amália. Born in Lisbon in 1920, the diva popularised the genre with her heartbreaking trills and poetic soul. Short tours take in portraits, glittering costumes and crackly recordings of her performances.

CEMITÉRIO DOS INGLESES

Overgrown with cypress trees, the **Cemitério dos Ingleses** (English Cemetery; Rua de São Jorge; ☽ daylight hrs) was founded in 1717. Expats at rest here include Henry Fielding (author of *Tom Jones*), who died during a fruitless visit to Lisbon to improve his health in 1754. At the far corner are the remains of Lisbon's old Jewish cemetery.

JARDIM BOTÂNICO

Nurtured by green-fingered students, the **Jardim Botânico** (Botanical Garden; ☎ 213 921 800; Rua da Escola Politécnica 58; adult/concession €1.50/0.75; ☽ 9am-6pm Mon-Fri, 10am-6pm Sat & Sun Oct-Apr, 9am-8pm Mon-Fri, 10am-8pm

Sat & Sun May-Sep) is a quiet pocket of lushness just north of Bairro Alto. Look out for Madeiran geraniums, sequoias, purple jacarandas and, by the entrance, a gigantic Moreton Bay fig tree.

JARDIM DA ESTRELA

Anyone seeking green respite should head for **Jardim da Estrela** (Largo da Estrela; admission free; ☽ 7am-midnight). Opposite the basilica, this garden is perfect for a stroll, with paths weaving past pine, monkey puzzle and palm trees, rose and cacti beds and the centrepiece – a giant banyan tree. Kids love the duck ponds and animal-themed playground.

MUSEU DA MARIONETA

Discover your inner child at the enchanting **Museu da Marioneta** (Puppet Museum; ☎ 213 942 810; Rua da Esperança 146; adult/concession €3/2; ☽ 10am-1pm & 2-6pm Tue-Sun), a veritable Geppetto's workshop housed in the 17th-century Convento das Bernardas. Alongside superstars like impish Punch and his Russian equivalent Petruschka are rarities such as Vietnamese water puppets, Sicilian opera marionettes and intricate Burmese shadow puppets. Tots can try their hand at puppetry.

MUSEU DO ORIENTE

Lisbon's new kid on the dock is the stunning **Museu do Oriente** (☎ 213 585 200; www.museudooriente .pt; Doca de Alcântara; adult/concession €4/2, admission free 6-10pm Fri; ☽ 10am-6pm Wed-Mon, 10am-10pm Fri), highlighting Portugal's ties with Asia from colonial baby steps in Macau to ancestor worship. The cavernous museum occupies a revamped 1940s *bacalhau* warehouse. Strikingly displayed in pitch-black rooms, the permanent collection focuses on Portuguese presence in Asia, and Asian gods. Standouts on the 1st floor feature rare Chinese screens and Ming porcelain, plus

---

FREE LISBOA

Lisbon is a superb city for euro-pinchers, as its biggest draws are outdoors: from astounding views at hilltop **miradouros** (see boxed text, opposite) to tranquil **squares** (see boxed text, p114) and urban treasure hunts in the warren-like **Alfama** (see boxed text, p115).

Many museums have free admission on Sunday mornings. For a free cultural fix on other days, make for Belém's **Museu Colecção Berardo** (p120), showcasing masterpieces by pop stars like Lichtenstein and Warhol gratis, **Museu do Teatro Romano** (p115) for Roman theatre ruins and, right opposite, the fortresslike **sé** (opposite). The **Museu Calouste Gulbenkian** (p119) gives free musical recitals at noon on Sundays in the library foyer. Try to catch one of the free jazz concerts on Thursdays in summer at **Cafeteria Quadrante** (p136).

BaixAnima (p126) entertains the crowds in Baixa on weekends from July to September with flamboyant street performers, centred on Rua Augusta.

East Timor curiosities such as the divining conch and delicately carved umbilical-cord knives. Upstairs, cult classics include peacock-feathered effigies of Yellamma (goddess of the fallen), Vietnamese medium costumes and an eerie, faceless Nepalese exorcism doll

MUSEU NACIONAL DE ARTE ANTIGA

Set in a lemon-fronted, 17th-century palace, the **Museu Nacional de Arte Antiga** (National Museum of Ancient Art; ☎ 213 912 800; www.mnarteantiga-ipmuseus .pt; Rua das Janelas Verdes 9; adult/concession €4/2, admission free 10am-2pm Sun; ☼ 2-6pm Tue, 10am-6pm Wed-Sun) is Lapa's biggest draw. It presents a star-studded collection of European and Asian paintings and decorative arts. Keep an eye out for highlights such as Nuno Gonçalves' naturalistic *Panels of São Vicente*, Dürer's *St Jerome*, Lucas Cranach's haunting *Salomé* and Courbet's bleak *Snow*. Other gems include golden wonder the *Monstrance of Belém*, a souvenir from Vasco da Gama's second voyage, and 16th-century Japanese screens depicting the arrival of the *namban* (southern barbarians), namely big-nosed Portuguese explorers.

PALÁCIO DA ASSEMBLEIA DA REPÚBLICA

The columned, temple-like **Palácio da Assembleia da República** (Assembly of the Republic; Rua de São Bento; closed to the public) is where the Assembleia da República, Portugal's parliament, makes its home. It was once the enormous Benedictine Mosteiro de São Bento. Its lofty Doric columns and graceful statues of temperance, prudence, fortitude and justice give visitors the shutterbug.

PONTE 25 DE ABRIL

Most people experience déjà vu the first time they clap eyes on bombastic suspension bridge **Ponte 25 de Abril** (Doca de Santo Amaro). It's hardly surprising given that it's the spitting image of San Francisco's Golden Gate Bridge, was constructed by the same company in 1966, and is almost as long, at 2.27km. The thundering bridge dwarfs Lisbon's docks and is dazzling when illuminated by night. It was called Ponte Salazar until the 1974 Revolution of Carnations (see p39), when a demonstrator removed the 'Salazar' and daubed '25 de Abril' in its place; the name stuck, the dictatorship crumbled.

Rato, Marquês de Pombal & Saldanha

Up north Lisbon races headlong into the 21st century with gleaming high-rises, dizzying roundabouts, shopping malls, and Parisian-

---

> **WATER FEATURE**
>
> The 109 arches of the **Aqueduto das Águas Livres** (Aqueduct of the Free Waters; Map p109) lope across the hills into Lisbon from Caneças, more than 18km away; they are most spectacular at Campolide, where the tallest arch is an incredible 65m high. Built between 1728 and 1835, by order of Dom João V, the aqueduct is a spectacular feat of engineering and brought Lisbon its first clean drinking water. Its more sinister claim to fame is as the site where 19th-century mass murderer Diogo Alves pushed his victims over the edge. No prizes for guessing why the aqueduct was closed to the public soon after.

---

style boulevard Avenida da Liberdade, which poet Fernando Pessoa dubbed 'the finest artery in Lisbon'. The contrast to the olde-worlde riverfront districts is startling.

Though often overlooked, these parts reveal some gems: from René Lalique glitterbugs at Museu Calouste Gulbenkian (opposite) to Hockney masterpieces at Centro de Arte Moderna (below), hothouses in Parque Eduardo VII (opposite) to the lofty arches of Aqueduto das Águas Livres (see boxed text, above). Foodies flock here to dine at top tables like Michelin-starred Eleven (p136).

The sights in this section are on Map p109 unless otherwise noted.

CENTRO DE ARTE MODERNA

Situated in a sculpture-dotted garden alongside Museu Calouste Gulbenkian, the **Centro de Arte Moderna** (Modern Art Centre; ☎ 217 823 474; adult/under 12yr/concession €4/free/2, admission free Sun; ☼ 10am-6pm Tue-Sun) reveals a stellar collection of 20th-century Portuguese and international art, including works by David Hockney, Anthony Gormley and José de Almada Negreiros. Feast your eyes on gems like Paula Rego's warped fairytale *Proies Wall* and Sonia Delaunay's geometrically bold *Chanteur Flamenco*. There's also a well-stocked bookshop and garden cafe.

MÃE D'ÁGUA

The king laid the aqueduct's final stone at **Mãe d'Água** (Mother of Water; ☎ 218 100 215; Praça das Amoreiras; admission €3; ☼ 10am-6pm Mon-Sat), the city's massive, 5500-cu-metre main reservoir. Completed in 1834, the reservoir's cool, echoing chamber (check out the start of the narrow aqueduct passage) now hosts art exhibitions.

MUSEU CALOUSTE GULBENKIAN

Famous for its outstanding quality and breadth, **Museu Calouste Gulbenkian** (☎ 217 823 461; www.museu.gulbenkian.pt; Av de Berna 45A; adult/under 12yr/concession €4/free/2, admission free Sun; ☷ 10am-6pm Tue-Sun) showcases an epic collection of Western and Eastern art. The chronological romp kicks off with highlights such as gilded Egyptian mummy masks, Mesopotamian urns, elaborate Persian carpets and Qing porcelain (note the grinning Dogs of Fo). Going west, art buffs bewonder masterpieces by Rembrandt (*Portrait of an Old Man*), Van Dyck and Rubens (including the frantic *Loves of the Centaurs*). Be sure to glimpse Rodin's passionate *Spring Kiss*. The grand finale is the collection of exquisite René Lalique jewellery, including the otherworldly *Dragonfly*. Don't miss the free classical concerts at noon on Sunday.

PARQUE EDUARDO VII

An urban oasis with British roots, **Parque Eduardo VII** (Alameda Edgar Cardoso; admission free; ☷ daylight hrs) is named after his highness Edward VII, who visited Lisbon in 1903. The sloping parterre affords sweeping views over the whizzing traffic of Praça Marquês de Pombal to the river. The **estufas** (greenhouses; adult/child under 12yr €1.61/free; ☷ 9am-4.30pm Oct-Apr, 9am-5.30pm May-Sep) are a highlight, with lush foliage and tinkling fountains. Look out for tree ferns and camellias in the *estufa fría* (cool greenhouse), coffee and mango trees in the *estufa quente* (hot greenhouse) and cacti in the *estufa doce* (sweet greenhouse).

Belém

Belém translates as Bethlehem but despite its villagey trappings, this is no little town. Picture stepping into a watercolour painting on the Age of Discovery: mighty caravels setting sail for Asia, coffers overflowing with spices, salt-bedraggled sailors washing up on distant shores and Manuel using his newfound wealth to parade on an elephant and send the Pope a rhino. Belém catapults you back to the nautical adventures and architectural exuberance of the 15th and 16th centuries, when the world was Portugal's oyster and Vasco da Gama's timely discovery of a sea route to India in 1498 kick-started the age of empires.

As well as Unesco World Heritage–listed Manueline stunners like Mosteiro dos Jerónimos (p120) and the whimsical Torre de Belém (p120), this district 6km west of the centre offers a tranquil botanical garden, fairytale golden coaches, Warhol originals, Lisbon's tastiest *pastéis de nata* (custard tarts) and a whole booty of other treasures.

The best way to reach Belém is on the zippy tram 15 from Praça da Figueira or Praça do Comércio. Note that most sights here close on Monday. Everything in this section is on Map p110 unless otherwise noted.

JARDIM DO ULTRAMAR

Far from the madding crowd, **Jardim do Ultramar** (Overseas Garden; Calçada do Galvão; adult/child €1.50/free; ☷ 9am-7.30pm) bristles with 4000 species from date palms to monkey puzzle trees. It's a peaceful, shady retreat on a sweltering summer's day. A highlight is the Macau garden complete with mini pagoda, where bamboo

---

INDIA AHOY!

Fed up with the Venetian monopoly on overland trade with Asia, Portuguese explorer Vasco da Gama set sail from Lisbon in 1497 for distant shores, with a motley crew aboard his handsome caravel. He skirted the coast of Mozambique and Mombasa before finally washing up on the shore of Calicut, India, in May 1498. The bedraggled crew received a frosty welcome from the Zamorin (Hindu ruler) and when tensions flared, they returned from whence they came. The voyage was hardly plain sailing – monsoon tides were fraught with danger, scurvy was rife and more than half of Vasco da Gama's party perished. For his pains and success at discovering a sea route to India, Manuel I made him a lord when he returned in 1499 and he was hailed 'Admiral of the Indian Ocean'.

But in 1502, mounting hostilities in Calicut meant Vasco da Gama was forced to return to establish control. No more mister nice guy, he seized an Arab ship and set it alight with hundreds of merchants onboard, then banished Muslims from the port. He returned to Europe with coffers full of silk and spices. Luís Vaz de Camões recounts the fascinating adventures of Portugal's *facundo Capitão* (eloquent captain) in the epic poem *The Lusiads*.

rustles and a cool stream trickles. Tots love to clamber over the gnarled roots of a banyan tree and spot the waddling ducks and geese.

MOSTEIRO DOS JERÓNIMOS

Belém's undisputed heart-stealer is the Unesco-listed **Mosteiro dos Jerónimos** (Hieronymites Monastery; ☎ 213 620 034; www.mosteirojeronimos.pt; Praça do Império; adult/under 14yr/concession €6/free/3, admission free 10am-2pm Sun; ☉ 10am-5pm Tue-Sun Oct-Apr, 10am-6pm daily May-Sep). The monastery is pure fantasy stuff; a fusion of Diogo de Boitaca's creative vision and the spice and pepper dosh of Manuel I, who commissioned it to trumpet Vasco da Gama's discovery of a sea route to India in 1498.

Wrought for the glory of God, Jerónimos was once populated by monks of the Order of St Jerome, whose spiritual job for four centuries was to comfort sailors and pray for the king's soul. When the order was dissolved in 1833, the monastery was used as a school and orphanage until about 1940.

Entering the **church** through the western portal, you'll notice tree-trunk-like columns seem to grow into the ceiling, which is itself a spiderweb of stone. Windows cast a soft golden light over the church. Superstar Vasco da Gama is interred in the lower chancel, just left of the entrance, opposite venerated 16th-century poet Luís Vaz de Camões. From the upper choir, there's a superb view of the church; the rows of seats are Portugal's first Renaissance woodcarvings.

There's nothing like the moment you walk into the honey-stone Manueline **cloisters**, dripping with organic detail in their delicately scalloped arches, twisting auger-shell turrets and columns intertwined with leaves, vines and knots. It's just wow. Keep an eye out for symbols of the age like the armillary sphere and the cross of the Military Order, plus gargoyles and fantastical beasties on the upper balustrade.

MUSEU DE MARINHA

The **Museu de Marinha** (Naval Museum; ☎ 213 620 019; Praça do Império; adult/under 6yr/concession €3/free/1.50, admission free 10am-1pm Sun; ☉ 10am-5pm Tue-Sun Oct-Mar, 10am-6pm Tue-Sun Apr-Sep) is a nautical flashback to the Age of Discovery with its armadas of model ships, canon balls and shipwreck booty. Dig for buried treasure such as Vasco da Gama's portable wooden altar, the polished private quarters of UK-built royal yacht *Amélia*, and ornate royal barges including a 1780 neo-Viking number.

PADRÃO DOS DESCOBRIMENTOS

Like a caravel frozen in mid-swell, the monolithic **Padrão dos Descobrimentos** (Discoveries Monument; ☎ 213 031 950; Av de Brasília; adult/under 12yr/concession €2.50/free/1.50; ☉ 10am-6pm Tue-Sun Oct-Apr, 10am-7pm May-Sep) was inaugurated in 1960 on the 500th anniversary of Henry the Navigator's death. The 52m-high limestone giant is chock-full of Portuguese bigwigs. At the prow is Henry, while behind him are explorers Vasco da Gama, Diogo Cão, Fernão de Magalhães and 29 other greats. The exhibition hails the triumphs of Portuguese explorers. Take the lift or puff up 267 steps to the top for 360-degree views over the river. The mosaic in front of the monument charts the routes of Portuguese mariners.

TORRE DE BELÉM

Jutting out onto the Rio Tejo, the World Heritage–listed fortress of **Torre de Belém** (☎ 213 620 034; Av da Índia; adult/under 14yr/concession €4/free/2, admission free 10am-2pm Sun; ☉ 10am-6.30pm Tue-Sun May-Sep, 10am-5pm Oct-Apr) epitomises the Age of Discovery. Francisco de Arruda designed the pearly-grey chesspiece in 1515 to defend Lisbon's harbour and nowhere else is the lure of the Atlantic more powerful. The Manueline show-off flaunts filigree stonework, meringue-like cupolas and – just below the western tower – a stone rhinoceros. The ungulate depicts the one Manuel I sent Pope Leo X in 1515, which inspired Dürer's famous woodcut. Breathe in to explore the poky former dungeons and climb a narrow spiral staircase to the tower, affording breathtaking views over Belém and the river.

MUSEU COLECÇÃO BERARDO

Culture fiends get their contemporary art fix for free at **Museu Colecção Berardo** (Berardo Collection Museum; ☎ 213 612 400; www.museuberardo.pt; Praça do Império; admission free; ☉ 10am-7pm, 10am-10pm Fri), the latest addition to the Centro Cultural de Belém (p143). The ultrawhite, minimalist gallery displays billionaire José Berardo's eye-popping collection of abstract, surrealist and pop art. Don't miss Warhol's blue-eyed girl *Judy Garland*, Lichtenstein's utterly dotty *Interior with Restful Painting*, Paula Rego's magical realism in *The Barn* and Magritte's fantastical *The Silvery Chasm*. Outside in the sculpture park, Niki de Saint Phalle's buxom *Swimmers* hog the limelight.

MUSEU NACIONAL DE ARQUEOLOGIA

It mightn't sound it, but the **Museu Nacional de Arqueologia** (National Archaeology Museum; ☎ 213 620 000; Praça do Império; adult/under 14yr/concession €3/free/1.50, admission free 10am-1pm Sun; ☺ 10am-5pm Tue-Sun Oct-Mar, 10am-6pm Apr-Sep) is a fascinating way to spend an hour. Housed in Mosteiro dos Jerónimos' western wing, the intriguing stash contains mesolithic flintstones, mummified crocodiles and Bronze Age torques. Even more curious is the collection of Roman phallic amulets and exorcism tables.

MUSEU NACIONAL DOS COCHES

Cinderella wannabes feel right at home at the palatial **Museu Nacional dos Coches** (National Coach Museum; ☎ 213 610 850; Praça Afonso de Albuquerque; adult/concession €4/2, admission free 10am-2pm Sun; ☺ 10am-6pm Tue-Sun), which dazzles with its world-class collection of 17th- to 19th-century coaches. The stuccoed, frescoed halls of the former royal riding stables display gold coaches so heavy and ornate, it's a wonder they could move at all. Stunners include Pope Clement XI's scarlet-and-gold *Coach of the Oceans*.

Parque das Nações

Parque das Nações blossomed out of an industrial estate for Expo 98. Polluting factories were demolished and progressive architects from Nick Jacobs to Santiago Calatrava pooled their creative vision to shape a futuristic glass-and-steel playground with an ocean theme and impeccable eco credentials. Today, the waterfront is a cocktail of contemporary style with sci-fi edifices, public art installations, riverfront cafes, lush gardens and kiddie wonderlands like the Oceanário (p122). It's proof that Lisbon is not beyond the reaches of modernisation.

Sights in this section are on Map pp102-3 unless otherwise noted. The riverfront promenade is great for two-wheel adventures. To rent your own set of wheels, check out Tejo Bike (p149).

GARE DO ORIENTE

Designed by acclaimed Spanish architect Santiago Calatrava, the space-age **Gare do Oriente** (Oriente Station; Av D João II; ♿) is an extraordinary vaulted structure, with slender columns fanning out into a concertina roof to create a kind of geometric, crystalline forest. The *Starship Enterprise*–like entrance adds a sci-fi dimension to the organic edifice. Calatrava, it seems, is a trainspotter at heart, having put his signature on other stations in Zurich, Lyon and Valencia. Keep an eye out for bold murals by celebrated artists like Friedensreich Hundertwasser, Antonio Seguí and Arthur Boyd at the metro station.

JARDIM GARCIA DE ORTA

Bristling with exotic foliage from Portugal's former colonies, the **Jardim Garcia de Orta** (Garcia de Orta Garden; Rossio dos Olivais; admission free) is named after a 16th-century Portuguese naturalist and pioneer in tropical medicine. Botanical rarities feature Madeira's bird of paradise and serpentine dragon tree. Stroll the Brazilian garden, shaded by bougainvillea, silk-cotton, frangipani and Tabasco pepper trees. There's

---

OUTDOOR ART

You can feast your eyes on some weird and wonderful public art in Parque das Nações. Commissioned pieces for Expo 98 comprise works by prolific sculptors such as Antony Gormley (of *Angel of the North* fame) and the late Jorge Vieira. All of the artworks listed here are on Map pp102-3. As you wander, look for the famous five:

- Amy Yoes' loopy *Cursiva*, two lime-green iron squiggles that apparently symbolise the capitulary of a medieval manuscript
- Antony Gormley's loose-limbed frenzy *Rhizome* on Rossio dos Olivais – the abstract iron sculpture represents nine life-sized human figures that harmoniously slot together
- Jorge Vieira's iron-oxide *Homem-Sol* (Sun Man), a 20m anthropomorphic giant whose sharp, angular bulk rises above Alameda dos Oceanos
- Fernando Conduto's ocean-inspired *Mar Largo* on Rossio dos Olivais, a wavy mosaic pathway reflecting the tides of the Tejo
- João Cutileiro's saucy *Lago das Tágides*, partially submerged marble sculptures of voluptuous female nudes evoking poet Luís de Camões' mythical *Tágides* (nymphs of the Tejo).

CENT SAVER

Save euros by buying the **Cartão do Parque** (adult/concession €17.50/9) offering admission to Parque das Nações' top attractions including the Oceanário and Pavilhão do Conhecimento, plus a 20% discount on bike rental. The pass is valid for one month and allows you to jump the queues at ticket offices. Buy yours at the **Posto de Informação** (Information Point; ☎ 218 919 333; www.parqueda snacoes.pt; Alameda dos Oceanos; ☿ 10am-8pm Apr-Oct, 10am-6pm Nov-Mar).

---

also a music garden where kids (and kids at heart) can bash out melodies on giant triangles and gongs.

OCEANÁRIO

The closest you'll get to scuba-diving without a wetsuit, Lisbon's **Oceanário** (Oceanarium; ☎ 218 917 002; www.oceanario.pt; Doca dos Olivais; adult/under 3yr/under 12yr/concession/family €11/free/5.50/11/26.50; ☿ 10am-7pm Apr-Oct, 10am-6pm Nov-Mar; ☖) is mind-blowing. No amount of hyperbole about it being Europe's second-largest aquarium, where 8000 species splash in 7 million litres of seawater, does it justice.

Huge wraparound tanks make you feel underwater, as you eyeball zebra sharks, honeycombed rays, gliding mantas and schools of neon fish. Keep your peepers open for oddities such as filigree seadragons, big 'n' dopey ocean sunfish and flying saucer–like moon jellyfish. The superstars, though, are frolicsome sea otters Eusebio and Amália. You'll also want to see the recreated rainforest, Indo-Pacific coral reef and Magellan penguins on ice. The conservation-oriented oceanarium arranges family activities from behind-the-scenes marine tours to sleeping – yeah right! – with the sharks.

PAVILHÃO DO CONHECIMENTO

Kids won't grumble about science at the interactive **Pavilhão do Conhecimento** (Knowledge Pavilion; ☎ 218 917 100; www.pavconhecimento.pt; Alameda dos Oceanos; adult/concession/family €7/3/15; ☿ 10am-6pm Tue-Fri, 11am-7pm Sat & Sun; ☐ ☖), where they can launch hydrogen rockets, don spacesuits for a walking-on-the-moon experience and get dizzy on a high-wire bicycle. Budding physicists have fun whipping up tornadoes and blowing massive soap

bubbles, while tots run riot in the adult-free unfinished house.

PONTE VASCO DA GAMA

Vanishing into a watery distance, **Ponte Vasco da Gama** (Vasco da Gama Bridge; Parque do Tejo) is Europe's longest bridge, stretching a head-spinning 17.2km across the Rio Tejo. Its incredible scale makes everything around it seem toy-town tiny. The architects took every last detail into account when building the six-lane, cable-style bridge for Expo 98, from the curvature of the earth to its rock-solid 85m foundations, which can withstand a major earthquake and winds of up to 250km/h.

TORRE VASCO DA GAMA

Nope, you're not in Dubai, even if it feels like it gazing up at the 145m-high, concrete-and-steel **Torre Vasco da Gama** (Vasco da Gama Tower; Rua Cais das Naus; closed to the public), shaped like the sail of explorer Vasco da Gama's mighty caravel. The brainchild of architects Leonor Janeiro and Nick Jacobs, the emaciated tower is about to be fed, with plans already under way to convert it into a swish five-star hotel.

ACTIVITIES
Birdwatching

Birdwatchers will want their binoculars handy for **Reserva Natural do Estuário do Tejo** (☎ 212 348 021; Av dos Combatentes da Grande Guerra 1, Alcochete), upriver from Lisbon. The vast wetland nature reserve hosts more than 120,000 migrant wading birds, including black cowbirds and flocks of pink flamingos. It's accessible from Montijo, a ferry ride from Lisbon's Terreiro do Paço (p148).

Golf

You can master your swing at six major courses (p85), plus the **Lisbon Sports Club** (Map p151; ☎ 214 310 077; Casal da Carregueira, Belas), just north of Queluz.

Swimming

When temperatures rise, cool off with a dip in the rooftop, indoor **Ateneu Comercial Complexo de Piscinas** (Map pp104-5; ☎ 213 430 947; Rua das Portas de Santo Antão 102; admission €4; ☿ 1.30-4.30pm & 9-10pm Mon-Fri, 3.30-7pm Sat). Professional-standard **Complexo de Piscinas do EUL** (Map pp102-3; ☎ 217 994 970; Av Professor Gama Pinto; admission €4.45; ☿ 7.30am-9pm Mon-Fri, 8am-7pm Sat) is part of the university's sports complex; head north 400m from Cidade Universitária metro.

Tennis

Also at the university sports complex are **tennis courts** (☎ 217 816 568). You can practise your stroke at **Instalações de Ténis de Monsanto** (Map p108; ☎ 213 648 741; Parque Florestal de Monsanto); to get there take bus 24 from Alcântara or bus 29 from Belém. You'll need to reserve at both places.

WALKING TOUR

This viewpoint-to-viewpoint route starts on tram 28 from Largo Martim Moniz or the Baixa, taking in the city's best tram route *and* avoiding uphill slogs. Take the tram up

to Largo da Graça. From here, stroll north and turn left behind the barracks for breathtaking views from Lisbon's highest lookout, **Miradouro da Senhora do Monte** (**1**; see boxed text, p116). Or, walk south and turn right to pine-shaded **Miradouro da Graça** (**2**; see boxed text, p116), where central Lisbon spreads out before you. Retrace your steps and head east

---

WALK FACTS

Start Largo Martim Moniz or Baixa
Finish near Praça do Comércio
Distance 2km
Duration Two to three hours

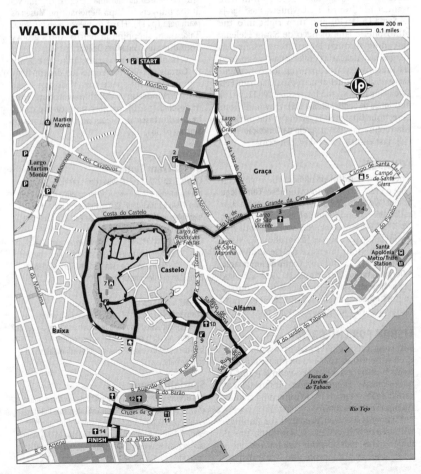

WALKING TOUR

to admire the exquisitely tiled cloisters of **Igreja de São Vicente de Fora** (3; p115), and the cool, echoing **Panteão Nacional** (4; p116). If it's Tuesday or Saturday, make a detour to the buzzy **Feira da Ladra** (Thieves Market; 5; p146) to hunt for buried treasure. Otherwise, go west along Arco Grande da Cima until you reach Largo de Rodrigues de Freitas. Take the Costa do Castelo fork, continuing west to skirt the castle battlements along narrow cobbled streets affording stunning views. Pass in front of **Solar dos Mouros** (6; p129), then turn left up to the **Castelo** (7; p115) and a **viewpoint** (8). Next, head down the steep lanes to Largo das Portas do Sol, and another fine vista from bougainvillea-clad **Miradouro de Santa Luzia** (9; see boxed text, p116). From here wander northward, past whitewashed **Igreja de Santa Luzia** (10) and turn right into the atmospheric lane of Beco de Santa Helena, threading through labyrinthine Alfama to Largo de São João da Praça westwards, pausing for coffee and flaky apple strudel at arty, Austrian-run **Pois Café** (11; p134), to the fortresslike **sé** (12; p116) and **Igreja de Santo António** (13). Downhill from here, your final stop is gazing at the intricate Manueline facade of **Igreja da Conceição Velha** (14), just east of Praça do Comércio.

COURSES

There is a handful of places where you can take a crash course in Portuguese. **Cambridge School** (Map p109; ☎ 213 124 600; www.cambridge.pt; Av da Liberdade 173) and **Centro de Línguas** (CIAL; Map p109; ☎ 217 940 448; www.cial.pt; Av da República 41) both give group language courses (from about €320 for a 30- to 40-hour intensive course; individual lessons cost €25 and up). **Centro de Informação e Documentação** (CIDAC; ☎ 021 317 28 60; www.cidac.pt; Rua Pinheiro Chagas 77) runs accredited courses in Portuguese, which start at €26.50 for individual and €13 for group lessons per hour.

LISBON FOR CHILDREN

Amusing kids is child's play in Lisbon, where even little things spark their imaginations – from bumpy rides on bee-yellow trams to gooey *pastéis de nata*, acting out fairytales at **Castelo de São Jorge** (p115) to munching colourful *pipocas* (popcorn).

Lisboetas are well prepared for families, with free or half-price tickets for little 'uns at major sights, half portions (ask for *uma meia dose*) at many restaurants, and free transport

for under-fives. Hotels will often squeeze in cots or beds for tots at no extra charge.

Prime kiddie territory is **Parque das Nações** (p121), where little nippers love to spot toothy sharks and sea otters at the eye-popping **Oceanário** (p122), launch rockets and ride the high-wire bicycle at the hands-on **Pavilhão do Conhecimento** (p122), then get utterly soaked at the splashy **Jardins d'Água** (Map pp102–3).

Most of Lisbon's squares and parks have playgrounds for tykes to let off excess energy, including **Parque Eduardo VII** (p119) and an animal-themed one at **Jardim da Estrela** (p117).

Go west to relive the nautical adventures of the Age of Discovery in Belém's barge-stuffed **Museu do Marinha** (p120), or marvel at the puppets in Lapa's enchanting **Museu da Marioneta** (p117). Hard-to-please teens in tow? Take them shopping in Bairro Alto's groovy boutiques like **Sneakers Delight** (p146).

When weather warms, take the train to **Cascais** (p160) for some ice-cream-licking, bucket-and-spade fun. Kids can make finny friends on a dolphin-watching tour in **Setúbal** (p170), or play king of the castle in the fantastical turrets and woodlands of **Sintra** (p150).

TOURS
Bus & Tram Tours

Carris (☎ 213 582 334; www.carris.pt) Tram 28 covers the major sights, but if you'd prefer to join a group, Carris runs 1½-hour tram tours (adult/child €17/8.50) of city highlights in Alfama and Baixa or Belém. Hop aboard at Praça do Comércio.

Cityrama (☎ 213 191 090; www.cityrama.pt) This outfit runs sightseeing bus tours of Lisbon, including a city tour (€15), plus Sintra and the Estoril coast (€39). All depart from Marquês de Pombal (Map p109).

River Cruises

Transtejo (Map pp104–5; ☎ 218 824 671; www.transtejo.pt; Terreiro do Paço terminal; adult/child €20/10; ☼ 3pm Apr-Oct) These 2½-hour river cruises are a laid-back way to enjoy Lisbon's sights with multilingual commentary.

Speciality Tours

Naturway (☎ 213 918 090; www.naturway.pt; tours €50; ☼ 8.30am pick-up) Naturway offers two full-day excursions, taking visitors by four-wheel drive to either Sintra (p150) or Parque Natural da Arrábida (p174). Tours take in coastal scenery and include hotel pick-up and drop-off.

Sidecar Touring (☎ 963 965 105; www.sidecartouring
.co.pt; tours €60-120) These madcap drivers offer sidecar
tours, from giddying spins of Sintra to night rides over
Ponte 25 de Abril.

Walking Tours

Lisbon Walker (Map pp104-5; ☎ 218 861 840; www
.lisbonwalker.com; Rua dos Remédios 84; 3hr walk adult/
under 12yr/concession €15/free/10; ☙ 10am & 2.30pm)
This excellent company, with well-informed, English-
speaking guides, offers themed walking tours through
Lisbon such as the Old Town (the history and lore of the
Alfama) and Lisbon Legends and Mysteries. They depart
from the northeast corner of Praça do Comércio.

Papa-Léguas (☎ 218 452 689; www.papa-leguas.com,
in Portuguese; Rua Conde de Sabugosa 3F) Offers rambles
in and around Lisbon such as a six-hour walk through
Parque Florestal de Monsanto from May to September,
costing €19 per person.

Walks on the Art Side (☎ 214 141 055; www.walk
sontheartside.com) Arranges walks through Lisbon with
an arty twist, from Chiado architecture to Belém *azulejos*.
Check the website for times and itineraries.

FESTIVALS & EVENTS

Lisboetas celebrate their seasons with fervour.
Rio-style carnivals and indie flicks heat up the
cooler months, while summer spells high-
octane concerts, sparkly pride parading and
saintly celebrations of feasting and indecent
proposals. *Fazer a festa* (partying) is considered a birthright in Portugal's livewire capital.
For up-to-date listings, pick up the tourist
board's free magazine *Follow Me Lisboa*.

February

Lisbon Carnival (www.visitlisboa.com) Wiggle to samba
as Rio's rhythms and party spirit fuel Lisbon's pre-Lenten
celebrations of merrymaking and flamboyant parades.

March

Moda Lisboa (www.modalisboa.pt) Lisbon strikes a pose
for this four-day catwalk fest, where Portuguese designers
flaunt their latest collections on the runway.

April

Dias da Música (www.ccb.pt) Classical-music buffs see
world-renowned orchestras perform at this three-day
festival held at Centro Cultural de Belém (p143).

Indie Lisboa (www.indielisboa.com) This spring filma-
thon brings 10 days of indie features, documentaries and
shorts to Lisbon's big screens.

May

Alkantara Festival (www.alkantarafestival.pt) The
cutting-edge Alkantara Festival lures theatregoers with a
fortnight of innovative, boundary-crossing performances.

Lisboa Downtown (http://lisboadowntown.sapo.pt)
Lisbon's wackiest race is this downhill boneshaker through
Alfama. Competitors rattle across the cobbles, negotiate
hairpin bends and perform gravity-defying jumps. First
down gets the crown…

Rock in Rio (http://rockinrio-lisboa.sapo.pt) Lisbon's
biggest music bash, the biannual Rock in Rio takes over
Parque da Bela Vista with a star-studded lineup; 2008
headliners featured Metallica, Bon Jovi, Kaiser Chiefs
and Lenny Kravitz. The Cidade do Rock spins nonstop
electronica.

June

Festa do Fado (Fado Festival; www.egeac.pt) Classic
and new-generation *fadistas* perform in the atmospheric
setting of an illuminated Castelo de São Jorge. Catch free
fado performances on trams every Thursday and Sunday
in June.

Lisbon Pride (www.portugalpride.org) Feel the pride as
whistling, rainbow flag-waving gays and lesbians parade
from Marquês de Pombal to Praça do Municipio. Expect
sizzling pink after-parties.

SAINTLY CELEBRATIONS

Come all ye faithful lovers of *vinho*-swigging, sardine-feasting, dancing and merrymaking to
June's **Festas dos Santos Populares** (Festivals of the Popular Saints), three weeks of midsummer
madness. In Lisbon, the key saintly festivities are:

- **Festa de Santo António** (Festival of St Anthony) This lively fest is celebrated with particular
  fervour in Alfama and Madragoa from 12 to 13 June, with feasting, drinking, *bailes* (balls)
  and some 50 *arraiais* (street parties). St Anthony has a bit of a reputation as a matchmaker.
  Lisboetas declare their undying love by giving *manjericos* (basil plants) with soppy poems.
  Around 300 hard-up couples get hitched for free!

- **Festa de São Pedro** (Festival of St Peter) Lisbon pulls out all the stops for St Peter, the patron
  saint of fishermen, from 28 to 29 June. There are slap-up seafood dinners and river processions in his barnacled honour.

July

BaixAnima Baixa's summertime shindig entertains the crowds for free on weekends from July to September with circus acts and live music, improvised theatre and mime.

Delta Tejo (www.deltatejo.com) Alto Ajuda's environmentally sustainable festival stages three days of live music under a starry sky – from reggae and fado to mellow Brazilian grooves.

Super Bock Super Rock (www.superbock.pt) Rocking all over Parque das Nações in mid-July, this is Lisbon's biggest beer-guzzling, head-banging shindig. Concerts are of the ZZ Top, Iron Maiden and Beck ilk.

August

Festival dos Oceanos (http://festivaldosoceanos.com) Dive into Lisbon's seafaring heritage at this two-week festival of swashbuckling parades, world beats, regattas and riverside fireworks.

Jazz em Agosto (www.musica.gulbenkian.pt) Fundação Calouste Gulbenkian (p144) welcomes established and fresh talent to the stage at this soulful jazz fest.

September

Festival de Cinema Gay e Lésbico (www.lisonfilmfest .org) Lisbon's pinkest 10-day flick fest screens 100 home-grown and international gay and lesbian films in late September.

November

Arte Lisboa (www.artelisboa.fil.pt) In the spotlight: the contemporary art of 60 Portuguese and international galleries at this massive art fair in Parque das Nações.

Dia de São Martinho Join Lisboetas to scoff hot chestnuts and drink fruity água-pé (young wine) on 11 November in celebration of good ol' Saint Martin.

December

Lisbon Marathon (www.lisbon-marathon.com) 'Tis the season to work up a festive appetite at Lisbon's pre-Yuletide dash from Praça do Comércio to Belém.

New Year's Eve Ring in the ano novo (new year) with fireworks, free concerts and DJs down by the river.

SLEEPING

Finally waking up to smell those tourist euros, Lisbon has seriously raised the slumber stakes recently with a new crop of design-conscious boutique hotels and upmarket backpacker digs. Be sure to book ahead during the high season (July to mid-September). If you arrive without a reservation, head to a tourist office, where staff can call around for you.

Rossio, Restauradores, Baixa & Chiado

Sandwiched between Alfama and Bairro Alto, this central area attracts budget travellers to its bare-bones *pensões* (guest houses) and snazzy new-generation hostels. It's within staggering distance of the main sights, shops and nightlife yet slightly quieter than Bairro Alto by night.

BUDGET

Pensão Galicia (Map pp104-5; ☎ 213 428 430; Rua do Crucifixo 50; s/d with shared bathroom €15/40) Central for Baixa, this homey, no-frills guest house exudes crusty charm. Its 11 small rooms are decked out in chintzy pastels, rag rugs and old-style furnishings; the best have little balconies. Ring the bell after 10pm.

   Poets Hostel (Map p107; ☎ 213 461 058; www.lis bonpoetshostel.com; Rua Nova da Trindade 2; dm €20; ▢) Backpackers wax lyrical about this poetry-themed hostel in well-heeled Chiado. The 17th-century town house has been lovingly reincarnated as a charming hostel with high-ceilinged, light-flooded dorms. There's a relaxed lounge with free internet and original blue-and-white *azulejos*.

   Travellers House (Map pp104-5; ☎ 210 115 922; http://travellershouse.com; Rua Augusta 89; dm from €22; ▢) Our readers enthuse about this super-friendly hostel set in a converted 250-year-old house on Rua Augusta. As well as cosy dorms, there's a retro lounge with beanbags, an internet corner and a communal kitchen. Tiago and Goncalo know what makes travellers tick – from scrambled eggs for breakfast to activities like wine-tasting and – like it! – an honour system for the minibar.

   Pensão Brasil-África (Map pp104-5; ☎ 218 869 266; www.pensaobrasilafrica.com; Travessa das Pedras Negras 8; s/d €25/35) Tucked down a quiet street, this old-school guest house near the *sé* offers sunny, wood-floored rooms with floral prints. Shared bathrooms are spotless. There's everything you need to rustle up a light breakfast in the lounge.

   Pensão Imperial (Map pp104-5; ☎ 213 420 166; Praça dos Restauradores 78; s/d with shower €25/40) Cheery Imperial has a terrific location, but you'll need to grin and lug it, as there's no lift. The high-ceilinged rooms with rickety '70s-style furniture are nothing flash, but some have flower-draped balconies overlooking the *praça*.

   Pensão Duque (Map p107; ☎ 213 463 444; duquelis boa@yahoo.com; Calçada do Duque 53; d €28-40) Up the steep cobbled steps, this amiable guest house gets rave reviews because of its rock-bottom rates and five-star location between Rossio and Bairro Alto. Pick a small back room to snooze soundly or a sunny front room if decibels don't affect your sleep. Bruno, the eccentric Breton, might even lend you his Celtic CDs.

MIDRANGE

our pick **Goodnight Hostel** (Map pp104-5; ☎ 213 430 139; http://goodnighthostel.com; Rua dos Correeiros 113; dm/d €20/50; 🖳) Set in a converted 18th-century town house, this glam hostel rocks with its fab location, retro design and friendly owner João. Goodnight has everything backpackers crave: from free wi-fi and breakfast (all hail the homemade cinnamon iced tea) to a communal kitchen and lounge. The high-ceilinged dorms offer vertigo-inducing views over Baixa.

Lounge Hostel (Map pp104-5; ☎ 213 462 061; www .lisbonloungehostel.com; Rua de São Nicolau 41; dm/d incl breakfast €20/60; 🖳) These ultrahip Baixa digs have a party vibe. Bed down in immaculate dorms and meet like-minded travellers in the hip lounge watched over by a wacky moose head. The fun team regularly organises events such as the Portuguese dinner with wine for €7. Free internet and breakfast sweeten the deal.

Pensão Gerês (Map pp104-5; ☎ 218 810 497; www .pensaogeres.com; Calçada do Garcia 6; d with/without bathroom €55/45; 🖳) This petite, family-run guest house overlooks bustling Largo de São Domingos, great for sundown tipples of *ginjinha*. Decorated in pastels with dark wood furniture, rooms are basic but immaculate, with titchy bathrooms and hardish beds.

Residencial Florescente (Map pp104-5; ☎ 213 426 609; www.residencialflorescente.com; Rua das Portas de Santo Antão 99; s/d/tw/tr €45/55/70/80; 🔀 🖳) On a vibrant street lined with alfresco restaurants, lemon-fronted Florescente has comfy rooms in muted tones with shiny new bathrooms and free wi-fi. It's a two-minute walk from Rossio.

Residencial Duas Nações (Map pp104-5; ☎ 213 460 710; Rua da Vitória 41; d with/without bathroom €75/45) Bang in the heart of pedestrianised Baixa, this bright guest house makes a good sightseeing and shopping base. Painted in blues and yellows, rooms are decent, though the microscopic bathrooms are a blast from the '70s. Rooms on upper floors are quieter and open onto verandas.

Residencial Roma (Map pp104-5; ☎ 213 460 557; www.residencialroma-lisbon.com; Travessa da Glória 22A; s/d/apt €50/60/70; 🔀 🖳) Close to Avenida da Liberdade boulevard, Roma's spacious rooms have modern bathrooms, but otherwise decor is lacklustre and furniture dated. The 20 sunny apartments with kitchenettes are a better deal.

VIP Eden (Map pp104-5; ☎ 213 216 600; www.viphotels.com; Praça dos Restauradores 24; apt €70; 🔀 🖳 🖳) The art-deco Eden theatre has morphed into this aparthotel on buzzy Praça dos Restauradores. Studios with kitchenettes are functional and clean. The biggest draw, though, is the rooftop pool, where you can splash, sunbathe and enjoy dreamy Lisbon views.

TOP END

Hotel Lisboa Tejo (Map pp104-5; ☎ 218 866 182; www .evidenciahoteis.com; Rua dos Condes de Monsanto 2; s/d €108/125; 🔀 🖳) Once a broom-maker, this town house has scrubbed up nicely into a contemporary hotel, combining original features like brick vaulting with quirks like wavy ceilings. Wood-floored rooms are cushy with cornflower-blue hues, theatrical chairs and satellite TV. Don't miss the Roman *poço* (well) near the entrance.

Hotel Avenida Palace (Map pp104-5; ☎ 213 218 100; www.hotelavenidapalace.pt; Rua 1 de Dezembro 123; s/d €180/205; 🔀 🖳) Palatial certainly sums up this belle-époque hotel with its blingy chandeliers, polished marble and skylight. Rooms are lavish with plump beds, high-thread-count sheets and gilt mirrors. There's a tiny gym, a wood-panelled bar and a sublime lounge where high tea is served. Van Morrison and Martin Sheen are among the hotel's celebrity guests.

Lisboa Regency Chiado (Map pp104-5; ☎ 213 256 100; www.regency-hotels-resorts.com; Rua Nova do Almada 114; s/d €197/216; 🔀) Fusing 19th-century charm with 21st-century cool, Regency offers plush rooms with perks like cable TV and fluffy bathrobes. Go for a top-floor room with a bougainvillea-clad terrace affording views to the river and castle; room 712 is most wanted. Open from noon to midnight, the 7th-floor bar offers superb vistas for all.

Bairro Alto & Around

If you want to be central for nightlife, crash in loud and lively Bairro Alto, which is better for all-night partying than quality shut-eye. Still, a few Sagres should pave the way to slumberland. Light sleepers should pack earplugs. The hip Santa Catarina district is giving rise to a new breed of stylish hostels.

SELF-CATERING IN STYLE

If you're travelling with family or a group of friends in high season (July to mid-September), it may work out cheaper to rent a self-catering apartment, particularly if you're staying for more than a few nights. Rates for modern, fully equipped apartments in central districts like Alfama, Baixa and Chiado range between €50 and €150 per night, with many places offering substantial discounts for stays of more than a week. There are some excellent deals out there, but you'll need to do your homework online. Good websites to try include www.travelingtolisbon.com, www.lisbon-apartments.com and www.lisbon-holiday-apartments.com.

BUDGET

Albergue Popular (Map p107; ☎ 213 478 047; Rua da Rosa 121; s/d with shared bathroom €15/25) If you don't mind street noise, coffee stains and the smell of dope, this grungy guest house is ideal. Rooms are well worn with rickety furnishings and microscopic bathrooms, but they're *very* cheap.

Lisbon Calling (Map pp104–5; ☎ 213 432 381; www.lisboncalling.net; 3rd fl, Rua de São Paulo 126; dm incl breakfast €20; ▯) This all-new backpacker favourite near Santa Catarina is the brainchild of Rita and Sofia, who have lovingly restored its original frescos, *azulejos* and hardwood floors. It's a charming pad with bright, spacious dorms, a groovy lounge with internet and a brick-vaulted kitchen where breakfast is served.

Oasis Lisboa (Map pp104–5; ☎ 213 478 044; www.oasislisboa.com; Rua de Santa Catarina 24; dm incl breakfast €20; ▯) Behind yellow wonder walls, this self-defined backpacker mansion offers wood-floored dorms, a sleek lounge and kitchen, and a rooftop terrace with stunning views to the river. There's free breakfast, internet and coffee. The young team arranges activities from cocktail hours to barbecues. Play ping pong or snuggle by an open fire.

MIDRANGE

Pensão Globo (Map pp104–5; ☎ 213 462 279; pensaoglobo@hotmail.com; Rua do Teixeira 37; s/d €30/50) Tucked down a quietish street, this guest house offers 17 tidy, individually decorated rooms – from scarlet ones with postage-stamp-sized courtyards to lime-green and leafy jobs; all have ultramodern bathrooms. Payment is cash only.

Pensão Luar (Map p107; ☎ 213 460 949; www.pensaoluar.com; Rua das Gáveas 101; s/d €40/45) The moon lights the way to Luar, a decent cheapie just steps from the nightlife. Recently revamped, the well-lit rooms in juicy fruit shades have parquet floors, TVs and little wrought-iron balconies. Nice touch: coat hangers shaped like dogs' backsides! You'll receive a warm *bemvindo* (welcome) here.

Anjo Azul (Map p107; ☎ 213 478 069; www.anjoazul.com; Rua Luz Soriano 75; d €50-80; ▯) You can't miss the dazzling blue-tiled facade of this gay-friendly hotel, named after smouldering Blue Angel Marlene Dietrich. Adorned with homoerotic artwork, its rooms stretch from scarlet-and-black love nests with heart pillows to chocolate-caramel numbers. All have squeaky-clean bathrooms and teeny balconies.

Pensão Londres (Map pp104–5; ☎ 213 462 203; www.pensaolondres.com.pt; Rua Dom Pedro V 53; s/d €52/72) Opposite Miradouro de São Pedro de Alcântara lookout, Londres oozes art-nouveau charm with its cage elevator and stuccowork. Its high-ceilinged rooms feature decorative balconies and polished wood furniture; those on the 4th floor afford sweeping city views.

Residencial Alegria (Map pp104–5; ☎ 213 220 670; www.alegrianet.com; Praça da Alegria 12; d incl breakfast €58-68; ❄) Overlooking a palm-dotted plaza, this lemon-fronted belle-époque gem is ablaze with pink geraniums in summer. Rooms are peaceful and airy with plaids and chunky wood, while corridors reveal stucco and antiques. Breakfast is a substantial affair.

TOP END

Casa de São Mamede (Map p108; ☎ 213 963 166; www.casadesaomamede.com; Rua da Escola Politécnica 159; s/d incl breakfast €100/120; ❄) This 18th-century, family-run villa has class: from the red carpet gracing the stone staircase to the tinkling chandeliers in the exquisitely tiled breakfast room. Large and serene, rooms sport period furnishings. It's a short stroll from Bairro Alto and the botanical gardens.

Hotel Príncipe Real (Map pp104–5; ☎ 213 407 350; www.hotelprincipereal.com; Rua da Alegria 53; s/d incl breakfast €119/149; ❄ ▯) Hidden in a quiet pocket of Bairro Alto, this boutique hotel has stylish rooms with flat-screen TVs and marble bathrooms; most have balconies with superb views. Wake up to a full English breakfast.

Bairro Alto Hotel (Map p107; ☎ 213 408 288; www.bairroaltohotel.com; Praça Luís de Camões 2; s/d from €290/310; ❄ ▯) Bairro Alto's funkiest boutique hotel bears the hallmark of interior designer José Pedro Vieira. Note the esoteric Rui Chafes' sculptures in the lobby. Decked out in bold colours, the plush rooms offer five-star trappings like plasma TVs, wi-fi and shiny marble bathrooms. A Ferrero Rocher–style gold lift zooms to the 6th-floor lounge, a great place to sip cocktails as Lisbon starts to twinkle.

Alfama, Castelo & Graça

Alfama's cobbled lanes generally offer peaceful slumber, though choose wisely or else you might find yourself being serenaded to sleep by a warbling *fadista*. On its hilltop perch above Lisbon, leafy Graça has dramatic views.

BUDGET & MIDRANGE

Casa de Hóspedes Estrela (Map pp104–5; ☎ 218 869 506; 1st fl, Rua dos Bacalhoeiros 8; s/d with shower €30/37) Our favourite waterfront cheapie, this homely place is run by a kindly Brazilian woman. The simple, tiled-floor rooms in chintzy pastels have tiny en suite showers. Ask for a room facing the plaza.

Pensão Ninho das Águias (Map pp104–5; ☎ 218 854 070; Costa do Castelo 74; s/d/tr with shared bathroom €30/40/60) It isn't called 'eagle's nest' for nothing: this guest house has a Rapunzel-esque turret affording magical 360-degree views over Lisbon. Let your hair down in the light and breezy rooms, or on the flowery terrace watched over by Pantufos (literally 'slippers'), the resident dachshund. Book well ahead.

Pensão São João da Praça (Map pp104–5; ☎ 218 862 591; 218862591@sapo.pt; 2nd fl, Rua de São João da Praça 97; d with/without bathroom €50/35) So close to the *sé* you can almost touch the gargoyles, this 19th-century guest house has a pick-and-mix of clean, sunny rooms with fridges and TVs; the best have river-facing verandas.

Sé Guesthouse (Map pp104–5; ☎ 218 864 400; 1st fl, Rua de São João da Praça 97; d with shared bathroom €70) This shrine to wanderlust brims with Mr and Mrs Belmira's worldly knick-knacks, from pharaohs to Bolivian throws. The bright rooms have karma-chameleon red, gold and green colours and technicolour lights; many feature little balconies facing the *sé*. Expect a tail-wagging reception from Muki the spaniel in the cosy lounge.

TOP END

Albergaria Senhora do Monte (Map pp104–5; ☎ 218 866 002; senhoradomonte@hotmail.com; Calçada do Monte 39; s/d €98/130; P) Don't judge this '60s hotel on face value. Though views are slightly dated, the views are stunning. Photographers and romantics swoon over the vistas from the patio. Shell out extra for a veranda to indulge in horizontal sightseeing from your lounger. Tram 28 runs close by.

Solar dos Mouros (Map pp104–5; ☎ 218 854 940; www.solardosmouros.pt; Rua do Milagre de Santo António 4; d €120–240; 🕸) Blink and you'll miss this boutique pad near the castle. Its art-slung interior reveals a passion for Africa and primary colours. Affording river or castle views, the 14 rooms bear the imprint of artist Luís Lemos and offer trappings like flat-screen TVs and minibars. There's a water garden for catnapping between sights.

Olissippo Castelo (Map pp104–5; ☎ 218 820 190; www.olissippohotels.com; Costa do Castelo 112–126; d incl breakfast from €190; 🕸 🖵) Up the cobbled hill lies this bubble-gum-pink hotel offering sweeping views and silent nights. The spacious rooms are classically elegant with huge windows, deep-pile carpets and sparkly marble bathrooms; pick one on the 3rd floor for a private veranda. Wi-fi and a hearty breakfast are other pluses.

Palácio Belmonte (Map pp104–5; ☎ 218 816 600; www.palaciobelmonte.com; Páteo Dom Fradique 14; ste from €400; 🕸 🖵) Nestled beside Castelo de São Jorge, this 15th-century palace turns on the VIP treatment in its 11 suites, named after Portuguese luminaries and lavishly adorned with 18th-century *azulejos*, silks, marble and antiques. There's a pool framed by herb gardens, a wood-panelled library where classical music plays and numerous other luxuries that justify the hefty price tag.

Estrela & Lapa

Lisbon's sleek, leafy diplomatic district has some top-notch boutique hotels and is ideal for escapists that prefer pin-drop peace to central bustle.

Maná Guesthouse (Map p108; ☎ 213 931 060; pensaomana@sapo.pt; Calçada do Marquês de Abrantes 97; d incl breakfast €50–70) Small and welcoming, Maná has ultraclean rooms with polished wood floors, high ceilings and homey chintz like porcelain animals and plastic flowers. Breakfast is served under the fruit trees in the garden.

York House (Map p108; ☎ 213 962 435; www.yorkhouselisboa.com; Rua das Janelas Verdes 32; s/d from €200/230; 🖵) Steps twist up past ivy-clad walls to this

17th-century convent turned boutique stunner, with art-slung vaulted corridors and a sun-dappled courtyard. Its born-again cells blend old-world with contemporary style: antique chests contrast with funky lighting, deep-blue hues with snowy-white linen. Lather up with Molton Brown suds in your eggshell-hued marble bathroom. The chandelier-lit restaurant serves Portuguese cuisine with a French twist.

As Janelas Verdes (Map p108; ☎ 213 968 143; www .heritage.pt; Rua das Janelas Verdes 47; s/d/tr €220/240/307; ✷ 💻) This romantic 18th-century mansion inspired Eça de Queirós's novel *Os Maias*. Spacious and classically elegant, the rooms feature perks like flat-screen TVs, DVD players, shiny marble bathrooms and complimentary port. Retreat to the wood-panelled library for sweeping views to the river and a stargazing telescope. When the sun's out, take breakfast in the bougainvillea-draped courtyard.

our pick Lapa Palace (Map p108; ☎ 213 949 494; www.lapapalace.com; Rua do Pau de Bandeira 4; d from €340; ✷ 💻 ⊠ 🚿) Set in landscaped gardens, this belle-époque mansion offers the red-carpet treatment in swanky quarters with five-star trimmings: from precious porcelain to Oscar-winning flicks and marble bathrooms with toasty towels. Flash the cash to upgrade to the Count of Valenças suite complete with a turret affording 360-degree views. The outdoor pool, Zen-style treatment rooms, cocktail lounge and Italian restaurant are, as befits a palace, first class.

Rato, Marquês de Pombal & Saldanha

Pousada da Juventude de Lisboa (Map p109; ☎ 213 532 696; lisboa@movijovem.pt; Rua Andrade Corvo 46; dm/d incl breakfast €16/43; ⏱ 24hr; 💻 🚿) Well located and expertly run, this hostel is in a fine mansion near Parque Eduardo VII. The single-sex dorms are plain but clean; one is fully wheelchair accessible. Free breakfast, a bar with happy hour and luggage storage are bonuses. The friendly crew speaks excellent English.

Fontana Park Hotel (Map p109; ☎ 210 410 600; www .fontanaparkhotel.com; Rua Engenheiro Vieira da Silva 2; d from €100; ✷ 💻) The new design kid on Saldanha's block is this 1908 iron factory turned cutting-edge hotel, flaunting smooth contours, space-age lighting and sylvan flourishes. The monochrome rooms are temples to minimalism, with wall-mounted flat-screen TVs, wi-fi and granite bathrooms with transparent

walls (forget modesty!). Zen is the word in the Japanese restaurant and the bamboo-fringed garden where a fountain gurgles.

Hotel Britania (Map p109; ☎ 213 155 016; www .heritage.pt; Rua Rodrigues Sampaio 17; s/d €165/175; ✷ 💻) Art deco rules the waves at Britania, a boutique gem near Avenida da Liberdade. Cassiano Branco put his modernist stamp on the rooms with chrome lamps, plaid fabrics and shiny marble bathrooms. Hobnob over a G&T at the bar, chat with the affable staff and let this 1940s time capsule work its charm. Free wi-fi.

Belém

Pensão Residencial Setúbalense (Map p110; ☎ 213 636 639; www.pensaosetubalense.pt; Rua de Belém 28; s/d from €30/40; ✷) A short toddle east of the monastery, this 17th-century guest house has twee but comfy rooms with tiled floors, floral fabrics and modern bathrooms. Corridors are a tad dark, but *azulejos* and pot plants add a homely touch.

Jerónimos 8 (Map p110; ☎ 213 600 900; www.jeronimos8hotel.com; Rua dos Jerónimos 8; d €118; ✷ 💻) Belém's first boutique hotel, Jerónimos 8 ups the style ante with clean lines, floor-to-ceiling windows and designer flourishes aplenty. The slick rooms, dressed in cream and caramel hues with natural fabrics, feature cable TV, minbar and wi-fi. Chill in the peppered bar or on the deck. The monastery views are superb.

Greater Lisbon

Clube de Campismo de Lisboa (off Map pp102-3; ☎ 219 623 960; www.clubecampismolisboa.pt; sites per adult/tent/car €1.30/4.50/1.30; 💻 🚿) Open to Camping Card International (CCI) cardholders only, and 16km northwest of Lisbon at Almornos, this shady site is great for families, with a restaurant, bar, sandy playground and tree-fringed pool (admission €3.50 for noncampers).

Lisboa Camping (Map pp102-3; ☎ 217 628 200; www.lisboacamping.com; sites per adult/tent/car €6/6/3; ✷ 🚿) Pitch a tent at this well-equipped site in forested Parque Florestal de Monsanto, 6km west of Rossio. Facilities include tennis courts, a playground and restaurant. Bungalows are also available. Take bus 43 from Cais do Sodré or bus 50 from Gare do Oriente.

Pousada da Juventude de Lisboa Parque Nações (Map pp102-3; ☎ 218 920 890; www.pousadasjuventude .pt; Via de Moscavide 47; dm/d €13/37; ⏱ reception 8am-midnight) Despite its nondescript decor, this

HI hostel is a decent base for exploring Parque das Nações (it's 1km north of Gare do Oriente). Four-bed dorms are clean and spacious. It has a restaurant, cooking and laundry facilities, and internet.

There are other *pousadas da juventude* (youth hostels) across the Tejo at **Almada** (off Map pp102-3; ☎ 212 943 491; almada@movijovem.pt; Quinta do Bucelinho, Pragal; dm/d €14/38), and near the beach at **Catalazete** (off Map pp102-3; ☎ 214 430 638; catalazete@movijovem.pt; Estrada Marginal, Oeiras; dm/d €13/38), 12km west of central Lisbon, accessible by frequent trains from Cais do Sodré. Both of these have bargain four-person apartments (€60). Reservations are essential – at least a month ahead in summer.

EATING

Sparky new-generation chefs at the stove, first-rate raw ingredients and a generous pinch of world spice means Lisbon no longer makes diners meow with *bacalhau*. Today's exciting, varied offer spans everything from ubercool dockside sushi lounges to designer Michelin-starred restaurants. Gourmet trailblazers like Olivier, Joachim Koerper and Henrique Sá Pessoa have put the Portuguese capital back on the gastro map with boldly creative, seasonally inspired cuisine.

With the Atlantic on the doorstep, fish is big on most menus and tastes terrific served with a glass of Alentejo white on the cobbles. Even vegetarians find more to like

---

LET THEM EAT PASTÉIS!

Londoners have pubs, Parisians boulangeries and Lisboetas *pastelerias* (pastry and cake shops) – temples to cream-filled treats that are never more than a few paces away. Everywhere, you'll see locals devouring flaky *pastéis de nata* or whiling away afternoons sipping *bicas*. Take this as your cue to follow those whiffs of butter, sugar and freshly roasted coffee. You can kiss the diet goodbye in this sugar-coated city, which sees *pastelerias* as life-enriching rather than waistline-expanding. But calorie counters take heart: for every blob of cream, there's another step to climb in Lisbon's steeply twisting streets, so you can counteract the indulgence with a vigorous urban workout.

---

about Lisbon nowadays. Euro-economisers should check out daily specials costing as little as €6. Many one-pan, family places close on Sunday or Monday.

Baixa, Chiado & Rossio

Many of Baixa's old-school bistros and outdoor cafes heave with tourists, but tiptoe away from the main drag Rua Augusta and you'll find some gems in streets like Rua dos Correeiros and Rua dos Sapateiros. Chiado's tree-fringed plazas and backstreets are more relaxed. For alfresco dining with dazzling castle views, make for the cobbled steps of Calçada do Duque.

BUDGET

Fragoleto (Map pp104-5; ☎ 218 877 971; Rua da Prata 74; scoops €1.80; ☑ 9am-8pm Mon-Sat, 10am-7pm Mon-Sat winter; ☑) For the tastiest gelato this side of Genoa, head for pint-sized Fragoleto. Manuela makes authentic ice cream (even vegan options) using fresh, seasonal fruit. Our favourites: pistachio and green tea.

Chá do Carmo (Map pp104-5; ☎ 213 421 301; Largo do Carmo 21; snacks €2-4; ☑ 10am-8pm Mon-Sat) Overlooking one of Chiado's loveliest squares, where jacaranda trees bloom in spring, this is a great spot to refuel over teas, toasties and ice cream.

Vertigo Café (Map pp104-5; ☎ 213 433 112; Travessa do Carmo 4; snacks €4-7; ☑ 10am-midnight; ☑) Artists lap up the boho vibe at this glam Chiado cafe, where they can relax, read the papers and play draughts. Speciality teas like violet and jasmine pair nicely with bagels or smoked salmon salads.

Royale Café (Map p107; ☎ 213 469 125; Largo Rafael Bordalo Pinheiro 29; snacks €4-6; ☑ 10am-midnight Mon-Sat, 10am-8pm Sun; ☑) Media types and yummy mummies flock to this chichi cafe – all monochrome walls and funky chandeliers. When the sun comes out, retreat to the vine-clad courtyard for zingy gooseberry juices, wild-rosebud teas and create-your-own sandwiches.

Confeitaria Nacional (Map pp104-5; ☎ 213 461 720; Praça da Figueira 18; lunches from €5.50; ☑ 8am-8pm Mon-Sat) Expanding waistlines since 1829, this stuccoed patisserie entices with strong *bica*, macaroons and *pastéis de nata*. Upstairs, the restaurant dishes up hearty quiches and soups.

Celeiro (Map pp104-5; ☎ 213 422 463; Rua 1 de Dezembro 65; lunches around €6; ☑ 8.30am-8pm Mon-Fri,

8.30am-7pm Sat; V) The midday crowds pile into this veggie cafe for freshly squeezed OJ and daily specials like quiche and pizza. It's next to a well-stocked health food store.

El Rei D'Frango (Map pp104-5; ☎ 213 424 066; Calçada do Duque 5; dishes €6-8; ☒ lunch & dinner Mon-Sat) Grill goddesses Luciana and Carla rustle up enormous and delicious portions of salmon and *febras* (sautéed pork strips) for pocket money. You'll *roll* down the cobbles after eating at this simple local haunt.

MIDRANGE
Nood (Map p107; ☎ 213 474 141; Largo Rafael Bordalo Pinheiro 20; dishes €6.50-9; ☒ noon-midnight Sun-Thu, noon-2am Fri & Sat; V) Young and buzzy, this Japanese newcomer is Chiado's hippest nosh spot. The scene: chilli-red walls, communal tables and flaming woks. The menu: well-prepared sushi, sashimi and noodles. No reservations – turn up and queue.

Mega Vega (Map pp104-5; Rua dos Sapateiros 113; lunches €6.50-10; ☒ 8.30am-11pm Mon-Fri, 10am-11pm Sat; V) This cheery vegetarian cafe rustles up fresh salads, tasty tarts and juices, and spreads a fine lunch buffet.

Everest Montanha (Map pp104-5; ☎ 218 876 428; Calçada do Garcia 15; dishes €7-9.50; ☒ lunch & dinner Mon-Sat; V)) Tucked just north of Praça da Figueira, this unassuming restaurant reaches Himalayan heights with flavourful lamb kormas, gobis and so-smooth mango lassis.

Oriente Chiado (Map pp104-5; ☎ 213 431 530; Rua Ivens 28; dishes €8-15; ☒ lunch & dinner; V) A rarity in Lisbon, this Feng Shui–inspired restaurant serves 100% vegan and macrobiotic food. Tasty dishes include polenta, hummus and tofu curries. There's a salad and juice bar.

Amo.te Chiado (Map pp104-5; ☎ 213 420 668; Calçada Nova de São Francisco 2; dishes €8-16; ☒ 10am-midnight Mon-Thu, 10am-2am Fri & Sat; V)) Giggly Lisboetas adore this *Sex and the City*–style haunt, kissed with silver and jazzed up with bubble-shaped lights. Lounge music plays as hipsters sip strawberry-vodka cocktails and devour veggie couscous or octopus with roast peppers.

Cervejaria da Trindade (Map p107; ☎ 213 423 506; Rua Nova da Trindade 20C; dishes €8-20; ☒ lunch & dinner) This 13th-century monastery turned clattering beer hall oozes atmosphere with its vaults and *azulejos* of quaffing clerics and seasonal goddesses. Feast away on humungous steaks or lobster stew, washed down with foaming beer.

Bonjardim (Map pp104-5; ☎ 342 43 89; Travessa de Santo Antão 11; dishes €9-15; ☒ lunch & dinner) Juicy, spit-roast *frango* (chicken) is served with a mountain of fries at this local favourite. Add piri-piri for extra spice. The pavement terrace is elbow-to-elbow in summer.

Tentaçoes de Goa (Map pp104-5; ☎ 218 875 824; Rua São Pedro Mártir 23; dishes €10-15; ☒ lunch & dinner Mon-Sat) Friendly and usually full, this family affair is tucked down a backstreet near Martim Moniz. Reserve a table to munch on spicy Goan nosh such as crab curry with perfectly fluffy basmati.

Café no Chiado (Map pp104-5; ☎ 213 460 501; Largo do Picadeiro 10; dishes €11-15; ☒ noon-2am Tue-Sun) Theatregoers applaud this laid-back cafe for its jazzy music, people-watching terrace and flavoursome specials like salmon burgers with asparagus.

TOP END
Tamarind (Map pp104-5; ☎ 213 466 080; Rua da Glória 43; dishes €12-18; ☒ lunch Sun-Fri, dinner daily; V) Dave Walia cooks up an Indian storm at this calm restaurant in Ayurveda-inspired pink and blue tones. His rich prawn kormas and lamb curries are inflected with chilli, ginger and fresh herbs.

O Fumeiro (Map pp104-5; ☎ 213 474 203; Rua da Conceição da Glória 25; dishes €12-20; ☒ lunch & dinner) This cosy blue-and-white–tiled restaurant specialises in the earthy, aromatic cuisine of the mountainous Beira Alta. Suckling pig and seafood *cataplana* (stew) pair well with Portuguese wines.

Café Buenos Aires (Map p107; ☎ 342 07 39; Calçada do Duque 31; dishes €14-20) Your tastebuds will tango at this boho Argentine gem, perched high on the cobbled steps of Calçada do Duque. Candles flicker, loved-up couples coo and amigos tuck into Argentine steaks and chocolate cake with *dulce de leche* (caramel spread).

Martinho da Arcada (Map pp104-5; ☎ 218 879 259; Praça do Comércio 3; dishes €14-25; ☒ breakfast, lunch & dinner Mon-Sat) Sizzling and stirring since 1782, this old-world restaurant was once a haunt of poet Fernando Pessoa. Dapper waiters bring pepper steak and grilled cod to the outdoor tables beneath a colonnade; prime people-watching territory.

Terreiro do Paço (Map pp104-5; ☎ 210 312 850; Praça do Comércio; dishes €22-28; ☒ lunch & dinner Mon-Fri, dinner only Sat) Sitting pretty on Lisbon's grandest square, this swish restaurant was once part

TOP 10 APPETISING VIEWS

Whether you want to soak up Lisbon's
street life or see the castle twinkle after
dark, these are our favourite places to dine
with a view.

- **Bica do Sapato** (p135)
- **Café Buenos Aires** (opposite)
- **Chá do Carmo** (p131)
- **Confeitaria Nacional** (p131)
- **Doca Peixe** (p136)
- **Eleven** (p136)
- **Martinho da Arcada** (opposite)
- **O Faz Figura** (p135)
- **Panorama** (p136)
- **Restô** (p135)

of the royal palace. Today brick vaults and
soft jazz set the scene for creative Portuguese
flavours such as Azores tuna with mango
compote and ginger soufflé.

Gambrinus (Map pp104–5; ☎ 213 421 466; Rua das
Portas de Santo Antão 23–25; dishes €20–35; ✆ noon–2am)
Since opening in the 1930s, this wood-panelled beer hall (named after the patron saint
of brewing) has been serving *the* best seafood in Lisbon. Book ahead to savour delicacies like steamed clams and shellfish bisque,
rounded out with vintage port. Service is
discreet, the crowd dressy.

Bairro Alto & Around

For a preclubbing vibe, caipirinhas and a
side order of cool, it has to be loud and lively
Bairro Alto. The rhythmic sizzle of grills,
wafts of garlic and pumping music fill the
narrow lanes come twilight. Late-night nibblers are *bemvindo*.

BUDGET

Pastelaria São Roque (Map pp104–5; Rua Dom Pedro V;
pastries €1–3; ✆ 7am–7.30pm) This wedding cake
of a patisserie drips with exquisite *azulejos*, gold-topped columns and mirrors.
Bag a seat in one of the alcoves to indulge
in buttery rock cakes, freshly made bread
and window-watching.

Mar Adentro (Map pp104–5; ☎ 346 91 58; Rua do
Alecrim 35; snacks €3–5; ✆ 10am–11pm Mon-Thu, 1pm-
midnight Fri & Sat; **V**) Gay-friendly Mar Adentro
reveals a razor-sharp industrial design with

a stainless steel arch, concrete walls and
moulded plastic chairs. Lisbon creatives
flock here for healthy breakfasts, yummy
sandwiches like feta, pepper and olive, and
free wi-fi.

Adamastor (Map p107; ☎ 213 471 726; Rua Marechal
Saldanha 24; dishes €4.50–7; ✆ lunch & dinner Mon-Sat)
Wedge-shaped Adamastor serves inexpensive
specials like roast chicken and sardines with
refreshing homemade lemonade. Try to snag
an outdoor table.

Esplanada (Map p108; ☎ 962 311 669; Praça do Príncipe
Real; mains €6–10; ✆ 9am-8pm Mon, 9am-11pm Wed-Sun)
This indoor–outdoor cafe is ideal for a coffee
break among the palms and twittering birds.
Sweet-toothed folk love the sharp lemon tart
and homemade ice cream.

Toma Lá-Dá-Cá (Map p107; ☎ 213 479 243; Travessa
do Sequeiro 38; dishes €6–12; ✆ lunch & dinner) Get your
tongue in a twist pronouncing the name of
this Santa Catarina gem, where there's often
an anaconda of a queue. The inviting haunt
rolls out Portuguese fare such as baked carp,
plus Alpine classics like fondue – adding do-
re-mi to the lá-dá-cá.

MIDRANGE

El Gordo II (Map p107; ☎ 213 426 372; Travessa dos Fiéis de
Deus 28; tapas €3.25–28; ✆ dinner Tue-Sun) Lit with a rosy
glow from cloth lanterns, Lisbon's 'fat boy'
churns out lip-smacking tapas such as octopus
in smoked paprika, pimento peppers and cod
pastries. Go alfresco on the cobbled steps.

A Camponesa (Map p107; ☎ 213 464 791; Rua Marechal
Saldanha 23; dishes €7.50–15; ✆ lunch & dinner Mon-Fri,
dinner only Sat; **V**) This Santa Catarina hot spot
attracts arty types with its poster-plastered
walls, jazzy grooves and tables full of holiday
snapshots. Savour home-grown flavours like
Algarve oysters and cuttlefish with fried egg.
There's always one veggie option.

Lisbona Italiana (Map p107; ☎ 213 432 184; Rua das
Gáveas 15; mains €9.50–18; ✆ lunch & dinner Mon-Sat, dinner Sun) Entering this bistro is like stepping
into a Michelangelo painting: cherubs beam
down from the bar, rosé wine flows and eye-
candy staff flutter around with heavenly pizzas – thin, crisp and with inventive toppings
like prawn, curry and banana.

Cravo e Canela (Map p107; ☎ 213 431 858; Rua da
Barroca 70; dishes €10–18; ✆ dinner Tue-Sun) Pure theatre with its maroon walls, teardrop chandeliers and gilt mirrors, this newcomer's name
translates as 'cloves and cinnamon'. Its innovative menu indeed adds spice to Bairro

Alto – think Asian-style beef and tender duck breast with pomegranate.

Louro & Sal (Map p107; ☎ 213 476 275; Rua da Atalaia 53; dishes €10-15; ☼ dinner) Smiley staff, a slick black-tiled decor and Med-style soul food ensure full tables at this bistro. Funky jazz plays and garlic wafts from the kitchen as you await heart-warming dishes like onion soup and game sausage with roast vegetables.

O Barrigas (Map p107; ☎ 213 471 220; Travessa da Queimada 31; dishes €10-18; ☼ dinner Thu-Tue) With a name meaning 'the bellies', there are no prizes for guessing what you'll be nursing at this low-lit bistro. Red-and-white tiles and candles create the backdrop for flavours like braised rabbit and fluffy *bacalhau espiritual* (salt-cod soufflé).

Terra (Map p108; ☎ 707 108 108; http://terra.vg; Rua da Palmeira 15; veg buffet €12.50; ☼ lunch & dinner; V) Our readers sing the praises of Terra for its superb vegetarian buffet (including vegan options) of salads, kebabs and curries, plus organic wines and juices. A fountain gurgles in the tree-shaded courtyard, lit by tealights after dark.

TOP END

Sul (Map p107; ☎ 213 462 449; Rua do Norte 13; dishes €12-16; ☼ dinner) Quirkily lit by ostrich-egg lamps, Sul is a fixture on Lisbon's late-night dining circuit. The mint-walled, gallery-style restaurant churns out Italian treats such as shitake risotto, plus more exotic fare like zebra steaks.

Lisboa á Noite (Map p107; ☎ 213 468 557; Rua das Gáveas 69; dishes €14-24; ☼ dinner Mon-Sat) Dinner is plucked from the tanks at this smart haunt, glammed up with tangerine-and-white hues and night shots of Lisbon. Sea-foodies lap up the Algarve clams with octopus.

Pap'Açorda (Map p107; ☎ 213 464 811; Rua da Atalaia 57; dishes €15-25; ☼ lunch & dinner) Way too sexy for Bairro Alto, Pap'Açorda lures the beauty set with its cascading chandeliers, pink-champagne walls and Right Said Fred lookalike waiters. The signature dish is *açorda* (bread and shellfish stew), washed down with Moët, sweetie.

La Brasserie de l'Entrecôte (Map p107; ☎ 213 428 344; Rua do Alecrim 117; steaks €16.50; ☼ lunch & dinner) So, sir, would you like steak and chips or chips and steak? Served high and mighty on a gut-busting plate, entrecôte steak with herby sauce is the only thing on the menu at this high-ceilinged, Parisian-style brasserie. It's more than enough.

our pick Olivier (Map pp104-5; ☎ 213 431 405; Rua do Teixeira 35; tasting menus €35; ☼ dinner Mon-Sat) Nathalie, the sister of Lisbon masterchef Olivier da Costa, is the perfect host at this intimate, low-ceilinged Bairro Alto restaurant. The Med-inspired tasting menu features delicacies such as thinly sliced octopus carpaccio and fall-off-the-bone osso buco (veal shank) in port sauce. Save room for the legendary chocolate coulant (a small cake with a liquid centre). Advance reservations are essential.

Tavares Rico (Map p107; ☎ 213 421 112; Rua da Misericórdia 37; dishes €32-37, tasting menus €75; ☼ lunch & dinner Tue-Sat) Tavares is the fairest of them all, with its all-gold 18th-century interior lit by chandeliers. Signature dishes such as scallops with Alentejo bacon are beautifully cooked, artfully presented and marry well with Portuguese wines.

Alfama, Graça & Santa Apolónia

Peppered with hobbit-sized family bistros where the owners might spontaneously break out in song, Alfama's twisting, lantern-lit lanes are made for romantic tête-à-têtes. Come for alfresco dining on the cobbles, views of the castle illuminated and impromptu *fado vadio* (street fado).

BUDGET

Botequim São Martinho (Map pp104-5; ☎ 218 860 215; Largo de São Martinho 1; snacks €2-8; ☼ 3pm-midnight) Plastered with Tricona sardine labels and lit by a dressmaker's model, this retro tapas bar is great for cheese and chorizo grazing between sights.

Pois Café (Map pp104-5; ☎ 218 862 497; Rua de São João da Praça 93; dishes €4-12; ☼ 11am-8pm Tue-Sun; V) All hail Austrian-run Pois for its laid-back boho vibe. Its sofas invite lazy afternoons spent reading novels and guzzling coffee. Creative salads and sandwiches with names like Sepp (olive, pesto and Emmental) go nicely with tangy juices. There's a kids' play area.

A Tasca da Sé (Map pp104-5; ☎ 218 875 551; Rua Augusto Rosa 62; dishes €6-12; ☼ lunch & dinner) This bijou restaurant opposite the *sé* rustles up simple yet tasty home cooking – try the garlicky prawns and squid kebabs.

Malmequer Bemmequer (Map pp104-5; ☎ 218 876 535; Rua de São Miguel 23; dishes €6-12.50; ☼ lunch & dinner Wed-Sun) Look for the daisy at this bright check-tablecloth-and-tile number, overlooking a pretty square. It rolls out charcoal-grilled dishes such as lamb with rosemary.

Casanova (Map pp104-5; ☎ 218 877 532; Cais da Pedra á Bica do Sapato; dishes €6-13; ☽ lunch & dinner Tue-Sun) Casanova seduces with wood-fired pizza that's thin, crisp and authentically Italian. Bag a table on the riverside terrace (heated in winter).

Porta d'Alfama (Map pp104-5; ☎ 218 864 536; Rua de São João da Praça 17; dishes €6-10; ☽ lunch & dinner) Tiny Porta d'Alfama serves simple fare like grilled sardines. But food is secondary at Saturday afternoon's free *fado vadio*, where the family gathers for a gutsy warble. Take a pew on the sunny terrace with a pitcher of white wine and enjoy.

MIDRANGE

Santo Antonio de Alfama (Map pp104-5; ☎ 218 881 328; Beco de Saõ Miguel 7; dishes €8-16; ☽ lunch & dinner Wed-Mon) Shoehorned between Alfama's candy-bright houses, this bistro wins the award for Lisbon's loveliest courtyard: all vines, twittering budgies and fluttering laundry. The interior is a silver-screen shrine, while the menu stars its own creations such as Sophia Loren salad (pesto, rocket and salmon).

Grelhador de Alfama (Map pp104-5; ☎ 218 886 298; Rua dos Remédios 135; mains €8.50-12; ☽ lunch & dinner Mon-Sat) Follow your nostrils to this no-fuss grill house. Exposed stone and fado paraphernalia create a cosy-meets-kitsch setting for barbecued fish or steak. The pocket-sized terrace fills up fast in summer.

Viagem de Sabores (Map pp104-5; ☎ 218 870 189; Rua de São João da Praça 103; dishes €8.50-12.50; ☽ dinner Mon-Sat) Travel your tastebuds at this worldly haunt behind the sé. Your affable host is João Baptista, the design industrial cool with quirks like an illuminated zeppelin. From tender Moroccan lamb to chocolate cannelloni – globetrotting here is moreish, we swear.

Restô (Map pp104-5; ☎ 218 867 334; Costa do Castelo 7; tapas €4-5, restaurant dishes €10-16; ☽ 7.30pm-2am Mon-Fri, noon-2am Sat & Sun) Part of the Chapitô arts cooperative (p143), Restô's tree-filled courtyard hums with arty types tucking into tapas or barbecued steaks. Zebra and giraffe prints glam up the top-floor restaurant, affording mesmerising views over Lisbon.

Senhora Mãe (Map pp104-5; ☎ 218 875 599; Largo de São Martinho 6-7; dishes €11-16; ☽ lunch & dinner) Senhora flaunts minimalist chic with blonde wood, clean lines and zinc flourishes. Seasonally inspired dishes might include ravioli in cuttlefish ink or game in chestnut and *ginjinha* sauce.

TOP END

Bica do Sapato (Map pp104-5; ☎ 218 810 320; Cais da Pedra á Bica do Sapato; sushi €3-10, restaurant dishes €24-35; ☽ lunch Tue-Sat, dinner Mon-Sat) Part-owned by John Malkovich, this uberhip dockside venue is all glass walls, UFO-style lighting and chocolate-black hues. Upstairs hipsters nibble sushi in the spacey bar, while downstairs the design-conscious restaurant serves highlights like tender roast lamb with citrus jelly.

O Faz Figura (Map pp104-5; ☎ 218 868 901; Rua do Paraíso 15B; dishes €17-33; ☽ lunch & dinner Tue-Sun, dinner Mon) This stylish restaurant feels like a well-kept secret. Polished wood, white linen and art-slung walls set the scene for seasonal Portuguese fare like stewed boar with wild mushrooms. The views from the conservatory are stunning.

Estrela, Lapa & Doca de Alcântara

There's a string of waterfront restaurants around the Docas area, near thundering Ponte 25 de Abril. Take a stroll to see what takes your fancy. After dark, the riverfront switches into party mode, while Estrela and Lapa offer a low-key ambience.

O Chá da Lapa (Map p108; ☎ 213 957 029; Rua da Olival 6; snacks €1.50-8; ☽ 9am-7pm) This ever-so-British tearoom catapults you back to Victorian times with its flock wallpaper and matronly staff. Relax over a cuppa, warm scones and dainty finger sandwiches.

Estado Líquido (Map p108; ☎ 213 972 022; Largo de Santos 5A; sushi €4-10; ☽ 8pm-2am Sun-Wed, to 3am Thu, to 4am Fri & Sat) A Feng Shui–inspired lounge, club and sushi bar rolled into one, Estado Líquido is currently *the* place to be. Get your back rubbed, nibble sushi, sip kiwi caipirinhas, then shake your sumo belly to house and electro on the dance floor.

Espalha Brasas (Map p108; ☎ 213 962 059; Doca de Santo Amaro; dishes €9-15; ☽ lunch & dinner Mon-Sat). A dockside favourite, Espalha is set in a converted 1910 warehouse. When the weather warms, bag a seat on the waterfront terrace for salads and grilled nosh like chops with rosemary.

Montado (Map p108; ☎ 213 909 185; Calçada Marquês de Abrantes 40A; dishes €11-18; ☽ dinner Tue-Sat) Holy cow! Montado specialises in organic beef from green Alentejo pastures, served in charming brick-vaulted surrounds. Antler chandeliers and a bovine Mona Lisa add a wacky touch.

Flor de Sal (Map p108; ☎ 213 975 065; Praça das Flores 40; dishes €13.50-17.50; ☽ lunch & dinner) Bringing a cool new breeze to Praça das Flores, Flor de Sal flaunts a glam design with white leather, bold colours and blown-up shots of Lisbon. The menu stars are 'forest' salads such as couscous with ginger and scallops with radish.

Doca Peixe (Map p108; ☎ 213 973 565; Doca de Santo Amaro; dishes €15-30; ☒ lunch & dinner Tue-Sun). Famous for its market-fresh seafood, Doca Peixe is practically under Ponte 25 de Abril. Savour lemony oysters or cod with clams on the terrace.

Alcântara Café (Map p108; ☎ 213 621 226; Rua Maria Luisa Holstein 15; dishes €16-30; ☒ 8pm-1am) This one-time printing factory now rolls out innovative cuisine in industrial-baroque surrounds. Lisbon's fashionistas love the celebrity treatment and decor: a fusion of red velvet, dark wood and steel pipework.

Rato, Marquês de Pombal & Saldanha

Head north of the centre to splurge at some of Lisbon's top restaurants, including master chef trio: Eleven (right), Panorama Restaurant (right) and Olivier Avenida (below).

Versailles (Map p109; ☎ 213 546 340; Av da República 15A; pastries €2-4; ☒ 7.30am-10pm) A marble, chandelier and icing-sugar stucco confection, this sublime patisserie is where well-coiffed ladies devour cream cakes and gossip. The grouchy waiters are the spitting image of the *Muppet Show*'s Statler and Waldorf. Honest.

Os Tibetanos (Map p109; ☎ 213 142 038; Rua do Salitre 117; dishes €7-12; ☒ lunch & dinner Mon-Fri; Ⓥ) Part of a Tibetan Buddhism school, the mantra here is fresh vegetarian food, with daily specials like quiche and curry. Sit in the serene courtyard if the sun's out and save room for rose-petal ice cream.

Cervejaria Ribadouro (Map p109; ☎ 213 549 411; Rua do Salitre 2; dishes €9-20; ☒ lunch & dinner) Bright, noisy and full to the gills, this bustling beer hall is popular with the local seafood fans. The shellfish are plucked fresh from the tank, weighed and cooked to lip-smacking perfection.

Luca (Map p109; ☎ 213 150 212; Rua Santa Marta 35; dishes €11-20; ☒ lunch Mon-Fri, dinner Mon-Sat) Luca is Lisbon's favourite Italian job, with speedy service, good vibrations and black-and-white shots of Hollywood divas. Nibble antipasti at the bar or feast on creative fare such as king prawn ravioli and fettuccini with wild boar ragout.

Olivier Avenida (Map p109; ☎ 213 174 105; Rua Júlio César Machado 7; dishes €14-60; ☒ breakfast, lunch & dinner) Star chef Olivier's latest venture is this gorgeous pearl-kissed restaurant, lit by teardrop chandeliers and centred on a horseshoe-shaped bar where DJs spin lounge music in the evening. Signatures such as tender kobe beef are polished off nicely with tangy apple sorbet.

Panorama Restaurant (Map p109; ☎ 213 120 000; Rua Latino Coelho 1; dishes €22-36; tasting menus €65; ☒ lunch & dinner) Towering above Lisbon on the Sheraton's 25th floor, this glass-walled restaurant basks in the glow of Henrique Sá Pessoa, aka Portugal's Jamie Oliver. His cuisine is fresh, seasonal and big on texture – think octopus carpaccio with watermelon vinaigrette and rack of veal with truffle polenta.

Eleven (Map p109; ☎ 213 862 211; Rua Marquês da Fronteira; tasting menus €85; ☒ lunch & dinner Mon-Sat) Michelin-starred Eleven lives up to the hype. Perched above Parque Eduardo VII, this aesthetically stunning restaurant is a fusion of glass walls and Joana Vasconcelos art. Chef Joachim Koerper conjures up inventive flavours such as sardine delight with artichoke and olive oil ice cream.

Belém

our pick **Antiga Confeitaria de Belém** (Map p110; ☎ 213 637 423; Rua de Belém 84-92; pastel de belém €0.80; ☒ 8am-midnight May-Oct, 8am-11pm Nov-Apr) Since 1837, this patisserie has been transporting locals to sugar-coated nirvana with heavenly *pastéis de belém*: crisp pastry nests filled with custard cream, baked at 400 degrees for that perfect golden crust, then lightly dusted with cinnamon. Admire *azulejos* in the vaulted rooms or devour a still-warm tart at the counter to try to guess the secret ingredient. And another, and another…

Pão Pão Queijo Queijo (Map p110; ☎ 213 626 369; Rua de Belém 124; snacks €3-6.50; ☒ 8am-midnight Mon-Sat, 8am-8pm Sun; Ⓥ) Join the snaking queue for Belém's tastiest falafel (both hands required), sardine baguettes and Mexican salads.

Cafetaria Quadrante (Map p110; ☎ 213 622 722; Centro Cultural de Belém; dishes €5-8; ☒ 10am-8pm Mon-Fri, 10am-9pm Sat & Sun; Ⓥ) Revive museum-weary eyes over salads and soups at this light-filled cafe. Don't miss the Henry Moore sculpture on the terrace. There are free jazz concerts on Thursdays in summer.

Floresta (Map p110; ☎ 213 636 307; Praça Afonso de Albuquerque 1A; dishes €5-8; ☒ lunch & dinner Tue-Sun) Floresta's sunny patio facing the park is a magnet to lunchtime crowds, who refuel over salads and generous portions of sardines.

Estrela de Belém (Map p110; ☎ 213 625 100; Rua do Embaixador 112; dishes €5.50-9; ☒ lunch & dinner Mon-Sat) Far from the madding crowd, this rustic place serves cold beer and soulful Portuguese grub, including herby *salsichas* (sausages) from the local butcher.

Parque das Nações

Many of the waterfront cafes and restaurants have outdoor seating and do double duty as pulsating bars after dark.

Art Cafe (Map pp102-3; Alameda dos Oceanos; snacks €1.50-5; ☒ 8am-8pm Tue-Fri, noon-8pm Sat & Sun; **V**) Scarlet walls and vibrant paintings give this high-ceilinged cafe an arty feel. It's a relaxed spot for a *bica* or light bites like quiches and salads. Free wi-fi.

Origami (Map pp102-3; ☎ 218 967 132; Alameda dos Oceanos; sushi €4.50-20; ☒ dinner Mon-Sat) Blonde wood and clean lines define this gallery-style restaurant. Between mouthfuls of great sushi and sashimi, try your hand at folding paper animals to add to the origami zoo.

Real Indiana (Map pp102-3; ☎ 218 960 303; Alameda dos Oceanos; dishes €12-18; ☒ lunch & dinner) With its brushed gold walls, photos of India and shiny black tiles, Real Indiana is a far cry from your bog-standard curry house. The aromatic biryanis and feisty vindaloos are authentically spicy.

DRINKING

All-night street parties in Bairro Alto, sunset *ginjinhas* on Rossio's sticky cobbles, drinks and gigs with indie kids in precipitous Santa Catarina – Lisbon is swiftly establishing a reputation as having one of Europe's liveliest and most eclectic nightlife scenes.

Most bars offer free admission, are open from 10pm until 3am, and have a relaxed dress code. For the clubbing lowdown, see p141.

Baixa, Chiado & Rossio

A Brasileira (Map p107; Rua Garrett 120-122; ☒ 8am-2am) All gold swirls and cherubs, this art-deco cafe has been a Lisbon institution since 1905. Sure it's touristy, but the terrace is brilliant for watching street entertainers beside the bronze statue of poet Fernando Pessoa. Order a *bica*, which takes its name from A Brasileira's 1905

catchphrase: *beba isto com açúcar* (drink this with sugar).

A Ginjinha (Map pp104-5; Largo de São Domingos 8; ☒ 9am-10.30pm) Loved-up couples and old men in flat caps, office workers and tourists, all meet at this microscopic *ginjinha* bar for that moment of cherry-licking, pip-spitting pleasure their euro buys. Watch the owner line 'em up at the bar under the beady watch of the drink's 19th-century inventor, Espinheira. It's less about the grog, more about the event.

Nectar Wine Bar (Map pp104-5; ☎ 912 633 368; Rua dos Douradores 33; ☒ 12.30-3pm Mon-Thu, to midnight Fri & Sat) This attitude-free bar attracts a young crowd with modern art, Portuguese wines by the glass and relaxed lounge music. Order a tasting plate to make an evening of it.

ViniPortugal (Map pp104-5; ☎ 342 06 90; Praça do Comércio; ☒ 11am-7pm Tue-Sat) This vaulted showroom is an ingenious initiative to promote Portuguese wine, from citrusy Alentejo whites to full-bodied Douros. Taste them for free, learn about their geography and give your (much-valued) feedback to the cheery staff.

Bairro Alto & Around

Bairro Alto is like a student at a house party: wasted on cheap booze, flirty and everybody's friend. At dusk, the nocturnal hedonist rears its head with bars trying to out-decibel each other, hash-peddlers lurking in the shadows and kamikaze taxi drivers forcing kerbside sippers to leap aside. Grab your plastic cup of Sagres, slosh it over your amigos and crawl till you can crawl no more – congratulations, you've got the hang of Bairro.

Bairro Alto Hotel (Map p107; Praça Luís de Camões 2; ☒ 12.30pm-midnight) Rise in the gold-mesh lift to the 6th floor of Bairro Alto Hotel (p128) for sundowners and dazzling views over the rooftops to the river. It's a smart, grown-up

---

CHERRY OH BABY

Come dusk, the area around Largo de São Domingos and the adjacent Rua das Portas de Santo Antão buzzes with locals getting their cherry fix in a cluster of *ginjinha* bars. A Ginjinha (above) is famous as the birthplace of the syrupy tipple thanks to a quaffing cleric named Espinheira, but there are many more postage-stamp-sized bars to try. Order your ginjinha *sem* (without) or, for a kick, *com* (with) the cherry.

lounge for cocktails and conversing as Lisbon starts to sparkle.

Bedroom (Map p107; Rua do Norte 86) It's a bedroom, but these beauties aren't sleeping. Join them on the dance floor for electro and hip-hop, or recline on the beds in the lounge shimmering with gold wallpaper and chandeliers.

Bicaense (Map p107; Rua da Bica de Duarte Belo 42A) Indie kids have a soft spot for this chilled Santa Catarina haunt, kitted out with retro radios, projectors and squishy beanbags. DJs spin house to the preclubbing crowd and the back room stages occasional gigs.

Catacumbas (Map p107; Travessa da Água da Flor 43) Moodily lit and festooned with portraits of legends like Miles Davis, this den is jam packed when it hosts live jazz on Thursday night. Musicians bash out bluesy rhythms on the piano, as the relaxed crowd sip *vinho tinto* (red wine).

Clandestino (Map p107; Rua da Barroca 99) Keep your eyes peeled for this well-hidden, old-skool Bairro Alto den. Battered and lovable, its walls are smothered in scribblings of the 'X luvs Y 4ever' and 'hasta la victoria siempre' variety. The playlist: Pearl Jam, Manu Chao, The Ramones…

Ginjinha das Gáveas (Map p107; Rua das Gáveas 17A) This hole-in-the-wall *ginjinha* bar is a popular hang-out for young Lisboetas and travellers, with plenty of buzz and incredibly cheap drinks (€1 for a *ginjinha* or beer).

Majong (Map p107; Rua da Atalaia 3) Bairro Alto's gay-friendly cabbage patch kid, Majong oozes shabby chic with pak-choi lights, deep-red walls and school chairs. Mojitos flow as DJs spin minimalist techno, rock and reggae.

our pick **Noobai Café** (Map pp104–5; Miradouro de Santa Catarina; ☻ noon-midnight) Three words: Lisbon's best-kept secret. Though it's next to Miradouro de Santa Catarina, you don't realise this bar is here until you descend the steps and a terrace unfurls before you. The vibe is laid-back, the music funky jazz and the views – wow the views! – magical, sweeping from the castle to Cristo Rei.

Portas Largas (Map p107; Rua da Atalaia 105) Once a *tasca* (tavern), this well-loved Bairro Alto linchpin retains original fittings including black-and-white tiles, columns and porticos. It throws open *portas largas* (big doors) to a mishmash of gays, straights and not-sures, who prop up the marble bar or spill onto the cobbles with zingy caipirinhas.

BAIRRO ALTO BAR-CRAWL

Still fizzing with energy? Test your stamina bar-hopping the rest of the best:

- **A Tasca** (Map p107; Travessa de Queimada 13) Sloshed stags, Latino grooves and tequila till the sun rises.
- **Bar 21** (Map p107; Rua da Atalaia 9) Friendly '80s kid with chart-toppers from The Clash to Culture Club.
- **Café Suave** (Map p107; Rua do Diário de Notícias 6) Futuristic forest decor, cubby holes and a preclubbing vibe.
- **Chueca** (Map p107; Rua da Atalaia 97) You've-been-Tangoed lounge popular with mojito sippers and lesbians.
- **Clube da Esquina** (Map p107; Rua da Barroca 30) DJs playing hip-hop and house to an eye-candy crowd.
- **Cuba a la Vista** (Map p107; Rua do Diário de Notícias 6) Caipirinhas, booty-shaking to merengue and Che beaming down from the wall.
- **Jürgen's Bar** (Map p107; Rua do Diário de Notícias 68) Big-screen sports, killer cocktails and people-watching.
- **Nova Tertúlia** (Map p107; Rua do Diário de Notícias 60) Low-lit den with house beats and a laid-back feel.
- **Páginas Tantas** (Map p107; Rua do Diário de Notícias 85) Relaxed soul man with live jazz and NYC style.
- **Sétimo Céu** (Map p107; Travessa da Espera 54) Old-school and upbeat gay favourite with a Latin twist.

LOCALS' FAVOURITE PARTY HAUNTS

Catacumbas (opposite) 'Catacumbas is tiny and cosy – it feels like you're part of the family. Drinks are a bit expensive, but it's the best place for live shows, chilling with friends and enjoying music.' *Alexandre, Fine Art student*

Cinco Lounge (below) 'Cinco Lounge is my favourite in Príncipe Real for quality, exotic cocktails. It's run by a guy from London and perfect for a relaxed evening.' *Jorge Moita, designer*

Music Box (p142) 'I love to hang out with friends here because of the easygoing atmosphere, diverse live music and DJs. Turn up at 3am and stay till 8am if you can!' *Marta Galamba, wine expert at ViniPortugal*

Ginjinha das Gáveas (opposite) 'It's typically Portuguese. Everyone buys cheap drinks and heads out onto the street to socialise.' *Nuno Ramos, computer engineer and (self-proclaimed) Lisbon Couchsurfing ambassador*

Jamaica (p141) 'DJs play pop, reggae, rock, disco, '80s – everything. It's fun, lively and has an interesting mix of people.' *Caspar, student*

Europa Club (p141) 'It's the never-ending sound of the city, filtered and polluted with rock, machines and thick walls.' *Rafa Vieira, architect*

Solar do Vinho do Porto (Map p107; Rua São Pedro de Alcântara 45; 11am-midnight Mon-Fri, 2pm-midnight Sat) The glug, glug of a 40-year-old tawny being poured is music to port lovers' ears here. Part of an 18th-century mansion, the low-lit, beamed cavern is ideal for nursing a glass of Portugal's finest.

Príncipe Real

Just north of Bairro Alto, Príncipe Real is the epicentre of Lisbon's gay scene and home to some quirky drinking dens.

Pavilhão Chinês (Map pp104-5; Rua Dom Pedro V 89-91) Pavilhão Chinês is an old curiosity shop of a bar with oil paintings and model spitfires dangling from the ceiling, and cabinets brimming with glittering Venetian masks and Action Men. Play pool or bag a comfy armchair to nurse a port or beer. Prices are higher than elsewhere, but such classy kitsch doesn't come cheap.

Cinco Lounge (Map p108; Rua Ruben António Leitão 17; 9pm-2am Tue-Sat) Take an award-winning London-born mixologist named Dave, add a candlelit, gold-kissed setting and give it a funky twist – et voilà – you have Cinco Lounge. Come here to converse and sip legendary cocktails – from Milli Vanillis (hazelnut-vanilla mojitos) to Bloody Shames (vodka-free Bloody Marys).

Alfama & Graça

Alfama and Graça are perfect for a relaxed drink with a view.

Bar das Imagens (Map pp104-5; Calçada Marquês de Tancos 1; 11am-2am Tue-Sat, 3-11pm Sun) With a terrace affording vertigo-inducing views over the city, this cheery bar serves potent cuba libres and other well-prepared cocktails. Jazz plays in the background.

Miradouro da Graça (Map pp104-5; 10.30am-3am) There are far-reaching vistas from this terrace, with soothing music during the day that gets heavier as the night wears on.

Última Sé (Map pp104-5; Travessa do Almargem 1) Hidden behind the Casa dos Bicos, Última Sé is an atmospheric haunt with arched stone walls, a fun crowd and DJs. It features nights of world beats and reggae.

Chapitô (Map pp104-5 Costa do Castelo 7; noon-midnight) This alternative theatre offers fantastic views from its bar and is a top choice for a sundowner or a late-night drink overlooking the city.

Cais do Sodré

Locals hit this upbeat nightlife area when they feel like a change from Bairro Alto. During the Salazar years, it was the only place for a bit of night-time sleaze, and some areas retain this seedy feel, particularly Rua Nova do Carvalho.

Ginjinha da Ribeira (Map pp104-5; Av 24 de Julho 2B; 8am-9pm Mon-Sat) Get your predinner *ginjinha* fix on the terrace of this dinky bar opposite Cais do Sodré.

O'Gilins (Map pp104-5; Rua dos Remolares 10) To be sure the best craic in Lisbon, O'Gilins serves Guinness, big-screen sports and live music from Wednesday to Saturday. 'Tis a lively affair with fiddles, singing and the odd punter jigging on the table.

GAY & LESBIAN LISBON

Take a look at www.portugalgay.pt for more pink listings.

The Scene

From camp bars to cruisy clubs, Praça do Príncipe Real, just north of Bairro Alto, is king of Lisbon's gay and lesbian scene.

Bar 106 (Map p108; www.bar106.com; Rua de São Marçal 106) Young and fun with an upbeat, preclubbing vibe and crazy events such as Sunday's message party.

Bar Água No Bico (Map p108; Rua de São Marçal 170) Cheery bar with art exhibitions, shows and music from jazz to chillout.

Bric-a-Bar (Map p108; Rua Cecilio de Sousa 82-84) Cruisy with resident DJs and a dark room.

Finalmente (Map p108; Rua da Palmeira 38) This popular club has a tiny dance floor, nightly drag shows and wall-to-wall crowds.

Memorial (Map p108; Rua Gustavo de Matos Sequeira 42A) Mainly lesbian with dance music, camp comedy and drag shows.

Trumps (Map p108; www.trumps.pt; Rua da Imprensa Nacional 104B) Lisbon's hottest gay club with cruisy corners, a sizeable dance floor and events from live music to drag.

Organisations & Events

Lisbon Pride (www.portugalpride.org) is in June, and the **Festival de Cinema Gay e Lésbico** (www.lisonfilmfest.org) is in late September.

Centro LGBT (Lisbon Gay & Lesbian Community Centre; Map pp104-5; ☎ 218 873 918; ilga-portugal@ilga.org; Rua de São Lazaro 88; ☟ 6-11pm Wed & Thu, 8.30pm-midnight Fri, 6pm-midnight Sat; ▣) Has a cafe, library, internet and counselling facilities.

Grupo de Mulheres (Women's Group; ☎ /fax 218 873 918; gmulheres@yahoo.com) Part of ILGA-Portugal, it organises regular social gatherings and lesbian film screenings.

Opus Gay (Map p109; ☎ 213 151 396; www.opusgay.org; 2nd fl, Rua da Ilha Terceira 34; ☟ 5-8pm Wed-Sat; ▣) Also has a visitors centre, including internet cafe.

Hennessy's (Map pp104-5; Rua Cais do Sodré 32-38) This is another relaxed Irish pub with banter, occasional live music and Kilkenny on tap.

British Bar (Map pp104-5; Rua Bernardino Costa 52; ☟ Mon-Sat) Resembling an early-20th-century railway bar, this bottle-lined watering hole has an old-fashioned clientele and a backwards clock. There's even a resident shoeshiner.

Docas & Alcântara

The dockside duo of Doca de Alcântara and Doca de Santo Amaro harbour wall-to-wall bars with a preclubbing vibe. Many occupy revamped warehouses, with terraces facing the river and the lit-up, rumbling Ponte 25 de Abril. Most people taxi here, but you can also take the train from Cais do Sodré to Alcântara Mar or catch tram 15 from Praça da Figueira.

Art (Map p108; Av 24 de Julho 66) Kate Moss wannabes and Moët-guzzling all-comers sway to house at this ubercool lounge before sashaying over to Kremlin (p142). The monochrome decor is fabulously OTT – think feather-filled columns, black velvet and teardrop chandeliers.

Belém Bar Café (Map pp102-3; Av Brasília, Pavilhão Poente; ☟ 10pm-2am Tue & Wed, midnight-5am Fri & Sat) The self-consciously cool BBC attracts fashionistas to its glass-walled lounge bar and terrace with cracking views of Ponte 25 de Abril. DJ Espírito Santo fills the dance floor with hip-hop and R 'n' B at the weekend.

Hawaii (Map p108; Doca de Santo Amaro; ☟ 11pm-5am) Chavs and bootylicious 18- to 30-somethings flock to loud and flirty Hawaii, one of a clan of similar dockside joints. Cheap mojitos and Latino hip-wiggling fuel the party under the giant surfboard.

Op Art Café (Map p108; Doca de Santo Amaro) On the water's edge, this slightly hidden glass-and-wood cafe attracts a more laid-back bunch than other Docas bars. On Saturday nights, DJs spin house and lounge till dawn.

Taberna e Artes (Map p108; Rua do Poço dos Negros 2; ☟ 4pm-4am) Ideal for quaffing a cold one and nattering with the bearded owner Antônio, Taberna e Artes is an eccentric little bar full of dog-eared poetry books and Franco-era posters. Note the mini spitfires above the bar and vinyl placemats.

ENTERTAINMENT

Lisbon entertains with high culture, high-octane clubbing and everything in between. One minute it's alternative gigs by upcoming bands in Bairro Alto and Rossio, the next sumptuous strings and street theatre in Chiado. Feel the melancholic soul of fado in Alfama's higgledy-piggledy, lantern-lit lanes, or get your groove on at Docas' bass-loaded clubs.

For event listings during your stay, grab a copy of the free monthly *Follow Me Lisboa* from tourist offices. If you speak Portuguese, click onto **Time Out Lisboa** (http://timeout.sapo.pt), **Guia da Noite** (www.guiadanoite.com) and **Agenda Cultural Lisboa** (www.lisboacultural.pt) for info on performances and screenings; cinema listings can also be found in the daily *Diário de Notícias*. Tickets are available in a number of outlets:

ABEP (Map pp104–5; ☎ 213 475 824; Praça dos Restauradores)

Fnac Greater Lisbon (Map pp102–3; ☎ 217 114 200; Centro Comercial Colombo); Baixa Chiado (Map pp104–5; ☎ 213 221 800; Armazéns do Chiado, Rua do Carmo 3)

Ticket Line (☎ 210 036 300; www.ticketline.pt)

Nightclubs

Superstar DJs heating up dance floors at clubbing temples like Lux (right) have put Lisbon firmly on Europe's must-party map. Sleep is overrated in a city where locals don't even think about showing up at a club before 2am. Clubbing here is not late-night, it's all-night, with waterfront haunts pumping out grooves from electro to deep house really warming up at 4am.

Though getting in is not as much of a beauty contest as in other capitals, you'll stand a better chance of slipping past the fashion police if you dress smartish and don't rock up on your lonesome. Most clubs charge entry (particularly on weekends – around €5 to €20, which usually includes a drink or two), and some operate a card-stamping system to ensure you spend a minimum amount. Many close Sunday and Monday.

BAIRRO ALTO, CAIS DO SODRÉ & SÃO BENTO

A Lontra (Map p108; Rua de São Bento 155) Near Bairro Alto, A Lontra attracts mostly African-Portuguese clubbers bumping and grinding to African sounds, R 'n' B and hip-hop. It fills up about 2am and stays open late.

Cabaret Maxime (Map pp104–5; www.cabaret-maxime.com; Praça da Alegria 58) Formerly a strip joint and Parisian-style cabaret, Maxime has bid farewell to the leggy showgirls. Nowadays, young Lisboetas flock here for club nights where DJs play old-school tunes, or loud, sweaty gigs of both established and upcoming local bands.

Capela (Map p107; Rua da Atalaia 45) Once a Gothic chapel, today Capela's gospel is an experimental line-up of electronica and funky house. Get there early (before midnight) to appreciate the DJs before the crowds descend. Frescos, Renaissance-style nude murals and dusty chandeliers add a boho-chic touch.

Europa Club (Map pp104–5; Rua Nova do Carvalho 18) Lisbon's hottest afterparties happen here at the weekend. Lisboetas descend from 6am to 10am for a 'breakfast' of Portuguese DJs spinning rock, house, electro and techno.

Frágil (Map p107; Rua da Atalaia 126) In the beginning there was Frágil, Manuel Reis' first love before Lux. This small, loud and sweaty club has been rocking Bairro Alto for 25 years and shows no signs of waning. DJs spin progressive house and electronica to a mixed gay/straight crowd.

Incógnito (Map p108; Rua Poiais de São Bento 37) No-sign, pint-sized Incógnito offers an alternative vibe and DJs thrashing out indie rock and electropop. Sweat it out with a fun crowd on the tiny basement dance floor, or breathe more easily in the loft bar upstairs.

Jamaica (Map pp104–5; Rua Nova do Carvalho 8) Yep, most dancing on this street involves laps but not at Jamaica, man. Gay and straight, black and white, young and old – everyone has a soft spot for this offbeat club. It gets going around 2am at weekends with DJs pumping out reggae, hip-hop and retro.

Lounge (Map pp104–5; Rua da Moeda 1) Little miss popular on the Cais do Sodré circuit, this laid-back indie club is jam-packed and pumping most nights. DJs, live acts and rock gigs are first-rate.

our pick Lux (Map pp104–5; www.luxfragil.com; Av Infante Dom Henrique) Lisbon's ice-cool, must-see club, Lux is run by ex-Frágil maestro Marcel Reis and part-owned by John Malkovich. The wacky design features an oversized shoe, mirrored tunnels and violet light. Special but not snooty, Lux hosts big-name DJs like Leonaldo de Almeida and Pinkboy spinning electro and house. Grab a spot on the roof terrace to see the sun rise over the Tejo. Style policing is heartwarmingly lax but get here after 4am on a Friday or Saturday and you might have trouble getting in because of the crowds.

Music Box (Map pp104–5; Rua Nova do Carvalho 24; www .musicboxlisboa.com) Under the brick arches on Rua Nova do Carvalho lies one of Lisbon's hottest clubs. The pulsating Music Box hosts loud and sweaty club nights with music shifting from electro to rock, plus ear-splitting gigs by up-and-coming bands.

DOCAS, ALCÂNTARA & AVENIDA 24 DE JULHO

Buddha Bar (Map p108; www.buddha.com.pt; Gare Marítima de Alcântara, Doca de Santo Amaro) Paris it ain't, but this Buddha still rocks. Slick and Oriental, the decor is a blend of red lanterns, gauzy curtains, exotic wood and fountains. A young, good-looking crowd shimmies to chillout tunes, then cools down on the breezy outdoor terrace with stunning river views.

Blues Café (Map p108; Rua Cintura do Porto) Decked out with gold, red velvet, dark wood and tassel lamps, this high-ceilinged warehouse fuses 1920s glamour with industrial cool. Music skips from lounge to house and dance, with the party mood picking up after 1am. The dockside terrace is perfect for chilling.

Dock's Club (Map p108; Rua Cintura do Porto) Blues Café's sibling rival, Dock's is another people-packed place, with mirrors, glitterballs, pop hits and dudes looking to score. Tuesday is ladies' night.

Kapital (Map p108; Av 24 de Julho 68) Being young, gorgeous and loaded helps you to get the nod from the picky doormen at Kapital. It's the super-slick haunt of 20- to 30-something Lisboetas out spending daddy's pension on cocktails in the VIP lounge. The too-cool crowd defrosts in the *madrugada* (wee hours) grooving to '80s and garage tunes.

Kremlin (Map p108; Escadinhas da Praia 5) Until Lux pinched its crown, Kremlin was Lisbon's undisputed megaclub. It's still the home of house, though slipping past the Stalin-esque bouncers can be a challenge. A pick 'n' mix of gays, straights, models and wannabes come to bop to deep house in wacky Oriental surrounds. Heats up around 3am.

Paradise Garage (Map p108; Rua João Oliveira Miguens 38–48) For garage freaks this *is* paradise. Resident DJs Enrage and VJ Water keep the dance floor rammed, particularly at Saturday

night's Baby Loves Disco party. It also hosts some of Lisbon's hottest live gigs.

The Loft (Map p108; www.theloft.pt; Rua do Instituto Industrial 6) Hipsters love the ultraglam design of this dockside newbie – think violet lighting, polka-dot walls, beanbags, primary-colour cube stools and mirrors for slyly checking your look. Grab a caipirinha and join the house party.

Fado

Infused by Moorish song and the ditties of homesick sailors, bluesy, bittersweet fado encapsulates the Lisbon psyche like nothing else. Ask 10 Lisboetas to explain it and each will give a different version because it's deeply personal and hinges on the mood of the moment. Recurring themes are love, destiny, death and the omnipresent *saudade* (p44) or 'nostalgic longing'; a kind of musical soap opera.

Though a *fadista* is traditionally accompanied by a classical and 12-string Portuguese guitar, many new-generation stars such as Mariza, Ana Moura and Joana Amendoeira are putting their own spin to the genre, giving it a twist of Cuban Son or a dash of Argentine tango. For more, see p53.

At Bairro Alto's touristy, folksy performances, you'll only be skating the surface. For authentic fado, go to where it was born – Alfama. You'll be serenaded by mournful ballads wandering the narrow lanes here by night. There's usually a minimum cover of €15 to €25 and, as food is often mediocre, it's worth asking if you can just order a bottle of wine. Book ahead at weekends. If you prefer a spontaneous approach, seek out *fado vadio* where anyone can – and does – have a warble.

ALFAMA & LAPA

A Baîuca (Map pp104–5; ☎ 218 867 284; Rua de São Miguel 20; minimum €25; ☽ dinner Thu-Mon) On a good night, walking into A Baîuca is like gatecrashing a family party. It's a special place with *fado vadio*, where locals take a turn and spectators hiss if anyone dares to chat during the singing. The food stops around 10pm but the fado goes on until midnight. Reserve ahead.

Clube de Fado (Map pp104–5; ☎ 218 852 704; www .clube-de-fado.com; Rua de São João da Praça; minimum €10; ☽ 9pm-2.30am Mon-Sat) Clube de Fado hosts the cream of the fado crop in vaulted, dimly lit surrounds. Big-name *fadistas* performing here include Joana Amendoeira and Miguel

Capucho, alongside celebrated guitarists like José Fontes Rocha.

Mesa de Frades (Map pp104-5; ☎ 91 702; Rua dos Remédios 139A; minimum €15; ☿ dinner Wed-Mon) A magical place to hear fado, tiny Mesa de Frades used to be a chapel. It's tiled with exquisite *azulejos* and has just a handful of tables. The show begins around 11pm.

Parreirinha de Alfama (Map pp104-5; ☎ 218 868 209; Beco do Espírito Santo 1; minimum €15; ☿ 8pm-2am) Owned by fado legend Argentina Santos, this place offers good food and ambience; it attracts an audience that often falls hard for the top-quality *fadistas*. Book by 4pm.

Senhor Vinho (Map p108; ☎ 213 972 681; Rua do Meio á Lapa; minimum €15; ☿ 8pm-2am) Fado star Maria da Fé owns this small place, welcoming first-rate *fadistas*. Even the legendary Mariza (see p92) has performed here.

Alternative Culture

Lisbon may flirt with high culture and embrace fado, but she also has an ongoing relationship with the underdog. Individuality trumps conformity and alternative culture rules in these offbeat cultural centres.

Bacalhoeiro (Map pp104-5; ☎ 218 864 891; Rua dos Bacalhoeiros 125; 🖳) Nonconformist, laid-back Bacalhoeiro shelters a cosy bar and hosts everything from alternative gigs to film screenings, salsa nights and themed parties. Free wi-fi.

Chapitô (Map pp104-5; ☎ 218 855 550; www.chapito .org; Costa do Castelo 1-7; 🖳) Chapitô offers physical theatre performances, with a theatre school attached. There's a jazz cafe downstairs with dentist-chair decor, with live music Thursday to Saturday. Come for the spectacular views and excellent restaurant.

Crew Hassan (Map pp104-5; ☎ 213 466 119; Rua das Portas de Santo Antão 159; 🖳 V) Grungy Crew Hassan smells like teen spirit. Alternative types dig its graffiti, threadbare sofas, cheap veggie fare and free internet. Its line-up spans films, gigs, exhibitions and DJs playing music from reggae to minimalist techno.

Culturgest (Map p109; ☎ 217 905 155; www.culturgest .pt; Rua do Arco do Cego) Culturgest's experimental and occasionally provocative line-up encompasses exhibitions, dance, poetry, music and theatre.

Zé dos Bois (Map p107; ☎ 213 430 205; www.zedosbois .org; Rua da Barroca 59) Focusing on tomorrow's performing arts and music trends, Zé dos Bois is an experimental venue with a graffitied courtyard for chilling. The boho haunt has

welcomed bands like Black Dice and Animal Collective to its stage.

Cinemas

For blockbusters try the multiplexes in **Complexo das Amoreiras** (Map p109; ☎ 213 810 200), **Centro Comercial Colombo** (Map pp102-3; ☎ 217 113 222) and **Centro Vasco da Gama** (Map pp102-3; ☎ 218 922 280) malls. More-traditional cinemas are the grand **São Jorge** (Map p109; ☎ 213 579 144; Av da Liberdade 175) and, just around the corner, **Cinemateca Portuguesa** (National Film Theatre; Map p109; ☎ 213 596 200; www.cinemateca.pt; Rua Barata Salgueiro 39), screening offbeat, art-house, world and old films.

For details of screen times and venues, visit www.7arte.net.

Theatre

Teatro Nacional de Dona Maria II (Map pp104-5; ☎ 213 250 835; www.teatro-dmaria.pt; Rossio) Rossio's graceful neoclassical theatre has a somewhat hit-and-miss schedule because of underfunding. There's a charming cafe on site.

Teatro Nacional de São Carlos (Map pp104-5; ☎ 213 253 045; www.saocarlos.pt; Rua Serpa Pinto 9) Worth visiting just to see the sublime gold-and-red interior, this theatre has opera, ballet and theatre seasons.

Teatro Municipal de São Luís (Map pp104-5; ☎ 213 257 640; Rua António Maria Cardosa 38) This venue stages opera, ballet and theatre.

Teatro Taborda (Map pp104-5; ☎ 218 854 190; Costa do Castelo 75; 🖳) This cultural centre shows contemporary dance, theatre and world music. It also has spectacular views and an excellent restaurant.

Teatro da Trindade (Map p107; ☎ 213 420 000; http:// teatrotrindade.inatel.pt; Largo da Trindade 7) Bairro Alto's early-20th-century gem stages an assortment of national and foreign productions.

Music & Dance

Centro Cultural de Belém (CCB; Map p110; ☎ 213 612 444; www.ccb.pt; Praça do Império, Belém) CCB presents a diverse program, spanning experimental jazz, contemporary ballet, boundary-crossing plays and performances by the Portuguese Chamber Orchestra.

Coliseu dos Recreios (Map pp104-5; ☎ 213 240 580; www.coliseulisboa.com; Rua das Portas de Santo Antão 96) This concert hall stages big-name concerts, theatre, dance and opera. The recent roll-call has included *fadista* Ana Moura and flamenco star Rafael Amargo.

Fundação Calouste Gulbenkian (Map p109; ☎ 217 935 131; www.musica.gulbenkian.pt; Av de Berna) Home to the Gulbenkian Orchestra under the baton of Lawrence Foster, this classical music heavyweight stages first-rate concerts and ballets.

Hot Clube de Portugal (Map pp104-5; ☎ 213 467 369; www.hcp.pt; Praça da Alegria 39) As hot as its name suggests, this small, poster-plastered cellar has staged top-drawer jazz acts since the 1940s. Shows are at 11pm and 12.30am.

Onda Jazz Bar (Map pp104-5; www.ondajazz.com; Arco de Jesus 7) This vaulted cellar features a menu of mainstream jazz, plus more-eclectic beats of bands hailing from Brazil and Africa. Don't miss Wednesday's free jam session.

Pavilhão Atlântico (Map pp102-3; ☎ 218 918 409; www.pavilhaoatlantico.pt; Parque das Nações) Sporting an energy-efficient zinc roof, this UFO-shaped arena is Portugal's largest. It hosts big international acts from Moby to Madonna.

Teatro Camões (Map pp102-3; ☎ 218 923 477; www.cnb.pt; Parque das Nações) Teatro Camões is home to the Portuguese National Ballet Company under the direction of innovative choreographer Vasco Wellenkamp.

Sport
FOOTBALL
Lisboetas are mad about football. It's hardly surprising given that the capital is home to two of Portugal's 'big three' clubs – SL Benfica and Sporting Club de Portugal. Lisbon's main stadiums were given a multimillion-euro facelift for Euro 2008.

The season runs September to mid-June, with most league matches on Sunday; check details in the papers (especially *Bola*, the daily football paper) or ask at the tourist office. Tickets cost €20 to €55 at the stadium on match day or, for higher prices, at the **ABEP ticket agency** (Map pp104-5; ☎ 213 475 824; Praça dos Restauradores).

Estádio da Luz (Map pp102-3; ☎ 217 219 555; www.slbenfica.pt) SL Benfica plays at this 65,000-seat stadium in the northwestern Benfica district. The nearest metro station is Colégio Militar-Luz.

Estádio Nacional (off Map pp102-3; ☎ 214 197 212; Cruz Quebrada) The national stadium hosts the Portuguese Cup Final each May. Take the train from Cais do Sodré.

Estádio José de Alvalade (Map pp102-3; ☎ 217 514 069) Sporting's state-of-the-art stadium, which hosted Euro 2004 matches, seats 54,000 and is just north of the university. Take the metro to Campo Grande.

BULLFIGHTING
Whether it makes your pulse race or blood boil, you can't ignore *tauromaquia* (bullfighting). The red-brick, neo-Moorish **Campo Pequeno** (Bullring; Map p109; ☎ 217 932 442; Av da República; tickets €10-75) reopened in 2006 following six years of restoration. Fights are held on Thursday from May to October. Tickets are sold outside the bullring, or at higher prices from the **ABEP ticket agency** (Map pp104-5; ☎ 213 475 824; Praça dos Restauradores). For the bullfighting lowdown, see p47.

SHOPPING
Le freak, c'est retro chic in grid-like Bairro Alto, attracting vinyl lovers and vintage devotees to its cluster of late-opening boutiques. Remember those days spent shopping with dear old gran? You can relive them in the backstreets of Alfama, Baixa and Rossio, where stuck-in-time stores deal exclusively in buttons and kid gloves, tawny port and tinned fish. Literary Chiado is the go-to place for high-street and couture shopping to the backbeat of buskers, while Santos is upping the design ante with avant-garde galleries.

Crafts & Souvenirs
A Arte da Terra (Map pp104-5; ☎ 212 745 975; Rua Augusto Rosa 40) In the stables of a centuries-old bishop's palace, this cobbled store brims with authentic Portuguese crafts including Castelo Branco embroideries, love hankies and hand-painted *azulejos*.

A Vida Portuguesa (Map pp104-5; ☎ 213 465 073; Rua Anchieta 11) A flashback to the late 19th century with its high ceilings and polished cabinets, this store lures nostalgics with all-Portuguese products from retro-wrapped Tricona sardines to lime oil soap and Bordallo Pinheiro porcelain swallows.

Fábrica Sant'Anna (Map pp104-5; ☎ 213 422 537; Rua do Alecrim 95) Hand-making and painting *azulejos* since 1741, this is the place to add some porcelain pizzazz to your home with classics from blue-and-white geometric tiles to cherubs and candlesticks.

O Peregrino (Map p107; ☎ 213 433 181; Rua da Bica de Duarte Belo 64) This Santa Catarina pipsqueak showcases contemporary work by local creatives including funky wicker bags, hand-carved marionettes and quirky fairytale wall hangings.

Ponte Lisboa (Map pp104-5; Rua Augusto Rosa 21) Kids love Joana Areal's bright, touchy-feely felt animals at this hole-in-the-wall workshop, presenting crafts by 15 Brazilian and Portuguese artists. Also look out for Sebastião Lobo's glittering silver dragonflies.

Santos Ofícios (Map pp104-5; ☎ 218 872 031; Rua da Madalena 87) If you've always fancied a hand-embroidered fado shawl, check out this brick-vaulted store. It's a must-shop for Portuguese folk art including Madeira lace, blingy Christmas decorations and glazed earthenware.

The Wrong Shop (Map pp104-5; ☎ 213 433 197; Calçada do Sacramento 25) Sick of Barcelos cockerels and 'I love Lisbon' tees? This Chiado shop gets it right with tongue-in-cheek souvenirs. Our favourites: gay roosters emblazoned with the rainbow flag, ever-so-friendly fly-catchers (with an escape route), and the blank-paged books Pessoa never wrote.

Vista Alegre (Map p107; ☎ 213 461 401; Largo do Chiado 20) Vista Alegre produces exquisitely crafted ceramics that have graced the tables of royalty and heads of state since 1824.

Design & Concept Stores

Embaixada Lomográfica (Map p107; ☎ 213 421 075; Rua da Atalaia 31) This shrine to Lomos (mass-produced, Soviet-era cameras) helps happy snappers achieve bizarre photographic effects with everything from coloured flashes to fisheye lenses.

our pick Fabrico Infinito (Map pp104-5; ☎ 212 467 629; Rua D Pedro V 74A) Set in a former coach house, this virginal white gallery showcases avant-garde designs that give recycled items a luxury twist. Keep an eye out

for pearl-studded toothpick necklaces, Marcela Brunken's born-again chandeliers, Jorge Moita's funky skirt-shaped La. Ga bags (see interview on p95) and Lidija Kolovrat's zesty armbands. There's a cafe at the back, where decadent desserts are served on golden crockery.

Loja CCB (Map p110; ☎ 213 612 410; Centro Cultural de Belém) Belém's progressive concept store tempts design lovers with gadgets and knick-knacks from snazzy Eva Solo crockery to Mr P bathplugs.

Yron (Map p108; ☎ 969 117 422; Rua de São Bento 170) This hip new gallery stages rotating exhibitions of mostly eco-friendly design by local creatives. On our last visit this meant a 21st-century take on Portuguese crafts with glam lacework, sculpted cork stools and bold cockerels.

Fashion & Accessories

Agência 117 (Map p107; ☎ 213 461 270; Rua do Norte 117) No place for wallflowers, Agência revamps wardrobes with tartan wellies, candy-bright dresses and Miss Sixty garb. Marilyn Monroe, velvet crucifixes, a hair salon – it's all at this eccentric Bairro boutique.

Articula (Map pp104-5; ☎ 934 113 225; Rua dos Remédios 102) This anticonformist gallery-cum-workshop displays Teresa Milheiro's rebellious, recycled creations made from bones, medical tubes and aluminium. Look out for doll's-eye necklace 'Big Brother is watching you' and syringe chain 'be botox, be beautiful'.

Bad Luck (Map p107; ☎ 213 460 888; Rua do Norte 81) Rock 'n' roll is king at Bad Luck, where a gyrating Elvis greets you. Be whisked back to '50s and '60s America with cow-print boots, polka-dot rockabilly dresses, oversized shades

---

THE KITSCH COLLECTION

Seeking quality kitsch? Look no further than cock-a-doolally Rua Augusta, where souvenir shops and stalls will help you part with your euros. Top of the tacky pops:

- **Galo de Barcelos** Portugal's beloved feathered friend is this punk cockerel with a heart, who miraculously escaped a piri-piri fate. Keyrings, coasters, watches, you name it – the rooster's there.

- **'I love Pessoa' T-shirt** Show poetic soul wearing a T-shirt graced with Fernando Pessoa's mug.

- **Lisbon landmark boxer shorts** Hmmm, what could be more entertaining than planning your next sightseeing trip on the loo? There's tram 28, the castle, Elevador de Santa Justa…

- **Fado shawl** Ignore the fashion slaves and set the trend with your very own embroidered lace creation; perfect for those warble-in-front-of-the-mirror moments.

- **Virgin Mary** Day-Glo or sprayed gold, a porcelain Virgin Mary is a must for the mantelpiece.

and grease for super-slick hair. You can even get tattooed and pierced next door.

El Dorado (Map p107; ☎ 213 423 935; Rua do Norte 23) A gramophone plays vinyl classics as divas bag vintage styles from psychedelic prints to 6in platforms and pencil skirts at this Bairro Alto hipster. There's also a great range of clubwear.

Happy Days (Map p107; ☎ 213 421 015; Rua do Norte 60) Sadly no Fonz, but this boutique still rocks with its collection of glittering bauble necklaces, sequin clutch bags, FLY London footwear and shimmery gold pumps. Kids' toys from toy cars to plastic fish give grown-up styles a wacky twist.

Kinky Store (Map pp104-5; ☎ 096 845 2041; Rua das Flores 24) Not as kinky as it sounds, this store lures with lacy lingerie, itsy-bitsy bikinis and the ever-popular 'bad-ex' voodoo dolls.

Outra Face da Lua (Map pp104-5; ☎ 218 863 430; Rua da Assunção 22) Vintage divas make for this retro boutique in Baixa, crammed with puffball dresses, lurex skirts and 1920s hats. There's even a trunk full of old Barbie dolls. Jazz and electronica play overhead. Revive over cosmic tea at the in-store cafe.

Sneakers Delight (Map p107; ☎ 213 479 976; Rua do Norte 30) Funk up your feet with limited edition Adidas trainers at this groovy store, where ogres and monsters beam down from the walls. DJs spin on weekends.

Story Tailors (Map pp104-5; ☎ 213 432 306; Calçada do Ferragial 8) Luís and João bewitch with floaty, feminine polka-dot, gingham and ruffle designs at their enchanted forest of fashion, bedecked with chandeliers and gnarled wood. Ask the mirror on the wall what it thinks.

The Loser Project (Map pp104-5; ☎ 213 421 861; Rua do Ferragial 1) Metrosexuals and gays love Rui Duarte's designer threads at this uber-trendy Chiado boutique, where slick creations include quilted robe-style coats and star-spangled shoes.

Zed's Dad (Map p107; Rua da Barroca 7) German-born designer Nicole puts her own stamp on vintage at this boutique-cum-workshop in Bairro Alto, with bold prints, lurex, denim and faux snakeskin.

Markets

Feira da Ladra (Thieves Market; Map p104-5; Campo de Santa Clara; 7am-5pm Sat & 8am-noon Tue) Browse for back-of-the-lorry treasures at this lively flea market. You'll find old records, coins, baggy pants, dog-eared poetry books and other attic junk. Haggle hard and watch your wallet – it isn't called 'thieves market' for nothing.

Mercado da Ribeira (Map p104-5; ☎ 210 312 600; Av 24 de Julho; 6am-2pm Mon-Sat) Lisbon's premier food market buzzes with locals shopping for fruit and veg, crusty bread and silvery sardines fresh from the Atlantic.

Music

Fnac (Map pp104-5; ☎ 213 221 800; Armazéns do Chiado) Fnac sells a vast array of music and audiovisual gear.

Discoteca Amália (Map pp104-5; ☎ 213 421 485; Rua Áurea 272) This shrine to *fadista* Amália Rodrigues stocks an excellent range of fado and classical CDs.

Louie Louie (Map p107; ☎ 213 472 232; Rua Nova da Trinidade 8) Clued-up DJs head for this funky music store stocking secondhand vinyl and the latest house, dance and electronica grooves.

Shopping Malls

Most malls and department stores open daily until 10pm or midnight.

Armazéns do Chiado (Map pp104-5; Rua do Carmo 2) Fashion, books, music and cosmetics in the heart of Chiado.

CATWALK QUEENS

Make way for Lisbon's trio of catwalk queens, revamping wardrobes with their majestic collections:

- **Ana Salazar** (Map pp104-5; ☎ 213 472 289; Rua do Carmo 87) Ana's sassy, feminine styles reveal a passion for stretchy fabrics, bold prints and earthy hues. Her flagship boutique, with a striking arched glass ceiling, is in the heart of Chiado.

- **Fátima Lopes** (Map p107; ☎ 213 240 545; Rua da Atalaia 36) Divas love Fátima's immaculate collection of figure-hugging, Latin-inspired threads – from slinky suits to itsy-glitzy prom dresses and hot-pink ball gowns.

- **Lena Aires** (Map p107; ☎ 213 461 815; Rua da Atalaia 96) Lena's funky Bairro Alto boutique brims with citrus-bright knits and fresh-faced fashion.

SHOP 'N' STROLL

If you prefer to mooch rather than target specific shops, Lisbon has some terrific streets for walking. Baixa's pedestrianised main drag, **Rua Augusta**, is a mix of high-street stores and souvenir kitsch; pause for chestnuts (winter) or popcorn (summer) and street entertainment between purchases. Nearby, olde-worlde **Rua da Conceição** is a classic stitch-up, where thimble-sized, wood-panelled haberdasheries recall an era when folk still used to darn their stockings. Chiado's well-heeled **Rua do Carmo** harbours designer names and smart cafes, while leafy boulevard **Avenida da Liberdade** cranks up the swank-o-meter with labels from Gucci to Louis Vuitton. Divas live out vintage dreams in the alleys of boho **Bairro Alto**, peppered with idiosyncratic boutiques playing scratchy vinyl and selling everything from glittering platforms to glam hairdos and tattoos. It's out with the old at the all-new **Santos Design District** (www.santosdesigndistrict.com), luring design fiends to its forward-thinking galleries.

Centro Comercial Colombo (Map pp102-3; Av Lusíada) Colossal with 420 shops, cinemas, restaurants and a health club.

Centro Vasco da Gama (Map pp102–3) Glass-roofed mall at Parque das Nações, sheltering high-street stores, a food court and cinema.

Complexo das Amoreiras (Map p109; Av Duarte Pacheco) Modernist mall with 275 stores.

El Corte Inglês (Map p109; Av António Augusto de Aguiar 31) Spanish giant with nine floors of fashion, design and food.

Speciality Stores

A Carioca (Map p107; ☎ 213 420 377; Rua da Misericórdia 9) Little has changed since this old-world store opened in 1924: brass fittings still gleam, the coffee roaster is still in action and home blends, sugared almonds and toffees are still lovingly wrapped in green paper.

Azevedo Rua (Map pp104-5; ☎ 213 427 511 Praça Dom Pedro IV 73) Lisbon's maddest hatters have been covering bald spots since 1886. Expect old-school service and wood-panelled cabinets full of flat caps and Ascot-worthy headwear.

Conserveira de Lisboa (Map pp104-5; ☎ 218 864 009; Rua dos Bacalhoeiros 34) In Rua dos Bacalhoeiros (cod-vessel street) lies a store dedicated wholly to tinned fish, whose walls are a mosaic of retro wrappings. An elderly lady and her son tot up on a monstrous old till and wrap purchases in brown paper.

Luvaria Ulisses (Map pp104-5; ☎ 213 420 295; Rua do Carmo 87A) So tiny it's almost an optical illusion, this magical art-deco store is chock-full of soft handmade leather gloves in kaleidoscope shades. Breathe in and squeeze in to find a glove that fits.

Manuel Tavares (Map pp104-5; ☎ 213 424 209; Rua da Betesga 1A) For a lingering taste of Lisbon,

nip into this wood-fronted store, tempting locals since 1860 with *pata negra* (cured ham), pungent cheeses, *ginjinha*, port and other Portuguese treats.

Napoleão (Map pp104-5; ☎ 218 861 108; Rua dos Fanqueiros 70) This family-run cellar is the go-to place for Portuguese wines and ports, with hundreds of bottles to choose from. Ships worldwide.

Saboeiro (Map p107; ☎ 914 284 538; Rua das Salgadeiras 32) Saboeiro has all you need for a scrub-a-dub-dub in the tub, from clove-and-cinnamon bath tea to rosehip oil and citrusy exfoliating soap bars.

Silva & Feijó (Map pp104-5; Rua dos Bacalhoeiros 117) Planning a picnic? Stop by this beamed store for sheep's cheese from the Seia mountains, sardine pâté, rye bread, *salsichas* and other Portuguese goodies.

Vellas Loreto (Map p107; ☎ 213 425 387; Rua do Loreto 53) Lisboetas have been waxing lyrical about this specialist candle maker since 1789. The wood-panelled, talc-scented store sells myriad candles, from cherubs and peppers to Christmas trees and water lilies.

Zotter (Map pp104-5; ☎ 213 462 253; Rua de Santa Justa 84) This Austrian chocolatier swears to *faz te feliz* (make you happy) with fair-trade and organic chocolate, including 100%-cocoa bars plus unusual varieties like port, pineapple-chilli and tofu.

GETTING THERE & AWAY
Air

Situated around 6km north of the centre, the ultramodern **Aeroporto de Lisboa** (Lisbon Airport; Map pp102-3; ☎ 218 413 500; www.ana.pt) operates direct flights to major international hubs including London, New York and Berlin. For details on airlines, see p504).

Boat

The **Transtejo ferry line** (www.transtejo.pt) has several riverfront terminals. From the eastern end of the Terreiro do Paço terminal (Map pp104–5), catamarans zip across the Tejo to Montijo (€2.10, 30 minutes) and Seixal (€1.75, 30 minutes, half-hourly weekdays, every hour or so weekends). From the main part of the terminal, called Estação do Sul e Sueste, Soflusa ferries run very frequently to Barreiro (€1.75, 30 minutes), for rail connections to the Alentejo, Algarve and Setúbal. From Cais do Sodré ferry terminal (Map pp104–5), passenger ferries go to Cacilhas (€0.81, 10 minutes, every 10 minutes all day). Car (and bicycle) ferries also go from Cais do Sodré to Cacilhas.

From Belém, ferries depart for Trafaria and Porto Brandão (€0.85, every 30 to 60 minutes), about 3.5km and 5km respectively from Costa da Caparica town.

Bus

Lisbon's new long-distance bus terminal is **Sete Rios** (Map p109; Rua das Laranjeiras), linked to both Jardim Zoológico metro station and Sete Rios train station. The big carriers, **Rede Expressos** (☎ 213 581 460; www.rede-expressos .pt) and **Eva/Mundial Turismo** (☎ 213 581 466; www .eva-bus.com), run frequent services to almost every major town. Destinations with 10 or more services a day include Coimbra (€13, 2½ hours), Évora (€11.50, 1½ hours), Porto (€17.50, 3½ to four hours) and Faro (€19, 3½ to four hours). You can buy your ticket up to seven days in advance.

The other major terminal is **Gare do Oriente** (Map pp102–3), concentrating on services to the north and to Spain. On the 1st floor are bus company booths (mostly open 9am to 5.30pm Monday to Saturday, to 7pm Friday, closed for lunch; smaller operators only open just before arrival or departure). The biggest companies operating from here are **Renex** (☎ 218 956 836; www.renex.pt) and the Spanish operator **Avanza** (☎ 218 940 250; www.avanz abus.com).

Many Renex buses take passengers 20 minutes early at Campo das Cebolas in Alfama, before Gare do Oriente.

Several regional companies with destinations in the north include **Mafrense** (www.ma frense.pt) for Ericeira & Mafra and **Barraqueiro Oeste** (www.barraqueiro-oeste.pt) for Malveira & Torres Vedras. These companies operate from **Terminal Campo Grande** (Map pp102–3; ☎ 217 582 212) outside Campo Grande metro station.

Buses to Sesimbra and Costa da Caparica go from a terminal (Map p109) at Sete Rios bus station.

Eurolines (Map pp102-3; ☎ 218 957 398; www .eurolinesportugal.com; Loja 203, Gare do Oriente) runs coaches to destinations all over Europe.

Information and tickets for international departures are scarce at weekends, so try to avoid that last-minute Sunday dash out of Portugal.

Car & Motorcycle

The nearest place to rent a motorbike is Cascais (see p164). The big-name car-hire companies are all on hand, though you can often save by using local agencies; most offer pick-up and delivery service to your hotel.
Autojardim (☎ 213 549 182; www.auto-jardim.com)
Avis (☎ 800 201 002; www.avis.com.pt)
Europcar (☎ 219 407 790; www.europcar.pt)
Hertz (☎ 219 426 300; www.hertz.com)
Holidays Car (☎ 217 150 610; www.holidayscar.com)
Sixt (☎ 218 407 927; www.e-sixt.com)

Train

Lisbon is linked by train to other major cities. See p513 for domestic services and p508 for international services. Check www.cp.pt for schedules. Some sample 2nd-class direct journeys to/from Lisbon are below. The abbreviations relate to comfort class (AN) on international train services (IN) and express services (*intercidade*; IC).

Lisbon has several major train stations. Santa Apolónia (Map pp104–5) is the terminal for trains from northern and central

TRAINS FROM LISBON				
Destination	Service	Price (€)	Duration	Frequency (per day)
Coimbra	IC/IN	15	2	10
Faro	IC	18	4	3
Porto C	IC	19.50	3	7

Portugal. It has a helpful **information desk** (☎ 808 208 208; ☺ 7.30am-9pm Mon-Fri, 8pm-4.30pm Sat & Sun) at door 8.

All of Santa Apolónia's services also stop at the Gare do Oriente (Map pp102–3), where there are departures to the Algarve and international destinations. Ticket booths are on the 1st floor (platforms are on the 2nd) and car-rental offices, banks and shops are at street level. Left-luggage lockers are on the basement metro level.

Another major terminal is Sete Rios (Map p109), which is connected to the Jardim Zoológico metro station and serves the northern suburbs. Most services continue on to Entrecampos station (Map p109). Either of these stations provides services across the Ponte 25 de Abril to Setúbal, among other destinations.

Cais do Sodré (Map pp104–5) is the terminal for train services to Cascais and Estoril.

Reopened in all its neo-Manueline glory in 2008, **Rossio** (Map pp104–5) is the most central station operating frequent services to Sintra via Queluz.

GETTING AROUND
To/From the Airport
The AeroBus (91) departs from outside Arrivals (€3.35, 25 to 35 minutes, roughly every 20 minutes from 7.45am to 8.15pm). It goes via Marquês de Pombal, Avenida Liberdade, Restauradores, Rossio and Praça do Comércio to Cais do Sodré. The ticket gives free passage on the entire city bus network for the rest of the day.

Local buses 43, 44 and 45 (single €1.35) also run from central stops including Cais do Sodré and Praça dos Restauradores and are a better deal if you arrive in the afternoon. They take slightly longer than the AeroBus and are best avoided during rush hour if you have a lot of luggage.

Expect to pay about €10 for a taxi into central Lisbon, plus €1.60 if your luggage needs to be placed in the boot. Avoid long queues by flagging down a taxi at Departures.

Bicycle
Traffic, trams, hills, cobbles and disgruntled drivers equal a cycling nightmare. You're better off stashing your bike with the left-luggage office at the bus station, airport or your hotel and seeing the city by public transport.

A pleasant place to cycle in Lisbon is the riverfront promenade at Parque das Nações, where **Tejo Bike** (Map pp102–3; ☎ 218 919 333; www.tejobike.pt; ☺ 10am-8pm Mar-Oct, 11am-6pm Nov-Feb) rents quality mountain bikes, kids' bikes, go-carts and inline skates.

Car & Motorcycle
Lisbon can be quite stressful to drive around, thanks to heavy traffic, maverick drivers, narrow one-way streets and tram lines, but the city is at least small. There are two ring roads useful for staying out of the centre: the inner Cintura Regional Interna de Lisboa (CRIL); and the outer Cintura Regional Externa de Lisboa (CREL).

Once in the centre, parking is the main issue. Spaces are scarce, parking regulations complex, pay-and-display machines often broken and car-park rates expensive (about €10 to €12 per day). On Saturday afternoon and Sunday parking is normally free.

Upmarket hotels usually have their own garages. If you need to park for more than a few days, there are cheaper car parks near Parque das Nações (metro Gare do Oriente – the multistorey here costs around €5 per day) or Belém (free car parks), then catch a bus or tram to the centre. Always lock up and don't leave any valuables inside, as theft is a risk.

Public Transport
BUS, TRAM & FUNICULAR
Companhia Carris de Ferro de Lisboa (Carris; ☎ 213 613 054; www.carris.pt) operates all transport except the metro. Its buses and trams run from about 5am or 6am to 1am; there are some night bus and tram services.

Pick up a transport map, *Planta dos Transportes Públicos da Carris* (including a map of night-time services) from tourist offices or Carris kiosks, which are dotted around the city. The Carris website has timetables and route details.

Individual tickets cost €1.35 on board or €0.81 if you buy a *bilhete único de coroa* (BUC; a one-zone city-centre ticket) beforehand. These prepaid tickets are sold at Carris kiosks – most conveniently at Praça da Figueira, at the foot of the Elevador de Santa Justa, and at Santa Apolónia and Cais do Sodré train stations.

The Carris kiosks also sell a one-day (€3.70) Bilhete Carris/Metro valid for buses, trams, funiculars *and* the metro.

The Lisboa Card (see boxed text, p113) is good for most tourist sights as well as bus, tram, funicular and metro travel.

Don't leave the city without riding tram 28 from Largo Martim Moniz or tram 12 from Praça da Figueira through the narrow streets of the Alfama.

Two other useful lines are tram 15 which runs from Praça da Figueira and Praça do Comércio via Alcântara to Belém, and tram 18 from Praça do Comércio via Alcântara to Ajuda. Tram 15 features space-age articulated trams with on-board machines for buying tickets and passes. Tram stops are marked by a small yellow *paragem* (stop) sign hanging from a lamppost or from the overhead wires.

METRO

The expanding **metropoitano** (underground; www .metrolisboa.pt; 1-zone single/return €1.25/1.55, 2-zone single/return €1.95/2.45, 1-/2-zone caderneta €7.40/10.35; ☽ 6.30am-1am) system is useful for short hops and to reach the Gare do Oriente and nearby Parque das Nações.

Buy tickets from metro ticket offices or machines. The Lisboa Card (see boxed text, p113) is also valid. Buy a *caderneta* (10-ticket booklet) if you'll be using the metro often.

Entrances are marked by a big red 'M'. Useful signs include *correspondência* (transfer between lines) and *saída* (exit to the street). There is some impressive contemporary art on the metro, including Angelo de Sousa at Baixa-Chiado and Hundertwasser at Oriente.

Watch out for pickpockets in rush-hour crowds.

Taxi

Táxis are reasonable and plentiful. If you can't hail one, try the ranks at Rossio, Praça dos Restauradores, near stations and ferry terminals, and at top-end hotels, or try **Rádio Táxis** (☎ 218 119 000) or **Autocoope** (☎ 217 932 756).

The fare on the meter should read €2.50 (daytime flag-fall). You will be charged an extra €1.60 for luggage and an additional 20% for journeys between 9pm and 6am. Rip-offs occasionally occur (the airport route is the main culprit). If you think that you have been cheated, get a receipt from the driver, note the registration number and talk to the tourist police.

For more information about taxis, see p512.

AROUND LISBON

Most frazzled urbanites hop on a plane when the sun-and-sea urge hits them. Not Lisboetas. When the city sizzles in summer, they don't have to go far to keep their cool – it's all in their backyard. A whopper of a pond for a start, the Atlantic, where the surf's always up and day trippers can tank rays on miles of gold-sand beaches. There are also rippling woods brushed with pine, palms and eucalyptus that say 'walk me', marshy reserves where bottlenose dolphins splash, hills studded with fanciful palaces that look like Disney blueprints, vineyards, fish restaurants, and limestone cliffs where dinosaurs created their own wall of fame 150 million years ago. And all within an hour of the capital.

Drenched in shades of green, Sintra (below) is often touted as the must-do day trip and you can believe the hype – it's stunning. Moors, blue-blooded eccentrics and even Lord Byron let their vivid imaginations loose in above-the-clouds palaces, woods scattered with enormous boulders and subtropical gardens; Unesco applauded. To the southwest, Cascais (p160) is a cocktail of beach, culture and lively bars, and neighbouring Estoril (p165) might tempt you to have a flutter at its ritzy casino of 007 fame. Go northwest for royal decadence in Mafra's (p166) baroque palace of Versailles proportions.

SINTRA
pop 26,400 / elev 280m

With its rippling mountains, dewy forests thick with ferns and lichen, exotic gardens and fairytale palaces affording top-of-the-beanstalk views, Sintra has a pinch-me quality. Its Unesco World Heritage centre, Sintra-Vila, is a storybook of pastel-hued manors folded into luxuriant hills that roll down to the blue Atlantic. And when Lisbon swelters, Sintra acts like a wet wipe with its cool microclimate.

Celts worshipped their Moon god here, the Moors built a precipitous castle and 18th-century Portuguese royals swanned around its dreamy gardens. Even Lord Byron waxed lyrical about Sintra's charms: 'Lo! Cintra's glorious Eden intervenes, in variegated maze of mount and glen', which inspired his epic poem *Childe Harold's Pilgrimage*. Extravagant and exquisite, Sintra

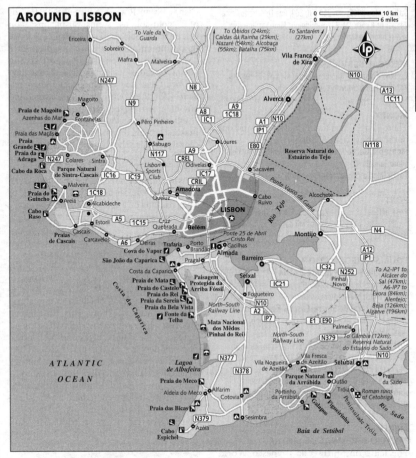

AROUND LISBON

0   10 km
0   6 miles

has ivy-clad Rapunzel-esque turrets, nature-gone-wild botanical gardens and forests strewn with megalithic granite boulders like giant's marbles.

It's the must-do day trip and, if time's not an issue, has enough allure to keep you there for several days. Try to come midweek to avoid the masses.

Orientation

There are four parts to Sintra: the old town is called Sintra-Vila; the new-town district of Estefânia, where the railway terminates, lies 1.5km northeast of there; the modern Portela de Sintra, 1km east of Estefânia, is where you'll find Sintra's bus station, Portela Interface (located beside the Portela

de Sintra train station); and tiny São Pedro de Penaferrim slumbers 2km southeast of Sintra-Vila.

The Parque Natural de Sintra-Cascais encompasses both the Serra de Sintra and nearby coastal attractions, including Cabo da Roca, Europe's most westerly point.

Information

EMERGENCY
Police station (Map p155; ☎ 219 230 761; Rua João de Deus 6)

INTERNET ACCESS
Loja do Arco (Map p155; Rua Arco do Teixeira 2; per hr €6; ⏰ 11am-7.30pm) Internet access, and also stocks a wide range of Portuguese literature, music and crafts.

Sabot (Map p155; ☎ 219 230 802; Rua Dr Alfredo Costa 74; per hr €2.50; ☼ 11am-midnight Mon-Sat) Internet access near the station.

MEDICAL SERVICES

Centro de saúde (medical centre; Map p155; ☎ 219 247 770; Rua Dr Alfredo Costa 34)

MONEY

There's an ATM at the train station, or try one of the banks (with ATMs):

Montepio Geral (Map p153; ☎ 214 248 000; Av Heliodoro Salgado 42)

Totta (Map p155; Rua das Padarias 4)

POST

Post office Sintra-Vila (Map p155; Rua Gil Vicente); Portela de Sintra (Map p153; Av Movimento das Forças Armadas) Has NetPost.

TOURIST INFORMATION

Parques de Sintra – Monte da Lua (☎ 219 237 300; www.parquesdesintra.pt) Runs the gardens and parks, most of which have visitors centres.

Parque Natural de Sintra-Cascais Headquarters (Map p153; ☎ 219 247 200; Rua Gago Coutinho 1) Opens usual business hours.

Turismo (☼ 9am-7pm Oct-May, 9am-8pm Jun-Sep); Main office (Map p155; ☎ 219 231 157; www.cm-sintra .pt; Museu Regional, Praça da República 23); Train station (Map p155; ☎ 219 241 623) These *turismos* (tourist offices) provide a free, information-packed map, and will also help with accommodation.

Sights

PALÁCIO NACIONAL DE SINTRA

The icing on Sintra-Vila's Unesco World Heritage cake is this **palace** (Sintra National Palace; Map p155; ☎ 219 106 840; Largo Rainha Dona Amélia; adult/under 14yr/concession €5/free/2, admission free 10am-2pm Sun; ☼ 10am-5.30pm Thu-Tue), whose iconic twin conical chimneys set imaginations into overdrive and cameras snapping. Of Moorish origins, the palace was first expanded by Dom Dinis (1261–1325), enlarged by João I in the 15th century (when the kitchens were built), then given a Manueline twist by Manuel I in the following century.

The whimsical interior is a mix of Moorish and Manueline styles, with arabesque courtyards, barley-twist columns and 15th- and 16th-century geometric *azulejos* that figure among Portugal's oldest. Highlights include the octagonal Sala dos

Cisnes (Swan Room), adorned with frescos of 27 gold-collared swans. Suspicious? You will be in the Sala das Pegas (Magpie Room), its ceiling emblazoned with magpies. Lore has it that the queen caught João I kissing one of her ladies-in-waiting. The cheeky king claimed the kisses were innocent and all '*por bem*' ('for the good'), then commissioned one magpie for every lady-in-waiting.

Other standouts feature the wooden Sala dos Brasões, bearing the shields of 72 leading 16th-century families, the shipshape Galleon Room and the Palatine chapel featuring an Islamic mosaic floor. Finally, you reach the kitchen of twin-chimney fame, where the flutes work their magic. You can almost hear the crackle of a hog roasting on a spit for the king – he didn't only have an appetite for infidelity!

CASTELO DOS MOUROS

Soaring 412m above sea level, this mist-enshrouded ruined **castle** (Map p153; ☎ 219 107 970; adult/under 5yr/concession €5/free/3; ☼ 9.30am-8pm May–mid-Sep, 10am-6pm mid-Sep–Apr, last admission 1hr before closing) is a Great Wall of China in miniature. Like a dragon's backbone, this 9th-century Moorish castle's dizzying ramparts wriggle across the mountain ridges and past moss-clad boulders the size of small buses. When the clouds peel away, the vistas over Sintra's palace-dotted hill and dale to the glittering Atlantic are – like the climb – breathtaking.

The best walking route here from Sintra-Vila is not along the main road but the quicker, partly off-road route via Rua Marechal Saldanha. The steep trail is around 2km, but quiet and rewarding.

PARQUE DA PENA

A further 200m up the road from Castelo dos Mouros is **Parque da Pena** (Map p153; ☎ 219 237 300; adult/under 5yr/concession €5/free/3, combined ticket with Palácio Nacional da Pena €11/9; ☼ 9.30am-8pm May–mid-Sep, 10am-6pm mid-Sep-Apr, last admission 1hr before closing), filled with tropical plants, huge redwoods and fern trees, camellias, rhododendrons and lakes (note the castle-shaped duck houses for web-footed royalty!). It's cheaper to buy a combined ticket if you want to visit Palácio Nacional da Pena too.

PALÁCIO NACIONAL DA PENA

Rising up from a thickly wooded peak and often enshrouded in swirling mist, **Palácio Nacional da**

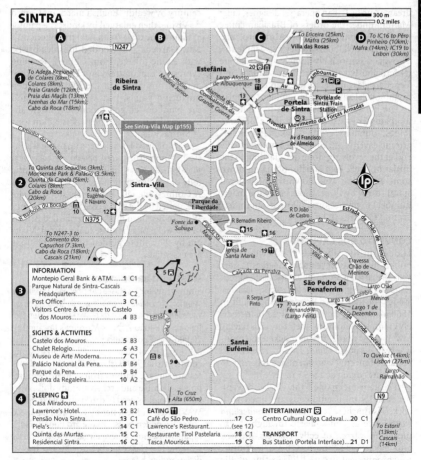

SINTRA

INFORMATION
Montepio Geral Bank & ATM......**1** C1
Parque Natural de Sintra-Cascais
  Headquarters...........................**2** C2
Post Office..................................**3** C1
Visitors Centre & Entrance to Castelo
  dos Mouros.............................**4** B3

SIGHTS & ACTIVITIES
Castelo dos Mouros.....................**5** B3
Chalet Relogio............................**6** A3
Museu de Arte Moderna..............**7** C1
Palácio Nacional da Pena............**8** B4
Parque da Pena...........................**9** B4
Quinta da Regaleira....................**10** A2

SLEEPING
Casa Miradouro..........................**11** A1
Lawrence's Hotel.........................**12** B2
Pensão Nova Sintra.....................**13** C1
Piela's..**14** C1
Quinta das Murtas......................**15** C2
Residencial Sintra.......................**16** C2

EATING
Café do São Pedro......................**17** C3
Lawrence's Restaurant............(see 12)
Restaurante Tirol Pastelaria **18** C1
Tasca Mourisca...........................**19** C3

ENTERTAINMENT
Centro Cultural Olga Cadaval....**20** C1

TRANSPORT
Bus Station (Portela Interface)...**21** D1

Pena (Pena National Palace; Map p153; ☎ 219 105 340; adult/ under 5yr/concession €6/free/4; ⏰ 10am-6.30pm Tue-Sun, 10am-5pm Nov-May, last admission 1hr before closing) is pure fantasy stuff. The wacky confection is a riot of onion domes, Moorish keyhole gates, writhing stone snakes, and crenellated towers in sherbet-bonbon pinks and lemons. Ferdinand of Saxe Coburg-Gotha, the artist-husband of Queen Maria II, commissioned Prussian architect Ludwig von Eschwege in 1840 to build the Bavarian-Manueline epic (and as a final flourish added an armoured statue of himself, overlooking the palace from a nearby peak).

The kitsch, extravagant interior is equally extraordinary, brimming with precious Meissen porcelain, Eiffel-designed furniture, trompe l'oeil murals and Dom Carlos' unfin-ished nudes of buxom nymphs. The ballroom has a chandelier holding 72 candles, and just in case those didn't do it, there are four statues of Turks bearing electric candles. A bas-relief showing a terrible cholera outbreak dominates Queen Amélia's teak-furnished tearoom.

Buses to the park entrance leave from Sintra train station and near the *turismo*. A taxi costs around €8 one way. The steep, zigzagging walk through pine and eucalyptus woods from Sintra-Vila is around 3km.

QUINTA DA REGALEIRA
This magical **villa and gardens** (Map p153; ☎ 219 106 650; Rua Barbosa du Bocage; adult/under 14yr/concession €6/3/4; ⏰ 10am-8pm Apr-Sep, to 6.30pm Feb-Mar & Oct, to 5.30pm Nov-Jan) is a neo-Manueline extravaganza,

dreamed up by Italian opera-set designer, Luigi Manini, under the orders of Brazilian coffee tycoon, António Carvalho Monteiro, aka Monteiro dos Milhões (Moneybags Monteiro). The villa is surprisingly homely inside, despite its ferociously carved fireplaces, frescos and Venetian glass mosaics. Keep an eye out for mythological and Knights Templar symbols.

The playful gardens are fun to explore – footpaths wriggle through the dense foliage to follies, fountains, grottoes, lakes and underground caverns. All routes seem to eventually end at the revolving stone door leading to the initiation well, **Poço Iniciáto**, plunging down some 30m. You walk down the nine-tiered spiral (three by three; three being the magic number) to mysterious hollowed-out underground galleries, lit by fairy lights.

CONVENTO DOS CAPUCHOS

Hidden in the woods is the bewitchingly hobbit-hole-like **Convento dos Capuchos** (Capuchin Monastery; off Map p153; ☎ 219 237 300; adult/under 5yr/ concession €5/free/3; ☼ 9am-8pm May–mid-Sep, 10am-6pm mid-Sep–Apr, last admission 1hr before closing), built in 1560 to house 12 monks who lived in incredibly cramped conditions, their tiny cells having low, narrow doors. Byron mocked the monastery in his poem *Childe Harold*, referring to recluse Honorius who spent a staggering 36 years here (dying at age 95 in 1596).

It's often nicknamed the Cork Convent, because its miniscule cells are lined with cork. Visiting here is an *Alice-in-Wonderland* experience as you squeeze through to explore the warren of cells, chapels, kitchen and cavern. The monks lived a simple, touchingly well-ordered life in this idyllic yet Spartan place, hiding up until 1834 when it was abandoned.

You can walk here – the monastery is 7.3km from Sintra-Vila (5.1km from the turn-off to Parque da Pena) along a remote, wooded road. There's no bus connection (taxis charge around €16 return; arrange for a pickup ahead). Admission is by guided visit (lasting 45 minutes), and it's preferable to book in advance.

MONSERRATE PARK

Wild and rambling **Monserrate Park** (off Map p153; ☎ 219 237 300; www.parquesdesintra.pt; adult/under 5yr/concession €5/free/3; ☼ 9.30am-8pm May–mid-Sep, 10am-6pm mid-Sep–Apr, last admission 1hr before closing) is a 30-hectare garden created in the 18th

century by wealthy English merchant Gerard de Visme, then enlarged by landscape painter William Stockdale (with help from London's Kew Gardens). Its wooded hillsides bristle with exotic foliage, from Chinese weeping cypress to dragon trees and Himalayan rhododendrons. Seek out the Mexican garden nurturing palms, yuccas and agaves, and the bamboo-fringed Japanese garden abloom with camellias. The park is 3.5km west of Sintra-Vila.

A manicured lawn sweeps up to the whimsical, Moorish-inspired **palácio** (☼ guided visits 10am-1pm & 2-6.30pm), the 19th-century romantic folly of English millionaire Sir Francis Cook. A Gothic-style villa previously stood on the site, rented by the rich, eccentric British writer William Beckford in 1794 after he fled Britain in the wake of a homosexual scandal. Visits are by 90-minute guided tour; reservations are essential.

MUSEU DO BRINQUEDO

Sintra's toy story is **Museu do Brinquedo** (Toy Museum; Map p155; ☎ 219 242 171; www.museu-do-brinquedo.pt; Rua Visconde de Monserrate; adult/concession €4/2; ☼ 10am-6pm Tue-Sun;). João Arbués Moreira's fascinating 20,000-piece collection presents a chronological romp, from 3000-year-old Egyptian stone counters to a 1999 Barbie Burberry. Standouts feature vintage Barbies from a more demure, housewifely era and archrival Sindy dolls. Also note tin soldiers used to drum up Nazi support, WWII Action Men, penny toys and Japanese kokeshi wooden dolls. On the 3rd floor is a toy-repair workshop, where a man sits studiously working in a glass case, beside a bizarre tray of disembodied heads.

The museum also has a cafe, a small shop and disabled access.

MUSEU DE ARTE MODERNA

The world-class **Museu de Arte Moderna** (Map p153; ☎ 219 248 170; www.berardocollection.com; Av Heliodoro Salgado; adult/under 18yr €3/free, admission free 10am-2pm Sun; ☼ 10am-6pm Tue-Sun;) hosts rotating exhibitions covering the entire modern art spectrum – from kinetic and pop art to surrealism and expressionism. Sheltering Hockney, Lichtenstein and Warhol originals, the permanent collection is part of billionaire José Berardo's stash, which also graces the walls of Museu Colecção Berardo (p120). Exhibits change frequently because of space limitations.

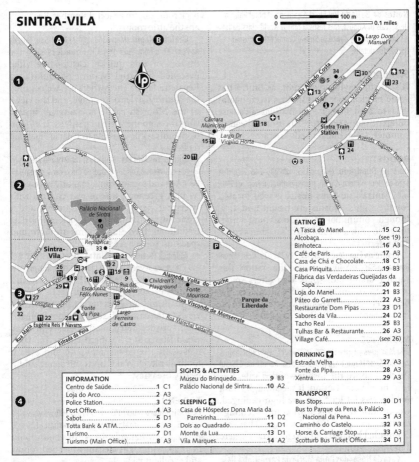

SINTRA-VILA

0 — 100 m
0 — 0.1 miles

EATING 🍴
A Tasca do Manel.....................**15** C2
Alcobaça...............................(see 19)
Binhoteca...............................**16** A3
Café de Paris...........................**17** A3
Casa de Chá e Chocolate..........**18** C1
Casa Piriquita..........................**19** B3
Fábrica das Verdadeiras Queijadas da
  Sapa.....................................**20** B2
Loja do Manel..........................**21** B3
Páteo do Garrett.......................**22** A3
Restaurante Dom Pipas..............**23** D1
Sabores da Vila........................**24** D2
Tacho Real..............................**25** B3
Tulhas Bar & Restaurante..........**26** A3
Village Café.............................(see 26)

DRINKING 🍷
Estrada Velha..........................**27** A3
Fonte da Pipa..........................**28** A3
Xentra...................................**29** A3

TRANSPORT
Bus Stops...............................**30** D1
Bus to Parque da Pena & Palácio
  Nacional da Pena....................**31** A3
Caminho do Castelo...................**32** A3
Horse & Carriage Stop................**33** A3
Scotturb Bus Ticket Office..........**34** D1

SIGHTS & ACTIVITIES
Museu do Brinquedo....................**9** B3
Palácio Nacional de Sintra..........**10** A2

INFORMATION
Centro de Saúde..........................**1** C1
Loja do Arco...............................**2** A3
Police Station.............................**3** C2
Post Office.................................**4** A3
Sabot..**5** D1
Totta Bank & ATM.......................**6** A3
Turismo.....................................**7** D1
Turismo (Main Office)...................**8** A3

SLEEPING 🛏
Casa de Hóspedes Dona Maria da
  Parreirinha..............................**11** D2
Dois ao Quadrado........................**12** D1
Monte da Lua..............................**13** D1
Vila Marques..............................**14** A2

Activities

Sintra is a terrific place to get out and stride, with waymarked (look for red-and-yellow stripes) **hiking trails** that corkscrew up into densely wooded hills strewn with giant boulders. Justifiably popular is the gentle 50-minute trek from Sintra-Vila to Castelo dos Mouros. You can continue to Palácio Nacional da Pena (another five minutes). From here you can ascend the Serra de Sintra's highest point, the 529m Cruz Alta (High Cross) named after its 16th-century cross, with amazing views all over Sintra. It's possible to continue on foot to São Pedro de Penaferrim and loop back to Sintra-Vila. Click onto www.cm-sintra.pt for basic trail maps.

If you're up for a challenge, Sintra is great terrain for **mountain biking**, with uphill climbs and exhilarating downhill rushes.

Ozono Mais (☎ 219 619 927; www.ozonomais.com) offers a variety of excursions, including canoeing, rafting, mountain-biking and jeep tours. Call ahead for times and prices.

Cabra Montêz (☎ 917 446 668; www.cabramontez .com), or 'mountain goat', arranges all kinds of adventurous pursuits including trekking/rafting/canyoning trips for €25/45/40 per person.

Festivals & Events

Festival de Música Classical music fans flock to Sintra for this string and soprano fest from mid-June to mid-July.

Noites de Bailado Held in the gardens of hotel Palácio de Seteais in August, this festival brings world-class ballet and contemporary dance to Sintra. Contact the *turismo* (p152) for details.

Sleeping

It's worth staying overnight, as Sintra has some magical places to snooze, from quaint villas to lavish manors. The *turismo* can advise on apartments (€50 to €70). Book ahead in summer, when budget beds are rare.

BUDGET

Dois ao Quadrado (Map p155; ☎ 219 246 160; Rua João de Deus 68; dm/d with shared bathroom from €15/40; 🖳) Sintra's no-frills hostel is well located for the sights. Dorms are bright and airy, though communal bathrooms could sometimes do with a scrub. There's a games room and internet.

Monte da Lua (Map p155; ☎ 219 241 029; Av Dr Miguel Bombarda 51; d €35-40) Opposite the station, this squat marshmallow-pink villa offers spick-and-span rooms decorated with plaids; the best overlook the wooded valley at the back. It's a quaint, silent spot.

MIDRANGE

Vila Marques (Map p155; ☎ 219 230 027; www.vilamarques.net; Rua Sotto Mayor 1; s/d with shared bathroom from €35/50) Perched above the lushly wooded vale, this rose-hued villa is a find. It's as though Laura Ashley was let loose on the high-ceilinged, wood-floored rooms with country-cottage dressers and pastel floral fabrics. There's a communal kitchen and serene terrace where a fountain gurgles.

Casa de Hóspedes Dona Maria da Parreirinha (Map p155; ☎ 219 232 490; Rua João de Deus 12-14; d €40-45; 🅿) This small, homely guest house is run by a charming elderly couple. Doubles are old-fashioned but spotless, with big windows, dark-wood furnishings and floral fabrics.

Piela's (Map p153; ☎ 219 241 691; Av Dr Cambournac 1-3; s/d €40/50) Look for the sign of a man wheelbarrowing his beer belly to find Piela's. The rooms are nothing flash, but they're clean and comfy. There's a cafe downstairs.

Pensão Nova Sintra (Map p153; ☎ 219 230 220; www.novasintra.com; Largo Afonso de Albuquerque 25; s/d incl breakfast €50/80; 🍴 🖳) This renovated late-19th-century mansion is set above the main road. The big drawcard is the sunny terrace overlooking Sintra, where you can take breakfast. Front-facing doubles offer dreamy views,

back rooms more peaceful slumber. Best of all are the attic rooms.

Chalet Relogio (Map p153; ☎ 219 241 550; Estrada da Pena 22; d from €60; 🅿) Our readers sing the praises of this quirky, castle-style villa, designed by Luigi Manini of Quinta da Regaleira fame. The owners are welcoming, the country-style rooms huge, and the views of the Moorish castle amazing. A stream runs through the verdant gardens. It's 700m from Sintra-Vila en route to Palácio Nacional da Pena.

Quinta das Murtas (Map p153; ☎ 219 240 246; www.quinta-das-murtas.com; Rua Eduardo Van Zeller 4; d from €75; 🐾) A grand salmon-pink manor surrounded by lush greenery, this retreat charms with sweeping views, a tinkling fountain and a grand sitting room with peacock mural. The traditional, tiled-floor rooms are light and spacious; some have kitchenettes.

our pick Residencial Sintra (Map p153; ☎ 219 230 738; www.residencialsintra.blogspot.com; Travessa dos Avelares 12; d incl breakfast from €75; 🐾 🖳) Sintra's greatest escape is this stately 1850s manor, set in rambling gardens with captivating views to the castle. The bright, high-ceilinged rooms are decorated in crisp hues with shiny wood floors. It's a superb choice for families with a large terrace, pool and even a football pitch! Wake up to birdsong and a hearty breakfast.

TOP END

Casa Miradouro (Map p153; ☎ 219 107 100; www.casa-miradouro.com; Rua Sotto Mayor 55; s/d incl breakfast €125/135) An imposing Battenberg cake of a house, built in 1890, with eight elegant, stuccoed rooms and excellent views.

Quinta da Capela (off Map p153; ☎ 219 290 170; s/d incl breakfast €130/140; ☿ mid-Mar–mid-Oct; 🐾) Slip into your role as lord or lady of the manor at this sublime 16th-century estate just beyond Monserrate Park. Its nine antique-filled rooms offer complimentary port and superb views. Stroll the manicured gardens, populated by peacocks and gliding swans, or take a dip in the pool with vistas over the valley to the Atlantic.

Quinta das Sequóias (off Map p153; ☎ 219 243 821; www.quintadasequoias.com; d incl breakfast €160; 🐾 🖳 🅿) Nestled among redwood forest with views of rolling hills, this sublime five-bedroom manor is near Monserrate Park. The owner, Candida, extends a sincere welcome and has tastefully decorated her home with art and antiques. The elegant rooms all have enchanting views. No children under 12.

Lawrence's Hotel (Map p153; ☎ 219 105 500; www .lawrenceshotel.com; Rua Consiglieri Pedroso 38; s/d €127/178; ✗ 🖳 ♿) Lord Byron once stayed at this 18th-century mansion turned boutique hotel. It oozes charm in its lantern-lit, vaulted corridors and snug bar (note the White House golf ball in the cabinet). Wood floors creak in the individually designed rooms, decorated with *azulejos* and antique trunks; some have views over the wooded valley. There's an excellent restaurant (p158).

Eating
BUDGET

Loja do Manel (Map p155; Rua do Arco do Teixeira) Stock up on picnic supplies at this tiny grocery (it even has plastic cutlery).

Restaurante Tirol Pastelaria (Map p153; Largo Afonso de Albuquerque 9; snacks €1-4.50; ✹ 7.30am-8.30pm) This buzzy cafe tempts with scrummy cream-filled desserts and almond biscuits. Sit on the terrace when the sun's out.

Binhoteca (Map p155; ☎ 219 240 849; Rua das Padarias 16; tapas €2-14; ✹ noon-10pm) Jazzy music and exposed stone set the scene at this glam wine bar, serving Portugal's finest, from full-bodied Douros to woody Madeira whites. Nibblers graze on goodies such as *pata negra*, cumin-and-apple blood sausage and pungent cheeses with pumpkin chutney. It's untouristy despite being smack in the centre.

Café do São Pedro (Map p153; Rua Serpa Pinta 5; mains €4-8; ✹ 9am-7pm Tue-Sun) Gold-framed prints and a Victrola lend an old-world air to this inviting cafe. You'll find coffees, teas and good-value lunch specials.

A Tasca do Manel (Map p155; ☎ 219 230 215; Largo Dr Virgílio Horta 5; mains €5-6.50; ✹ breakfast, lunch & dinner Mon-Sat) The smell of sizzling sardines and garlic draws locals to this good-value, TV-and-tiles place.

Tasca Mourisca (Map p153; Calçada de San Pedro 28; mains €6-8; ✹ lunch & dinner Mon-Sat) This small, unassuming tavern rustles up tasty Portuguese fare from grilled squid to steak.

Village Café (Map p155; ☎ 219 213 013; Rua Gil Vicente 21; mains around €6; ✹ daily) Popular with a young crowd, this laid-back, barn-style cafe makes a great pit stop for inexpensive lunch specials, salads and pastries.

Sabores da Vila (Map p155; ☎ 219 241 040; Av Augusto Freire 2; lunch buffet €7; ✹ lunch Mon-Sat; Ⓥ) Painted

---

SWEET DREAMS

Sintra is famous for its luscious sweeties. **Fábrica das Verdadeiras Queijadas da Sapa** (Map p155; ☎ 219 230 493; Alameda Volta do Duche 12; ✹ closed Mon) has been rotting the teeth of royalty since 1756 with bite-sized *queijadas* – crisp pastry shells filled with a marzipan-like mix of fresh cheese, sugar, flour and cinnamon. Since 1952, **Casa Piriquita** (Map p155; ☎ 219 230 626; Rua das Padarias 1-5; ✹ closed Wed) has been tempting locals with another sweet dream – the *travesseiro* (pillow), light puff pastry turned, rolled and folded seven times, then filled with delicious almond-and-egg yolk cream and lightly dusted with sugar.

---

in zesty lemon-and-lime tones, this modern cafe attracts lunchtime locals with its wallet-pleasing lunch buffet (with vegetarian options). The price includes a drink and coffee.

MIDRANGE & TOP END

Café de Paris (Map p155; ☎ 219 232 375; Praça da República 32; mains €6-14; ✹ 10am-8pm) This opulent cafe is a pink marble, stucco and chandelier confection facing the palace. *Oui*, the crunchy baguettes, bistro specials, light crepes and even the snooty service are indeed very Parisian.

Tacho Real (Map p155; ☎ 219 235 277; Rua da Ferraria 4; mains €6.50-19; ✹ closed Wed) Take a pew on the cobbled patio or retreat to the 17th-century vaulted interior, bedecked with century-old *azulejos*, at this charming haunt. Dapper waiters bring specialities from juicy steaks to stuffed king crab to the table.

Alcobaça (Map p155; ☎ 219 231 651; Rua das Padarias 7; mains €7.50-13; ✹ lunch & dinner) This simple, busy place is one of the best-value and most traditional restaurants in the old town. It serves hearty Portuguese fare including tasty *caldo verde* (cabbage soup), grilled sardines and garlicky clams.

Restaurante Dom Pipas (Map p155; ☎ 219 234 278; Rua João de Deus 60, Estefânia; mains €8.50-10; ✹ Tue-Sun) Tucked down a sleepy backstreet near the train station, little Dom Pipas keeps locals coming with favourites such as *arroz de marisco* (seafood rice).

Tulhas Bar & Restaurante (Map p155; ☎ 219 232 378; Rua Gil Vicente 4; mains €9-14; ✹ closed Wed) This converted grain warehouse is dark, tiled and quaint, with twisted chandeliers and a relaxed, cosy atmosphere. It's renowned for its *bacalhau com natas* (shredded cod with cream and potato).

Páteo do Garrett (Map p155; ☎ 219 243 380; Rua Maria Eugénia Reis F Navarro 7; mains €10-22; ☺ lunch & dinner Thu-Tue) Don't be put off by the rustic-meets-kitsch decor; the major draw here is the patio, shaded by a huge plane tree and affording far-reaching views over Sintra's rooftops. Home-cooked classics include spicy black sausage and garlicky clams with coriander.

Casa de Chá e Chocolate (Map p155; ☎ 219 234 825; Rua Dr Alfredo Costa 8; mains around €11; ☺ lunch & dinner Tue-Sat, dinner Sun; Ⓥ) Maria uses fruit and veg from her own garden to whip up vegetarian dishes, salads and the like. But it's her wicked desserts that shine, from chocolate fondue to yoghurt-and-berry torte. The mint-and-ginger iced tea is refreshing.

Lawrence's Restaurant (Map p153; ☎ 219 105 500; Rua Consiglieri Pedroso 38; set 3-course lunch €19.50; ☺ lunch & dinner) Perfect for romantic tête-à-têtes with its classical music, candlelight and rose-clad terrace, the restaurant at Lawrence's Hotel (p157) serves modern Portuguese cuisine. Signatures such as veal with turnip tops and tarragon sauce are beautifully cooked and presented.

Drinking

Sintra is no party town, but there are several bars in the side streets where you can converse over a cold one. Rua das Padarias and Rua Fonte da Pipa are quite buzzy in summer.

Fonte da Pipa (Map p155; ☎ 219 234 437; Rua Fonte da Pipa 11-13) A hip tiled bar, this has craggy, cavelike rooms and comfy seats.

Estrada Velha (Map p155; ☎ 219 234 355; Rua Consiglieri Pedroso 16) Jazzy music place at this popular den with a laid-back, pubby vibe. Its sign of a fallen angel, guzzling beer and smoking, causes a few giggles.

Xentra (Map p155; ☎ 219 240 759; Rua Consiglieri Pedroso 2A) This cellar bar has a vaguely medieval feel with stone walls and an arched ceiling.

Entertainment

Sintra's major cultural venue, staging concerts, theatre and dance, is the **Centro Cultural Olga Cadaval** (Map p153; ☎ 219 107 110; www.ccolgaca daval.pt; Praça Francisco Sá Carneiro), beautifully converted from an old cinema.

Getting There & Away

Buses run by **Scotturb** (Map p155; ☎ 214 699 100; www.scotturb.com; Av Dr Miguel Bombarda) or **Mafrense** (☎ 261 816 150; www.mafrense.pt) leave regularly for Cascais (€3.35, 60 minutes), sometimes via Cabo da Roca (€3.35). Buses also head to Estoril (€3.35, 40 minutes), Mafra (45 minutes) and Ericeira (45 minutes). Most services leave from Sintra train station (which is *estação* on timetables) via Portela de Sintra. Scotturb's useful information office, open from 9am to 1pm and 2pm to 8pm, is opposite the station.

Train services (€1.70, 40 minutes) run every 15 minutes between Sintra and Lisbon's Rossio station. Bikes travel free on weekends and holidays (€2.50 return weekdays, not permitted from 7am to 10am Sintra to Lisbon, 4pm to 8pm Lisbon to Sintra).

Getting Around

BUS

From the station, it's a 1.5km scenic walk into Sintra-Vila – a good way to get your bearings – or you can hop on bus 433, which runs regularly from Portela Interface to São Pedro (€0.90, 15 minutes, at least half-hourly from 7am to 8pm) via Estefânia and Sintra-Vila. Unless you fancy an uphill hike, it's well worth buying the Scotturb Bilhete Diário Circuito da Pena (€4.50), a hop-on, hop-off day pass for bus 434, which runs from the train station via Sintra-Vila to Castelo dos Mouros (10 minutes), Palácio da Pena (15 minutes) and back. It operates every 15 minutes from 9.15am to 7.50pm.

HORSE & CARRIAGE

Horse-driven carriages clip-clop all over Sintra, even as far as Monserrate. The *turismo* has a full list of prices (€30 to €100). The best place to pick up a carriage is by the *pelourinho* (stone pillory) below Palácio Nacional de Sintra.

TAXI & CAR

Taxis are available at the train station or opposite Sintra-Vila post office. They are metered, so fares depend on traffic. Count on about €8 one way to Palácio Nacional da Pena, or €16 return to Convento dos Capuchos.

There's a free car park below Sintra-Vila; follow the signs by the *câmara municipal* (town hall), in Estefânia. Alternatively, park at Portela Interface and take the bus.

WEST OF SINTRA

Precipitous cliffs and crescent-shaped bays pummelled by the Atlantic lie just 12km west of Sintra. Previous host of European Surfing Championships, **Praia Grande** lures surfers and body-boarders to its big sandy beach with ripping breakers. Clamber over the cliffs to spot dinosaur fossils. Family-friendly **Praia das Maçãs** has a sweep of gold sand, backed by a lively little resort. **Azenhas do Mar**, 2km further, is a cliff-hanger of a village, where a jumble of white-washed, red-roofed houses tumble down the crags to a free saltwater pool (only accessible when the sea is calm).

En route to the beaches, ridgetop **Colares** makes a great pit stop with its panoramas, stuck-in-time village charm and wines dating back to the 13th century. The vines grown today are the only ones in Europe to have survived the 19th-century phylloxera plague, saved by their deep roots and sandy soil. Call in advance to arrange a visit to **Adega Regional de Colares** (☎ 219 291 210; Alameda Coronel, Linhares de Lima 32) to taste some of its velvety reds.

Wild and wonderful **Cabo da Roca** (Rock Cape) is a sheer 150m cliff, facing the roaring sea, 18km west of Sintra. It's Europe's westernmost point and a terrific sunset spot. Though it receives a steady trickle of visitors that come to see the lighthouse and buy an I've-been-there certificate at the *turismo*, it still has an air of rugged, windswept remoteness.

Sleeping

Residencial Real (☎ 219 292 002; Rua Fernão Magalhães, Praia das Maçãs; s/d incl breakfast €40/45) For spacious, immaculate rooms with expansive ocean views, you can't beat this homely guest house right on the beach at Praia Grande.

Village Praia Grande (☎ 219 290 581; www.villagepraiagrande.com; Av Atlântico; 2-/4-/6-bedroom apt €80/104/135; ▢ ⊜) Just 500m from the beach, these rustic bungalows come equipped with kitchens, TV and telephone. Cool off in the pine-fringed pool.

Estalagem de Colares (☎ 219 282 942; estalagemdecolares@yahoo.com; Estrada Nacional 247, Colares; s/d €80/120; ⊠ Ⓟ) Peeking above lush greenery, this whitewashed villa is a calm retreat with large, clean rooms and a peaceful garden.

Hotel Arribas (☎ 219 292 145; www.hotelarribas.com; Av Alfredo Coelho, Praia Grande; s/d/tr/q €95/118/157/191;

⊠ ▢ ⊛) While this 39-room, scallop-shaped hotel isn't a pretty face, its sea views over Praia Grande and 100m-long oceanwater pool are magnificent. Light, breezy rooms feature fridges, TVs, and balconies ideal for watching surfers ride the waves.

Casal St Virginia (☎ 219 283 198; www.casalstvirginia.com; Av Luis Augusto Colares 17; d €125; ⊜) On a cliff facing the Atlantic, this manor house near the small village of Azenhas do Mar exudes charm with its antique-filled corridors and sunny terrace. The individually designed rooms include one with a skylight where you can stargaze by night. Sunbathe on the lawns or swim laps in the pool.

Eating

Many cafes and seafood restaurants are scattered along Praia Grande and Praia das Maçãs.

Azenhas do Mar (☎ 219 280 739; Azenhas do Mar; mains €10-18; ⊙ lunch & dinner) This smart restaurant, next to the saltwater pool in Azenhas do Mar, serves fresh fish caught by the owner – the clams and steamed barnacles are delicious with a glass of house white. The sea views are wonderful, especially from the deck. Step up to the bar to glimpse the old water mill.

ourpick Colares Velho (☎ 219 292 406; Largo Dr Carlos França 1-4; mains €15-25; ⊙ lunch & dinner Tue-Sat, lunch Sun) Clued-up foodies make sure there's rarely an empty table at this restaurant and tearoom, set in a converted grocery store and tavern. The country-style dining room, bedecked with 200-year-old pinewood dressers, is an elegant setting for flavours like Roquefort steak and seafood *cataplana*, accompanied by full-bodied wines. Alternatively, sip Earl Grey and nibble on divine pastries in the tearoom. The vine-strewn courtyard is ideal for summertime dining.

Getting There & Away

Bus 441 from Portela Interface goes frequently via Colares to Praia das Maçãs (€2.75, 25 minutes) and on to Azenhas do Mar (€2.75, 30 minutes), stopping at Praia Grande (€2.75, 25 minutes) three times daily (more in summer). Bus 440 also runs from Sintra to Azenhas do Mar (€2.75, 35 minutes).

Bus 403 to Cascais runs regularly via Cabo da Roca (€3.55, 45 minutes) from Sintra station.

CASCAIS

pop 33,255

Cascais (kush-*kaish*) has rocketed from sleepy fishing village to much-loved summertime playground of shiny, happy Lisboetas ever since King Luís I slipped on his bathing togs for a dip in 1870. Its trio of golden bays attracts sun-worshipping day trippers and ice-cream-licking holidaymakers that come to flop, sizzle and splash in the ice-cold Atlantic. Don't expect much sand to yourself at the weekend, though.

And there's plenty of post-beach life, with winding lanes leading to one-off museums, cool gardens, a shiny new marina and a pedestrianised old town dotted with designer boutiques and alfresco fish restaurants. After dark, lively bars and clubs fuel the party. Active bods can ride the waves at Praia do Guincho, 9km northwest, or pedal along the palm-fringed coastline to Estoril.

Orientation & Information

The train station and nearby bus station are about 250m north of the main pedestrianised drag, Rua Frederico Arouca.

BOOKSHOPS

Livraria Galileu (☎ 214 866 014; Av Valbom 24A) Good source of secondhand English, Spanish, Italian, French and German books.

EMERGENCY

Main police station (☎ 214 861 127; Rua Afonso Sanches)
Tourist police post (☎ 214 863 929; Rua Visconde da Luz) Next to the *turismo*.

INTERNET ACCESS

Golfino (Rua Sebastião J Carvalho e Melo 17; per hr €4; ☻ 9.30am-8pm Mon-Sat)

MEDICAL SERVICES

Cascais Hospital (☎ 214 827 700; Rua Padre JM Loureiro)
International Medical Centre (☎ 214 845 317; Instituto Médico de Cascais, Av Pedro Álvares Cabral 242)

MONEY

Banco Espírito Santo (☎ 214 864 302; Largo Luís de Camões 40) Has an ATM.

POST

Post office (Av Marginal; ☻ 8.30am-6pm Mon-Fri) Also has NetPost.

TOURIST INFORMATION

Turismo (☎ 214 868 204; www.visiteestoril.com; Rua Visconde da Luz 14; ☻ 9am-7pm Mon-Sat Sep-Jun, to 8pm Mon-Sat Jul-Aug, 10am-6pm Sun year-round) Can assist with accommodation. Hands out free maps and brochures.

Sights

OLD CASCAIS

The hubbub of the **fish market** near Praia da Ribeira races you back to when Cascais was but a little fishing village. An auctioneer sells the day's catch in rapid-fire lingo at about 5pm Monday to Saturday.

Weave through the back alleys west of the *câmara municipal* to the palm-fringed square that is home to the whitewashed **Igreja de Nossa Senhora da Assunção** (Largo da Assunção; admission free; ☻ 9am-1pm & 5-8pm), adorned with *azulejos* predating the 1755 earthquake.

The **citadel** is where the royal family used to spend the summer. It's currently occupied by the military, but plans are under way to transform it into a new cultural space. Beyond lies the modern **Marina de Cascais** with its postcard-perfect lighthouse, sleek yachts and too-cool lounge bars.

PARKS & MUSEUMS

Escape the crowds at wild and shady **Parque Marechal Carmona**, speckled with birch and pine trees, palms and eucalyptus, rose gardens and flowering shrubs. Kids love the duck pond and playground with a sandpit, but the cramped and grimy mini zoo is a letdown.

The grounds harbour the **Museu Condes de Castro Guimarães** (☎ 214 815 304; admission €1.80; ☻ 10am-5pm Tue-Sun), the whimsical early-19th-century mansion of Irish aristocrat Jorge O'Neill, complete with castle turrets and Arabic cloister. But the clover leaves inside didn't bring him luck – he went bankrupt and had to sell up. His successor, Count of Castro Guimarães, lavishly decorated the abode with 17th-century Indo-Portuguese cabinets, Oriental silk tapestries and 17th-century *azulejos*. Don't miss the rare 16th-century manuscript depicting pre-earthquake Lisbon. Admission is with half-hourly guided tours.

Nearby, the colourful **Centro Cultural de Cascais** (☎ 214 848 900; Av Rei Humberto II de Itália; admission free; ☻ 10am-6pm Tue-Sun), in what was a barefooted Carmelite convent, hosts contemporary exhibitions and cultural events. It has a great cafe.

CASCAIS

0   300 m
0   0.2 miles

INFORMATION
Banco Espirito Santo ATM.......1 C3
Cascais Hospital.....................2 B1
Golfinho..............................3 D2
Livraria Galileu......................4 D2
Main Police Station................5 C2
Post Office...........................6 D1
Tourist Police Post............(see 7)
Turismo...............................7 C2

SIGHTS & ACTIVITIES
Centro Cultural de Cascais.......8 C4
Citadel................................9 C4
Fish Market.........................10 C2
Igreja de Nossa Senhora da
  Assunção..........................11 C3
Marina de Cascais................12 D4
Museu Condes de Castro
  Guimarães........................13 B4
Museu do Mar.....................14 B3
Parque Marechal Carmona....15 B4

SLEEPING
Albergaria Valbom................16 D2
Casa da Pergola...................17 C2
Cascais Beach Hostel............18 B2
Hotel Albatroz.....................19 D2
Residencial Avenida.............20 C2
Residencial Parsi..................21 C3
Residencial Solar Dom Carlos.22 C3
Villa Albatroz.......................23 C3

EATING
A Carvoaria........................24 B2
A Económica.......................25 D2
A Tasca..............................26 C2
Apeadeiro..........................27 B3
Confraria Sushi....................28 C3
Jardim dos Frangos..............29 C2
Kwantha............................30 C2
Mariazinha.........................31 C1
Paradox..............................32 D1
Pastelaria Bijou....................33 C2
Santini...............................34 D2

DRINKING
Baluarte.............................35 C3
Buvigis..............................36 C3
Esplanada Rainha................37 D2
O Luain's...........................38 C2
O'Neill's.............................39 C3
Rock'n'Shots..................(see 1)

SHOPPING
Cascais Villa Shopping Centre.40 D1
Ceramicarte........................41 C3
Mercado Municipal..............42 C1

TRANSPORT
Ausocar.............................43 D1
Bus Station.........................44 D1
Centro Comercial Cisne.........45 D1
Free Bikes...........................46 D2
Transrent.......................(see 45)

To Sintra (14km)
Avenida 25 de Abril
Rua Padre
  M Lourenço
Rua da Bela Vista
Rua Vic da Luz
Avenida do Ultramar
Rua Manuel de Avelar
Rua da Vista Alegre
Praça Dr
Francisco de Sá
Cameiro
Largo da
Estação
Train
Station
To Estoril
(2km)
Avenida Marginal
Praia da
Conceição
To John
David's Bar
(100m);
John David's
Watersports
Centre (100m);
Exclusive
Divers (100m);
Praia da
Duquesa (100m)
Jardim
Visconde
da Luz
Largo
Luís de
Camões
Rua Visconde da Luz
Combatentes da Grande Guerra
Avenida Valbom
Rua Frederico Arouca
Largo
Cidade de
Vitória
Praia
da
Rainha
To Agarre o
Momento
(300m)
To Praça de Touros (600m);
Open-Air Market (600m)
Rua dom Luís
de Moura
Avenida
Emidio Navarro
Rua João Luís
de Moura
Rua Luís Xavier
Rua Afonso Sanches
Rua Alm Cochia Ferreira
Avenida Vasco da Gama
Câmara
Municipal
Praia da Ribeira
ATLANTIC
OCEAN
To International
Medical Centre
(800m)
Largo 5
de Outubro
Tv da Vitória
To Bikes (100m);
Praça de Touros (1km);
Open-Air Market (1km)
Avenida Dom Carlos
To Esplanada
Santa Marta (100m);
Farol Design Hotel (200m);
Coconuts (200m); Furnas do
Guincho (1km); Boca do
Inferno (2km); Praia do
Guincho (9km);
Orbitur do Guincho
(9km); Cabo
da Roca (23km)
Av Rei Humberto II de Itália
Estrada da Boca do Inferno

Set in Jardim da Parada, the small **Museu do
Mar** (☎ 214 825 400; admission €2.85, Sun free; ⏰ 10am-5pm
Tue-Sun) spells out Cascais' maritime history with
costumes, tools, nets and boats, accompanied
by quotes (in English) from the fisherfolk.

BOCA DO INFERNO

Atlantic waves pummel craggy **Boca do Inferno**
(Mouth of Hell), 2km west of Cascais. Taxis
charge €6 return, or you can walk along the
coast (about 20 minutes). Expect a mouthful
of small splashes unless a storm is raging.

Activities

Cascais' three sandy bays – Praia da
Conceição, Praia da Rainha and Praia da
Ribeira – are great for a sunbake or a tingly

Atlantic dip, but don't expect much towel
space in summer.

The best beach is wild, windswept **Praia do
Guincho**, 9km northwest, a Mecca to surfers
and windsurfers (the site of previous World
Surfing Championships) with massive crashing rollers. The strong undertow can be dangerous for swimmers, but Guincho still lures
nonsurfers with powder-soft sands, fresh
seafood and magical sunsets.

If you're keen to ride the waves, grab your
boardies and check out the surfing courses
available at **Moana Surf School** (☎ 964 449 436;
www.moanasurfschool.com; introductory 75min lesson €20,
4 x 75min classes €75) and **Guincho Surf School** (☎ 965
059 421), or rent a board from **Aerial Wind e Surf**
(☎ 917 890 036).

John David's Watersports Centre (☎ 214 830 455; 10am-7.30pm May-Sep) at Praia da Duquesa, midway between Cascais and Estoril, rents out pedaloes (€15 per hour) and canoes (€12 per hour) and arranges water-skiing jaunts (€30 per 15 minutes), banana-boat rides (€30 per five people) and windsurfing (€25 per hour). Next door, **Exclusive Divers** (☎ 214 868 099; www.exclusive-divers.net) can take you scuba-diving around the Cascais coastline and beyond with equipment rental and courses.

Festivals & Events

Festas do Mar This festival in late August celebrates Cascais' maritime heritage with nautical parades, fireworks and fado. Wackier events include placing bets on which hole a mouse will run down and a bull race on the beach.

Estoril Jazz This 10-day jazz fest takes place in Cascais and Estoril in July.

Festival de Música da Costa do Estoril This festival brings classical and jazz concerts to both towns in July.

Free outdoor entertainment Cascais and Estoril entertain the summertime crowds from July to mid-September with live bands nightly, usually at Estoril's Praia de Tamariz and/or Cascais' Praia de Moitas, and fireworks on Saturdays around midnight.

Sleeping

It's worth booking in advance if you're visiting in summer, as the best places fill up in a flash.

BUDGET

Camping Orbitur do Guincho (☎ 214 870 450; www.orbitur.pt; sites per adult/tent/car €4.80/5.40/4.70; ♿) Set back behind the dunes of Praia do Guincho, 9km from Cascais, this pine-shaded site has a restaurant and tennis court. It gets busy in July and August. Buses run frequently to Guincho from Cascais.

Agarre o Momento (☎ 214 821 834; Rua Joaquim Ereira 458; dm/d €20/35; 💻) These groovy new backpacker digs in a bubblegum-pink house, 10 minutes' walk north of the station, offer clean, airy dorms, plus other perks such as a garden, free wi-fi, shared kitchen and bike rental.

Cascais Beach Hostel (☎ 309 906 421; www.cascaisbeachhostel.com; Rua da Vista Alegre 10; dm/d €20/49; 💻 🏊) This funky newcomer is central for Cascais' beaches and nightlife. Dorms and doubles sport shiny wood floors and citrus hues. There's a lounge with DVDs, beanbags and a PlayStation, a modern communal kitchen, and a small pool in the garden. Other pluses include bike rental and free wi-fi.

MIDRANGE

Residencial Avenida (☎ 214 864 417; Rua da Palmeira 14; d with shared bathroom €40) Blink and you'll miss the sign for Avenida. It's like staying in someone's flat, with just four plain but comfy, clean and quiet doubles decorated in pastel shades.

Residencial Parsi (☎ 214 861 309; www.residencial-parsi.com; Rua Afonso Sanches 8; d with/without bathroom €90/40) In a crumbling, characterful building near the waterfront, Parsi's rooms have recently been spruced up with zingy colours, parquet floors and flat-screen TVs. The stuccoed front room has sea views. It's intimate and friendly.

Residencial Solar Dom Carlos (☎ 214 828 115; www.solardomcarlos.com; Rua Latino Coelho 104; s/d €55/70; P 💻) Hidden down a sleepy alley, this 16th-century former royal residence turned guest house retains lots of original features from chandeliers to wood beams, *azulejos* and a frescoed breakfast room. The high-ceilinged rooms are spacious and traditional. Don't miss the 400-year-old chapel where Dom Carlos used to pray.

Albergaria Valbom (☎ 214 865 801; albergariavalbom@mail.telepac.pt; Av Valbom 14; s/d €58/73) Centrally located Valbom reveals a contemporary design ethic in its chocolate-and-lime breakfast room and mulberry-hued lounge. Unfortunately, the drab, '70s-style rooms don't live up to first impressions. Word has it, though, that the entire place will soon get a makeover.

TOP END

our pick **Casa da Pergola** (☎ 214 840 040; Av Valbom 13; d incl breakfast with/without balcony €129/119) An oasis of calm with its lush garden and bougainvillea-draped facade, this century-old manor is a family heirloom. A marble staircase sweeps up to six classically elegant rooms with stucco, dark wood trappings and sparkling bathrooms; several have garden-facing balconies. Relax in the antique-filled sitting room or with a glass of complimentary port in the evening.

Villa Albatroz (☎ 214 863 410; www.albatrozhotels.com; Rua Fernandes Tomás 1; s/d incl breakfast from €182/224; ❄ 🏊 💻 ♿) Facing the bay, this smaller sibling of Hotel Albatroz (opposite) has just 11 individually decorated rooms – some flowery, some with ornamental fireplace. The best rooms sport terraces, Jacuzzi tubs and ocean views.

Hotel Albatroz (☎ 214 847 380; www.albatrozho tels.com; Rua Frederico Arouca 100; s/d from €200/240; P ※ 🖴 🕱) Take a 19th-century clifftop villa, give it an avant-garde twist with glass walls and streamlined aesthetic and you get this boutique gem. The snazzy rooms feature wi-fi, complimentary port, and bathrooms with copper basins and Molton Brown cosmetics. Upgrade for a free-standing tub or private tower. There's a saltwater pool overlooking the bay and a panoramic restaurant serving Mediterranean-style cuisine.

Farol Design Hotel (☎ 214 823 490; www.farol .com.pt; Av Rei Humberto II de Itália 7; s €280, d €300-370; P ※ 🕱) Self-consciously cool, this hotel reveals a razor-sharp design – picture chillired walls, floor-to-ceiling windows facing the Atlantic, a poolside chillout lounge and a creative restaurant with Med-sushi fusion cuisine. The more expensive rooms have sea views and were designed by Portuguese fashion royalty like Ana Salazar and Fátima Lopes.

Eating

You'll find a glut of restaurants with alfresco seating along pedestrianised Rua Frederico Arouca and cobbled Largo Cidade de Vitória. For seafood and sunsets, make for the beach-shack restaurants by the waterfront in Guincho.

BUDGET

Santini (☎ 214 833 709; www.geladosantini.com; Av Valbom 28F; ice creams €2.10; ⏱ 11am-11pm Tue-Sat, 11am-8pm Sun) All hail Santini for its yummy 100% natural *gelati*, made to an age-old family recipe. Grab a cone and skedaddle to the beach before it melts.

John Davids Bar (☎ 214 830 455; Praia da Duquesa; light meals €3-10; ⏱ 10am-7.30pm May-Oct) Slow service, dirty glasses, poor food, rude staff, expensive…thankfully, this sign is just cracking English humour. If you're missing Blighty, this beachfront cafe is the go-to place for tasty cooked breakfasts, daily papers and a natter with John, who also runs the watersports centre (opposite) next door.

Paradox (☎ 214 843 004; Av Costa Pinto 91; mains €5-7; ⏱ lunch Mon-Sat; V) This good-value cafe rustles up organic and veggie fare, from sushi to buffets.

Mariazinha (☎ 1936 530 520; Rua Visconde da Luz 43; light meals €5-8; ⏱ 8am-8pm Mon-Fri, 8am-7pm Sat) An injection of cool with its spidery wire lights and turquoise paintjob, this sassy cafe is run by the young, bubbly Patricia. Take a seat for appetising baguettes and homemade sweets like tiramisu.

A Económica (☎ 214 833 524; Rua Sebastião JC Melo 11; mains €5.50-8; ⏱ lunch & dinner Fri-Wed) This buzzy, unassuming spot whips up generous portions of Portuguese staples from sardines to stew. Plant yourself outside when the sun's out.

Pastelaria Bijou (☎ 214 830 283; Largo Luis de Camões 55; mains €6; ⏱ 8am-7pm) Head to this jewel-box patisserie for sweets and inexpensive lunch specials. Be sure to try the Cascais speciality, buttery *areias* (sands) cookies.

MIDRANGE

A Tasca (☎ 214 821 382; Rua Afonso Sanches 61; mains €6-9; ⏱ lunch & dinner Mon-Sat) This simple, friendly tavern serves good-value specials like grilled squid and hake.

Jardim dos Frangos (☎ 214 861 717; Av Marginal; mains €6-11; ⏱ lunch & dinner Mon-Sat) Whiffs of grilled chicken and piri-piri lure hungry locals to the pavement terrace of this no-frills joint. Waiters can be moody, but the *frangos* is first-class.

Apeadeiro (☎ 214 832 731; Av Vasco da Gama 252; mains €6.50-11; ⏱ lunch & dinner) With chequered tablecloths, big windows and walls hung with fishing nets, this sunny restaurant is known for its superb chargrilled fish – shrimp piri-piri is delicious.

Esplanada Santa Marta (☎ 214 837 779; Praia de Santa Marta; mains €7.50-10; ⏱ 9am-10pm Tue-Sun) Perched above a bay, this cute place is a family favourite because of its after-dinner paddling potential. Tuck into dishes like shrimp kebabs and halibut on the palm-shaded terrace with lighthouse views.

Kwantha (☎ 214 865 507; Rua Afonso Sanches 54; mains €8-12; ⏱ lunch & dinner Thu-Tue; V) Flavoursome curries (including some vegetarian options) are polished off nicely with mango sticky rice and Singha beer at this Thai newcomer.

Confraria Sushi (☎ 214 834 614; Rua Luís Xavier Palmeirim 16; mains €8-13; ⏱ noon-midnight Tue-Sun) It's hard to know where to look first at this Smartie-bright, art-slung cafe, jazzed up with flower prints, zebra stripes and technicolour glass chandeliers. It's a fun spot for sushi and yummy salads such as goat's cheese with forest fruits. There's a handful of tables on the sunny patio.

TOP END

Furnas do Guincho (☎ 214 869 243; Estrada da Guincho; mains €10-16; ☼ lunch & dinner; ⏚) Straddling a rocky outcrop looking out to the Atlantic, this smart seafood restaurant is about 1km along the road to Guincho. Savour house specials like goose barnacles and lobster over dramatic sea views.

A Carvoaria (☎ 214 830 406; Rua João Luís de Moura 24; mains €10-20; ☼ dinner Mon-Sat) A well-kept local secret, this rustic South African haunt is always packed thanks to its friendly service and terrific food. On the menu: spicy *boerewors* (sausage), garlicky ostrich fillet, oxtail stew and the roll-me-out-the-door 'steak big boss'.

Drinking

Bars huddling around Largo Luís de Camões are publike, lively and packed with a good-time crowd that gets crazy after too many rays.

Baluarte (☎ 214 865 157; Av Dom Carlos I 6) Ubercool Baluarte draws a see-and-be-seen crowd with its glam-meets-retro decor of swirly gold wallpaper, tub chairs and bold purple splashes. It offers sea views, well-mixed cocktails and regular events from DJ nights to karaoke.

Buvigis (☎ 214 868 717; Rua do Poço Novo) A hip new lounge bar close to the waterfront, Buvigis is packed with 20- to 30-somethings that just wanna have fun sipping cocktails, playing pool and grooving to everything from chillout to old-skool tunes.

Rock 'n' Shots (☎ 919 057 946, Largo Luís do Camões 36) This funky new bar does what the label says – expect thumping Portuguese rock, a dash of reggae and potent shots and cocktails. Sip a cool Rui Veloso (vodka, peach and pineapple juice).

O Luaín's (☎ 214 861 627; Rua da Palmeira 4A) For the craic in Cascais, it has to be this cheery Irish watering hole, run by Ivor and Karen. Pull up a stool for Guinness and – at 10.30pm from Thursday to Sunday – live music, including the popular banjo jam sessions.

O'Neill's (☎ 214 868 230; Rua Afonso Sanches 8) Another Irish number with banter and a passion for the pint, O'Neill's has live music at around 11pm from Thursday to Saturday.

Coconuts (☎ 214 844 109; www.nuts-club.com; Av Rei Humberto II de Itália 7; ☼ 11pm-4am) Young, touchy-feely, dressed-up and nutty at times, this ever-

popular club has DJs heating up two dance floor, seven bars and an esplanade by the sea.

Esplanada Rainha (Largo da Rainha; ☼ 10am-10pm) For sundowners with a sea view, head to this outdoor place overlooking Praia da Rainha beach.

Shopping

Label lovers head down Rua Frederico Arouca for boutiques from Max Mara to Hugo Boss.

Cascais Villa shopping centre (Av Marginal) Near the bus station, this mall shelters a cinema, supermarket and a string of other shops.

Mercado Municipal (Av Dom Pedro I; ☼ Wed & Sat morning) Cascais' bustling municipal market tempts with fresh local produce such as juicy Algarve nectarines, glossy olives, wagon-wheel-sized cheeses and bread. An entire hall is given over to fish.

Ceramicarte (☎ 214 840 170; Largo da Assunção 3) This eye-catching gallery showcases Luís Soares' bright, abstract fused-glass creations from jewellery to tableware.

Getting There & Away

Buses go frequently to Sintra from both Estoril and Cascais (€3.35, 40 minutes) and to Cabo da Roca (€2.60, 30 minutes). You pay more on board than at the kiosk. If you're planning on travelling a lot by bus, it's worthy buying a day pass for €4.

Trains from Lisbon's Cais do Sodré run to Cascais via Estoril (€1.70, 40 minutes, every 20 minutes daily). Bikes travel free on this line on weekends.

It's only 2km to Estoril, so it doesn't take long to walk the seafront route.

Getting Around

Since parking is tricky, a good option is to park for free on the outskirts (for instance at Praça de Touros) and take the **BusCas minibus** (☎ 214 699 100; tickets €0.55) into town. It does a circular route via the centre every 10 minutes from 7.30am to 9.20pm (to 10.20pm July to September) Monday to Thursday and Sunday, and to 12.20am on Friday and Saturday.

Transrent (☎ 214 864 566; www.transrent.pt; basement level, Centro Comercial Cisne, Av Marginal) rents bikes/scooters/cars/motorbikes for €10/16.50/25/46.50 a day. Buses 405 and 415 go to Guincho (€2.60, 20 minutes, seven daily).

Often waiting at Jardim Visconde da Luz are horse-drawn carriages, which do half-hour trips to Boca do Inferno.

FREE WHEELS

Cascais has recently boosted its eco-credentials by offering **free bike hire**. The bikes are available from 8am to 7pm daily at various points around town, including Largo da Estação near the train station. Demand is naturally high, so arrive early and bring some form of ID. There's a bicycle path that runs the entire 9km stretch from Cascais to Guincho. A shorter route is along the attractive seafront promenade to Estoril, 2km east.

Near the bus station are numerous car-rental agencies including **Ausocar** (☎ 214 822 472; www.ausocar-rentacar.pt; loja D, Edificio Sol de Cascais, Av 25 de Abril 16). For a taxi, call ☎ 214 660 101.

Free bike hire (see above) offers a more eco-friendly way to explore Cascais.

ESTORIL

pop 23,770

With its swish hotels, turreted villas and glitzy casino, Estoril (shtoe-*reel*) once fancied itself as the Portuguese Riviera. The rich and famous came here to frolic in the sea, stroll palm-fringed landscaped gardens and fritter away their fortunes. Though it still has a whiff of faded aristocracy, those heady days of grandeur have passed and the sedate vibe today is more Bournemouth than Monaco. Estoril's big draw is the sandy bay of Praia de Tamariz, which tends to be slightly quieter than the beaches in neighbouring Cascais in summer.

Estoril was where Ian Fleming hit on the idea for *Casino Royale*, as he stalked Yugoslav double agent Dusko Popov at its casino. During WWII, the town heaved with exiles and spies (including Graham Greene, another intelligence man turned author).

Orientation & Information

The bus and train stations are a stone's throw from the beach on Avenida Marginal, opposite shady Parque do Estoril. The casino is at the north end of the park, while the **turismo** (☎ 214 663 813; 🕑 9am-7pm Mon-Sat Sep-Jun, to 8pm Mon-Sat Jul & Aug, 10am-6pm Sun year-round) faces the train station.

Sights & Activities

The glitzy, temple-like **casino** (☎ 214 667 700; www.casino-estoril.pt; Praça José Teodoro dos Santos; gaming room/slot machine room €4/free; 🕑 3pm-3am; 🔥) has

everything from roulette to poker, blackjack and the ubiquitous slot machines. Its cavernous main restaurant, **Preto e Prata** (☎ 214 684 521; show with/without dinner €58/22.50), stages a sparkly floor show nightly at 11pm.

Estoril's sandy Praia de Tamariz tends to be quieter than the bays in Cascais and has showers, cafes, beachside bars and a free ocean **swimming pool**, east of the train station.

For details on Estoril's world-famous golf scene, see p85.

Sleeping

Casa Londres (☎ 214 682 383; www.casalondres.com; Av Fausto Figueiredo 7; s/d €35/60) A five-minute walk from the beach, this immaculate guest house has light, high-ceilinged rooms with white-washed walls, hardwood floors and decorative blue-and-white panels.

Pica-Pau (☎ 214 667 140; www.picapauestoril.com; Rua do Afonso Henriques 48; s/d €55/80; 🔥) Occupying a white-fronted, red-roofed villa 400m west of the casino, Pica Pau's big draw is its pool framed by sunloungers. The marble-floored rooms with cable TV and safes are spacious and well kept, though beds can be on the springy side.

Residencial Smart (☎ 214 682 164; www.residencialsmart.com; Rua Maestro Laçerda 6; s/d €60/70; 🔥 P) This little guest house is smart alright. The affable owner runs the place with pride – think manicured lawns, a clean swimming pool and gleaming marble floors. The light-filled rooms have lots of polished wood and tiny balconies.

Hôtel Inglaterra (☎ 214 684 461; www.hotelinglaterra.com.pt; Rua do Porto 1; s/d €192/200; 🔥 🖥 🔥) Estoril's swankiest option is this lavishly renovated mansion. The contemporary rooms have been glammed up with pearl-tinged wallpaper, stripy furnishings and shiny marble bathrooms. It also offers spa treatments, a top-notch restaurant and a palm-fringed pool.

Eating

Garrett do Estoril (☎ 214 680 365; Av de Nice 54; snacks €1-4) Overlooking the park, this old-world *pastelaria* impresses the small-dog-toting clientele with its teas, sandwiches and sticky pastries.

Praia de Tamariz (☎ 214 681 010; Praia de Tamariz; mains €10-14; 🕑 lunch & dinner) Sure, the faded menu pictures are past their prime, but thankfully the kitchen at this beachfront restaurant is more inspiring. Tasty options include pepper sirloin steak and paella.

Costa do Estoril (☎ 214 681 817; Av Amaral; mains €12-20; ☺ noon-3.30pm & 7pm-5am Tue-Sun) Yep, you read those times right: this restaurant next to the casino feeds ravenous gamblers to the wee hours. The chargrilled seafood is superb, especially the Setúbal red mullet and salt-crusted cod.

Getting There & Away
Bus 412 goes frequently to Cascais (€1.80; five minutes), or it's a pleasant 2km walk or cycle along the seafront. For other train and bus services, see p164.

QUELUZ
Versailles' fanciful cousin-once-removed, the powder-puff **Palácio de Queluz** (☎ 214 343 860; adult/under 14yr/concession €5/free/2.50; ☺ 9.30am-5pm Wed-Mon; ⚿) was once a hunting lodge, converted in the late 1700s to a royal summer residence. It's surrounded by queen-of-hearts formal gardens, with oak-lined avenues, fountains (including the Fonte de Neptuno, ascribed to Italian master Bernini) and an *azulejo*-lined canal where the royals went boating.

The palace was designed by Portuguese architect Mateus Vicente de Oliveira and French artist Jean-Baptiste Robillon for Prince Dom Pedro in the 1750s. Pedro's niece and wife, Queen Maria I, lived here for most of her reign, going increasingly mad. Her scheming Spanish daughter-in-law, Carlota Joaquina, was quite a match for eccentric British visitor William Beckford. On one occasion she insisted that Beckford run a race with her maid in the garden and then dance a bolero, which he did 'in a delirium of romantic delight'.

Inside is like a chocolate box, with a gilded, mirror-lined Throne Room and Pedro IV's bedroom where he slept under a circular ceiling, surrounded by *Don Quixote* murals. The palace's vast kitchens now house a palatial restaurant, **Cozinha Velha** (☎ 214 356 158; lunch & dinner Wed-Mon).

You've seen the palace, now live the life. The Royal Guard of the Court quarters in this ice-cream-pink rococo palace have been converted into the dazzling **Pousada de Dona Maria I** (☎ 214 356 158; recepcao.dmaria@pousadas.pt; s/d incl breakfast €173/185; ⚿), with high-ceilinged rooms that will make you feel as if you're at home with the royals.

Getting There & Away
Queluz (keh-*loozh*) is 5km northwest of Lisbon and makes an easy day trip. Frequent trains from Rossio station stop at Queluz-Belas (€1.20; 15 minutes).

MAFRA
pop 11,276 / elev 250m
Mafra, 39km northwest of Lisbon, makes a superb day trip from Lisbon, Sintra or Ericeira. It is home to Palácio de Mafra, Portugal's extravagant monastery/palace hybrid with 1200 rooms. Nearby is the beautiful former royal park, Tapada de Mafra, once a hunting ground and still teeming with wild animals and plants.

Orientation
The monumental palace facade dominates the town. Opposite is a pleasant square, Praça da República, which is lined with cafes and restaurants. Mafra's **bus terminal** (☎ 261 816 152) is 1.5km northwest but buses also stop in front of the palace. A Mafrense bus **ticket office** (Terreiro Dom João V 21) is located near the square.

A WOLF IN THE WOODS
There's no need to be afraid of the wolves at the **Centro de Recuperação do Lobo Ibérico** (Iberian Wolf Sanctuary; ☎ 261 785 037; http://lobo.fc.ul.pt, Vale da Guarda, Picão; adult/concession €5/2.50; ☺ 4-8pm Sat & Sun May-Sep, 2.30-6pm Sat & Sun Oct-Apr) located near Malveira, 10km east of Mafra. The centre is home to a pack of around 20 wolves that can no longer live in the wild. Set in a forested valley, the centre aims to boost the rapidly dwindling numbers of Portugal's Iberian wolf population (now just 300 in the wild) by affording them safe shelter in a near-to-natural habitat. As the wolves are free to roam in their large enclosures, there's no guarantee that you'll spot them, but encounters are frequent. Advance bookings are essential. The sanctuary is best reached by private transport.

Information

The **turismo** (☎ 261 817 170; Terreiro Dom João V; ☺ 9.30am-1pm & 2.30-6pm) is in part of the palace. It has a picturesque (though outdated) map of the Mafra area and a bilingual *Mafra Real* booklet describing the palace and park.

Sights

PALÁCIO NACIONAL DE MAFRA

Wild-spending Dom João V poured pots of Brazilian gold into this baroque **palace** (☎ 261 817 550; adult/under 14yr/concession €4/free/2, admission free 10am-2pm Sun, ☺ 10am-5pm Wed-Mon), covering a mind-boggling 4 sq km and comprising a monastery and basilica. Begun in 1717, the exuberant mock-marble confection is the handiwork of German master Friedrich Ludwig, who trained in Italy and clearly had a kind of Portuguese Vatican in mind. No expense was spared: around 45,000 artisans worked on building its 1200 rooms and two bell towers to shelter the world's largest collection of bells (92 in total).

When the French invaded Portugal in 1807, Dom João VI and the royals skedaddled to Brazil, taking most of Mafra's furniture with them. Imagine the anticlimax when the French found nothing but 20 elderly Franciscan friars. General Junot billeted his troops in the monastery, followed by Wellington and his men. From then on the palace became a military haven. Even today, most of it is used as a military academy.

On the one-hour visit, escorted by a guard, you'll take in treasures such as the antler-strewn hunting room and a walled bed for mad monks (maybe sent over the edge by all those corridors!). The biggest stunner is the 83.6m-long barrel-vaulted library, housing some 40,000 15th- to 18th-century books, many handbound by the monks. It's an appropriate fairy-tale coda to all this extravagance that they're gradually being gnawed away by rats. The basilica of twin bell tower fame is strikingly restrained by comparison, featuring multihued marble floors and Carrara marble statues.

Guided English-language tours usually set off at 11am and 2.30pm. A leaflet (€1) helps if you catch a non-English tour. If it's a Sunday, stay till 4pm to hear a **Concerto de Carrilhão**, a concert of the basilica's infamous bells (preceded by a free guided bell-tower tour at 3.15pm). The palace's **Jardim do Cerco** (Enclosed Garden; admission free; ☺ 10am-5pm) at the northern end of the palace, where the queen once picked her flowers, is a charming place to wait.

TAPADA NACIONAL DE MAFRA

The palace's 819-hectare park, **Tapada Nacional de Mafra** (☎ 261 817 050; www.tapadademafra.pt; walker €4.50-6, cyclist €10) is where Dom João V used to go a-hunting. Enclosed by an original 21km wall, the grounds are now an environmentally aware game park home to free-roaming wild board and red deer, plus smaller numbers of foxes, badgers and eagles.

To appreciate the different ecosystems, hike through its woodlands of Portuguese oak, cork oak and pine; don't miss the 350-year-old cork oak saved from fire in 2003. The 4km trail (€4.50) is a good introduction to the park, but you have a greater chance of spotting animals on the more remote 7.5km route (€6). For walking trails, gates open between 9.30am and 11am as well as between 2pm and 3.30pm daily; you can stay until 6pm. There's also a 15km **mountain-bike trail** (ride with/without own bike €10/20; ☺ 10am-4pm), with bikes available.

The Tapada is about 7km north of Mafra, along the road to Gradil. It's best reached by private transport, as buses are erratic; from Mafra, taxis charge around €8 one way.

SOBREIRO

At the village of Sobreiro, 4km northwest of Mafra (take any Ericeira-bound bus), sculptor José Franco has created an enchanting miniature, vaguely surreal **craft village** (admission free; ☺ 9.30am-around 7.30pm; ♿) of windmills, watermills and traditional shops. José himself can often be seen crafting clay figures at the entrance. Kids love it here; so do adults, especially when they discover the rustic *adega* (winery) serving good red wine and snacks. Ramped walkways make it accessible for wheelchair users.

Sleeping & Eating

Hotel Castelão (☎ 261 816 050; Av 25 de Abril; s/d incl breakfast €55/75) If you want to stay overnight, Castelão offers comfy, though corporate, rooms with minibar and satellite TV. It has a pizzeria and bar.

Café Paris (☎ 261 815 797; Praça da República 14; mains €6-9; ☺ lunch & dinner Mon-Sat) This smartish, genteel pink place is among several cafe-restaurants around Praça da República and rustles up decent Portuguese dishes.

If you want something lighter, there are lots of nice *pastelarias* around the square selling local crusty Mafra bread and traditional cakes, such as *pastéis de feijão*, a concoction of eggs, sugar and almonds.

Getting There & Around

There are regular **Mafrense** (☎ 261 816 159; Av Dr Francisco Sá Carneiro) buses to/from Ericeira (€1.95, 20 minutes, at least hourly), Sintra (€3.75, 45 minutes) and Lisbon's Campo Grande terminal (€3.75, 75 minutes, at least hourly). Mafra's train station is 6km away from the town centre with infrequent buses (taxis charge around €9 between the train station and the town centre); go to Malveira station instead for easier connections (20 minutes) to Mafra.

Taxis (☎ 261 815 512) are available in Praça da República.

SETÚBAL PENINSULA

As the mercury rises, the promise of sun, sea and mouth-watering grilled fish lures Lisboetas south to the Setúbal Peninsula for weekends of ozone-enriched fun. Beach bums make for the Costa da Caprica's (right) 8km sweep of golden sand to laze on a lounger, dip in the freezing Atlantic and unwind over sundowners in beachside cafes. The coast gets wilder the further south you venture and Cabo Espichel (p177) is wildest of all – a vertiginous cape thrashed by the Atlantic, where you can trace the footprints of dinosaurs.

Edging further south, the vibrant port of Setúbal (p170) provides a tonic for a UV overdose. It's a fine place to munch *choco frito* (fried cuttlefish) and spot bottlenose dolphins on a breezy cruise of the marshy Sado estuary. To the west lies Parque Natural da Arrábida (p174), lined with scalloped bays flanked by sheer cliffs that are home to birds of prey. It leads to the fishing town and bay of Sesimbra (p175), laced with cobbled backstreets and overshadowed by a Moorish castle. The coast is great for outdoorsy types, offering activities from scuba-diving and surfing to hiking and canyoning.

CACILHAS

This sleepy seaside suburb lies just across the Rio Tejo from the capital. Its star attraction, visible from almost everywhere in Lisbon, is 110m-high **Cristo Rei** (☎ 212 751 000). Perched on a pedestal, the statue of Christ with outstretched arms is the spitting image of Rio de Janeiro's Christ the Redeemer. It was erected in 1959 to thank God for sparing Portugal from the horrors of WWII. A **lift** (adult/concession €4/2; ⏰ 9.30am-6pm Apr-Sep, 9.30am-5pm Oct-Mar) zooms you up to a platform, from where Lisbon spreads out like a patchwork before you. It's a fantastic place for photos.

Lisboetas also flock to Cacilhas for the *cervejarias* (beer halls) serving fresh seafood, refreshing brews and fine views of the sun setting over the river.

Near the ferry terminal, **Cervejaria O Farol** (☎ 212 765 248; Largo Alfredo Diniz Alex 1; mains €7-12; ⏰ 9am-midnight Thu-Tue) is a buzzy haunt that cooks crustaceans, including garlicky clams and shrimps, to finger-licking perfection. Note the tiled panel depicting the *farol* (lighthouse) that once stood here.

A 15-minute stroll along the waterfront brings you to Brazilian restaurant **Atira-te ao Rio** (☎ 212 751 380; Cais do Ginjal 69; mains €12-15; ⏰ 1-4pm & 8pm-midnight Tue-Sun). Its terrace is a wonderful spot to feast on coconut-rich shrimp bobo and sip expertly mixed caipirinhas, as Ponte 25 de Abril starts to twinkle.

Getting There & Away

Ferries to Cacilhas (€0.81, 10 minutes) run frequently from Lisbon's Cais do Sodré. A car-ferry service (€2.30 to €4 depending on the size of the car) runs every 40 minutes between 4.30am and 2.30am; from Cais do Sodré and back, or you can take bus 101 from the bus station beside the Cacilhas terminal.

COSTA DA CAPARICA

Costa da Caparica's seemingly never-ending 8km beach attracts sun-worshipping Lisboetas craving all-over tans, surfer dudes keen to ride Atlantic waves, and day-tripping families seeking clean sea and soft sand. It hasn't escaped development, but head south and the high-rises soon give way to pine forests and mellow beach-shack cafes. The town has the same name as the coastline, and is a cheery place with shops and lots of inflatable seaside tack.

During the summer a narrow-gauge railway runs most of the length of the beach and you can jump off at any one of 20 stops. The nearer beaches, including **Praia do Norte** and **Praia do São Sebastião**, are great for families, while the further ones are younger and trendier. **Praia do Castelo** (stop 11) and **Praia da Bela Vista** (stop 17) are more-secluded gay and nudist havens.

Continuing along the coast all the way to Lagoa de Albufeira is the Paisagem Protegida da Arriba Fóssil, a protected fossilised cliff of geological importance backed by the Mata Nacional dos Mêdos (aka Pinhal do Rei), a 600-hectare pine forest originally planted by Dom João V to stop the encroaching sand dunes.

Orientation & Information

Costa da Caparica town focuses on Praça da Liberdade. West of the *praça*, pedestrianised Rua dos Pescadores, with hotels and restaurants, leads to the seaside. The main beach (called Praia do CDS, or Centro Desportivo de Surf), with cafes, bars and surfing clubs along its promenade, is a short walk north. The **bus terminal** (Av General Humberto Delgado) is 400m northwest of the Praça da Liberdade; additional stops are by the *praça*.

The **turismo** (☎ 212 900 071; Av da República 18; ☾ 9.30am-1pm & 2-5.30pm Mon-Fri, 9.30am-1pm Sat) is just off the *praça*.

Activities

Atlantic rollers pounding the shore are all the encouragement surfers need to grab their boards and hit the waves, particularly along the northern stretch of coast.

Among the hottest **surfing** spots are São João da Caparica, Praia da Mata and Praia da Sereia. **Fonte da Telha** (where the train terminates) is the best beach for **windsurfing** and has plenty of water-sports facilities. Check the handy *Tabela de Marés* booklet (available at the *turismo*), listing tide times, surf shops and clubs.

Caparica Surfing School (☎ 212 919 078; www.caparicasurf.com; Praia do CDS; ☾ 10am-6pm Sat & Sun) is the main surfing school. Brian Trigg runs the excellent **Hooked Surf School** (☎ 913 615 978; http://hookedsurf.com; intro lesson €25; 4 lessons €80), offering lessons and a kids' surf club at Costa da Caparica, Praia do Guincho (p161) and Praia Grande (p159). Call ahead for a pickup from your accommodation. It also rents boards and wetsuits.

Cabana Divers (☎ 212 977 711, 919 390 278; www.cabanadivers.com; Fonte da Telha), with a nicely setup bar and wicker basket chairs by the beach, provides diving lessons and equipment.

Sleeping

Costa da Caparica (☎ 212 901 366; sites per adult/tent/car €4.80/5.40/4.70; ♿) Orbitur's campsite, 1km north of town, is the closest and best. Situated 200m from the beach, the pine-shaded site has excellent facilities such as a cafe, tennis court and playground.

Residencial Mar e Sol (☎ 212 900 017; www.residencialmaresol.com; Rua dos Pescadores 42; s/d €45/65; ▢) Recently given a facelift, this guest house offers simple yet comfy rooms in warm hues. There is free internet, bike hire and an Italian restaurant, Napoli, in case you get the pizza munchies.

Residencial Real (☎ 212 918 870; www.hotel-real.pt; Rua Mestre Manuel 18; s/d €50/80; 😺) A young crew runs this bright guest house, 30m from the beach. The light-filled rooms with blonde-wood furnishings feature cable TV, minibars and squeaky-clean en suite bathrooms.

Eating & Drinking

In Costa da Caparica town, seafood restaurants line Rua dos Pescadores. You'll find a mix of restaurants and bars on the beach, which crank up during the summer months.

A Merendeira (☎ 212 904 527; Rua dos Pescadores 20; mains €1.50-6) This cafe on the main drag serves fresh sandwiches (chorizo or cod) and filling daily soups and desserts.

Carolina do Aires (☎ 212 900 124; Av General Humberto Delgado; mains €7-12; ☾ lunch & dinner) A big shady greenhouse of a restaurant, this indoor/outdoor spot serves up tasty seafood dishes and cold Sagres. It's along the footpath to the beach.

Napoli (☎ 212 903 197; Rua dos Pescadores 42; mains €7-13; ☾ dinner) Pizzas, pasta dishes and other Italian fare draw hungry locals to this unassuming Italian joint at Residencial Mar e Sol.

Bar Waikiki (☎ 212 962 129; Praia da Sereia; snacks €2.50-7; ☾ 10.30am-7.30pm May-Sep) Nicely on its own, this beachfront bar is popular with surfers and has a cool lounge vibe. It's great for sundowners. You'll find it at stop 15 on the train.

Another beachside haunt is **Kontiki** (☎ 212 914 391; Praia de Sao Joao).

Getting There & Away

Transportes Sul do Tejo (TST; ☎ 217 262 740; www.tsuldotejo.pt) runs regular buses to Costa da Caparica from Lisbon's Praça de Espanha (€2.50, 20 to 60 minutes).

The best way to get here is by ferry to Cacilhas (every 15 minutes) from Lisbon's Cais do Sodré, where bus 135 runs to Costa da Caparica town (€2.75, 30 to 45 minutes, every 30 to 60 minutes); buses 124 and 194 also run here but are slower, also stopping at the train station. Bus 127 runs from Cacilhas to Fonte da Telha (50 minutes, at least hourly). Bus 130 runs from Trafaria to Fonte da Telha (45 minutes, at least hourly) via Costa da Caparica and Pinhal do Rei (near Praia do Rei).

Getting Around

The train along the beach operates daily from 9am to 7.30pm between Praia Nova and Fonte da Telha (€5 return, every 15 minutes from June to September, weekends from Easter to May, depending on the weather), about 1km before the end of the county beach. Although this is the end of the line, the beaches continue along the coast.

SETÚBAL
pop 114,000

Though hardly a classic beauty, the thriving port town of Setúbal (*shtoo-bahl*) makes a terrific base for exploring the region's sublime natural assets. Top of the must-do list is a cruise to the marshy wetlands of the Sado estuary, the splashy playground of around 30 bottlenose dolphins, flocks of white storks (spring and summer), and 1000 wintering flamingos that make the water fizz like pink champagne. Outdoorsy types can hike or bike along the dramatic, pine-brushed coastline of Parque Natural da Arrábida, while sun-seekers can bliss out on nearby sandy beaches.

Back in town, it's worth taking a stroll through the squares in the pedestrianised old town, seeking out Igreja de Jesús, Portugal's first-ever Manueline church, and clambering up to the hilltop fortress for giddy views over the estuary. The fish reeled the Romans to Setúbal in 412, so it's no surprise that seafood here is delicious. On Avenida Luísa Todi, locals happily while away hours polishing off enormous platters of *choco frito* and carafes of white wine.

Orientation

The mostly pedestrianised centre focuses on Praça de Bocage and Largo da Misericórdia, with most sights within easy walking distance. The bus station is about 150m northwest of the municipal *turismo*. The main train station is 700m north of the centre. Frequent ferries shuttle across the Rio Sado to the Tróia peninsula from terminals around Doca do Comércio.

Information
EMERGENCY & MEDICAL SERVICES
Hospital (☎ 265 549 000) Near the Praça de Touros (bullring), off Avenida Dom João II.
Police station (☎ 265 522 022; Av 22 de Dezembro)

INTERNET ACCESS
Cyber Tody (Av Rua de São Cristóvão 7; per hr €1.65; ☽ 10am-midnight Mon-Fri, 2.30pm-midnight Sat & Sun) Good central location.
Instituto Português da Juventude (IPJ; ☎ 265 532 707; Largo José Afonso; free internet access; ☽ 9am-5pm Mon-Fri) Maximum 30 minutes.

MONEY
Caixa Geral de Depósitos (☎ 265 530 500; Av Luísa Todi 190) Has an ATM.

POST
Branch post office (Praça de Bocage)
Main post office (Av Mariano de Carvalho; ☽ 8.30am-6.30pm Mon-Fri, 9am-12.30pm Sat) Has NetPost.

TOURIST INFORMATION
Municipal turismo (☎ 936 515 845; www.mun-setu bal.pt; Av Luísa Todi 486; ☽ 9am-9pm daily)
Regional turismo (☎ 265 539 130; www.costa-azul .rts.pt; Travessa Frei Gaspar 10; ☽ 9.30am-7pm Tue-Fri, 9.30am-12.30pm Sun May-Sep, to 6pm Mon-Fri, closed Sun Oct-Apr) Has a glass floor revealing the remains of a Roman *garum* (fish condiment) factory. The office hands out a free booklet, *Parques e Reservas Naturais* (Parks & Natural Reserves), with an English translation, plus many other leaflets on the area.

Sights
IGREJA DE JESUS

Setúbal's architectural stunner is the sand-coloured **Igreja de Jesus** (Praça Miguel Bombarda; admission free; ☽ 9am-1pm & 2-5.30pm Tue-Sun), one of the earliest examples of Manueline architecture, adorned with gargoyles and twirling turrets. The facade, however, is eclipsed by its interior of twisted pillars, like writhing snakes, that spiral upwards to the ceiling. Nebulous-seeming and organic, they are made from pink-tinged Arrábida marble. Around the altar, 18th-century blue-and-white geometric *azulejos* contrast strikingly with the curling arches of the roof.

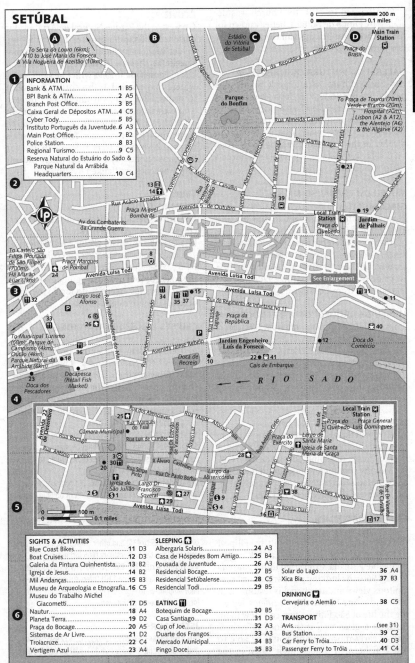

SETÚBAL

Constructed in 1491, the church was designed by Diogo de Boitaca, better known for his later work on Belém's fantastical Mosteiro dos Jerónimos (p120).

GALERIA DA PINTURA QUINHENTISTA

Art buffs should take a peek inside this **gallery** (Rua do Balneário Paula Borba; admission €1.10; ⏰ 9am-noon & 1.30-5.30pm Tue-Sat), dedicated to 16th-century painting. Star pieces include a set of 14 intricate panels that were once on display in the adjacent Igreja de Jesus. Also on display is the stained glass of the church's main window.

MUSEU DO TRABALHO MICHEL GIACOMETTI

How does the sardine get in the tin and 1001 other fishy mysteries are solved at this quirky yet often empty **museum** (Largo Defensores da República; admission €1.10; ⏰ 9.30am-6pm Tue-Sat), set in a cavernous former sardine-canning factory. In pride of place is an entire 1920s grocery, transported from Lisbon wholesale.

MUSEU DE ARQUEOLOGIA E ETNOGRAFIA

This small, rambling **museum** (Museum of Archaeology & Ethnography; ☎ 265 239 365; Av Luísa Todi 162; admission free; ⏰ 9am-12.30pm & 2-5.30pm Tue-Sat) showcases several intriguing pieces such as Roman mosaics and 19th-century devotional paintings on wood, showing invalids having holy visions.

PRAÇA DO BOCAGE

All streets in the pedestrianised old town seem to lead to this mosaic-cobbled **square**, presided over by the arcaded pink-and-white town hall. It's a sunny spot for a wander amid the palms and fountains, or for coffee and people-watching on one of the pavement terraces.

CASTELO SÃO FILIPE

Worth the 500m schlep uphill to the west, the **castle** (⏰ 7am-10pm) was built by Filipe I in 1590 to fend off an English attack on the invincible Armada. Converted into a *pousada* in the 1960s, its hulking ramparts afford precipitous views and its chapel is festooned in blue-and-white 18th-century *azulejos* depicting the life of São Filipe – you can view them through a glass wall if the door is locked. Arrive early morning and you'll be able to watch fishermen unload their catch in the harbour below.

Activities

Go west to the Parque Natural da Arrábida for chiselled cliffs, pine-brushed hills and long, golden beaches including windsurfer hot spot **Figueirinha**, sheltered **Galapos** and the stunning bay of **Portinho da Arrábida** with fine sand, azure waters and a small 17th-century fort built to protect the monks from Barbary pirates. There are some *quartos* (private rooms) right on the beach here. Buses from Setúbal run to Figueirinha in the summer. Alternatively, it's an easy 20-minute ferry ride – look out for dolphins on the way – to **Tróia**, where the soft sandy beaches are flanked by dunes.

Tours

CYCLING TOURS

For two-wheel adventures in the Setúbal area, check out the new and highly recommended **Blue Coast Bikes** (☎ 965 339 103; www.bluecoastbikes .com; Rua das Fontaínhas 82; 4hr bike hire €25, half-day tours €45-85; ⏰ 8am-8pm). Hire a bike to pedal along the coast, or join one of the guided tours (advance bookings essential) to local vineyards, beaches or native cork forests.

CRUISES & DOLPHIN-WATCHING

A highlight of any trip to Setúbal is the chance to spot resident bottlenose dolphins on a cruise of the Sado estuary. The frolicsome fellas show off their dorsal fins to a happy-snappy crowd; listen for their high-pitched clicking. Plenty of companies run half-day trips around the estuary (leaving from Doca do Comércio). Book ahead.

Nautur (☎ 265 532 914; www.nautur.com; Rua Praia da Saúde 15E) Offers cruises with lunch, starting on the estuary, then visiting Arrábida beach, returning to the river for dolphin-spotting (€44).

Mil Andanças (☎ 265 532 996, 265 532 979; www .mil-andancas.pt; Av Luísa Todi 121) Runs dolphin-spotting river tours (€30 per person).

Troiacruze (☎ 265 228 482; www.troiacruze.com; Rua das Barroças 34) Offers dolphin-spotting (five-hour trip per person €25 to €35) and other cruises, such as a sailing galleon along the Sado estuary (€65 incl meals).

Vertigem Azul (☎ 265 238 000; www.vertigemazul .com; Rua Praia da Saúde 11D) Offers sustainable three-hour dolphin-watching tours in the Sado estuary (€30). It's located 500m west of the centre.

JEEP TOURS

Mil Andanças (☎ 265 532 979, 265 532 996; www .mil-andancas.pt; Av Luísa Todi 121; half-day €30) Offers jeep tours in Arrábida.

Planeta Terra (☎ 919 471 871; www.planetaterra.pt; Praça General Luís Domingues 9) Jeep safaris in Arrábida include half-day options such as a nature and wine tour (€35) or the birdwatching- and culture-focused Storks Route (€35).

WALKING

The ecotourism company **Sistemas de Ar Livre** (SAL; ☎ 265 227 685; www.sal.pt; Av Manuel Maria Portela 40; per person Sat/Sun €6/7; ☼ 10am Sat & Sun Sep-Jun) arranges activities including three-hour guided walks in or around Setúbal.

WINE TOURS

Wine-lovers shouldn't miss the cellar tours of **José Maria da Fonseca** (☎ 212 198 940; www.jmf.pt; Rua José Augusto Coelho 11; €2.50 Mon-Fri, €3.50 Sat & Sun; ☼ 10am-12.15pm & 2-5.30pm), the oldest Portuguese producer of table wine and Moscatel de Setúbal, in nearby Vila Nogueira de Azeitão. The winery is now run by the sixth generation of the family. Ring ahead to arrange a visit to the house and museum. From Setúbal, buses leave frequently to Vila Nogueira de Azeitão (20 minutes).

The tourist office has a free useful leaflet, *Rota de Vinos da Costa Azul*, detailing all the wine producers in the area you can visit.

Sleeping
BUDGET

Parque de Campismo (☎ 265 238 318; Outão; sites per adult/tent/car €3.60/4.40/5.90) Situated 4km west of Setúbal, this green and shady site is right on the coast, perfect for those who want to snorkel or windsurf. It's accessible by regular bus (25 minutes).

Pousada de Juventude (☎ 265 534 431; setubal@ movijovem.pt; Largo José Afonso; dm/d €9/32; ☼ curfew 11pm-7am) Attached to the IPJ, this curved building is near the busy fishing harbour. The dorms are spick and span.

Residencial Todi (☎ 265 220 592; Av Luísa Todi 244; s/d with shared bathroom €20/30, with bathroom €25/35) If street noise doesn't affect your shut-eye, this is a decent cheapie on the main drag. The bare-bones rooms with TV and tiny bathrooms are tidy and clean. Reception is a hatch in the wall.

Casa de Hóspedes Bom Amigo (☎ 265 526 290; 2nd fl, Rua do Concelho 7; d with/without shower €30/25) Anyone who believes silence is golden is *bem-vindo* at this homely pad, where 'silêncio' signs rule out late-night shenanigans. Still, it's a bargain and the chintzy rooms – think lace doilies, plastic roses and baby pinks and blues – are immaculate.

MIDRANGE

Residencial Bocage (☎ 265 543 080; www.residencialbocage.pt; Rua de São Cristóvão 14; s/d incl breakfast €38/50; ✻) A recent makeover has brought the rooms at this central guest house bang up to date. Decorated inside with earthy hues and striped curtains, the renovated rooms sport parquet floors, comfy beds and squeaky-clean bathrooms.

Residencial Setúbalense (☎ 265 525 790; Rua Major Afonso Pala 17; s/d incl breakfast €39/49; ✻ 🖳) Tucked down a quiet backstreet, Setúbalense's old-style rooms are nothing flash but they're clean and comfy with wood furnishings and cable TV. Other bonuses include a hearty breakfast, free parking and internet access.

Albergaria Solaris (☎ 265 541 770; albergaria.solaris@ netc.pt; Praça Marquês de Pombal 12; s/d incl breakfast €50/60; ✻ 🖳) Overlooking a lively square, Solaris is a small and friendly option. Though rooms are plain and corporate, they're well kept and feature perks like cable TV, minibar and small balconies. Breakfast is above-par, with eggs and fresh fruit.

TOP END

Há Mar ao Luar (☎ 265 220 901; www.hamaraoluar.com; Alto S Filipe; apt/windmill €90/125) Romantic types love this peach-hued villa near the castle for its large, strikingly decorated apartments with plump beds, tranquil shaded terraces and sea views. Book ahead to stay in the windmill.

Pousada de São Filipe (☎ 265 550 070; recepcao .sfilipe@pousadas.pt; d €200; ✻) Perched high and mighty above Setúbal is this green-shuttered retreat, hidden inside the town's hilltop fortress. Expect vaulted corridors filled with antiques, spacious quarters and dramatic ocean panoramas.

Eating & Drinking

Head to the western end of Avenida Luísa Todi for lip-smacking, fresh-from-the-Atlantic seafood. Here you'll find a cluster of simple, buzzy restaurants with alfresco seating. Be sure to sample local specialities such as *caldeirada*, a hearty fish stew prepared in a covered brass pot, or *choco frito* washed down with sweet Moscatel de Setúbal wine.

Botequim de Bocage (☎ 265 534 077; Praça de Bocage 128; pastries €2-3) Pull up a chair at this cafe terrace on Setúbal's sunny main square. Light bites include quiche, pizza and sweets such as almond tart. It makes a good coffee pit stop.

Cup of Joe (Av Luísa Todi 558; ☯ 3pm-2am; snacks €3-5) A young crowd gathers at this funky cafe to chill on the decked terrace, or bag a spot on the sofa to watch MTV. As well as potent cappuccinos, you'll find toasties, crepes, bagels and other snacks.

Duarte dos Frangos (☎ 265 522 603; Av Luísa Todi 285; roast chicken for 1/2 people €5.50/8.50; ☯ lunch Fri-Wed, dinner Fri-Tue) This cosy spot just south of the old town whips up succulent roast chicken. The yellow-and-blue decor is cheery, but service can border on matronly.

Cervejaria o Alemão (☎ 965 798 764; Rua Dr Antóniu Joaquim Granjo 32; light meals €5.50-8; ☯ noon-2am Sun-Fri) Günther runs this totally cuckoo German enclave. His bar resembles a Black Forest clock shop, with walls smothered in antique timepieces and pocket watches. Stop by for Franziskaner beer, schnitzel and cheesy schlager music.

ourpick **Casa Santiago** (☎ 265 221 688; Av Luísa Todi 92; mains €7-12; lunch & dinner Mon-Sat) Wafts of fish sizzling on the grill will reel you into this local favourite, where the hungry lunchtime crowds feast on huge portions of *choco frito*, served with a squirt of lemon and mounds of fries, rice and salad. It's the best along the strip with a covered terrace and plenty of buzz.

Solar do Lago (☎ 265 238 847; Parque das Escolas 40; mains €7.50-15; ☯ lunch & dinner) This high-ceilinged restaurant exudes rustic charm with its chunky wooden tables and terracotta tiles. Tasty seafood dishes include garlicky *caldeirada* and grilled squid. A handful of outdoor tables overlook a quiet plaza.

Xica Bia (☎ 265 522 559; Av Luísa Todi 131; mains €9-12; ☯ lunch & dinner Mon-Sat) Fado shawls, wrought-iron chandeliers and copper pots jazz up this brick-vaulted restaurant. It serves market-fresh seafood alongside other flavoursome fare like herby *salsichas*.

Verde e Branco (☎ 265 526 546; Rua Maria Batista 33; mains around €9; ☯ lunch Tue-Sun Oct-Aug) Beside the Praça de Touros and famous for miles around, this traditional hot spot serves only grilled fish: simple and superb.

Pousada de São Filipe (☎ 218 442 001; mains €17-23; ☯ lunch & dinner) Great for special occasions, this smart restaurant has a top-of-the-world sea-view terrace. Service is attentive and food beautifully presented – try the monkfish stew or tender lamb.

For self-caterers there's the supermarket **Pingo Doce** (Av Luísa Todi 149; ☯ 8am-9pm) and the large mercado municipal market next door selling excellent fish and fresh produce.

Getting There & Away
BOAT
Car and passenger ferries to Tróia depart half-hourly to hourly every day (car and driver €5.70, passenger €1.15). Note that car ferries, cruises and passenger ferries all have different departure points.

BUS
Buses run between Setúbal and Lisbon's Praça de Espanha (€3.90, 45 to 60 minutes, at least hourly) – or from Cacilhas (€3.60, 50 minutes, every 15 minutes Monday to Friday, at least every two hours Saturday and Sunday). Services also run to Évora (€3.50, 1¾ hours) and Faro (€16.80, four hours, two daily), and to Santarém (€12.30, three hours 20 minutes, six daily Monday to Friday, three daily Saturday and Sunday).

TRAIN
From Lisbon's Terreiro do Paço terminal there are ferries to Barreiro station (€1.75, 30 minutes, every 10 to 20 minutes), from where there are hourly *suburbano* (suburban) trains to Setúbal (€1.70, 45 minutes, at least hourly).

Getting Around
Cycling is a great way to discover the coast at your own pace. Hire a bike from Blue Coast Bikes (p172).

Car-rental agencies include **Avis** (☎ 265 538 710; Av Luísa Todi 96).

PARQUE NATURAL DA ARRÁBIDA
Thickly green, hilly and edged by gleamingly clean, golden beaches and chiselled cliffs, the Arrábida Natural Park stretches along the southeastern coast of the Setúbal Peninsula from Setúbal to Sesimbra. Covering the 35km-long Serra da Arrábida mountain ridge, this is a protected area rich in Mediterranean plants, from olive, pistachio and strawberry to lavender, thyme and camomile, with attendant butterflies, beetles and birds (especially birds of prey such as eagles and kestrels) and even 70 types of seaweed. Its pine-brushed hills are also home to deer and wild boar.

In 2004 it suffered huge fire damage, when 700 hectares were scorched and Portugal had to appeal to the EU for assistance to put out blazes across the country, but there is still much to visit.

Local honey is delicious, especially that produced in the gardens of the whitewashed, red-roofed **Convento da Arrábida** (☎ 212 180 520), a 16th-century former monastery overlooking the sea just north of Portinho (best days to visit are Tuesday or Thursday, but call ahead). Another famous product is Azeitão ewe's cheese, with a characteristic flavour that owes much to lush Arrábida pastures and a variety of thistle used in the curdling process.

Public transport through the middle of the park is nonexistent; some buses serve the beach from July to September (around four daily to Figueirinha). Your best option is to rent a car or motorcycle, or take an organised trip by jeep and/or boat (p172). Be warned: parking is tricky near the beaches, even in the low season.

Headquarters for both this park and the **Reserva Natural do Estuário do Sado** (Sado Estuary Nature Reserve; ☎ 265 541 140; fax 265 541 155) are on Praça da República, Setúbal. They're not much use if you don't speak Portuguese – guided walks can be arranged here, but only in Portuguese. However, you can buy a useful map of the park (€4).

SESIMBRA
pop 37,570

Sesimbra has been reeling in nets for centuries and today the picture-perfect town also hooks day-tripping Lisboetas and holidaymakers. But the fishermen haven't hung up their salt-encrusted boots yet. As well as fine sands, turquoise waters and a Moorish castle slung high above the centre, Sesimbra offers mighty tasty seafood in its waterfront restaurants. So when you're done topping up the lobster tan, you can see lunch sizzling on an open grill.

Though it can be cheek by jowl on the beach in summer, the town has kept its low-key charm with narrow lanes lined with terracotta-roofed houses, outdoor cafes and a palm-fringed promenade for lazy ambles. Cruises, guided hikes and scuba-diving activities here include trips to Cabo Espichel, where dinosaurs once roamed. It's 30km southwest of Setúbal, sheltering under the Serra da Arrábida at the western edge of the beautiful Parque Natural da Arrábida.

Orientation & Information

The **bus station** (Av da Liberdade) is about 250m north of the seafront. Turn right when you reach the bottom of the *avenida* and pass the small 17th-century Forte de Santiago to the helpful **turismo** (☎ 212 288 540; www.mun-sesimbra.pt; Largo da Marinha 26; 9am-8pm Jun-Sep, 9am-12.30pm & 2-5.30pm Oct-May), set back slightly from the seafront.

Sights

CASTELO

For sweeping views over dale and coast, roam the snaking ramparts of the Moorish **castle** (admission free; 7am-8pm Mon-Wed, Fri & Sat, 7am-7pm Sun & Thu), rising 200m above Sesimbra. It was taken by Dom Afonso Henriques in the 12th century, retaken by the Moors, then snatched back by Christians under Dom Sancho I. The hilltop battlements glow gold when illuminated by night.

The ruins harbour the 18th-century, chalk-white **Igreja Santa Maria do Castelo**; step inside to admire its heavy gold altar and exquisite blue-and-white *azulejos*. The shady castle grounds are ideal for picnics.

The grandest castle on the sand is 17th-century **Fortaleza de Santiago** (admission free; 8am-8pm). Once part of Portugal's coastal defences and the summertime retreat of Portuguese kings, the fort is now open to the public and boasts fine views out to sea.

PORTO DE ABRIGO

Brightly painted boats bob on the water at **Porto de Abrigo**, 1km west of town, where grizzled fishermen unload, gut and auction their catch at the bustling fish market in the early morning and late afternoon.

Activities

Sesimbra is a great place to get into the outdoors with a backyard full of cliffs for climbing, clear water for diving, Atlantic waves for windsurfing and miles of unspoilt coastal trails for hiking and cycling. Adrenaline junkies get their thrills with vigorous pursuits from canyoning to rappelling.

Aquarama (☎ 965 263 157; Av dos Náufragos; adult/child €15/9; 10am-6pm) runs two to four trips per day to Cabo Espichel on a glass-bottomed partially submerged boat. Buy tickets at the office or on the boat.

Nautilus (☎ 212 281 769; www.nautilus-sub.com; Porto de Abrigo) is a PADI Dive Centre offering courses (including some for kids) and dives in the Sesimbra area. **Tridacna** (☎ 936 233 313; Rua da Casa Nova 2) is another reputable diving school.

Surf Clube de Sesimbra (☎ 210 875 139; www.scs.pt; Edifício Mar de Sesimbra, Rua Navegador Rodrigues Soromenho, Lote 1A, Loja 5) offers lessons and board hire. Or you can windsurf with **O Lagoa** (☎ 212 683 109; Lagoa de Albufeira).

Vertente Natural (☎ 210 848 919; www.vertente natural.com; Santana; mountain biking/diving/canoeing/climbing/canyoning from €20/20/18.50/18/70), an eco-aware, one-stop shop for adventure sports, offers excursions from trekking and canyoning to canoeing, diving and rappelling. It's headquartered a few kilometres northwest of town.

Festivals & Events

Cabo Espichel festival Spectacularly set, this festival celebrates an apparition of the Virgin during the 15th century; an image of the Virgin is carried through the parishes, ending at the Cape. It takes places on the last Sunday in September.

Senhor Jesus das Chagas In early May, a procession stops twice to bless the land and four times to bless the sea, carrying an image of Christ that is said to have appeared on the beach in the 16th century (usually kept in Misericórdia church).

Sleeping

Forte do Cavalo (☎ 212 288 559; www.mun-sesim bra.pt; sites per adult/tent/car €2.60/4.40/1.40) Camp under the pines at this hilltop municipal site, 1km west of town. It's a shady, quiet spot with sea views, an on-site restaurant and kids' playground.

Parque de Campismo de Valbom (☎ 212 687 545; sites per adult/tent/car €3.55/3.10/3.10; 🏊 ♿) Situated 5km north of Sesimbra in Cotovia, this leafy, well-equipped site has excellent facilities for families including a swimming pool, playground and minigolf. To get here from Sesimbra, take any Lisbon-bound bus.

Senhora Garcia (☎ 212 233 227; Travessa Xavier da Silva 1; s/d with shared bathroom €30/40) This place has well-advertised *quartos* that are Spartan and a tad dark. They are, however, cheap and right in the centre of town.

Quinta do Rio (☎ 212 189 343; www.estalagemquinta dorio.com; Alto das Vinhas; s/d €45/70; 🐕) Nestled among orange groves and vineyards, this converted *quinta* (estate), 7km from Setúbal, is a calm hideaway with light, spacious rooms and mountain views. Ideal for families, the country retreat offers horse riding, tennis and minigolf.

Residencial Náutico (☎ 212 233 233; www.residencial nautico.com; Av dos Combatentes 19; d incl breakfast from €80; 🏊) Set 500m uphill from the waterfront, this cheery guest house has airy tiled-floor doubles in citrus shades. The best have terraces that overlook Sesimbra's sun-bleached red rooftops.

Sesimbra Hotel & Spa (☎ 212 289 800; www.sesimbra hotelspa.com; Praça da Califórnia; s/d from €165/180; 🏊 🍴 💻) Entering the lobby at this beachside spa hotel is like stepping into a Hundertwasser painting with its vivid sea-themed mosaics. The slick rooms sport groovy pebble-and-marble bathrooms and balconies with ocean views. There's an infinity pool, a kids' club, gym and restaurant. Get scrubbed, rubbed and steamed in the spa, which pampers with treatments from Vichy showers to aroma facials.

Eating & Drinking

Sea-foodies are in heaven in Sesimbra, where what swims in the Atlantic in the morning lands on plates by midday. Check out the fish restaurants by the waterfront just east of the fort.

Isaías (☎ 914 574 373; Rua Coronel Barreto 2; mains around €6-8; 😋 lunch & dinner Mon-Sat) No menu, no frills, just *the* tastiest grilled fish and cheapest plonk in town at this *tasca* run with love and prowess by Senhor Isaías, his son Carlos and chip maven Maria. You might well share your table with a band of merry fishermen. Sole, sardines, swordfish – it's all uniformly delicious.

DINO PAWS

Step back in time 150 million years hunting for the footprints of dinosaurs on the craggy limestone cliffs just north of Cabo Espichel. The clearly visible imprints are near the small cove of Praia dos Lagosteiros. Rare and remarkably well preserved, the tracks date back to the Late Jurassic Age when this area was the stomping ground of four-legged, long-necked, herbivorous sauropods. Apparently, they were first discovered by fishermen in the 13th century who believed they were made by a giant mule that carried Our Lady of the Cape. Kids and dino fans should take a short ramble to see how many footprints they can find.

Rodízio (☎ 212 231 009; Largo da Marinha 13; mains €7-12; ◐ lunch & dinner Tue-Sun) Locals head to this friendly nosh spot for grilled seafood, particularly the all-you-can-eat *rodízio* feasts (€12.50). Save room for scrummy, cream-loaded desserts. There's outdoor seating.

Tony Bar (☎ 212 233 199; Largo de Bombaldes 19; mains €8-16; ◐ lunch & dinner) This smart restaurant on the square serves deliciously fresh fish. Menu standouts include the swordfish with tomatoes and succulent lobster. Portions are generous and service is attentive.

Ribamar (☎ 212 234 853; Av dos Náufragos 29; mains €15-20; ◐ lunch & dinner) One of Sesimbra's best, this sleek restaurant faces the beach. Feast away on well-cooked, artfully presented specialities such as Arrábida spider crab and monkfish in lobster sauce. Choosing a bottle from the arm-long wine list is quite a challenge.

For evening snacks and late-night drinks, mosey down Avenida dos Náufragos.

Getting There & Away
Buses leave from Lisbon's Praça de Espanha (€3.90, 60 to 90 minutes, at least 10 daily); from Setúbal (€3.15, 45 minutes, at least nine daily Monday to Saturday, six Sunday); and from Cacilhas (€3.40, around one hour, at least hourly). There are runs to Cabo Espichel (€2.30, 25 minutes, two daily) and more frequent runs to the village of Azóia (€2.30, 10 daily Monday to Saturday, six Sunday), about 3km before the cape.

AROUND SESIMBRA
Aldeia do Meco
Like nearby Alfarim, this tiny village 12km northwest of Sesimbra is famous for its seafood restaurants. Praia do Meco is an unspoilt sweep of golden sand, flanked by low-rise cliffs; try to catch one of its mesmerising sunsets.

SLEEPING & EATING
Campimeco (☎ 212 683 393; sites per adult/tent/car €3.55/3.10/3.10; 🖴 ♿) Right up on the clifftop and offering lots of shade, this large camp site is 3km from the village, above Praia das Bicas and close to several beaches. Its facilities include barbecue areas and a kids' playground.

Country House (☎ 212 685 001; www.countryhouse -meco.com; Rua Alto da Carona, Alfarim; d €50, 2-/4-person apt €65/80) In a wooded setting 1.4km north of the village, this big, fairly modern whitewashed house offers four spacious rooms (with coffeemakers and fridge) and three apartments, most with balconies. It's 2km from the beach and well signposted.

Bar do Peixe (☎ 212 684 732; Praia do Meco; mains €7-11; ◐ lunch & dinner Wed-Mon, daily Jul & Aug) This beachfront restaurant, north of Praia das Bicas, has a chilled vibe and a sea-facing terrace. It serves light bites and fresh seafood.

Other top seafood spots are scattered throughout the village, particularly on the main street Rua Central do Meco.

GETTING THERE & AWAY
Buses run from Sesimbra (€2.30, 25 minutes, four to eight daily).

Cabo Espichel
At strange, bleak Cabo Espichel, frighteningly tall cliffs plunge down into piercing blue sea, some met by swaths of beach. The only building on the cape is a huge church, the 18th-century Nossa Senhora do Cabo, flanked by two arms of desolately empty pilgrims' lodges.

It's easy to see why Wim Wenders used this windswept spot as a location when he was filming *A Lisbon Story*, with its lonely, brooding, outback atmosphere. It's worth your while trying to catch the Cabo Espichel festival if you are visiting in September (opposite).

Buses run direct from Sesimbra (€2.30, 25 minutes, two daily), more frequently terminating at the village of Azóia (€2.30, 10 daily Monday to Saturday, six Sunday), about 3km before the cape.

The Algarve

Love it or loathe it, it's easy to see the allure of the Algarve: breathtaking cliffs, golden sands, scalloped bays and long sandy islands. And let's not forget (as too many do) the stunning inland area, which boasts beautiful countryside and pretty castle towns.

Coastal Algarve, Portugal's premier holiday destination, sold its soul to tourism in the sixties and, it seems, it's still for sale... Just behind the beachscape, especially along the south coast, loom some monstrosities: huge conglomerations of bland, modern holiday villas and brash resorts. For some it's paradise, for others it's an abhorrence.

Whatever your view, there's no doubting the Algarve's personality. Underrated Faro boasts beautiful assets, especially the Parque Natural da Rio Formosa; Lagos is the Algarve's carnival queen; and elegant Tavira boasts a beautiful island beach. The rugged west coast is more relaxed; this enchanting place is more about nature and less about construction (for now, anyway). The laid-back villages of Sagres and Carrapateira attract surf- and sun-loving visitors.

But it's the inner Algarve that really shines. To bypass this area is to miss the Algarve proper: cork tree– and flower-covered hillsides, historic villages (many with restaurants serving intoxicating cuisine), walking tracks and birdlife. Highlights include stunning Silves above the banks of the Rio Arade, sleepy Alcoutim on the picture-perfect Rio Guadiana, and quaint Monchique. The region has some excellent walking opportunities and the Via Algarviana passes through the area.

If you're not keen on crowds or high-season prices, avoid hitting the coastal region in the European holiday season (July to mid-September). Spring and autumn are wonderful alternatives, especially for inland adventures.

HIGHLIGHTS

- Winding your way up the stunning – and secluded – west coast, after peering over the cliffs of **Cabo de São Vicente** (p226)
- Lounging in waters off untouched sand islands in the **Parque Natural da Ria Formosa** (p192)
- Strolling the historic streets and exploring the castle of **Silves** (p209)
- Finding your inner hedonist at the beaches and nightclubs of **Lagos** (p216)
- Unwinding in the spas of **Monchique** (p231) after hiking in the surrounding hills

★ Monchique
★ Lagos   ★ Silves
★ Cabo de São Vicente
★ Parque Natural da Ria Formosa

- POPULATION: 396,000
- AREA: 4995 SQ KM

History

British residents in Portugal are following a long tradition of settlement. Phoenicians came first and established trading posts some 3000 years ago, followed by the Carthaginians. Next came the industrious Romans, who, during their 400-year stay, grew wheat, barley and grapes and built roads and palaces. Check out the remains of Milreu (p189), near Faro.

Then came the Visigoths and, in 711, the North African Moors. They stayed 500 years, but later Christians obliterated what they could, leaving little trace of the era. Many place names come from this time, easily spotted by the article 'al' (eg Albufeira, Aljezur, Alcoutim). The Syrian Moors called the region in which they settled (east of Faro to Seville, Spain) 'al-Gharb al-Andalus' (western Andalucía), later known as 'Algarve'. Another Arabic legacy is the flat-roofed house, originally used to dry almonds, figs and corn, and to escape the night heat.

Trade, particularly in nuts and dried fruit, boomed, and Silves was the mighty Moorish capital, quite independent of the large Muslim emirate to the east.

The Reconquista (Christian reconquest) began in the early 12th century, with the wealthy Algarve as the ultimate goal. Though Dom Sancho I captured Silves and territories to the west in 1189, the Moors returned. Only in the first half of the 13th century did the Portuguese claw their way back for good.

Two centuries later the Algarve had its heyday. Prince Henry the Navigator chose the appropriately end-of-the-earth Sagres as the base for his school navigation, and had ships built and staffed in Lagos for the 15th-century exploration of Africa and Asia – seafaring triumphs that turned Portugal into a major imperial power.

The Algarve coastline is 155km long, with five regions: the leeward coast (Sotavento), from Vila Real de Santo António to Faro, largely fronted by a chain of sandy offshore *ilhas* (islands); the central coast, from Faro to Portimão, featuring the heaviest resort development; the increasingly rocky windward coast (or Barlavento), from Lagos to Sagres, culminating in the wind-scoured grandeur of the Cabo de São Vicente, Europe's southwesternmost corner; and the hilly, thickly green interior, which rises to two high mountain ranges, the Serra de Monchique and less-visited Serra do Caldeirão. The Costa do Ouro (Golden Coast) borders the Costa de Sagres (Bay of Sagres), while the Costa

Vicentina stretches north of here on the windy, wild rim of a national park.

Climate

Blessed with good weather, the Algarve has a mild winter and sunshine almost year-round, with 12/six hours' sunshine on a typical summer/winter day. Summertime temperatures average between 25°C and 30°C, sometimes reaching as high as 40°C. In January and February almond blossoms cover the countryside, while March is orange blossom time; April is the best month to visit to see wildflowers.

Dangers & Annoyances

This is Portugal's most touristed area, and petty theft is prevalent. Never leave valuables unattended in the car or on the beach.

Swimmers should beware of the temperamental coast conditions, especially on the west coast. This means dangerous ocean currents, strong winds and sometimes fog. Check the coloured flags: chequered means the beach is unattended, red means don't even dip your toe in, yellow means wade but don't swim, and green means go: wade, swim. Blue is an international symbol that means the beach is smashing – safe, clean and with good facilities.

Orientation

One of the clearest Algarve maps, including six town maps, is published by Freytag & Berndt (1:150,000).

Information

There are several Algarve-specific newspapers and magazines, including *Algarve Resident* (www.portugalresident.com) and the trilingual classified newspaper *Algarve 123* (www.algarve123.pt), which has informative features. *Essential Algarve* (www.essential-algarve.com) and *The Good Life* (www.vistaiberica.com) are leisure and lifestyle magazines.

Turismos (tourist offices) dole out information, maps and free leaflets, including the monthly *Algarve Guide*, which covers what's on, and the quarterly *Welcome to the Algarve*. Major towns have a monthly *Agenda Cultural* magazine. *Algarve Tourist Yellow Pages* is another freebie, with town maps and local information. Useful for up-to-date tips on local spots are privately produced *Free Maps*, often available at resorts, bars and shops.

THE ALGARVE

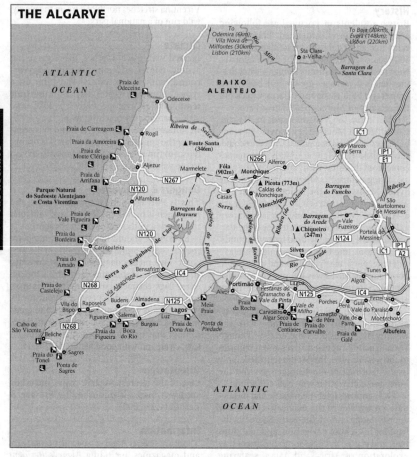

Far and away the best of many websites is www.visitalgarve.pt, with information on hidden beaches, upcoming events and festivals, activities and more.

Shopping

Look out for warm woollens, brassware and Moorish-influenced ceramics.

Buzzy local markets include the following:

Every Saturday Loulé, Olhão, São Brás de Alportel
Every Wednesday Quarteira
First Saturday Lagos
First Sunday Almancil, Azinhal, Portimão
First and third Tuesday Albufeira
Second Friday Monchique
Third Monday Aljezur, Silves
Third Thursday Alte

The Algarve for Children

The Algarve is one of the best places in Portugal for kids, with loads of attractions, family-friendly beaches and cultural activities. Try thrilling water parks (p206 and p208); a great zoo in Lagos (p219); and, at Silves, an imagination-firing castle (p209) and the Fábrica do Inglês (p212), with kinetic fountains and a playground. There are some excellent museums, too. In São Bras de Alportel there's a simple cork display in the Museu Etnográfico do Trajo Algarvio (p190), and in Portimão there's the wonderful new Museu de Portimão, which re-creates a former fish cannery (p213).

Many towns along the coast run boat trips (see individual sections), and many

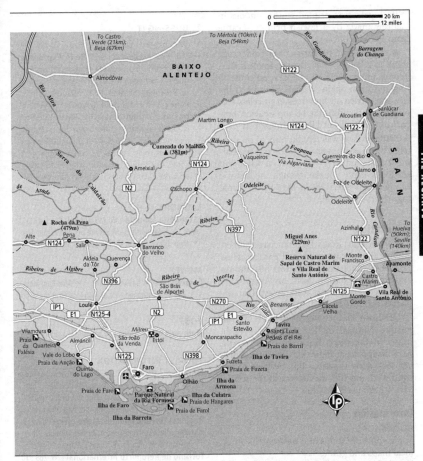

THE ALGARVE

have little trains. Horse riding is another option (see p206 and p205). See the Directory chapter (p495) for more details on keeping little ones happy.

FARO & THE LEEWARD COAST

FARO
pop 52,000

Algarve's capital has a more distinctly Portuguese feel than most resort towns. Many visitors only pass through, but it makes an enjoyable stopover. It has an attractive marina, well-maintained parks and plazas

and a historic old town full of pedestrian lanes and outdoor cafes. Its student population of 8000 ensures a happening nightlife, and its theatre scene is strong. Marvellously preserved medieval quarters harbour curious museums and churches (and a bone chapel). Nearby beaches, including the island sands of Ilha da Barreta, add to Faro's allure.

History

After the Phoenicians and Carthaginians, Faro boomed as the Roman port Ossonoba. During the Moorish occupation, it became the cultured capital of an 11th-century principality.

Afonso III took the town in 1249 – making it the last major Portuguese town to be recaptured from the Moors – and walled it.

THE ALGARVE

Portugal's first printed works – books in Hebrew made by a Jewish printer – came from Faro in 1487.

A city from 1540, Faro's brief golden age slunk to a halt in 1596, during Spanish rule. Troops under the Earl of Essex, en route to England from Spain in 1597, plundered the city and carried off hundreds of priceless theological works from the bishop's palace, now part of the Bodleian Library in Oxford.

Battered Faro was rebuilt, only to be shattered by an earthquake in 1722 and then almost flattened in 1755. Most of what you see today is post quake, though the historic centre largely survived. In 1834 Faro became the Algarve's capital.

Orientation

The town hub, Praça Dr Francisco Gomes, adjoins the marina and small garden called Jardim Manuel Bívar. The Eva bus station and the train station, both on Avenida da República, are a short walk away. The airport is about 6km west, off the N125.

Offshore is the widest stretch of the Parque Natural da Ria Formosa. While many of the near-shore sand bars along here disappear at high tide, two of the bigger sea-facing islands – Ilha de Faro to the southwest and Ilha da Culatra to the southeast – have good beaches.

Information

BOOKSHOPS

Some souvenir shops and newsagents stock local maps and guides.

Livraria Bertrand (☎ 289 828 147; Rua Dr Francisco Gomes 27) Faro's main bookshop. Ask for maps (they are not on display).

EMERGENCY & MEDICAL SERVICES

Faro district hospital (☎ 289 891 100; Rua Leão Penedo) Over 2km northeast of the centre.

Police station (☎ 289 822 022; Rua da Polícia de Segurança Pública 32)

Tourist support line (☎ 808 781 212)

INTERNET ACCESS

Café Aliança (Rua Dr Francisco Gomes; per hr €2.50; ☺ 10am-11.45pm)

Instituto Português da Juventude (IPJ; Rua da Polícia de Segurança Pública; ☺ 9am-8pm Mon-Fri) Free internet access; next to the Pousada da Juventude (p186).

BUSSING IT

Two big bus companies, **Eva** (☎ 289 899 760; www.eva-bus.com) and **Rede Expressos** (☎ 289 899 760; www.rede-expressos.pt) zip frequently between the Algarve and elsewhere in Portugal. Smaller lines include Caima, Renex and Frota Azul. If you're travelling by bus, consider buying the Passe Turístico (€23.30), available from major bus stations and good for three days of unlimited travel on most main routes between Lagos and Loulé. Bus service slows down considerably on weekends – particularly on Sunday.

LAUNDRY

Lavandaria Sólimpa (☎ 289 822 891; Rua Batista Lopes 30; 1-day wash-&-dry service per kg €2, min 4kg; ☺ 9am-1pm & 3-7pm Mon-Fri, 9am-1.30pm Sat)

MONEY

Cotacâmbios (Av da República 16; ☺ 9am-8pm Mon-Sun) A private exchange bureau. Also located at the airport.

POST

Main post office (Largo do Carmo) ATM available here.

TOURIST INFORMATION

Municipal Turismo (☎ 289 803 604; www.cm-faro.pt; Rua da Misericórdia 8; ☺ 9.30am-1pm & 2.30-5.30pm Mon-Fri) The chief information office run by the regional tourism administrative office: efficient, busy and helpful.

Regional Turismo administrative office (☎ 289 800 400; rtalgarve@rtalgarve.pt; Av 5 de Outubro 18; ☺ 8.30am-8pm Mon-Fri) Provides a map and leaflets.

Turismo de Aeroporto Internacional (☎ 289 818 582; ☺ 8am-11.30pm) Based at the airport; good for basic information on arrival.

TRAVEL AGENCIES

Abreu Tours (☎ 289 870 900; www.abreu.pt; Av da República 124; ☺ 9am-6pm Mon-Fri)

Tagus (☎ 289 805 483; www.taguseasy.pt; Av 5 de Outubro 24C; ☺ 9.30am-7pm Mon-Fri, 10am-1pm Sat) The best student-oriented agency. ISIC cards (with proof of student ID) cost €6.

Sights & Activities

CIDADE VELHA

Within medieval walls, the picturesque Cidade Velha (Old Town) consists of winding, peaceful cobbled streets and squares, reconstructed in a mélange of styles following successive batterings – first by marauding British and then two big earthquakes.

Enter through the neoclassical **Arco da Vila**, built by order of Bishop Francisco Gomes, Faro's answer to the Marquês de Pombal (see p36), who oversaw Faro's reconstruction after the 1755 earthquake. The top of the street opens into the orange tree–lined Largo da Sé, with the *câmara municipal* (town hall) on the left, the Paço Episcopal (Bishop's Palace) on the right and the ancient *sé* (cathedral) in front of you.

The **sé** (admission €3; ⏲ 10am-6pm Mon-Fri, 10am-1pm Sat) was completed in 1251, on what was probably the site of a Roman temple, then a Visigoth cathedral and then a Moorish mosque. Only the tower gate and several chapels remain of the original Romanesque-Gothic exterior – the rest was devoured in 1755. It was rebuilt in a polygamy of Gothic, Renaissance and baroque styles, with intense gilded carving alongside elaborate tilework inside. The baroque organ is worth noting. Climb up to the rooftop *miradouro* (lookout) for views across the pretty walled town to the sea. If you're lucky, you might see storks nesting in the bell towers. The cathedral buildings also house the **Museu Capitular**, with an assortment of sacred artwork (vestments, chalices, saint statues in glass boxes), and a small 18th-century shrine built of bones to remind you of your mortality.

Facing the cathedral is the 18th-century **Paço Episcopal** (no longer open to visitors), with a pointy roof and finished in multicoloured *azulejos* (hand-painted tiles), successor to the previous Episcopal dwelling trashed by British troops in 1596. At the southern end of the square is a small 15th-century town gate, the **Arco da Porta Nova**, leading to the ferry pier.

Next to the cathedral is the stately 16th-century **Convento de Nossa Senhora da Assunção**, now housing the Museu Municipal, also known by its former name, Museu Arqueológico (right).

From here you can leave the old town through the medieval **Arco de Repouso**, or Gate of Rest (apparently Afonso III, after taking Faro from the Moors, put his feet up and heard Mass nearby). Around the gateway are some of the town walls' oldest sections – Afonso III's improvements on the Moorish defences.

IGREJA DE NOSSA SENHORA DO CARMO & CAPELA DOS OSSOS

The twin-towered, baroque **Igreja de Nossa Senhora do Carmo** (Our Lady of Carmel; Largo do Carmo; ⏲ Mass times) was completed in 1719 under João V and paid for (and gilded to death inside) with Brazilian gold. The facade was completed after the 1755 earthquake.

A more ghoulish attraction lies behind the church. The 19th-century **Capela dos Ossos** (admission €1) was built from the bones and skulls of over 1000 monks as a blackly reverent reminder of earthly impermanence, and the ultimate in recycling. There's a similar chapel at Évora (p242).

OTHER CHURCHES

For more dazzling woodwork, head to the frenzied 18th-century baroque interior of the **Igreja de São Francisco** (Largo de São Francisco; ⏲ Mass 6.30pm), with tiles depicting the life of St Francis.

The 16th-century **Igreja de Misericórdia** (⏲ Mass 9am), opposite the Arco da Vila, has a remarkable Manueline portico, the only remnant of an earlier chapel to withstand the 1755 earthquake.

At the southern end of Largo do Carmo is the 16th-century **Igreja de São Pedro** (⏲ 10am-1pm & 3-5pm). The plain exterior hides an interesting interior of 18th-century *azulejos* and fine-carved woodwork.

MUSEU MUNICIPAL

Faro's domed and splendid 16th-century Renaissance Convento de Nossa Senhora da Assunção, in what was once the Jewish quarter, houses the **Museu Municipal** (☎ 289 897 400; Largo Dom Afonso III; adult/student €2/1; ⏲ 10am-6pm Tue-Fri, 10.30am-5pm Sat & Sun Oct-May, 11.30am-5.30pm Tue-Fri, 10am-7pm Sat & Sun Jun-Sep), formerly called the Museu Arqueológico. Highlights are the 3rd-century *Mosaic of the Ocean*, found in 1976 on a building site; 9th- to 13th-century domestic Islamic artefacts; and works by a notable Faro painter, Carlos Filipe Porfírio, depicting local legends. Ask for the informative pamphlets in English about some of the exhibits, including the interesting *Paths of the Roman Algarve*, an atmospheric display of large rocks and plinths, and *Walks Around the Historic Centre (The Inward Village)*.

MUSEU REGIONAL DO ALGARVE

Elements of old peasant life – such as a small fishing boat and a wooden water cart (used until the owner's death in 1974) – are on display at the **Museu Regional do Algarve** (☎ 289 827 610; Praça da Liberdade; admission €1.50; ⏲ 9am-12.30pm & 2-5.30pm Mon-Fri). There are also enigmatically

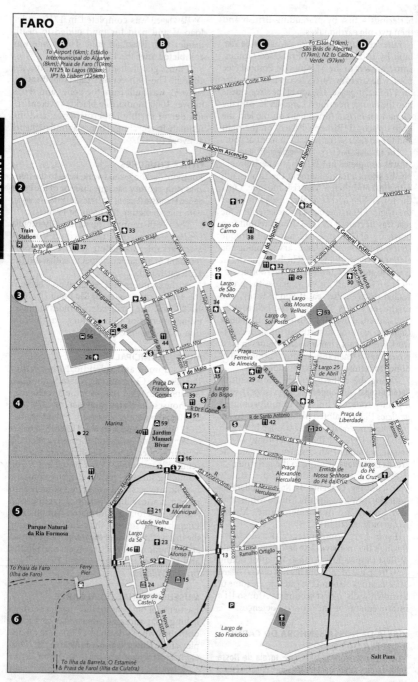

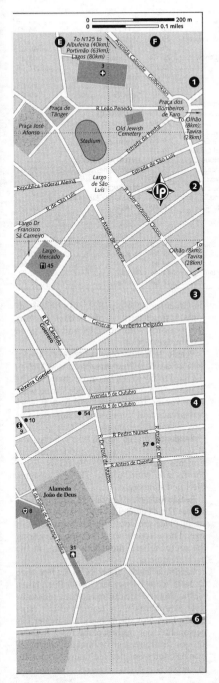

labelled displays of ceramics, fabrics and dioramas of typical interiors.

TREM MUNICIPAL GALLERY OF ART

In the old town, the interesting and attractively converted **Trem Gallery** (Rua do Trem; admission free; 🕙 10am-6pm Tue-Fri, 10.30am-5pm Sat & Sun) houses temporary exhibitions by known locals and international artists – painters, photographers, installation artists and sculptors. It's worth popping in here to see what's on.

BEACHES

The town's beach, **Praia de Faro**, with miles of sweeping sand, windsurfing operators and some cafes, is on the Ilha de Faro, 10km away. It's crammed in July and August. Take bus 14 or 16 from opposite the bus station (€1.55, half-hourly in summer, via the airport). Ferries go out to **Praia de Farol** (Ilha da Culatra) and **Ilha da Barreta** (aka Ilha Deserta; see p189), a stunning, remote and long narrow strip of sand just off the mainland. Here, there is a new environmentally friendly restaurant, **O Estaminé**, built on boardwalks and run by solar power.

Courses

You can have group and private lessons in Portuguese at **Centro de Linguas** (CIAL; ☎ 289 807 611; www.cial.pt; Rua Almeida Garrett 44). Prices are around €350 for a 30-hour intensive course.

Tours

Two companies under the umbrella name Formosamar, **Ria Formosa** and **Lands** (☎ 289 817 466, 967073846; www.formosamar.pt, www.lands .pt; Clube Naval, Faro Marina) are highly recommended outfits that work together to genuinely embrace and promote environmentally friendly, responsible tourism. Among their excellent tours are two-hour birdwatching trips around the Parque Natural da Rio Formosa (€25, minimum four people; see p192), guided cycling tours (€17, 2½ hours), and numerous guided walking tours inland from Faro. Accompanying guides may include a marine biologist and raptor specialist. Their boat trips take small boats (up to eight people) in some of the narrower channels in the lagoon (€20, two hours), providing participants with a close-to-nature experience.

THE ALGARVE

INFORMATION		
Abreu Tours.................................**1** A3	Museu Capitular...................(see 23)	Gengibre e Canela..................**43** C4
Café Aliança...........................(see 39)	Museu Municipal...................(see 15)	La Pizza..................................**44** B3
Cotacâmbios..............................**2** B4	Museu Regional do Algarve.....**20** D4	Mercado
Faro District Hospital **3** E1	Paço Episcopal.........................**21** B5	Municipal............................**45** E3
Instituto Português da	Ria Formosa and Lands............**22** A4	Mesa dos Mouros....................**46** B5
Juventude.........................(see 31)	Sé...**23** B5	Minipreço...............................**47** C4
Lavandaria Sólimpa....................**4** C3	Trem Gallery............................**24** B6	Restaurante A
Livraria Bertrand........................**5** C4		Taska..................................**48** C3
Main Post Office & ATM.............**6** B2	SLEEPING	Sushi Ya..................................**49** C3
Municipal Turismo.....................**7** B5	Hotel Dom Bernardo **25** C2	
Police Station.............................**8** E5	Hotel Eva................................**26** A4	DRINKING
Regional Turismo Administrative	Hotel Faro...............................**27** B4	A Capelinha.............................**50** B3
Office....................................**9** E4	Hotel Santa Maria....................**28** C4	Columbus Bar..........................**51** B4
Tagus......................................**10** E4	Pensão Residencial Central.......**29** C4	Taverna da Sé..........................**52** B5
	Pensão Residencial Oliveira.....**30** D3	
SIGHTS & ACTIVITIES	Pousada da Juventude.............**31** E5	ENTERTAINMENT
Arco da Porta Nova.................**11** B5	Residencial Adelaide................**32** C3	Teatro Lethes..........................**53** D3
Arco da Vila............................**12** B5	Residencial Algarve..................**33** B2	
Arco de Repouso **13** C5	Residencial Dandy...................**34** C3	TRANSPORT
Capela dos Ossos ....(see 17)	Residencial Oceano..................**35** C4	Automóvel Club de Portugal
Cidade Velha...........................**14** B5	São Filipe Hospedária...............**36** A2	(ACP)...................................**54** E4
Convento de Nossa Senhora da		Buses to Airport & Praia de
Assunção............................**15** B6	EATING	Faro....................................**55** B3
Igreja de Misericórdia **16** B5	Adega Nova............................**37** A3	Eva Bus Station.......................**56** A3
Igreja de Nossa Senhora do	Alisuper..................................**38** C2	Intersul (Eurolines) Ticket
Carmo................................**17** C2	Café Aliança............................**39** B4	Megasport............................**57** F4
Igreja de São Francisco............**18** C6	Café do Coreto.......................**40** B4	Office.................................(see 56)
Igreja de São Pedro..................**19** C3	Faro e Benfica Restaurante.......**41** A5	Renex.....................................**58** B3
	Gardy.....................................**42** C4	Taxi Rank................................**59** B4

Other short tours are available through **Animaris** (☎ 917 811 856; www.ilha-deserta.com); see p189.

Festivals & Events

Festival Internacional de Músic do Algarve (FIMA; Algarve Music Festival) Brings together an impressive range of international artists who perform in Faro's Teatro Lethes and the modern Teatro Figuras. Usually around April and May.

FolkFaro The city's big folk festival features lots of dance (with local and international folk groups), live music and street fests. It's held in late August over a week at various venues around town.

Feira de Santa Iria Held in late October, Faro's biggest traditional event honours St Irene with fairground rides, stalls and entertainment. It takes place in a temporary fairground to the northeast, by the municipal fire station.

Sleeping

Unless stated otherwise, rates for the budget options listed here do not include breakfast.

BUDGET

Pousada da Juventude (☎ 289 826 521; www.pousadasjuventude.pt; Rua da Polícia de Segurança Pública; dm incl breakfast €13, d with/without bathroom €38/30; reception ⏱ 24hr) Part of the Instituto Português

da Juventude (IPJ; p182), this hostel adjoins a small park. It offers basic visitors clean rooms with no frills and is a good ultrabudget option.

Pensão Residencial Oliveira (☎ 289 812 154; Rua Horta Machado 28; s/d/tr without bathroom from €20/30/45) It's hard to say which has more character: the house or the owner. This place's nine well-worn rooms are cluttered and have flowery bedspreads and floral odours. Some rooms have (leaning) balconies.

Residencial Oceano (☎ 289 805 591; Travessa Ivens 21; s/d/tr €37/47/61) This simple and friendly option has tidy rooms with tile floors. Some rooms are windowless. There's a steep, tile-lined stairway.

Pensão Residencial Central (☎ 289 807 291; Largo do Bispo 12; s/d €40/50) The eight rooms in this small place are cool and tiled and vary in size. Those rooms with balconies overlook the pretty square, though the rooms at the back are quieter.

Residencial Dandy (☎ 289 824 791; Rua Filipe Alistão 62; d with/without bathroom from €50/40) Pot plants, plastic flowers, African masks and museum-style paraphernalia are features of this rambling place. Not surprisingly, the owner has personality, too. The best of the 18 rooms have antique furniture, high ceilings and wrought-iron balconies. Smaller, tile-floored rooms are in the back.

MIDRANGE

Residencial Adelaide (☎ 289 802 383; www.adelaid eresidencial.com; Rua Cruz dos Mestres 7; s/d incl breakfast €45/50; 🔀) This modern and pleasant guest house is one of the best-value places in Faro. It has clean and light rooms, some with terraces and all with cable TV. A cheap laundry service is available.

São Filipe Hospedária (☎ /fax 289 824 182; www .guesthouse-saofilipe.com; Rua Infante Dom Henrique 55; s/d/tr €45/55/65; 🔀) The 11 rooms in this friendly place are small but shipshape and spotlessly clean. Great out-of-season deals available.

Residencial Algarve (☎ 289 895 700; www.residencial algarve.com; Rua Infante Dom Henrique 52; s/d/tr €55/70/85; 🅿 🖳) This efficiently run place has 36 bright, spick-'n-span motel-style rooms, some with balconies. Parking costs €5 per night.

TOP END

Hotel Dom Bernardo (☎ 289 889 800; www.hoteldomb ernardo.com; Rua General Teófilo da Trindade 20; d from €85; 🔀) Part of the Best Western chain, rooms here are spotless and modern, if a little 'a là eighties'. The brown decor is offset by the light large windows overlooking a busy street. Beware, though: it's a popular group option.

Hotel Santa Maria (☎ 289 898 080; www.jcr-group .com; Rua de Portugal, 17; s/d €92/113) Don't be fooled by the exterior of this plain place. Renovated in 2006, this modern motel-style option offers clean rooms with contemporary, stylish decor. Rooms are cramped, however. Low-season prices are significantly cheaper.

Hotel Faro (☎ 289 830 830; www.hotelfaro.pt; Praça Dr Francisco Gomes 2; s/d €127/147; 🔀) We're not sure how this modern cubist block made it past the town planners. But it has comfortable, sleek rooms with large beds and marble-filled bathrooms and flat-screen TV. The small top-floor bar-restaurant with terrace is great for a sunset cocktail.

Hotel Eva (☎ 289 001 000; www.tdhotels.pt; Av da República 1; s/d/ste €123/144/190; 🔀 🖳) This 134-room hotel has spacious, pleasant rooms. Those facing east have balconies and views. There's a rooftop swimming pool for more marina-gazing. An extra €10 gets you a more upmarket 'superior' room – worth it for the extra space, but there's no balcony.

Eating

BUDGET

Café Aliança (Rua Dr Francisco Gomes; snacks €1.50-10; 🕑 breakfast, lunch & dinner) Head for this dog-eared, old-fashioned place for coffee, snacks and people-watching from the tables spilling into the square.

Café do Coreto (Jardim Manuel Bívar; mains €3-8; 🕑 10am-11pm) Overlooking the marina and with pleasant outdoor seating area, this casual cafe is a popular place for afternoon tea or lighter bites and drinks. Hamburgers and pizzas cater to a tourist crowd.

Gardy (☎ 289 824 062; Rua de Santo António 16 & 33; mains €3-10; 🕑 8.30am-8.30pm Tue-Fri, 8.30am-7.30pm Sat & Mon) The place to head for your patisserie fix and *the* place to be seen. Has a wide variety of homemade specialities.

Faro's big, daily *mercado municipal* (municipal market) is in Largo Mercado. Two central supermarkets are **Alisuper** (Largo do Carmo) and small **Minipreço** (Praça Ferreira de Almeida 8).

MIDRANGE

Several midrange eateries are clustered around Praça Ferreira de Almeida. They serve similar fare in similar settings, mainly to tourists.

Adega Nova (☎ 289 813 433; Rua Francisco Barreto 24; mains €6-12; 🕑 lunch & dinner) This popular place buzzes with tourists and country charm. It has a lofty beamed ceiling, rustic cooking implements on display and long, communal tables and bench seats. The meat and fish dishes are reliable and service is efficient.

Restaurante A Taska (☎ 289 824 739; Rua do Alportel 38; mains €6-13; 🕑 lunch & dinner Mon-Sat) Popular with locals, this cosy, busy trattoria-style restaurant serves delicious regional food such as *xarém* (corn meal), and has daily specials on a blackboard.

La Pizza (☎ 289 806 023; Travessa José Coelho 13; mains €6.50-11; 🕑 lunch & dinner) On a narrow pedestrian lane near the bars (follow your nose), this small pizzeria whips up delicious tasty thin-crust pizzas plus other dishes. Plate of the day is around €6.

Gengibre e Canela (☎ 289 882 424; Travessa da Mota 10; buffet €7.50; 🕑 lunch Tue-Sat; 🅥) Give the taste-buds a break from meat and fish dishes, and veg out (literally) at this Zenlike vegetarian restaurant. The buffet changes daily; there may be vegetable lasagne, *feijoada* (bean casserole) and tofu dishes.

O Farol Cervejaria (☎ 289 813 394; www.ofarol cervejaria.com; Largo Dr Francisco Sá Carneiro; mains €9-13; 🕑 10.30am-1am Tue-Sun) This clean, modern blue-and white-themed beacon is located by the market complex and attracts many locals. It serves traditional Portuguese cuisine – fish and meat dishes – in a pleasant, airy environment. Generous and tasty plates of the day are around €9.

Faro e Benfica Restaurante (☎ 289 821 422; Marina; mains €9-20; ☺ lunch & dinner) Candlelit at night, with a marina-side setting, big open windows and a plant-filled terrace, this is a classy and romantic seafood choice.

Sushi Ya (☎ 289 821 196; Rua Cruz das Mestras 36; mains €9-20; ☺ dinner Tue-Sun) This small place is decked out in black, red and yellow, and there's a simple, airy courtyard. Serves decent sushi, sashimi and noodle dishes. A platter for two costs €42.

Mesa dos Mouros (☎ 966 784 536; Largo da Sé 10; mains €11-18; ☺ lunch & dinner Mon-Sun) With cosy indoor seating and a small outdoor terrace right by the cathedral, this place is blessed with high-quality cuisine (as confirmed both by us and the comments book!). Excellent choices include the seafood dishes or hearty gourmet-style mains such as rabbit with chestnuts.

Drinking

Faro's student-driven nightlife clusters around Rua do Prior and surrounding alleys, with bars and clubs open most days till late, though things pick up considerably on weekends.

A Capelinha (Largo da Madalena 8; ☺ 8pm-2am Tue-Sat; ▢) An attractive low-key bar, with outdoor tables scattered around a fountain. You'll also find good sangria and computers for web-browsing.

Taverna da Sé (Praça Afonso III 26; ☺ 11am-2am Mon-Sat) This small in-crowd taverna in the old town comes alive at night. There are some outdoor tables in its very quaint square.

Columbus Bar (Rua Dr Francisco Gomes) A popular place for drinks, parties, music and events.

Entertainment

Estádio Intermunicipal do Algarve (www.parquedidades-eim.pt, in Portuguese) This 30,000-seat, state-of-the-art stadium, built for Euro2004, is located at São João da Venda, 8km northwest of Faro. Here you can watch Faro's own team, SC Farense, and Loulé's Louletano.

Teatro Lethes (☎ 289 820 300; www.teatrolethes.pt; Rua Lethes) This tiny and exquisite Italianate theatre hosts drama, music and dance. Adapted into a theatre in 1874 (from a building dating to 1603), it was once the Jesuit Colégio de Santiago Maior and is now owned by the Portuguese Cruz Vermelha (Red Cross). Ask the tourist office for a list of what's on. Other

performances are often held in the modern Teatro Figuras.

Getting There & Away
AIR

Portugália and TAP (Air Portugal) provide multiple daily Lisbon–Faro flights (40 minutes), as well as Lisbon–Porto connections (45 minutes). For international services, see p505.

For flight inquiries call the **airport** (☎ general inquiries 289 800 800, flight information 289 800 801). An office of **TAP** (☎ 707 205 700; www.tap.pt) is located at the airport.

BUS

Buses arrive at and depart from the **Eva bus station** (☎ 289 899 760; www.eva-bus.com; Av da República 5). Express coaches run to Lisbon (€18, five hours, at least hourly, one night service). Opposite the bus station, **Renex** (☎ 289 812 980; ☺ 9-11.15am & 1.30-8pm Mon-Sat, 12.30-8pm Sun) sells tickets for the Renex Lisbon express bus (€17, eight daily).

Buses run to Vila Real de Santo António (€4.75, 1¾ hours, seven to 11 daily), via Tavira (€3, one hour, eight to 11 daily); and to Albufeira (€4, 1¼ hours, at least hourly), with some going on to Portimão (€5.75, 1½ hours, seven daily weekdays, two daily weekends) and Lagos (€5.35, 1¾ hours). For Sagres, change at Lagos. There are regular buses to Olhão (€1.75, 20 minutes, every 15 minutes weekdays) and buses to São Bras de Alportel (€3.35, 35 minutes, nine to 10 daily) via Estói (€2.60, 15 minutes).

Eva services run to Seville in Spain (€16, four hours, two daily) via Huelva (€12, 3½ hours). For further details, see p507.

CAR

The most direct route from Lisbon to Faro takes about five hours. A nonmotorway alternative is the often traffic-clogged N125. Tollways on this route cost around €18.

Major car-rental agencies are at the airport. Local heroes include **Auto Rent** (☎ free call 800 212 011, 289 818 580; www.autorent.pt), **Gerin** (☎ 289 889 445; www.guerin.pt) and **Auto Jardim** (☎ 289 800 881). Portugal's national auto club, **Automóvel Club de Portugal** (ACP; ☎ 289 898 950; www.acp.pt; Av 5 de Outubro 42; ☺ 9am-5pm Mon-Fri) has an office here.

Faro's easiest parking is in Largo de São Francisco (free).

TRAIN

There are trains from Lisbon (€18 to €19.50 – slightly more for 1st-class, three to 3¾ hours, five daily). You can also get to Porto (€38 to €47, six to eight hours, three daily), usually changing at Lisbon.

Trains also run daily to Albufeira (€2.50, 30 minutes, 11 daily); Vila Real de Santo António (€4.90, 1¼ hours, 10 daily) via Olhão (€1.10, 10 minutes); Lagos (€6.40, 1¾ hours, nine daily, fewer on weekends); and Loulé (€1.35, 20 minutes, 10 daily).

Getting Around

TO/FROM THE AIRPORT

Eva (☎ 289 899 740; www.eva-bus.com) buses 14 and 16 run to the bus station (€1.55, 20 minutes, half-hourly in summer, every couple of hours on weekends and in winter). From here it's an easy stroll to the centre.

A taxi into town costs about €10 (€11.50 after 10pm and on weekends).

BICYCLE

You can rent bikes (including kids' bikes) from **Megasport** (☎ /fax 289 393 044; www.megasport .pt; Rua Ataíde de Oliveira 39C; per day from €9; ⏱ 10am-1pm & 3-7.30pm Mon-Sat). It offers free delivery between Faro and Albufeira.

BOAT

From May to September, **Ilha Deserta** (Animaris; ☎ 917811856; www.ilha-deserta.com) operates five ferries a day to/from Ilha da Barreta (€5 one way). The same company also runs 2½-hour year-round boat trips (€20) through Parque Natural da Ria Formosa (p192). Boats leave from the pier next to Arco da Porta Nova. Taxi boats also operate from here, or from the nautical centre.

TAXI

Ring for a **taxi** (☎ 289 895 790) or find one at the taxi rank on Jardim Manuel Bívar.

MILREU & ESTÓI

The Roman ruins at Milreu make a pleasant brief excursion from Faro, 10km to the south. Several hundred metres up the road is the sleepy but attractive village of Estói. Estói boasts a charming derelict 18th-century rococo palace and gardens. Unfortunately, these were closed at time of research; the palace is being renovated into a posh *pousada* (inn).

Milreu Ruins

Set in beautiful countryside, **Milreu** (adult/under 25yr €2/1; ⏱ 9.30am-12.30pm & 2-6pm Tue-Sun Apr-Sep, 9.30am-12.30pm & 2-5pm Oct-Mar), the ruins of a grand Roman villa, provides a rare opportunity to get something of an insight into Roman life. The 1st-century AD ruins reveal the characteristic form of a peristyle villa, with a gallery of columns around a courtyard. In the surrounding rooms geometric motifs and friezes of fish were found, but these have now been removed for restoration.

THE ALGARVE

TOP 10 BEACHES OF THE ALGARVE

From small, secluded coves to wide stretches of rugged, dune-backed shores, the Algarve has enticing choices when it comes to sunbaking and wave frolicking. Our top 10, highly subjective picks:

- **Odeceixe** (p230) Small and pretty, with decent swimming and good surfing.
- **Meia Praia** (p219) Vast, popular and sceney, with options for water sports.
- **Ilha de Tavira** (p198) Crown jewel of the east-coast beaches, with a nudist area.
- **Ilha da Barreta** (Ilha Deserta; p185) – In the Parque Natural da Rio Formosa, this sandy island is accessed by boat through nature-filled lagoons.
- **Vale Figueira** (p230) Long stretch of wild coast that's little frequented.
- **Praia da Galé** (p206) Attractive cove beach with striking rock formations.
- **Praia da Bordeira** (p229) Wild untamed beauty (and surfing).
- **Praia da Arrifana** (p230) Lovely setting along a bay framed by black cliffs.
- **Alcoutim** (p234) Novel because it's a tiny riverside beach; it comes with life guard!
- **Praia de Dona Ana** (p219) Enchanting, golden rock formations make this cove beach a photographer's favourite.

Tantalising glimpses of the villa's former glory include the **fish mosaics** in the bathing chambers, which are located to the west of the villa's courtyard.

The remains of the bathing rooms include the **apodyterium**, or changing-room (note the arched niches and benches for clothes and postbath massage), and the **frigidarium**, which had a marble basin to hold cold water for cooling off postbath.

Other luxuries were underground heating and marble sculptures (now in Faro and Lagos museums).

To the right of the entrance is the site's **nymphaerium**, or water sanctuary, a temple devoted to the cult of water. The interior was once decorated with polychrome marble slabs and its exterior with fish mosaics. In the 3rd century the Visigoths converted it into a church, adding a baptismal font and a small mausoleum.

Eating

Several simple local cafes front Estói's small main square. Alternatively, next to the old Roman bridge at Milreu, **V Terra** (☎ 289 997 198; Sítio do Guelhim; mains €11-16; 🕑 lunch & dinner Mon-Fri, dinner Sat), a cheery spot, serves a range of international dishes. There's a sunny terrace on the top floor.

Getting There & Away

Buses run from Faro to Estói (€2.10, 20 minutes, four to 10 buses daily Monday to Friday), continuing to São Brás de Alportel. To get to Milreu, ask the bus from Faro to stop outside Estói.

SÃO BRÁS DE ALPORTEL
pop 10,030 / elev 210m

Seventeen kilometres north of Faro, this quiet country town provides a welcome break from the coast. São Brás de Alportel has few attractions in the town proper, but it's a pleasant place to stroll. There are some excellent DIY activities in the surrounds, including walks and a cork route. The town was a hot spot in the 19th-century heyday of cork and has stayed true to its agricultural roots. It lies in a valley in the olive-, carob-, fig- and almond-wooded Barrocal region, a lush limestone area sandwiched between the mountains and the sea.

Orientation & Information

The bus station is only a couple of blocks from the town centre, around Largo de São Sebastião.

The **turismo** (☎ 289 843 165; www.cm-sbras.pt; Largo de São Sebastião; 🕑 9.30am-1pm & 2-5.30pm Mon-Fri) distributes maps and information on the town and region. Ask for copies of the excellent *Percursos Pedestres* (Pedestrian Routes) or of the São Brás Municipality, including self-guided walking tours in the surrounding valleys and countryside.

Sights & Activities
MUSEU ETNOGRÁFICO DO TRAJO ALGARVIO

This constantly expanding and beautifully maintained **museum** (☎ 289 846 100; Rua Dr José Dias Sancho 61; admission €2; 🕑 10am-1pm & 2-5pm Mon-Fri, 2-5pm Sat, Sun & holidays), 200m east of the Largo (along the Tavira road, known as Rua Dr José Dias Sanco), is a labour of love of the curator and Friends of the Museum. It's housed in a former cork magnate's mansion (which is stunning in itself – note the original kitchen). The building displays a rambling collection of local costumes, while the garden has agricultural implements. In the stables, there is a fascinating exhibit, including video, of the town's once buoyant cork industry (see below). Very kid friendly.

OLD TOWN

For a fine stroll, follow Rua Gago Coutinho south from the Largo to the 16th-century **igreja matriz** (parish church), which has breezy views of orange groves and surrounding valleys. Nearby, below what was once a bishop's palace, is **Jardim da Verbena**, a pretty garden with an interesting fountain. Here, also, is the **municipal swimming pool** (☎ 289 841 243; 🕑 Jun-Sep) and children's playground.

The **Calçadinha de São Brás de Alportel** is an ancient road constructed in Roman times, possibly linking Faro (Ossonoba) with Beja (Pax Julia). It was used by mules and shepherds until the 19th century. You can wander along two branches – one is around 100m, the other half a kilometre. It starts alongside the municipal library.

At the time of research, the municipality was in the process of promoting a **cork trail**. The idea is excellent – to educate visitors about the cork industry – from the extraction of cork from the trees to its production, processes and use. The trail's practical aspects were still being arranged. While primarily intended as a guided tour for larger groups, it would make a fascinating and enjoyable DIY car tour into the Serra do Caldeirão. Ask at the tourist office for information and maps.

Sleeping

Residencial São Brás (☎ /fax 289 842 213; Rua Luís Bívar 27; s/d €30/50) Around the corner from the bus station (along the Loulé road), this delightful guest house is jam-packed with attractive antiques (note the gramophone), pretty *azulejos* and plants. The delightful owner is happy to show you the full range of eclectic rooms.

Estalagem Sequeira (☎ 289 843 444; fax 289 841 457; Rua Dr Evaristo Gago 9; s/d €35/55) Although the facade is uninspiring and the decor is a bit dated, the rooms here are decent, with a trim, modern design.

Pousada de São Brás (☎ 289 842 305; www.pousadas .pt; s/d from €158/170; 🖳 🅰) Located on a hilltop, this recently (re)renovated 1950s low-riser is Portugal's second-oldest *pousada*. It offers stylish, spacious rooms, most with terraces; a pool with a panoramic view; and a good restaurant. There's a 40% discount in price for those aged over 55 years.

Eating

Pastelaria Ervilha (Largo de São Sebastião 7; pastries from €1; 🕑 breakfast, lunch & dinner) In the centre of town and overlooking the square, this São Bras institution (it's been around since 1952) sells tasty homemade pastries, many made on the premises. It's one of the few places in Portugal you'll find a reasonable cappuccino.

Luís dos Frangos (☎ 289 842 635; Estrada de Tavira 8150; mains €4.50-8.50; 🕑 lunch & dinner Tue-Sun) Five hundred metres east of the Largo (beyond the museum), this is another local institution, and is famous for its grilled mains – particularly its chicken. It's a large, busy and friendly place.

Villa Velha (☎ 289 098 520; Rua Gago Coutinho 45; mains €13-17; 🕑 lunch & dinner Mon-Sat) Just south of the Largo, this warm and intimate restaurant has tasteful decor and a tasty menu of regional specialities such as *lombinho de porco aromatizado come ameixas* (pork with prunes; €14). Alternatively, opt for a drink in the small, modern lounge area in the front room.

Getting There & Away

Buses run from Faro (€3.55 via Estói, 30 minutes, four to 10 daily) and Loulé (€2.75, 25 minutes, five weekdays).

OLHÃO

pop 40,800

A short hop east of Faro, Olhão (ol-*yowng*) is the Algarve's biggest fishing port, with an active waterfront and pretty, bustling lanes in its old quarters. There aren't many sights, but the flat-roofed Moorish-influenced neighbourhoods and North African feel make it a pleasant place to wander. The town's excellent fish restaurants draw the crowds, as does the morning fish and vegetable **market** (Av 5 de Outubro), best visited on Saturday.

Olhão is also a springboard for Parque Natural da Ria Formosa's sandy islands, Culatra and Armona, plus the park's environmental centre in Quinta Marim.

Orientation

From the small **Eva bus station** (Rua General Humberto Delgado), turn right (west) or, from the train station, left (east) and it's a block to the town's main avenue, Avenida da República. Turn right, and then 300m down the *avenida* you will reach the parish church, at the edge of the central, pedestrianised shopping zone.

At the far side of this zone is waterfront Avenida 5 de Outubro. Here is the twin-domed market and to the left (east) is the town park, Jardim Patrão Joaquim Lopes.

Information

Centro de saúde (medical centre; ☎ 289 722 153; Rua Associação Chasfa)

Espaço Internet (Rua Teófilo Braga; 🕑 10am-10pm Mon-Fri, 10am-8pm Sat) Free internet access.

Police (☎ 289 710 770; Av 5 de Outubro 176)

Post office (☎ 289 700 600; Av da República) A block north of the parish church, opposite a bank with an ATM.

Turismo (☎ 289 713 936; Largo Sebastião Martins Mestre; 🕑 9.30am-7pm May-Sep, 9.30am-1pm & 2-5.30pm Mon-Fri) In the centre of the pedestrian zone; from the bus station bear right at the fork beside the parish church.

Sights & Activities

BAIRRO DOS PESCADORES

Just back from the market and park is the Bairro dos Pescadores (Fishermen's Quarter), a knot of whitewashed, cubical houses, often with tiled fronts and flat roofs. Narrow lanes thread through the *bairro* (neighbourhood), and there's a definite Moorish influence, probably a legacy of longstanding trade links with North Africa. Similar houses are found in Fuzeta (10km east).

THE ALGARVE

BEACHES

Fine beaches nearby, sparsely sprinkled with holiday chalets, include **Praia de Farol** (the best); **Praia de Hangares** on Ilha da Culatra; and **Praia de Armona** and **Praia de Fuzeta** on Ilha da Armona. There are ferries to both islands from the pier just east of Jardim Patrão Joaquim Lopes (opposite). You can also reach Armona from Fuzeta, and it is less busy, but narrower.

PARQUE NATURAL DA RIA FORMOSA

Ria Formosa Natural Park is mostly a lagoon system stretching for 60km along the Algarve coastline and encompassing 18,000 hectares, from west of Faro to Cacela Velha. It encloses a vast area of *sapal* (marsh), *salinas* (salt pans), creeks and dune islands. To the west there are several freshwater lakes, including those at Ludo and Quinta do Lago; the marshes are an important area for migrating and nesting birds. You can see a huge variety of wetland birds here, along with ducks, shorebirds, gulls and terns. This is the favoured nesting place of the little tern and rare purple gallinule (see boxed text, below).

You'll find some of the Algarve's quietest, biggest beaches on the sandbank *ilhas* of Faro, Culatra, Armona and Tavira. For transport there, see opposite.

The **park headquarters and visitor interpretation centre** (☎ 289 700 210; www.icn.pt; Quinta de Marim; ☺ 11am-1pm, 2-4pm) is 3km east of Olhão, within the 60-hectare Centro Educação Ambiental de Marim (Environmental Education Centre of Marim; commonly known as Quinta Marim). A 3km nature trail takes you through various ecosystems – dunes, saltmarshes, pine woodlands. Don't miss visiting the refuge kennels of the remarkable Portuguese water-dog. These were formerly fishermen's helpers – known for their distinctively matted waterproof coats, they helped herd the fish into nets.

To get to Quinta Marim, take a municipal bus to the camp site (200m before the visitor centre).

Festivals & Events

The **Festival do Marisco**, a seafood festival with food and folk music, fills the Jardim Patrão Joaquim Lopes during the second week of August.

Sleeping

There are few places to stay and they fill up quickly in summer.

Parque de Campismo de Fuzeta (☎ 289 793 459; fax 289 793 285; sites per adult/tent/car €3.20/2.50/3.40; ☺ year-round) This small, shady municipal site is on the waterfront in peaceful Fuzeta, about 10km east

---

WILDLIFE OF THE ALGARVE

Although not the most fauna-rich region of the country, the Algarve is home to some fascinating wildlife. The purple gallinule (aka the purple swamp-hen or sultan chicken) is one of Europe's rarest and most nattily turned-out birds – a large violet-blue water creature with red bill and legs. In Portugal it only nests in a patch of wetland spilling into the exclusive Quinta do Lago estate, at the western end of the Parque Natural da Ria Formosa, 12km west of Faro. Look for it near the lake at the estate's São Lourenço Nature Trail.

Another bizarre Algarve resident is the Mediterranean chameleon *(Chamaeleo chamaeleon)*, a 25cm-long reptile with independently moving eyes, a tongue longer than its body and skin that mimics its environment. It only started creeping around southern Portugal about 75 years ago, and is the only chameleon found in Europe, its habitat limited to Crete and the Iberian Peninsula. Your best chance of seeing this shy creature is on spring mornings in the Quinta Marim area of the Parque Natural da Ria Formosa or in Monte Gordo's conifer woods, now a protected habitat for the species.

Bird lovers should consider a trip to the Serra do Caldeirão foothills. Approximately 21km northwest of Loulé, the dramatic Rocha da Pena, a 479m-high limestone outcrop, is a classified site because of its rich flora and fauna. Orchids, narcissi and native cistus cover the slopes, where red foxes and Egyptian mongooses are common. Among many bird species seen here are the huge eagle owl, Bonelli's eagle and the buzzard.

There's a *centro ambiental* (environmental centre) in Pena village, and you can walk up to the top of Rocha itself (see p204).

of Olhão. You can go canoeing from the beach, and there are ferries to the offshore islands.

Camping Olhão (☎ 289 700 300; www.sbsi.pt; sites per adult/tent/car €4.10/3/3.30, family bungalow €45; 🐾) This large, well-equipped, shady camping ground is 2km east of Olhão. The upside: it's near Quinta Marim. The downside: it's by a train line and trains run between 6.45am and midnight. To get here, you can catch a municipal bus from the bus station.

Pensão Bela Vista (☎ 289 702 538; Rua Teófilo Braga 65; s/d €30/40/50) A short walk west of the *turismo*, this friendly and efficient place has clean, tiled rooms and a plant-filled courtyard. Some singles don't have a bathroom or external-facing window.

Pensão Bicuar (☎ 289 714 816; www.pension-bicuar .net; Rua Vasco da Gama 5; s €30-35, d €40-45, ste €65, all with shower) Run by a welcoming expat couple, this guest house offers a range of pleasant rooms, which feature old-fashioned details. There's also a kitchen for guests, a roof terrace and a book exchange. Head to the left (east) of the parish church.

Pensão Boémia (☎ /fax 289 714 513; Rua da Cerca 20; r €50; 🐾) This quaint spot has clean, colourful rooms with tile floors and small fridges. Several rooms have a terrace with views over the old town.

Eating
Avenida 5 de Outubro is lined with excellent seafood restaurants; this is also where you'll find the **market** (⊗ 7am-2pm Mon-Sat).

Aroma Cafetaria (Rua do Comércio 35; snacks €2-6; ⊗ 8.30am-7pm) A pleasant place for good coffee and snacks, and popular meeting place for the gals. Seats outside on the pedestrian street.

Horta Restaurante (☎ 289 714 215; Av 5 de Outubro 146; mains €7-11) A mix of locals and travellers crowd the outdoor tables at this popular seafood restaurant. Grilled fish, *cataplanas* (seafood stews) and *xerém* are tops here.

Catedral do Marisco (☎ 289 714 532; Av 5 de Outubro 10; mains for 2 people €12.50-18; ⊗ Wed-Sun) You can't miss the marine theme here, with a small lobster-filled pool and boat. Besides novelty, the real value is in the quality seafood dishes. Price for seafood is by weight.

Getting There & Away
BUS
Eva express buses run to Lisbon (€18, four hours, four to five daily), as do **Renex** (Av da República 101).

Buses run frequently from Faro (€1.65, 20 minutes), some continuing to the waterfront at Bairro dos Pescadores, and from Tavira (€2.40, 40 minutes).

TRAIN
Regular trains connect to Faro (€1.05, 10 minutes, every one to two hours) or east to Fuzeta (€1.05, 10 minutes) and Tavira (€1.65, 30 minutes).

Getting Around
Handy municipal buses run 'green and yellow routes' around town, including to the camp site and supermarkets.

Ferries run out to the *ilhas* from the pier at the eastern end of Jardim Patrão Joaquim Lopes. Boats run to Ilha da Armona (€2.90 return, 15 minutes, at least nine daily June to mid-September, hourly July and August, four daily mid-September to May); the last trip back from Armona in July and August leaves at 8.30pm.

Boats also go to Ilha da Culatra (€2.90, 30 minutes) and Praia de Farol (€3.20, one hour), with six daily from June to September and four daily from mid-September to May. Ferries also run from Fuzeta to the offshore islands.

TAVIRA
pop 12,600
Set on either side of the meandering Rio Gilão, Tavira is a charming town. The ruins of a hilltop castle, an old Roman bridge and a smattering of Gothic and Renaissance churches are among Tavira's historic attractions. Its enticing assortment of restaurants and guest houses make it an excellent base for exploring the Algarve's eastern section.

Tavira is ideal for wandering; the warren of cobblestone streets hides pretty, historic gardens and shady plazas. There's a small, active fishing port and a modern market. Only 3km from the coast, Tavira is the launching point to the stunning, unspoilt beaches of Ilha de Tavira.

History
The Roman settlement of Balsa was just down the road from Tavira, near Santa Luzia (3km west). The seven-arched bridge the Romans built at Tavira (which was then called Tabira) was an important link in the

TAVIRA

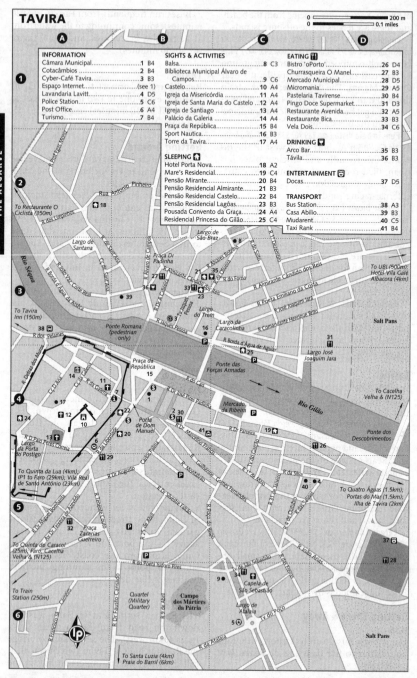

INFORMATION
Câmara Municipal	1	B4
Cotacâmbios	2	B4
Cyber-Café Tavira	3	B3
Espaço Internet	(see 1)	
Lavandaria Lavitt	4	D5
Police Station	5	C6
Post Office	6	A4
Turismo	7	B4

SIGHTS & ACTIVITIES
Balsa	8	C3
Biblioteca Municipal Álvaro de Campos	9	C6
Castelo	10	A4
Igreja da Misericórdia	11	A4
Igreja de Santa Maria do Castelo	12	A4
Igreja de Santiago	13	A4
Palácio da Galeria	14	A4
Praça da República	15	B4
Sport Nautica	16	B3
Torre da Tavira	17	A4

SLEEPING
Hotel Porta Nova	18	A2
Mare's Residencial	19	C4
Pensão Mirante	20	B4
Pensão Residencial Almirante	21	B3
Pensão Residencial Castelo	22	B4
Pensão Residencial Lagôas	23	B3
Pousada Convento da Graça	24	A4
Residencial Princesa do Gilão	25	C4

EATING
Bistro 'oPorto'	26	D4
Churrasqueira O Manel	27	B3
Mercado Municipal	28	D5
Micromania	29	A5
Pastelaria Tavirense	30	B4
Pingo Doce Supermarket	31	D3
Restaurante Avenida	32	A5
Restaurante Bica	33	B3
Vela Dois	34	C6

DRINKING
Arco Bar	35	B3
Távila	36	B3

ENTERTAINMENT
Docas	37	D5

TRANSPORT
Bus Station	38	A3
Casa Abilio	39	B3
Mudarent	40	C5
Taxi Rank	41	B4

0 _____ 200 m
0 _____ 0.1 miles

THE ALGARVE

route between Baesuris (Castro Marim) and Ossonoba (Faro).

In the 8th century, the Moors occupied Tavira. They built the castle, probably on the site of a Roman fortress, and two mosques. In 1242 Dom Paio Peres Correia reconquered the town. Those Moors who remained were segregated into the *mouraria* (segregated Moorish quarter) outside the town walls.

As the port closest to the Moroccan coast, Tavira became important during the Age of Discoveries (p33), serving as a base for Portuguese expeditions to North Africa, supplying provisions (especially salt, wine and dried fish) and a hospital. Its maritime trade also expanded, with exports of salted fish, almonds, figs and wine to northern Europe. By 1520 it had become the Algarve's most populated settlement and was raised to the rank of city.

Decline began in the early 17th century when the North African campaign was abandoned and the Rio Gilão became so silted up that large boats couldn't enter the port. Things got worse when the plague struck in 1645, followed by the 1755 earthquake.

After briefly producing carpets in the late 18th century, Tavira found a more stable income in its tuna fishing and canning industry, although this too declined in the 1950s when the tuna shoals sensibly moved elsewhere. Today, tourists have taken the place of fish as the biggest money-earners.

Orientation

The train station is on the southern edge of town, 1km from the centre. The bus station is a 200m walk west of central Praça da República.

Most of the town's shops and facilities are on the southern side of the river.

Information

EMERGENCY & MEDICAL SERVICES

Police station (☎ 281 322 022; Campo dos Mártires da Pátria)

Riverside International Medical Centre Clinic (☎ 289 997 742; 🕓 24 hr); Hotel Vila Galé Albacora (☎ 919 657 860; 🕓 9am-noon & 4-6pm Mon-Fri) A private clinic.

INTERNET ACCESS

Biblioteca Municipal Álvaro de Campos (Rua Comunidade Lusiada 21; 🕓 2-7.30pm Mon & Sat, 10am-7pm Tue-Fri) Free access.

Cyber-Café Tavira (Rua Jacques Pessoa 4; per hr €3; 🕓 10.30am-9pm Mon-Sat)

Espaço Internet (Câmara municipal, Praça da República; 🕓 9am-noon, 12.30-5pm & 5.30-9pm Mon-Fri, 10am-1pm Sat) Free access.

LAUNDRY

Lavandaria Lavitt (☎ 281 326 776; Rua das Salinas 6; 🕓 9am-6pm Mon-Fri, 9am-5pm Sat) Charges around €4 for up to 6kg wash and dry.

MONEY

Banks with ATMs lie around Praça da República and Rua da Liberdade.

Cotacâmbios (Rua Estácio da Veiga 21; 🕓 9am-8.30pm) Private exchange bureau.

POST

Post office (Rua da Liberdade)

TOURIST INFORMATION

Turismo (☎ 281 322 511; Rua da Galeria 9; 🕓 9.30am-1pm & 2.30-5.30pm Mon-Fri Sep-Jun, 9am-7pm Mon-Fri Jul & Aug) Provides local and some regional information and helps with accommodation.

Sights

IGREJA DA MISERICÓRDIA

Built in the 1540s, this **church** (Rua da Galeria; admission free; 🕓 10am-1pm Mon, Wed & Fri) is the Algarve's most important Renaissance monument, with a magnificent carved, arched doorway topped by statues of Nossa Senhora da Misericórdia, São Pedro and São Paulo. The church's stone mason, André Pilarte, also worked on Mosteiro dos Jerónimos (p120).

IGREJA DE SANTA MARIA DO CASTELO

This 13th-century **Gothic church** (admission free; 🕓 9.30am-noon & 2.30-5pm), beside the castle, was built on the site of a Moorish mosque but rebuilt by an Italian neoclassicist following earthquake damage 500 years later. However, the architect retained traces of the former church – namely the main doorway, two side chapels and Arabic-style windows in the clock tower.

Inside is a plaque marking the tomb of Dom Paio Peres Correia, who won the town back from the Moors, as well as those of the seven Christian knights whose murder by the Moors precipitated the final attack on Tavira.

CASTELO

What's left of the **castle** (admission free; 🕓 8am-5pm Mon-Fri, 9am-5pm Sat & Sun) is surrounded

THE ALGARVE

by a decidedly unwarlike, small and very appealing garden.

The defence might date back to Neolithic times; it was rebuilt by Phoenicians in the 8th century and later taken over by the Moors. What stands today dates mostly from 17th-century reconstruction. The restored octagonal tower offers fine views over Tavira. Note: don't set the kids free here – ramparts and steps are without railing.

OTHER OLD TOWN ATTRACTIONS

Enter the old town through the Porta de Dom Manuel (by the *turismo*), built in 1520 when Dom Manuel I made Tavira a city. Around the back, along Calçada da Galeria, the elegant **Palácio da Galeria** (gallery; admission free; 10am-12.30pm & 2-5.30pm Tue-Sat) holds occasional exhibitions.

Nearby, the **Torre da Tavira** (admission €4; 10am-5pm Mon-Sat), which was formerly the town's water tower (100m), now houses a camera obscura. A simple but ingenious object, the camera obscura reveals a 360-degree panoramic view of Tavira, its monuments and local events, in real time – all while you are stationary.

Just south of the castle is the whitewashed 17th-century **Igreja de Santiago** (Mass 8.30am Mon-Fri, 6pm Sun), built where a small mosque probably once stood. The area beside it was formerly the Praça da Vila, the old town square.

Downhill from here is the **Largo da Porta do Postigo**, at the site of another old town gate and the town's Moorish quarter.

PONTE ROMANA

This seven-arched **bridge** that loops away from Praça da República may pre-date the Romans but is so named because it linked the Roman road from Castro Marim to Tavira. The structure you see dates from a 17th-century reconstruction. The latest touch-up job was in 1989, after floods knocked down one of its pillars.

PRAÇA DA REPÚBLICA

For centuries, this sociable town **square** on the riverfront served as promenade and marketplace, where slaves were traded along with less ignominious commodities such as fish and fruit. The market moved to Jardim do Coreto in 1887 to improve hygiene, only moving again in 2000 to a new riverside location. The *mercado municipal* is held on Monday to Saturday mornings.

BIBLIOTECA MUNICIPAL ÁLVARO DE CAMPOS

Aspiring architects or anyone who appreciates modern design should pay a visit to Tavira's municipal **library** (10am-7pm Tue-Fri, 2-7.30pm Mon & Sat), which was originally the town prison. Architect João Luís Carrilho da Graça sympathetically and cleverly converted the former prison's facade and cells into a fabulous modern and harmonious cultural space. Opened in 2006, the building now houses books, exhibitions and computers.

SALT PANS & QUATRO ÁGUAS

You can walk 2km east along the river, past the fascinating, snowlike salt pans to Quatro Águas. The salt pans produce tiptop table salt and in summer attract feeding birds, including flamingos. As well as being the jumping-off point for Ilha de Tavira, the seaside hub of Quatro Águas has a couple of seafood restaurants and a former tuna-canning factory – now a luxury hotel, across the river.

For information on buses to Quatro Águas, see p199.

Activities

You can rent kayaks for a paddle along the river at **Sport Nautica** (281 324 943; Rua Jacques Pessoa 26; kayak per hr/day €6.50/25; 9.30am-1pm & 3.30-7.30pm Mon-Fri, to 6pm Sat).

Tours

Riosul (281 510 200; www.riosultravel.com; Rua Tristão Vaz Teixeira 15C, Monte Gordo) Has a pick-up point in Tavira for its jeep tours and Rio Guadiana cruises.

Tourist Train (40min tours €3; hourly 10am-7pm Sep-May, to 8pm Jun, to midnight Jul & Aug) Starts from Praça da Republica and visits the main sights.

Festivals & Events

You can't go wrong with free sardines, and that's what you'll get at Tavira's biggest festival, the **Festa de Cidade**, held on 23 to 24 June. Myrtle and paper flowers decorate the streets, and the dancing and festivities carry on till late.

Sleeping

BUDGET

Rates for the budget places listed here do not include breakfast.

Ilha de Tavira (☎ 281 321 709; www.campingta
vira.com; sites per 1/2 people incl tent €9/14; ☺ May-Oct)
Tavira's nearest camp site has a great location
on the island (see p198). It gets crowded and
noisy in the high season (mid-June to mid-
September). There's no car access.

Pensão Residencial Lagôas (☎ 281 322 252; Rua
Almirante Cândido dos Reis 24; s/d with shared bathroom
€20/30, s with bathroom €40, d with bathroom €40-50) A
long-standing favourite, Lagôas has endearing
owners and small (some cramped), spotless
rooms. There's a plant-filled courtyard and
good terrace views.

Pensão Residencial Almirante (☎ 281 322 163; Rua
Almirante Cândido dos Reis 51; d with shared bathroom from
€25) One block from the river, this cosy family
house is full of clutter, but its six rooms are
spacious and charmingly old-fashioned.

MIDRANGE

Pensão Mirante (☎ 281 322 255; Rua da Liberdad 83;
s/d €40/45) This centrally located option is the
oldest place in town…and it shows. The 11
rooms have high doors, well-worn decor and
a sense of history. Some rooms are windowless. Nevertheless, there's no dismissing
olde-world atmosphere.

Residencial Princesa do Gilão (☎ /fax 281 325 171;
Rua Borda d'Água de Aguiar 10; s/d/tr €45/55/65; ☒) This
eighties-style place on the river has tight but
neat rooms with identical decor. Go for a
room with a river view.

Pensão Residencial Castelo (☎ 281 320 790; fax 281
320 799; Rua da Liberdade 22; s/d/apt €50/70/70; ☒ ☒)
Castelo offers nicely furnished rooms with
spotless tile floors. Some also have balconies
and castle views. It has wheelchair access.

Mare's Residencial (☎ 281 325 815; www.resi
dencialmares.com; Rua Dr José Pires Padinha 134; s/d/tr
€70/80/90) Decorated with seafaring themes,
this 24-room riverside place has neat, if dated,
rooms – the best have balconies overlooking
the river (although the river can be a little
smelly at times).

TOP END

Hotel Vila Galé Albacora (☎ 281 380 800; www.vila
gale.pt; Quatro Águas; r from €99; ☒ ☒ ☒) Two
kilometres east, overlooking Ilha de Tavira,
this four-star 162-room hotel was converted
from a tuna-canning factory. It has cheerful
modern rooms with terraces, plus health club,
expansive pool and restaurant, and wheelchair
access. The hotel runs a private boat service
to Ilha da Tavira.

Quinta do Caracol (☎ 281 322 475; www.quin
tadocaracol.com; São Pedro; s/d €100/130; ☒ ☒)
Overlooking a large exotic garden (sadly
consumed by new development next door),
this 17th-century farmhouse has maintained
its patch of paradise. Each of its nine individual apartments is tastefully designed with
traditional Algarve furnishings and rustic
artwork; all have kitchenettes. It's child-
and pet-friendly.

Tavira Inn (Casa do Rio; ☎ 917 356 623; www.tavira
-inn.com; Rua Chefe António Afonso 39; d €110; ☒ ☒)
In a quirky spot nestled by the train bridge
and in front of the river, the five rooms in
this comfortable place have style…and effective double-glazed windows. There's lots of
terracotta, interesting artwork, a small saltwater swimming pool and a bar. Children
not permitted.

Hotel Porta Nova (☎ 281 329 700; www.hotelpor
tanova.com; Rua António Pinheiro; d €120; ☒ ☒ ☒) On
a hill in a newer area above town, this modern whitewashed hotel offers a predictably
safe, international hotel style experience,
complete with pleasant top-floor bar. Rooms
with fine views over the pool and town cost
another €25.

Quinta da Lua (☎ 281 961 070; www.quintadalua
.com.pt; Bernardinheiro, Santo Estevão; d/ste €165/185)
Set among orange groves 4km northwest of
Tavira, this peaceful place has eight bright,
airy, serene rooms set around a large, saltwater swimming pool. The extensive gardens
feature an outdoor lounge area.

Pousada Convento da Graça (☎ 281 329 040; www
.pousadas.pt; Rua Dom Paio Peres Correia; s/d €238/250;
☒ ☒) If you can get past the front door
(there's a bit of attitude here), you'll find an
elegant converted convent, with attractive
and plush rooms – some with modern four-
poster beds – a pool and pricey restaurant.

Eating

BUDGET

The old marketplace is now filled with cafes
and upmarket places.

Micromania (Rua da Liberdade; mains €3.50; ☺ 8am-
7pm Mon-Fri, 8am-2pm Sat) This small and new
casual spot serves bargain meals of the
day (€3.50) plus snacks. Frequented by the
working locals.

Churrasqueira O Manel (☎ 281 323 343; Rua
Dr António Cabreira 39; mains €5-8) Great takea-
way *frango no churrasco* (grilled chicken)
on offer.

THE ALGARVE

There are plenty of cafes in town and around the plaza. **Pastelaria Tavirense** (☎ 281 323 451; Rua Dr Marcelino Franco 17; ☺ 8am-midnight) serves up the nicest indoor experience and has the town's best pastries.

There's also a modern **mercado municipal** (☺ most stalls morning only) on the eastern edge of town, and a Pingo Doce Supermarket.

MIDRANGE & TOP END
Restaurante Bica (☎ 281 323 843; Rua Almirante Cândido dos Reis 24; mains €6-16; ☺ lunch & dinner) Deservedly popular. Here you can eat splendid food, such as fresh grilled fish, and down cheap bottles of decent Borba wine.

Restaurante O Ciclista (☎ 281 325 246; Rua João Vaz Corte Real; mains €5.50-10, fish per kg €25-50; ☺ lunch & dinner Tue-Sun) Just beyond the EN125 bridge, this isolated barnlike spot rightly stands out on its own. Seafood here is among the best in town (and don't the locals know it). It's packed to the gills serving up fresh catches by the kilo.

Restaurante Avenida (☎ 281 321 113; Av Dr Mateus Teixeira de Azevedo; mains €7-12.50; ☺ lunch & dinner Wed-Mon) This charming, well-maintained Portuguese place with fleur-de-lis table-cloths has an air of the sixties decade, and a loyal clientele. Good home-style Portuguese plates include the seafood risotto and the monk fish.

Portas do Mar (☎ 281 321 255; Quatro Águas; mains €8.50-17; ☺ lunch & dinner Wed-Sun) This place has attentive service and good seafood. Try the spaghetti with shrimp.

Bistro 'oPorto' (☎ 968991401; Rua de José Pires Padinha 180; mains €9.50-13.50; ☺ lunch & dinner Tue-Sat) An intimate bar and a pleasant riverside setting make for a pleasant time at this French-owned spot. The menu is varied – think samosas to *bacalhau* (dried salt-cod).

Vela Dois (☎ 281 323 661; €10; ☺ lunch & dinner Mon-Sat) Soccer fanatics will love this Benfica-crazy restaurant (which looks like it's raided the Benfica fan club premises). The other extraordinary thing is the ideal meals: €10 for all-you-can-eat (very good) seafood feast. This restaurant is opposite the main police station.

Quatro Águas (☎ 281 325 329; Quatro Águas; mains €12.50-22.50; ☺ lunch & dinner Tue-Thu) Next to Portas do Mar, there's a touristic hum at this pleasant restaurant, which serves good seafood, fish and meat dishes. You can eat inside or out.

Drinking & Entertainment
The main bar areas in town are along Rua Almirante Cândido dos Reis and Rua Poeta Emiliano da Costa, which have relaxing, welcoming places.

Arco Bar (Rua Almirante Cândido dos Reis 67; ☺ Tue-Sun) This small bar is fairly stock-standard (let's face it, there's not much choice), although fired-up by the owner and patrons. On Monday nights there's a drag show.

Távila (Praça Dr António Padinha 50) Overlooking a small tree-filled plaza, this low-key spot has outdoor tables, ideal for an afternoon or evening drink. Other similar cafe-bars are nearby.

For a higher-velocity night, the Docas, an extension of the *mercado municipal*, hosts a row of dancier, preclub bars that play music from hands-in-the-air house to African. The area buzzes in July and August.

After that, head to **UBI** (Rua Almirante Cândido dos Reis; ☺ midnight-6am Tue-Sun May-Sep, Sat & Sun Nov-Apr), an extraordinary nightclub, in a former tuna factory, that churns out music (and an experience) across umpteen sleek spaces and bar areas. Join the party with up to 3999 others.

Getting There & Around
Frequent buses (☎ 281 322 546) go to Faro (€3, one hour, 12/seven daily weekdays/weekends), via Olhão (€2.30), as well as to Vila Real (€2.85, 40 minutes). Express buses also go to Lisbon (€18, up to five hours) and Huelva (Spain; €11, two hours, twice daily), with connections to Seville (€15, three hours).

Trains run daily to Faro (€2.30, 40 minutes, nine daily) and Vila Real (€1.70, 35 minutes).

You can rent a car from **Mudarent** (☎ 281 326 815; Rua da Silva 18D).

Bike rental is available through the professional **Casa Abilio** (☎ 281 323 467; www.tavira -tours.com; Rua João Vaz Corte Real 21-23; per day around €7). Other options are **Sport Nautica** (☎ 281 324 943; Rua Jacques Pessoa 26; per day from €6) and **Balsa** (☎ 281 322 882; Rua Álvares Botelho 51; normal/tandem per day €6/12), although this place is more interesting for the ceramics shop and the friendly owner than the bike quality.

Taxis (☎ 281 321 544, 281 325 746) gather near the cinema on Rua Dr Marcelino Franco.

AROUND TAVIRA
Ilha de Tavira
Sandy islands (all part of the Parque Natural da Ria Formosa) stretch along the coast from Cacela Velha to just west of Faro, and

this is one of the finest. The huge beach at the island's eastern end, opposite Tavira, has water sports, a camp site (p197) and cafe-restaurants. Outside high season, the island feels wonderfully remote and empty, but during July and August it's busy. There's a designated nudies area. Be aware that mosquitoes may be a problem.

Heading west from the jetty, in 1km you'll reach the nudist area of the island. A few kilometres further west along the island is **Praia do Barril**, accessible by a miniature train that trundles over the mud flats from **Pedras d'el Rei**, a resort 4km southwest of Tavira. There are some eateries where the shuttle train stops, then sand, sand, sand as far as the eye can see.

GETTING THERE & AWAY

Ferries make the five-minute hop to the *ilha* (€1.80 return, from 8am to 8pm) from Quatro Águas, 2km southeast of Tavira. Times are subject to change – ask the crew when the last one runs! In July and August they usually run till midnight. From July to mid-September a boat normally runs direct from Tavira from around 8am (€1.80 return; 15 minutes) – ask at the *turismo* for details.

In addition to the local ferry, **Áqua-Taxis** (☎ 964515073, 917035207) operates 24 hours a day from July to mid-September, and until midnight from May to June. The fare from Quatro Águas/Tavira to the island is €6/15 for six people.

A bus goes to Quatro Águas from the Tavira bus station from July to mid-September (eight daily).

A taxi to Quatro Águas costs about €7. For Praia do Barril, take a bus from Tavira to Pedras d'el Rei (€1.80, 10 minutes, eight daily weekdays), from where the little train runs regularly to the beach from March to September. Out of high season the timetable depends on the operating company's mood.

Cacela Velha

Enchanting, small and cobbled, Cacela Velha is a huddle of whitewashed cottages edged with bright borders, and has a pocket-sized fort, orange and olive groves, and gardens blazing with colour. It's 12km east of Tavira, above a gorgeous stretch of sea, with one cafe-restaurant, splendid views and a meandering path down to the long, white beach.

GETTING THERE & AWAY

There's no direct bus from Tavira, but Cacela Velha is only 1km south of the N125 (2km before Vila Nova de Cacela; €1.75), which is on the Faro–Vila Real de Santo António bus route. Coming from Faro, there are two sign-posted turn-offs to Cacela Velha; the second is more direct.

VILA REAL DE SANTO ANTÓNIO
pop 11,000

Perched on the edge of wide Rio Guadiana, low-key but pleasant Vila Real de Santo António stares across at Spanish eyes. Its small pedestrian centre is architecturally

---

VIA ALGARVIANA & ECOVIA DO LITORAL

Covering some of the most beautiful scenery in the Algarve, the 300km Via Algarviana walking trail crosses the breadth of Portugal from Alcoutim to Cabo de São Vicente, taking in the wooded hillsides of the Serras de Caldeirão and Monchique. It takes about 14 days to walk the trail. You may hear the contrary, but a local resident who completed the trail in April 2008 assures us that the Via Algarviana is definitely *not* yet fully marked. New military maps are accurate. The best times to walk the trail are between March and May (note: hunting season takes place on Thursday and Sunday from October to June – *do not walk* on these days). For more information, visit www.viaalgarvia.org (run by environmental group Almargem) or www.algarveway.com (a private website run by enthusiasts).

Cyclists might like to check out Algarve Tourism's latest activity idea, the Ecovia do Litoral, a proposed cycling route that links Cabo de Sao Vicente and Sagres in the west to Vila Real de São António on the Spanish border. Spanning 214km, it encompasses both secondary roads and rural paths across 12 Algarve municipalities. The initiative was launched in 2008, but at the time of writing, several municipalities were still officially approving their patches – so to save a bumpy (or traffic-clogged) ride, check with tourism authorities before heading out.

impressive; in five months in 1774, the Marquês de Pombal stamped the town with his hallmark gleaming grid-pattern of streets (like Lisbon's Baixa district) after the town was destroyed by floods. From here you can head off to Castro Marim or on boat or biking trips along the Rio Guadiana (see boxed text, opposite).

Orientation & Information

The seafront Avenida da República is one of the town's two main thoroughfares; the other is the pedestrianised Rua Teófilo Braga, which leads straight from the seafront and past the main square, Praça Marquês de Pombal. The train station lies 350m north of the riverfront. Buses stop beyond the ferry terminal on Avenida da República.

Espaço Internet (Rua Candid do Reís; ☼ 9am-9pm) Free internet access.

Turismo (☎ 281 542 100; Rua Teófilo Braga; ☼ vary) A support office in high season to the principal *turismo* (☎ 281 544 495; Av Marginal) at Monte Gordo, 4km west

Sleeping

Parque de campismo (☎ 281 510 970; sites per adult/tent/car €3.40/2.35/3.75; ♿) Frequent buses go to this mammoth municipal camping ground outside the built-up Monte Gordo, 3km west of town. It has shade and beach access but gets jam-packed in summer. There are wheelchair facilities, a restaurant and bar.

Residência Matos Pereira (☎ 281 543 325; Rua Dr Sousa Martins 57; s/d €35/60) This family home-cum–guest house near the *turismo* has lace-filled, small rooms, some with a terrace.

Residência Baixa Mar (☎ 281 543 511; Rua Teófilo Braga 3; s/d €35/60) This decent guest house has a promising marble-lined entrance, but gives way to a mishmash of 10 clean but uninspiring rooms. The front one overlooks the river, while the back ones open onto a tiny, viewless terrace.

Villa Marquês (☎ 281 530 420; Rua Dr José Barão 61; s/d €55/60) Two streets back from the waterfront, near the bus station, this modern, yellow place has bright and airy – if a little cramped – rooms and a rooftop terrace with views over town. The best value in town.

Hotel Guadiana (☎ 281 511 482; www.hotelguadiana.com.pt; Av da República 94) Vila Real's grand old mansion was undergoing a facelift at the time of research, but should be worth checking out.

Eating

Snack-Bar Mira (☎ 281 544 773; Rua da Princesa 59; mains €6-10; ☼ lunch & dinner Mon-Sat) This cheery, pocket-sized place with blue-chequered tablecloths serves good-value daily dishes.

Snack-Bar Cuca (☎ 281 513 625; Rua Dr Sousa Martins 64; mains €7-12; ☼ lunch & dinner) Small, friendly and with outdoor tables, this is by far the elderly locals' choice for fish.

O Pescador (☎ 281 543 473; Av da República 48-51; mains €8-12; ☼ lunch & dinner Tue-Sun) 'The Fisherman' prides itself on its seafood theme (note the boat models), but this unpretentious place also serves up okay home-style meat and chicken meals.

Caves do Guadiana (☎ 281 544 498; Av da República 90; mains €8-12; ☼ lunch & dinner Fri-Wed, lunch Thu) With outdoor seats and a tiled interior, this posher, but ever-so-slightly tired waterfront 'Dame' pulls in the clients for her seafood dishes.

Getting There & Away

BOAT

Ferries cross the river border every 20 minutes to whitewashed Ayamonte; buy tickets (€1.45/4.50/0.80 per person/car/bike) from the waterfront office, open from 8.30am to 7pm Monday to Saturday, 9.15am to 5.40pm Sunday. Note: there is a one-hour time difference between Portugal and Spain.

BUS

Buses (☎ 281 511 807) run daily to Tavira (€2.80, 30 to 45 minutes, six to nine daily) and Faro (€4.75, 1½ hours), some going on to Lisbon (normal/express €17.50/18, 4¾ hours, four to five daily). A service runs to Mértola (€9.40, one hour, one daily). Regular buses go to Monte Gordo (€1.80, 10 minutes, eight to nine daily) and Huelva (Spain; €10, one hour, two daily), with connections on to Seville (€15 total from Vila Real de Santo António, 3½ hours).

TRAIN

Trains to Lagos (€8.25, 3½ hours, nine daily) require changes at Faro and/or Tunes. There are regular train services to Faro (€4.55, 1¼ hours, nine daily).

Getting Around

The nearest place to rent bikes is in Monte Gordo, from **Riosul** (☎ 281 510 200; www.riosultravel .com; Rua Tristão Vaz Teixeira 15C).

GLIDING ALONG THE GUADIANA

One of the major rivers of Portugal, the slow-flowing Rio Guadiana makes an idyllic setting for a bit of adventure. Several outfits offer excursions along the river, which forms the border with Spain for some 50km.

Riosul (☎ 281 510 200; www.riosultravel.com; Monte Gordo) runs small-scale trips from Vila Real de Santo António to Foz de Odeleite at least four times weekly in summer and twice-weekly the rest of the year. The trips cost €41, including lunch and a stop for a swim. Periodically, Riosul also offers night-time cruises, which cost €40 including dinner.

Lands – Turismo na Natureza (☎ 289 817 466; www.lands.pt; Clube Naval, Marina), based in Faro, arranges walks around the Rio Guadiana (€22) and, in the Parque Natural da Ria Formosa, trips in a traditional fishing boat (€25) and bird-spotting tours (€20).

The quiet back road along the river from Foz de Odeleite to Alcoutim (14km) is also popular with bikers. Along this scenic route are several villages worth visiting, including Álamo, with its Roman dam, and Guerreiros do Rio, with its small **Museu do Rio** (River Museum; ☎ 281 547 380; admission €1; 9am-12.30pm & 2-5.30pm Tue-Sat) about traditional river life.

CASTRO MARIM
pop 3100

Slumbering in the shadows of a 14th-century castle, Castro Marim is a picturesque village that sees few foreign visitors, but deserves to see more. It has a quaint, tree-shaded centre, several restaurants and impressive fortifications. These afford views across salt pans, the bridge to Spain, and the marshes of the Reserva Natural do Sapal de Castro Marim, which is famous for its flamingos. For walkers, there are some good trails around the area. It's 3km north of Vila Real de Santo António.

Information

Odiana (☎/fax 281 531 171; www.odiana.pt; Rua 25 de Abril; 9.30am-1pm & 2.30-6pm) This excellent organisation promotes the more rural Baixo (lower) Guadiana region. It distributes an excellent guide (published in 1999, but still useful in the most part) covering regional culture, with suggestions for day trips. A must for keen walkers are the recently published trail brochures of 19 signposted trails within the region. The trails encompass diverse areas from salt pans and river areas, to ruins and villages.

Turismo (☎ 281 531 232; Rua Dr José Alves Moreira; 9.30am-1pm & 2-5.30pm Mon-Fri) Below the castle in the village centre, the *turismo* sells the excellent *Algarve Guides* (€5).

Sights

CASTELO & AROUND

In the 13th century, Dom Afonso III built Castro Marim's **castle** (admission free; 9am-7pm Apr-Oct, 9am-5pm Nov-Mar) on the site of Roman and Moorish fortifications in a dramatic and strategic position for spying on the Spanish frontier. In 1319 it became the first headquar-

ters of the religious military order known as the Order of Christ, the new version of the Knights Templar (see boxed text, p318). Until they moved to Tomar in 1334, the soldiers of the Order of Christ used this castle to keep watch over the estuary of the Rio Guadiana and the border with Spain, where the Moors were still in power.

The grand stretch of ruins today, however, dates from the 17th century, when Dom João IV ordered the addition of vast ramparts. At the same time a smaller fort, the **Forte de São Sebastião**, was built on a nearby hilltop (currently closed to the public as it is being excavated, cleaned and repaired). Much of the area was destroyed in the 1755 earthquake, but the ruins of the main fort are still amazing.

Inside the wonderfully derelict castle walls is a 14th-century church, the **Igreja de Santiago**, where Henry the Navigator, also Grand Master of the Order of Christ, is said to have prayed. A fun spectacle, the **Feira Medieval**, takes place at the castle for four days encompassing the last weekend of August. There's a parade on the first (from the village to the castle) and last days (from the castle to the village, emulating medieval times). Food stalls with local products, music, fencing competitions and a medieval banquet create an authentic atmosphere.

RESERVA NATURAL DO SAPAL DE CASTRO MARIM E VILA REAL DE SANTO ANTÓNIO

Established in 1975, this nature reserve is Portugal's oldest, covering 20 sq km of marshland and salt pans bordering the Rio Guadiana north of Vila Real. Important winter visitors are greater flamingos, spoonbills and Caspian terns. In spring it's busy with white storks.

The park's **administrative office** (☎ 281 510 680; Sapal de Venta Moínhos; ◑ 9am-12.30pm & 2-5pm Mon-Fri) is 2km from Monte Francisco, a five-minute bus ride north of Castro Marim; get directions from the *turismo* at Castro Marim, as there are few signs.

There are two accommodation centres in the park but you need to book ahead, as they are used by groups (mainly scientists and schools). Birdwatchers should also head to Cerro do Bufo, 2km southwest of Castro Marim, another rewarding area for spotting the park's birdlife. There are three short walks in the area (all unsigned). Ask staff at the park office or at Castro Marim's *turismo* for details.

Getting There & Away

Buses from Vila Real run to Castro Marim (€1.70, eight minutes) and go on to Monte Francisco, a short distance north. Weekend buses are extremely limited.

THE CENTRAL COAST

LOULÉ

pop 21,700 / elev 160m

One of the Algarve's largest inland towns, and only 16km northwest of Faro, Loulé (*lo-lay*) is a reasonable base from which to explore the inland Algarve. A busy commercial centre, it is one of the fastest-growing towns in Portugal, as people use this as a base to work (or seek work) in the Algarve. Loulé has an attractive old quarter and Moorish castle ruins and its history spans back to the Romans. A few of Loulé's artisan traditions still survive; crafty folk toil away on wicker baskets, copperworks and embroidery at hole-in-the-wall workshops about town. Loulé's small university lends it some verve, as does its wild Carnaval (Carnival, just before Lent) and FestivalMed, an annual music festival.

Orientation

The bus station is about 250m north of the centre. The train station is 5km southwest (take any Quarteira-bound bus).

Information

Biblioteca Municipal de Loulé (Rua José Afonso; ◑ 2-7pm Mon, 9.30am-7pm Tue-Fri, Sat 2.30-6pm 15 Sep–15 Jun, Mon-Fri 16 Jun–14 Sep) Free internet in smart, new library.

Bookshop (Praça da República) Has an excellent range of guidebooks and maps.

Espaço Internet (☎ 289 417 348; Largo de São Francisco; per hr €2; ◑ 9am-noon Mon-Sat) Provides internet access.

Turismo (☎ 289 463 900; Av 25 de Abril; ◑ 9.30am-1pm, 2-5.30pm Mon-Sat Oct-Jun, 9.30-5.30pm Mon-Sat Jul-Sep) Get maps and the lowdown on Loulé at this friendly, efficient office.

Sights & Activities

The restored castle ruins house the **Museu Municipal** (☎ 289 400 600; Largo Dom Pedro I; admission €1.05; ◑ 9am-5.30pm Mon-Fri, 10am-2pm Sat), which currently contains beautifully presented fine fragments of Bronze Age and Roman ceramics (exhibitions change every few years). A glass floor exposes excavated Moorish ruins. The admission fee includes entry to a stretch of the castle walls and the **Cozinha Tradicional Algarvia** (◑ 9am-5.30pm Mon-Fri, 10am-2pm Sat), a re-creation of a traditional Algarve kitchen, featuring a cosy hearth, archaic implements and burnished copper.

Opposite the castle, **Nossa Senhora da Conceição** (closed for renovations at time of research) dates from the mid-17th century. It's a small chapel with a plain facade nonchalantly hiding a heavily decorated mid-18th-century interior with a magnificent gold altarpiece.

An environmental group, **Almargem** (☎ 289 412 959; www.almargem.org; admission free) welcomes visitors on its Sunday walks. Each year it tries to cover every area of the Algarve.

Festivals & Events

Carnaval Just before Lent, Loulé shimmies into something sexy and sequinned, with parades, tractor-drawn floats and lots of musical high jinks. Friday is the children's parade, and Sunday the big one. Held in late February or early March.

FestivalMed (www.festivalmed.com.pt) Having been an attraction since 2006, this is fast gaining a reputation as a quality world music festival, attracting the likes of Jamaican performer Jimmy Cliff and international performers. Held in late June.

Loulé International Jazz Festival (www.ccloule.com) In July the town dons jazz boots on selected evenings; international and Portuguese musicians jam in the convent and castle.

Nossa Senhora da Piedade Linked to ancient maternity rites, this *romaria* (religious festival) is the Algarve's most important. On Easter Sunday a 16th-century image of

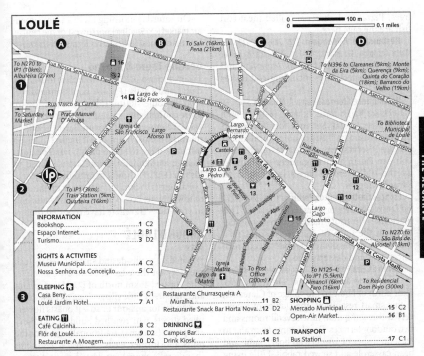

LOULÉ

INFORMATION	
Bookshop...1	C2
Espaço Internet......................................2	B1
Turismo..3	D2

SIGHTS & ACTIVITIES	
Museu Municipal....................................4	C2
Nossa Senhora da Conceição................5	C2

SLEEPING	
Casa Beny..6	C1
Loulé Jardim Hotel................................7	A1

EATING	
Café Calcinha..8	C2
Flôr de Loulé...9	D2
Restaurante A Moagem.......................10	D2

Restaurante Churrasqueira A	
Muralha...11	B2
Restaurante Snack Bar Horta Nova...12	B1

DRINKING	
Campus Bar...13	C2
Drink Kiosk..14	B1

SHOPPING	
Mercado Municipal..............................15	C2
Open-Air Market..................................16	B1

TRANSPORT	
Bus Station...17	C1

Our Lady of Pity (or Piety) is carried down from its hilltop chapel, 2km north of town, to the parish church. Two weeks later, a procession of devotees lines the steep route to the chapel to witness its return.

Sleeping

Residencial Dom Payo (☎ 289 414 422; Rua Dr Francisco Sá Carneiro; s/d incl breakfast €30/50; ⊠ ⊒) This orange-and-brown place is as basic as they come. There are no decorations nor frills, and mattresses are slightly saggy. But it's clean and cheap.

Quinta do Coração (☎ /fax 289 489 959; www .algarveparadise.com; Carrasqueiro; r incl breakfast €50, self-catering studio €55, 2-person cottage €59) Set into a wooded hill and surrounded by eucalypts, olive groves and cork trees, this remote, converted farmhouse is rustic-with-a-wee-touch-of-hippy paradise. The range of accommodation includes rooms, studios and a cottage with fireplace and kitchenette. There are hammocks and shade for relaxing, and great walks for the energetic (it's near Rocha da Pena; see p204). It's located in tiny Carrasqueiro, 18km north of Loulé, between Salir and Barranco do Velho.

Loulé Jardim Hotel (☎ 289 413 094; www.loulejardim hotel.com; Praça Manuel D'Arriaga; s/d/tr €56/73/94, d with terrace €78; ⊠ ⊒) A late-19th-century building with tasteful, airy and spacious rooms, this well-run place overlooks a pretty square. Book ahead for a terrace.

Casa Beny (☎ 289 417 702; casabeny@portugalmail .com; Travessa de São Domingos 13; s/d €60/65; ⊠) In a pleasantly restored mansion dating from 1897, Casa Beny offers nine peachy rooms, each with Brazilian hardwood floors, a touch of eighties-style pine, tall ceilings and French doors. The rooftop terrace has castle views.

Eating & Drinking

Café Calcinha (☎ 289 415 763; Praça da República 67; snacks €1-7; ☯ breakfast, lunch & dinner Mon-Sat) This traditional 1920s-style cafe has marble-topped tables and sidewalk tables. The statue outside depicts António Aleixo, an early 20th-century poet and former regular of the cafe.

Restaurante Snack Bar Horta Nova (☎ 289 462 429; Rua Major Manuel do Olival; mains €6-11; ☯ lunch & dinner Mon-Fri) Offers open-air, cheap-and-cheerful dining in a large, walled garden under orange trees. Pizzas and charcoal-grilled meat and fish are the rage here.

Restaurante A Moagem (☎ 289 412 629; Rua Maria Campina 37; mains €8-13; ☺ lunch & dinner Mon-Sat) Recommended for its Algarvian and Alentejana specialities including cod dishes to rabbit.

Restaurante Churrasqueira A Muralha (☎ 289 412 629; Rua Martim Moniz 41; mains €8-17; ☺ lunch Tue-Sat, dinner Mon-Sat) Set in a former bakery, quaint A Muralha is full of olde-world knick-knacks. It serves tasty regional favourites, and you can eat in a small garden, surrounded by the old ovens. There's live music on Saturday nights.

Espaços Gastronómicos Perdição (☎ 289 413 257; Rua Camilo Castelo Branco; mains €6-15; ☺ lunch) This place lives up to its name: gastronomic delights in the form of daily vegetarian, fish, meat and pasta dishes. Good selection of juices, teas and desserts, too.

Monte da Eira (☎ 289 438 129; Clareanes; mains €9-15; ☺ lunch & dinner Tue-Sat; lunch Sun) On Route 396, 5km north of Loulé in the village of Clareanes, is this smart restaurant, the stables of a converted threshing mill, now several rooms and two outdoor terraces. People come from afar to feast on dishes of *javali* (wild boar), lamb and bean casserole and stewed rabbit. Little living beasts (err, children) also welcome. To top it off, choose from one of 94 wines – *hic* – and that's the red alone. Vegetarians catered for, too.

Flôr de Loulé (☎ 289 416 581; Rua Ramalho Ortigão 1; buffet per kg €13; ☺ breakfast, lunch & dinner Mon-Sun;) Boasting a funky lime-green-and-white interior, this cafeteria-style *pastelaria* (pastry and cake shop) boasts a new self-service buffet, serving up meats and salads, plus cakes and ice-creams. It's air-conditioned.

Campus Bar (Praça da República; ☺ 11.30am-2pm & 8pm-2am Mon-Sat) Next to the university, this lively student bar is a good spot for a pick-up game of table soccer or hearing the latest uni gossip. Outdoor tables are set on the plaza.

Another good open-air spot is the drink kiosk on Largo de São Francisco.

Shopping

Loulé's excellent arts and crafts are made and sold in craft shops along Rua da Barbaca (behind the castle). Here, look out for O Senhor Ilídio António Marques; he is the last coppersmith to make *cataplana* dishes by hand. The *mercado municipal* also has traditional craft stalls.

On Saturday morning there's a large open-air **market** (☺ 9am-1pm) northwest of the centre, selling clothes, shoes, toys and souvenirs.

Getting There & Around

Trains to Faro (€1.35, 15 minutes, four to six daily) and Lagos (€5, 1½ hours, nine daily) stop at Loulé station (5km south of town). More conveniently, there are regular **bus** (☎ 289 416 655) connections to/from Faro (€2.60, 40 minutes, almost hourly), Albufeira (€3.55, 50 minutes, three to seven daily). For Portimão change at Albufeira. Express buses head to Lisbon (€18, 3¾ hours, four to five daily).

Parking is tricky in Loulé – park on the edge of town. Note, however, never leave valuables in your car – travellers have reported theft.

AROUND LOULÉ
Alte

Perched on a hillside and surrounded by lush greenery on the edge of Serra do Caldeirão, Alte, located 45km north of Loulé, is a quaint and very pretty little village. It's a pleasant place to wander for an hour or so – it boasts flower-filled streets, whitewashed buildings and several *fontes* (streams), traditionally used for the mills and former wells. Several *artesanatos* (handicrafts shops) are dotted around town. The helpful **tourist office-cum-'museum'** (☎ 289 478 666) is on the main road and provides a suggested walking 'tour'. There's a restaurant and a couple of cafes, and one large and incongruously modern hotel 1km out of town (you are better off staying in Carrasqueiro near Salir; see p203). In high season visitors are disgorged from buses for a quick-see experience.

Rocha da Pena

Just east of Alte and around 30km north of Loulé, Rocha da Pena, a limestone rock, sits just off the N124, within the Serra do Caldeirão, a beautiful protected area of undulating hills, cork trees and harsh scrubland. The area is renowned for its bird varieties. In some ways Rocha da Pena resembles Tabletop Mountain in Capetown, South Africa; the views from the top are superb. Keen walkers can do a 4.7km circuit walk up the mountain; drop into the tourism office at **Salir** (☎ 289 489 733; Rua José Viegas Guerreiro) or **Alte** (☎ 289 478 666). They have basic maps; follow road signs to the mountain. A return walk takes about two to three hours. Carry water and snacks; there's a small shop-cum-cafe at the base but no other

---

(OVER) EXPOSING THE ALGARVE

Tourism accounts for 80% of Portugal's GDP, and much of this comes from the Algarve. Tourists are not international travellers alone; local visitors comprise a large part of the industry, numerous Portuguese have homes in this sun-kissed region, and many foreigners have moved here permanently. The massive influx of visitors has led to ongoing heavy development in the region – large (mainly concrete) hotels, apartments, shops and restaurants – along much of the Algarve's southern coastline. Some say the Algarve's tourist industry provides work – albeit seasonal – to thousands of people, especially the young, thereby enhancing their skills and improving service mentality. But, others argue, the departure of Portuguese from their villages has devastating consequences – it is causing an irreversible disintegration of traditions and village life. Then there are the obvious environmental problems caused by heavy construction: destruction of coastal areas including cliffs and beaches, pressure on water resources, and the building of major roads. Construction is said to be controlled (although it is not always sensitive to its surrounds).

More recently, tourism authorities have focused their efforts on promoting special-interest activities beyond sun, surf and sand. While this is a positive initiative – with the region's spectacular nature, walks and inland villages being increasingly highlighted – it also means that thousands flock to visit some of the Algarve's 30-plus golf courses. These have a major environmental impact on an already stretched region, although some courses are adopting environmentally friendly maintenance practices.

Visitors to the Algarve should think carefully about their impact on this sensitive region: don't stick only to the coast – head inland (responsibly), be discriminate about which enterprises you select, and consider the impact of the type of activities you undertake.

The Algarve Tourism Board has some excellent publications to help you get off the beaten track. These include *Rotas: tours around the Algarve* (ideal for those with their own wheels) and *Trails in the Algarve*, which outlines some nature trails and cross-country day (or shorter) hikes. Both cost €5.

---

refreshment stops for miles. Note fire danger times – bushfires occur in this area, too. If in a car, it's worth heading on to the small, sleepy and attractive town of **Salir**. Although there's not much here, it's a pleasant, very genuine village.

Almancil

It's worth making a detour here, 13km northwest of Faro and about 6km south of Loulé, to visit the marvellous **Igreja de São Lourenço de Matos** (Church of St Lourenço; admission free). The church was built on the site of a ruined chapel after local people, while digging a well, had implored the saint for help and then struck water.

The resulting baroque masterpiece, which was built by fraternal master-team Antão and Manuel Borges, is smothered in *azulejos* – even the ceiling is covered in them. The walls depict scenes from the life of the saint. In the earthquake of 1755, only five tiles fell from the roof.

One of the Algarve's longest-established horse-riding centres is here too: **Paraíso dos Cavalos** (☎ 289 394 189; Almancil; rides per hr €20).

Buses between Albufeira (40 minutes) and Loulé (15 minutes) stop here.

ALBUFEIRA
pop 20,200

Once a scenic fishing village, Albufeira started to sell its soul to mass-market tourism in the 1960s. The problem is, it didn't stop. Today, much of the old town – and its pretty cobblestone streets and Moorish influences – is concealed by neon signs, English menu boards and rowdy bars. It is the destination for cheap package deals, mainly catering to Brits and Germans focused on cheap food, grog and fine nearby beaches. Tragically, travellers will be hard pushed to find any vestiges of the local fishing industry of former times, the few remaining fishermen's boats are now moored at the ultramodern new marina southwest of town.

Albufeira is useful for its handy transport links to good beaches, such as Praia da Galé to the west. To explore the pretty inland villages and the area's high-quality restaurants, you will need your own transport.

Orientation

Albufeira's old town lies below the N526 (Avenida dos Descobrimentos). Largo Engenheiro Duarte Pacheco is a central focal point, with bars and restaurants. Three kilometres to the town's east is 'the Strip', a road with more shops and bars, leading up from crowded Praia da Oura. The new marina 'tourist complex' is at the southwestern edge of town.

Sprawled to the north and east is modern-day Albufeira: the market, the bus station and main police station are almost 2km north. The train station is 6km north at Ferreiras.

Information

EMERGENCY & MEDICAL SERVICES

Centro de saúde (medical centre; ☎ 289 585 899; ☻ 24hr) Two kilometres north of the old town.

Clioura Clinic (☎ 289 579 790; ☻ 24hr) A private clinic in Montechoro.

GNR police station (☎ 289 590 790; Estrada Vale de Pedras) North of town, near the *mercado municipal*.

INTERNET ACCESS

Unnamed Internet (☎ 966 977 850; 2nd fl, Centro Comercial California, Rua Cândido dos Reis 1; per hr/10min €3.50/1; ☻ 10am-1pm & 2-10pm) Look for the Vodafone TMN sign.

TOURIST INFORMATION

Turismo (☎ 289 585 279; www.cm-albufeira.pt; Rua 5 de Outubro 8; ☻ 9.30am-5.30pm Mon-Sat) By a tunnel that leads to the beach. Helpful, multilingual staff.

Sights

BEACHES

Besides strolling cheek-to-jowl with others along the pedestrianised seafront, most come here for the beaches. **Praia do Peneco**, through the tunnel near the *turismo*, is usually head-to-toe with sun loungers. East and west of town are beautifully rugged coves and bays, though the nearest are heavily developed and often crowded. These include **Praia da Oura**, at the bottom of 'The Strip' 3km to the east; **Praia da Falésia**, a long beach 10km to the east; **Balaia** and **Olhos de Água**. Buses run to Olhos de Água (€1.60, 10 minutes, half-hourly), mostly continuing to Praia da Falésia (20 minutes).

One of the best beaches to the west, **Praia da Galé**, about 6km away, is long and sandy, not so crowded and is a centre for jet-skiing and water-skiing. It's easily accessible by car, but there's no direct bus service to this beach or the others en route, though local buses to Portimão do run along the main road about 2km above the beaches (get off at Vale de Parra).

MUSEUMS

If you have time to kill while waiting for transport, the **Museu Municipal de Arqueologia** (admission €1; ☻ 10.30am-4.30pm winter, 2-8pm summer) is worth a visit. Its four well-presented rooms showcase items excavated from the municipality and surrounds (such as the castle in the village of Paderne). Pieces date from the prehistoric era to the 16th century. A highlight is a beautifully complete Neolithic vase from 5000 BC. Ask for the English printouts. The museum is 50m east of the tourist office up the hill. The tiny **Museum of Sacred Art** (☻ 10am-4.30pm winter, 10am-noon summer) is housed in the beautifully restored 18th-century Chapel of San Sebastian. It has a stunning gold wood altar and exhibits sacred art from surrounding churches that survived the 1775 earthquake.

Activities

A plethora of agencies around town sell a variety of action-packed trips, from cruising on pirate ships to diving. Most boat trips leave from the marina.

Albufeira Riding Centre (☎ 289 542 870; Vale Navio Complex; 1hr ride €25) On the road to Vilamoura. Offers one- to three-hour horse rides for all ages and abilities.

Aqualand (☎ 282 320 230; www.aqualand.pt; Alcantarilha; adult/child €18.50/15; ☻ 10am-6pm Jun-Sep) Huge loop-the-loop slide and rapids.

Aqua Show (☎ 289 389 396; www.aquashowpark.com; adult/child €20/15; ☻ 10am-5.30pm May-Sep, to 7pm Aug) In Quarteira, 10km east of Albufeira, with flamingos, parrots and a wave pool.

Dolphins Driven (☎ 913 113 095; www.dolphines.pt; Marina de Albufeira) Offers three boat trips from Albufeira, between 2½ hours to full day trips including to caves, beaches, up the Arade river and to Ria Formosa.

Indigo Divers (☎ 289 587 013; www.indigo-divers .pt; Rua Alexandre Herculano 16) PADI qualified, and offers courses and dives (prices start at around €70).

Zoomarine (☎ 289 560 306; www.zoomarine.com; adult/child €23/14; ☻ 10am-7.30pm Jul–mid-Sep, to 6pm mid-May–Jun & mid-Sep–Oct, to 5pm Tue-Sun Jan–mid-May & Nov, closed Dec) Will satisfy all desires for aqua-entertainment, with huge swimming pools and slides, as well as lakes, an aquarium and dolphin shows. Located At Guia, 8km northwest of Albufeira.

Sleeping

Most places are associated with travel companies – bagging a room in July and August is impossible without reservations. Many places close in low season (November to March).

Pensão Restaurante Silva (☎ 289 512 669; Rua 5 de Outubro 23; d with shower €45) Rooms at this small-scale centrally located spot are clean, bright and nicely kept.

Pensão Dianamar Residencial (☎ 289 587 801; www.dianamar.com; Rua Latino Coelho 36; s/tr from €50/70, d €60-65, incl breakfast) If you must stay in Albufeira, this is one good reason to do so. Friendly, Scandinavian-run Dianamar has lovely details, with fresh flowers and attractive rooms, many with balconies and two with sea views. Excellent and oh-so-generous breakfasts and afternoon teas. Best to reserve ahead.

Vila São Vicente (☎ 289 583 700; www.sao-vicente-hotel.com; Largo Jacinto D'Ayet; s/d from €85/110; 🖾 🖳) This peaceful, classically decorated boutique-style hotel has handsome rooms with polished-wood floors. It's a welcome relief from the town's theme-park atmosphere.

Vila Joya (☎ 289 591 795; www.vilajoya.com; Apt 120 Praia da Galé; d €490-750, ste €810-2200) This luxury resort and spa located right on the beachfront near Praia da Galé, several kilometres from Albufeira (yet a planet away in every respect), is smart and plush, yet ultra-relaxing. The decor and surrounds have a touch of Africa and there are pool areas, lush green lawn, views of the sea and a Michelin-star restaurant (right).

Eating & Drinking

British breakfasts? Thai curries? Tasty? Bland? Albufeira has every conceivable range of dining options. The small market has fruits, vegetables and fish.

You can bar-hop (drink) your brain cells away in Albufeira. Bars throng the area around Largo Engenheiro Duarte Pacheco and nearby Rua Cândido dos Reis. Nearly all offer happy hours (at various times of the day), similar cocktails and open until at least 4am in summer.

Snack Bar Ti Rosa (Rua Diogo Cão; mains €1.50-6; 🕑 lunch & dinner) This tiny restaurant has many local admirers for its simple but tasty home-cooked meals (in the form of one or two daily specials).

Rei dos Frangos (☎ 289 512 981; Travessa dos Telheiros 4; mains €6-18; 🕑 lunch & dinner) It's true, the owner is indeed 'King of Chickens' – good, inexpensive grilled chicken is the dish of choice (the owner is known to launch into song, and might squawk out a few notes).

Restaurante Tipico A Ruína (☎ 289 512 094; Largo Cais Herculano; mains €15-20; 🕑 lunch daily, dinner Mon-Sat)

This restaurant has a romantic setting – with views – on Albufeira's highest point. You can choose the rooftop terrace, a pleasantly rustic setting or beachside tables. It offers good seafood and fish options.

our pick Vila Joya (☎ 289 591 795; Apt 120 Praia da Galé; mains €45-100; 🕑 lunch & dinner) Part of the renowned Vila Joya (left), this stylish haunt boasts a setting by the beach (near Praia da Galé), impeccable service, exquisite locally sourced produce and the best of the best cuisine from chef Dieter Koschina. This is one experience you'll want to linger over.

There is an **Alisuper supermarket** (🕑 8am-8.30pm) in the town centre, at the end of Rua Cândido dos Reis.

Getting There & Away

The **main bus station** (☎ 289 580 611; Rua dos Caliços) is 2km north of town. Passengers travelling to Lisbon can purchase tickets at a more conveniently located **bus shop** (☎ 289 588 122; Av da Liberdade); outside the bus shop, buses go to the main bus station (€1.10) every 30 minutes from 7am to 10pm.

Buses run to Lagos (€4.70, 65 to 75 minutes, 12 daily) via Portimão; Faro (€4, 40 minutes, hourly); Silves (€3.55, 40 minutes to one hour, seven daily); and Loulé (€3.55, 40 minutes, four to seven daily). There are two to Huelva in Spain (€13, 4¼ hours, via Faro), and on to Seville (€17, 5½ hours). Services shrink from October to May. Trains run to Lagos (€4.90, 1¼ hours, nine daily) and Faro (€2.50, 35 minutes, nine daily).

Getting Around

To reach the train station, take the *estação* (station) Eva bus (€2, 20 minutes, at least hourly 6.45am to 8pm) from the main bus station.

A major car-rental agency is **Auto Jardim** (☎ 289 580 500; www.auto-jardim.com; Edifício Brisa, Av da Liberdade). Another option with competitive rates is **Auto Prudente** (☎ 289 542 160; Estrada de Santa Eulália, Edifíccio Ondas do Mar, Loja 1).

CARVOEIRO

Carvoeiro is a cluster of whitewashed buildings rising up from tawny, gold and green cliffs and backed by hills. Shops, bars and restaurants rise steeply from the small arc of beach that is the focus of the town, and beyond lie hillsides full of sprawling holiday villas. This diminutive seaside resort 5km south of Lagoa is prettier and more laid-back than many of

THE ALGARVE

the bigger resorts, but its size means that it gets full to bursting in summer.

Orientation & Information

Buses from Lagoa stop right by the beach, beside the **turismo** (☎ 282 357 728; 9.30am-1.30pm & 2-5.30pm Fri-Mon, 9.30am-6pm Tue-Thu). The post office and several banks are on Rua dos Pescadores (the one-way road in from Lagoa).

Sights & Activities

The town's handkerchief-sized sandy beach, **Praia do Carvoeiro**, is surrounded by the steeply mounting town. About 1km east on the coastal road is the bay of **Algar Seco**, a favourite stop on the tour-bus itinerary thanks to its dramatic rock formations.

If you're looking for a stunning swimming spot, continue east along the main road, Estrada do Farol, to **Praia de Centianes**, where the secluded cliff-wrapped beach is almost as dramatic as Algar Seco. Buses heading for **Praia do Carvalho** (nine daily from Lagoa, via Carvoeiro) pass nearby – get off at Colina Sol Aparthotel, the Moorish-style clifftop hotel. The nearest water park is **Slide & Splash** (☎ 282 341 685; adult/child €18/14.50; www.slidesplash.com; Estrada Nacional 125), situated 2km west of Lagoa.

Golfers can be choosy: there's the **Pestana Gramacho** (☎ 282 340 900; www.pestanagolf.com) and **Pestana Vale da Pinta** (☎ 282 340 900; www.pestanagolf.com), both at Pestana Golf Resort; and the challenging **Vale de Milho** (☎ 282 358 502; www.valedemilhogolf.com) near Praia de Centianes, which is good for all levels.

The (German) family-run **Divers Cove** (☎ 282 356 594; www.diverscove.de; Quinta do Paraíso; 9am-7pm) diving centre provides equipment, dives and PADI certification (three-hour introduction €60, one-day discovery €120, two-day scuba diver/four-day open water €220/405).

Sleeping

In July and August it may be impossible to find a room, so reserve well ahead. Some guest houses may require a minimum three-night stay.

Casa von Baselli (☎ 282 357 159; Rua da Escola; s with shared bathroom €25, d €45-50) This homely, antique-filled five-room place is run by a delightful German owner. A shared terrace, high above the bay, is a highlight for breakfast and sunset.

O Castelo (☎ 282 357 416; www.ocastelo.net; Rua do Casino 59; d without view €46, d with view €53-74) To the west of the bay, behind the *turismo*, this welcoming guest house gets the sunrise view and offers spotless well-kept rooms with parquetry floors. Some rooms share a large terrace and sea views.

Casa Luiz (☎ 282 354 058; ww.casaluiz.com; Rampa da Nossa Senhora da Encarnação; d/studio €60/75) Unless you're serious about staying, it can be hard to get your foot in this well-situated place (the owner refers you to the internet), but once ensconced, you'll enjoy clean and modern rooms or studios (with kitchen) overlooking the beach.

Vivenda Brito (☎ 282 357 222; www.vivendabbrito.com; Beco dos Navegadores; r/studio/apt; €60/80/120;) In a quiet location, northeast of the beach, this place has a variety of attractive, modern sleeping options nestled around a small garden and pool.

Eating & Drinking

There is a handful of restaurants clustered near the beach and scattered along Estrada do Farol.

Marisqueira (☎ 282 358 695; Estrada do Farol; mains €6.50-14; lunch & dinner Mon-Sat) This local, well-established place has an outdoor terrace and is known for its seafood and grilled dishes.

Julio's Bar Restaurante (☎ 282 358 368; Vale do Milho; mains €11-15; dinner Mon-Sat) This smart but unstuffy place is set in a pretty garden around 2km east of town. Its clientele are mainly tourists who come here for the excellent international cuisine. Try the noisettes of lamb with mint (€16). Best to reserve.

Restaurante Boneca Bar (☎ 282 358 391; 10am-midnight) Hidden in the rock formations out at Algar Seco, this is a novel spot for a cocktail.

Getting There & Around

Buses run on weekdays from Portimão to Lagoa (€1.90, 20 minutes, half-hourly) and on to Carvoeiro (€2.75, 10 minutes).

You can rent scooters from **Motorent** (☎ 282 356 551; Rua do Barranco; 50/125cc per 3 days from €50/65) on the road back to Lagoa. Several car-rental agencies are also along this road. There's a taxi rank at the bottom of Estrada do Farol.

SILVES

pop 10,800

Silves is a gorgeous town of jumbling orange rooftops scattered above the banks of the Rio Arade. It boasts one of the best-preserved castles in the Algarve, attractive red-stone walls and winding sleepy backstreets on a hillside. After dark, not much happens around town (except one lively cafe), but it's the perfect place to base yourself if you're after a less hectic, non-coastal Algarvian pace. Around Silves, there are some lovely rural accommodation options. It's 15km northeast of Portimão.

History

The Rio Arade was long an important route into the interior for the Phoenicians, Greeks and Carthaginians, who wanted the copper and iron action in the southwest of the country. With the Moorish invasion from the 8th century, the town gained prominence due to its strategic hilltop, riverside site. From the mid-11th to the mid-13th centuries, Shelb (or Xelb), as it was then known, rivalled Lisbon in prosperity and influence: according to the 12th-century Arab geographer Idrisi, it had a population of 30,000, a port and shipyards, and 'attractive buildings and well-furnished bazaars'.

The town's downfall began in June 1189, when Dom Sancho I laid siege to it, supported by a horde of (mostly English) hooligan crusaders who had been persuaded (with the promise of loot) to pause in their journey to Jerusalem and give Sancho a hand. The Moors holed up inside their impregnable castle with their huge cisterns, but after three hot months of harassment they ran out of water and were forced to surrender. Sancho was all for mercy and honour, but the crusaders wanted the plunder they were promised, and stripped the Moors of their possessions (including the clothes on their backs) as they left, tortured those remaining and wrecked the town.

Two years later the Moors recaptured the town. It wasn't until 1249 that Christians gained control once and for all. But by then Silves was a shadow of its former self. The silting up of the river – which caused disease and stymied maritime trade – coupled with the growing importance of the Algarvian ports hastened the town's decline. Devastation in the 1755 earthquake seemed to seal its fate. But in the 19th century, local cork and dried-fruit industries revitalised Silves, hence the grand bourgeois architecture around town. Today tourism and agriculture are the town's lifeblood.

Orientation & Information

The centre of Silves is 2km north of the train station, a mostly downhill walk on a busy highway. Buses stop on the riverfront road at the bottom of town, crossing the Rio Arade on a modern bridge slightly upriver from a picturesque 13th-century version (for pedestrians only).

IT Connect (Rua Pintor Bernardo Marques; per hr €1.50; ☾ 10am-1.30pm, 3-7.30pm) Near the *turismo*, this place has reasonable machines.

Post office (Rua Samora Barros)

Turismo (☎ 282 442 255; www.cm-silves.pt; Rua 25 de Abril; ☾ 9.30am-1pm & 2-5.30pm Mon-Fri) It's a short climb from the bottom of town to the *turismo*.

Sights & Activities

CASTELO

The russet-coloured, Lego-like **castle** (☎ 282 445 624; adult/under 12yr €2.50/free; ☾ 9am-6.30pm mid-Jul–mid-Sep, 9am-6pm mid-Sep–mid-Jul) has great views over the town and surrounding countryside. It was restored in 1835 and you can walk around its chunky sandstone walls, which today enclose unfinished archaeological digs that reveal the site's Roman and pre-Roman past. In the north wall you can see a treason gate (an escape route through which turncoats would sometimes let the enemy in), typical of castles at the time. The Moorish occupation is recalled by a deep well and a rosy-coloured water cistern, 5m deep. Inside, the cistern's four vaults are supported by 10 columns. Probably built in the 11th century, by the 16th century the castle was abandoned. Recently the castle has been restored – an interior walkway has been constructed, as has a modern brick cafe. Tragically, this incongruous building is unsympathetic to the surrounds (what *were* they thinking?); it was yet to be opened at time of research. Prices may increase once it's finally completed.

SÉ & IGREJA DA MISERICÓRDIA

Just below the castle is the **sé** (cathedral; admission €1; ☾ 10am-noon & 3-7pm), built in 1189 on the site of an earlier mosque, then rebuilt after the 1249 Reconquista and subsequently restored several times following earthquake damage. The stark, fortresslike building has a multi-arched Portuguese-Gothic doorway,

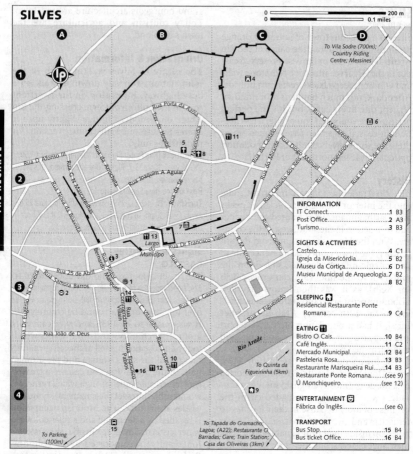

SILVES

0   200 m
0   0.1 miles

To Vila Sodre (700m);
Country Riding
Centre; Messines

INFORMATION	
IT Connect.............................**1**	B3
Post Office...........................**2**	A3
Turismo................................**3**	B3

SIGHTS & ACTIVITIES	
Castelo...............................**4**	C1
Igreja da Misericórdia..........**5**	B2
Museu da Cortiça.................**6**	D1
Museu Municipal de Arqueologia.**7**	B2
Sé.......................................**8**	B2

SLEEPING ☐	
Residencial Restaurante Ponte	
Romana.............................**9**	C4

EATING ☐	
Bistro O Cais.......................**10**	B4
Café Inglês..........................**11**	C2
Mercado Municipal..............**12**	B4
Pasteleria Rosa....................**13**	B3
Restaurante Marisqueira Rui..**14**	B3
Restaurante Ponte Romana....(see 9)	
Ú Monchiqueiro.................(see 12)	

ENTERTAINMENT ☐	
Fábrica do Inglês................(see 6)	

TRANSPORT	
Bus Stop.............................**15**	B4
Bus ticket Office.................**16**	B4

To Quinta da
Figueirinha (5km)

To Parking
(100m)

To Tapada do Gramacho;
Lagoa; (A22); Restaurante O.
Barradas; Gare; Train Station;
Casa das Oliveiras (3km)

and some original Gothic touches left, including the nave and aisles and a dramatically tall, strikingly simple interior. There are several fine tombs, one of which is purported to be of João do Rego, who helped to settle Madeira. Nearby is the 16th-century **Igreja da Misericórdia** (☑ 9am-1pm & 2-5pm), plain apart from its distinctive, fanciful Manueline doorway (not the main entrance) decorated with curious heads, pine cones, foliage and aquatic emblems.

MUSEU MUNICIPAL DE ARQUEOLOGIA
Just below the cathedral is the impressive, well laid-out **Museu Municipal de Arqueologia** (☎ 282 444 832, Rua das Portas de Loulé; adult/under 14yr €1.50/free; ☑ 9am-5.30pm Mon-Sat). In the centre is a well-preserved 4m-wide, 18m-deep Moorish

well surrounded by a spiral staircase, which was discovered during excavations. The find, together with other archaeological discoveries in the area, led to the establishment of the museum on this site; it shows prehistoric, Roman and Moorish antiquities. One wall is of glass, showing a section of the fort wall (also of Almohad origin) that is used to support the building.

MUSEU DA CORTIÇA
The **Museu da Cortiça** (Cork Museum; ☎ 282 440 480; www.fabrica-do-ingles.com; Rua Gregório Mascarenhas; adult/7-12yr €2/1; ☑ 9.30am-12.45pm & 2-6pm) is housed in the **Fábrica do Inglês** (English Factory; p212), a large complex unashamedly catering to large groups. The museum, with

the former workshops, machine room and press room, has good bilingual displays on the process and history of cork production. Cork was a major industry in Silves for 150 years, until the factory's closure in the mid-1990s, largely due to the silting-up of the Rio Arade.

HORSE RIDING & ANIMAL PARK

Country Riding Centre (www.countryridingcenter.com; Y daily), about 4km east of Silves, left off the road to Messines (it is signposted), offers hour-long to half-day hacks at all levels, with swimming opportunities as well.

Near São Bartolomeu de Messines, about 17km northwest, there's **Krazy World** (☎ 282 574 134; www.krazyworld.com; adult/child €15/8; Y 10am-6pm), an animal and crocodile park with minigolf, pony rides and two swimming pools.

Festivals & Events

Over one week each August (dates vary annually), Silves relives its past at its **Medieval Fair**. The town's important events and people are reconstructed, from Al Muthamid, the Governor of Silves, to the town being awarded its charter. Think bawdy costumes, dances, jesters, feasts…almost anything goes, as long as it evokes life in the 11th to 13th centuries.

Sleeping

BUDGET & MIDRANGE

Residencial Restaurante Ponte Romana (☎ 282 443 275; Horta da Cruz; s/d €20/30) At the end of the old bridge on the other side of the river from town, this long-standing guest house has clean rooms with frilly bedspreads. Some of the rooms have idyllic views across the river to the castle. There's a cheery restaurant, too (right). To get here by car, drive over the larger bridge towards Portimão and take the first right (west) after the big bridge.

Vila Sodre (☎ /fax 282 443 441; Estrada de Messines; s incl breakfast €45, d €50-60; ✂ ☎) This modern blue-and-white villa is 1.4km east of the newer bridge. It's good value, with smart, if faded, rooms that overlook orange orchards. The highlight is the owner – ask to see his extraordinary wine collection.

Quinta do Rio (☎ /fax 282 445 528; d incl breakfast €58) This charming restored farmhouse, set among orange groves and rolling hills, has six plain and pleasant rooms. Some have their own small terrace. To get here, head 5.5km northeast (en route to São Bartolomeu de Messines) to Sítio São Estevão.

Casa das Oliveiras (282 342 115; www.casa-das.ol iveiras.com; d incl breakfast €60; ☎ ⅏) This peaceful place offers an old-style B&B (the owners are British), with five slightly dated rooms in a relaxed setting. There's a lovely garden and pool area. It's 2.5km from Silves train station. Ring for directions.

Quinta da Figueirinha (☎ 282 440 700; www.qdf.pt; 2-/4-/6-person apt €62/90/122; ☎) This 36-hectare organic farm and botanic (drought-resistant) garden, run by the kindly agro-economist Dr Gerhard Zabel, offers simple apartments in peaceful farm-like surroundings. Leaving Silves and crossing the bridge, take the first left to Fagura and continue for 4km. The *quinta* (estate) is signposted. You can self-cater, or there is a basic restaurant serving delicious, wholesome buffet-style food (note: not always open).

TOP END

Tapada do Gramacho (☎ 919667048; www.tapada dogramacho.com; r incl breakfast €85, apt 1-week min €650) This hot-off-the-press Dutch-run place shouts 'contemporary', although it's a renovated farmhouse with beautiful original features. There's a choice of themed rooms, from the bohemian room to the funky. It gets full sun – there's not a lot of greenery or shade – and is a good, if hip, villa experience at any time of year. It's several kilometres from Silves; ring for directions.

Eating

There are plenty of cafe-restaurants in the pedestrianised streets leading up to the castle or down by the river, where you'll also find a reasonable *mercado municipal* (just west of the old pedestrian bridge).

Pastelaria Rosa (Largo do Município; Y 7.30am-11pm Mon-Sat) On the ground floor of the town hall building, this long-standing, tile-lined place is lovely for coffee and pastries. You can sit outside next to a small tree-shaded plaza or inside for rustic charm.

Restaurante Ponte Romana (☎ 282 443 275; Horta da Cruz; mains €4-8) Adjoining the Ponte Romana *residencial* (guest house; left), this basement restaurant has decorations – keys, cowbells and harnesses – as antiquated as its prices (which haven't moved in years). Great value, hearty country fare.

Ú Monchiqueiro (☎ 282 442 142; mercado municipal; mains €5-10; Y lunch & dinner Thu-Tue) By the river and near the market, this casual spot serves

THE ALGARVE

ALGARVE FOOD FESTIVALS

Epicureans shouldn't miss a chance to eat and drink their way into a tizzy – Algarve-style.

- **Feira Concurso Arte Doce** (Lagos) Dessert is elevated to high art at this three-day sweets fair, with marzipan, an Algarvian favourite, taking centre stage. The fair takes place in July.
- **Feira da Serra** (São Brás de Alportel) This down-home country fair held in late July sells locally produced cheese and meats, cakes, wine and other belly fillers; there are also games for the kiddies and plenty of folkloric song and dance performances.
- **Feiras dos Enchidos Tradicionais** (Monchique) Head for the hills in early March if you want to get a taste of Monchique's country cooking at this traditional sausage festival. You'll also catch performances by folklore troops and find handicrafts for sale.
- **Festival da Cerveja** (Silves) Usually held around July/August, this spirited fest is dedicated to beer, though you'll also find traditional cuisine and singing and dancing to accompany all that beer-guzzling.
- **Festival do Marisco** (Olhão) Held in mid-August, this lively seafood festival features all the great Algarvian oceanic dishes, including *caldeirada* (fish stew) and *cataplana*. Bands add to the fun – the Village People played in 2006.

grilled meats (there's an outdoor grill), and punchy piri-piri chicken.

Bistro O Cais (☎ 282 448 098; Rua José Estevão 2; mains €5-12; ⏰ lunch & dinner Sun-Fri) This restored waterfront town house has a relaxed setting with a changing menu. It has jazz jam sessions on a Sunday afternoon, and fado during the week.

Café Inglês (☎ 282 442 585; mains €6-14; ⏰ 9am-midnight Tue-Sun, 9am-5.30pm Mon) Below the castle entrance, this cafe has a wonderful shady terrace and is everyone's favourite spot. The food is excellent (don't miss the Chocolate St Emilion dessert). One of the Algarve's liveliest restaurants north of the coast, it has an elegant interior and in summer has occasional live jazz, fado and African music.

Restaurante Marisqueria Rui (☎ 282 442 682; Rua Commendatory Villain 27; mains €6-15; ⏰ lunch & dinner Wed-Mon) Situated in the old town, this place is Sagres' finest seafood restaurant. Join the locals – it gets busy – and savour plates of cockles, clams and crabs to bass and seafood rice.

Restaurante O Barradas (☎ 282 443 308; Palmeirinha; mains €8.50-21; ⏰ dinner Thu-Tue) The star choice for fine dining is this delightful spot, 3km south of Silves, past the Silves train station on the road to Lagoa. The German chef creates her own Portuguese wonders, always using Mediterranean ingredients, sourced where possible from local suppliers. Organic meats and fresh, not farmed, fish are used. Desserts use seasonal fruits (don't miss the figs with muscatel). An elegant atmosphere, gourmet dishes, and too many fine wines (did we mention her husband is a winemaker?) make for a taxi booking (seriously, think about it).

Entertainment

Fábrica do Inglês (English Factory; ☎ 282 440 480; www.fabrica-do-ingles.pt; Rua Gregório Mascarenhas) In the surroundings of the converted 19th-century English Museu da Cortiça (cork factory; p210), 300m northeast of the new bridge, this complex has restaurants and bars. From July to mid-September, it hosts a nightly show with dancers and singers.

Getting There & Around

Buses travel daily between Silves and its train station (€1.80, three to four daily). Trains head to/from Lagos (€2.10, 35 minutes, eight daily) and Faro (€4.90, one hour, eight daily). There are buses to Albufeira (€3.55, 40 minutes, seven daily), and to Portimão (€2.60, 20 minutes, two to five daily). For Lagos (40 minutes) change at Portimão. All buses leave from the riverfront, with fewer running at weekends. The **bus ticket office** (☎ 282 442 338; ⏰ 8am-noon & 2-5pm Mon-Fri, 8am-1pm Sat & 11am-noon Sun) is on the western side of the market.

Much of the hilly and compact centre of Silves is easily done on foot; many streets are pedestrianised areas only. Drivers are advised to park their car in the large car park on the city side (north) of the river and southwest of the city centre (no charge).

PORTIMÃO
pop 37,000

Bustling Portimão is the western Algarve's main commercial centre and the second most populous city in the Algarve. It used to be the region's fishing and canning centre but, although it still has a sprawling port, only a small fishing fleet remains. The messy outskirts of the city hide a small, friendly hub, with manicured parks and plazas along the waterfront, an assortment of outdoor cafes, and sizzling fish restaurants in the old quarter and quayside. You can also arrange a boat trip up the Rio Arade. Most tourists only pass through en route to Praia da Rocha.

Portimão's strategic position has long been recognised. It was an important trading link for Phoenicians, Greeks and Carthaginians (Hannibal is said to have visited). It was called Portos Magnus by the Romans and was fought over by Moors and Christians. In 1189 Dom Sancho I and a band of crusaders sailed up the Rio Arade from here to besiege Silves. Almost destroyed in the 1755 earthquake, it regained its maritime importance in the 19th century. Since the 1970s, the fishing and related industries have been in decline, but recently there has been much investment into marina and waterfront redevelopment for tourism and leisure boats.

Orientation

The town's focal point is the Praça Manuel Teixeira Gomes, next to a smart riverside promenade. There's no bus station, but buses stop at various points. The train station is a 15-minute walk (1.1km) north of the centre – follow the pedestrianised Rua Vasco da Gama and its continuation, Rua do Comércio.

Information

There are several banks with ATMs around the riverside Praça Manuel Teixeira Gomes. The **Municipal turismo** (☎ 282 470 732; www.cm-portimao.pt; Av Zeca Afonso; 🕒 9am-6pm Mon-Fri, 9am-1pm Sat Jun-Aug, 9am-12.30pm & 2-5.30pm Mon-Fri Sep-May) is opposite the football stadium, about 600m west of the river. A handy same-day laundry service is at **Sodeal** (☎ 282 424 061; Rua Mouzinho de Albuquerque 39; 🕒 9am-1pm & 3-7pm Mon-Fri, 9am-1pm Sat).

Sights

The town's parish church, the **igreja matriz** (admission free), stands on high ground to the north of the town centre and features a 14th-century Gothic portal – all that remains of the original structure after the 1755 earthquake. Other echoes of the past can be found in the narrow streets of the **old fishing quarter**, around Largo da Barca, just before the old highway bridge.

The modern **Museu de Portimão** (☎ 282 405 230; €2; 🕒 2.30-6pm Tue & 10am-6pm Wed-Sun 15 Sep–14 Jul, 7.30-11pm Tue & 3-11pm Wed-Sun 15 Jul–14 Sep), housed in a converted fish cannery, is one excellent reason to visit Portimão. Opened in 2008, the museum focuses on three areas: archaeology, underwater finds and, the most fascinating, the re-creation of the fish cannery (mackerel and sardines). The museum re-creates former production lines, complete with sound effects – clanking and grinding and the like. An excellent video (in Portuguese) of the fishing industry reveals each step in the process, from netting the shoals to packaging.

Activities

Operators galore line the riverside promenade offering boat trips. These include cruises up coast and/or the Rio Arade, visiting caves along the way. Prices start at around €23. There are also dolphin-spotting opportunities. Avoid being netted on the promenade – the tourist office has a booklet outlining all the operators. Some trips are in fishing boats for 10 people, others are in sailing boats for 35. **Santa Bernarda** (☎ 282 422 791, 967023840; www.santa-bernarda.com; trips adult/child from €30/15; 👍) runs trips visiting the caves and coast on a 23m wooden sailing ship with wheelchair access. The full-day trip includes a beach barbecue and time to swim.

The nearest place to go for a gallop is **Centro Hípico Vale de Ferro** (☎ 282 968 444; www.algarvehorseholidays.com; per hr €25), near Mexilhoeira Grande (4.2km west of Portimão), which also offers riding-holiday packages.

Ask at the tourist office for a copy of *Get in touch with Nature*, which outlines several self-guided nature walks, bikes and boat trips in the region.

Courses

Centro de Linguas (☎ 282 430 250; www.clcc.pt; Rua Dom Maria Luísa 122) offers lessons in Portuguese for groups and individuals.

Sleeping

Residencial Arabi (☎ 282 460 250; Praça Teixeira Gomes 13; s/d €35/65) Overlooking the main square on the waterfront, this pleasant *residencial*

BUSES FROM PORTIMÃO

Destination	Price	Duration	Frequency (weekdays/weekends)
Albufeira	€3.85	1hr	14/6
Cabo São Vicente	€5.15	2½hr	2/0
Faro	€4.70	1½hr	7/2
Lagos	€2.45	40min	19 daily
Lisbon	€18	3¾hr	6/4
Loulé	€5.10	1¾hr	2/4 (Saturday only; change in Albufeira)
Monchique	€2.80	45min	9/5
Sagres	€5.10	1¼hr	2/0
Salema	€3.55	1hr	2/0
Silves	€2.60	35min	8/5

has small neat rooms with linoleum 'wood' floors. The best (slightly pricier) rooms face the square and have French doors opening onto decorative balconies.

Globo Hotel (☎ 282 405 030; www.hoteisalgarvesol.pt; Rua 5 de Outubro 26; s/d €81.50/108.50) Recently renovated, rooms here have a snazzy design, with contemporary fittings and abundant natural light. Each floor has a colour scheme, from lilac to green.

Eating & Drinking

The fountain-lined pedestrian street Rua Direita, about 300m west of the river, is a good destination for restaurant browsing. For open-air seafood grub, head for the strip of restaurants by the bridge, where charcoal-grilled sardines and barbecued fish are the specialities.

Casa Inglesa (Praça Manuel T Gomes; mains €2-6; ⏱ 8am-11pm) Central to Portimão life, this large cafe on the main square has a charming 1950s feel, with lots of snacks on offer, as well as tasty marzipan. Outdoor tables are pleasant.

Taberna de Maré (☎ 282 414 614; Largo da Barca; mains from €4.50) This restaurant is off the main strip, with a cluster of other terrace restaurants in the old fishing quarter, under the arches of the bridge; it's known for its Algarve seafood specialities and serves excellent *bacalhau com natas* (salted cod with cream and potatoes) on Friday.

Snack-Bar Porta Velha (☎ 918 053 169; Travessa Manuel Dias Barão; snacks €3-8; ⏱ 10pm-4am Mon-Sat) This atmospheric bar is the kind of place you can kick back and relax in. It's been lovingly restored and decorated; spread across several

rooms are antique knick-knacks and modern artworks. The tables are made of wood and stone slabs and in one room, the ceiling is made entirely of corks. *Petiscos* (snacks) and drinks only. It's near the modern square (an extension of Rua Direita).

Shopping

A big open-air market is held behind the train station on the first Monday of each month. A flea market also takes place on the first and third Sunday of the month (mornings only) in the Feiras (exhibition) area.

Getting There & Around

Six daily trains connect Portimão with Tunes (via Silves) and Lagos. Change at Tunes for Lisbon.

Portimão has excellent bus connections.

Buses shuttle between Praia da Rocha and Portimão (€1.20 on the bus, €10 for 10 pre-purchased tickets, at least half-hourly).

You can get information and tickets for Eva and Intersul (Eurolines) services at the **Eva office** (☎ 282 418 120; Largo do Duque 3), located by the riverside. Buses leave from near the Repsol petrol station along the riverside on Avenida Guanaré.

The easiest parking is a free riverside area by the Galp station.

Local buses cover some inner-city routes.

PRAIA DA ROCHA

One of the Algarve's finest beaches, Praia da Rocha is a wide stretch of sand backed by ochre-red cliffs and a petite 16th-century fortress.

Behind the beach looms the town; this has long known the hand of development, with high-rise condos and luxury hotels sprouting like weeds along the cliffside, and a row of restaurants, bars and dance clubs packed along the one main thoroughfare. If you look hard beyond the ugly concrete facade, Praia da Rocha has several vestiges from an elegant past, including some 19th-century mansions, now atmospheric guest houses.

There's also a sleek marina painted weirdly autumnal colours (to match the cliffs) and a casino where you can double (or deplete) your savings.

Orientation

Set high above the beach, the esplanade, Avenida Tomás Cabreira, is the resort's main drag and is lined with shops, hotels and restaurants. At the eastern end is the shell of the **Fortaleza da Santa Catarina**, built in the 16th century to stop pirates and invaders from sailing up the Rio Arade to Portimão. Down below is the Marina de Portimão, with more restaurants and bars.

Information

The post office is near the *turismo*.

Police (9am-12.30pm & 2-5pm Mon-Fri) Next door to the *turismo*.

Turismo (☎ 282 419 132; 9.30am-7pm Jul & Aug, 9.30am-1pm & 2-5.30pm Mon-Fri Sep-Jun) In the centre of the esplanade, opposite Restaurant Sol.

Western Union (9.30am-9pm) Next door to the *turismo*, this has telephone booths and internet (per hr €2.50).

Activities

Marina-based **Dolphin Seafaris** (☎ 282 799 209; dolphinseafaris.com; trips €40; Apr-Oct) offers dolphin-spotting trips.

Sleeping

Accommodation is almost impossible to find in the high season if you don't have a prior reservation.

Residencial Toca (☎ 282 418 904; residencialtoca.iol .pt; Rua Engenheiro Francisco Bívar; d €75; P) One of Praia's more affordable spots, this friendly guest house has tidy rooms with sizable windows, wood floors and frilly bedspreads. Low-season prices are less.

Albergaria Vila Lido (☎ 282 241 127; fax 282 242 246; Av Tomás Cabreira; d from €100; P) Near the fort, this hotel was converted from a 19th-century mansion and has a slightly

Brighton (UK) guest house feel, with great sea views and 10 bright rooms, most of which have terraces.

Hotel Oriental (☎ 282 480 800; www.oriental@tdho tels.pt; s/d €190/210; P) One of a growing number of immense hotels rising over the beach, the Oriental is big, slightly brash and a bit like a Moorish theme park. It has a lavish foyer, inviting pools with kitchenettes, and spacious rooms with splashes of colour. Most rooms have sea views and some feature balconies.

Eating

Snack Bar Scorpíus (Rua Bartolomeu Dias; mains €6-12; 10am-1am) A bit off the beaten path, this popular local cafe is a good spot to enjoy simple but nicely prepared plates of seafood, omelettes and desserts.

Cervejaria e Marisqueira (☎ 282 416 541; mains €7-17, 3-course menu €14.50; lunch & dinner Mon-Sat) An unusually traditional restaurant for Praia da Rocha, this popular and low-key *cervejaria* (beer house) on a road opposite the casino offers decent Portuguese fare, with a hearty array of daily specials.

La Dolce Vita (☎ 282 419 444; Av Tomás Cabreira; mains €7-10; lunch & dinner) A good Italian restaurant with olde-world charm (herbs, garlic bulbs and bench seating), this serves mamma-style pasta dishes and pizzas.

Restaurante Almeida (☎ 282 424 304; mains €12-15) Almeida has a pleasant setting on the marina and is a safe, conservative bet for your standard fish and meat cuisine. *Cataplanas* also on offer.

Titanic (☎ 282 422 371; Edifício Colúmbia, Rua Engenheiro Francisco Bívar; mains €15-18; dinner) An old-fashioned classic, Titanic cooks up some of Praia's best seafood and steak dishes.

The marina has a row of romantic, upmarket dining and drinking spots.

Entertainment

Praia da Rocha bristles with bars that are packed with sun-kissed faces, satellite TV, live music and karaoke. Many are owned or run by foreign residents. You might as well be in Dublin, for the plethora of Irish bars, including **Ireland's Eye**, **Kerri's Bar** and **Celt Bar** (bar-hopping directions not needed, just follow the *cráic*). They're open all day (and nearly all night).

Well-situated bars string along the main strip, most with outdoor seating. Try **Pé de**

Vento (☿ 4pm-4am), a two-floor disco bar. **The Waterfront Bar** (www.thewaterfrontbar.com; ☿ 2pm-4am) at the marina is a sleek, fun alternative. It has karaoke on Thursday evening, and regular live music.

Voxx (Av Tomás Cabreira) is a sleek discotheque that makes good use of its waterside setting and plays anything from pop to African to hip hop. Monster **Discoteca Katedral** (Rua António Feu) gets busy to pop house, until 6am nightly during summer.

Many locals-in-the-know hit the bar scene in Alvor, several kilometres away.

The glitzy **casino** (☎ 282 402 000; Av Tomás Cabreira), midway along the esplanade in Hotel Algarve, has slot machines (admission free, open 4pm to 3am) and a gambling room (admission €4, plus passport and smart attire; open 7.30pm to 3am).

Getting There & Around

Buses shuttle to Portimão (€2 on the bus, €10 for 10 prepurchased tickets, every 15 to 30 minutes). There are services to Albufeira (€3.70), Lagos (€3.40, four to six daily) and Lisbon (€17, four daily). The bus terminus in Praia da Rocha is by Club Praia de Rocha.

Auto Rent (☎ 282 417 172; www.autorent.pt; Av Tomás Cabreira) offers good car-rental deals.

THE WINDWARD COAST & COSTA VICENTINA

LAGOS
pop 17,500

As far as touristy towns go, Lagos (*lah-goosh*) has, fortunately – or unfortunately – got the lot. It lies along the bank of the Rio Bensafrim, with 16th-century walls enclosing the old town's pretty, cobbled streets and picturesque plazas and churches. Beyond these lie a modern, but not overly unattractive, modern sprawl. The town's good restaurants and range of fabulous beaches nearby add to the allure. With every activity under the sun (literally) on offer, plus a pumping nightlife, it's not surprising that people of all ages are drawn here. In season, with all the crowds and action, the town can feel hectic and claustrophobic.

Aside from its hedonistic appeal, Lagos has historical clout, having launched many naval excursions during Portugal's extraordinary Age of Discoveries (see p33).

History

Phoenicians and Greeks set up shop at this port (which later became Roman Lacobriga) at the mouth of the muddy Rio Bensafrim. Afonso III recaptured it from the Moors in 1241, and the Portuguese continued harassing the Muslims of North Africa from here. In 1415 a giant fleet set sail from Lagos under the command of the 21-year-old Prince Henry the Navigator to seize Ceuta in Morocco, thereby setting the stage for the Age of Discoveries.

The shipyards of Lagos built and launched Prince Henry's caravels, and Henry split his time between his trading company here and his navigation school at Sagres. Local boy Gil Eanes left here in 1434 in command of the first ship to round West Africa's Cape Bojador. Others continued to bring back information about the African coast, along with ivory, gold and slaves. Lagos has the dubious distinction of having hosted (in 1444) the first sale of black Africans as slaves to Europeans, and the town grew into a slave-trading centre.

It was also from Lagos in 1578 that Dom Sebastião, along with the cream of Portuguese nobility and an army of Portuguese, Spanish, Dutch and German buccaneers, left on a disastrous crusade to Christianise North Africa, which ended in a debacle at Alcácer-Quibir in Morocco. Sir Francis Drake inflicted heavy damage on Lagos a few years later, in 1587.

Lagos was the Algarve's high-profile capital from 1576 until 1755, when the earthquake flattened it.

Orientation

The town's main drag is the riverfront Avenida dos Descobrimentos. The administrative hub is the pedestrianised Praça Gil Eanes (zheel *yan*-ish), centred on a statue of Dom Sebastião with what looks like a space helmet at his feet.

The bus station is roughly 500m north of Praça Gil Eanes off Avenida dos Descobrimentos; the train station is on the other side of the river, accessible by a footbridge.

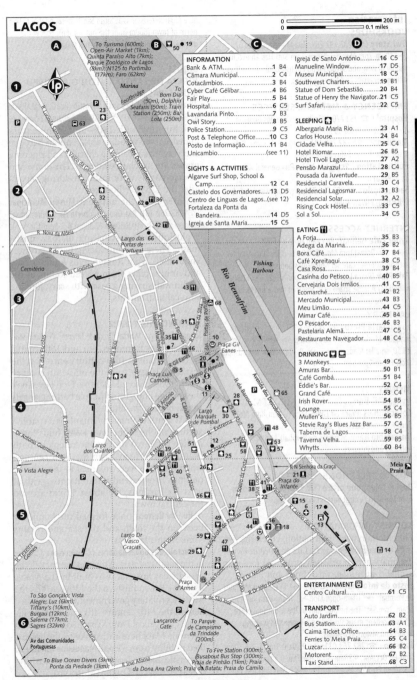

LAGOS

INFORMATION

Bank & ATM..................................1	B4
Câmara Municipal.........................2	B4
Cotacâmbios..................................3	B4
Cyber Café Gélibar........................4	B6
Fair Play...5	B4
Hospital..6	C5
Lavandaria Pinto...........................7	B3
Owl Story.......................................8	B5
Police Station................................9	C3
Post & Telephone Office.............10	C3
Posto de Informação....................11	B4
Unicambio...............................(see 11)

SIGHTS & ACTIVITIES

Algarve Surf Shop, School & Camp.....12	C4
Castelo dos Governadores........13	D5
Centro de Linguas de Lagos..(see 12)
Fortaleza da Ponta da Bandeira.....14	D5
Igreja de Santa Maria.................15	C5

Igreja de Santo António...........16	C5
Manueline Window....................17	D5
Museu Municipal.......................18	C5
Southwest Charters...................19	B1
Statue of Dom Sebastião...........20	B4
Statue of Henry the Navigator....21	C5
Surf Safari.................................22	C5

SLEEPING

Albargaria Maria Rio.................23	A1
Carlos House.............................24	B4
Cidade Velha.............................25	C4
Hotel Riomar.............................26	B5
Hotel Tivoli Lagos.....................27	A2
Pensão Marazul........................28	C4
Pousada da Juventude..............29	B5
Residencial Caravela.................30	C4
Residencial Lagosmar...............31	B3
Residencial Solar......................32	A2
Rising Cock Hostel....................33	C5
Sol a Sol...................................34	C5

EATING

A Forja.......................................35	B3
Adega da Marina......................36	B2
Bora Café..................................37	B4
Café Xpreitaqui.........................38	C5
Casa Rosa.................................39	B4
Casinha do Petisco...................40	B5
Cervejaria Dois Irmãos.............41	C5
Ecomarché................................42	B2
Mercado Municipal...................43	B3
Meu Limão................................44	C5
Mimar Café...............................45	B4
O Pescador...............................46	B3
Pastelaria Alemã.......................47	C5
Restaurante Navegador............48	C4

DRINKING

3 Monkeys................................49	C5
Amuras Bar...............................50	B1
Café Gombá..............................51	B4
Eddie's Bar................................52	C4
Grand Café...............................53	C4
Irish Rover................................54	B5
Lounge......................................55	C4
Mullen's....................................56	B5
Stevie Ray's Blues Jazz Bar........57	C4
Taberna de Lagos.....................58	C4
Taverna Velha...........................59	B5
Whytts......................................60	B4

ENTERTAINMENT

Centro Cultural.........................61	C5

TRANSPORT

Auto Jardim..............................62	B2
Bus Station...............................63	A1
Caima Ticket Office..................64	B3
Ferries to Meia Praia................65	B2
Luzcar......................................66	B2
Motorent..................................67	B2
Taxi Stand................................68	C3

THE ALGARVE

Information

BOOKSHOPS

Owl Story (☎ 282 792 289; Rua Marreiros Neto 67; ☯ 10am-7pm Mon-Fri, 10am-1pm Sat) Has an excellent supply of new and secondhand English books as well as sailing almanacs and boating books.

EMERGENCY & MEDICAL SERVICES

Hospital (☎ 282 770 100; Rua Castelo dos Governadores) Just off Praça do Infante.

Medilagos (☎ 282 760 181; Amejeira de Cima, Bela Vista, Lote 2; ☯ 24hr) Private clinic.

Police station (☎ 282 762 930; Rua General Alberto da Silveira)

Saó Gonçalo (☎ 282 790 700; www.hppsaude.pt; Av D Sebastião) Private clinic.

INTERNET ACCESS

Cyber Café Gélibar (Rua Lançarote de Freitas 43A; per hr €3; ☯ 9am-11pm Mon-Sat, 9am- 8pm Sun) Another friendly internet cafe serving drinks and snacks.

Fair Play (Praça Luís Camões 23; per hr €2; ☯ 11.30am-midnight) A large space with internet and a drinks cafe.

LAUNDRY

Lavandaria Pinto (☎ 282 762 191; Rua Conselheiro Joaquim Machado 28; 1-day wash & dry service per 5kg €8.50, smaller loads min €5; ☯ 9.30am-1pm & 3.30-6pm Mon-Fri, to 1pm Sat)

MONEY

Praça Gil Eanes has banks with ATMs.

Cotacâmbios (Praça Gil Eanes 11; ☯ 9am-8pm Mon-Sun) A private exchange bureau.

Unicambio (Largo Marquês de Pombal) Also has telephones and internet.

POST & TELEPHONE

Post & telephone office (☎ 282 770 240; ☯ 9am-6pm Mon-Fri) Central, just off Praça Gil Eanes.

TOURIST INFORMATION

For entertainment information, check the listings in the *Best of Lagos, Luz & Burgau* (www .freemaps.net), a privately produced free map available at *residencials*, shops and bars.

Posto de informação (☎ 282 764 111; Largo Marquês de Pombal; ☯ 10am-6pm Mon-Fri, 10am-8pm Jul-Aug, 10am-2pm Sat) The helpful staff at the municipal office offers excellent maps (including a suggested walking route) and historical leaflets.

Turismo (☎ 282 763 031; ☯ 9.30am-1pm & 2-5.30pm Mon-Fri Oct-Apr, 9.30am-5pm Tue-Thu, 9.30am-1pm & 2-5.30pm Fri-Mon May-Sep) The less handy and less reli-able Algarve *turismo* is at Situo São João roundabout, 1km north of town (600m from the bus station). Follow the *avenida* until you see the Galp petrol station.

Sights

IGREJA DE SANTO ANTÓNIO & MUSEU MUNICIPAL

The little **Igreja de Santo António** (Rua General Alberto da Silveira; admission €2; ☯ 9.30am-12.30pm & 2-5pm Tue-Sun), bursting with 18th- and 19th-century gilded, carved wood, is a stupendous baroque extravaganza. Beaming cherubs and ripening grapes are much in evidence. The dome and *azulejo* panels were installed during repairs after the 1755 earthquake.

Enter from the adjacent **Museu Municipal** (☎ 282 762 301; Rua General Alberto da Silveira; adult/concession €2/1; ☯ 9.30am-12.30pm & 2-5pm Tue-Sun), a glorious and fascinating historic mishmash. There's an entrancing haphazardness about it all, from Roman nails found locally and opium pipes from Macau to bits of the Berlin wall sharing a case with scary-looking surgical instruments.

AROUND THE TOWN

Igreja de Santa Maria (Praça do Infante; ☯ 9am-noon & 3-6pm) dates from the 15th and 16th centuries and retains a 16th-century entrance; the rest dates largely from the mid-19th century when it was restored after fire. Don't overlook the strange orange and purple battling angels mural behind the altar.

Just south of Praça do Infante is a restored section of the stout **town walls**, built (atop earlier versions) during the reigns of both Manuel I and João III in the 16th century, when the walls were enlarged to the existing outline. They extend intermittently, with at least six bastions, for about 1.5km around the central town.

Rua da Barroca once formed the boundary between the town and the sea and retains some Arabic features.

Castelo dos Governadores (Governors Castle; in the southeast part of town at the back of the present-day hospital) was built by the Arabs. After the Reconquista in the 13th century, the Algarve's military government was established here in the 14th century. It's said that the ill-fated, evangelical Dom Sebastião attended an open-air Mass here and spoke to the assembled nobility from a small **Manueline window** in the castle, before leading them to a crushing defeat at Alcácer-Quibir (Morocco).

Near Praça do Infante is a less-than-glorious site – where slaves were auctioned off in Portugal in the 15th century. It now houses an art gallery.

FORTALEZA DA PONTA DA BANDEIRA
This little **fortress** (Av dos Descobrimentos; adult/concession €2/1; ☼ 9.30am-12.30pm & 2-5pm Tue-Sun), at the southern end of the avenue, was built in the 17th century to protect the port. Restored, it now houses a museum on the Portuguese discoveries.

PONTA DA PIEDADE
Protruding south from Lagos, Ponta da Piedade (Point of Piety) is a stunning, dramatic wedge of headland. Three windswept kilometres out of town, the point is well worth a visit for its contorted, polychrome sandstone cliffs and towers, complete with lighthouse and, in spring, hundreds of nesting egrets. The surrounding area is brilliant with wild orchids in spring. On a clear day you can see east to Carvoeiro and west to Sagres.

PARQUE ZOOLÓGICO DE LAGOS
This **zoo** (☎ 282 680 100; www.zoolagos.com; Quinta Figueiras; adult/child €10/6; ☼ 10am-7pm Apr-Sep, 10am-5pm Oct-Mar, restaurant closed Mon) is a shady 3-hectare kid-pleaser, with many small primates, and a children's farm housing domestic animals. It's near the village of Barão de São Miguel, 8km west of Lagos.

Activities
BEACHES & WATER SPORTS
Meia Praia, the vast expanse of sand to the east of town, has outlets offering sailboard rental and water-skiing lessons, plus several laid-back restaurants and beach bars. South of town the beaches – **Batata**, **Pinhão**, **Dona Ana**, **Camilo** among others – are smaller and more secluded, lapped by calm waters and punctuated with amazing grottoes, coves and towers of coloured sandstone. It's best to avoid swimming at Batata, the closest beach to Lagos (and therefore the dirtiest). A ferry runs from the waterfront in Lagos to Meia Praia.

Lagos is a popular surfing centre and has good facilities; surfing companies head to the west coast for the waves.

Surf Safari (☎ 282 764 734; Rua da Silva Lopes 31; 1-/3-/5-day courses €45/120/180) will help you catch a wave and head to where there are suitable swells. Children under 14 must be accompanied by a family member (not necessarily an adult).

Another swell option is **Algarve Surf Shop, School & Camp** (☎ 282 767 853; www.algarvesurfcamp.com; Rua Dr Joaquim Tello 32; equipment hire & B&B €55 per day, 1-/3-/5-day course or safari €45/120/180).

If you want to go diving or snorkelling, contact **Blue Ocean Divers** (☎ 964665667; www.blue-ocean-divers.de; Motel Ancora, Porto de Mos), which offers a half-day 'Snorkelling Safari' (€30), a full-day diving experience (€90) and a three-day PADI scuba course (€250). It also offers kayak safaris (€30/45 half/full day, child under 12 years €15/22.50).

BOAT TRIPS & DOLPHIN SAFARIS
Numerous operators have ticket stands at the marina or along the promenade opposite the marina. They operate a bit like sausage factories but offer some fun outings.

Bom Dia (☎ 282 764 670; www.bomdia.info) The oldest operator and based at the marina, Bom Dia runs trips on traditional schooners, including a five-hour barbecue cruise (€49/25 adult/child), with a chance to swim; a two-hour grotto trip (€25/12.50, four daily) or family fishing (€39/29).

Espadarte do Sul (☎ 282 761 820; espadartedosul@yahoo.com.br) offers one- or two-hour trips to the grottoes beneath Ponta da Piedade (€10/17.50), a three-hour coastal cruise (€20) and fishing trips (€35).

Kayak Adventures (☎ 913 262 200; ☼ Apr-Oct) has kayaking trips from Batata Beach, including snorkelling. Trips last around 2½ hours (€25).

Southwest Charters (☎ 282 792 681; www.southwestcharters.com; Marina de Lagos) offers powerboat or yacht charters carrying eight people for €220 to €385 per half-day, €300 to €565 per full day. Larger boats and weekly rentals are available. A skipper costs €60/100 per half-/full day.

Local fishermen offering jaunts to the grottoes by motorboat trawl for customers along the promenade and by the Fortaleza da Ponta da Bandeira.

Some outfits offer dolphin-spotting trips:
Algarve Dolphins (☎ 282 087 587; www.algarve-dolphins.com; trips from €30) Also supports the research and protection of dolphins.
Dolphin Seafaris (☎ 282 799 209; www.dolphinseafaris.com; trips €35; ☼ Apr-Oct)

OTHER ACTIVITIES
About 10km west of Lagos, **Tiffany's** (☎ 282 697 395; www.valegrifo.com/tiffanysriding/; Vale Grifo, Almádena;

THE ALGARVE

(☼ 9am-dusk) charges €30 an hour for horse riding and has other options, including a three-/five-hour trip (€80/125); the latter includes a champagne picnic. Another centre with similar activities is **Quinta Paraíso Alto** (☎ 282 687 596; www.qpahorseriding.com; Fronteira), 7km north of Lagos.

Courses

Centro de Linguas de Lagos (☎ 282 761 070; www.centrodelinguas.com; Rua Dr Joaquim Telo 32) offers classes in Portuguese. Students can choose from one of five levels, and can arrange private classes or intensive group lessons (four to eight students per class).

Sleeping

BUDGET

Accommodation options are extensive in Lagos, with more places out on Meia Praia and on Praia da Dona Ana. Rooms are pricier and scarcer from July to mid-September. Locals often meet the buses to tout their private homes; head to the tourist office for a list of officially approved individuals.

Parque de Campismo da Trindade (☎ 282 763 893; cfelagos@clix.pt; sites per adult/tent/car €3.10/4.80/4.50) A small site 200m south of the Lançarote gate beyond the town walls (but still surrounded by buildings), this camping ground has shade and good facilities.

Pousada da Juventude (☎ 282 761 970; www.pousadasjuventude.pt; Rua Lançarote de Freitas 50; dm/d €16/43, d with shared bathroom €35; ☼ 24hr; 💻) One of Portugal's best, this well-run hostel is a great place to meet other travellers. There's a kitchen and pleasant courtyard, and the reception is very helpful.

Carlos House (☎ 916 594 225; carloshousez@yahoo.com; Rua do Jogo da Bola 8; dm from €19.50; 💻) Another popular privately run hostel, this one's uphill from the centre and has a guest kitchen and a rooftop terrace.

Rising Cock Hostel (☎ 969 411 131; Travessa do Forno 14; dm €28; 💻) The name is nothing to crow about, but the rooms in this privately run establishment are more tasteful and nicely designed, and there's a comfy lounge, a terrace and free internet. It's the coop for party animals.

Residencial Caravela (☎ 282 763 361; Rua 25 de Abril 16; s/d €30/40) In the central pedestrian zone, Caravela has ageing but breezy rooms, most with wood floors. Some rooms have their own showers, but none have toilets.

MIDRANGE

Pensão Marazul (☎ 282 770 230; www.pensaomarazul.com; Rua 25 de Abril 13; s/d with shared bathroom €40/50; 💻) Also central, this well-run place has comfortable, well-kept rooms with either sea views or inner balconies.

Hotel Riomar (☎ 282 763 091; Rua Cândido dos Reis 83; s/d €45/65; P 🐾) Rooms here are small but comfortable, with parquetry wood floors and balconies (no view). It's in need of a facelift but it's still good value.

Residencial Solar (☎ 282 762 477; residencial-solar@netvisao.pt; Rua António Crisógono dos Santos 60; d €40-60; 🐾) On a quiet street near the bus station and the waterfront, this place has slightly stuffy and dated, but clean, rooms.

Cidade Velha (☎ 282 762 041; www.cidadevelha.info; Rua Dr Joaquim Tello 7; s/d/tr from €45/65/75; 🐾 💻) This friendly, welcoming guest house has light, airy and tidy rooms with tile floors and balconies. Top-floor rooms are best, with peeks of the ocean and town. Excellent value.

Sol a Sol (☎ 282 761 290; Rua Lançarote de Freitas 22; d/tr from €60/85) This central, small hotel has rooms with tiny balconies and views over the town; it's a bit dated on the outside but, inside, the rooms are neat and clean. Cheap singles available outside high season.

Residencial Lagosmar (☎ 282 763 722; Rua Dr Faria da Silva 13; s/d €65/75) Lagosmar has a slightly musty – read cigarette – odour and ageing rooms, each of which has a sizable terrace (but check out those built-in radios).

TOP END

Albergaria Marina Rio (☎ 282 780 830; www.marinario.com; Av dos Descobrimentos; d €104; P 🐾 🐾 💻) Overlooking the harbour, this recently renovated hotel has comfortable rooms with contemporary decor and balconies. On the downside, it faces the road and backs onto the bus station. Most rooms are twins. There's a tiny pool and roof terrace.

Hotel Tivoli Lagos (☎ 282 790 079; www.tivolihotels.com; Rua Nova da Aldeia; d €180-190; P 🐾 🐾) This is Lagos' finest hotel, offering many creature comforts, including a health club and a lovely pool. It's popular with busloads of tour groups.

Eating

Lagos has some great dining spots, serving both Portuguese and international cuisine. Budget travellers should focus their attentions on lunchtime *pratos do dia* (daily specials), which often cost around €6.

BUDGET

Many excellent cafes are dotted around town.

Bora Café (Rua Conselheiro Joaquim Machado 17; mains €3-5; ☎ 8.30am-7pm Wed, Thu & Sun, 8.30am-11pm other days; 🖳) Tiny Bora is the ideal place for your healthy fruit and veggie fix, delicious *batidos* (fruit and milk drinks) and a cool setting. The downsides are that outdoor tables cost more, smoking is allowed, and the computers' fashionable rubber keyboards are impractical.

Café Xpreitaqui (☎ 282 762 758; Rua da Silva Lopes 14; salads €3-6; ☻ 10am-2am Mon-Sat) The glass tabletops cover spices and coffee beans; this creative cafe serves up healthy juices, smoothies, salads and good coffee.

Casa Rosa (☎ 966884317; Rua do Ferrador 22; dishes €3-7; ☻ 5pm-midnight) Backpacker-favourite Casa Rosa serves up simple, good-value mains such as veggie stir-fry, chilli con carne and fajitas.

Cervejaria Dois Irmãos (☎ 282 181 100; Travessa do Mar 2; tapas €5 per plate; ☻ lunch & dinner). Hordes of local businessfolk head to this relaxing and stylish place – which is housed in a quaint historical building and overlooks the beautiful Praça do Infante. The sublime selection of *petisco* plates (Portuguese tapas) includes everything from pipis to pork ear.

Café Gombá (☎ 282 762 188; Rua Cândido dos Reis 56; ☻ 8am-7pm) This place has been around since 1964 and the friendly owner has a loyal local clientele for its coffee and cakes. It's hard to miss for its display of two massive wine glasses.

Pastelaria Alemã (Rua São Gonçalo 10; snacks €1.50-4; ☻ 8am-6pm Mon-Fri, 8am-1pm Sat) This delightful, German-run patisserie sells a variety of tempting fresh-baked goods, including cheesecakes, *sachertorte* and flaky croissants.

Mimar Café (Rua António Barbosa Viana 27; snacks €3-8; ☻ 7.30am-8pm Mon-Sat, to midnight in summer) One of the few places to open early, this is excellent for coffees, breakfasts and snacks. The quiche and salad is a scrumptious luncheon special (€3.50).

Écomarché (Av dos Descobrimentos 2; ☻ 8am-9pm) is an accessible supermarket.

MIDRANGE & TOP END

Adega da Marina (☎ 282 764 284; Av dos Descobrimentos 35; mains €6-9; ☻ lunch & dinner) This barnlike place

is a bit like a Portuguese grandmother – she hasn't changed her hairstyle in a while. But she dishes out generous portions of reliable (and economical) tasty grilled chicken and seafood favourites to grateful guests. Her accessories include iron chandeliers and farming implements.

Bar Lota (☎ 282 764 048; Fish Dock; mains €6-10; ☻ lunch & dinner Mon-Sat) One of the few traditional authentic 'what-you-see-is-what-you-get' fish places around. Think wooden benches with paper tablecloths, loads of clients, and piles of fabulously fresh seafood daily plates. Head to opposite the 'new' train station entrance, beyond the marina.

O Pescador (☎ 282 767 028; Rua Gil Eanes 6; mains €6.50-13; ☻ lunch & dinner Mon-Sat) Don't let the pictures of dishes in the menu display put you off. This plain and unpretentious place is far from a fast-food joint, but can be recommended for its blackboard specials.

ourpick A Forja (☎ 282 768 588; Rua dos Ferreiros 17; mains €6.50-14; ☻ lunch & dinner, closed Sat) The secret is out. This buzzing place pulls in the crowds for its over-hearty, top quality traditional food served in a bustling environment at great prices. Plates of the day are always reliable, as are the fish dishes.

Casinha do Petisco (☎ 282 084 285; Rua da Oliveira 51; mains €6.90-12; ☻ lunch & dinner Mon-Sat) Blink – or be late – and you'll miss this tiny traditional gem. It's cosy and simply decorated and comes highly recommended by locals for its seafood grills and shellfish dishes.

Meu Limão (☎ 282 767 946; Rua Silva Lopes 40; mains €8.50-12.50; ☻ lunch & dinner) This handsome international-style tapas bar has a trendy feel, a smart crowd and a postcard view of Igreja Santo António from the outdoor tables. Tapas choices (€3.50 to €6) include shrimp with coconut, lemon chicken and mussels. It also serves heartier plates and good wines.

Restaurante Navegador (☎ 282 767 162; Rua da Barroca; mains €12.50-17; ☻ lunch & dinner) With a sea view and pretty roof terrace, this smart, slightly olde-world restaurant rustles up some elaborately flambéed food, with lots of meat and fish dishes and port- and brandy-based sauces.

Vista Alegre (☎ 282 792 151; Rua Ilha Terceira 19B; mains €13-17; ☻ lunch & dinner Tue-Sun) Beyond the town walls is this warm, intimate eatery. The chef is French, his wife Portuguese, and the menu an enticing mix of both. Think lamb *provençal* and quail (with a *jus* to die for). True panache.

Drinking

Dozens of bars litter the streets of Lagos, with some of the Algarve's most diverse and most clichéd drinking holes on hand.

Stevie Ray's Blues Jazz Bar (Rua da Senhora da Graça 9; ☺ 9pm-4am) This intimate two-level candlelit joint is the best live music bar in town. On weekends it has live blues, jazz and oldies. It attracts a smart-casual older crowd.

Taberna de Lagos (Rua Dr Joaquim Tello 1) Boasting a stylish space and brooding electronic music, this airy and atmospheric bar attracts a somewhat savvier bar-goer (higher cocktail prices also keep some punters away). It's set in a handsome town house, complete with high ceilings and old stone walls hung with vibrant paintings.

Taverna Velha (Rua Lançarote de Freitas 34) The snug Old Tavern is an old favourite and continues to haul in a lively crowd with its feel-good cocktail of pop classics.

Mullen's (Rua Cândido dos Reis 86) It may have lost some of its former energy, but this long-established *adega típica* (wine bar) still attracts a crowd. The restaurant turns into a bar later in the evening.

Eddie's Bar (Rua 25 de Abril 99) A good-natured and buzzing local beer stop, this busy dark-wood bar gathers plenty of surfers and backpackers.

Irish Rover (Rua do Ferrador 9) This local boozer serves up Guinness and the quintessential karaoke experience.

Whytts (Rua do Ferrador 7A) The full-on booze-bin where guys and gals can compete in a Deadly Sins competition (think speed drinking of hard liquor).

3 Monkeys (Rua Lançarote de Freitas) This is a backpacker's favourite for a good time. This classic bar has friendly staff who dish out plenty of shots and glasses to its jolly clientele. Its gimmick is a funnel-full of whatever you want to scull.

Grand Café (Rua N Senhora da Graça; ☺ 9pm-4am) This classy place has three bars, lots of gold leaf, kitsch, red velvet and cherubs, over which are draped dressed-up local and foreign hipsters.

Lounge (Travessa Senhora da Graça 2) Small and sleek, Lounge plays a good range of, you guessed it, lounge music and more commercial-style house music.

Amuras Bar (Marina; ☺ 10am-2am) One of half a dozen restaurant-bars overlooking the marina, this one attracts a slightly more staid crowd, who come for fruity cocktails and live music most nights.

Duna Beach Club (☎ 282 762 091; Meia Praia; ☺ 9-2am) Chill out with the smart set at this new bar-restaurant, open day and night. It's located bang on the beach, with a pool and attitude. At night it's the bar for A-listers.

Meia Praia has some beachfront gems just seconds from sun, swimming and sand, including Linda's Bar, with fab food, good salads, cocktails and tunes; and Bahia Beach Bar, an essential hang-out with live music on Friday and Sunday. Further around the beach and side by side are Bar Quim, renowned for their prawn dishes, and Pôr do Sol, a great place to enjoy the Angolan dish, *muamba de galinha*, chicken in palm oil.

Entertainment

Centro Cultural (☎ 282 770 450; Rua Lançarote de Freitas 7; ☺ 10am-8pm) Lagos' main venue for classical performances, including popular fado concerts, as well as contemporary art exhibitions.

Getting There & Away

BUS

From the **bus station** (☎ 282 762 944; www.eva-bus.com; Rua Vasco da Gama) buses travel to Portimão (€2.45, 20 minutes, 14 daily) and Albufeira (€4.70, one hour, four to six daily). Connections to Sagres run regularly (€3.40, one hour, nearly hourly on weekdays, seven daily Saturday and Sunday), via the crossroads to Salema (€2.15, 20 minutes; several run into Salema) from where you must walk around 1km down a narrow road; and a couple go on to Cabo de São Vicente (€3.55, one hour, three on weekdays only).

Eva express buses run to Lisbon (€18, 4¼ hours, six daily). To get to/from Carrapateira or Monchique, change at Aljezur (€3, 50 minutes, one to two daily) or Portimão. Buses to Aljezur serve Odeceixe (€3.80, 1½ hours). Renex operates an express service from Lagos to Lisbon (€17); tickets are available from the **Caima ticket office** (☎ 282 768 931; Rua das Portas de Portugal 101; ☺ 7am-1.30pm & 3-7.15pm daily, plus 10.30pm-12.30am Sun-Fri), which can also arrange minibus transfers to Faro airport (€20-28).

Buses also go to Seville (via Huelva) in Spain (€20, 5½ hours, two to four times daily Monday to Friday; more frequently in summer).

TRAIN
Lagos is at the western end of the Algarve line, with direct regional services to Faro daily (€6.40, 1¾ to two hours, eight daily), via Albufeira and Loulé (1½ hours), with onward connections from Faro to Vila Real de Santo António (€6.70, 3¼ hours) via Tavira (2¼ to 2¾ hours). Trains go daily to Lisbon (all requiring a change at Tunes; €25, 3½ hours, four daily).

Getting Around
BOAT
In summer, ferries run to and fro across the estuary to the Meia Praia side from a landing just north of Praça do Infante.

BUS
A recently introduced local bus service provides useful connections around town, as well as to Meia Praia, Luz, Odeceixe and the zoo in Barão de São Miguel. Tickets cost between €1 and €1.30. Buses run from Monday to Saturday between 7am and 8pm (2pm on Saturdays).

CAR, MOTORCYCLE & BICYCLE
Local agencies offering competitive car-rental rates:

Auto Jardim (☎ 282 769 486; www.auto-jardim.com; Rua Victor Costa e Silva 18a; ⊗ 8.30am-1pm & 2.30-7pm)

Luzcar (☎ 282 761 016; www.luzcar.com; Largo das Portas de Portugal 10; ⊗ 9am-1pm & 3-6pm)

Motorent (☎ 282 769 716; www.motorent.pt; Rua Victor Costa e Silva) You can hire both bicycles (€10/21 per one/three days) and scooters (50/125cc per three days from €50/65).

Drivers are advised to leave their cars in one of the free car parks on the outskirts (look for the large parking signs). The parking area along the riverfront on Avenida dos Descobrimentos is usually congested. Parking spaces closer to the centre are metered – watch out or you'll be wheel-clamped.

TAXI
You can call for **taxis** (☎ 282 763 587) or find them on Rua das Portas de Portugal.

LAGOS TO SAGRES
West of Lagos, the coast is sharp and ragged, and much less developed, though it's certainly not undiscovered. Once-sleepy fishing villages set above long beaches have now woken up to the benefits of tourism and, in some cases, developers have moved in. Out of high season, these places are bewitchingly calm.

Luz
Six kilometres west of Lagos, the small resort of Luz is packed with Brits and fronted by a sandy beach that's ideal for families. Unless you're part of the package deal mob, Luz is most conveniently done as a day trip from Lagos. Buses arrive at the central Praça da República.

SLEEPING & EATING
If you do end up here for the night, there are a few basic options.

Camping de Espiche (☎ 282 789 265; sites per adult/tent/car €5.80/6/4.90; 🔊 ⚙) Turiscampo-run, this shady site – one of the two nearest camping grounds – is only 2km from Luz.

Bella Vista (☎ 282 788 655; www.belavistadaluz .com; s/d €130/150; ✹ 🔊) This sizable place offers pleasant tiled rooms with verandas, a sunny terrace and pool. It's 500m up from the beach, off a busy road.

Pastelaria Chicca (☎ 282 761 334; Rua Direita) While the British-run Chicca's doesn't boast prime position (near the post office), the excellent range and quality of quiches, salads and cakes, all made on the premises, is worth writing home about.

GETTING THERE & AWAY
Buses run frequently from Lagos (around €1.90, 15 minutes).

Salema
This charmingly small coastal resort has an easygoing atmosphere; it's set on a wide bay 17km west of Lagos, surrounded by developments that manage not to overwhelm it. It's ideal for families, and there are several small, secluded beaches within a few kilometres – **Praia da Salema** by the village, **Praia da Figueira** to the west and **Boca do Rio** to the east.

THE ALGARVE

THE ALGARVE

The role of **Salema Property and Services** (☎ /fax 282 695 855), opposite Hotel Residencial Salema, is not primarily that of a tourist office, but it has some basic tourist material and is happy to organise bike rental and general services.

SLEEPING & EATING
Private rooms are plentiful along the seaside Rua dos Pescadores; expect to pay €40 or more for a double.

Quinta dos Carriços (☎ 282 695 201; www.quinta doscarricos.com; sites per adult/tent/car €4.90/4.90/4.90, studio/apt from €65/74; 🖳) Just 1.5km north of Salema, this camping ground is in a peaceful, tree-filled setting with abundant birdlife (no radios allowed!). It has studios and apartments and a designated naturist camping area.

Hospedaria Maré (☎ 282 695 165; www.algarve.co.uk; s/d €53/70) Just off the main road into town, this welcoming blue-and-white guest house has light and bright rooms, some with sea views, a pretty garden and a guests' kitchen. It's a short stroll downhill to the beach.

Hotel Residencial Salema (☎ 282 695 328; www .hotel.salema.pt; s/d incl breakfast €81/91; 🏊) Fifty metres from the beach, Salema offers comfortable rooms with terraces (most with sea views) in a modern whitewashed building.

There's a good selection of eateries along the beach and in the streets behind. **Boia** (☎ 282 695 382; Rua dos Pescadores 101; mains €7.50-15; 🕑 lunch & dinner) is an attractive fish eatery with a sea-facing terrace. Nearby, **A Casinha** (☎ 282 697 339; Rua dos Pescadores 101; mains €7-12.50; 🕑 Tue-Sun) has a tasty *feijoada de choco* (cuttlefish with beans), while the unpretentious **Restaurante Lourenço** (☎ 282 698 622; Rua 28 de Janeiro) behind the car park place, is recommended for fish (the owner is a keen hobby fisherman).

GETTING THERE & AWAY
At least six buses daily connect Lagos and Salema (€2.20, 30 minutes).

SAGRES
pop 1940

Overlooking some of the Algarve's most dramatic scenery, the small, elongated village of Sagres has an end-of-the-world feel with its sea-carved cliffs and empty, wind-whipped fortress high above the ocean. Despite its connection to Portugal's rich nautical past, there isn't much of historical interest in town. Its appeal lies mainly in its sense of isolation (refreshing after the hectic Algarve), plus access to fine beaches. It has a laid-back vibe, and simple, cheery cafes and bars. It's especially popular, particularly in the last decade, with a surfing crowd. Outside of town, the striking cliffs of Cabo de São Vicente make for an enchanting visit.

Sagres is where dashing Prince Henry the Navigator built a new, fortified town and a semimonastic school of navigation that specialised in cartography, astronomy and ship design, steering Portugal on towards the Age of Discoveries.

At least, that's according to history and myth. Henry was, among other things, governor of the Algarve and had a residence in its primary port town, Lagos, from where most expeditions set sail. He certainly did put together a kind of nautical think-tank, though how much thinking went on out at Sagres is uncertain. He definitely had a house somewhere near Sagres, where he died in November 1460.

In May 1587 the English privateer Sir Francis Drake, in the course of attacking supply lines to the Spanish Armada, captured and wrecked the fortifications around Sagres. The Ponta de Sagres was refortified following the earthquake of 1755, after which there was little of verifiable antiquity left standing.

Sagres has milder temperatures than other parts of the Algarve, with Atlantic winds keeping the summers cool.

Orientation
From Vila do Bispo, the district's administrative centre at the western end of the N125, a 9km line of villas runs along the N268 to Sagres city centre.

From a roundabout at the end of the N268, roads go west for 6km to the Cabo de São Vicente, south for 1km to the Ponta de Sagres and east for 250m to little Praça da República at the head of unassuming Sagres town. One kilometre east of the square, past holiday villas and restaurants, is the port, still a centre for boat building and lobster fishing, and the marina.

Note that there is no car rental in Sagres; it's advisable to hire cars in Lagos instead.

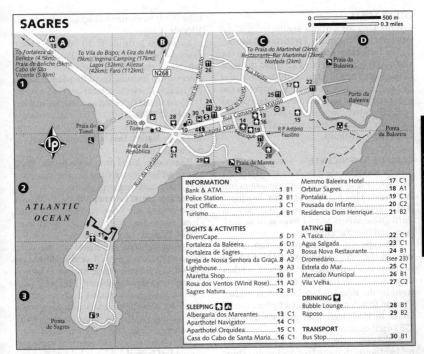

SAGRES

| 0 | 500 m |
| 0 | 0.3 miles |

To Fortaleza do Beliche (4.5km); Praia de Beliche (5km); Cabo de São Vicente (5.8km)

To Vila do Bispo (9km); A Eira do Mel (9km); Ingrina Camping (17km); Lagos (32km); Aljezur (42km); Faro (112km)

N268

To Praia do Martinhal (2km); Restaurante-Bar Martinhal (2km); Nortada (2km)

Praia da Baleeira

Rua do Mercado

Rua Mestre

Rua Comandante Matoso

Rua da Mareta

Porto da Baleeira

Praia do Tonel

Sítio do Tonel

Rua Infante Dom Henrique

R P António Faustino

Ponta da Baleeira

Praça da República

Rua da Fortaleza

ATLANTIC OCEAN

Praia da Mareta

Ponta de Sagres

INFORMATION		
Bank & ATM	1	B1
Police Station	2	B1
Post Office	3	C1
Turismo	4	B1

SIGHTS & ACTIVITIES		
DiversCape	5	D1
Fortaleza da Baleeira	6	D1
Fortaleza de Sagres	7	A3
Igreja de Nossa Senhora da Graça	8	A2
Lighthouse	9	A3
Maretta Shop	10	B1
Rosa dos Ventos (Wind Rose)	11	A2
Sagres Natura	12	B1

SLEEPING		
Albergaria dos Mareantes	13	C1
Aparthotel Navigator	14	C1
Aparthotel Orquidea	15	C1
Casa do Cabo de Santa Maria	16	C1

Memmo Baleeira Hotel	17	C1
Orbitur Sagres	18	A1
Pontalaia	19	C1
Pousada do Infante	20	C2
Residencia Dom Henrique	21	B2

EATING		
A Tasca	22	C1
Agua Salgada	23	C1
Bossa Nova Restaurante	24	B1
Dromedário	(see	23)
Estrela do Mar	25	C1
Mercado Municipal	26	B1
Vila Velha	27	C2

DRINKING		
Bubble Lounge	28	B1
Raposo	29	B2

TRANSPORT		
Bus Stop	30	B1

THE ALGARVE

Information

There's a bank and ATM just beyond the *turismo*, and a post office just east of there. Internet is available at a couple of the town cafes; bike rental is available through Sagres Natura (see p226).

Turismo (☎ 282 624 873; Av Comandante Matoso; ⏱ 9.30am-12.30pm & 1.30-5.30pm Tue-Sat) Situated on a patch of green lawn, 100m east of Praça da República.

Sights

FORTALEZA DE SAGRES

Blank, hulking and prisonlike, Sagres' **fortress** (☎ 282 620 140; adult/child €1.50/free; ⏱ 9.30am-8pm May-Sep, 9.30am-5.30pm Oct-Apr) has a forbidding front wall balanced by two mighty bastions. Inside, a few buildings dot the vast, open expanse, but otherwise a visit here is mostly about the striking views over the sheer cliffs, and all along the coast to Cabo de São Vicente.

Splash out on the printed guide (€1) that's sold at the entrance. In high season, there are occasional tours, but don't hold your breath for them.

Inside the gate is a curious, huge stone pattern that measures 43m in diameter. Named the **rosa dos ventos** (literally translating as 'wind rose'), this strange paving pattern is believed to be a mariner's compass. Excavated in 1921, the paving may date from Prince Henry's time – probably the only thing that does other than the foundations.

The village's oldest buildings, which include a cistern tower to the east; a house and the small, whitewashed, 16th-century **Igreja da Nossa Senhora da Graça**, with its worn golden altar, to the west (at time of research this was closed for renovations); and the remnants of a wall, are possibly replacements for what was there before.

Many of the gaps you'll see between buildings are the result of a 1960s spring-clean of 17th- and 18th-century ruins, organised to make way for a reconstruction (later aborted) that was to coincide with the 500th anniversary of Henry's death.

Smack in the centre is a modern, rather unsightly exhibition hall (closed at time of research). Near the southern end of the promontory is a **lighthouse**. Death-defying anglers balance on the cliffs below the walls, hoping to land bream or sea bass.

THE ALGARVE

OTHER FORTS

Overlooking the harbour are the ruins of the small mid-16th-century **Fortaleza da Baleeira**.

The **Fortaleza do Beliche**, built in 1632 on the site of an older fortress, is 4.5km to the west of the Sagres roundabout on the way to Cabo de São Vicente. Inside is a small chapel on the site of the ruined Igreja de Santa Catarina (and possibly an old convent). It was once a hotel, but sadly it's crumbling, along with the cliff, and is now off-limits.

CABO DE SÃO VICENTE

A trip to Cabo de São Vicente (Cape St Vincent), Europe's southwesternmost point, is a must. This barren, thrusting headland is the bleak last piece of home that nervous Portuguese sailors would have seen as they launched into the unknown.

The cape – a revered place even in the time of the Phoenicians and known to the Romans as Promontorium Sacrum – takes its present name from a Spanish priest martyred by the Romans (see boxed text, p228). The old fortifications, trashed by Sir Francis Drake in 1587, were later pulverised by the 1755 earthquake.

At the end of the cape are a wind-whipped red lighthouse (hundreds of oceangoing ships round this point every day) and a former convent. Henry the Navigator's house is believed to have been in a small castle to the right of the lighthouse.

The best time to visit is at sunset, when you can almost hear the hissing as the sun hits the sea. It's a fantastic cycle along a quiet road, though it's 6km each way, and windy.

There are cafes and restaurants along the way.

Activities

There are four good beaches a short drive or long walk from Sagres: **Praia da Mareta**, just below the town; lovely **Praia do Martinhal** to the east; **Praia do Tonel** on the other side of the Ponta de Sagres; and the isolated **Praia de Beliche**, on the way to Cabo de São Vicente. **Praia da Baleeira**, adjacent to the harbour, gets polluted from all the boat traffic. Praia do Tonel is especially good for surfing.

BOATING, SURFING & DIVING

Mar Ilimitado (☎ 916 832 625; www.marilimitado.com), a team of marine biologists, offers a variety of 'educational' boat trips from dolphin-spotting

trips (€30) to excursions up to Cabo de São Vicente (€20).

Surfing is possible at all beaches except Praia do Martinhal. Praia da Baleeira is not suitable for either swimmers or surfers. Several places offer lessons, including **Sagres Natura** (☎ 282 624 072; www.sagresnatura.com; Rua São Vicente; 1-/3-/5-day courses €45/120/180) and **International Surf School** (☎ 914482407, 919262773; www.international surfschool.com; 1-/3-/5-day courses €45/120/180); visit the surf shop, **Maretta Shop** (Av Comandante Matoso), for further details.

Bikes can be hired from **Sagres Natura** (☎ 282 624 072; Rua São Vicente; per day €15). The company also offers canoeing trips (€30).

Free Ride Sagres Surfcamp (☎ 916 089 005; www .freeridesurfcamp.com; 1-/3-/5-day lessons €45/120/180) gives lessons and offers free transport from Sagres, Praia da Luz and Lagos.

Diving centres are based at the port. Recommended is the PADI-certified **DiversCape** (☎ 965 559 073; www.diverscape.com; Porto da Baleeira). It organises dives between 12m and 30m around shipwrecks. A dive and equipment costs €40/200/320 for one/six/10 days, while the four-day PADI open-water course is €320. Beginners courses (from €60) are available.

Sleepy Sagres goes into overdrive during its annual **Surf Festival**, which is held during one weekend in mid-August and features music (with reggae bands taking centre stage) and surfy crowds.

Sleeping

Sagres fills up in summer, though it's marginally easier to find accommodation here than in the rest of the Algarve during the high season, thanks partly to the number of private houses in Sagres which advertise private rooms or apartments. Doubles generally cost around €40 and flats cost €45 to €80. As for elsewhere, prices can halve outside high season, including the top-end options.

BUDGET

Ingrina Camping (☎ 282 639 242; sites per adult/tent/car €4.50/4.50/3.70) About 17km northeast of Sagres, this is a small site, 600m from the beach south of Raposeira, with shade, a restaurant and bike hire.

Orbitur Sagres (☎ 282 624 371; www.orbitur.pt; sites per adult/tent/car €4.50/5/4.20) Some 2km from town, just off the road to Cabo de São Vicente, this is a shady, well-maintained camping ground with lots of trees. You can hire bikes here.

THE ALGARVE

MIDRANGE & TOP END

Casa do Cabo de Santa Maria (☎ /fax 282 624 722; casacabosantamaria@sapo.pt; Rua Patrão António Faustino; r from €50-60, apt from €60) You could eat off the floors of these squeaky-clean, welcoming rooms and apartments. They might not have sweeping views, but they are handsome and nicely furnished rooms – excellent value (breakfast not included).

Albergaria dos Mareantes (☎ 282 620 260; www .mareantes.com.sapo.pt; Rua Patrão António Faustino; s/d €60/75; P) This unpretentious place offers neat, adequate motel-style rooms with wooden floors and features TV, telephone and air-con trimmings.

Aparthotel Orquidea (☎ 282 624 257; apartho telorquidea@sapo.pt; Rua das Naus; d/apt €65/74) This worn and dated place has spacious, carpeted apartments, each with a mishmash of furniture. Outside August, the price is appealing, as are the verandas – some with views over the marina.

Aparthotel Navigator (☎ 282 624 354; www.hotel -navigator.com; Rua Infante Dom Henrique; 1-/2-person apt €88/93; P) It certainly ain't five-star (and breakfast isn't included), yet it's large (think groups), and has spacious, cheaply furnished apartments with million-dollar views over the cliffs. Each has a balcony and satellite TV. Prices halve outside high season.

Residencia Dom Henrique (☎ 282 620 003; fax 282 620 004; Praça da República; P) This friendly three-storey guest house was closed for renovations at time of research, but is worth checking out for its favourable traveller and reader reviews. It has wonderful sea views and an excellent location near the old plaza.

Pontalaia (☎ 282 620 280; www.pontalaia.pt; Rua Infante Dom Henrique; apt from €110; P) Next door to Navigator, this small, condo-like complex opened in 2005 offers attractive airy apartments set with blonde woods and stylish furnishings, each with a balcony.

our pick Memmo Baleeira Hotel (☎ 282 624 212; www.memmobaleeira.com; €140; P) Reopened in 2008 with a facelift, and not a wrinkle onsite. Think clean, smooth, white and minimalist design, from the contemporary glass reception area, to the retro foot rests in brown, white and powder blue coverings. The wide corridors kind of resemble a morgue, though you'd be pretty pleased to be entombed in one of the contemporary-style rooms, decked out in stylish white interiors and flat-screen TV. Heaven comes at a price; ask about promotional deals. Also has its own restaurant.

Pousada do Infante (☎ 282 624 222; fax 282 624 225; Rua P Antonio Faustino; d €250-300; P) This modern *pousada* has large, luscious rooms in a great setting near the clifftop. Count on bright, rich colours, handsome furnishings and picture-perfect views from the terraces.

Eating

Many places close or operate shorter hours during the low season (November to April). The *mercado municipal* provides great supplies for long beach days. You might need it – Sagres isn't the cheapest place to eat on the Algarve.

Dromedário (☎ 282 624 219; Rua Comandante Matoso; mains €3.50-7; 10.30am-2am;) Decked out in camels sent by enthusiastic patrons, this friendly place is indeed for those who enjoy a relaxed pace and reasonable, tasty snacks and drinks, including good coffee. There's free internet for patrons.

Agua Salgada (☎ 282 624 297; Rua Comandante Matoso; mains €5-9; 10am-2am; V) On the main drag, this two-storey bar-cafe serves a range of pizzas (try the mozzarella, tomato, ham, egg and banana selection) and veggie burgers and plenty of cocktails when evening arrives. Service can be slow and the music varies – lucky or not, Sting seemed to dominate when we were there. There's free internet.

Estrela do Mar (☎ 282 624 065; Rua Comandante Matoso; mains €5.50-11.50; lunch & dinner) This popular local restaurant offers good honest grilled fare (such as chicken or swordfish) that won't break the bank.

Bossa Nova Restaurante (☎ 282 624 566; off Rua Comandante Matoso; mains €6-17; lunch & dinner) The owner of the attractive Dromedário runs this pizza place. Here, the decor is nonexistent – it's a bit shedlike and impersonal, but the pizzas are good.

A Tasca (☎ 282 624 177; Porto da Baleeira; dishes €7-23; lunch & dinner) Overlooking the marina and out to sea, this place – a converted fish warehouse – specialises in, you guessed it, seafood. The cosy interior is filled with hanging strands of dried garlic and chillies, and bottles and clay jugs are embedded in the walls. The kitchen is open and there's a sunny terrace. Note – solo travellers – one of the few places in Portugal where you can have a *cataplana* for one person (rather than two).

DOUBLE DIVINITY

Although not much is known about the life of the Spanish-born St Vincent, his death is of such legendary stuff that both Spain and Portugal claim him as their own. In Portugal he is considered the patron saint of wine and sea voyages.

Born in the 4th century AD, St Vincent was a Spanish preacher killed by the Romans in 304. During his torturous death (by burning at the stake), he is said to have maintained such composure, praising God all the while, that he converted several of his torturers on the spot. Following his martyrdom, his remains were gathered, at which point two differing accounts emerge. Spain claims his final resting place is in Ávila. Portugal claims his remains washed up on the shores of the Algarve, near Sagres, in a boat watched over by two protective ravens. A shrine, which Muslim chronicles refer to as the Crow Church, became an object of Christian pilgrimage, though it was destroyed by Muslim fanatics in the 12th century.

Afonso Henriques, Portugal's first king, had the remains moved by ship to Lisbon in 1173, again accompanied by ravens. St Vincent became Lisbon's patron saint (his remains now rest in the Igreja de São Vicente de Fora). A raven features in the city's coat of arms – some Lisboêtas claim that ravens inhabited the church's bell tower for years afterwards.

Vila Velha (☎ 282 624 788; Rua António Faustino; mains €10-23; ⏰ dinner Tue-Sun; **V**) In a house with a lovely rose garden in front, the more upmarket Vila Velha offers rich seafood mains, rabbit, grilled salmon and good vegetarian dishes.

Praça da República has several small eateries.

There are several inviting restaurants on the sands of Praia do Martinhal, including **Nortada** (☎ 918 613 410; mains €5-25; ⏰ 10am-10pm), which serves grilled pizzas, omelettes, pasta and fish. Nearby is the more traditional **Restaurante-Bar Martinhal** (☎ 282 624 032; Praia do Martinhal; dishes €10-15; ⏰ 10am-9pm Tue-Sun), offering snacks and fish of the day.

It's worth driving 10km further north to Vila do Bispo to enjoy the fine foods of Chef José Pinheiro at **A Eira do Mel** (☎ 282 639 016; www.eiradomel.com; Estrada do Castelejo, Vila do Bispo; mains €12-30; ⏰ lunch & dinner Sun-Fri), a charming, Michelin-listed restaurant. The meat leans to the Algarvian; the seafood has a more contemporary touch. Think rabbit in red wine sauce, octopus *cataplana* with sweet potatoes (€31 for two people), curried Atlantic wild shrimps (€16) and lamb stew (€14). Mouthwatering stuff.

Drinking
Raposo (⏰ 10am-9pm) On the beach, laid-back Raposo enjoys an ideal setting, with lapping waves a few steps from the terrace.

Bubble Lounge (☎ 282 624 494; Rua Senhora da Graça; ⏰ 6pm-2am Tue-Sun) Bright walls, beanbags, low seating, Indian lanterns and wall hangings: boho Bubble Lounge has an easy vibe and good beats. It's friendly and there's a small streetside terrace. Movies are screened here on some nights.

Getting There & Around
The bus stop is by the *turismo*. You can buy tickets on the bus. For more information call ☎ 282 762 944.

Buses come from Lagos (€3.40, one hour, around 12 daily), via Salema, and Portimão (€5.10, 1¾ hours). On weekends there are fewer services. It's only 10 minutes to Cabo de São Vicente (one daily on weekdays).

Near the *turismo*, bike rental is available at Sagres Natura (see p226).

For a taxi, call ☎ 282 624 501.

NORTH OF SAGRES
Heading north along the Algarve's western coast you'll find some amazing beaches, backed by beautiful wild vegetation. Thanks to building restrictions imposed to protect the Parque Natural do Sudoeste Alentejano e Costa Vicentina, it's relatively well preserved (but there's the odd shock – construction is occurring – although it's said to be 'controlled'). Protected since 1995, it's rarely more than 6km wide, and runs for about 120km from Burgau to Cabo de São Vicente and up nearly the entire western Algarve and Alentejo shore. Here there are at least 48 plant species found only in Portugal, and around a dozen or so found only within the park.

It's home to otters, foxes and wild cats, and some 200 species of birds enjoy the coastal wetlands, salt marshes and cliffs, including Portugal's last remaining ospreys. Although the seas can be dangerous, the area has a growing reputation for some of Europe's finest surf and attracts people from all over the world.

Carrapateira

Surf-central Carrapateira is a tranquil, pretty, spread-out village, with two exhilarating beaches nearby whose lack of development, fizzing surf and strong swells attract a hippy, surf-dude crowd. The coast along here is wild, with copper-coloured and ash-grey cliffs covered in speckled yellow and green scrub, backing creamy, wide sands.

Praia da Bordeira (aka Praia Carrapateira) is a mammoth swath merging into dunes, 2km off the road on the north side of the village, while the similarly stunning **Praia do Amado** (more famous for its surf) is at the southern end of the village. Note: despite the number of campervans you see around the place, camping here is illegal.

For surfing courses contact Algarve Surf (p219). Or try the less official **Carrapateira Surf School & Camp** (☎ 964432324, 962681478; www .surfcamp-algarve.com; 1-week accommodation, equipment hire & lessons €395, €295 if camping; lessons per day €45; boards per hr/day €10/25), run by two local brothers who are passionate and experienced surfers. They built the camp (made up of basic but well-made three-bed wooden huts, with a communal kitchen) on family farmland, in a beautiful remote setting. They also hire out boards on both beaches from May to September.

Opened in May 2008, the compact **museum** (☎ 282 947 000; Rua de Pescador; ☽ 10am-5pm) is a must for visitors – surfers or otherwise. Its contemporary design space has small exhibits covering everything from the fishing industry to daily life of the locals, and stunning photograph collages depicting Carrapateira of yesteryear (there's minimal English labelling). The vista from the museum's ingenious viewing window is sublime.

SLEEPING & EATING

Pensão das Dunas (☎ /fax 282 973 118; Rua da Padaria 9; d with shared bathroom €28, 1-/2-room apt €39/58) This pretty guest house has tidy, colourful rooms overlooking a flower-filled courtyard. It's 100m from the road at the southern end of the village. At the time of research it was up for sale as a *pensão* so its status is unclear.

Bamboo (☎ 282 973 323; Sítio do Rio; d €50) About 500m from Praia da Bordeira, on the main road, this friendly, ecologically minded guest house has four attractive, colourful rooms.

Monte Velha (☎ 282 973 207; www.wonderfulland .com; r/ste €120/160) As far from the hippy-dude image as you can get, this luxurious place provides the *Out of Africa* experience with a Buddhist touch; think minimalist and contemporary design with a touch of Asia. It's 5km south of town; ring for directions.

Restaurante do Cabrito (☎ 282 973 128; mains €7-14; ☽ lunch & dinner Tue-Sun) Near the main N268 and specialising in seafood grills, Cabrito is a big, friendly restaurant with lots of country charm and outdoor seating.

Restaurante Torres (☎ 282 973 222; Rua da Padaria 7; mains €7.50-10; ☽ 8am-midnight) This very basic eatery has a few tables and serves up everything from toasted sandwiches to rabbit.

O Sítio do Forno (☎ 282 973 914; mains €8-18; ☽ noon-9pm Tue-Sun) On the cliff overlooking Praia do Amado and formerly a tiny fishermen's cabana, today this is a large place and *the* eatery to visit for magnificent ocean views. A variety of grilled fish is on offer; best is probably the fresh fish of the day, usually bream or bass.

O Sítio do Rio (☎ 282 973 119; mains €9-14; ☽ lunch & dinner; Ⓥ) Right on the dunes near Praia da Bordeira, this restaurant cooks up excellent grilled fish and meat mains; there are also vegetarian choices. It has an appealing indoor area, with fishing nets on the walls, and outdoor seating under large brollies. It's hugely popular with Portuguese at weekends.

Aljezur

Some 20km further north, Aljezur is an attractive, if uneventful, village that straddles a river. The western part is Moorish, with a collection of cottages below a ruined 10th-century hilltop castle; the eastern side, called Igreja Nova (meaning 'new church'), is 600m up a steep hill. Aljezur is close to some fantastic beaches, edged by black rocks that reach into the white-tipped, bracing sea – surfing hotspots. The countryside around, which is part of the natural park, is a tangle of yellow, mauve and green wiry gorse and heather.

ORIENTATION & INFORMATION

The high-up, pretty Largo Igreja Nova is the new town's focus, with some small cafes.

THE ALGARVE

Banks with ATMs, shops and restaurants can all be found on Rua 25 de Abril.

Espaço Internet (Largo Igreja Nova) Internet access

Post office (Rua 25 de Abril)

Turismo (☎ 282 998 229; ☒ 9.30am-7pm Tue-Thu, 9am-1pm & 2-5.30pm Fri-Mon May-Sep, 9.30am-5.30pm Tue-Thu, 9.30am-1pm & 2-5.30pm Fri-Mon Oct-Apr) The *turismo* is next to a small covered market, just before the bridge leading to the Lagos N120 road (Rua 25 de Abril). Buses stop near here.

SIGHTS & ACTIVITIES

Nearby wonderful, unspoilt beaches include **Praia da Arrifana** (10km southwest, near a tourist development called Vale da Telha), a dramatic curved black-cliff-backed bay with one restaurant, balmy pale sands and some big northwest swells (a surfer's delight); and **Praia de Monte Clérigo**, about 8km northwest. **Praia de Amoreira**, 6km away, is a wonderful beach where the river meets the sea. More difficult to reach but worth the effort getting there is the more remote **Praia de Vale Figueira**, about 15km southwest of Aljezur on rugged dirt roads.

SLEEPING

Parque de Campismo Serrão (☎ 282 990 220; www .parque-campismo-serrao.com; sites per adult/tent/car €5/4.50/4; ☐ ☒ ☒) This calm, shady site is 4km north of Aljezur, then 1km off the main road (follow the official 'campismo' signs; do not take the turn-off to Praia da Amoreira). It has wheelchair access, tennis courts, a playground and apartments, plus bike rental.

Restaurante Oceano (☎ 282 997 300; Praia Arrifana; d €35) The friendly owners here rent cosy rooms, with carved wooden beds and big windows overlooking palms and flowers. Brilliant seafood is just downstairs.

Residencial Dom Sancho II (☎ 282 997 070; turimol@ iol.pt; Largo Igreja Nova; s/d €35/45) In Igreja Nova, just off the main square, this friendly guest house has handsome rooms and a great restaurant below. It's excellent value.

Hospedaria O Palazim (☎ 282 998 249; N120; s/d €40/50) There are a few cracks here and there, but this modern two-storey place has rooms with verandas (and views over the hillsides and the road). It's 2km north of Aljezur on the busy Lisbon road.

Restaurante-Bar A La Reira (☎ 282 998 440; Rua 3 de Janeiro; d €60-70) Also in Igreja Nova, this place has 12 clean and tidy rooms with wood details, and each opens onto a shared terrace with lovely views.

In Praia da Arrifana locals sometimes rent out private rooms (look for '*quartos*' signs). There are a few other options outside town.

EATING & DRINKING

Snack Bar Acepipe (Largo Igreja Nova) This casual spot in Igreja Nova has outdoor tables overlooking the main square and makes a good spot for coffee, cakes and other light fare.

Pontá Pé (☎ 282 998 104; Largo da Liberdade; mains €7.50-12; ☒ lunch & dinner Mon-Sat) Friendly, with wooden floors and a beamed ceiling, Pontá Pé does tasty fish dishes and good barbecue chicken. Adjoining it is a cheery bar with live music on Friday and Saturday evenings.

Two casual, popular places near Pontá Pé are the nautically themed **Restaurante Ruth o Ivo** (☎ 282 998 534; Rua 25 de Abril 14; mains €8-11; ☒ lunch & dinner) and Palmeira, a friendly English-speaking cafe, that's right beside the bridge.

Facing Igreja Nova's main square, there's **Alisuper** (Largo Igreja Nova; ☒ 9am-8pm Mon-Sat, 9.30am-1.30pm Sun), a small but adequate supermarket. Next to the *turismo*, the town **market** (☒ 8am-2pm Tue-Sun) is a good place to buy fresh fruits and veggies.

Just past the fire-station is **Restaurante Portal da Várzea** (☎ 282 995 443; mains €9.50-14; ☒ lunch & dinner Wed-Mon), a friendly and popular restaurant with a friendly feel and lovely garden area. Serves up everything from fish dishes to *feijoada* delights. Has a great-value tourist menu (€8.50).

In Praia da Arrifana there's a string of seafood restaurants (packed with Portuguese at weekends) on the road above the beach, where you can expect to pay around €10 for grilled fish.

At Praia da Amoreira try **Restaurante Paraíso do Mar** (☎ 282 991 088; mains from €6.50-14, fish from €38 per kg; ☒ lunch & dinner), which offers fantastic panoramas overlooking the beach.

GETTING AROUND

If you're driving, there's a free car park next to the *turismo*.

Odeceixe

Around here the countryside rucks up into rolling, large hills. As the Alentejo turns into the Algarve, the first coastal settlement is Odeceixe, an endearing small town clinging to the southern side of the Ribeira de Seixe valley, and so snoozy it's in danger of falling off, apart from during high season, when Portuguese and European visitors pack the place.

The sheltered **Praia de Odeceixe**, 3.5km down the valley, is a wonderful bite of sand surrounded by gorse- and tree-covered cliffs. There's a **turismo** (☎ 961624596; ☯ 10am-12.30pm & 2-6pm) near the car park. **Lokko Surfing** (☎ 963170493; 1-/3-/5-day courses €45/120/180) offers surfing classes (and board and wetsuit rental) – look for their signs on the beach.

SLEEPING
There is a handful of well-advertised *quartos* (private rooms) in the village, especially along Rua Nova (en route to the beach). Expect to pay at least €35 to €40 for a double.

Parque de Campismo São Miguel (☎ 282 947 145; www.campingsaomiguel.com; sites per adult/tent/car €6/5.50/5; ⌨) Facility-loaded and pine-shaded, this camping ground-cum-miniresort is 1.5km north of Odeceixe; wooden bungalows are also available.

Restaurante Dorita (☎ 282 947 581; d with/without bathroom €60/40) You pay for the gorgeous beach view – but not much more – at this small place. Most rooms are worn and basic; the best have terraces with a vista.

Casa Hospedes Celeste (☎ 282 947 150; www .casaceleste.web.pt; Rua Nova 9; d incl breakfast €50) This renovated, clean and bright spot is excellent value, in a great central location and run by delightful owners. Rooms are smallish, but have colourful bedspreads and TV.

Pensão Luar (☎ 282 947 194; Rua da Várzea 28; d €65) At the western edge of the village, this friendly place is an excellent bargain (prices are almost half outside high season), with modern and white spick-and-span rooms.

Casa Vicentina (☎ 282 947 447; www.casavicentina .pt; Monte Novo; d €115-130, ste €155) For a touch of indulgence, head to this stylish complex, set in tranquil, rural surrounds. The interior decorator owner has gone to town in the rooms and suites; these are arranged around lush green lawn, with pool and lily ponds. Some rooms have kitchenettes. It's 2km from Odeceixe near Maria Vinagre – ring for directions.

EATING
Taberna do Gabão (☎ 282 947 549; Rua do Gabão 9; mains €6.50-13.50; ☯ lunch & dinner Wed-Mon) Next to the fire station, this welcoming restaurant features good-value traditional dishes served in a charming old-fashioned wooden dining room. There's outdoor seating.

Restaurante Chaparro (☎ 282 947 304; Rua Estrada Nacional; mains €7-8.50; ☯ lunch & dinner Tue-Sun) Opposite the post office, Chaparro has reliable standard fare, cheery service and yellow interior.

You'll find several pleasant restaurants around Largo 1 Mai, a great spot to sit and watch the world amble by.

Esplanada do Mar (Praia de Odeceixe) by the beach serves up some quality snacks.

GETTING THERE & AWAY
Express buses run from Lagos to Odeceixe (€8.80, 80 minutes, two daily) via Aljezur (€5.20, 35 minutes). Buy tickets at the *papelaria* (newsagent) next to the market.

One daily bus connects Vila do Bispo with Carrapateira (€3.80, one hour). There's a twice-weekly service to Praia de Arrifana from Aljezur (€2, 35 minutes).

THE INTERIOR

MONCHIQUE
pop 2800 / elev 410m

High up above the coast, in cooler mountainous woodlands, the picturesque hamlet of Monchique makes a lovely base for exploring, with some excellent options for walking, biking or canoeing.

An enticing spa town nearby is another alluring factor. It's set in the forested Serra de Monchique, the Algarve's mountain range, lying some 24km north of Portimão. Monchique is also known for having the best brews of the fiery *medronho*, a locally made liqueur (read firewater; see boxed text, p69)

Fires regularly affect this area in the summertime – the last major one was in 2003–04. These cause widespread damage and ongoing frustration at the lack of measures to prevent the devastation.

Orientation & Information
Buses will drop you off in the central Largo dos Chorões, with its cafes and large waterwheel sculpture.

Espaço Internet (☎ 282 910 235; Largo dos Chorões; ☯ 3-9pm Mon-Fri, 9am-9pm Sat)

Turismo (☎ 282 911 189; Largo da São Sebastião; ☯ 9.30am-1pm, 2-5.30pm Mon-Fri) A useful spot for picking up maps, but limited (or no) information on walks. It's uphill from the bus stop up Rua Engenheiro Duarte Pacheco.

Sights

A series of brown pedestrian signs starting near the bus station directs visitors up into the town's narrow old streets and major places of interest.

The **igreja matriz** (parish church; admission free; ⓨ 9am-5pm) has an extraordinary, star-shaped Manueline porch decorated with twisted columns that look like lengths of knotted rope, and a simple interior, with columns topped with more stony rope, and some fine chapels, including one whose vault contains beautiful 17th-century glazed tiles showing Sts Francis and Michael killing the devil.

Keep climbing and you'll eventually reach the ruins of the 17th-century Franciscan monastery of **Nossa Senhora do Desterro**, which overlooks the town from its wooded hilltop.

Activities

All of the activities listed here require advance reservations.

The German-run **Nature Walk** (☎ 966 524 822) organises one-day walking trips to nearby 773m Picota peak (€20 per person) and full-moon walks during summer.

Dutch-run **Outdoor Tours** (☎ 282 969 520, 916 736 226; www.outdoor-tours.com; Mexilhoeira Grande) offers biking (€24 to €35), kayaking (€23) and walking trips (€19) both in and around the Serra Monchique.

Alternativtour (☎ 282 913 204, 965004337; www.alternativtour.com) offers many activities, including guided walks (€20), mountain-biking tours (€35), canoeing trips (€25) or combined mountain-biking and canoeing trips (€55). Minimum persons apply, however.

Volunteers are welcome to help the reforestation project **Monchique Verde** (☎ 282 418 881). Launched after the big forest fires of 2003–04, the group meets on Saturday mornings at 9.30am in Monchique's Café O Lanche to clear, plant and water.

Sleeping

BUDGET

Residencial Estrela de Monchique (☎ 282 913 111; Rua do Porto Fundo 46; s/d €20/35) Near the bus station, this central spot has good-value rooms above a cafe.

Residencial Miradouro (☎ 282 912 163; Rua dos Combatentes do Ultramar; s/d €35/50) Up steep Rua Engenheiro Duarte Pacheco (signposted to Portimão), near the *turismo*, this 1970s hilltop place, run with great seriousness, offers

sweeping, breezy views and neat rooms, some with balcony.

MIDRANGE

Estalagem Abrigo da Montanha (☎ 282 912 131; www .abrigodamontanha.com; s €60, d €75-85, ste €90-105) This large granite-rock inn has 16 rooms and several contemporary and comfortable suites, as well as a well-set pool with a panoramic view, and a restaurant. It's a worthwhile alternative if you want comfort without the spa experience.

Albergaria Bica-Boa (☎ 282 912 271; d incl breakfast €70; ⓢ ⓟ) One kilometre out of town on the Lisbon road, this pretty four-room place overlooks a wooded valley. There's a decent restaurant here, too.

Eating & Drinking

Barlefante (Travessa das Guerreiras; mains €2.70-4; ⓨ noon-2am Mon-Thu, 1pm-4am Fri-Sun) Signposted off the town's main drag, this fun place has a touch of the burlesque, with hot-pink walls, red-velvet alcoves, ornate mirrors and green chandeliers. Excellent tapas (aka sandwiches). It's young Monchique's hippest haunt.

Restaurante O Parque (mains €6-12.50; ⓨ lunch & dinner) Directly opposite the tourist office, this cosy local haunt serves good, honest down-to-earth dishes. Many workers head here for lunch.

A Charrete (☎ 282 912 142; Rua Dr Samora Gil 30-34; mains €7.50-13; ⓨ lunch & dinner) Touted as the town's best eatery for its regional specialities, this place serves reliably good cuisine amid country rustic charm. A few favourites include cabbage with spicy sausages and award-winning honey flan for dessert.

Jardim das Oliveiras (☎ 282 912 874; mains €10-25; ⓨ lunch & dinner) About 2km from Monchique just off the road to Fóia (signposted), this atmospheric place, with beamed ceilings, serves up regional dishes. Outdoors, the garden, shady trees, hammocks and seating scream 'long lunch'. It is known for its *javali* (wild boar), wild rabbit and game dishes.

Also on the road to Fóia, many restaurants offer piri-piri chicken.

Shopping

Distinctive, locally made 'scissor chairs' – wooden folding stools – are a good buy here (smaller children's versions start at €25). Try shops along Rua Estrada Velha and Rua Calouste Gulbenkian.

Getting There & Away

Buses run from Portimão (€2.80, 45 minutes, five to nine daily).

AROUND MONCHIQUE

Fóia

The 902m Fóia peak, 8km west of Monchique, is the Algarve's highest point. The road to the summit climbs through eucalyptus and pine trees and opens up vast views over the rolling hills. On the way are numerous piri-piri pit stops offering spicy chicken. Telecommunication towers spike the peak, but ignore them and look at the panoramic views. On clear days you can see out to the corners of the western Algarve – Cabo de São Vicente to the southwest and Odeceixe to the northwest.

Caldas de Monchique

Caldas de Monchique is a bit like the filmset of *The Truman Show*. It's a slightly sanitised, faintly fantastical place, with a therapeutic calm, and pastel-painted buildings nestling above a delightful valley full of birdsong, eucalyptus, acacia and pine trees, 6km south of Monchique. It has been a popular spa for over two millennia – the Romans loved its 32°C, slightly sulphurous waters, which are said to be good for rheumatism and respiratory and digestive ailments. Dom João II came here for years in an unsuccessful attempt to cure his dropsy.

Floods in 1997 led to the closure of the spa hospital, after which it was redeveloped into a spa resort, and its picturesque buildings repainted pale pink, green and yellow.

ORIENTATION & INFORMATION

The hamlet is 500m below the main road. At reception (the first building on your left) you can book accommodation. Spa treatments and other luxuries are available at the spa.

SIGHTS

The most peaceful patch is a pretty, streamside garden above the hamlet's central square. Down the valley is the spa itself and below this is the huge unattractive bottling plant where the famous Caldas waters are bottled.

In the wooded valley below town, at the **Termas de Monchique Spa** (☎ 282 910 910; www.monchiquetermas.com; admission €25, hotel guests €15; 10.30am-7pm Tue, 9am-7pm Wed-Mon), admis-

sion allows access to the sauna, steam bath, gym and swimming pool with hydromassage jets. You can then indulge in special treatments, from a Cleopatra bath to a chocolate mask wrapping.

SLEEPING & EATING

There are two private accommodation options here: **Restaurante & Residencial Granifóia** (☎ 282 910 500; fax 282 912 218; s €30, d €35-40, tw €43-58;), set in a quiet location, has small rooms with dated, sixties-era decor. Some rooms have balconies and views. Coming from Monchique, you'll find it 400m past the turn-off to the hamlet, in a modern, unattractive building. In the village, **Albergaria Lageado** (☎ 282 912 616; www.albergariadabagado.com; s/d €45/55;) is an attractive hotel with a red-sloped roof and cosy ambience. It provides spotless rooms, a small plant-surrounded pool and a restaurant. Packages with board are also available.

The four other hotels all belong to Termas de Monchique. **Hotel Termal** (s/d €100/130), situated next to the spa, is the oldest, biggest (and least modern) of them; **Hotel Central** (s/d €100/130), next to Termas' main reception, has 13 beautifully furnished rooms; **Estalagem Dom Lourenço** (s/d €100/130), opposite reception, is the most luxurious option. The newest and most contemporary in style is **Hotel Dom Carlos** (s/d €100/130). The Termas also runs the self-catering **Apartamentos Turísticos D Francisco** (apt €160). Rates include breakfast, and you can book weekend or weeklong packages that include treatments. Prices are cheaper in low season.

The upmarket **Restaurante 1692** (mains €9-18; lunch & dinner) has tables in the tree-shaded central square, and a classy interior.

From the outside there's nothing particularly hot about **Café Imperio** (☎ 282 912 290; lunch & dinner Wed-Mon), although the view it offers of the valley is lovely. Locals flock to this place for what is reputedly the best piri-piri chicken in the region. Heading north, it's 700m on the left-hand side past the turn-off to Caldas.

GETTING THERE & AWAY

The Monchique to Portimão bus service goes via Caldas de Monchique (€1.25); the bus stop is on the road above the hamlet near Restaurant Rouxinol. It's easy to miss – ask the driver to alert you.

THE ALGARVE

ALCOUTIM
pop 1100 / elev 334m

Strategically positioned along the idyllic Rio Guadiana, Alcoutim (ahl-ko-*teeng*) is a small village just across the river from the Spanish town of Sanlúcar de Guadiana. What-are-you-looking-at fortresses above both villages remind one of testier times. Phoenicians, Greeks, Romans and Arabs have barricaded themselves in the hills here, and centuries of tension have bubbled across the river, which forms the Algarve's entire eastern boundary. In the 14th century, Dom Fernando I of Portugal and Don Henrique II of Castile signed a tentative peace treaty in Alcoutim. Tragically, today Alcoutim is said to be one of the fastest-diminishing towns in Portugal, as younger people leave the village to find jobs elsewhere. Tourism authorities are desperately trying to maintain this pleasant spot, as they well should. It boasts a lovely riverside beach, a fascinating castle and museum, and some interesting sites.

Orientation & Information

Alcoutim has a new town development 500m north of the square across the Ribeira de Cadavais stream.

Casa dos Condes (☎ 281 546 104; ☽ 9am-12.30pm & 2-5.30pm) Opposite the *turismo*; has free internet access (including wi-fi), a small display of local crafts; the Municipality has a desk here which offers guided visits of Alcoutim.

Turismo (☎ 281 546 179; Rua 1 de Maio; ☽ 9.30am-1pm & 2-5.30pm Oct-Jun, 9.30am-7pm Jul-Sep) Behind the central square, just a few steps from the river, this office distributes maps and *Walking in the Algarve* booklets (€5).

Sights & Activities

The main attraction for most day-trippers is the small riverside **beach**, equipped with sand, palm-leaf umbrellas, and even a life guard! The setting is breathtaking, but in summer it's hot, hot, hot. At the bridge, follow the signs to Praia Fluvial. The flower-ringed 14th-century **castelo** (admission €2.50; ☽ 10am-7pm) has sweeping views. Inside the grounds are the small, excellent **Núcleo Museológico de Arqueologia** (archaeological museum), displaying ruined medieval castle walls and other artefacts and a recent addition, an exhibition on Islamic board games.

You can cross the river on the small local **ferry** (€1, ☽ 9am-1pm & 2-7pm) but you might have to wait a while; it's a casual affair – wave your arms to attract the ferryman's attention if he's on the other side. Rent bikes or canoes from the Pousada da Juventude (see below).

Entrance fee to the castle also includes entry to small museums (*núcleos museológicos*) in Alcoutim and around. Ask at the tourist office for a brochure; some museums are by appointment only. In Alcoutim, this includes **Igreja de Nossa Senhora da Conceição** (☽ 10am-1pm & 2-6pm) and **Museu de Arte Sacra in Capela de Santo António** (☽ 10am-1pm & 2-6pm).

Inland Adventures (☎ 964993446; www.inland-adventures.com; Apartado 24) offers riverboat trips and bicycle tours along the Guadiana and surrounds.

Sleeping & Eating

Sleeping options are extremely limited in Alcoutim.

Pousada da Juventude (☎ 281 546 004; www.pousadasjuventude.pt; dm/d/apt €14/43/70; ☽ reception 8am-noon & 6pm-midnight; ⬚) On the river, 1km north of the square, past the new town and fire station, is this well-appointed hostel, with an excellent pool and kitchen facilities, plus bikes and canoes for rent.

Ilda Afonso (Rua Dr João Dias; r €35) This is the only private house that rents rooms. Rooms are plain and the plumbing can be a bit on the nose, but the owners are friendly and, hey, it's a bed.

Estalagem do Guadiana (☎ 281 540 120; www.grupofbarata.com; s/d €65/80) Below the *pousada da juventude*, this eighties-style place has reasonable but unremarkable rooms. Large windows overlook the river. Has a refreshing pool.

Snack Bar Restaurante O Soeiro (☎ 281 546 241; Rua do Município; daily specials €6-7; ☽ lunch Mon-Fri) This cheap and cheerful place serves hearty lunch plates. It has plastic outdoor tables overlooking the river.

Alcatiã (☎ 281 546 606; Mercado Municipal, 1st fl; mains €6.50-15; ☽ lunch & dinner Tue-Sat, lunch Sun) In the new part of town, in Centro Comercial (turn right after the bridge), is this modern, air-conditioned restaurant. It is distinguished by its seasonal dishes, which include lamprey and wild boar, fried eels and partridge.

Getting There & Around

Bus services run from Vila Real de Santo António (€3.40, 1¼ hours, one to two daily Monday to Friday); on Monday and Friday these go on to Beja (two hours) via Mértola (50 minutes).

The Alentejo

Alentejo is like Portuguese fado music: ultra-traditional, intriguingly diverse and lingeringly sentimental. Covering one-third of the country, Portugal's largest region – divided into Alto (upper) and Baixo (lower) – is bewitching, with its dry, golden plains, rolling hillsides and lime-green vines, rugged coastline, tiny whitewashed villages and majestic medieval cities. Its people are fiercely proud, yet somewhat melancholic.

A journey into the heart of the Alentejo reveals a tradition of centuries-old farming: cork plantations, vineyards and olive groves, the region's ongoing economic stalwarts in this otherwise poor, and very beautiful, area. Alentejo's rich past offers mystical stone carvings of Palaeolithic tribes, fragments from Roman conquerors, and stolid Visigothic churches. There are Moorish-designed neighbourhoods and the awe-inspiring fortresses built at stork's-nest heights, peering over the edge of Spanish-speaking Castile, Portugal's former nemesis.

For the visitor, Alentejo has further high notes, especially the enchanting medieval city of Évora. But the region's true soul extends beyond tourist enclaves. Experience traditional village life in the flower-filled towns of Marvão and Castelo de Vide; absorb the peaceful river views in Mértola; and glimpse the local craftsmanship in the marble towns of Estremoz, Vila Viçosa or Borba. The region, too, is rich in birdlife and rare plants, and walking opportunities abound.

As for the cuisine? It's commonly acknowledged that Alentejo is 'it' for traditional food. Village-based gastronomic delights abound, especially pork and game dishes, breads, cheeses and wines. Seafood is popular along the Alentejan coastline, where lovely stretches of beach – plus the pretty town of Zambujeira do Mar – attract a mixed summertime crowd after sun, surf and a laid-back nightlife scene.

HIGHLIGHTS

- Sampling the history, culture and cuisine of historically rich **Évora** (p236), a Unesco World Heritage–listed city
- Soaking up the sun and sunset cocktails of **Vila Nova de Milfontes** (p283)
- Gazing out over the countryside from the castle perch of enchanting **Marvão** (p268)
- Strolling with spirits of past civilisations and religions in **Mértola** (p270) and at the nearby **Convento de São Francisco** (p273)
- Watching the shadows play on the megaliths at **Cromeleque dos Almendres** (p247) and **Monsaraz** (p249)

- POPULATION: 770,000
- AREA: 31,483 SQ KM

THE ALENTEJO

History

Prehistoric Alentejo was a busy place, and today's landscape is covered in megaliths. But it was the Romans who stamped and shaped the landscape, introducing vines, wheat and olives, building dams and irrigation schemes and founding huge estates called *latifúndios* (that still exist today) to make the most of the region's limited rivers and poor soil.

The Moors, arriving in the early 8th century, took Roman irrigation further and introduced new crops such as citrus and rice. By 1279 they were on the run to southern Spain or forced to live in *mouraria* (segregated Moorish quarters) outside town walls. Many of their hilltop citadels were later reinforced by Dom Dinis (p32), who threw a chain of spectacular fortresses along the Spanish border.

Despite Roman and Moorish development, the Alentejo remained agriculturally poor and backward, increasingly so as the Age of Discoveries (p33) led to an explosive growth in maritime trade and seaports became sexy. Only Évora flourished, under the royal patronage of the House of Avis, but it too declined once the Spanish seized the throne in 1580.

During the 1974 revolution (p39) the Alentejo suddenly stepped into the limelight; landless rural workers who had laboured on the *latifúndios* for generations rose up in support of the communist rebellion and seized the land from its owners. Nearly 1000 estates were collectivised, although few succeeded and all were gradually re-privatised in the 1980s. Most are now back in the hands of their original owners.

Today Alentejo remains among Europe's poorest and emptiest regions. Change here has occurred rapidly. Portugal's entry into the EU (and its demanding regulations), increasing mechanisation, successive droughts and greater opportunities elsewhere have had a major effect on the region: young people have headed for the cities (many to the Algarve and Lisbon), leaving villages – and their traditions – to die out. Although its cork, olives, marble and granite are still in great demand, and the deep-water port and industrial zone of Sines is of national importance, this vast region contributes only a small fraction to the gross national product. Locals are still waiting for the benefits promised by the construction of the huge Barragem do Alqueva (Alqueva Dam) and its reservoir (p250). Currently the hydroelectric dam provides energy to the national grid, but the effects of tourism and 'greenifying' the region (providing water in an effort to make the region green and productive) are hard to determine.

ALTO ALENTEJO

The northern half of the Alentejo is a medieval gem, with a scattering of walled fortress towns (like Elvas and Estremoz) and remote cliff-top castles (like Marvão and Castelo de Vide). Only a handful of visitors to Alto Alentejo travel beyond Évora, so once outside the city you'll see traditional life at its most authentic.

ÉVORA

pop 56,500 / elev 250m

One of Portugal's most beautifully preserved medieval towns, Évora is an enchanting place to delve into the past. Inside the 14th-century walls, Évora's narrow, winding lanes lead to striking architectural works: an elaborate medieval cathedral and cloisters; the cinematic columns of the Templo Romano (near the intriguing Roman baths); and a picturesque town square, once the site of some rather gruesome episodes courtesy of the Inquisition. Aside from its historic and aesthetic virtues, Évora is also a lively university town, whose students nicely dilute the tourist population, and its many attractive restaurants serve up hearty Alentejan cuisine. Outside of town, Neolithic monuments and rustic wineries make for fine day trips.

History

The Celtic settlement of Ebora had been established here before the Romans arrived in 59 BC and made it a military outpost, and eventually an important centre of Roman Iberia, when it was known as 'Ebora Liberalistas Julia'.

After a depressing spell under the Visigoths, the town got its groove back as a centre of trade under the Moors. In AD 1165 Évora's Muslim rulers were hoodwinked by a rogue Portuguese Christian knight known as Giraldo Sem Pavor (Gerald the Fearless). The well-embellished story goes like this: Giraldo single-handedly stormed one of the town's watchtowers by climbing up a ladder of spears driven into the walls. From there

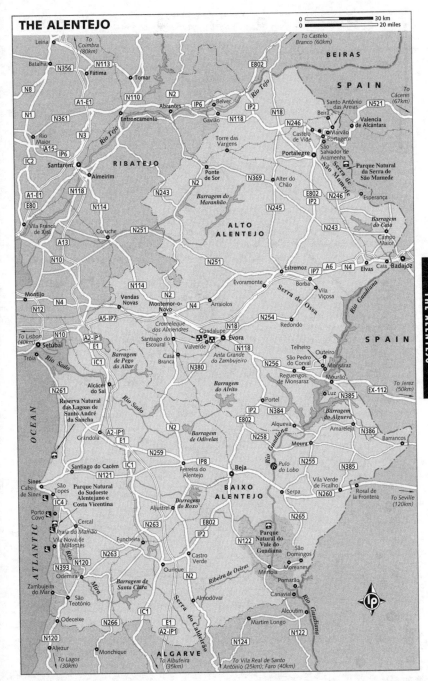

ÉVORA

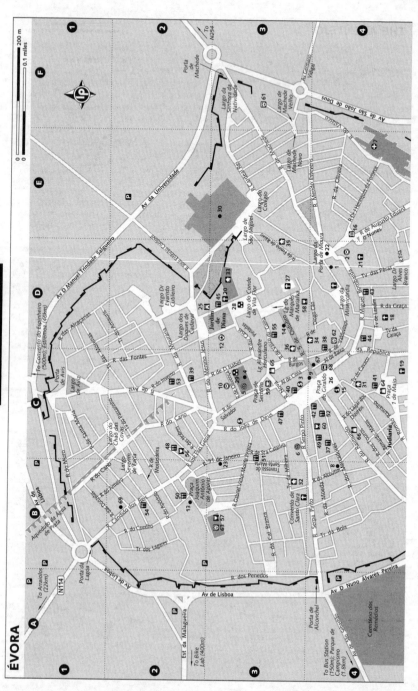

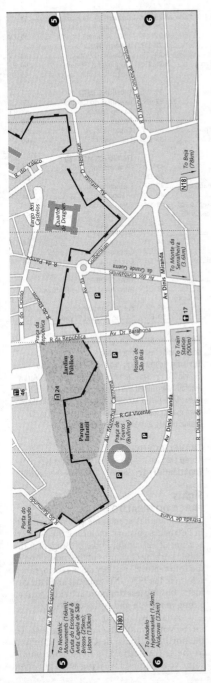

he distracted municipal sentries while his companions took the town with hardly a fight. The Moors took it back in 1192, clinging on for another 20 years or so.

The 14th to 16th centuries were Évora's golden age, when it was favoured by the Alentejo's own House of Avis, as well as by scholars and artists. Declared an archbishopric in 1540, it got its own Jesuit university in 1559.

When Cardinal-King Dom Henrique, last of the Avis line, died in 1580 and Spain seized the throne, the royal court left Évora and the town began wasting away. The Marquês de Pombal's closure of the university in 1759 was the last straw. French forces plundered the town and massacred its defenders in July 1808.

Ironically, as in many other well-preserved ancient cities, it was decline itself that protected Évora's very fine old centre – economic success would have led to far greater redevelopment. Today the population is smaller than it was in the Middle Ages.

Orientation

Évora climbs a gentle hill above the Alentejo plain. Around the walled centre runs a ring road from which you can enter the town on one of several 'spoke' roads.

The town's focal point is Praça do Giraldo, 700m from the bus station to the southwest. The train station is outside the walls, 1km south of the square.

If you're driving, it's advisable to park outside the walls at one of the many signposted car parks (eg at the southern end of Rua da República). Except on Sunday, spaces inside the walls are limited and usually metered; pricier hotels have some parking.

Information

BOOKSHOPS

Livraria Nazareth (☎ 266 741 702; Praça do Giraldo 46) Head up the stairs for maps, including *Alentejo & Évora* (€4.95), and some books in English.

EMERGENCY

PSP police station (☎ 266 746 977; Rua Francisco Soares Lusitano) Near the Templo Romano.

INTERNET ACCESS

Câmara municipal (town hall; Praça de Sertório; ⏲ 9am-12.30pm & 2-5pm Mon-Fri) Free internet access in the same building as the old Roman baths.

THE ALENTEJO

INFORMATION		
Abreu	1	D4
Branch Post Office	2	D4
Caixa de Crédito Agrícola	3	C3
Câmara Municipal	4	C3
Câmara Municipal Internet	5	C3
Cybercenter	6	C3
Évora District Hospital	7	E4
Lavandaria Olimpica	8	B4
Livraria Nazareth	9	C4
Main Post Office	10	C3
Oficin@Bar	11	C4
PSP Police Station	12	D3
Rota dos Vinhos do Alentejo Headquarters	13	B2
Top Atlântico	14	D3
Turismo	15	C4

SIGHTS & ACTIVITIES		
Agia	(see 15)	
Capela dos Ossos	(see 19)	
Casa Cordovil	16	E4
Convento dos Lóios	(see 33)	
Ermida de São Brás	17	D6
Galeria das Damas	(see 24)	
Igreja da Nossa Senhora da Graça	18	D4
Igreja de São Francisco	19	C4
Igreja de São João	20	D3
Igreja do Carmo	21	D4
Largo da Porta de Moura	22	D4
Mendes & Murteira	23	B3
Palácio de Dom Manuel	24	C5

Palácio dos Duques de Cadaval.	25	D2
Praça do Giraldo	26	C4
Sé	27	D3
Templo Romano	28	D3
Termas Romanas	29	C3
Universidade de Évora	30	E3

SLEEPING		
Casa dos Teles	31	C4
Hotel Santa Clara	32	B3
Pousada dos Lóios	33	D3
Residencial Diana	34	D4
Residencial Policarpo	35	D3
Residencial Riviera	36	D3

EATING		
Adega do Neto	37	C4
Aquário	38	D4
Botequim da Mouraria	39	C2
Café Arcada	40	C3
Café Restaurante Repas	41	C4
Cafetaria Cozinha de Santo Humberto	42	C4
Casa dos Sabores	43	D4
Gelataria Zoka	44	D4
Jardim do Paço	45	D3
Mercado Municipal	46	C5
O Antão	47	C3
Restaurante Cervejaria São Domingos	48	C2
Restaurante Cozinha de Santo Humberto	49	C4
Restaurante o Fialho	50	B2

Restaurante Taverna	51	C3
Snack-Bar Restaurante A Choupana	52	C4
Taberna Típica Quarta-Feira	53	C2
Tasquinha d'Oliveira	54	B2
Vasco da Gama Cafetaria	55	D3

DRINKING		
Bar Amas do Cardeal	56	C2
Bar do Teatro	57	B3
Bar UÉ	58	B3
Cup of Joe	59	C3
Oficin@Bar	60	C4

ENTERTAINMENT		
Casa dos Bonecos	61	F3
Praxis	62	D4
Sociedade Harmonia Eborense	(see 15)	
Teatro Garcia de Rezende	63	B3

SHOPPING		
Feiras no Largo	64	C4
Oficina da Terra	65	C3
Oficina da Terra	66	C4

TRANSPORT		
Automóvel Club de Portugal (ACP)	67	C4
Bus to Camp Site	68	C4
Silvano Manuel Cégado	69	B2

Cbercenter (Rua Serpa Pinto 36; per hr €2; 10.30am-11pm Mon-Fri, 2-10pm Sat & Sun)

Oficin@Bar (☎ 266 707 312; Rua da Moeda 27; per hr €3; 9pm-3am Tue-Sat, 9pm-2am Sat)

LAUNDRY
Lavandaria Olimpica (☎ 266 705 293; Largo dos Mercadores 6; 9am-1pm & 3-7pm Mon-Sat) Offers next-day service; €5 per kilo wash, dry and iron.

MEDICAL SERVICES
Évora district hospital (☎ 266 740 100; Largo Senhor da Pobraza) East of the centre.

MONEY
There are several banks with ATMs on and around Praça do Giraldo, including **Caixa de Crédito Agrícola** (Praça do Giraldo 13).

POST
Branch post office (Largo da Porta de Moura)
Main post office (Rua de Olivença)

TOURIST INFORMATION
Rota dos Vinhos do Alentejo headquarters (Wine Route Office; ☎ 266 746 498; Praça Joaquim António de Aguiar 20-21; 9am-12.30pm & 2-5.30pm Mon-Fri)

Head here for details of a *rota dos vinhos* (wine route) to *adegas* (wineries) in the Alentejo.

Turismo (tourist office; ☎ 266 777 071; Praça do Giraldo 73; 9am-7pm Apr-Oct, 9am-6pm Nov-Mar) A fabulously organised and helpful place that has a *Historical Itineraries* leaflet (€1.05) and a range of free publications – town map, a spiral tourist guide and a couple of useful listings guides, *Viva por Cá* and *Sapatoraso*.

TRAVEL AGENCIES
Abreu (☎ 266 769 180; Rua da Misericórdia 16)
TopAtlântico (☎ 266 746 970; Rua 5 de Outubro 63)

Sights
PRAÇA DO GIRALDO
This square has seen some potent moments in Portuguese history, including the 1483 execution of Fernando, Duke of Bragança; the public burning of victims of the Inquisition in the 16th century; and fiery debates on agrarian reform in the 1970s. Nowadays it's still the city focus, hosting less dramatic activities such as sitting in the sun and coffee drinking.

The narrow lanes to the southwest were once Évora's *judiaria* (Jewish quarter). To the northeast, Rua 5 de Outubro, climbing to the *sé* (cathedral), is lined with handsome town houses wearing wrought-iron

THE ALENTEJO

balconies, while side alleys pass beneath Moorish-style arches.

SÉ

Évora's **cathedral** (Largo do Marquês de Marialva; admission €1; ⏰ 9am-12.20pm & 2-4.50pm) looks like a fortress, with two stout granite towers. It was begun around 1186, during the reign of Sancho I, Afonso Henriques' son – there was probably a mosque here before. It was completed about 60 years later. The flags of Vasco da Gama's ships were blessed here in 1497.

You enter the cathedral through a portal flanked by 14th-century stone apostles, flanked in turn by asymmetrical towers and crowned by 16th-century roofs. Inside, the Gothic influence takes over. The chancel, remodelled when Évora became the seat of an archdiocese, represents the only significant stylistic change since the cathedral was completed. Golden light filters through the window across the space.

The cool **cloister** (admission with cathedral & museum €3; ⏰ 9am-noon & 2-4.30pm Tue-Sun) is an early-14th-century addition. Downstairs are the stone tombs of Évora's last four archbishops. At each corner of the cloister a dark, circular staircase (at least one will be open) climbs to the top of the walls, from where there are good views.

Climb the steps in the south tower to reach the choir stalls and up to the **museum**, which demonstrates again the enormous wealth poured into the church, with fabulous ecclesiastical riches, including a revolving jewelled reliquary (containing a fragment of the true cross): encrusted with emeralds, diamonds, sapphires and rubies, it rests on gold cherubs that would dazzle Liberace, is flanked by two Ming vases and topped by Indo-Persian textiles.

TEMPLO ROMANO

Opposite the museum are the remains of a Roman **temple** (Largo do Conde de Vila Flor) dating from the 2nd or early 3rd century. It's among the best-preserved Roman monuments in Portugal, and probably on the Iberian Peninsula. Though it's commonly referred to as the Temple of Diana, there's no consensus about the deity to which it was dedicated, and some archaeologists believe it may have been dedicated to Julius Caesar. How did these 14 Corinthian columns, capped with Estremoz marble, manage to survive in such good shape for some 18 centuries? The temple was apparently walled up in the Middle Ages to form a small fortress, and then used as the town slaughterhouse. It was uncovered late in the 19th century.

TERMAS ROMANAS

Inside the entrance hall of the *câmara municipal* on Praça de Sertório are more Roman vestiges, discovered only in 1987. These impressive **Roman baths** (admission free; ⏰ 9am-5.30pm Mon-Fri), which include a *laconicum* (heated room for steam baths) with a superbly preserved 9m-diameter circular pool, would have been the largest public building in Roman Évora. The complex also includes an open-air swimming pool, discovered in 1994.

IGREJA DE SÃO JOÃO & CONVENTO DOS LÓIOS

The small, fabulous **Church of St John the Evangelist** (admission €3, plus Salas de Exposição do Palácio €5; ⏰ 9am-12.30pm & 2-6pm Tue-Sun), which faces the Templo Romano, was founded in 1485 by one Rodrigo Afonso de Melo, count of Olivença and the first governor of Portuguese Tangier, to serve as his family's pantheon. It's still privately owned, by the Duques de Cadaval, and notably well kept.

Behind its elaborate Gothic portal is a nave lined with glorious floor-to-ceiling *azulejos* (hand-painted tiles) created in 1711 by one of Portugal's best-known tile-makers, António de Oliveira Bernardes. The grates in the floor reveal a surprising underworld: you'll see a deep Moorish cistern that predates the church and an ossuary full of monks' bones. In the sacristy beyond are fragments of even earlier *azulejos*.

The former **Convento dos Lóios**, to the right of the church, has elegant Gothic cloisters topped by a Renaissance gallery. A national monument, the convent was converted into a top-end *pousada* (upmarket inn), the Pousada dos Lóios (p243), in 1965. If you want to wander around, wear your wealthy-guest expression – or have dinner at its upmarket restaurant.

PALÁCIO DOS DUQUES DE CADAVAL

Just northwest of the Igreja de São João is the 17th-century facade of a much older palace and castle, as revealed by the two powerful square towers that bracket it. The Palácio dos Duques de Cadaval (Palace of the Dukes of Cadaval) was given to Martim Afonso de

THE ALENTEJO

Melo, the governor of Évora, by Dom João I, and it also served from time to time as a royal residence. A section of the palace still serves as the private quarters of the de Melo family; the other main occupant is the city's highway department.

UNIVERSIDADE DE ÉVORA

Just outside the walls to the northeast is the university's main building (Colégio do Espírito Santo), a descendent (reopened in 1973) of the original Jesuit institution founded in 1559 (which closed when the Jesuits got shooed out by Marquês de Pombal in 1759). Inside are arched, Italian Renaissance-style **cloisters**, the Mannerist-style **Templo do Espírito Santo** and beautiful *azulejos*.

TOWN WALLS

About one-fifth of Évora's residents live within the town's old walls, some of which are built on top of 1st-century Roman fortifications. Over 3km of 14th-century walls enclose the northern part of the old town, while the bulwarks along the southern side, such as those running through the *jardim público* (public gardens), date from the 17th century.

LARGO DA PORTA DE MOURA

The Largo da Porta de Moura (Moura Gate Square) stands just southeast of the cathedral. Near here was the original entrance to town. In the middle of the square is a strange-looking, globular 16th-century Renaissance **fountain**. Among the elegant mansions around the square is **Casa Cordovil**, built in Manueline-Moorish style. Across the road to the west have a look at the extraordinary knotted Manueline stone doorway of the **Igreja do Carmo**.

IGREJA DE SÃO FRANCISCO & CAPELA DOS OSSOS

Évora's best-known **church** (Praça 1 de Maio) is a tall and huge Manueline-Gothic structure, completed around 1510 and dedicated to St Francis. Exuberant nautical motifs celebrating the Age of Discoveries deck the walls and reflect the confident, booming mood of the time. It's all topped by a cross of Christ's order and dome. Legend has it that the Portuguese navigator Gil Vicente is buried here.

What draws the crowds, though, is the mesmerising **Capela dos Ossos** (Chapel of Bones; admission €1.50; ☉ 9am-12.50pm & 2.30-5.40pm Mon-Sat, from 10am Sun). A small room behind the altar

has walls and columns lined with carefully arranged bones and skulls of some 5000 people. Visitors here describe the sight as macabre, artistic, ghoulish or beautiful (and, tasteful or not, we even heard several people humming 'Dem bones, dem bones, dem dry bones'). According to records, 17th-century Franciscan monks constructed this as a *memento mori* (reminder of death) to meditate on the human condition. An inscription over the entrance translates as: 'We bones await yours'.

Adding a final ghoulish flourish are two hanging mummified corpses; explanations in English highlight a legend. The entrance is to the right of the main church entrance. Pay €0.50 extra to take photos.

JARDIM PÚBLICO

For a lovely tranquil stroll, head to the light-dappled public gardens (with a small outdoor cafe) south of the Igreja de São Francisco. Inside the walls of the 16th-century **Palácio de Dom Manuel** is the **Galeria das Damas** (Ladies' Gallery), an indecisive hybrid of Gothic, Manueline, neo-Moorish and Renaissance styles. It's open when there are (frequent) temporary art exhibitions.

From the town walls you can see, a few blocks to the southeast, the crenellated, pointy-topped Arabian Gothic profile of the **Ermida de São Brás** (Chapel of St Blaise), dating from about 1490. It's possibly an early project of Diogo de Boitaca, considered the originator of the Manueline style.

IGREJA DA NOSSA SENHORA DA GRAÇA

Down an alley off Rua da República is the curious baroque facade of the Igreja da Nossa Senhora da Graça (Church of Our Lady of Grace), topped by four ungainly stone giants – as if they've strayed from a mythological tale and landed up on a religious building. An early example of the Renaissance style in Portugal is found in the cloister of the 17th-century **monastery** next door.

AQUEDUTO DA ÁGUA DE PRATA

Jutting into the town from the northwest is the beguilingly named Aqueduto da Água de Prata (Aqueduct of Silver Water), designed by Francisco de Arruda (better known for Lisbon's Tower of Belém) to bring clean water to Évora and completed in the 1530s. At the end of the aqueduct, on Rua do Cano, the neighbourhood feels like a self-contained village, with houses, shops and cafes built right into its perfect arches, as if nestling against the base of a hill.

Tours

Agia (☎ 963702392; agia@iol.pt; adult/child under 12yr €12/free, minimum 2 people; ☷ 10am) Agia offers daily 90-minute guided tours of Évora from outside the *turismo* on Praça do Giraldo.

Mendes & Murteira (☎ 266 739 240; www.evora-mm .pt; Rua 31 de Janeiro 15a) Operating out of the Barafunda boutique, this company offers flexible three- to four-hour tours (price negotiable) of surrounding megaliths or around the city itself.

Festivals & Events

Rota de Sabores Tradicionais A gastronomic festival that lasts from January to May, celebrating game in January, pork in February, soups in March, lamb in April and desserts in May – traditional restaurants throughout the city serve specialities accordingly.

Feira dos Ramos Palm Fair is celebrated with a large market on the Friday before Palm Sunday.

Festas Populares Évora's biggest, bounciest annual bash, and one of the Alentejo's best country fairs is held in late June.

Évora Classical Music Festival This five-day event (usually held in early July) formerly featured a strictly classical program, but today encompasses a wide range of contemporary and world musical styles. Concerts are held at various indoor and outdoor venues in Évora.

Sleeping

In high season it's essential to book ahead. Budget choices are limited.

BUDGET

Parque de campismo (☎ 266 705 190; www.orbitur .pt; adult/tent/car €4.80/5.40/4.70) Flat, grassy and tree-shaded, with disabled access, Orbitur's well-equipped camp site is 2km southwest of town. Urban Sitee bus 5 or 8 (€1.20) from Praça do Giraldo, via Avenida de São Sebastião and the bus station, goes close by.

Casa dos Teles (☎ 266 702 453; Rua Romão Ramalho 27; s €25, d with shared bathroom €30-35, r with bathroom €40; ☷) Run by a delightful owner, these 10 mostly light and airy rooms are the best of the *quartos* (rooms in private houses); quieter rooms at the back overlook a pretty courtyard; the 'apartment' has its own bathroom.

MIDRANGE

Residencial Policarpo (☎ 266 702 424; www.pensao policarpo.com; Rua da Freiria de Baixo 16; s/d with bathroom €52/57, without bathroom €30/35; ℗) This hotel is the former holiday home of a 16th-century count – the family was purged by the Pombals in the 18th century. While charming and atmospheric (with the odd musty wall), it's somewhat faded. Rooms have a mix of carved wooden and traditionally hand-painted Alentejan furniture. Room 101 features 17th-century *azulejos*.

Residencial Diana (☎ 266 702 008; Rua de Diogo Cão 2; s/d with bathroom €60/65, without bathroom €45/55; ☷) Diana is slightly long in the tooth now, with saggy mattresses and grannylike decor. Nevertheless, it's charming in a high-ceilinged-wood-floored kind of way.

Residencial Riviera (☎ 266 737 210; Rua 5 de Outubro 49; s/d/ste €62/77/92; ☷) Only one block from the *praça* (town square), this charming and well-renovated place has bright, stylish rooms with *boveda* (brick-arched) ceilings and carved bedheads. Bathrooms are gleamingly tiled.

Hotel Santa Clara (☎ 266 704 141; www.hotel santaclara.pt; Travessa da Milheira 19; r €74; ℗ ☷) A whitewashed building tucked away in a quiet back street, this efficiently run Best Western hotel has plain but comfortable rooms.

There are 10 converted *quintas* (estates) around Évora, including **Monte da Serralheira** (☎ 266 741 286; www.monteserralheira.com; 2-/4-person apt €58/98; ☷), a big, blue-bordered farm, 4km south of town, offering self-catering or B&B, with horses and bikes to ride. The Dutch owner is a qualified local guide.

TOP END

Convento do Espinheiro (☎ 266 788 200; www.con ventodoespinheiro.com; r from €200) Housed in a restored 15th-century convent and located by the doors to the old city, is this elegant hotel and spa complex with facilities galore (heliport, anyone?). Rooms feature heavy fabrics and rugs. A vaulted restaurant, Divinus, serves high-class Alentejan cuisine.

Pousada dos Lóios (☎ 266 730 070; recepcao.loios@ pousadas.pt; Largo do Conde de Vila Flor; d €230; ℗ ☷) Occupying the former Convento dos Lóios, opposite the Templo Romano, this beautiful *pousada* has gorgeously furnished rooms in a contemporary style (mint green and white) set around the pretty cloister. Note the original walkie-talkie 'devices' in the room doors.

THE ALENTEJO

There's a flash restaurant on the ground floor of the cloister (mains €22 to 25).

Eating

Scattered around Praça do Giraldo are a handful of attractive cafes with outdoor seating – a good spot for coffee or an early evening drink.

BUDGET

Gelataria Zoka (Largo de São Vicente 14, Rua Miguel Bombarda; ice creams from €1.65; ☺ 8am-midnight) Ice-cream lovers can head here for heaven-in-a-cone – experienced at tables on the pedestrianised street.

Casa dos Sabores (☎ 266 701 030; Rua Miguel Bombarda 50; snacks €2-4; ☺ 8am-7pm Mon-Fri, to 1pm Sat) A sleek cafe with solid, small wood tables, marble floors and nice sandwiches. You can buy local wines, cheeses and meats here, too.

ourpick Snack-Bar Restaurante A Choupana (☎ 266 704 427; Rua dos Mercadores 18; mains €5-12; ☺ lunch & dinner Mon-Sat) This is a tiled, busy place where many locals opt to sit on stools at a long bar. There's a TV, lots of knick-knacks and tasty daily mains. Attached is an appealing restaurant served by efficient bow-tied waiters.

Cafe Restaurante Repas (☎ 266 708 540; Praça 1 de Maio 19; mains €5-12; ☺ breakfast, lunch & dinner) Repas may be nothing special cuisine-wise, but its location near the Igreja São Francisco is pleasant.

Aquário (☎ 266 785 055; Rua de Valdevinos 7; mains €5.50-8; ☺ lunch & dinner Tue-Sun; Ⓥ) This small, quaint spot serves well-prepared dishes, including one vegetarian special per day. Checked tablecloths and a stone support within the restaurant add to the ambience.

You can pick up fruit and vegetables at the **mercado municipal** (municipal market; Praça 1 de Maio; ☺ 8am-5pm Tue-Sun) and eat them in the adjacent *jardim público*. Or try Modelo Hypermarket, a supermarket just beyond the town limits on the road to Alcáçovas.

MIDRANGE

Adega do Neto (☎ 266 209 916; Rua dos Mercadores 46; mains €6-7; ☺ lunch & dinner) This cheap and cheerful eatery has daily specials, such as fried chicken and *feijoada* (pork and bean casserole). There are a handful of tables and counter service.

Café Arcada (Praça do Giraldo 10; meals €6.50-10; ☺ breakfast, lunch & dinner) This busy, barn-sized cafe is an Évora institution, serving up coffee,

crêpes and cakes. You can sit at an outdoor table on the lovely plaza.

Restaurante Taverna (☎ 266 700 747; Travessa de Santa Marta 5; mains €7-10; ☺ lunch & dinner Tue-Sun) Set in a former chapel (note the vaulted ceiling), and with drawings of Évora's plazas along the stone walls, Taverna serves a solid menu (pork with Madeira, chicken with roasted capsicums) at fair prices.

Vasco da Gama Cafetaria (Rua de Vasco da Gama 10; mains €7.50-10; ☺ breakfast, lunch & dinner Mon-Sat, lunch Sun) This laid-back place has a menu which seems to have been translated by one of its student patrons – it has some amusing menu translations. Basic and filling food.

Restaurante Cervejaria São Domingos (☎ 266 703 173; Rua Amas do Cardeal 9; mains €7.50-12.50) This unpretentious and pleasant family-style place has beautiful *azulejos*, wooden chairs, white tablecloths and robust Portuguese fare.

O Antão (☎ 266 706 459; Rua do João de Deus 5; mains €10-15; ☺ lunch & dinner Thu-Tue) With a white, arched, leafy interior, this prize-winning restaurant offers beautifully cooked rural fare such as braised lamb, and partridge with bacon.

TOP END

Restaurante Cozinha de Santo Humberto (☎ 266 704 251; Rua da Moeda 39; mains €9-16; ☺ lunch & dinner Fri-Tue) This is a traditional, long-established place, in a grand arched, whitewashed cellar hung with brass and ceramics. It offers hearty servings of rich regional fare – try the *arroz com pato* (duck risotto). It has an excellent plaza-side cafe serving similar (but lighter) bites.

Dom Joaquim (☎ 266 731 105; Rua dos Penedos 6; €10.50-13; ☺ lunch & dinner Thu-Tue) Housed in a renovated building, Dom Joaquim offers fine dining in a contemporary setting. Modern artworks line the stone walls, and cane chairs grace clothed tables. While it's smart and trendy, it offers excellent traditional meat-based (including game) and seafood dishes, such as *perdiz* (partridge) and *caçao* (dogfish). For dessert, we dare you to try the *toucinho ransoso dos santos* – literally translated as 'rancid lard of the saint'. Oh so sweet.

Taberna Típica Quarta-Feira (☎ 266 707 530; Rua do Inverno 16; mains €12-20; ☺ lunch & dinner Mon-Sat) A jovial spot in the heart of the Moorish quarter, this place is decked with wine jars and serves up hearty dishes.

Botequim da Mouraria (☎ 266 746 775; Rua da Mouraria 16A; mains €12.50-14; ☺ lunch & dinner Mon-

Fri, lunch Sat) The town's culinary shrine may be O Fialho (below), but some gastronomes believe this place is better. Poke around the old Moorish quarter to find this cosy spot serving some of Évora's finest food and wine (the owner currently stocks more than 150 wines from the Alentejo alone). There are no reservations, nor tables – just 12 stools at a counter.

our pick **Tasquinha d'Oliveira** (☎ 266 744 841; Rua Cândido dos Reis 45A; mains €12-17; ☾ lunch & dinner Mon-Sat) This delightful, intimate restaurant (14 places) has tables decked out with crisp white tablecloths and is decorated with ceramic plates. The menu features a small selection of well-prepared Alentejan cuisine. Judging by the framed write-ups on the wall, this restaurant has already been noticed.

Restaurante O Fialho (☎ 266 703 079; Travessa dos Mascarenhas 16; mains €14.50-18; ☾ lunch & dinner Tue-Sun) People talk in awed tones of O Fialho, such is the quality of its food. Spread over several small rooms and with wood panelling and white tablecloths, this restaurant manages to be smart yet unpretentious. It serves up professional service and top-quality Alentejan cuisine.

Drinking

Most bars open late and don't close until at least 2am (4am at weekends). There are no cover charges at these places.

Bar do Teatro (Praça Joaquim António de Aguiar; ☾ 8pm-2am) Next to the theatre, this small, inviting bar has high ceilings and old-world decor that welcomes a friendly mixed crowd. The music tends toward lounge and electronica.

Oficin@Bar (☎ 266 707 312; Rua da Moeda 27; ☾ 8pm-2am Mon-Fri, 9pm-3am Sat) Attracting all ages, this is an appealing, relaxed bar with little wooden tables in a white-arched cave-like space. It's convivial, with jazz and blues playing gently in the background.

Bar UÉ (☎ 266 706 612; Rua de Diogo Cão 21; ☾ Mon-Sat) At the Associação de Estudantes da Universidade de Évora, this is the main central student hang-out with a laid-back atmosphere.

Bar Amas do Cardeal (☎ 266 721 133; Rua Amas do Cardeal 4A; ☾ 10pm-3am) Popular, darkly lit and weirdly decorated, this bar attracts a chilled, eclectic crowd for post-1am drinking, and weekend dancing on the small dance floor. Regular DJs play cool and funky house.

Cup of Joe (Praça de Sertório 3; ☾ noon-2am; **V**) Part of a coffee chain, this attractive cafe has a peaceful outdoor seating overlooking a plaza, and a good selection of lighter fare (mains from €3.50 to €5) – crêpes, salads, wraps and plenty of caffeine. Electronic music and a friendly cocktail-sipping crowd arrive by night.

Entertainment

For theatre, film, concerts and art expositions, stop in at the imaginative cultural centre **Sociedade Harmonia Eborense** (☎ 266 746 874; Praça do Giraldo 72) to see what's on.

Praxis (☎ 266 707 505; Rua de Valdevinos; ☾ midnight-6am) Praxis has one big dance floor, one small dance floor and DJs spinning house, R&B and hip-hop. It's a lively, good-time crowd, but the place doesn't get busy until around 2am after the other places have closed.

THEATRE & PUPPET THEATRE

Casa dos Bonecos (☎ 266 703 112) Actors from the grand municipal Teatro Garcia de Resende studied for several years with the only surviving master of a traditional rural puppetry style called *bonecos de Santo Aleixo* (Santo Aleixo puppets). They occasionally perform this, other styles, and hand-puppet shows for children at this little theatre off Largo de Machede Velho. Ask at the tourist office for their schedule.

BULLFIGHTS

Évora has a *praça de touros* (bullring; Aréna de Evora) outside the southern walls, near the *jardim público*. Several bullfights take place generally between March and October.

Shopping

Rua 5 de Outubro has rows of *artesanatos* (handicrafts shops) selling pottery, knick-knacks and cork products of every kind. A couple of shops in the modern *mercado municipal* sell pottery. There are more up-market shops along Rua Cândido dos Reis, northwest of the centre.

On the second Tuesday of each month a vast open-air market, with everything from shoes to sheep's cheese, sprawls across the big Rossio de São Brás, just outside the walls on the road to the train station.

Oficina da Terra (☎ 266 746 049; www.oficinada terra.com; Travessa do Sertorio 26; ☾ 10am-7pm Mon-Fri,

THE ALENTEJO

BUSES FROM ÉVORA

Destination	Price*	Duration*	Frequency**
Beja	€7	1½hr	10
Coimbra	€14.80	4½hr	10-27 (Express only; most change in Lisbon)
Elvas	€5.90/10	2¼/1¼hr	2-6
Estremoz	€3.80/7.80	1½hr/30min	6-14
Faro	€15	5¼hr	3 (via Albufeira)
Lisbon	€11.50	1½-2hr	13
Portalegre	€6.20/10.50	2½/1½hr	3
Reguengos de Monsaraz	€3.20/6.90	1¼/¾hr	7-8 (weekdays)
Vila Viçosa	€5	1½/1hr	2 (weekdays)

* normal/express
** services per day

to 3pm Sat) You might see resident artists in action at this award-winning handicraft and clay-figure (read contemporary and quirky) workshop and gallery.

Feiras no Largo (Praça 1 de Maio; ☾ 8am-2pm Sat & Sun) Each weekend sees one of four different markets – antiquities, used books and collectables, art and *artesenato* – near the aqueduct.

Getting There & Away
BUS
The **bus station** (☎ 266 769 410) is off Avenida de São Sebastião.

TRAIN
The **Évora station** (☎ 266 742 336), 600m south of the Jardim Público, is on a branch of the Lisbon–Funcheira (via Beja) train line. There are daily trains to/from Lisbon (€10, 2½ hours, three daily). Trains also go to/from Beja (€6.40, 1¼ hours, four daily), Lagos (€14.50, five hours, two daily) and Faro (€12.80, five hours, two daily).

Getting Around
CAR & BICYCLE
If you want to rent a car, get in touch with Abreu or TopAtlántico (p240).

Évora has a branch of the **Automóvel Club de Portugal** (ACP; ☎ 266 707 533; fax 266 709 696; Alcárcova de Baixo 7).

You can rent a bike from **Bike Lab** (☎ 266 735 500; www.bike-lab.com; Centro Comercial da Vista Alegre, Lote 14; per day €8-15), 800m northwest of the centre, or from **Silvano Manuel Cégado** (☎ 266 703 434; Rua Cándido dos Reis 66; per day €15; ☾ 9am-1pm & 3-7pm Mon-Fri, to 1pm Sat).

TAXI
Taxis (☎ 266 734 734) congregate in Praça do Giraldo and Largo da Porta de Moura. On a weekday you can expect to pay about €6 from the train station to Praça do Giraldo.

AROUND ÉVORA
Megaliths – derived from the Ancient Greek for 'big stones' – are found all over the ancient landscape that surrounds Évora. Such prehistoric structures, built around 5000 to 6000 years ago, dot the European Atlantic coast, but here in Alentejo there is an astounding amount of Neolithic remains. Dolmens (Neolithic stone tombs, or *antas* in Portuguese) were probably temples and/or tombs, covered with a large flat stone and usually built on hilltops or near water. Menhirs (individual standing stones) point to fertility rites – as phallic as skyscrapers, if on a smaller scale – while *cromeleques* (cromlechs, stone circles) were also places of worship.

Évora's *turismo* sells a *Historical Itineraries* leaflet (€1.05) that details many sites. Dolmen devotees can buy the book *Paisagens Arqueologicas A Oeste de Évora,* which has English summaries.

You can see more megaliths around Reguengos de Monsaraz, Elvas and Castelo de Vide.

GETTING THERE & AWAY
To get to this area, your only option is to rent a car or bike (note that about 5km of the route is rough and remote), or hire a taxi for the day (around €60).

With your own wheels, head west from Évora on the old Lisbon road (N114) for 10km, then turn south for 2.8km to Guadalupe.

Follow the signs from here to the Cromeleque dos Almendres (4.3km).

Return to Guadalupe and head south for 5km to Valverde, home of the Universidade de Évora's school of agriculture and the 16th-century Convento de Bom Jesus. Following the signs to Anta Grande do Zambujeiro, turn into the school's farmyard and onto a badly potholed track. After 1km you'll see the Great Dolmen.

Continue west from Valverde for 12km. Before joining the N2, turn right for the cave at Santiago do Escoural.

Cromeleque dos Almendres

Set within a beautiful landscape of olive and cork trees (unfortunately the dirt road almost impinges onto the site) stands the Cromeleque dos Almendres (Almendres Cromlech). This huge, spectacular oval of standing stones, 15km west of Évora, is the Iberian Peninsula's most important megalithic group and an extraordinary place to visit.

The site consists of a huge oval of some 95 rounded granite monoliths – some of which are engraved with symbolic markings – spread down a rough slope. They were erected over different periods, it seems with geometric and astral consideration, probably for social gatherings or sacred rituals.

Two and a half kilometres before Cromeleque dos Almendres stands **Menir dos Almendres**, a single stone about 4m high, with some very faint carvings near the top. Look for the sign; to reach the menhir you must walk for a few hundred metres from the road.

Anta Grande do Zambujeiro

The Anta Grande do Zambujeiro (Great Dolmen of Zambujeiro), 13km southwest of Évora, is Europe's largest dolmen and a

rather neglected one at that. Under a huge sheet-metal shelter in a field of wildflowers and yellow broom, seven stones, each 6m high, form a huge chamber more than 50m in diameter. Unfortunately, you cannot enter; the entrance is blocked, but the setting is pretty.

Archaeologists removed the capstone in the 1960s. Most of the site's relics are in the Museu de Évora (currently closed).

Feeling peckish? **Restaurante O Ricardo** (☎ 266 711 115; Valverde; €6.80-12; ☯ lunch & dinner Tue-Sat, lunch Sun) is the perfect place to sate your menhir-like appetite. The owner cooks seasonal dishes, carrying on the tradition of her grandparents. Summer dishes include asparagus and gaspacho; winter feasts include *feijoadas* (rich kidney- or butter-bean-and-meat stews) and *açorda* (bread soup). Organic produce is used where possible. The restaurant is on your return leg (after you visit Zambujeiro) in the village of Valverde.

ÉVORAMONTE
pop 700 / elev 474m

Northeast of Évora, this tiny hilltop village with its quaint 16th-century castle makes an interesting detour on your way through the region. There are fine views all around across the low hills. A small *turismo* is just beyond the castle.

The **castle** (admission €1.50; ☯ 10am-1pm year-round, 2-5pm Tue-Sun, closed last weekend of every month) dates from 1306, but was rebuilt after the 1531 earthquake. Exterior stone carving shows unwarlike small bows, the symbol of the Bragança family – the knot symbolises fidelity. The interior is neatly restored, with impressively meaty columns topped by a sinuous arched ceiling on each cavernous floor. The roof provides sweeping panoramas.

THE ALENTEJO

THE WINE ROUTE

Wines here, particularly the reds, are fat, rich and fruity. But tasting them is much more fun than reading about them, so drop in on some wineries. The Rota dos Vinhos do Alentejo (Alentejan Wine Route) splits the region into three separate areas – the Serra de São Mamede (dark reds, full bodied, red fruit hints), Historic (around Évora, Estremoz, Borba and Monsaraz; smooth reds, fruity whites), and the Rio Guadiana (scented whites, spicy reds). Some wineries also have accommodation options.

You'll see the brown signs announcing that you are on the wine trail all over the place, and can pick up the booklet that lists wineries and their details at any local tourist office. Otherwise visit the helpful **Rota dos Vinhos do Alentejo headquarters** (☎ 266 746 498; Praça Joaquim António de Aguiar 20-21, Évora; ☯ 9am-12.30pm & 2-5.30pm Mon-Fri).

ARRAIOLOS: THE GREAT CARPETS OF PORTUGAL

About 20km north of Évora, the small town of Arraiolos is famed for its exquisite *tapetes* (carpets). These hand-woven works show a marked influence from Persian rugs, and they have been in production here since the 12th century. It seems half the town is involved in this artistry, and on a casual stroll through town, you might encounter several women stitching in front of their homes. Rug patterns are based on abstract motifs, *azulejo* designs or flower, bird or animal depictions. Shops are abundant, and you can pay anything from €50 for a tiny runner to €2000 for the most beautiful pieces, which feature more elaborate designs.

The village itself dates from the 2nd or 3rd century BC, and is laid out along traditional lines, with whitewashed blue-trimmed houses topped with terracotta roofs and the ruins of a castle overlooking the town. The plain facade of the **Igreja da Misericórdia** hides a beautiful interior with a golden altar and 18th-century *azulejo*-lined walls.

Take a peak at the centuries-old dye chambers in the main square, which is also where you'll find the **turismo** (☎ 266 490 254; www.cm-arraiolos.pt). There are cafes in town for lingering, and a flashy **pousada** (☎ 266 419 340; www.pousadas.pt; d €240) just outside Arraiolos.

You can stay at **A Convenção** (☎ 268 959 217; Rua de Santa Maria 26; d with/without terrace €35/30), where the three rooms – particularly the one with a terrace – have fantastic views from this peaceful spot.

It's also an unexpectedly smart **restaurant** (mains €9-12; �½ Sun) with indoor-outdoor seating and views matched by good traditional specialities.

Nearby are also some rural tourism options, including the attractive **Quinta do Serafim** (☎ 268 959 360; quintadoserafim@portugalmail.pt; r €90-150; ☒) with an attractive array of quirky, antiques-filled rooms and self-contained 'villas', and **Monte da Fazenda** (☎ 268 959 172; montefazendater@ mail.telepac.pt; d with breakfast €80; ☒).

One to two buses a day stop in Évoramonte from Évora (€1.40, 30 minutes), though it's a long uphill walk (1km) from the bus stop to the castle.

SÃO PEDRO DO CORVAL

Known for its fine pottery traditions, this tiny village, 5km east of Reguengos de Monsaraz, has dozens of workshops where you can see both the potters and artists in action and purchase a few pieces of cheap and cheerful plates, pots, jugs, candlesticks and floor tiles.

With more than 20 *olarias* (pottery workshops) the village is one of Portugal's largest pottery centres. It's difficult to recommend one *olaria* over the other; wander along Rua da Primavera and the nearby streets (follow the '*olarias*' signs). At **Olaria José Cartaxo** (☎ 266 549 681, Rua da Primavera 23) you can see artists painstakingly painting pieces near the showroom. The booklet *Guia de Turismo de*

Reguengos de Monsaraz, from the Reguengos and Monsaraz tourist offices, locates the *olarias*. Buses between Reguengos and Monsaraz stop here.

REGUENGOS DE MONSARAZ

pop 11,300 / elev 200m

This small working-class town, once famous for its sheep and wool production, is a stopping point and transport hub for Monsaraz. It's also close to the pottery centre of São Pedro do Corval as well as to an impressive half-dozen dolmens and menhirs (out of around 150 scattered across the surrounding plains). Near here, too, are some excellent wineries.

The rocket-like local church (built in 1887) was designed by José António Dias da Silva, who was also responsible for Praça de Touros, the Lisbon bullring.

Orientation

The town's focal point is Praça da Liberdade, 200m northeast of the bus station.

Information

Espaço Internet (☎ 266 519 424; Rua do Conde de Monsaraz 32; �½ 10am-1pm & 2-8pm Mon-Fri, 10am-1pm & 2-4pm Sat) About 100m northeast of the *praça*. Free internet access.

Saberes & Encantos (☎ 962501397; www.saberese encantos.org) Offers personalised tours around the region including bike, vineyard and lake tours.

Turismo (☎ 266 503 052; Rua 1 de Maio; �½ 9am-12.30pm & 2-5.30pm Mon-Fri, from 10am Sat & Sun) Just off the *praça*. Has a good brochure on the Reguengos de Monsaraz *concelho* (municipality).

THE ALENTEJO

Sights

There are several wineries around Reguengos (part of the wine route), including the acclaimed **Herdade do Esporão** (☎ 266 509 280; www .esporao.com), 7km south of town. The property's border was defined in 1267 and it has vestiges of Roman times. Under the direction of oenologist David Baverstock, it produces a wide variety of wines for the domestic and overseas markets. There are tours through the extraordinary wine cellars, among the largest in Portugal (parts of the cellars were sourced from the same factory that supplied the underground in Lisbon). It's worth splurging at the wine cellar shop or the restaurant. Phone ahead to arrange a tour.

Sleeping & Eating

Casa da Palmeira (☎ 266 502 362; fax 266 502 513; Praça de Santo António 1; s/d with shared bathroom €23/36) This place, 200m northwest of the main square, is about atmosphere, not luxury (although its former opulence is reflected in its chandeliered rooms). It's a huge, run-down old mansion, with high ceilings, peeling gold trimmings and decorative wrought-iron balconies.

Pensão O Gato (☎ /fax 266 502 353; Praça da Liberdade 11; s/d €25/35; 🖭) This friendly guest house has pleasant rooms that are nicely maintained. The best have small balconies (with flower boxes) overlooking the sleepy *praça*.

Restaurante Central (☎ 266 502 219; Praça da Liberdade; mains €8.50-12) Since 1918, Central has been in the same family, has offered tasty Portuguese mains and still keeps up a busy trade. The original wooden tables and chairs are still in use, although covered in crisp cloths. Legacies, too, are the fabulous metal bar stools in the small bar-cafe next door.

Shopping

The local handicraft is *mantas alentejanas* (hand-woven woollen blankets). The making of these beautiful pieces is, sadly, a declining craft.

Fabrica Alentejana de Lanificios (☎ 266 502 179; Rua Mendes; 🕑 9am-5pm Mon-Fri) This extraordinary factory is the last remaining hand-loom producer of *mantas alentejanas*. Only two women are at the looms these days. It's worth visiting, if only to support the craft (purchases can be made). The weavers are happy to show you around. The factory is southeast of the *praça* (take the road to Monsaraz and turn right at Rua Mendes). The factory's shop is in Monsaraz (see p251).

Getting There & Away

Buses run daily to Évora (€3.50/6.90 normal/express, 1¼ hours/45 minutes, two to nine daily) and direct to Lisbon (€12, 2½ hours, two daily).

MONSARAZ

pop 950 / elev 190m

Perched high over the surrounding countryside, tiny Monsaraz is a charming village with a looming castle at its edge, great views over the winding roads and olive groves sprinkling the landscape. The narrow streets here are lined with uneven-walled, whitewashed cottages. Sadly, as with other villages in the region, Monsaraz struggles to maintain its inhabitants; permanent residents are mainly elderly people. But it has not lost its magic or community feel. In the streets, you'll see flat-capped men watch the day unfold and women chatting on stoops.

Today, the village prospers on tourism, with a handful of restaurants, guest houses and artisan shops. It's worth coming here to taste a slice of traditional Portugal, wander the slumbering streets and sample Alentejan cuisine. It's at its best as it wakes up in the morning, in the quiet of the evening, or during a wintry dusk.

Settled long before the Moors arrived in the 8th century, Monsaraz was subsequently recaptured by the Christians under Giraldo Sem Pavor (Gerald the Fearless) in 1167, and then given to the Knights Templar as thanks for their help. The castle was added in 1310.

Orientation

Coaches or cars have to be parked outside the walled village, so your arrival at one of the four arched entrances will be as it should be – on foot. From the main car park, the Porta da Alcoba leads directly onto the central Praça Dom Nuno Álvares Pereira.

Porta da Vila, the main entrance to Monsaraz, is at the northern end of town (the castle is at the other end) and leads into Rua São Tiago and the parallel Rua Direita, Monsaraz' two main streets.

Information

Multibanco ATM (Travessa da Misericórdia 2) Off the main square.

Turismo (☎ 266 557 136; Praça Dom Nuno Álvares Pereira; 🕑 9.30am-1pm & 2-5.30pm) Stocked with some regional information, including bus timetables and basic maps of the area's megalithic monuments.

THE ALENTEJO

DAM STATISTICS

The 250-sq-km Alqueva reservoir, Europe's largest, created by an enormous dam (Barragem do Alqueva) near Moura, is undeniably beautiful. But there is something strange and otherworldly about it: it's not so much a lake as drowned land, with islands poking out of the water and roads disappearing into nowhere.

It is hoped that this huge water mass will save the arid Alentejo. One of Portugal's major agricultural regions, and its poorest, it employs a host of irrigation schemes and reservoirs to bring water to the soil. The most important source of water is the Rio Guadiana, which rises in Spain and flows through the Alentejo. Various agreements with Spain were meant to ensure that its waters were fairly shared. But successive droughts strained the arrangement. Although the idea for the dam was first mooted in 1957, the Portuguese finally took matters into their own hands in 1998 and started work on the giant dam to guarantee both irrigation water and electricity for years to come. It flooded 2000 properties, including those of the village of Luz (rebuilt elsewhere but strangely antiseptic). The project cost €1.7 billion.

Critics say that the dam may not even fulfil its remit, that irrigation schemes are vastly expensive, and that it is an ecological disaster (many birds and animals had to be moved as part of the initial agreement). Ancient rock art was enveloped in the waters and menhirs were moved elsewhere. Plans are afoot for tourism projects, including resorts and associated activities.

Completed in 2002, the dam created an 83km-long reservoir, with a perimeter of 1100km. It's well worth driving to the dam for a look if you have your own transport. Better still, take a boat trip (below). There are no buses running here.

Sights & Activities

IGREJA MATRIZ

The parish **church** (2-7pm), near the *turismo*, was rebuilt after the 1755 earthquake and again a century later. Inside (if you can get in, hours can be vague) is an impressive nave and a 14th-century marble tomb carved with 14 saints. An 18th-century *pelourinho* (stone pillory) topped by a Manueline globe stands outside. The 16th-century **Igreja da Misericórdia** is opposite, but is rarely open.

MUSEU DE ARTE SACRA

Housed inside a fine Gothic building beside the parish church, the **Museu de Arte Sacra** (Museum of Sacred Art; admission €1.70; 10am-7pm) houses a small collection of 14th-century wooden religious figures and 18th-century vestments and silverware. Its most famous exhibit is a rare example of a 14th-century secular fresco, a charming piece depicting a good and a bad judge, the latter appropriately two-faced.

CASTELO

The **castle** (24hr) at the southwestern end of the village was one in the chain of Dom Dinis' defensive fortresses along the Spanish border. It's now converted into a small bullring, and its ramparts offer a fine panoramic view over the Alentejan plains.

BARRAGEM DO ALQUEVA

A great way to explore the lake is by boat. **Capitão Tiago** (962653711; www.sem-sim.com; Telheiro) runs excellent voyages in his 17m Dutch sail boat. Several trips are available – the standard is a two-hour trip with the chance to swim and visit some of the islands (€50 per person if alone, less if in a group). Other packages include a meal at Tiago's restaurant, **Sem Sim** (962653711; Telheiro), and a boat trip (€30). You can also rent bikes and canoes (each costs €25 per day). Ultra-keen campers can be dropped on an island for the night (prices negotiable). Telheiro is about 2km from Monsaraz; call in advance for advice on mooring on the lake.

Festivals & Events

Accommodation must be booked far in advance at these times.

Bullfights If you want to see a bullfight, Easter Sunday is a good time to visit.

Music festival Monsaraz heaves with jollity during its week-long Museu Aberto (Open Museum) music festival, held in July in even-numbered years.

Festa de Nosso Senhor Bullfights and processions feature in this festival on the second weekend of September.

Sleeping

Some villagers have converted their ancient cottages to guest houses, although several of these seem to have closed in the last few years.

Unless otherwise mentioned, all the following rates include breakfast. Book ahead in high season. There are some excellent rural alternatives close by.

BUDGET

Casa Paroquial (☎ 266 557 181; Rua Direita 4; s/d/tr/ste €35/40/50/70) Owned by a *padre* and managed by a friendly local, this charming place has five cool rooms (great when the mercury hits 40 degrees) with wooden trimmings, white-washed walls and heavy wooden furniture. There's an upstairs suite.

Casa Modesta (☎ 266 557 388; Rua Direita 5; s/d from €35/50) This friendly place has several rooms of various sizes. The best have high ceilings, tile floors, traditional hand-painted furniture and flower boxes; the downstairs one is a bit stuffy. The welcoming family owners run the adjoining cafe.

MIDRANGE & TOP END

Casa do Embaixador (☎ 266 557 432; honorata.mas sano@hotmail.com; Rua Direita; s €45, d €50-60) This dollhouse-sized place, with its low door-ways and whitewashed walls, has three rooms of varying quality. The downstairs rooms don't have views, but one has a lovely wooden bedstead.

Casa Dona Antónia (☎ 266 557 142; www.casadant onia-monsaraz.com; Rua Direita 15; d €50-60, ste €70; ✦) The four pleasant rooms here vary in size, but all are pleasant and comfortable; the suite is huge and includes a terrace.

ourpick **Casa Saramago de Monsaraz** (☎ 266 557 494; www.casasaramago-monsaraz.com.pt; Telheiro; s/d €50/60; ✦ ✦) Unpretentious, yet charming with easy-going owners, this delightfully converted blue and white *quinta* is great value for money. Rooms are tastefully decorated in old-style – but not too twee – furniture. Those in the former *celeiros* (silos) have verandas and face Monsaraz. Four-legged friends are welcome too – a horse hotel and *cão* (dog) kennels are on the premises.

Monte Alerta (☎ 266 550 150; fax 266 557 325; Telheiro; s/d €65/85; ✦) Very beautiful, and not the type of place in which you'd kick back on the sofa with your smelly socks on, this rather formal blue-bordered *quinta* is only 2.5km away from Monsaraz, at Telheiro. Inside are family antiques, Persian-style carpets and eight double rooms with heavy fabrics; outside are wind chimes, a small lake and a pretty garden.

Estalagem de Monsaraz (☎ 266 557 112; www .estalagemdemonsaraz.com; Largo São Bartolomeu 5; s/d/ste €67/84/90; ✦ ✦) Just outside the village walls, this atmospheric place has handsomely deco-rated rooms across three areas. The older sections have dark-wood furniture and shuttered windows; the more recent ones have unusual touches, such as recycled door bedheads. All rooms have glorious views. Other bonuses include the restaurant, pool and playground, as well as a lounge area with an open fire.

Eating

Monsaraz has a handful of restaurants, all offering traditional Alentejan mains such as *borrego assado* (roast lamb).

Café-Restaurante Lumumba (☎ 266 557 121; Rua Direita 12; mains €6.50-8.50; ✦ lunch & dinner) This small place has a more local, less touristy, atmos-phere than other cafes. TV forms a backdrop – it's a good place to watch football.

Café Restaurante O Alcaide (☎ 266 557 168; Rua São Tiago 15; mains €8-12; ✦ lunch & dinner Fri-Wed) This is Monsaraz' best and most popular restaurant, especially on weekends. Clients who are put off by the mounted wild boar head on the wall can distract themselves with lovely sunset views over the plains. This restaurant prides itself on seasonal meat and herb dishes.

A Casa do Forno (☎ 266 557 190; Travessa da Sanabrosa; mains €9-12.50; ✦ lunch & dinner Wed-Mon) The menu is fairly standard here (although the walls display lots of prizes for cuisine from previous dec-ades), but the ambience is pleasant – there are checked tablecloths, attractive wooden chairs and an outdoor terrace with 'those' views.

There are also a couple of cafes, includ-ing **Casa Modesta** (Rua Direita 11) with a patio and **Pastelaria Cisterna** (Rua Direita 25). Self-catering options are limited to bread and cheese from a **grocery shop** (Rua São Tiago 29) at the Porta da Vila end of the street and wines from **Castas & Castiços** (Rua São Tiago 31; ✦ 10am-2pm & 3-7.30pm Tue-Sun), next door.

Shopping

Loja da Mizette (☎ 266 557 159; Rua do Celeiro) sells beautiful Alentejano *mantas* made by one of two workers in its factory in nearby Reguengos, the last of its kind (p249). Well worth a visit.

Getting There & Away

Buses run to/from Reguengos de Monsaraz (€2.50; 35 minutes, four daily on weekdays). The last bus back to Reguengos, where

THE ALENTEJO

you can pick up connections to Évora, is around 5.15pm.

AROUND MONSARAZ

Neolithic megaliths are scattered throughout the landscape around Monsaraz – it is great to explore and discover these (they're signposted, but finding each one is an adventure) amid the tangles of olive groves and open fields of wildflowers. Most spectacular is **Cromeleque do Xerez**, an ensemble with the triumphant 7-tonne menhir at its centre. The rocks once stood 5km south of Monsaraz but were moved before flooding by the massive Barragem do Alqueva. A remaining highlight is the Menhir de Bulhoa, another phallic stone with intriguing carved circles and lines, 4km north of Monsaraz off the Telheiro-Outeiro road. A sketch map of several other accessible megaliths is available at the tourist office.

ESTREMOZ

pop 9000 / elev 420m

Along with neighbouring Borba and Vila Viçosa, Estremoz is one of the region's well-known marble towns. Because there is so much fine marble in this region – rivalling that in Carrara, Italy – it's used all over the place: even the cobbles are rough chunks of marble.

Ringed by an old protective wall, Estremoz has an attractive centre set with peaceful plazas, orange tree-lined lanes and a hilltop castle and convent. This simple provincial town is a busy trading centre, with lots of shops selling farm tools, though visitors can also load up on crafts, earthenware pottery and gourmet delights – all of which are available at the great market that fills the huge central square on Saturday.

Orientation

The lower, newer part of town, enclosed by 17th-century ramparts, is arranged around a huge square, Rossio Marquês de Pombal (known simply as 'the Rossio'). Here you'll find most accommodation, restaurants and shops. A 10-minute climb west of the Rossio brings you to the old quarter, with its 13th-century castle (now a luxurious *pousada*) and keep.

The bus station is the former ticket office of the disused train station, 400m east of the Rossio and is covered in stunning *azulejos*.

Information

Caixa Geral de Depósitos Bank & ATM (Rossio Marquês de Pombal 43)

Centro de saúde (medical centre; ☎ 268 332 042; Av 9 de Abril) At the northeastern end of town.

Espaço Internet (Rossio Marquês de Pombal; ☎ 2-8pm) Free internet access inside the Centro Ciência Viva.

Police station (☎ 268 334 141) In the *câmara municipal*.

Post office (Rua 5 de Outubro; ☎ 9am-6pm Mon-Fri)

Turismo (☎ 268 339 200; www.cm-estremoz.pt; Casa de Estremoz/câmara municipal, Rossio Marquês de Pombal; ☎ 10am-1pm & 2-6pm)

Sights

LOWER TOWN

On the fringes of the Rossio are imposing old churches, former convents and, just north of the Rossio, monastic buildings converted into cavalry barracks. Opposite these, by Largo General Graça, is a marble-edged water tank, called the **Lago do Gadanha** (Lake of the Scythe) after its scythe-wielding statue of Neptune. Some of the prettiest marble streets in town are south of the Rossio, off Largo da República.

Museu de Arte Sacra

Overlooking the Rossio is the floridly bell-towered 17th-century **Convento dos Congregados**, which now leads a multiple life housing the police station, *câmara municipal*, *turismo* and **Museu de Arte Sacra** (admission €1; ☎ 9.30am-12.30pm & 2.30-5.30pm Tue-Fri, 2.30-5.30pm Sat & Sun), with stately 17th- to 18th-century ecclesiastical silverware and religious statues. You also get to see the restored marble church and, best of all, a rooftop view from the bell towers themselves. The stairway to the top is lined with *azulejos*.

UPPER TOWN

The upper town is surrounded by dramatic zigzagging ramparts and contains a gleaming white palace. The easiest way to reach it on foot is to follow narrow Rua da Frandina from Praça Luís de Camões and pass the inner castle walls through the Arco da Frandina.

Royal Palace & Torre das Três Coroas

At the top of the upper town is the stark, glowing-white, fortress-like former royal palace, now the Pousada de Santa Rainha Isabel (p254).

Dom Dinis built the palace in the 13th century for his new wife, Isabel of Aragon.

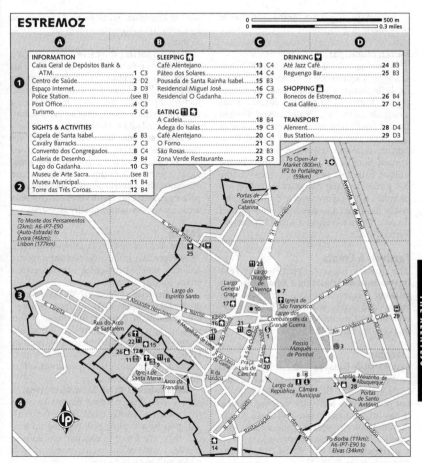

ESTREMOZ

0 — 500 m
0 — 0.3 miles

INFORMATION			SLEEPING			DRINKING		
Caixa Geral de Depósitos Bank &			Café Alentejano	13	C4	Até Jazz Café	24	B3
ATM	1	C3	Páteo dos Solares	14	C4	Reguengo Bar	25	B3
Centro de Saúde	2	D2	Pousada de Santa Rainha Isabel	15	B3			
Espaço Internet	3	D3	Residencial Miguel José	16	C3	SHOPPING		
Police Station	(see 8)		Residencial O Gadanha	17	C3	Bonecos de Estremoz	26	B4
Post Office	4	C3				Casa Galileu	27	D4
Turismo	5	C4	EATING					
			A Cadeia	18	B4	TRANSPORT		
SIGHTS & ACTIVITIES			Adega do Isaías	19	C3	Alenrent	28	D4
Capela de Santa Isabel	6	B3	Café Alentejano	20	C4	Bus Station	29	D3
Cavalry Barracks	7	C3	O Forno	21	C3			
Convento dos Congregados	8	C4	São Rosas	22	B3			
Galeria de Desenho	9	B4	Zona Verde Restaurante	23	C3			
Lago do Gadanha	10	C3						
Museu de Arte Sacra	(see 8)							
Museu Municipal	11	B4						
Torre das Três Coroas	12	B4						

THE ALENTEJO

After her death in 1336 (Dinis had died 11 years earlier) it was used as an ammunition dump. An inevitable explosion, in 1698, destroyed most of the palace and the surrounding castle, though in the 18th century João V restored the palace for use as an armoury. The 27m-high keep, the Torre das Três Coroas (Tower of the Three Crowns), survived and is still the dominant feature. It's so-called because it was apparently built by three kings: Sancho II, Afonso III and Dinis.

Visitors are welcome to view the public areas of the *pousada* and climb the keep, which offers a superb panorama of the old town and surrounding plains. The holes at the keep's edges were channels for boiling oil – a good way of getting rid of uninvited guests.

Capela de Santa Isabel

This richly adorned **chapel** (admission free) behind the keep was built in 1659. The narrow stairway up to the chapel, and the chapel itself, are lined with 18th-century *azulejos*, most of them featuring scenes from the saintly queen's life.

Isabel was famously generous to the poor, despite her husband's disapproval. In one legend, the king demanded to see what she was carrying in her skirt; she let go of her apron and the bread she had hidden to donate to the poor was miraculously transformed into roses.

To visit the chapel, ask for the custodian in the Galeria de Desenho.

Museu Municipal

This **museum** (☎ 268 333 608; adult €1.50; ☺ 9am-12.30pm & 2-5.30pm Tue-Sun) is housed in a beautiful 17th-century almshouse near the former palace. Pretty hand-painted furniture sits alongside endearing, locally carved wooden figures (charming rural scenes by Joaquim Velhinho) and a collection of typical 19th-century domestic Alentejan items. On the ground floor is an amazing display of the unique Estremoz pottery figurines – some 500 pieces covering 200 years, including lots of ladies with carnivalesque outfits, explosively floral headdresses and wind-rippled dresses. There's even an entire 19th-century Easter Parade.

Festivals & Events

The town's biggest event is the **Feira Internacional de Artesanato e Agro-Pecuária de Estremoz** (Fiape), a baskets, ceramics, vegetables and livestock bonanza, held for several days at the end of April in an open-air market area east of the bus station.

Sleeping

Residencial O Gadanha (☎ 268 339 110; www.residencialogadanha.com; Largo General Graça 56; s/d/tr €20/32.50/42.50; ⊠) This whitewashed house is one of Portugal's best-value sleeping options. It has bright, fresh, white and clean rooms that overlook the square. Rooms come with satellite TV (and even hairdryers).

Residencial Miguel José (☎ 268 322 326; Travessa da Levada 8; s/d from €20/35; ⊠) Along the marble-lined corridors of this labyrinthine place are small, simple, rooms with wooden furniture and clean, compact bathrooms.

Café Alentejano (☎ 268 337 300; Rossio Marquês de Pombal 14; s/d/tr €25/35/40) The giant antique coffee mill on the landing indicates big things here, but standards soon come to a grind. The rooms come in a variety of shapes and sizes and, while they have ageing character (the odd spoke is missing from the brass bedsteads), it might pay to be choosy. There's a wonderful cafe downstairs.

Monte dos Pensamentos (☎ 268 333 166; monte dospensamentos@yahoo.com; Estrada da Estação do Ameixal; d/apt with breakfast €80/90; ⊠) This lovely manor house offers attractive, traditionally furnished apartments in a pretty setting 2km

west of Estremoz. There's a pool surrounded by citrus trees. Mountain bikes are available to guests.

Páteo dos Solares (☎ 268 338 400; www.pateosolares.com; Rua Brito Capelo; s/d from €170/180; ⊠ ⊠) This sumptuous guest house, partly situated on the old city walls, is housed in a converted bread factory. Spacious, well-furnished rooms, a charming sitting room, large terrace, restaurant and pool add to the appeal.

Pousada de Rainha Santa Isabel (☎ 268 332 075; www.pousadas.pt; d €230; ⊠ ⊠) In the restored former palace, this lavish *pousada* offers spacious rooms with antique furnishings and views over the Alentejo plains. There are lovely palace gardens, a pool with views and common areas set with museum-quality tapestries.

Eating

O Forno (Rua 1 de Dezembro 21; pastries & cakes €2-8; ☺ 7am-7pm) This is the local *pastelaria* (pastry and cake shop) of choice for a local breakfast snack (or any excuse!).

Café Alentejano (☎ 268 337 300; Rossio Marquês de Pombal 14; mains €7-11; ☺ lunch & dinner) Generations of country folk meet at this pleasant spot, which has art-deco wood and mirror panels and tiled tabletops. Outdoor tables face the square. Upstairs, a wood-floored, white-tablecloth restaurant offers heartier traditional fare.

Adega do Isaías (☎ 268 322 318; Rua do Almeida 21; mains €7.50-10; ☺ lunch & dinner Mon-Sat) To enter this award-winning, rustic *tasca* (tavern), you pass by a sizzling grill cooking up tender fish, meat and Alentejan specialities. Inside, a wine cellar awaits, crammed with tables and huge wine jars.

Zona Verde Restaurante (☎ 268 324 701; Largo Dragões de Olivença 86; mains €7.50-14; ☺ lunch & dinner Fri-Wed) This smart restaurant may have done a modern renovation (it replaced the original *azulejos*), but thankfully, it hasn't changed its traditional cuisine. It serves massive portions of excellent regional specialities, including *ensopado de borrego* (lamb stew). Warning: even the half servings are massive.

A Cadeia (☎ 268 323 400; www.cadeiaquinhentista.com; Rua Rainha Santa Isabel; mains €11.50-19.50; ☺ lunch & dinner) Unlock your purses at this classy place, housed in the former judicial jail, which dates from the 16th century; the two storeys of the quadrangle separated male and female prisoners. The restaurant serves *petis-*

BUSES FROM ESTREMOZ

Destination	Price*	Duration*	Frequency**
Borba	€2/5.20	15min	4-9
Elvas	€3.55/7	1½hr/45min	6-8
Évora	€3.80/5.45/7.80	1½/1hr	5-16
Évoramonte	€2.15	30min	4 Mon-Fri
Faro	€15.50	6hr	3-5
Lisbon	€7/12	2½hr	6-10
Portalegre	€5.50/8	1¼/1hr	7-9 (fewer on weekends)
Vila Viçosa	€2.45	45min	3 Mon-Fri

*normal/express
** services per day

cos (snacks; €4.50 to €6.50) plus free-range meat dishes. There's also an area for coffee and drinks under the building's arch. The dessert menu is delectable.

São Rosas (☎ 268 333 345; Largo de Dom Dinis; mains €13-18; ⊙ lunch & dinner Tue-Sun) White tablecloths under whitewashed arches equal rustic meets smart, and the food is great, featuring some unusual starters (such as smoked salmon and buttery, garlic-covered clams), pork and clams, and gaspacho in summer. It's near the former palace.

Drinking

Reguengo Bar (Rua Serpa Pinta 126; ⊙ 8am-2am Tue-Sun) This big barnlike space with a vaulted ceiling is where Estremoz' youth kick their heels up. Live bands play most Friday nights. In summer the party continues in the garden outside.

Até Jazz Café (Rua Serpa Pinta 65) This cosy bar delivers a varied schedule of jazz or fado most weekends to an arty, older crowd than Reguengo's.

Shopping

Turismo can provide a list of artisans who work with cork, clay, wood, iron, making figurines, bells, sculptures and unique pieces (most work from their homes, but many are happy to receive customers).

The weekly Saturday market held on the Rossio provides a great display of Alentejan goodies and Estremoz specialities, from goat's- and ewe's-milk cheeses, to a unique style of unglazed, ochre-red pots.

Casa Galileu (☎ 268 323 130; Rua Victor Cordon 16) If you miss the Saturday market, visit this shop southeast of the Rossio. It is crammed

with locally made ceramic figurines, as well as other essentials such as flat caps and cowbells.

Bonecos de Estremoz (Rua do Arco de Santarém 4) If you're after contemporary, Estremoz-style ceramic figurines, have a look at this workshop near the Museu Municipal.

Getting There & Around

Car rental is available at **Alenrent** (☎ 268 333 929; alenrent@iol.pt; Rua Capitão Mouzinho de Albuquerque 11). The **bus station** (☎ 268 322 282) is on the east side of town.

AROUND ESTREMOZ

Borba
pop 7800

The least visited of the marble towns, Borba glows with a peculiar rosy light. Its marble wealth hasn't brought it many obvious riches, so its marble-lined houses and public buildings have a remarkable simplicity. Locals here are particularly welcoming.

This quiet small town is encircled by marble quarries and is famous for its great red wines.

ORIENTATION & INFORMATION

Borba's main square, Praça da República, is the town focus, with its ornate 18th-century marble fountain, Fonte das Bicas, a rare sojourn into fanciness. The town comes to life once a year in early November, when it hosts a huge country fair. Access the net for free at **Celeiro da Cultura** (Rua Fernão Penteado; ⊙ 2-7pm Sun-Fri, 10am-1pm & 3-7pm Sat). The **turismo** (☎ 268 891 630; ⊙ 10am-12.30pm & 2-6.30pm Mon-Fri, 10am-1pm Sat) is half a block from Praça da República.

SIGHTS

The Alentejo Wine Route lists several *adegas* in this region (see p247). The **Adega Cooperativa de Borba** (☎ 268 891 660; www.adegaborba.pt; Rua Gago Coutinho Sacadura Cabral; ⏰ 9am-12.30pm & 2-5pm Mon-Fri) is one of the region's largest *adegas*, producing the famous Borba full-bodied red and white *maduro* (mature) and rosé wines. You can buy wine at the Adega's large **shop** (☎ 268 891 660; ⏰ 9am-7pm Mon-Sat), 100m further up the road from the coop.

SLEEPING & EATING

Residencial Inaramos (☎ 268 894 563; Av do Povo 22; s/d without breakfast €25/30) Up a marble staircase, this pleasant option offers bright, good-value rooms. It's nicely located on a street sprinkled with cafes, 1½ blocks east of the *praça*.

Casa de Borba (☎ 268 894 528; www.casadeborba .com; Rua da Cruz 5; s/d with breakfast €70/80; 🏊) An aristocratic 18th-century mansion, this place has five high-ceilinged rooms filled with antiques – carved beds and canopies, rich rugs and marble-topped tables. There's also a peaceful garden and pool.

A Talha (☎ 268 894 473; Rua Mestre Diogo de Borba 12; mains €6.50-8.50; ⏰ lunch & dinner Mon-Sat) Unsigned and unpretentious, this delightful place is housed in an arched cellar, and is lined with enormous urns. Its specialities are punchy new wine and lashings of home-cooked food. To get here, walk down Rua Antonio Joaquim da Guerra (off Avenida do Povo). Take the first left (Rua Visconde Gião), then the first right. Look for the green door.

GETTING THERE & AWAY

Daily buses connect Borba with Estremoz (€5.20, 15 minutes, around five buses daily) and Vila Viçosa (around €1.30). Buses stop just east of the *praça*. For bus times to Estremoz, ask at **Café Brinquete** (Av do Povo 31); tickets to Vila Viçosa are purchased on the bus.

Vila Viçosa
pop 9100

If you visit just one marble town in the region, Vila Viçosa is the one to hit. It has a long attractive plaza, set with orange trees, a fountain and a few outdoor cafes, and a marvellous marble palace – one of the country's largest.

This was once home to the Bragança dynasty, whose kings ruled Portugal until it became a republic (Dom Carlos spent his last night here before his assassination). There is also a fine castle – one of the few nonmarble structures in town – an excellent archaeological museum, appealing churches and a friendly laid-back citizenry who are proud of their sparkling town.

ORIENTATION & INFORMATION

The huge, sloping Praça da República is the attractive heart of town, with the *mercado municipal* and gardens 200m to the southeast. At the top of the *praça* is the 17th-century Igreja de São Bartolomeu; at the bottom is Avenida Bento de Jesus, which lies at the foot of the castle.

The Paço Ducal (Ducal Palace) is 300m northwest of the *praça* (follow Rua Dr Couto Jardim). Pick up a town map and other info at the **turismo** (☎ 268 881 101; www.cm-vilavicosa .pt; Praça da República 34; ⏰ 9.30am-noon, 1-6pm). Free web access is available around the corner at **Espaço Internet** (Rua Padre Joaquim Espanca 19; ⏰ 9am-7.30pm Mon-Sat).

SIGHTS
Terreiro do Paço & Paço Ducal

The **palace square** covers 16,000 sq metres, and it's ringed by the palace, the heavy-fronted Agostinhos Convent and graceful Chagas Nunnery. In the centre is a statue of Dom João IV.

The dukes of Bragança built their **palace** (☎ 268 980 659; adult/child under 10yr €5/free; ⏰ 2.30-5.30 Tue, 10am-1pm & 2.30-5.30pm Wed-Fri, 8.30am-1pm & 2.30-6pm Sat & Sun Apr-Sep, 2-5pm Thu-Tue, 10am-1pm & 2-5pm Wed Oct-Mar) in the early 16th century when the fourth duke, Dom Jaime, decided he had had enough of his uncomfortable hilltop castle. The wealthy Bragança family, originally from Bragança in Trás-os-Montes, had settled in Vila Viçosa in the 15th century. After the eighth duke became king in 1640, it changed from a permanent residence to just another royal palace, but the family maintained a special fondness for it and Dom João IV and his successors continued to visit the palace.

The best furniture went to Lisbon after Dom João IV ascended the throne, and some went on to Brazil after the royal family fled there in 1807, but there are some stunning pieces, such as a huge 16th-century Persian rug in the Dukes Hall. Lots of royal portraits put into context the interesting background on the royal family.

The private apartments hold a ghostly fascination – toiletries, knick-knacks and clothes of Dom Carlos and his wife, Marie-Amélia, are laid out as if the royal couple were about to return (Dom Carlos left one morning in 1908 and was assassinated in Lisbon that afternoon).

A Portuguese-speaking guide leads the hour-long tours (note: all tours are accompanied; visitors cannot enter alone). English guidebooks cost €5.

Other parts of the Ducal Palace, including the 16th-century cloister, house more museums containing specific collections and with separate admission fees (armoury/coach collection/Chinese Porcelain/treasury €2.50/1.50/2.50/2.50).

Castelo

The fascinating Dom Dinis' walled hilltop castle was where the Bragança family lived before the palace was built. It has been transformed into the **Museu de Arqueologia and Museu de Caça** (Archaeological Museum & Game & Hunting Museum; admission €3; 2.30-5.30pm Tue, 10am-1pm & 2.30-5.30pm Wed-Fri, 8.30am-1pm & 2.30-6pm Sat & Sun Apr-Sep, 2-5pm Thu-Tue, 10am-1pm & 2-5pm Wed Oct-Mar). A visit to these museums is a must – if only for an excuse to wander through the castle itself (think 'secret' tunnels, giant fire places and wonderful vaulted ceilings). The extraordinary (and under-promoted) archaeological collection is housed in the castle's many rooms and spans various eras from the Palaeolithic to the Roman. It even has ancient Egyptian treasures. Portuguese speakers should chat about the collection with the knowledgeable and modest museum minder, Sr Loper. The less interesting hunting museum is stuffed with guns and the dukes' animal trophies.

Surrounding the castle is a cluster of village houses and peaceful overgrown gardens. There's a 16th-century Manueline *pelourinho* (the prison used to be nearby), with sculpted frogs. Also near the castle is the brilliantly tiled 15th-century **Igreja de Nossa Senhora da Conceição**.

Marble Museum

The modest **marble museum** (268 889 314; admission €1; 9.30am-12.30pm & 2-5pm Tue-Sun) is worth going for its location alone – it's housed in the town's former train station, which is covered in stunning tiles. Spanning seven

small rooms, the museum's basic exhibits illustrate the marble industry and its processes (see p258).

FESTIVALS & EVENTS

On the second weekend of September the **Fiesta dos Capuchos** takes place, with a bullfight and a *vacada* (a bull is released and locals try to jump over it to show how brave they are) in the main square.

SLEEPING

Casa da Mariquinhas (268 980 523; Av Duques de Bragança 56; s/d without breakfast €20/30) On the main road into town opposite the castle, this welcoming spot offers three small, nicely furnished rooms with wood floors in a private house.

Hospedaria Dom Carlos (/fax 268 980 318; Praça da República 25; s/d/tr without breakfast €30/35/45;) In an excellent location on the main square, this offers tidy and comfortable rooms with wood finishing and a small, fancy lobby.

Quinta do Colmeal (919569751, 651 536 575; www.quintadocolmeal.net; 2-/4-person apt €100, house €150-250) This pretty *quinta* has two apartments and a house, set in a delightful flower and sculpture garden. It is surrounded by olive trees and has a large swimming pool. Interiors are decked in antique wooden furniture. It's located 3km from Vila Viçosa on the road to São Roman.

Hotel Convento de São Paulo (266 989 160; www.hotelconventospaulo.com; Aldeia da Serra; d from €160;) A marvellously romantic huge monastery on a 240-hectare estate, this hotel has big, grand, striking rooms and a restaurant with a lofty painted ceiling.

Pousada de Dom João IV (268 980 742; www.pousadas.pt; d €250;) Next to the Ducal Palace, this former royal convent was once the 'House of the Ladies of the Court'. Today, this regal spot offers spacious rooms – one with original frescos – terraces and classic furnishings. Rooms open onto a striking inner courtyard.

EATING

Os Cucos (268 980 806; mains €5.90-8.30; lunch & dinner Mon-Sat) Hidden in the pretty gardens near the *mercado municipal*, this is the pick for quality food and position. It has an airy, semicircular interior, and you can eat snacks at garden tables. The changing daily specials feature regional cuisine. To get here head

---

USING YOUR MARBLES

The marble towns gleam with rosy-gold or white stone, but the effect is enhanced by the houses, which have a Hollywood-smile brightness. As if locals hadn't found enough uses for the stone stuff, with their marble doorsteps, pavements and shoes (OK, we made that last one up) a process has been cooked up to create marble paint: marble is recrystallised limestone, so if you heat marble chips in a clay oven for three days they turn into calcium oxide which is mixed with water to become whitewash. Cheaper than paint. People take pride in their houses' whiteness and retouch them annually.

While we're on the subject of colour, apparently the yellow borders keep away fever, while blue is the bane of flies (you can add these colours to the oxide). The blue theory may have some truth, or at least international adherents – in Rajasthan (India) local people also apply pale blue to their houses to ward off mosquitoes.

Vila Viçosa has an interesting little marble museum (see p257), housed in the quaint former train station, the walls of which are covered with stunning blue and white *azulejos*.

---

uphill from the *praça*, then turn left after a block.

O Safari (☎ 268 980 414; Largo Mariano Prezado 17, mains €6-10 ☺ lunch & dinner Sun-Fri) For those on a budget, this is your no-frills, home-cooking option.

Café Restauração (☎ 268 980 256; Praça da República; mains €7.50-11; ☺ lunch & dinner) This is the best and buzziest of several cafe-restaurants that sit on the square just below the *turismo*. It has decent mains inside, and has pleasant outdoor seating for snacks.

ENTERTAINMENT

Classical **concerts** (admission free) are held in the chapel of the Ducal Palace on the last Friday of the month at 9pm year-round.

GETTING THERE & AWAY

There are **buses** (☎ 268 989 787) to/from Évora (€4.80/7.20 normal/express, 1¾/one hour, three to six daily on weekdays), or Estremoz (€2.80, 35 minutes, three to five daily on weekdays).

ELVAS

pop 23,400 / elev 280m

The impressive fortifications zigzagging around this pleasant little town reflect some of the most sophisticated military technology of 17th-century Europe. Its moats, fort and heavy walls would indicate a certain paranoia if it weren't for Elvas' position, only 15km west of Spain's Badajoz. Inside the stout town walls, you'll find a lovely town plaza, some quaint museums and very few foreign visitors – aside from the occasional flood of Spanish day-trippers.

Although there's not much to hold your attention beyond a day, Elvas is a fascinating place to visit, with its evocative frontier-post atmosphere, its narrow medina-like streets and its extraordinary, forbidding walls and buttresses.

History

In 1229 Elvas was recaptured from the Moors after 500 years of fairly peaceful occupation. The following centuries saw relentless attacks from Spain, interrupted by occasional peace treaties. Spain only succeeded in 1580, allowing Felipe II of Spain (the future Felipe I of Portugal) to set up court here for a few months. But the mighty fortifications were seldom breached: in 1644, during the Wars of Succession (1640–68), the garrison held out against a nine-day Spanish siege and, in 1659, just 1000 (an epidemic had wiped out the rest) withstood an attack by a 15,000-strong Spanish army.

The fortifications saw their last action in 1811, when the Duke of Wellington used the town as the base for an attack on Badajoz during the Peninsular War.

Orientation

Praça da República is at its heart, with all major sights a short walk away. Those arriving by train will find themselves disembarking at Fontaínhas, 4km northeast of town off the Campo Maior road.

It's possible to find central parking, but not always easy; if you don't like narrow one-way streets, park on the outskirts of town (or just inside Portas de Olivença).

ELVAS

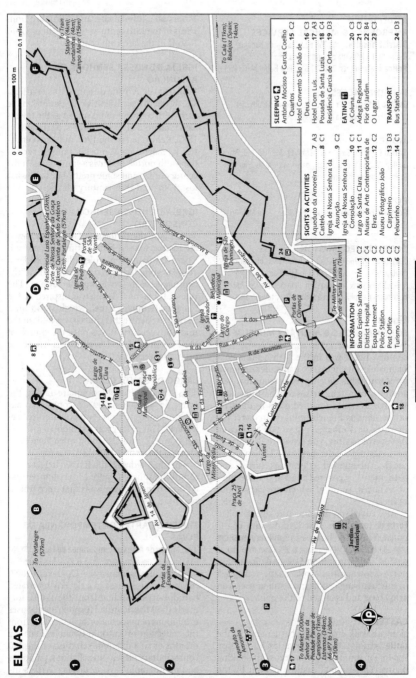

INFORMATION
Banco Espírito Santo & ATM......1	C2
District Hospital.........................2	C4
Espaço Internet.........................3	C2
Police Station...........................4	C2
Post Office................................5	C2
Turismo....................................6	C2

SIGHTS & ACTIVITIES
Aqueduto da Amoreira...............7	A3
Castelo....................................8	C1
Igreja de Nossa Senhora da Assunção....9	C2
Igreja de Nossa Senhora da Consolação....10	C1
Largo de Santa Clara.................11	C1
Museu de Arte Contemporânea de Elvas....12	C2
Museu Fotográfico João Carpinteiro....13	D3
Pelourinho..............................14	C1

SLEEPING 🛏
António Mocisso e Garcia Coelho Quartos....15	C2
Hotel Convento São João de Deus....16	C3
Hotel Dom Luís.......................17	A3
Pousada de Santa Luzia............18	C4
Residência Garcia de Orta.........19	D3

EATING 🍴
A Coluna................................20	C3
Adega Regional.......................21	C3
Flor do Jardim.........................22	B4
O Lagar.................................23	C3

TRANSPORT
Bus Station............................24	D3

Information

EMERGENCY & MEDICAL SERVICES

District hospital (☎ 268 622 225; Av de Badajoz) Opposite the Pousada de Santa Luzia.
Police station (☎ 268 622 613; Rua Isabel Maria Picão)

INTERNET ACCESS

Espaço Internet (Praça da República) Free internet access. Enter from Rua dos Sapateiros.

MONEY

Banco Espirito Santo & ATM (☎ 268 939 240; Praça da República) There are many banks with ATMs around town, including this one.

POST

Post office (Rua da Cadeia; ⏰ 8.30am-6pm Mon-Fri, 9am-12.30pm Sat)

TOURIST INFORMATION

Turismo (☎ 268 622 236; www.cm-elvas.pt; Praça da República; ⏰ 9am-7pm Mon-Fri, 10am-12.30pm & 2-5.30pm Sat & Sun May-Sep, 9am-5.30pm Oct-Apr) distributes pamphlets and a rudimentary town map.

Sights

FORTIFICATIONS & MILITARY MUSEUM

Walls encircled Elvas as early as the 13th century, but it was in the 17th century that Flemish Jesuit engineer Cosmander designed the formidable defences that you now see, adding moats, ramparts, seven bastions, four semibastions and fortified gates in the style of the famous French military architect the Marquis de Vauban. To give you an idea of the level of security, you cross a drawbridge to get to the main gate; inside is a 150-sq-metre square, surrounded by bastions, turrets and battlements, a covered road and three lines of trenches, some of which are carved out of rock.

Also added was the miniature zigzag-walled **Forte de Santa Luzia**, just 1.4km south of the *praça*. This now houses the **military museum** (☎ 268 628 357; ⏰ 9am-noon & 2-5.30pm Mon-Thu, to 4pm Fri). The **Forte de Nossa Senhora da Graça**, 3km north of town, with a similar shape, was added in the following century; it's still in use as an army base and is closed to the public.

CASTELO

You can walk around the battlements at the **castle** (admission €1.50; ⏰ 9.30am-1pm & 2.30-5.30pm Mon-Fri) for dramatic views across the baking plains. The original castle was built by the Moors on a Roman site, and rebuilt by Dom Dinis in the 13th century, then again by Dom João II in the late 15th century.

IGREJA DE NOSSA SENHORA DA ASSUNÇÃO

Francisco de Arruda designed this fortified, sturdy **church** (Praça da República; admission free) in the early 16th century, and it served as the town's cathedral until Elvas lost its episcopal status in 1882. Renovated in the 17th and 18th centuries, it retains a few Manueline touches, such as the south portal. Inside is a sumptuous 18th-century organ and some pretty, but somewhat lost, 17th- and 18th-century tiling.

IGREJA DE NOSSA SENHORA DA CONSOLAÇÃO

This plain **church** (Largo de Santa Clara; admission free, donations welcome) hides a thrilling interior. There are painted marble columns under a cupola, gilded chapels and fantastic 17th-century *azulejos* covering the surface. The unusual octagonal design was inspired by the Knights Templar chapel, which stood on a nearby site before this church was built in the mid-16th century. It was once the church of the Dominicans, and is all that is left of the original monastery.

LARGO DE SANTA CLARA

This delightful cobbled square facing the Igreja de Nossa Senhora da Consolação has a whimsical centrepiece – a polka-dotted **pelourinho**. This pillory was a symbol of municipal power: criminals would once have been chained to the metal hooks at the top.

The fancy **archway** with its own loggia at the top of the square is pure Moorish artistry – a flourish in the town walls that once trailed past here.

MUSEU DE ARTE CONTEMPORÂNEA DE ELVAS

The **Museu de Arte Contemporânea de Elvas** (☎ 268 637 150; www.cm-elvas/mace; ⏰ 3-6.30pm Tue, 10am-1pm & 3-6pm Wed-Sun) is a must see. Opened in 2007, the museum is housed in a cleverly renovated baroque-style building from the 1700s, formerly the Misericórdia Hospital, and houses exhibitions of modern Portuguese artists from the collection of António Cachola. Each six months or so a different selection of the 300 contemporary pieces – installations, paintings and photographs – is on display. Artists include the likes of Franciso Vidal, Rui Patacho and Ana Pinto. One of the rooms contains the original chapel with exquisite tiles. Upstairs is a small funky all-white cafe with a stunning city vista from the terrace.

AQUEDUTO DA AMOREIRA

It took an unsurprising 100 years or so to complete this breathtakingly ambitious **aqueduct**. Finished in 1622, these huge cylindrical buttresses and several tiers of arches stalk from 7km west of town to bring water to the marble fountain in Largo da Misericórdia. It's best seen from the Lisbon road, west of the centre.

MUSEU FOTOGRÁFICO JOÃO CARPINTEIRO

Housed in the old town cinema is the **Photography Museum João Carpinteiro** (☎ 268 636 470; Largo Luis de Camões; adult/child €2/1; ☼ 10am-1pm & 2-5pm Oct-Mar, 10am-1pm & 3-7pm Apr-Sep Tue-Sun), with an impressive collection of cameras, the oldest a pocket-vest number dating from 1912. Changing photography exhibits, however, are often the highlight of a visit here.

Tours

Agia (☎ 933 259 036; agia@iol.pt), a licensed guide association, organises two-hour walking tours (€12) that explore Elvas' historic sites. Call to arrange a time and meeting place.

Festivals & Events

Elvas starts to tap its blue suede shoes in late September, celebrating the **Festas do Senhor da Piedade e de São Mateus**, with everything from agricultural markets and bullfights to folk dancing and religious processions (especially on the last day). Book accommodation well in advance.

Sleeping

BUDGET

Senhor Jesus da Piedade Parque de Campismo (☎ 268 628 997; adult/tent/car €3.50/4.50/3.50; ☼ Apr–mid-Sep) Elvas' nearest camping ground is on the southwestern outskirts of Elvas, off the N4 Estremoz road. It's a small tree-shaded camp, with a municipal pool 1km away.

António Mocisso e Garcia Coelho Quartos (☎ 268 622 126; Rua Aires Varela 15; s/d/tr €20/30/35; ☒) The best of the budget places in the town centre has 20 small but clean rooms. Some have a musty, basement feel and very small windows.

MIDRANGE

Residencial Luso Espanhola (☎ /fax 268 623 092; Rua Rui de Melo; s/d €25/40; ☒) A short way from town (2km north on the Portalegre road), this friendly 14-room hostelry has smallish, modern rooms with balconies giving a fine view of the countryside. There are two restaurants next door. You'll need your own transport to get here.

Residência Garcia de Orta (☎ 268 623 152; Av Garcia de Orta 3a; s/d/tr €30/40/50) Although the pine-clad rooms in this beautiful old building are worn and stuffy and the floors slope, they are nonetheless clean and offer good value. Each room has views to Spain or of the streetscape.

Hotel Dom Luís (☎ 268 622 710; fax 268 620 733; Av de Badajoz; s/d with breakfast €59/69; ☒) An efficient, modern establishment, this hotel is 700m west of the centre, just outside the town walls and near the aqueduct. There are two sections – the older rooms have traditional floral Alentejano decor, while the newer rooms boast contemporary decor in browns and beiges.

Quinta de Santo António (☎ 268 636 460; www .qsa.com.pt; Estrada de Barbacena; s/d with breakfast €84/105; ☒ ☐) This beautiful, stately old house sits in lush gardens 7km northwest of Elvas. There are tennis courts and horses to ride. You'll need your own transport to get to this place.

Hotel Convento São João de Deus (☎ 268 639 220; www.hotelsaojoadeus.com; Largo João de Deus 1; s/d Sun/Thu €64/70, Fri & Sat €74/80; ☒ ☒) Spanish-owned and operating since 2004, this is Elvas' finest hotel. It is a grand but not always sympathetic conversion of a 17th-century convent. Each room is different in size and decor – the larger ones are lovely, a couple of smaller ones less so. Most, however, have handsome wood floors and heavy fabrics. One has a bedhead made of tiles. There's also a good restaurant.

TOP END

Pousada de Santa Luzia (☎ 268 637 470; www.pousadas .pt; Av de Badajoz; s/d €158/170; ☒ ☒) Dating from 1942, this is a comfortable, though relatively modern and characterless, *pousada* – the first in Portugal.

Eating

A Coluna (☎ 268 623 728; Rua do Cabrito 11; mains €5.50-8, tourist menu €9; ☼ lunch & dinner Wed-Mon) This whitewashed cavern is a cut above its competitors, with *azulejos* on the walls and lots of pork and *bacalhau* (cod fish) dishes on the menu.

O Lagar (☎ 969413152; Rua Nova da Vedoria 7; mains €6.50-15; ☽ lunch & dinner Fri-Wed) Smart and buzzing, O Lagar dishes up excellent regional cooking. Its high-quality *açordas* and *bacalhau* and meat dishes are great value, but steer clear of the expensive and not-so-nice salads. Service can be a bit slow, but this is a place to linger over a meal.

Adega Regional (☎ 268 623 009; Rua João Casqueiro 22B; mains €7-10.50) Locals love this small place where it's all about the food – lashings of *plumas de porco preto* (pork) and *choquinhos á alentejana* (squid), or a great value three-course daily meal for €6.50.

Flor do Jardim (☎ 268 623 174; Av António Sardinho; mains €9.50-18; ☽ lunch & dinner) Set in the Jardim Municipal, this restaurant has a peaceful terrace where you can have drinks; the smart, traditional dining room inside serves nicely prepared meat and seafood dishes. Spaniards come for the *bacalhau* dishes while locals love the *bife da vazia a casa* (beef with a creamy, egg-based salsa).

Shopping

On alternate Mondays there's a big lively market around the aqueduct, just off the Lisbon road west of town. The weeks it's not on, there's a flea market in Praça da República.

Getting There & Around

The bus station is outside the city walls, on the road to Spain. It's an 800m walk mostly uphill (or a €4.50 taxi ride) to the main *praça*. There are buses to Estremoz (€7, 45 minutes, five daily), Évora (€10, 1¼ to 1¾ hours, three daily), Portalegre (€11.50, 1¼ hours, one daily), Faro (€17, 6½ hours, one daily) and Lisbon (€11.70, 3¼ to 3½ hours, nine daily). Cheaper but considerably slower 'carreira normal' (bus) services are also available to these destinations.

Two train services run daily to Lisbon (€13, 4¼ to 5¼ hours), with a transfer necessary at Entroncamento.

Taxis (☎ 268 623 526) charge around €5 from the train station at Fontaínhas into town.

PORTALEGRE

pop 26,800 / elev 520m

Alto Alentejo's capital, Portalegre, is bunched up on a hilltop at the foot of Serra de São Mamede. This pretty, whitewashed, ochre-edged city makes a charming, low-key, off-the-beaten-track experience. A lively student population and handy transport links to nearby mountaintop villages add to its appeal.

Inside the city walls, faded baroque mansions – relics of the town's textile-manufacturing heyday – are all dressed up with no place to go. In the 16th century, the town boomed through tapestry; in the 17th, silk. Bust followed boom after the 1703 Treaty of Methuen brought English competition. But, even today, Portalegre stays true to its legacy of natty threads – there is a factory here producing extraordinary tapestries of artworks by famous modern artists, and an impressive museum showcasing the work.

Orientation

Portalegre has an hourglass shape, with the new town to the northeast and the old town spread across a hilltop to the southwest. The 'waist' is a traffic roundabout – the Rossio, which is close to the bus station, from where it's about 400m to the old town via the pedestrianised Rua 5 de Outubro.

Information

EMERGENCY

Hospital (☎ 245 301 000) About 400m north of town.
Police station (☎ 245 300 620; Praça da República) Just outside Porta de Alegrete.

INTERNET ACCESS

Espaço Internet (Praça da República; ☽ 10.30am-8pm Mon-Fri, 2-6pm Sat) Free access, but often packed.
Instituto Português de Juventude (Estrada do Bonfim; ☽ 9am-12.30pm & 2-5.30pm Mon-Fri) Free access; 700m north of the Rossio.

MONEY

In the Rossio, the Millennium, BPI and Montepio banks all have ATMs.
Caixa Geral de Depósitos & ATM (☎ 245 339 100; Rua de Elvas) Bank with ATM in the old town.

POST

Branch post office (Rua Luís de Camões 39) In the old town.
Main post office (cnr Av da Liberdade & Rua Alexandre Herculano; ☽ 8.30am-6pm Mon-Fri, 9am-12.30pm Sat) About 250m north of the Rossio.

TOURIST INFORMATION

Turismo (☎ 245 307 445; Rua Guilherme Gomes Fernandes 22; ☽ 9.30am-1pm & 2.30-6pm Mon-Sun) Has an excellent town map with suggested walking route

PORTALEGRE

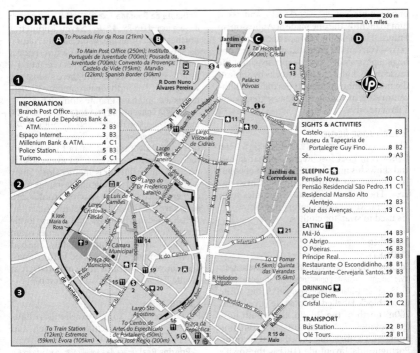

INFORMATION
Branch Post Office...........................1 B2
Caixa Geral de Depósitos Bank &
ATM...2 B3
Espaço Internet..............................3 B3
Millenium Bank & ATM.................4 C1
Police Station.................................5 B3
Turismo...6 C1

SIGHTS & ACTIVITIES
Castelo..7 B3
Museu da Tapeçaria de
Portalegre Guy Fino.................8 B2
Sé...9 A3

SLEEPING
Pensão Nova.................................10 C1
Pensão Residencial São Pedro..11 C1
Residencial Mansão Alto
Alentejo.....................................12 B3
Solar das Avenças.......................13 C1

EATING
Má-Jó..14 B3
O Abrigo.......................................15 B3
O Poeiras......................................16 B3
Príncipe Real................................17 B3
Restaurante O Escondidinho...18 B1
Restaurante-Cervejaria Santos.19 B3

DRINKING
Carpe Diem...................................20 B3
Crisfal..21 C2

TRANSPORT
Bus Station...................................22 B1
Olé Tours......................................23 B1

and other brochures on the region, including the recently formulated *Ruta dos Sabores*, a route promoting local products that have been declared 'Protected Designation of Origin (PDO)'. The monthly *Agenda Cultural* promotes concerts which are sometimes held in the Jardim do Tarro.

Sights

SÉ

In 1550 Portalegre became the seat of a new diocese and soon got its own **cathedral** (☎ 245 330 322). The pyramid-pointed, twin-towered 18th-century facade, with a broken clock, sombrely presides over the whitewashed Praça do Município. The sacristy contains an array of fine *azulejos*.

CASTELO

Portalegre's **castle** (admission free; 10am-1pm & 2-5pm Mon-Fri, 10am-1pm & 3-6pm Sat & Sun), off Rua do Carmo, dates from the time of Dom Dinis, with three restored towers that offer good views across the town. In the 1930s, part of the castle walls were destroyed to open the streets to traffic. In 2006, a controversial renovation was completed – a modern wooden structure now links the walls of the castle to the tower.

Designed by Portuguese architect Cândido Chuva Gomes, the you-either-love-it-or-hate-it construction is intended to resemble rocks, marking the difference between the 13th and 21st centuries. There is a temporary exhibition gallery on the 1st floor.

MANSIONS

The town's former glory is recorded in stone: faded 17th-century baroque town houses and mansions dot Rua 19 de Junho to the southeast.

MUSEU DA TAPEÇARIA DE PORTALEGRE GUY FINO

If there's one thing you must visit in Portalegre, it's this splendid **museum** (☎ 245 307 530; Rua da Figueira 9; admission €2; 9.30am-1pm & 2.30-6pm Tue-Sun). Opened in 2001, it contains brilliant contemporary creations from Portalegre's unique tapestry factory. It's named after the factory founder, who created an innovatory 'stitch' by hand weaving. The museum shows a selection of the 7000 colours of thread used. French tapestry artist Jean Lurçat at first dismissed the technique, then the factory made a copy of one of his works – a cockerel – and asked him to identify the one made at Aubusson, in France. He chose the more perfect Portalegre copy – you can see them juxtaposed here. The huge tapestries are vastly expensive, and the museum includes copies of works by some of the most famous names in Portuguese 20th-century art, including Almada Negreiros and Vieira de Silva.

MUSEU JOSÉ REGIO

This small **museum** (☉ 9.30am-12.30pm & 2-6pm Tue-Sun) is in poet José Regio's former house, and shows his magpie-like collection of popular religious art, with around 400 Christ figures. There are lots of rustic ceramics from Coimbra, which 18th-century migrant workers used to swap for clothes.

Sleeping
BUDGET
Pousada da Juventude (☎ 245 330 971; www.pousadas juventude.pt; Estrada do Bonfim; dm/d with shared bathroom €9/18; ☉ 8am-10am & 6pm-midnight) A big white tower block labelled 'Centro de Juventude', 700m north of the Rossio, this youth hostel provides the usual not-fancy-but-fine bunks and bathrooms; the adjacent Instituto Português da Juventude (IPJ) is the town's main youth centre.

Pensão Nova (☎ 245 331 212; fax 245 330 493; Rua 31 de Janeiro 26; s/d €25/35; ☒) A friendly place in the old part of town, Pensão Nova has pretty rooms with large pieces of wooden furniture and shuttered windows. Bathrooms are a bit cramped, but overall it's good value. If it's full, guests are housed in the proprietors' other hotel, Pensão Residencial São Pedro.

MIDRANGE & TOP END
Residencial Mansão Alto Alentejo (☎ 245 202 290; www.mansaoaltoalentejo.com.pt; Rua 19 de Junho 59; s/d €35/45; ☒) The stone staircase is steep and it's a bit of a labyrinth, but it's centrally located and has small, bright rooms with traditional hand-painted furniture and a charming lounge area.

Solar das Avenças (☎ 245 201 028; www.rtsm .pt/solardasavencas; Jardim da Corredoura 11; s/d/ste €55/65/90; ☒ ☐) Near the park, this extraordinary 18th-century manor house has five ornate rooms, with antique furnishings. Some rooms have fireplaces. The spacious and luxurious suites will take you back a few centuries.

Quinta da Dourada (☎ 937218654; www.quinta dourada.com; d €65-85; ☒ ☒) Seven kilometres northeast of Portalegre, in the Parque Natural da Serra de São Mamede, this picture-perfect place is surrounded by glorious vegetation – lime trees and flowers – and there's a historic water tank. The individual rooms are smartly furnished and have granite stone floors.

our pick Convento da Provença (☎ 245 337 104; www.provenca.pt; Monte Paleiros; s/d/ste €85/95/105 ☒ ☒) Mother Superior may not have approved of this luxury sleeping option, but we do. This renovated former convent has a white, austere exterior, but its interior is another story. Shiny sabres and suits of armour fill the lounge room and entrance hall. The spacious rooms and suites are decked out in masculine hues and stylish wooden trimmings, and all have lovely green views. There's a massive games room (and kids' nursery). Unfortunately, one bad habit – smoking – is permitted in the rooms. The Convento is located north of Portalegre at Monte Paleiros on the road to Marvão.

Eating
Portalegre has some excellent restaurants. Cheap eats include sandwich and pizza places.

Príncipe Real (Praça da República 2; snacks from €2; ☉ 8am-2am Mon-Sat) One of several attractive outdoor cafes on Praça da República, this place serves up good baguette sandwiches, pastries and coffee. A garrulous young crowd arrives in the evenings.

Restaurante-Cervejaria Santos (☎ 245 203 066; Largo Serpa Pinto 4; mains €4-6.50; ☉ lunch & dinner Thu-Tue) This little place has a small outdoor wooden terrace under green umbrellas, and great migas (pork and fried bread) and so on.

Má-Jó (Rua Dom Augusto Eduardo Nunes 1; ☉ 9am-1pm & 3-6pm Mon-Fri, 9am-1pm Sat) This tiny wine shop sells smoked meats, cheeses and velvety rich reds.

Poeiras Restaurante (☎ 245 201 862; Praça da República 9-15; mains €5-10) This great value, popular restaurant has a meaty smell and whips up fabulous Alentejano cuisine, including bacalhau dishes.

O Abrigo (☎ 245 331 658; Rua de Elvas; mains €7.50-9; ☉ lunch & dinner Wed-Mon) This smart restaurant with crimson and cream decor is renowned for its delicious local dishes, including açorda miolada (€7.50).

Restaurante O Escondidinho (☎ 245 202 728; Travessa das Cruzes 1; mains €7-14; ☉ lunch & dinner Mon-

Sat) A Portalegre charmer, this cosy spot has quaint country-style dining areas, a bar lined with tiles and a massive selection of traditional mains. Try the *espetados de toreiro bravo* (wild bull kebabs; €14). Half servings are available.

Drinking
Portalegre's student population adds some life to the old streets, with outdoor drinking spots around Praça da República and to a lesser extent Largo do Dr Frederico Laranjo.

Carpe Diem (Rua 19 de Junho 33; ☺ noon-3pm & 7pm-2am) This nicely designed bar and bistro has a good mixed crowd. Cocktails and beer are served as are flavourful soups and sandwiches (the kitchen stays open late).

Crisfal (Av George Robinson) This recently renovated former cinema is the place to join the late-night disco crowd.

Entertainment
Overlooking Praça da República, the **Centro de Artes do Espectáculo de Portalegre** (☎ 245 307 498; www.caeportalegre.blogspot.com in Portuguese; Praça da República 39) is Portalegre's major performance space with a line-up of fado singers, rock, jazz and acoustic groups, as well as dance and theatre. Ask at the tourist office or check the latest *Agenda Cultural* for current shows.

Getting There & Around
The **bus station** (☎ 245 330 723) has regular services to Lisbon (€13, 4½ hours), Estremoz (€4.85/8 normal/express, 80/50 minutes, two daily weekdays), Évora (€6.50 to €9.50, 1½ hours, two daily weekdays), Castelo Branco (€9.50, one hour 50 minutes, one daily), Elvas (€5, 1½ hours, two daily weekdays), Marvão (€4, two daily, 45 minutes) and Castelo de Vide (€4.60, two daily).

Trains from Lisbon run daily (€11.50; 3½ to four hours, two daily); change at Entroncamento. The station is 12km south of town. There are sometimes **taxis** (☎ 245 203 842) outside the bus station and in the nearby Rossio. Car rental is available from **Olé Tours** (☎ 245 205 000; Rua Dom Nuno Álvares Pereira) opposite the bus station.

CASTELO DE VIDE
pop 4100 / elev 570m
High up above lush, rolling countryside, Castelo de Vide is one of Portugal's most attractive and underrated villages. Its fine hilltop vantage point, dazzlingly white houses, flower-lined lanes and proud locals are reason alone to visit. There aren't many attractions in town, but there don't need to be. Absorb this pleasant place for a day and night; at dusk and early morning you can experience the town at its most disarming. You'll see elderly ladies crocheting on doorsteps, children playing in the narrow streets, and neighbours chatting out of upper-storey windows.

By the castle is a small *judiaria* – the former Jewish district, strongest here in the early 15th century after the expulsion of the Jews from Spain. A small synagogue is the main memento of this era. Castelo de Vide is famous for its crystal-clear mineral water, which spouts out of numerous pretty public fountains; several of these are surrounded by hedged gardens.

Orientation
At the heart of town are two parallel squares backed by the Igreja de Santa Maria da Devesa. The *turismo* is in Rua Bartolomeu Álvares da Santa.

The castle, old quarter and *judiaria* lie to the northwest. Buses stop beside the garden to the east; the train station is 4km northwest.

Information
Caixa Geral de Depósitos (☎ 245 339 100; Praça Valência de Alcántara)

Centro de Interpretação (☎ 245 905 299; Rua de Santo Amaro 27; ☺ 9am-12.30pm & 2-5.30pm Mon-Fri) Information centre for the Parque Natural da Serra de São Mamede.

Centro de saúde (medical centre; ☎ 245 900 160; EN246-1 on the southern exit out of town)

Police station (☎ 245 901 314; Av da Aramenha)

Post office (Rua de Olivença; ☺ 9am-12.30pm & 2-5.30pm Mon-Fri)

Turismo (☎ 245 901 361; www.cm-castelo-vide.pt, turismo.cmcv@gmail.com; Praça Dom Pedro V; ☺ 9am-5.30pm Oct-Apr, to 7pm May-Sep) Stocks some excellent printed matter, including maps and leaflets; disinterested staff, however.

Sights
OLD TOWN & JUDIARIA
A sizeable community of Jews settled here in the 12th century, then larger waves came in the 15th. At first they didn't have an exclusive district, but Dom Pedro I restricted them to specific quarters. Closed at the time of research but worth walking past, the tiny **synagogue** looks just like its neighbouring cottages,

THE ALENTEJO

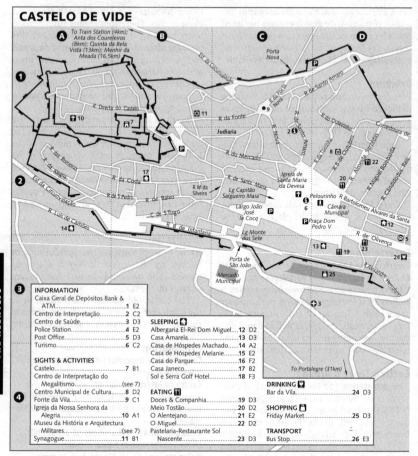

CASTELO DE VIDE

INFORMATION
Caixa Geral de Depósitos Bank & ATM	**1** E2
Centro de Interpretação	**2** C2
Centro de Saúde	**3** D3
Police Station	**4** E2
Post Office	**5** D3
Turismo	**6** C2

SIGHTS & ACTIVITIES
Castelo	**7** B1
Centro de Interpretação do Megalitismo	(see 7)
Centro Municipal de Cultura	**8** D2
Fonte da Vila	**9** C1
Igreja da Nossa Senhora da Alegria	**10** A1
Museu da História e Arquitectura Militares	(see 7)
Synagogue	**11** B1

SLEEPING
Albergaria El-Rei Dom Miguel	**12** D2
Casa Amarela	**13** D3
Casa de Hóspedes Machado	**14** A2
Casa de Hóspedes Melanie	**15** E2
Casa do Parque	**16** F2
Casa Janeco	**17** B2
Sol e Serra Golf Hotel	**18** F3

EATING
Doces & Companhia	**19** D3
Meio Tostão	**20** D2
O Alentejano	**21** E2
O Miguel	**22** D2
Pastelaria-Restaurante Sol Nascente	**23** D3

DRINKING
Bar da Vila	**24** D3

SHOPPING
Friday Market	**25** D3

TRANSPORT
Bus Stop	**26** E3

as it was adapted from an existing building. It's divided into two rooms: one for women and one for men. In the bare interior is a wooden tabernacle and Holy Ark for Torah scrolls. Following Manuel I's convert-or-leave edict in 1496, many Jews returned to Spain, though some headed to Évora.

CASTELO
Originally Castelo de Vide's inhabitants lived within the castle's sturdy outer walls; even now there remains a small inner village with a church, the 17th-century **Igreja da Nossa Senhora da Alegria**.

You can take in some brilliant views from here over the town's red roofs, surrounded by green and olive hills. The **castle** (admission free; ☺ 9.30am-12.30pm & 2-6pm), built by Dom Dinis and his brother Dom Afonso between 1280 and 1365, is topped by a 12m-high brick tower, thought to be the oldest part. Feel like the king of the castle and catch the great views from the roof of the tower's fine vaulted hall (the hall itself is unfortunately covered in graffiti).

The castle houses the **Centro de Interpretação do Megalitismo**. Its wordy information boards explain the background, history and characteristics of the area's megaliths, and there are some ancient stone tools. In the room above, the **Museu da História e Arquitectura Militares** outlines the chronology of the castle's kings between the 12th and 14th centuries, and displays a few muskets, cannon

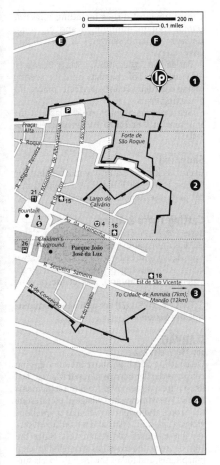

ANTA DOS COURELEIROS & MENHIR DA MEADA

In the wild, boulder-strewn landscape around Castelo de Vide are dozens of ancient megaliths. The two most impressive are the Anta dos Coureleiros, 8km north of town (with three other megaliths nearby making up what's called a Parque Megalítico), and the 7m-high Menhir da Meada, 8.5km further on – supposedly the tallest menhir in the Iberian Peninsula – a large phallus for keeping the fields fertile.

Both megaliths are easily accessible by car or on foot. *Turismos* here and in Marvão, plus the helpful Centro de Interpretação should have *Paisagens Megalíticas Norte Alentejana* (Megalithic Landscapes North of Alentejo) a free, glossy photographic leaflet (English versions available) to help you track down these and other megaliths; follow the small wooden 'Antas' signs en route.

TRAIN STATION

Trains have stopped running through Castelo de Vide. However, if you are passing by, this quaint place, with its beautiful *azulejos* is worth a look. The station is 4km northwest of town.

Festivals & Events

Carnaval Held in February/March, this festival is great fun, with everyone out to watch processions of fantastically costumed folk, many in drag.

Easter festival Castelo de Vide's big bash is the four-day fair in March/April when hundreds of lambs go through the highs and lows of blessings and slaughter; processions, folk dances, band music and much revelry all take place.

Sleeping

BUDGET

Casa de Hóspedes Melanie (☎ 245 901 632; Largo do Paça Novo 3; s/d/tr €25/35/45; ✿) Situated near a leafy square, this clean spot has five plain but neat and light, good-value rooms with cork-tile floors.

Casa de Hóspedes Machado (☎ 245 901 515; Rua Luís de Camões 33; s €28-30, d €35) On the western edge of town, this friendly and efficiently run place has airy, modern and spotless rooms. There's a small, shared kitchen and outdoor patio.

Casa Janeco (☎ 245 901 211; Rua da Costa 56a) The elderly and sweet Senhora Janeco is in the process of renovating a small apartment in her private residence in the narrow cobbled heart of town. Prices will be around the €30 mark.

balls and stone tools. All information is in Portuguese only.

FONTE DA VILA

In a pretty square just below and east of the *judiaria* is the worn-smooth 16th-century marble Fonte da Vila, with a washing area. This, along with several other fountains in the village, spouts out the delicious mineral water for which Castelo de Vide is known.

CENTRO MUNICIPAL DE CULTURA

This **cultural centre** (Rua 5 de Outubro 21; free admission; ☼ 9am-4pm Mon-Fri) hosts a range of temporary exhibitions – photographs of traditional and rural life in the Alentejo and the like. There's also a carving from a menhir on display.

THE ALENTEJO

MIDRANGE & TOP END

Albergaria El-Rei Dom Miguel (☎ 245 919 191; fax 245 901 592; www.albdmiguel.com; Rua Bartolomeu Álvares da Santa 19; s/d €30/60) This central seven-room guest house is extraordinarily good value. It has an upmarket but not snobby feel with tasteful, modern rooms and smart bathrooms in an 1875 house. Antiques and beautiful artefacts – all from the owner's family – fill the stunning communal area.

Casa do Parque (☎ 245 901 250; www.casadoparque .net; Av da Aramenha 37; s/d €35/48) Overlooking the park, and in a historic building (a former girls' school), this lovely spot has inviting, slightly worn, rooms with tile floors and big windows. A decent restaurant adjoins the lobby.

Sol e Serra Golf Hotel (☎ 245 900 000; www.grupof barata.com; Estrada de São Vicente 73; s/d €50/80; 🏊 🍴) About 100m towards Marvão, this large, attractive hotel has many amenities, including a children's pool and a bar-restaurant.

Casa Amarela (☎ 245 905 878; www.casaamarelath .com; Praça Dom Pedro V; s/d/ste €75/100/140) This beautifully restored 18th-century building on the main square, with views over the *praça*, is a luxurious choice. It has stone staircases and antiques-filled common areas. The 10 rooms drip with rich fabrics and feature massive, marble-filled bathrooms.

Quinta da Bela Vista (☎ 245 968 125; Póvoa e Meadas; d €80; 🍴) This is an olde-worlde country house 13km north of Castelo de Vide. It's been in the same family since the 1920s and is a lovely choice.

Eating & Drinking

Doces & Companhia (☎ 245 901 408; Praça Dom Pedro V 6; mains €3-5; 🕐 breakfast, lunch & dinner Mon-Sat) Serving great cakes and ice-creams, this is the place to ease your sugar cravings. Also on offer are set-menu lunches and a lovely terrace (head through the restaurant to find it).

Pastelaria-Restaurante Sol Nascente (☎ 245 901 789; Rua do Olivença; mains €6.50-8; 🕐 breakfast, lunch & dinner Tue-Sun) This pleasant central cafe has a massive menu selection, from soups and sandwiches to three-course lunch specials (€5 to €7.50).

O Miguel (☎ 245 901 882; Rua Almeida Sarzedas 32; mains €6.50-8; 🕐 lunch & dinner Mon-Sat) This casual place with blue and white tiles is a great-value eatery with daily specials and generous portions of regional cuisine.

O Alentejano (☎ 245 901 355; Largos dos Mártires de República 14; mains €6-10.50) Another excellent choice for local dishes including *migas de batata* (potato dumplings) and *espetadas de barrego* (lamb skewers) in a warm and cosy eatery.

Bar da Vila (☎ 245 905 433; Rua de Olivença 11; 🕐 11am-11pm) This bar has outdoor seating facing a garden square – perfectly placed for a relaxing drink.

Self-catering supplies are available at the minimarket **Meio Tostão** (Rua Bartolomeu Álvares da Santa 52).

Shopping

Every week there's a Friday market (but the biggest is the last Friday of the month) in a car park just outside the old walls.

Getting There & Away

Buses (☎ 245 901 510) run to/from Portalegre (€2.45/5 normal/express, 20 minutes, one to four daily) and Lisbon (€15, 4¼ hours, two daily). All buses stop beside the garden (Praça Valéncia de Alcántara). Ask at the *turismo* for bus times.

Taxis (☎ 245 901 271) are available from outside the *turismo*.

MARVÃO

pop 150 / elev 862m

On a jutting crag high above the surrounding countryside, the narrow lanes of Marvão feel like a retreat far removed from the settlements below. The whitewashed village of picturesque tiled roofs and bright flowers has marvellous views, a splendid castle and a handful of low-key guest houses and restaurants. Since the 16th century, the town has struggled to keep inhabitants, and today, the friendly locals survive mainly on tourism. It's worth spending a night here.

History

Not surprisingly, this garrison town just 10km from the Spanish frontier has long been a prized possession. Romans settled here, and Christian Visigoths were on the scene when the Moors arrived in 715. It was probably the Moorish lord of Coimbra, Emir Maraun, who gave the place its present name.

In 1160 Christians took control. In 1226 the town received a municipal charter, the walls were extended to encompass the whole summit, and the castle was rebuilt by Dom Dinis.

Marvão's importance in the defence against the Castilians was highlighted during the

17th-century War of Restoration, when further defences were added. But by the 1800s it had lost its way, a garrison town without a garrison, and this lack of interest is why so many 15th- and 16th-century buildings have been preserved. Its last action was at the centre of the tug-of-war between the Liberals and Royalists; in 1833 the Liberals used a secret entrance to seize the town – the only time Marvão has ever been captured.

Orientation

Arriving by car or bus you'll approach Portas de Ródão, one of the four village gates, opening onto Rua de Cima, which has several shops and restaurants. Drivers can park outside or enter this gate and park in Largo de Olivença, just below Rua de Cima. The castle is up at the end of Rua do Espiríto Santo.

Information

There's a Caixa Geral do Depósitos bank (with ATM) on Rua do Espiríto Santo. Access the internet for free at the **Casa da Cultura** (Largo do Pelourinho; 🕑 9.30am-1pm & 2-5.30pm Mon-Fri). Near the castle and selling jams and souvenirs is the helpful **turismo** (☎ 245 909 131; www.cm-marvao .pt; Largo de Santa Maria; 🕑 9am-noon & 2-5.30pm Sep-Jun, 9am-7pm Jul & Aug). Also on sale is the excellent book, *Norte Alentejano Walking Excursions* (€10), which includes maps. It has a complete list of accommodation options.

Sights & Activities

CASTELO

The formidable **castle** (admission free; 🕑 24hr), built into the rock at the western end of the village, dates from the end of the 13th century, but most of what you see today was built in the 17th century. The views from the battlements are staggering. There's a huge vaulted cistern (still full of water) near the entrance and it's landscaped with hedges and flowerbeds. You can walk around the town on the castle walls. At the far end, the **Núcleo Museológico Militar** (Military Museum; adult/student €1/0.80; 🕑 10am-1pm & 2-5pm Tue-Sun) offers a fine little display of Marvão and its castle's embattled history with an accompanying flourish of 17th- to 18th-century muskets and bayonets.

MUSEU MUNICIPAL

Just east of the castle, the Igreja de Santa Maria provides graceful surroundings for the small **museum** (adult/child under 12 €1/free; 🕑 9am-12.30pm

& 2-5.30pm Tue-Sun). The approach to history is a bit scattershot, with displays of medieval grave markers, carved stonework dating from the 3rd millennium BC, costumes and Roman pottery shards.

CASA DA CULTURA

In a restored building, this **cultural centre** (Largo do Pelourinho; free admission; 🕑 9.30am-1pm & 2-5.30pm) hosts changing exhibitions, and you can check out the rustic upstairs court room, dating from 1809. There's also a small handicrafts **shop** on site.

WALKING TRAIL

Ask at the tourist office for instructions on the interesting 7.5km circuit walk from Marvão to Portagem via Abegoa and Fonte Souto (or 2.5km direct to Portagem), following a medieval stone-paved route (note: the return journey is steep).

MEGALITHS

You can make a brilliant 30km round-trip via Santo António das Areias and Beirã, visiting nearby *antas* (dolmens). Pick up the free *Paisagens Megalíticas Norte Alentejana* leaflet from the *turismo*. Follow the wooden *'antas'* signs through a fabulously quiet landscape of cork trees and rummaging pigs. Some of the megaliths are right by the roadside, while others require a 300m to 500m walk. Be sure to bring refreshments: there's no village en route. You can continue north of Beirã to visit the megaliths in the Castelo de Vide area (p267). Ask at the *turismo* about bikes to rent.

CIDADE DE AMMAIA

This excellent little **Roman museum** (admission €2.50; 🕑 9am-1pm & 2-5pm Mon-Fri, 10am-1pm & 2-5pm Sat & Sun) lies between Castelo de Vide and Marvão in São Salvador de Aramenha. From São Salvador head 700m south along the Portalegre road, then turn left, following the signs to Ammaia.

In the 1st century AD this area was a huge Roman city called Ammaia, flourishing from the area's rich agricultural produce (especially oil, wine and cereals). Although evidence was found (and some destroyed) in the 19th century, it wasn't until 1994 that thorough digs began.

Here you can see some of the finds, including engraved lintels and tablets, jewellery, coins and some incredibly well-preserved glassware. You can also follow paths across the fields to where the forum and spa once stood and see several impressive columns and ongoing excavations.

Sleeping

Casa da João (☎ 245 993 437; Travessa de Santiago 1; d €30) This welcoming little house offers two clean rooms. Look for the bright red door.

Casa das Portas de Ródão (☎ 245 992 160; Largo da Silveirinha 2; r with shared bathroom €35) At the entrance to town, this two-storey, three-bedroom house has a rustic, old-fashioned feel with curly iron bedsteads and original knick-knacks. There's a kitchen and a terrace. You can rent by room or the whole house. For info, ask at the handicraft shop Muralhas da Vila nearby.

Casa Dom Dinis (☎ 245 993 957; www.casaddinis.pa-net.pt; Rua Dr Matos Magalhães 7; s/d €45/55, d with terrace €60) Near the *turismo*, the friendly Dom Dinis has eight imaginatively decorated rooms of varying sizes, one of which has a terrace.

Casa da Árvore (☎ 245 993 854; Rua Dr Matos Magalhães 3; s/d with breakfast €50/70) This elegant guest house has five country-home-style rooms and an attractive lounge area with a stunning view. It boasts a Roman funerary stone and a João Tavares tapestry (see p263).

Albergaria El Rei Dom Manuel (☎ 245 909 150; www.turismarvao.pt; Largo da Olivença; s/d €63/70) Rooms in this charming, friendly guest house have tiled floors and sizeable windows. The best rooms have great views and there's a restaurant (mains €8.50 to €12).

Pousada de Santa Maria (☎ 245 993 201; www.pousadas.pt; Rua 24 de Janeiro; d €150; ⚥) Converted from two village houses, this is the most elegant and intimate option in town, with marvellous views from some rooms.

Eating

Marvão is light on for great quality restaurant options. If cuisine rates over views, then you're better off heading to Portagem on the Rio Sever, several kilometres down the road.

Restaurante Casa do Povo (☎ 245 993 160; Rua de Cima; mains €7-10; ⚥ 9am-midnight Fri-Wed) Boasting the town's loveliest terrace, Casa do Povo has wonderful views across the countryside. The menu includes shark with garlic and coriander. Readers have reported surly service.

Bar-Restaurante Varanda do Alentejo (☎ 245 993 272; Praça do Pelourinho 1; mains €7.50-10; ⚥ lunch & dinner) This popular place serves up lots of pork-based regional specialities, which you can enjoy with a sangria on the terrace.

Restaurante Sever (☎ 245 993 318; Portagem; mains €7.50-17.10; ⚥ lunch & dinner) This smart place is in a beautiful location, just over the bridge in Portagem, on the Rio Sever. It comes highly recommended by locals and serves first-class Alentejan cuisine. For both price and quality, it's at the higher end of the scale. Specialities include *arroz de lebre* (hare risotto).

Bar O Castelo (☎ 245 993 957; Rua Dr Matos Magalhães; snacks €2-3; ⚥ 9am-10pm) This cosy, local snack bar serves daily simple specials (pasta and sandwiches) and is recommended for its soups.

Getting There & Away

Two buses run daily between Portalegre and Marvão (€4, 45 minutes). There are two services from Castelo de Vide, but the first requires a change of buses at Portagem, a major road junction 7.5km northeast.

The nearest train station, Marvão-Beirã, is 9km north of Marvão, and has beautiful *azulejo* panels. Two trains run daily to/from Lisbon (€13, 4½ hours); change at Abrantes and Torre das Vargens. Taxis charge around €6 to the station. The daily Lisbon–Madrid *Talgo Lusitânia* train stops here en route to Valencia de Alcántara (Spain), and on the journey to Lisbon (3¼ hours).

Taxis (☎ 245 993 272; Praça do Pelourinho) charge around €13 to Castelo de Vide.

BAIXO ALENTEJO

MÉRTOLA

pop 8700 / elev 70m

Spectacularly set on rocky hills, high above the peaceful Rio Guadiana, the cobbled streets of medieval Mértola are a delightful place to roam. A small but imposing castle stands high over town, overlooking the jumble of dazzlingly white houses and a picturesque church that was once a mosque. A long bout of economic stagnation at this remote town has left many traces of Islamic occupation intact, so much so that Mértola is considered a *vila museu* (open-air museum). To let Mértola's magic do its thing, you need more than a quick visit here.

In the heat of the day – up to 47°C – the only sound is insects buzzing. Nearby is an enchanting botanic garden in the grounds of a restored convent, and further afield, the

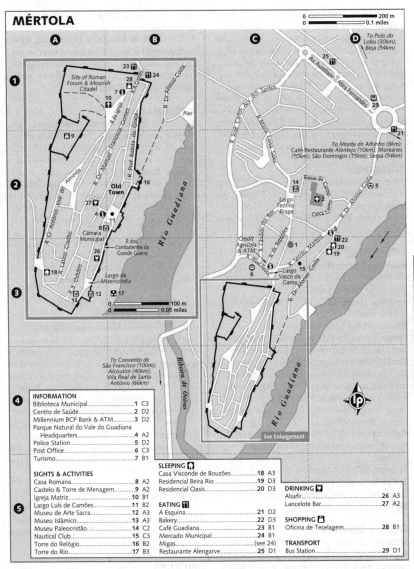

MÉRTOLA

THE ALENTEJO

beautiful, bleak, disused copper mines of São Domingos. The pretty gorge and cascades of **Pulo do Lobo** are around 30km away.

History

Mértola follows the usual pattern of settlement in this area: Phoenician traders, who sailed up the Guadiana, then Carthaginians, then Romans. Its strategic position, as the northernmost port on the Guadiana, and the final destination for many Mediterranean routes, led the Romans to develop Mértola (naming it Myrtilis) as a major agricultural and mineral-exporting centre. Cereals and olive oil arrived from Beja, copper and other metals from Aljustrel and São Domingos. It was a rich merchant town.

Later the Moors, who called it Martulah and made it a regional capital, further fortified Mértola and built a mosque. Dom Sancho II and the Knights of the Order of Santiago captured the site in 1238. But then, as commercial routes shifted to the Tejo, Mértola declined. When the last steamboat service to Vila Real de Santo António ended and the copper mines of São Domingos (the area's main employer) closed in 1965, its port days were over.

Orientation

From the bus station in the new part of town, it's about 600m southwest to the historic old walled town. Everything is close here; don't even think about driving in the narrow, bumpy streets of Old Mértola.

Information

Biblioteca Municipal (town library; Rua 25 de Abril 16; ☽ 10.30am-12.30pm Mon-Wed & Fri, 2-7pm Mon-Fri) Provides free internet access.

Centro de saúde (☎ 286 612 254; Cerca Carmo) Medical centre.

Millennium BCP Bank (Rua Dr Afonso Costa) Has an ATM.

Parque Natural do Vale do Guadiana headquarters (☎ 286 610 090; ☽ 9am-12.30pm & 2-5.30pm Mon-Fri, 10am-1pm, 3-6pm Sat) In smart new premises by the câmara municipal, displays information on the fauna and flora of the 600-sq-km park, plus brochures on walks (note: these are fairly basic; serious walkers should buy the Serviço Cartográfico do Exército (ie army maps) labelled 'Mertola' from papelierias.

Police station (☎ 286 612 127; Rua Dr Afonso Costa)

Post office (Rua Alves Redol; ☽ 9am-12.30pm & 2-5.30pm)

Turismo (☎ 286 610 109; Rua da Igreja 31; ☽ 9am-12.30pm & 2-5.30pm) Just inside the walled town; this helpful place has a good town map with sights, a list of quartos and offers free internet access.

Sights & Activities

Stepping through the thick outer walls into the old town makes you feel as if you have stepped back in time. It's enchanting just to wander around the snoozy, sun-baked streets (but take plenty of water).

LARGO LUÍS DE CAMÕES

This is the administrative heart of the old town, a picturesque square lined with orange trees, with the câmara municipal at its western end. To reach the largo (small square), enter

the old town and keep to the left at the fork in the road.

The **Torre do Relógio**, a little clock tower topped with a stork's nest and overlooking the Rio Guadiana, is northeast of the square. Alongside it is a municipal building with a rooftop worthy of Van Gogh.

IGREJA MATRIZ

Mértola's striking parish **church** (Rua da Igreja; admission free; ☽ Tue-Sun) – square, flat-faced and topped with whimsical little conical decorations – is most well known because in a former incarnation it was a mosque, one of the few in the country to have survived the Reconquista. It was reconsecrated as a church in the 13th century. Look out for an unwhitewashed cavity in the wall, behind the altar; in former times this served as the mosque's mihrab (prayer niche). Note also the goats, lions and other figures carved around the peculiar Gothic portal and the typically Moorish horseshoe arch in the north door.

CASTELO & TORRE DE MENAGEM (NUCLEO DO CASTELO)

Above the parish church looms Mértola's fortified **castle** (☽ 9am-12.30pm & 2-5.30pm Tue-Sun), most of which dates from the 13th century. It was built upon Moorish foundations next to an Islamic residential complex and alcáçova (citadel), which itself overlaid the Roman forum. For centuries the castle was considered western Iberia's most impregnable fortress.

From its prominent tower, the Torre de Menagem, there are fabulous views – you can look down on archaeological digs outside the castle on one side, and the old town and the river on the other.

TORRE DO RIO

At the river's edge, near its confluence with the Ribeira de Oeiras, is the ruined, Roman-era Torre do Rio (River Tower), which once guarded the vital port.

MUSEUMS

Mértola's wonderful group of **museums** (1 museum adult/concession €2/1, combined ticket €5/2.50; ☽ 9am-12.30pm & 2-5.30pm Tue-Sun) have the same opening hours and form an excellent tour of the town.

In the cellar of the câmara municipal is the enchanting **Casa Romana** (Roman House; Largo Luís de Camões). This clever display allows the visitor to walk 'through' the foundations of the Roman house upon which the building rests, and brings it to life with its small collection of pots, sculpture and other artefacts.

At the southern end of the old town, the **Museu Islâmico** (Islamic Museum) is a small but dramatic display (with atmospheric sound effects) of inscribed funerary stones, jewellery, pots and jugs from the 11th to the 13th centuries.

The nearby **Museu de Arte Sacra** (Museum of Ecclesiastical Art; Largo da Misericórdia) exhibits religious statuettes from the 16th to the 18th centuries (the oldest is the torso of São Sebastiano) and three impressive 16th-century retables, originally in the parish church, portraying the battle against the Moors.

North of the old town is the **Museu Paleo-cristão** (Palaeo-Christian Museum; Rossio do Carmo), an attractive exhibition space that has a partly reconstructed line of 6th-century Roman columns and poignant funerary stones, some of which are beautifully carved with birds, hearts and wreaths. This was the site of a huge palaeo-Christian basilica, and its adjacent cemetery was used over the centuries by both Roman-era Christians and medieval Moors.

CONVENTO DE SÃO FRANCISCO

This 400-year-old former **convent** (www.con ventomertola.com/en; adult/student €3/2; 10am-7pm Fri-Sun), across the Ribeira de Oeiras, 500m southwest of Largo Vasco da Gama, has been owned since 1980 by Dutch artist Geraldine Zwanikken and her family. In a true labour of love, they have gradually transformed the ruins into an extraordinary place, most simply described as a nature reserve and art gallery. The organic garden is full of herbs, rare plants and flowers, watered by a re-stored Islamic irrigation system. Highlights include Geraldine's modern artworks, and, gracing the former chapel (if they are not in temporary exhibitions elsewhere), the kinetic installations of renowned artist Christiaan Zwanikken, Geraldine's eldest son. The nearby riverside is devoted to specially con-structed nests for storks and lesser kestrels. Don't miss the detour to the *nora* (well) en route to the convent building (follow the signs and enter the door underneath – we won't spoil the surprise). Go with time up your sleeve – there is more than meets the eye in this inspiring place.

PARQUE NATURAL DO VALE DO GUADIANA

Created in 1995, this zone of hills, plains and deep valleys around Serpa and Mértola shelters the Rio Guadiana, one of Portugal's largest and most important rivers. Among its rich variety of flora and fauna are several rare or endangered species, including the black stork (sightings of the shy creatures are rare), lesser kestrel (most likely around Castro Verde and at Convento do São Francisco), Bonelli's eagle, royal owl, grey kite, horned viper and Iberian toad. The park also has many prehis-toric remains. Ask at the park headquarters (opposite) for details of walking trails and where to spot wildlife – they can advise you and provide you with a basic map. Note: hunt-ing takes place in the park throughout the year; this not only creates controversy about the park's status (and frightens birds away) but can be dangerous for walkers; check with headquarters before venturing out.

CANOEING

You can rent canoes for trips down the lazy river at the **Nautical Club** (286 612 044; www .guadianatrainingcentre.com; Rua Serrão Martins 16; 1 day €15) below the Restaurante O Naútico.

Sleeping

Residencial Oasis (286 612 404; Rua Dr Afonso Costa 104; d without breakfast €30-35;) Overlooking the river and run by a delightful owner, this is among the best value places in town. Rooms are basic but tidy (some have superb views), and one has a kitchenette. Downstairs rooms are cool and spacious.

Residencial Beira Rio (286 611 190; Rua Dr Afonso Costa 108; s/d/tr from €35/45/60;) Great at self-pro-motion, Beira Rio offers slightly more polished rooms than Oasis, but lacks the same charac-ter and some rooms are cramped. Most have river views and some have breezy terraces.

Casa Visconde de Bouzões (965351979; casa .visconde@iol.pt; Rua António José de Almeida 12; d €45-50) In this lovely ancient house in the old town, rooms have a personality, even if they are decorated in a hotchpotch of the modern and the antique. Basic breakfasts are provided for in your rooms (including percolated coffee machines).

our pick **Convento de São Francisco** (286 612 119; www.conventomertola.com; r & apt with breakfast €50-65, cottage €65) This hauntingly beautiful and rustic former convent overlooking Mértola and the Rio Guadiana should be a mandatory sleepover for all tranquil souls. It has a variety of accommodation options, including monks' cells, a funky studio and a lovely room with a veranda. There's a cottage (solar powered) on the grounds for those looking for complete seclusion. Minimum stays apply, and prices are lower for long-term stays and self-caterers. An artist-in-residence program is also available.

There are also some rural tourism options around: try the appealing **Monte do Alhinho** (☎ 286 655 115; www.montedoalhinho.com; Estrada Nacional 265; s/d €50/60; 🏊 🔲), 8km from Mértola on the road to São Domingos. This tastefully converted farmhouse-cum-hacienda has massive rooms, fluffy white towels, and a superb kitchen, where breakfast – an onslaught of Alentejan delights – is served. Discounts apply for long-term stays.

The *turismo* has a brochure listing more accommodation options in rural areas.

Eating

Mértola's specialities are game, including *javali* (wild boar) and the regional pork dish *migas* – great labouring fuel, but perhaps heavier than necessary for sightseeing.

Café Guadiana (☎ 286 612 186; Praça Vasco da Gama; snacks €1-4; 🕓 8am-10pm) This focus of local social life has the advantage of an excellent raised vantage point and outdoor terrace.

Restaurante Alengarve (☎ 286 612 210; Av Aureliano Mira Fernandes; mains €5-10; 🕓 lunch & dinner Tue-Thu) This popular place has been run by the same family for over 40 years and serves up filling, traditional (and often seasonal) cuisine. A small terrace overlooks the street.

our pick **Café-Restaurante Alentejo** (☎ 286 655 133; Moreanes; mains €6-10; 🕓 lunch & dinner Tue-Sun) This attractive place in Moreanes, 10km from Mértola on the way to São Domingos, is almost a museum thanks to its antique exhibits (including the local clients themselves!). It serves great-value, hearty helpings of true Alentejan cuisine.

Migas (mercado municipal; mains €8) This long-standing place within the market complex is very much at home. It serves up serious Alentejan specialities, most with a touch of, you guessed it... *oink*.

A Esquina (☎ 286 611 081; Rua Dr Afonso Costa 2; mains €9-12; 🕓 lunch & dinner Wed-Mon) Several boars' heads mounted on the wall (not to mention the array of *presuntos* – hams –hanging at the bar) attest to this eatery's hearty Alentejan cuisine, which is of high quality and served with gusto. It's situated on the roundabout into town.

Self-caterers should head to the **mercado municipal** (municipal market; Praça Vasco da Gama; 🕓 8am-4pm Mon-Sat), which sells fresh fruit and vegetables and other produce. There's also an unsigned **bakery** (Rua Dr Afonso Costa 96) where you can buy fresh-baked bread (go in the evening for hot rolls).

Drinking

Lancelote Bar (Rua Nossa Senhora da Conceição; 🕓 9pm-4am) This vaguely medieval-feeling bar has friendly barkeeps and eclectic decor (colourful paintings and a wall of skeleton keys), with a shady wooden terrace attached.

Alsafir (☎ 286 618 049; Rua dos Combatentes da Grande Guerra 9; 🕓 9pm-4am) This more tavern-like bar hosts occasional dance-party nights.

Shopping

Oficina de Tecelagem (Rua da Igreja; 🕓 9am-5.30pm) A small wool-weaving workshop next to the *turismo*, this place hangs on by a thread through tourist sales of beautiful handmade products, including rugs and ponchos.

Getting There & Away

There are **buses** (☎ 286 611 127; www.rodalentejo.pt) to Lisbon (€13.80, 4¼ hours, one or two daily) and Vila Real de Santo António (€9.40, 1½ hours); and a slower local Vila Real service (€5.85, two hours) via Alcoutim (50 minutes), which runs on Monday and Friday. Three weekday services run to/from Beja (normal/express, €5/9, 75 minutes/one hour). During summer a bus runs the locals to Monte Gordo beach every Sunday (€10 return; 1¼ hours one way).

AROUND MÉRTOLA

The ghost town of **São Domingos** consists of desolate rows of small mining cottages. Once the mine closed in the 1960s, many miners emigrated or moved to Setúbal. But the nearby contemporary village is set amid beautiful countryside and next to a huge lake, where you can swim or rent a paddleboat or canoe.

The São Domingos mine itself is over 150 years old – though mining has been taking place here since Roman times – and is a deserted, fascinatingly eerie place to explore, with crumbling old offices and machinery. The rocks surrounding it are clouded with different colours, and the chief mine shaft is

THE ALENTEJO

filled with deep, unnatural dark-blue water, shot through with it-doesn't-bear-thinking-about-substances (read contaminated). Locals have no fondness for the firm that established the mines, which kept its workers in line with a private police force.

Set in some of the mine's former administrative buildings, the grand new **Estalagem São Domingos** (☎ 286 640 000; www.hotelsaodomingos.com; s/d from €128/160; ☒) features extensive facilities. The hotel's rooms are bright and spacious, with attractive furnishings. There's a saltwater pool, games room and elegant common areas, including a library. Packages are available.

Best visited with your own transport, São Domingos is 15km east of Mértola.

BEJA
pop 36,200 / elev 240m

Baixo Alentejo's principal town is easy-going, welcoming and untouristed, with a walled centre and some beguiling sights. Often dismissed as Évora's 'plainer cousin', it has an inferiority complex, but it shouldn't. Its inexpensive guest houses, quaint plazas and excellent eateries make for a relaxing stop and a very genuine Portuguese experience.

Beja is at the heart of the regional tourist area called Planície Dourada (Golden Plain) – meaning it's surrounded by an endless sea of wheat fields. On Saturday there's the bonus of a traditional market, spread around the castle.

History

Settlements have existed on the site of Beja since the Iron Age. Vestiges of this period have been discovered as recently as the 1990s, and some of these finds are proudly displayed in the town's archaeological museum. During Roman and Muslim times, Beja was considered an important administrative centre (wrongly, as locals will stress, attributed to Évora alone). The Romans called the city Pax Julia (shortened to Pax, which then became Paca, Baca, Baju and finally Beja), after Julius Caesar restored peace between the Romans and rebellious Lusitanians. It became an important agricultural centre, booming on wheat and oil.

Little evidence remains of the 400 years of subsequent Moorish rule, except for some distinctive 16th-century *azulejos* in the Convento de Nossa Senhora da Conceição

(now the Museu Regional). The town was recaptured from the Moors in 1162.

Orientation

Beja's historic core is circled by a ring road and surrounded by modern outskirts. The train station is about 500m northeast of the town centre, the bus station 400m southeast. The main sights are all within an easy walk of each other and often follow old Roman routes. Drivers are advised to park near the bus station.

Information

Several banks near the *turismo* have ATMs.

Biblioteca Municipal (Rua Luís de Camões; ☒ 2.30-10.30pm Mon, 10.30am-12.30pm & 2.30-10.30pm Tue-Fri, 2.30-8pm Sat) Free internet access.

Casa da Cultura (Rua Luis de Camões; ☒ 2-5.30pm Mon-Fri) Free internet access.

Hospital (☎ 284 310 200; Rua Dr António Covas Lima)

Lavandaria Bandeira (☎ 284 329 957; Rua Dr Brito Camacho 11; ☒ 9.30am-1pm & 3-7.30pm Mon-Fri, 9.30am-1pm Sat; €4.50 per kg wash, dry & iron)

Planície Dourada (☎ 284 310 150; www.rt-planicie dourada.pt; Praça da República 12, 1st fl; ☒ 9am-12.30pm & 2-5.30pm) Knowledgeable staff in the regional *turismo* have information on the Baixo Alentejo region.

Police station (☎ 284 322 022; Largo Dom Nuno Álvares Pereira)

Post office (Rua Luís de Camões; ☒ 8.30am-6.30pm Mon-Fri) Has NetPost.

Turismo (☎ /fax 284 311 913; Rua Capitão João Francisco de Sousa 25; ☒ 10am-1pm & 2-6pm Mon-Sat) Provides a good city map and information on Beja. There is talk of the office moving to the Castle premises.

Sights
PRAÇA DA REPÚBLICA

This renovated attractive **town square** with a *pelourinho* (stone pillory) is the historic heart of the old city. Dominating the square is the 16th-century **Igreja de Misericórdia**, a hefty church with an immense porch – its crude stonework betrays its origins as a meat market. The Planície Dourada building features an elegant Manueline colonnade.

CASTELO

Dom Dinis built the castle on Roman foundations in the late 13th century. There are grand views from the top of the impressive 42m-high **Torre de Menagem**. The ticket office has free bilingual leaflets on Beja's culture, arts and heritage.

THE ALENTEJO

THE ALENTEJO

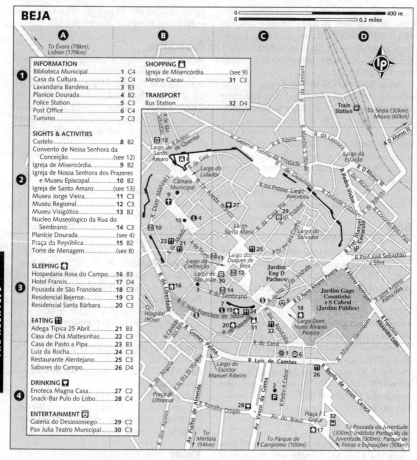

BEJA

0   400 m
0   0.2 miles

To Évora (78km);
Lisbon (179km)

CONVENTO DE NOSSA SENHORA DA CONCEIÇÃO & MUSEU REGIONAL

Founded in 1459, this Franciscan **convent** (Largo da Conceição; adult/child €2/free, admission free 9.30am-12.30pm Sun; 9.30am-12.30pm & 2-5.15pm Tue-Sun) was the location for the romance between a nun and soldier that inspired *Letters of a Portuguese Nun* (see opposite).

Indeed a romantic setting, it's a delicate balance between no-nonsense Gothic and Manueline flights of fancy. The interior is lavish – amazing highlights are the rococo chapel with 17th- and 18th-century gilded woodwork, and a chapel inlaid with intricate marble. The chapterhouse is incongruously Arabian, with a beautiful ceiling painted with unfurling ferns, 16th-century tiles and a

carved doorway. The cloister has some splendid 16th- and 17th-century *azulejos*.

Tucked inside this convent is the **Museu Regional**, displaying Roman lamps, glass bottles and stelae, and 16th- and 17th-century paintings. The admission fee includes entry to the Museu Visigótico.

MUSEU VISIGÓTICO

Found just beyond the castle, the unusual Visigothic **museum** (Largo de Santo Amaro; admission adult/concession €2/1; 9.30am-12.30pm & 2-5pm Tue-Sun) is housed in the former **Igreja de Santo Amaro**, parts of which date from the early 6th century when it was a Visigothic church – so it's one of Portugal's oldest standing buildings. Inside, the original columns display intrigu-

---

BEJA'S LOVE LETTERS

A series of scandalous, passionate 17th-century love letters came from Beja, allegedly written by one of the convent's nuns, Mariana Alcoforado, to a French cavalry officer, Count Chamilly. The letters immortalised their love affair while the count was stationed here during the time of the Portuguese war with Spain.

The *Letters of a Portuguese Nun* first emerged in a French translation in 1669 and subsequently appeared in English and many other languages. Funnily enough, the originals were never found.

In 1972 three Portuguese writers, Maria Isabel Barreno, Maria Teresa Horta and Maria Velho da Costa published *The Three Marias: New Portuguese Letters*, a collection of stories, poems and letters that formed a feminist update of the letters – for which they were prosecuted under the Salazar regime.

---

ing, beautiful carvings. The admission fee includes entry to the Museu Regional.

MUSEU JORGE VIEIRA

A charming, small **museum** (Rua do Touro 33; admission free; 10am-12.30pm & 2-6.30pm Tue-Fri, 2-6pm Sat & Sun), devoted to the work of renowned Portuguese sculptor Jorge Vieira, who donated his works to Beja. His monumental bulbous figures and strange creatures capture the imagination, calling to mind Maurice Sendak's *Where the Wild Things Are*. Look out for Viera's linked ellipses on Praça Diogo Fernandes de Beja.

NÚCLEO MUSEOLÓGICO DA RUA DO SEMBRANO

Opened in 2008, there is more to this modern **museum** (Rua do Sembrano; admission free; 9.45am-12.30pm, 2-5.45pm) than meets the eye – the exhibition is underfoot and displayed through a glass floor. Iron Age finds were discovered here during building works in the 1980s, and the site was deemed important enough to excavate and protect. Peer through the glass floor at 2200-year-old remains, over which were laid subsequent Roman walls, indicating that this location was important for millennia. A curator will explain the site.

SACRED ART MUSEUMS

Several museums of religious artworks opened in 2008. So great was the wealth of the Catholic Church that no single space can display all of the paintings and other items. The most attractive, for its church, is housed in the restored and recently re-opened **Igreja de Nossa Senhora dos Prazeres** and the attached **Museu Episcopal** (admission €1.50; 10am-12.30pm & 2.30-6pm summer, 10am-12.30pm, 2pm-5pm winter, Wed-Sun). While the church is stunning, perhaps only those interested in religious art might appreciate the museum (enter from near the altar).

Festivals & Events

The nine-day **Ovibeja agricultural fair** (starts last weekend Apr) one of the largest in the country's south, has music by day and a show every night. Held in the Parque de Feiras e Exposições on the town's southeastern outskirts, the fair has grown from a livestock market to a music, handicrafts and cuisine bonanza.

Sleeping

BUDGET

Hospedaria Rosa do Campo (284 323 578; Rua da Liberdade 12; s €25, d €35-40;) This sparkling guest house has polished floors and mostly spacious rooms, each with a small refrigerator. There are even fly-wire window coverings. Breakfast is included.

Pousada da Juventude (284 325 458; www.pousadasjuventude.pt; Rua Professor Janeiro Acabado; dm €11, d with/without bathroom €28/26) Next to the Instituto Português da Juventude (IPJ), 300m southeast of the bus station, this yellow-and-blue, spick-and-span hostel is one of the cleanest and best around. A decent continental breakfast is included. There are male and female dorms.

MIDRANGE

Residencial Santa Bárbara (284 312 280; www.residencialsantabarbara.pt; Rua de Mértola 56; s/d/tw €30/42/45;) This reliable and good-value choice has neat, motel-style rooms set in masculine tones – all dark woods and plaid curtains – and it's well located in the pedestrianised town centre.

Residencial Bejense (284 311 570; www.residencialbejense.com; Rua Capitão João Francisco de Sousa 57; s/d €30/45;) This pleasant family-run option, with bright and airy rooms and tasteful decor, is hard to beat for value. The front rooms have

THE ALENTEJO

small balconies. The hallways are trimmed with tiles and fresh flowers.

Hotel Francis (☎ 284 315 500; www.hotel-francis.com; Praça Fernando Lopes Graça; s/d €60/70; ❄) Sporting a sleek and modern look, this is a favourite among local business people. The colourful rooms have balconies, and there's a fitness centre, a small Jacuzzi and a sauna. It's slightly out of the historic centre.

TOP END

Pousada de São Francisco (☎ 284 313 580; recepcao .sfrancis@pousadas.pt; Largo Dom Nuno Álvares Pereira; d €230; ❄ ☒) Located in the 13th-century São Francisco Convent, this *pousada* provides gorgeous rooms, formerly cells, and a restaurant with a magnificent vaulted ceiling. A Gothic chapel and Chapter House (with billiards table) add to the unique and luxurious atmosphere.

Eating

ourpick Casa de Chá Maltesinhas (☎ 284 321 500; Rua dos Açoutados 12; snacks €1-5; ❄ 9am-7.30pm Mon-Sat) This not-to-be-missed serene tearoom serves delicious regional *doces conventuais* (desserts traditionally made by nuns). Try the *pasteis de toucinho,* a delicious thin pastry and almond creation with, believe it or not, a smidgeon of pork lard. Well worth the pig out.

Luiz da Rocha (☎ 284 323 179; Rua Capitão João Francisco de Sousa 63; mains €5.50-10; ❄ lunch & dinner) Founded in 1893, this is one of Beja's oldest cafes and best known institutions. It gathers a chatty neighbourhood crowd day and night and is justly famous for its cakes: *trouxas de ovos* (literally 'sweet egg yolks') and *porquinhos de doce* ('sweet little pigs'). It also serves up Alentejan staples.

Casa de Pasto a Pipa (☎ 284 327 043; Rua da Moeda 8; mains €6-9; ❄ lunch & dinner Mon-Sat) This rustic eatery has a wood-beamed ceiling, bright blue wooden chairs and checked tablecloths. It dishes up the usual standards such as *migas alentejana* (a tasty bread mix with pork).

Restaurante Alentejano (☎ 284 323 849; Largo dos Duques de Beja 6; mains €6-10; ❄ lunch & dinner Sat-Thu) This lively local eatery is a good bet for filling Alentejan plates of roasted pork or cod dishes. Its plain exterior hides a dapper but relaxed interior.

Adega Típica 25 Abril (☎ 284 325 960; Rua da Moeda 23; mains €6-11; ❄ lunch & dinner Tue-Sun) Packed to the basket-lined rafters with locals, this cavernous, rustic *adega* serves typical food, with good daily specials.

Sabores do Campo (Rua Bento de Jesus Caraça 4; ❄ lunch & dinner Mon-Thu, lunch Fri Ⓥ) This simple place serves 100% vegetarian food – perfect for those in need of a tasty fill of pork-free tarts, vegetables and salads. Prices are by weight (€13 per kilo).

Drinking

Snack-Bar Pulo do Lobo (Av Vasco da Gama; ❄ noon-10pm) A cafe-restaurant with outdoor seating, this is a favourite for an evening get-together over snails and *petiscos* and cold beer. Plates of the day €9 to €15.

Enoteca Magna Casa (Rua Dr Aresta Branco 45; snacks €1-7; ❄ 6pm-midnight Mon-Sat) An atmospheric, contemporary wine bar (note the fabulous green-tiled exterior). The passionate owner serves delicious *petiscos* to match his long list of Portuguese wines.

Entertainment

Galeria do Desassossego (Rua da Casa Pia 26-28; www.myspace.com/galeriadodesassossego; ❄ 7pm-4am Tue-Sat) Try saying 'desassossego' after a few drinks. Literally meaning 'unquiet', this gallery is anything but. This unique concept brings a bar and snacks, shows and exhibitions together in the one place. *Petiscos* are sometimes shared with neighbours, live music ranges from jazz to rock (no covers allowed!) and creativity is in the air. There is no signage – follow the vibe. Concerts cost €3.

Pax Julia Teatro Municipal (☎ 284 315 090; www .paxjulia.org; Largo de São João 1) This cinema and theatre hosts regular concerts, dance performances and film screenings. A program guide is available at the *turismo* or the theatre's box office.

Shopping

An *artesenato* cooperative has a range of goods for sale within the **Igreja de Misericórdia** (Praça da República), a unique style of store.

Mestre Cacau (www.mestrecacau.pt; Rua da Branca 16) This chocolate shop is the initiative of a group of bright young locals who have created a fabulous range of homemade chocolates (they trained in Belgium). Experimental chocolate fillings include olive oil, *medronho* (liquor) and Earl Grey tea. The results are sublime.

Getting There & Away

BUS

From the **bus station** (☎ 284 313 620) buses run to Évora (€5.45, 1¼ hours, seven daily); Mértola (€5, 1¼ hours, three daily except weekends); and Serpa (€3, 40 minutes, five daily); some continue to Moura (€4.50, 65 minutes, four daily). Around half this number operates on weekends. Buses run to Faro daily (€11.90, three hours, three daily) via Albufeira (€11.50, three hours), and to Lisbon (€12, 3¼ hours, eight daily).

On weekdays, buses also run to the Spanish border town of Vila Verde de Ficalho (€4.85, one hour, three daily).

TRAIN

Beja is on the Lisbon–Funcheira (near Ourique) railway line. There are four direct *intercidade* (IC) services from Lisbon (€15.50, 2½ hours).

SERPA

pop 8000 / elev 230m

Planted among the rolling hills of vineyards and dusty fields, Serpa is a sleepy and atmospheric town of bleached-white walls and narrow cobblestone streets. At its medieval heart is a small, pretty plaza carefully guarded by the elderly folk who have long called Serpa home. Locals are renowned for their love of food, and several factory outlets produce the town's culinary jewel, *queijo Serpa*, a cheese made from curdled sheep's milk.

Orientation

Those arriving by car must brave tight gateways into the old town and breathtakingly narrow streets (or park outside the walls).

The bus station, *mercado municipal* and *parque de campismo* are in the new town area, southwest of the old town. From the bus station, turn left and then take the first right and keep walking till you see the walls.

Information

On the fourth Tuesday of the month a country market sprawls beside Rua de Santo António on the town's northeastern outskirts.

C@fe (Rua Dr Eduardo Fernando de Oliveira 18; per hr €1.20; ☺ 10am-6pm, 8pm-midnight) Bar with internet access; 250m east of the *mercado municipal*.

Caixa Geral de Depósitos Bank & ATM (Largo Conde de Boavista) Around the corner from the *turismo*.

Espaço Internet (Rua Pedro Anes 14; ☺ 10am-5pm Mon-Fri, 10am-1pm Sat) Free internet access with helpful staff.

Post office (Rua dos Lagares)

Turismo (☎ 284 544 727; www.cm-serpa.pt; Largo Dom Jorge de Melo 2; ☺ 10am-7pm) In the centre; helpful staff provide a map of the old town with good listings, and sell local handicrafts.

Sights

CASTELO

You enter the small **castle** (admission free; ☺ 9am-12.30pm & 2-5.30pm) through a dramatic entrance: a heavy cracked piece of wall. Inside it feels domestic in scale. You can walk around the battlements for long views over the flat plains, the aqueduct, town walls, rooftops and orange trees, and the slow life of Serpa residents. Also inside the walls the small **Museu de Arqueologia** (closed for site excavations; check status with the tourist office) houses a small collection of archaeological remnants that reveal bits of Serpa's history, including the presence of the Celts over 2000 years ago.

TOWN WALLS & AQUEDUTO

Walls still stand around most of the inner town. Along the west side (follow Rua dos Arcos) run the impressive remains of an 11th-century **aqueduct**. At the southern end is a huge 17th-century wheel pump (aka noria), once used for pumping water along the aqueduct to the nearby **Palácio dos Condes de Ficalho** (still used by the de Ficalho family as a holiday home).

MUSEU ETNOGRÁFICO

No traditional rural trade is left unturned in the exquisite exploration of Alentejan life found at Serpa's **Museu Etnográfico** (Ethnographic Museum; Largo do Corro; admission free; ☺ 9am-12.30pm & 2-5.30pm Tue-Sun). Occupying the former town market (in use from 1887 to 1986), the museum beautifully presents restored items donated by locals. Polished tools used by former wheelwrights, saddle makers, cheese makers, barrel makers and ironmongers are on display.

MUSEU DO RELÓGIO

This **museum** (☎ 284 543 194; www.museudorelogio .com; Rua do Assento 31; adult/child under 10yr €2/free; ☺ 2-5pm Tue-Fri, 10am-noon & 2-5pm Sat & Sun) houses an amazing collection of watches and clocks, dating from 1630 to the 2008 Guimarães 1143 wristwatch. Napoleonic gilded timepieces and Swiss cuckoo clocks are among the 1800 models ticking away in the cool surroundings of the former Convento do Mosteirinho.

THE ALENTEJO

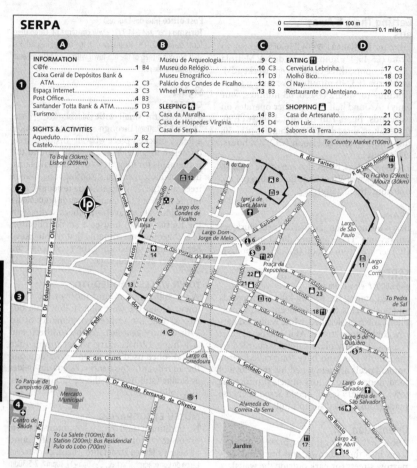

SERPA

INFORMATION		
C@fe	1	B4
Caixa Geral de Depósitos Bank & ATM	2	C3
Espaça Internet	3	C3
Post Office	4	B3
Santander Totta Bank & ATM	5	D3
Turismo	6	C2

SIGHTS & ACTIVITIES		
Aqueduto	7	B2
Castelo	8	C2

Museu de Arqueologia	9	C2
Museu do Relógio	10	C3
Museu Etnográfico	11	D3
Palácio dos Condes de Ficalho	12	B2
Wheel Pump	13	B3

SLEEPING		
Casa da Muralha	14	B3
Casa de Hóspedes Virgínia	15	D4
Casa de Serpa	16	D4

EATING		
Cervejaria Lebrinha	17	C4
Molhó Bico	18	D3
O Nay	19	D2
Restaurante O Alentejano	20	C3

SHOPPING		
Casa de Artesanato	21	C3
Dom Luis	22	C3
Sabores da Terra	23	D3

Festivals & Events

Festas de Senhora de Guadalupe Celebrations of Serpa's patron saint take place in March/April from Good Friday to the following Tuesday – there is a pilgrimage to bring the saint's image down to the parish church, and on the last day a procession takes it back to the chapel. On the Tuesday roast lamb is the traditional meal.

Noites na Nora Held in July and the first week of August, this festival features nightly local theatre and music shows on a terrace tucked behind the aqueduct.

Sleeping

Parque de campismo (☎ 284 544 290; Largo de São Pedro; adult/tent/car €2/1.80/1.50) The municipal camp site is on dusty ground 400m northeast of the bus station. There's a restaurant and disabled access; rates include admission to the nearby pool.

Casa de Hóspedes Virgínia (☎ 284 549 145; Largo 25 de Abril; s/d €20/35) This small guest house has basic and frilly rooms, recently renovated bathrooms, and somewhat thin walls. It faces a square dotted with orange trees.

Residencial Pulo do Lobo (☎ 284 544 664; www .residencialpulodolobo.com; Estrada de São Bras 9; s/d €30/45) Handy to the bus station, this new, sparkling place and its house-proud owner provide plain but modern rooms. Excellent value if you don't mind being out of the centre.

Casa de Serpa (☎ 284 549 238; www.casadeserpa .com; Largo do Salvador 28; s €40, d €56-67) This friendly guest house has handsomely furnished rooms and a fine location near the centre. Rooms at the back open onto a courtyard. Homemade breakfasts include local produce.

Casa da Muralha (☎ 284 543 150; www.casadamuralha.com; Rua das Portas de Beja 43; s/d €55/65) Nestled beside the town walls, which loom overhead, this place is atmospheric, although one senses it's seen better days. Its whitewashed rooms have arched or beamed ceilings, and are set with traditional, elegant wooden furniture. Most rooms face onto an overgrown courtyard with lemon and orange trees.

Eating & Drinking

All the local restaurants serve *tapas de queijo de Serpa*, the salty and creamy local cheese, or *queijadas*, small cheesecakes.

La Salete (☎ 284 543 475; Av da Paz, Bloco 24; mains €5; 🕙 9am-9pm Mon-Fri) Near the bus station, this place dishes out home-style eat-in or take-away feeds, including vegetarian dishes. Nearby, also around the roundabout, there are three low-key cafes serving drinks and snacks.

O Nay (☎ 284 543 247; Rua de Santo António 10; mains €5.50-8; 🕙 lunch & dinner Mon-Sat) A small, cheerful *churrasqueira*, serving up basic grills. It's one of the few places open on a Monday.

Molhó Bico (☎ 284 549 264; Rua Quente 1; mains €5.50-13; 🕙 lunch & dinner Thu-Tue) This enticing place pulls a crowd; kitchen odours hit you on entry to its arched, rustic space. It has wagon wheel lights, huge wine urns, and a friendly ambience. Eating here is a pure, traditional gastronomic experience. There are hearty half serves.

Cervejaria Lebrinha (☎ 284 549 311; Rua do Calvário 6; mains €6-9; 🕙 lunch & dinner Wed-Mon) Popular with the locals, Lebrinha is a no-nonsense joint that's touted as Serpa's choice spot for quality beer (but less so for food).

Restaurante O Alentejano (☎ 284 544 335; Praça da República; mains €8-15; 🕙 lunch & dinner Tue-Sun) This handsome place, above a cafe of the same name, in a former mansion, serves local specialities. The braised hare in red wine is a treat.

Pedra de Sal (☎ 284 543 436; Estrada da Circunvalaçao s/n; mains €10-15; 🕙 lunch & dinner Tue-Sun) This smart place is a win-win food-lover's scenario. The owner-chef conjures up Alentejana specialities using quality produce, including her own home-grown greens. Modern art, candelabra and wood trim grace the interior, and there's an attractive bamboo-covered outdoor patio.

Shopping

Small artisan shops and delicatessens are dotted around town. You can buy good *queijadas* and a range of oils, honey, herbs and handicrafts at the unsigned **Dom Luis** (Praça da República

15), as well as **Sabores da Terra** (Rua dos Fidalgos), and **Casa de Artesenato** (Rua dos Cavalos 33; 🕙 10am-6pm).

Getting There & Away

Buses (☎ 284 544 740) run to/from Lisbon (€12.50, four hours, two to four daily) via Beja (normal/express €3/5.20, 35 minutes, one to six daily). There are no direct buses to Évora. A daily service goes to the Spanish frontier east of Vila Verde de Ficalho (€7, 35 minutes, one daily).

MOURA

pop 17,600 / elev 180m

This pleasant working-class city – a flattish fortified town – has an ageing castle, graceful buildings and a well-preserved Moorish neighbourhood. Well placed near water sources and rich in ores, Moura has been a farming and mining centre and a fashionable spa in previous incarnations. Previously a backwater, Moura is currently experiencing a new lease of life; the world's largest solar power generation plant is located nearby. Moura is also the nearest large town to the Barragem do Alqueva, 15km to the north.

The Moors' 500-year occupation came to an end in 1232 after a Christian invasion. Despite the reconquest, Moorish presence in the city remained strong – they only abandoned their quarter in 1496 (after Dom Manuel's convert-or-leave edict).

The town's name comes from a legend related to the 13th-century takeover. Moorish resident Moura Salúquiyya opened the town gates to Christians disguised as Muslims. They sacked the town, and poor Moura flung herself from a tower.

Orientation

The bus station is by the defunct train station at the newer, southern end of town, around 500m from the old town and the main square, Praça Sacardo Cabral. Places of interest are within easy walking distance.

Information

There are banks on the *praça* and along Rua Serpa Pinto, directly north of the *turismo*.

Espaço Internet (☎ Rua 5 de Outubro 18; 🕙 8.30am-midnight Mon-Fri, 12.30pm-midnight Sat) Free internet access.

Post office (Rua da República) East of Rua Serpa Pinto.

Turismo (☎ 285 251 375; www.cm-moura.pt; Largo de Santa Clara; 🕙 9am-12.30pm & 2-5.30pm Mon-Fri, 10am-1pm & 2.30-5.30pm Sat) Some 400m downhill from

THE ALENTEJO

the bus station; turn left into the first main street, Rua das Forças Armadas, and right at the end (at the cemetery).

Sights & Activities

MUSEU MUNICIPAL

In an appealing residential quarter off a lane about 200m east of the *praça* (head up Rua do Espírito, south of the swimming pool), this tiny **museum** (☎ 285 253 978; Rua da Romeira; admission free; ✆ 9.30am-12.30pm & 2.30-5.30pm Tue-Fri, 10am-noon & 2-4pm Sat & Sun) contains local prehistoric and Roman remains, such as 1st- and 2nd-century needles, as well as Moorish funerary tablets.

LAGAR DE VARAS DO FOJO (MUSEU DO AZEITE)

With a system of production that would have been similar to that of Roman times, the **oil press** (Rua João de Deus 20; admission free; ✆ 9.30am-12.30pm & 2.30-5.30pm Tue-Sun) re-creates the oil-pressing factory that functioned here between 1841 and 1941, with giant wooden and stone-wheel presses, vats and utensils.

IGREJA DE SÃO BAPTISTA

This 16th-century **church** (admission free) has a remarkable Manueline portal. Set against the plain facade, it is a twisting, flamboyant bit of decoration, with carvings of knotted ropes, crowns and armillary spheres. Inside, the church has some fine deep-blue and yellow 17th-century Sevillian *azulejos*. It's just outside Jardim Dr Santiago.

JARDIM DR SANTIAGO & SPA

The lovely, shady Jardim Dr Santiago, at the eastern end of Praça Sacadura Cabral, is a delightful place to wander. There are good views, a bandstand, shady, flowering trees and it's a favourite spot for elderly men to sit and chat. The **thermal spa**, at the entrance to the garden, is open and you can join the locals for a soak in a basic bath. Bicarbonated calcium waters, said to be good for rheumatism, burble from the richly marbled **Fonte das Três Bicas** (Fountain with Three Spouts) by the entrance to the *jardim*.

MOURARIA

The old **Moorish quarter** (Poço Árabe) lies at the western end of Praça Sacadura Cabral. It's a well-preserved tight cluster of narrow, cobbled lanes and white terraced cottages with chunky or turreted chimneys.

The **Núcleo Árabe** (Travessa da Mouraria 11; admission free) just off Largo da Mouraria is a pocket collection of Moorish ceramics and other remains, such as carved stone inscriptions and a 14th-century Arabic well. Visits here must be arranged through the Museu Municipal.

CASTELO

The **castle** (admission free) offers fabulous views across the countryside. One of the towers is the last remnant of a Moorish fortress. Rebuilt by Dom Dinis in the 13th century and again by Dom Manuel I in 1510, the castle itself was largely destroyed by the Spanish in the 18th century. There's a ruined convent inside the walls.

Sleeping

There are some great-value places around town.

Residencial Santa Comba (☎ 285 251 255; www.residencialsantacomba.com; Praça Sacadura Cabral 34; s/d from €24/35; ✦) On the main square, this smart place opened in 2004 and has clean rooms overlooking the square. There's disabled access and a pleasant dining room.

Residencial Alentejana (☎ 285 250 080; www.residencialalentejana.com.pt; Largo José Maria dos Santos 40; s/d €26/38; ✦) The key holders – jugs embedded into walls – are the most novel things in this modern, but comfortable and spotless place. It's near the bus station – look for an ordered, green-shuttered house.

Hotel de Moura (☎ 285 251 090; www.hoteldemoura.com; Praça Gago Coutinho; s/d from €43/45; ✦) Moura's loveliest hotel is housed in a former military hospital and overlooks a pretty square. It's a grand place, covered in tiles on the outside, and with sweeping staircases and tall windows on the inside. Rooms, however, vary considerably, from the classically furnished to the rather sterile. It's worth paying extra for a superior room. Prices increase slightly on weekends and 'special' days.

Eating & Drinking

There are several cafes with outdoor seating around Praça Sacadura Cabral, where you'll also find the *mercado municipal* in a huge glass building. Some good restaurants are located in the streets further south from the Praça.

O Túnel (☎ 285 253 384; Rua dos Ourives 13; mains €7-12; ✆ lunch & dinner Mon-Fri) This down-to-earth grill house serves up a big daily feed (locals tend to head here for lunch).

O Trilho (☎ 285 254 261; Rua 5 de Outubro 5; mains €7.50-12.50; ✆ lunch & dinner Tue-Sun) Three streets east of Rua Serpa Pinto, O Trilho is a local favourite, with excellent regional mains and cheap specials in pleasant surroundings.

Forum Bar (☽ 2pm-4am Tue-Sun) This small bar with attached patio is most notable for its location – in the castle complex. It has a rock-solid following with a younger crowd, but there are reports that it can get a bit rough.

Getting There & Away
Buses run to/from Beja (€5, one hour, three to five daily) via Serpa (€3.20, 40 minutes). Rede Expressos run to Lisbon (€14.20, four hours, daily) via Évora (€9.50, 1½ hours); these leave from Praça Sacadura Cabral.

COASTAL ALENTEJO

PORTO CÔVO
pop 1100

Perched on low cliffs with views over the sea, Porto Côvo is the first enticing coastal town you'll reach after heading south of the Setúbal Peninsula. The old town, a former fishing village, has a pretty square and cobbled streets lined with sun-bleached houses. Modern (but not imposing) summer houses are spread outside the small centre. The town hosts an annual music festival, which morphs into the well-known festival in nearby Sines.

Paths along the cliffs lead down to the harbour at the town's southern end and to interesting rock formations to the north, with access down to various beaches such as Praia do Somouqueira. The official nudist beach is Praia do Salto.

The **turismo** (☎ 269 959 124; www.freguesiadeporto covo.com ☽ 9am-noon & 1-5pm Mon-Fri winter; 10am-1pm & 3-7pm summer) is on the edge of the old town, just one block north of the main square and next to a car park. Diving trips can be arranged through **Ecoalga** (☎ 964620394; www.ecoalga.com). In summer, a boat shuttles between Porto Côvo and the diminutive island of Ilha do Pessegueiro (adult/child €8/4).

Sleeping & Eating
The tourist office has a good list of accommodation options.

Parque do Campismo (☎ 269 905 136; camping -portocovo@gmail.com; Estrada Municipal 554; adult/tent/car €3.40/4.90/3.70, bungalows €55) This good, well-equipped camp site is just outside of town on the road to Vila Nova de Milfontes. Bungalows are also available (minimum two days).

Zé Inácio (☎ 269 959 124; www.zeinacio.com; Rua Vasco da Gama; d €40-70) Above a restaurant of the same name, these attractive rooms have contemporary decor, tile floors, bamboo ceilings and white stucco walls.

Quartos Abelha (☎ 934755293; s/d €25/50) This place has simple clean rooms, fine if you are only after a bed. The owners also have apartments.

Refúgio da Praia (☎ 963528496; Praia do Queimado; d €90) Located several kilometres outside of town, this remote house (a converted restaurant) is a slice of beach paradise, sitting in countryside just 50m from the water's edge. It has neat, pine-filled rooms.

Restaurante Miramar (☎ 269 905 449; Rua Cândido da Silva 57; mains €11-15; ☽ lunch & dinner Fri-Wed) Located above the narrow harbour, this excellent restaurant has the best views in town from its terrace. In addition to seafood, there are tasty desserts, including lemon meringue pie.

Restaurante Marquês (☎ 269 905 036; Largo Marquês de Pombal; mains €12-19; ☽ lunch & dinner Wed-Mon) Porto Côvo's overwhelmingly favourite dining spot is set on the town's main square, with inviting outdoor tables and scrumptious plates of grilled fish and seafood salads.

Getting There & Away
During summer at least five buses a day travel to/from Lisbon (€12.20, 2¾ hours). There are also regular connections to Vila Nova de Milfontes (around €5.20, 25 minutes).

VILA NOVA DE MILFONTES
pop 3200

One of the loveliest towns along this stretch of the coast, Vila Nova de Milfontes has an attractive, whitewashed centre, sparkling beaches nearby and a laid-back population that couldn't imagine living anywhere else. Vila Nova remains much more low-key than most resort towns in the Algarve, except in August when it's packed to the hilt with surfers and sun-seekers. It's located in the middle of the beautiful Parque Natural do Sudoeste Alentejano e Costa Vicentina and is still a port (Hannibal is said to have sheltered here) alongside a lovely, sand-edged limb of estuary.

Vila Nova's narrow lanes and tiny plazas harbour varied eating and drinking options, with even more scenic restaurants out on the beach.

THE ALENTEJO

Orientation & Information

The main road into town from Odemira and Lisbon, Rua Custódio Bras Pacheco, is lined with restaurants, banks, shops and the post office.

Police station (☎ 283 998 391; Rua António Mantas)

Turismo (☎ 283 996 599; Rua António Mantas; ☺ 10am-1pm & 2-6pm Tue-Sat) Off the main road, opposite the police station. Buses stop a bit further along the same road.

Beaches

Praia do Farol, the lighthouse beach just by the town, is sheltered but gets busy. Beaches on the other side of the estuary are less crowded. Be careful of the strong river currents running through the estuary. If you have your own transport, you could head out to the fantastic **Praia do Malhão**, backed by rocky dunes and covered in fragrant scrub, around 7km to the north (travel 2.5km to Bruinheras, turn left at the roundabout just before the primary school, then travel another 3km until you see a series of successive lines and a painted arrow on the road – no signage – where you turn left; the road is mostly unpaved). The more remote parts of the beach harbour nudist and gay areas. The sea can be quite wild here, but the rugged coast is strikingly empty of development.

Activities

There are some gorgeous beaches around, both near the town and extending out along the coast. Scuba diving is possible through **Ecoalga** (☎ 964620394; www.ecoalga.com) in nearby Porto Côvo.

Sudaventura (☎ 283 997 231; www.sudaventura.com; Rua Custódio Brás Pacheco; ☺ 10am-7pm) offers a range of excursions, including canoe trips, river boat outings and bike hire. Surf lessons are available through **Surf Milfontes** (☎ 969483334; www.surfmilfontes.com; Rua António Mantas 26).

Sleeping

The tourist office has a list of official sleeping options. High season (August) prices are listed here; at other times of the year prices are significantly lower. In August, you'll need to book in advance.

BUDGET

Campiférias (☎ 283 996 409; www.roteiro-campista.pt; Rua da Praça; adult/tent/car €3.95/3.20/4; ☒) A camp site 500m northwest of the *turismo*, this is only 800m from the beach, with disabled access and lots of shade.

Parque de Campismo Milfontes (☎ 283 996 140; www.campingmilfontes.com; adult/tent/car €4/3.80/4.40; ☒) Near Campiférias, this is an even better equipped site in a pine forest close to the beach. It has a cafe and grocery, small bungalows (€55 to €75) and disabled access.

Casa Amarela (☎ 283 996 632; www.casaamarela milfontes.com; Rua Dom Luis Castro e Almeida; dm €22.50, d/tr/q €60/80/90; ☐) This privately run, cheery yellow place is set with eclectic knick-knacks belonging to the genial English-speaking owner, Rui. You'll find bright rooms, a lounge space and shared (if slightly backpacker-style-messy) kitchens. The annexe nearby has attractive dorm rooms, a courtyard and solar-heated showers.

MIDRANGE & TOP END

Quinta das Varandas (☎ 283 996 155; fax 283 998 102; d €55, 1-/2-bedroom apt €65/85) In a peaceful setting 700m west of the *turismo* (and 300m from the beach), this blue-and-white complex offers handsome rooms with cork floors and verandas. It also has simply furnished apartments. Many other similar apartment hotels are nearby.

Casa da Eira (☎ 283 990 010; www.alentejoadventures .com; Rua Casa da Pedra; r €60, apt €120-240) Housed in a refurbished building, this lovely place boasts a range of contemporary-style rooms and apartments (two to four person), each decked out in a funky colour scheme and fun decor. Stripes, squares and tasteful touches from lamps to cushions add to a colourful experience. Prices are significantly lower outside high season.

Casa dos Arcos (☎ 283 996 264; fax 283 997 156; Rua do Cais; d €70; ☒) Jauntily painted in blue and white, this airy, spotless guest house has comfortable beds, tiled floors and small balconies. There's disabled access.

Casa do Adro (☎ 283 997 102; www.casadoadro.com; Rua Diário de Notícias 10; d €85; ☐) Set in a house dating from the 17th century, this Turismo Rural option is chock-a-block with antiques and artwork. It has six elegantly furnished bedrooms, some with private balconies (others have access to shared terraces). Each guest gets to request the hour of breakfast – a nice touch.

Castelo de Milfontes (☎ 283 998 231; s/d €130/147) Entering this atmospheric 16th-century castle is a bit difficult – there's fortlike privacy. But it all adds to a safe and very private stay, surrounded by antique furniture, suits of armour, *azulejos* and superb views. Reservations are essential.

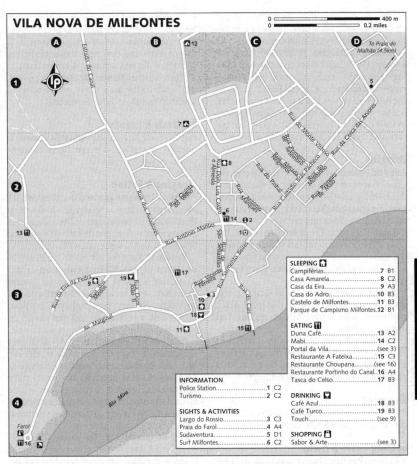

VILA NOVA DE MILFONTES

Eating

Mabi (Largo de Santa Maria 25A; 8am-2am Tue-Sun) Something of a Milfontes institution, this cheery and inviting cafe is known particularly for its flavoured croissants and pastries (€0.75 to €1.50).

Restaurante A Fateixa (283 996 415; Largo do Cais; mains €6.50-12; lunch & dinner Thu-Tue) A Fateixa delivers good grills and seafood dishes – try the *tamboril* (monkfish) rice for two – and it has breezy outdoor tables. It's excellent value given its perfect setting down by the river.

Restaurante Portinho do Canal (283 996 255; mains €6.50-14; lunch & dinner Fri-Wed) Up from the fishing harbour, this old-school, family-run place is a bit like a museum it's been around for so long. It has superb sea views and good seafood dishes.

Portal da Vila (283 996 823; Largo do Rossio; mains €8-12; lunch & dinner Tue-Sun) A cosy restaurant decorated in colourful tiles, this place serves up sizzling grilled fish as well as *porco na pedra* (pork served on a hot stone) and other unusual plates.

Duna Café (283 996 451; Eira da Pedra; mains €10-14; lunch & dinner) Despite its setting off the main drag and in a modernish apartment complex, this cafe gets great reviews for its international cuisine. The interior – think funky 1960s-style perspex seating and coloured tablecloths – is as busy as its menu, from duck breast to beef steaks *na pedra* (cooked on a sizzling stone.)

Tasca do Celso (283 996 753; Rua dos Aviadores; mains €10-22; lunch & dinner Tue-Sun) *The* choice. Locals and travellers rave about the excellent cuisine produced within the kitchen of this charming, traditional blue-and-white building. You're safe trying anything here.

Restaurante Choupana (☎ 283 996 643; Praia do Farol; dinner for 2 €55; ☼ lunch & dinner) In a wooden building right on the beach, this rustic, lovely spot is renowned for its fresh grilled fish. You pay by the kilo here so you feel it in your hip pocket, but the quality is top-notch. You can just stop in for a drink on a pleasant little open-air terrace and watch the grill master in action.

Drinking
Café Azul (Rossio 20) Always lively, whatever the time of year, even if the rest of the town is dead, this is a jovial bar with a pool table and lots of papier-mâché sharks, octopuses and squid hanging from the ceiling.

Touch (Travessa da Eira da Pedra) A nightclub with a more cosmopolitan touch. Outside, the walls feature incongruous giant black and white photographs, while inside there's more colour and fun.

Discoteca SudWest (Estrada do Canal; ☼ midnight-6am) In season this is the local disco nightspot, with a packed dance floor and diverse crowds.

Café Turco (Rua Dom João II) With a touch of Moorish atmosphere, this yellow spot gathers a fun, slightly more bohemian crowd. It has a partly outdoor and candlelit setting.

Shopping
For tasteful (and tasty) local products, it's worth checking out **Sabor & Arte** (Largo do Rossio 18).

Getting There & Away
Vila Nova has three bus connections daily on weekdays to/from Odemira (€5.20, 20 minutes). There are Rede Expresso buses daily from Lisbon (€13, four hours, three daily) via Setúbal (€10.80, three hours) and one daily from Portimão (€11, two hours) and Lagos (€10.70). The ticket office for **Rede Expresso** (☎ 917790634; www.rede.expresso.pt) is a few doors down from the *turismo* in Rua Custódio Brás Pacheco.

ZAMBUJEIRA DO MAR
pop 850

Enchantingly wild beaches backed by rugged cliffs form the setting to this sleepy seaside village. The main street terminates at the cliff; paths lead to the attractive sands below. Quieter than Vila Nova, Zambujeira attracts a backpacker, surfy crowd, though in August the town

is a party place and hosts the massive music fest, Festa do Sudoeste. The high-season crowds obscure Zambujeira's out-of-season charms: fresh fish in mom-and-pop restaurants, blustering cliff-top walks and a dramatic, empty coast.

There's a small **turismo** (☎ 283 961 144; ☼ 10am-6pm Tue-Sat) on the main street, which closes to traffic from July to mid- September.

Festivals & Events
Held in early August, the **Festival do Sudoeste** is one of Portugal's best international contemporary music festivals.

Sleeping & Eating
Parque de Campismo Zambujeira (☎ 283 961 172; www.campingzambujeira.com.sapo.pt; adult/tent/car €4.50/5/4.50) Just 800m east of the village, this is a wooded, well-appointed site. It's near the beach and also has bungalows for rent.

Residencial Mar-e-Sol (☎ 283 961 171, 283 961 193; Rua Miramar 17A; d €30-50) In Zambujeira's main street, this is run by a real character. Rooms in the attic section are cheap, but are a bit unappealing. Newer, spick-and-span 1st-floor rooms have a private (though not always en suite) bathroom; a shared kitchen is available.

Quinta do Sardanito de Trás (☎ 964180430; www .quinadosardanito.com; r €75, 2-, 4-person apt €115-155; ⌨). Four kilometres northeast of Zambujeira do Mar are these tastefully decorated rural apartments, located in two places – one around the original *quinta* building, the others about 600m away in new stone *casinhas* (little house-cum-bungalows).

Café-Restaurant Rita (Rua Miramar 1; mains €7-14; ☼ lunch & dinner Fri-Wed) Has a fine vantage point, with raised terraces (including one indoors) overlooking the sea. The menu offers grilled 'everything'.

For a sumptuous seafood meal, head 3km out of town to Entrada Das Barcas (boat ramp) where the simple **Restaurante Sacas** (☎ 283 961 151; meals €10-15; ☼ lunch & dinner Thu-Tue) delivers sublime seafood dishes. The fish and shellfish make up for the car park view.

Getting There & Away
In summer, Zambujeira has one to three daily connections with Vila Nova (€7, 45 minutes) and Lisbon (€14, 3¾ hours) through **Rede Expresso** (www.rede.expresso.pt) – buy tickets at the **bookshop** (Rua Miramar 9). Buses also run to Odemira (40 minutes) and Beja (three hours); for these you buy your ticket on the bus.

Estremadura & Ribatejo

Stretching from the mighty Rio Tejo to the Atlantic Ocean, Estremadura and Ribatejo constitute Portugal's heartland, but their central importance goes well beyond geography. These fertile lands have formed the backdrop for every major chapter in Portuguese history, from the building of key fortified settlements in the 12th century to bolster the fledgling nation-state, to the release of Salazar's political prisoners at Peniche in 1974. Two of medieval Portugal's most critical battles for autonomy – against the Moors at Santarém and the Spaniards at Aljubarrota – were fought and won here, and remain commemorated to this day in the magnificent monasteries at Alcobaça and Batalha, both Unesco World Heritage Sites. A third Unesco site, the Convento de Cristo in Tomar, is one of central Portugal's not-to-be-missed gems, its medieval core embellished with later architectural flourishes ranging from the Manueline to the Renaissance.

Estremadura and Ribatejo play an equally central role in contemporary Portuguese life. Within easy striking distance for day-tripping Lisboêtas, the beaches of Estremadura boast countless attractions. Epicures feast on seafood at Ericeira, surfers flock to the sands of Ribeira d'Ilhas and Baleal, families head for the sheltered shores of São Martinho do Porto, and campers bask in sunlight filtered through fragrant pines at Pinhal de Leiria. Nazaré's cliffs and narrow cobbled streets form one of the region's most picturesque beach-party settings, while the Ilhas Berlengas nature reserve shows off coastal Portugal's wilder, less-developed side.

Inland, gorgeous medieval Óbidos is home to some of the country's most colourful festivals, while the brand-new cathedral at Fátima continues to draw pilgrims from around the world to modern Portugal's premier religious shrine.

ESTREMADURA & RIBATEJO

HIGHLIGHTS

- Balancing your way across the narrow arched bridge to the 17th-century fort on ruggedly beautiful **Berlenga Grande** (p294)

- Riding the waves or just catching some rays at Ericeira's **Ribeira d'Ilhas beach** (p289), an international favourite with surfers

- Surveying the Rio Tejo from the crenellated heights of **Castelo de Almourol** (p317), a 12th-century island fortress

- Exploring Unesco World Heritage Sites – prowling the extraordinary monasteries at **Batalha** (p304) and **Alcobaça** (p302) or watching theatre by torchlight at **Tomar** (p323)

- Sampling *ginja* (cherry liqueur) in a chocolate cup while strolling the flowery lanes and medieval walls of **Óbidos** (p295)

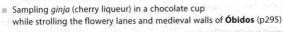

★ Batalha ★ Tomar
Berlenga Grande ★ ★ Alcobaça
                   Castelo de Almourol
          ★ Óbidos
★ Ericeira

| POPULATION: 1.1 MILLION | AREA: 11,500 SQ KM |

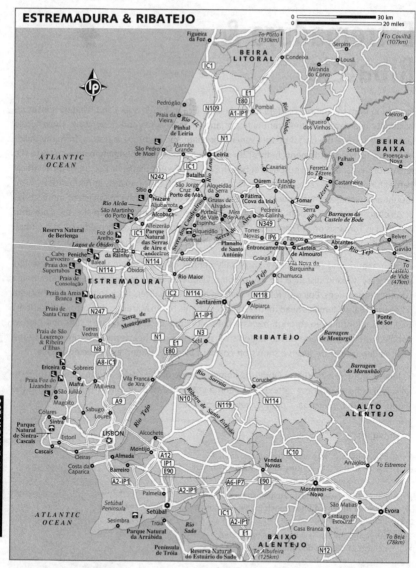

ESTREMADURA & RIBATEJO

ESTREMADURA

Running up the Atlantic coast from the mouth of the Rio Tejo almost to the Rio Mondego, Estremadura has long been a land of plenty, its rolling hills and valleys offering up some of Portugal's richest farmland. For proof, visit the elaborate kitchens that fattened up the monks at Alcobaça's extraordinary monastery. The coast is blessed with miles-long strands, which also catch some of Europe's best surf.

Estremadura earned its name the same way as Spain's Extremadura: for a time, it represented the furthest reaches of the Reconquista.

ERICEIRA

pop 6700

Picturesquely draped across sandstone cliffs above the blue Atlantic, sunny, whitewashed Ericeira is popular with Lisboêtas seeking a quick weekend getaway. It's renowned as much for its spectacular ocean vistas as for its excellent seafood restaurants, where you choose your own fresh-caught fish from the case and watch it grilled on the spot. Ericeira is also a mecca for surfers, who come here for the great waves and camaraderie of beaches like São Sebastião and Ribeira d'Ilhas – witness the amusing surfer-dude statue catching a wave just north of town!

The town's old centre is clustered around Praça da República, with the chaos of newer development spreading south and north.

Information

Ericeira Online (Centro Comercial de Ericeira, Praça da República; per hr €2; ⏰ 9am-10pm Sep-Jun, 8am-midnight Jul & Aug)

Lavandaria Fonte do Cabo (☎ 261 864 203; Rua do Caldeira 12; per kg €3; ⏰ 9am-1pm & 3-7pm Mon-Sat)

Police station (☎ 261 863 533, 261 866 700; Largo Domingos Fernandes)

Post office (☎ 261 860 501; Rua do Paço 2; ⏰ 9am-12.30pm & 2.30-6pm Mon-Fri)

Turismo (tourist office; ☎ 261 863 122; www.ericeira .net; Rua Dr Eduardo Burnay 46; ⏰ 10am-1pm & 2.30-6.30pm Mon-Fri, 10am-1pm & 3-7pm Sat & Sun)

Sights & Activities

There are three beaches within walking distance of the *praça* (town square). **Praia do Sul**, also called Praia da Baleia, is easiest to get to and has a protected pool for children. **Praia do Norte** (also called Praia do Algodio) and **Praia de São Sebastião** lie to the north. Some 5km north is unspoilt **Praia de São Lourenço**, while **Praia Foz do Lizandro**, a big bite of beach backed by a small car park and a couple of restaurants, is 3km south.

The big attraction in Ericeira is **surfing**. Serious aficionados congregate 3km north of town at **Praia da Ribeira d'Ilhas**, a WQS (World Qualifying Series) site and home to Portugal's annual national championships in late August; most amateurs will find the waves at the nearer Praia de São Sebastião challenging enough.

Recommended surfing outlets:

Ribeira d'Ilhas Surf Camp (☎ 261 869 590; 914444626, 968026577; www.ribeirasurfcamp.com; Praia da Ribeira d'Ilhas; lesson/lesson plus lodging & 2 meals €15/45) Runs surf classes and camps from its privileged location directly across from central Portugal's premier surfing beach.

XXS Surf Shop & Surf School (☎ 261 867 771; www.xxs.pt; Av São Sebastião, Loja 14; group/private lesson per person €25/30, surfboard/wetsuit rental per day €20/10) This well-established surf school has special family lessons (€70 for two adults and two children).

Sleeping

Book ahead in July and August. During the low season, expect discounts of 30% to 50%.

BUDGET

Ericeira Camping (☎ 261 862 706; www.ericeiracamping .com; sites per adult/child/car/tent €5/2.50/5/6) Just off the coastal highway 800m north of Praia de São Sebastião, this relatively expensive but high-quality site has lots of trees, a playground, disabled access and a municipal swimming pool next door. It also offers trim, two-bedroom cabins (from €105).

MIDRANGE

Hospedaria Bernardo (☎ /fax 261 862 378; hospedaria bernardo@iol.pt; Rua Prudêncio Franco da Trindade 11; d with/without bathroom €55/35) If saving money is your prime objective, consider the claustrophobic downstairs rooms with shared bathroom here – among Ericeira's cheapest. Upstairs is better, especially the front room with balcony overlooking the street. The proprietor can also arrange private home rentals in town. No breakfast.

Pensão Gomes (☎ /fax 261 863 619; Rua Mendes Leal 11; d with/without bathroom €50/40) This old-fashioned boarding house, once featured in a popular Portuguese soap opera, has smallish rooms and creaky floors but still charms guests with homey touches like its plant-filled courtyard and friendly watchdog.

Residencial Vinnu's (☎ /fax 261 863 830; www .residencialvinnus.pt; Rua Prudêncio Franco da Trindade 19; d/tr €50/60) Friendly, bright, modern and centrally located, Residencial Vinnu's offers great value, with simple and comfortable whitewashed rooms, some with pretty, blue-tiled bathrooms. Triples with kitchenette are especially nice.

Residencial Fortunato (☎ 261 862 829; www .pensaofortunato.com; Rua Dr Eduardo Burnay 7; d €55; ℗) A well-run, well-kept place with light, bright and all-white rooms. The best digs upstairs have small terraces with lovely sea views for

ESTREMADURA & RIBATEJO

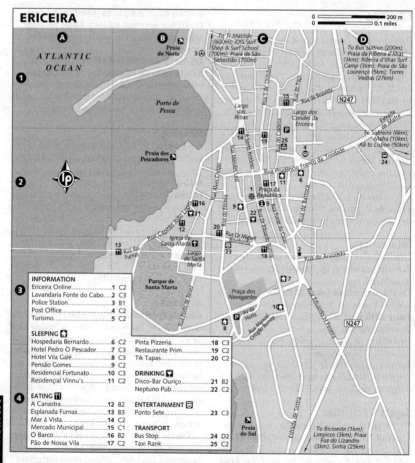

ERICEIRA

INFORMATION	
Ericeira Online	1 C2
Lavandaria Fonte do Cabo	2 C3
Police Station	3 B1
Post Office	4 C2
Turismo	5 C2

SLEEPING	
Hospedaria Bernardo	6 C2
Hotel Pedro O Pescador	7 C3
Hotel Vila Galé	8 C3
Pensão Gomes	9 C2
Residencial Fortunato	10 C3
Residençial Vinnu's	11 C2

EATING	
A Canastra	12 B2
Esplanada Furnas	13 B3
Mar á Vista	14 C2
Mercado Municipal	15 C1
O Barco	16 B2
Pão de Nossa Vila	17 C2

Pinta Pizzeria	18 C3
Restaurante Prim	19 C2
Tik Tapas	20 C2

DRINKING	
Disco-Bar Ouriço	21 B2
Neptuno Pub	22 C2

ENTERTAINMENT	
Ponto Sete	23 C3

TRANSPORT	
Bus Stop	24 D2
Taxi Rank	25 C2

only €7.50 extra. Parking under the building costs €2.50 per night.

Hotel Pedro O Pescador (☎ 261 869 121; www .hotelpedropescador.com; Rua Dr Eduardo Burnay 22; d/tr €70/80) An acceptable backup if you can't find a room elsewhere, this place features a few front rooms with ocean views.

TOP END

Hotel Vila Galé (☎ 261 869 900; www.vilagale.pt; Praça dos Navegantes; d from €144; P X 🖳 🚲) Proudly advertising itself as Europe's westernmost four-star hotel, the spiffy Vila Galé is an imposing edifice whose green mansard roof dominates Ericeira's skyline. Although its classic fin de siècle core has been rendered unrecognisable by recent remodelling,

modern amenities compensate for the lost historic charm, and they include comfortable bedrooms, a fine cliffside pool and panoramic vistas.

Eating

Tik Tapas (☎ 261 869 235; Rua do Ericeira 15; tapas €2-7.50; 🕒 lunch & dinner Fri-Wed) Decked out with orange walls, colourful wooden tables and a brightly lit bar area glowing blue through the window to lure you in, this place sells meat, fish and vegie tapas, full meals, sangria and draft beer.

Ti Matilde (☎ 261 862 734; Rua Dr Manuel Arraiga 29; mains €6-12; 🕒 lunch & dinner Tue-Sun) Perched above Praia do Norte (also called Praia do Algodio) at the north end of the old town, this unfussy place specialises in grilled seafood and *caldeirada de peixe* (seafood stew). There's a great back patio where you can gaze at the blue-green ocean, listen to the crackle of the outdoor grill and catch a few rays while awaiting your meal.

Mar á Vista (☎ 261 862 928; Rua Santo António 16; mains €7-11; ☕ lunch & dinner Thu-Tue) A hearty local place known for its shellfish. Its cosy dining room looks out over the sea, while the bar pulls in the local tipplers.

Restaurante Prim (☎ 261 865 230; Rua 5 de Outubro 12; mains €8-13; ☕ lunch & dinner) This bright, contemporary place with outdoor seating dishes up high-quality, Brazilian-style grilled meats, potent caipirinhas, and intriguing desserts such as mango and passionfruit mousse. Side dishes such as rice and black beans make welcome alternatives to the ubiquitous Portuguese potato. Try the all-inclusive €8.50 lunch special.

Pinta Pizzeria (☎ 261 862 842; Calçada da Baleia 7A; individual pizzas from €6.50, mains €8-13.50; ☕ dinner Tue, lunch & dinner Wed-Sun) This corner pizzeria with twin entrances regularly draws crowds for pizza, calzone, pasta, steaks and – a rarity in Portugal – imaginative salads.

O Barco (☎ 261 862 759; Rua Capitão João Lopes; mains from €12; ☕ lunch & dinner Wed-Mon) Just across from the sea, O Barco serves the highest-quality seafood, including grilled fish and *caldeiradas*, in its snug, nautical-rustic dining room and at some rather windswept outside tables.

A Canastra (☎ 261 865 367; Rua Capitão João Lopes 8A; mains around €15; ☕ lunch & dinner Thu-Tue) O Barco's twin and near-neighbour delivers the other 'best' seafood in town (and yes, you really can eat at that alluring lone table on the ocean side of the footpath).

Esplanada Furnas (☎ 261 864 870; Rua das Furnas; mains from €15; ☕ lunch & dinner) As close to the sea as you can get without a boat, Furnas is all about fresh-caught fish and spectacular ocean views. They'll show you the catch of the day and then barbecue your choice on the spot. The per-kilogram price on the board covers the fish, plus all the accompaniments.

Self-caterers can find tasty bread, pastries, croissants and mini-quiches at **Pão da Nossa Vila** (Praça da República 12; ☕ 7am-9pm Wed-Mon, to 11pm summer weekends). For fresh produce and other foodstuffs, head to the **mercado municipal** (municipal market; Largo dos Condes da Ericeira).

Drinking & Entertainment

Neptuno Pub (☎ 261 862 017; Rua Mendes Leal 12; ☕ 8pm-2am) As the name suggests, this place is decked out like an underwater cavern – one that hasn't been redecorated since the early '60s, we're guessing. It attracts fishermen and city types in search of realness, and sometimes features fado (traditional, melancholic Portuguese singing) in summer.

Disco-Bar Ouriço (Rua Caminho Novo 9; ☕ 11pm-6am Fri & Sat, nightly Jul & Aug) One of Portugal's oldest discos caters to night owls of all ages, with a mix of pop, dance, oldies and disco standards.

Ponto Sete (cnr Rua do Ericeira & Rua Dr Miguel Bombarda; ☕ 10.30pm-2am) This laid-back little club specialises in jazz and blues.

Limpicos (Praia Foz do Lizandro) Closed for remodelling at time of writing, this popular beachfront bar was scheduled to reopen shortly.

Getting There & Away

The bus station is situated 800m north of the *praça*, off the N247 highway. Buses arriving from Lisbon and Sintra will sometimes stop to let passengers off at other bus stops more convenient to the centre along the N247.

Regular **Mafrense** (☎ 261 816 152; www.rodoeste .pt, in Portuguese) buses travel roughly hourly from 6am to 8pm to/from Sintra (€2.80, 50 minutes), and to/from Lisbon's Campo Grande station (€5.10, 1¼ hours) via Mafra (€1.85, 25 minutes). Connections to northern destinations such as Peniche and Coimbra are best made through Torres Vedras (€3.20, one hour, several daily).

There is paid parking under Praça dos Navegantes and by the sea just north of the town centre near Praia de São Sebastião.

Getting Around

Regular local buses to Torres Vedras go past Praia da Ribeira d'Ilhas (€1.05). For Praia Foz do Lizandro (€1.05), take any Sintra-bound bus to a stop on the N247 above the beach.

You can rent bicycles from **Bicioeste** (☎ 261 867 029; Rua Egas Moniz 2; per day €16; ☕ 10am-1pm & 3-6.30pm), just south of Ericeira on the coastal road towards Sintra. There's a taxi stand in Largo Conde da Ericeira.

PENICHE

pop 15,600

Popular for its nearby surfing beaches and also as a jumping-off point for the beautiful Ilhas Berlengas nature reserve, the coastal city of Peniche remains a working port, giving it a slightly grittier and more 'lived-in' feel than its beach resort neighbours. The town's walled historic centre makes for pleasant strolling, and the seaside fort where Salazar's regime detained political prisoners is a must-see for anyone with an interest in Portuguese history. Outdoors enthusiasts will love the beaches east of town, where lessons and rentals for every sport under the sun are available.

Orientation

From the bus station, it's a 10-minute walk west to the historic centre. Cross the Ponte Velha (Old Bridge) into the walled town, then turn left on Rua Alexandre Herculano towards the *turismo*. The fort, harbour and Avenida do Mar – where you'll find most of the seafood restaurants – are just a short distance further south. Passenger boats for Ilha Berlenga leave from the harbour.

Driving into Peniche, the main highway (N114/IP6) reaches a roundabout shortly before town, where you can bear left towards the centre, right for Baleal and the eastern beaches, or straight for 3km along the northern cliffs to Cabo Carvoeiro and its lighthouse.

Information

Espaço Internet (☎ 969195895; Rua Dr João de Matos Bilhau; ⊙ 10am-1pm & 3-10pm Mon-Sat, 10am-noon & 3-8pm Sun) Free internet access.

Hospital (☎ 262 780 900; Rua General Humberto Delgado) About 600m northwest of the market.

Police station (☎ 262 790 310; Rua Heróis Ultramar) About 400m west of the market.

Turismo (☎ /fax 262 789 571; turismo@cm-peniche.pt; ⊙ 9am-8pm Jul & Aug, 10am-1pm & 2-5pm Sep-Jun) In a shady public garden alongside Rua Alexandre Herculano.

Sights

FORTALEZA

Dominating the southern end of the peninsula, Peniche's imposing 16th-century **fortress** (admission free; ⊙ 2-5.30pm Tue, 9am-12.30pm & 2-5.30pm Wed-Fri, 10am-12.30pm & 2-5.30pm Sat & Sun) was in military use as late as the 1970s, when it was converted into a temporary home for refugees from the newly independent African colonies.

Twenty years earlier it served as one of dictator Salazar's infamous jails for political prisoners. By the entrance, where prisoners once received visitors – the stark booths with their glass partitions are all preserved – is the **Núcleo- Resistência**, a grim but fascinating display about those times. It includes the flimsy leaflets of the Resistance; educational materials for schools where pupils would learn phrases such as 'Viva Salazar!'; prisoners' poignant, beautifully illustrated letters to their children; and some secret letters, written in incredibly small handwriting.

Housed in another part of the fort is the **Museu Municipal** (☎ 262 780 116; admission €1.40; ⊙ 2-5.30pm Tue, 9am-12.30pm & 2-5.30pm Wed-Fri, 10am-12.30pm & 2-5.30pm Sat & Sun). Outside is the desolate prison yard, and the top floor reveals the chilling, sinister interrogation chambers and cells, some used for solitary confinement. Floors below this contain a municipal mishmash, from Roman archaeological artefacts to shipwreck finds.

LACE-MAKING SCHOOLS

Like Vila do Conde – another of Portugal's Atlantic fishing ports – Peniche is famous for lace. You can watch the nimble (and chatty) ladies in action at **Escola de Rendas de Bilros** (⊙ 9am-12.30pm & 2-5.30pm Mon-Fri) in the *turismo* building. The chaos of their bobbins produces some of the world's most exquisite lace.

BALEAL

About 4km to the northeast of Peniche is this scenic island-village, connected to the mainland village of Casais do Baleal by a causeway. The fantastic sweep of sandy beach here offers some fine surfing. Surf schools dot the sands, as do several bar-restaurants.

Activities

SURFING

The beach at Baleal, northeast of Peniche, is a paradise of challenging but, above all, consistent waves, making it ideal for learners. Depending on the season, camps charge from €269 to €465 for a week of classes, including equipment and shared, self-catering lodging. You can also take individual two-hour classes (€50) and rent boards and wetsuits (from €25/119 per day/week). There are various surf schools:

Baleal Surfcamp (☎ 262 769 277, 963982899; www .balealsurfcamp.com; Rua Amigos do Baleal 2)

Maximum Surfcamp (☎ 933240472; www.maximum
surfcamp.com; Rua do Gualdino 7)
Peniche Surfcamp (☎ 962336295; www.penichesurf
camp.com; Av do Mar 162)

DIVING
There are good diving opportunities around
Peniche, and especially around Berlenga.
Expect to pay about €60 for two dives (less
around Peniche) with **Berlenga Sub** (☎ 965107728;
www.berlengasub.com; Largo da Ribeira Velha 4).

OTHER ACTIVITIES
Kitesurfing is big in Peniche. On the far side
of high dunes about 500m east of the walled
town, **Peniche Kite Center** (☎ 919424951; www
.penichekitecenter.com; Praia de Peniche de Cima) gives lessons (three hours with equipment for €70).

For fishing trips, contact **Nautipesca**
(☎ 262 789 648, 917358358), which has a kiosk at
the harbour.

Sleeping
Prices are for high season; expect discounts of
up to 30% outside July and August.

Parque de Campismo Municipal (☎ 262 789 696;
campismo-peniche@sapo.pt; sites per adult/child/tent/car
€2.35/1.40/1.95/1.95) The small municipal site is
2km east of town (next to Sportagua, Peniche's
giant outdoor water park). It has disabled facilities and is only 500m from the beach, but
there's constant traffic noise from the adjacent
superhighway and virtually no shade.

Parque de Campismo Peniche Praia (☎ 262 783
460; www.penichepraia.pt; sites per adult/child/car/tent
€3.45/1.75/3.10/3.45; 🐾) On the high, windy,
north side of the peninsula, 1.7km from town
and the beach, and 2km from Cabo Carvoeiro,
this site has decent facilities but lacks shade.

ourpick Peniche Hostel (☎ 969008689; www
.penichehostel.com; Rua Arquitecto Paulino Montês 6; dm/d
€18/40; 🖳) This brand-new hostel only steps
from the tourist office is a delight. The small
but breezy dorm rooms are colourfully decorated and have tall windows overlooking the
town wall. The friendly owners immediately
make you feel at home, as do the comfortable
common areas and small sundeck.

Residencial Rimavier (☎ 262 789 459; www.rimavier
.com; Rua Castilho 6; d €40) This immaculate *pensão*
(guest house) – run by the helpful couple in
the souvenir shop downstairs – has small but
spruce rooms, nautically themed linens and
hallways decorated with lovely tile paintings
of Peniche.

Residencial Popular (☎ 262 790 290; residencial
.popular@netvisao.pt; Largo da Ribeira 40; d Jul/Aug €35/50)
Simple, clean rooms above the excellent restaurant of the same name deliver great value
near the Berlenga ferry dock.

Casa das Marés (☎ 262 769 371/200/255; casadas
mares@sapo.pt; Praia do Baleal; d €80) At the picturesque, windswept tip of Baleal stands one of the
area's most unique accommodation options.
Three sisters inherited this imposing house
from their parents and divided it into three
parts – each of which now serves as its own
little B&B. The breezy, inviting rooms all have
great sea views, the downstairs sitting areas are
extremely cosy and the entire place is loaded
with character. Worth reserving ahead.

Eating
Restaurante A Sardinha (☎ 262 781 820; Rua Vasco da
Gama 81; mains €6-14; 🕑 lunch & dinner) This simple
place on a narrow street parallel to Largo da
Ribeira does a roaring trade with locals and
tourists alike. The fixed-price menu, featuring
soup, main course, dessert, wine and coffee,
is a good deal at €7.50.

Restaurante Popular (☎ 262 790 290; Largo da Ribeira
40; mains €6.25-17; 🕑 lunch & dinner) This harbour-
side spot serves up delicious, freshly caught
fish grilled before your eyes.

Restaurante O Pedro (☎ 262 785 626; Av do Mar 26;
mains €7-14; 🕑 lunch & dinner Wed-Mon) Also down
near the harbour, this place serves reliably
good seafood without an excessive price tag.

Hó Amaral (☎ 262 785 095; Rua Dr Francisco Seia 7;
mains €8-15; 🕑 lunch & dinner Fri-Wed) It may be a
little more expensive, but snug Hó Amaral
reliably does the best seafood in Peniche.

Drinking
The area around Igreja de São Pedro is the
centre of the town's nightlife (think four walls,
cold beer and a home stereo system). In Baleal
you'll find several laid-back surfer bars right
on the beach, including the rather stylish
wood-and-glass **Danau Bar** (☎ 262 709 818; 🕑 lunch
& dinner), offering hot snacks, ocean views and
sometimes live music or karaoke on weekends.
It's closed Mondays in the low season.

Getting There & Away
Peniche's **bus station** (☎ 968903861) is located
400m northeast of the *turismo* (cross the Ponte
Velha connecting the town to the isthmus).
It's served by **Rodotejo** (www.rodotejo.pt) and **Rede
Expressos** (www.rede-expressos.pt). Buses run to/from

ESTREMADURA & RIBATEJO

Lisbon (€7.50, 1¾ hours, hourly) via Torres Vedras, to Coimbra (€11.80, 3½ hours, four daily) via Leiria (€10.70, two hours), and every few hours to Óbidos (€2.60, 40 minutes). Service drops off at weekends.

Most days you can find ample free parking along Largo da Ribeira, the road that runs along the harbour.

Getting Around

Local buses connect Peniche with Baleal (€1.40, 10 minutes) during the week, but service is very spotty on weekends outside summer.

Cycling is a great way to get to the eastern beaches. Bikes can be rented from **Duas Rodas** (☎ 262 781 385; Zona Industrial de Prageira; per day €5; ꔷ 9am-1pm & 3-7pm Mon-Fri) near the bus station.

RESERVA NATURAL DA BERLENGA

Sitting about 10km offshore from Peniche, Berlenga Grande is a spectacular, rocky and remote island, with twisting, shocked-rock formations and gaping caverns. It's the only island of the Berlenga archipelago you can visit – the group consists of three tiny islands surrounded by clear, calm, dark-blue waters full of shipwrecks that are great for snorkelling and diving (see p293).

In the 16th century Berlenga Grande was home to a monastery, but now the most famous inhabitants are thousands of nesting sea birds, especially guillemots. The birds take priority over human visitors: the only development that has been allowed includes housing for a small fishing community, a lighthouse, a shop and a restaurant-*pensão*. You can camp here – book at the *turismo* in Peniche. Paths are clearly marked to stop day trippers trespassing on the birds' domain.

Linked to the island by a narrow causeway is the 17th-century **Forte de São João Baptista**, now one of the country's most dramatic (but barren) hostels.

The reserve's **headquarters** (☎ 262 787 910; fax 262 787 930; Porto da Areia Norte, Estrada Marginal) are in Peniche.

Tours

A number of companies offer day tours to Berlenga, plus other activities like fishing and diving. Tickets and information are available at Peniche's harbour, at the kiosks in Largo da Ribeira.

Barco-Noa (☎ 969134534; per person €18) Runs three boat trips a day, depending on demand and weather.

TurPesca (☎ 963073818; adult/child €18/12, minimum 6 people) Runs privately organised cruises on demand throughout the year. There's usually a 10am trip, plus at least two more daily during the summer, when you may have to book a few days ahead. Cruises last four to five hours.

Sleeping & Eating

If you want to sleep on the island, you'll need to book well ahead. The two park facilities can only be reserved starting in May. Most places are already booked solid by the end of May.

Berlenga campsite (2-/3-/4-person tent sites €9.25/13/16.50; ꔷ May-Sep) This simple camping area is just above a pretty beach near the boat dock; book in advance at the Peniche *turismo*.

Forte de São João Baptista Hostel (☎ 912631426, reservations taken 6.30-10pm Mon-Fri; r €18-81; ꔷ Jun-Sep) This was once a fine historic inn, but was abandoned for many years – and you can feel it. It's a dramatic but dead-basic hostel, with antiquated bathrooms; you need to bring your own sleeping bag and cooking equipment (though there is a small shop and a bar). To get a place in summer you'll have to make reservations in May. Bring a torch, as the generator goes off at midnight.

Mar e Sol (☎ 262 750 331; www.restaurantemaresol .com; d €78-100; ꔷ Apr-Oct) The decent, if simple, rooms at Mar e Sol would seem overpriced anywhere else, but when you consider the location just a few steps above Berlenga's boat dock and directly adjacent to its only restaurant, the place starts looking a bit more appealing. Advance reservations essential.

There's also a small grocery store on the island for self-catering.

Getting There & Away

Viamar (☎ 262 785 646; fax 262 783 847; adult/child €18/10; ꔷ 20 May-15 Sep) does the 45-minute trip to the island three times daily during July and August, at 9.30am, 11.30am and 5.30pm, returning at 10.30am, 4.30pm and 6.30pm. During the remainder of the season there's one sailing daily, departing at 10am, returning at 4.30pm. Tickets tend to sell out quickly in summer, as only 300 visitors are allowed each day. All sailings are weather-dependent.

If you're prone to seasickness, choose your day carefully – the crossing to Berlenga can be rough.

ESTREMADURA & RIBATEJO

ÓBIDOS

pop 3100 / elev 80m

Surrounded by a classic crenellated wall, Óbidos' gorgeous historic centre is a labyrinth of cobblestoned streets and flower-bedecked, whitewashed houses livened up with dashes of vivid yellow and blue paint. It's a delightful place just to pass an afternoon, but there are plenty of reasons to stay overnight, including atmospheric medieval bars and a hilltop castle now converted into one of Portugal's most luxurious *pousadas* (upmarket inns).

It's especially enjoyable to visit during one of the town's festivals – celebrating everything from opera to chocolate to Óbidos' medieval heritage – when you'll find yourself rubbing shoulders with Portuguese tourists as much as those from other countries.

European hill-town aficionados looking to savour Óbidos' 'lost in time' qualities may find the nearby superhighway a bit jarring. For a more bucolic approach, visitors can arrive at the sleepy Óbidos train station just west of town and walk up the zigzagging country lanes to the town gate, through a rural landscape more in keeping with the town's medieval flavour.

History

When Dom Dinis first showed Óbidos to his wife Dona Isabel in 1228, it must have already been a pretty sight, because she fell instantly in love with the place. The king decided to make the town a wedding gift to his queen, initiating a royal tradition that lasted until the 19th century.

Any grace it had in 1228 must be credited to the Moors, who had laid out the streets and had only recently abandoned the strategic heights. The Moors had chased out the Visigoths, who in turn had evicted the Romans, who also had a fortress here.

Until the 15th century Óbidos overlooked the sea; the bay gradually silted up, leaving the town landlocked.

Information

Espaço Internet (☎ 262 955 537; Rua Direita 107; ☺ 10am-7pm Mon-Fri, 11.30am-6.30pm Sat & Sun Sep-Jun, 10am-10pm Jul & Aug) Free internet access.

Post office (Praça de Santa Maria; ☺ 9am-12.30pm & 2.30-6pm Mon-Fri)

Região de Turismo do Oeste (☎ 262 955 060; www .rt-oeste.pt; Rua Direita 45; ☺ 10am-1pm & 2-6pm Mon-Fri) Regional tourism headquarters.

Turismo (☎ 262 959 231; posto.turismo@cm-obidos.pt; ☺ 9.30am-6pm Mon-Fri, 9.30am-12.30pm &1.30-5.30pm Sat & Sun) Town tourist office, just outside Porta da Vila near the bus stop.

Sights

CASTELO, WALLS & AQUEDUCT

You can walk around the unprotected **muro** (wall) for uplifting, if nail-biting, views over the town and surrounding countryside. The walls date from the time of the Moors (later restored), but the **castelo** (castle) itself is one of Dom Dinis' 13th-century creations. It's a stern edifice, with lots of towers, battlements and big gates. Converted into a palace in the 16th century, it's now a deluxe *pousada*.

ESTREMADURA & RIBATEJO

JOSEFA DE ÓBIDOS

In an age when the only acceptable vocations for a woman were as nun, or wife and mother, Josefa de Óbidos managed to establish herself not just as one of 17th-century Portugal's best artists but also as one of its most respected. The daughter of minor Portuguese painter Baltazar Gomes Figueira, she was born in Seville but returned to Portugal as a child after the country regained its independence from Spain. She studied at the Augustine Convento de Santa Ana but left the convent and eventually settled in Óbidos, where she remained famously chaste and religious until her death in 1684.

A number of factors enabled Josefa to carve out her unlikely public position. First, her father was a painter, so she was able to receive an education within her home – the only 'respectable' place a woman might have received training. Second, she allied herself closely with the church without ever taking vows. In this way, she never subjected her talents to the whims of a nay-saying mother superior, yet still could appear as a humble representative of the Mother Church rather than an independent woman hawking her own works. Finally, there was the sheer appeal of her paintings. Often they ignore established iconography in favour of a certain domestic sweetness, but at the same time they combine a masterful use of colour and form.

THE PERFECT VALENTINE'S DAY GIFT

Really want to impress your sweetheart next Valentine's Day? How about taking her, or him, to Óbidos' annual Festival Internacional do Chocolate? This scrumptiously decadent 12-day celebration draws over 200,000 people to Óbidos each February. Events for every age and taste include an international chocolate recipe contest, a chocolate-themed fashion show, the Portuguese Chocolatier of the Year awards, a chocolate sculpture exhibit and a kids' play-house made entirely of chocolate (sorry, older kids, only the youngest toddlers get to taste the merchandise!).

If your trip to Óbidos doesn't coincide with the festival, no worries. A gaggle of shops open year-round along Óbidos' main street will be happy to ease your pain with a chocolate cup full of *ginja* (the local cherry liqueur).

The **aqueduct**, southeast of the main gate, dates from the 16th century and is 3km long.

IGREJA DE SANTA MARIA

The town's elegant main **church** (Praça de Santa Maria; ☺ 9.30am-12.30pm & 2.30-7pm May-Sep, to 5pm Oct-Apr), near the northern end of Rua Direita, stands on the foundations of a Visigothic temple later converted into a mosque. Begun in the 12th century but restored several times since, it dates mostly from the Renaissance. It had its 15 minutes of fame in 1444 when 10-year-old Afonso V married his eight-year-old cousin Isabel here.

Inside is a wonderful painted ceiling and walls done up in beautiful blue-and-white 17th-century *azulejos* (hand-painted tiles). Paintings by the renowned 17th-century painter Josefa de Óbidos (see p295) are to the right of the altar. There's a fine 16th-century Renaissance tomb on the left, probably carved by the French sculptor Nicolas Chanterène.

MUSEU MUNICIPAL

Located in an 18th-century manor house just next to Igreja de Santa Maria, the town's **mu-seum** (☎ 262 955 557; Solar da Praça de Santa Maria; admission €1.50; ☺ 10am-1pm & 2-6pm) houses a small collection of paintings spanning several centuries. The highlight is a haunting portrait by Josefa de Óbidos, *Faustino das Neves* (1670), remarkable for its dramatic use of light and shade.

Festivals & Events

Óbidos celebrates **Semana Santa** (Holy Week) with religious re-enactments and processions.

In July a 10-day **Mercado Medieval** (Medieval Market) held in the castle grounds and below the town's western wall includes live enter-

tainment, jousting matches, plenty of grog and pigs roasting on spits, and the chance to try your hand at scaling the town walls (with the help of harness and rope). Dress in medieval attire and the €5 admission fee is waived.

For almost two weeks following Valentine's Day, Obidos' **Festival Internacional do Chocolate** (see the boxed text, above) celebrates the sweet temptation of the cocoa bean.

Sleeping
BUDGET

The two places listed below display duelling 'rooms available' signs on the town's main thoroughfare. Several less official places also rent private rooms.

Casa dos Castros (☎ 262 959 328; Rua Direita 83; s/d with shared bathroom €30/35) Be short or at least prepared to stoop at this place near the church. The ceilings of its simple rooms are unbelievably low, but then again so are the prices. No breakfast.

ÓbidoSol (☎ 262 959 188; Rua Direita 40; d €40) This neatly kept old town house, with cosy and comfortable rooms surrounding a snug living room, is one of Óbidos' best-value options. It's worth booking ahead for the two east-facing rooms, with views across town to the adjacent hills.

MIDRANGE

Casa do Relógio (☎ 262 959 282; www.casadorelogio .com; Rua da Graça 12; s/d/tr €45/60/80) Just east of the town walls, this 18th-century house (named for a nearby sundial) has eight smallish, but spotless, traditionally furnished rooms with handsome tile floors – plus a pretty shared terrace.

Casa de São Thiago (☎ 262 959 587; www.ca sas-sthiago.com; Largo de São Thiago; s/d €65/80; (P)) This ridiculously charming labyrinth of snug, 18th-century rooms and tiled, flower-filled courtyards in the shadow of the castle has its own wine cellar and billiards room. Rooms vary, but all offer standard midrange comforts, plus some nice antique touches.

Casa d'Óbidos (☎ 262 950 924; www.casadobidos.com; Quinta de São José; s/d €69/80, 2-/4-/6-person apt €80/130/160; P ⅏) In a whitewashed, 19th-century villa at the foot of the old town, this delightful place is clearly a labour of love for its friendly owners. It features spacious, breezy rooms with good new bathrooms and period furnishings, plus tennis courts, a swimming pool and lovely grounds with sweeping views of Óbidos' bristling walls and towers. Home-raised honey and fruit are served at breakfast, and trails lead through the orchards up to town.

TOP END

Casa das Senhoras Rainhas (☎ 262 955 360; www .senhorasrainhas.com; Rua Padre Nunes Tavares 6; s/d €132/144; ⅏) This classy inn with a flowery courtyard directly abutting the town walls is more luxurious than most lodgings in the historic centre and has an excellent restaurant attached.

Pousada do Castelo (☎ 262 955 080; www.pousadas .pt; d €220; ⅏) One of Portugal's best *pousadas* occupies a charming convent hidden within the town's forbidding 13th-century castle. The whitewashed rooms are mostly done up with sleek contemporary furnishings. Book well in advance for the split-level rooms in the two castle towers – especially room 203, which is popular with honeymooners.

Eating & Drinking

Touristy Óbidos has few budget dining options – visitors with limited funds can grab a sandwich outside the town gate or snack at one of the bars below. The larger inns, including the *pousada*, have good, if pricey, dining rooms.

Bar Lagar da Mouraria (☎ 919937601; Rua da Mouraria; snacks €2-8; ⅏ 6pm-2am) Enjoy the simple menu of tapas, cheese, sausage, sandwiches or fish soup in this lovely traditional bar behind the post office. It's housed in a former winery, with beamed ceiling, a flagstone floor and seats around a massive old winepress.

Bar Taberna d'Óbidos (☎ 967179341; Rua do Hospital 5; sandwiches & snacks €2-10; ⅏ 1pm-2am Tue-Sun) For sandwiches or a drink with a little atmosphere thrown in, this medieval-style bar with stone walls and a spiral staircase makes a fun stop. It's especially cosy at night when there is an open fire roaring in the giant fireplace.

Alcaide (☎ 262 959 220; Rua Direita 60; mains €11-16; ⅏ lunch & dinner) This upstairs restaurant with wrought-iron chandeliers and windows overlooking town features creative dishes like *requinte de bacalhau* (salt-cod with cheese, chestnuts and apples).

Cozinha das Rainhas (☎ 262 955 360; Rua Padre Nunes Tavares 6; mains €12-15; ⅏ lunch & dinner Tue-Sun) Attached to the Casa das Senhoras Rainhas hotel, this elegant restaurant offers some of the finest dining in Óbidos, and award-winning desserts like *pêra escarlate* – pears with panna cotta in a *ginjinha* (cherry liqueur) reduction.

Getting There & Away

The town's main gate, Porta da Vila, leads directly into the main street, Rua Direita. Buses stop on the main road just outside Porta da Vila. There is a fee-charging car park just outside the gate, while the one just across the road is free.

Buses run frequently to Caldas da Rainha (€1.40, 15 minutes) and Peniche (€2.60, 45 minutes). There are eight weekday runs to Lisbon (€7, 70 minutes), with fewer on Saturday and Sunday. Otherwise change at Caldas da Rainha.

Óbidos' train station has at least six daily trains to Lisbon (€7.65, 2½ hours) via connections at Mira Sintra-Meleças station on the suburban Lisbon line. The station is located at the foot of the castle end of town. It's rather a hoof uphill.

CALDAS DA RAINHA

pop 25,300 / elev 90m

Now that its sulphurous waters are restricted to hospital patients, dowdy Caldas da Rainha is of limited interest to the traveller, though its old centre – particularly the leafy Parque Dom Carlos I – is pleasant enough.

If ceramics are your bag, the **Museu de Cerâmica** (☎ 262 840 280; Ilídio Amado; admission €2, 10am-12.30pm Sun free; ⅏ 10am-12.30pm & 2-5pm Tue-Sun) makes an interesting stop. In a delightful, 19th-century holiday mansion, it features fantastic works by native son Rafael Bordalo Pinheiro, whose intricate creations often involve effusions of flora and fauna. Most

ESTREMADURA & RIBATEJO

memorable are the fabulous jars and bowls encrusted with animals, lobsters and snakes.

The **turismo** (☎ 262 839 700; fax 262 839 726; 9am-7pm Mon-Fri, 10am-1pm & 3-7pm Sat & Sun) is on Praça 25 de Abril, a block from the bus station and five blocks east of the train station. Free internet access is available on several computers in the adjacent room.

Sleeping & Eating

Pensão Residencial Central (☎ 262 831 914; www .residencialcentral.com; Largo Dr José Barbosa 22; s/d €27.50/35) This pink-hued old building has tall French windows overlooking a cobbled square in the old town.

Casa dos Plátanos (☎ 262 841 810; fax 262 843 417; Rua Rafael Bordalo Pinheiro 24; s/d €40/60) At the park's edge, this whitewashed, 18th-century manor house has huge but simple rooms with terracotta-tile floors, rustically elegant common areas and an impressive library.

Pastelaria Baía (Rua da Liberdade 33; 7.30am-8.30pm) This appealing little cafe has a small terrace overlooking the street alongside the park. The local speciality is the sweet *cavacas* (air-filled tarts covered with icing).

Incógnito (☎ 262 841 258; Rua General Amílcar Mota; mains around €14; 12.30-2.30pm & 6.30-11pm Tue-Sat) This elegant place 700m south of the park specialises in French delicacies such as scallops with asparagus in Vermouth sauce, or caramelised apple tart with green apple sorbet. Best to go at lunch for the €8 fixed price menu.

Getting There & Away

Rápida Verde buses run frequently to Lisbon (€7, 1¼ hours) and twice daily to Alcobaça (€3.55, 30 minutes). Regular buses also run to/from Óbidos (€1.40, 15 minutes), Peniche (€3, 45 minutes), Nazaré (€3, 45 minutes) and Leiria (€7.50, 50 minutes).

Four to six regional trains run daily to/from Óbidos (€1.04, four minutes), continuing to Lisbon (€7.65, 2½ hours) via connections at Mira Sintra-Meleças station on the suburban Lisbon line.

There is ample metered street parking around Parque Dom Carlos I.

FOZ DO ARELHO
pop 1300

With a vast, lovely beach backed by a lagoon ideal for windsurfing, Foz do Arelho remains remarkably undeveloped. It makes a fine place to laze in the sun, and outside July and August it'll often be just you and the local fishermen.

Escola de Vela da Lagoa (☎ 262 978 592; www .escoladeveladalagoa.com; Marginal da Lagoa) rents out sailboards and sailboats (each €16 per hour), kayaks (€8 per hour) and catamarans (€20 per hour). The school also provides group kayak lessons (€14 per person for a three-hour session), private windsurfing and sailing lessons (two hours, €60 each), and an initiation to kitesurfing (two three-hour lessons with equipment €150). It's located 2.5km down the road that runs inland along the lagoon. From the village, turn left when you approach the lagoon.

Sleeping

Parque de Campismo Foz do Arelho (☎ 262 978 683; www.orbitur.pt; sites per adult/child/car/tent €4.80/2.50/4.70/5.40, 4-person cabins €87;) This good, shady campsite, 2km from the beach, is run by Orbitur. It has a restaurant, a bar, shade, and bikes for rent.

Residencial Penedo Furado (☎ 262 979 610; www .penedo-furado.web.pt; Rua dos Camarções 3; s/d €65/80;) Situated in the village, this smart, efficient and modern *residencial* (guest house) offers simple, bright rooms with tiled floors, some with verandas and lagoon views.

O Facho (☎ 262 979 110; ofachoguesthouse@hotmail .com; Rua Francisco Almeida Grandela; rear-view/ocean-view d €65/85) Just above the beach past the cluster of cafes, this new pink confection has airy, bright rooms, many with terrific ocean views. There's also a cool bar and shady veranda on the ground floor.

Eating

Restaurante-Bar Atlântica (☎ 262 979 213; Av do Mar; mains €4-10; lunch & dinner) The oldest and scruffiest of the restaurants along Avenida do Mar, Atlântica has a typically fish-heavy menu and good views.

Cabana do Pescador (☎ 262 979 451; Av do Mar; mains €11-23) This renowned restaurant with an ocean-view terrace serves every manner of sea life, plus inventive specials like *tornedó à Cabana* (tenderloin steak with fruit, vegetables, potatoes and shrimp).

Getting There & Away

Buses connect Foz do Arelho with Caldas da Rainha (€1.75, 20 minutes, nine times daily weekdays, fewer on weekends).

SÃO MARTINHO DO PORTO

pop 2700

Families seeking a safe place for their kids to swim can't do much better than São Martinho do Porto. The town's moon-shaped bay is ringed by sandy beaches, and cradled between twin headlands that shield it from the open Atlantic's notorious undertow. Midrise development isn't making the place any more charming, but São Martinho still has a small centre of cobbled streets and open-air seafood restaurants to remind you of quieter days.

Orientation & Information

The **turismo** (☎ 262 989 110; pit-smporto@rt-leiriafatima .pt; Largo Vitorino Fróis; ⏱ 10am-1pm & 3-7pm May-Sep, 10am-1pm & 2-6pm Tue-Sat Oct-Apr) is in the middle of the little town, a block back from the beach.

The train station is about 700m to the southeast. Buses stop on Rua Conde de Avelar, a block inland.

Sleeping & Eating

Colina do Sol (☎ 262 989 764; www.colinadosol.net; sites per adult/child/car/tent €4.50/2.30/4/4.50; ⚡) This well-equipped, friendly campsite is 2km north of town, but only 1km from the beach, with disabled access, a children's playground, a pool and some sections shaded by pine trees.

Residencial Atlântica (☎ 262 980 151; www.visit -sao-martinho-do-porto.com/html/ing-hotel.html; Rua Miguel Bombarda 6; s/d €50/75; 🖳) In a modern building, Residencial Atlântica has spotlessly white rooms with tiled floors to match. Friendly staff and large breakfasts are nice bonuses.

Palace do Capitão (☎ 262 985 150; www.palacecapitao .com; Rua Capitão Jaime Pinto 6; d from €100, ste €150; ⚡ 🖳) This perfectly preserved, 19th-century sea captain's home directly across from the beach is the town's only place of distinction, with much of its original Victoriana still intact. The upstairs suite (room 6) has its own sun terrace, accessed by a whimsical spiral staircase.

Restaurante Carvalho (☎ 262 980 151; Rua Miguel Bombarda 6; mains €7-12; ⏱ 8am-late) On the ground floor of the Residencial Atlântica, this place serves simple but good fish and meat dishes. The speciality is *bife na pedra* (sizzling beefsteak).

Getting There & Away

There are five daily trains northbound to Leiria (€2.85, 45 minutes) and southbound to Caldas da Rainha (€1.25, 15 minutes), with onward connections in both directions. Rede Expressos runs at least five buses daily to/from Lisbon (€9.50, 1½ hours).

Street parking is plentiful, though it can grow competitive on summer weekends.

NAZARÉ

pop 14,900

With a warren of narrow, cobbled lanes running down to a wide, cliff-backed beach, Nazaré is Estremadura's most picturesque coastal resort. The sands are packed wall-to-wall with multicoloured umbrellas in July and August, but the party atmosphere isn't limited to the summer beach scene – Nazaré is one of Portugal's top draws for New Year's Eve and Carnaval celebrations as well.

The town centre is jammed with seafood restaurants, bars and local women in traditional dress hawking rooms for rent. To escape the crowds and get a different perspective on the town, take the funicular up to Promontório do Sítio, where picture-postcard coastal views unfold from the clifftops.

Orientation

Until the 18th century the sea covered the present-day site of Nazaré; the locals lived inland at the hilltop Pederneira and the nearer Promontório do Sítio. Today, both places play second fiddle to Nazaré and its seafront Avenida da República. The former fisherfolk's quarter of narrow lanes now hosts restaurants and cafes.

Information

Centro de saúde (☎ 262 569 121; Urbanização Caixins) Medical centre on the eastern edge of town.

Espaço Internet (cnr Avs Manuel Remígio & do Municipio; ⏱ 9.30am-1pm & 2-7pm Mon-Fri, 3-7pm Sat) Free internet and wi-fi in Nazaré's Centro Cultural.

Police station (☎ 262 550 070; Rua Sub-Vila)

Post office (Av da Independência Nacional; ⏱ 9am-12.30pm & 2.30-6pm Mon-Fri)

Turismo (☎ 262 561 194; www.cm-nazare.pt; Av da República; ⏱ 9am-9pm Jul & Aug, 9.30am-1pm & 2.30-6pm Oct-Mar, to 7pm Apr-Jun & Sep)

Sights

The **Promontório do Sítio**, the clifftop area 110m above the beach, is popular for its tremendous views and, among Portuguese devotees, its mystical associations. According to legend it was here that a long-lost statue of the Virgin, brought back from Nazareth

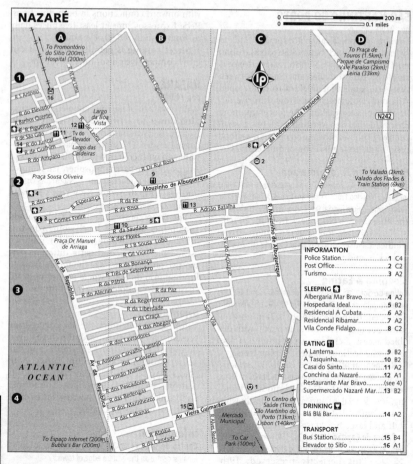

NAZARÉ

INFORMATION	
Police Station...............................1	C4
Post Office..................................2	C2
Turismo......................................3	A2

SLEEPING	
Albergaria Mar Bravo...................4	A2
Hospedaria Ideal..........................5	B2
Residencial A Cubata....................6	A2
Residencial Ribamar.....................7	A2
Vila Conde Fidalgo.......................8	C2

EATING	
A Lanterna..................................9	B2
A Tasquinha..............................10	B2
Casa do Santo...........................11	A2
Conchina da Nazaré....................12	A1
Restaurante Mar Bravo.........(see 4)	
Supermercado Nazaré Mar....13	B2

DRINKING	
Blá Blá Bar................................14	A2

TRANSPORT	
Bus Station...............................15	B4
Elevador to Sítio 16	A1

in the 4th century, was finally rediscovered in the 18th century.

Even more famously, it's said the Virgin appeared here on a foggy day in 1182. Local nobleman Dom Fuas Roupinho was in pursuit of a deer when the animal disappeared off the edge of the Sítio precipice. Dom Fuas cried out to the Virgin for help and his horse miraculously stopped right at the cliff's edge.

Dom Fuas built the small **Hermida da Memória** chapel on the edge of the belvedere to commemorate the event. It was later visited by a number of VIP pilgrims, including Vasco da Gama. The nearby 17th-century, baroque **Igreja de Nossa Senhora da Nazaré** replaced an earlier church, and is decorated with attractive Dutch *azulejos*.

From Rua do Elevador, north of the *turismo*, an **elevador** (funicular; adult/child €0.90/0.65; 7am-2am Jul & Aug, to midnight Sep-Jun) climbs up the hill to Sítio.

Festivals & Events

Carnaval (www.carnavaldanazare.com) One of Portugal's brashest Mardi Gras celebrations, with lots of costumed parades and general irreverence.

Festa do Mar Held every year on the first weekend in May, this festival features fireworks at midnight, a parade with floats dedicated to local fishermen's patron saints and a procession of decorated boats around Nazaré's harbour.

Nossa Senhora da Nazaré This annual pilgrimage, held in Sítio on 8 September and the following weekend, is Nazaré's big religious festival, featuring sombre processions, folk dances and bullfights.

Bullfights Fights take place in the *praça de touros* (bullring) about every other weekend from August to mid-September; check with the *turismo* for times and ticket availability.

Sleeping

You'll likely be hit up by local women offering rooms for rent. It never hurts to bargain and see what the going rate is. Places listed below are more formal business establishments. Prices are for July and August. Expect a 30% to 50% discount at other times.

BUDGET

Parque de Campismo Valado (☎ 262 561 111; www .orbitur.pt; sites per adult/child/car/tent €4.10/2.10/3.80/4.50) This shady, well-equipped Orbitur site has a restaurant and bar. It's 2km east of town, off the Alcobaça road.

Parque de Campismo Vale Paraíso (☎ 262 561 546; www.valeparaiso.com; sites per adult/child/car €4.50/2.30/3.50, tent €4-5.50; 🔊) This well-equipped, security-conscious site, 2km north off the N242 Leiria road, has lots of shade, disabled access and bikes for hire. There are rustic chalets for two/four people for €75/85. Buses to/from Alcobaça and Leiria pass in front.

Hospedaria Ideal (☎ 262 551 379; Rua Adrião Batalha 98; d with shared bathroom €40, with full board €75) The gracious French-speaking landlady has a little restaurant downstairs and six humbly old-fashioned rooms upstairs that are little bigger than the beds. Booked solid in August, when full board is sometimes mandatory.

MIDRANGE & TOP END

Vila Conde Fidalgo (☎ /fax 262 552 361; http://conde fidalgo.planetaclix.pt; Av da Independência Nacional 21A; 2- /4-person apt €45/75) This pretty little complex uphill a few blocks from the beach is built around a series of courtyards and patios decorated with broken-china mosaics and adorned with flowers and plants. Rooms all have kitchenettes.

Residencial A Cubata (☎ 262 561 706; www .residencialcubata.com; Av da República 6; d €60) Rooms at the front of this small hotel have pictur-esque tiled balconies with full-on views of Nazaré's beach, ocean and cliffs.

Residencial Ribamar (☎ 262 551 158; www.ribamar .pa-net.pt; Rua Gomes Freire 9; d €80) Rooms at this seafront hotel are brighter, frillier and airier than the musty and lugubrious halls might suggest. Bathrooms are clean and nicely tiled, and the two corner rooms have little balconies with great ocean views.

Albergaria Mar Bravo (☎ 262 569 160; www.mar bravo.com; Praça Sousa Oliveira 71; d from €100; [P] [✗] [⊒]) Facing Nazaré's busiest square on one side and the sea on the other, this four-star hotel offers calmly luxurious, if not tremendously large, rooms, all with verandas and ocean views. Completely remodelled in 2008, Mar Bravo offers in-room wireless internet and free parking at its sister hotel a few blocks away.

Eating & Drinking

Seafood is the star here.

Casa do Santo (☎ 262 085 128; Travessa do Elevador 11; seafood appetizers from €5; ⏲ noon-late Tue-Sun) An immensely enjoyable *cervejaria* (beer house) serving beer, wine and tasty seafood snacks – especially recommended are the garlicky steamed *ameijoas* (clams). Grab a table on the pavement, or eat under the stone arches of the cosy interior rooms beside the bustling bar.

Bubba's Bar (☎ 262 086 069; Av Manuel Remígio Marginal; mains €5-12; ⏲ 8am-late) For a beer or a bite without leaving the beach, Bubba's is the place. Serving everything from morning cof-fee to standard beach-bar fare, it's got a big sunny outdoor deck, with plexiglass windows to block the wind and sand.

Conchina da Nazaré (☎ 262 186 156; Rua de Leiria 17D; mains €5.50-10; ⏲ lunch & dinner) This simple place with outdoor seating on a backstreet square serves good-value seafood, including wood-grilled fish and delicious *açorda de marisco* (thick bread soup with seafood). Many nights there are more locals than tourists.

A Tasquinha (☎ 262 551 945; Rua Adrião Batalha 54; mains €6.50-10; ⏲ lunch & dinner Tue-Sun) This snug family operation serves…you guessed it – seafood! High prices and reasonable prices make it hugely popular. Expect queues on summer nights.

A Lanterna (☎ 262 562 215; Rua Mouzinho de Albuquerque 59; mains for 2 €18-30; ⏲ lunch & dinner Wed-Mon) This cosy if touristy place specialises in paella-like *cataplana* (seafood simmered with herbs, tomatoes, onions and wine), served in its low-ceilinged dining room.

Restaurante Mar Bravo (☎ 262 569 160; Praça Sousa Oliveira; mains €11-20; ⏲ lunch & dinner) On the ground floor of the town's top hotel you'll find its most upscale restaurant, with high-quality seafood simply prepared, plus ocean views.

Blá Blá Bar (☎ 262 558 968; cnr Av da República & Rua de Guilhim; ⏲ 9pm-6am) Serving drinks late into

ESTREMADURA & RIBATEJO

the night, Blá Blá sits near the cliffs at the northern end of the beachfront promenade.

Self-caterers can head to **Supermercado Nazaré Mar** (cnr Ruas Sub-Vila & Adrião Batalha; 9am-8.30pm Mon-Sat, to 1pm Sun). To drink with the locals, check out the bars around Travessa do Elevador.

Getting There & Away

There are several buses daily to Lisbon (€8.60, 1¾ hours), Leiria (express/local €7/3.20, 40/60 minutes), Caldas da Rainha (express/local €5.20/3, 40/45 minutes) and Alcobaça (€1.75, 20 minutes). Rede Expressos also runs to Peniche four times daily (€8, 70 minutes).

Parking and, in summer, even driving, can be frustrating. There's a large, free car park one block south of the municipal market.

ALCOBAÇA
pop 6300

Only 100km north of Lisbon, the little town of Alcobaça is pleasant but unassuming, yielding centre stage to the magnificent 12th-century Mosteiro de Santa Maria de Alcobaça, one of Portugal's most easily accessible Unesco World Heritage Sites. Prominent bell towers provide the only guidance needed to reach the grand square before the church. Hiding behind the imposing if uninspired baroque facade lies a bright forest of unadorned 12th-century Cistercian arches rising to ethereal heights, adjoined by a graceful ensemble of courtyards, kitchens and former monks' living quarters.

Orientation

From the bus station and car park in the new town, descend 500m along Avenida dos Combatentes to cross the Rio Alcôa and reach the monastery. The *turismo,* restaurants and hotels are all near the monastery.

Information

Hospital (262 590 400; Rua Hospital) On the eastern edge of the new town, off Rua Afonso de Albuquerque.
Police station (262 595 400; Rua de Olivença)
Post office (262 590 351; Praça 25 de Abril; 8.30am-6pm Mon-Fri) Almost next door to the *turismo.*
Turismo (262 582 377; Praça 25 de Abril; 10am-1pm & 3-7pm Jun-Sep, 10am-1pm & 2-6pm Oct-May) Opposite the monastery's main entrance, providing useful bus timetables and free internet access for 15 minutes.

Sights
MOSTEIRO DE SANTA MARIA DE ALCOBAÇA

This **monastery** (262 505 126; admission cloisters, kitchen & refectory adult/senior/child under 14 yr €5/2.50/ free, 9am-2pm Sun & holidays free; 9am-7pm Apr-Sep, 9am-5pm Oct-Mar) was founded in 1153 by Dom Afonso Henriques, first king of Portugal, to honour a vow he'd made to St Bernard after the capture of Santarém from the Moors in 1147. The king entrusted the construction of the monastery to the monks of the Cistercian order, also giving them a huge area around Alcobaça to develop and cultivate.

Building started in 1178 and by the time the monks moved in, some 40 years later, the monastery estate had become one of the richest and most powerful in the country. In those early days the monastery is said to have housed 999 monks, who held Mass nonstop in shifts.

Switching from farming to teaching in the 13th century, the monks used the estate's abundant rents to carry out further enlargements and changes to the monastery to suit the fashions of the day. Towards the 17th century, the monks turned their talents to pottery and the sculpting of figures in stone, wood and clay.

Revived agricultural efforts in the 18th century made the Alcobaça area one of the most productive in the land. However, it was the monks' growing decadence that became famous, thanks to the writings of 18th-century travellers such as William Beckford, who, despite his own tendency to exaggerate, was shocked at the 'perpetual gormandising...the fat waddling monks and sleek friars with wanton eyes...'. The party ended in 1834 with the dissolution of the religious orders.

Church

Much of the original facade was altered in the 17th and 18th centuries (including the addition of wings), leaving only the main doorway and rose window unchanged.

However, once you step inside, the combination of Gothic ambition and Cistercian austerity hits you immediately: the nave is a breathtaking 106m long but only 23m wide, with huge pillars and truncated columns. It is modelled on the French Cistercian abbey of Clairvaux.

LOVE, POLITICS & REVENGE

As moving as *Romeo and Juliet* – and far more gruesome – is the tragic story of Dom Pedro. The son of Dom Afonso IV, he fell madly in love with his wife's Galician lady-in-waiting, Dona Inês de Castro. Even after the death of his wife, Pedro's father forbade his son from marrying Inês, wary of her Spanish family's potential influence. Various suspicious nobles continued to pressure the king until finally he sanctioned her murder in 1355, unaware that the two lovers had already married in secret.

Two years later, when Pedro succeeded to the throne, he exacted his revenge by ripping out and eating the hearts of Inês' murderers. He then exhumed and crowned her body, and ordered the court to pay homage to his dead queen by kissing her decomposing hand.

Tombs of Dom Pedro & Dona Inês

Occupying the south and north transepts are two intricately carved 14th-century tombs, the church's greatest possessions, which commemorate the tragic love story of Dom Pedro and his mistress (see the boxed text, above).

Although the tombs themselves were badly damaged by rampaging French troops in search of treasure in 1811, they still show extraordinary narrative detail and are embellished with a host of figures and scenes from the life of Christ. The Wheel of Fortune at the foot of Dom Pedro's tomb and the gruesome Last Judgment scene at the head of Inês' tomb are especially amazing. The tombs are inscribed *Até ao Fím do Mundo* (Until the End of the World) and, on Pedro's orders, placed foot to foot so that, when the time comes, they can rise up and see each other straight away.

Kitchen & Refectory

The grand kitchen, described by Beckford as 'the most distinguished temple of gluttony in all Europe', owes its immense size to alterations carried out in the 18th century, including a water channel built through the middle of the room so that a tributary of the Rio Alcôa could provide a constant source of fresh fish to the monastery – they swam directly into a stone basin. The water was also useful for cooking and washing.

Even now, it's not hard to imagine the scene when Beckford was led here by the abbey's grand priors ('hand in hand, all three together'). He saw:

> …pastry in vast abundance which a numerous tribe of lay brothers and their attendants were rolling out and puffing up into a hundred different shapes, singing all the while as blithely as larks in a corn field.

The adjacent refectory, huge and vaulted, is where the monks ate in silence while the Bible was read to them from the pulpit. Opposite the entrance is a 14th-century *lavabo* (bathroom) embellished with a dainty hexagonal fountain. The monks entered through a narrow door on their way to the refectory. Those who could not pass through were forced to fast.

Claustro do Silencio & Sala dos Reis

The beautiful Cloister of Silence dates from two eras. Dom Dinis built the intricate lower storey, with its arches and traceried stone circles, in the 14th century. The upper storey, typically Manueline in style, was added in the 16th century.

Off the northwestern corner of the cloister is the 18th-century Sala dos Reis (Kings' Room), so called because statues of practically all the kings of Portugal line the walls. Below them are *azulejo* friezes depicting stories relevant to the abbey's construction, including the siege of Santarém and the life of St Bernard.

MUSEU NACIONAL DO VINHO

This national **wine museum** (☎ 262 582 222; www .ivv.min-agricultura.pt), in an atmospheric old *adega* (winery) 1.2km east of town, was closed indefinitely at the time of writing.

Sleeping

Parque de Campismo (☎ 262 582 265; Av Professor Vieira Natividade; sites per adult/child/tent/car €2/1.40/1.40/1.50; ⓨ Feb-Dec) The small, simple municipal site is 500m north of the bus station. It has some tree shade and disabled access.

Hotel Residencial Santa Maria (☎ 262 590 160; www.hotelsantamaria.com.pt; Rua Dr Francisco Zagalo 20-22; s/d/tr €40/50/60; P ✖) Popular with tour groups, this well-appointed, modern place sits just across from the monastery. Book ahead for the front rooms with impressive views of the monastery's facade and square.

Challet Fonte Nova (☎ 262 598 300; www.challet fontenova.pt; Rua da Fonte Nova; s/d €85/120; P ☒ ⬜) Set amid pretty gardens, this elegant and charming 19th-century chalet has grand common areas with gleaming wood floors, carpets and period furnishings. The main house is especially attractive, with sumptuously decorated rooms, tall French windows, and a downstairs self-serve bar with billiards table; there's also a whitewashed modern annexe.

Eating & Drinking

Pastelaria Saraiva (Praça Dom Afonso Henriques; pastries €1; ☺ 8am-7.30pm) One of a cluster of cafes on pretty Praça Dom Afonso Henriques – just to the left of the monastery's facade – where you can enjoy local pastries under the shade of umbrellas and leafy trees.

Ti Fininho (☎ 262 596 506; Rua Frei António Brandão 34; mains €5-6.50; ☺ lunch Wed, lunch & dinner Thu-Tue) On a side street off the monastery square, this folksy, family-run place serves simple, traditional dishes at good value, including the local speciality, *frango na púcara* (stewed chicken).

Festivals & Events

Now in its second decade, the **Cistermúsica festival** (☎ 262 580 890) runs from mid-May to mid-June, featuring classical concerts in the monastery and other local venues.

Getting There & Away

BUS

There are about six daily weekday buses (fewer on weekends) to Lisbon (€9.80, two hours). There is also service about hourly to Nazaré (€1.75, 20 minutes), and about eight buses daily to Batalha (€2.60, 30 minutes) and Leiria (€3.20, 50 minutes). Coming from Leiria it's possible to see both Batalha and Alcobaça in a single, carefully timed day.

There is a public car park near the roundabout at the end of Avenida dos Combatentes da Grande Guerra, as you arrive from the EN8 from Leiria.

BATALHA

pop 7500 / elev 120m

Among the supreme achievements of Manueline architecture, Batalha's monastery nowadays looks strangely out of place, surrounded by a rather nondescript modern town, and flanked by a national highway passing 100m from its facade. But walk through the doors and you're immediately transported to another world, where solid rock has been carved into forms as delicate as snowflakes and as pliable as twisted rope.

Beyond the monastery, the town's charms are limited to a pleasant pedestrian zone, a couple of nice hotels and an excellent new wine bar/restaurant. For anyone disinclined to linger, Batalha makes an easy day trip from Leiria, Alcobaça or other places along the N8.

Orientation & Information

Buses stop in Largo 14 de Agosto, 200m east of the abbey. Facing the eastern end of the abbey, the **turismo** (☎ 244 765 180; ☺ 10am-1pm & 3-7pm May-Sep, 10am-1pm & 2-6pm Oct-Apr) is beside a modern complex of shops and restaurants.

Sights

MOSTEIRO DE SANTA MARIA DA VITÓRIA

This extraordinary **abbey** (☎ 244 765 497; admission cloisters & Capelas Imperfeitas adult/child under 14 yr/senior €5/free/2.50, 9am-2pm Sun & holidays free; ☺ 9am-6pm Apr-Sep, to 5pm Oct-Mar) was built to commemorate the 1385 Battle of Aljubarrota (fought 4km south of Batalha), when 6500 Portuguese, commanded by Dom Nuno Álvares Pereira and supported by a few hundred English soldiers, repulsed a 30,000-strong force of Juan I of Castile, who had come claiming the throne of João d'Avis.

João called on the Virgin Mary for help and vowed to build a superb abbey in return for victory. Three years later he made good on his promise, as work began on the Dominican abbey.

Most of the monument – the church, Claustro Real, Sala do Capítulo and Capela do Fundador – was completed by 1434 in Flamboyant Gothic, but Manueline exuberance steals the show, thanks to additions made in the 15th and 16th centuries. Work at Batalha only stopped in the mid-16th century when Dom João III turned his attention to expanding the Convento de Cristo in Tomar.

Exterior

The glorious ochre-limestone building bristles with pinnacles and parapets, flying buttresses and balustrades, and Gothic and Flamboyant carved windows, as well as octagonal chapels and massive columns, after the English perpendicular style. The western doorway positively boils over – layers of arches pack in the apostles, various angels, saints and prophets, all topped by Christ and the Evangelists.

Interior

The vast, vaulted Gothic interior is plain, long and high like Alcobaça's church, warmed by light from the deep-hued stained-glass windows. To the right as you enter is the intricate Capela do Fundador (Founder's Chapel), a beautiful, achingly tall, star-vaulted square room lit by an octagonal lantern. In the centre is the joint tomb of João I and his English wife, Philippa of Lancaster, whose marriage in 1387 established the cement alliance that still exists between Portugal and England. If you stand on tiptoes, you can see that the two monarchs' sculpted figures are still holding hands. The tombs of their four youngest sons line the south wall of the chapel, including that of Henry the Navigator (second from the right).

Claustro Real

Afonso Domingues, the master of works at Batalha during the late 1380s, first built the Claustro Real (Royal Cloisters) in a restrained Gothic style, but it's the later Manueline embellishments by the great Diogo de Boitac that really take your breath away. Every arch is a tangle of detailed stone carvings of Manueline symbols, such as armillary spheres and crosses of the Order of Christ, entwined with exotic flowers and marine motifs – ropes, pearls and shells. Four graceful cypresses in the central courtyard echo the shape of the Gothic spires atop the adjacent chapter house.

Claustro de Dom Afonso V

Anything would seem austere after the Claustro Real, but the simple Gothic Claustro de Dom Afonso V is like being plunged into cold water – sobering you up after all that frenzied decadence.

Sala do Capítulo

To the east of the Claustro Real is the early-15th-century chapter house, containing a beautiful 16th-century stained-glass window. The huge, unsupported, 19-sq-metre vault was considered so outrageously dangerous to build that only prisoners on death row were employed in its construction. The Sala do Capítulo contains the tomb of the unknown soldiers – one killed in France in WWI, the other in Mozambique – now watched over by a constant guard of honour and by the 'Christ of the Trenches', a partially shattered statue that also fell victim to war.

Capelas Imperfeitas

The roofless Capelas Imperfeitas (Unfinished Chapels) at the eastern end of the abbey are perhaps the most astonishing, and certainly the most tantalising, aspect of Batalha. Only accessible from outside the abbey, the octagonal mausoleum with its seven chapels was commissioned by Dom Duarte (João I's eldest son) in 1437. However, the later Manueline additions by the architect Mateus Fernandes overshadow everything else, including the Renaissance upper balcony.

Although Fernandes' original plan for an upper octagon supported by buttresses was never finished, the staggering ornamentation gives a hint of what might have followed, and is all the more dramatic for being open to the sky. Most striking is the 15m-high doorway, a mass of stone-carved thistles, ivy, flowers, snails and all manner of 'scollops and twistifications', as William Beckford noted. Dom Duarte can enjoy it for all eternity: his tomb, and that of his wife, lie opposite the door.

Sleeping & Eating

Pensão Gladius (☎ 244 765 760; fax 244 767 259; Praça Mouzinho de Albuquerque; s/d €25/30) In the square right next to the abbey, this snug but attractive place has a vaguely Alpine feel, with flower-filled window boxes and spotless, modern rooms tucked under the eaves. Some upstairs rooms overlook the equestrian statue in the abbey square.

Residencial Casa do Outeiro (☎ 244 765 806; www.casadoouteiro.com; Largo Carvalho do Outeiro 4; s/d €50/65; P ✖ 🖵 🐾) This colourful contemporary place sits just uphill from the town centre. The airy rooms, some with balconies overlooking the abbey and one equipped for guests with disabilities, are individually decorated with flair. Lobby walls are plastered with praise from former guests. Book ahead in summer.

Churrasqueira Vitória (☎ 244 765 678; Largo da Misericórdia; mains €6-9; ✆ lunch & dinner) In the square adjacent to the bus stop, this simple, friendly place serves excellent grilled meat and other Portuguese standards.

our pick **Vinho em Qualquer Circunstância** (☎ 244 768 777; www.circunstancia.com.pt; Estrada de

Fátima 15; mains €9-15; 5pm-1am Mon-Fri, noon-1am Sat, noon-4pm Sun) Sleek and stylish, this wine bar serves delicious tapas and full meals along with an amazing array of Portuguese wines.

Getting There & Away

Frequent buses serve Leiria (€1.65, 25 minutes). There are three daily runs to Alcobaça (€2.80, 30 minutes), Nazaré (€3.70, one hour), Fátima (€2.80, 30 minutes) and Tomar (€4.75, 1½ hours). There is no direct service to Lisbon.

There is street parking just east of the abbey, as well as a marked paying public car park a little further on.

LEIRIA
pop 42,800

Leiria is an agreeable mixture of medieval and modern influences, a lively university town built at the foot of a promontory fortified since Moorish times. The town's dramatically sited castle is a commanding presence above the narrow streets and red-tiled roofs of the historic centre, built along the lazy curves of the Rio Liz.

Dom Afonso III convened a *cortes* (Portugal's early parliament) here in 1254; Dom Dinis established his main residence in the castle in the 14th century; and in 1411 the town's sizeable Jewish community built Portugal's first paper mill.

Modern-day Leiria has a pleasant, low-key urban buzz. Good restaurants, bars and cafes abound, and back alleys hide a bevy of shops selling skateboards and clubwear to the town's student population.

Leiria makes a convenient base for visiting several nearby sights, including Alcobaça, Batalha, Fátima, and the beaches and pine forests of the Pinhal de Leiria. All are easily accessible by bus.

Orientation

The old town is focused on Praça Rodrigues Lobo, with hotels and restaurants nearby. The castle is perched on a wooded hilltop a short walk to the north.

Information

Espaço Internet (Largo de Sant'Ana; 9am-7pm Mon-Fri, 2-7pm Sat) Free internet access (one hour per person daily).

Lavandaria Ingom (969052671; Centro Comercial Dom Dinis; wash & dry per kg €2.50; 9am-8pm Mon-Fri, to 5pm Sat) Laundry near the youth hostel.

Police station (244 859 859; Largo Artilharia 4) By the castle.

Post office (Av Heróis de Angola 99; 8.30am-6.30pm Mon-Fri, 9am-12.30pm Sat)

St André District Hospital (244 817 000) About 1.5km east of town in the Olhalvas-Pousos district (follow the signs to the A1 motorway).

Turismo (244 848 771; 10am-1pm & 3-7pm May-Sep, 10am-1pm & 2-6pm Oct-Apr) Provides a free town map, plus reams of information about attractions and events in Leiria and Fátima.

Sights

This long-inhabited clifftop site got its first **castelo** (244 813 982; castle €1.18, castle & museum adult/child under 12 yr €2.37/free; 10am-6pm Apr-Sep, 9.30am-5.30pm Oct-Mar) in the time of the Moors. Captured by Afonso Henriques in 1135, it was transformed into a royal residence for Dom Dinis in the 14th century. Inside the walls is a peaceful garden, overgrown with tall trees, and the ruined but still lovely Gothic **Igreja de Nossa Senhora da Penha**, originally built in the 12th century and rebuilt by João I in the early 15th century. It has beautiful leaflike carvings over one arch. The castle's most spectacular feature, however, is a gallery with small corner seats. It provides a fantastic vantage point over the town's red-tiled roofs, though the current structure is largely the result of overeager restoration by early-20th-century Swiss architect Ernesto Korrodi.

The **sé** (cathedral), to the southeast of the castle, was started in the 16th century, and the cloister, sacristy and chapter houses date from 1583 to 1604. It's a plain, cavernous place. Opposite is the wonderfully tiled **Pharmácia Leonardo Paiva** – the beautiful *azulejos* depict Hippocrates, Galen and Socrates. Novelist Eça de Queirós used to live in Rua da Tipografia next to the cathedral, and he and his literary group met regularly in the pharmacy. These days, it's a Dutch-owned, Irish-style pub (p308).

Festivals & Events

Leiria celebrates the joy of eating with the nine-day **Festival de Gastronomia** in early September. Expect folk dancing, as well as stalls of mouth-watering traditional food.

ESTREMADURA & RIBATEJO

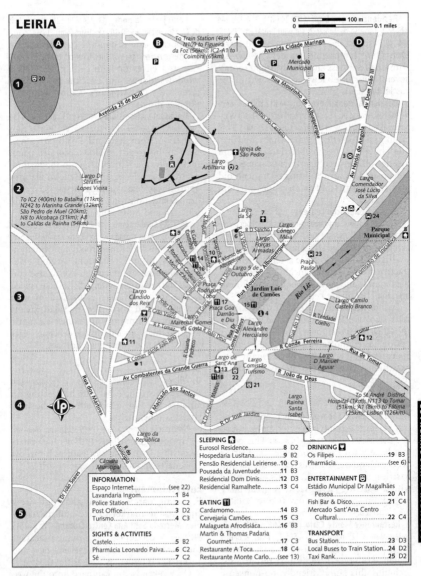

LEIRIA

INFORMATION
Espaço Internet..................(see 22)
Lavandaria Ingom.....................1 B4
Police Station............................2 C2
Post Office...............................3 D2
Turismo.....................................4 C3

SIGHTS & ACTIVITIES
Castelo......................................5 B2
Pharmácia Leonardo Paiva.....6 C2
Sé..7 C2

SLEEPING 🛏
Eurosol Residence......................8 D2
Hospedaria Lusitana..................9 B2
Pensão Residencial Leiriense...10 C3
Pousada da Juventude.............11 B3
Residencial Dom Dinis.............12 D3
Residencial Ramalhete............13 C4

EATING 🍴
Cardamomo............................14 B3
Cervejaria Camões..................15 C3
Malagueta Afrodisíaca............16 B3
Martin & Thomas Padaria
    Gourmet...........................17 C3
Restaurante A Toca.................18 C4
Restaurante Monte Carlo.....(see 13)

DRINKING 🍷
Os Filipes...............................19 B3
Pharmácia.............................(see 6)

ENTERTAINMENT 🎭
Estádio Municipal Dr Magalhães
    Pessoa.............................20 A1
Fish Bar & Disco......................21 C4
Mercado Sant'Ana Centro
    Cultural.............................22 C4

TRANSPORT
Bus Station.............................23 D3
Local Buses to Train Station....24 D2
Taxi Rank................................25 D2

Sleeping

Pousada da Juventude (☎ 244 831 868; www.movi jovem.pt; Largo Cândido dos Reis 9; dm €11, d with/without bathroom €28/26) In an attractive, 18th-century town house on a charming central square, this friendly hostel offers kitchen and TV privileges, a filling breakfast, and high-ceilinged (if basic) doubles and dorms.

Hospedaria Lusitana (☎ 244 815 698; Rua Dom Afonso Henriques 24; s/d €25/30) Tucked down a side street on the slopes leading up to the castle, this well-maintained and unpretentious lodging features tiled hallways and simple rooms with pretty wood floors, tall windows and solid old furniture. Discounts of 10% are offered after the first night.

Residencial Dom Dinis (☎ 244 815 342; fax 244 823 552; Travessa de Tomar 2; s/d with breakfast €25/35; ✗ ☐) Across the river from the old town, Dom Dinis is a friendly, modern *residencial* with small, spotless and mostly bright rooms; several have fine views across town to the castle. French is spoken.

Residencial Ramalhete (☎ 244 812 802; res.ramal hete@mail.telepac.pt; Rua Dr Correia Mateus 30; s/d without breakfast €23/32, with breakfast €25.50/37; ☐) This clean and efficient, if somewhat careworn, guest house has been cobbled together from a series of late-deco apartments, some with balconies. The corner sitting room with old leather armchairs and piano exudes a certain retro charm.

Pensão Residencial Leiriense (☎ 244 823 054; fax 244 823 073; Rua Afonso de Albuquerque 6; s/d without breakfast €35/36, with breakfast €40/42; ✗) In the historic centre, on a cobbled street just off pretty Praça Rodrigues Lobo, this place is replete with attractive period features, including decorative tiles, marble and parquet wood floors. Rooms are small but all are kept in fine fettle.

Eurosol Residence (☎ 244 860 460; www.euro sol.pt; Rua Commissão da Iniciativa 13; s/d from €81/92; ℙ ✗ ☐ ✈) Downtown Leiria's only luxury option has comfortable business-class mini-apartments, all with kitchens and many with exceptional views across the riverside park to the castle.

Eating

Martin & Thomas Padaria Gourmet (Praça Rodrigues Lobo 8-9; snacks & pastries from €1; ☺ 8am-8pm Sun & Mon, to midnight Tue-Thu, to 2am Fri & Sat) This gourmet bakery with outdoor tables on Leiria's prettiest square features tasty bread and pastries, as well as light meals, all served with a dazzling castle view. A great place to pick up snacks for a day trip to Batalha or Alcobaça.

Restaurante Monte Carlo (☎ 244 825 406; Rua Dr Correia Mateus 32; mains €3.50-4.50; ☺ lunch & dinner Mon-Sat) Along pedestrianised Rua Dr Correia Mateus are several traditional restaurants, including this family-friendly, no-nonsense spot popular for its great-value menu and filling Portuguese fare.

Restaurante A Toca (☎ 244 832 221; Rua Dr Correia Mateus 42; mains around €6.50; ☺ lunch & dinner Sun-Fri) Just next door to Restaurante Monte Carlo is this slightly more upmarket place, with a pretty tiled interior and a long menu featuring meat and fish prepared on a wood grill.

Cervejaria Camões (☎ 244 838 628; Jardim Luís de Camões; mains €5.50-10; ☺ 10am-2am) This contemporary cafe-restaurant-cum-beerhouse in the *jardim* (park) has lots of terrace seating, as well as floor-to-ceiling plate-glass windows looking out over the town's little riverside park. Upstairs, Club Glam is a popular disco.

Malagueta Afrodisíaca (☎ 244 831 607; Rua Gago Coutinho 17; mains €9-13; ☺ dinner; Ⓥ) For a rare deviation from standard Portuguese fare, head to this trendy, slinkily decorated place, tucked down a narrow street in the historic centre. The eclectic 15-page menu features aphrodisiac teas, flaming desserts, mixed drinks, and a dizzying collection of Brazilian, Mexican and other ethnic dishes.

our pick Cardamomo (☎ 244 832 033; Rua Barão de Viamonte 43; mains around €10; ☺ lunch & dinner Tue-Sun; Ⓥ) The owner's Goan roots are evident at this new upstairs restaurant serving a delightful fusion of Indian and Portuguese cuisine. Start with intriguing dishes like spiced lentils in crème fraiche, pappadam with grapefruit and coriander, or salad greens with sliced almonds in honey-balsamic dressing, then move on to the delicious vegetarian, fish and curry main courses.

Drinking

Os Filipes (Largo Cândido dos Reis 1A; ☺ 11am-2am Mon-Sat) This simple bar-cafe has seating on an attractive old square, attracting hosts of students most nights.

Pharmácia (Largo da Sé 9; ☺ 9.30pm-2am Mon-Sat) Set inside a marvellous 19th-century pharmacy, this Irish-style bar features a mellow vibe, darts and a vast universe of drinks.

Entertainment

Featuring dance, theatre and high-brow cinema, the market-turned-cultural complex **Mercado Sant'Ana Centro Cultural** (☎ 244 815 091; Largo de Sant'Ana) is built around a pleasant courtyard, where you'll find several cafes and an Espaço Internet, as well as the theatre.

On weekends you can party into the wee hours at Leiria's popular **Fish Bar & Disco** (Rua Machado dos Santos; www.fishnightclub.net; ☺ bar 10pm-3am Fri & Sat, disco 2-5am Sat).

Leiria hosted some of the 2004 European Football Championships in its 35,000-seat **Estádio Municipal Dr Magalhães Pessoa** (☎ 244 831 774), home ground for local team União de Leiria.

Getting There & Around

Street parking is fairly easy along Rua João de Deus. The train station is 4km northwest of town, while the bus station is right in the historic centre.

BUS

From the **bus station** (☎ 244 811 507) there are almost hourly services to Batalha (€1.65, 20 minutes), Alcobaça (€3.20, 50 minutes), Fátima (€2.80, 25 minutes), Coimbra (€8, 50 minutes) and Lisbon (€10, two hours). In addition there are multiple daily runs to Tomar (€3.70, one hour) and Nazaré (€3.20, 50 minutes).

TRAIN

Leiria is on the line that runs from Figueira da Foz (€4.60, one hour) to the Mira Sintra-Meleças station (€11.60, three to 3½ hours) – between Sintra and Lisbon – about three times daily. Local bus 1 runs frequently to Leiria's train station from Largo José Lúcio da Silva near the downtown bus station (€1.25, 15 minutes, schedule posted at bus stop). A taxi from downtown to the train station costs about €4.

PINHAL DE LEIRIA

First planted by a forward-looking monarch some 700 years ago, the Pinhal de Leiria is a vast forest of towering pines whose fragrance and stippled shade make this one of the most enchanting stretches of Portugal's Atlantic coast. Dom Dinis expanded it significantly as a barrier against encroaching dunes and also as a source of timber for the maritime industry – a great boon during the Age of Discoveries.

Today, the protected forest covers more than 100 sq km along the coast west of Leiria. Narrow roads cut through the serene stands of pine, leading to a number of excellent beaches around the resort towns of **São Pedro de Moel**, **Praia da Vieira** and **Pedrógão**.

Be aware that here, as elsewhere on the Atlantic coast, seas and currents can be strong; ask around before venturing into the waters.

Orientation & Information

São Pedro de Moel is 20km west of Leiria. Praia da Vieira and Pedrógão are 16km to the north, along the coastal highway. Each town's **turismo** (☎ São Pedro de Moel 244 599 633, Praia da Vieira 244 695 230, Pedrógão 244 695 411) opens in summer only.

Sleeping & Eating

SÃO PEDRO DE MOEL

Parque de Campismo Orbitur (☎ 244 599 168; www .orbitur.pt; sites per adult/child/car/tent €4.80/2.50/4.70/5.40; 🖳) In among the pine trees 500m above town, this well-equipped, pretty site includes swimming pool, disabled facilities and playground. You can also rent two-/four-/six-person bungalows for €62/69/95.

Pensão Miramar (☎ 244 599 141; fax 244 599 199; Rua Serviços Florestais 2; s/d/q €40/50/65) Bland but conveniently located, Miramar is halfway between the bus stop and the beach.

Hotel Mar e Sol (☎ 244 590 000; www.hotelmaresol .com; Av da Liberdade 1; s/d from €70/80) This recently refurbished seafront hotel is comfortable and sparkling clean, with minimalist modern decor. The best rooms, with grand views over the tussling sea, cost €25 to €35 extra.

Bambi Café (☎ 244 599 020; 🕑 11am-3am Jun-Sep, to 2am Fri-Sun Oct-May) Guinness on tap, wi-fi, and comfy couches on an outdoor deck are the big draws at this cool glass-walled cafe behind the *turismo*.

O Pai dos Frangos (☎ 244 599 158; mains €9-13; 🕑 lunch & dinner Wed-Mon) At Praia Velha, 'The Father of Chickens' sits in splendid isolation above the sands, just north of the lighthouse. Specialities include *arroz de marisco* (paella-like rice and seafood stew) and, naturally, grilled chicken.

Estrela do Mar (☎ 244 599 245; Av Marginal; mains €12-19; 🕑 lunch & dinner) Food prices here reflect the unbeatable view; the restaurant is perched on wave-battered cliffs above São Pedro's town beach.

PRAIA DA VIEIRA & PEDRÓGÃO

Parque de Campismo Pedrógão (☎ 244 695 403; www.leirisport.pt/parque.html; sites per adult/child/tent/ car €3/1.50/2.50/4) Just inland from the beach at Pedrógão is this well-equipped municipal ground with a market, hot water, partial shade and air scented sweetly by the surrounding pines.

Hotel Estrela do Mar (☎ 244 695 762; www.hoteis coelho.com; Av Marginal; s/d/tr/q €45/60/94/116; 🍴 🖵 🖳) Right on the beach in Praia da Vieira, this place offers good value with decently furnished, neatly kept rooms with tile floors. Angle for a front room with veranda and sea view.

Hotel Cristal (☎ 244 699 060; www.hoteiscristal.pt; Av Marginal; s/d €95/125; 🍴 🖵 🖳) This, the most up-market option in this stretch of coast, has large rooms with midrange comforts, plus a full-service spa for pampering. Almost all rooms have at least a lateral sea view onto Praia da Vieira; an extra €5 gets a frontal sea view.

Solemar (☎ 244 695 404; Av Marginal; mains €9-14; ☽ lunch & dinner Wed-Mon) On the ground floor of the Hotel Estrela do Mar, this place serves up excellent seafood, managing to stay crowded even in the low season with admiring locals.

Getting There & Away

From Leiria there are at least six daily buses to São Pedro de Moel (€2.60, 40 minutes). During July and August there are also at least seven daily buses to Praia da Vieira (€2.90, 45 minutes).

FÁTIMA

pop 10,300 / elev 320m

What you see in Fátima will depend on what you come looking for. Aesthetically, it's hard to get past the town's bland and monolithic architecture, and outside the main pilgrimage dates (the 12th and 13th of each month from May to October) the vast parking lots ringing the basilicas have the feel of a forlorn desert. Yet for Catholic pilgrims Fátima has a magnetic appeal like few places on earth, and a visit here is necessary to fully understand Portugal's religious culture. If you're travelling anywhere within a 100km radius near the dates of the important May and October pilgrimages, you'll find the highways lined with throngs of fluorescent-clad wanderers, making the spiritual journey to Fátima from all over Portugal and the world.

Whatever your beliefs, you can't help but be impressed by the vast reserves of faith that every year lead as many as six million people to the glade where, on 13 May 1917, the Virgin Mary is said to have first appeared to three awe-struck peasant children. The site of the apparition has been given over to two huge churches on opposite ends of a courtyard twice the size of St Peter's: the earlier 1953 basilica topped with a golden crown and a cross; and the modernist Basilica da Santíssima Trindade, inaugurated on 12 October 2007, with room for 9000 worshippers.

The town itself is packed with boarding houses and restaurants for the pilgrim masses, and shop windows crowded with glow-in-the-dark Virgins and busts of John Paul II.

Orientation & Information

The focus of the pilgrimages is Cova da Iria, site of the visions, just east of the A1 motorway. Where sheep once grazed there's now a vast 1km-long esplanade dominated by the twin basilicas.

Several major roads ring the area, including Avenida Dom José Alves Correia da Silva to the south, where the bus station is located. To reach the sanctuary, turn right from the bus station and walk 300m, then left along Rua João Paulo II for 500m. The **turismo** (☎ 249 531 139; ☽ 10am-1pm & 3-7pm May-Sep, 2-6pm Oct-Apr) is also on Avenida Dom José Alves Correia da Silva, 300m beyond this turning.

Sights

At the east end of the sanctuary is the 1953 **basilica**, a triumphantly sheer-white building with a *praça* and a colonnade reminiscent of St Peter's in Rome. On the left side, the **Capela das Apariçoes** (Chapel of the Apparitions) marks the site where the Virgin appeared. It is the focus of intense devotion, and suppliants who have promised penance (for example, in return for helping a loved one who is sick, or to signify a particularly deep conversion) regularly shuffle on their knees across the vast

---

THE FÁTIMA APPARITION

On 13 May 1917, three children from Fátima – Lúcia, Francisco and Jacinta – claimed to have seen an apparition of the Virgin 'more brilliant than the sun'. Only 10-year-old Lúcia could hear what she said, including her request that the children return on the 13th of each month for the next six months. Word spread and by 13 October some 70,000 devotees had gathered. Lúcia asked the Virgin for a sign, and just at that moment rainy skies opened and thousands of pilgrims reported seeing the sun turn into a whirling disc of colours that seemed to shoot its rays down to the very earth. The Vatican, which had hitherto tried to squelch enthusiasm about the appearances, decided it wisest to embrace them wholeheartedly. The home-grown miracle also proved a great boon to the coming Salazar dictatorship, with its strategic melding of nationalism, Catholicism and fascism.

esplanade, following a long marble runway polished smooth by thousands of previous penitents. Near the chapel is a blazing pyre and a candle-lighting area. Here people can throw offerings on the fire, leave gifts – which are collected at the end of the day and donated to charities – or simply light candles in prayer. As you approach, the sound of melting wax from so many hundreds of candles is like a rushing waterfall.

Inside the basilica are 15 altars dedicated to the 15 mysteries of the rosary. Attention is focused on the tombs of Blessed Francisco (died 1919, aged 11) and Blessed Jacinta (died 1920, aged 10), both victims of the flu epidemic, who were beatified in 2000. Lúcia, the third witness of the apparition, entered a convent in Coimbra in 1928, where she died in 2005.

At the entrance of the sanctuary, to the south of the rectory, is a segment of the **Berlin Wall**, donated by a Portuguese resident of Germany and a tribute to God's part in the fall of communism, as some say was predicted at Fátima.

Eight Masses are held daily in the basilica, and seven daily in the Capela das Aparições. (At least two Masses daily are held in English; check at the information booth by the chapel for details.)

The new **Basílica da Santíssima Trindade** (Basilica of the Holy Trinity), inaugurated in October 2007, sits at the west end of the esplanade. A central passageway hung with golden angels leads to a long etched-glass window spelling out scriptural verses in dozens of languages. Twelve 30ft bronze doors run around the edges of the monumental round marble structure, each with a Biblical quote dedicated to one of Jesus' disciples. Inside, the church's cavernous and impersonal feel is redeemed by Irish artist Catherine Green's striking altarpiece depicting a wild-haired and gaunt Jesus on the cross, backed by the beautiful gold-and-terracotta mosaic work of Slovenian artist Marko Ivan Rupnik.

Fátima's several Catholic-themed museums include the **Museu de Arte Sacra e Etnologia** (☎ 249 539 470; Rua Francisco Marto 52; adult/child €2.50/1.50; ☼ 10am-7pm Tue-Sun Apr-Oct, to 5pm Nov-Mar) – displaying religious art and artefacts from around the world – and duelling wax museums on either side of the basilica: the **Museu de Cera de Fátima** (☎ 249 539 300; www .mucefa.pt; Rua Jacinta Marto; adult/child aged 6-12 yr €6/3.50; ☼ 9.30am-6.30pm Apr-Oct, 10am-5pm Nov-Mar), which

gives a blow-by-blow, starry-eyed account of the story of Fátima; and the **Museu Vida de Cristo** (☎ 249 530 680; www.vidadecristo.pt; Rua Francisco Marto; adult/child €7/4; ☼ 9am-7pm), representing 33 scenes from the life of Christ.

Sleeping & Eating

There are dozens of restaurants, *pensões* (guest houses) and interchangeable pilgrim lodges in the thick of the shops east of the basilica, most geared for visiting groups of hundreds and very few with any character.

Residencial Aleluia (☎ 249 531 540; www.residencial aleluia.com; Av Dr José Silva 120; s/d/tr/q with bathroom €35/42/54/60, breakfast per person €3) Budget travellers will rejoice at the reasonably priced rooms at this place. As bland as everything else in Fátima but squeaky clean and directly across from the basilica, it offers a few spartan rooms with shared bathrooms on the top floor for €15 to €25. The friendly English-speaking owner is also a plus.

Hotel Coração de Fátima (☎ 249 531 433; fax 249 531 157; Rua Cônego Formigão; s/d €45/75) Next to the post office and not far from the *turismo*, this place offers comfortable, cookie-cutter rooms with midrange comforts, and brisk, efficient service.

Getting There & Away

Fátima is a stop on most major north–south bus runs, with at least hourly services between Lisbon (€10, 1½ hours) and points north such as Coimbra (€10, 1½ hours) and Porto (€15.50, two to three hours). There are also at least hourly buses to Leiria (€2.95, 45 minutes). Note that Fátima is sometimes referred to as Cova da Iria on bus timetables.

PORTO DE MÓS
pop 6200 / elev 260m

Dominated by a 13th-century hilltop castle, Porto de Mós is an untouristy town on the little Rio Lena that makes a good base for exploring the mountains and caves of the adjacent Parque Natural das Serras de Aire e Candeeiros.

Porto de Mós became a major Roman settlement whose residents used the Lena to ferry millstones from a nearby quarry and, later, iron from a mine 10km northeast at Alqueidão da Serra. Today, the region remains an important centre for quarrying the black and white stones used in *calçada portuguesa*, the mosaic-style pavements seen throughout Portugal.

The windswept plateaus surrounding town are dotted with ancient stone windmills alongside sleek modern ones generating electricity for Portugal's power grid.

Orientation & Information

The town spreads south from a cluster of streets just below the castle to a newer area around the *mercado municipal* on Avenida Dr Francisco Sá Carneiro, where buses also stop. Walk west from here towards the river and you'll hit Alameda Dom Afonso Henriques, the main road through town. The **turismo** (☎ 244 491 323; ☯ 10am-1pm & 3-7pm Tue-Sun May-Sep, 10am-1pm & 2-6pm Tue-Sun Oct-Apr) is near the town's main roundabout in the *jardim público* (public park) and offers 15 minutes' free internet access.

Sights

CASTELO

The green-towered **castle** (admission free; ☯ 10am-12.30pm & 2-6pm Tue-Sun May-Sep, to 5pm Oct-Apr) was originally a Moorish stronghold. Conquered definitively in 1148 by Dom Afonso Henriques, it was largely rebuilt in 1450 and again after the 1755 earthquake. These days it's too pristine to be convincingly medieval, especially the overneat green tiles of its pitched roof. Still, it's fun to climb around and has pleasant views across the valley to the Serras de Aire e Candeeiros. Stick around till closing and watch 'em lock up with a key the size of your forearm!

MUSEU MUNICIPAL

This little **museum** (☎ 244 499 615; Travessa de São Pedro; admission free; ☯ 10am-12.30pm & 2-5.30pm Tue-Sat), in a pink building beneath the *câmara municipal* (town hall), contains a hodgepodge of highly local treasures: dinosaur fossils, Neolithic stones, Palaeolithic flints, Roman columns, *azulejos*, millstones, butterflies, spinning wheels and, just for fun, a few old typewriters.

ESTRADA ROMANA

Fifteen minutes northeast of Porto de Mós by car, a section of ancient Roman road has been converted into a walking trail. Marked with red and yellow blazes, the old road bed meanders through the hills for 9km; the most impressive section is at the signposted trailhead just above the town of Alqueidão da Serra.

Sleeping & Eating

Residencial O Filipe (☎ 244 401 455; www.ofilipe.com; Largo do Rossio 41; s/d/ste €30/45/60) Porto de Mós' only *pensão* offers 13 trim if slightly grandmotherly rooms at the town's main intersection.

our pick Quinta de Rio Alcaide (☎ 244 402 124; rio-alcaide@mail.telepac.pt; d from €45; ☒) One kilometre southeast of Porto de Mós, this terrific inn is set in a converted 18th-century paper mill. The rooms and apartments are charming, including one in a hilltop windmill, and another that in 1973 served as a meeting place for Portuguese captains plotting the Revolution of the Carnations. The lovely grounds feature a pool, citrus trees, hiking trails and a cascading stream. Many languages spoken.

Esplanada Jardim (☎ 244 403 004; lunch €4.50-6.50; ☯ 10am-2am) This pleasant cafe in the leafy municipal gardens near the *turismo* serves excellent, reasonably priced lunches on weekdays.

Adega do Luis (☎ 244 401 196; www.adegadoluis.pt; Rua Principal, Livramento; mains €6.50-12.50; ☯ lunch & dinner Wed-Mon) Three kilometres southeast of town, this delightful place with high ceilings, stone walls and a roaring fire in the brick oven serves grilled bacon, Iberian pork and *picanha* (rump steak), with pear tart for dessert.

Getting There & Away

There are five daily weekday buses to/from Leiria (€3.20, 45 minutes) via Batalha (€1.70, 15 minutes). There are also two daily buses to Alcobaça (€2.80, 35 minutes). You can buy tickets in the municipal market.

PARQUE NATURAL DAS SERRAS DE AIRE E CANDEEIROS

With its barren limestone heights criss-crossed by hiking trails, this natural park east of Porto de Mós is a popular place for outdoor pursuits. While more easily reached by car than by public transit, it has recently become more accessible to budget travellers thanks to the opening of a new hostel at Alvados in 2007.

Once the haunt of dinosaurs (see opposite), the park is famous for its cathedral-like caves, but above ground it's also scenic, particularly the high Planalto de Santo António (starting 2km south of the Grutas de Santo António). Gorse- and olive grove–covered hills are divided by dry-stone walls and threaded by cattle trails, all making for tempting rambles. Numerous *percursos pedestres* (walking trails), ranging from 1km to 17km, are described in the English-language *Guide to Walking Tours*

DINOSAUR FOOTPRINTS

For years a huge quarry 10km south of Fátima yielded nothing more interesting than chunks of limestone. But when the quarry closed in 1994 a local archaeologist discovered huge footprints embedded in the sloping rock face. These, the oldest and longest sauropod tracks in the world, record a 147m walk in the mud a trifling 175 million years ago.

The sauropods (those nice herbivorous dinosaurs with small heads and long necks and tails) would have been stepping through carbonated mud, later transformed into limestone. As you walk across the slope you can clearly see the large elliptical prints made by the *pes* (feet) and the smaller, half-moon prints made by the *manus* (hands).

Another major dinosaur discovery – a partial skeleton of a flesh-eating *Allosaurus fragilis* – was made in April 1999 at nearby Pombal (26km northeast of Leiria). It proved to be the same species as fossils found in the western USA, throwing into disarray the theory that the Atlantic Ocean opened only during the late Jurassic period.

You can follow in the footsteps of the dinosaurs, through Fátima's **Monumento Natural das Pegadas dos Dinossáurios** (☎ 249 530 160; www.pegadasdedinossaurios.org; adult/child €1.50/0.50; 10am-5pm Tue-Sun) at Pedreira do Galinha, 9km east of the N360 running south of Fátima; follow the brown signs marked 'Pegadas da Serra de Aire'.

---

in the Aire and Candeeiros Mountain Ranges, available for €5 from the park offices.

Information

Ecoteca (☎ 244 491 904; fax 244 403 555; 9.30am-12.30pm & 2-6pm Tue-Sun) Main information office near the Porto de Mós *turismo*, where you can pick up information and hiking maps.

Head office (☎ 243 999 480; www.icn.pt, in Portuguese; Rua Dr Augusto César da Silva Ferreira) In Rio Maior, at the south of the park.

Sights

MIRA DE AIRE

Portugal's largest **cave system** (☎ 244 440 322; adult/child €5/3; 6pm Apr & May, to 5.30pm Oct-Mar), at Mira de Aire, 14km southeast of Porto de Mós, was discovered in 1947 and opened to the public in 1971. The 45-minute guided tour apparently hasn't changed much since, although the caves themselves are impressive. A spiralling 110m descent leads through psychedelically lit chambers with names like the Spaghetti and Organ Pipe Rooms to a final cavern containing a lake with a rather hokey fountain display.

There are three buses daily on weekdays from Porto de Mós to Mira de Aire (€2.30, 30 minutes), plus one on Sunday. In July and August there is one additional bus daily.

GRUTAS DE ALVADOS & GRUTAS DE SANTO ANTÓNIO

These **caves** (☎ 244 440 787, 249 841 876; adult/child per cave €4.80/3, both caves €8/5; 9.30am-8.30pm Jul & Aug, to 7pm Jun & Sep, to 6pm Apr & May, to 5.30pm Oct-Mar) are about 15km southeast of Porto de Mós, and 2km and 3.5km, respectively, south of the N243 from Porto de Mós to Mira de Aire. They were discovered by workmen in 1964, and are the spiky smaller cousins of Mira de Aire, with similarly disco-flavoured lighting.

Buses between Porto de Mós and Mira de Aire can drop you at the caves turnoff on the N243, but it's a steep uphill walk from there. A **taxi** (☎ 244 491 351) from Porto de Mós costs about €15 return, including an hour's wait at the caves.

Sleeping

The park operates four rustic *centros de acolhimento* (lodging centres) in its southern section, geared to groups of four to eight and starting at about €60 per night in the high season. This accommodation should be booked at least a week in advance at the park's ecoteca in Porto de Mós. They are available June through September.

Parque de campismo (☎ 244 450 555, reservations 244 449 700; sites per adult/tent €2.50/0.75 May-Sep) Remote, basic, and beautifully set at Arrimal, 17km south of Porto de Mós, this place has only 50 pitches, and is accessible by a weekday bus to Porto de Mós (€2.80, 35 minutes).

Alvados Hostel (☎ 244 441 202; www.pousadasjuventude.pt; dm €13, r with/without bathroom €38/30; **P**), This The friendly, sparkling new place 8km southeast of Porto de Mós, has four-bed dorms, doubles with and without private bathroom, a guest kitchen, a cafe serving meals (€6 each, advance notice required) and wheelchair-accessible facilities. Buses from Leiria (€3.70, 55 minutes) stop at the Alvados traffic circle in front of the hostel twice daily.

RIBATEJO

Literally meaning 'Above the Tejo', Ribatejo is the only Portuguese province that doesn't border either Spain or the open ocean. A string of Templar castles are proof of its strategic importance, though these days its clout is economic, thanks both to industry along the Tejo and to rich agricultural plains that spread out from the river's banks. This is also bull country – most of the country's fighters are bred in and around the capital, Santarém.

SANTARÉM
pop 28,900 / elev 110m

Contemplating the staggering views from Santarém's Portas do Sol garden atop the old town walls, it's easy to understand why Roman, Visigoth, Moorish and Portuguese armies all wanted to claim this as their strategic stronghold above the Rio Tejo. Dom Afonso Henriques' storming of these heights in 1147 marked a turning point in the Reconquista and quickly became the stuff of Portuguese national legend. The city's name refers to Santa Iria, the martyred saint who washed up on these shores after being thrown into the Tejo upstream near Tomar.

A group of beautiful Gothic buildings recalls Santarém's glory days, though it was quickly eclipsed by Lisbon. These days, the Ribatejan capital's main claims to fame are bullfights and a large June agricultural fair.

History

One of the most important cities of Lusitania under Julius Caesar, and prized by the Moors under the name Xantarim for almost 400 years, Santarém already had centuries of history under its belt before passing to Portuguese rule in 1147. So great was Dom Afonso Henriques' joy at conquering this legendarily impenetrable citadel that he built the magnificent Mosteiro de Santa Maria de Alcobaça (p302) in gratitude.

Under the Portuguese, Santarém became a favourite royal residence (hunting was the main draw), and its palace served as the meeting place of the *cortes* during the 13th, 14th and 15th centuries. A 400-year royal hiatus ended in 1833 – when Dom Miguel used it as his base during his brief (unsuccessful) war against his brother Pedro.

Orientation

Pedestrianised Rua Serpa Pinto and Rua Capelo e Ivens constitute the heart of Santarém's old town, where you'll find the *turismo* and most of the restaurants, shops and cheap accommodation. Signposts to the Portas do Sol lookout lead visitors on a walk past most of the churches of interest.

Information

Esp@çonet (Rua João Afonso 6; ☺ 10am-8pm Mon-Fri, 2.30-8pm Sat) Free internet access in the upstairs lobby of the Teatro Sá da Bandeira.

Hospital (☎ 243 300 200; Av Bernardo Santareno) On the northern edge of town.

Police station (☎ 243 322 022; Campo Sá da Bandeira)

Post office (☎ 243 309 730; Rua Dr Teixeira Guedes; ☺ 8.30am-6.30pm Mon-Fri, 9am-12.30pm Sat)

Turismo (☎ 243 304 437; pturismo.santarem@mail .telepac.pt; Rua Capelo e Ivens 63; ☺ 9am-7pm Tue-Fri, 10am-12.30pm & 2.30-5.30pm Sat & Sun, 9am-12.30pm & 2-5.30pm Mon)

Sights

IGREJA DE NOSSA SENHORA DA CONCEIÇÃO

This baroque, 17th-century Jesuit **church** (☺ 9am-12.30pm & 2-5.30pm Wed-Sun), built on the site of the former royal palace, looms over the town's most impressive square, Praça Sá da Bandeira. The church now serves as the town's cathedral. Inside is a lush baroque ceiling bursting with angels, plus a number of elaborately gilded altars.

IGREJA DE MARVILA

Dating from the 12th century but with 16th-century additions, this endearing little **church** (☺ 9am-12.30pm & 2-5.30pm Wed-Sun) has a fine, twisted Manueline doorway, while the interior is completely awash in brilliant, dramatically patterned *azulejos* dating from the 17th century.

IGREJA DA GRAÇA

Just south of the Igreja de Marvila is Santarém's early-15th-century **church** (☺ 9am-12.30pm & 2-5.30pm Wed-Sun), with its delicately carved facade

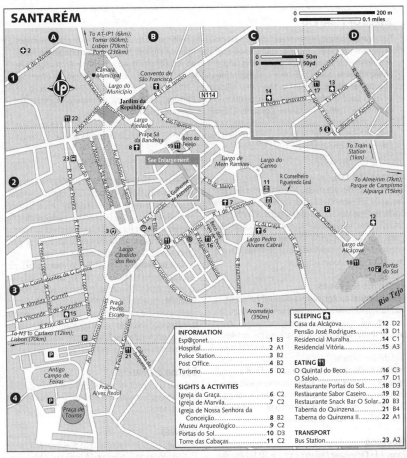

SANTARÉM

of multilayered arches. Inside, a rose window spills light across the beautifully spare interior of stone columns and white walls. Note especially the tombs of Pedro Álvares Cabral (the 'discoverer' of Brazil, who lived in Santarém) and Dom Pedro de Menezes (the first governor of Ceuta, who died in 1437). The de Menezes family founded the church, which explains why Dom Pedro's funerary monument – supported by a pride of lions – is considerably more ornate than that of the more prominent explorer.

MUSEU ARQUEOLÓGICO

This **archaeological museum** (admission €1; 9am-12.30pm & 2-5.30pm Wed-Sun) is housed in the enchanting, 12th-century Igreja de São João

de Alporão. Among the stone carvings, *azulejos* and rotating exhibits is the elaborate tomb of Dom Duarte de Menezes, who died in 1464 in a battle against the Moors in North Africa. It's quite grand – especially considering that once the Moors had finished with him, all that was left for burial was a tooth!

TORRE DAS CABAÇAS

This 15th-century bell tower opposite the Museu Arqueológico houses the Núcleo Museológico do Tempo (Museum of Time). Closed at the time of writing, the museum's collection includes everything from ancient sundials to an intricate, glass-sheathed, 19th-century clock.

WINES OF RIBATEJO

For years, Ribatejo wines were considered good, honest jug stuff, while the really good vintages came from Alentejo. Indeed, alluvial soil and a temperate climate have made these wines fruity and eminently drinkable, if unexciting, and prone to rough, tannic edges. However, things have changed as vintners pursue more experimental techniques and exploit more labour-intensive but higher-quality terrains in the stony hillsides. In 2000 the region won DOC (Denominação de Origem Controlada; the best wine certification in Portugal) status, with six regions of particular distinction: Tomar, Santarém, Coruche, Chamusca, Cartaxo and Almeirim.

For more information about vineyards and suggested do-it-yourself itineraries, head to www .rotavinhoribatejo.pt, or pick up one of Vini Portugal's free wine-route maps, available at tourist offices throughout the region.

PORTAS DO SOL

Occupying the site of the Moorish citadel, the **Portas do Sol** (Gates of the Sun; admission free; 9am-6pm Oct-Apr, to 10pm May-Sep) garden proffers by far the town's best views over the Rio Tejo and the great spread of plains that surround it. The garden's shady walks make a fine place for a picnic or afternoon linger.

Festivals & Events

Feira Nacional da Agricultura (National Agriculture Fair) Famous nationwide for its merriment, horse races, bullfights and night-time bull-running in the streets. It lasts for 10 days in the first half of June and mostly takes place 2km west of the town centre. There are lots of associated children's events.

Festival Nacional de Gastronomia Held over a fortnight in October at the Casa do Campino, it encourages you to eat as much traditional Portuguese fare as you can. Stalls sell regional specialities, and selected restaurants from 18 different regions present their finest cuisine.

Sleeping

Parque de Campismo Alpiarça (/fax 243 557 040; sites per adult/child/car/tent €3.50/2/3/4;) The nearest camp site is at Alpiarça, 15km to the east. It's well equipped and close to a reservoir, with pool, restaurant and some shade.

Pensão José Rodrigues (243 110 079; Travessa do Frois 14; r per person €15) On a quiet cobbled alley between Santarém's two pedestrianised thoroughfares, Dona Arminda rents out a few simple rooms, most with shared bathroom. Look for the 'quartos/dormidas' sign out front. No breakfast.

Residencial Muralha (243 322 399; Rua Pedro Canavarro 12; s/d €30/35) By the old town walls, this simple and centrally located place offers cheerful, good-value rooms with tiled floors and rather eclectic ornaments. Breakfast is not included.

Residencial Vitória (243 309 130; Rua 2 Visconde de Santarém 21; s/d €25/45;) This night-at-your-great-aunt's-type place is run by Dona Vitória herself, who is also helped by various elderly hangers-on. It has clean and well-kept rooms with old-fashioned amenities, including parquet wood floors and writing desks.

Casa da Alcáçova (243 304 030; www.alcacova.com; Largo da Alcáçova 3; d from €115;) Worth the splurge, this 17th-century manor house has an enviable position near the Portas do Sol garden, with the same remarkable vistas. Rooms are impeccable, large, bright and beautifully furnished, while the handsome, walled garden includes an inviting pool.

Eating & Drinking

As you'd expect of a student-packed agricultural town, Santarém is well off for good-value restaurants.

BUDGET

O Saloio (243 327 656; Travessa do Montalvo 11; mains €5-6.50; lunch & dinner Mon-Fri, lunch Sat) This cosy, tiled, family-friendly *tasca* (tavern) is a neighbourhood favourite thanks to its authentic Portuguese dishes. Drop your inhibitions and discover local specialities like *enguias de caldeirada* (eel stew).

Restaurante Snack Bar O Solar (243 322 239; Rua Elias Garcia 6-10; mains €5-7; lunch & dinner Sun-Fri) With a terracotta floor, exposed brick walls and lace curtains, O Solar is a pleasantly traditional eatery serving Portuguese standards, with a few upmarket touches thrown in.

Taberna do Quinzena (mains €5-8; lunch & dinner Mon-Sat); Bullring branch (243 322 804; Rua Pedro de Santarém 93); Bus station branch (243 333 110; Cerca da Mecheira 20) If you don't mind drawing a few locals' stares, this atmospheric neighbourhood hang-out is well worth a visit. Walls plastered with brightly coloured bullfighting posters are a reminder that this was once a macho refuge, though women can now join the boys for a simple plate of grilled meat or fish, washed down with local Ribatejo wine straight from the barrel. The new branch near the bus station is slightly less intimidating for tourists squeamish about sticking out like a sore thumb.

O Quintal do Beco (☎ 243 391 247; Beco dos Fiéis de Deus 15; mains €5-10; ☯ lunch & dinner Mon-Sat) This cheerful, modern place with lots of natural light draws in local crowds for its €7 midday specials including main dish, beer and dessert.

MIDRANGE

Restaurante Portas do Sol (☎ 969040316; mains €9-14; ☯ 10am-2am Tue-Sun) The backdrop is unbeatable at this outdoor terrace grill in the Portas do Sol garden. Fragrant flowers, hilltop breezes and panoramic views make fine accompaniments to a menu emphasising pasta, grilled meats and fish.

Aromatejo (☎ 917598861; Travessa do Bairro Falcão 21; mains €9-12; ☯ dinner Wed-Sun) Overlooking the Tejo, this is another garden restaurant with a fantastic river-and-rural view from its outside terrace. The house speciality is aromatically grilled wild game, from partridge to deer to wild boar.

Restaurante Sabor Caseiro (☎ 243 329 211; Beco do Feleijo 13-15; mains €9-11; ☯ 10am-2am) Tucked away in a tiny back square, this new arrival features Brazilian favourites such as fish with shrimp and coconut sauce. It's a great place to sit on the cobblestones on a sunny afternoon, listening to music while sipping a caipirinha.

Getting There & Away

The train station is 2.4km northeast of town, while the **bus station** (Av do Brasil) is near the historic centre. Regular buses run between the two stations on weekdays and Saturday mornings (€1.25, 10 minutes). Taxis (☎ 243 322 919) charge about €4 for the trip. There is usually sufficient street parking; there are also a few public car parks near the bullring.

BUS

Buses run at least hourly to Lisbon (€6.70, one hour) and several times daily to Coimbra (€11.80, two hours), Leiria (€9.50, 1¼ hours) and Fátima (€7.80, 45 minutes).

TRAIN

Very frequent IC (€9) and IR (€6.40) trains go to Lisbon (50 minutes).

CONSTÂNCIA & CASTELO DE ALMOUROL

pop 3800

Constância's compact cluster of whitewashed houses, cobbled lanes and narrow staircases spills picturesquely down a steep hillside to the confluence of the Rios Tejo and Zêzere. Its leafy riverfront promenade, main square and gardens make a lovely place for lunch or a stroll before moving on to the biggest draw in these parts, the neighbouring Castelo de Almourol. Constância's **turismo** (☎ 249 730 052; turismo@cm-constancia.pt) is beside the river in the centre of town.

Sights

CASTELO DE ALMOUROL

Like the stuff of legend, the 10-towered Castelo de Almourol seems to have broken away from the land and floated out into the middle of the Rio Tejo. Set on an island that was once the site of a Roman fort, this remarkable sight was built by Gualdim Pais, Grand Master of the Order of the Knights Templar, in 1171. It's no surprise that Almourol has long caught the imagination of excitable poets longing for the Age of Chivalry.

The **castelo** (☯ 10am-7.30pm Apr-Oct, to 5.30pm Nov-Mar) is 5km from Constância. Boats (€1.25, five minutes) leave regularly from a riverside landing directly opposite the castle. Once on the island, a short walk leads up to the ramparts, where you're free to linger as long as you like.

Sleeping & Eating

Casa João Chagas (☎ 249 739 403; www.constancia .info; Rua João Chagas, Constância; s/d €40/52; ☒) Once past the town hall, this 18th-century house offers rather plain but neat, high-ceilinged rooms just off the main square near the river. João Chagas also runs the Café da Praça nearby; try the fantastic *queijinhos do Céu* (sweets from heaven), still made by local nuns.

Restaurante Esplanada (Constância; mains about €6; ☯ lunch & dinner Fri-Wed) With a pleasantly leafy bar-restaurant right on the river serves simple Portuguese fare. The bar stays open until 2am on Friday and Saturday.

Remédio d'Alma (☎ 249 739 405; Largo 5 de Outubro, Constância; mains €10-14; ☯ lunch & dinner Tue-Sun) For fine regional cooking, try this

THE ORDER OF THE KNIGHTS TEMPLAR

Founded in about 1119 by French crusading knights to protect pilgrims visiting the Holy Land, the Templars got their name when King Baldwin of Jerusalem housed them in his palace, which had once been a Jewish temple. The Knights soon became a strictly organised, semireligious gang. Members took vows of poverty and chastity, and wore white coats emblazoned with a red cross – a symbol that eventually came to be associated with Portugal itself. By 1139 the Templars came under the pope's authority and were the leading defenders of the Christian crusader states in the Holy Land.

In Portugal, Templar knights played a key role in expelling the Moors. Despite their vows of poverty, they gladly accepted land, castles and titles in return for their military victories. Soon the order had properties not just in Portugal but all over Europe, the Mediterranean and the Holy Land. This geographically dispersed network enabled them to take on another influential role: bankers to kings and pilgrims.

By the early 14th century, the Templars had grown so strong that French King Philip IV – eager for their wealth or afraid of their power – initiated an era of persecution (supported by the French pope Clement V). He arrested all of the knights, accusing many of heresy and seizing their property. In 1314 the last French Grand Maître (Master) was burned at the stake.

In Portugal, Dom Dinis followed the trend by dissolving the order in 1314, but a few years later he cannily re-established it as the Order of Christ, though now under the royal thumb. It was largely thanks to the order's wealth that Prince Henry the Navigator (Grand Master from 1417 to 1460) was able to fund the Age of Discoveries. In the 16th century, Dom João III took the order into a humbler phase, shifting it towards monastic duties. In 1834, together with all of the other religious orders, it was finally dissolved.

elegant little place, set in a pretty stucco house with a lovely garden shaded by orange trees. It's 200m upriver from Constância's main square.

Getting There & Away

If travelling by car, exit the A23/IP6 at Constância and follow signs to the riverside ferry landing directly opposite Castelo de Almourol. Access by public transit is a bit trickier, as described below.

Constância is best reached by bus from Tomar (€2.30, 40 minutes), as the Constancia–Praia do Ribatejo train station is 2km outside town.

To visit the castle only, take a local train (changing at Entroncamento) from Tomar (€2.35, one hour) or Santarém (€2.75, 45 minutes) to tiny Almourol station, then walk 1km downhill to the ferry landing.

Visitors wanting to take in both Constância and the castle by public transport can theoretically link the two routes above with an intermediate rail leg between Constância's Praia do Ribatejo station and Almourol station (€1.04, five minutes), but note that there's a substantial walk involved at either end of this short train journey.

TOMAR
pop 15,800

Tomar is one of central Portugal's most appealing small cities. With its pedestrian-friendly historic centre, its pretty riverside park frequented by swans, herons and families of ducks, and its charming natural setting adjacent to the lush Mata Nacional dos Sete Montes (Seven Hills National Forest), it wins lots of points for aesthetics.

But to understand what makes Tomar truly extraordinary, cast your gaze skyward to the crenellated walls of the Convento de Cristo, which forms a beautiful backdrop from almost any vantage point. Eight-and-a-half centuries after its founding, this venerable headquarters of the legendary Knights Templar still rules the hill above town, casting Tomar in the role of supporting actor. Now a Unesco World Heritage Site, Tomar's crown jewel is a rambling concoction of Gothic, Manueline and Renaissance architecture that bears extravagant witness to its integral role in centuries of Portuguese history, from the founding of Portugal as a nation-state to the Age of Discoveries.

Given the good train connections from Lisbon, Tomar makes a very appealing place to base yourself for a few days, or

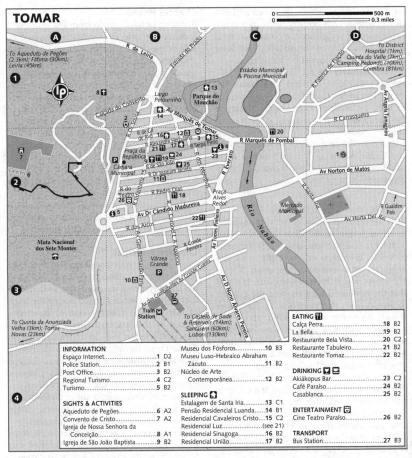

TOMAR

even a pleasant first destination to get over your jet lag.

Orientation
The Rio Nabão neatly divides the town, with new developments largely concentrated on the east bank and the old town to the west. The monastery looks down on it all from a wooded hilltop above the town to the west.

Information
District hospital (☎ 249 320 100; Av Maria de Lourdes Mello e Castro) A new hospital 1km east of town.
Espaço Internet (☎ 249 312 291; Rua Amorim Rosa; ☻ 10.30am-12.30pm & 2.30-7pm Mon-Sat) Free internet access.
Police station (☎ 249 313 444; Rua Dr Sousa)

Post office (☎ 249 310 400; Av Marquês de Tomar; ☻ 8.30am-6pm Mon-Fri, 9am-12.30pm Sat)
Regional turismo (☎ 249 329 000; fax 249 324 322; Rua Serpa Pinto 1; ☻ 9.30am-12.30pm & 2-6pm Mon-Fri) Head here for information about other places in the region.
Turismo (☎ /fax 249 322 427; turismo.tomar@sapo.pt; Av Dr Cândido Madureira; ☻ 10am-1pm & 2-6pm) Offers a good map of the town and an accommodation list with prices.

Sights
CONVENTO DE CRISTO
Wrapped in equal parts splendour and mystery, the Knights Templar held enormous power in Portugal from the 12th to 16th centuries, and largely bankrolled the Age of Discoveries. Their headquarters, set

ESTREMADURA & RIBATEJO

on wooded slopes above the town and enclosed within 12th-century walls, is a stony expression of magnificence combined with the no-holds-barred theatricality that long lent the order its particular fascination.

The **monastery** (☎ 249 313 481; adult/senior/child under 14 yr €5/2.50/free, 9am-2pm Sun & holidays free; ❧ 9am-6pm Jun-Sep, to 5pm Oct-May) was founded in 1160 by Gualdim Pais, Grand Master of the Templars. It has chapels, cloisters and chapter houses in widely diverging styles, added over the centuries by successive kings and Grand Masters. You can follow a short route (45 minutes) or take a more comprehensive 90-minute tour.

Charola

This 16-sided Templar church, thought to be in imitation of the Church of the Holy Sepulchre in Jerusalem, dominates the complex. The interior is otherworldly in its vast heights – an awesome combination of simple forms and rich embellishment. It's said that the circular design enabled the knights to attend Mass on horseback. In the centre stands an eerily Gothic high altar, like a temple within a temple. Restored wall paintings date from the early 16th century. A huge funnel to the left is an ancient organ pipe (the organ itself is long gone).

Dom Manuel was responsible for tacking the nave on to the west side of the Charola and for commissioning the architect Diogo de Arruda to build a chapter house with a *coro alto* (choir) above it. The main western doorway into the nave – a splendid example of Spanish plateresque style (named after the ornate work of silversmiths) – is the work of Spanish architect João de Castilho. The same team repeated its success at Belém's Mosteiro dos Jerónimos (p120).

Claustro do Cemitério & Claustro da Lavagem

Two serene, *azulejo*-decorated cloisters to the east of the Charola were built during the time when Prince Henry the Navigator was Grand Master of the order in the 15th century. The Claustro do Cemitério (Burial-Ground Cloisters) contains two 16th-century tombs and some pretty citrus trees, while the two-storey Claustro da Lavagem (Ablutions Cloisters) affords nice views of the crenellated ruins of the Templars' original castle.

Chapter House

Seeming to have grown from the wall like a frenzied barnacle, the window on the western side of the chapter house is the most famous and fantastical feature of the monastery. It's the ultimate in Manueline extravagance, a celebration of the Age of Discoveries: a Medusa tangle of snaking ropes, seaweed and cork boats, on top of which floats the Cross of the Order of Christ and the royal arms and armillary spheres of Dom Manuel. These days it's covered in ochre-coloured lichen – appropriate given the seaworthy themes. It's best seen from the roof of the adjacent Claustro de Santa Bárbara. Follow signs to the *janela* (window).

Unfortunately obscured by the Claustro Principal is an almost equivalent window on the southern side of the chapter house.

Claustro Principal

The elegant Renaissance Claustro Principal (Great Cloisters) stands in striking contrast to the flamboyance of the monastery's Manueline architecture. Commissioned during the reign of João III, the cloisters were probably designed by the Spaniard Diogo de Torralva but completed in 1587 by an Italian, Filippo Terzi. These foreign architects were among several responsible for introducing a delayed Renaissance style into Portugal. The Claustro Principal is arguably the country's finest expression of that style: a sober ensemble of Greek columns and Tuscan pillars, gentle arches and sinuous, spiralling staircases.

The outlines of a second chapter house, commissioned by João III but never finished, can be seen from the cloisters' southeast corner.

AQUEDUTO DE PEGÕES

This impressive aqueduct, striding towards the monastery from the northwest, was built from 1593 to 1613, to supply water to thirsty monks. Its 180 arches, some of which are double-decker, are thought to have been designed by Italian Filippo Terzi. It's best seen just off the Leiria road, 2.3km from town.

IGREJA DE NOSSA SENHORA DA CONCEIÇÃO

Downhill from the monastery is this strikingly simple, small, pure Renaissance basilica, built in the 16th century. It's believed to have been designed by Diogo de Torralva, who is also responsible for the Convento

---

FESTA DOS TABULEIROS

Tomar's Festival of the Trays is a weeklong celebration with music, drinking, dancing and fireworks. But the highlight is definitely the procession of about 400 young, white-clad women (traditionally virgins) bearing headdresses of trays stacked as tall as they are with loaves of bread and ears of wheat, decorated with colourful paper flowers and, finally, topped with a crown, cross or white paper dove. Young male attendants, dressed in black and white, help the girls balance the load, which can weigh up to 15kg. The following day, bread and wine are blessed by the priest and handed out to local families. The festival is believed to have roots in pagan fertility rites, though officially it's related to the saintly practices of 14th-century Dona Isabel (Dom Dinis' queen).

The festival is held every four years during the first two weeks of July; the next one is scheduled for 2011.

---

cloisters. At the time of writing it was closed for restoration.

IGREJA DE SÃO JOÃO BAPTISTA

The old town's most striking **church** (☾ 10am-7pm Tue-Sun Jun-Sep, 11am-6pm Tue-Sun Oct-May) faces Praça da República, itself an eye-catching ensemble of 17th-century buildings. The recently restored church dates mostly from the late 15th century. It has an octagonal spire and richly ornamented Manueline doorways on its northern and western sides. Inside are 16th- and 17th-century *azulejos*; Gregório Lopes, one of 16th-century Portugal's finest artists, painted the six panels hanging inside.

MUSEU LUSO-HEBRAICO ABRAHAM ZACUTO

On a charming cobbled lane in the old town, you'll find the country's best-preserved medieval **synagogue** (Rua Dr Joaquim Jacinto 73; admission free; ☾ 10am-1pm & 2-6pm). Built between 1430 and 1460, it was used for only a few years, until Dom Manuel's convert-or-leave edict of 1496 forced most Jews to do the latter. The synagogue subsequently served as a prison, chapel, hayloft and warehouse until it was classified as a national monument in 1921.

Mostly thanks to the efforts of Luís Vasco (who comes from one of two Jewish families left in Tomar and is often present), the small, plain building has been remodelled to look something like it would have in the 15th century. It's named after the Jewish mathematician and royal astrologer who helped Vasco da Gama plan his voyages. Inside, among various stones engraved with 13th- and 14th-century Hebraic inscriptions, is a rose-colored limestone block from the Great Synagogue of Lisbon, dating from 1307. The walls are adorned with gifts and contributions from international Jewish visitors. The upturned jars high in the wall were a device to improve acoustics.

MUSEU DOS FÓSFOROS

This **museum** (admission free; ☾ 10am-2pm Jun-Sep, 2-5pm Oct-May), reached via the lovely courtyard of the Convento de São Francisco, contains Europe's largest collection of matchboxes. Amassed by local 'phillumenist' Aquiles da Mota Lima, the 40,000-plus matchboxes from countries around the world depict everything from bullfighters to bathing beauties, and from dinosaurs to French cuisine.

NÚCLEO DE ARTE CONTEMPORÂNEA

This recently opened **museum** (Rua de Gil de Avô; admission free; ☾ noon-5pm Wed-Sun Oct-Jun, 10am-7pm Wed-Sun Jul-Sep) showcases the work of modern artists from all over Portugal.

Activities

Via Aventura (☎ 919641425; www.via-aventura.com) organises canoe trips on the Rio Nabão as well as to Constância and Castelo de Almourol (€15 per person).

Festivals & Events

Festa dos Tabuleiros Tomar's most famous event is this quadrennial tray-toting spectacle, next scheduled for early July 2011 (see above).

Nossa Senhora da Piedade Another important religious festival, this one features a candlelit procession and a parade of floats decorated with paper flowers. It's held on the first Sunday in September.

Sleeping

BUDGET

Camping Redondo (☎ 249 376 421; www.camping redondo.com; sites per adult/child/car/tent €3.50/2/2.10/2.80,

ESTREMADURA & RIBATEJO

4-person bungalow €60-75; �"ᵂ) This lovely Dutch-run campground with three bungalows and a stone cottage is 10km northeast at Poço Redondo. Amenities include a bar, pool and sun terrace.

Residencial Luz (☎ 249 312 317; www.residencialluz .com; Rua Serpa Pinto 144; s/d €20/33; 🖳) Threadbare but central, this place occupies a once-lovely town house in the historic heart of town. Rooms are somewhere between grandmotherly and doleful, with spongy faux-wood linoleum floors. Angle for a front balcony with views of Tomar's main pedestrian thoroughfare and the castle beyond.

Residencial União (☎ 249 323 161; www.residencial uniao.verportugal.com; Rua Serpa Pinto 94; s/d/q €25/38/45; 🛄) Tomar's most atmospheric budget choice, this once-grand town house features large and sprucely maintained rooms with antique furniture and fixtures. Especially pleasant are the expansive old-fashioned parlor and bright breakfast room – both with wireless internet access.

MIDRANGE

Pensão Residencial Luanda (☎ 249 323 200; Av Marquês de Tomar 15; s/d €25/45; 🛄) Run by a jovial owner who once lived in Angola, this simple little establishment has neat, well-maintained rooms in an undistinguished modern building. Double-paned windows help block noise from the busy street below.

Residencial Sinagoga (☎ 249 323 083; resi dencial.sinagoga@clix.pt; Rua de Gil de Avô; s/d €34/49; 🛄) In the centre but tucked away on a quiet residential street, this place offers tidy, if undistinguished, modern rooms with satellite TV and unrepentantly 1970s furniture.

Residencial Cavaleiros Cristo (☎ 249 321 203; residencialcavcristo@sapo.pt; Rua Alexandre Herculano 7; d €52; 🛄) In a newer building near the river, this place offers trim, modern rooms with writing desks and minibars. Somewhat sterile, but comfortable and good value.

TOP END

Estalagem de Santa Iria (☎ 249 313 326; www.esta lagemiria.com; Mouchão Parque; s/d/ste €65/85/125; 🛄) Centrally located on an island in Tomar's lovely riverside park, this slightly kitschy, '40s-style country inn has large comfortable rooms, most with balconies overlooking the leafy grounds or the river. Downstairs are a restaurant and bar, both with roaring fireplaces in the winter.

Quinta do Valle (☎ 249 381 165; www.quintadovalle .com; 2-/4-person apt €89/109; 🅿 🛄) With parts dating back to the 15th century, this manor house 7km south of Tomar, together with its outbuildings, has been turned into an upmarket inn, with large grounds, chapel, swimming pool and quaint two- to four-bedroom apartments featuring fireplaces and kitchenettes.

Eating

Restaurante Tomaz (☎ 249 312 552; Rua dos Arcos 31; mains €4-7; 🕑 lunch & dinner Mon-Sat) Popular with locals, this simple, appealing place has a cosy tiled dining room and outdoor seating on a wide, leafy street. Specialities include Portuguese dishes such as *bacalhau à brás* (salt-cod fried with onions and potatoes).

Restaurante Tabuleiro (☎ 249 312 771; Rua Serpa Pinto 140; mains from €5; 🕑 lunch & dinner Mon-Sat) Located just off Tomar's main square, this undistinguished-looking eatery with multilingual menus posted out front doesn't immediately inspire confidence, but step inside and you'll discover a family-friendly local hang-out with warm, attentive service, great food and ample portions.

La Bella (☎ 249 322 996; Rua Serpa Pinto 149; mains €5-10; 🕑 lunch & dinner Tue-Sun) People flock to this brightly lit, mirror-walled pizzeria just behind Igreja de São João Baptista. Pasta and meat dishes are excellent.

Restaurante Bela Vista (☎ 249 312 870; Rua Marquês de Pombal 68; mains €6-10; 🕑 lunch & dinner Wed-Sun, lunch Mon) The views are lovely from Bela Vista's wisteria-bedecked terrace overlooking the river, but service and food (standard Portuguese fare) are somewhat less dependable.

Calça Perra (☎ 249 321 616; Rua Pedro Dias 59; mains €8-13; 🕑 lunch & dinner Tue-Sun) Eat in the pretty pink-walled dining room or the breezy courtyard below. Best in the off-season, when €7 lunch specials include beer or wine, soup, main course and coffee.

Drinking

Café Paraíso (Rua Serpa Pinto 127; snacks €1-4; 🕑 9.30am-2am Mon, 7.30am-2am Tue-Sat, 7.30am-8pm Sun) This old-fashioned, high-ceilinged deco cafe serves as a refuge for the town's alternative scene, as well as for anyone in need of a snack and a shot of caffeine or whisky.

Casablanca (Rua de São João 85; 🕑 10pm-3am Wed & Thu, to 4am Fri & Sat) A charming side-street bar with movie stills of Bogie.

THEATRE IN THE MONASTERY

For a completely different take on Tomar's Convento de Cristo, catch a performance of Umberto Eco's *The Name of the Rose* by hometown theatre troupe Fatias de Cá. From the first strains of Gregorian chants wafting through the monastery's entry hall, to the torch-lit finale in the Great Cloisters, this performance takes you to places (literally and figuratively) that you won't get to during a daytime tour.

Not for the faint of heart or weak of leg, the play is a five-hour workout. Although performed in Portuguese, its plot is easy enough to follow for anyone who has read the novel, and roaming the monastery by night is a wonderful experience regardless of your linguistic abilities. As the drama unfolds, actors lead you from room to room and back again, eventually taking you to almost every corner of the monastery. The presentation is punctuated by five meal breaks, each taking place in the old refectory, where chanting black-robed monks preside at the head of long stone tables. The first course involves a little tongue-in-cheek medieval humour: diners are presented with a rock and a pile of walnuts and left to their own devices. Subsequent courses are more substantial and accompanied by free-flowing wine.

As the sun sets, a mood of meditative contemplation creeps in with the crepuscular light. Walking the hallways in this altered state, it's easier to summon up images from centuries past: the Knights Templar mounted on horseback in their torch-lit octagonal chapel, or the royal wedding that took place in the half-finished chapter house under a roof improvised from sailcloth. The play's last few scenes, staged in obscure atticlike spaces off the public tour circuit, are guaranteed to jolt you out of this reverie.

Fatias de Cá stages performances in other atmospheric sites throughout Portugal, including the Sete Montes national forest, the Roman ruins of Conimbriga and the old quarry full of fossilised dinosaur footprints near Porto de Mós. For full details, see www.fatiasdeca.com.

Akiákopus Bar (Rua de São João 28; ☼ 9.30pm-4am) This place looks intimidating because you have to ring the doorbell, but inside it's a cosy little drinking hole with stone walls, beamed ceilings and a surprisingly good margarita.

Entertainment

Fatias de Cá (☎ 249 314 161; www.fatiasdeca.com) This Tomar-based theatre company presents highly innovative and entertaining weekend performances such as *The Name of the Rose* and *The Tempest*, often in amazing locations (see above).

Cine Teatro Paraíso (☎ 249 329 190; cnr Ruas Infantaria 15 & do Teatro) Showing movies five nights a week, this community-run theatre also hosts occasional live music and drama performances.

Getting There & Away

From the **bus station** (☎ 249 312 738) at least two daily buses go to Fátima (€3.20, one hour), Batalha (€4.75, 1½ hours), Alcobaça (€6.15, two to 2½ hours) and Nazaré (€6.40, 2½ to three hours), and four to Leiria (€3.70, one hour). Regular trains run to Lisbon's Santa Apolónia and Oriente stations (€8.20, two hours, several daily) via Santarém (€4.90, one hour).

The bus and train stations are next door to each other, about 500m south of the *turismo*. You will also find several large car parks here.

The Beiras

Once the southern frontier of the Portuguese kingdom but now firmly entrenched in the north, the Beiras are three worlds rolled into one, offering as much diversity as any region in Portugal.

Along the Atlantic, the Beira Litoral (Coastal Beira) encompasses miles of sandy beaches, punctuated in the north by the Ria de Aveiro – an extraordinary network of wetlands teeming with bird life – and in the south by the fertile lowlands at the mouth of the Rio Mondego. At Figueira da Foz, where the Mondego meets the ocean sands, surfers catch waves by day and the casino shines brightly on summer nights. Further upstream along the Mondego lies Coimbra, an early Portuguese capital and military stronghold whose prominence over the centuries has shifted into the scholarly realm – it's now Portugal's greatest university town, with student-fuelled nightlife to match.

Moving inland, the Beira Alta (Upper Beira) region is home to exquisite stone villages such as Piódão and Linhares, the lovely city of Viseu and the high mountains of the Serra da Estrela, where a diminishing number of traditional shepherds still graze their flocks alongside a burgeoning crop of outdoor adventure outfitters offering everything from paragliding to downhill skiing.

East of the mountains, in the sparsely populated and hypnotically beautiful Beira Baixa (Lower Beira), vast expanses of olive and cork oak forest spread across a wide-open landscape interrupted by dramatic rocky outcrops. Here the medieval Portuguese built fortresses to drive out the Moors and ward off Spanish incursions; even now, as you survey the borderlands from the castle ramparts in Sortelha or Monsanto, it's easy to feel transported to those earlier times.

HIGHLIGHTS

- Hiking alongside the glistening Rio Zêzere outside **Manteigas** (p364), through a landscape of stone shepherd's huts and soaring peaks

- Conjuring up a vanished civilisation at **Conimbriga** (p339), whose extensive Roman ruins include beautifully preserved mosaics and working fountains

- Sipping fine Dão wine, strolling flowery civic gardens, or enjoying carnival rides at the month-long summer fair in **Viseu** (p373)

- Savouring the golden light in the cork oak forest as you climb from ancient **Idanha-a-Velha** (p356) to the craggy cliff-top castle at **Monsanto** (p355)

- Listening intently for the first notes of the *serenata*, a midnight fado performance staged annually by black-caped students in **Coimbra** (p327)

★ Viseu

Coimbra ★
★Conimbriga
★ Manteigas
★ Monsanto
Idanha-a-Velha ★

THE BEIRAS

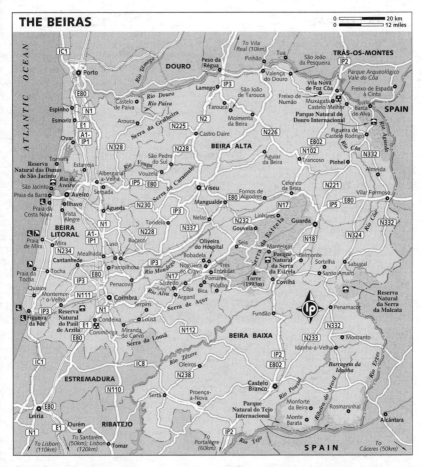

THE BEIRAS

BEIRA LITORAL

COIMBRA
pop 101,000 / elev 150m

The medieval capital of Portugal for over 100 years, and site of the country's greatest university for the past five centuries, Coimbra wears its weighty importance in Portuguese history with gritty dignity. Its historic core straggles down a hillside on the east bank of the Rio Mondego, a multicoloured collage of buildings spanning nearly a millennium, from the Moorish Arco de Almedina at the base of town to the 18th-century clock tower crowning the courtyard of the old university.

If you visit during the academic year, you'll be sure to feel the university's influence. Students throng the bars and cafes of the old town and Praça da República; posters advertise talks on everything from genetics to genocide, and graffiti scrawled outside *repúblicas* (communal student dwellings) addresses the political issues of the day. If you can, come during the Queima das Fitas (see boxed text, p327) in early May, a raucous 10-day celebration featuring live music every night. Or stroll the streets on a summer evening, when the city's old stone walls reverberate with the haunting metallic notes of the Portuguese *guitarra* (guitar) and the full, deep voices of fado singers.

Take a few steps outside the historic centre and you'll also see the city's modern side – a

THE BEIRAS

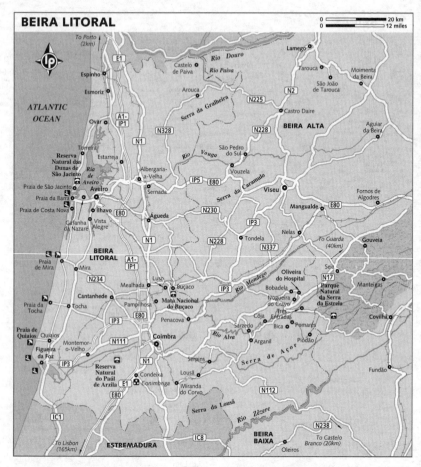

BEIRA LITORAL

0 ———— 20 km
0 ———— 12 miles

To Porto
(2km)

Espinho

Esmoriz

ATLANTIC
OCEAN

Ovar

Torreira

Reserva
Natural das
Dunas de
São Jacinto

Estarreja

Ria
de
Aveiro

Praia de São Jacinto

Praia da Barra

Praia de Costa Nova

Gafanha
da Nazaré

Ílhavo

Vista
Alegre

BEIRA
LITORAL

Praia
de Mira

Mira

Cantanhede

Praia da
Tocha

Tocha

Praia de
Quiaios

Quiaios

Figueira
da Foz

Montemor-
o-Velho

Reserva
Natural
do Paúl
de Arzila

Condeixa

Conimbriga

Miranda
do Corvo

Serra da Lousã

Rio Douro

Castelo
de Caiva

Rio Paiva

Arouca

Serra da Gralheira

São Pedro
do Sul

Rio Vouga

Vouzela

Albergaria-
a-Velha

Sernada

Serra da Caramulo

Águeda

Luso

Mealhada

Buçaco

Mata Nacional
do Buçaco

Pampilhosa

Penacova

Coimbra

Rio Alva

Serpins

Lousã

Tarouca

São João
de Tarouca

Castro Daire

BEIRA ALTA

Viseu

Tondela

Oliveira
do Hospital

Bobadela

Nogueira
do Cravo

Côja

Sárzedo

Arganil

Serra de Açor

Lamego

Moimenta
da Beira

Aguiar
da Beira

Fornos de
Algodres

Mangualde

Nelas

To Guarda
(40km)

Gouveia

Seia

Parque
Natural
da Serra
da Estrela

Manteigas

Covilhã

Três
Entradas

Bica

Pomares

Piódão

Fundão

Rio Zêzere

BEIRA
BAIXA

To Castelo
Branco (20km)

Oleiros

To Lisbon
(165km)

ESTREMADURA

Rio Mondego

brand new riverfront park with terrace bars and restaurants, a spiffy pedestrian bridge across the Mondego, and vast shopping complexes offering everything you'd expect in a major European city.

Coimbra makes a fine base for day visits to the remarkable Roman ruins at Conimbriga (p339), the medieval hilltop fortress of Montemor-o-Velho (p342), or the outlandishly ornate Palace Hotel do Buçaco (see p340).

History

The Romans founded a city at Conimbriga, though it was abruptly abandoned in favour of Coimbra's more easily defended heights. The city grew and prospered under the Moors,

who were evicted definitively by Christians in 1064. The city served as Portugal's capital from 1139 to 1255, when Afonso III decided he preferred Lisbon.

The Universidade de Coimbra, Portugal's first university (and among the first in Europe), was actually founded in Lisbon by Dom Dinis in 1290 but settled here in 1537. It attracted a steady stream of teachers, artists and intellectuals from across Europe. The 16th century was a particularly heady time thanks to Nicolas Chanterène, Jean de Rouen (João de Ruão) and other French artists who helped create a school of sculpture here that influenced styles all over Portugal.

Today Coimbra's university remains Portugal's most prestigious – and one of its

THE BEIRAS

FIRED UP

In the first week of May, Coimbra marks the end of the academic year with **Queima das Fitas** (www.queimadasfitas.org) – a weeklong party that serves as the country's biggest and best excuse to get roaring drunk. Literally, the name means 'Burning of the Ribbons', because graduates ritually torch the colour-coded ribbons worn to signify particular courses of study.

The Queima kicks off with a hauntingly beautiful midnight fado performance on the steps of the Sé Velha (traditionally on a Thursday, but moved to Friday in 2008, to the great displeasure of many traditionalists). The agenda continues with sports events, private black-tie balls, nightly concerts at the so-called Queimodromo across the Ponte de Santa Clara, and a beer-soaked afternoon parade from the university down to Largo da Portagem (traditionally held on Tuesday but moved to Sunday in 2008).

In their rush to sponsor the various festivities, Portuguese breweries provide ultracheap beer, which is distributed and drunk in liberal quantities. Relations between students and police are amazingly friendly, but the strain on local hospitals is heavy, with a strong emphasis on stomach pumping.

---

most traditional. Students still attend class in black robes and capes – often adorned with patches signifying course of study, home town or other affiliation – while a rigorously maintained set of rites and practices called the *codigo de praxe* (praxe code) governs all aspects of student life, including the schedule of the annual Queima das Fitas (see boxed text, above).

Orientation

Crowning Coimbra's steep hilltop is the university, around and below which lies a tangle of lanes marking the limits of the old town. The new town, locally called 'Baixa', sprawls at the foot of the hill and along the Rio Mondego.

From the main bus station on Avenida Fernão de Magalhães it's about 1.2km to the old centre. There are three train stations: Coimbra B (also called *estação velha*, or old station), 2km northwest of the centre; central Coimbra A (also called *estação nova*, or new station, and on timetables called just 'Coimbra'); and Coimbra Parque, south of the centre. Coimbra A and B are linked by a rail shuttle, free for those with an inbound or outbound long-distance ticket.

Pick up a map of the city centre in any of Coimbra's tourist offices.

Information
BOOKSHOPS

For English-language books, try Livraria Bertrand or FNAC, both in the Forum shopping centre (off Map p329) on the Mondego's west bank (look for the giant C on the hillside opposite Coimbra's bus sta-

tion). There's a cluster of bookshops on Rua Ferreira Borges.

Livraria Bertrand (Map pp330-1; ☎ 239 823 014; Rua Ferreira Borges 11)

CULTURAL CENTRES

British Council (Map pp330-1; ☎ 239 823 549; Rua de Tomar 4; ⏱ library 2.30-8.30pm Tue-Wed, 2.30-7pm Thu & Fri, 10am-12.30pm & 2.30-4.30pm Sat, closed Aug) Catch up with British newspapers at the library here.

EMERGENCY

Police station (Map pp330-1; ☎ 239 822 022; Rua Olímpio Nicolau Rui Fernandes)

INTERNET ACCESS

Casa Municipal da Cultura (Map p329; ☎ 239 702 630; Rua Pedro Monteiro; ⏱ 10am-7.30pm Mon-Fri, 2-6.30pm Sat) Free access near the youth hostel.

Ciberespaço (Map pp330-1; ☎ 239 948 570; Galerias Avenida, Loja 4, Av Sá da Bandeira; per hr €2; ⏱ 10am-midnight Mon-Sat, 1pm-midnight Sun) Paid access on ground floor of shopping centre.

Ponto Ja (Map pp330-1; AAC, Av Sá da Bandeira; ⏱ 10am-12.30pm & 2-6pm Mon-Fri, 10am-10pm Sat & Sun) Free access at the Associação Acadêmica de Coimbra (AAC), the university's student union.

LAUNDRY

Lavandaria Lucira (Map pp330-1; ☎ 239 825 701; Av Sá da Bandeira 86; wash & dry per kg €2; ⏱ 9am-7pm Mon-Fri, 9am-1pm Sat)

MEDICAL SERVICES

Hospital da Universidade de Coimbra (☎ 239 400 400; Praceta Mota Pinto) Located 1.5km northeast of the centre.

POST

Post office Main branch (Map p329; Av Fernão de Magal-hães 223; 🕘 8.30am-6.30pm Mon-Fri); Praça da República (Map pp330-1; 🕘 9am-6pm Mon-Fri); Rua Olímpio Nicolau Rui Fernandes (Map pp330-1; 🕘 8.30am-6.30pm Mon-Fri, 9am-12.30pm Sat)

TOURIST INFORMATION

Good town maps as well as a very detailed bimonthly cultural agenda are available from tourist offices.

Municipal turismo (Map pp330-1; ☎ 239 859 884; coimbraviva@cm-coimbra.pt; Praça da Porta Férrea; 🕘 9am-7pm Mon-Fri, 9.30am-1pm & 2.30-6pm Sat & Sun) Adjacent to the Velha Universidade ticket office, just outside the Porta Férrea.

Regional turismo (Map pp330-1; ☎ 239 488 120; atendimento@turismo-centro.pt; Largo da Portagem; 🕘 9am-6pm Mon-Fri, 10am-1pm & 2.30-5.30pm Sat & Sun)

TRAVEL AGENCIES

Intervisa (Map pp330-1; ☎ 239 823 873; intervisa coimbra@mail.telepac.pt; Av Fernão de Magalhães 11; 🕘 9am-12.30pm & 2.30-6.30pm Mon-Fri)

Tagus (Map pp330-1; ☎ 239 834 999; coimbra@via genstagus.pt; Rua Padre António Vieira) In the Associação Académica de Coimbra (AAC); head here for student cards and youth travel discounts.

Top Atlântico (Map pp330-1; ☎ 239 855 970; coimbra .ta@topatlantico.com; Av Sá da Bandeira 62; 🕘 9.30am-7pm Mon-Fri, 10am-1pm Sat)

Sights

Compact Coimbra is best toured on foot. Sights of interest across the river are also accessible on foot via the Ponte de Santa Clara.

Unless otherwise noted, the following sights are all on Map pp330–1

UPPER TOWN

Long a Moorish stronghold and for a century the seat of Portugal's kings, Coimbra's upper town rises abruptly from the banks of the Rio Mondego. The most picturesque way to enter Coimbra's labyrinth of lanes is via **Arco de Almedina** – the city's heavy-duty Moorish gateway – and up the staggered stairs known as **Rua Quebra Costas** (Backbreaker). People have been gasping up this hill (and falling down it) for centuries; local legend says that it was the 19th-century writer Almeida Garrett who persuaded the mayor to install the stairs.

To the left up Rua Sub Ripas is the grand Manueline doorway of the early-16th-century **Palácio de Sub Ripas**; its Renaissance windows and stone ornaments are the work of Jean de Rouen, whose workshop was nearby. Further on is the **Torre de Anto**, a tower that once formed part of the town walls.

Backtrack and climb past Largo da Sé Velha up to the Museu Nacional Machado de Castro (p331) and the 'new' campus, much of it founded by the Marquês de Pombal in the 18th century. Dominating Largo da Sé Nova in front of the museum is the severe **Sé Nova** (new cathedral; ☎ 239 823 138; admission free; 🕘 9.30am-12.30pm & 2-6.30pm Tue-Sat), started by the Jesuits in 1598 but only completed a century later.

The **Museu Acadêmico** (☎ 239 827 396; Colégio de São Jerónimo; adult/student/senior €1/0.50/0.50; 🕘 10am-12.30pm & 2-5.30pm Mon-Fri), just uphill from Largo Dom Dinis, has some interesting displays on Coimbra student life, including vintage Queima das Fitas posters from decades past (especially noteworthy is the 27 May 1926 poster showing hordes of student revellers one day before the coup d'état that ushered in the Salazar era). The museum is also adorned with some grand *azulejos* (hand-painted tiles).

For a glimpse of student life, stroll along any of the alleys around the *sé velha* (old cathedral) or below the *sé nova*. Flags and graffiti mark the cramped houses known as *repúblicas*, each housing a dozen or so students from the same region or faculty.

Velha Universidade

In every way the university's high point, the Old University consists of a series of remarkable 16th- to 18th-century buildings, all set around the vast **Patio das Escolas**. You enter the patio by way of the elegant 17th-century **Porta Férrea**, which occupies the same site as the main gate to Coimbra's Moorish stronghold. In the square is a **statue of João III**, who turns his back on a sweeping view of the city and the river. It was he who re-established the university in Coimbra in 1537 and invited big-shot scholars to teach here.

The square's most prominent feature is the much-photographed 18th-century **clock tower**. This tower is nicknamed *a cabra* (the goat) because, when it chimed to mark the end of studies, the first-year undergrads were pounced upon by swaggering elder students

COIMBRA

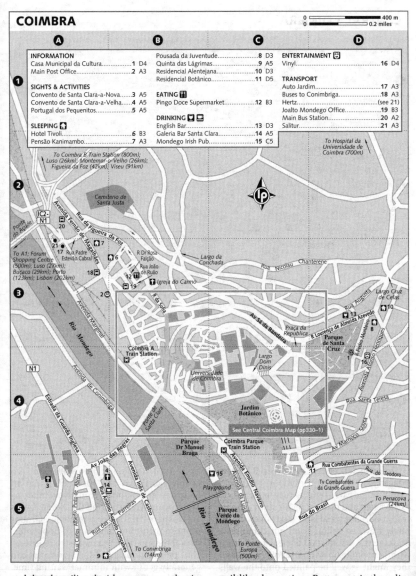

and then humiliated without mercy – that is, unless they leapt their way home like mountain goats in order to avoid them.

From the courtyard gate take the stairway on the right up to the rather grand **Sala dos Capelos** (Graduates' Hall), a former examination room hung with dark portraits of Portugal's kings and heavy patchwork,

quiltlike decoration. Better yet is the adjacent catwalk, which affords visitors excellent city views.

Back outside, take a peek to the left below the clock tower, where you'll find the entrance to the fanciful **Capela de São Miguel**, an ornate baroque chapel with a brightly painted ceiling and a gilded baroque organ.

THE BEIRAS

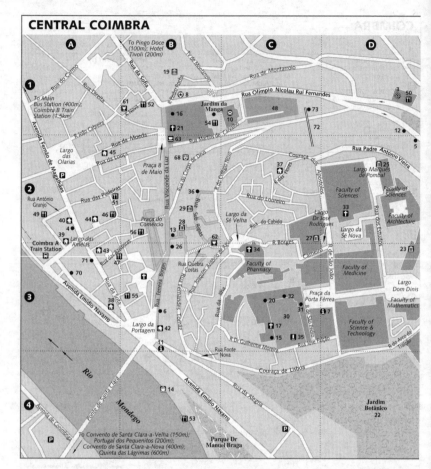

CENTRAL COIMBRA

However, all else pales before **Biblioteca Joanina** (João V Library) next door. A gift from João V in the early 18th century, it seems too extravagant and distracting for study with its rosewood, ebony and jacaranda tables, elaborately frescoed ceilings and gilt chinoiserie bookshelves. Its 300,000 ancient books deal with law, philosophy and theology, though they might as well be painted onto the walls for all the study they receive now.

Admission to both the Biblioteca Joanina and the Sala dos Capelos is €6/4.20/4.20 for adults/seniors/students, or you can visit just one for €3.50/2.45/2.45. Entry to the Capela de São Miguel is free.

Visitors are only admitted in small numbers and on a timetable (from 9am to 7pm from April to October; from 9.30am to 5pm Monday to Friday and 10.30am to 4pm on Saturday and Sunday from November to March), and you may find that some rooms are closed during degree ceremonies. Groups of more than four may want to book a few days ahead by emailing a request to reservas@ci.uc.pt; individuals and smaller groups can generally get in with minimal waiting time. The **ticket office** (Map pp330-1; ☎ 239 859 884) is adjacent to the municipal *turismo* (tourist office), in the square just outside the Porta Férrea.

Sé Velha

Coimbra's stunning **old cathedral** (☎ 239 825 273; Largo da Sé Velha; admission free; ☑ 10am-1pm & 2-6pm

Mon-Thu, 10am-1pm Fri, 10am-5pm Sat) is considered to be one of the finest examples of Romanesque architecture in all of Portugal. Its crenellated exterior and narrow, slit-like lower windows serve as reminders of the nation's embattled early days, when the Moors were still a threat. Since its construction in the late 12th century, the building has been only slightly altered. Even the 16th-century Renaissance portal in the northern wall is so eroded you hardly notice it. The austere majesty of the interior is broken only by a 16th-century gilded altarpiece.

Museu da Ciência

This wonderful **museum** (☎ 239 854 350; www .museudaciencia.pt; Largo Marquês de Pombal; adult/student/ senior €3/1.50/1.50; ☺ 10am-6pm Tue-Sun) occupies a centuries-old former monastery converted by Pombal into the university's chemical engineering building. With a couple of awards under its belt since opening in 2006, it features intriguing state-of-the-art interactive science displays coexisting with 18th-century lab sinks. Don't miss the frogs-in-underwear display, the giant glowing globe in a room paved with medieval stones, or the psychedelic insect's-eye view of flowers. Displays are English/Portuguese bilingual.

Museu Nacional Machado de Castro

Housed in a former bishop's palace, with a 16th-century loggia overlooking the *sé velha* and the old town, this **museum** (☎ 239 823 727;

www.ipmuseus.pt; Largo Dr José Rodrigues) houses one of Portugal's most important collections of 14th- to 16th-century sculpture. Unfortunately, this gem will remain closed for renovations until 2010.

BAIXA & AROUND

Igreja de Santa Cruz

From the trendy shops out on Praça 8 de Maio, this **church** (☎ 239 822 941; adult/student/senior €2.50/1.50/1.50; ☉ 9am-noon & 2-5pm Mon-Sat, 4-5pm Sun) plunges you back to Manueline and Renaissance times. Step through the Renaissance porch and flamboyant 18th-century arch to discover some of the Coimbra School's finest work, including an ornate pulpit and the elaborate tombs (probably carved by Nicolas Chanterène) of Portugal's first kings, Afonso Henriques and Sancho I. The most striking Manueline work is in the restrained 16th-century cloister.

Behind the church is the Jardim da Manga (once part of the cloister) and its curious fountain: a lemon-yellow, four-buttressed affair.

Núcleo da Cidade Muralhada/Torre de Almedina

Housed in the medieval tower directly above the Arco de Almedina, this new **museum** (☎ 239 833 771; cidade.muralhada@cm-coimbra.pt; Pátio do Castilho; adult/student/senior €1.70/1.05/1.05; ☉ 11am-1pm & 2-7pm Tue-Sat Apr-Sep, 10am-1pm & 2-6pm Tue-Sat Oct-Mar) displays a plaster reproduction of Coimbra's old town layout, complete with castle. A multilingual audiovisual presentation traces the fate of the many towers that used to line Coimbra's walls, each lit in red on the map as its story is told. There are fine city views upstairs, but the real fun is looking down through the *matacães* (dog-killers), big holes cut in the watchtower's stone floor, through which hot oil was traditionally poured on unsuspecting enemies below.

Museu da Cidade Edifício Chiado

This sunlit confection of rippling, coiling iron opened in 1910 as Coimbra's largest commercial emporium. It now houses a **gallery** (☎ 239 840 754; chiado@cm-coimbra.pt; Rua Ferreira Borges; adult/student/senior €1.70/1.05/1.05; ☉ 11am-7pm Tue-Sat Apr-Sep, 10am-6pm Tue-Sat Oct-Mar, closed for lunch1-2pm Sat year-round) with a permanent collection of paintings, sculpture, ceramics, furniture and splendid silverware donated by local collector José Carlos Telo de Morais, plus temporary exhibitions.

CAV (Centro de Artes Visuais)

This **museum** (Centre of Visual Arts; ☎ 239 826 178; Pátio da Inquisição; admission free; ☉ 2-7pm Tue-Sun) hosts cutting-edge contemporary photographic and video exhibitions within a whitewashed cloister that once served as a prison during the Spanish Inquisition. It's hidden in the backstreets west of Igreja de Santa Cruz.

PRAÇA DA REPÚBLICA & AROUND

Leafy Praça da República is the unofficial student social centre. The surrounding neighbourhood, laid out in the 19th century and still dominated by prim bourgeois homes of the period, is a relaxing break from the high density of both the university and the Baixa area.

Casa Museu Bissaya Barreto

Bissaya Barreto was a local surgeon, scholar and obsessive hoarder of fine arts, and his handsome, late-19th-century mansion has been turned into a **museum** (☎ 239 853 800; www.fbb.pt, in Portuguese; Rua Infantaria 23; admission €2.50; ☉ 3-6pm Tue-Sun Apr-Oct, 3-6pm Tue-Fri Nov-Mar). A guide (not necessarily English-speaking) accompanies guests through rooms jam-packed with Portuguese sculpture and painting, Chinese porcelain, old *azulejos* and period furniture.

Jardim Botânico

A serene place to catch your breath, the lovely **botanical garden** (☎ 239 855 233; ☉ 9am-8pm Apr-Sep, 9am-5.30pm Oct-Mar) sits in the shadow of the 16th-century Aqueduto de São Sebastião. Founded by the Marquês de Pombal, the gardens combine formal flowerbeds, meandering paths and elegant fountains. The green-fingered can also visit the lush **greenhouses** (admission €0.50) and the adjacent **Museu Botânico** (Botanical Museum; ☎ 239 855 210; adult/under 6yr/student & senior €2/free/1.50; ☉ 9am-noon & 2-5pm Mon-Fri).

ALONG & ACROSS THE RIVER

In a kind of ecclesiastical counterweight to the university, a cluster of convents, together with several other sights, sits on the far side of the Rio Mondego. A new pedestrian bridge connects these west-bank attractions to one of the city's prettiest green spaces, stretching south from the historic centre along the east side of the river.

Convento de Santa Clara-a-Velha

Slowly being cleared of the river ooze that has drowned it since the 17th century, this Gothic **convent** (Map p329; ☎ 239 801 160; admission €3; ☽ tours 10am, 11am, 3pm & 4pm Tue-Sun, plus 5pm & 6pm Apr-Sep) was closed for renovation at the time of writing. Founded in 1330 by the saintly Dona Isabel, Dom Dinis' wife, it served as her final resting place until flooding and mud forced her to move uphill to Convento de Santa Clara-a-Nova (below).

Convento de Santa Clara-a-Nova

Begun on higher ground in the 17th century to replace its flooded twin, this **convent** (Map p329; ☎ 239 441 674; admission cloister €1.50; ☽ 8.30am-6pm) is devoted almost entirely to the saintly Isabel's memory. Aisle panels tell her life story, while her solid-silver casket is enshrined above the altar. Even her clothes hang in the sacristy. Her statue is the focus of the Festa da Rainha Santa (p334).

Quinta das Lágrimas

Legend says Dona Inês de Castro met her grisly end in the gardens of this private estate. It's now a deluxe hotel (see p335; Map p329), although anyone can take a turn about the **gardens** (admission €2; ☽ 10am-7pm Tue-Sun Apr-Oct, 10am-5pm Thu-Sun Nov-Mar, closed Jan) and track down the Fonte dos Amores (Lovers' Fountain), which marks the spot where the king's unwitting mistress was struck down. Also note the sequoia tree planted by English hero the Duke of Wellington.

Parque Dr Manuel Braga & Parque Verde do Mondego

Lovely green spaces stretch south from the Ponte de Santa Clara along the eastern bank of the river. Parque Dr Manuel Braga provides a haven of serene shade under stately rows of old sycamores, while the newer Parque Verde do Mondego, opened in June 2004, features riverfront bars and eateries, a pedestrian bridge across the Rio Mondego and a small playground for kids.

Activities

Several organisations offer opportunities for canoeing, rafting and other outdoor sports in the region surrounding Coimbra.
Capitão Dureza (off Map p329; ☎ 239 918 148; www.capitaodureza.com; Rua Principal 64C, Penacova) This well-regarded outfit organises rafting, canoeing trips, biking, hiking and more.
Geoaventura (off Map p329; ☎ 914982651, 919485976; www.geoaventura.pt, in Portuguese; Penacova) Conducts rafting, kayaking, rock-climbing and more.
O Pioneiro do Mondego (off Map p329; ☎ 239 478 385; www.opioneirodomondego.com; Penacova; ☽ Jun-Sep, call 8-10am, 1-3pm & 8-10pm) Rents out kayaks for paddling the Rio Mondego between Penacova and Coimbra, a 25km, four-hour trip costing €20 per person; a shorter version to Torres de Mondego, with transport back to Coimbra, costs the same.

Coimbra for Children

Portugal dos Pequenitos (Map p329; ☎ 239 801 170; Rossio de Santa Clara; adult/under 5yr/5-12yr/senior €9/free/4.50/4.50; ☽ 9am-8pm Jun–mid-Sep, 10am-5pm mid-Sep–Feb, 10am-7pm mid-Sep–May), the brainchild of local collector Bissaya Barreto, is an impossibly cute theme park where kids clamber over, into and through doll's-house versions of Portugal's most famous monuments, while parents clutch cameras at the ready. There's an extra charge to visit the marginally interesting mini-museums of marine life, clothing and furniture. You can also hop aboard one of the frequent river trips with Basófias (p334).

Coimbra is short on children's play spaces. The best bet near the city centre is the small playground in the Parque Verde do Mondego. Across the river, via the new pedestrian bridge, there's also a fun zip line. Both can be incorporated into a walking route from Largo da Portagem to Portugal dos Pequenitos.

Tours

BUS TOURS

Carristur (Map pp330-1; ☎ 239 801 100; www.carristur.pt, in Portuguese; adult/child €8/4; ☽ Sat & Sun mid-Mar–mid-May, Tue-Sun mid-May–Oct) runs hour-long hop-on, hop-off bus tours of Coimbra with recorded multilingual commentary. The double-decker open-top buses originate near the *turismo* at Largo da Portagem. The bus ticket (available at the *turismo* and SMTUC ticket office, as well as at some local hotels) entitles you to a Basófias boat tour (see p334) and free admission to municipal museums.

THE BEIRAS

QUEEN-SAINT ISABEL

One of Portugal's most popular saints, Isabel is most often depicted with a scattering of roses falling across her garments. Legend has it that one day while she was bringing food to the poor, her less-than-saintly husband (Dinis I) accused her of stealing food from the royal kitchens. When the king angrily demanded to see the contents of her apron, out fell nothing but flowers. Rainha Isabel – not surprisingly, given the tenor of the apocryphal tale – is credited with founding homes for abused wives and abandoned children. When eldest son Afonso challenged Dom Dinis for the throne, Isabel rode on horseback between the two lines of opposing forces, daring both father and son to attack her first.

BOAT TOURS

Basófias (Map pp330-1; ☎ 969830664; www.basofias.com, in Portuguese; ⌚ Tue-Sun) runs boat trips (€8, 55 minutes) on the Rio Mondego. They depart from beside Parque Dr Manuel Braga hourly from 3pm to 7pm May to September, and at 3pm and 4pm only from October to April.

Festivals & Events

QUEIMA DAS FITAS

Coimbra's biggest bash celebrates the end of the academic year in great style. The festivities take place every year during the first week in May.

FESTA DA RAINHA SANTA

Held around 4 July in even-numbered years, this festival commemorates Santa Isabel (see boxed text, above). A Thursday-night candlelit procession carries her statue from the Convento de Santa Clara-a-Nova across the Ponte de Santa Clara to Largo da Portagem and through the streets of Coimbra to Igreja do Carmo; a second procession the following Sunday returns her to the convent. The festival also coincides with the Festa da Cidade (Town Festival), celebrated with music, folk dancing and fireworks.

OTHER EVENTS

Coimbra hosts international festivals of music in July and magic in mid-September (Coimbra is the home of Luís de Matus, Portugal's most famous magician).

From late June to mid-September, there's folk music and dancing in Praça 8 de Maio and open-air fado at the Arco de Almedina and along Rua Quebra Costas.

Sleeping

BUDGET

Pousada da Juventude (Map p329; ☎ 239 822 955; coimbra@movijovem.pt; Rua Dr António Henriques Seco 14; dm €11, d with/without bathroom €28/26, all incl breakfast) Occupying a fine old house in a quiet, leafy neighbourhood, Coimbra's HI-affiliated hostel is 500m northeast of Praça da República. No meals other than breakfast are served, but there are self-catering kitchen facilities. Do your best to avoid the gloomy basement dorms. From Coimbra A station take northbound bus 6, 7 or 29.

Pensão Kanimambo (Map p329; ☎ 239 827 151; fax 239 828 408; Av Fernão de Magalhães 484; s/d from €12/22, with bathroom from €16/27; 🔁) In a '70s concrete apartment block with decor to match, this cheapie offers clean, basic rooms to rest a weary head just arrived from the nearby bus station.

Pensão-Restaurante Flôr de Coimbra (Map pp330-1; ☎ 239 823 865; flordecoimbrahr@sapo.pt; Rua do Poço 5; s/d/tr €30/35/40, with bathroom €40/45/50) This once-grand 19th-century home with its own restaurant (mains around €10) offers loads of character in a great location. It's clean and friendly, if occasionally a bit behind on maintenance. The low-ceilinged upstairs rooms, popular with Fátima pilgrims (see p21) and partially occupied by foreign students during the academic year, have wi-fi, shared bathrooms and a community kitchen for self-catering. Main floor rooms are larger, with private bathrooms.

MIDRANGE

Residencial Domus (Map pp330-1; ☎ 239 828 584; residencialdomus@sapo.pt; Rua Adelino Veiga 62; s/d €30/40; 🔁) Domus is a family-run place in a quiet pedestrian shopping zone near Coimbra A. It has clean, well-maintained rooms, all with wi-fi. Upstairs rooms at the front get plenty of natural light.

Pensão Residencial Larbelo (Map pp330-1; ☎ 239 829 092; residencialarbelo@sapo.pt; Largo da Portagem 33; s/d €30/40; 🔁) In a pleasant and impeccably maintained 19th-century building, Larbelo is bang in the centre and boasts high-ceilinged rooms with wooden floors and modern furnishings. Front rooms with windows opening onto the Largo da Portagem are especially nice.

Residencial Moeda (Map pp330–1; ☎ 239 824 784; www.residencialmoeda.com; Rua da Moeda 81; s/d incl breakfast €35/40, €30/40 without breakfast; 🔀) On a narrow Baixa street above the owner's hole-in-the-wall seashell-and-charms shop, this friendly place offers snug but modern rooms at good value. Two 2nd-floor rooms have small balconies, and the elevator is an unexpected plus.

Residencial Botânico (Map p329; ☎ 239 714 824; residencialbotanico@mail.telepac.net; Bairro de São José 15; s/d €35/45; 🔀) This irreproachably kept guest house sits at the bottom of Alameda Dr Júlio Henriques. It has spacious, elegantly sparse rooms, including some family suites. There's wi-fi in the lobby and double-paned glass to keep out street noise.

Residencial Alentejana (Map p329; ☎ 239 825 903; www.residencialalentejana.com; Rua Dr António Henriques Seco 1; s/d €35/55; 🔀) Worth the uphill walk, this prominent old town house offers wood-panelled, high-ceilinged older rooms, plus some less charming but still comfortable newer ones.

Hotel Bragança (Map pp330–1; ☎ 239 822 171; www.hotel-braganca.com; Largo das Ameias 10; s/d/tr/q from €35/55/70/85; 🔀) Unpromising on the outside, this '60s concrete hotel has large and rather elegant rooms, all with parquet floors and many with river views.

Pensão Residencial Antunes (Map pp330–1; ☎ 239 854 720; residencialantunes.pt.vu; Rua Castro Matoso 8; s/d/tw €36/46/50; 🅿) A few steps from the aqueduct and botanical gardens, this large old guest house in a 19th-century building offers charming, creaky doubles, wi-fi in the downstairs parlour, and that Coimbra rarity: free, off-street parking.

ourpick Casa Pombal Guesthouse (Map pp330–1; ☎ 239 835 175; www.casapombal.com; Rua das Flores 18; d with/without bathroom €62/52, all incl breakfast; 🕑 closed mid-Dec–mid-Jan) Hidden down a narrow lane near the university, this winning, Dutch-run guest house squeezes tons of charm into a small space. The cosy wood-floored rooms are simple, fresh and brightly coloured, and a couple of attic eyries boast superb views. The friendly owners provide multilingual advice about local cultural events, plus an ample morning buffet in the gorgeous blue-tiled breakfast room. Singles cost €5 less.

Hotel Oslo (Map pp330–1; ☎ 239 829 071/2/3; www.hotel-oslo.web.pt; Av Fernão de Magalhães 25; s/d/tr/ste €55/70/90/110; 🅿 🔀 💻) This otherwise bland, modern hotel block redeems itself with well-maintained rooms, a free parking garage, satellite TV, double-paned windows and a popular 5th-floor bar with views up to the university. Newly remodelled 'superior' rooms (€85) have larger bathrooms, big-screen TVs and balconies.

TOP END

Hotel Tivoli (Map p329; ☎ 239 858 300; www.tivolihotels.com; Rua João Machado; s/d €85/95, superior d €150; 🅿 🔀 💻 🈂) If you require unimpeachable 'business-class' comforts and are willing to give on aesthetics, consider the Tivoli. Occupying an ugly modern building in a rather unappealing and trafficky stretch of the Baixa, it has huge rooms with all the expected frills, a pool and a small gym. Superior rooms upstairs were completely remodelled in 2008 with big-screen LCD TVs, broadband wi-fi and (ahem!) electric blinds.

Hotel Astória (Map pp330–1; ☎ 239 853 020; www.almeidahotels.com; Av Emídio Navarro 21; s/d/ste €90/110/135; 🅿 🔀 💻) The Astória's unmistakable art-nouveau facade contemplates the river and Largo da Portagem. It has bags of personality and professional staff, though some of the quiet, plush rooms are a tad dog-eared. The round tower suites (room numbers ending in 9) score fabulous panoramic views from the Mondego up to the university.

Quinta das Lágrimas (Map p329; ☎ 239 802 380; www.quintadaslagrimas.pt; Rua António Augusto Gonçalves; s/d from €149/177; 🅿 🔀 🈂) This splendid historical palace is now one of Portugal's most enchanting upper-crust hotels. Choose between richly furnished rooms in the old palace, or Scandinavian-style minimalist rooms in the modern annexe – complete with Jacuzzi. A few rooms look out onto the garden where Dona Inês de Castro reputedly met her tragic end (see p333).

Eating

BUDGET

Mercado Municipal Dom Pedro V (Map pp330–1; Rua Olímpio Nicolau Rui Fernandes; 🕑 Mon-Sat) This modern market is a colourful stop for self-caterers. It's full of lively fruit and vegetable stalls and butcher shops displaying Portuguese cuts of meat, hooves, claws and all. Watch out for the bunny eyes!

Porta Larga (Map pp330–1; ☎ 239 823 619; Rua das Padeiras 35; sandwiches €3.75; 🕑 8.30am-8pm Mon-Sat) For a quick snack with a hefty dose of local

THE BEIRAS

flavour, António's *sandes de leitão* (roast pork sandwich) can't be beat, although it's best avoided if you're squeamish about little piggies turning on spits.

Adega Paço dos Condes (Map pp330-1; ☎ 239 825 605; Rua do Paço do Conde 1; mains €4-7; ☽ lunch & dinner Mon-Sat) Usually crowded with students and Coimbra locals, this straightforward grill is one of the city's best affordable eateries.

Restaurante Jardim da Manga (Map pp330-1; ☎ 239 829 156; Rua Olímpio Nicolau Rui Fernandes; dishes €5-7.50; ☽ lunch & dinner Sun-Fri) Student-friendly and tailored to tight budgets, this cafeteria-style restaurant serves up tasty meat and fish dishes, with pleasant outdoor seating beside the Jardim da Manga fountain.

Cheap and filling cafeteria food abounds at the university's student **cantinas** (Map pp330-1; AAC, Av Sá da Bandeira; meals €3.70; ☽ lunch & dinner), off the courtyard of the AAC – one upstairs at the back (southern) end and one down a flight of steps on the eastern side. The downstairs restaurant generally has better food but is also more likely to ask to see student ID. There's another cantina nearby on the campus proper, just off Largo Dom Dinis. This one tends to have longer hours and is also most likely to admit nonstudents.

Coimbra has many supermarkets. Two options:

Minipreço (Map pp330-1; Rua António Granjo 6C; ☽ 9am-8pm Mon-Sat, 9am-1pm & 3-7pm Sun)

Pingo Doce (Map p329; Rua João de Ruão; ☽ 8.30am-8.30pm)

MIDRANGE

Restaurante Democrática (Map pp330-1; ☎ 239 823 784; Travessa da Rua Nova 5; mains €5-10; ☽ lunch & dinner Mon-Sat) A down-to-business, family-friendly place offering good-value standards, Democrática is a Coimbra classic and always filled with hungry students.

Churrasqueira Giro (Map pp330-1; ☎ 239 833 020; Rua das Azeiteiras 39; mains €5-8; ☽ lunch & dinner Mon-Sat) This back-alley place serves wonderful traditional Portuguese fare in a pleasant tiled dining room.

Molho de Brócolos (Map pp330-1; ☎ 966645913; Galerias Avenida, Av Sá da Bandeira 33, 2nd fl, Loja 230; mains €6-7; ☽ noon-2pm & 8-10pm Mon-Sam; ⓥ) Feijoada with vegan 'sausage'? Miso soup in Portugal? It's enough to make a vegetarian swoon! Hidden on the 4th floor of a movie theatre-turned-shopping mall, this new ar-

rival serves reasonably priced organic and vegetarian food.

Restaurante Zé Neto (Map pp330-1; ☎ 239 826 786; Rua das Azeiteiras 8; mains €6-9; ☽ lunch & dinner Mon-Sat) This marvellous family-run place specialises in homemade Portuguese standards, including *cabrito* (kid). Come in the late morning and you'll catch the elderly owner tapping out the menu on a typewriter of similar vintage.

Restaurante Zé Manel (Map pp330-1; ☎ 239 823 790; Beco do Forno 12; mains €7-9; ☽ lunch & dinner Mon-Fri, lunch Sat) Tucked down a nondescript alleyway, this little gem, which is papered with scholarly doodles and scribbled poems, is easy to miss. Despite its location, it's highly popular, so come early or be ready to wait. Try the good *feijoada á leitão* (a stew of beans and suckling pig).

Restaurante Italia (Map pp330-1; ☎ 239 838 863; Parque Dr Manuel de Braga; mains €7-14; ☽ noon-midnight) Cheery Italia serves reasonably good Italian food, but what really draws the crowds is its incomparable location. The sunny glass-walled dining room is cantilevered out over the Rio Mondego, while breezy outdoor tables bask in the shade of giant sycamores in the adjacent riverside park.

ⓞⓤⓡⓟⓘⓒⓚ Zé Carioca (Map pp330-1; ☎ 239 835 450; Av Sá da Bandeira 89; mains €13-15; ☽ lunch & dinner) Set in a series of colourfully decorated rooms in a handsome old town house, this Brazilian eatery is both relaxed and elegant. The grilled meats, *moqueca de camarão* (shrimp stewed with coconut milk, tomatoes and cilantro) and caipirinhas are all superb. The weekday per-kilo lunch buffet is a good deal, as is the *rodizio de carnes* on Sunday afternoon (€11.90 for all the meat you can eat and still waddle home).

Drinking

Praça da República is the epicentre of student nightlife. The big nights are Thursday to Saturday – but during university term time, any night is game.

CAFES

Café Teatro (Map pp330-1; Praça da República; ☽ 10am-1am Mon-Fri, 2pm-1am Sat) With huge windows, minimalist decor and a long zinc bar overlooking leafy Praça da República, the cafe in the upstairs lobby of the university theatre is the place where alternative types congregate for their caffeine fix or first drink of the evening. Ticket-holders only during performances.

ourpick **Café Santa Cruz** (Map pp330-1; ☎ 239 833 617; Praça 8 de Maio; ✆ Mon-Sat 9am-late) Few cafes in Portugal offer such an atmospheric backdrop. The interior, set in a dramatically beautiful high-vaulted former chapel, features stained-glass windows and graceful stone arch, while the outdoor patio area affords one of the city's best vantage points over the popular Praça 8 de Maio. Popular with tourists and locals alike, the cafe periodically hosts free evening music events and talks. You'll pay a bit extra here for the atmosphere, but it's worth it.

Cartola Esplanada Bar (Map pp330-1; Praça da República; ✆ 8am-2am Mon-Sat; 9am-1am Sun) Equally popular for morning coffee and late-night beers, this perennially packed cafe with a great plaza-side location is the ideal place for a spot of student-watching.

Galeria Bar Santa Clara (Map p329; ☎ 239 441 657; Rua António Augusto Gonçalves; ✆ 2pm-2am Sun-Thu, 2pm-3am Fri & Sat) Arty tearoom by day and chilled-out bar at night, this terrific place has good art on the walls, a series of sunny rooms and a fine, riverfront terrace.

BARS

Bar Quebra Costas (Map pp330-1; ☎ 239 821 661; www .quebra.eu; Rua Quebra Costas 45-49; ✆ noon-4am Mon-Sat year-round, plus Sun Jun-Sep) In the perfect position to sip a cold beer as you watch people puff and pant up the Quebra Costas, this Coimbra classic has a great terrace as well as a recently updated interior with sharp art on the walls. Thursday through Saturday there's music into the wee hours, from chilled-out electronica to jazz (see website for details).

Feitoconceito (Map pp330-1; Rua Alexandre Herculano 16A; ✆ 2pm-3am Mon-Sat) Entered through the Tabacaria Pavão downstairs, this ultrahip hideaway near Praça da República is comprised of three colourfully lit high-ceilinged rooms. The intimate vibe is best appreciated when you're sitting cross-legged on cushions at the low tables in the innermost room. Beers cost €0.70, and caipirinhas are €14 for a tray of eight. The vintage barbershop and design store next door are equally fun.

Mondego Irish Pub (Map p329; ☎ 239 837 092; Parque Verde do Mondego; ✆ noon-3am Sun-Thu, noon-4am Fri & Sat) It may be a tad overpriced, but you can't argue with this pub's prime riverfront location, Guinness and Kilkenny on draught and live music from midnight to 3am three nights a week.

English Bar (Map p329; Rua Lourenço de Almeida Azevedo 24; ✆ Mon-Sat) This British-style pub serves light meals downstairs and offers a bar in which to knock back draught Murphy's upstairs. There's a very popular Latin night on Wednesdays.

Café Tropical (Map pp330-1; Praça da República 35; ✆ 10am-2am Mon-Sat) Another bare-bones student place with pleasant outdoor seating, bohemian wall decor, cheap beers and lively crowds – a favourite place to start out the night.

AAC pub (Map pp330-1; Av Sá da Bandeira; ✆ 9.30am-4am) Join the black-cape-clad students at their student-union bar, where beers are under €1 and everyone is welcome.

Bar Diligência (Map pp330-1; ☎ 239 827 667; Rua Nova 30; ✆ 6pm-2am) This bar hosts live music of varying quality, including occasional fado, from about 10.30pm most nights.

Entertainment

MUSIC
If Lisbon represents the heart of Portuguese fado music, Coimbra is its head. The local style is more cerebral than the Lisbon variety, with a greater emphasis on *guitarra*-led instrumental pieces. Its adherents are also staunchly protective: a fracas erupted in Coimbra in 1996 when a woman named Manuela Bravo decided to record a CD of Coimbra fado, which is traditionally sung only by men.

Free fado performances take place periodically at Café Santa Cruz (left) – consult the weekly schedule of events posted at the cafe. Free open-air fado can also be heard at Arco de Almedina (p328), nightly in summer at 9pm. You can also hear live music most nights at other venues.

ourpick **Á Capella** (Map pp330-1; ☎ 239 833 985; www.acapella.com.pt; Rua do Corpo de Deus; admission incl 1 drink €10; ✆ 10pm-2am) A tiny, 14th-century chapel transformed into a candlelit cocktail lounge, Á Capella regularly hosts the city's most renowned fado musicians. The setting is as intimate as the music itself, with heart-rendingly good acoustics. Be forewarned that these shows cater directly to a tourist crowd, but the atmosphere and music are both superb.

NIGHTCLUBS

Via Latina (Map pp330-1; ☎ 916433432; Rua Almeida Garrett 1; ☼ midnight-6am Tue-Sat) Students swear by the DJs at this simple, sweaty, excellent dance club. Fridays are particularly good, when there's occasional live music.

Vinyl (Map p329; Av Afonso Henriques 43; ☼ midnight-4am Tue-Sat) Another perennial favourite, where a mostly student crowd does the soft shake to predictable pop tunes.

Getting There & Away

BUS

From the main **bus station** (Map p329; Av Fernão de Magalhães), **Rede Expressos** (☎ 239 827 081) runs at least a dozen buses daily to Lisbon (€12, 2½ hours) and to Porto (€10.70, 1½ hours), with almost as many to Braga (€11.90, 2¾ hours) and to Faro (€21.50, six to seven hours). There's also regular service (more frequent in summer) that runs to Seia (€10, 1¾ hours), Guarda (€11.80, three hours) and other points around the Parque Natural da Serra da Estrela.

Joalto Mondego (Map p329; ☎ 239 820 141; Rua João de Ruão 18; ☼ 9am-12.30pm, 2-6.30pm Mon-Fri) has bus service to the Roman ruins at nearby Conímbriga (opposite).

CAR

The local branch of the **Automóvel Club de Portugal** (ACP; Map pp330-1; ☎ 239 852 020; Av Emídio Navarro 6) is by Coimbra A.

Several car-rental agencies are concentrated just south of the bus terminal. These include:

Auto Jardim (Map p329; ☎ 239 827 347; Rua Abel Dias Urbano 6)

Hertz (Map p329; ☎ 239 834 750; Edifício Tricana, Rua Padre Estevão Cabral)

Salitur (Map p329; ☎ 239 820 594; Edifício Tricana, Rua Padre Estevão Cabral)

TRAIN

Most trains stop only at Coimbra B. Cross the platform for quick, free connections to more-central Coimbra A (called just 'Coimbra' on timetables). There's no left-luggage office at either station.

Coimbra is linked by regular Alfa Pendular (AP) and *intercidade* (IC) trains to Lisbon (AP/IC €20.50/15, two/2½ hours) and Porto (€15/10.50, 1¼/1½ hours). Additional *inter-regional* (IR) services cost slightly less but take at least 30 minutes longer. IR trains also run about four times a day to Luso/Buçaco (€1.61,

30 minutes) and at least hourly to Figueira da Foz (€1.88, one hour).

Getting Around

If you come by car, prepare for snarled traffic and scarce parking. The best free parking near the Baixa is on the west bank of the river, in a dirt lot just across Ponte de Santa Clara from Largo da Portagem. Nearer the university, free street parking is available on side streets around Praça da República. If you're willing to pay, look for the blue 'P' signs in the Baixa district, and buy your ticket from the machine. Make sure you're legal, as enforcement is strict. There are also parking garages along Avenidas Fernão de Magalhães and Emídio Navarro.

BICYCLE

For mountain bike rental, **Centro Velocipédico de Sangalhos** (Map pp330-1; ☎ 239 824 646; Rua da Sota 23; ☼ 9am-1pm & 2-7pm Mon-Fri, 9am-1pm Sat) charges €7.50 per day.

BUS

Between them, buses 27, 28 and 29 run about every half-hour from the main bus station and the Coimbra B train station to Praça da República. Bus 40 makes an anticlockwise loop that takes in the stations as well as the Baixa district.

You can purchase multiuse tickets (three/11 trips €1.90/6), also usable on the *elevador* (see below), at the **SMTUC office** (Map pp330-1; ☎ 239 801 100; www.smtuc.pt, in Portuguese; Largo do Mercado; ☼ 7.30am-7.30pm Mon-Fri, 8am-1pm Sat) at the foot of the *elevador*, at official kiosks and also at some *tabacarias* (tobacconists-cum-newsagents). Tickets bought on board cost €1.50 per trip.

You'll also see *patufinhas* (electric mini-buses) crawling around pedestrian areas in the centre of Coimbra, between Baixa and Alta Coimbra and through the medieval heart of the city. These accept the same tickets as other SMTUC buses.

ELEVADOR DO MERCADO

The **elevador** (Map pp330-1; ☼ 7.30am-10pm Mon-Sat, 10am-10pm Sun) – a combination of elevator, walkway and funicular between the market and the university – can save you a tedious uphill climb. See under 'Bus', above, for details of tickets, which you punch once for each ascent or descent. You can't buy tickets at the top.

AROUND COIMBRA
Conimbriga

Hidden amid humble olive orchards in the rolling country southwest of Coimbra, Conimbriga boasts Portugal's most extensive and best-preserved Roman ruins, and ranks with the best-preserved sites on the entire Iberian Peninsula. It tells the poignant tale of a town that, after centuries of security, was first split in two by quickly erected walls and then entirely abandoned as the Roman Empire disintegrated.

HISTORY

Though Conimbriga owes its celebrity to the Romans, the site actually dates back to Celtic times (*briga* is a Celtic term for a defended area). However, when the Romans settled here in the 1st century AD, it blossomed into a major city on the route from Lisbon (Olisipo) to Braga (Bracara Augusta). Its prosperity is revealed by well-to-do mansions floored with elaborate mosaics and scattered with fountains.

In the 3rd century the townsfolk, threatened by invading tribes, desperately threw up a huge defensive wall right through the town centre, abandoning the residential area. But this wasn't enough to stop the Suevi seizing the town in 468. Inhabitants fled to nearby Aeminius (Coimbra) – thereby saving Conimbriga from destruction.

SIGHTS
Museum

To get your head around Conimbriga's history, begin at the small but well-organised and informative **museum** (☎ 239 944 100; admission incl ruins adult/under 14yr/student, teacher & senior €4/free/2, admission free 10am-1pm Sun; ☼ 10am-6pm Tue-Sun Oct-May, 9am-8pm Tue-Sun Jun-Sep). Displays present every aspect of Roman life from mosaics to medallions. There's a sunny cafe-restaurant at the back.

Ruins

The sprawling **Roman ruins** (☼ 10am-6pm daily Oct-May, 9am-8pm Jun-Sep), included in museum admission, tell a vivid story. On the one hand, their domesticity is obvious, with elaborate mosaics, heated baths and trickling fountains that evoke delightful, toga-clad dalliances. But smack through the middle of this scene runs a massive defensive wall, splitting and cannibalising nearby buildings in its hasty erection to fend off raids.

It's the disproportionately large wall that will first draw your attention, followed by the patchwork of exceptional mosaic floors below it. Here you'll find the so-called **Casa dos Repuxos** (House of Fountains); though partly destroyed by the wall, it contains cool pond-gardens, fountains and truly extraordinary mosaics showing the four seasons and various hunting scenes.

The site's most important **villa**, on the other side of the wall, is said to have belonged to one Cantaber, whose wife and children were seized by the Suevi in an attack in 465. It's a palace of a place, with baths, pools and a sophisticated underground heating system.

Excavations continue in the outer areas. Eye-catching features include the remains of a 3km-long aqueduct, which led up to a hilltop bathing complex, and a forum, once surrounded by covered porticoes.

GETTING THERE & AWAY

You can catch a **Joalto** (☎ 239 823 769) bus from Coimbra directly to the ruins site (€2, 30 minutes) at 9am or 9.35am (only 9.35am on weekends). Buses depart for the return trip at 1pm and 5pm (only 5pm on weekends). Joalto also runs buses to Condeixa (€1.85) about every half-hour (less often on weekends). But note that from Condeixa to the site it's a poorly signposted 2km walk, some of it along the hard shoulder of a high-speed road.

Luso & Mata Nacional do Buçaco

A retreat from the world for almost 2000 years, the slopes of the Serra do Buçaco are now home to the 105-hectare Mata Nacional do Buçaco (or Bussaco). Harbouring an astounding 700 plant species, from huge Mexican cedars to tree-sized ferns, this national forest is equally fecund in terms of the poetry it has inspired. Generations of Coimbra's literary types have enshrined the forest in the national imagination with breathless hymns to its mystical marriage of natural and spiritual beauty.

The high stone walls that for centuries have encircled the forest have no doubt helped reinforce its sense of mystery. And in the midst of the forest stands a royal palace completed in 1907; despite the extravagance of its fairy-tale neo-Manueline facade, the dynasty fell just three years later.

Outside the forest walls lies the old-fashioned little spa town of Luso, whose waters are considered a balm for everything from gout to asthma. The forest and spa make an easy day trip from Coimbra. If you want to linger, Luso has a handful of *residenciais* (guest houses). Those with the wherewithal can stay at the astonishing royal palace, right in the forest (see right).

HISTORY

The Luso and Buçaco area probably served as a Christian refuge as early as the 2nd century AD, although the earliest known hermitage was founded in the 6th century by Benedictine monks. In 1628 Carmelite monks embarked on an extensive program of forestation. They planted exotic species, laid cobbled paths and enclosed the forest within high stone walls. The forest grew so renowned that in 1643 Pope Urban VIII decreed that anyone damaging the trees would be excommunicated.

The peace was briefly shattered in 1810, when Napoleon's forces under Masséna were soundly beaten here by the Anglo-Portuguese army of the future Duke of Wellington (the battle is re-enacted here every 27 September). In 1834, when religious orders throughout Portugal were abolished, the forest became state property.

ORIENTATION & INFORMATION

From the Luso/Buçaco train station it's a 15-minute walk into town. Turn left (uphill) and climb gradually to the N234 before descending via Rua Dr António Granjo to the *turismo* and spa in the centre of Luso.

Buses from Coimbra stop on Rua Emídio Navarro, near the *turismo*.

By road the Portas das Ameias, the nearest gate into the forest, is 900m south of the *turismo*. From May to October there's a charge of €2.50 per car entering the forest, though walkers go in free.

The **turismo** (☎ 231 939 133; jtluso-bussaco@mail.telepac.pt; Rua Emídio Navarro 136; ☻ 9.30am-12.30pm & 2-6pm Mon-Fri, 10am-1pm & 3-5pm Sat) has accommodation information, town and forest maps, and leaflets (in English) detailing flora and points of historical interest. It also offers internet access on a single terminal.

SIGHTS & ACTIVITIES

Forest

The aromatic forest is crisscrossed with trails, dotted with crumbling chapels and graced with ponds, fountains and exotic trees ranging from palms to sequoias. Popular paths lead to the pretty **Vale dos Fetos** (Valley of Ferns) and the **Fonte Fria**, where swans float on a pond beneath a grand staircase. Among several fine viewpoints is **Cruz Alta** (545m), reached by a route called the Via Sacra.

What most visitors come to see is the fairy-tale **Palace Hotel do Buçaco**. Now a luxury hotel (opposite), it was originally built in 1907 as a royal summer retreat on the site of a 17th-century Carmelite monastery. This wedding cake of a building is over the top in every way: outside, its conglomeration of turrets and spires is surrounded by rose gardens and swirling box hedges in geometrical patterns; inside you'll find neo-Manueline carving, suits of armour on the grand staircases and *azulejos* illustrating scenes from *Os Lusíados* (The Lusiads; see p49), in which Portuguese armies win glorious battles at sea amid the dismayed looks of their stupefied opponents. By road, the hotel is 2.1km from the Portas das Ameias. Staff are generally tolerant of gawping nonguests.

Spa

Just the ticket after a long walk in the forest, the **Termas de Luso** (☎ 231 937 910; Rua Alvaro; ☻ 9am-noon & 4-7pm) welcomes drop-in visitors from May to October – preferably in the afternoon. Therapies for day visitors include a general massage (€17), and a kind of high-velocity shower, called *duche de Vichy,* followed by a short massage (€15.75).

Fonte de São João

People come from far and wide to fill their bottles for free at this crystal-clear natural **spring** adjacent to the spa. A glass skylight allows you to peer down and see the limpid waters rippling over pretty grey and white stones.

SLEEPING

Luso's glut of accommodation places, coupled with a struggling Portuguese economy, tends to drive down prices for visitors staying in town.

Budget

Orbitur Camping Ground (☎ 231 930 916; www.orbitur.pt; Bairro do Comendador Melo Pimenta; sites per adult/child/car €4.10/2.10/3.80, tent €4.50-6; ☻ year-round) This small, lush site is a 1.5km walk south of the *turismo*. Wooden bungalows with kitchen are also available (two-/four-/six-person cabins €59/66/77).

Astória (☎ 231 939 182; pensaoastorialuso@sapo.pt; Rua Emídio Navarro 144; s/d/tr €25/35/45; **P**) Beside the *turismo*, this rambling, homely place feels more like grandma's house than a guest house. Its clean, comfortable rooms feature wood floors, slightly tired-looking beds and frilly decor.

Casa de Hóspedes Familiar (☎ 231 939 612; paulocoelho@sapo.pt; Rua Ernesto Navarro 34; d/tr €35/40) You feel (and are) a guest of the family at this handsome, late-Victorian country house just above town. Personal touches include lacy bedspreads and curtains made by the owner's mother, homemade jams at breakfast and eclectic amenities such as room 6's huge bathroom filled with house plants or room 5's extra bedroom under the eaves for kids.

Midrange

Central (☎ 231 939 254; www.pensaocentral.no.sapo.pt; Rua Emídio Navarro; s/d/tr/q €35/45/70/80; **P** &) A workaday but welcoming *pensão* (guest house), Central has exceptionally spacious rooms with parquet wood floors, some with verandas.

Pensão Alegre (☎ 231 930 256; www.alegrehotels.com; Rua Emídio Navarro 2; r from €55; **P** 🕱 🖵 🖭) This grand, peach-coloured 19th-century town house wears its age much better than Luso's other in-town lodgings. Replete with period touches, its large doubles boast plush drapes, decorative plaster ceilings and highly polished period furniture. Its appeal is enhanced by an elegant entryway, formal parlour and pretty vine-draped garden with pool.

Vila Aurora (☎ 232 479 816, 231 930 150; www.vilaaurora.com; Rua Barbosa Collen; r from €60; **P** 🕱 🖭) On a hillside west of the centre, this castle-like old mansion features several grand common areas, a swimming pool and Jacuzzis in the more expensive (€85) rooms.

Top End

Vila Duparchy (☎ 231 930 790; principe.santos@clix.pt; Rua José Figueiredo; s/d €69/80; **P** 🖵 🖭) Home to French railway engineer Jean Alexis Duparchy while he constructed the Beira Alta railway, this rather genteel house is set back from the road on a woody hilltop, 2km outside the centre of Luso off the EN234. English is spoken and meals are available on request.

Palace Hotel do Buçaco (☎ 231 937 970; www.palacehoteldobussaco.com; Mata Nacional do Buçaco; s/d from €150/180; **P** 🕱) If you can afford it, treat yourself to a night at this delightfully ostentatious king's palace. Rooms abound in varying degrees of period finery, some of it a touch threadbare. Common areas are stunning and will put you in a royal mood, and the meals here are truly memorable (see boxed text, below). Significant discounts are sometimes available for bookings via the hotel's website.

EATING

Most *pensões* have reasonable restaurants of their own.

Salão de Chá (Praça Fonte São João; 🕾 9am-2am Sun-Thu, 9am-4am Fri & Sat) Conveniently located above the Fonte de São João, this snack bar serves run-of-the-mill sandwiches, drinks and coffee, but its outdoor terrace makes a pleasant place to sip a beer or sample *chá de limão*, a delightful infusion made from fresh lemon peel and boiling water.

Restaurante Imperial (☎ 231 937 570; Rua Emídio Navarro 25; meals €4.90-8.50; 🕾 lunch & dinner Tue-Sun) The grilled meats and other simple Portuguese fare are good value here, but steer clear of the vinegary house red and be prepared for lacklustre service.

DINNER AT THE PALACE

For a truly memorable dinner, it's hard to beat the elegant spread at the **Palace Hotel do Buçaco**'s dining room. Better come hungry – the meal spans seven to eight courses: appetisers, soup, pasta, fish and/or meat, a salad trolley, a selection of local cheeses, the dessert trolley and finally an evening *cafezinho* (espresso). Specialities on offer at the time of writing included cold melon soup with crunchy Serrano ham, suckling pig ravioli with candied orange zest, marinated sardines with raspberry vinaigrette and kiwi mousse, and codfish confit with sautéed scallops, corn bread, turnip sprouts and black-eyed peas. The dining room itself is a work of art, with natural light pouring over the parquet wood floors through a graceful faux-Manueline window studded with rosettes and overlapping arches.

You'll probably be too full to move afterwards, but never fear – the palace also rents out rooms, for a 'mere' €150 (and up; see above).

Restaurante Lourenços (☎ 231 939 474; Av Emídio Navarro; mains €8.50-10; ☻ lunch & dinner Thu-Tue) This blandly bright modern place serves surprisingly good regional specialities with amusing if unintelligible English translations (really, who could resist a plate of 'sweated skrimp'?).

Palace Hotel do Buçaco (☎ 231 937 970; Mata Nacional do Buçaco; 7-/8-course meals €35/40) Hands down the region's spiffiest dining option, this royal retreat-turned-hotel serves a blow-out seven-to eight-course menu offering a creative take on regional dishes (see boxed text, p341).

GETTING THERE & AWAY
Buses (more convenient than the train) run four times each weekday and twice daily on weekends from Coimbra's main bus station to Luso (€3, 40 minutes) and the Palace Hotel do Buçaco (€3.20, 50 minutes).

IR trains run four times daily from Coimbra A to Luso/Buçaco station (€1.61, 30 minutes), from where it's a solid 15-minute walk to the Luso *turismo,* plus another half-hour uphill through the forest to the Palace Hotel do Buçaco.

Montemor-o-Velho
Perched high atop a rugged hill 25km west of Coimbra, the glowering walls of the **Castelo do Montemor-o-Velho** (admission free; ☻ 9am-9pm Jun-Aug, 10am-6.30pm Apr, May & Sep, 10am-5pm Oct-Mar) dominate the surrounding marshland far out to the horizon. Whether seen from a distance or from atop the castle walls themselves, it's easy to imagine this site as an early bastion in the Reconquista. Ferdinand I of Castile and León recaptured Montemor-o-Velho from the Moors in 1064, and within less than a century his great-grandson Afonso Henrique claimed it as part of his new Kingdom of Portugal. Over the intervening centuries the castle was rebuilt and expanded several times, with most of the current structure dating from the 14th century.

Today you can walk around the castle's crenellated battlements, explore the 'killing ground' between the inner and outer perimeter, and survey the lush rice fields lying alongside the Rio Mondego far below. Inside the walls almost no buildings remain except for a small portion of the ruined **Paço das Infantas** (Princesses' Palace), which was built by Afonso Henrique's aunt Urraca,

and the beautifully tiled **Igreja de Santa Maria de Alcáçova,** a small Romanesque church that was founded in 1090 and was rebuilt most recently with Manueline touches in the 16th century. The site's strategic importance as a fortification dates back at least two millennia, and archaeologists have identified elements of Roman stonework in the castle's keep.

A stylish-looking snack bar provides a scenic spot for a drink, but avoid the stale sandwiches and pastries, which seem to pre-date the castle itself.

The village below is small, though there are restaurants and parking beneath the castle's southern and eastern walls. **Residencial Abade João** (☎ 239 687 010; burgomedieval@sapo.pt; Rua dos Combatentes da Grande Guerra 15; s/d/tr €30/40/55) is a beautiful old town house for anyone looking to hang their hat.

Trains between Coimbra (€1.40, 40 minutes) and Figueira da Foz (€1.65, 30 minutes) stop every hour or two at Montemor station, 4km southeast of the castle. Moisés Correia de Oliveira buses between Coimbra (€2.75, 55 minutes) and Figueira (€2, 30 minutes) stop closer to the castle, five to eight times daily (fewer on Sunday).

Reserva Natural do Paúl de Arzila
Birdwatchers and other nature fans may wish to make a detour to the 535-hectare Reserva Natural do Paúl de Arzila. Halfway between Coimbra and Montemor-o-Velho, this marshy natural reserve is home to some 120 species of resident and migratory birds, as well as otters. The **on-site centre** (☎ 239 980 500; rnpa.san tosmf@icn.pt) serves as the base for a two-hour interpretive walk.

FIGUEIRA DA FOZ
pop 27,700
Popular with Portuguese holidaymakers for over a century, the beach resort of Figueira da Foz (fi-*guy*-ra da *fosh*; Figueira) continues to attract big summer crowds – including increasing numbers of Spaniards lured by the easy superhighway access, as well as surfers drawn to the championship-calibre waves at Cabedelo. For most visitors, the star attractions are Figueira's outlandishly wide beach and a casino featuring big-name acts on summer evenings. The local sands are so vast that it takes a five-minute walk across creaky boardwalks simply to reach the sea.

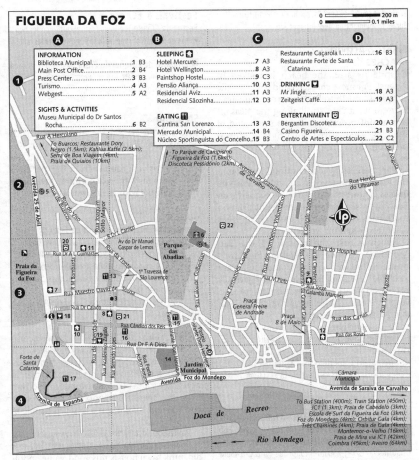

FIGUEIRA DA FOZ

INFORMATION		
Biblioteca Municipal	1	B3
Main Post Office	2	B4
Press Center	3	B3
Turismo	4	A3
Webgest	5	A2

SIGHTS & ACTIVITIES		
Museu Municipal do Dr Santos Rocha	6	B2

SLEEPING		
Hotel Mercure	7	A3
Hotel Wellington	8	A3
Paintshop Hostel	9	C3
Pensão Aliança	10	A3
Residencial Aviz	11	A3
Residencial Sãozinha	12	D3

EATING		
Cantina San Lorenzo	13	A3
Mercado Municipal	14	B4
Núcleo Sportinguista do Concelho	15	B3

Restaurante Caçarola I	16	B3
Restaurante Forte de Santa Catarina	17	A4

DRINKING		
Mr Jingle	18	A3
Zeitgeist Caffé	19	A3

ENTERTAINMENT		
Bergantim Discoteca	20	A3
Casino Figueira	21	B3
Centro de Artes e Espectáculos	22	C2

Out of season, the place feels a bit desolate, but come here in summer and things are much more upbeat, with sizzling bodies and candy-striped beach huts filling every square inch of beach.

Orientation
Just inland from the beach and the 16th-century Forte de Santa Catarina is a knot of streets with the *turismo*, accommodation and restaurants, and the casino. Seafront development continues clear to Buarcos, a former fishing village 3km to the north.

The train and bus stations are right next to each other, 1.5km east of the beach. High-season parking is a headache in the centre, even in the evenings, thanks to the casino. A good bet for street parking is the area between the Jardim Municipal and the train station.

Information
Biblioteca Municipal (Rua Calouste Gulbenkian; ⏰ 2-7.15pm Mon, 10am-7.15pm Tue-Fri, 2-6.45pm Sat) Free internet on four computers at town library.

Main post office (Passeio Infante Dom Henrique; ⏰ 8.30am-6.30pm Mon-Fri)

Press Center (Rua Bernardo Lopes 113; ⏰ 9am-11pm Sep-May, 8am-1am Jul-Aug) Newsagent stocking foreign newspapers.

Turismo (☎ 233 422 610; www.figueiraturismo.com; Av 25 de Abril; ⏰ 9am-midnight 1 Jun–15 Sep, 9am-12.30pm & 2-5.30pm Mon-Fri, 10am-12.30pm & 2.30-6.30pm Sat & Sun 16 Sep-31 May)

Webgest (Av 25 de Abril 74; per hr €2; ☺ 10.30am-10pm, to midnight Jul-Aug) Internet access.

Sights & Activities

BEACHES

Despite its size, the beach is packed in August. For more character and some terrific surf, head north to **Buarcos**. From Figueira's *turismo* it's a 2km stroll along the pleasant beachfront promenade to the south end of Buarcos. Alternatively you can take a Joalto bus from the train station (€1.05) every hour or so.

For more seclusion, continue on around the Cabo Mondego headland to **Praia de Quiaios**, about 10km north of Figueira da Foz. Joalto services run from the bus station to Quiaios (€2.10, 30 minutes) seven times daily (less often on weekends).

South across the mouth of the Rio Mondego is **Praia de Cabedelo**, Figueira's prime surfing venue; classes and rentals are available here from **Escola de Surf da Figueira da Foz** (☎ 233 412 413; www.surfingfigueira.com; Rua Adolfo Gonçalves Santiago, Cabedelo; group/individual class €25/35, short-/longboard rental per day €35/40).

A little further on (4km from Figueira) is **Praia de Gala**. Joalto buses marked 'Cova' run from the train station via the *mercado municipal* to Cabedelo and Gala (both €1.05) every hour or so on weekdays (less often on weekends).

MUSEU MUNICIPAL DO DR SANTOS ROCHA

This modern **museum** (☎ 233 402 840; Rua Calouste Gulbenkian; adult/under 12yr/student/senior €1.30/free/1/1; ☺ 9.30am-5.15pm Tue-Fri & 2-6.45pm Sat year-round, plus 2-6.45pm Sun Jul-Aug), beside Parque das Abadias, houses a wonderfully wide-ranging collection featuring local archaeological finds, Roman coins, medieval statues, outlandish Indo-Portuguese furniture, objects documenting Portugal's early African explorations, and rotating art exhibits.

SERRA DE BOA VIAGEM

For those with wheels, this headland, found 4km north of Figueira and carpeted in pines, eucalyptus and acacias, is a fine place for panoramas, picnics and cool walks. Take the coastal road to Buarcos, turn right at the lighthouse and follow the signs to Boa Viagem.

Festivals & Events

Festas da Cidade The Town Festival carries on for two weeks at the end of June, with folk music, parades and concerts.

Mundialito de Futebol de Praia The town is mobbed for about a week in late July or August most years for the World Beach-Football Championships.

Sleeping

Prices listed are for the high season (July and August). Expect discounts of up to 40% in winter. The *turismo* has details of a few *quartos* (private rooms) from €25 per double. Touts may approach you at the bus or train stations with their own offers.

BUDGET

Parque de Campismo Figueira da Foz (☎ 233 402 810; www.figueiracamping.com, in Portuguese; Quinta da Calmada; sites per adult/child/car €4.60/2.40/3.50, tent €3-3.50; ☺ year-round) Northeast of the centre and 2km inland from Buarcos beach, this camping ground has a pool, tennis courts and a supermarket. To get here, take a Casal de Areia bus (€1.05, six to 10 daily) from the train station or the *mercado municipal*.

Orbitur Gala (☎ 233 431 492; info@orbitur.pt; Praia de Gala; sites per adult/child/tent/car €4.80/2.50/5.40/4.70; ☺ year-round) The best of the local camp sites, flat and shady Orbitur Gala is next to a great beach. It's south of Foz do Mondego and 1km from the nearest bus stop. Bungalows here cost €59 to €103 for three to seven people in the high season.

Paintshop Hostel (☎ 233 105 044; www.paintshophostel.com; Rua da Clemência 9; dm/tw/d €18/40/45; 🖳) In an old, pink town house, this good-value option offers small, attractive rooms, plush quilts, free wi-fi, a great bar out back, and a nice shared kitchen and barbecue for self-caterers. Bike, skateboard and bodyboard rentals are available for €5 per day.

MIDRANGE

Residencial Aviz (☎ 233 422 635; www.residencialaviz.pt.to; Rua Dr AL Lopes Guimarães 16; s/d €45/55; ⊠) This squeaky-clean guest house two blocks from the beach has a slightly grandmotherly aesthetic, although a recent remodel has everything shining. Reserve ahead in summer.

Residencial Sãozinha (☎ 233 425 243; www.hospedariasaozinha.com; Ladeira do Monte 43; d Jul/Aug €50/60) Hidden away on a backstreet, this restored 1940s art-deco building has snug, spotless rooms with tiled floors and tiny balconies. The only downside is the annoying buzzer that goes off every time you cross the threshold.

Pensão Aliança (☎ 233 422 197; www.residenciala lianca.com; Rua Miguel Bombarda 12; d from €60) The spacious rooms at this central guest house have wood floors polished to a shine, although they've lost some character during enthusiastic renovations.

TOP END

Hotel Wellington (☎ 233 426 767; www.lupahoteis .com; Rua Dr Calado 23-27; s/d/ste €75/85/120; ⚡) Near the beach and casino action, the run-of-the-mill Wellington offers off-street parking at a nearby car park (€5 per night).

Hotel Mercure (☎ 233 403 900; www.mercure .com; Av 25 de Abril 22; d with city/ocean view €115/155; P ⚡ 🖥) This is the only four-star hotel in town. Row upon row of balconies boast sweeping views of the vast beach.

Eating

Restaurante Caçarola I (☎ 233 424 861; Rua Cándido dos Reis 65; daily specials €5.50-6, mains €7-15; lunch & dinner) Locals belly up to the bar all day long for good-value *combinados do dia balcão* (daily lunch-counter specials) at this popular seafood restaurant. In addition to the counter seating, there are plenty of tables on the pedestrian boulevard outside.

Nucleo Sportinguista do Concelho (☎ 233 434 882; Rua Praia da Fonte 14; all-you-can-eat €7.50; lunch & dinner) Sitting on the cobblestones under the awning here, surrounded by enthusiastic locals and a sea of tables draped in checked tablecloths, feels a bit like crashing a Portuguese family's private barbecue. The waitresses bring round plate after plate of grilled meat and fish and you eat as much as you like of everything. With wine at €1 a pitcher, it's an unbeatable deal.

Cantina San Lorenzo (☎ 965754527; Rua São Lourenço 23; mains from €7.50; lunch & dinner Tue-Sun) Offering reasonably authentic (albeit underspiced) Mexican treats like mole, enchiladas and shrimp taquitos, this cantina also features kick-ass margaritas, vividly colourful decor, and Latin dance parties every Friday from 11pm.

Restaurante Dory Negro (☎ 233 421 333; Largo Caras Direitas 16, Buarcos; mains €8-12; lunch & dinner Wed-Mon) This unassuming restaurant in Buarcos specialises in crab, lobster, shrimp, clams and deep-sea fish.

Restaurante Forte de Santa Catarina (☎ 233 428 530; Tennis Club, Av 25 de Abril; all-you-can-eat seafood per person €16; lunch & dinner Wed-Mon) At this wildly popular seafront eatery, crowds pack in nightly for the all-you-can-eat *rodizio de mariscos* and to chat with the turbaned owner, who is something of a local celebrity. Dinner reservations are recommended in summer and on weekends.

Self-caterers will find everything they need at the **mercado municipal** (☎ Passeio Infante Dom Henrique; Mon-Sat) opposite the Jardim Municipal.

Drinking

Mr Jingle (Esplanada Silva Guimarães; 2pm-4am Fri & Sat year-round, to 2am Sun-Thu Jul-Aug, to 10pm Sun-Thu Sep-Jun) The beachfront patio here is an unbeatable spot for a pint at sundown.

Kahlua Kaffe (Praça do Mar Português; 10am-4am) This classy joint by the waterfront in Buarcos keeps everyone happy with a ridiculously long drinks menu and a front patio perfect for sunbathing. Everything's artfully done – check out the unique presentation of a simple espresso. Netheads will also appreciate the free wi-fi.

Zeitgeist Caffé (Rua Francisco António Dinis 82; 4pm-4am) Glamorous Zeitgeist features lounge, ambient and jazz (plus live music most Sundays).

Entertainment

Discoteca Pessidónio (☎ 233 435 637; Condados, Tavarede; midnight-4am Fri & Sat) Still going strong after four decades, Pessidónio is in the suburbs east of the municipal campground. Its four distinct dance venues include the Capela Club, whose poolside Sala da Piscina is popular for tropical drinks on hot summer nights.

Bergantim Discoteca (☎ 967647910; www.ber gantim.com, in Portuguese; Rua Dr AL Lopes Guimarães 28; 2.30pm-8am Fri & Sat) This lively disco/nightclub spinning mostly '80s and '90s tunes has a party atmosphere and a perfect downtown location one block from the beach.

Três Chaminés (☎ 233 407 920; www.3chamines .com, in Portuguese; Caceira; disco midnight-6am Friday & Sat, bowling 6pm-1am Mon-Thu, 6pm-3am Fri, 3pm-4am Sat, 3pm-1am Sun) Four kilometres east of town on the EN111, this huge industrial-looking place encompasses bowling, paintball and a Latin-American-flavoured disco on Fridays and Saturdays.

Casino Figueira (☎ 233 408 400; www.casino figueira .pt; Rua Bernardo Lopes; ◷ 3pm-3am) Shimmering in neon and acrylic, Figueira's casino is crawling with cash-laden holidaymakers in search of a quick buck. It has roulette and slot machines, plus a sophisticated piano bar with live music after 11pm most nights. Dress up at night – beach attire, thongs (flip-flops) or sports shoes may keep you out.

Centro de Artes e Espectáculos (☎ 233 407 200; www.cae.pt, in Portuguese) Behind the museum, CAE hosts big-name bands, theatre and art-house cinema. Check the website or pick up a schedule at the *turismo*.

Getting There & Away
BUS
Figueira's bus terminal is served by two long-distance companies. **Moisés Correia de Oliveira** (☎ 233 426 703) has at least hourly service (fewer on weekends) via Montemor-o-Velho to Coimbra (€3.70, 1½ hours).

Rede Expressos (www.rede-expressos.pt) has buses to Lisbon (€12.50, 2¾ hours, three daily), Aveiro (€9, 1¼ hours, at least two daily) and Leiria (€8.40, one hour, three daily).

TRAIN
Train connections to/from Coimbra (€1.88, 70 minutes, hourly) are superior to buses. There are also direct trains to Leiria (€4.60, one hour, two to three daily), with connecting service to Mira Sintra-Meleças station on the suburban Lisbon line.

Getting Around
For information on **Joalto** (☎ 233 422 648) buses to local beaches, see p344.

PRAIA DE MIRA
For a few days of sunny, windblown torpor, head for Praia de Mira, the best-equipped town along the mostly deserted 50km coastal strip between Figueira da Foz and Aveiro (opposite). Sandwiched between a long, clean beach and a canal-fed lagoon, this small resort has little – aside from the candy-striped Igreja da Nossa Senhora Conceição on the beachfront – to distract you from the main business at hand: sun, sea and seafood. You may still glimpse local fishermen hauling in their

colourful *xavega* boats in summer, though they're a vanishing species.

Orientation & Information
Praia de Mira is 7km west of Mira on the N109, itself 35km north of Figueira da Foz.

Praia de Mira's axis is Avenida Cidade de Coimbra (also called the N342). The **turismo** (☎ 231 472 566; turismo@cm-mira.pt; Av da Barrinha; ◷ 9am-7pm daily Jul-Aug, 9am-12.30pm & 2-5.30pm Mon-Fri, 10am-1pm & 2-6pm Sat & Sun Sep-Jun), 450m south of Avenida Cidade de Coimbra beside the lagoon, shares a wooden house with a little ethnographic exhibition.

Sleeping
Rates given here are for the high season (mid-July to August). At other times the rates drop by up to 40%. The town abounds in summer *quartos*, typically €30 to €40 per double. Watch for signs, or ask at the *turismo*.

Orbitur (☎ 231 471 234; info@orbitur.pt; sites per adult/child/tent/car €4.50/2.50/5/4.20; ◷ Feb-Nov) This well-equipped, shady site is at the southern end of the lagoon. Bungalows are available from €54. Bikes can also be hired here.

Pousada da Juventude (☎ 231 471 199; mira@movi jovem.pt; dm/d €9/22; ◷ Jun-Aug) Super-cheap but bare-bones – no kitchen or restaurant. It's near Orbitur, about 200m from the beach in a pine area south of town. Reception is open from 8am to noon and 6pm to midnight.

Residencial Senhora da Conceição (☎ 231 471 645; www.residencial-sra-conceicao.pt.vu, in Portuguese; Av Cidade de Coimbra; s/d from €40/45; P ▢) Only a few blocks back from the beach, this hotel on the lagoon side of the main road into Mira offers simple but bright and impeccable rooms.

Residencial Maçarico (☎ 231 471 114; www.residen cial-macarico.com; Av Arrais Batista Cêra; r €65; P) Mira's best lodging option, this attractive yellow villa sits back from the beachfront promenade, a stone's throw from the Atlantic. It's clean and friendly, and front rooms have little balconies with sea views.

Eating & Drinking
Marisqueira Tezinho (☎ 231 471 162; Av da Barrinha 9; mains €7-13; ◷ lunch & dinner) Bustling and friendly, with only two small rooms, Tezinho is recommended for its ultrafresh seafood.

Restaurante A Cozinha (☎ 231 471 190; Av da Barrinha 13; mains €7.50-13; ◷ lunch & dinner Tue-Sun) This slightly upmarket, lagoon-side place is another good choice for seafood, just down the street from Marisqueira Tezinho (opposite).

Restaurante Caçanito (☎ 231 472 678; Av do Mar; mains €8-15; ☒ lunch & dinner) Right on the beach, Caçanito is decorated predictably with rough timber and fishnets, but recompenses with great views and good grilled seafood.

Sixties Irish Pub (☎ 231 472 475; Travessa Arrais Manuel Patrão 14; ☒ 12.30pm-4am) Tucked into a classic pub crawler's alley a block back from the beachfront, this cosy spot has multiple beers on tap and a lively old-school Irish atmosphere.

Polar Cervajaria (☎ 231 471 171; Av Arrais Batista Cera 34; ☒ noon-4am) Featuring seafood and occasional live music, ever-popular Polar is an inviting bar with a breezy terrace just across the street from the Atlantic.

Getting There & Away
Joalto runs direct Praia de Mira buses from Aveiro's train station (€3.15, 50 minutes, at least two daily). However, most coastal transport stops inland only at Mira (7km east). There's also service from Figueira da Foz to Mira (€2.90, one hour, about five daily).

Taxis (☎ 231 471 257; Praia de Mira) can ferry you between Mira and Praia de Mira.

AVEIRO
pop 55,300

Hugging the edge of the Ria, a shallow coastal lagoon rich in bird life, Aveiro (uh-*vey*-roo) has occasionally been dubbed the Venice of Portugal thanks to its high-prowed boats, humpbacked bridges and a small network of canals. It's certainly not Venetian in scale, but Aveiro and its surroundings make a pleasant day trip from Porto or Coimbra. The town is best explored on foot, on a free municipal bicycle, or aboard a *moliceiro* – the traditional seaweed-harvesting boat that has now been converted to tourist use.

A prosperous sea port in the early 16th century, Aveiro suffered a ferocious storm in the 1570s that blocked the mouth of the Rio Vouga, closing it to ocean-going ships and creating fever-breeding marshes. Over the next two centuries, Aveiro's population shrunk by three-quarters. But in 1808 the Barra Canal forged a passage back to the sea, and within a century Aveiro was rich once more, as evidenced by the spate of art-nouveau houses that still define the town's old centre.

Orientation
From the *azulejo*-clad train station it's a 1km stroll southwest down the main street, Avenida Dr Lourenço Peixinho and Rua Viana do Castelo (together called Avenida by all), to Praça Humberto Delgado, straddling the Canal Central. Nearby are the *turismo* and a pedestrianised centre dominated by the flashy Forum Aveiro shopping mall.

Information
Aveiro Digital (Praça da República; ☒ 9am-7pm Mon-Fri, 10am-6pm Sat) Free internet.
Hospital (☎ 234 378 300; Av Artur Ravara)
Police station (☎ 234 302 510; Praça Marquês de Pombal)
Net7 (Av 5 de Outubro 45; per hr €3; ☒ 9.30am-midnight Mon-Sat, 3pm-midnight Sun)
Main post office (Praça Marquês de Pombal; ☒ 8.30am-6.30pm Mon-Fri)
Regional turismo (☎ 234 423 680; www.rotadaluz.pt; Rua João Mendonça 8; ☒ 9am-8pm) Extremely helpful office with multilingual staff in an art-nouveau gem beside the Canal Central.

Sights
MUSEU DE AVEIRO
This fine, if somewhat single-minded, **museum** (☎ 234 423 297; Av Santa Joana; adult/child/14-25yr & senior €2/free/1, admission free 10am-2pm Sun; ☒ 10am-1pm & 2-5.30pm Tue-Sun), in the former Mosteiro de Jesus opposite the Catedral de São Domingos, owes its finest treasures to Princesa (later beatified as Santa) Joana, daughter of Afonso V. In 1472, 11 years after the convent was founded, Joana 'retired' here and, though forbidden to take full vows, she stayed until her death in 1490.

Her tomb, a 17th-century masterpiece of marble mosaic, sits in an equally lavish baroque chancel decorated with *azulejos* depicting her life. The museum's paintings include a late-15th-century portrait of her, attributed to Nuno Gonçalves.

RESERVA NATURAL DAS DUNAS DE SÃO JACINTO
Stretching north from São Jacinto to Ovar, between the sea and the N327, is an excellent little 6.7-sq-km wooded nature reserve, equipped with trails and birdwatching hides. Entry is via an **interpretive centre** (☎ 234 331 282; http://camarinha.aveiro-digital.net, in Portuguese; ☒ 9am-noon & 2-5pm Fri-Wed) on the N327. To minimise the impact on wildlife, you can only enter

THE BEIRAS

AVEIRO

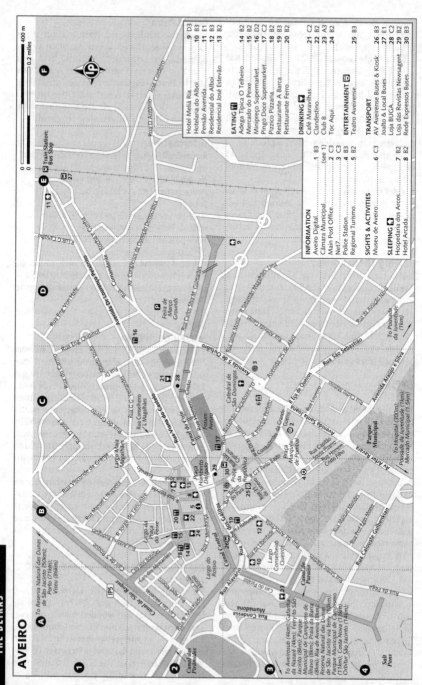

		0 400 m
		0 0.2 miles
		⊞ E Train Station; Bus Stop

EATING 🍴		
Hotel Meliá Ria..........................	9	D3
Hotelaria do Alboi....................	10	B3
Pensão Avenida........................	11	E1
Residencial do Alboi.................	12	B3
Residencial José Estevão..........	13	B2

EATING 🍴		
Adega Típica O Telheiro...........	14	B2
Mercado do Peixe....................	15	B2
Minipreço Supermarket............	16	D2
Pingo Doce Supermarket..........	17	C2
Pizzico Pizzaria.......................	18	B2
Restaurante A Barca................	19	B3
Restaurante Ferro...................	20	B2

DRINKING 🍷		
Café Maravilhas......................	21	C2
Clandestino............................	22	B2
Club 8...................................	23	A3
Toc Aqui................................	24	B2

ENTERTAINMENT 🎭		
Teatro Aveirense......................	25	B3

TRANSPORT		
AV Aveirense Buses & Kiosk.......	26	B3
Joalto & Local Buses................	27	E1
Loja BUGA.............................	28	C2
Loja das Revistas Newsagent.....	29	B2
Rede Expressos Buses...............	30	B3

INFORMATION		
Aveiro Digital..........................	1	B3
Câmara Municipal...................	(see 1)	
Main Post Office......................	2	C3
Net7.....................................	3	C3
Police Station..........................	4	B3
Regional Turismo.....................	5	B2

SIGHTS & ACTIVITIES		
Museu de Aveiro......................	6	C3

SLEEPING 🛏		
Hospedaria dos Arcos...............	7	B2
Hotel Arcada...........................	8	B2

between 9am and 9.30am or between 2pm and 2.30pm for a maximum stay of 2½ hours, and you must book ahead. There's usually a guide on hand to give a free tour, or materials available to help you make the best of a visit on your own.

To get here, take a Forte da Barra bus from the **AV Aveirense kiosk** (☎ 234 423 513; Rua Clube dos Galitos) to the end of the line, from where a small passenger ferry crosses to the port of São Jacinto (combined boat-and-bus ticket: adult €3.10, child aged four to 10 years and seniors €1.55). Ask at the *turismo* for current timetables.

From São Jacinto port the reserve entrance is 1.3km down the Torreira road. Note that by road the entrance is 50km from Aveiro!

Activities

Though not the Costa de Prata's finest beaches, the surfing venues of **Praia da Barra** and **Costa Nova**, 13km west of Aveiro, are good for a day's outing. The prettier Costa Nova has a beachside street lined with cafes, kitsch gift shops and picturesque candy-striped cottages.

AV Aveirense buses go via Gafanha da Nazaré to Costa Nova (€2, hourly) from the kiosk on Rua Clube dos Galitos; the last bus returns at around midnight.

Wilder and more remote is **Praia de São Jacinto**, on the northern side of the lagoon. The vast beach of sand dunes is a 1.5km walk from São Jacinto port, through a residential area at the back of town.

Aveirosub (☎ 234 367 666, 961 409 489; www.aveirosub .com; Av José Estevão 724, Gafanha da Nazaré) offers scuba-diving classes (36 50-minute sessions, about half in the sea, for around €400) as well as individual dives (from €18).

One-hour private **moliceiros trips** (adult/under 6yr/7-12yr €8/free/5) around the Ria are available subject to passenger numbers; tickets are available at the *turismo*. Two-hour *moliceiros* trips to São Jacinto may also be on offer in July and August; ask at the *turismo*.

Festivals & Events

Feira de Março Held from 25 March to 25 April, this festival dates back 5½ centuries. Nowadays it features everything from folk music to rock concerts.

Festa da Ria Aveiro celebrates its canals and *moliceiros* from mid-July to the end of August. Highlights include folk dancing and a *moliceiros* race.

Festas do Município Aveiro sees two weeks of merry-making around 12 May in honour of Santa Joana.

Sleeping

Summer accommodation is even tighter than parking here; consider booking a week or so ahead in peak season.

BUDGET

Parque Municipal de Campismo (☎ /fax 234 331 220; sites per adult/tent & car €2/1; ☼ Mar-Nov) The cheapest camping ground is this city-run and slightly tatty park at São Jacinto, 2.5km from the pier along the Torreira road.

Parque Municipal de Campismo de Ílhavo (☎ 234 369 425; www.campingbarra.com, in Portuguese; Rua Diogo Cão, Praia da Barra; sites per adult/car €3.05/2.70, tent €3.30-4.85; ☼ year-round) A well-equipped, sandy and flat site next to the beach about 10km from Aveiro.

Orbitur São Jacinto (☎ 234 838 284; info@orbitur.pt; sites per adult/child/car €4.10/2.10/3.80, tent €4.50-6; ☼ Feb-Nov) Orbitur is a very nice site with more shade and better facilities (including an ATM) and is close to the sea. There's no bus service along this road; see Reserva Natural das Dunas de São Jacinto (left) for transport details.

Pousada da Juventude (☎ 234 420 536; aveiro@movi jovem.pt; Rua das Pombas 182; dm €9, d with/without bathroom €22/18; ▣) Aveiro's youth hostel, 1.5km south of the centre, is basic and rather clinical.

Pensão Avenida (☎ 234 423 366; Av Dr Lourenço Peixinho 256; d with/without bathroom €40/35) This handsome art nouveau building is conveniently located just across from the train station. The owners, who also run the adjacent *pastelaria*, have fixed up the bright rooms simply but tastefully.

Hospedaria dos Arcos (☎ 234 383 130; Rua José Estevão 47; d incl breakfast €40) This place has a just-like-grandma's-house atmosphere, with several floors of spotless little rooms and a generous breakfast.

MIDRANGE

Residencial do Alboi (☎ 234 380 390; www.residencial -alboi.com; Rua da Arrochela 6; s/d €45/65; ▣) Down a quiet lane in the heart of town, this place has standard midrange digs, with polished granite lending an air of dignity.

Hotelaria do Alboi (☎ 234 404 190; Rua da Liberdade 10; s/d €45/65) Sister hotel of and just around the corner from Residencial do Alboi (above), this place has identical prices and some rooms with canal views.

Hotel Arcada (☎ 234 423 001; www.hotelarcada.com; Rua Viana do Castelo 4; s/d/ste €49/59/89; 🕭) Right in the heart of things, the faded but still pleasant Arcada boasts some of Aveiro's best canal views.

Residencial José Estevão (☎ 234 383 964; info@ hotelasamericas.com; Rua José Estevão 23; s/d €55/65; 🕭) This fine old town house offers up a dozen gleaming, snug and comfortable rooms.

TOP END

Hotel Meliá Ria (☎ 234 401 000; www.solmelia.com; Cais da Fonte Nova; s/d €104/116; P 🕭 🖳) Aveiro's newest and spiffiest hotel sits alone along the main canal. Its cubelike exterior is shrouded in intriguing brises-soleil, while inside it's all contemporary lines and business-friendly comforts. Check online for specials as low as €70 (without breakfast).

Eating

Pizzico Pizzaria (☎ 234 424 509; Largo da Praça do Peixe 24; pizzas €6-8; 🕭 lunch & dinner) This affordable Italian eatery, serving designer pizza and a €5.50 lunch special, caters to a younger crowd.

Restaurante Ferro (☎ 234 422 214; Rua Tenente Resende 30; dishes €6-12; 🕭 lunch & dinner Mon-Sat, lunch Sun) Popular, bustling Ferro makes a great lunch stop, with a diverse menu of fish, meat and egg dishes.

Adega Típica O Telheiro (☎ 234 429 473; Largo da Praça do Peixe 20-21; mains €8-14; 🕭 lunch & dinner Sun-Fri) This cosy, reasonably priced place has hams hanging from the low wooden ceiling, red wine by the jug, grilled seafood and a long bar where locals convene.

our pick Mercado do Peixe (☎ 234 383 511; Largo da Praça do Peixe; mains €8-18; 🕭 lunch daily, dinner Mon-Sat) Perched above the city's homely fish market, this industrial-chic restaurant has large windows overlooking the canal and the adjacent square. The seafood is excellent, and €6 lunch specials Monday to Friday include homemade bread, soup, and a main course.

Restaurante A Barca (☎ 234 426 024; Rua José Rabumba 5; mains €9-13; 🕭 lunch & dinner Mon-Fri, lunch Sat) This restaurant has a casual atmosphere and a choice of fish, fish and more fish – all fresh from the nearby market, of course.

Self-caterers can choose from the **mercado municipal** (🕭 Tue-Sat) about 500m further south beyond the *pousada da juventude* (youth hostel), and supermarkets including **Pingo Doce** (🕭 9am-10pm) in the Forum Aveiro

mall and **Minipreço** (🕭 9am-8pm Mon-Sat, 9am-1pm & 3-7pm Sun) on the Avenida.

Drinking & Entertainment

With a big student population and a generally party-friendly culture, nightlife is quite raucous in this small city.

Café Maravilhas (☎ 234 383 064; Largo do Mercado 4; 🕭 9am-3am) Drawing a mixed crowd of students and older folks, this place with its showy neon sign features pool tables in the back, plus live Cape Verdean and Brazilian music Wednesday to Friday.

Toc Aqui (Largo da Praça do Peixe; 🕭 9pm-2am Sep-Jun, 2pm-3am Jul-Aug) This raucous, friendly pub opposite the fish market regularly hosts live music of various types.

Clandestino (Rua do Tenente Resende 35; 🕭 9pm-2am Mon-Sat) A cosy little pub attracting an alternative crowd with chilled-out music and imported DJs.

Club 8 (Cais do Paraíso 19; 🕭 Wed-Sat) The town's all-purpose disco, with varying music and clientele.

Teatro Aveirense (☎ 234 400 920; www.teatroaveir ense.pt, in Portuguese) Celebrating 125 years at the heart of Aveiro's cultural scene, this newly renovated historic theatre regularly hosts dance, music and theatre performances.

Getting There & Away

BUS

Few long-distance buses terminate here – there isn't even a bus station.

Rede Expressos has about three daily services to/from Lisbon (€14, three to four hours) and Coimbra (€5.20, 45 minutes). Get tickets and timetables at the **Loja das Revistas newsagent** (Praça Humberto Delgado; 🕭 7am-8pm) and catch the bus around the corner.

Joalto goes three to four times a day to Figueira da Foz (€4.15, one hour) from Rua Viana do Castelo and the train station. Two daily buses also serve Praia de Mira (€3.15, 50 minutes).

TRAIN

Aveiro is within Porto's *suburbano* network, which means there are commuter trains to/from Porto at least every half-hour (€2.05, 50 to 60 minutes); much pricier IC/AP links (€9/12.50) are only slightly faster. There are also at least half-hourly links to Coimbra

(€4.90, one hour) and several daily IC trains to Lisbon (€16, 2½ hours).

Getting Around

Parking is awful and isn't getting any better. Fight your way into the centre, past the *turismo* to the Largo do Rossio car park, and leave your car there for the duration. The *turismo* can give you a map showing other car parks.

Local bus routes converge on the Avenida and the train station. It's an easy 15-minute walk southwest from the station into town.

Aveiro runs a pioneering free-bike scheme, Bicicleta de Utilização Gratuita de Aveiro (BUGA). Give your ID details at the **Loja BUGA** (10am-7pm) kiosk beside the Canal do Cojo, take a bike and ride it within the designated town limits, and return it to the kiosk before it shuts, all for free.

PIÓDÃO

pop 225 / elev 690m

Remote Piódão (*pyoh*-down) offers a chance to see rural Portugal at its most pristine. This tiny traditional village clings to a terraced valley in a beautiful, surprisingly remote range of vertiginous ridges, deeply cut valleys, rushing rivers and virgin woodland called the Serra de Açor (Goshawk Mountains).

Until the 1970s you could only reach Piódão on horseback or by foot, and it still feels as though you've slipped into a time warp. The village is a serene, picturesque composition in schist stone and grey slate; note the many doorways with crosses over them, said to offer protection against curses and thunderstorms.

Orientation & Information

Houses descend in terraces to Largo Cônego Manuel Fernandes Nogueira – smaller than its name. Here you'll find the fairy-tale parish church, the Igreja Nossa Senhora Conceição. Across the square, the village **turismo** (235 732 787; geral@cm-arganil.pt; 10am-1pm & 2-6pm Jun-Sep, 9am-1pm & 2-5pm Oct-May) provides info on Piódão itself and walks in the surrounding area – check upstairs in the museum if nobody's minding the *turismo* below.

Sights & Activities

The tiny **Núcleo Museológico de Piódão** (admission €1; 10am-1pm & 2-6pm Jun-Sep, 9am-1pm & 2-5pm Oct-May), just upstairs from the *turismo*, offers a glimpse of traditional village life in Piódão, displaying reconstructions of typical rooms in local homes, complete with tools, pottery and furniture. There are also historic photos of Piódão and its residents.

A signposted network of **hiking trails** connects Piódão to the nearby villages of Foz d'Égua (6.3km, two-hour loop hike) and Chãs d'Égua (4km, one hour each way). Foz d'Égua has some lovely old stone bridges, schist houses and a precarious-looking footbridge over the river gorge. Chãs d'Égua is home to over 100 examples of rock art spanning the period from the Neolithic to the Iron Age.

Festivals & Events

The area's patron saint, São Pedro do Açor, is honoured with a Mass, religious procession, ball, and a handicrafts fair during the **Santos Populares no Piódão** on the last weekend in June.

Sleeping & Eating

There are *quartos* everywhere, but quality is uneven; the most dependable options are listed below. A full list is available from Piódão's *turismo* (left).

Campismo de Ponte de Três Entradas (238 670 050; www.pontedas3entradas.com; sites per adult/child/tent/car €3/1.50/2.60/2.60) This shady riverside site 22km from Piódão near Avô also has bungalows from €45 for two people.

Parque de Campismo de Côja (235 729 666; www.coja.no.sapo.pt, in Portuguese; Côja; sites per adult/tent/car €3.90/2.55/2.55) A well-equipped, shady facility near the river, 27km west on the Rio Alva. It also has bungalows (€50 for up to four people).

Casas da Aldeia (235 731 424; d €25, d with kitchenette €40, 2-room house €65) Two schist houses just outside the centre have been kitted out with help from the village improvement committee. You can rent just a room, or an entire house with TV, private bathroom, kitchenette and fireplace.

Estalagem do Piódão (235 730 100; est.piodao@inatel.pt; s/d €57/71; P) Run by Inatel, this mammoth caricature of a local schist house looms over everything on a ridge above the village. The hotel has rather luxurious, modern rooms and the town's only decent restaurant.

In the same vein as Casas da Aldeia (above), Turihab (a nationwide organisation marketing private accommodation; see p494) rents rooms with breakfast from €35 to €40 in properties such as **Casa da Padaria** (☎ 235 732 773; casa. padaria@sapo.pt) – a former bakery within the village limits – and **Casa do Malhadinho** (☎ 235 731 464), on a hillside west of town.

Several cafes around the *largo* (central square) serve pastries and toasted sandwiches.

Getting There & Away
The only transport other than car or bicycle is a bus from Arganil (41km to the west) that stops in Piódão's *largo* (€2.80, 1¼ hours) on Thursday and Sunday. Check current times with Piódão's *turismo* (p351) or by calling Arganil's **turismo** (☎ 235 732 787).

The area's breathtaking views, narrow roads and sheer drops are a lethal combination for drivers. Note that side roads marked '4WD' are axle-breakers for ordinary cars.

BEIRA BAIXA

Beira Baixa closely resembles neighbouring Alentejo, with hospitable locals, fierce summer heat and rolling plains that stretch out to the horizon. It's also home to sprawling agricultural estates, humble farming hamlets and several stunning fortress towns that for centuries guarded the vulnerable plains from Spanish aggression.

CASTELO BRANCO
pop 30,600 / elev 360m
With its sweltering heat and a current wave of construction projects that has torn up half the town's streets, the provincial capital of Castelo Branco probably won't charm you at first glance. The best reasons to visit nowadays are the town's excellent museum and gardens, but it's also worth walking up to the town's ruined *castelo* (castle) for a better appreciation of the town's historic importance – these once-strategic heights afforded views across the surrounding plains to the Spanish border 20km away. Unfortunately, Castelo Branco's position made it a regular target of aggression, and as a result much of its historic fabric has been destroyed. Still, there are some charming medieval streets clustered in the centre, and the town's modern development includes an attractive series of tree-lined squares and boulevards.

Orientation
From the bus station, turn right down Rua do Saibreiro to central Alameda da Liberdade. From the train station the Alameda is 500m north on Avenida Nuno Álvares.

Information
Cyber Centro Municipal (Praça do Município; internet per hr €1; ⏰ 9am-11pm Mon-Fri) Across the plaza from the *turismo* in a courtyard behind the yellow facade.
Parque Natural do Tejo Internacional office (☎ 272 348 140; www.icn.pt, in Portuguese; 3rd fl, Av 1 de Maio 99) One block southwest of the *turismo*.
Police station (Rua Espírito Santo) Just west of the *turismo*.
Post office (Rua da Sé; ⏰ 8.30am-6.30pm Mon-Fri, 9am-12.30pm Sat)
Turismo (☎ 272 330 339; turismo.cmcb@mail.telepac .pt; Alameda da Liberdade; ⏰ 9.30am-7.30pm Mon-Fri, 9.30am-1pm & 2.30-6pm Sat & Sun) Slick new quarters on the town's main square.

Sights
PALÁCIO EPISCOPAL
The Palácio Episcopal (Bishop's Palace), in the north of town, is a sober 18th-century affair housing the **Museu de Francisco Tavares Proença Júnior** (☎ 272 344 277; www.ipmuseus.pt; Largo Dr José Lopes Dias; adult/under 14yr/student €2/free/1; ⏰ 10am-12.30pm & 2-5.30pm Tue-Sun). Downstairs, the museum's centrepiece is an excellent display of archaeological finds from the surrounding area.

If you're a fan of embroidery you'll also be wowed by the upstairs exhibition of Castelo Branco's famous *colchas*: silk-embroidered linen bedspreads and coverlets made with patterns and techniques inspired by fabrics brought back by early Portuguese explorers. The museum has a stunning collection of Indian and Chinese originals, as well as a workshop where you can watch women practising the art.

Beside the museum is the **Jardim Episcopal** (Bishop's Garden; adult/under 10yr/senior €2/free/1; ⏰ 9am-7pm Apr-Sep, 9am-5pm Oct-Mar), a baroque whimsy of clipped box hedges and little granite statues. Notice that the statues of Portugal's Spanish-born kings Felipe I and II are smaller than those of the Portuguese monarchs!

Watch your back at the bottom of the kings' stairway, as there's a hidden, clap-activated fountain. It was built by a loutish 18th-century bishop who liked to surprise

THE BEIRAS

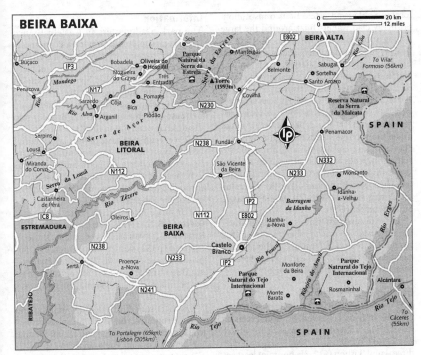

BEIRA BAIXA

maidens by soaking their petticoats. The attendant will show you where to clap.

CASTELO
There's little left of the castle, which was built by the Knights Templar in the 13th century and extended by Dom Dinis. However, the Miradouro de São Gens garden, which has supplanted the walls, offers grand views over town and countryside. The old lanes that lead back down to the town centre are very picturesque.

Sleeping
Parque de Campismo de Castelo Branco (☎ 272 322 577; sites per adult/child/tent/car €2/1.30/1.75/2; ☻ Jan-Nov) About 3km north of the town centre, this dusty site has scattered trees, mostly grassy pitches and basic facilities.

Pousada da Juventude (☎ 272 321 363; caste lobranco@movijovem.pt; Rua Dr Francisco José Palmeiro; dm/d €11/28; ♿) This friendly, recently renovated hostel is lost in a sea of unsightly high-rise development west of the centre. It has basic dorms plus two double rooms (one wheelchair-equipped).

Pensão Residencial Arraiana (☎ 272 341 637; fax 272 331 884; Av 1 de Maio 18; s/d/tr €25/40/50; ✕) A few blocks south of the *turismo*, Arraiana provides good value, with large, clean, well-kept rooms and generously stocked minibars for weary business travellers.

Tryp Colina do Castelo (☎ 272 349 280; www.sol melia.com; Rua da Piscina; s/d/ste €79/89/110; ⓟ ✕ ▢ ▨) Soulless but nicely positioned on the hillside northwest of the *castelo*, the city's top choice is a huge, modern business hotel affording fine views from most of its comfy, bright rooms. Amenities include a gym and indoor pool.

Eating & Drinking
Restaurante O Jardim (☎ 272 342 850; Rua Figueira 29; meals €7-9.50; ☻ lunch & dinner Mon-Sat) Given the sheer volume of helpings (order pork and expect half a pig!), this cosy, friendly restaurant down a backstreet near Largo da Sé is fantastic value. Daily specials include soup, main course, drink, dessert and coffee for under €10; sangria goes for €6.50 a litre.

Kalifa (☎ 272 344 246; Rua Cadetes de Toledo 10; mains €7.50-11; ☻ lunch & dinner) Bustling, centrally

THE BEIRAS

located Kalifa is a Castelo Branco institution. Formally clad waiters buzz around the large dining room, serving generous portions of hearty, regional fare. Especially pleasant is the lively grapevine-shaded patio on the cobblestones out back. It's just off Alameda da Liberdade near the *turismo*.

Praça Velha (☎ 272 328 640; Praça Luís de Camões 17; dishes €11-16, tasting menus €26-39; ☷ lunch & dinner Tue-Sat, lunch Sun) For a proper treat, make a beeline for this former Knights Templar abode in the old town. The atmospheric setting includes a medieval wooden ceiling, stone floors and pillars, and a long buffet table heaped with platters. Try the all-inclusive lunch specials (€13.50) or the fantastic Sunday buffet (€19).

Self-caterers can find supplies, including the *queijo de ovelha* (sheep's cheese) for which this region is famous, in the **mercado municipal** (Av 1 de Maio) or nearby **Pingo Doce supermarket** (Av 1 de Maio; ☷ 8.30am-9pm).

Getting There & Away
BUS
Castelo Branco is served by **Rede Expressos** (☎ 272 340 120; www.rede-expressos.pt), with direct service to Coimbra (€12.30, 2½ hours, about three daily), Lisbon (€12, 3½ hours, at least six daily), Guarda (€9.20, 1½ hours, at least six daily) and Covilhã (€4.20, one hour, at least six daily).

TRAIN
Castelo Branco is on the Lisbon–Covilhã line. Three daily IC trains to Lisbon (€13.50, 2¾ hours) are supplemented by four slower regional services (€11.60, 3¾ hours). IC/regional trains also serve Covilhã (€7.50/€5.90, 55 minutes/1½ hours).

PARQUE NATURAL DO TEJO INTERNACIONAL
Still one of Portugal's wildest landscapes, this 230-sq-km natural park shadows the Rio Tejo and the watersheds of three of its tributaries: the Rio Ponsul, Ribeira do Aravil and Rio Erges. While not aesthetically remarkable, it shelters some of the country's rarest bird species, including black storks, Bonelli's eagles, royal eagles, Egyptian vultures, black vultures and griffon vultures. The park was established in 2000, after a major push by private environmental organisation Quercus (see p81).

Information
The park headquarters in Castelo Branco (p352) can sometimes provide a Portuguese-language brochure with general background information, although supplies are limited.

The park's best-marked hiking trail, known locally as the Rota dos Abutres (Route of the Vultures), descends from Salvaterra do Extremo (60km east of Castelo Branco) into the dramatic canyon of the Rio Erges.

Drivers can get a taste of the park's natural beauty by following the unnumbered road between Monforte da Beira and Cegonhas (southeast of Castelo Branco), which passes through a beautiful cork oak forest on either side of the Ribeira do Aravil.

For more information, your best bet is **Quercus** (☎ 272 324 272; www.quercus.pt; Travessa da Ferradura 14, Castelo Branco). At Castelo Branco's *turismo* (p352) you can buy Quercus' 250-page *Guia de Percursos Tejo Internacional*, a guide (in Portuguese) to regional geology, climate, flora and fauna, villages, trails and transport.

Quercus runs birdwatching, walking and other programs. Basic accommodation is available at Rosmaninhal and Monte Barata; for details contact **Paulo Monteiro** (☎ 277 477 463) at Quercus.

MONSANTO
pop 200 / elev 600m
Like an island in the sky, the stunning village of Monsanto towers high above the surrounding plains. A stroll through its steeply cobbled streets, lined with stone houses that seem to merge together with the boulder-strewn landscape, is reason enough to come. But to fully appreciate Monsanto's rugged isolation, climb the shepherds' paths above town to the abandoned hilltop castle, whose crumbling walls command vertiginous views in all directions. Walkers will also appreciate the network of hiking trails threading through the vast cork oak–dominated expanses below.

Orientation & Information
Monsanto is so small that you need only follow the very steep path uphill to reach the castle. A handy brochure and map from the *turismo* helps to identify routes and sights and describes historic details.

Post office (Largo do Cruzeiro; ☷ 9am-12.30pm Mon-Fri) Near the town centre.

Turismo (☎ 277 314 642; Rua Marquês da Graciosa; ⊙ 10am-1pm & 2-6pm May-Sep, 9.30am-1pm & 2-5.30pm Oct-Apr) A few doors east of the post office.

Sights

VILLAGE
Since winning a national competition in 1938 as the country's most 'Portuguese' village, Monsanto has been largely shielded from modernisation. Several houses near the village entrance are surprisingly grand, some sporting Manueline doorways and stone crests. Halfway to the castle you'll come across the **gruta**, a snug cavern apparently once used as a drinking den – and still used as such, judging by the half-empty glasses of beer inside. Other caves around town double as barns for the local sheep and goats.

CASTELO
This formidable stone fortress seems almost to have grown out of the boulder-littered hillside that supports it. It's a beautiful site, windswept and populated by lizards and wildflowers. Immense vistas (marred only by mobile-phone masts) include Spain to the east and the Barragem da Idanha dam to the southwest.

There was probably a fortress here even before the Romans arrived, but after Dom Sancho I booted out the Moors in the 12th century it was beefed up. Dom Dinis refortified it, but after centuries of attacks from across the border it finally fell into ruin.

Just below the castle stands what's left of the Romanesque **Capela de São Miguel**, with its cluster of sarcophagi carved into solid rock eerily lying just outside the chapel portal.

HIKING TRAILS
Monsanto is crisscrossed by long-distance hiking trails, including the GR-12 from Lisbon to Constancia, Bulgaria, and the GR-22, a 540km circuit of Portugal's historic villages. For a beautiful, relatively easy walk (one hour round trip), descend the GR-12 along the stone road to the **Capela de São Pedro de Vir-a-Corça**, a medieval chapel surrounded by giant boulders. You can follow this same trail all the way to Idanha-a-Velha (p356), a beautiful but exposed 7km walk best undertaken in cooler weather.

Festivals & Events
On 3 May each year Monsanto comes alive in the **Festa das Cruzes**, commemorating a medieval siege. The story goes that the starving villagers threw their last lonely calf over the walls, taunting their besiegers as if they had plenty to spare. And apparently, their attackers were hoodwinked, because they promptly abandoned the siege. These days, young girls throw baskets of flowers instead, after which there's dancing and singing beside the castle walls.

Sleeping & Eating
At the time of writing, high demand and low supply meant there were no real budget accommodation options in Monsanto.

Casa da Maria (☎ 965624607; Av Fernando Ramos Rocha 11; r incl breakfast €50; ⊠) Depending on group size, you can rent one, two or all three rooms in this well-equipped house just below town, with optional access to a kitchen and living room. Advance reservations are required.

Divino Monsanto (☎ 277 314 471; www.divinomonsanto.com; s/d €60/70; ⊠ 🖳) Understaffed and with crumbling infrastructure, this place doesn't live up to its price or setting, but it's the only hotel in the old town. The best reason to stay here (aside from the sheer pleasure of being in Monsanto overnight) is room 103, whose large balcony commands fabulous views of the town and surrounding countryside. Staff are good-natured and helpful, albeit overworked.

Restaurante O Jovem (☎ 277 314 590; Av Fernando Ramos Rocha 21; mains €7.50-10; ⊙ lunch & dinner) Right at the town entrance, this humble restaurant cheerfully dishes up good-value Portuguese fare, including good *ensopado de borrego* (lamb stew with mint and parsley).

Petiscos e Granitos (☎ 277 314 029; Rua do Castelo 15; mains €8.50-12.50; ⊙ lunch & dinner) Wedged between gigantic boulders, Petiscos e Granitos' back terrace provides a fantastic backdrop for sipping a *copo de vinho* (glass of wine) at sunset, with incomparable views over the plains below. Waiters sometimes move at a geological pace, but the food is excellent. Specialities like grilled lamb chops with roasted potatoes are delicious, and even the salads are done to perfection.

There are also souvenir shops selling homemade honey cakes, some laced with a wicked *aguardente* (alcoholic 'firewater').

Getting There & Away
Without a car, Monsanto can be difficult to reach. **Rede Expressos** (☎ 272 340 120; www.rede-expressos.pt) usually has one bus daily to

Castelo Branco (€3.50), but departure times change often (and can be inconveniently early, usually at 6.30am). There is often additional service during the school year, and an extra afternoon bus on Sundays. Ask at the *turismo* in either Monsanto or Castelo Branco for the latest schedules.

IDANHA-A-VELHA

While very different from hilltop Monsanto, neighbouring Idanha-a-Velha is just as extraordinary. Nestled in a remote valley of patchwork farms and olive orchards, Idanha-a-Velha was founded as the Roman city of Igaeditânia. Rome's ramparts still define the town, though it only reached its apogee under Visigothic rule. They built a cathedral and made Idanha their regional capital. It's also believed that their legendary King Wamba was born here.

Moors were next on the scene, and the cathedral was turned into a mosque during their tenure. They, in turn, were driven out by the Knights Templar in the 12th century. The mystical knights constructed the town's small but imposing keep, which sits on the remarkably preserved pedestal of a Roman temple.

How has such a tiny village managed to preserve such a grand sweep of history? It's believed that a 15th-century plague virtually wiped out its population, with survivors going on to found Idanha-a-Nova about 30km to the southwest. However, the townspeople's misfortune is our luck, since they left the town virtually intact. A few brave souls eventually returned, and today a small but hardy population of shepherds and farmers live amid the Roman, Visigothic and medieval ruins.

Information

The **turismo** (☎ 277 914 280; Rua da Sé; 🕒 10am-1pm & 2-6pm May-Sep, 9.30am-1pm & 2-5.30pm Oct-Apr) is built on a see-through floor over ruins of the old settlement. Staff lead free guided town visits at 11am and 4.30pm whenever there's enough interest (10 people or more). English-language and/or smaller group tours are also available by prior arrangement.

Sights

From the *turismo* it's a short walk to the 6th-century Visigothic **cathedral**, surrounded by a jigsaw puzzle of scattered archaeological remains. The church has undergone heavy restoration, but its early roots are evident everywhere: foundation stones bearing Latin inscriptions, Moorish brick arches (now plastered over), salvaged Roman columns along the right side of the nave and Visigothic elements such as the baptistry visible through glass near the entrance. Of the frescos within, the best-preserved features São Bartolomeu with a demon at his feet.

The nearby **Lagar de Varas** (admission free; 🕒 by request at turismo 10.30am-11.30am & 3-5pm) hosts an impressive olive-oil press made in the traditional way with ruddy great tree trunks providing the crushing power.

The only evidence of the Knights Templar is the **Torre des Templários**, made of massive chunks of stone and now surrounded by clucking hens. It sits on top of what was likely the pedestal of a Roman temple. Other Roman remains include the gracefully arched **Roman bridge** on the east side of town, the old **Roman wall and gate** on the north side (accessible via a metal catwalk) and a row of stones on the south side used for two purposes: crossing the river on foot and measuring river depth to ensure safe passage of horse-drawn carts.

After all this history it's a delight to come across the **Forno Comunitário** (communal bakery; Rua do Castelo) and discover villagers sliding trays of biscuits and enormous loaves of bread into the huge stone oven, blackened from use.

Sleeping & Eating

Idanha-a-Velha has traditionally been without tourist accommodation. There are long-term plans to convert the giant Salazar-era residence near the *turismo* into a hotel, but in the meantime Monsanto remains the best bet for a hot meal and a place to bed down.

Café Lafiv (☎ 277 914 180; Rua da Amoreira 1; 🕒 8am-late) Near the *turismo*, this is the village's most dependable cafe, serving sandwiches and smoked sausage.

Getting There & Away

Getting to Idanha-a-Velha by bus can be difficult indeed. On school days, there's generally one bus daily to/from Idanha-a-Nova (40 minutes), from where you can catch onward buses to Castelo Branco (€3.20, 55 minutes, two to three daily). Alternatively, the *turismo* can arrange a taxi to Idanha-a-Nova or Monsanto, but prices are steep (about €30).

SORTELHA
pop 800 / elev 760m

Perched on a rocky promontory, Sortelha is the oldest of a string of fortresses guarding the frontier east of Guarda and Covilhã. Its fortified 12th-century castle teeters on the brink of a steep cliff, while immense walls encircle a village of great charms. Laid out in Moorish times, it remains a winning combination of stout stone cottages, sloping cobblestone streets and diminutive orchards.

These days the walled village has few permanent residents, giving it an eerie silence. A scramble along the ramparts affords views over a landscape of steep valleys and forbidding, boulder-strewn peaks that is just as beautiful and just as haunting as the town itself.

Orientation & Information

'New' Sortelha lines the Santo Amaro–Sabugal road, along which are several Turihab properties and a restaurant. The medieval hilltop fortress is a short drive, or a 10-minute walk, up one of two lanes signposted 'castelo'.

The town's **turismo** (☎ 800 262 788; turismo@sabugalmais.com; Largo do Corro; 🕑 10am-1pm & 2-6pm Apr-Sep, 9.30am-1pm & 2-5.30pm Oct-Mar) is an incongruous one-room wooden structure (air-conditioned in summer) in Largo do Corro, just inside the old town gate. It provides a wide range of brochures on Sortelha and the surrounding area.

Sights

The entrance to the fortified old village is a grand, stone **Gothic gate**. From here, a cobbled lane leads up to the heart of the village, with a *pelourinho* (stone pillory) in front of the remains of a small **castle** to the left and the parish **church** to the right. Higher still is the **bell tower**. Climb it for a view of the entire village (but heed the sign begging visitors not to ring the bells). For a more adventurous and scenic climb, tackle the **ramparts** around the village (beware precarious stairways and big steps!). As you walk, keep your eyes open for the weather-worn Arabic script above the doorway of the **Casa Árabe** at the very top of town.

Sleeping

Sortelha boasts several atmospheric Turihab properties, complete with kitchens, thick stone walls and heating. Calling a week or two ahead is essential in July and August. There's no true budget accommodation.

Casa da Villa (☎ 271 388 113; Rua Direita; 2-8 people €60-180) This delightful stone cottage has a privileged place within the village walls. It's owned by the same people that run Casa da Cerca (below) and Casa do Páteo (below).

Casas do Campanário (☎ 271 388 198; Rua da Mesquita; d €60) Sortelha's other 'inside-the-walls' lodging option, the Casas do Campanário include a house for two people and another for up to six; ask at Bar Campanário, at the top of the village just beyond the bell tower.

Casa da Cerca (☎ /fax 271 388 113; casadacerca@clix.pt; Largo de Santo António; d €85; 🅿 🐾) Just off the main road, below the old town, this 17th-century house is Sortelha's top choice. Rooms are comfortable and attractive if not luxurious, with wood floors and traditional furnishings. The same owners rent out apartments just across the courtyard in the Casa do Páteo (two/four people with kitchen €60/80).

Eating & Drinking

Bar Forno Esplanada (☎ 271 388 034; Travessa do Forno; snacks from €3; 🕑 lunch & dinner) Suitable for a simple afternoon snack, this terrace cafe directly below the castle walls commands sweeping views of the rugged landscape below.

Restaurante O Celta (☎ 271 388 291; mains €7-15; 🕑 lunch & dinner Wed-Mon) On the main road, this place serves mountain specialities such as *costeletas de javali* (wild boar chops); the €12.50 *ementa turística* (tourist menu) includes wine, dessert and coffee.

Restaurante Dom Sancho I (☎ 271 388 267; Largo do Corro; mains €11-17; 🕑 lunch & dinner) Sortelha's favourite eatery sits just inside the main Gothic gates. Prices for the regional cuisine are high, but the food is renowned and the dining room rustically elegant. For lighter snacks and drinks, head to the beamed, stone-walled bar downstairs.

Bar As Boas Vindas (🕑 2pm-late Fri-Sun) Uphill and to the right of the *turismo*, this cosy little stone house with couches, rustic farm decor and a well-stocked bar makes a good place to cool off on a hot summer afternoon.

Getting There & Away

Regional trains on the Covilhã–Guarda line (three to four daily) stop at Belmonte-Manteigas station, 12km to the northwest, where you can catch a local **taxi** (☎ 271 388 182) to Sortelha (around €12). There's no regular bus service.

THE BEIRAS

PARQUE NATURAL DA SERRA DA ESTRELA

Fascinating both for its natural and cultural history, Parque Natural da Serra da Estrela was one of Portugal's first designated natural parks, and at 1011 sq km remains the country's largest protected area. The rugged boulder-strewn meadows and icy lakes of its high country form one of Portugal's most unique and unexpected landscapes. On the slopes below, rushing rivers historically provided hydro power to spin and weave the Serra's abundant wool into cloth. Nowadays, shepherds still roam a landscape of terraced fields and traditional one-room, stone *casais* (huts) thatched with rye straw, but traditional sheep-herding is fast giving way to a service economy catering to weekending tourists.

The presence of 1993m Torre – Portugal's highest peak – at the centre of the park is both a blessing and a curse. It forms an undeniably dramatic backdrop, but as the only place in Portugal where snow dependably falls, it also tends to lure vast winter hordes with little consciousness of their impact on the high country's ecosystems. The fragility of the mountain environment is underscored by the devastation wrought by forest fires in recent years, while the fragility of the economy is evidenced by the large numbers of local residents who have emigrated elsewhere, leading to a notable greying of the population in small mountain villages like Linhares.

The Serra abounds in hiking and climbing opportunities. Although the underfunded park service struggles to keep trails marked, and the best books and maps on the region regularly go out of print due to lack of funding, these mountains remain one of Portugal's most alluring destinations for outdoors enthusiasts. Hikers – and everyone else – will also appreciate the Serra's excellent mountain cheese and hearty rye bread.

Information

There are park offices at Manteigas (headquarters), Seia, Gouveia and Guarda, though not all staff speak English. Some local *turismos* can also provide park information.

Finding up-to-date printed information about the park can be frustrating. A free pamphlet (last published in 2006) offers a general introduction in English to the park as well as two suggested walks, but supplies are scarce due to lack of funds.

Likewise, the best resource for serious hikers – the 1:50,000 topographic map *Carta Turística: Parque Natural da Serra da Estrela* – has been out of print for years. Until the government's **Instituto de Conservação da Natureza e da Biodiversidade** (icnb@icnb.pt) provides funding for a reprint, your best bet is to snap a digital photo of the map at one of the park offices.

An English-language booklet, *Discovering the Region of the Serra da Estrela* (€4.25), has trail profiles, walking times, historic notes and flora and fauna basics, but is of limited use due to its 1992 publication date. A recommended, more-scientific guide to local flora and fauna is *Geobotanical Guide of the Serra* (€10), published in 2002. Park offices offer other books and brochures in Portuguese on geography, geology, medicinal plants and archaeology.

The best bets for understanding the Serra's natural history are the state-of-the-art Centro de Interpretaçaõ da Serra da Estrela (CISE; Serra da Estrela Interpretive Centre; p361) in Seia and the park service's small but well-done natural and cultural history exhibit atop Torre, both newly opened at the time of writing.

ACCOMMODATION

While Seia, Gouveia, Manteigas, Covilhã and Guarda all provide useful bases with comfortable accommodation options, those wanting a true mountain experience should opt for Manteigas, because the others – situated as they are on the Serra's outer slopes – feel as if they are more a part of the surrounding plains.

Whereas camping grounds drop their rates or close in winter, many hotels, *pensões* and *residenciais* actually increase their rates, typically from late December to March.

The park has also begun to rent out basic cabins near Manteigas in **Penhas Douradas** (cabins per 2/4 people €30/60). For reservations, contact the park office in Manteigas (p364).

There are hostels at Penhas da Saúde and Guarda, and at least eight camping grounds near the centre of the park. Turismo Habitação properties, which are concentrated on the western slopes, can be booked through local *turismos*.

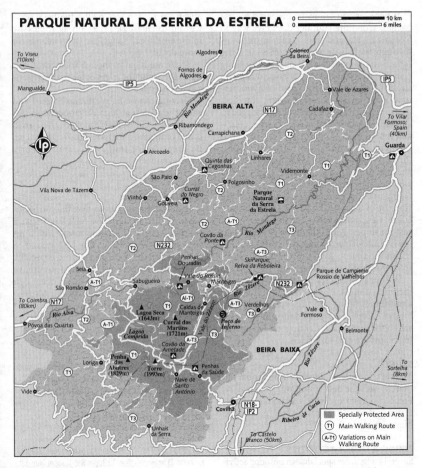

Sights & Activities
WILDLIFE

The park harbours many endangered or vulnerable species – especially feathered ones. These include the black stork, Montagu's harrier, chough, turtle dove and 10 species of bats.

Unusual animals also include the mountain gecko, and if you're lucky you may catch a glimpse of more rare birds such as the peregrine falcon, eagle owl and black-shouldered kite.

The flora, too, is interesting. Popularity as medicinal remedies has put several of the park's plants in the list of endangered or vulnerable species, including mountain thrift *(Armeria transmontana)*, great yellow gentian *(Gentiana lutea)* and juniper *(Juniperus communis)*.

WALKING

Crisp air and immense vistas make this a trekking paradise for those willing to make the effort. In part because of limited infrastructure, surprisingly few people get off the main roads. Even in summer, walkers will generally feel they have the park to themselves.

While still very chilly and possibly damp, late April has the hillsides bright with wildflowers. The weather is finest from May to October. Winter is harsh, with snow at the higher elevations from November or December to April or May.

THE BEIRAS

Whenever you come, be prepared for extremes: scorching summer days give way to freezing nights, and chilling rainstorms blow through with little warning. Mist is a big hazard not only because it obscures walking routes and landmarks, but because it can also stealthily chill you to the point of hypothermia. You may set out on a warm, cloudless morning and by noon find yourself fogged in and shivering, so always pack for the cold – and the wet, too.

There are three main 'official' routes through the park, as well as branches and alternative trails. T1 runs the length of the park (about 90km) and is the easiest to follow, taking in every kind of terrain, including the summit of Torre. T2 and T3 (both around 80km) run respectively along the western and eastern slopes. All of the trails pass through towns and villages, each of which offers some accommodation. Many of the finest walks start around Manteigas (p364).

Within a zone of special protection (which includes almost everything above 1200m altitude), camping and fires are strictly prohibited except at designated sites, all of which are on the main trails. Cutting trees and picking plants are also forbidden.

SKIING

The ski season typically runs from January to March, with the best conditions in February. For a rundown on what's available for skiers, see the listings on Torre (p367) and Manteigas (p364).

BIKING & OTHER ACTIVITIES

Several companies specialise in outdoor activities in the park, including **Adriventura** (☎ 275 325 919, 919 462 183; www.adriventura.com), which organises groups for biking, rock-climbing, hiking and more. **Turistela** (☎ 275 319 120; www.turistela.pt) also organises biking adventures and can offer information about the new Vodaphone Bike Park around Torre (half-/full day €15/20). SkiParque (p366), east of Manteigas, offers many activities, including paragliding, rock-climbing, canoeing, biking and horse riding.

Getting There & Around

Express buses run daily from Coimbra to Seia, Guarda and Covilhã, and from Aveiro, Porto and Lisbon to Guarda and Covilhã. There are daily IC trains from Lisbon and Coimbra to Guarda (plus IR services calling at Gouveia) and from Lisbon to Covilhã (with IR services on to Guarda). Prices on all routes are in the €10 to €15 range; see town listings for more details.

There are regular, though infrequent, bus services around the edges of the park but none directly across it.

Driving can be hairy, thanks to mist and wet or icy roads at high elevations, and stiff winds. The Gouveia–Manteigas N232 road is one of the most tortuous in all of Portugal. Be prepared for traffic jams around Torre on weekends.

SEIA

pop 5700 / elev 532m

Despite its sweeping views over the surrounding lowlands, modern Seia feels largely like a charmless strip of contemporary buildings slapped onto a hillside. The best reason to come is for the local museums, especially the brand-new Serra da Estrela Interpretive Centre (CISE). The town also has enough restaurants and hotels to make it a convenient stop if you're arriving from the west and aren't quite ready for switchbacking drives into the mountains.

Information

Espaço Internet (☺ 10am-6pm Tue-Sun) Free internet adjacent to the CISE interpretive centre (opposite).
Parque Natural da Serra da Estrela office (☎ 238 310 440; fax 238 310 441; Praça da República 28; ☺ 9am-12.30pm & 2-5.30pm Mon-Fri)
Post office (Av 1 de Maio; ☺ 8.30am-12.30pm & 2-6pm Mon-Fri)
Turismo (☎ 238 317 762; turismo@cm-seia.pt; Rua Pintor Lucas Marrão; ☺ 9am-12.30pm & 2-5.30pm Mon-Sat, 9am-1pm Sun)

Sights & Activities

Museu do Pão (Museum of Bread; ☎ 238 310 760; www.museudopao.pt; admission €2; ☺ 10am-6pm Tue-Sun) has all the information you'll ever need on local bread production. The museum's highlight is the traditional-style shop, which sells local goodies (including freshly ground flour and bread baked on the premises). It's 1km northeast of the centre on the road to Sabugueiro.

Near the *turismo*, the **Museu do Brinquedo** (Toy Museum; ☎ 238 082 015; museu.brinquedo@cm-seia.pt; Largo de Santa Rita; admission €1.50; ☺ 10am-6pm Tue-Sun) traces the history of toys in Portugal, from the Victorian to the contemporary. There's a playroom, a collection of toys from other

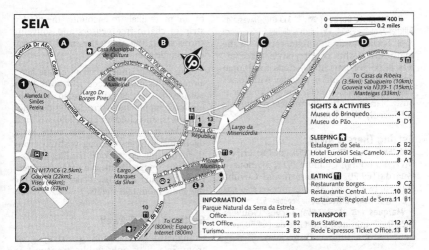

SEIA

SIGHTS & ACTIVITIES
Museu do Brinquedo...............4 C2
Museu do Pão.........................5 D1

SLEEPING
Estalagem de Seia...................6 B2
Hotel Eurosol Seia-Camelo.....7 B2
Residencial Jardim..................8 A1

EATING
Restaurante Borges.................9 C2
Restaurante Central...............10 B2
Restaurante Regional de Serra.11 B1

TRANSPORT
Bus Station...........................12 A2
Rede Expressos Ticket Office.13 B1

INFORMATION
Parque Natural da Serra da Estrela
Office.................................1 B1
Post Office.............................2 B2
Turismo.................................3 B2

countries and a workshop where kids can watch toys being made or repaired.

Opened in 2007 with partial EU funding, the state-of-the-art **Centro de Interpretaçaõ da Serra da Estrela** (CISE; Serra da Estrela Interpretive Centre; ☎ 238 320 300; www.cise-seia.org.pt; Rua Visconde Molelos; admission adult/child €2/1.50; ☼ 10am-6pm Tue-Sun) provides an excellent introduction to the Serra da Estrela region. A nine-minute film in English or Portuguese (don your 3D glasses at the door!) takes you flying around the mountains' main points of interest. Multimedia displays in the museum next door include a topographic scale model of the Serra with push buttons allowing you to light up rivers and fault lines, or see which features are granite and which are schist. CISE also provides free information on local hikes.

Sleeping

Residencial Jardim (☎ 238 311 414; fax 238 310 091; Edifício Jardim II, Av Luís Vaz de Camões; s/d €17.50/30) Hidden in the basement of a modern apartment block across from the Casa Municipal de Cultura, this squeaky-clean but rather dreary place offers Seia's most affordable accommodation. It's a stiff uphill walk to the centre.

Hotel Eurosol Seia-Camelo (☎ 238 310 100; www.eurosol.pt; Av 1 de Maio 16; s/d/tr €46/64/86; P X ⊠ ⊠) This well-functioning but nondescript business-class hotel has large rooms, pink-marble bathrooms with abundant hot water, a large sandy children's play area, a pool with lounge chairs and free off-street parking. Inquire about discounts for longer stays.

Estalagem de Seia (☎ 238 315 866; fax 238 315 538; Av Dr Afonso Costa; s/d €48/53; P X ⊠) This elegant 17th-century mansion of thickset stone has a grand parlour and a breakfast terrace with good views. Closed for remodelling in 2008, its reopening date remains uncertain – check with the *turismo*.

Casas da Ribeira (☎ 238 311 221, 919660354; www.casasdaribeira.com; Póvoa Velha; 2-/4-person cottages incl breakfast & firewood from €70/85) In the hills above Seia, this charming collection of vine-draped, stone cottages equipped with kitchenettes and fireplaces is highly recommended if you have your own vehicle. There's a two-night minimum stay, but prices drop significantly for additional nights. From Seia, climb the Sabugueiro road for about 5km, then follow signs into the tiny hamlet of Póvoa Velha, where you'll find the rental office. Call ahead to arrange your visit.

Eating

Restaurante Central (☎ 238 314 433; Av 1 de Maio 12B; mains €6-10; ☼ lunch & dinner) Family-friendly, with warm and attentive service, this plain-faced restaurant near Hotel Carmelo serves dependably good if basic Portuguese fare.

Restaurante Regional de Serra (☎ 238 312 717; Av dos Combatentes da Grande Guerra 14; mains €7-11; ☼ lunch & dinner) Hugely popular at lunchtime, this trim place is well known for hearty regional specialities, including local cheeses and sausages as well as *chanfana à serrana* (highland goat).

THE BEIRAS

Restaurante Borges (☎ 238 313 010; Travessa do Funchal 7; mains €9-14; ☿ lunch & dinner Fri-Tue, lunch Wed) Tucked away in a tight corner off the main street, this country-style place offers large portions of delicious traditional Portuguese fare and is popular with locals celebrating special events. The TV conspicuously blaring in other Portuguese restaurants is blessedly absent here.

Getting There & Away
Rede Expressos (☎ 238 313 102) goes to Lisbon (€17, 4½ hours), Coimbra (€10, 1½ hours), Guarda (€9.20, 70 minutes) and Covilhã (€11.50, two hours). Rede Expressos also has a central **ticket office** (Rua da República 52).

Marques (☎ 238 312 858) serves Gouveia (€2.30, 25 minutes) and Guarda (€4.50, two hours) several times each weekday.

SABUGUEIRO
pop 700 / elev 1050m
Attracting tourists from far and wide thanks to its title as Portugal's highest village, Sabugueiro is more noteworthy as a place to shop for *queijo da serra* (mountain cheese) and Serra da Estrela dogs (see boxed text, below) than as a destination in itself. While the hills around town are still inhabited by sturdy farmer-shepherd families living in slate-roofed granite houses, casual passers-

by are more likely to encounter the motley strip of charm-free *pensões* and souvenir shops straggling along the main highway between Seia and Torre.

You can buy some excellent cheese here, although it's mostly made with milk from outside the Serra da Estrela due to diminishing local supply and skyrocketing demand. Pet lovers, and children especially, will find it hard to resist stopping to look at the Serra da Estrela puppies peering wistfully from their roadside cages. Local families also sell delicious smoked ham, rye bread, juniper-berry firewater and cosy fleece slippers for the chilly mountain nights.

Getting There & Away
Sabugueiro is a 15-minute drive uphill from Seia. The only public transport is a single bus that runs to/from Seia each Wednesday (Seia's market day), departing from Sabugueiro at about 8am and returning from Seia at about noon. A taxi from Seia costs around €10.

GOUVEIA
pop 3800 / elev 650m
Gouveia (goh-*vay*-ah), draped across a hillside 5km from the N17, is a charming blend of the contemporary and historic in a

---

A SHEPHERD'S BEST FRIEND

Any animal lover travelling through the Serra da Estrela will be hard pressed to resist the 'take-me-home-now!' feeling prompted by the region's indigenous Cão da Serra da Estrela, or **Estrela mountain dog** (EMD). It's not just the adorable fuzzy golden and black puppies; the massive adults are as handsome as they are reputed to be strong and smart, loving and loyal.

The importance of these beautiful animals to local culture is epitomised in the bronze statue outside Gouveia depicting a shepherd with his faithful dog. Widely recognised as one of the most ancient breeds on the Iberian Peninsula, the EMD is thought to have descended from dogs brought by the Romans or Visigoths. Over the centuries, shepherds chose the best dogs to guard their goats and sheep and perform in harsh mountain conditions. The dogs are massive, with males weighing over 100lb; they have a warm coat to protect against the frigid mountain winters, can survive on minimal diets, and possess the endurance and agility to trek over boulder-strewn terrain. Fiercely resisting any predator daring enough to attack its flock, the EMD can also be gentle as a lamb, especially in its nurturing attitude towards the young of both the human and goat/sheep variety. Traditionally the dogs were outfitted with spiked collars to protect their throats against an attacking wolf or bear.

While today the EMD is one of the most popular pets in Portugal, its traditional use has declined drastically. In an ironic twist, the wolf recovery organisation Grupo Lobo (http://lobo.fc.ul .pt) has become one of Portugal's leading advocates for reviving the EMD's role as herd guardian. Biologists worldwide now see herd-guarding dogs as one of the best strategies for protecting flocks while promoting wolf recovery.

smaller-town setting. Pleasantly laid out, with parks and public gardens, it offers sufficient accommodation, food and transport to be a good base for exploring the western side of the *parque natural*.

Orientation & Information

From the bus station, it's 450m south via Avenida 1 de Maio and Rua da República to Praça de São Pedro, the town centre.

Biblioteca Municipal (☎ 238 490 230; Praça de São Pedro 5; ⊙ 9.30am-12.30pm & 2-6pm Mon-Fri, 9.30am-12.30pm Sat) Free internet.

Centro do Cidadão Espaço Net (Rua da República; ⊙ 10am-12.30pm & 2-6.30pm Tue-Sat) Free internet across the square from the *turismo*.

Parque Natural da Serra da Estrela office (☎ 238 492 411; fax 238 494 183; Av Bombeiros Voluntários 8; ⊙ 9am-12.30pm & 2-5.30pm Mon-Fri) A block south of the centre.

Post office (Av 1 de Maio 3; ⊙ 9am-12.30pm & 2-6pm Mon-Fri) Between Praça de São Pedro and the Hotel de Gouveia.

Turismo (☎ 238 083 930; gouveia.postodeturismo@gmail.com; Jardim da Ribeira; ⊙ 9.30am-12.30pm & 2-6pm Mon-Sat, 10am-12.30pm & 2-5pm Sun) On a pleasant square just downhill from Praça de São Pedro.

Sights

The former manor house of the Condes de Vinhós now houses the paintings of favourite son Abel Manta (1888–1982) at the eponymous **Abel Manta Museu de Arte Moderna** (☎ 238 493 648; Rua Direita 45; admission free; ⊙ 9.30am-12.30pm & 2-6pm Tue-Sun), south off Praça de São Pedro. Along with occasional special exhibits, this small museum also features paintings and drawings by Manta's wife and son, and a small glass case containing his black beret, pipe, bow ties and wooden artist's palette.

Sleeping

Parque de Campismo Curral do Negro (☎ /fax 238 491 008; www.fcmportugal.com; sites per adult/tent/car €3.70/2.65/2.65; ⊙ Jan-Nov; ☢) Generously shaded with oaks, pine and chestnuts, this scenically located camp site has picnic tables and a small playground. It's a steeply winding climb 3km southeast of town.

Quinta das Cegonhas (☎ 238 745 886; www.cegonhas.com; Nabainhos; sites per adult/child/tent/car €3.90/2/3.90/2.90, r/apt from €46/62; ☢) Meaning 'House of the Storks', this restored 17th-century *quinta* (country estate) 6km northeast of

Gouveia has nice views, terraced tent sites and a few private rooms and self-catering apartments (minimum three days). Meals are available by arrangement (adult/child €10/5).

Residencial Monteneve (☎ 238 490 370; www.monteneveresidencial.com; Av Bombeiros Voluntários 12; s/d/tr €45/60/78; P ✕) This old granite building in the heart of town has been converted into a rigorously clean and surprisingly stylish hotel with comfortable rooms and a pretty breakfast room.

Casas do Toural (☎ 238 492 132, 963023893; www.casasdotoural.com; Rua Direita 74; 2-person cottages €60-74, 4-person cottages €100-108; 6-person cottages €151; ☢) This gorgeous ensemble of restored houses surrounds an immaculately kept hillside garden near the centre of town. Most rooms feature exposed stone walls, kitchens, fireplaces and living rooms. Book in advance on weekends. Owner Maria José offers a guided hike into the Serra da Estrela as part of your stay.

Eating

Restaurante O Júlio (☎ 238 498 016; Travessa do Loureiro 11A; dishes €7.50-11; ⊙ lunch & dinner) Tucked away in a narrow downtown street, this place is popular for its regional cuisine. House specialities include *cabrito à serrana* and *batatinhas do céu* (heavenly potatoes).

Lá em Casa (☎ 238 491 983; Sítio de Barreiros; mains €7.50-16.95; ⊙ lunch & dinner Tue-Sat, lunch Sun) It doesn't look like much from the outside, but this excellent restaurant near a roundabout northwest of town serves some of Gouveia's best food, including treats such as shrimp crêpes or grilled veal with mushroom–port-wine sauce.

Self-caterers will find the **mercado municipal** (⊙ Mon-Sat morning), straight uphill from the *turismo*, at its best on Thursday.

Shopping

O Mundo Rural (☎ 238 490 180; Largo Dr Alípio de Melo; ⊙ 9am-12.30pm & 2-5.30pm Mon-Fri) This outlet for regional artisans, affiliated with ADRUSE – a nonprofit organisation supporting rural development – has fair-priced ceramics, fabrics, cheese, Dão wines, sausages and more.

Getting There & Away

Rede Expressos (☎ 238 493 675) and **Marques** (☎ 238 312 858) stop at Gouveia's **bus station** (Rua Cidade da Guarda), a 10-minute walk north of the centre. Marques runs to Seia (€2.30, 25 minutes, four per weekday) and Guarda (€4.10, 1½ hours, one daily). Rede Expressos goes once or twice

---

HILL TOWNS OF THE NORTHERN SERRA

Two of the Serra da Estrela's prettiest towns are tucked high in the hills between Gouveia and Guarda. Neither **Linhares** nor **Folgosinho** has much in the way of tourist infrastructure – which is part of their appeal.

Linhares, designated an *aldeia histórica* (historic village) by the Portuguese government, is best known for its imposing castle, which commands remarkable bird's-eye views over the surrounding countryside. Aside from that, it's the kind of place where shepherds still drive their flocks down the middle of the road and older women come out to chat in their gardens at sunset. Poke around in the warren of stone houses, terraced hillsides and twisting lanes below the castle and you'll find signs advertising rooms for rent, including those at **Casa Pissarra** (☎ 271 776 180; fax 271 776 010; r from €35, house €100); weekend visitors can eat and drink at **Taberna do Alcaide** (☎ 271 776 578; www.cvrdao.pt; Rua Direita, Linhares; mains €8-10; 🕑 9am-midnight Sat & Sun).

Folgosinho's biggest draw, aside from its miniature hilltop castle, is its pretty main square, where you'll find **O Albertino** (☎ 238 745 266; prix fixe menus €11; 🕑 lunch & dinner Tue-Sat, lunch Sun), a cosy stone-walled restaurant specialising in down-to-earth mountain cuisine. Dinner is an all-you-can-eat affair, featuring gamey favourites like *feijoada de javeli* (beans stewed with wild boar). Albertino also rents rooms around town from €40.

---

daily to Coimbra (€12, two hours) and twice to Lisbon (€17, 4¾ hours).

The Gouveia railway station, 14km north near Ribamondego, is on the Beira Alta line from Lisbon to Guarda – regional trains stop here four times daily. A taxi between Gouveia and the station will cost around €10.

MANTEIGAS
pop 3400 / elev 720m

Cradled at the foot of the beautiful Vale do Zêzere, with high peaks and forest-draped slopes dominating the horizon in all directions, Manteigas feels more like a true mountain town than any of the other major Serra da Estrela gateways. There has been a settlement here since at least Moorish times, probably because of the hot springs at the nearby spa of Caldas de Manteigas (opposite).

As headquarters for the Parque Natural da Serra de Estrela, Manteigas also makes an excellent base for hikers looking to explore the region. Walk through the glacial valley above town and you'll still encounter terraced meadows, stone shepherds' *casais* and tinkling goatbells, while in Manteigas itself cobblestoned streets and older homes still hold their own against the high-rise development that has taken root elsewhere on the Serra's fringes.

Orientation & Information

From Seia or Gouveia you approach Manteigas down a near-vertical switchback, the N232. South of town, the N338 snakes up the Zêzere valley into the high country between Torre and Penhas da Saúde.

Manteigas has no real centre, but buses will set you down between the Galp petrol station and the *turismo*, near the park headquarters and a cluster of hotels and restaurants.

Parque Natural da Serra da Estrela office (☎ 275 980 060; pnse@icn.pt; Rua 1 de Maio 2; 🕑 9am-12.30pm & 2-5.30pm Mon-Fri)

Turismo (☎ /fax 275 981 129; Rua Dr Esteves de Carvalho; 🕑 9am-12.30pm & 2-5.30pm Tue-Sat)

Sights & Activities
POÇO DO INFERNO

In springtime, this **waterfall** in the craggy gorge of the Ribeira de Leandres – about 10km outside of Manteigas by car – makes a beautiful sight. From Manteigas town centre, drive approximately 4km along the signposted main road towards Torre. Just beyond Caldas de Manteigas, look for a sign on your left for Poço do Inferno (Hell's Well) and climb up a narrow road 6km further to the falls, passing through a lush remnant of evergreen forest that was spared by the 2004 forest fire.

There's also a hiking trail from Manteigas to the falls, starting with a long descent along the cobbled road between the *turismo* and the Galp petrol station. However, at the time of writing it was extremely poorly marked.

In summer the waterfall slows to a trickle, and with trash and misuse the site's beauty is considerably dampened.

HOT SPRINGS

Just south (uphill) from the town centre is the privately run **Caldas de Manteigas** (☎ 275 980 300; cf.manteigas@inatel.pt), where for a €30 consultation with a medical practitioner you can get a prescription for various treatments, from bathing in water from the natural hot springs to massage and other kinds of physiotherapy (€3.20 to €9.60). Singles/doubles in the comfortable if slightly workaday hotel start at €45/56 (plus €16 per person for full board).

WALKING

Following are the outlines of three recommended walks in the mountains surrounding Manteigas. For details and more walks, inquire at the park office (opposite).

Vale do Zêzere

The relatively easy ramble through this magnificent, glacier-scoured valley at the foot of Torre is a highlight of any trip to Manteigas. Its only drawback: the trail is shadeless and baking in clear summer weather. The valley suffered a massive forest fire in 2004, and recovery has been very slow. Still, the Zêzere valley remains one of the park's most beautiful and noteworthy natural features.

From the park office, follow the N338 for 2.8km towards Caldas de Manteigas, leaving the road at the brown-and-white 'Roteiro Rural Palhotas' sign just beyond the spa hotel. From here, a part-cobbled, part-dirt road leads upstream through irrigated fields dotted with typical stone *casais*. About 4km along, the unpaved road crosses the Rio Zêzere just above a popular local swimming hole. A park service sign here (marked 'Reserva Biogenética') signals the beginning of a trail closed to vehicles. Drivers can park in the small dirt lot beside the road.

The 4km trail follows the Zêzere upstream along its eastern bank, climbing gradually through a wide-open landscape dotted with stone shepherds' huts and backed by spectacular views of the looming mountains on either side. Eventually the path narrows and steepens – it is marked with cairns and red and yellow paint – as you scramble up to meet the N338 at trail's end (11km from Manteigas).

Once at the N338, backpackers wanting to overnight amid this dazzling scenery can continue uphill on the paved road 1.1km to the Covão da Ametade camp site (p366).

Thirsty day trippers should descend 900m along the pavement to Fonte Paulo Luís Martins, a crystalline spring whose delightfully cold water (constantly 6ºC) is bottled in Manteigas and sold nationally as Glacier mineral water – but you can drink as much as you want here at the source for free! If you've left a car at the swimming hole, you can walk an additional 3.2km back downhill along the N338, although it's usually easy to hitch a ride from someone filling their bottles at the springs.

Penhas Douradas & Vale do Rossim

A more demanding walk goes to Penhas Douradas, a collection of windblown holiday houses. The track climbs northwest out of town via Rua Dr Afonso Costa to join a sealed, switchback forestry road and, briefly, a wide loop of the Seia-bound N232. Branch left off the N232 almost immediately, on another forestry road to the Meteorological Observatory. From there it's a short, gentle ascent to Penhas Douradas.

You're about 700m above Manteigas here, and you mustn't miss the stunning view from a stub of rock called Fragão de Covão; just follow the signs. You can also drive up the N232 just for the view: about 18km from Manteigas, then left at the first turning after the one marked *observatório,* and 1km to the sign for Fragão de Covão. Save your car's oilpan and walk the rest of the way.

Walking back the same way makes for a return trip of about 5½ hours.

Vale do Rossim to Lagoa Comprida

If you've got a vehicle and want a taste of the high country without having to climb on foot from Manteigas, consider this trek through the boulder-strewn hillsides and sheep-grazing meadows between two artificial lakes: the Vale do Rossim reservoir and Lagoa Comprida. To reach the trailhead, drive up the steep N232 to Penhas Douradas, where signs on your left will point to the Vale do Rossim.

From the trailhead, follow the T1 trail towards Torre, then veer off onto the T13. Total hiking time to Lagoa Comprida is approximately three hours each way. Elevation gain is relatively moderate, starting at 1425m on the Vale do Rossim side and climbing to 1700m before descending to 1600m at Lagoa Comprida.

SKIING & OTHER ACTIVITIES

A rather surreal-looking dry-ski run 7.5km east of Manteigas, **SkiParque** (☎ 275 980 090; www .skiparque.pt, in Portuguese; N232; ☺ 10am-6pm Sun-Thu, 10am-10pm Fri & Sat) has a lift, gear rental, snowboarding, a cafe and a treeless, functional camp site. The all-inclusive price for lifts and equipment rental is €10/22 per hour/day in low season, €14/26 in high season. Group lessons are also available.

When the weather's good SkiParque also organises increasingly popular lessons in **paragliding** for first-timers, including one 15- to 30-minute ride.

To further compensate for the lack of snow in summer, SkiParque organises other outdoor activities such as **canoeing**, **rock-climbing**, **biking** and **horse riding**.

Sleeping

BUDGET

Parque de Campismo Rossio de Valhelhas (☎ 275 487 160; jfvalhelhas@clix.pt; Valhelhas; sites per adult/child/tent/ car €2.50/1.25/2/2; ☺ May-Sep) About 15km from Manteigas, in a pretty grove of cottonwood trees near the Rio Zêzere, this municipal camp site just off the N232 is flat and shady, if a bit dusty. It enjoys distant views of the Serra and access to a river beach nearby.

Two idyllic, bare-bones camp sites are tucked away in the mountains surrounding Manteigas. The wilder-feeling, tents-only **Covão da Ametade** (officially closed at the time of writing, but expected to reopen in 2009; inquire at the park office, p364) sits in a grove of birch trees near the head of the Vale do Zêzere, with awe-inspiring views up to the looming Cántaro Magro. It's signposted at a hairpin bend 12km west of Manteigas along the N338.

Covão da Ponte (sites per adult/child/tent/car €1.50/1/1.50/1) provides a gentle shaded spot along the Mondego where you can wade, picnic or simply relax by the river's tranquil headwaters. Hikers can also explore the surrounding fields and mountains on three loop trails of varying lengths described on a park service sign at the camp site entrance. To get here, take the N232 5.4km uphill from Manteigas, then continue an additional 5km from the signposted turn-off. The poorly marked park entrance is on the right.

Both of these basic camp sites are open from 15 June to 15 September. There are toilets, picnic tables, cement barbecues, an intermittently open snack bar and (at Covão da Ponte) showers, but don't expect electricity or hot water. Contact the park office in Manteigas for information (p364).

MIDRANGE

Pensão Serradalto (☎ /fax 275 981 151; Rua 1 de Maio 15; s/d/ste €35/45/60 winter, €25/35/50 summer) In a renovated stone house, the Serradalto offers rooms with wood floors and simple antique furnishings, plus fine valley views from a sunny upstairs terrace shaded by young grapevines.

Casa de São Roque (☎ 275 981 125, 965357225; Rua de Santo António 51; s/d €40/50 August & Dec-Mar, €30/40 rest of year) This beautiful, creaky old house filled with cosy lounges, antique furnishings and religious artwork is lovingly kept by its elderly owner. From the *turismo* take the second left beyond Pensão Serradalto.

Residencial Estrela (☎ 275 981 288; Rua Dr Sobral 5; s/d €42.50/52.50) Just uphill from the park office, Estrela provides comfortable, carpeted doubles in a boarding-house atmosphere; a few rooms have fine valley views. Beware the neighbouring church bells at 7am (as effective as any alarm clock!).

Casa das Obras (☎ 275 981 155; www.casadasobras.pt; Rua Teles de Vasconcelos; d incl breakfast €70; [P] [≋]) Manteigas' nicest in-town lodging, this lovely 18th-century town house has been carefully renovated to preserve its original grandeur and stonewalled charm. The antique-filled rooms are well kept, and breakfast includes local cheese, honey and jams. Other pluses include the friendly hotel dog, the cave-like stone bar and the pool in a grassy courtyard across the street.

TOP END

Pousada de São Lourenço (☎ 275 980 050; www.pousa das.pt; d €170; [P]) Pitching for the Beiras' most stupendous view, but right on the busy main road, this luxurious modern hotel features plush rooms with a woodsy, alpine feel. It's 13km above and north of town, topping the wiggly switchbacks on the N232. The restaurant (open to nonguests) shares the hotel's glorious views; on a clear day, you can see all the way into Spain.

Eating

Most eateries listed here are within a block of the park office.

Pastelaria Padaria Floresta (Rua 1 de Maio; ☺ 6am-7pm Mon-Sat, 6am-1pm Sun) Open bright and early, this little bakery is a hiker's best friend, with simple sandwiches on homemade bread plus delicious trail snacks for sale for around €1. Taste the *empadas de frango* (pastry dough filled with chicken), *queijadas de requeijão* (half-sweet, half-savoury cheese tarts) and the house speciality *pasteis de feijoca* (bean cakes).

Cervejaria Central (☎ 275 982 787; Rua Dr Bernardo Marcos Leitão; mains €6.50-10; ⊗ lunch & dinner) This no-nonsense eatery is popular with locals for its short, good-value menu, which includes fresh trout and interestingly translated meat specials like 'veal prick' and 'lamb outlet' (veal kebabs and lamb chops, respectively).

Luso Pizza (☎ 275 982 628; Rua Dr Bernardo Marcos Leitão; pizzas from €7; ⊗ noon-11pm) This tiny place makes great pizza, although locals tend to get preferential treatment over visitors. Pasta appears on the menu but isn't always available.

Dom Pastor (☎ 275 982 920; Rua Sá da Bandeira; mains €9.50-12.50; ⊗ lunch & dinner Wed-Mon) Set idyllically on the parklike banks of the town's millstream, Manteigas' top-rated restaurant puts fine local ingredients, from cheese and produce to mountain-raised meats, to creative use.

Clube de Compras (Rua 1 de Maio; ⊗ 9am-1pm & 2-8pm Mon-Fri, 9am-8pm Sat, 9am-6pm Sun) Provides groceries for self-caterers, just up the street from the park office.

Getting There & Away

Two regular weekday buses connect Manteigas with Guarda. Getting from Manteigas to Covilhã by bus is also possible, but more complicated. It's best to check with Manteigas' *turismo* (p364) for up-to-the-minute details.

Manteigas is a fairly easy, 20-minute drive from the IP2, or a more winding 40-minute drive from Covilhã.

TORRE

In winter, Torre's road signs are so blasted by freezing winds that horizontal icicles barb their edges. Portugal's highest peak at 1993m, Torre ('Tower') produces a winter freeze that's so reliable you'll also find the small **Estancia Vodaphone ski resort** (☎ 275 314 727; www.turistrela.pt/pistas; half-/full day €15/25; ⊗ 9am-4.30pm during ski season), with three creaky lifts that serve a small set of beginner's slopes. Ski-gear rental is also available, including skis, poles and

boots (€25 per day) and snowboards (€15 per day).

If you come outside of the snowy season (mid-December to mid-April), Portugal's windy pinnacle is rather depressing – occupied by several ageing golf-ball radar domes, and a sweaty, smelly shopping arcade. And then there's the 7m-high, neoclassical obelisk, erected by João VI in the early 19th century so that Portugal could cheekily claim its highest point was exactly 2000m.

The complex's one saving grace is the park service's new visitor's centre, opened in summer 2008. The **Centro de Interpretação do Parque Natural da Serra da Estrela** (admission €1.50) is filled with interesting maps, photos and informational displays about the natural and cultural history of the region.

Even if you decide to give Torre itself a miss, it's worth making the trip up in this direction just to survey the astoundingly dramatic surroundings. The drive from Manteigas or Covilhã is especially breathtaking, passing as it does through the Nave de Santo António – a traditional high-country sheep-grazing meadow – before climbing abruptly through a surreal moonscape of crags and gorges. The area's most remarkable rock formation, visible near the turn-off for Torre, is Cántaro Magro. Rising 500m straight up from the valley below, it forms a dramatic and popular spot for rock-climbers.

A taxi to Torre costs about €25 from Covilhã, €30 from Seia or €20 from Manteigas.

PENHAS DA SAÚDE

Penhas, the closest spot in which to hunker down near Torre (about 10km from Covilhã), isn't a town but a weather-beaten collection of chalets sited strip-like along the N339 at an elevation of about 1500m. It sits just uphill from a burned-out tuberculosis sanatorium and downhill from the Barragem do Viriato dam. Supplies are limited; if you plan to go walking, do your shopping in Covilhã (p368).

Sleeping & Eating

Pousada da Juventude (☎ 275 335 375; penhas@movijovem.pt; summer/winter dm €9/14, d €22/32, d with bathroom €28/43; P) Penhas' first-rate mountaintop hostel has a communal kitchen and cafeteria, giant stone fireplaces and a games room featuring billiards and table tennis.

THE BEIRAS

Hotel Serra da Estrela (☎ 275 310 300; www .turistrela.pt; summer/winter s €60/100, d €75/130, tr €120/180; P) Regarded as Portugal's fanciest mountain hotel, this place offers travellers handsome rooms, tennis courts, a disco and woodsy six-bed chalets (summer/winter €150/240) sporting kitchenettes, verandas and great views. However, the gigantic scale of this and other properties owned by the Turistrela corporation (including the Torre ski run) seems ill-fitting in this fragile mountain environment, as do the package deals including mountain tours that are organised by Humvee.

There are several cafes along the N339.

Getting There & Away
At the weekends from mid-July to mid-September and daily during August, local **Transcovilhã** (☎ 275 336 017) buses (€1.70) climb to Penhas from the kiosk on Rua António Augusto d'Aguiar in Covilhã, twice daily. Otherwise, you must take a taxi (€20), hitch, cycle or walk.

COVILHÃ
pop 34,800 / elev 700m
Easily accessible from Lisbon by train and superhighway, modern Covilhã is awash in suburban sprawl, its 18th-century textile factories having given way to 20th-century high-rise apartment blocks. Even so, its pleasant historic core – of unlikely if modest elegance – remains intact, and the presence of the Universidade da Beira Interior lends it an air of modern urban vitality. The town's geographic setting – on steeply canted terraces directly below Penhas da Saúde and Torre – provides phenomenal views eastward towards Spain.

Orientation
From the train and long-distance bus stations, it's a punishing 1.5km climb to Praça do Município, the town centre – for local transport, see opposite.

Information
Police station (☎ 275 320 922; Rua António Augusto d'Aguiar)
Post office (⏰ 8.30am-6.30pm Mon-Fri, 9am-12.30pm Sat)
PostWeb (Rua Comendador Campos Melo 27; per hr €2; ⏰ 9am-1pm & 3-7pm Mon-Fri, 9.30am-1pm Sat) Internet access.

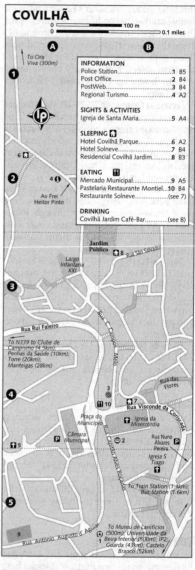

COVILHÃ

INFORMATION	
Police Station.....................1	B5
Post Office........................2	B4
PostWeb............................3	B4
Regional Turismo................4	A2

SIGHTS & ACTIVITIES	
Igreja de Santa Maria...........5	A4

SLEEPING	
Hotel Covilhã Parque..............6	A2
Hotel Solneve......................7	B4
Residencial Covilhã Jardim......8	B3

EATING	
Mercado Municipal.................9	A5
Pastelaria Restaurante Montiel..10	B4
Restaurante Solneve...........(see 7)	

DRINKING	
Covilhã Jardim Café-Bar...........(see 8)	

Regional turismo (☎ 275 319 560; turismo.estrela@ mail.telepac.pt; Av Frei Heitor Pinto; ⏰ 9am-5.30pm Mon-Fri, 9am-12.30pm & 2-5.30pm Sat)

Sights
The narrow, winding streets to the west of Praça do Município have a quiet charm, and set in the midst of them is the **Igreja de**

THE BEIRAS

Santa Maria, with a startling facade covered in *azulejos*.

Covilhã used to be the centre of one of Europe's biggest wool-producing regions. However, it has fallen on hard times. Stray outside the centre and you'll see the town's ghostly mills standing empty and forlorn.

Sited in the former royal textile factory, founded in 1764 by the Marquês de Pombal, the **Museu de Lanifícios** (Museum of Wool-Making; ☎ 275 319 700, ext 3131; adult/under 15yr/15-25yr €2/free/1; 🕑 9.30am-noon & 2.30-6pm Tue-Sun) traces the proud but vanishing history of wool production and cloth dyeing in the Serra da Estrela. A map shows the 100-plus wool producers that once thrived in this region, while other displays demonstrate how cochineal and indigo from the New World were used to dye Portuguese soldiers' uniforms red and blue. Even if yarn makes you yawn, you may be impressed by the gigantic old looms and dyeing vats.

Sleeping

Clube de Campismo e Caravanismo da Covilhã (☎ 275 314 312; www.ccccovilha.no.sapo.pt; sites per adult/tent/car €2.85/3.45/2.10, 2-/4-person bungalows from €45/60; 🕑 year-round) Some 4km up the N339 towards Penhas da Saúde, this snug, wooded municipal camp site also offers bungalows with kitchen facilities.

Residencial Covilhã Jardim (☎ 275 322 140; www.residencialcovilhajardim.com; Jardim Público 40; s/d €25/42; 🔌 🖳 🚫) This recently opened, family-run place is pleasantly situated on the quietest corner of the municipal gardens. All rooms have leafy views of the park or sweeping panoramas of the surrounding mountains. The cafe downstairs (right) is another plus.

Hotel Solneve (☎ 275 323 001/2; www.solneve.pt; Rua Visconde da Coriscada 126; s/d/tr/ste €35/53/63/80 Fri & Sat Nov-Mar, €25/43/53/65 rest of year; 🅿 🔌 🖳) With photogenic views of Covilhã's main square, this grand pink hotel in the heart of the town has spotless, stylish rooms. There's free wi-fi on offer, a great restaurant and off-street parking (€2). Pricier rooms include jet baths.

Hotel Covilhã Parque (☎ 275 329 320; www.naturaimbhotels.com; Av Frei Heitor Pinto; s/d/tr €44/63/90 winter, €22/44/49 summer; 🔌 🖳) Ten floors of un-inspired but comfortable rooms enjoy nice city views in this modern apartment block next to the *turismo*. Internet is available but expensive.

Eating & Drinking

Covilhã Jardim Café-Bar (☎ 275 322 140; Jardim Público 40; 🕑 all day) With comfy couches inside and tree-shaded tables on its parkside terrace, this trendy little cafe makes an enjoyable place to watch the world go by.

Restaurante Solneve (☎ 275 323 001/2; Rua Visconde da Coriscada 126; mains €6-8; 🕑 lunch & dinner Mon-Sat, Sun morning) This cavernous eatery sits below street level at the back of Hotel Solneve (left). Its elegantly dressed waiters proffer quality Portuguese fare ranging from garlicky pork medallions to grilled squid with clams and shrimp. Hotel guests get a 10% discount.

Pastelaria Restaurante Montiel (☎ 275 322 086; Praça do Município 33-37; daily specials €6.50-7; 🕑 cafe all day, restaurant lunch & dinner) This corner bakery is good for basking in the sun over coffee and a pastry. The upstairs dining room serves up decent regional cooking, with an emphasis on meat dishes.

Ora Viva (☎ 275 325 102; www.oraviva.org; Rua Indústria; 🕑 4pm-6am) This gritty DJ bar and club is one of a cluster of late-night venues popular with students, set in the abandoned-looking mill zone north of the municipal gardens.

Self-caterers will find abundant fruit and vegetables most mornings at the **mercado municipal** (Rua António Augusto d'Aguiar).

Getting There & Away

From the **bus station** (☎ 275 336 700), Joalto and Rede Expressos run jointly to Guarda (€4.20, 45 minutes, three times daily), and via Castelo Branco (€4.20, one hour) to Lisbon (€13, 3½ hours) about three times a day. There are also multiple daily services to Porto (€14, 4½ to 5½ hours).

Two daily IC trains run to/from Lisbon (€15, four hours) via Castelo Branco (€7.50, one hour). Regional trains serving this same route are slower and only slightly cheaper. There are two regional trains daily to Guarda (€3.05, 1¼ hours).

Getting Around

Bus 7 (Teixoso/Estação) runs every 30 to 60 minutes from the bus and train stations to the Transcovilhã kiosk by the police station (€1.10). Taxis from either station are about €5 to the centre.

Parking is available at several public garages along Rua Visconde da Coriscada.

BEIRA ALTA

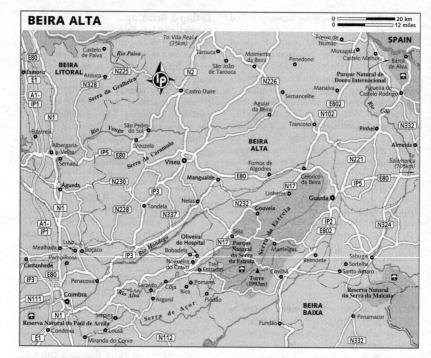

BEIRA ALTA

Heading north and west from the Serra da Estrela, mountains give way quickly to rolling plains that stretch up to the Douro valley and east to Spain. Threat of invasion from its not-always-friendly neighbour marks both the region's history and its landscape. A series of fearsome fortress-towns are the biggest draw for travellers, though the cities of Viseu and Guarda also have their charms, from excellent local wines to troves of Renaissance art.

VISEU

pop 47,300 / elev 480m

One of the Beiras' most appealing cities, Viseu easily rivals the more visited Coimbra for sheer charm and vitality. Its well-preserved historical centre offers numerous enticements to pedestrians: cobbled streets, meandering alleys, leafy public gardens and a central square (Praça da República, aka 'O Rossio', the Rossio) graced with bright flowers and fountains. Sweeping vistas over the surrounding plains unfold from the town's

highest point, the square fronting the late-Gothic and Manueline cathedral, built on the site of a former mosque.

Nowadays capital of the Beira Alta province, and a bishopric since Visigothic times, Viseu has a proud and multilayered history. The former bishop's palace now houses a museum dedicated to the works of Renaissance painter Vasco Fernandes and his contemporaries. Viseu is also a great place to eat and drink: the reds from the surrounding Dão region (see boxed text, p374) are considered to be some of Portugal's finest.

History

According to legend, Viriato, chief of the Lusitani tribe (see p30), took refuge in a cave here before the Romans hunted him down in 139 BC, though there's no cave now.

The Romans did build a fortified camp just across the Rio Pavia from Viseu, and some well-preserved segments of their roads survive nearby. The town, conquered and reconquered in the struggles between Christians and Moors, was definitively taken by Dom Fernando I, King of Castile and León, in 1057.

Afonso V completed Viseu's sturdy walls in about 1472. The town soon spread beyond them, and grew fat from agriculture and trade. An annual 'free fair' declared by João III in 1510 carries on today as one of the region's biggest agricultural and handicrafts expositions.

Orientation

Viseu sits beside the Rio Pavia, a tributary of the Mondego. In the middle of town is Praça da República, known to all as the Rossio. From here the shopping district stretches east along Rua Formosa and Rua da Paz, and then north into the historic centre along Rua do Comércio and Rua Direita. At the town's highest point and historical heart is the cathedral.

The bus station is 500m northwest of the Rossio along Avenida Dr António José de Almeida.

Information

Espaço Internet (Solar dos Condes de Prime, Rua dos Andrades; ✆ 10am-7pm Mon-Fri, 10am-1pm & 2-7pm Sat, 2-7pm Sun) Free internet in a centrally located historic mansion.

Espaço Internet Pórtico do Fontelo (Rua Aristides Sousa Mendes; ✆ 8am-11.30pm Mon-Fri, 8am-10pm Sat & Sun) Free internet, newly opened near the youth hostel.

Lavandaria 5 à Sec (☎ 232 422 820; Av Calouste Gulbenkian 32; wash & dry per kg €2.50; ✆ 8am-8pm Mon-Sat)

Main post office (Rua dos Combatentes da Grande Guerra; ✆ 8.30am-6.30pm Mon-Fri, 9am-12.30pm Sat)

Police station (☎ 232 480 380; Rua Alves Martins)

Regional turismo (☎ 232 420 950; www.rtdaolafoes .com; Av Calouste Gulbenkian; ✆ 9.30am-12.30pm & 2-6pm Mon-Fri, 9.30am-12.30pm & 2.30-5.30pm Sat, 9.30am-12.30pm Sun)

São Teotónio Hospital (☎ 232 420 500; Av Dom Duarte)

Sights

AROUND THE ROSSIO

At the southern end of Praça da República is the late-18th-century **Igreja dos Terceiros** (admission free), all heavy, gilded baroque but for the luminous *azulejos* portraying the life of St Francis.

Fine modern *azulejos* at the northern end of the Rossio depict scenes from regional life, and beyond these is the *azulejo*-adorned **Museu Almeida Moreira** (☎ 232 422 049; Rua Soar de Cima; admission free; ✆ 10am-12.30pm & 2-5.30pm Wed-Sun, 2-5.30pm Tue), genteel home to the first director of the Museu de Grão Vasco, with fine furnishings and art.

From here the grandest route into the old town is through the **Porta do Soar de Cima**, a gate set into a section of Afonso V's town walls.

SÉ

Resplendent on a rock above town is the 13th-century granite **cathedral** (admission free; ✆ 9am-noon & 2-7pm), whose gloomy Renaissance facade conceals a splendid 16th-century interior, including an impressive Manueline ceiling.

Stairs in the northern transept climb to the **Museu de Arte Sacra** (adult/14-26yr €2.50/1.25; ✆ 9am-noon & 2-5pm Tue-Sat, 2-5pm Sun). The museum itself is a lacklustre assemblage of vestments and religious paraphernalia, but its lofty setting offers a nice perspective on the church's architecture; sweeping panoramas of Viseu's historic centre are also available from the upper gallery of the adjacent **Claustro Jónico** (Ionian Cloister).

The original lower level of the cloister is one of Portugal's earliest Italian Renaissance structures. Note the Romanesque-Gothic portal on one corner, rediscovered during restoration work in 1918.

Facing the cathedral is the 1775 **Igreja da Misericórdia**, whose bright rococo exterior contrasts markedly with its neoclassical, severe and rather dull interior.

MUSEU GRÃO VASCO

Adjoining the cathedral is the severe granite box of the Paço de Três Escalões (Palace of Three Steps), probably a contemporary of the cathedral and originally built as the bishop's palace. In 1916 it reopened as a splendid **museum** (☎ 232 422 049; mgv@ipmuseus .pt; admission €4; ✆ 2-6pm Tue, 10am-6pm Wed-Sun) featuring Viseu's own Vasco Fernandes, known as Grão Vasco, 'the Great Vasco' (1480–1543) – one of Portugal's seminal Renaissance painters.

The recently renovated museum houses other bright lights of the so-called Viseu School. Vasco's colleague, collaborator and rival Gaspar Vaz merits special attention. Together they spurred each other on to produce some of Portugal's finest artwork. After five centuries their rich colours and luminous style are still as striking as ever.

THE BEIRAS

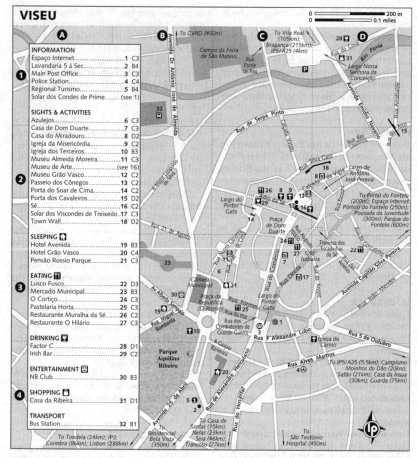

VISEU

AROUND THE SÉ

North of the cathedral along Rua Silva Gaio is the longest remaining stretch of the old **town walls**. To the east, across Avenida Emídio Navarro, is another old town gate, the **Porta dos Cavaleiros**.

South of the cathedral beneath the **Passeio dos Cônegos** (Curates Walk, on part of the old wall) is **Praça de Dom Duarte**, named after the Portuguese monarch (brother of Prince Henry the Navigator) born in Viseu. Several of the square's mansions show off wrought-iron balconies and genteel contours.

Southward is **Casa de Dom Duarte** (Rua Dom Duarte; closed to public), a house with a beautiful Manueline window and traditionally regarded as the king's birthplace.

Rua Augusto Hilário runs southeast through the former **judiaria** (14th- to 16th-century Jewish quarter). **Rua Direita**, Viseu's most appealing street and once the most direct route to the hilltop, is a lively melee of shops, souvenir stands, restaurants and old town houses.

MANSIONS

The most handsome of Viseu's many old town houses is the 18th-century **Solar dos Condes de Prime** (Rua dos Andrades), currently used by Espaço Internet (p371).

Among other stately homes are the 18th-century **Solar dos Viscondes de Treixedo** (Rua Direita), now a bank, and the 16th-century **Casa do Miradouro** (Calçada da Vigia), just off Largo de António José Pereira. Neither is open to the public.

PARQUE DO FONTELO
A haven of woodland and open space sprawls beyond the Portal do Fontelo. Here are the 16th-century **Antigo Paço Episcopal** (former Bishop's Palace), now home to the Dão Regional Vintners' Commission (CVRD; see boxed text, p374), together with once-lovely Renaissance gardens, a stadium and a recreation complex.

Festivals & Events
Viseu's biggest annual get-together is the **Feira de São Mateus** (St Matthew's Fair), a jamboree of agriculture and handicrafts from mid-August to mid-September, augmented by folk music, traditional food, amusement park rides and fireworks. This direct descendant of the town's old 'free fair' still takes place in the riverside Campo da Feira de São Mateus, set aside for the event by João III in 1510.

Sleeping
Campismo Moinhos do Dão (☎ 232 610 586; www .moinhosdodao.nl, in Dutch; Tibaldinho, Mangualde; sites per adult/child/car €3.50/1.75/4, tent €3-4) This tranquil spot at the end of a dirt road 20km southeast of Viseu offers camping on the banks of the Rio Dão, plus rustic indoor lodgings with pro-pane stoves and fridges (per week from €275). Built amid a cluster of restored water-mills, it's a place where you truly get away from it all – swimming and boating by day, dining by candlelight at outdoor tables by night (three-course dinners including Dão wine run at €15/7.50 per adult/child). Clientele is almost exclusively Dutch, but the hosts speak excel-lent English; call ahead for directions.

Pousada da Juventude (☎ 232 435 445; www.movi jovem.pt; Rua Aristides Sousa Mendes; dm €9, d with/without toilet €22/18; P) A short walk from the centre is this modern, boxy, rather basic hostel. There are no cooking facilities, but staff are friendly and helpful, and there's a decent restaurant and free internet next door.

Residencial Bela Vista (☎ 232 422 026; fax 232 428 472; Rua de Alexandre Herculano 510; s/d/tr €25/37/45; P ⊠) In a modern apartment block south of the centre, Bela Vista is extremely plain but well run, offering spick-and-span rooms, some with verandas.

Pensão Rossio Parque (☎ 232 422 085; Praça da República 55; s/d €30/45) Directly above the Rossio,

this small old-fashioned hotel features a bright, bustling restaurant downstairs and nice views from the front rooms. One interior room without bathroom rents for €10 less.

Hotel Avenida (☎ 232 423 432; www.hotelave nida.com.pt; Av Alberto Sampaio 1; s/d/tr €45/55/65; ⌨) Proudly proclaiming its presence with a vintage neon sign visible from the Rossio, this friendly, modestly elegant hotel has a grand spiral staircase, stately common areas and slightly creaky rooms decorated in regal colours.

Hotel Grão Vasco (☎ 232 423 511; www.hotel graovasco.pt; Rua Gaspar Barreiros; s/d/ste €64/74/97; P ⊠ ⌨ 🖤) Top of the scale in central Viseu, this handsome, if slightly pompous, modern granite hotel is set back in leafy grounds above the Rossio. Rooms are prop-erly plush, though a little shy of luxurious.

Eating
Viseu is awash in good food for any budget.

Pastelaria Horta (Rua Formosa 22; ⏰ 7am-7pm Mon-Sat) This popular bakery serves traditional sweets made of egg yolk and almonds, and offers pleasant outdoor seating on Viseu's main pedestrian thoroughfare.

Restaurante O Hilário (☎ 232 436 587; Rua Augusto Hilário 35; mains around €3.50-6.90; ⏰ lunch & dinner Mon-Sat) Named for the 19th-century fado star who once lived down the street, this highly recommended eatery wins points for its excellent food, cosy atmosphere, righteous prices and attentive service.

Lusco Fusco (☎ 965310804; Rua do Gonçalinho 48; mains €6.50-8; ⏰ 5pm-midnight Mon-Sat; 🅥) Using organic produce in vegan and vegetarian offerings such as *bife de seitan com molho de cogumelos* (seitan steak with mushroom sauce), Lusco Fusco also serves mixed drinks with natural fruit juices at its sleek modern bar and hosts occasional live music and poetry readings.

O Cortiço (☎ 232 423 853; Rua Augusto Hilário 45; mains €9-17.50; ⏰ lunch & dinner) This heartily recom-mended stone-walled eatery specialises in traditional recipes collected from surround-ing villages. Generous portions are served in heavy tureens, and the good house wine comes in medieval-style wooden pitchers. Finish your meal with a glass of the local firewater made from olives.

Restaurante Muralha da Sé (☎ 232 437 777; Adro da Sé 24; mains €11-20; ⏰ lunch & dinner Tue-Sat, lunch Sun) Go ahead: bust your budget at this una-bashedly upper-crust spot under the looming

THE BEIRAS

WINES OF THE DÃO REGION

The velvety red wines of the Dão region (within the Rio Mondego and tributary Rio Dão, south and east of Viseu) have been cultivated for over 2000 years, and are today among Portugal's best. Vineyards are mostly sheltered in valleys at altitudes of 200m to 900m just west of the Serra da Estrela, thus avoiding the rain of the coast but also the harsh summer heat further inland. This, together with granitic soil, helps the wines retain their natural acidity. They are often called the burgundies of Portugal because they don't overpower but, rather, are subtle and full of finesse.

Some three-dozen Dão vineyards and producers offer multilingual cellar tours and tasting; most require advance bookings. You can pick up a list in Viseu's *turismo*. Two popular wineries near Viseu are **Casa da Ínsua** (☎ 232 642 222; Penalva do Castelo), 30km east on the IP5 and N329-1, and **Casa de Santar** (☎ 232 942 937; Santar), 15km southeast on the N231. Both have fine grounds and lovely architecture.

Coordinating them all is the **Comissão Vitivinícola Regional do Dão** (CVRD; ☎ 232 410 060; www.cvrdao.pt; Av Capitão Homem Ribeiro 10, Viseu), which eventually plans to open its headquarters – Viseu's 16th-century Antigo Paço Episcopal (p373) – as a posh Solar do Dão where the public can sample a range of Dão wines.

White Dão wines are also available, though the full-bodied reds are the best (and the strongest). Also try the sparkling white wines of the separate, small Lafões region, northwest of Viseu.

Igreja da Misericórdia. It boasts fine regional cuisine made with ingredients from the nearby Serra da Estrela, plus cathedral views from its terrace.

Self-caterers will find fruit, vegetables and other goodies at the **mercado municipal** (Rua 21 de Agosto; ☺ Mon-Sat).

Drinking & Entertainment

A clutch of bars near the cathedral overflows onto the streets and makes for a merry atmosphere on summer nights.

Irish Bar (☎ 967130270; Largo do Pintor Gata 8; ☺ 9am-2am Mon-Sat, 1pm-2am Sun) Guinness on tap, occasional live Irish music and terrace seating on a charming square near the old town gate.

Factor C (☎ 232 415 808; Rua do Coval 39-43; ☺ 9pm-4am Mon-Sat) Viseu's trendiest disco, with distinct rooms playing pop, rock and alternative sounds to keep everyone happy.

NB Club (☎ 232 435 535; www.noitebiba.pt; Rua Conselheiro Afonso de Melo 31; ☺ midnight-6am Thu-Sat) Centrally located one block from the Rossio, popular NB spins a mix of house, pop, hip-hop and rock.

Shopping

Handicrafts here are cheaper than in more-touristy towns.

Casa da Ribeira (☎ 232 429 761; Largo Nossa Senhora da Conceição; ☺ 9am-12.30pm & 2-5.30pm Tue-Sat) In this municipal space north of the river, local arti-sans work and sell their products, including lace, ceramics and the region's distinctively black earthenware.

Getting There & Around

Operators at the bus station include **Rede Expressos** (☎ 232 422 822) and **Joalto** (☎ 232 426 093).

Rede Expressos heads to Vila Real (€9.80, 75 minutes, three daily), Trancoso (€6.30, 1½ hours, two daily), Coimbra (€7.50, 75 minutes, 10 daily), Bragança (€13, 3¼ hours, three daily) and Lisbon (€14.50, 3½ hours, at least 14 daily).

Joalto heads to Braga (€12.30, three hours, one daily) and Porto (€9.50, two hours, five daily).

Parking is available just north of the Rio Pavia around the town's fairgrounds and at an underground garage adjacent to Igreja do Carmo, east of the Rossio.

GUARDA

pop 26,100 / elev 1056m

Fria, farta, forte e feia (cold, rich, strong and ugly): such is the popular description of Portugal's highest fully fledged city. Hunkered down on a hilltop, it was founded in 1197 to guard young Portugal against both Moors and Spaniards (hence the name).

Nowadays stripped of its military functions, this granite-grey district capital is a delightful place to spend an afternoon.

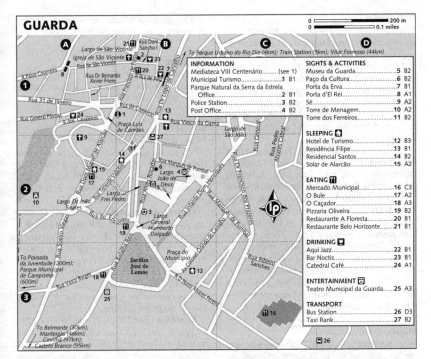

GUARDA

Highlights include the looming cathedral and its enormous square, the narrow lanes and town gates of the historic Jewish quarter, a good museum and sweeping views of the plains stretching all the way to Spain.

Orientation

Old Guarda is perched on a steep hill, a rambling climb from the IP5 or the train station; the latter is 5km northeast of the old centre, linked by a shuttle bus.

From the bus station on Rua Dom Nuno Álvares Pereira, it's 800m northwest to Praça Luís de Camões (also called Praça Velha), heart of the old town. Most things of interest to visitors are near the *praça*.

Information

Mediateca VIII Centenário (☎ 271 205 531; Praça Luís de Camões; ◷ 9am-12.30pm & 2-5.30pm Mon-Fri) Free internet. Upstairs from the *turismo*.

Municipal turismo (☎ 271 205 530; postodeturismo@ mun-guarda.pt; Praça Luís de Camões; ◷ 9am-12.30pm & 2-5.30pm)

Parque Natural da Serra da Estrela office (☎ /fax 271 225 454; Rua Dom Sancho I 3; ◷ 9am-12.30pm & 2-5.30pm Mon-Fri) Modestly helpful.

Police station (☎ 271 222 022; Rua Alves Roçadas 15)

Post office (☎ 271 221 754; Largo João de Deus; ◷ 8.30am-6pm Mon-Fri, 9am-12.30pm Sat)

Sights

SÉ

Powerful in its sobriety, this Gothic fortress of a **cathedral** (Praça Luís de Camões; ◷ 9am-noon & 2-5pm Tue-Sat) squats heavily by a large square in the city centre. The earliest parts date from 1390 but it took 150 years to finish; it's dotted with Manueline doors and windows and Renaissance ornamentation, while its facade is girded by two handsomely hexagonal bell towers.

The most striking feature in the immense, granite interior is a four-storey Renaissance altarpiece attributed to Jean de Rouen (João de Ruão), one of a team of 16th-century French artists who founded an influential school of sculpture at Coimbra. Also impressive are the twisted Manueline columns at each transept.

OLD TOWN

With its 16th- to 18th-century **mansions** and its overpowering cathedral, Praça Luís de Camões is the town's centrepiece.

Little remains of Guarda's 13th-century castle except the simple **Torre de Menagem** (castle keep; closed to public), on a hilltop above the cathedral. However, plenty of medieval atmosphere survives in the cobblestone lanes and huddled houses north of the cathedral, centred around Rua de São Vicente.

Of the old walls and gates, the stalwart **Torre dos Ferreiros** (Blacksmiths' Tower; Rua Tenente Valadim) is still in good condition. Two other surviving gates are the **Porta d'El Rei**, the steps of which you can still climb for views over town, and the **Porta da Erva**. A walk between these two gates takes you through the heart of Guarda's historic **judiaria** (Jewish quarter; see boxed text, opposite). Sharp-eyed visitors will notice crosses and other symbols scratched into a few 16th-century vaulted doorframes – look for examples along Ruas Rui de Pina and Dom Sancho I – which identified the homes of *marranos* (New Christians) during the Inquisition (p35).

MUSEU DA GUARDA

The **museum** (☎ 271 213 460; museudaguarda.imc-ip.pt; Rua Alves Roçadas 30; admission €2, admission free 10am-12.30pm Sun; ⏲ 10am-12.30pm & 2-5.30pm Tue-Sun) occupies the severe, 17th-century Episcopal Seminary, adjacent to the old bishop's palace. The collection runs from Bronze Age swords to Roman coins, from Renaissance sculpture to 19th- and 20th-century Portuguese painting. Particularly interesting are the upstairs rooms focusing on traditional rural culture, including sheep-herding and olive oil production.

In the adjacent, 18th-century courtyard, the handsome **Paço da Cultura** (admission free; ⏲ irregular hrs) features temporary art exhibitions.

Guarda for Children

The new **Parque Urbano do Rio Diz**, set in 21 hectares of green space by Guarda's train station, was inaugurated in November 2007. It has an astoundingly large, modern playground that can keep kids happily engaged for hours.

Festivals & Events

Guarda hosts a jazz festival called **Ciclo de Jazz de Guarda**, with several performances each week from March to May.

The *turismo* hands out a free calendar of events.

Sleeping

There's no winter high-price season here, though Guarda is almost as close to the snow as the park's other main towns.

BUDGET

Parque Municipal de Campismo (☎ 271 221 200; fax 271 210 025; Rua do Estádio Municipal; sites per adult/child/tent/car €1.90/1.40/1.90/1.90; ⏲ year-round) Very close to the town centre and next to a leafy park, this municipal site has hot water and plenty of shade.

Pousada da Juventude (☎ 271 224 482; www.pousadasjuventude.pt; Av Alexandre Herculano; dm €9, d with/without toilet €22/18; P ♿) The modern, rather clinical youth hostel is a short walk to the centre. Reception is open 8am until noon and 6pm until midnight. The dorms have only four beds each, and some upper rooms enjoy nice vistas; on the downside, there's no guest kitchen.

Residência Filipe (☎ 271 223 658; fax 271 221 402; Rua Vasco da Gama 9; s/d/tr €20/35/45; P) This funny mix of old and new offers mostly bright, attractive rooms, brisk service and garage parking (€2.50).

MIDRANGE

Residencial Santos (☎ 271 205 400; www.residencialsantos.com; Rua Tenente Valadim 14; s/d incl breakfast €30/45/55) Santos is warmly recommended for its spotless, newly furnished rooms, good prices, generous breakfast and welcoming staff. Its ultramodern interior resembles an Escher drawing, with interconnecting walkways, stairs and glass walls that incorporate both a handsome 19th-century granite building and the town's medieval walls. For nice views of the cathedral, book ahead for room 307 on the top floor.

Hotel de Turismo (☎ 271 223 366; www.hturismoguarda.com; Praça do Município; s/d €45/60; P ✖) This art-deco-style hotel with large rooms and handsome common areas had just changed owners at the time of writing. Closed for remodelling in 2009, it plans to reopen as a four-star in 2010.

Solar de Alarcão (☎/fax 271 214 392; Rua Dom Miguel de Alarcão 25-27; d €80; P) Easily Guarda's most refined choice, this beautiful 17th-century granite mansion has its own courtyard and loggia, sits within spitting distance of the cathedral, and offers a handful of gorgeous rooms stuffed with antique furniture and drapes.

Eating

Pizzaria Oliveira (☎ 271 214 446; Rua do Encontro; pizzas €5-10.50, mains €4.50-9.50; ☻ lunch & dinner) This pizzeria serves standard Italian fare in a rather sterile upstairs dining room.

Restaurante A Floresta (☎ 271 212 314; Rua Francisco de Passos 40; mains €5-10; ☻ lunch & dinner) Just north of the cathedral, this snug and friendly (if well-touristed) place serves up hearty regional cuisine, including the marvellous *chouriçada:* a heaping portion of grilled sausages from the nearby Serra da Estrela.

O Caçador (☎ 271 211 702; Rua Batalha Reis 121; mains €5.50-12.50; ☻ lunch & dinner Tue-Sun) Drawing in dinner guests with a happy red neon sign and a glass-walled front room vaguely reminiscent of Parisian brasseries, O Caçador serves both meat and seafood.

Restaurante Belo Horizonte (☎ 271 211 454; Largo de São Vicente 1; mains €6.50-14; ☻ lunch & dinner Sun-Fri) Granite-fronted Belo Horizonte packs them in for lunch and dinner, with regional specialities such as *chouriçada* and *cabrito gelada* (grilled kid).

O Bule (☎ 271 211 275; Rua Dom Miguel de Alarcão; ☻ 8am-8pm Mon-Sat, 10am-8pm Sun) This lovely, traditional cafe near the cathedral specialises in local pastries, including the delicious *queijadas de canela,* cinnamon-tinged tarts made with sheep's milk.

Self-caterers can head to the *mercado municipal* near the bus station.

Drinking

Guarda's historic centre has a surprising number of nightspots for its size – all small and unlikely looking from the outside, but welcoming within. **Aqui Jazz** (Rua Rui de Pinha 29; ☻ 10pm-3am) attracts alternative and arty types with live jazz. Just around the corner, **Bar Noctis** (Rua Dom Sancho I 9; ☻ 10.30pm-3am) is another popular hang-out. Serious night owls will appreciate **Catedral Café** (Rua dos Cavaleiros 11; ☻ midnight-5am), a bar with occasional DJ-and-dancing gigs lasting into the wee hours.

Entertainment

Teatro Municipal da Guarda (☎ 271 205 240; www .tmg.com.pt; Rua Batalha Reis 12) Guarda's shiny new theatre complex, a boxy modern building of grayish-green glass just south of the historic centre, regularly hosts high-quality theatre, dance and music.

THE JEWS OF BELMONTE

When the Moors ruled Portugal, it's estimated that 10% of the country's population was Jewish. Jews remained vital to the young Christian state, serving as government ministers and filling key roles in Henry the Navigator's school devoted to overseas exploration. Even the current Duke of Bragança, hereditary king of Portugal, proudly acknowledges his own Jewish parentage.

When Portugal embraced Spain's Inquisitorial zeal beginning in the 1490s, thousands of Jews from both Portugal and Spain fled to northeast Portugal, including the Beiras and Trás-os-Montes, where the arm of the Inquisitors had not yet reached. Eventually the Inquisitors made their presence felt even here, and Jews once again faced conversion, expulsion or death.

However, in the 1980s it was revealed that in the town of Belmonte, 30km south of Guarda, a group of families had been practising Jewish rites in secret since the Inquisition – more than 500 years. While it's believed that many such communities continued in secrecy well into the Inquisition, most slowly died out. But Belmonte's community managed to survive five centuries by meticulously ensuring marriages were arranged only among other Jewish families. The transmission of Jewish tradition was almost exclusively oral and passed not from father to son but from mother to daughter. Each Friday night families descended into basements to pray and celebrate the Sabbath. Now that the community is out in the open, they have embraced male-dominated Orthodox Judaism, though the women elders have not forgotten the secret prayers that have been doggedly transmitted these past 500 years.

The modest **Museu Judaico de Belmonte** (☎ 275 913 505; Rua Portela 4; admission free; ☻ 9.30am-12.30pm & 2-6pm Tue-Sun) tells the story of the Belmonte families and Judaism generally. Ask here about visits to the town's synagogue.

There are frequent daily bus connections between Belmonte and Guarda.

Getting There & Away

BUS

Rede Expressos (☎ 271 221 515) runs services at least three times daily via Covilhã (€4, 45 minutes) to Castelo Branco (€9.20, 1¾ hours) and Lisbon (€14.50, 5½ hours), and several times daily to Viseu (€7.80, 1¼ hours), Porto (€11.80, three hours) and Coimbra (€11.80, three hours).

Marques (☎ 238 312 858) goes daily via Gouveia (€4.10, 1½ hours) to Seia (€4.50, two hours). Rede Expressos also goes to Seia (€9.20, 1¼ hours) once daily Sunday to Friday.

TRAIN

Guarda's spiffy modern train station is served by at least two fast IC trains lines from Lisbon (€17, 4¼ hours). There are also direct trains to Coimbra (€10, 2½ hours). Trains to Porto change at Pampilhosa (€18.20, four hours).

Getting Around

Shuttle buses run between the train station and the bus station (€0.80), with a stop at Rua Marquês de Pombal, every half-hour during the day. Call for a **taxi** (☎ 271 221 863) or board one at the rank on Rua Alves Roçadas. A taxi to/from the train station costs about €5.

Parking is competitive in the centre. Try your luck around Largo Dr João Soares.

TRANCOSO

pop 3500 / elev 870m

A warren of cobbled lanes squeezed within Dom Dinis' 13th-century walls make peaceful, hilltop Trancoso a delightful retreat from the modern world. The town also served as a refuge of Spanish Jews fleeing the Inquisition – until Portugal, too, adopted Spain's persecutory zeal. As elsewhere along the border, you can generally spot Jewish houses by looking for a pair of doors: a smaller one for the private household and a larger one for a shop or warehouse.

Although it's predominantly a medieval creation, the town's castle also features a rare, intact Moorish tower, while just outside the walls are what are believed to be Visigothic tombs.

Dinis underscored the importance of this border fortress by marrying the saintly Dona Isabel of Aragon here in 1282. But the town's favourite son is Bandarra, a lowly 16th-century shoemaker and fortune-teller who put official noses out of joint by foretelling the end of the Portuguese monarchy.

Sure enough, shortly after Bandarra's death, the young Dom Sebastião died, heirless, in the disastrous Battle of Alcácer-Quibir in 1558. Soon afterwards, Portugal fell under Spanish rule.

Information

Espaço Internet (☎ 271 829 300; ☾ 9am-12.30pm & 1.30-6pm Mon-Fri) Free internet in Trancoso's Centro Cultural, two blocks south of the *turismo*.

Police station (Largo Luis Albuquerque; ☎ 271 811 212)

Post office (Av da República; ☾ 9am-12.30pm & 2-6pm Mon-Fri)

Turismo (☎ 271 811 147; pttrancoso@hotmail.com; ☾ 9am-12.30pm & 2-5.30pm Mon-Fri, 10am-12.30pm & 2-5.30pm Sat & Sun)

Sights

The **Portas d'El Rei** (King's Gate), surmounted by the town's ancient coat of arms, has always been its principal entrance, and its guillotine-like door long sealed out unwelcome visitors. The **town walls** run intact for over 1km around the medieval core, which is centred on the main square, Largo Padre Francisco Ferreira (also called Largo do Pelourinho, or Largo Dom Dinis). The square, in turn, is anchored by an octagonal **pelourinho** dating from 1510.

Like many northern towns, Trancoso acquired a sizeable Jewish community following the expulsion of Jews from Spain at the end of the 15th century.

The **old judiaria** covered roughly the southeast third of the walled town. Among dignified reminders of that time is a former rabbinical residence called the **Casa do Gato Preto** (House of the Black Cat; Largo Luís Albuquerque), decorated with the gates of Jerusalem and other Jewish images. It's now private property.

On a hill in the northeast corner of town is the now-tranquil, 10th- to 13th-century **castelo** (admission free; ☾ 9am-5.30pm Mon-Fri, 10am-5.30pm Sat & Sun), with its crenellated towers and the distinctively slanted walls of the squat, Moorish **Torre de Menagem**.

Across the road from the Portas do Prado, beside the courthouse, is an untended rock outcrop carved with eerie, body-shaped cavities, thought to be **Visigothic tombs** dating back to the 7th or 8th century.

About 150m northward is Trancoso's prettiest church, the 13th-century **Capela de Santa Luzia**, with heavy Romanesque door arches and unadorned dry-stone construction. Trancoso abounds with other churches heavy

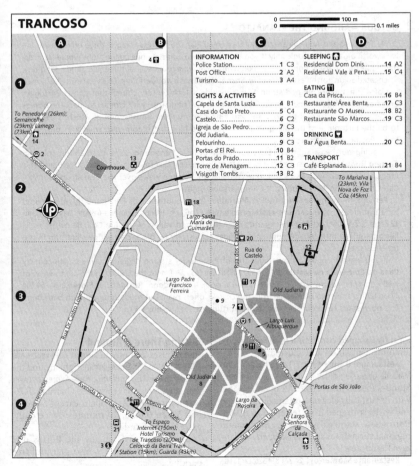

TRANCOSO

INFORMATION	
Police Station	1 C3
Post Office	2 A2
Turismo	3 A4

SIGHTS & ACTIVITIES	
Capela de Santa Luzia	4 B1
Casa do Gato Preto	5 C4
Castelo	6 C2
Igreja de São Pedro	7 C3
Old Judiaria	8 B4
Pelourinho	9 C3
Portas d'El Rei	10 B4
Portas do Prado	11 B2
Torre de Menagem	12 C3
Visigoth Tombs	13 B2

SLEEPING	
Residencial Dom Dinis	14 A2
Residencial Vale a Pena	15 C4

EATING	
Casa da Prisca	16 B4
Restaurante Área Benta	17 C3
Restaurante O Museu	18 B2
Restaurante São Marcos	19 C3

DRINKING	
Bar Água Benta	20 C2

TRANSPORT	
Café Esplanada	21 B4

with baroque make-up, most prominently the Igreja de São Pedro, behind the *pelourinho* on Largo Padre Francisco Ferreira.

Sleeping

Ask at the *turismo* about the possibility of *quartos* for rent.

Residencial Vale a Pena (☎ 271 811 951; Largo Senhora da Calçada; s/d €20/40) This simple, slightly grandmotherly place near the Portas de São João offers clean, modern rooms with tile floors and newish furnishings.

Residencial Dom Dinis (☎ 271 811 525; www.dom dinis.net Av da República 10; s/d/tr/q €29/39/56/70; P) In a drab apartment block behind the post office, the Dom Dinis has spotless, if spiritless,

carpeted modern rooms, plus a downstairs bar and restaurant.

Hotel Turismo de Trancoso (☎ 271 829 200; www .hotel-trancoso.com, in Portuguese; Rua Professora Irene Avillez; s/d/ste from €65/80/110; P ⊠ ☐ ⍩) Forming an anachronistic counterpoint to the walled city two blocks away, this brand-new, chalk-white monolith offers stylish modern rooms, most with verandas and rural vistas around a semicircular courtyard.

Eating & Drinking

Casa da Prisca (☎ 271 811 196; Rua da Corredoura 1; ⍩ 9am-7pm) This shop specialising in regional cheeses and smoked meats just inside the Portas d'El Rei is a fun place to browse. Try the *sardinhas doces* (sweet sardines), a

THE BEIRAS

DETOUR – AROUND THE PLANALTO

While Trancoso and Almeida are the quintessential Planalto fortress-villages, three other towns are well worth a gander, though only if you have your own wheels – bus connections would be maddening in this sparsely populated region. With a car, you could see all three in a single, long day.

Located 30km northwest of Trancoso, **Sernancelhe** has a wonderfully preserved centre fashioned out of warm, beige-coloured stone. Sights include a 13th-century church that boasts Portugal's only free-standing Romanesque sculpture; an old Jewish quarter with crosses to mark the homes of the converted; several grand 17th- and 18th-century town houses, one of which is believed to be the birthplace of the Marquês de Pombal; and hills that bloom with what are considered to be Portugal's best chestnuts.

Heading northeast another 16km, you arrive at little **Penedono**, with its small but splendid **Castelo Roqueiro** (Roqueiro Castle; admission free; 9am-6pm Mon-Fri, 10am-6pm Sat, 2.30-6pm Sun). This irregular hexagon, with its picturesque crenellation, has fine views over the Planalto. It probably dates back to the 13th century. It's a remarkable sight.

Perhaps most impressive of all is **Marialva**, 25km southeast of Penedono. It's dominated by a forbidding, 12th-century **castelo** (admission €1.50; 10am-1.30pm & 3-6.30pm May-Sep, 9am-12.30pm & 2-5.30pm Oct-Apr) that guards over the rugged valley of the Rio Côa. Below its walls lies a haunting little village populated almost exclusively by black-clad widows knitting in the timeless shade.

If you want to make an overnight trip of it, consider staying at Sernancelhe's 17th-century **Casa da Comenda de Malta** (☎ 254 559 189; d from €65; 🐾), near the church in the old town, with well-equipped rooms, walled gardens and a pool. In Penedono, **Residencial Flores** (☎ 254 504 411; d €30), a short walk downhill from the *castelo*, offers plain but modern rooms with bathroom. The downstairs restaurant serves hearty Portuguese fare (mains €4 to €7).

---

local fish-shaped confection made with eggs, almonds, cinnamon and chocolate.

Restaurante O Museu (☎ 271 811 810; Largo Santa Maria de Guimarães; dishes €6-13; lunch & dinner) Stone-walled O Museu goes for quaint appeal, with its rustically elegant upstairs dining room and wisteria-draped front terrace. Along with Portuguese standards, it serves fondue and regional specialities such as *ensopado de borrego* (lamb stew).

Restaurante São Marcos (☎ 271 811 326; Largo Luis Albuquerque; daily specials from €6, mains €7-12; lunch & dinner Mon-Sat, lunch Sun) This down-to-earth place next door to Casa do Gato Preto draws a local clientele with its tasty Portuguese fare.

Restaurante Área Benta (☎ 271 817 180; Rua dos Cavaleiros 30A; mains €7.50-15; lunch & dinner) For regional cuisine presented with contemporary flair, try this swish, minimalist restaurant in an ancient stone town house. Specialities include *feijoada à trasmontana* (a stew of red beans, pork and cabbage) and *cabrito assado com castanhas* (roast goat with chestnuts).

Bar Água Benta (Rua dos Cavaleiros 36A; noon-3am Sun-Fri, 9pm-4am Sat) Tucked away in the backstreets is this little cafe-bar, with a cheerful and youthful atmosphere, international beers, and occasional live music and karaoke.

Getting There & Around

Catch buses and buy tickets at **Café Esplanada** (☎ 271 811 188; 7am-midnight), right around the corner from the *turismo*. **Rede Expressos** (www .rede-expressos.com) has service to Guarda (€7.70, one hour, daily at 10.30am except Sunday) and Viseu (€6.30, 70 minutes, twice daily, extra bus on Sunday).

Buses stop just outside the Portas d'El Rei gate, where there is also plentiful free parking.

The closest train station is at Celorico da Beira, 15km to the south.

ALMEIDA

pop 1500 / elev 760m

After Portugal regained independence from Spain in the 1640s, the country's border regions were on constant high alert. Tiny Almeida, along with Elvas and Valença do Minho, became a principal defence again Spanish incursions. Almeida's vast, star-shaped fortress – completed in 1641 on the site of its medieval predecessor, 15km from Spain – is the least famous but the most handsome of the three.

When its military functions were largely suspended in 1927, Almeida settled into weedy obscurity. Nowadays, the fortified old village – designated as a national monument and recently scrubbed up for tourism – is a place of great charm, where you'll find flowery green spaces interspersed with old stone houses. The town may have the disquieting calm of a museum, but it also has enough history and muscular grandeur to set the imagination humming.

Orientation & Information
The fortress is on the northern side of 'new' Almeida. Most visitors arrive via the handsome Portas de São Francisco, two long tunnel-gates separated by an enormous dry moat.

The **turismo** (☎ 271 574 204; ⏱ 9am-12.30pm & 2-5.30pm, from 10am Sat & Sun) is impressively located in an old guard-chamber within the Portas de São Francisco. Here you can get a map of the fortress, though not much else.

Sights
The long arcaded building just inside the Portas de São Francisco is the 18th-century **Quartel das Estradas** (Infantry Barracks), which still serves as military housing.

In a bastion 300m northeast of the *turismo* are the **casamatas** (casemates or bunkers; ⏱ 9am-12.30pm & 2-5pm Oct-Mar, 10am-12.30pm & 2-5.30pm Apr-Sep), a labyrinth of 20 underground rooms used for storage, barracks and shelter for troops in times of siege. In the 18th century it also served as a prison. Piles of cannonballs fill a central courtyard, with British and Portuguese cannons strewn about nearby.

The fort's **castle** was blown to smithereens during a French siege in 1810, when Britain's and Portugal's own ammunition supplies exploded. You can still see the foundations, 300m northwest of the *turismo,* from an ugly catwalk. Below the ruins is the former Royal Riding Academy.

Sleeping & Eating
Pensão-Restaurante A Muralha (☎ /fax 271 574 357; Bairro de São Pedro; s/d €25/40; P ✗) This functional, modern place sits 250m outside the Portas de São Francisco on the Vilar Formoso road. It has quiet, personality-free rooms and a large restaurant serving straightforward, belly-filling platters (mains €6.50 to €9).

Pousada Nossa Senhora das Neves (☎ 271 574 283; pousadadealmeida@mail.telepac.net; d €170; P ✗) Ugly from the outside if entirely respectable on the inside, this modern *pousada* (upmarket inn) sits on the site of former cavalry quarters near the north bastion. Rooms are large and comfortable, all with giant windows and/or balconies. Rates drop considerably in winter. The dining room (mains €13 to €18) offers creative takes on regional cuisine, such as lamb stew fortified with egg yolks and pudding made from local almonds.

Casa Pátio da Figueira (☎ 271 571 133; ltqueiros@gmail.com; Rua Direita 48; house for up to 8 people €200-250; ✗) At the northern end of the village, this restored 18th-century town house of chunky stone and considerable charm is Almeida's only other lodging within the historic centre. Featuring four elegant double rooms and a lovely garden with a pool, it's scheduled to close for remodelling in 2009, reopening in 2010.

Getting There & Around
Rede Expressos (www.rede-expressos.pt) has weekday-only service to Celerico da Beira, with connections to Viseu (€9.80, three hours), Coimbra (€12, five hours) and Lisbon (€15.80, 7½ hours). On Sunday afternoons there's a faster direct service to Lisbon (€15.80, 5½ hours). Nondrivers will almost certainly have to stay the night due to limited bus connections.

If you do drive, you're better off parking outside the gates and negotiating the inner town on foot.

The Douro

The meandering Rio Douro has shaped both the geography and the history of this dramatic region. The Douro region is home to Portugal's most famous vineyards, including those of the Alto Douro, one of the oldest demarcated wine regions on the planet and a Unesco-declared World Heritage Site.

The gateway to the region is Porto, the historic city at the mouth of the river. Wealth from its wine trade has long powered the economy, leaving a legacy of intricately carved cathedrals, beaux-arts boulevards and Parisian-style squares. It is also a city with a burgeoning cultural scene, with cutting-edge modern architecture, forward-looking theatres and galleries, and uninhibited nightlife.

Upriver from Porto, the steeply terraced vineyards show vintners' Herculean efforts to shape this region over the centuries. The riverbanks stretch skyward at impossibly steep angles and are covered by vines. For the curious, there are numerous ways to delve into the Douro experience: visiting vineyards, sailing the Douro, embarking on scenic train journeys, staying in a chateau on a working wine estate, or sampling an aged port in an 18th-century wine-cellar.

The Douro is also a fascinating place to glimpse the artistic treasures left by previous inhabitants. Highlights include Stone Age petroglyphs, Visigothic churches and magnificent baroque churches slumbering in tiny villages. And while the coast isn't the Douro's big draw, there are some worthwhile stops here, including picturesque Vila do Conde, a once-important shipbuilding centre.

Note that this chapter includes a few towns that are technically in the Beira Alta and Trás-os-Montes regions but lie along the Rio Douro.

HIGHLIGHTS

- Wine-tasting in the picturesque vineyards of the **Alto Douro** (p420)

- Losing yourself amid the medieval alleys and riverfront promenades of Porto's cinematic **Ribeira district** (p389)

- Sampling a late-bottled vintage at a port-wine lodge in **Vila Nova de Gaia** (p393)

- Relaxing beside the Rio Tâmega and its medieval bridge in the charming town of **Amarante** (p409)

- Coming face to face with Palaeolithic artwork at **Vale do Côa** (p421), home to petroglyphs dating back over 10,000 years

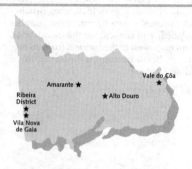

- POPULATION: 2.1 MILLION

- AREA: 3350 SQ KM

PORTO

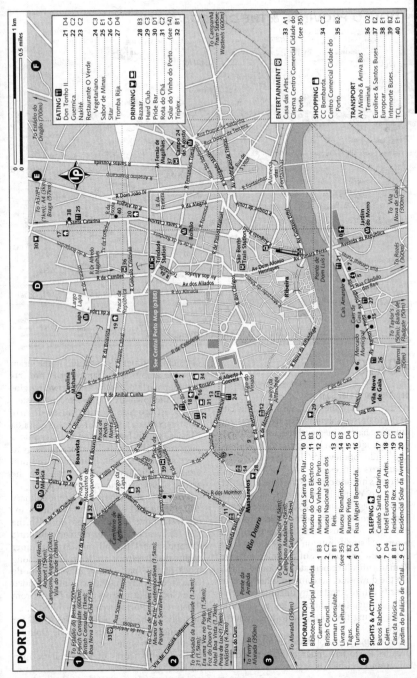

EATING 🍴
Don Tonho II..........................	21 D4
Guernica.................................	22 C2
Nakité....................................	23 C2
Restaurante O Verde Vegetariano.........................	24 C3
Sabor de Minas.......................	25 E1
Sitar.....................................	26 C4
Tromba Rija............................	27 D4

DRINKING 🍷
Bazaar...................................	28 B3
Hard Club..............................	29 C3
Pride Bar...............................	30 D1
Rota do Chá............................	31 C2
Solar do Vinho do Porto.............	(see 14)
Triplex..................................	32 B1

ENTERTAINMENT 🎭
Casa das Artes........................	33 A1
Cinema Centro Comercial Cidade do Porto.....................	(see 35)

SHOPPING 🛍
CC Bombarda...........................	34 C2
Centro Comercial Cidade do Porto.................................	35 B2

TRANSPORT
Av Minho & Arriva Bus Terminal..............................	36 D2
Eurolines & Santos Buses............	37 E2
Europcar................................	38 E1
Intermonte Buses.....................	39 B2
TCL......................................	40 E1

INFORMATION
Biblioteca Municipal Almeida Garrett.................................	1 B3
British Council.........................	2 C2
German Consulate.....................	3 B1
Livraria Leitura........................	(see 35)
Tagus....................................	4 B2
Turismo..................................	5 D4

SIGHTS & ACTIVITIES
Barcos Rabelos........................	6 C4
Calém....................................	7 D4
Casa da Música........................	8 B1
Jardim do Palácio de Cristal.......	9 C3
Mosteiro da Serra do Pilar.........	10 D4
Museu do Carro Eléctrico...........	11 B3
Museu do Vinho do Porto...........	12 C3
Museu Nacional Soares dos Reis..................................	13 C2
Museu Romântico.....................	14 B3
Ramos Pinto............................	15 D4
Rua Miguel Bombarda................	16 C2

SLEEPING 🛏
Castelo Santa Catarina..............	17 C4
Hotel Eurostars das Artes..........	18 C2
Residencial Rex.......................	19 D1
Residencial Solar da Avenida......	20 E2

To Matosinhos (4km);
To Estádio do Bessa (500m);
British Consulate (600m);
Porto Consulate (1km);
Boa Nova Casa-Chá (7.5km)

Campismo Angeiras (20km);
Vila do Conde (28km)

To Estádio do Dragão (700m)

Airport (15km);
A4 (3km);
Braga (57km)

See Central Porto Map (p388)

Rio Douro

DOURO PROVINCE & THE DOURO VALLEY

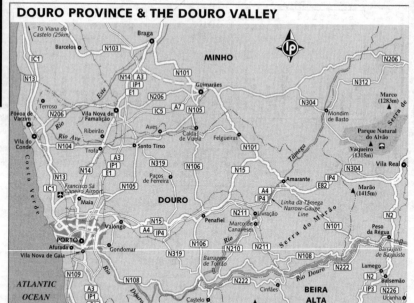

PORTO

pop 270,000 / elev 80m

At the mouth of the Rio Douro, the hilly city of Porto presents a jumble of styles, eras and attitudes: narrow medieval alleyways, extravagant baroque churches, prim little squares, and wide boulevards lined with stately beaux-arts edifices.

Porto's historic centre is the Ribeira district, a Unesco World Heritage zone of winding lanes, zigzagging staircases and tiled churches peering around every corner. Old traditions live on as *tripeiros* (Porto residents) mingle before old storefronts, on village-style plazas and in the old houses of commerce where Roman ruins lurk beneath the foundations. On the downside, here and in other parts of the city centre stand many dilapidated early-20th-century town houses, left to crumble as the young flee to the sprawling suburbs by the sea.

Yet despite signs of decay, in the last two decades Porto has undergone a remarkable renaissance – which is expressed in the hum of its efficient metro system and in the gleam of some ambitious urban renewal projects in other parts of town. The crowning glories of the town are the two recent masterworks, Álvaro Siza Vieira's Museu de Arte Contemporânea and Rem Koolhaas' Casa da Música, which have turned the city into a pilgrimage site for architecture buffs. And there are signs that an infusion of youthful vitality is returning to the centre, with the arrival of new galleries and boutiques.

Porto has also enjoyed a recent culinary renaissance, with a number of forward-leaning restaurants opening their doors in the last few years. The city regularly imports Europe's top DJs, and on warm summer nights the riverfront can seem like one long block party – particularly in Vila Nova de Gaia (technically another city but included here), located just across the Rio Douro from Porto itself. Porto's riverside sibling, incidentally, is the best place in the world for sampling the great fruits from the Douro – historic port-wine lodges jockey for attention, with scores of wine-cellars open for tastings.

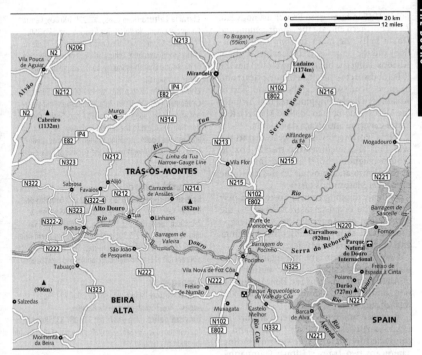

HISTORY

Porto put the 'Portu' in 'Portugal'. The name dates from Roman times, when Lusitanian settlements straddled both sides of the Rio Douro. The area was briefly in the hands of Moors but was reconquered by AD 1000 and reorganised as the county of Portucale, with Porto as its capital. British-born Henri of Burgundy was granted the land in 1095, and it was from here that Henri's son and Portuguese hero Afonso Henriques launched the Reconquista (Christian reconquest), ultimately winning Portugal its status as an independent kingdom.

In 1387 Dom João I married Philippa of Lancaster in Porto, and their most famous son, Henry the Navigator, was born here. While Henry's explorers groped around Africa for a sea route to India, British wine merchants – forbidden to trade with the French – set up shop, and their presence continues to this day, evidenced in port-wine labels such as Taylor's and Graham's.

Over the following centuries Porto acquired a well-earned reputation for rebelliousness. In 1628 a mob of angry women attacked the minister responsible for a tax on linen. A 'tipplers' riot' against the Marquês de Pombal's regulation of the port-wine trade was savagely put down in 1757. And in 1808, as Napoleon's troops occupied the city, Porto citizens arrested the French governor and set up their own short-lived junta. After the British helped drive out the French, Porto radicals were at it again, leading calls for a new liberal constitution, which they got in 1822. Demonstrations in support of liberals continued to erupt in Porto throughout the 19th century.

Meanwhile, wine profits helped fund the city's industrialisation, which began in earnest in the late 19th century, when elites in the rest of Portugal tended to see trade and manufacturing as vulgar. Today the city remains the economic capital of northern Portugal and is surpassed only by much-larger Lisbon in terms of economic and social clout.

ORIENTATION

Central Porto sits on a series of bluffs some 5km east of the mouth of the Rio Douro. The city's central axis is Avenida dos Aliados (aka Aliados), which is a handsome avenue carved out in 1915 in homage to French art nouveau. At its northern end are the *câmara municipal* (town hall), the main *turismo* (tourist office) and the central post office. Just south of Aliados along the banks of the Douro lies the Ribeira district – the city's historic heart and its most picturesque neighbourhood. East of Aliados is a lively shopping area that includes the Mercado do Bolhão (Bolhão Market), Rua Santa Catarina and Praça da Batalha.

'New' Porto sprawls out westward to the sea. This area includes the trendy Foz do Douro neighbourhood around the mouth of the Douro and, moving up the coast, the upmarket Matosinhos district.

Roughly dividing central Porto from new Porto is the Boavista district, home to the giant Praça de Mouzinho de Albuquerque roundabout, shopping malls, office buildings and the new Casa da Música.

Central hubs for city and regional buses include Praça da Liberdade (the southern end of Aliados), the adjacent São Bento train station, and Jardim da Cordoaria, about 400m west of Aliados.

Porto's Francisco Sá Carneiro airport lies 19km northwest of the city centre and is connected by the city's newest metro line. There are two train stations: Campanhã, 2km east of the centre, which handles intercity traffic; and central São Bento, which is only for commuter lines. Trindade station, just north of Aliados, is now the hub of Porto's metro system. Intercity bus terminals are scattered all over the city; see p405 for further information.

The city's World Heritage–listed historic centre reaches from the Torre dos Clérigos and São Bento train station down to the Cais da Ribeira. Also included are the Ponte de Dom Luís I and the Mosteiro da Serra de Pilar in Vila Nova de Gaia.

You can pick up free maps of the city, including bus and metro maps, at any of Porto's tourist offices (see p388).

INFORMATION
Bookshops

Newsagents close to Aliados and Rua Santa Catarina will usually stock at least a handful of foreign-language newspapers and periodicals.

Livraria Bertrand (Map p387; ☎ 222 080 638; Centro Comercial Via Catarina, Rua Santa Catarina; ❤ 10am-10pm) Has a selection of travel books and maps.

Livraria Leitura (Map p385; ☎ 220 100 006; Centro Comercial Cidade do Porto, Rua Gonçalo Sampaio 350; ❤ 10am-11pm) Inside the Centro Comercial Cidade do Porto shopping centre, Leitura stocks a decent selection of music and English-language books and periodicals. Live music occasionally.

Livraria Lello (Map p387; ☎ 222 002 037; Rua das Carmelitas 144; ❤ 10am-7pm Mon-Sat) Even if you're not after books, don't miss this 1906 neo-Gothic confection that's stacked to the rafters with new, secondhand and antique books, including foreign-language guidebooks and some literature. Up the curving staircase is a pleasant cafe.

Cultural Centres

British Council (Map p385; ☎ 222 073 060; Rua do Breiner 155; ❤ 2-8.30pm Mon & Wed, 10am-1pm & 2-8.30pm Tue & Thu, 2-7.30pm Fri, irregular hours Sat mid-Sep–mid-Jun, 2-5.30pm Mon, Wed & Fri, 10am-1pm & 2-5.30pm Tue & Thu mid-Jun–mid-Sep, closed Aug) Has a library full of English-language books and newspapers.

Emergency

Police station (Map p387; ☎ 222 006 821; Rua Augusto Rosa) South of Praça da Batalha.

Tourism police (Map p387; ☎ 222 081 833; Rua Clube dos Fenianos 11; ❤ 8am-2am) Multilingual station beside the main city *turismo*.

Internet Access

For free wi-fi access, try Plano B (p402).

Biblioteca Municipal Almeida Garrett (Map p385; Jardim do Palácio de Cristal; ❤ 2-6pm Mon, 10am-6pm Tue-Sat) Library with free internet access.

Laranja Mecânica (Map p387; Rua Santa Catarina 274, Loja V; per hr €1.50; ❤ 10am-midnight Mon-Sat, 2-8pm Sun)

On Web (Map p387; Praça General Humberto Delgado 291; per hr €1.80; ❤ 10am-2am Mon-Sat, 3pm-2am Sun)

Portugal Telecom Office (PT; Map p387; Praça da Liberdade 62; per hr €2.30; ❤ 8am-8pm Mon-Sat, 10am-8pm Sun) The telephone office also has a dozen pricey terminals.

Internet Resources

www.portoturismo.pt Useful and complete guide from the city's tourist office, with English- and Spanish-language versions.

www.portoxxi.com Cultural guide with restaurant listings, including a version in quirky English.

Medical Services

Hospital Geral de Santo António (Map p387; ☎ 222 077 500; Rua Prof Vicente J Carvalho) Has some English-speaking staff.

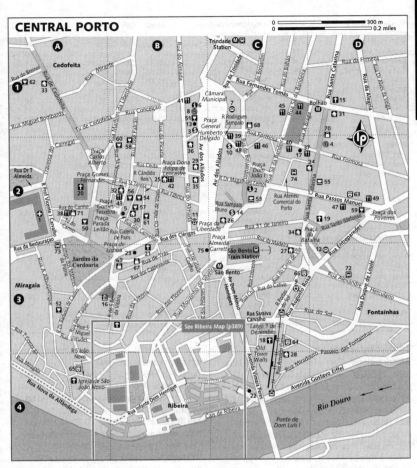

CENTRAL PORTO

Money
There is a currency exchange, open from 5am to 1am, as well as several 24-hour ATMs, in the airport arrivals hall. If you need a private exchange, consider the following:

Intercontinental (Map p387; ☎ 222 005 557; Rua de Ramalho Ortigão 8; ⏰ 9am-noon & 2-6.30pm Mon-Fri, 9am-noon Sat)

Portocâmbios (Map p387; ☎ 222 000 238; Rua Rodrigues Sampaio 193; ⏰ 9am-12.30pm & 1.30-6pm Mon-Fri, 9am-12.30pm Sat)

Western Union (Map p387; ☎ 213 429 760; Rua Sá da Bandeira 39; ⏰ 8.30am-6.45pm Mon-Fri, 9am-1pm & 2-5.45pm Sat & Sun) Currency exchange, plus internet access (€3 per hour) and phone booths for international calls (€0.25 per minute to Europe or the USA).

Post
Branch post offices Praça da Batalha (Map p387; ⏰ 8.30am-6pm Mon-Fri); Rua Ferreira Borges 67 (Map p389; ⏰ 8.30am-6pm Mon-Fri)

Main post office (Map p387; ☎ 223 400 200; Av dos Aliados; ⏰ 8am-9pm Mon-Fri, 9am-6pm Sat, 9am-12.30pm & 2-6pm Sun) Opposite the main city *turismo*.

Telephone
Post offices, kiosks and newsagents sell Portugal Telecom phonecards, which can be used from most public phones.

Portugal Telecom office (PT; Map p387; ☎ 225 001 117; Praça da Liberdade 62; ⏰ 8am-8pm Mon-Sat, 10am-8pm Sun) The handiest place for long-distance calls using cardphones or pay-afterward *cabines* (phone boxes).

INFORMATION
Hospital Geral de Santo António..1 A2
ICEP Turismo...........................2 C2
Intercontinental.......................3 B1
Laranja Mecânica......................4 D2
Livraria Bertrand...................(see 70)
Livraria Lello.........................5 B2
Loja da Mobilidade.................(see 6)
Main City Turismo.....................6 B1
Main Post Office.......................7 C1
On Web.................................8 B1
Police Station.........................9 C3
Portocâmbios.........................10 C2
Portugal Telecom Office.............11 B2
Post Office...........................12 D3
Top Atlântico........................13 B1
Tourism Police......................(see 6)
Western Union........................14 C2

SIGHTS & ACTIVITIES
Capela das Almas.....................15 D1
Centro Português de
  Fotografia..........................16 A3
Confeitaria do Bolhão Shop......17 C2
Igreja de Santa Clara................18 C3
Igreja de Santo Ildefonso............19 D2
Igreja do Carmo......................20 A2
Igreja dos Clérigos...................21 B3
Ribeira Negra.........................22 C4
Torre dos Clérigos...................23 B3

SLEEPING 🏠
Grande Hotel do Porto............24 D2

Hotel Infante de Sagres............25 B2
Hotel Peninsular......................26 C2
Mercure Praça da Batalha........27 C3
Pensão Astória.......................28 C4
Pensão Avenida.......................29 B2
Pensão Cristal.........................30 B2
Pensão do Norte.....................31 D1
Pensão Duas Nações................32 B2
Pensão-Residencial Estoril........33 A1
Quality Inn Praça da Batalha....34 C2
Residencial dos Aliados..........35 B2
Residencial Pão de Açucar.......36 B2

EATING 🍴
A Pérola do Bolhão.................37 C2
A Tasquinha...........................38 A2
Al Forno Baixa.......................39 C2
Confeitaria do Bolhão..............40 C2
Confeitaria Ricardo Jorge..........41 B1
Confeitaria Sical.....................42 B2
Leitaria Quinta do Paço 43 B2
Mercado do Bolhão.................44 C1
Minipreço............................45 C1
Modelo.............................(see 70)
O Caçula.............................46 C2
O Escondidinho.....................47 D2
Pedro dos Frangos.................48 C2
Pingo Doce..........................49 D2

DRINKING 🍷 🍸
Âncora d'Ouro.......................50 A2
Black Coffee..........................51 B1
Boys 'R' Us...........................52 A3

Café A Brasileira.....................53 C2
Café au Lait..........................54 B2
Café Guarany......................(see 35)
Café Majestic.........................55 D2
Casa do Livro........................56 B2
Galeria de Paris......................57 B2
Lusitano...............................58 B2
Maus Habitos........................59 D2
Moinho de Vento.....................60 B2
Plano B................................61 B2
Uptown...............................62 A1

ENTERTAINMENT 🎭
Coliseu do Porto.....................63 D2
Hot Five Jazz & Blues Club........64 C3
Restaurante O Fado.................65 A4
Teatro Nacional São João.........66 C3

SHOPPING 🛍
Artesanato dos Clérigos...........67 B3
Casa Januário........................68 C1
Casa Oriental........................69 B3
Centro Comercial Via Catarina
  Catarina............................70 D1
Garrafeira do Carmo...............71 A2

TRANSPORT
Paragem Atlântico Terminal
  Terminal..........................(see 72)
Rede Expressos.......................72 D3
Renex Buses..........................73 A3
Rodonorte Bus Terminal............74 C2
STCP Service Point..................75 B3

Tourist Information

Branch turismos Ribeira – City Tourist Office branch (Map p389; ☎ 222 060 412; Rua Infante Dom Henrique 63; ☽ 9am-7pm Jul & Aug, 9am-5.30pm Mon-Fri, 9.30am-4.30pm Sat & Sun Sep-Jun); Airport – ICEP branch (☎ 229 412 534, 229 432 400; ☽ 8am-11pm)

ICEP turismo (Investimentos, Comércio e Turismo de Portugal; Map p387; ☎ 222 057 514; Praça Dom João I 43; ☽ 9am-7.30pm Jul & Aug, 9am-7.30pm Mon-Fri, 9.30am-3.30pm Sat & Sun Sep & Apr-Jun, 9am-7pm Mon-Fri, 9.30am-3.30pm Sat & Sun Nov-Mar) For countrywide queries, visit this national *turismo*.

Loja da Mobilidade (Mobility Store; Map p388; loja.mobilidade@cm-porto.pt; Rua Clube dos Fenianos 25; ☽ 9am-5.30pm Mon-Fri) In the main city *turismo*. Dispenses a handy brochure, *Guia de Transportes* (English version available), sells tickets and passes, and can provide details on everything from bus timetables to car parks and metro stations.

Main city turismo (Map p387; ☎ 223 393 472; turismo.central@cm-porto.pt; Rua Clube dos Fenianos 25; ☽ 9am-7pm Jul & Aug, 9am-5.30pm Mon-Fri, 9.30am-4.30pm Sat & Sun Sep-Jun) Opposite the *câmara municipal*. This office has a detailed city map, a transport map and the *Agenda do Porto* cultural calendar.

Travel Agencies

When booking a tour, see p395 for details of government-run Porto Tours, which acts

as an impartial intermediary between tour operators and travellers.

Tagus (Map p385; ☎ 226 094 146; www.viagenstagus.pt; Rua Campo Alegre 261; ☽ 9am-6pm Mon-Fri, 10am-1pm Sat) Youth-oriented agency selling discounted tickets, rail passes and international youth and student cards.

Top Atlântico (Map p387; ☎ 222 074 020; aliados@topatlantico.com; Praça General Humberto Delgado 269; ☽ 9.30am-7pm Mon-Fri, 10am-1pm Sat)

Wasteels (off Map p385; ☎ 225 194 230; Rua Pinto Bessa 27-29; ☽ 9.30am-12.30pm & 1.45-6pm Mon-Fri) Another youth-oriented agency, near Campanhã train station.

DANGERS & ANNOYANCES

While Porto is generally quite safe, it's worth exercising caution after dark in the backstreets of the Ribeira district, as well as in the area between São Bento train station and the cathedral. In even the most central parks and squares, you may spy a few drunks and unsavoury characters lingering about.

SIGHTS

Most of Porto's sights are found in its compact centre and are in easy walking distance of each other, though the city's hills can turn an outing into a workout.

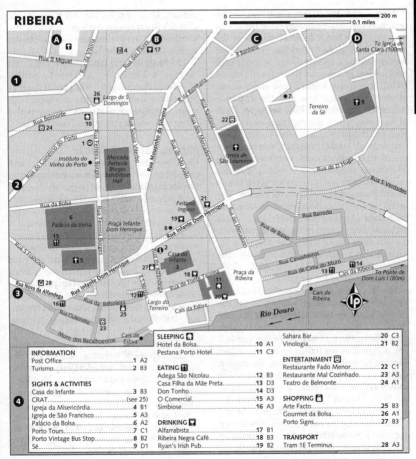

RIBEIRA

Ribeira

The Ribeira district – Porto's riverfront nucleus – is a remarkable window into Porto's history. Along the riverside promenade, *barcos rabelos* (the traditional boats used to ferry port wine down the Douro) bob beneath the shadow of the photogenic Ponte de Dom Luís I. From here you have a fine perspective of the sea of port-wine lodges across the river in Vila Nova de Gaia. Despite flocks of tourists, the neighbourhood remains easygoing and surprisingly ungentrified.

Just back from the river is the handsomely renovated **Casa do Infante** (Map p389; ☎ 222 060 400; Rua Alfândega 10; adult/senior & under 26yr €2/1, Sat & Sun free; ☉ 10am-noon & 2-5pm Tue-Sat, 2-5pm Sun). It's claimed Henry the Navigator was born here in 1394,

and the building later served as Porto's first customs house. Today it houses three floors of exhibits on the complex activities of the customs house throughout the centuries; there's also a model of Porto from its medieval days. In 2002 the complex was excavated, revealing Roman foundations as well as some remarkable mosaics – all of which are now on display.

Sitting on the nearby Praça Infante Dom Henrique, **Igreja de São Francisco** (Map p389; ☎ 222 062 100; Rua Infante Dom Henrique; adult/student €3/2.50; ☉ 9am-6pm) looks from the outside to be an austerely Gothic church, but inside hides one of Portugal's most dazzling displays of baroque finery. Hardly an inch escapes unsmothered, as unworldly cherubs and sober monks alike are drowned by nearly 100kg of gold leaf.

Next door to the church you'll see another temple – this one dedicated unabashedly to Mammon. The **Palácio da Bolsa** (Stock Exchange; Map p389; ☎ 223 399 000; Rua Ferreira Borges; ⊙ 9am-6.30pm May-Sep, 9am-1pm & 2-5.30pm Oct-Apr) is a splendid neoclassical monument (built from 1842 to 1910) honouring Porto's past and present money merchants. Just past the entrance hall is the glass-domed **Pátio das Nações** (Hall of Nations), where the exchange once operated. But this pales in comparison with rooms deeper inside, and to visit these you must join one of the €5 guided tours, which set off every 30 minutes and last for 30 minutes. You can usually join any group; tours are given in any two of Portuguese, English and French. The highlight is a stupendous ballroom called the **Salão Árabe** (Arabian Hall), with stucco walls that have been teased into complex Moorish designs, then gilded with some 18kg of gold. There's also a restaurant and wine bar (the appropriately named 'O Comercial'; p399) for lingering amid the elegance.

North of the square on the distinctly Parisian Rua das Flores, you'll find the rococo facade of the **Igreja da Misericórdia** (Map p389; ☎ 222 074 710; Rua das Flores 15; adult/student €1.50/free; ⊙ 9.30am-12.30pm & 2-5.30pm Tue-Fri, 9am-noon Sat & Sun), designed by the Italian baroque architect Nicolau Nasoni. Now a museum, the church shelters the superb Renaissance painting known as *Fons Vitae* (Fountain of Life), showing Dom Manuel I and his family around a fountain of blood from the crucified Christ.

Back down by the river, narrow streets open out onto **Praça da Ribeira**, which is framed by austerely grand, tiled town houses overlooking a picturesque stretch of the Rio Douro. From here you have fine views of the port-wine lodges across the river as well as the monumental, double-decker **Ponte de Dom Luís I**. Completed in 1886 by a student of Gustave Eiffel, the bridge's top deck is now reserved for pedestrians as well as one of the city's metro lines; the lower deck bears regular traffic, with narrow pedestrian walkways lining the road.

From Praça da Ribeira rises a tangle of medieval alleys and stairways that eventually reach the hulking, hilltop fortress of the **sé** (Map p389; ☎ 222 059 028; admission cloister €2; ⊙ cathedral 8.45am-12.30pm & 2.30-7pm daily, cloister 9am-12.15pm & 2.30-6pm Mon-Sat, 2.30-6pm Sun, both close 1hr earlier Nov-Mar). Founded in the 12th century, this cathedral was largely rebuilt a century later and then extensively altered in the 18th century. However, you can still make out the church's Romanesque contours. Inside, a rose window and a 14th-century Gothic cloister remain from its early days.

The **Igreja de Santa Clara** (Map p387; ☎ 222 054 837; Largo 1 de Dezembro; ⊙ 9.30-11.30am & 3-6pm Mon-Fri), east of the cathedral, was part of another Franciscan convent. Gothic in shape, with a fine Renaissance portal, its interior is also dense with elaborately gilded woodwork.

Aliados, Batalha & Bolhão

Lined with bulging, beaux-arts facades and capped by the stately **câmara municipal**, the **Avenida dos Aliados** may not be exactly Parisian, but it certainly recalls grand Parisian imitators like Buenos Aires and Budapest. Its central plaza was restored a few years back and if it weren't for all the buses (this is the city's transport hub) it would be a fine place to linger.

Just uphill from Aliados you can get your bearings and bird's-eye photographs from the vertigo-inducing **Torre dos Clérigos** (Map p387; Rua dos Clérigos; admission €2; ⊙ 9.30am-1pm & 2.30-7pm Apr-Jul & Sep-Oct, 10am-7pm Aug, 10am-noon & 2-5pm Nov-Mar). Italian-born baroque master Nicolau Nasoni designed the 76m-high tower in the mid-1700s. To reach the top you must scale its 225-step spiral staircase. Nasoni also designed the adjacent **Igreja dos Clérigos** (Map p387; ⊙ 8.45am-12.30pm & 3.30-6.30pm Mon-Sat, 9-10pm Sun), with its theatrical facade and unusual, oval-shaped nave.

Just east of Aliados lies the 19th-century, wrought-iron **Mercado do Bolhão** (Map p387; Rua Formosa; ⊙ 8am-5pm Mon-Fri, 8am-1pm Sat), where earthy vendors sell fresh produce, including cheeses, olives, smoked meats, fresh flowers and more. Uphill along Rua Formosa are **Confeitaria do Bolhão** (Map p387; Rua Formosa 305) and **A Pérola do Bolhão** (Map p387; Rua Formosa 279), two art-nouveau delicatessens stacked high with sausages and cheeses, olives, and dried fruits and nuts.

PORTO CARD

If you plan to do a lot of sightseeing, the **Porto Card** (1-/2-/3-day card €7.50/11.50/15.50) may save you money. It allows holders free or discounted admission to city museums, free travel on public transport and discounts on cruises, tours and cultural events, as well as at some restaurants and shops. The card is sold at *turismos* throughout Porto.

AZULEJO HUNTER'S GUIDE TO PORTO

Porto has some stunning tilework, with a wide range of stories unfolding on the city's old walls. One of the largest and most exquisite displays covers the **Igreja do Carmo** (Map p387; ☎ 222 078 400; Praça Gomes Teixeira; ☺ 8am-noon & 2-5pm Mon-Fri, 8am-noon Sat). Silvestre Silvestri's magnificent 1912 panel illustrates the legend of the founding of the Carmelite order.

Along pedestrianised Rua Santa Catarina, the **Capela das Almas** (Map p387; Rua Santa Catarina 428; ☺ irregular hours) is a close second to Igreja do Carmo. Magnificent panels here depict scenes from the lives of various saints, including the death of St Francis and the martyrdom of St Catherine. Interestingly, Eduardo Leite painted the tiles in a classic 18th-century style, though they actually date back only to the early 20th century.

Hidden inside the **Sé** (opposite), on the upper storey of the cloister (reached via a Nasoni-designed stairway), is Vital Rifarto's 18th-century masterpiece. *Azulejos* (hand-painted tiles) lavishly illustrate scenes from the *Song of Songs*.

Just off Aliados lies **São Bento train station** (Map p387). Completed in 1903, it seems to have been imported straight from 19th-century Paris, thanks to its mansard roof and imposing stone facade. But the dramatic *azulejos* in the front hall are the real attraction. Designed by Jorge Colaço in 1930, some 20,000 tiles depict historic battles scenes (including Henry the Navigator's conquest of Ceuta), as well as a history of transport.

Bringing the art of the *azulejo* up to date, the modernist, polychromatic **Ribeira Negra** (Map p387) by Júlio Resende celebrates life in the Ribeira district in a huge, tiled mural. Created in 1987, it's located at the mouth of the tunnel to the lower deck of the Ponte de Dom Luís I.

For more on the Portuguese art of tilework, see p62.

A little further east lies the pedestrianised **Rua Santa Catarina**, the main shopping district in the centre, with its trim boutiques and animated crowds. At its southern end, Rua Santa Catarina opens out onto the lovely, eclectic **Praça da Batalha**. It's anchored at one end by Nasoni's gracefully baroque **Igreja de Santo Ildefonso** (Map p387; ☎ 222 004 366; ☺ 9.30am-noon & 3-6.30pm Mon-Sat, 9am-12.30pm & 6-7.45pm Sun) and at the other by the lavishly romantic **Teatro Nacional São João** (p404), built in the style of Paris' Opéra-Garnier by the architect of São Bento train station.

Cordoaria

Uphill from Aliados and past the Torre dos Clérigos lies the pleasantly leafy **Jardim da Cordoaria** (simply called 'Cordoaria'; Map p388). Architecture buffs will want to check out the nearby **Hospital Geral de Santo António** (Map p388), whose neo-Palladian facade recalls an Oxfordshire manor house. Just north of the square stands the *azulejo*-covered **Igreja do Carmo** (see boxed text, above), one of Porto's best examples of rococo architecture.

On the south side of Cordoaria is a stately yet muscular building (1796) that once served as a prison and now houses the **Centro Português de Fotografia** (Portuguese Photography Centre; Map p387; ☎ 222 076 310; www.cpf.pt; Campo dos Mártires da Pátria; admission free; ☺ exhibition hall 3-6pm Tue-Fri, 3-7pm Sat & Sun). Multiple exhibitions feature the works of talented photographers from across the globe. Note that the rather gloomy lanes south of the museum were once part of Porto's *judiaria* (Jewish quarter).

A short walk west of Cordoaria lands you at **Museu Nacional Soares dos Reis** (Map p385; ☎ 223 393 770; www.mnsr-ipmuseus.pt, in Portuguese; Rua Dom Manuel II 44; admission €3, 10am-2pm Sun free; ☺ 2-6pm Tue, 10am-6pm Wed-Sun). The town's most comprehensive art collection, it ranges from Neolithic carvings to Portugal's take on modernism and is housed in the formidable Palácio das Carrancas. Requisitioned by Napoleonic invaders, the neoclassical palace was abandoned so rapidly that the future Duke of Wellington found an unfinished banquet in the dining hall. Transformed into a museum of fine and decorative arts in 1940, its best works date from the 19th century, including sculpture by António Soares dos Reis (see especially his famous *O Desterrado*, The Exile) and António Teixeira Lopes, and the naturalistic paintings of Henrique Pousão and António Silva Porto.

Boavista & West Porto

The sprawling roundabout at Praça de Mousinho de Albuquerque roughly marks the boundary between 'old' and 'new' Porto.

Here you'll find **Casa da Música** (see boxed text, below), Porto's extraordinary concert hall.

Three kilometres west, in a leafy, upmarket suburb off the grand Avenida da Boavista, is Porto's other great work of contemporary architecture. Designed by the eminent Porto-based architect Álvaro Siza Vieira, the **Museu de Arte Contemporânea** (Fundação de Serralves, Museum of Contemporary Art; off Map p385; ☎ 226 156 500; www .serralves.pt; Rua Dom João de Castro 210; admission museum & park €5, park or museum only €2.50, 10am-2pm Sun free; 🕒 10am-7pm Tue, Wed & Fri-Sun, 10am-10pm Thu Oct-Mar, 10am-7pm Tue-Thu, 10am-10pm Fri & Sat, 10am-8pm Sun Apr-Sep) is an arrestingly minimalist construction of vast, whitewashed spaces bathed in natural light. Most of the museum is devoted to cutting-edge exhibitions, though there's also a fine permanent collection featuring works from the late 1960s to the present day by artists such as Gerhard Richter, Ed Ruscha and Georg Baselitz. With a single admission fee, you can also visit the nearby **Casa de Serralves**, a delightful, pink, art-deco mansion (built by a forward-looking nobleman in the 1930s) that also hosts temporary exhibitions.

Both museums are located within the marvellous, 18-hectare **Parque de Serralves**. Lily ponds, rose gardens, formal fountains and more-whimsical touches – such as a bright-red sculpture of oversized pruning shears – make for a bucolic outing in the city.

The estate and museum are 4km west of the city centre; take bus 207 from in front of Praça Dom João I, one block east of Avenida dos Aliados.

Palácio de Cristal to Foz do Douro

Sitting atop bluffs just west of Porto's old centre, the leafy **Jardim do Palácio de Cristal** (Map p385; main entrance Rua Dom Manuel II; 🕒 8am-9pm Apr-Sep, 8am-7pm Oct-Mar) is home to a domed sports pavilion, the hi-tech **Biblioteca Municipal Almeida Garrett** (p386) and pleasant tree-lined footpaths with fantastic river views.

Nestled on the garden's south slopes is the Quinta da Macieirinha, the small but stately home where the exiled king of Sardinia spent his final days holed up in 1843. The upstairs has been turned into the modest **Museu Romântico** (Map p385; ☎ 226 057 033; Rua Entre Quintas 220; admission Tue-Fri €2, Sat & Sun free; 🕒 10am-12.30pm & 2-5.30pm Tue-Sat, 2-5.30pm Sun), featuring the king's belongings and dainty period furnishings. Downstairs is the wonderful **Solar do Vinho do Porto** (see p403).

Down by the river in a remodelled warehouse, the modest **Museu do Vinho do Porto** (Port Wine Museum; Map p385; ☎ 222 076 300; Rua do Monchique 45-52; adult/student & senior Tue-Sat €2/1, Sun free; 🕒 11am-7pm Tue-Sun) explores the impact

---

PORTO'S NEW MUSIC MECCA

Called 'insane' yet 'brilliant' by the *Times* and 'ruthlessly inventive' by the *Guardian*, Porto's **Casa da Música** (House of Music; Map p385; ☎ 220 120 220; www.casadamusica.com; Av da Boavista 604) finally opened its doors in 2005 – four years late but every bit worth the wait. Like a gigantic piece of raw crystal, the cloud-white concrete exterior is at once rigorously geometric and defiantly unsymmetrical. But that monolithic sheathing doesn't prepare you for the surprisingly varied delights inside.

At the building's heart is a classic shoe-box-style concert hall, meticulously engineered to accommodate everything from jazz duets to Beethoven's Ninth. It's also home to most of the building's right angles. The rest of the rooms, from classrooms and practice halls to a light-filled VIP lounge, wind around the central hall in a progression of trapezoids and acute angles. It's as if architect Rem Koolhaas has deliberately crushed and twisted the sombre geometry of high modernism, then added narrative touches such as *azulejos* (hand-painted tiles) and gilded furnishings – though always refracted through his own peculiar vision.

The hall holds concerts most nights of the year, from classical to jazz, fado to electronica, with occasional summer concerts staged outdoors in the adjoining plaza. It also offers guided tours led by students from Porto's highly regarded school of architecture. Tours in English are currently held at 11am and 3.30pm Monday to Friday, and at 10.30am and 4pm on weekends; tours cost €3.

Other ways to interact with the space: have a coffee or a light meal in the 1st-floor cafe **Bar dos Artistas** (🕒 10am-8pm), or head to the 7th floor for fine dining at the stylish **Restaurante Kool** (☎ 226 092 876; www.restaurantekool.com; mains €14-20; 🕒 12.30-3.30pm & 8-11pm Tue-Sat).

of the famous tipple on the region's history in a series of largely interactive displays, though it doesn't offer much insight into the wine itself.

Further east is the cavernous **Museu do Carro Eléctrico** (Tram Museum; Map p385; ☎ 226 158 185; http://museu-carro-electrico.stcp.pt; Alameda Basílio Teles 51; adult/child incl free Andante transport for 4hr €3.50/2; ☼ 9.30am-12.30pm & 2.30-6pm Tue-Fri, 3-7pm Sat & Sun). Housed in a former switching-house, it displays dozens of beautifully restored old trams. See p407 for details of Porto's surviving tramlines, and p406 for information on the Andante Card.

Vila Nova de Gaia

While technically its own municipality, Vila Nova de Gaia ('Gaia') sits just across the Rio Douro from Porto and is woven into the city's fabric both by a series of stunning bridges and by its shared history of port-wine making. Since the mid-18th century, port-wine bottlers and exporters have been obliged to maintain their 'lodges' – basically dressed-up warehouses – here.

Today some 60 of these lodges clamber up the steep riverbank, and at night the entire scene transforms itself into Portugal's version of Las Vegas, with huge neon signs clamouring for the attention of nonexperts and oenophiles alike.

From Porto's Ribeira district, a short walk across Ponte de Dom Luís I lands you on Gaia's inviting, riverside promenade. Lined with beautiful *barcos rabelos* – flat-bottomed boats specially designed to carry wine down the Douro's once-dangerous rapids – the promenade offers grandstand views of Porto's historic centre. Here you'll find Gaia's **turismo** (Map p385; ☎ /fax 223 751 902; turismo.vngaia@mail.cm-gaia.pt; Av Diogo Leite 242; ☼ 10am-6pm Mon-Sat, 10am-1pm & 2-6pm Sun Jul & Aug, 10am-6pm Mon-Fri, 10am-1pm & 2-6pm Sat Sep-Jun), which dispenses a good town map and a brochure listing all the lodges open for tours.

Most people come here to taste the tipple, of course, and about 20 lodges oblige them. If you come in high season (June to September), you may feel yourself rushed in the largest lodges. Then again, you won't have to wait long for a tour in your native tongue. Note that more and more large houses are charging for their tours (€2 to €3), though these invariably include free tastings.

Right on the riverfront you can visit the rather grand **Ramos Pinto** (Map p385; ☎ 223 707 000; www.ramospinto.pt; Av Ramos Pinto 380; tour & tasting €2; ☼ 10am-6pm Mon-Sat Jun & Sep, 10am-6pm Jul & Aug, 9am-1pm & 2-5pm Mon-Fri Oct-May), including a look at its historic offices and ageing cellars. The nearby **Calém** (Map p385; ☎ 223 746 660; www.calem.pt; Av Diogo Leite 26; tour & tasting €2; ☼ 10am-7pm May-Sep, 10am-6pm Oct-Apr) is a smaller, independent lodge.

Up from the river, British-run **Taylor's** (off Map p385; ☎ 223 742 800; www.taylor.pt; Rua do Choupelo 250; tour & tasting free; ☼ 10am-6pm Mon-Fri Sep-Jun, 10am-6pm Mon-Sat Jul & Aug) boasts lovely, oh-so-English grounds with fine views of Porto. Its tours are free and even include a tasting of one top-of-the-range (late-bottled vintage) wine – your reward for the short huff uphill.

Barros (off Map p385; ☎ 223 746 660; www.porto-barros.pt; Rua Dona Leonor de Freitas; tour & tasting free; ☼ 10am-6pm Jun-Sep, 10am-5.30pm Mon-Fri Oct-May) is also well worth seeking out, with some of the town's oldest surviving cellars and a more in-depth look at the process of making the wine itself.

Watching over the entire scene is the severe, 17th-century hilltop **Mosteiro da Serra de Pilar** (Map p385), with its striking, circular cloister. Requisitioned by the future Duke of Wellington during the Peninsular War (1807–14), it still belongs to the Portuguese military and is closed to the public. The church is open for Mass every Sunday morning from 10am to noon.

Afurada

Near the mouth of the Rio Douro, this picturesque fishing village clings to traditional ways – men fishing and women washing their laundry at communal fonts. Houses are decked with *azulejos* (hand-painted tiles) and cafes are redolent with hearty *caldeirada* (fish stew). This old-fashioned way of life is depicted in Pedro Neves' 2007 documentary *A Olhar O Mar* (Gazing out to Sea).

For the most scenic route, take a tram from the Ribeira to the stop just west of the Ponte da Arrábida. From here, catch a small ferry (€1) across the river to the village. Hours are not fixed, but if the ferry is not operating, fishing vessels regularly make the crossing and will generally accommodate visitors, so just ask around.

Alternatively, buses 93 and 96 from Cordoaria stop just across the bridge in Vila Nova de Gaia. From here, it's a short walk downhill to Afurada.

THE DOURO

WALKING TOUR

Begin at the baroque **Torre de Clérigos** (1; p390), which offers unrivalled views over Porto. Next, head down Rua dos Clérigos, passing the foot of **Avenida dos Aliados** (2; p390) and pausing to admire the avenue's beaux-arts splendour. Just ahead, you'll see the French-inspired **São Bento train station** (3; see boxed text, p391). Check out the astounding *azulejos* in its main hall. Now cross over to Rua das Flores, a lovely street dotted with second-hand booksellers, old-fashioned stationers and some enticing cafes.

Near the end of the street is Nicolau Nasoni's baroque masterpiece, the **Igreja da Misericórdia** (4; p390). Cross Largo São Domingos to Rua Ferreira Borges, where

you will pass the neoclassical **Palácio da Bolsa** (5; p390). You can check out its main courtyard – once Porto's stock exchange – for free or stay on for a tour of its elaborate interior. Just next door is the **Igreja de São Francisco** (6; p389), with a severe Gothic facade hiding a jaw-dropping golden interior.

Head back up Rua Infante Dom Henrique and turn right on Rua da Alfândega, where

---

WALK FACTS

Start Torre de Clérigos
End Vila Nova de Gaia's riverside esplanade
Distance 2km
Time Two to three hours

WALKING TOUR

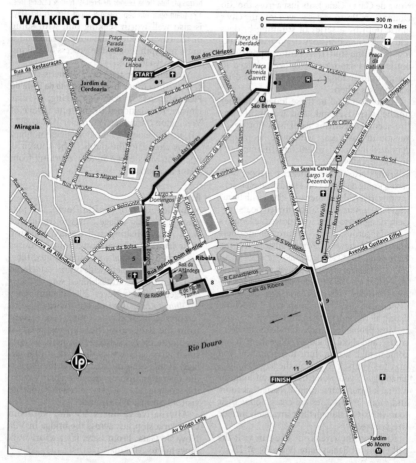

you'll find the medieval **Casa do Infante** (7; p389), the birthplace of Henry the Navigator and the site of some remarkable Roman ruins. Continue into the shadowy Ribeira district, following narrow, medieval Rua de Fonte Taurina as it opens onto the lovely **Praça da Ribeira** (8; p390). From here, take a stroll along the Douro, admiring Vila Nova de Gaia's port-wine lodges across the river. Next, walk across the Eiffel-inspired **Ponte de Dom Luís I** (9; p390) to **Gaia's waterfront esplanade (10)**. Finally, grab an outdoor table at one of the waterfront cafes – like **Dom Tonho II (11)** – where you can enjoy the splendid city views across the Ribeira over a much-deserved drink.

COURSES

CRAT (Centro Regional de Artes Tradicionais; Map p389; ☎ 223 320 201; crat@mail.telepac.pt; Rua da Reboleira 37) sometimes runs brief introductory workshops on *azulejo* painting and stamping, aimed at tourists. A lesson costs around €25, and you can usually pick up your freshly fired tiles a few days later.

PORTO FOR CHILDREN

The best spots for kids to let off some steam are Porto's numerous parks – the fenced, expansive Parque de Serralves (p392) is particularly kid-friendly. For beach fun, head to Praia da Luz at Foz do Douro (p401); kids might also enjoy a rattling journey in one of Porto's old trams (p407). The *turismo* offers a brochure called *Famílias Nos Museus* (Families in Museums), which lists a wide variety of activities designed just for kids throughout the city's museums.

TOURS

Eco Tours (☎ 800 207 906; www.ecotours.com.pt; Rua do Passeio Alegre 20; 4hr tour per person €20) This new outfit offers two English-language walking excursions

BOHEMIAN PORTO

For a glimpse of Porto's bohemian side, take a stroll two blocks north of Igreja do Carmo to Rua Miguel de Bombarda (Map p385). Heading west along this street, you'll soon pass a growing number of art galleries, a few cafes, curio and record shops and some edgy local designer boutiques. The neighbourhood is liveliest in the afternoon and early evening – particularly as the weekend nears.

each day (other languages available by advance booking). Tours take in the highlights of historical Porto (Igreja dos Clérigos, Livraria Lello, Sé and a dozen other sites) before heading to Vila Nova de Gaia for port-tasting. Tours depart from Praça Carlos Alberto.

Porto Tours (Map p389; ☎ 222 000 073; www.porto tours.com; Torre Medieval, Calçada Pedro Pitões 15; ⊙ 10am-7pm Mon-Fri, 10am-1pm & 2-6pm Sat & Sun Apr-Sep, 10am-5pm Mon-Fri, 10am-2pm Sat Oct-Mar) Situated next to the cathedral, this excellent municipal service provides details of all the recommended tour operators, from city walking tours and Douro cruises to private taxi tours or helicopter rides over the city. As well as providing impartial advice, Porto Tours will make bookings for you.

Porto Vintage (☎ 808 200 166) The city transport company offers hourly hop-on, hop-off city tours (€10; half-price for children aged five to 12). You can start at any of the chosen sights (eg Aliados), linger at others and then just catch the next bus, which runs hourly (approximately 9.30am to 6pm). The circuit includes virtually all of the city's sights, including Vila Nova de Gaia and Foz do Douro. You can buy tickets on the bus.

River Cruises

Several outfits offer cruises in ersatz *barcos rabelos*, the colourful boats that were once used to transport port wine from the vineyards. Cruises last 45 to 55 minutes and depart at least hourly on summer days. You can board at Porto's Cais da Ribeira or Cais da Estiva, or at Vila Nova de Gaia's Cais de Gaia or Cais Amarelo.

More interesting are full-day cruises that take you into the heart of port-wine country.

Most tours head upriver by boat and return by train or bus (or vice versa), and offer a snack and at least one full meal. Porto–Peso da Régua–Porto costs around €55 to €85, depending on the day of the week and the time of year you are travelling. Porto–Pinhão–Porto costs around €70 to €90. For multiday cruises, expect to pay upwards of €120 per day per person based on double occupancy with half-board. By far the largest carrier is **Douro Azul** (☎ 223 402 500; www.douroazul.pt).

For reservations and more information, your best bet is Porto Tours (see above).

FESTIVALS & EVENTS

There's a stream of cultural events throughout the year; check the main tourism website, www.portoturismo.pt/en/eventos, for more details. Some highlights:

Fantasporto (International Fantasy Film Festival; www .fantasporto.com) World-renowned two weeks of fantasy, horror and just plain weird films in February/March.

Festival Intercéltico do Porto (Festival of Celtic Music) Ten days of music in late March/early April exploring Portugal's Celtic roots.

Festival Internacional de Teatro de Expressão Ibérica (International Theatre Festival of Iberian Expressions; www.fitei.com) Two weeks of contemporary theatre in Spanish and Portuguese; held in late May/ early June.

Serralves em Festa (http://serralvesemfesta.com) This huge event runs for 40 hours nonstop over one weekend in early June. Parque de Serralves hosts the main events, with concerts, avant-garde theatre and kiddie activities; other open-air events happen all over town.

Festa de São João (St John's Festival) Porto's biggest party. For one night in June the city erupts into music, competitions and riotous parties; this is also when merrymakers pound each other over the head with squeaky plastic mallets (you've been warned).

Festival Internacional de Folclore (International Folk Festival) A weeklong festival in late July/early August attracting international groups.

Noites Ritual Rock (Festival of Portuguese Rock; www .noitesritual.com) A weekend-long rock extravaganza in late August.

SLEEPING
Camping

Porto's nearest camp sites are all located near the ocean, between 6km and 20km from town. Keep in mind that on summer weekends the crowds arrive.

Campismo Marisol (off Map p385; ☎ 227 135 942; fax 227 126 351; Rua Alto das Chaquedas 82, Praia de Canide; sites per adult/tent/car €2/3.50/2.75) This flat, grassy site is located 6km south of Porto.

Campismo Madalena (off Map p385; ☎ 227 122 520; www.orbitur.com; Rua do Cerro, Praia da Madalena; sites per adult/tent/car €4.80/5.40/4.70) Some 12km south of Porto is Orbitur's well-shaded and sandy option.

Campismo Angeiras (off Map p385; ☎ 229 270 571; www.orbitur.com; Rua de Angeiras, Lavra; sites per adult/tent/car €4.80/5.40/4.70) Popular camp site located 20km north of Porto, with shaded sites.

Ribeira

Hotel da Bolsa (Map p389; ☎ 222 026 768; www.hotel dabolsa.com; Rua Ferreira Borges 101; d with/without view from €110/87; ⊠) A few steps from the Instituto do Vinho do Porto, the three-star Hotel da Bolsa has an attractive facade, but spare carpeted rooms, with small windows and not

much space to move about. The front-facing rooms are brighter, with picturesque views of the Ribeira and the river.

Pestana Porto Hotel (Map p389; ☎ 223 402 300; www.pestana.com; Praça da Ribeira 1; d incl breakfast from €160; ⊠ ⊡) A clutch of colourfully haphazard buildings have been transformed into what is, hands down, Porto's most sophisticated sleep. Rooms are a fine balance between plush-contemporary and traditional. Be aware that they vary widely in terms of size, light and views (the best face the river). But everyone can tuck into the fine breakfast buffet.

Aliados

Pensão Duas Nações (Map p387; ☎ 222 081 616; www .duasnacoes.com.pt; Praça Gomes Fernandes 59; s/d/tr from €14/23/36; ⊡) Cheap? You'd better believe it. But it's also clean, friendly and centrally located, and even has double-glazing to shut out the city din. Rooms are basic but cosy, and the whole affair is packed into a narrow town house that has been modernised in some places and left to its creaky, 19th-century devices in others. No breakfast.

Residencial Solar da Avenida (Map p385; ☎ 222 084 196; Rua Santa Catarina 744; s/d €20/25) Among a string of cheap guest houses flowing north along Rua Santa Catarina, this place offers the best value for the money. Rooms here are carpeted and in fair condition despite the rock-bottom prices.

Pensão do Norte (Map p387; ☎ 222 003 503; Rua de Fernandes Tomás 579; s/d/tr from €30/40/55) Opened in 2008, the Pensão do Norte has simple but attractive rooms with wood floors and windows opening onto the brilliant *azulejo*-covered Capela das Almas across the street. Ruby-red carpeting lines the staircase leading up the old building (an elevator may eventually be added).

Pensão Avenida (Map p387; ☎ 222 009 551; http:// planeta.clix.pt/pensaoavenida; Av dos Aliados 141; s/d/tw €35/40/45; ⊠) A good budget option overlooking the main square, this small guest house has a handful of rooms on the upper two floors of a beaux-arts building. Rooms have high ceilings, wood floors and simple furnishings. Those in the front open onto the plaza; back rooms are small and a little dark.

Pensão Cristal (Map p387; ☎ 222 002 100; Rua Galeria de Paris 48; s/d/tw/tr €35/45/50/60; P ⊠ ⊡) The new budget favourite in town, Pensão Cristal lies

PORT WINE 101

With its intense flavours, silky textures and appealing sweetness, port wine is easy to love, especially when it is taken with its proper accompaniments: cheese, nuts and dried fruit. Ports are also wonderfully varied, and even nonconnoisseurs can quickly learn to tell an aged tawny from a late-bottled vintage (LBV). For a friendly primer on all things port, head to the convivial **Vinologia** (p401), where learned servers give an enlightening lesson with each glass they pour for their visitors (English and French spoken). From here, you can also head across the Douro to Vila Nova de Gaia to taste the output of particular houses (p393). Finally, impress friends and loved ones by leading your own tour through the offerings at the remarkable **Solar do Vinho do Porto** (p403).

Until you've become an authority, we've prepared this quick cheat sheet.

History

It was probably Roman soldiers who first planted grapes in the Douro valley some 2000 years ago, but tradition credits the discovery of port itself to 17th-century British merchants. With their own country at war with France, they turned to their old ally Portugal to meet their wine-drinking habits. The Douro valley was a particularly productive area, though its wines were dark and astringent. According to legend, the British threw in some brandy with grape juice, both to take off the wine's bite and to preserve it for shipment back to England – and port wine was the result. In fact, the method may already have been in use in the region, though what's certain is that the Brits took to the stuff. Their influence in the region has been long and enduring, a fact that is still evidenced in some of port's most illustrious names, including Taylor's, Graham's and Cockburn's.

The Grapes

Port-wine grapes are born out of adversity. They manage to grow on rocky terraces with hardly any water or even soil, and their roots must reach down as far as 30m, weaving past layers of acidic schist (shalelike stone) to find nourishment. In addition, the vines endure both extreme heat in summer and freezing temperatures in winter. It's believed that these conditions produce intense flavours that stand up to the infusions of brandy. The most common varietals are hardy, dark reds like *touriga, tinto cão* and *tinto barroca*.

The Wine

Grapes are harvested in autumn and immediately crushed (often still by foot) and allowed to ferment until alcohol levels reach 7%. At this point, one part brandy is added to every five parts wine. Fermentation stops immediately, leaving the unfermented sugars that make port sweet. The quality of the grapes, together with the ways the wine is aged and stored, determines the kind of port you get. The most common include the following:

- Ruby: made from average-quality grapes, and aged at least two years in vats; rich, red colours and sweet, fruity flavours.
- Tawny: made from average-quality grapes, and aged for two to seven years in wood casks; mahogany colours, drier than ruby, with nuttier flavours.
- Aged tawny: selected from higher-quality grapes, then aged for many years in wood casks; subtler and silkier than regular tawny;
- Late-bottled vintage (LBV): made from very select grapes of a single year, aged for around five years in wood casks, then bottled; similar to vintage, but ready for immediate drinking once bottled, and usually smoother and lighter-bodied;
- Vintage: made from the finest grapes from a single year (and only select years qualify), aged in barrels for two years, then aged in bottles for at least 10 years and up to 100 or more; dark ruby colours, fruity yet extremely subtle and complex.

on a quiet street near a few galleries and bars. Corridors are narrow, but decorated with artwork, and the rooms are clean and cosy with tile floors and simple wood furnishings. There's a tiny lift.

Hotel Peninsular (Map p387; ☎ 222 003 012; Rua Sá da Bandeira 21; s/d from €38/46) From a lobby decked out in *azulejos* and polished wood, an ancient lift carries you to a dizzying variety of rooms, architectural styles and pricing schemes that make this place hard to categorise – from poky, dark back rooms to bright, Jacuzzi-endowed, practically deluxe digs. But all offer one thing: value for money.

Residencial Rex (Map p385; ☎ 222 074 590; fax 222 083 882; Praça da República 117; s/d from €40/50; P ✖) Overlooking a peaceful plaza, Residencial Rex is set in a belle époque manor with a wide range of rooms. Floors two and three are best, with handsome old details, high ceilings and plenty of space. Fourth-floor rooms are small, carpeted and charmless. It's popular with a good mix of travellers.

Residencial Pão de Açucar (Map p387; ☎ 222 002 425; www.residencialpaodeacucar.com; Rua do Almada 262; s/d from €45/60) Occupying an imposing art-deco building just steps from Aliados, the Pão de Açucar offers two distinct choices: old-fashioned rooms with new beds and polished parquet floors; or, for a small premium, modern, top-floor rooms with huge, sliding glass doors that open onto a wide communal terrace.

Residencial dos Aliados (Map p387; ☎ 222 004 853; www.residencialaliados.com; Rua Elísio de Melo 27; s/d from €50/60; ✖) Set in one of Porto's marvellous beaux-arts buildings, this guest house offers spiffy rooms with polished wooden floors, decent beds and tasteful if vaguely austere furnishings of dark-stained wood. Plaza-facing rooms are bright, but can be noisy. Prices dip dramatically in the low season.

Hotel Infante de Sagres (Map p387; ☎ 223 398 500; www.hotelinfantesagres.pt; Praça Dona Filipa de Lencastre 62; s/d from €175/195; ✖ 💻) An exquisite time warp with well-coiffed doormen, crystal chandeliers and ornately decorated common areas, this place feels like a royal getaway in the heart of the city. Digs are modern but with all the trimmings, though standard rooms are a little careworn; superiors are quite up to scratch.

Batalha & Bolhão

ourpick **Pensão Astória** (Map p387; ☎ 222 008 175; Rua Arnaldo Gama 56; s/d from €20/30) In an austere but elegant town house atop vertiginous stairs that lead down to the Rio Douro, this spotless place has no frills but great charms. Rooms vary in size and equipment – only a few have full bathroom – but all are decorated with trim antiques, many have high ceilings, all are clean as whistles, and several have great river and bridge views. Reservations recommended.

Castelo Santa Catarina (Map p385; ☎ 225 095 599; www.castelosantacatarina.com.pt; Rua Santa Catarina 1347; s/d from €45/65; P) And now for something completely different: Castelo Santa Catarina is a whimsical, late-19th-century, pseudo-Gothic castle, a fabulously over-the-top hideaway in palm-shaded, *azulejo*-smothered gardens complete with its own chapel. Choose between more-elegant, period-furnished doubles in the castle and smaller rooms in a modern annexe. Reserve well in advance for summer weekends and holidays.

Quality Inn Praça da Batalha (Map p387; ☎ 223 392 300; www.choicehotels.eu; Praça da Batalha 127; d from €60; ✖ 💻) It may be part of a chain, but this place offers attractive, recently remodelled rooms. Many have balconies, and virtually all above the 2nd floor offer fine views.

Mercure Praça da Batalha (Map p387; ☎ 222 043 300; www.mercure.com; Praça da Batalha 116; s/d €80/120; P ✖) Near the Teatro São João, Porto's link in the Mercure chain has plush, modern, identically furnished rooms with fine views, and hallways decorated with theatre memorabilia. You'll also find a gleaming lobby and attentive service here.

Grande Hotel do Porto (Map p387; ☎ 222 076 690; www.grandehotelporto.com; Rua Santa Catarina 197; s/d from €115/125; P ✖) Open since 1880, this proud old institution preserves a good deal of its grandeur, especially in its cavernous dining room and gilded parlour. Its rooms are less distinguished but still large and plush.

Cordoaria & Around

Pensão-Residencial Estoril (Map p387; ☎ 222 002 751; www.pensaoestoril.com; Rua de Cedofeita 193; s/d €30/40) Set on a busy pedestrian strip (that's quiet at night), this dated but cosy family-run place has small, carpeted rooms that represent fair value for the area. It's close to the gallery and alternative scene along Rua Miguel Bombarda.

Hotel Eurostars das Artes (Map p385; ☎ 222 071 250; www.eurostarshotels.com; Rua do Rosário 160; d from €80; P ✖ 💻) This stylish new hotel has something of a boutique feel, with handsomely outfitted rooms featuring spare contemporary furnishings, sparkling bathrooms and nice touches like in-room wi-fi access. There's also a lounge and a peaceful terrace that's ideal for an afternoon drink.

West Porto

Pousada da Juventude (off Map p385; ☎ 226 177 257; www.pousadasjuventude.pt; Rua Paulo da Gama 551; dm/d €14/38; ⏰ 24hr; 🅿 🖳) In a bright, modern building on bluffs above the Rio Douro, the crown jewel of Portugal's hostels offers basic but handsome doubles with sweeping views of the river, as well as clean, well-maintained dorms. There's a decent restaurant and a supermarket across the street, but no open kitchen. The hitch: it's 4km from central Porto. Take bus 207 from Campanhã station or bus 500 from Aliados. Reservations are essential.

Hotel Boa Vista (off Map p385; ☎ 225 320 020; www.hotelboavista.com; Esplanada do Castelo 58; s/d from €72/€80) A classic, 19th-century seaside inn outside and a thoroughly modern if somewhat characterless hotel inside, the Boa Vista sits at the mouth of the Douro and one block from the beach in the tiny Foz do Douro neighbourhood.

EATING

Porto's restaurant scene has grown in leaps and bounds in recent years. Diners can enjoy traditional recipes from the north, contemporary Portuguese fusion fare or a medley of Italian, Indian and vegetarian dishes at new multicultural eateries. For dessert or breakfast, the cafes and patisseries around town keep locals in *pastéis de nata* (custard tarts). For the latest restaurant openings, pick up a copy of *Porto Menu* (www.portomenu.com) at the tourist office.

Those wanting to self-cater should check out Porto's municipal market, the Mercado do Bolhão (p390), as well as the nearby grocery-cum-bakery **Confeitaria do Bolhão** (Map p387; Rua Formosa 305) and the art-nouveau food shop **A Pérola do Bolhão** (Map p387; Rua Formosa 279). Among the central *supermercados* (supermarkets) are the well-stocked **Minipreço** (Map p387; Rua Sá da Bandeira 355; ⏰ 9am-8pm Mon-Sat), **Pingo Doce** (Map p387; Rua Passos Manuel 213; ⏰ 8.30am-9pm Mon-Sat, 9am-8.30pm Sun) and **Modelo** (Map p387; Centro Comercial Via Catarina, Rua Santa Catarina; ⏰ 10am-10pm).

Ribeira

Casa Filha da Mãe Preta (Map p389; ☎ 222 055 515; Cais da Ribeira 40; half-portions €6-9; ⏰ lunch & dinner Mon-Sat) Set smack on the Ribeira's riverfront, this is the most congenial of a long line of touristy riverside restaurants. Go early to bag an upstairs front table for views of the Douro.

Adega São Nicolau (Map p389; ☎ 222 008 232; Rua São Nicolau 1; mains €8-12; ⏰ lunch & dinner) Half-hidden down a narrow lane, this cosy place serves satisfying traditional seafood to a mix of locals and travellers. *Bacalhau a Gomes* (codfish with potatoes) and *polvo com arroz* (octopus with rice) are top picks.

Simbiose (Map p389; ☎ 222 030 398; Rua Infante Dom Henrique 133; mains €9-13; ⏰ lunch & dinner Tue-Sun) On two floors in an airy, quayside town house, Simbiose serves up decent traditional cuisine and lovely river views.

O Comercial (Map p389; ☎ 223 322 019; Palácio da Bolsa, Rua Ferreira Borges; mains €12-16; ⏰ lunch & dinner Mon-Fri, dinner Sat) Hidden at the back of the stock-exchange building, this one-of-a-kind restaurant boasts towering arches, old-world service and a stylish, fireside lounge. At dinner, the food has been known to disappoint, but the three-course lunch menu is great value.

Don Tonho (Map p389; ☎ 222 004 307; Cais da Ribeira 13-15; mains €12-22; ⏰ lunch & dinner) Built into ancient riverside ramparts, this elegant restaurant serves traditional Portuguese fare prepared with a contemporary twist. Opened by Rui Velosa, crown prince of Portuguese pop, it serves up superb seafood, including fine *bacalhau* (dried salt-cod), and also boasts one of Porto's most extensive wine lists. There's a second, newer restaurant, Don Tonho II (Map p385; ☎ 223 744 835) on the riverside in Vila Nova de Gaia.

Aliados, Batalha & Bolhão

Confeitaria Sical (Map p387; ☎ 222 056 148; Praça Dona Filipa de Lencastre 29; sandwiches €2-3, mains €5; ⏰ 7.30am-7.30pm Mon-Fri, 8am-12.30pm Sat) A mix of labourers and literary types from the neighbouring publishing houses rub elbows at this lunch-time joint. The design features a clever take on Portuguese *azulejos*.

Confeitaria do Bolhão (Map p387; Rua Formosa 339; mains €3.50-9; ⏰ 7am-9pm Sun-Fri, 7am-7.30pm Sat) This cheerful belle-époque cafe, popular with everyone but especially ladies of a certain age, serves good food at great prices, including a daily lunch special of soup, main course and freshly squeezed juice for €5. The front

THE DOURO

counter serves an irresistible array of local sweets to go.

Confeitaria Ricardo Jorge (Map p387; ☎ 222 057 869; Rua Dr Ricardo Jorge 67; mains €4-5; ⏰ 1-8pm Mon-Fri, 2-8pm Sat) This popular lunch-time spot has good, inexpensive daily specials. Fried or baked fish, codfish balls and vegie burgers are among the options in this simple but welcoming restaurant.

Pedro dos Frangos (Map p387; ☎ 222 008 522; Rua do Bonjardim 219; mains €4-7; ⏰ 11am-7pm Wed-Mon) *Frango no espeto* (spit-roasted chicken) is the name of the game at this extremely popular and inexpensive grill. Grab a spot at the stand-up counter and join the good old boys for a filling meal (abundant chips included). Other grills are nearby.

Leitaria Quinta do Paço (Map p387; ☎ 222 004 303; Praça Guilherme Gomes Fernandes 47; mains €4-7; ⏰ 9am-8pm Mon-Sat, 2-8pm Sun) Dine alfresco at tables on the tiny plaza, or inside the sleekly designed cafe. Neither will break the bank, with excellent lunch specials (chicken cordon bleu, grilled beef and the like) and a tempting dessert counter.

O Caçula (Map p387; ☎ 222 055 937; Travessa do Bonjardim 20; mains €7-9; ⏰ lunch & dinner Mon-Sat; Ⓥ) Tucked down a narrow lane, O Caçula serves healthy-tasting lighter fare in a trim, contemporary, bi-level space. In addition to a few vegetarian dishes (vegie lasagne, ratatouille), there are grilled items (chicken breast with Roquefort cheese), steak, and fresh juices and smoothies.

Sabor de Minas (Map p387; ☎ 914759473; Rua Santa Catarina 1198; lunch/dinner buffet €8/14; ⏰ lunch & dinner Mon-Sat) Specialising in the hearty dishes from Minas Gerais (Brazil), this small, inviting place offers decent value for its all-you-can-eat buffet. While the selection isn't huge, the dishes are nicely prepared, with salads, desserts and a few side dishes on offer. Friday night is dedicated to *churrasco* (grilled meat).

Al Forno Baixa (Map p387; ☎ 222 021 049; Rua Rodrigues Sampaio; mains €11-15; ⏰ lunch & dinner Mon-Sat) The stylish new favourite in town, Al Forno Baixa serves excellent thin-crust pizzas and hit-and-miss Italian fare in a sleek, contemporary space just off Aliados.

O Escondidinho (Map p387; ☎ 222 001 079; Rua Passos Manuel 144; mains €13-20; ⏰ lunch & dinner) Amid *azulejos*, dark wood furnishings and starched white place settings, O Escondidinho serves excellent traditional cuisine. Chefs here combine fresh ingredients and a wood-burning oven to create classic *bacalhau* dishes and flavourful baked octopus, while grilled seafood dishes are equally impressive.

Cordoaria

Nakité (Map p385; ☎ 226 002 536; Rua do Breiner 396; mains €6-8; ⏰ 9am-midnight Mon-Fri, 12.30-11pm Sat; Ⓥ) This pleasant vegetarian restaurant has satisfying daily specials featuring tofu, seitan and tempeh paired nicely with goat cheese, shiitake mushrooms and other fresh ingredients. Nakité also has fresh juices and good desserts. Dine inside (amid piped-in New Age tunes) or on the back patio next to a gurgling fountain. For more vegie cuisine, check out Maus Habitos (p403).

A Tasquinha (Map p387; ☎ 223 322 145; Rua do Carmo 23; mains €8-13; ⏰ lunch & dinner Mon-Sat) Tucked inside a rustic house, this touristy but pleasant place offers cask wines, garlicky appetisers and good northern specialities. The €13 tourist menu includes three courses, coffee and drink.

Restaurante O Verde Vegetariano (Map p385; ☎ 226 063 886; lower level, Edifício Crystal Park, Rua Dom Manuel II; per kg €10; ⏰ lunch & dinner Sun-Thu, lunch Fri; Ⓥ) This uncluttered little self-service restaurant has a varied selection of vegetarian dishes and an elegant, minimalist dining area that looks onto a pleasant green space.

our pick **Guernica** (Map p385; ☎ 226 062 179; Rua Miguel Bombarda 598; mains €14-18; ⏰ lunch Tue-Fri, dinner Mon-Sat) Guernica brings a self-conscious dash of style to Porto, with excellent international cooking in a slim Manhattan-style bistro. Recent favourites include lasagne with mushrooms and brie, codfish with sausage, wild boar and seafood pasta. For once, you can order wines by the glass.

Vila Nova de Gaia

Barão de Fladgate (off Map p385; ☎ 223 742 800; Rua do Choupelo 250; mains €10-14, set meals €26; ⏰ lunch & dinner Mon-Sat, lunch Sun) With excellent food, enviable views, and of course lots and lots of port, the restaurant in Taylor's port-wine lodge is a worthy splurge. The menu is long on seafood, the speciality being (surprise!) *bacalhau*.

Sitar (Map p385; ☎ 223 796 100; Av Ramos Pinto 244; mains €14-18; ⏰ lunch & dinner) High-end Sitar serves tasty Indian fare (with highlights from north and south) in a small evocative dining room. The pappadams and tandoori are standouts, but the lassis are best avoided.

Tromba Rija (Map p385; ☎ 223 743 762; Av Diogo Leite 102; prix fixe €27.50; ☺ dinner Mon, lunch & dinner Tue-Sat, lunch Sun) Porto's branch of Leiria's famous eatery offers a huge, soup-to-nuts buffet of classic, well-prepared Portuguese dishes – plus all the wine, port and homemade liqueur you can drink. Tromba Rija is a great introduction to Portuguese cuisine – and always festive thanks to all that free booze.

Foz do Douro

Praia da Luz (off Map p385; Av Brasil; mains €7-14; ☺ 9am-2am) Beautifully set along the rocky beach of the same name, Praia da Luz is a worthwhile stop when out exploring Porto's coastline. Sit outside on the wooden deck (but bring a sweater), and enjoy grilled seafood or meat dishes, snacks, salads, and of course a cocktail. It's about 500m north of the Castelo de São João.

DRINKING

They may have a strong work ethic, but that doesn't stop *tripeiros* from partying – the city has a club scene that is at once sophisticated and largely devoid of status jockeying. Porto also boasts a rich theatre and music scene. To keep pace, pick up *Agenda do Porto*, a monthly cultural events brochure, or scan the daily *Jornal de Notícias*.

Cafes

Café Majestic (Map p387; ☎ 222 003 887; Rua Santa Catarina 112; breakfast €15, afternoon tea €9.75; ☺ 9.30am-midnight Mon-Sat) Porto's best-known teashop is packed with prancing cherubs, opulently gilded woodwork, leather seats and gold-braided waiters who'll serve you an elegant set breakfast, afternoon tea or any number of snacks and beverages.

our pick Rota do Chá (Map p385; Rua Miguel Bombarda 457; tea €2; ☺ noon-8pm Mon-Thu, noon-midnight Fri & Sat, 1-8pm Sun; Ⓥ) This proudly bohemian cafe has a verdant but rustic back garden where students and the gallery crowd sit around low tables sampling from an enormous tea menu. Teas are divided by region and include addictive concoctions like iced matcha (green tea) latte and yerba mate. Tasty snacks include broccoli and cheese crêpes and vegie empanadas.

Café Guarany (Map p387; Av dos Aliados 89; mains €6-12; ☺ 9am-midnight) With a sunny, tiled interior, marble-top tables and an Afro-Brazilian mural, this classy affair has attracted the business and literary elite since

the 1930s. It regularly has live music, and serves full meals.

Café A Brasileira (Map p387; Rua Sá da Bandeira; ☺ 9am-midnight) This beaux-arts treasure is looking a little battered, but it's still great to linger amid its bowed windows and Corinthian columns.

Boa Nova Casa-Chá (off Map p385; ☎ 229 951 785; Leça da Palmeira; ☺ noon-10pm Mon-Sat) Designed by famed Portuguese architect Álvaro Siza Vieira and completed in 1963, this cliffside tea house and restaurant is set alluringly above a crashing sea. Massive boulders frame the white, low-rise building, while inside the Zenlike design continues as light floods the wood and stone interior. The restaurant is 20 minutes north of Porto along the coast. It's best reached by car or taxi.

Bars & Nightclubs

Porto's clubs usually don't charge admission, but require you to spend a minimum amount on drinks: usually between €4 and €6 in a bar and €5 to €15 in a club.

RIBEIRA

There are dozens of bars on Praça da Ribeira and along the adjacent quay. On warm nights the outdoor terraces get packed.

Ribeira Negra Café (Map p389; ☎ 222 005 366; Rua Fonte Taurina 66; ☺ 10pm-2am) A ragtag crowd of rock- and reggae-lovers gathers at this trim back-alley bar just off the plaza. As the weekend nears, punters spill out into the streets around the neighbouring bars (handy for checking out the crowd before committing).

Ryan's Irish Pub (Map p389; ☎ 222 005 366; Rua Infante Dom Henrique 18; ☺ 6pm-4am) Serves generous drams of whisky with its good ol' Irish tunes. And of course, English is spoken. Follow the Guinness signs.

Alfarrabista (Map p389; ☎ 222 012 892; Rua das Flores 46; ☺ 10am-2am Mon-Sat) The nicely designed contemporary lounge has style without the pretension, with DJs spinning world music most nights. There's tapas to go with the cocktails (and a full menu by day).

Sahara Bar (Map p389; ☎ 969206037; Caís da Estiva 4; ☺ 10pm-4am Mon-Sat) Decked out like an Arabian hideaway, this loungey place has hookahs, a young garrulous crowd, the occasional belly dancer (Friday at 11pm) and sidewalk seating for taking in the passing people parade.

Vinologia (Map p389; ☎ 936057340; www.lamai sondesporto.com; Rua de São João 46; ☺ 4-9pm Mon-Wed,

THE DOURO

GAY & LESBIAN PORTO

Porto's gays and lesbians keep it discreet in the streets, but are more than willing to let loose behind closed doors. Most venues are clustered around Jardim de Cordoaria. Gay Pride festivities take place in the first or second weekend in July. Consult http://portugalgay.pt for listings, events and other information.

Note that while there are no exclusively women's bars or clubs, all the places listed here are at least somewhat mixed.

■ **Boys 'R' Us** (Map p387; ☎ 917549988; Rua Dr Barbosa de Castro 63; ☉ 11pm-4am Wed & Fri-Sun) This long-standing favourite has pumping pop and electronica and raucous drag shows downstairs. Upstairs is a quieter lounge. It's usually best from 1am to 3am.

■ **Moinho de Vento** (Map p387; ☎ 222 056 883; Rua Sá Noronha 78; ☉ 11pm-4am Wed-Sun) This small but spiffy bar-disco has a dark room, drag and go-go boys. It usually picks up after 1am.

■ **Pride Bar** (Map p385; ☎ 964936791; Rua do Bonjardim 1121; www.pride-bar.net; ☉ midnight-late Fri-Sun) Porto's newest hot spot has live music, drag shows and go-go boys. It's open very late.

■ **Triplex** (opposite) This popular nightspot near Casa da Música draws a mixed gay/straight crowd.

■ **Lusitano** (Map p387; ☎ 222 011 067; Rua José Falcão 137; ☉ noon-1.30am Mon-Thu, noon-3.30am Fri & Sat) In a handsomely designed throwback to the 1950s, this intimate space hosts a good mixed gay/straight crowd.

4pm-midnight Thu-Sat, 6-9pm Sun) This cosy wine bar is an excellent place to sample the fine quaffs of Porto, with over 200 different ports on offer. If you fall in love with a certain wine, you can usually buy a whole bottle (or even send a case home).

ALIADOS

Nightlife has returned to central Porto, with some eclectic bar/gallery spaces leading the way. It's worth exploring the narrow cobblestone streets just north of Rua das Carmelitas. Nearby, there is also a lively (downmarket) scene at open-air cafe-restaurants around the corner from the Jardim da Cordoaria.

our pick **Plano B** (Map p387; ☎ 222 012 500; www .planobporto.com; Rua Cândido dos Reis 30; ☉ 2.30-8pm & 10pm-2am Tue & Wed, 2.30pm-2am Thu-Sat, closed Aug) This creative space has an art gallery in front, a tall-ceilinged cafe (with free wireless access) in back, and a cosy downstairs where DJs and live bands hold court. Much like the crowd, the programming is truly eclectic, with performance art, theatre and art openings held regularly.

Galeria de Paris (Map p387; ☎ 934210792; Rua Galeria de Paris 56; ☉ 6pm-3am Mon-Sat) New in 2008, the Galeria de Paris is a whimsically decorated spot, with toys, thermoses, old phones and other assorted memorabilia lining the walls. In addition to cocktails and draft beer, you'll find an expensive lunch buffet during the day and tapas at night.

Casa do Livro (Map p387; Rua Galeria de Paris 85; ☉ 11.30am-2am Mon-Sat) Vintage wallpaper, gilded mirrors and walls of books give a discreet charm to this nicely lit beer and wine bar. On weekends, DJs spin funk, soul, jazz and retro sounds in the back room.

Café au Lait (Map p387; ☎ 222 025 016; Rua Galeria de Paris 44; ☉ 11.30am-2am Mon-Sat) A narrow, intimate bar attracting a lively but unpretentious crowd. In addition to cocktails, there are snacks and salads, including vegetarian fare. DJs spin on Wednesday through Saturday nights, adding to the good cheer.

Âncora d'Ouro (Map p387; ☎ 222 003 749; Praça Parada Leitão 45; ☉ noon-2am Mon-Sat) Also known as O Piolho (The Louse), this unkempt place has been a regular student hang-out since the 19th century. The food and service are poor, but the prices are low and the vibe is festive/rowdy depending on the proximity to Saturday night. Outdoor seating.

Black Coffee (Map p387; ☎ 222 010 689; Av dos Aliados; ☉ 8pm-2am Mon-Sat) Film stills blanket the walls of this polished new place across from the *câmara municipal*. A youthful but mixed crowd gathers over cocktails and electronic music early in the evening before moving on to the dance clubs.

Uptown (Map p387; ☎ 225 021 360; Rua do Breiner 59; ☉ 10am-2am Tue-Sat) Uptown hosts a broad assortment of live music, with bands playing funk, jazz, indie rock and even a bit of esoterica (like medieval sounds). DJs pick up the slack (Afro-beat, classic disco) between sets.

Maus Habitos (Map p387; ☎ 222 087 268; 4th fl, Rua Passos Manuel 178; ☣ 10pm-2am Wed, Thu & Sun, 10pm-4am Fri & Sat; **V**) This creatively decorated multiroom space hosts a culturally ambitious agenda. Changing art exhibits and imaginative installations adorn the walls, while live bands and DJs work the back stage. Hidden within, there's also a design shop and an inexpensive vegetarian restaurant (open for lunch only Monday through Friday).

BOAVISTA & WEST PORTO

Triplex (Map p385; ☎ 226 098 968; www.triplex.com.pt; Av Boavista 911; ☣ 10pm-4am Thu-Sat) In a pink, three-storey mansion, the vaguely upmarket Triplex has a regular line-up of '80s, electronica and '60s sounds (plus karaoke on Thursday). A fairly mixed crowd gathers on the pleasant tree-shaded adjoining patio.

Indústria (off Map p385; ☎ 226 176 806; Av do Brasil 843; ☣ 11.30pm-4am Thu-Sat) Done up with silver-and-velvet wallpaper and beanbag chairs, this retro basement club serves up funk, house and, above all, electronica to a crowd that generally skews very young. Take the bus and get off at the Molhe stop.

RIVERFRONT TO FOZ DO DOURO
All of the places listed here can be reached via the night-time bus 1M from Aliados.

Bazaar (Map p385; ☎ 226 062 113; Rua de Monchique 13; ☣ from 4pm) One of the hottest clubs in Porto, Bazaar spins high-quality house to hundreds of pretty 20- and 30-somethings in their shiny best. The club spreads across three minimalist, whitewashed levels.

Era uma Vez no Porto (off Map p385; ☎ 226 164 793; www.eraumaveznoporto.com; Rua do Passeio Alegre 550; ☣ 6-9pm & 10pm-2am Mon-Fri, 4-8pm & 10pm-2am Sat & Sun) Part tearoom, part nightclub, part experimental art gallery and part vintage-clothing shop, this place in an airy riverfront town house feels as if you've entered a private party with a cash bar.

31 (off Map p385; ☎ 226 107 567; www.trintaeum .com; Rua do Passeio Alegre 564; ☣ 10pm-4am Thu-Sat) Beguilingly simple place with a large bar, comfortable seating, louche, '70s-inspired decor, a dance floor and some of the best DJs from Portugal.

Solar do Vinho do Porto (Map p385; ☎ 226 097 749; Rua Entre Quintas 220; ☣ 4pm-midnight Mon-Sat) In a 19th-century house near the Palácio de Cristal, this upmarket *solar* (manor house) has a manicured garden offering picturesque views of the Douro. There are hundreds of ports available as well as refreshing aperitifs, such as *portônico* (white port and tonic water).

VILA NOVA DE GAIA
Just across the river from the gritty Ribeira waterfront, Gaia's esplanade is trendier (though also more mainstream). A string of identical-looking chrome-and-glass bars and nightclubs are surrounded by open-air decks and designer fountains.

Hard Club (Map p385; ☎ 227 375 819; www.hard-club .com; Cais de Gaia 1158) Set above the waterfront in an old tannery, this industrial-inspired club hosts the cream of visiting international and home-grown DJs, plus it boasts a cool rooftop terrace.

ENTERTAINMENT
Cinemas
There are no cinemas in the centre, but you can head by metro to the multiscreen **Cinema Centro Comercial Cidade do Porto** (Map p385; ☎ 226 009 164; Rua Gonçalo Sampaio 350, Boavista).

Fado
Porto has no fado tradition of its own, but you can enjoy the Lisbon or Coimbra version of 'Portugal blues' into the wee hours at atmospheric haunts **Restaurante O Fado** (Map p387; ☎ 222 026 937; Largo de São João Novo 16; ☣ 8.30pm-3.30am Mon-Sat) and **Restaurante Mal Cozinhado** (Map p389; ☎ 222 081 319; Rua Outeirinho 11, Ribeira; ☣ 8.30pm-1am Mon-Sat). The food isn't the main attraction – and in any case is overpriced – but there's a minimum charge, equivalent to a light meal or several drinks. The more low-key **Restaurante Fado Menor** (Map p389; ☎ 222 010 991; Largo dos Grilos, Ribeira; ☣ noon-10pm Mon-Sat), overlooking a hidden plaza in the Ribeira, hosts fado several nights a week.

Music & Theatre
The Casa da Música (p392) has quickly become the city's premier music venue, with a line-up of classical, jazz, fado and world music.

Hot Five Jazz & Blues Club (Map p387; ☎ 919015374; www.hotfive.eu, in Portuguese; Largo Actor Dias 51;

THE DOURO

⊙ 10pm-3am Wed-Sun) True to its name, this new spot hosts live jazz and blues as well as the occasional acoustic, folk or all-out jam session. It's a modern but intimate space, with seating at small round tables, both fronting the stage and on an upper balcony.

Other venues:

Teatro Nacional São João (Map p387; ☎ 223 401 900; www.tnsj.pt, in Portuguese; Praça da Batalha) Porto's other premier performing-arts venue, hosting international dance, theatre and music groups.

Coliseu do Porto (Map p387; ☎ 223 324 940; www.coliseudoporto.pt; Rua Passos Manuel 137) Hosts major names in arena-style performances.

Teatro de Belmonte (Map p389; ☎ 222 083 341; www.marionetasdoporto.pt, in Portuguese; Rua Belmonte 57) Specialises in puppet shows.

Sport

The flashy, fairly new, 52,000-seat Estádio do Dragão (off Map p385) is home to heroes of the moment **FC Porto** (☎ 808 201 167; www.fcporto.pt). It's northeast of the centre, just off the VCI ring road (metro stop Estádio de Dragão).

FC Porto's worthy cross-town rivals are the under-funded **Boavista FC** (☎ 226 071 000; www.boavistafc.pt). Their home turf is the newly spruced-up Estádio do Bessa, which lies west of the entre just off Avenida da Boavista (take bus 3 from Praça da Liberdade).

Check the local editions of *Público* or *Jornal de Notícias* newspapers for upcoming matches.

SHOPPING

Porto boasts a diverse shopping scene, from quirky delicatessens to endless *sapatarias* (shoe shops). In addition, there are entire streets specialising in particular items (try Rua Galeria de Paris for fine art or Rua da Fábrica for bookshops). Rua Santa Catarina near Praça da Batalha is another bustling, all-purpose shopping street.

Amid the galleries along Rua Miguel Bombarda, the small, unique **CC Bombarda** (Map p385; Rua Miguel Bombarda) is well worth a peek. Inside this shopping gallery, you'll find stores selling locally designed urban wear, bonsai trees, stylish home knick-knacks, Portuguese indie rock and other hipster-pleasing delights. There's a shop (Frida) where you can order a doll made to your own likeness and a cafe (Pimenta Rosa) serving light fare on an inner courtyard.

A little more mainstream are the following shopping centres: **Centro Comercial Via Catarina** (Map p387; Rua Santa Catarina) and **Centro Comercial Cidade do Porto** (Map p385; Rua Gonçalo Sampaio) in Boavista.

Port & Other Wines

Gourmet da Bolsa (Map p389; ☎ 919088968; Largo de São Domingos 26). This small, atmospheric, friendly shop is a good place for wine and provisions, selling a well-curated selection of port as well as olives, spreads, truffles and other gourmet picnic items. The shop hosts occasional tastings; English is spoken.

It's great fun buying direct from the warehouses in Vila Nova de Gaia, but you can also try **Garrafeira do Carmo** (Map p387; ☎ 222 003 285; Rua do Carmo 17), specialising in vintage port and high-quality wines at reasonable prices. Other good sources are **Casa Januário** (Map p387; Rua do Bonjardim 352) and the photogenic **Casa Oriental** (Map p387; Campo dos Mártires da Pátria 111).

Handicrafts

Arte Facto (Map p389; Rua da Reboleira 37, Ribeira; ⊙ 10am-noon & 1-6pm Mon-Fri) Arte Facto sells high-quality handmade crafts, from textiles and toys to puppets and pottery, in CRAT's on-site boutique (p395).

Artesanato dos Clérigos (Map p387; ☎ 222 000 257; Rua Assunção 33) A modest but atmospheric shop, this old-school place is stacked high with pottery, tiles, embroidery, copper and pewter.

Porto Signs (Map p389; ☎ 220 160 359; Rua Alfândega 17; ⊙ 10am-8pm Mon-Sat, 2-7pm Sun) A nice twist on the traditional tourist shop, Porto Signs has unique, locally designed graphic T-shirts, as well as Portuguese wine, tea, photography books, cork products and that ever-present Barcelos rooster.

GETTING THERE & AWAY
Air

The gleaming new **Francisco Sá Carneiro airport** (☎ 229 432 400; www.ana.pt), ominously named after a beloved politician who was killed in a plane crash, is 19km northwest of the city centre. Portugália and TAP have multiple daily flights to/from Lisbon. There are also services by low-cost carriers such as Ryanair and Air Berlin. On most days there is nonstop service to London, Madrid, Paris, Frankfurt, Amsterdam, Brussels and Newark; see p504 for more details. Note that there is no left-luggage facility at the airport.

Bus

As in many Portuguese cities, bus service in Porto is regrettably dispersed. The good news is that there is frequent service to just about everywhere in northern Portugal, as well as express service to Coimbra, Lisbon and points south.

DOMESTIC

Renex (Map p387; ☎ 222 003 395; www.renex.pt; Campo dos Mártires da Pátria 37) is the choice for Lisbon (€16.50, 3½ hours), with the most direct routes and eight to 12 departures daily, including one continuing to the Algarve. Renex also has frequent services to Braga (€4.50, 1¼ hours).

Rede Expressos (Map p387; ☎ 222 052 459; www.rede-expressos.pt, in Portuguese) has services to the entire country from the smoggy **Paragem Atlântico terminal** (Map p387; Rua Alexandre Herculano 370).

For fast Minho connections, mainly on weekdays, three lines run from around Praceta Régulo Magauanha, off Rua Dr Alfredo Magalhães (Map p385). **Transdev-Norte** (☎ 222 006 954) runs chiefly to Braga (€4.30, one hour). **AV Minho** (☎ 222 006 121) goes mainly via Vila do Conde (€2.80, 55 minutes) to Viana do Castelo (€6.50, 2¼ hours). And **Arriva** (☎ 222 051 383) serves Guimarães (€4.50, 50 minutes).

Rodonorte (Map p387; ☎ 222 005 637; www.rodonorte .pt; Rua Ateneu Comercial do Porto 19) has multiple daily departures (fewer on Saturday) for Amarante (€6, one hour), Vila Real (€7.30, 1½ hours) and Bragança (€11.40, 3½ hours).

Santos (Map p385; ☎ 279 652 188; www.santosvia gensturismo.pt; Centro Comercial Central Shopping, Campo 24 Agosto) has frequent buses to Vila Real (€7.30, 1½ hours) and Bragança (€11.40, 3½ hours).

INTERNATIONAL

There are **Eurolines** (Map p385; ☎ 225 189 303; www.euro linesportugal.com; Centro Comercial Central Shopping, Campo 24 Agosto 215) services to/from cities all over Europe. Northern Portugal's own international carrier is **Internorte** (Map p385; ☎ 226 052 420; www.internorte.pt, in Portuguese; Praça da Galiza 96). Take bus 302 or 501 from Aliados. Most travel agencies (p388) can book outbound buses with either operator.

Car & Motorcycle

All major European and international rental-car companies have offices at the airport as well as in the centre. A handful of rental agen-

cies lie scattered along Rua Santa Catarina north of the pedestrian-only zone, including **TCL** (Map p385; ☎ 222 076 840; tcl.rentacar@netc.pt; Rua Santa Catarina 922; per day from €35) and **Europcar** (Map p385; ☎ 808 204 050, 222 057 737; www.europcar.com; Rua Santa Catarina 1158; per day from €60).

Other agencies offering good deals are **Budget** (☎ 808 252 627; www.budgetportugal.com), **Auto Jardim** (☎ 226 053 197; www.autocarhire.net; per day from €30) and **Sixt** (☎ 229 439 240; www.sixt.com).

Train

Porto is the principal rail hub for northern Portugal. Long-distance services start at Campanhã station, which is 2km east of the centre. Most *urbano*, regional and *interregional* (IR) trains depart from São Bento station, though all these lines also pass through Campanhã.

For destinations on the Braga, Guimarães and Aveiro lines, or up the Douro valley as far as Marco de Canaveses, take one of the frequent *urbano* trains. Don't spend extra money on *interregional*, *intercidade* (IC) or Alfa Pendular (AP) trains to these destinations (eg Porto to Braga costs €2.15 by *urbano*, but €12.50 by AP train).

Direct IC destinations from Porto include Coimbra (2nd class from €10.50, 1¼ hours, hourly) and Lisbon (2nd class €19.50, three hours, hourly).

There are information points at both **São Bento** (☉ 8.30am-8pm) and **Campanhã** (☉ 9am-7pm) stations. Alternatively, call toll-free ☎ 808 208 208 or consult www.cp.pt.

GETTING AROUND
To/From the Airport

The metro's 'violet' line provides a handy service to the airport. A one-way ride from the centre costs €1.45 and takes about 45 minutes.

A daytime taxi costs €20 to €25 to/from the centre. Taxis authorised to run *from* the airport are labelled 'Maia' and/or 'Vila Nova de Telha'; the rank is just outside the arrivals hall. In peak traffic time, allow an hour or more between the city centre and the airport.

Car & Motorcycle

Avoid driving in central Porto if possible. Narrow, one-way streets, construction and heavy traffic can turn 500m into half a morning. Street parking is tight, with a two-hour

THE DOURO

maximum stay on weekdays. There is no limit on weekends and parking spaces are more readily available. Most squares have underground, fee-charging lots – follow the blue Ps. Beware that men may guide you into places and then expect tips. They can be very disagreeable if you don't comply. They also may direct you into an illegal spot – be sure to double-check signs. The Loja de Mobilidade (p388) provides a map devoted exclusively to parking.

Public Transport

BUS

Porto's transport agency **STCP** (Sociedade de Transportes Colectivos do Porto; Map p387; ☎ information 808 200 166; www.stcp.pt, in Portuguese) runs an extensive bus system, with central hubs at Praça da Liberdade (the south end of Avenida dos Aliados), Praça Almeida Garrett (in front of São Bento train station) and Cordoaria. Special all-night lines also run approximately hourly, leaving Aliados on the hour and returning on the half-hour from 1am to 5.30am. City *turismos* have maps and timetables for day and night routes.

A ticket bought on the bus (one way to anywhere in the STCP system) costs €1.45. But you get steep discounts if you buy multiple tickets in advance from the STCP office or many newsagents and *tabacarias* (tobacconists). For two/10 trips within Porto city limits you pay €1.75/7.40; those to outlying areas cost €2.20/9.20, and longer trips (including to or from the airport) cost €2.55/11.30. Tickets

are sold singly or in discounted *cadernetas* (booklets) of 10. Many key lines accept the Andante Card (see boxed text, below).

Also available is the *bilhete diário* (day pass), valid for unlimited trips within the city on buses and the tram. For 24/72 hours, it costs €5/11.

FUNICULAR

The restored **Funicular dos Guindais** (one way €0.90; ⊙ 8am-10pm Sun-Wed, 8am-midnight Thu-Sat Jun-Sep, 8am-8pm Sun-Wed, 8am-midnight Thu-Sat Oct-May) shuttles up and down a steep incline from Avenida Gustavo Eiffel opposite Ponte de Dom Luís I, to Rua Augusto Rosa, near Batalha and the cathedral. The funicular is part of the Andante Card scheme (see boxed text, below).

METRO

Porto's fairly new metro system provides speedy service around town. The central hub is Trindade station, a few blocks north of the Aliados corridor. Three lines – Linha A (blue, to Matosinhos), Linha B (red, to Vila do Conde and Póvoa de Varzim) and Linha C (green, to Maia) – run from Estádio do Dragão via Campanhã train station through the city centre, and then on to far-flung northern and western suburbs. Linha D (yellow) runs north to south from Hospital São João to João de Deus in Vila Nova de Gaia, crossing the upper deck of Ponte de Dom Luís I. Key stops include Aliados and São Bento station. Linha E (violet) connects via Linha B with the airport.

ANDANTE CARD

For maximum convenience, Porto's transport system offers the rechargeable **Andante Card** (☎ 808 200 444; www.linhandante.com, in Portuguese), allowing smooth movement between tram, metro, funicular and many bus lines.

The card itself costs only €0.50 and can be recharged indefinitely. Once you've purchased the card, you must charge it with travel credit according to which zones you will be travelling in. It's not as complicated as it sounds. A Z2 trip covers the whole city centre east to Campanhã train station, south to Vila Nova de Gaia and west to Foz do Douro. And each 'trip' allows you a whole hour to move between different participating methods of transport without additional cost. Your time begins from when you first enter the vehicle or platform: just wave the card in front of a validation machine marked 'Andante'.

You can purchase credit at metro ticket machines and staffed TIP booths at central hubs such as Casa da Música and Trindade, as well as the STCP office, the funicular, the electric tram museum and a scattering of other authorised sales points.

One/11 'trips' in Z2 (including central Porto, Boavista and Foz do Douro) cost €0.95/9.50. Alternatively, you can choose to roam freely for 24 hours for €3.35. If you want to go further out than two zones, pick up a map and explanation of zones at any metro station.

Metro trains run from approximately 6am to 1am daily. For information on prices and tickets, see the boxed text, opposite.

TRAM

Porto's trams used to be one of its delights. Only three lines remain, but they're very scenic. The Massarelos stop, on the riverfront near the foot of the Palácio de Cristal, is the tram system's hub. From here, line 1 trundles along the river to near Praça Infante Dom Henrique (Ribeira). Line 1E (appears as a crossed-out '1') heads down the river in the opposite direction, towards Foz do Douro. And line 18 heads uphill to the Igreja do Carmo and Jardim do Cordoaria. Trams run approximately every 30 minutes from 9am to 7pm. For fare information see the boxed text, opposite.

Taxi

There are taxi ranks throughout the centre, or you can call a **radio taxi** (☎ 225 076 400, 225 029 898). Count on paying around €5 to €7 for trips within the centre during the day, with a 20% surcharge at night. There's an extra charge if you leave the city limits, which includes Vila Nova de Gaia.

AROUND PORTO

VILA DO CONDE
pop 26,000

Though a popular weekend getaway for Porto residents, the town of Vila do Conde – a prime shipbuilding port during the Age of Discoveries – retains much of its salty-dog, historical character. Looming over the town is the immense hilltop Mosteiro de Santa Clara, which, along with surviving segments of a long-legged aqueduct, lends the town an air of unexpected monumentality. At the same time, Vila do Conde's beaches are some of the best north of Porto, and a new metro link makes getting to the beaches an easy afternoon jaunt from downtown Porto. The town is also renowned for its ancient tradition of lace-making.

Orientation & Information

Vila do Conde sits on the north side of the Rio Ave, where it empties into the sea.

From the metro station, look for the aqueduct (about 100m) and follow it towards the large convent (another 400m). From here it's a few steep blocks downhill to the town's historic centre. From the centre it's another 1.25km via Avenida Dr Artur Cunha Araúja or Avenida Dr João Canavarro to Avenida do Brasil and the 3km-long beach.

Vila do Conde has two **turismos** (☎ 252 248 473; fax 252 248 422; Rua 25 de Abril 103 & Rua 5 de Outubro 207; ⊙ 9am-6pm Mon-Fri, 9.30am-1pm & 2.30-6pm Sat & Sun), just 150m apart. Free audio-guide tours in various languages are available here, which cover the major churches and museums of Vila do Conde (one guide per sight). The *turismo* opposite the bus stop shares a space with a small handicrafts gallery.

Sights & Activities

MOSTEIRO DE SANTA CLARA

Peering down over the town centre and the Rio Ave, the imposing Mosteiro de Santa Clara, founded in 1318, still has a severe-looking Gothic chapel, though the main building is a grand, 18th-century affair. Currently the entire complex remains closed to visitors. If you're lucky, you may find a side door of the church open.

Outside the convent are the poetic remains of a towering **aqueduct** that once brought water to the convent's 100 resident nuns from Terroso, 7km away.

TOWN CENTRE

At the heart of the old town is the Manueline **igreja matriz** (parish church; Rua 25 de Abril; ⊙ 9am-noon & 2-6pm Tue-Sun), which dates mostly from the early 16th century and has an ornate doorway carved by Basque artist João de Castilho. Outside is a *pelourinho* (stone pillory) topped by the sword-wielding arm of Justice. Inside is the **Museu de Arte Sacra** (☎ 252 631 424; admission free; ⊙ 10am-noon & 2-4pm Jun-Sep, 2-4pm Oct-May), with its modest collection of ecclesiastical art.

Yet more religious art, as well as antique furnishings, ceramics and popular art, can be glimpsed at the **Casa de José Régio** (☎ 252 248 400; admission free; ⊙ 10am-noon & 2-6pm Tue-Sat, 2-5pm Sun), named after the distinguished local-born poet and playwright José Régio (1901–69).

It's no accident that seafaring fingers, so deft at making nets, should also be good at lace-making. Vila do Conde is one of the few places in Portugal with an active school of the art, founded in 1918. Housed in a typical 18th-century town house in the town centre, the school includes the **Museu**

das Rendas de Bilros (Museum of Bobbin Lace; ☎ 252 248 470; Rua São Bento 70; admission free; ⏰ 9am-noon & 2-7pm Mon-Fri, 2-5pm Sat & Sun), with eye-popping examples of work from Portugal and around the world.

RIVERFRONT

On the banks of the Rio Ave, just west of Praça da República, stands the **Museu da Construção Naval** (Museum of Shipbuilding; ☎ 252 240 740; Largo da Alfândega; adult/child €1/0.50; ⏰ 9am-6pm Tue-Sun). Shipbuilding has been in Vila do Conde's bones since at least the 13th century; many of the stoutest ships of the Age of Discoveries were made here. The museum, occupying the former customs house, is mildly interesting, with exhibits on trade, and models of hand-built *nau* (a sort of pot-bellied caravel once used for cargo and naval operations). The real attraction, however, is the replica of a 16th-century *nau* moored opposite the museum. Visitors can wander across the various decks of the ship, peeking in rooms that give a faint taste of ship life of the 1500s.

Nearby is the tiny but striking 17th-century **Capela da Nossa Senhora de Socorro** (Largo da Alfândega; ⏰ irregular hours), with its crisp, mosquelike dome. The interior is covered in *azulejos* that date back to the church's founding.

BEACHES

The two best beaches, Praia da Forno and Praia de Nossa Senhora da Guia, have calm seas suitable for young children, while surfers often ride the swells near the *castelo* (see below). Buses marked 'Vila do Conde' from Póvoa de Varzim stop at the station and continue to the beach, about half-hourly all day.

At the river mouth is the 17th-century **Castelo de São João Baptista**, once a castle but now a small deluxe hotel (right).

Festivals & Events

Festa de São João The town's biggest event takes place on the days leading up to 23 June, with fireworks, concerts, a traditional boat parade and a religious procession through the streets.

Feira Nacional de Artesanato (http://fna.vconde.org, in Portuguese) A major fair of Portuguese handicrafts during the last week of July and the first week of August.

Sleeping

Parque de Campismo da Árvore (☎ 252 633 225; cnmporto@mail.telepac.pt; Rua do Cabreiro, Árvore; sites per adult/tent €5.50/5; 🏊) Tightly packed and well shaded, this camp site is 3km from town, right next to Praia da Árvore.

Restaurante Le Villageois (☎ 252 631 119; aliceclisson@netcabo.pt; Praça da República 94; d €35) Top pick among the budget choices, Le Villageois offers several pleasant but sparsely furnished rooms above a lively Franco-Portuguese restaurant. Some rooms lack windows. Book well ahead in summer.

Pensão Patarata (☎ 252 631 894; Cais das Lavandeiras 18; d/tw €35/40) Looking over the river, off the southwest corner of the square, this place has flowery en suite rooms, a few that are quite large with river views, and others that are rather dark and poky.

Residencial O Manco d'Areia (☎ /fax 252 631 748; Praça da República 84; d with/without view €45/40) Up an *azulejo*-clad staircase, this renovated old town house has clean, quiet, simply furnished rooms with wood floors.

Residencial Bento de Freitas (☎ 252 633 557; fax 252 633 077; Av Bento de Freitas 398; s/d €50/65; 🖳) In a refurbished, 19th-century, neo-Gothic town house, this spruce place offers spare but comfortable and spotless rooms done up in period style. There's also a pleasant dining room with exposed stonework and a trim garden.

Estalagem do Brasão (☎ 252 642 016; estalagembrazao@netcabo.pt; Av Dr João Canavarro; s/d/ste €57/81/98; Ⓟ 🖳) Set in a restored 16th-century nobleman's house, this guest house has been added onto at various times over the years, making it a patchwork of old and new. Rooms are comfortable but somewhat gloomy, with sea-green carpeting and marble-filled bathrooms. It is situated 200m west of the Rua 25 de Abril *turismo*.

Santana Hotel (☎ 252 640 460; www.santanahotel.net; Monte Santana, Azurara; s/d €83/109; Ⓟ 🖳 🏊) On a hillside across the river, this spry modern hotel has comfortable rooms boasting excellent views over town. The amenities are the best part of Santana, with a small gym, Jacuzzi, indoor pool, decent restaurant and spa. It's 1km from the centre; take Avenida José Régio across the bridge and turn left up Calçada de Sant'Ana.

Hotel Forte São João Baptista (☎ 252 240 600; www.hotelfortesjoao.com; Av Brasil; d from €160; Ⓟ 🖳 🖳) Hidden within the forbidding, metres-thick stone walls of a 17th-century fort is this small oasis of luxury. The hotel's rooms are cosy but plush, and sitting just across the small, pentagonal courtyard is the city's finest restaurant.

Eating & Drinking

Around the corner from the *turismo*, Praça José Régio has an assortment of outdoor cafes and restaurants. There are even more options by the waterfront (near Praça da República).

O Pesqueiro (☎ 933030038; Praça José Régio 113; mains €8-10; ☺ lunch & dinner Mon-Sat) On a cafe-filled plaza, O Pesqueiro is a local favourite for its fresh fish and seafood, with all-you-can-eat deals *(rodizio)* on most days.

Ramon (☎ 252 631 334; Rua 5 de Outubro 176; mains €9-10; ☺ lunch & dinner Wed-Mon) Near the *turismo*, Ramon serves decent fresh fish and even more-notable shellfish dishes, along with *cabrito no forno* (roast kid). Outside seating available.

Restaurante Le Villageois (☎ 252 631 119; Praça da República 94; mains for 2 €9-18; ☺ lunch & dinner Tue-Sun) The popular Villageois offers a huge menu of well-prepared French and Portuguese dishes, a full bar, an airy dining room appointed with *azulejos*, and an appealing sun-drenched patio.

Caximar (☎ 252 642 492; Av Brasil; mains €12-16; ☺ lunch & dinner Tue-Sun) Serving some of the best seafood in town, Caximar is a modern, unfussy place with tables overlooking the crashing waves. It sits right on the beach, roughly 1km west of Forte São João Baptista.

Seca Bar (☎ 919697501; Av Marquês Sá da Bandeira; cocktails €2-4; ☺ noon-2am Mon-Sat) A popular meeting place for Conde's young revellers, this sleek and modern drinking spot hosts periodic concerts and parties on summer weekends. The attractive esplanade is a fine open-air retreat on warm nights. It's located around the corner from the Forte São João Baptista. Nearby are a few cafes and drink stands on the beach itself.

Shopping

Centro de Artesanato (☎ 252 248 473; Rua 5 de Outubro 207; ☺ 10am-7pm Mon-Fri, 10am-noon & 1.30-5.30pm Sat) Sharing space with the *turismo* opposite the bus stop, this place has a small selection of pottery, wooden toys, basketry, embroidered linen and, of course, lace. Local lace-makers sometimes work here, too.

Getting There & Away

Vila do Conde is 33km from Porto, and it's a straight shot on the IC1 highway. It's now served by Porto's Linha B (red) metro line to Póvoa de Varzim, stopping about 400m from the town centre. A one-way trip from central Porto costs €1.40 and takes about one hour – the trip is a little faster if you catch the express service.

Buses stop near the *turismo* on Rua 5 de Outubro. AV Minho express buses stop about hourly (fewer on weekends) en route to Porto (€2.80, 50 minutes) and Viana do Castelo (€3.80, one hour). **Linhares** (☎ 252 298 300) also has regular services.

EASTERN DOURO

AMARANTE

pop 11,400 / elev 150m

Handsomely set on a bend in the Rio Tâmega, the sleepy village of Amarante is dominated by a striking church and monastery, which sit theatrically beside a rebuilt medieval bridge that still bears city traffic. The willow-lined riverbanks lend a pastoral charm, as do the balconied houses and switchback lanes that rise quickly from the narrow valley floor.

The town enjoys some small degree of fame for being the hometown of São Gonçalo. Portugal's Saint Valentine, he is the object of veneration among lonely hearts who make pilgrimages here in hope of finding true love.

Surrounded by prized vineyards, Amarante is a something of a foodie mecca. As well as wine, the region produces excellent cheeses, smoked meats *(fumeiros)* and richly eggy pastries.

The most appealing way to get here is on the narrow-gauge Linha da Tâmega railway (see p413 for details).

History

The town may date back as far as the 4th century BC, though Gonçalo, a 13th-century hermit, is credited with everything from the founding of the town to the construction of its first bridge.

Amarante's strategically placed bridge (Ponte de São Gonçalo) almost proved to be its undoing in 1809, when the French lost their brief grip on Portugal. Marshal Soult's troops retreated to the northeast after abandoning Porto, plundering as they went. A French detachment arrived here in search of a river crossing, but plucky citizens and troops

THE DOURO

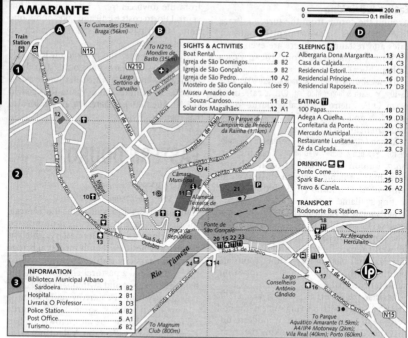

AMARANTE

SIGHTS & ACTIVITIES
Boat Rental.................................7 C2
Igreja de São Domingos........8 B2
Igreja de São Gonçalo..........9 B2
Igreja de São Pedro..............10 A2
Mosteiro de São Gonçalo....(see 9)
Museu Amadeo de
Souza-Cardoso..................11 B2
Solar dos Magalhães............12 A1

SLEEPING
Albergaria Dona Margaritta......13 A3
Casa da Calçada..................14 C3
Residencial Estoril................15 C3
Residencial Príncipe............16 D3
Residencial Raposeira..........17 D3

EATING
100 Papas............................18 D2
Adega A Quelha...................19 D3
Confeitaria da Ponte............20 C3
Mercado Municipal...............21 C2
Restaurante Lusitana............22 C3
Zé da Calçada......................23 C3

DRINKING
Ponte Come.........................24 B3
Spark Bar.............................25 D3
Travo & Canela....................26 A2

TRANSPORT
Rodonorte Bus Station..........27 C3

INFORMATION
Biblioteca Municipal Albano
Sardoeira...........................1 B2
Hospital.................................2 B1
Livraria O Professor...............3 D3
Police Station.........................4 B2
Post Office.............................5 A1
Turismo..................................6 B2

---

held them off, allowing residents to escape to the far bank. The French retaliated by burning down much of the town.

Amarante has also suffered frequent natural invasions by the Tâmega. Little *cheia* (high-water level) plaques in Rua 31 de Janeiro and Largo Conselheiro António Cândido tell the harrowing story.

Orientation

The Tâmega flows through the middle of town, spanned by the Ponte de São Gonçalo. On the northwest bank is Amarante's showpiece, the Igreja de São Gonçalo. The church's cloisters, opposite the market, house the *turismo*.

The little train station is about 800m southeast (and uphill) from the bridge. Nearly all coaches stop in Largo Conselheiro António Cândido, just across the river.

There is free parking just east of the *turismo* where the *mercado municipal* (municipal market) is held; avoid parking there overnight before crowded market days (Wednesday and Saturday).

Information

Banks with ATMs are along Rua 5 de Outubro and Rua António Carneiro.

Biblioteca Municipal Albano Sardoeira (☎ 255 420 236; Rua Capitão Augusto Casimiro; ☑ 10am-12.30pm & 2-6.30pm Mon-Sat) In the newly refashioned Casa da Cerca; provides free internet access.

Hospital (☎ 255 410 500; Largo Sertório de Carvalho) North of the centre.

Livraria O Professor (☎ 255 432 441; Rua António Carneiro; ☑ 9am-12.30pm & 2.30-7pm Mon-Fri, 9am-1pm & 3-7pm Sat) Stocks foreign-language newspapers.

Police station (☎ 255 432 015; Rua Capitão Augusto Casimiro)

Post office (Rua João Pinto Ribeiro; ☑ 8.30am-6pm Mon-Fri)

Turismo (☎ 255 420 246; Alameda Teixeira de Pascoaes; ☑ 9am-7pm Jul–mid-Sep, 9am-12.30pm & 2-5.30pm mid-Sep-Jun) In the former cloisters of São Gonçalo.

Sights & Activities
PONTE DE SÃO GONÇALO

Symbol of the town's heroic defence against the French (marked by a plaque at the south-eastern end), the granite Ponte de São Gonçalo is Amarante's visual centrepiece. It also offers one of the best views of town. The original bridge, allegedly built at Gonçalo's urging in the 13th century, collapsed in a flood in 1763; this one was completed in 1790.

MOSTEIRO DE SÃO GONÇALO & IGREJA DE SÃO GONÇALO

Founded in 1540 by João III, the **Mosteiro de São Gonçalo** (Monastery of São Gonçalo; ☎ 255 437 425; admission free; 🕑 8am-6pm) and its arresting church, the Igreja de São Gonçalo, were only finished in 1620. Above the church's photogenic, multitiered, Italian Renaissance side portal is an arcaded gallery, 30m up, with 17th-century statues of Dom João and the other kings who ruled while the monastery was under construction: Sebastião, Henrique and Felipe I. The bell tower was added in the 18th century. The best view of the royals is from the steep lane just west of the church entrance.

Within the lofty interior are an impressive gilded baroque altar and pulpits, an organ casing held up by fish-tailed giants, and Gonçalo's tomb in a tiny chapel (left of the altar). Tradition has it that those in search of a mate will have their wish granted within a year if they touch the statue above his tomb. Sure enough, its limestone toes, fingers and face have been all but rubbed away by hopefuls.

Through the north portal are a couple of peaceful Renaissance cloisters – one now occupied by the town hall. The sacristy is also worth a peek for its intricately painted ceiling and wall paintings hung in gilded cherub-filled frames.

MUSEU AMADEO DE SOUZA-CARDOSO

Hidden in one of the monastery's cloisters is the **Museu Amadeo de Souza-Cardoso** (☎ 255 420 233; Alameda Teixeira de Pascoaes; adult/under 15yr/student under 26yr/senior €1/free/0.50/0.50; 🕑 10am-12.30pm & 2-5.30pm Tue-Sun). Its delightfully eclectic collection of modernist and contemporary art is a pleasant surprise in a town this size. The museum is named after Amarante's favourite son, artist Amadeo Souza-Cardoso (1889–1918) – one of the best-known Portuguese artists of the 20th century. He abandoned naturalism for home-grown versions of Impressionism and cubism. This museum is full of his sketches, cartoons, portraits and abstracts. Notable works by other local artists include Acácio Lino's enormous *O Grande Desvairo,* depicting the burial of Dom Pedro I, and Carneiro's evocative 1901 painting of Ponte de São Gonçalo.

OTHER CHURCHES

Rising beside São Gonçalo are several impressively steep switchbacks topped by the round, 18th-century **Igreja de São Domingos** (🕑 irregular hours). Up on Rua Miguel Bombarda, the baroque-fronted **Igreja de São Pedro** (admission free; 🕑 2-5pm) has a nave decorated with 17th-century blue-and-yellow *azulejos.*

RIO TÂMEGA

For an idyllic river stroll, take the cobbled path along the north bank. A good picnic/daydreaming spot is the rocky outcropping overlooking the rapids, 400m east of the bridge.

You can potter about on the peaceful Rio Tâmega in a paddle or rowing **boat** (per half-/full hour €5/8; 🕑 9am-8pm), available for hire along the riverbank.

SOLAR DOS MAGALHÃES

This burned-out skeleton of an old manor house situated above Rua Cândido dos Reis, near the train station, has been left in ruins – a stark and uncaptioned memento from Napoleon's troops.

PARQUE AQUÁTICO AMARANTE

A good place for little kids (and big kids) to splash around, **Parque Aquático Amarante** (☎ 255 446 648; www.tamegaclube.com/pkaquatico; A4 exit 15; adult/child €13/7; 🕑 10.30am-7pm Jun-Sep) is located above the river, about 2km southwest of the centre. It has a choice of three chutes, plus swimming pools and sunbathing areas.

Festivals & Events

Held during the first weekend in June, **Festas de Junho** highlights include an all-night drumming competition, a livestock fair, a handicrafts market and fireworks, all rounded off with Sunday's procession in honour of the main man – São Gonçalo.

PRINCE OF LONELY HEARTS

Normally staid Amarante folk get a little frisky during the feast of São Gonçalo (13 January). Unmarried men and women swap phallic pastries as a sign of affection – a tradition that almost certainly pre-dates the 13th-century saint to earlier pagan times.

THE DOURO

Sleeping

Rooms are scarce during the Festas de Junho, though they're plentiful at other times.

Parque de Campismo de Penedo da Rainha (☎ 255 437 630; ccporto@sapo.pt; Rua Pedro Avelos; sites per adult/tent/car €3.30/2.20/2.10; ☯ Feb-Nov; ☒) This big, shady site cascades down to the river and has a *minimercado* (grocery shop) and bar. It's about 1km upstream (and uphill) from the town centre.

Residencial Raposeira (☎ 255 432 221; Largo Conselheiro António Cândido 41; s/d from €18/25) The best of the budget options, Raposeira has small but spotless modern rooms. Front-facing rooms are bright and look onto a pretty square. Noise from the busy bus station, however, may mean an early morning for light sleepers.

Residencial Príncipe (☎ 255 446 104; Largo Conselheiro António Cândido 78; d with/without bathroom €30/25) This perfectly average place sits above a simple restaurant of the same name. It offers small but cheery rooms with simple furnishings and creaky wood floors.

Residencial Estoril (☎ /fax 255 431 291; mnestoril@ hotmail.com; Rua 31 de Janeiro 49; d facing street/river €35/40, with balcony €45) Jutting out over the riverbank, Estoril has basic, wood-floored rooms with small bathrooms. The best feature: four rooms (two with balcony) offer sweet views of São Gonçalo's bridge.

Albergaria Dona Margaritta (☎ 255 432 110; www.albergariadonamargaritta.pa-net.pt, in Portuguese; Rua Cândido dos Reis 53; d €50; ☒) This faded but handsome town house has motherly service and pleasant, characterful quarters. Try to snag one of the rooms with river views.

Casa da Calçada (☎ 255 410 830; www.casada calcada.com; Largo do Paço 6; s/d Sun-Thu €155/170, Fri & Sat €200/220; ☒ ☒ ☒) Oozing class and boasting every creature comfort, this 16th-century palace (rebuilt following Napoleon's destructive campaign) rises royally above the Ponte de São Gonçalo. Past the antique-filled parlours lie spacious, elegantly furnished rooms, set with marble bathrooms. The Jacuzzi and pool overlook gardens and the hotel's vineyards.

Eating

Confeitaria da Ponte (Rua 31 de Janeiro; pastries €0.70; ☯ 8am-11pm) Boasting a peaceful, shaded terrace overlooking the bridge, this traditional bakery has the best ambience for enjoying Amarante's famous pastries and eggy custards.

Adega A Quelha (☎ 255 425 786; Rua de Olivença; mains €5-10; ☯ lunch & dinner Tue-Sun, lunch Mon) One of several low-key *adegas* (wine taverns) proffering Amarante's fine smoked meats and cheese, A Quelha is a good place to sample the local delicacies. Grab a bite and a jug of red wine at the bar, or sit down to a simple but filling meal.

Restaurante Lusitana (☎ 255 426 720; Rua 31 de Janeiro; mains €8-12; ☯ lunch & dinner Wed-Mon) Roasted kid and stewed tripe are house specialities at this traditional Portuguese restaurant with a pretty riverside terrace.

Zé da Calçada (☎ 255 426 814; Rua 31 de Janeiro; mains €9-10; ☯ lunch & dinner) Excellent northern cuisine is served in an elegant country-style dining room or on a veranda jutting out over the river. Top picks here include a remarkable *posta á marônesa* (grilled local beef), as well as the satisfying *açorda de camarãoes* (shrimp stew in bread bowl).

100 Papas (☎ 918312012; 2nd fl, Av Alexandre Herculano; mains €9-12; ☯ lunch & dinner) Amarante's best new restaurant features a dramatically set dining room, watched over by images of local luminaries (like artist Souza-Cardoso, second from left) superimposed on sliding glass walls. The cuisine, however, is the real draw, with tasty dishes such as grilled tuna on a bed of spinach, flaky filo pastry stuffed with cod, and steak with fig paste and goat cheese.

You can get picnic fixings at shops along Rua 31 de Janeiro or at the **mercado municipal** (Rua Capitão Augusto Casimiro), whose big days are Wednesday and Saturday.

Drinking & Entertainment

Open-air cafes/bars, like Ponte Come, pop up every summer on the riverside along Avenida General Silveira, opposite the monastery.

Spark Bar (Av Alexandre Herculano; ☯ 12.30pm-4am) This contemporary, multilevel bar-restaurant turns into a makeshift disco on Friday and Saturday nights.

Travo & Canela (Rua Cândido dos Reis; ☯ 1pm-2am) This inviting wine bar combines trim decor with festive red-and-yellow walls. Try the sandwiches, which are made with local ingredients.

Magnum Club (☯ 912302349; www.magnum-club .com; Av General Silveira; ☯ 11pm-4am) A bit out of place in sleepy Amarante, this sleek, modern club throws big dance parties on Saturdays, with DJs and bands playing throughout the night.

Getting There & Away

BUS

At the small but busy **Rodonorte bus station** (☎ 255 422 194; www.rodonorte.pt; Largo Conselheiro António Cândido), buses stop at least five times daily from Porto (€6, one hour) en route to Vila Real (€5.90, 40 minutes) and Bragança (€11.30, 2¾ hours). Rodonorte also runs daily to Braga (€7.40, 1½ hours), Coimbra (€11.40, two hours) and Lisbon (€17, 4¼ hours).

TRAIN

The journey on the narrow-gauge Linha da Tâmega, which runs from the Douro mainline at Livração up to Amarante, takes 25 minutes and costs €1.21 (buy tickets on board). There are six to nine trains a day, most with good connections to Porto.

LAMEGO

pop 9100 / elev 550m

Most people come to Lamego – a prim, prosperous town 10km south of the Rio Douro – to see (and possibly to climb) the astonishing baroque stairway that zigzags its way up to the Igreja de Nossa Senhora dos Remédios. The old town centre itself has a mix of winding narrow lanes and tree-lined boulevards, with a few other worthwhile sights sprinkled about town, including a small castle, a photogenic cathedral and a well-curated regional museum. Connoisseurs also swear by Lamego's *raposeira*, the town's famously fragrant sparkling wine, which provides a fine break between bouts of port.

Lamego is a natural base for exploring the half-ruined monasteries and chapels in the environs, one of which dates back to the time of the Visigoths. Though in the Beira Alta, in spirit Lamego belongs to the Douro region.

History

Lamego was an important centre even in the time of the Visigoths and has had a cathedral since at least the 6th century. The city fell to the Moors in the 8th century and remained in their hands until the 11th century. In 1143 Portugal's first *cortes* (parliament) was convened here to confirm Afonso Henriques as Portugal's first king. The little town grew fat thanks to its position on trading routes between the Douro and the Beiras, and also from its wines, already famous in the 16th century.

Orientation

The town's main axis is Avenida Visconde Guedes Teixeira (known as 'Jardim' and shaded by lime trees) and the wide Avenida Dr Alfredo de Sousa (called 'Avenida' and shaded by chestnut trees).

At the far end of Avenida, the immense stairway ascends to the Igreja de Nossa Senhora dos Remédios, on top of one of the two hills overlooking the town. Northwards, atop a more modest hill, stand the ruins of a 12th-century castle.

Parking can be tight, but there are free, shady spaces around Avenida (though you must pay along adjacent Jardim).

Information

C@fenet (Av 5 de Outubro 153; internet access per hr €1.50; ☺ 8am-midnight)

Hospital (☎ 254 609 980; Lugar da Franzia)

Laundry (Av 5 de Outubro; ☺ 8.30am-10pm)

Library (☎ 254 614 013; Rua de Almacave 9; ☺ 9.30am-12.30pm & 2-5.30pm Mon-Fri) Provides free internet access in 30-minute chunks.

Police station (☎ 254 612 022; Rua António Osório Mota)

Post office (Av Dr Alfredo de Sousa; ☺ 8.30am-6pm Mon-Fri)

Turismo (☎ 254 612 005; douro.turismo@mail.telepac .pt; Av Visconde Guedes Teixeira; ☺ 10am-12.30pm & 2-6pm Mon-Fri, 10am-12.30pm & 2-5pm Sat & Sun Jul-Sep, 9.30am-12.30pm & 2-5.30pm Mon-Fri, 10am-12.30pm Sat Oct-Jun)

Sights & Activities

IGREJA DE NOSSA SENHORA DOS REMÉDIOS

One of the country's most important pilgrimage sites, the twin-towered, 18th-century **church** (admission free; ☺ 7.30am-8pm May-Sep, 7.30am-6pm Oct-Apr) has a trim blue-and-white stucco interior vaguely reminiscent of Wedgwood Jasperware. The church, however, is quite overshadowed by the zigzagging theatricality of the monumental stairway that leads up to it. The 600-plus steps are resplendent with *azulejos*, urns, fountains and statues, adding up to one of the great works of Portuguese rococo.

It's a dramatic sight at any time, but the action peaks in late summer when thousands of devotees arrive and ascend the steps in search of miracles – or at least a little comfort – during the Festa de Nossa Senhora dos Remédios (p415).

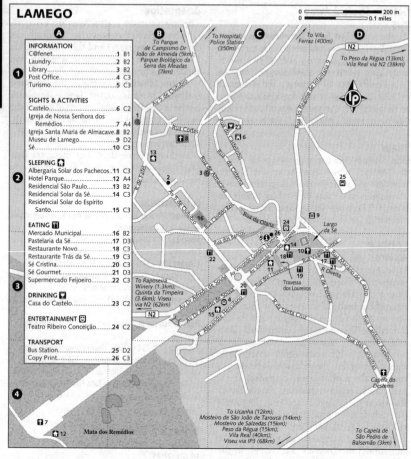

LAMEGO

INFORMATION	
C@fenet	1 B1
Laundry	2 B2
Library	3 B2
Post Office	4 C3
Turismo	5 C3

SIGHTS & ACTIVITIES	
Castelo	6 C2
Igreja de Nossa Senhora dos Remédios	7 A4
Igreja Santa Maria de Almacave	8 B2
Museu de Lamego	9 D2
Sé	10 C3

SLEEPING	
Albergaria Solar dos Pachecos	11 C3
Hotel Parque	12 A4
Residencial São Paulo	13 B2
Residencial Solar da Sé	14 C3
Residencial Solar do Espírito Santo	15 C3

EATING	
Mercado Municipal	16 B2
Pastelaria da Sé	17 D3
Restaurante Novo	18 C3
Restaurante Trás da Sé	19 C3
Sé Cristina	20 C3
Sé Gourmet	21 D3
Supermercado Feijoeiro	22 C3

DRINKING	
Casa do Castelo	23 C2

ENTERTAINMENT	
Teatro Ribeiro Conceição	24 C2

TRANSPORT	
Bus Station	25 D2
Copy Print	26 C3

If you can't face climbing by foot, a road (turn off 1km out on the Viseu road) winds up the hill for about 3km before reaching the top. You can make your way back down through cool, winding forest paths on either side of the steps.

SÉ

Older than Portugal itself, Lamego's striking **sé** (cathedral; ☎ 254 612 766; Largo da Sé; admission free; ☷ 8am-1pm & 3-7pm) has been declared a National Monument. There's little left of the 12th-century original except the base of its square belfry. The rest of the structure, including the brilliantly carved, flamboyant Gothic triple portal, dates mostly from the 16th and 18th centuries. Arresting biblical frescoes seem to leap off the ceiling. Both these and the high choir stalls are the work of the 18th-century Italian baroque architect Nicolau Nasoni, who left his mark all over Porto.

With luck you'll find the door open to the peaceful 16th-century cloisters, just around the corner.

IGREJA SANTA MARIA DE ALMACAVE

This unassuming little **church** (☎ 254 612 460; Rua de Almacave; ☷ 7.30am-noon & 4-7.30pm) is Lamego's oldest surviving building, much of it dating back to the 12th century. The church occupies the site of a Moorish cemetery; some of its grave markers are now in the Museu de Lamego (opposite). On the south side is a lovely Romanesque portal.

It's thought that an early version of the *cortes*, Portugal's proto-democratic assembly of nobles and clergy, met here from 1142 to 1144.

MUSEU DE LAMEGO

Occupying a grand, 18th-century episcopal palace, the **Museu de Lamego** (☎ 254 600 230; www.ipmuseus.pt; Largo de Camões; adult/youth €2/1, 10am-12.30pm Sun free; ☷ 10am-12.30pm & 2-5pm Tue-Sun) is one of Portugal's finest regional museums. The collection features some luminous pieces, including five entrancing works by renowned 16th-century Portuguese painter Vasco Fernandes (Grão Vasco), richly worked Brussels tapestries from the same period, and an extraordinarily diverse collection of heavily gilded 17th-century chapels rescued in their entirety from the long-gone Convento das Chagas.

CASTELO

Climb the narrow, winding Rua da Olaria to the modest medieval **castle** (Rua do Castelinho; admission by donation; ☷ irregular hours), which is encircled by a clutch of ancient stone houses. What little remains – some walls and a tower – has belonged to the Boy Scouts ever since their mammoth 1970s effort to clear the site after years of use as a glorified rubbish tip. Unfortunately, the site isn't always open; stop in the tourist office for the latest details.

Festivals & Events

Lamego's biggest party, the **Festa de Nossa Senhora dos Remédios**, runs for several weeks from late August to mid-September. In an afternoon procession on 8 September, ox-drawn carts rattle through the streets carrying *tableaux vivants* (religious scenes represented by costumed people), and devotees slowly ascend the stairway on their knees.

Less-pious events in the run-up include rock concerts, folk dancing, car racing, parades and at least one all-night party.

Sleeping

Parque de Campismo Dr João de Almeida (☎ /fax 254 613 918; Serra das Meadas; sites per adult/tent/car €3.20/3/3; ☷ Jun-Sep) A well-equipped camping facility about 5km west of town. Restaurant, market and some shade.

Residencial Solar da Sé (☎ 254 612 060; fax 254 615 928; Av Visconde Guedes Teixeira 7; s/d incl breakfast €24/39; ☒) Homely but comfortable rooms with tan carpeting, many with French windows and little verandas that face the cathedral's facade.

Residencial São Paulo (☎ 254 613 114; fax 254 612 304; Av 5 de Outubro 22; d €35; ℗) Although it's a bit out of the way, this is the best of the budget options. Rooms are clean and bright, with wood floors and somewhat dated bathrooms. Corner rooms have extra windows and verandas, and some rooms have views.

Residencial Solar do Espírito Santo (☎ /fax 254 655 060; Rua Alexandre Herculano 8; d incl breakfast €37; ℗ ☒) The common areas feature old-world touches like wood floors and *azulejo*-lined walls. Rooms are less inspiring, as they're a bit cramped, with ageing mattresses.

Albergaria Solar dos Pachecos (☎ 254 600 300; www.solar-pachecos.com; Av Visconde Guedes Teixeira 27; s/d incl breakfast €40/50; ☒) Occupying an impressive, 18th-century nobleman's city home, this central place combines exposed stone walls with bright, modern rooms done up rather stylishly in a crisp white.

Vila Ferraz (☎ 254 656 956; www.vilaferraz.com, in Portuguese; Av General Alves Pedrosa; d incl breakfast €60; ℗ ☒ ☖) Some 800m beyond the *castelo*, this converted, pink, 19th-century mansion boasts large rooms decked out in period furniture, plus a huge garden with swimming pool. Every inch is packed with antique character, and no two rooms are alike.

Quinta da Timpeira (☎ 254 612 811; www.quintadatimpeira.com; s/d €60/75; ℗ ☖) Surrounded by vineyards, this is an attractive modern place with bright and airy (if smallish) rooms, and lovely grounds with pool and tennis courts. It's located about 4km out on the Viseu road.

Hotel Parque (☎ 254 609 140; www.hotel-parque.com; d with/without view €65/55; ℗ ☒) Set in a former convent next to the Igreja de Nossa Senhora dos Remédios, the Hotel Parque offers tastefully decorated rooms with wood floors and a few antique flourishes. The best rooms overlook Lamego; others face onto the woods. Best to have your own car; the turn-off is 1km out on the Viseu road (N2).

Eating & Drinking

Like most regions that produce good wines, Lamego delivers food to match. Its *fumeiros* (smoked meats) are justly famous.

Pastelaria da Sé (☎ 254 612 463; Rua Virgílio Correia; pastries €1; ☷ 8am-8pm) Serving Lamego's best pastries, this inviting cafe lies just behind the cathedral.

Restaurante Trás da Sé (☎ 254 614 075; Rua Virgílio Correia 12; half-portions €5-6; ☽ lunch & dinner) Congratulations to the chef line the walls at this *adega*-style place, where the atmosphere is friendly, the menu short and simple, the food good and the *vinho maduro* (wine matured for more than a year) list long.

Restaurante Novo (☎ 254 613 166; Largo da Sé; mains €7-9; ☽ lunch & dinner) Occupying a fine vantage point beside the cathedral, this popular newcomer serves decent plates of grilled trout, squid and the usual meaty selections. Grab a seat outside or in the *azulejo*-filled dining room.

Sé Cristina (☎ 254 656 562; 1st fl, Rua do Mazeda 2; mains €8-12; ☽ lunch & dinner) Lamego's best restaurant occupies an elegantly set dining room, with outdoor tables above a small plaza. Here you'll find excellent traditional Portuguese recipes and attentive service.

The **mercado municipal** (Av 5 de Outubro; ☽ Mon-Fri, morning Sat) and grocery shops on Rua da Olaria sell Lamego's famous hams and wines – ideal picnic food. You'll find more-upmarket selections of wine, cheese and snacks at **Sé Gourmet** (☎ 254 688 263; Rua Macário de Castro 38; ☽ 11am-1pm & 2.30-7.30pm Tue-Sun). For wider selections, there's **Supermercado Feijoeiro** (Av 5 de Outubro 11; ☽ 9am-12.30pm & 2-8pm Mon-Sat).

Popular spots for a sundowner include the casual outdoor cafes located near the roundabout, where Avenida Visconde Guedes Teixeira meets Avenida Dr Alfredo de Sousa. Another youthful but more hidden drinking spot lies inside the walls of the *castelo:* the atmospheric **Casa do Castelo** (Rua do Castelinho 25; ☽ noon-2am Tue-Sun) is subdued during the week, but packs in a festive student crowd on weekends.

Entertainment

Teatro Ribeiro Conceição (☎ 962116119; Largo Camões; tickets €5-48) This handsomely restored theatre and cultural space reopened to much fanfare in 2007. It hosts a wide range of programs throughout the year, from children's puppet shows to classical concerts, fringe theatre with nights of fado, orchestral concerts and ballets. There's also a cafe with outdoor seating.

Getting There & Away

The most appealing route to Lamego from anywhere in the Douro valley is by train to Peso da Régua (p418) and by bus or taxi from there. A **taxi** (☎ 254 321 366) from Régua costs about €12 to €15.

From Lamego's bus station, **Joalto/EAVT** (☎ 254 612 116) goes about hourly to Peso da Régua (€1.85, 30 minutes) and daily to Viseu (€7.50, 1¼ hours), Coimbra (€11, three hours) and Lisbon (€15.30, 5¾ hours).

Rodonorte (www.rodonorte.pt) also stops here three times daily en route between Chaves (€10.50, 2¼ hours) and Vila Real (€5.50, one hour) to Lisbon (€15.30, five hours). **Rede Expressos** (www.rede-expressos.pt) stops twice daily en route between Vila Real and Viseu, where you can transfer to other destinations. **Copy Print** (☎ 254 619 447; Av Visconde Guedes Teixeira; ☽ 8am-8pm), a newsagent beside the *turismo*, sells tickets for these services.

AROUND LAMEGO
Capela de São Pedro de Balsemão

Older than Portugal itself, this extraordinary little **chapel** (admission free; ☽ 10am-12.30pm & 2-6pm Wed-Sun, 2-6pm Tue, closed 3rd weekend of month) has mysterious origins, but parts were probably built by Visigoths as early as the 6th century. With Corinthian columns, round arches and intriguing symbols etched into the walls, it certainly pre-dates the introduction of even Romanesque architecture to Portugal. More-ornate 14th-century additions were commissioned by the Bishop of Porto, Afonso Pires, who's buried under a slab in the floor. Check out the ancient casket dominating the entrance chamber: supported by lions and intricately engraved, it depicts the Last Supper on one side and the Crucifixion on the other.

The chapel is tucked away in the hamlet of Balsemão, 3km southeast of Lamego above the Rio Balsemão. It's a pleasant, downhill walk from Lamego (though a rather steep return trip). From the 17th-century Capela do Desterro at the end of Rua da Santa Cruz, head southeast over the river and follow the road to the left.

Mosteiro de São João de Tarouca

The skeletal remains of Portugal's first Cistercian monastery, the **Mosteiro de São João de Tarouca** (☎ 254 678 766; admission free; ☽ 10am-12.30pm & 2-5.30pm Wed-Sun, to 6pm May-Sep), founded in 1124, stand eerily in the wooded Barosa valley below the Serra de Leomil, 15km southeast of Lamego. The monastery fell into ruin after religious orders were abolished in 1834.

Only the church, considerably altered in the 17th century, stands intact among the ghostly ruins of the monks' quarters. Its treasures include the gilded choir stalls, 18th-century *azulejos*, and an imposing 14th-century tomb of the Conde de Barcelos (Dom Dinis' illegitimate son), carved with scenes from a boar hunt. The church's pride and joy is a luminous *São Pedro* painted by Gaspar Vaz, contemporary and colleague of Grão Vasco (p371).

From Lamego, Joalto/EAVT has eight services each weekday (fewer on weekends) to São João de Tarouca (€2).

Mosteiro de Salzedas

Another Cistercian monastery picturesquely mouldering, the **Mosteiro de Salzedas** (admission free; 9am-12.30pm & 2-5pm Wed-Sun Nov-Apr, 10am-12.30pm & 2-6pm Wed-Sun May-Oct) is located about 3km further up the Barosa valley from Ucanha. This was one of the grandest monasteries in the land when it was originally built in 1168 with funds from Teresa Afonso, governess to Afonso Henriques' five children. The enormous church, which was extensively remodelled in the 18th century, is today a bit scruffy with decay, particularly its roofless cloisters next door. Across from the church lies the old *judiara*, with dark narrow lanes skirting around the gloomy centuries-old dwellings.

From Lamego, Joalto/EAVT runs three buses each weekday to Salzedas (€2.30).

Parque Biológico da Serra das Meadas

This 50-hectare **biological park** (254 609 600; www.cm-lamego.pt, in Portuguese; adult/under 18yr/senior €1/0.50/0.50; 2-5pm Mon-Fri, 2-6pm Sat & Sun), in the hills 7km from Lamego, is a pleasant setting for short hikes (along 3km of trails) amid peaceful forests. You can also see the local fauna in captivity, including deer and wild boar. You'll need your own transport to get here.

PESO DA RÉGUA

pop 9800 / elev 125m

Lamego's businesslike alter ego, the sun-bleached town of 'Régua' abuts the Rio Douro at the western edge of the demarcated port-wine region. As the largest regional centre with river access, it grew in the 18th century

into a major port-wine entrepôt, though the unofficial title of 'capital of the trade' has now shifted 25km upstream to the prettier village of Pinhão (p419).

Régua remains an important transport junction – thanks in part to the hulking IP3 bridge that soars above the river valley. It makes a convenient base to visit the port-wine country, cruise the Rio Douro and ride the Corgo railway line to Vila Real.

The town itself, set along a busy highway above the river, doesn't have a lot of charm, and most visitors stop in just long enough to get directions to nearby wineries. Those willing to scratch beneath the surface, however, can learn about port wine at the Solar do Vinho do Porto (below), take a stroll along the riverbank or dine in one of several excellent restaurants in town.

Orientation & Information

While the older heart of the city lies further up the sloping riverbank, the main area of interest to travellers is ranged along the riverfront west of the train station and its adjacent bus stop. Pick up a town map and local information at the **Rota do Vinho do Porto** (254 324 774; Largo da Estação; 9am-12.30pm & 2-6pm Feb-Oct, Mon-Fri only Nov-Jan), conveniently located in a converted warehouse right next to the train station. You can ask here about the Museum of the Douro, which is scheduled to open in Régua in 2009. There's also a less useful **turismo** (254 312 846; fax 254 322 271; Rua da Ferreirinha 505; 9am-12.30pm & 2-5.30pm Jul–mid-Sep, 9am-12.30pm & 2.30-5.30pm Mon-Fri mid-Sep–Jun), 1km west of the station. For the *cais fluvial* (river terminal) bear left at the Residencial Império.

There is a public car park at the eastern end of the riverfront promenade, a few blocks from the *turismo*.

Sights & Activities

PORT

Port-wine enthusiasts can collect an armful of brochures from the **Instituto do Vinho do Porto** (254 320 130; Rua dos Camilos 90; 8.30am-12.30pm & 2-6pm Mon-Fri).

A good place to learn about the history of port is the small museum of the **Solar do Vinho do Porto** (254 320 960; Rua da Ferreirinha; admission with/without audio guide €4/2; 10am-12.30pm & 2-6pm Tue-Sun). Housed in an 18th-century warehouse, the museum illuminates the centuries-old traditions of winemaking in the Douro, with an ox cart, delicate decanters and an enormous, wondrously fragrant wine cask among the props. The Solar hosts free wine-tastings on Friday afternoons and Saturday mornings.

For more wine-tasting, visit the **Quinta de São Domingos** (☎ 254 320 262; www.castelinho-vinhos .com; ☽ noon-3pm & 7pm-midnight Tue-Sun), also called Quinta do Castelinho, the nearest grower to Régua offering free tours and tastings. It also has a good restaurant open Tuesday to Sunday. To reach the lodge from the train station, head 600m east on the Vila Real road, turn left and continue for 400m. On foot, look for the signed short cut across the train tracks, 400m east of the train station.

RIVER CRUISES & TRAIN RIPS

Peso da Régua is a major stop on the Douro cruise lines (see p395 for more information). Your best bet is to reserve through Porto Tours in Porto (p395). In Régua, you can inquire about trips at the Rota do Vinho do Porto (p417). You could also try hopping aboard one of the frequent daily 50-minute cruises offered by **Manos do Douro** (☎ 223 756 723; cruises €10).

Another option on Saturdays from May to October is a ride in a restored **steam train** (comboio vapor; ☎ 808 208 208, www.cp.pt; adult/child return €43/21.50), which travels along the Douro from Régua to Tua. Trips last four hours and depart at 2.45pm. Book at any train station or stop in at the Rota do Vinho do Porto (p417) for more information.

Sleeping

Accommodation is relatively pricey in Peso da Régua.

Dom Quixote (☎ 254 321 151; residencialdquixote@ sapo.pt; 1st fl, Av Sacadura Cabral 1; s/d €25/40; P ⊠) Located 1.5km west of the *turismo*, the modern Dom Quixote is the closest Régua comes to a decent budget option. It offers simple but comfortable rooms.

Hotel Régua Douro (☎ 254 320 700; www.hotelregua douro.pt; Largo da Estação; d from €75; P ⊠ ≋) This industrial-sized hotel sits by the river and is steps from the train station. It has plush, carpeted rooms in ruby (or is that tawny?) colour schemes and windows overlooking the Douro. The pool is much appreciated on hot days.

Pousada Solar da Rêde (☎ 254 890 130; www.pousadas .pt; Mesão Frio; d from €150; P ⊠ ⊟ ≋) This magnificent, 18th-century palace 12km west of Régua sits royally above a particularly stunning bend in the Douro. It preserves all its original glory, including period furnishings and terraced gardens, plus new features like tennis courts and swimming pool. Among Portugal's most regal sleeps.

Eating

Restaurante O Maleiro (☎ 254 313 684; Rua dos Camilos; mains €6-8; ☽ lunch & dinner) Situated opposite the post office, this brisk but friendly place offers roast lamb, fried squid and other Portuguese standards, served in a simple *azulejo*-covered dining room.

Taberna Jéréré (☎ 254 323 299; Rua Marquês de Pombal 38; mains €8-10; ☽ lunch & dinner) Excellent Portuguese dishes, including *bacalhau á Jéréré* (dried salt-cod with shrimp, mushroom and spinach), served in a tastefully rustic dining room with a beamed ceiling.

Restaurante Cacho d'Oiro (☎ 254 321 455; Rua Branca Martinho; mains €8-12; ☽ lunch & dinner) This large cottage-restaurant, 150m west of the *turismo*, offers a longer menu, a good wine list, a more upmarket atmosphere and excellent cuisine. The *cabrito no churrasco* (grilled kid; €12) is excellent.

Douro In (☎ 254 323 951; Av João Franco; mains €14-16; ☽ lunch & dinner) A big step up in price and quality from most Régua options is the stylish Douro In. Elegant place settings and sizeable windows overlooking the river set the scene for feasting on *arroz de tamboril* (monkfish rice), roast loin with asparagus risotto, and other flavourful dishes. Superb wine list.

Getting There & Around

Joalto buses run hourly to/from Lamego (€1.85, 30 minutes). AV Tâmega runs services to Vila Real (€2.90, 40 minutes) about hourly on weekdays and thrice daily on weekends, and Rodonorte goes four times each weekday.

There are around 12 trains daily from Porto (€8, two hours); some go up the valley to Pinhão (€1.70, 25 minutes, five daily) and Tua (opposite). Around five trains depart daily for Vila Real (€2.20, 55 minutes) on the narrow-gauge Corgo line.

If you've taken a train this far and suddenly realise you need a car to visit the vineyards, your best bet is **Europcar** (☎ 254 321 146; Av João Franco), with car rentals from €60 per day.

ALTO DOURO

Heading upriver from Peso da Régua, terraced vineyards cover every hillside, with whitewashed *quintas* (estates) perched high above the Douro. This dramatic landscape has been completely refashioned by 2000 years of winemaking. While villages are small and architectural monuments few and far between, it's worth the trip simply for the ride itself (scenic by car, train or boat), with panoramic vistas lurking around nearly every bend. Its allure has clearly not gone unnoticed. In 2001 Unesco designated the entire Alto Douro wine-growing region a World Heritage Site.

Further east towards Spain, the soil is drier, and the sculpted landscape gives way to more-rugged terrain. But despite the aridity – and the blusteringly hot summers – the land around Vila Nova de Foz Côa produces fine grapes and excellent olives and nuts.

Many port-wine *quintas* offer rural accommodation, though rooms grow scarce in late September and early October during the *vindima* (grape harvest).

Though not technically part of the Douro province, this section of the Douro valley is an integral part of the region and is most easily reached via Porto.

Daily trains run from Porto, with a change at Régua, up to Pinhão, Tua and Pocinho. Travellers with their own wheels can take the river-hugging N222 from Régua to Pinhão, beyond which the roads climb in and out of the valley. For information on river cruises, see p395.

Pinhão

pop 960 / elev 120m

Encircled by terraced hillsides that produce some of the world's best port, little Pinhão sits on a particularly lovely bend of the Rio Douro, about 25km upriver from Peso da Régua. The scene is dominated by port-wine lodges and their competing signs; even the delightful train station has *azulejos* depicting the wine harvest. The town itself is of little interest but makes a fine base for exploring the many vineyards blanketing the area.

In addition to drinking your fill of port, this is a good setting for country walks, and there are some fine day-trip possibilities, especially by train.

ORIENTATION & INFORMATION

The summer-only **turismo** (☎ 254 731 932; Largo do Estação; 🕙 10am-noon & 2-6pm Tue-Sun) is open from May to September and is housed in the train station.

Except on high-season weekends, street parking is straightforward. Look around the train station or down by the river (first left after passing the train station).

SIGHTS & ACTIVITIES
Train Trips

The most beautiful of Portugal's narrow-gauge lines is the **Linha da Tua**, from the sun-blasted backwater of Tua (13km upriver) for 52km up the Tua valley to the pretty market town of Mirandela (p486). The two-hour Pinhão–Mirandela journey (€10.50 return, change at Tua) is just feasible as a day trip, departing about 11.30am, arriving in Mirandela at 2pm and returning from Mirandela about 4pm. There were serious accidents on this line in 2008 and you should inquire locally about the safety of this line before embarking on a journey. There's also talk of building a dam in the area that would submerge much of the line.

Alternatively, take the mainline train for another hour, past dams and vineyards, to the end of the line at Pocinho (single/return trip €2.85/5.30), visiting the Pocinho dam (Barragem de Pocinho) and returning the same day, or travelling on up to Vila Nova de Foz Côa (p420).

SLEEPING & EATING

Residencial Ponto Grande (☎ 254 732 456; Rua António Manuel Saraiva 41; s/d €25/38; 🍴) This place just across from the station offers clean but snug rooms with tile floors above a humble but well-regarded restaurant. Try to snag one of the bright front rooms with river views.

Residencial Douro (☎ /fax 254 732 404; Largo do Estação 39; d €50; 🍴) This cheery, well-kept guest house has several river-facing rooms, other large rooms facing a quiet rear courtyard, and a mini terrace covered with flowering vines.

Quinta de la Rosa (☎ 254 732 254; www.quinta delarosa.com; d incl breakfast from €85; 🅿 🍴) This lovely hillside *quinta* overlooks terraced vineyards just above the river 2km west of Pinhão. Rooms have wood floors and charming farmhouse-style furnishings, and most have exceptional river views. There's a lovely terrace for enjoying the delicious breakfasts, a pool,

DRINKING IN THE DOURO

Pinhão offers some enticing exploring for wine-lovers, with picturesque 18th-century manor houses overlooking steeply terraced vineyards leading down to the Douro. To explore the *quintas* (estates) on your own, you'll need your own vehicle. Ask the tourist office about lodges open for tours and tastings. It's worth shelling out €2 for a map (*Rota do Vinho do Porto*; www.rvp.pt) – available at most *turismos* in the Douro – listing 50 or so vineyards accepting visitors. A few good places to start the viticultural journey are listed here:

■ **Quinta do Panascal** (☎ 254 732 321; www.fonseca.pt; ✆ 10am-6pm Mon-Fri Nov-May, daily Jun-Oct) Producer of Fonseca ports, this lovely estate offers free self-guided audio tours (in English, French or Portuguese) through some beautifully situated vineyards. It's located about 10 minutes' drive west of Pinhão, well signed from the N222.

■ **Quinta do Portal** (☎ 259 937 100; www.quintadoportal.com; ✆ 10am-1pm & 2-6pm) Quinta do Portal is an award-winning vineyard producing ports, red and white table wines, and a little-known muscatel wine. The surrounding region is one of the only places in the country producing muscatel (the other is Setúbal). There's a restaurant and guest house (doubles from €125). The winery lies about 12km north of Pinhão, along EN323, direction Vila Real.

■ **Quinta Nova** (☎ 254 732 430; www.quintanova.com; ✆ tours 11am & 4pm Tue-Sun) This 120-hectare vineyard offers tours and tastings in a historic estate on the north side of the Douro. There's a restaurant (open by reservation only) and wine bar (open from 10.30am to midnight), with lodging (doubles from €120) available in a restored 18th-century manor house. It also has several walking trails, including a 12km trail past ancient vineyards. To get here, head 9km west of Pinhão, along the north bank of the Douro (EN322-2).

wine-tastings and classic meals by advance notice. Book well ahead.

Vintage House (☎ 254 730 230; www.relais chateaux.com; d from €150; P ✆ ▢ ▢ ▣) Occupying a string of 19th-century buildings right on the river, this luxurious sleep is actually very modern once you get past the distinctly English facade (a reminder of the key role Brits played in the port trade). Vintage House also boasts the best restaurant (mains €19 to €36) in town, with an elegant riverside setting and delicious seafood.

Veladouro (☎ 254 731 794; Rua Praia; mains €6-8; ✆ lunch & dinner Mon-Sat) Simple Portuguese food, such as wood-grilled meats, is served inside this quaint schist building or outside under a canopy of vines. From the train station, turn left and go along the main road for 150m, then left again under a railway bridge, and right at the river.

Restaurante Ponte Romana (☎ 254 732 978; Rua Santo António 2; mains €8-10; ✆ lunch & dinner Mon-Sat) For nicely prepared traditional Portuguese food, Ponte Romana is the place, with tasty *arroz de tamboril* (monkfish rice), *cataplana de marisco* (seafood stew) and *cabrito assado* (roasted kid). From the train station, turn left and follow the main road for 600m; cross the stone bridge, and you'll see it on the right.

DOC (☎ 254 858 123; EN222; mains €15-30; ✆ lunch & dinner) A bit of a drive from Pinhão, DOC is a stylish newcomer serving haute cuisine on an outdoor deck over the Douro. The changing menu features delectable dishes such as scallops with wild mushrooms, and lamb with vegetable ragout. It's located 13km west of Pinhão, on the south side of the river.

GETTING THERE & AWAY

Regional trains go from Peso da Régua (€1.70, 30 minutes, five daily). From Porto you must change at Régua; the quickest links (€9.05, two hours, four daily) are by IC train as far as Régua.

Vila Nova de Foz Côa
pop 3200 / elev 420m

In the heart of the Douro's *terra quente* (hot land), this once-remote, whitewashed town has been on the map since the 1990s. That's when researchers – during an environmental impact study for a proposed dam – stumbled across an astounding collection of Palaeolithic art. These mysterious rock engravings, which number in the thousands, blanket the nearby Rio Côa valley. Yet they were very nearly lost when the power company tried to insist on completing the dam. Archaeologists brought the petroglyphs to the world's attention, and the dam builders finally backed down when the whole valley was declared a Unesco World Heritage Site.

As it turns out, the region has been popular with human beings ever since those Upper Palaeolithic days (10,000 to 40,000 years ago), and around 'Foz' you can also find remains of Bronze Age, Roman and Visigothic civilisations.

You may find the climate startlingly Mediterranean if you've just come from the mountains. Summers here are infernally hot, with temperatures regularly exceeding 45°C. But if you come in late March, you'll be treated to cooler climes as well as the sight of entire hillsides in blossom thanks to the highest density of flowering almond trees in Portugal.

ORIENTATION

Long-distance coaches stop at the bus station about 150m north of the *turismo* at Avenida Gago Coutinho. From here the town stretches eastward along Avenida Gago Coutinho, pedestrianised Rua Dr Juiz Moutinho de Andrade, Rua São Miguel and Rua Dr Júlio de Moura to the old town's centre, Praça do Município.

There is usually plenty of free street parking along Avenida Gago Coutinho between the *turismo* and the park headquarters.

INFORMATION

Biblioteca Municipal de Vila Nova de Foz Côa
(☎ 279 760 300; Av Cidade Nova 2; ☷ 9am-noon & 2-5.30pm Mon-Fri) Free internet access in the same building as the *turismo*.

Municipal Turismo (☎ 279 760 329; Av Cidade Nova 2; ☷ 9am-12.30pm & 2-5.30pm) Opposite Albergaria Foz Côa.

Parque Arqueológico office (☎ 279 768 260; www.ipa.min-cultura.pt/coa; Av Gago Coutinho 19A; ☷ 9am-12.30pm & 2-5.30pm Tue-Sun) The helpful first point of contact for those interested in touring the Palaeolithic sites.

Post office (Av Dr Artur de Aguilar 6; ☷ 9am-12.30pm & 2-5.30pm Mon-Fri) Three blocks north of the park office via Largo do Rossio.

SIGHTS & ACTIVITIES

Parque Arqueológico do Vale do Côa

Most visitors to Vila Nova de Foz Côa come for one reason: to see its world-famous gallery of rock art.

Although the park is currently an active research zone, three sites are open to the public: Canada do Inferno from the **park office** (☷ daily, trips Tue-Sun) in Vila Nova de Foz Côa; Ribeira de Piscos from the **Muxagata visitor centre** (☎ 279 764 298; ☷ 9.30am-3pm Tue-Sun) on the western side of the valley; and Penascosa from the **Castelo Melhor visitor centre** (☎ 279 713 344; ☷ 2-5.30pm Tue-Sun) on the eastern side. While Castelo Melhor has some of the most significant etchings, Canada do Inferno – which sits by the half-constructed dam – is the ideal place to understand just how close these aeons-old drawings came to disappearing.

Near Ribeira de Piscos there is also a private site (owned by the Ramos Pinto port-wine lodge) at **Quinta da Ervamoira** (☎ 279 759 229; www.ramospinto.pt; ☷ Tue-Sun). It has vineyards, wine-tastings, a restaurant and a small museum featuring Roman and medieval artefacts. Visits must be arranged by advanced booking; visitors are met at Muxagata and taken by 4WD to the estate.

Because the entire valley is a working archaeological site, all visitors must enter with a guided tour. Visitors gather at the various visitors centres, where they're taken, eight at a time, in the park's own 4WDs, for a guided tour of one of the sites (1½ hours at Canada do Inferno and Penascosa, 2½ hours at Ribeira de Piscos). Visitors with mountain bikes may go on guided bike tours in similar-sized groups. The price in either case is €7 per person.

Visitor numbers are strictly regulated, so from July to September book a tour well in advance or you may miss out. Likewise, you must book at least a few weeks ahead for bicycle trips at any time. You can make bookings through the park office (left).

For a bit more adventure, you can sign up for an excursion with **Ravinas do Côa** (☎ 279 762 832, 966746423; www.ravinasdocoa.lda.pt, in Portuguese; Bairro Flor da Rosa 34), a private local tour operator offering organised hiking, biking and canoeing trips, as well as rappelling and other activities.

Old Town

The sleepy old quarter makes for a pleasant stroll in the early evening. Highlights are the Praça do Município, with its impressive granite *pelourinho* topped by an armillary sphere, and the elaborately carved portal of the Manueline-style parish church. Inside, the nave recalls a banqueting hall, with glimmering chandeliers and a painted ceiling (supported by perilously pitched columns). Just east off the square is the tiny Capela de Santa Quitéria, once the town's synagogue.

Other Attractions

Archaeological finds from the Stone Age to the 18th century have been uncovered in the region around Freixo de Numão, 12km west of Vila Nova de Foz Côa. A good little display can be viewed at Freixo de Numão, in the **Museu da Casa Grande** (☎ 279 789 573; www .acdr-freixo.pt, in Portuguese; adult/under 12yr/under 26yr €1.50/0.75/1; ☉ 9am-noon & 2-6pm Tue-Sun), a baroque town house with Roman foundations. Some English and French are spoken here. Free with entrance is a leaflet on the museum and the rich neolithic/Roman/medieval site at Prazo, about 3km west of Freixo de Numão. Guided tours are available by arrangement with the museum.

The *turismo* in Vila Nova de Foz Côa (p421) also offers free brochures for a **self-guided archaeological tour** of the region.

SLEEPING

Pousada da Juventude (☎ 279 768 190; www.pousadas juventude.pt; Caminho Vicinal Currauteles 5; dm/d/apt €13/38/60; ℗) This fairly new hostel in a modern, pink-brick building is well worth the 800m walk north from the town centre (1.4km by road). Its basic but handsome doubles have views over a rugged valley; four-bed dorms are clean and well maintained; and there's an apartment with kitchen that sleeps four. Amenities include bar, open kitchen, laundry, cafeteria, games room and large patio with sweeping views.

Residencial Avenida (☎ 279 762 175; Av Gago Coutinho 10; d €30) Across from the *turismo*, Avenida is a good budget pick, with fairly large rooms that are decently furnished. It can sometimes be noisy, however, from the neighbouring cafe.

Albergaria Vale do Côa (☎ 279 760 010; www .albergariavaledocoa.net, in Portuguese; Av Cidade Nova 1A; s/d €38/50; ℗ 🐕) This modern hotel opposite the tourist office offers comfortable, air-conditioned rooms with clean-swept wood floors. Most rooms have verandas with views of the hilly countryside.

Quinta do Chão d'Ordem (☎ 279 762 427; www .chaodordem.com; N102; d incl breakfast €60; ℗ 🐕 🍷) This working farm offers a warm welcome

and rather grand rooms in a new wing off the old villa. Breakfasts are wonderful, and amenities include a pool, tennis court, lounge and a remarkable wine-cellar in a converted dovecote. The farm is about 6km from Foz Côa, just past Muxagata on the N102 towards Guard. Some English spoken.

Casa Vermelha (☎ 279 765 252; www.casavermelha .com; Av Gago Coutinho 3; s/d €70/90; 🐕 🍷) A splendid new option near the *turismo*, this fire-engine-red place has bright, handsome rooms with squeaky-clean wood floors and antique furnishings. The beautifully restored 1920s-era mansion is fronted by gardens and a pool – a welcome relief on hot days.

EATING

Terrinca (Rua de São Miguel; mains €4-6; ☉ 7am-7pm, tea-room to midnight) An excellent bakery downstairs and a popular, tricked-up tearoom upstairs.

António & Julia (Rua de São Miguel) Top-quality local hams, sausages, cheese and honey are available for picnics in this charming shop near A Marisqueira and Terrinca.

Restaurante A Marisqueira (☎ 279 762 187; Rua de São Miguel; mains €8-12, daily specials under €5; ☉ lunch & dinner Mon-Sat) Located on a pleasant pedestrian street in the old town, this cheery place serves good Portuguese meat dishes and just enough *mariscos* (shellfish) to justify the name in a small but bright contemporary dining room.

Apeadeiro (☎ 279 764 393; Rua das Atafonas; mains €6-8; ☉ lunch & dinner Thu-Tue) Apeadeiro is a bright and cheery spot serving nicely prepared regional favourites, with inexpensive daily specials. It's a short walk 300m north of the *turismo* (take Avenida Misericórdia past the bus station).

ENTERTAINMENT

Although there isn't a lot going on in Foz Côa, the **Centro Cultural** (☎ 279 760 324; www.fozcoactiva .pt, in Portuguese; Av Cidade Nova 2) hosts concerts, temporary art exhibitions and film screenings throughout the year. It's in the same building as the *turismo*.

GETTING THERE & AWAY

Several daily Rede Expressos and Joalto buses connect Vila Nova de Foz Côa with Bragança (€7.50, 1¾ hours). Rede Expressos buses come once daily from Miranda do Douro (€5.70, 2½ hours) and two times daily via Trancoso (€4.20) from Viseu (€9.20, two hours).

Five daily trains run to Pocinho, at the end of the Douro valley line, from Porto (€11.40, 3½ hours) and Peso da Régua (€5.60) through Pinhão (€2.85). A taxi between Pocinho and Vila Nova de Foz Côa costs about €6 to €8, and there are infrequent buses, too (€1.30, 10 minutes).

GETTING AROUND

There are no direct buses to Muxagata or Quinta da Ervamoira. However, a twice-daily bus passes the outskirts of Castelo Melhor (€1.70, 15 minutes); it's an easy walk to the visitor centre. Alternatively, there is a taxi stand on the square in front of the parks office.

The Minho

Tucked beneath the edge of Spanish Galicia, the Minho enjoys an exceptional reputation among the Portuguese. Its natural beauty encompasses lush river valleys, sparkling beaches, granite peaks and virgin forests. Villages seem particularly in tune with the scenery, whether straddling the banks of an idyllic river or overlooking flower-strewn valleys from mountainous heights.

For the Portuguese, the Minho's charms go beyond mere aesthetics. This is, after all, the birthplace of the Portuguese kingdom, an idea first conceived in the beautifully preserved medieval centre of Guimarães. It's also home to one of Portugal's most impressive Celtic sites, the sprawling Citânia de Briteiros. North of there, the majestic and vibrant city of Braga provides a window into ecclesiastical history, with dozens of baroque churches and a magnificent cathedral that dates back a thousand years.

The Minho remains one of Europe's most tradition-bound provinces. Old-fashioned market days still draw crowds to small country towns, and the calendar is packed with fervently observed saints' days – a cause for solemn processions followed by music, dancing, feasting and merriment late into the night.

Yet it's not all ox-drawn carts and Romanesque churches. The Costa Verde (Green Coast), which stretches roughly from the mouth of the Rio Cávado in the south to the mouth of the Rio Minho in the north, has a blend of old settlements and modern-day resorts. Lovely Viana do Castelo has an old centre filled with 16th-century architecture and sparkling new condos overlooking nearby beaches. The duality continues at the eastern end of the province: inside Parque Nacional da Peneda-Gerês, old stone villages slumber not far from lively spa resorts – all set amid the breathtaking mountain scenery of Portugal's biggest nature reserve.

HIGHLIGHTS

- Visiting historic monuments, followed by dinner at a top restaurant in **Braga** (opposite)
- Strolling the atmospheric streets of **Viana do Castelo** (p441), then catching a sunset over the beach
- Lounging at a cafe overlooking the medieval bridge and lush countryside beyond in **Ponte de Lima** (p450)
- Delving into medieval history inside the striking old quarter of **Guimarães** (p436)
- Hiking the boulder-strewn peaks and gorse-clad moorlands of the **Parque Nacional da Peneda-Gerês** (p457)

- POPULATION: 1.4 MILLION
- AREA: 5265 SQ KM

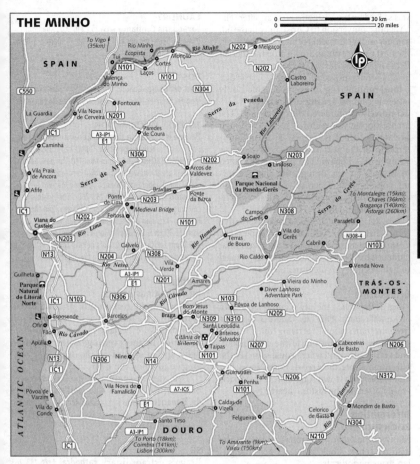

THE MINHO

SOUTHERN MINHO

BRAGA
pop 120,000 / elev 200m

Portugal's third-largest city boasts an astounding array of churches, their splendid baroque facades looming above the old plazas and narrow lanes of the historic centre. Braga's crown jewel is an extraordinary 12th-century cathedral, with its intricately carved facade, atmospheric little chapels and intriguing hidden relics. The constant chiming of bells is a reminder of Braga's age-old devotion to the spiritual world. Its religious festivals – particularly the elaborately staged Semana Santa (Holy Week) – are famous throughout Portugal.

But don't come expecting piety alone: Braga's old centre is packed with lively cafes and trim little boutiques, with some excellent restaurants and low-key bars catering to students from the Universidade do Minho.

Just outside the city stands the magnificent, much-visited hillside church and sanctuary of Bom Jesus do Monte (p431).

History
Founded by Celts, Braga first attracted Roman attention in 250 BC. The Romans named it Bracara Augusta and made it capital of their province Gallaecia, stretching all the way up into Spain. Braga's position at the intersection of five Roman roads helped it grow fat on trade. Braga fell to the Suevi around AD 410, and

was sacked by the Visigoths 60 years later. The Visigoths' conversion to Christianity in the 6th century and the founding of an archbishopric in the next century put the town atop the Iberian Peninsula's ecclesiastical pecking order.

The Moors moved in around 715, sparking a long-running tug of war that ended only when Fernando I, king of Castilla y León, definitively reconquered the city in 1040. The archbishopric was restored in 1070, though prelates bickered with their Spanish counterparts for the next 500 years over who was Primate of All Spain. The pope finally ruled in Braga's favour, though the city's resulting good fortune began to wane in the 18th century, when a newly anointed Lisbon archdiocese stole much of its thunder.

Not surprisingly, it was from conservative Braga that Salazar, with his unique blend of Catholicism and fascism, gave the speech that launched his 1926 coup, introducing Portugal to half a century of dictatorship.

Orientation

Praça da República, the city's central square, is a 500m walk south of the bus station, or 1km east from the train station (if arriving from the train station, walk straight out to the roundabout, and veer to the right, where you'll soon see the old entrance gate, the Arco da Porta Nova). Just east of the *praça* (town square) lie the pedestrianised streets of the historic heart.

Information

BOOKSHOPS

Many of the *tabacarias* (tobacconists) in the historic centre stock at least a few foreign-language periodicals.

Centésima Página (☎ 253 267 647; Av Central 118; ☾ 9am-7.30pm Mon-Sat) A splendid new bookshop with foreign-language titles and a backyard cafe.

EMERGENCY & MEDICAL SERVICES

Hospital de São Marcos (☎ 253 209 000; Rua 25 Abril) A block west of Avenida da Liberdade.

Police station (☎ 253 200 420; Rua dos Falcões)

INTERNET ACCESS

Casa da Juventude (Instituto Português da Juventude; ☎ 253 204 250; Rua de Santa Margarida; ☾ 9am-6.30pm Mon-Fri) Free internet access at the southern end of the *pousada da juventude* (youth hostel).

Espaço Internet (☎ 253 267 484; Praça Conde de Agrolongo 177; ☾ 9am-12.30pm & 2.30-5.30pm Mon-Fri, 9am-1pm Sat) Free internet access.

LAUNDRY

Lavandaria Confiança (☎ 253 216 907; Rua Dom Diogo de Sousa 46; per kg €3; ☾ 9am-1.30pm & 3-8pm Mon-Fri, 9am-2pm Sat)

POST

Post office (Rua Gonçalo Sampaio; ☾ 8.30am-6pm Mon-Fri, 9am-12.30pm Sat) Just off Avenida da Liberdade.

TOURIST INFORMATION

Parque Nacional da Peneda-Gerês headquarters (☎ 253 203 480; pnpg@icn.pt; Quinta das Parretas; ☾ 9am-12.30pm & 2-5.30pm Mon-Fri) The park headquarters are 800m west of the town centre and reached via a tunnel under busy Avenida António Macedo.

Turismo (tourist office; ☎ 253 262 550; turismo@ cm-braga.pt; Praça da República; ☾ 9am-7pm Mon-Fri, 9am-12.30pm & 2-5.30pm Sat & Sun Jun-Sep, 9am-12.30pm & 2-6.30pm Mon-Fri, 9am-12.30pm & 2-5.30pm Sat Oct-May) Braga's helpful tourist office is in an art-deco-style building facing the fountain.

Sights

PRAÇA DA REPÚBLICA

The cafes and restaurants on this broad plaza are a pleasant place to start or finish your day. An especially mellow atmosphere descends in the evening, when coloured lights spring up and people of all ages congregate to enjoy the night air.

The square-shaped, crenellated tower behind the cafes is the walled-up **Torre de Menagem** (castle keep; Largo Terreiro do Castelo), which is all that survives of a fortified medieval palace.

SÉ

Braga's extraordinary **cathedral** (☎ 253 263 317; www.se-braga.pt; Rua Dom Paio Mendes; ☾ 8.30am-6.30pm) is the oldest in Portugal, begun when the archdiocese was restored in 1070 (probably on the ruins of a mosque) and completed in the following century. It's a rambling complex made up of differing styles, and architectural buffs could spend half a day happily distinguishing the Romanesque bones from Manueline musculature and baroque frippery. The original Romanesque style is the most interesting and survives in the cathedral's overall shape, the southern entrance and the marvellous west portal, which is carved with scenes from the medieval legend of Reynard the Fox (now sheltered inside a Gothic porch).

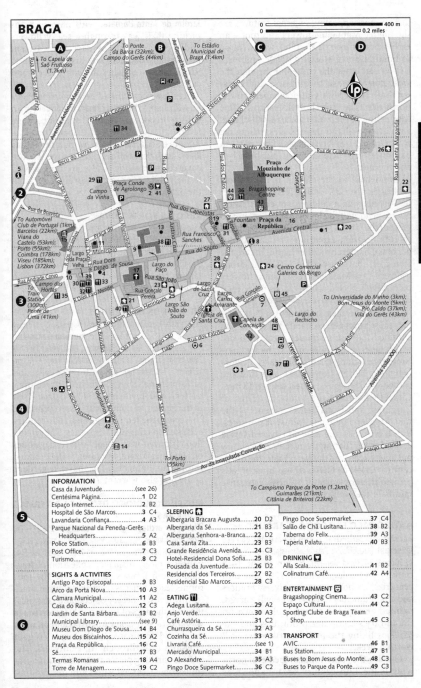

BRAGA

THE MINHO

The most appealing external features are the filigree Manueline towers and roof – an early work by João de Castilho, who went on to build Lisbon's Mosteiro dos Jerónimos.

You can enter the cathedral through the west portal or via a courtyard and cloister that's lined with Gothic chapels on the north side. The church itself features a fine Manueline carved altarpiece, a tall chapel with *azulejos* (hand-painted tiles) telling the story of Braga's first bishop, and fantastic twin baroque organs held up by formidable satyrs and mermen.

Connected to the church is the **treasury** (adult/under 12yr €2/1; ☉ 9am-12.30pm & 2-5.30pm Tue-Sun), housing a goldmine of ecclesiastical booty, including the lovely *Nossa Senhora do Leite* of the Virgin suckling Christ, attributed to 16th-century, expatriate French sculptor Nicolas Chanterène. Other highlights are the iron cross that was used in 1500 to celebrate the very first Mass in Brazil, and a flowery pair of high-heeled (10cm) shoes made for a particularly diminutive archbishop.

To visit the **choir** (adult/under 12yr €2/1), visitors must purchase a separate ticket and join a guided tour (some guides speak English), which gives an up-close look at the mesmerising organs and gilded choir stalls. Visitors will then be led downstairs and into the cathedral's showpiece **Capela dos Reis** (Kings' Chapel), home to the tombs of Henri of Burgundy and Dona Teresa, parents of the first king of Portugal, Afonso Henriques. You'll also visit the *azulejo*-covered **Capela de São Geraldo** (dating from the 12th century but reworked over the years) and the 14th-century **Capela da Glória**, whose interior was painted in unrepentantly Moorish geometric motifs in the 16th century.

ANTIGO PAÇO EPISCOPAL & AROUND

Facing the cathedral is the severe **Antigo Paço Episcopal** (Archbishop's Palace; admission free; ☉ 9am-12.30pm & 2-7.30pm Mon-Fri). Begun in the 14th century and enlarged in the 17th and 18th centuries, it's now home to university offices and the municipal library. A heavily carved, painted and gilded ceiling looks down on the library's computer room; this and the *azulejos* lining the main stairway are well worth a peek.

Outside the spiky-topped, medieval north wing is the 17th-century square known as

Jardim de Santa Bárbara, with narrow paths picking their way through a sea of flowers and topiary. On sunny days, the adjacent pedestrianised streets Rua Justino Cruz and Rua Francisco Sanches fill with buskers and cafe tables.

At the western end of neighbouring Praça do Município, Braga's **câmara municipal** (town hall) sports one of Portugal's finest baroque facades, designed by André Soares da Silva. A more extroverted Soares work is the **Casa do Raio** (Casa do Mexicano; Rua do Raio), its rococo face covered in *azulejos*. These are both closed to the public, but are still worth seeing from the outside.

ARCO DA PORTA NOVA

West of the old centre on Rua Dom Diogo de Sousa, this diminutive but elegant, 18th-century 'arch of the new gate' once served as the city's main entrance. It displays the ostentatious coat of arms of the archbishop who commissioned it, Dom José de Bragança.

MUSEU DOS BISCAÍNHOS

An 18th-century aristocrat's palace is now home to the enthusiastic **municipal museum** (☎ 253 204 650; Rua dos Biscaínhos; adult/under 14yr/14-25yr/senior €2/free/1/1, 10am-12.15pm Sun free; ☉ 10am-12.15pm & 2-5.30pm Tue-Sun), with a nice collection of Roman relics and 17th- to 19th-century pottery and furnishings. The palace itself is the reason to come, with its polychrome, chestnut-panelled ceilings and 18th-century *azulejos* depicting hunting scenes. The ground floor is paved with deeply ribbed flagstones on which carriages would have once rattled through to the stables. The mazelike gardens at the rear also warrant a visit.

MUSEU DOM DIOGO DE SOUSA & TERMAS ROMANAS

The new **archaeological museum** (☎ 253 273 706; http://mdds.imc-ip.pt; Rua dos Bombeiros Voluntários; adult/child €3/1.50, before 2pm Sun free; ☉ 10am-5.30pm Tue-Sun) houses a nicely displayed collection of fragments from Braga's earliest days. The four rooms feature pieces from Palaeolithic times (arrowheads, funerary objects and ceramics) through the days of Roman rule (when Braga was known as Bracara Augusta) and on up to the period dominated by the Suevi-Visigoth kingdom (5th through 7th centuries). The most fascinating pieces are the huge *miliários* (milestones), carved with Latin inscriptions,

---

EASTER IN BRAGA

Braga hosts the most-elaborate Easter celebrations in Portugal. It kicks off with **Semana Santa** (Holy Week), when Gregorian chants are piped throughout the city centre, and makeshift, candlelit altars light the streets at night. The action heats up during Holy Thursday's **Procissão do Senhor Ecce Homo**, when barefoot, hooded penitents – members of private Catholic brotherhoods (think Opus Dei) – march through the streets spinning their eerie rattles. The **Good Friday Mass** in the cathedral is a remarkable, elaborately staged drama with silk canopies, dirgelike hymns, dozens of priests and a weeping congregation. On Saturday evening, the **Easter Vigil Mass** begins dourly, the entire cathedral in shadow, only to explode in lights and jubilation. Finally, on Sunday, the people of Braga blanket their thresholds with flowers, inviting passing priests to enter and give their home a blessing.

---

that marked the Roman roads. There is also a section of mosaic flooring recovered from a local site, which dates from the 1st century AD.

A short walk from the museum are the **Termas Romanas** (Roman Baths; ☎ 253 278 455; Rua Dr Rocha Peixoto; ☒ 9am-12.30pm & 2-5.30pm Tue-Fri, 11am-5pm Sat & Sun), ruins of an extensive bathing complex dating from the 2nd century AD.

Festivals & Events

Semana Santa See boxed text, above.

Festas de São João A pre-Christian solstice bash dressed up to look like holy days, this festival still bursts with pagan energy. Held on 23 and 24 June, it features medieval folk plays, processions, dancing, bonfires, fireworks – and thousands of little pots of basil. Basil is the symbol of São João (John the Baptist), and traditionally people write poems to loved ones and then conceal them in little pots of the stuff. Locals also bust out the squeaky plastic hammers and whack each other mercilessly.

Sleeping

Reservations are essential during Semana Santa.

BUDGET

Campismo Parque da Ponte (☎ 253 273 355; sites per adult/tent/car €2.60/2.20/2.40; ☒ year-round) On a hillside 1.5km south of the centre, this basic municipal camping ground is little more than a clutch of weedy caravan pitches, but it does have nice vistas of the city. Buses 9, 18 and 56 from Avenida da Liberdade run four services hourly (fewer at weekends), stopping at the camp site.

Pousada da Juventude (☎ 253 616 163; www .pousadasjuventude.pt; Rua de Santa Margarida 6; dm €7, d with bathroom €22) Braga's rather institutional but lively youth hostel (with pool table), a 700m walk from the *turismo*, has frill-free,

eight-bed dorms as well as very basic en suite doubles – most with high ceilings and huge windows. Reception here is open from 8am to noon and from 6pm to midnight.

ourpick Casa Santa Zita (☎ 253 618 331; Rua São João 20; s/d €25/38) This high-ceilinged, impeccably kept pilgrim's lodge (look for the small tile plaque reading 'Sta Zita') has an air of palpable serenity. The sisters offer bright, spotless rooms, nice touches such as ironed cotton sheets, and excellent meals in the dining room. Very warmly recommended.

Grande Residência Avenida (☎ 253 609 020; www .residencialavenida.net; 2nd fl, Av da Liberdade 738; s/d from €26/33; ☒) Cobbled together from a few big apartments in an art-deco building, this friendly, family-run place offers carpeted, simply furnished accommodation. Rooms have frilly decor and vary widely in size and light; some have verandas.

Residencial São Marcos (☎/fax 253 277 177; Rua de São Marcos 80; s/d from €30/35; ☒) This welcoming place in a fine old town house has large, comfortable, recently refurbished rooms with high ceilings, parquet floors and a touch of grandeur in the furnishings. Good value.

MIDRANGE

Residencial dos Terceiros (☎ 253 270 466; www .terceiros.com; Rua dos Capelistas 85; s/d/tr €29/40/49) On a quiet pedestrianised street near Praça da República, Terceiros offers simple carpeted rooms with elderly mattresses. Front rooms are bright, and some sport small verandas; rooms in back are dark and depressing.

Albergaria Senhora-a-Branca (☎ 253 269 938; www.albergariasrabranca.pt; Largo da Senhora-a-Branca 58; s/d €38/50; ☒) A little removed from the city centre, this converted town house has well-kept, carpeted rooms (some on the small side), all with full bathroom and double-glazed windows. It's above a pastry shop (bonus), overlooking a busy little square.

Albergaria da Sé (☎ 253 214 502; www.albergaria-da-se.com.pt; Rua Gonçalo Pereira 39; s/d/ste €45/55/75; **P** **☒**) As the name promises, this simple, friendly, three-storey guest house is around the corner from the cathedral. It has dark wood floors, airy rooms and a scattering of *azulejos* to recommend it. The bright breakfast room and veranda are particularly pleasant.

Hotel-Residencial Dona Sofia (☎ 253 263 160; www.hoteldonasofia.com; Largo São João do Souto 131; s/d €45/60; **☒** **▣**) On a pretty, central square, prim little Dona Sofia has spotless, carpeted rooms of varying sizes, with all the midrange comforts, including very good beds. Aim for one of the airy rooms with big windows overlooking the square.

Albergaria Bracara Augusta (☎ 253 206 260; www.bracaraaugusta.com; Av Central 134; s/d/ste from €59/69/99; **☒** **▣**) This stylish, self-consciously upmarket place occupies a grand town house, and offers bright, modern rooms with parquet floors and French doors opening onto decorative balconies. It has an excellent breakfast buffet and one of Braga's top restaurants, serving classic Portuguese fare at midrange prices (with open-air dining by a gurgling fountain in back).

Eating

Some of Braga's best restaurants lie along a narrow alley (Largo da Praça Velha) just west of the cathedral.

Livraria Café (☎ 253 267 647; Av Central 118; mains €4; ⏱ 9am-7.30pm Mon-Sat) Tucked inside the bookshop Centésima Página (p426), this charming cafe serves a changing selection of tasty quiches (tomato with camembert, broccoli and brie) along with salads and desserts. Has outdoor tables in the pleasantly rustic garden.

Cozinha da Sé (☎ 253 277 343; Rua Dom Frei Caetano Brandão 95; mains €4; ⏱ lunch & dinner Tue-Sun) Contemporary artwork hangs from the exposed stone walls at this handsome Braga newcomer. Sé serves traditional, high-quality dishes (including one vegetarian selection), with flavourful standouts liked baked *bacalhau* (dried salt-cod) and *açorda de marisco* (seafood stew in bread bowl).

Salão de Chá Lusitana (Rua Justino Cruz 119; mains €4-6; ⏱ 8am-8pm) Next to sweet-smelling Jardim de Santa Bárbara, this sunny, well-preserved art-deco teashop is a local favourite with all, but especially ladies who lunch.

Churrasqueira da Sé (☎ 253 263 387; Rua Dom Paio Mendes 25; mains €6-8; ⏱ lunch & dinner) This no-nonsense restaurant is an extremely popular local dining spot, with an assortment of grilled dishes at low prices.

Anjo Verde (☎ 253 264 010; Largo da Praça Velha 21; mains €6-8; ⏱ lunch & dinner Mon-Sat; **Ⓥ**) Braga's best vegetarian restaurant serves up generous, elegantly presented plates in a lovely, airy dining room with ancient stone walls splashed with colour. Vegetarian lasagne, soy burgers and vegetable tarts are among the tasty selections.

Taberna do Felix (☎ 253 617 701; Largo da Praça Velha 17; dishes €7-10; ⏱ dinner Mon-Sat) Situated near the Arco da Porta Nova, this attractive country-style tavern prepares unusual Franco-Portuguese dishes; try the tapas or delicious *pataiscas* (fish fritters).

Café Astória (☎ 253 273 944; Praça da República; mains €7-17; ⏱ lunch & dinner) Set beneath a grand old portico, with tables on the plaza, Café Astória has a diverse menu of salads, pastas, grilled meats and seafood. Daily lunch specials (€8) are better value than the mains. The upstairs bar and dining room (with veranda seating) opens from 7pm to 2am.

ourpick **Taperia Palatu** (☎ 253 279 772; Rua Dom Afonso Henriques 35; tapas €8-12; ⏱ lunch & dinner Mon-Sat) A Spanish/Portuguese couple serves up delectable Spanish tapas and classic Portuguese dishes in a pleasantly minimalist dining room or the airy courtyard in front. Top picks include *gambas ao olho* (grilled shrimp), *secretos de porco preto* (wild boar) and grilled calamari.

O Alexandre (☎ 253 614 003; Campo das Hortas; mains €12-14; ⏱ lunch & dinner) A handsomely appointed dining room sets the stage for the top-notch cuisine at one of Braga's best Portuguese restaurants. Grilled meats, *bacalhau com nata* (baked codfish) and an excellent *cabrito assado* (roasted kid) are particularly recommended.

Adega Lusitana (☎ 253 215 147; Campo da Vinha 115; mains €17-20; ⏱ lunch & dinner) This new restaurant has a traditionally decorated dining room, a wine bar and a lush outdoor patio. Tapas, trusty *bacalhau* dishes and wild boar are among the varied offerings. Saturday nights feature live fado (reservations recommended), with DJs spinning some other nights.

The **mercado municipal** (municipal market; Praça do Comércio; ⏱ 8am-3pm Mon-Fri, 6am-1pm Sat) buzzes on weekdays and Saturday mornings. There are Pingo Doce supermarkets in the **Bragashopping centre** (⏱ 10am-11pm) and on Avenida da

Liberdade (🕒 9am to 9pm). Several fruit-and-vegetable shops are open during the day along Rua de São Marcos.

Drinking

Colinatrum Café (☎ 253 215 630; Rua dos Bombeiros Voluntários; 🕒 8am-2am) On a hill overlooking the countryside, this airy cafe is a fine meeting spot for a coffee or sunset cocktail. From the outdoor terrace, you'll have a splendid view of Bom Jesus do Monte.

Alla Scala (☎ 961915467; Praça Conde de Agrolongo; 🕒 8pm-midnight Mon-Thu, 8pm-1am Fri & Sat) Buried in a kind of bunker in the middle of an old square, this bar has a contemporary-lounge feel and features live music and the odd DJ from time to time.

Entertainment

PERFORMING ARTS

Espaço Cultural (☎ 963619816; Rua dos Chãos 14; 🕒 4-7pm & 9.30pm-2am) Just north of the Praça da República, this youthful new arts space hosts exhibitions, concerts, film screenings and other cultural fare. There's also a shop selling fair-trade items and a cafe where you can linger over a bite or a drink.

Theatro Circo de Braga (☎ 253 203 800; Av da Liberdade 697) One of the most dazzling theatres in the country reopened in late 2006 following a lengthy restoration. Inside the grand fin de siècle building, you can catch concerts, theatre and dance, with offerings ranging from the staid to the truly avant-garde.

CINEMAS

Bragashopping Cinema (☎ 253 217 819; Av Central) Has the usual Hollywood fare, with the occasional art film.

FOOTBALL

Now home to Braga's football team (Sporting Clube de Braga), the city's 30,000-seat Estádio Municipal de Braga was built to host the European Football Championships (Euro2004). It's 2km north of the centre off the northbound N 101; you can buy match tickets at the **team shop** (☎ 253 271 320; Av da Liberdade; 🕒 10am-1pm & 2.30-7pm Mon-Fri, 10am-1pm Sat) in the Centro Comercial Galeries do Bingo.

Getting Around

Because of one-way and pedestrian-only streets, driving in central Braga is difficult, and parking is maddening. There is a large, fee-charging lot

under Praça da República. You might also try side streets east of Avenida da Liberdade.

BUS

Braga has a centralised bus station that serves as a major regional hub. Within the Minho, **Transdev Norte/Arriva** (☎ 253 209 401) has at least eight buses per day to Viana do Castelo (€4, 1½ hours), Barcelos (€2.15, one hour), Guimarães (€2.60, 50 minutes) and Porto (€4.30, one hour), plus four per day to Campo do Gerês (€3.30, 1½ hours). Service drops by half at weekends.

Rede Expressos (☎ 253 209 401; www.rede-expressos .pt) has up to seven buses daily to Viseu (€12.30, three hours) and 12 to Lisbon (€18, 4½ hours).

Empresa Hoteleira do Gerês (☎ 253 262 033) also serves Rio Caldo (€3.60, 1¼ hours) and Campo do Gerês (€3.80, 1½ hours) about hourly during the week and six times on Saturday and Sunday.

CAR & MOTORCYCLE

Braga has a branch of **AVIC** (☎ 253 203 912; Rua Gabriel Pereira de Castro 28; 🕒 9am-12.30pm & 2.30-6.30pm Mon-Fri), a highly efficient agency for several car-rental companies, with prices starting at €30 per day.

The A3-IP1 motorway makes Braga an easy day trip from Porto. The N101 from Braga to Guimarães is congested and poorly marked.

TRAIN

Braga is at the end of a branch line from Nine and also within Porto's *suburbano* network, which means commuter trains travel every hour or so from Porto (€2.05, about one hour); don't waste €12.50 on an Alfa Pendular (AP) train.

Useful AP links include Coimbra (€18.50, 2¼ hours, five to seven daily) and Lisbon (€30, four hours, two to four daily).

AROUND BRAGA
Bom Jesus do Monte

The goal of legions of penitent pilgrims every year, Bom Jesus do Monte is one of the country's most recognisable icons. Lying 5km east of central Braga just off the N103, this sober neoclassical church, completed in 1811, stands atop a forested hill that offers grand sunset views across Braga. However, most people don't come for the church or even the view. They come to see what lies below: the extraordinary baroque staircase, **Escadaria do Bom Jesus**.

The photogenic climb is made up of various tiered staircases, dating from different decades of the 18th century. The lowest is lined with chapels representing the Stations of the Cross and eerily lifelike terracotta figurines. **Escadaria dos Cinco Sentidos** (Stairway of the Five Senses) features allegorical fountains with water gurgling from ears, eyes, nose and mouth of different statues. Highest is the **Escadaria das Três Virtudes** (Stairway of the Three Virtues), with chapels and fountains representing Faith, Hope and Charity.

The area around the church has become something of a resort, with sumptuous hotels, tennis courts and flower gardens. It's choked with tourists on summer weekends.

SLEEPING

Reservations are recommended in summer.

Grande Hotel (☎ 253 281 222; grandehotelbomjesus@ gmail.com; Largo Mãe da Água Bom Jesus, Tenões; d from €55; P 🔀) This handsome new hotel has spacious modern rooms with ruby-red carpeting and verandas with magnificent views. It's 1km from the church (at the fork before reaching Bom Jesus, veer left).

Hotel do Elevador (☎ 253 603 400; www.hoteisbom jesus.web.pt; Bom Jesus do Monte; d €99; P 🔀 🖥 🍴) This modern hotel offers fairly plush rooms, many with gorgeous mountain views, and has a restaurant (mains €10 to €16).

Castello Bom Jesus (☎ 253 676 566; www.armilar worldusa.com; N103; d from €120; P 🍴) With fantastic views over the area, this neo-Gothic castle has whimsical gardens, gazebos, grottoes, pool and peacocks. The grand rooms, most with views of Braga and the surrounding mountains, are a worthy splurge.

The same company that operates Hotel do Elevador (above) runs one midrange option and two other high-end hotels in the same area:

Hotel do Lago (☎ 253 603 020; Bom Jesus do Monte; d €65; P 🔀 🖥)

Hotel do Parque (☎ 253 603 470; Bom Jesus do Monte; d €99; P 🔀 🖥 🍴)

Hotel do Templo (☎ 253 603 610; Bom Jesus do Monte; d €99; P 🔀 🖥 🍴)

EATING

Aside from the hotel restaurants, eating options are scarce.

Esplanada Bom Jesus (☎ 253 676 695; mains €3-4; 🕙 10am-8pm) Near the top of the stairs, this outdoor place serves sandwiches, hamburgers, ice cream and other basic snack food.

Restaurante Casavelha (☎ 253 281 222; Lugar Mãe da Água; mains €9-11; 🕙 lunch & dinner Tue-Sun) For something a little more satisfying, this new restaurant next door to the Grande Hotel (left) offers good traditional Portuguese dishes, with live music on Friday and Saturday nights.

GETTING THERE & AWAY

City bus 2 runs from Braga's Avenida da Liberdade to the bottom of the Bom Jesus steps (€1.30, 20 minutes) – the end of the line – every half-hour all day (hourly on Sunday). From here you can hoof it up the steps, or hop aboard the newly restored **ascensor** (funicular; ☎ 253 281 222; Lugar Mãe da Água; 1 way €1.20; 🕙 8am-8pm), which whisks visitors up to the top every half-hour. Alternatively, a taxi from central Braga to the top of the steps costs around €12 to €15.

BARCELOS

pop 21,000 / elev 100m

The Minho is famous for its sprawling outdoor markets, but the largest, oldest and most celebrated is the Feira de Barcelos, held every Thursday in this ancient town on the banks of the Rio Cávado. Tourist buses now arrive by the dozen, spilling their contents into the already brimming marketplace. Even if you don't come on a Thursday, you'll find that Barcelos has a pleasant medieval core, with its old stone towers perched over the river. It also harbours an ancient but still-thriving pottery tradition.

Orientation

Campo da República (Campo da Feira), an immense shady square where the market is held, is approximately 1km southwest of the train station, and around 2km northwest from the bus station. On market day (Thursday), most buses stop alongside the Campo da República. The medieval town is on the slopes above the river, just southwest of the Campo.

Information

Hospital Santa Maria Maior (☎ 253 809 200; Campo da República)

Police station (☎ 253 802 570; Av Dr Sidónio Pais)

Post office (☎ 253 811 711; Av Dr Sidónio Pais; 🕙 8.30am-6.30pm Mon-Fri, 9am-12.30pm Sat)

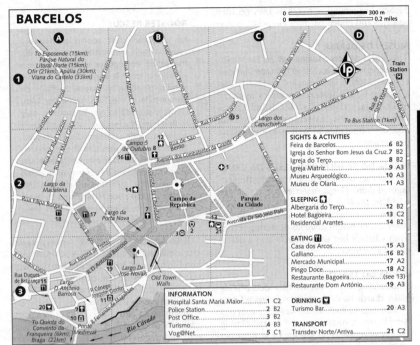

BARCELOS

THE MINHO

Turismo (☎ 253 811 882; turismo@cm-barcelos.pt; Largo Dr Jose Novais 8; ✆ 9.30am-6pm Mon-Fri, 10am-1pm & 2-5pm Sat, 10am-1pm & 2-4pm Sun Mar-Sep, 9.30am-5.30pm Mon-Fri, 10am-1pm & 2-5pm Sat Oct-Feb) Free internet access (two computers available).

Vog@Net (☎ 253 812 799; Rua Francisco Torres; per hr €1.50; ✆ 9am-midnight) A backstreet games hall with internet access.

Sights

FEIRA DE BARCELOS

You'll need at least a couple of hours to see all the goods in this sprawling market. Despite attracting travellers, the **market** (Campo da República; ✆ 7am-6pm Thu) retains its rural soul. Villagers hawk everything from scrawny chickens to hand-embroidered linen, and Roma women bellow for business in the clothes section. Snack on sausages and homemade bread as you wander among the brass cowbells, hand-woven baskets and carved ox yokes.

Pottery is what outsiders come to see, especially the yellow-dotted *louça de Barcelos* ware and the gaudy figurines à la Rosa Ramalho, a local potter (known as the Grandma Moses of Portuguese pottery) whose work put Barcelos on the map in the 1950s. The trademark Barcelos cockerel motif (see boxed text, p434) is everywhere.

MUSEU ARQUEOLÓGICO & AROUND

On a ledge above Barcelos' 14th-century bridge over the Rio Cávado are the roofless ruins of the former palace of the counts of Barcelos and dukes of Bragança. Practically obliterated by the 1755 earthquake, they now serve as an alfresco **archaeological museum** (admission free; ✆ 9am-5.30pm).

Among the mysterious phallic stones, Roman columns and medieval caskets, you'll find a 14th-century stone cross, the Crucifix O Senhor do Galo, depicting the gentleman of the cockerel story and said to have been commissioned by the lucky pilgrim himself. Near the entrance is a late-Gothic *pelourinho* (stone pillory) topped by a granite lantern.

Eastward along the bluffs is a remnant of the medieval **town walls**.

Peek inside the **igreja matriz** (✆ 10am-5.30pm Tue-Fri, 9.30-11.45am & 3.30-7.30pm Sat & Sun), the stocky Gothic parish church behind the

Museu Arqueológico, to see its 18th-century *azulejos* and gilded baroque chapels.

MUSEU DE OLARIA

This good **pottery museum** (☎ 253 824 741; Rua Cónego Joaquim Gaiolas; adult/under 14yr/under 26yr/senior €1.40/free/0.70/0.70, Sun morning free; ☺ 10am-12.30pm & 2-5.30pm Tue-Sun) features ceramics in many of Portugal's regional styles, from Azores pots to Barcelos, Estremoz and Miranda do Corvo figurines, as well as some striking pewterware.

IGREJA DO SENHOR BOM JESUS DA CRUZ

On a corner of the Campo, this arresting octagonal **church** (Templo do Bom Jesus; ☺ 8.30am-noon & 2-5.30pm Wed-Mon), built in 1704, overlooks a garden of obelisks. Its baroque interior includes some bright *azulejos* depicting scenes from Christ's last days; there's also a grand gilded altarpiece.

IGREJA DO TERÇO

Smothering the walls of this deceptively plain **church** (Av dos Combatentes da Grande Guerra; ☺ 10am-noon & 2-4pm), which was once part of a Benedictine monastery, is an overwhelming display of *azulejos* on the life of St Benedict by the 18th-century master António de Oliveira Bernardes. In what little space escapes the *azulejos,* a carved, gilded pulpit and a ceiling with other saintly scenes compete for attention.

Festivals & Events

Festa das Cruzes (Festival of the Crosses) For one week, in the first week of May, this festival turns Barcelos into a fairground of flags, flowers, coloured lights and open-air concerts. The biggest days are generally 1 to 3 May.

Festival de Folclore This celebration of folk song and dance in this tradition-loving town takes place on the last weekend in July or the first weekend in August.

Sleeping

Most travellers visit Barcelos as a day trip from Porto or Braga, but accommodation is always tight on Wednesday and Thursday in the run-up to the market.

Residencial Arantes (☎ 253 811 326; residencial arantes@sapo.pt; Av da Liberdade 35; d €40) Fronting Campo da República, this friendly, family-run spot offers clean, tidy rooms with parquet floors. Some rooms have nice views over the green plaza (and market tents on Thursday).

ROOSTER RESCUE

His colourful crest adorns a thousand souvenir stalls, but just how and why did the proud Portuguese cockerel become a national icon? It seems that a humble pilgrim, plodding his way to Santiago de Compostela in the 16th (some say 14th) century, stopped to rest in Barcelos, only to find himself wrongfully accused of theft and then swiftly condemned to be hanged. The outraged pilgrim told the judge that the roast on the judge's dinner table would affirm the pilgrim's innocence. As it would happen, just as the judge was about to tuck in, the cooked cock commenced to crow. The pilgrim, needless to say, was set free.

Hotel Bagoeira (☎ 253 809 500; www.bagoeira.com; Av Dr Sidónio País 495; s/d from €45/55) A business-class hotel just across from the market site, with tastefully done-up, contemporary digs with carpeting and shiny new bathrooms. Prices rise significantly in August.

Albergaria do Terço (☎ 253 808 380; www.arterco .com; Edifício do Terço; d €55; Ⓟ ✗) This sleek, modern, midrange option sits atop its namesake shopping centre (take the lift round the back). The stylish, squeaky-clean rooms feature dark wood floors, tiny verandas and furnishings straight out of an Ikea catalogue.

Quinta do Convento da Franqueira (☎ 253 831 606; www.quintadafranqueira.com; s/d/apt €80/110/110; ☺ May-Oct; Ⓟ ✗) Six kilometres from Barcelos, south off the N205, lies this remarkable 16th-century convent turned vineyard and up-market inn. The complex includes cloisters, a bell tower and a gatehouse (now a self-catering apartment). Rooms are prim, antique affairs, and all have garden views, while the surrounding property yields a fine *vinho verde* (a young, slightly sparkling wine). Minimum two-night stay.

Eating & Drinking

Casa dos Arcos (☎ 253 811 975; Rua Duques de Bragança 185; mains €6-9; ☺ lunch & dinner Tue-Sun) Set in an old stone-walled dining room, this cosy restaurant has been around for 50 years. All the traditional favourites are here, including eight cod dishes, suckling pig and *picanha* (rump steak).

Restaurante Dom António (☎ 253 812 285; Rua Dom António Barroso 85; mains €7-8; ☺ lunch & dinner) Down a short passageway from the busy pedestrianised street outside, this locally popular choice has lots of inexpensive daily plates. House specialities include roast kid and grilled game meat, including wild boar and deer.

Galliano (☎ 253 815 104; Campo 5 de Outubro 20; mains €8-14; ⏲ lunch & dinner) Near the Campo da República, Galliano serves up some of Barcelos' best cuisine. The menu features regional delicacies like *barrosã grelhado* (grilled steak), *costeletas* (ribs) and other grilled meats, as well as seafood and salads. Lunch specials (€7) are excellent value. There are pavement tables and an airy, elegant dining room.

Restaurante Bagoeira (☎ 253 811 236; Av Dr Sidónio País 495; dishes €9-16; ⏲ lunch & dinner) With an open kitchen and attractive dining room, this place serves regional specialities made with the best fresh ingredients, including very good grilled meats and fish. The staff deal admirably with the jovial chaos of market day.

Two stops for self-caterers are the **mercado municipal** (Largo da Madalena; ⏲ 7am-7pm Mon-Fri, 7am-1pm Sat) and a nearby **Pingo Doce** (Rua Filipa Borges 223) supermarket.

Barcelos has little nightlife to speak of, but you could while away summer evenings on the picturesque, riverside patio of **Turismo Bar** (Rua Duques de Bragança; ⏲ 11.30am-3am).

Getting There & Away
Parking is very tight on Thursdays, so avoid driving if you can. Other days, look for spots around Campo da República.

BUS
There's a new, centralised bus terminal 1km east of the centre. Many buses also depart from Av Dr Sidónio País across from the Campo da República. Check times at the **Transdev Norte/Arriva** (☎ 253 209 401; Av Dr Sidónio País 445) office, which has at least eight buses to Braga (€2.15, one hour) on weekdays, and about four on weekends. It also has services to Ponte de Lima (€3, one hour).

Caetano Cascão Linhares (☎ 253 811 571) has a service every hour or two to Braga and Porto (€3.80, two hours) daily, and to Viana do Castelo (€3, one hour). Service drops to about four daily on weekends.

TRAIN
Barcelos station is on the Porto–Valença do Minho line. There are three to five direct trains a day to/from Porto (€3.75, 55 minutes), and commuter trains every hour or two that change at Nine (€3.20, 1¼ hours). There is similar service via Nine to Braga (€2.60 to €3.60, 45 to 60 minutes).

AROUND BARCELOS
Parque Natural do Litoral Norte
Embracing the Braga district's entire 18km of seashore, this protected area was set aside in order to safeguard its unstable sand dunes, delicate vegetation and the remnants of an ancient way of life – symbolised by the Minho's photogenic if decrepit coastal windmills.

The partnership of land and sea is illustrated by the area's agricultural fields immediately behind the dunes, watered by ocean spray and fertilised with algae and crustaceans from the sea. However, it's an area that continues to be nibbled away by the sea on one side and by humans on the other.

Attempts are being made to stabilise the dunes with fencing and plants, and access is largely restricted to elevated walkways. For more information, contact the **area office** (☎ 253 965 830; pnln@icnb.pt; Rua 1 de Dezembro 65, Esposende; ⏲ 9am-12.30pm & 2-5.30pm Mon-Fri).

SLEEPING
Basic accommodation is available at Esposende, some 15km west of Barcelos, and at Ofir and Apúlia.

At Fão, 3km south of Esposende, there's a level, shaded **camping ground** (☎ 253 981 777; cccb@esoterica.pt; Rua São João de Deus; sites per adult/tent/car €3.40/3.45/2.60; ⏲ year-round; ♿) with hot showers, laundry, services for travellers with disabilities, and a bar-restaurant. There's also an attractive pink villa-turned-youth hostel, **Foz do Cávado Pousada da Juventude** (☎ 253 981 790; www.pousadasjuventude.pt; Alameda Bom Jesus; dm/d/apt €13/38/70; P 🖳), which has bikes for hire, a grassy garden, proximity to the beach, and an outdoor pool. Reserve well in advance during summer and holidays.

GETTING THERE & AWAY
AV Minho (☎ 253 962 369) has three to five buses daily that run to/from Porto (€3, one hour) on their way to Viana do Castelo (€2.70, 40 minutes), with two to three buses continuing on to Valença do Minho and Monção. All of these buses make stops at towns along the coast.

THE MINHO

THE MINHO

GUIMARÃES

pop 54,000 / elev 400m

The proud birthplace of the Portuguese kingdom, Guimarães has beautifully preserved its illustrious past. Its medieval centre is a warren of labyrinthine lanes and picturesque plazas framed by 14th-century edifices, while on an adjacent hill stands a 1000-year-old keep and, next to it, the massive palace built by the first duke of Bragança in the 15th century. Guimarães' glory was officially recognised in 2001, when Unesco declared its old centre a World Heritage Site. It has also been chosen by Portugal to be the European capital of culture in 2012.

The city, however, is more than just the sum total of its historical treasures. Guimarães is a university town, and its students lend much vitality to the place – particularly during the celebratory Festas de Cidade e Gualterianas (p439) in August.

For visitors, the old streets of Guimarães are great for exploring, and its cafe-filled plazas, atmospheric guest houses and delightful restaurants make for a rewarding overnight stay.

History

Guimarães is the famed birthplace of Afonso Henriques, the first independent king of Portugal. He was born here in 1110 and later used the city to launch the main thrust of the Reconquista against the Moors. Guimarães caught the royal eye as early as AD 840, when Alfonso II of León convened a council of bishops here, but it only started to grow in the 10th century after the powerful Countess Mumadona Dias, widowed aunt of another king of León, gave it her attention, founding a monastery here and building a castle to protect it. Henri of Burgundy chose Guimarães for his court, as did his son Afonso Henriques until 1143, when he shifted the capital to Coimbra.

Orientation

Old Guimarães is in the northeast of the modern city. Most points of interest lie within a demarcated tourist zone stretching south from the castle to an arc of public gardens at Alameda de São Dâmaso. Guimarães' commercial heart is Largo do Toural.

The main *turismo* is about 1km north up Avenida Dom Afonso Henriques from the train station. It is a 1km slog up Avenida Conde de Margaride from the main bus station, which is beneath the Centro Comercial Guimarães Shopping.

Information

There's free wi-fi in the main squares.

Espaço Internet (Praça de Santiago; ☎ 9am-12.30pm & 2-10pm Mon-Fri, to 7pm Sat, to noon Sun) Free internet access. It's up a flight of stairs near Largo da Oliveira.

Hospital (☎ 253 512 612; Rua dos Cotileros, Creixomil) Opposite the bus station.

Livraria Ideal (☎ 253 422 750; Rua da Rainha 34; ☎ 9am-1pm & 3-7pm Mon-Fri, 9am-1pm Sat) The city's best bookshop.

Police station (☎ 253 519 598; Av Dr Alfredo Pimenta)

Post office (Largo Navarros de Andrade 27; ☎ 8.30am-6.30pm Mon-Fri, 9am-12.30pm Sat)

Turismo (☎ 253 518 790; Praça de Santiago; ☎ 9.30am-6.30pm Mon-Fri, 10am-6pm Sat, 10am-1pm Sun)

Sights

PAÇO DOS DUQUES

Looming over the medieval city, the crenellated towers and brick chimneys of the **Paço dos Duques** (Ducal Palace; ☎ 253 412 273; adult/under 14yr/under 26yr/senior €4/free/1.60/2, 9am-12.30pm Sun free; ☎ 9.30am-5.30pm Mon-Fri, 9.30am-6.30pm Sat & Sun) have pushed the palace into the foreground on Guimarães' hilltop. Built in 1401 by a later and equally famous Afonso (the future first Duke of Bragança), it fell into ruin after his powerful family upped sticks to Vila Viçosa in the Alentejo (p256). Pompously restored – often too perfectly – as a presidential residence for Salazar, it still contains a clutch of original treasures. Visitors can wander freely through the rooms, which house a collection of Flemish tapestries, furniture of Indo-Portuguese manufacture, porcelain, weapons from the 15th and 16th centuries, and a chapel with glittering stained-glass windows. The real treasures, however, are reproductions: four enormous tapestries originally made by Pastrana, which relate various episodes in the Portuguese attempt to conquer North Africa.

CASTELO & IGREJA DE SÃO MIGUEL DO CASTELO

Built in the 11th century and still in fine form, the seven-towered **castle** (☎ 253 412 273; admission castle keep €1.50, Sun morning free; ☎ 9.30am-12.30pm & 2-5.30pm Tue-Sun) is thought to be the birthplace of the great man himself, Afonso Henriques. It's free to walk around the windswept ram-

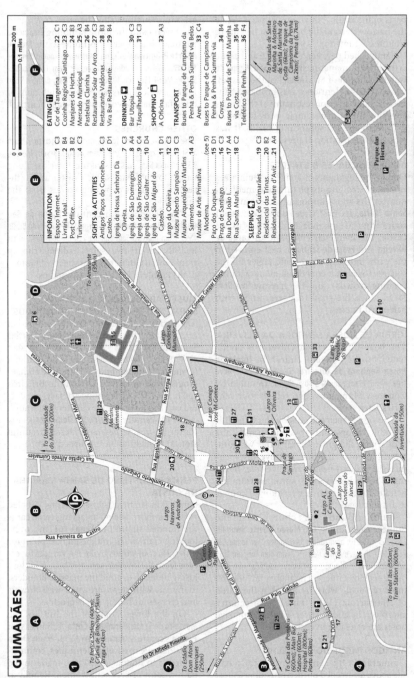

GUIMARÃES

THE MINHO

INFORMATION	
Espaço Internet...........................	1 C3
Livraria Ideal..............................	2 B4
Post Office.................................	3 B2
Turismo.....................................	4 C3

SIGHTS & ACTIVITIES	
Antigos Paços do Concelho.........	5 C3
Castelo.....................................	6 D1
Igreja de Nossa Senhora Da	
Oliveira..................................	7 C3
Igreja de São Domingos...............	8 A4
Igreja de São Francisco................	9 C4
Igreja de São Gualter..................	10 D4
Igreja de São Miguel do	
Castelo...................................	11 D1
Largo da Oliveira.......................	12 C3
Museu Alberto Sampaio...............	13 C3
Museu Arqueológico Martins	
Sarmento................................	14 A3
Museu de Arte Primitiva	
Moderna................................	(see 5)
Paço dos Duques.........................	15 D1
Praça de Santiago.......................	16 C3
Rua Dom João I..........................	17 A4
Rua Santa Maria..........................	18 C2

SLEEPING	
Pousada de Guimarães................	19 C3
Residencial das Trinas..................	20 B2
Residencial Mestre d'Aviz.............	21 A4

EATING	
Cor de Tangerina.........................	22 C1
Cozinha Regional Santiago...........	23 C3
Manjares da Horta.......................	24 B3
Mercado Municipal......................	25 A3
Pastelaria Clarinha......................	26 B4
Restaurante Solar do Arco............	27 C3
Restaurante Valdonas..................	28 B3
Vira Bar Restaurante...................	29 B4

DRINKING	
Bar Utopia.................................	30 C3
Tásquilhado Bar..........................	31 C3

SHOPPING	
A Oficina...................................	32 A3

TRANSPORT	
Buses to Parque de Campismo da	
Penha & Penha Summit via	
Ares......................................	33 C4
Buses to Parque de Campismo da	
Penha & Penha Summit via	
Covas....................................	34 B4
Buses to Pousada de Santa Marinha	
via Costa...............................	35 B4
Teleférico da Penha.....................	36 F4

parts of the castle, but you must pay to scale the narrow steps to the bird's-nest heights of Countess Mumadona's keep.

Sandwiched between the palace and castle is the little Romanesque **Igreja de São Miguel do Castelo** (Church of St Michael of the Castle), where Afonso Henriques was probably baptised. Under its floor rest many of the king's companions-at-arms, their graves marked with worn crosses, spears and shields. It was closed for restoration at press time.

ANCIENT SQUARES & STREETS

One of the highlights of a visit to Guimarães is simply strolling its picturesque medieval quarter. Its most important areas are **Rua Santa Maria**, its first street and the ancient route from Mumadona's monastery to the castle; the medieval ensemble of **Largo da Oliveira** and **Praça de Santiago**, best enjoyed in the early morning before cafe tables fill the squares (or with a cool drink along with the evening crowds); and the narrow **Rua Dom João I**, once the road to Porto, lined with balconied houses.

IGREJA DE NOSSA SENHORA DA OLIVEIRA

The beautiful Largo da Oliveira is dominated by the convent church of **Igreja de Nossa Senhora da Oliveira** (Our Lady of the Olive Tree; 7.15am-noon & 3.30-7.30pm), founded by Countess Mumadona and rebuilt four centuries later.

The odd **monument** outside the church is a Gothic canopy and cross said to mark the spot where the great Wamba the Visigoth, victorious over the Suevi, drove his spear into the ground beside an olive tree, refusing to reign unless a tree sprouted from the handle. In true legendary fashion, of course, it did just that.

Built around the church's serene Romanesque cloister, the **Museu Alberto Sampaio** (☎ 253 423 910; adult/under 14yr/under 26yr/senior €3/free/1.50/1.50, Sun morning free; 10am-6pm Tue-Sun) has an excellent collection of ecclesiastical art and other religious finery. Highlights include the tunic reputedly worn by João I at the Battle of Aljubarrota (1385) and a 14th-century altarpiece in gilded silver. English-language notes are available in each room.

ANTIGOS PAÇOS DO CONCELHO

Guimarães' 14th-century former town hall sits above an arcaded portico providing a most graceful communication between cosy Largo da Oliveira and the more rambling Praça de Santiago. It also serves as home to the **Museu de Arte Primitiva Moderna** (Museum of Modern Primitive Art; ☎ 253 414 186; admission free; 9am-12.30pm & 2-5.30pm Mon-Fri Sep-Jun, 10.30am-12.30pm & 3-6pm Sat & Sun Jul & Aug), which hosts temporary exhibitions of often fascinating works by self-taught artists.

OTHER CHURCHES

The 13th-century **Igreja de São Francisco** (Church of St Francis of Assisi; 9.30am-noon & 3-5pm Tue-Sat, 9.30am-1pm Sun) has a striking interior, along with a lovely Renaissance cloister and 18th-century *azulejos* depicting scenes from the saint's life.

The slender 18th-century **Igreja de São Gualter** (Church of St Walter; Largo da República do Brasil; 7.30am-noon & 3-5pm Mon-Sat, 7.30am-noon Sun), with its 19th-century twin spires and huge run-up from central Guimarães, has the most harmonious facade of all the city's churches.

MUSEU ARQUEOLÓGICO MARTINS SARMENTO & IGREJA DE SÃO DOMINGOS

The curious collection of mostly Celtiberian artefacts of the **Museu Arqueológico Martins Sarmento** (☎ 253 415 969; Rua Paio Galvão; admission €2; 9.30am-noon & 2-5pm Tue-Sun) is housed in a former convent and named after the archaeologist who excavated Citânia de Briteiros (p440) in 1875. Hefty stone artefacts are dotted carelessly around the cloister of the adjacent 14th-century **Igreja de São Domingos** – look for the impressive *pedras formosas* (beautiful stones) thought to have adorned Celtiberian bathhouses in the surrounding region.

PENHA & MOSTEIRO DE SANTA MARINHA DA COSTA

Some 7km southeast up a twisting, cobbled road or a short ride on an ageing cable car is the wooded summit of **Penha** (617m), overlooking Guimarães and the highest point for miles. Its cool woods make it a wonderful escape from the city and summer heat. Kids love losing themselves amid the massive boulders, many cut with steps, crowned with flowers and crosses, or hiding secret grottoes.

On the lower slopes of the hill lies the **Mosteiro de Santa Marinha da Costa**, 1.5km east of Penha's centre. It dates from 1154, when Dona Mafalda, wife of Afonso Henriques, commissioned it to honour a vow she made to the patron saint of pregnant women. Rebuilt in the 18th century, it's now a flagship Pousada de Portugal (right). Nonguests can still snoop around the chapel and gardens.

The easiest route to the monastery and *pousada* (upmarket inn) is on municipal bus 51 or 52 to São Roque (€1.30, every half-hour Monday to Saturday, hourly on Sunday), which departs from the south side of the public gardens; get off at Costa. But the finest way to the top is on the **Teleférico da Penha** (cable car; ☎ 253 515 085; return €3.80; ◷ 10.30am-6.30pm Mon-Fri, 10.30am-7.30pm Sat, Sun & holidays May-Sep, 10am-5pm Fri-Sun Oct-Apr), which starts from Parque das Hortas, 600m east of Guimarães' old centre.

Festivals & Events

Encontros de Primavera This series of classical and early music concerts is held at historical venues in late May and June.

Festas de Cidade e Gualterianas (www.aoficina.pt) Marked by a free fair (held in Guimarães since 1452 to honour its patron saint), this festival also features folk dancing, rock concerts, bullfights, fireworks and parades. It takes place on the first weekend in August.

Jazz Festival One of the country's top festivals, this jazz extravaganza runs for about three weeks in November.

Sleeping

BUDGET & MIDRANGE

Parque de Campismo da Penha (☎ 253 515 912; www.turipenha.pt; sites per adult/tent/car €2.50/2/2; ◷ May–mid-Sep; ⊛) With a terrific position near the top of Penha, this is a well-equipped and densely wooded municipal camping ground. It has an outdoor pool for hot days and a TV room with a fireplace for cool nights. Take the *teleférico* (see above) to get there.

Pousada da Juventude (☎ 253 421 380; www.pousadasjuventude.pt; Largo da Cidade; dm/d/apt €13/32/60; ⊛) In the home of a prosperous factory owner, this terrific hostel has hardwood floors, clean, bright dorms and doubles that are downright stylish. It also has kitchen and laundry facilities, and two wheelchair-accessible rooms.

Residencial das Trinas (☎ 253 517 358; www.residencialtrinas.com; Rua das Trinas 29; s/d €25/30; ⊛) This renovated house in the historical zone offers likeable little rooms with double glazing, satellite TV and patterned ceramic-tile floors. You won't get a better position for the price.

Residencial Mestre d'Aviz (☎ 253 422 770; r_mestre_aviz@iol.pt; Rua Dom João I 40; s/d/tr €25/38/50; ⊛) Fronted by curlicue ironwork, this renovated town house has small, somewhat worn rooms with wood floors and sparse furnishings. It

has slick modern touches, a stone-slab bar and minimal street traffic on the narrow old lane outside.

Hotel Ibis (☎ 253 424 900; www.ibishotel.com; Av Conde de Margaride 12; d €37, incl breakfast €47; ⊛) Just across from the bus station, the Hotel Ibis has small, simple rooms that are comfortably outfitted, if a bit on the boxy side. Double-pane windows ensure quiet despite the noisy avenue below.

TOP END

Pousada de Guimarães (☎ 253 514 157; www.pousadas.pt; d from €170; Ⓟ ⊛) Offering the most atmospheric stay in medieval Guimarães, this small, elegant *pousada* is set in a converted manor house overlooking the Largo da Oliveira. The spacious rooms are set with wide plank floors, dark-panelled wood and classical furnishings. Guests here can use the beautifully sited pool at the Pousada de Santa Marinha (below).

ourpick Pousada de Santa Marinha (☎ 253 511 249; www.pousadas.pt; d from €230; Ⓟ ⊛ ⊛) This is the real deal: history, beauty and an unbeatable location. A restored former monastery overlooking the city from the slopes of Penha, the *pousada* is now a far cry from past frugality. Guests may wander round the cloister past dribbling fountains and masterful *azulejos*, and sleep in now-luxurious converted monks' cells. For transport information, see opposite.

Eating

Pastelaria Clarinha (☎ 253 516 513; Largo do Toural 86; pastries €1; ◷ 7am-midnight Tue-Sun) Guimarães' best pastry shop has a window of fresh-baked tarts and cakes to tempt passers-by. There are a few pavement tables and heavenly *toucinho do ceu* (almond cake).

Cozinha Regional Santiago (☎ 253 516 669; Praça de Santiago 16; half-portions €5-8; ◷ lunch & dinner Mon-Sat) Among the handful of restaurants sprinkled about the central plaza, Santiago always seems to pack a crowd. There's outdoor seating, an extensive menu and good-value lunch specials (around €7).

ourpick Cor de Tangerina (☎ 253 542 009; Largo Martins Sarmento 89; mains €6-10; ◷ 11am-11pm Tue-Sat, 11am-7pm Sun; Ⓥ) This charming restaurant sits above a co-op and whips up a good selection of cuisine you won't find elsewhere in Guimarães. Among the standouts: vegetarian pizza, carrot and orange soup, and vegetable fusilli. Changing art exhibitions decorate the walls, while the garden (with tangerine tree) makes a sweet setting for a pick-me-up.

Manjares da Horta (☎ 253 413 277; Rua João Lopes Faria 71; mains €6-10; ☯ lunch & dinner; **V**) A splendid new addition to Guimarães, this restaurant serves tasty vegetarian dishes (vegie lasagne, crêpes, tofu *feijoada*) and fresh juices, as well as meat and fish plates. Dine in the airy upstairs dining room or on the back patio.

Vira Bar Restaurant (☎ 253 518 427; Alameda de São Dâmaso 27; mains €8-12; ☯ lunch & dinner Tue-Sun) This genteel venue features a vaulted ceiling and stained-glass windows. Specialities include wood-grilled meat and fish and *sopa de nabos* (turnip soup).

ourpick **Restaurante Valdonas** (☎ 253 511 411; Rua Val de Donas 4; mains €9-13; ☯ lunch & dinner) A long wine list, chalk-white minimalist decor, and a changing menu based on market-fresh availability have generated buzz at this stylish restaurant. It's set in a 17th-century manor house, with outdoor seating in the courtyard.

Restaurante Solar do Arco (☎ 253 513 072; Rua Santa Maria 50; mains €10-20; ☯ lunch & dinner Mon-Sat, lunch Sun; ✇) With a handsomely panelled dining room under a graceful arcade, this is a top central choice. Portuguese classics made with straight-from-the-market ingredients add to the allure.

Self-caterers will like the **mercado municipal** (Rua Paio Galvão; ☯ 7am-1pm Mon-Sat).

Drinking & Entertainment

One of a swath of bar-hopping venues in the historic centre, the cosy, ever-popular **Tásquilhado Bar** (Rua Santa Maria 42; ☯ 2pm-midnight Sun-Tue, to 2am Wed-Sat) plays alternative sounds and offers enticing drink specials during the week. Another bar with a more mainstream pop-and-rock bias is **Bar Utopia** (Praça de Santiago; ☯ 9am-midnight Mon-Sat).

Shopping

Today, as in medieval times, Guimarães is renowned for its linen. Other crafts contributing to its prosperity are embroidery, worked gold and silver, and pottery. For quality work by Guimarães artisans, visit the municipal outlet **A Oficina** (☎ 253 515 250; Rua Paio Galvão 11; ☯ 9am-6pm Mon-Sat).

A big flea market takes over Praça de Santiago and Largo da Oliveira on the first Saturday of each month.

Getting There & Away

There is street parking in front of the Convento do Carmo at the foot of the Paço dos Duques.

BUS

Transdev/Arriva (☎ 253 423 500) has buses leaving at least hourly for Braga (€2.60, 50 minutes) on Monday through Saturday, and eight buses on Sunday. It also has services to Porto (€4.50, 50 minutes) running approviximately hourly on weekdays but less often at weekends, and to Lisbon (€15.50, five hours) daily. **Rodonorte** (☎ 253 514 476; www.rodonorte.pt) heads for Amarante (€6.10, one hour, two to five daily), Vila Real (€7.40, two hours, two to six daily – but none Saturday) and Bragança (€12.20, four hours, one to four daily).

TRAIN

Guimarães is the terminus of a branch of Porto's wide *suburbano* network. Commuter trains potter out to Guimarães from Porto (€2.15, 80 minutes) 11 to 15 times daily. Try to avoid the once-daily *intercidade* (express) train, which costs €10.

AROUND GUIMARÃES

Citânia de Briteiros

One of the most evocative archaeological sites in Portugal, **Citânia de Briteiros** (admission incl museum €3; ☯ 9am-6pm), 15km north of Guimarães, is the largest of a liberal scattering of northern Celtic hill settlements, called *citânias* (fortified villages), dating back at least 2500 years. It's also likely that this sprawling 3.8-hectare site, inhabited from about 300 BC to AD 300, was the Celtiberians' last stronghold against the invading Romans.

When archaeologist Dr Martins Sarmento excavated the site in 1875, he discovered the foundations and ruins of more than 150 rectangular, circular and elliptical stone huts, linked by paved paths and a water distribution system, all cocooned by multiple protective walls. Highlights include two reconstructed huts that evoke what it was like to live in the settlement, and – further back down the hill – a bathhouse with a strikingly patterned stone doorway.

Ask at the entrance for a detailed plan, keyed to markers around the site, with information in French and English.

Some artefacts are on display in the Museu Arqueológico Martins Sarmento in Guimarães (p438), but the **Museu da Cultura Castreja** (Museum on Pre-Roman Culture; ☎ 253 478 952; Solar da Ponte, Briteiros Salvador; ◷ 9.30am-12.30pm & 2-6pm Tue-Sun) also has important artefacts from various sites, housed in Sarmento's 18th- and 19th-century manor house. It's about 2km back down the hill towards Guimarães in the village of Briteiros Salvador.

GETTING THERE & AWAY

From Guimarães, **Transdev/Arriva** (☎ 253 516 229) has about six weekday buses that pass within 1km of the site; get off between the towns of Briteiros Salvador and Santa Leocádia. Check with the Guimarães *turismo* (p436) or at the bus station for current schedule information.

COASTAL & NORTHERN MINHO

VIANA DO CASTELO

pop 37,500

The jewel of the Costa Verde, Viana do Castelo is blessed with both an appealing medieval centre and lovely beaches just outside the city. The old quarters seem downright sophisticated, with leafy, 19th-century boulevards and narrow lanes crowded with Manueline manors and rococo palaces. It's also the place where conservative Minho comes to let its hair down, with raucous traditional festivals complemented by a few sleek local nightclubs. The town's setting just by the Rio Lima estuary means that Viana do Castelo is only a short hop from some excellent beaches, and it also makes it a handy base for exploring the lower Lima valley.

Viana do Castelo also whips up some excellent seafood – among the region's best.

History

There are remains of Celtic hill settlements on Monte de Santa Luzia, overlooking the contemporary town centre, while Rome's only lasting mark was to call its settlement Diana, which, over the years, evolved into Viana.

Manueline mansions and monasteries attest to Viana's 16th-century prosperity as a major port for cod-fishing off Newfoundland. By the mid-17th century it had become Portugal's biggest port, with merchants trading as far afield as Russia.

More riches arrived in the 18th century, with the advent of the Brazilian sugar and gold trade. But with Brazil's independence and the rising importance of Porto, Viana's golden age stuttered and faded. These days it is still a deep-sea-fishing centre, though it earns much of its living as the Minho's favourite resort town.

Orientation

From the adjoining train and bus stations, the main axis down to the river is Avenida dos Combatentes da Grande Guerra (often just called 'Avenida'). East of here is the old town, centred on Praça da República. West lies the old fishing quarter.

Information

Foreign-language newspapers are available at many of the *tabacarias* around the centre.

EMERGENCY & MEDICAL SERVICES

Hospital (☎ 258 829 081; Estrada de Santa Luzia) North of the train station.
Police station (☎ 258 822 022; Rua de Aveiro)

INTERNET ACCESS

Esp@ço.net (Rua General Luis do Rego 21; per hr €1; ◷ 9am-7pm Mon-Fri, 9am-6pm Sat)

LAUNDRY

LAV (☎ 936546825; Rua do Marquês 17; ◷ 9am-10pm) Self-service laundry near the *Gil Eannes* ship (p443).

POST

Post office (Av dos Combatentes da Grande Guerra; ◷ 8.30am-6pm Mon-Fri, 9am-12.30pm Sat)

TOURIST INFORMATION

Regional turismo (☎ 258 822 620; fax 258 827 873; Rua Hospital Velho; ◷ 9am-12.30pm & 2-5.30pm Mon-Fri, 9.30am-1pm & 2-5.30pm Sat, 9.30am-1pm Sun Oct-Apr, 9am-12.30pm & 2.30-6pm Mon-Fri, 9.30am-1pm & 2-6pm Sat, 9.30am-1pm Sun May-Jul & Sep, 9am-7pm daily Aug) Housed in a 15th-century inn.
Viana Welcome Centre (☎ 258 098 415; www .vivexperiencia.pt; Rotunda da Liberdade; ◷ 10am-7pm) This private outfit offers adventure activities such as canyoning, rafting and kayaking. Unfortunately, it's geared mostly to groups. Bike rental is also available (€2.50/6 per hour/day).

THE MINHO

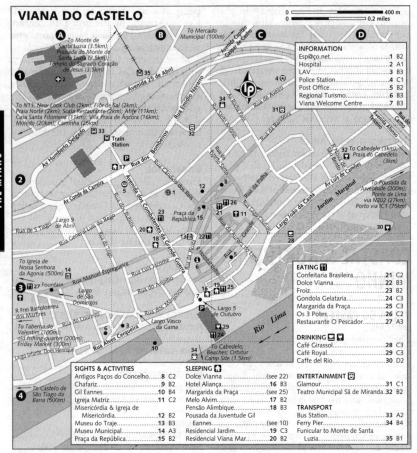

VIANA DO CASTELO

0 — 400 m
0 — 0.2 miles

INFORMATION

Esp@ço.net.................................**1** B2	
Hospital....................................**2** A1	
LAV..**3** B3	
Police Station..........................**4** C1	
Post Office...............................**5** B2	
Regional Turismo.....................**6** B3	
Viana Welcome Centre............**7** B3	

SIGHTS & ACTIVITIES

Antigos Paços do Concelho......**8** C2	
Chafariz...................................**9** B2	
Gil Eannes..............................**10** B4	
Igreja Matriz..........................**11** C2	
Misericórdia & Igreja de	
Misericórdia.......................**12** B2	
Museu do Traje......................**13** B3	
Museu Municipal....................**14** A3	
Praça da República.................**15** B2	

SLEEPING

Dolce Vianna.....................(see 22)	
Hotel Aliança.........................**16** B3	
Margarida da Praça..............(see 25)	
Melo Alvim............................**17** B2	
Pensão Alimbique..................**18** B3	
Pousada da Juventude Gil	
Eannes.............................(see 10)	
Residencial Jardim.................**19** C3	
Residencial Viana Mar............**20** B2	

EATING

Confeitaria Brasileira..............**21** C2	
Dolce Vianna..........................**22** B3	
Froiz......................................**23** B2	
Gondola Gelataria..................**24** C3	
Margarida da Praça.................**25** C3	
Os 3 Potes..............................**26** C3	
Restaurante O Pescador..........**27** A3	

DRINKING

Café Girassol.........................**28** C3	
Café Royal.............................**29** C3	
Caffe del Rio.........................**30** D2	

ENTERTAINMENT

Glamour.................................**31** C1	
Teatro Municipal Sã de Miranda.**32** B2	

TRANSPORT

Bus Station............................**33** A2	
Ferry Pier...............................**34** B4	
Funicular to Monte de Santa	
Luzia................................**35** B1	

Sights & Activities

PRAÇA DA REPÚBLICA & AROUND

The fine Praça da República is at the heart of the old town's well-preserved zone of mansions and monuments – the city's most picturesque quarter. Especially elegant is the *praça*'s **Chafariz**, a Renaissance fountain that was built in 1554 by João Lopes the Elder. It is topped with Manueline motifs of an armillary sphere and the cross of the Order of Christ. The fortresslike **Antigos Paços do Concelho** is the old town hall – another 16th-century creation.

Situated at right angles to this is the striking former **Misericórdia** almshouse, designed in 1589 by João Lopes the Younger, its loggias supported by monster caryat-ids. Adjoining the almshouse is the **Igreja de Misericórdia** (10am-12.30pm & 2-5pm Mon-Fri Aug, 11am-12.30pm Sun year-round), which was re-built in 1714 and is adorned with some of Portugal's finest *azulejos,* created by the master António de Oliveira Bernardes and his son Policarpo.

IGREJA MATRIZ

This elegant **parish church** (Rua da Aurora do Lima; irregular hours) – also known as the *sé* – dates back to the 15th century, although it has since been through several reincarnations. Check out its unusually sculpted Romanesque towers and Gothic doorway, carved with figures of Christ and the Evangelists.

MUSEU MUNICIPAL

The 18th-century Palacete Barbosa Maciel, home of the **museu municipal** (☎ 258 820 377; Largo de São Domingos; admission €2; ⊗ 9am-noon & 2-5pm Tue-Sun), bears witness to Viana's affluent past. It houses an impressive collection of 17th- and 18th-century ceramics (especially blue Portuguese china) and furniture. Most impressive are three 2nd-floor rooms lined with *azulejos*, depicting scenes of hunting, palace life and the anthropomorphic allegory of the four continents.

MUSEU DO TRAJE

Still under construction at the time of research, the **costume museum** (Praça da República) is set to house the traditional wear used for farming, fishing and seaweed harvesting in centuries past. It will also contain costumes worn during the Romaria de Nossa Senhora d'Agonia (see boxed text, right); a video (available in English, Spanish and Portuguese) about the festival explains what all the fuss is about.

CASTELO DE SÃO TIAGO DA BARRA

You can still scoot around the ramparts of this squat **castle** (⊗ 9am-5pm Mon-Fri), a short walk west of the centre, which began in the 15th century as a smallish fort. It was integrated into a larger fort, commissioned by Felipe II of Spain (Felipe I of Portugal) in 1592, to guard the prosperous port against pirates.

MONTE DE SANTA LUZIA

There are two good reasons to visit Viana's 228m, eucalyptus-clad hill. One is the wondrous **view** down the coast and up the Lima valley. The other is the fabulously over-the-top, 20th-century, neo-Byzantine **Templo do Sagrado Coração de Jesus** (Temple of the Sacred Heart of Jesus; ☎ 258 823 173; ⊗ 8am-7pm Apr-Sep, 8am-5pm Oct-Mar). You can get a little closer to heaven on its windy, graffiti-covered roof, via an elbow-scrapingly tight stairway (€0.50) – take the entrance marked *zimbório* (dome) – or the lift (€0.80).

There's an over-the-top Pousada de Portugal (Pousada do Monte de Santa Luzia; p445) up here, too, behind and above the basilica. Behind that is another attraction, the poorly maintained ruins of a Celtiberian **citânia** from around the 4th century BC, though these remained closed for redevelopment at the time of writing. You can also make the short walk onwards to the summit.

CELEBRATION OF SORROWS

Streets decorated with coloured sawdust. Women decked out in traditional finery of scarlet and gold. Men drinking till they keel over. Viana do Castelo's Romaria de Nossa Senhora d'Agonia (Festival of Our Lady of Sorrows) is one of the Minho's most spectacular festivals. Expect everything from emotive religious processions to upbeat parades with deafening drums and lumbering carnival *gigantones* (giants) and *cabeçudos* (big heads). The festival takes place for three or four days around 20 August. Accommodation is very tight at this time, so book well ahead.

You can get up the mountain by the restored **funicular** (1 way/return €2/3; ⊗ 8am-8pm Jun-Sep, 8am-6pm Oct-May), which departs from near the train station. You can also drive or take a taxi (3.5km) to the top, or walk the often steep, 2km climb (only for the fit and/or penitent). The road starts by the hospital, and the steps begin about 200m up the road.

GIL EANNES

Demanding attention on the waterfront near Largo 5 de Outubro is a pioneering naval hospital ship, the *Gil Eannes* (zheel *yan*-ish). Now restored, the **ship** (☎ 258 809 710; admission €2; ⊗ 2-7pm Mon-Fri Jul-Sep, 9am-noon & 2-7pm Sat, Sun & holidays Apr-Sep, 9am-noon & 2-5.30pm Sat, Sun & holidays Oct-Mar) once provided on-the-job care for those fishing off the coast of Newfoundland. Visitors can clamber around the steep decks and cabins, though a scattering of old clinical equipment may make your hair stand on end. The ship even houses a novel – if cramped – youth hostel (p444).

BEACHES

Viana's enormous arcing beach, **Praia do Cabedelo**, is one of the Minho's best, with little development to spoil its charm. It's across the river from town, and one way to get there is by passenger **ferry** (1 way adult/child €1.10/0.60) from the pier south of Largo 5 de Outubro. The five-minute trip goes about hourly between 8.15am and 7pm daily.

Alternatively, **TransCunha** (☎ 258 821 392) has multiple daily buses to Cabedelo (€0.75) from the bus station. Check at the station or *turismo* for current schedules.

There's a string of fine beaches north of Viana for 25km to Caminha, including good **surfing** at Afife. Four daily regional trains (€1.05, 12 minutes) make their way up the coast to Afife.

RIVER TRIPS
If there are enough passengers, boats run up and down the Rio Lima daily in summer, from the pier south of Largo 5 de Outubro. The most common trip takes 45 minutes (€5), but longer excursions, with lunch, are available in midsummer. For details call **Portela & Filhos** (☎ 258 842 290) or check at the pier.

Festivals & Events
Viana has a knack for celebrations. The **Romaria de Nossa Senhora d'Agonia** (www.festas -agonia.com), held in August, is the region's biggest annual bash (see boxed text, p443), and **Carnaval** festivities here are considered northern Portugal's best. The town also goes a little nuts in mid-May during **Semana Académica** (or Queima das Fitas), a week of student end-of-term madness similar to Coimbra's (see boxed text, p327).

And that's not all. Almost every Saturday from May to September sees traditional dancing and a photogenic food market on Praça da República.

The *turismo* has details of other annual events, which include the following:

Encontros de Viana A weeklong festival of documentaries and short films; held in the first half of May.

Festival Maio A national folk-dance extravaganza that takes place at the end of May.

Sleeping
Accommodation options in Viana do Castelo are a little old-fashioned, with an armful of basic rooms for budget travellers and a few higher-end options, but nothing too impressive in the midrange. Those with wheels can ask at the *turismo* about nearby cottages and manor houses (Turismo Rural options), with doubles in fine country settings running from €60 to €90.

BUDGET
Orbitur (☎ 258 322 167; info@orbitur.pt; Praia do Cabedelo; sites per adult/tent/car €4.80/5/4.20; ☉ year-round; ☎) This beachside site is within walking distance of the ferry pier on the Cabedelo side, and also has different types of bungalows (€80 to €100). It heaves with holidaymakers in summer.

Pousada da Juventude Gil Eannes (☎ 258 821 582; www.pousadasjuventude.pt; Gil Eannes; dm/d from €8/16) Ever slept in the oily bowels of a huge, creaky hospital ship? In Viana, on the same ship where men were stitched up and underwent emergency dentistry, you can partake in this slightly surreal experience. The floating *pousada da juventude* scores well for novelty, but don't expect easy access, luxury or more natural light than fits through a few portholes. While discouraged for fusspots and claustrophobes, it's certainly memorable for some. Reception is open from 8am to noon and from 6pm to midnight.

Pensão Alimbique (☎ 258 823 894; Rua Manuel Espregueira 88; d €35; ☒) Another budget basic, Alimbique has a warren of carpeted, sparsely furnished rooms (some of which are too gloomy to recommend) set over a decent traditional restaurant (mains €5 to €7).

Pousada da Juventude (☎ 258 800 260; www .pousadasjuventude.pt; Rua da Argaçosa; dm €13, d with/ without bathroom €38/30; ☒ 🖳) For landlubbers, Viana has a second hostel 1km east of the town centre, with neat dorms and doubles, some with balconies overlooking the marina.

Hotel Aliança (☎ 258 829 498; Av dos Combatentes da Grande Guerra; d from €38) Near the waterfront, Aliança offers low prices for its simple accommodation. The rooms are small and ageing, with tatty wallpaper, stiff beds and wood floors; the best rooms have partial river views.

MIDRANGE
Dolce Vianna (☎ 258 824 860; pizzariadolcevianna@gmail .com; Rua do Poço 44; d €40; ☒) Set above a popular pizzeria (opposite), the quiet rooms at Dolce Vianna are spick and span, with tile floors and sturdy furnishings. It's decent value for being in the town centre.

Residencial Viana Mar (☎ /fax 258 828 962; Av dos Combatentes da Grande Guerra 215; s/d from €30/40) This well-worn place has rooms with thin carpeting, tall ceilings and simple furnishings. Rooms in back are gloomy, while front rooms are at least bright and have balconies.

our pick Casa Santa Filomena (☎ 258 981 619; soc.com.smiths@mail.telepac.pt; Estrada de Cabanas, Afife; d incl breakfast from €50) Located 11km north of Viana, this stone-walled B&B offers simple but pleasant rooms that open onto a beautiful garden setting. Breakfast is served on the grassy lawn amid fruit trees, sunflowers and twittering birds.

Residencial Jardim (☎ 258 828 915; www.residencial jardim.com.sapo.pt; Largo 5 de Outubro 68; d €55; ⊠ 🖳) In a stately 19th-century town house, this quirky place has cosy carpeted rooms that are ready for a refresh, though most are at least bright. Several rooms have delightful views of the riverfront, while others look onto the historic centre.

Margarida da Praça (☎ 258 809 630; www.margarida dapraca.com; Largo 5 de Outubro 58; d €75; ⊠ 🖳) At the highest end of the midrange options, this hotel offers remodelled rooms in a handsome town house with a pleasant riverfront location. Rooms are trim and stylish, but somewhat expensive for the small size.

TOP END

Melo Alvim (☎ 258 808 200; www.meloalvimhouse.com; Av Conde da Carreira 28; d from €140; 🅿 ⊠) Near the train station, Melo Alvim offers handsomely furnished rooms in a stately 16th-century mansion. It's worth the extra €15 for the deluxe rooms, which have huge ceilings and ornately carved beds. There's a top-notch Portuguese restaurant (mains €12 to €18) on the ground floor.

Flôr de Sal (☎ 258 800 100; www.hotelflordesal.com; Av de Cabo Verde 100, Praia Norte; d with/without sea view from €180/150; 🅿 ⊠ 🖳 🐾) Perched on a windswept stretch of rocky coastline, this sleek, contemporary, three-storey hotel has designer rooms with all the modern touches, plus huge balconies. There's a spa, a workout centre, two heated pools and a pleasant restaurant on site. It's located 2km west of the centre.

Pousada do Monte de Santa Luzia (Pousada de Viana do Castelo; ☎ 258 800 370; www.pousadas.pt; d with/without sea view from €215/170; 🅿 ⊠ 🖳 🐾) This regal 1918 hotel sits squarely atop Monte de Santa Luzia, peering down at the basilica's backside and beyond it to some of the best coastal views in Portugal. Common areas are splendid, and the rooms themselves are bright and luxurious, if less inspired than the views.

Eating

The newest destination for dining or drinking is the waterfront Praça da Liberdade, with its open-air cafes and restaurants. For a quick meal before or after the journey, head to the top floor (nice views) of the shopping mall next to the bus and train stations.

Confeitaria Brasileira (☎ 258 822 637; Rua Sacadura Cabral 23; pastries €1; ⏲ 8am-7pm Mon-Sat) Around the corner from the main plaza, this pastry shop delivers flaky fresh-baked delights as well as decent coffee.

Gondola Gelataria (Praça da Liberdade; ice-cream scoops €1.25; ⏲ noon-8pm) For creamy rich gelato (known in these parts as 'gelado'), Gondola delivers the goods. Mango, blood orange, banana and pistachio are among the flavour temptations at this indoor/outdoor spot by the water.

Dolce Vianna (☎ 258 824 860; Rua do Poço 44; pizzas €6-7) This pleasant local favourite cooks up thin-crust, cheese-heavy pizzas in a wood-burning oven. Lasagne, calzones and fettuccine provide a nice respite from Portuguese standards.

Scala Restaurante (☎ 258 808 060; Av do Atlântico 813, Praia Norte; mains €7-14; ⏲ lunch & dinner) Overlooking the rugged Praia Norte, Scala has unrivalled views of the sea. The interior is less exciting, but livened up perhaps by the broad menu of salads, crêpes, seafood and the usual Portuguese favourites. Scala is 2km west of the centre.

Os 3 Potes (☎ 258 829 928; Rua Beco dos Fornos 7; mains €8-12; ⏲ lunch & dinner) Set in the former public kiln, this cosy restaurant serves traditional Minho delicacies such as oven-roasted lamb, lamprey (in season) and grilled fish. An ample wine cellar adds to the appeal.

our pick Margarida da Praça (☎ 258 809 630; Largo 5 de Outubro 58; mains €9-12; ⏲ lunch & dinner Mon-Fri, dinner Sat; Ⓥ) Bringing a bit of bohemian chic to the scene, this intimate restaurant has a small selection of tasty, lovingly made dishes. Pasta with monkfish and seafood, vegetable goulash and shrimp with guacamole are among recent selections. There's always a good vegetarian option or two.

Restaurante O Pescador (☎ 258 826 039; Largo de São Domingos 35; mains €9-13; ⏲ lunch & dinner Tue-Sat, lunch Sun) A simple, friendly, family-run restaurant admired by locals for its good seafood.

Taberna do Valentim (☎ 258 827 505; Rua Monsignor Daniel Machado 180; mains €12-14; ⏲ lunch & dinner Mon-Sat) Hidden among the humble abodes of the old fishermen's neighbourhood you'll find this fantastic seafood restaurant. Fresh grilled fish is available by the kilo, while the equally well-loved dishes are the rich seafood stews – *arroz de tamboril* (monkfish rice) and magnificent *caldeirada* (fish stew).

The **mercado municipal** (Av Capitão Gaspar de Castro; ⏲ 7am-1pm Mon-Sat) is just northeast of the centre. Rua Grande and its eastward extension have numerous small food shops.

For picnic items and self-catering, **Froiz** (Av dos Combatentes da Grande Guerra 236; 🕙 9am-9pm Mon-Sat, 9.30am-1pm & 3-8pm Sun) is the best supermarket in the centre.

Drinking

There is a handful of upmarket bars, and some more-casual, open-air spots, on the waterfront across from the Jardim Marginal.

Caffe del Rio (☎ 258 822 963; Caís de Viana; 🕙 1pm-2am Sun-Thu, 1pm-4am Fri & Sat) Imported DJs spin house and hip-hop as well as pop and R&B here. The sleek glass-and-chrome, '60s-style bar upstairs has great river views.

Café Royal (Praça da Liberdade; 🕙 noon-midnight) A small, stylish spot on the waterfront with outdoor tables and nicely mixed cocktails.

Café Girassol (🕙 8am-8pm Wed-Mon, to midnight Jun-Sep) A greenhouse-like cafe in the Jardim Marginal, with tables spilling out into the park.

Entertainment

Teatro Municipal Sá de Miranda (☎ 258 809 382; Rua Sá de Miranda) Viana do Castelo's cultural epicentre, this neoclassical theatre hosts a regular line-up of music, theatre, dance and the occasional opera.

New Look Club (☎ 914956080; Av de Cabo Verde, Praia Norte; 🕙 11pm-4am Thu-Sat) A popular newcomer to the club scene, this boxy space has a spacious dance floor ringed by an upstairs gallery for checking out the scene below. It's next door to Flôr de Sal hotel (p445) on Praia Norte.

Glamour (Rua da Bandeira 179-185; 🕙 7.30pm-4am Mon-Sat) This nightlife mainstay is Viana's longest-running disco, with a menu of commercial house and pop, as well as the odd band thrown in the mix.

Getting There & Away

Parking can be a challenge; most locals opt for paid underground lots sprinkled about the centre (including lots on either end of Avenida dos Combatentes da Grande Guerra); there's also ample free parking next to the Castelo de São Tiago da Barra.

BUS

Long-distance *expresso* buses operate from the shiny, centralised bus station (inside a shopping mall), which is just across the tracks from the train station.

AV Minho (☎ 258 800 341) runs a line from Porto (€6.50, 2¼ hours) at least four times daily, passing through Esposende (€2.80, 40 minutes); there are also one to three daily buses to Valença do Minho (€3.60, 1¼ hours) and Monção (€4, 1½ hours).

Transdev Norte (☎ 253 209 410) has at least eight weekday and four weekend runs to Braga (€4, 1½ hours).

AV Cura/Transcolvia (☎ 258 800 340) runs up the Lima valley to Ponte de Lima (€3, 50 minutes), Ponte da Barca (€3.60, 1½ hours) and Arcos de Valdevez (€3.80, 1½ hours) at least hourly on weekdays (fewer at weekends).

TRAIN

Daily direct services from Porto include five IR/international trains (€7.95, 1¾ hours) and five regional services (€7.35, two hours). For Braga (€4.15, 1½ to two hours, 12 daily), change at Nine. There are also seven to 10 daily trains to Valença do Minho (€3.15, 45 minutes to one hour).

VALENÇA DO MINHO

pop 5200

Occupying strategic heights above the picturesque Rio Minho, Valença do Minho (Valença) sits just a cannonball shot from Spain. Its impressive pair of citadels long served as the Minho's first line of defence against Spanish aggression. But history insists on repeating itself, and these days the town is regularly overrun by Spanish hordes. They come armed with wallets and make away with volumes of towels and linens that are stacked high along the cobbled streets of the fortresses.

The good news is that on even the busiest days, you can sidestep the towel touts and discover that these two interconnected forts also contain a fully functioning village where locals shop, eat, drink and gossip among pretty squares and narrow, medieval lanes. And when in the evening the weary troops retreat back to Spain with their loot, the empty watchtowers return once again to the silent contemplation of their ancient enemy – the glowering Spanish fortress of Tui just across the river.

Visitors can easily see the sights of Valença as a day trip, but there are several atmospheric guest houses within the fortress walls that make for a worthy splurge.

GREENWAY ALONG THE RIO MINHO

For fine views of the Rio Minho, walkers and cyclists can go along the **Ecopista**, a paved path along the former railway tracks running east from Valença. The path currently extends for 13km to Cortes, but plans are under way to connect it all the way to Monção (another 5km). Part of the journey follows the river, with delightful views of vineyards, countryside and vestiges of distant centuries (including Valença's fortress, the cathedral of Tui across the river in Spain, and the stolid medieval tower of Lapela). The converted railway-to-greenway is Portugal's first, but by no means its last. The south of the country has ambitious plans for greenways in coming years, with plans to add 500km of greenways to the Alentejo by 2013. There's even talk of creating a 215km-long *ecopista* coursing the breadth of the Algarve, from Sagres in the west to Vila Real de Santo António in the east.

Orientation & Information

An uninspiring new town sprawls at the foot of the fortress. From the bus station it's 800m north via Avenida Miguel Dantas (the N13) and the Largo da Trapicheira roundabout (aka Largo da Esplanada) to the **turismo** (☎ /fax 251 823 374; Av de Espanha; ♥ 9.30am-12.30pm & 2-5.30pm Mon-Sat year-round). The train station is just east of Avenida Miguel Dantas.

The fortress has its own **post office** (Travessa do Eirado; ♥ 9am-12.30pm & 2pm-5.30pm Mon-Fri). **Espaço Internet** (☎ 251 809 588; ♥ 10am-12.30pm & 2-6.30pm Mon-Fri), by the bus station, has free internet access.

Sights & Activities

There are in fact two **fortresses**, bristling with bastions, watchtowers, massive gateways and defensive bulwarks, and connected by a single bridge. The old churches and Manueline mansions inside testify to the success of the fortifications against several sieges, some as late as the 19th century. The earliest fortifications date from the 13th-century reign of Dom Afonso III, though largely what you see today was built in the 17th century, its design inspired by the French military architect Vauban.

Press on through the gift shops and towel merchants along the cobbled lanes to the far end of the larger northern fortress, which incorporates Dom Afonso's original stronghold and contains almost everything that's of interest.

From Praça da República bear right, then left, into Rua Guilherme José da Silva. On the left, opposite the post office, is the **Casa da Eira**, with a handsome Manueline window. The 14th-century **Igreja de Santo Estevão**, with its neoclassical facade, is at the end of the

street. Nearby is a 1st-century **Roman milestone** from the old Braga–Astorga road.

From the milestone continue north to the end of Rua José Rodrigues and the now decrepit Romanesque parish church, **Igreja de Santa Maria dos Anjos** (Church of St Mary of the Angels), dating from 1276. At the back is a tiny **chapel** with leering carved faces and Romano-Gothic inscriptions on the outside, though this is in an appalling state of disrepair and closed to the public.

To the left of the parish church is the **Capela da Misericórdia** and beyond it the Pousada de São Teotónio (p448). All around this area there are picturesque ramparts and sweeping views to Tui.

Turn right by the *pousada* and descend the atmospheric lane through one of the 13th-century **original gates**, with a trickling stream running below, and an impressive echo. Keep going and you'll pass through several thick onion-skin fortress layers to the outside world.

Sleeping

Val Flores (☎ 251 824 106; fax 251 824 129; Av dos Bombeiros; d from €30) On a busy road facing the fortress, Val Flores is a boxy hotel that has clean, trim rooms graced with cork-tiled floors and sizeable windows. It's the top pick for new-town options.

Residencial Rio Minho (☎ 251 809 240; fax 251 809 248; Largo da Estação; d from €40) Located just a few steps from the train station, this quiet place has a mix of battered, gloomy back rooms with worn carpeting, and airier high-ceilinged chambers overlooking a vine-covered terrace.

Casa da Eira (☎ 251 921 905; www.casaeira.net; Laços Gondomil; d €80; P ☎) Occupying an 18th-century farmhouse with lustrous wood floors, this place offers handsomely furnished rooms with sparkling, tiled bathrooms, plus a grassy garden with pool. It's 8km east of Valença towards Monção. Turn off the N101 towards Laços and follow the signs.

our pick Pousada de São Teotónio (☎ 251 800 260; www.pousadas.pt; Rua de Baluarte do Socorro; d from €100; P ⚒) Perched on the outermost post of the fortress and surrounded by green ramparts, this bright, modern *pousada* has large, rather luxurious rooms, most with prime views overlooking the walls and river to Spain; a few have verandas.

Casa do Poço (☎ 251 825 235; www.casadopoco .fr.fm; Travessa da Gaviarra 4; ste from €120) Also inside the citadel, this gorgeously restored 17th-century house has contemporary European art, a library, a billiard room and six antique-appointed, silk-wallpapered suites.

Eating

Restaurante Baluarte (☎ 251 824 042; Rua Apolinário da Fonseca; mains €8-11; ☯ lunch & dinner Sat-Thu) Baluarte enjoys a peaceful fortress setting with outdoor tables fronting a plaza. A decent assortment of Minho specialities are on hand, including *truta* (trout), salmon and seafood rice.

Solar do Bacalhau (☎ 251 822 161; Rua Mouzinho Albuquerque 99; mains €8-20; ☯ lunch & dinner Tue-Sun) True to its name, this contemporary restaurant in the fortress serves good *bacalhau* in dozens of forms – along with other Portuguese fare.

Restaurante Mané (☎ 251 823 402; Av Miguel Dantas 5; mains €10-15; ☯ lunch Tue-Thu, lunch & dinner Fri & Sat) Hidden in a plain modern building in the new town (near the roundabout), Mané cooks up Valença's best cuisine. The menu features classic Minho specialities, including the seasonal, eel-like lamprey. It also has a popular bar-cafe with terrace seating, serving satisfying snacks.

Getting There & Away

There is free parking in lots just west of the fortresses, though they can fill to capacity at weekends.

BUS

AV Minho (☎ 251 652 917) has two daily weekday runs and one daily weekend run beginning in Monção (€2, 20 minutes) and going all the way to Porto (€7.50, 3½ hours) via Viana do Castelo (€3.60, 1¼ hours).

TRAIN

Five to 10 trains run daily to Valença from Porto (€9 to €10.50, 3½ hours), two of which continue on as far as Vigo in Spain.

MONÇÃO

pop 2600

Like Valença do Minho to the west, Monção (mohng-*sowng*) was once an important fortification along the border with Spain. Although not as well preserved as its hilltop brother, Monção has a modest but attractive historic centre that sees fewer visitors than Valença's, with the remains of its 14th-century fortifications still watching over the river. The town's big claim to fame is its fine *vinho verde*, with signs touting Monção as the cradle of the refreshing Alvarinho wine (Galicia makes similar claims). In 2008 it reopened its once well-regarded town spa.

It's said that during a siege by Castilian soldiers in 1368, a local townswoman named Deu-la-Deu Martins managed to scrabble together enough flour from starving citizens to make a few loaves of bread, and in a brazen show of plenty tossed them to the enemy with the message, 'if you need any more, just let us know'. The disheartened Spaniards immediately withdrew.

Orientation

From the bus station it's 600m east to the defunct train station, then another two blocks north up Rua General Pimenta de Castro to the first of the town's two main squares, Praça da República. Praça Deu-la-Deu and the heart of the old town lie just one block further on.

Information

Post office (Praça da República; ☯ 9am-12.30pm & 2-5.30pm Mon-Fri)

Turismo (☎ 251 652 757; Praça Deu-la-Deu; ☯ 9.30am-12.30pm & 2-6pm Mon-Sat) Housed in the Casa do Curro, the *turismo* also sells a small but high-quality selection of pottery and lacework from artisans of northern Portugal.

Sights & Activities

OLD MONÇÃO

In chestnut-shaded Praça Deu-la-Deu, a hand-on-breast statue of its namesake tops a **fountain** and looks hungrily down over the surrounding cafes. The Senhora da Vista bastion at the northern end offers a gentle view across the Rio Minho into Spain – a mere slingshot's throw away. The **Capela da Misericórdia** at the

GOING GREEN IN VINHO VERDE COUNTRY

Outside Portugal, *vinho verde* (literally, 'green wine') gets a bum rap, but often for good reason – exports tend to sit on shelves far too long. The stuff is made to be drunk 'green' – that is, while it is still very young, preferably less than one year old.

While the wine is made from fully ripe rather than still-green grapes as is sometimes believed, the straw-coloured whites can indeed achieve greenish tints – a visual reminder of the green landscape from which they come. Served well chilled on a hot summer day, its fruity nose, fine bubbles and acidic bite make *vinho verde* one of the great delights of travelling in northern Portugal.

Vinho verde is grown in a strictly demarcated region of the Minho that occupies the coastal lowlands between the Rio Douro and the Spanish border. Traditionally, the vines are trained high both to conserve land and to save the grapes from rot, and you can still see great walls of green in the summer months. Like German wines, *vinho verde* tends to be aromatic, light-bodied and low in alcohol. There are red *vinho verdes*, though you may find them chalky and more of an acquired taste. White is both the most common and the easiest to appreciate. Alvarinho grapes, grown around Monção, are also used to make a delightful *vinho verde*.

For more information about the wine, its history and visiting particular regions and vineyards, check out www.vinhoverde.pt.

square's southern end has a coffered ceiling painted with cherubs.

East of the square is the snug, cobbled old quarter. Two blocks along Rua da Glória is the pretty little Romanesque **igreja matriz**, where Deu-la-Deu is buried (look for the stone-carved alcove to the left of the entrance).

WINE-TASTING

Alvarinho is a delicious, full-bodied variety of white *vinho verde* produced around Monção and neighbouring Melgaço. If you'd like a free tasting, stop by the **Adega Cooperativa de Monção** (☎ 251 652 167; 10am-noon & 2-5pm Mon-Fri), 1.8km south of Monção on the N101 to Arcos de Valdevez.

Otherwise, the clutch of bars around Monção's principal squares will be happy to oblige.

THERMAL BATHS & POOL

Monção's **termas** (thermal baths; ☎ 911036919; www.tesal.com, in Portuguese; Av das Caldas) reopened in 2008 under Galician management. This modern centre has a large aquatic area with Jacuzzis, tiny waterfalls and a children's swimming area. There's also a wide variety of spa treatments available, with day packages starting at €55.

Those wanting the aquatic experience without the fuss can head across the road to the newly inaugurated **piscina municipal** (Largo das Caldas), a handsomely designed

25m indoor pool, with a smaller pool for younger swimmers.

RAFTING

Fugas Lusas Aventuras (☎ 251 656 215; www.fugaslusas.com, in Portuguese; Veiga Velha, Cortes; 1-day rafting/canyoning/trekking from €35/35/15) offers a range of adrenaline-charged activities, including rafting, canyoning, rappelling and trekking. It's located west of Monção in Cortes.

Festivals & Events

Feira do Alvarinho (www.feiraalvarinho.pt.vu) The self-described cradle of Alvarinho, Monção hosts a five-day fair in honour of its fine-flavoured wine. Music, folkloric dancing and much eating and drinking rule the day. It's held in late May.

Festa do Corpo de Deus The town's biggest party, held on Corpus Christi (the ninth Thursday after Easter). Events include a religious procession and medieval fair, with a re-enactment of St George battling the dragon.

Festa da Nossa Senhora das Dores A big five-day celebration in the third week of August, headed by a pious procession.

Sleeping

Residencial Esteves (☎ 251 652 386; Rua General Pimenta de Castro; d with/without bathroom from €25/20) Around the corner from the Praça da República, this *residencial* (guest house) has a certain old-fashioned cosiness. You'll find simple, quiet rooms with tan carpeting and a friendly welcome from the accommodating couple that runs it. No breakfast.

THE MINHO

Croissanteria Raiano (☎ 251 653 534; raiano4950@hotmail.com; Praça Deu-la-Deu 34; s/d €25/35) A handful of the small but cheerful rooms above this chirpy cafe have limited views across to Spain. The waste-not-want-not decor uses the same chintzy material for bedspreads, tablecloths and curtains. Good value.

Hospedaria Beco da Matriz (☎ 251 651 909; Beco da Matriz; d €40) Just left of the facade of the *igreja matriz* (parish church), this place offers simple but impeccable rooms, with comfortable beds and spotless tile floors. Some rooms have excellent views over the adjacent ramparts to Spain.

Fonte da Vila (☎ 251 651 909; Beco da Matriz; s/d/ste €40/65/80) A handsome newcomer to Monção, the Spanish-owned Fonte da Vila has cheerfully painted rooms with wooden floors and an overall clean, contemporary look. You'll find an excellent restaurant on the ground floor.

Solar de Serrade (☎ 251 654 008; www.solardeserrade.pt; Mazedo; d from €70; P) One of two manor houses on estates producing Alvarinho grapes, this rather magnificent, 17th-century mansion has whimsical gardens and a few suites with elaborately furnished digs. Good for romantic getaways.

Casa de Rodas (☎ 251 652 105; rodas@solaresdeportugal.pt; Lugar de Rodas; d incl breakfast €85; P 🐾) One kilometre south of the town centre, this elongated, 17th-century manor house – a few kilometres before Solar de Serrade, and also producing Alvarinho grapes – offers mostly large, antique-appointed rooms, with breakfast served in a fine dining room around a common table. English and French are spoken.

Eating

The pick of local specialities is fresh shad, salmon and trout from the Rio Minho, and lamprey eels in spring.

O Escondinho (Praça Deu-la-Deu; pastries €1; 6am-2am) Monção's best pastry shop has tempting fresh-baked goods as well as other snacks, with outdoor tables overlooking the plaza.

Deu-La-Deu (☎ 251 652 137; Praça da República; mains €6-9; lunch & dinner) This typical local joint sees the most lunchtime traffic. It does good regional dishes such as *cabrito à Monção* (stewed kid).

Sete á Sete (☎ 251 652 577; Rua João da Cunha; mains €10-17; lunch & dinner Tue-Sat) Located about 600m south of the old centre, this

place serves up top-notch *bacalhau* as well as Minho specialities, made with the finest, freshest ingredients.

Fonte da Vila (☎ 251 651 909; Beco da Matriz; mains €14-17; lunch & dinner) The chef at Fonte da Vila prepares a mix of Spanish tapas and Minho favourites at this elegant, upmarket restaurant. Marinated octopus, endive salad with anchovies and Roquefort and Iberian dried meats and cheeses are among the many excellent choices. Dine inside or in the minimalist garden.

Getting There & Away

You'll find street parking around Praça da República.

Salvador/Renex (☎ 251 653 881) makes six weekday runs and one weekend run to Arcos de Valdevez (€3.60, 45 minutes), plus four weekday runs and one weekend run to Braga (€5.60, two hours). **AV Minho** (☎ 251 652 917) operates one weekend and two weekday runs that begin in Monção and go all the way to Porto (€8, four hours) via Viana do Castelo (€4, 1½ hours).

PONTE DE LIMA
pop 2800 / elev 175m

This photogenic town by the Rio Lima springs to life every other Monday, when a vast market spreads along the riverbank, offering farm-fresh fruit and cheese, farm tools, wine barrels and – these days – made-in-China electronics. And it all takes place in the shadow of Portugal's finest medieval bridge.

Even if you can't make the market, Ponte de Lima is well worth visiting, with a small, historic centre dotted with cafes, shops and restaurants, while gardens and greenways line the banks of the river.

When a Roman regiment first passed through here, soldiers were convinced that the Rio Lima was Lethe itself – the mythical 'river of oblivion'. Alas, no such luck. Decimus Junius Brutus forced his men to plunge ahead, and yet they still remembered all their sins upon reaching the far side. The impressive Ponte Romana (Roman Bridge) – part of the Roman road from Braga to Astorga in Spain and the town's namesake – supposedly marks their crossing. Though largely rebuilt in medieval times, it still contains traces of its Roman antecedent.

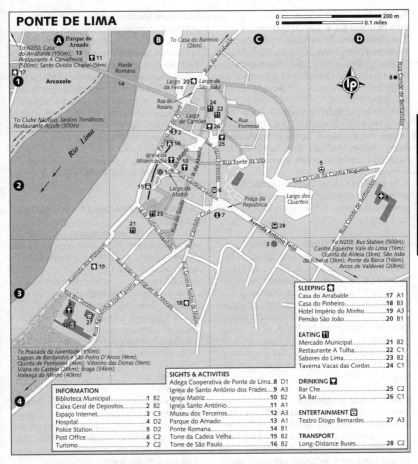

PONTE DE LIMA

0 ———————— 200 m
0 ———————— 0.1 miles

THE MINHO

Ponte de Lima is an appealing overnight stop. This is the heartland of Turismo de Habitação (Turihab; p494), and the surrounding countryside is packed with appealing manor houses.

Orientation

The bus station is 800m uphill from the town centre, though all long-distance buses loop down to within a block of the *turismo* on Praça da República. Most places of interest are located in the short strip between the *turismo* and the riverbank.

Information

Biblioteca municipal (☎ 258 900 411; Largo da Matriz; ☽ 10am-12.30pm & 2-6.30pm Mon-Fri) Provides free internet access.

Caixa Geral de Depósitos (☎ 258 909 300; Rua Inácio Perestrelo 40) ATMs and currency exchange.

Espaço Internet (☎ 258 900 400, ext 415; Av António Feijó; ☽ 1-8pm Mon-Fri, 10am-8pm Sat) Free internet access.

Hospital (☎ 258 909 500; Rua Conde de Bertiandos)

Police station (☎ 258 941 113; Rua Dr Luís da Cunha Nogueira)

Post office (Praça da República; ☽ 8.30am-5.30pm Mon-Fri)

Turismo (☎ 258 942 335; Praça do Marquês; ☽ 9.30am-12.30pm & 2.30-6pm Mon-Sat, 10am-12.30pm Sun Jun-Aug, 9.30am-12.30pm & 2-5.30pm Mon-Sat, 10am-12.30pm Sun Sep-May) This well-organised tourist office shares an old tower with a small handicrafts gallery. The lower floor has glass walkways over the excavated layers of an ancient tower.

Sights

PONTE ROMANA & ARCOZELO

The city's pièce de résistance, this elegant, 31-arched bridge across the Rio Lima is now limited to foot traffic. Most of it dates from the 14th century, though the segment on the north bank by the village of **Arcozelo** is bona fide Roman.

In down-at-heel Arcozelo you'll find the extremely photogenic little **Igreja Santo António** and the kitsch **Parque do Arnado** (admission free; ⏰ 10am-7pm), an architecturally themed park that crams in styles from all around the world.

In Ponte de Lima, **Largo de Camões**, with a fountain resembling a giant bonbon dish, makes a fine spot to watch the sun set over the bridge.

MUSEU DOS TERCEIROS & AROUND

Down river, the 18th-century Igreja de São Francisco dos Terceiros is now a rambling **museum** (☎ 258 942 563; Av dos Plátanos) full of ecclesiastical and folk treasures, although the highlight is the church itself, with its gilded baroque interior. The Renaissance-style **Igreja de Santo António dos Frades**, once a convent church, is adjacent to the museum. Both church and museum were shut for renovations at the time of writing, but scheduled to reopen by 2009.

TOWN WALLS & TOWERS

Two crenellated towers (part of the fortifications made in the 14th century) face the river at the end of Rua Cardeal Saraiva. The **Torre da Cadeia Velha** (Old Prison Tower; admission free; ⏰ 2-6pm Tue-Sun) now houses temporary art exhibitions, plus a host of pigeons on its window ledges.

Fragments of the walls survive behind and between this and the other tower, the **Torre de São Paulo**. Note the somewhat bizarre *azulejo* image on its front wall, entitled *Cabras são Senhor!* (They're goats m'lord!) – a reference to a local story in which Dom Afonso Henriques almost attacked a herd of goats, apparently mistaking them for Moors!

Behind the tower is the rather staid, mostly 15th-century **igreja matriz** (Rua Cardeal Saraiva; ⏰ daily), sporting a pretty Romanesque doorway.

GARDENS & RIVERSIDE PATHS

Green space is abundant in Ponte de Lima, with several peaceful gardens near the river.

The **Jardins Temáticos** (admission €1; ⏰ 10.30am-7pm) is a small, intriguing garden with rose bushes and lemon-filled trellises next to a public swimming pool on the west side of the river. Each summer, it hosts a competition where 12 artists create temporary gardens built around a theme. You can reach it by following the **ecovia** (greenway) on the western bank of the Rio Lima. Incidentally, this riverside path continues along another 4.5km to the south, making for a pleasant stroll along the water.

On the opposite bank and parallel to this path is another *ecovia*, which follows the river for 5km to the settlement of Vitorino das Donas.

LAGOAS DE BERITANDOS E SÃO PEDRO D'ARCOS

This 350-hectare **nature reserve** (☎ 258 733 553; www.lagoas.cm-pontedelima.pt, in Portuguese; admission €1; ⏰ 9am-12.30pm & 2-5.30pm Mon-Fri, 2.30-6pm Sat & Sun) is set in a wildlife-rich humid zone just north of the Rio Lima. There's a wildlife interpretation centre and five hiking trails, ranging from an easy lakeside loop (1.6km) to a longer 12.5km hike. To get there, take the A27 4km west from Ponte de Lima, taking exit 3. There's lodging (camping, bungalows, house rental) at Quinta de Pentieiros (opposite).

Activities

WALKING

In addition to the riverside paths (left), there are charming walks all round the area – through the countryside, past ancient monuments and along cobbled lanes trellised with vines. The *turismo* has descriptions of walks ranging from 5km to 14km. Pack water and a picnic – cafes and restaurants are rare.

A steep climb north of Arcozelo yields panoramic views up and down the Lima valley. A steep climb up a hill north, about 5km from Ponte de Lima, is a tiny and bizarre **chapel** (⏰ irregular hours) dedicated to Santo Ovídio, patron saint of ears. Yes, you read that right. The interior is covered with ear-shaped votive candles offered in hope of, or as thanks for, the cure of an ear affliction. You can also drive up; the turning off the N202 is about 2.5km upstream of the N201 bridge.

BOATING

The **Clube Náutico** (☎ 258 944 499; ⏰ 10am-1pm & 2.30-7pm Jul-Sep, 10am-1pm & 3-7pm Sat & Sun Oct-Jun), across the river and 400m downstream by the

N201 bridge (you can walk via Arcozelo), rents canoes and plastic kayaks for gliding around the river, for €3 per person for 1½ hours.

HORSE RIDING

You can hire horses (from around €20 per hour) at the **Centro Equestre Vale do Lima** (☎ 258 943 873; 🕙 9am-7pm), about 1km south of Ponte de Lima off the N201.

WINE-TASTING

For a taste of both red and white varieties of *vinho verde*, as well as two brands of *aguardente* (firewater) at their source, head to the **Adega Cooperativa de Ponte de Lima** (☎ 258 909 700; Rua Conde de Bertiandos; 🕙 9am-noon & 1-5pm Mon-Fri).

Festivals & Events

Vaca das Cordas & Corpus Christi Another tradition that probably dates back at least to Roman times, and possibly with Phoenician origins. Held on the ninth Wednesday and Thursday after Easter, it features a kind of bull-running in which young men goad a hapless bull (restrained by a long rope) as it runs through the town. It's followed the next day by the more pious Festa do Corpo de Deus, with religious processions and flowers carpeting the streets.

Feiras Novas (New Fairs) Held here since 1125, this is one of Portugal's most ancient ongoing events. Stretching over three days in the third week in September, it centres on the riverfront, with a massive market and fair, and features folk dances, fireworks, brass bands and all manner of merry-making. Book accommodation well ahead.

Sleeping

There are dozens of Turihab properties in the Ponte de Lima area, from humble farmhouses to enormous mansions: pick up a list at the *turismo* (p451).

Quinta de Pentieiros (☎ 258 733 553; www.lagoas .cm-pontedelima.pt, in Portuguese; sites per adult/tent/car €5.40/3.60/4.20, bungalows/cottages from €40/55; P 🔁) Inside the Lagoas nature reserve (opposite), this estate has campgrounds, bungalow rental and more-comfortable houses with kitchen units. There's also an inviting swimming pool, horse riding and bike rental available. Prices are lower (and crowds fewer) on weekdays.

Pousada da Juventude (☎ 258 943 797; www .pousadasjuventude.pt; Rua Agostinho José Taveira; dm/d €11/30; P 🖥) Built of glass, metal and pink stone, this new, contemporary youth hostel is a pleasant 800m walk from the centre of town along the river. Facilities are limited, but the rooms are clean and attractive.

Reception is open from 8am to noon and from 6pm to midnight.

Pensão São João (☎/fax 258 941 288; Largo de São João; d with/without bathroom €30/25) This welcoming guest house offers the town's best budget accommodation, with clean, serviceable and mostly bright rooms (no TV) with wood floors. Ask at the restaurant on the ground floor.

Hotel Império do Minho (☎ 258 741 510; hotel imperio@sapo.pt; Av dos Plátanos; s/d from €35/43; P 🔁 🛜) In an uninspiring modern building by the river, this ageing hotel has serviceable rooms, all with parquet floors and small balconies overlooking the trees and river beyond. There is a refreshing outdoor pool, and a billiards table/bar area overlooking it.

our pick **Casa do Pinheiro** (☎ 258 943 971; Rua General Norton de Matos 50; d €65; 🛜 🔁) The unsigned Casa do Pinheiro is set in a painstakingly restored private house, whose seven elegant rooms boast high ceilings, antique beds and touches of religious art. Some rooms have verandas, while others open onto the splendid back garden with pool and fruit trees.

Casa do Barreiro (☎ 258 948 137; www.casadobarreiro .com; Quinta de Pias, Fornelos; d €70, 1-/2-bedroom cottages €70/120; P 🔁) Particularly elegant, this 17th-century manor house features original details, including stone mantles and *azulejos*. Rooms are spare but lovely, and the walled garden has a pool and tennis courts.

Casa do Arrabalde (☎ 258 742 442; www.casado arrabalde.com; d €80, 1-/2-bedroom cottages €80/130; P 🔁) This terrific option sits conveniently just across the Ponte Romana in Arcozelo. The main quarters are still inhabited by the family who built the place in the 18th century. Rooms are grand and furnished with period antiques; cottages are more contemporary. There are huge grounds and an inviting pool.

Eating

Restaurante A Tulha (☎ 258 942 879; Rua Formosa; mains €6-10; 🕙 lunch & dinner Tue-Sat, lunch Sun; 🛜) All dark wood, stone and terracotta tiles inside, this restaurant serves excellent meat and fish dishes with plenty of vegetables. Try the *medalhão á Tulha* – a deliciously thick steak wrapped in bacon.

Sabores do Lima (☎ 258 931 121; Largo de António Magalhães 64; mains €8-13; 🕙 lunch & dinner) A few steps from the river, the inviting Sabores do Lima has exposed stone walls that give a dash of style to its open dining room. The first-rate cooking features grilled meats, cod dishes and a few assorted seafood plates.

Restaurante A Carvalheira (☎ 258 742 316; N202; mains €12-18; ☽ lunch & dinner Tue-Sun; 🅿 🗷) On the N202 at the northern end of Arcozelo, country-style A Carvalheira is generally agreed to serve the area's best food. Order ahead if you want the regional favourite – *arroz de sarrabulho* (stewed rice with pork and pork blood).

Restaurante Açude (☎ 258 944 158; Arcozelo; mains €14-18; ☽ lunch & dinner Tue-Sun; 🅿 🗷) Beside the Clube Náutico (p452), this place has lots of knotty-pine floors and walls, and big windows onto the river. Try the fresh fish or *bacalhau com broa* (dried salt-cod in cornbread).

Taverna Vacas das Cordas (☎ 258 741 167; Rua Padre Francisco Pacheco 39; mains for 2 €16-20; ☽ 11am-2am Mon-Sat) On a narrow lane near Largo de Camões, you'll find a nicely set two-level restaurant and bar that serves juicy grilled steaks, tasty *açorda de marisco* and lots of meaty appetisers. Bull-fighting murals and cowboy accoutrements adorn the walls.

For fresh fruit, vegies and other regional goodies, stop in at the modern **mercado municipal** (Av dos Plátanos; ☽ 7am-7pm Mon-Fri, 7am-2pm Sat).

Drinking

Bar Che (Rua Formosa; ☽ 4pm-2am) Images of the bar's namesake revolutionary decorate this cosy place, which attracts alternative types.

SA Bar (Rua Formosa; ☽ 1pm-2am) A pleasant terrace and snug indoor bar pull in an eager, younger crowd most nights – especially when there's a big football match.

Entertainment

Behind the Museu dos Terceiros (p452), the galleried **Teatro Diogo Bernardes** (☎ 258 900 414; Rua Agostinho José Taveira), built in 1893, is the pride of the town, with interesting music and theatre performances throughout the year.

Getting There & Away

There is street parking uphill from Praça da República; higher up, it's free.

Board long-distance buses on Avenida António Feijó (buy tickets on board) or at the bus station. All services thin out on Sunday.

AV Cura/Transcolvia (☎ 258 800 340) has a service to Viana do Castelo (€3, 50 minutes). **Rede Expressos** (☎ 258 942 870) has one daily run to Braga (€7.20, 30 minutes), Valença do Vinho (€6.30, 25 minutes) and Lisbon (€19, 6½ hours) via Porto (€9.80, 2¼ hours).

PONTE DA BARCA

pop 2100 / elev 178m

Peaceful Ponte da Barca, named after the *barca* (barge) that once ferried pilgrims and others across the Rio Lima, has an idyllic, willow-shaded riverfront, a handsome 16th-century bridge, a tiny old centre and appealing walks in the surrounding countryside. It's also the home of the best source of information on the Parque Nacional da Peneda-Gerês.

The town erupts in activity every other Wednesday (alternating with Arcos de Valdevez), when a large market spreads along the riverside.

Orientation

The old town, just east of the bridge, is packed into narrow lanes on both sides of the main road, Rua Conselheiro Rocha Peixoto. Uphill and away from the river, where the main road becomes Rua António José Pereira and Rua Dr Joaquim Moreira de Barros (and eventually the N101 to Braga), is the less picturesque new town.

Information

Adere-PG (Parque Nacional da Peneda-Gerês Regional Development Association; ☎ 258 452 250; www .adere-pg.pt; Largo da Misericórdia 10; ☽ 9am-12.30pm & 2.30-6pm Mon-Fri) Park information and bookings (see p457).

Post office (Rua das Fontaínhas; ☽ 9am-12.30pm & 2-5.30pm Mon-Fri)

Turismo (☎ /fax 258 452 899; Rua Dom Manuel I; ☽ 9.30am-12.30pm & 2.30-6pm Mon-Sat) The tourist office is about 750m east of the bridge down a small street, and has a town map and accommodation information. The adjacent shop has local wine, honey and jam.

Sights & Activities

The riverfront is the focal point of the town (and a good place for a picnic), with picturesque weeping willows lining the banks of the Rio Lima. The lovely, 10-arched **ponte** (bridge) originally dates from the 1540s. Beside it is the old arcaded marketplace and a little garden, **Jardim dos Poetas**, dedicated to two 16th-century poet brothers, Diogo Bernardes and Agostinho da Cruz, who were born in Ponte da Barca.

The *turismo* has a booklet called *Historia, Patrimonia & Cultura* (€3), with regional information, including **hikes** in the surrounding valley, some of them punctuated with ancient sites.

You could take a simple stroll westwards for 4km to Bravães, a village famous for its lovely, small Romanesque **Igreja de São Salvador**, once part of a Benedictine monastery. Its west portal is adorned with intricate carved animals, birds and human figures; its interior shelters simple frescoes of the Virgin and of the Crucifixion.

Festivals & Events

The **Festa de São Bartolomeu**, held from 19 to 24 August, sees folk music and dancing aplenty, not to mention parades and fireworks.

Sleeping

Parque de Campismo de Entre Ambos-os-Rios (☎ 258 588 361; Entre Ambos-os-Rios; sites per adult/tent/car €3.20/3.10/3.10; ☼ mid-May–Sep) This basic, pine-shaded, riverside site is 11km upriver from town. It can be booked through Adere-PG (opposite). Take any Lindoso-bound bus to reach it (see right).

Pensão Restaurante Gomes (☎ 258 452 288, 258 454 016; Rua Conselheiro Rocha Peixoto 13; d with shared bathroom €25) This guest house has homely old rooms, many with sloping roofs and quaint old-fashioned furnishings (stuffy in summer); they and the rooftop terrace offer privileged views of the river and bridge.

Residencial San Fernando (☎ 258 452 580; Rua Heróis da Índia; d incl breakfast €35; P) At the very top of the new town, about 800m beyond Pensão Restaurant e Gomes (right), this more modern, businesslike *residencial* has smart, bright rooms with more up-to-date comforts. Very good value.

Residencial Os Poetas (☎ 258 453 578; Jardim dos Poetas; d from €50; ☼ Jul-Sep) A short stroll east of the bridge, this summer-only place has 10 pleasant rooms and an excellent riverside location.

Residencial Frei Agostinho (☎ 258 480 240; www .residencialfreiagostinho.com; Av Dr Francisco Sá Carneiro; s/d from €32/58; P 💥 🖳) Ponte de Barca's sparkling new option is a boxy, brick four-storey with trim, modern (somewhat bland) rooms. The best quarters have verandas overlooking the river. It's about 300m east of the Praça da República.

Casa do Correio Mor (☎ 258 452 129; correiomor@ solaresdeportugal.pt; Rua Trás do Forno 1; d from €90; P 🐾) Lovingly restored, this 17th-century manor house on the street above the town hall offers 10 graceful old rooms, some with four-poster beds, that are well worth the price tag. Bonuses include a Jacuzzi, steam bath and sauna.

There are four more Turismo Rural properties within 5km of town, including the red-tiled and whitewashed villa **Quinta da Prova** (☎ 258 452 163; www.quintadaprova.com; ste with 2/4 beds €60/100), located just across the old bridge. Guests stay in new buildings that are undistinguished, though they do have fireplaces, kitchenettes and little patios with the town's finest views.

Eating & Drinking

our pick **Belião Bar** (☎ 258 454 195; Jardim dos Poetas; mains €6-8; ☼ 10am-2am Sun-Thu, 10am-4am Fri & Sat; V) On a pretty plaza overlooking the bridge, diners can enjoy vegetable lasagne, Mexican burritos, vegetable quiche, hamburgers and big salads made with market-fresh ingredients. At night, the inside bar sometimes hosts DJs spinning pop, rock and electronica.

Pensão Restaurant e Gomes (☎ 258 452 288; Rua Conselheiro Rocha Peixoto 13; mains €7-12; ☼ lunch & dinner) This large, airy restaurant serves up tasty regional fare, including the flavourful *truta à Rio Lima* (River Lima trout).

Restaurante O Moinho (☎ 258 452 035; Largo do Côrro; mains €9-14; ☼ lunch & dinner Tue-Sat) O Moinho serves respectable traditional plates, including two of Portugal's best meat treats: *posta de barrosã* (grilled steak of locally raised veal) and *porco preto* (Alentejan pork). Nearby, you'll find a handful of other low-key eating/drinking spots. To get here, turn left just before reaching the bridge.

Getting There & Away

You'll find free parking in the shady square at the western end of the bridge.

AV Cura buses run to Arcos de Valdevez (€1, 10 minutes), Ponte de Lima (€2.10, 40 minutes) and Viana do Castelo (€3.40, 1½ hours) four to five times daily from Monday to Friday, and once or twice a day on weekends.

Salvador buses travel through Ponte da Barca twice a day Monday to Friday on their way from Arco de Valdevez to Soajo (€2.10, 45 minutes) and Lindoso (€2.20, one hour) in Parque Nacional da Peneda-Gerês. Buses stop in front of Pensão Restaurant e Gomes, just west of the old bridge. Inquire at the *turismo* for information on the current schedule.

ARCOS DE VALDEVEZ
pop 2300 / elev 200m

Drowsy little Arcos is home to a couple of interesting old churches and several stately homes in a small, almost tourist-free old centre. It also has a willow-shaded riverfront, and on warm days youths splash about in the river and sunbathe on the sandy banks facing the town. While it doesn't merit a special trip, it's a handy gateway to the northern Parque Nacional da Peneda-Gerês (opposite).

The bus station is almost 1km north of the town centre, but regional buses will stop on request in front of the **turismo** (☎ 258 510 260; Campo do Trasladário; ⏰ 9.30am-noon & 2.30-6pm Mon-Sat), which is across from the town fountains (legless horses); it's on the N101 just north of where the road crosses the river.

The **national park office** (☎ 258 515 338; Rua Padre Himalaya; ⏰ 9am-12.30pm & 2-5.30pm Mon-Fri), uphill on the right about two blocks west of the riverfront fountain, sells books and maps for the national park.

Sleeping

Tavares Residencial (☎ 965181226; Rua Padre MJ Cunha Brito; d €30; ✦) In the historic centre, Tavares is excellent value for its clean, bright rooms, though the building itself is modern and unappealing. Some rooms have verandas. It's near the *câmara municipal*.

Residencial Dona Isabel (☎ 258 520 380; residencial .disabel@simplesnet.pt; Rua Mário Júlio Almeida Costa; d €40; ✦) A short hop from the tourist office and near the town bridge, Dona Isabel has clean, tidy rooms with wood floors and a warm design. Some rooms have river views. There's also a bright, breezy restaurant (mains €5 to €7) that's open to nonguests.

Hotel Ribeira (☎ 258 510 240; hotelribeira@sapo.pt; Largo dos Milagres; d incl breakfast €55; ✦ ✦ ✦ ✦) Except for its picturesque fairy-pink facade, this early-1900s town house has, unfortunately, been largely gutted of its original character, but it does have spotless, comfortable rooms and an excellent position by the river. One room has been adapted for wheelchair access and use.

Casa dos Confrades Espírito Santo (☎ 258 515 234; www.casadosconfrades.com; Praça Municipal 10; s/d/ apt €40/60/70; ✦ ✦ ✦) Set in a bright-pink 16th-century manor, this guest house has five sparsely furnished rooms, with polished wood floors. Some rooms overlook the pool and surrounding lawn. There's

also an apartment with fine views over the neighbouring hillsides.

Casa de Cortinhas (☎ 258 522 190; mpulrich@ hotmail.com; d €65; ✦ ✦) Just off the road to Ponte da Barca, 1km south of town, this pink manor house looks out on a classic, green Minho landscape and offers rather grand rooms. It also has a winning parlour with a fireplace and original fittings.

Eating & Drinking

Doçaria Central (☎ 258 515 215; Rua General Norton de Matos 47; pastries €1; ⏰ 9am-5.30pm) Founded in 1830, this confectioner stocks the town's favourite sweet – *rebuçados dos arcos* (enormous, jaw-breaking, hard-boiled sweets). To get here take the street to the right of the tourist office, past the post office.

DNA Cafeteria (Campo do Trasladário; snacks €3-5; ⏰ 9am-2am) One of a handful of cafes on the riverfront, DNA is a sleek, modern, all-glass box with outdoor tables just a few steps from the water. In addition to libations, the menu features sandwiches, hamburgers, simple salads and the like. It's near the legless horse fountains.

Restaurante Minho Verde (☎ 258 516 296; Rua Mário Júlio Almeida Costa 37; mains €6-12; ⏰ lunch & dinner Mon-Sat) Arcos de Valdevez' finest restaurant is in an unlikely location in an ugly block down the waterfront from the *turismo*. However, it serves excellent Minho specialities, ranging from *posta de vitela* (veal steak) to *arroz de sarrabulho*.

O Lagar (☎ 258 516 002; Rua Dr Vaz Guedes; mains for 2 €14-18; ⏰ 8am-10pm) This cosy spot has its local boosters. The menu has a fair range of Minho specialities, with a focus on cod. Follow the street to the left of the *turismo* and take the first left.

Azenha Bar (☎ 964061290; Campo do Trasladário; ⏰ 10pm-4am) In an old stone house perched over the river, this bar is a popular destination for the young partiers of Arcos de Valdevez. DJs heat things up (house, world, pop) on Saturday nights.

Getting There & Away

AV Cura buses run to Ponte da Barca (€1, 10 minutes), Ponte de Lima (€2.80, 40 minutes) and Viana do Castelo (€4.10, 1½ hours) four to five times daily Monday to Friday, and once or twice at weekends.

Salvador buses head at least twice on weekdays to Soajo and Lindoso (€2.60, one hour) in Parque Nacional da Peneda-Gerês. There is no weekend service into the park.

PARQUE NACIONAL DA PENEDA-GERÊS

Spread across four impressive granite massifs in Portugal's northernmost reaches, this 703-sq-km park encompasses boulder-strewn peaks, precipitous valleys, gorse-clad moorlands and lush forests of oak and fragrant pine. It also shelters more than 100 granite villages that, in many ways, have changed little since Portugal's founding in the 12th century. Established in 1971, Peneda-Gerês – Portugal's first and most important national park – has helped preserve not just a unique set of ecosystems but also a highly endangered way of life.

The horseshoe-shaped park is blessed (or cursed) with more rain than anywhere else in Portugal, swelling its rivers and five sizeable reservoirs. Within the southern park in particular, you'll find exceptional hiking through forests and over high plateaux dotted with beehives and archaeological sites. The northwest is known for its idyllic rural accommodation in far-flung cottages and stone shelters.

Villages are dwindling as young residents leave for the cities, but so far they're still able to offer a glimpse into a vanishing way of life. Meanwhile, the heights close to the Spanish border (especially in the Serra do Gerês, where several peaks rise over 1500m), are almost free of human activity, other than the shifting of livestock to high pastures in summer.

The park shares 80km of frontier with Spain and embraces a corresponding Spanish reserve. The main base is spa town Vila do Gerês. Portuguese day trippers swarm up here on summer weekends, but if you go beyond the main camping areas you'll quickly give crowds the slip.

Many of the park's oldest villages remain in a time warp, with oxen trundled down cobbled streets by black-clad widows, and horses shod in smoky blacksmith shops. The practice of moving livestock, and even entire villages, to high pastures for up to five months still goes on in the Serra da Peneda and Serra do Gerês.

Despite joint governmental and private initiatives, this rustic scene is fading away as young people head for the cities, and village populations continue to shrink.

Information

An EU-assisted consultancy formed to spur development in the region, **Adere-PG** (Parque Nacional da Peneda-Gerês Regional Development Association; ☎ 258 452 250; www.adere-pg.pt; Largo da Misericórdia 10, Ponte da Barca; ✆ 9am-12.30pm & 2.30-6pm Mon-Fri) is the best resource on the park. Materials available include pamphlets on the park's natural, architectural and human landscapes; village-to-village walks on marked trails; and a booklet on accommodation.

Adere-PG is also the booking agent for many camping grounds, shelters and rural houses located in the park. You can book online as well as see pictures of, and read about, accommodation (in Portuguese) at www.adere-pg.pt.

Somewhat less user-friendly are the park information centres at Braga (p426), Arcos de Valdevez and Montalegre (p465). However, they should have pamphlets and brochures available.

It's best to buy topographical maps at home or in Lisbon (p498).

ACCOMMODATION

Camping grounds include basic, park-run sites at Entre Ambos-os-Rios (p455), Lamas de Mouro and Vidoeiro (open from mid-May to September). There are also private sites at Campo do Gerês (p464) and Cabril (p465).

You can book restored rural houses in Soajo, in Lindoso, around Arcos de Valdevez and in Ponte da Barca through Adere-PG (above). Prices for cottages are currently fixed at €50/90/180 for two/four/eight occupants. Most include some kind of cooking facilities for self-catering. Adere-PG also maintains extensive listings of other country lodging, including rural hotels, village inns and private rooms in B&Bs. It also rents rustic, self-catering casas de abrigo (shelter houses) that sleep four to eight people and cost €70 to €140 per night (minimum of two nights). You can read descriptions and book online at www.adere-pg.pt.

THE MINHO

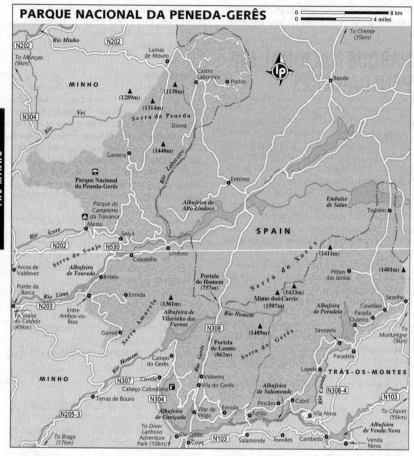

There is also a rustic youth hostel in Campo do Gerês (p464).

Vila do Gerês has many mainstream *pensões* (guest houses), though they overflow in summer.

SHOPPING

Local honey is on sale everywhere. The best – unpasteurised, unadulterated and with a faint piney taste – is from small dealers; look for signs on private homes.

Environment

WILDLIFE

The Serra da Peneda gets more rain than anywhere else in Portugal – it's little wonder that it supports a diversity of flora and fauna.

In the more remote areas a few wolves still roam, as do wild boar, badgers, polecats and otters. With luck, you may catch a quick glimpse of roe deer and a few wild ponies. Closer to the ground are grass snakes and the very occasional venomous black viper. Bird-fanciers can also be on the lookout for red kites, buzzards, goshawks, golden eagles and several species of owl.

But it's not just the wild animals that get all the glory here; the park's domestic animals are also of interest – and don't tend to run away so fast. In particular, primitive local breeds of long-horned cattle (the mahogany-coloured *barrosã* and darker *cachena*), goats, sheep, and the huge, sturdy Castro Laboreiro sheepdog are all unique to the area.

In terms of flora, sheltered valleys hold stands of white oak, arbutus, laurel and cork oak. Forests of black oak, English oak and holly give way at higher elevations to birch, yew and Scots pine, and in alpine areas to juniper and sandwort. In a small patch of the Serra do Gerês grows the Gerês iris, found nowhere else in the world.

PROTECTED AREAS

The government is doing all it can to ensure that Peneda-Gerês' largely undisturbed ecosystems remain that way. The park has a high-elevation inner zone, partly set aside for research and closed to the public, and an outer buffer zone, where development is controlled. Most villages, roads, tracks and trails are in the latter area.

The most assiduously protected area is the Mata de Albergaria, north of Gerês. Ironically, it's crossed by the N308 highway, which, because it serves an EU-appointed border crossing, cannot simply be closed. Motorised traffic is tolerated on a 6km stretch of road above Gerês but forbidden to linger. At checkpoints at either end, drivers must pay €1.50 to enter the road from June to September. Daily patrols ensure that motorists don't park on the road. Two side roads are also no-go areas for nonresidents: southwest down the Rio Homem valley and east from Portela do Homem into the high Serra do Gerês.

Campers must use designated sites or risk the wrath of park rangers. There are also restrictions on the type of boats in the park's *albufeiras* (reservoirs), and no boats at all are allowed on the Vilarinho das Furnas and Paradela. Even swimming is prohibited in Vilarinho das Furnas.

Sights & Activities

The ancient, remote granite villages, still inhabited by farmers and shepherds (and now small doses of tourists), are the park's real treasure. So are their distinctive *espigueiros* (see boxed text, p460).

There is a scattering of **Stone Age dolmens** and **antas** (megaliths) on the high plateaux of the Serra da Peneda and Serra do Gerês, near Castro Laboreiro, Mezio, Paradela, Pitões das Júnias and Tourém. Not all are easily accessible, however. For details ask at Adere-PG (p457).

Mountain bikes can be hired from adventure outfits and some private accommodation for around €8/13 per half-/full day.

For **water sports** there are the park's reservoirs, the best spot being Rio Caldo, 8km south of Vila do Gerês (p463).

There are a number of **horse-riding** facilities in Campo do Gerês (p464).

Some local outfits long involved in the park's outdoor activities:

Diver Lanhoso (☎ 253 635 763; www.diverlanhoso.pt; off N103, Póvoa de Lanhoso) Although 10km southwest of the park, this adventure theme park makes a good trip for outdoor enthusiasts. Geared mainly towards groups, it has everything from rappelling and rock climbing to mountain biking.

Jav Sport (☎ 252 850 621; www.javsport.pt; Fafião, Cabril) Hiking, adventure sports.

HIKING

Scenery, crisp air and the rural panorama make walking a pleasure in Peneda-Gerês. Adere-PG has pioneered nine marked loop trails from 5km to 16km, described in free, illustrated foldout maps available at park offices.

Day walks around Vila do Gerês are popular but crowded (see p462 for details).

Elsewhere in the park there's a certain amount of dead reckoning involved, although tracks of some kind (animal or vehicle) are everywhere in the populated buffer zone, nearly all within a half-day's walk of a settlement or a main road.

Getting There & Around

BUS

Empresa Hoteleira do Gerês (☎ 253 262 033) buses go from Braga to Vila do Gerês (€3.50, 1½ hours) hourly during the week and six times on Saturday and Sunday.

Salvador buses pass through Ponte da Barca twice on weekdays on their way from Arco de Valdevez to Soajo (€2.10, 45 minutes) and Lindoso (€2.20, one hour) in Parque Nacional da Peneda-Gerês.

CAR & MOTORCYCLE

Note that the back roads can be axlebreakers, even when maps suggest otherwise. There's no practical way to travel by car or motorcycle between the Peneda and Gerês sections of the park, except from outside of it – most conveniently via Spain, or back through Braga.

THE MINHO

ESPIGUEIROS

They look hauntingly like mausoleums, but *espigueiros* are in fact the stuff of life. New World corn was a great innovation in these low-yielding lands when it was introduced in the 18th century. But there was a catch – it ripened late, when autumn rains threatened harvests with rot. *Espigueiros* – granite caskets on stilts with slotted sides – were created to dry and store the valuable kernels. Usually built in clusters, covered with moss and topped with little crosses, they look like the village graveyard. Neither the washing lines lashed to them nor the squat, long-horned cattle grazing at their feet can entirely dispel their eerie charm.

SOAJO

pop 500 / elev 300m

Sturdy, remote Soajo (soo-*ahzh*-oo), high above the upper Rio Lima, is best known for its photogenic *espigueiros* (stone granaries; see boxed text, above). It has splendid views over the surrounding countryside, with scenic walks providing a fine opportunity to take in the beauty of this protected region. Thanks to village enterprise and the Turismo de Aldeia, you can stay in one of Soajo's restored stone houses and look out onto a vanishing way of life.

Orientation & Information

Soajo is 21km northeast of Ponte da Barca on the N203 and N530, or the same distance from Arcos de Valdevez via the scenic N202 and N304. Buses stop by Restaurante Videira at the intersection of these two roads. A few hundred metres down the N530 towards Lindoso are Soajo's trademark *espigueiros*.

Soajo's small main square, Largo do Eiró – with a *pelourinho* topped by what can only be described as an ancient smiley face – is down a lane in the opposite direction from the bus stop. There's an ATM below the parish council office, off the far side of the square.

The **Turismo de Aldeia office** (Adere-Soajo; ☎ 258 576 427; Largo da Cardeira, Bairros; ☺ 9am-noon & 2-7pm Mon-Fri, 9am-1pm Sat) is the village's de facto *turismo*; follow the signs west from the bus stop for 150m. Here you can book a room, get tips on good walks and pick up a basic map of the region.

Activities

Soajo is filled with the sound of rushing water, a resource that has been painstakingly managed over the centuries. A steep **walk** above Soajo shows just how important these streams once were.

On the N304, 250m north of the bus stop, is a signed trail, marked 'Lage'. Look for a 'P Taxis' sign next to a roofed pool for communal laundry. The trail is paved with immense stones and grooved by centuries of ox-cart traffic. It ascends though a landscape shaped by agriculture, taking in granite cottages, *espigueiros* and superb views.

Further up are three derelict **watermills** for grinding corn, stone channels that once funnelled the stream from one mill to the next, and the reservoir that fed them. This much of the walk takes half an hour.

Above here a network of paths, often overgrown, leads to more mills and the abandoned **Branda da Portelinha**. (A *branda* was a settlement of summer houses for villagers, who drove their livestock to high pastures and lived with them all summer.)

Another walk, a steep two-hour round trip, takes you down to the **Ponte da Ladeira**, a simple medieval bridge. The path drops down to the right from the Lindoso road, about 150m down from the *espigueiros*, then forks to the right further down.

Sleeping & Eating

Eating options are extremely limited in Soajo.

Parque do Campismo da Travanca (☎ 258 526 105; www.adere-pg.pt; Cabana Maior; sites per adult/tent/car €3.20/3.10/3.10; ☺ Jul & Aug) This newly reopened campground offers grassy plots about 6km northwest of Soajo.

Village houses (2- to 8-person cottages €50-180) About a dozen houses are available for tourist accommodation under the Turismo de Aldeia scheme. Each has a fireplace or stove (with firewood in winter) and a kitchen stocked with breakfast food, including fresh bread on the doorstep each morning. Stays of more than one night are preferred on weekends. You can book through Adere-PG in Ponte da Barca (p454).

ourpick Casa do Adro (☎ /fax 258 576 327; www.casa doadroturismorural.com; d €50; P 🖵) This manor house (rather than a cottage), located off Largo do Eiró by the parish church, dates to the 18th century. Rooms are old-fashioned and modest but comfortable. There is a minimum three-night stay in July and August.

Restaurante Videira (☎ 258 576 205; mains €7-10; ☺ lunch Thu-Tue Jul-Sep, Sat & Sun only Oct-Jun) Situated by the bus stop, Videira serves authentic regional snacks such as ham, sausage, cheese and other *petiscos* (snacks).

Restaurante Espigueiro de Soajo (☎ 258 576 136; mains €7-10; ☺ lunch & dinner Tue-Sun) Just out of town, this modern place serves pleasant Minho fare, with outdoor seating on a vine-covered terrace. Top picks include the hearty *arroz de frango caseiro* (stewed rice with chicken) as well as the *cabrito* (goat). It's about 200m north of the centre on the N304. The restaurant also rents out several simple but clean rooms (€30 per night).

Saber ao Borralho (☎ 258 577 296; mains for 2 €17-20; ☺ lunch & dinner Wed-Mon) A further 200m beyond Restaurante Espigueiro, the handsomely set Saber ao Borralho serves Soajo's best cuisine. The menu features excellent local dishes like the Minho *barrosã* steak as well as three codfish dishes and a tempting dessert counter. Village house rentals are available here (€50 per night).

Soajo also has several cafes and a *minimercado* (grocery shop), all found near the bus stop.

Getting There & Away

On weekdays there are two Salvador buses from Arco de Valdevez (€2.50, 45 minutes) via Ponte da Barca (€2.30, 35 minutes). A taxi from Arcos or Ponte da Barca costs about €15 to €20.

LINDOSO

pop 500 / elev 380m

Across the deep valley cut by the upper Rio Lima lies the little-visited settlement of Lindoso (leen-*doze*-oo). This hardscrabble village provides a glimpse of traditional life, with stone houses, chickens pecking on the paths, black-clad women washing at communal fonts, and untethered cows grazing amid the *espigueiros* (see boxed text, opposite). Crowning this rustic settlement is a small, hilltop fortress that has guarded the strategic Lima valley pass since medieval times.

Sights

The village and a cluster of *espigueiros* sit at the foot of a small, restored **castle**, which was under restoration when we passed

through. First built in the 13th century by Afonso III, it was beefed up by Dom Dinis, occupied by the Spanish from 1662 to 1664, and used as a military garrison until 1895. These days it's under the dominion of the national park, and should contain exhibitions on the castle and the village when it reopens.

Sleeping & Eating

Lindoso has about half a dozen restored village houses, with prices similar to those in Soajo. These must be booked through Adere-PG in Ponte da Barca (p454).

Casa do Destro (☎ 258 577 534; d €45; ☒) The first building after the turn-off into the village, this modern *pensão* has a good restaurant downstairs (mains for two €10 to €15; open for lunch and dinner Thursday to Tuesday) with *cabrito serrano assado* (grilled mountain kid) as the house speciality. Upstairs are prim, spotless little rooms, most with fine views.

Restaurante Lindoverde (☎ 258 578 010; mains for 2 €10-15; ☺ lunch & dinner Sat-Thu, lunch Fri) On the N304-1, about 900m east of the turning to the village, Lindoverde doubles as a restaurant serving standard Portuguese fare and an early-bird bar (open till midnight Saturday to Thursday).

Getting There & Away

On weekdays there are two Salvador buses from Arco de Valdevez (€2.40, one hour) via Ponte da Barca (€2.20, 50 minutes). A taxi from Arcos or Ponte da Barca costs about €20.

VILA DO GERÊS

pop 800 / elev 350m

The small but bustling tourist resort town of Vila do Gerês is the busiest settlement in the national park. Sandwiched tightly into the wooded valley of the Rio Gerês, this spa town has a rather charming fin de siècle core surrounded by a ring of less-appealing, modern *pensões*. Many accommodation places close from October to April, as does the spa itself. By the same token, it's packed to the brim in July and August.

Vila do Gerês is more commonly referred to simply as Gerês or, to confuse matters further, Caldas do Gerês (*caldas* means hot springs).

THE MINHO

Orientation

The town is built on an elongated, one-way loop of road, with the *balneário* (spa centre) in the pink buildings on the lower road. The original hot spring, some baths and the *turismo* are in the staid colonnade at the northern end (where the road takes a sharp U-turn). Buses stop at a traffic circle just south of the loop.

Information

Espaço Internet (☺ 9am-12.30pm & 2-5.30pm Mon-Fri) Free internet access up the stairs across from Hotel Universal.

Park office (☎ 253 390 110; Centro de Educação Ambiental do Vidoeiro; ☺ 9am-noon & 2-5.30pm Mon-Fri) About 1km north of the village on the track leading to the camping ground.

Post office (☺ 9am-12.30pm & 2-5.30pm Mon-Fri) By the roundabout at the southern end of the village.

Turismo (☎ 253 391 133; fax 253 391 282; ☺ 9.30am-12.30pm & 2.30-6pm Mon-Wed, Fri & Sat) Located in the colonnade.

Activities

WALKING

Miradouro Walk

About 1km up the N308 is a picnic site, which is the start of a short, popular stroll with good views to the south.

Gerês Valley

A park-maintained loop trail, the **Trilho da Preguiça**, starts on the N308 about 3km above Gerês, by a lone white house, the Casa da Preguiça. For 5km it roller-coasts through the valley's oak forests. A leaflet about the walk is available from the park office (€0.60).You can also carry on – or hitch – to the **Portela de Leonte**, 6km north of Gerês.

Further on, where the Rio Homem crosses the road (10km above Gerês), a walk east up the river takes you to a picturesque **waterfall**. (See p459 for driving and parking restrictions in the Mata de Albergaria.)

An 8km walk heads southwest from the Mata de Albergaria along the Rio Homem and the Albufeira de Vilarinho das Furnas to Campo do Gerês. This route takes you along part of an ancient **Roman road** that once stretched 320km between Braga and Astorga (in Spain), and now has World Heritage status. Milestones – inscribed with the name of the emperor during whose rule they were erected – remain at miles XXIX, XXX and

XXXI; the nearest to Campo do Gerês is 1km above the camping ground. Others have been haphazardly collected at the Portela do Homem border post, 13km from Gerês.

Trilho da Cidade da Calcedónia

A narrow, sealed road snakes over the ridge from Vila do Gerês to Campo do Gerês, offering short but spectacular, high-elevation walks from just about anywhere along its upper reaches. One of these walks is the Cidade da Calcedónia trail, a moderate, Adere PG–signposted, 7km (four-hour) loop that climbs a 912m **viewpoint** called the Cabeço Calcedónia, with views to knock your socks off.

The road is easy to find from Campo but trickier from Gerês; the turning is about 700m up the old Portelo do Homem road from Pensão Adelaide.

TERMAS & SPA

After a long hike, finish the day by soaking away aches and pains in the **spa** (☎ 253 391 113; www.aguasdogeres.pt; ☺ 9am-noon & 2.30-6pm Mon-Sat May-Oct). In addition to the sauna, steambath and pool, there's a full range of treatments available, including massages, aromatherapy, facials and shiatsu. You can even subject your body to vulcanised rock therapy (for placating that inner masochist).

WATER SPORTS

Gerês looks down on a stunning pair of reservoirs in Rio Caldo, 8km to the south, where you can swim and also engage in other water sports (see opposite).

Sleeping

Gerês has plenty of *pensões*, though in summer you may find some are block-booked for spa patients and other visitors. The upper loop road is lined with simple guest houses costing around €40 to €50. Outside July and August, prices plummet and bargaining is in order.

BUDGET

Parque de Campismo de Vidoeiro (☎ 253 391 289; www.adere-pg.pt; sites per adult/tent/car €3.20/3.10/3.10; ☺ mid-May–mid-Oct) This cool and shady, hillside, park-run facility is next to the river, about 1km north of Vila do Gerês. Book ahead through Adere-PG (p457).

Pensão Flôr de Moçambique (☎/fax 253 391 119; d from €30) The best budget option in town, this guest house offers modern rooms, most with verandas and nice views. Some rooms, however, are small and cramped. It's off the upper loop of town.

MIDRANGE

Pensão Adelaide (☎ 253 390 020; www.pensao adelaide.com.pt; d from €40; ✗) This big lemon-yellow, modern place wins for value. Rooms have nice tiled (or wood) floors and new beds, some with valley views. Guests also have access to a great outdoor pool at Quinta Souto-Linho (below). It's uphill from the southern end of the town loop. There's an enticing restaurant with picturebook views.

Pensão Baltazar (☎ 253 391 131; www.pensao baltazar.com; N308; d from €40) In a fine old granite building, this ultrafriendly, family-run place just up from the *turismo* has well-kept if not deluxe rooms, many of which look out onto a pleasant wooded park. The downstairs restaurant (right) is excellent.

Hotel Apartamentos Gerês Ribeiro (☎ 253 900 060; www.ehgeres.com; Av Manuel F Costa; s/d €40/55; P ✗ ☰) The newest link in the Hoteleira do Gerês chain offers polished modern suites with kitchen units, high ceilings and wood floors.

Hotel Universal (☎ 253 390 220; www.ehgeres.com; Av Manuel F Costa; s/d €43/58; P ✗ ☰) In a solid 19th-century edifice, the Universal offers rather plain carpeted rooms, which are comfortable enough. There is one grace note – the bright central atrium.

Quinta Souto-Linho (☎ 253 392 000; www.geocities .com/souto_linho; d €50-60; P ✗ ☰) This delightful little Victorian manor house has been simply but tastefully remodelled into the town's one genuinely nonbland option. The four rooms are cosy and spotless with hardwood floors; some also have views. There's also a large swimming pool with fine vistas.

Hotel Águas do Gerês (☎ 253 390 190; www .aguasdogeres.pt; Av Manuel F Costa; s/d €55/72; P ✗) In a grandly fin de siècle building, this up-market place has spacious, carpeted rooms with high ceilings and modern decor. The hotel also runs the *termas* and offers special packages.

Eating & Drinking

Churrasqueira Geresino (☎ 253 391 574; Lugar de Brufe; mains €6-11; ✗ lunch & dinner) Grilled meats are the speciality at this family-run place about 1km uphill from the *turismo* in a little mall. It does a pretty mean *frango* (chicken).

Vai Vai 2 (☎ 253 391 226; Rua Augusto Sérgio Almeida; mains €6-12; ✗ lunch & dinner) Near the Hotel Águas do Gerês, this trim modern place serves a decent selection of traditional fare (trout, grilled meats and salmon).

Pensão Baltazar (☎ 253 392 058; N308; mains €7-11; ✗ lunch & dinner) Gerês' best-value restaurant, this family-run place is always brimming with customers. Its small menu always includes one daily regional special, plus lots of local dishes such as *truta com presunto* (trout with ham), as well as *porco preto* (roasted pork) and a tasty *bacalhau* dish. Helpings are wholesome, vegetable-heavy and quite ample.

Café Torga (Rua de Arnaço; mains €7-11; ✗ 10am-2am) This small cafe-bar has an outdoor terrace with refreshing views of the countryside. It's a good spot for an afternoon drink; things get lively on big game nights.

Getting There & Away

Empresa Hoteleira do Gerês (☎ 253 615 896) runs between six and 10 buses daily from Braga to Gerês (€3.80, 1½ hours), passing through Rio Caldo (1¼ hours).

RIO CALDO
pop 1000 / elev 160m

Just below Vila do Gerês, this tiny town sits on the back of the stunning Albufeira de Caniçada, making it the park's centre for water sports.

English-run **AML** (Água Montanha e Lazer; ☎ 253 391 779, 968021142; www.aguamontanha.com; Lugar de Paredes) rents single/double kayaks for €4.50/7.50 for the first hour (€22/35 for the day), plus pedal boats, rowing boats and small motorboats. It will also take you waterskiing (€40 per 20 minutes), or organise kayaking trips along the Albufeira de Salamonde. AML also rents three attractively furnished **cottages** (d €75-140), all with verandas, kitchen units and water views. The shop is 100m from the N304 roundabout, but staff are often down by the water on the other side of the bridge to Vila do Gerês.

High above the Albufeira de Caniçada, the lovely **Pousada do Gerês-Caniçada/São Bento** (☎ 253 649 150; www.pousadas.pt; Caniçada; d from €100; P ✗ ☰) offers a splendid retreat at eagle's-nest heights. The rooms have wood-beamed ceilings and comfy furnishings, and some have verandas with magnificent views. There's a pool, gardens, a tennis court and an excellent restaurant serving local delicacies (trout, roasted goat). To get there, head south 3km from Rio Caldo, along the N304, following signs to Caniçada.

ERMIDA & FAFIÃO

From the picnic site above Vila do Gerês, a newly paved and impossibly scenic road runs 11km southeast to Ermida, a village of smallholdings and sturdy stone houses that cling to the steep hillsides.

Casa do Criado (☎ 253 391 390; Ermida; d incl breakfast/full board €27/65) is a modern building in a bucolic spot, with chirpy hosts, six homely rooms (book ahead) and a simple restaurant (mains €6 to €10). The village also has a few **private rooms** (from around €25), several cafes and a *minimercado*.

You can also continue east for 6km to Fafião, another village surrounded by terraced farms with rooms and a cafe or two.

CAMPO DO GERÊS

pop 200 / elev 690m

Campo do Gerês (called São João do Campo on some maps, and just Campo by most) was once a humble hamlet in the middle of a wide, grassy basin. These days it has more tourists than shepherds once the weather turns warm, which makes sense since it's a good base for hikes into the surrounding peaks.

Orientation & Information

Coming from Vila do Gerês, you first arrive at a little traffic circle and, adjacent, the town's museum. The tiny village centre is another 1.5km straight on, while the youth hostel is 1km up the road to the left.

Sights

The neighbouring village of **Vilarinho das Furnas** was for centuries a remarkably democratic and fiercely independent village, with a well-organised system of shared property and decision-making. But the entire town was submerged by the building of a dam in 1972. In anticipation of the end of their old way of life, villagers collected stories, and objects for a moving memorial that has been fashioned into the **Museu Etnográfico** (☎ 253 351 888; adult/under 12yr/student €2/free/1; ☉ 10am-12.30pm & 2-5pm Tue-Fri, 10am-7pm Sat & Sun). All exhibit explanations are in Portuguese.

In late summer and autumn when the reservoir level falls, the empty village walls rise like spectres from the water. You can visit

the spooky remains about 2.5km beyond the dam, which is a comfortable three-hour return hike.

Activities

There are several well-marked **hiking** trails around Campo do Gerês, lasting from three to six hours. You can pick up free maps and trail information at the Parque Campismo de Cerdeira (below) or at the information desk of the Museu Etnográfico (left).

There are also several adventure outfits based nearby, including **Equi Campo** (☎ 253 357 022; www.equicampo.com; ☉ 10am-7pm), located on the right just before you arrive in town. Guides here lead horse-riding trips (one/two hours €17/30), hikes (half-/full day €7/12 per person) and combination hiking/climbing/rappelling excursions (€20 per person). You can also rent mountain bikes here, if you'd like to head off on your own (per hour/day €5/17.50).

Sleeping & Eating

The road to Cerdeira is lined with signs advertising **houses for rent** (4 people €40 to €60).

Parque Campismo de Cerdeira (☎ 253 351 005; www.parquecerdeira.com; sites per adult/tent/car €4.60/3.90/4.30, 2-/4-person bungalows with kitchenette €63/85; ☉ year-round; P ☺) This privately run facility has oak-shaded sites, laundry, pool, *minimercado*, tennis, a particularly good restaurant (open to the public) and bikes to hire. Best of all are the lovely new eco-friendly bungalows, with French doors opening onto unrivalled mountain views. Book ahead, especially in August. Look for the turn-off just before you reach the village.

Pousada da Juventude de Vilarinho das Furnas (☎ 253 351 339; www.pousadasjuventude.pt; dm/d €13/38, bungalows €80; P ☺) Campo's woodland hostel began life as a temporary dam-workers' camp and now offers a spotless selection of spartan dormitories, simply furnished doubles (with bathrooms) and roomier bungalows with kitchen units. It's a popular place, despite the vaguely institutional vibe. There's also a cafeteria on hand.

Albergaria Stop (☎ 253 350 040; www.albergariastop.com; Rua de São João 915; d €50; P ☺) This peremptorily named modern guest house has spotless and comfy rooms with verandas, pleasant common areas and nice little touches (heated towel racks for one). There's also a modest restaurant (mains around €7 to €12). It's located just before the village.

ourpick O Abocanhado (☎ 253 352 944; www.abo
canhado.com; Brufe; mains €15-18) This beautifully
sited restaurant is a temple to the finest ingredients that the surrounding countryside
has to offer, including *javali* (wild boar),
veado (venison) and *coelho* (rabbit), as well
as beef and goat raised in the adjacent fields.
Finish with *requeijão* – a soft goat's cheese
so fresh it's actually sweet. The only drawback: the restaurant keeps irregular hours,
so call ahead before making the trip. It's located 6km east of Campo do Gerês (across
the dam) on a panoramic spot above the
Rio Homem.

Getting There & Away
From Braga, REDM has three daily buses
(€3.70, 1½ hours; fewer at weekends), stopping at the museum crossroad and the
village centre.

EASTERN PENEDA-GERÊS
Cabril, on the eastern limb of the national
park, and Montalegre, just outside the park,
are actually in Trás-os-Montes (p467), but
you're unlikely to visit either unless you're
coming in or out of the park.

Cabril
pop 700 / elev 400m
Although it hardly looks the part, peaceful
Cabril – set with its outlying hamlets in a
wide, fertile bowl – is the administrative
centre of Portugal's biggest *freguesia* (parish), stretching up to the Spanish border.
Your best reference point is **Largo do Cruzeiro**,
with its old *pelourinho*. To one side is the
little **Igreja de São Lourenço**, said to have been
moved five centuries ago, brick by brick,
by villagers of nearby São Lourenço. Some
400m southwest is a bridge over an arm of
the Albufeira de Salamonde.

SLEEPING & EATING
Parque de Campismo Outeiro Alto (☎ 253 659
860; www.geocities.com/campingouteiroalto; Eiredo; sites
per adult/tent/car €3/3/1; year-round) This hilly
woodland facility, over the bridge and
800m up the Pincães road, has 48 tent sites
and a patch for caravans, plus a lovely old
granite cafe-bar with fine views from its
stone terrace.

Café Águia Real (☎ 253 659 752, 962935691; d
€25) Plain and cosy, this place is 300m up
the Paradela road, and offers simple rooms

above the restaurant. The cafe (open 7am to
midnight) does light meals and carries on in
the evening as a bar.

Restaurante Ponte Nova (☎ 253 659 882; mains €7-
12; 7am-midnight) At a picturesque spot next
to the bridge, this place does good river trout
and, if you order ahead, *cabrito* or *javali as-
sada* (roast wild boar). There's an outdoor
deck right over the water that makes a great
destination for an afternoon pick-me-up.

GETTING THERE & AWAY
There are no buses to Cabril, but you could
take any Braga–Montalegre or Braga–Chaves
bus and get off at the Ruivães bus stop, then
hike the last 4km.

Drivers can cross into the park from the
N103 via the Salamonde dam; a longer but far
more scenic route is via the Venda Nova dam,
14km east of Salamonde at Cambedo.

Montalegre
pop 2100 / elev 1000m
Technically in Trás-os-Montes, Montalegre
is the park's eastern gateway. Presiding over
the town and the surrounding plains is a small
but particularly striking castle, part of Dom
Dinis' 14th-century ring of frontier outposts.
The future Duke of Wellington made use of
it in his drive to rid Portugal of Napoleon's
troops in 1809. Today visitors can wander
around its perimeter, taking in lovely views
(amid circling swifts) of the countryside.
Just below the castle lies the tiny old town
centre, with narrow streets that maintain an
old-fashioned charm.

ORIENTATION
From the bus station it's 500m uphill on Rua
General Humberto Delgado to a five-way
roundabout, beside which you'll find the town
hall and *turismo*. Keep heading uphill to reach
the picturesque castle.

INFORMATION
Biblioteca Municipal (☎ 276 510 200; Rua General
Humberto Delgado; 1-7pm Mon, 9am-12.30pm &
2-5.30pm Tue-Fri) Free internet access.
Park information office (☎ 276 518 320; Rua do
Reigoso 17; 9am-12.30pm & 2-5.30pm Mon-Fri) This
gruff office is two blocks north beyond the town hall (on
Rua Direita), then right at the *pelourinho*.
Post office (9am-12.30pm & 2-5.30pm Mon-Fri)
Located 400m northeast of the roundabout, down Avenida
Dom Nuno Álvares Pereira.

THE MINHO

Turismo (☎ 276 511 010; fax 276 510 201;
⏰ 9am-12.30pm & 2-5.30pm Mon-Fri, 10am-5.30pm Sat,
10am-4pm Sun Jul & Aug, 9am-12.30pm & 2-5.30pm Mon-
Fri Sep-Jun). Just off the roundabout at the top of town.

SIGHTS & ACTIVITIES

Next to the castle, the new **Barroso Eco Museu**
(☎ 276 518 645; www.ecomuseu.org; Praça do Município;
⏰ irregular hours) hosts changing exhibits that
showcase the local history, rural traditions
and folklore of the region. The museum
sometimes hosts thematic nights, and has also
helped create a well-marked trail network for
exploring the region. Inquire here about hikes
through the surrounding countryside, ranging
in length from 12km to 40km.

Natur Barroso (☎ 276 518 125; www.naturbarroso.net;
Rua João Rodrigues Cabrilho 265) is a local outfit that
organises hiking and canyoning trips as well
as other outdoor adventures.

SLEEPING & EATING

Casa Zé Maria (☎ 276 512 457; www.centrobarrosao
.com/zemaria; Rua Dr Victor Branco 10; d €45; Ⓟ) This
converted 19th-century granite manor features old-fashioned charm in its wood-floored
rooms with lacy bedspreads and dark wood
furnishings. It's located just down the street
opposite the *turismo*.

Quality Inn Montalegre (☎ 276 510 220; Rua do
Avelar 2; d from €58; Ⓟ 🏺 🍴) Just southwest of
the roundabout at the top of town, this somewhat out-of-place business hotel has spacious,
high-quality rooms with wood floors and fine
views of the mountains. It also features a relaxing and tropically heated indoor swimming
pool, sauna and gym. Oh, and did we mention
that it used to be a political prison during
Salazar's reign?

Tasca do Açougue (☎ 276 511 164; Terreiro do Açougue;
mains €7-10; ⏰ lunch & dinner Tue-Sun) In a charming
stone cottage just below the castle, Tasca do
Açougue serves tasty Iberian tapas dishes,
including grilled octopus and smoked meats,
as well as heartier plates. It's a lively place for
a drink in the evening.

O Castelo Piano Bar (☎ 276 511 237; Terreiro
do Açougue; mains €7-10; ⏰ noon-10pm Tue-Sun) O
Castelo serves a good selection of the regional
hits, including smoked meats, trout from the
Rio Cávado, roast pork and the like. Diners
can enjoy the peaceful setting at outdoor tables, and there's live music on most weekend
nights.

GETTING THERE & AWAY

REDM/AV Tâmega (☎ 276 512 131) buses stop at
Montalegre between Braga (€5.80, 2½ hours)
and Chaves (€4.60, 1¼ hours) four times daily
Monday to Friday; they run less frequently on
weekends. Change at Chaves for Bragança
or Vila Real.

Trás-os-Montes

If Portugal often feels like Europe's forgotten corner, Trás-os-Montes takes things a step further. This remote region sometimes feels like the land that even Portugal forgot.

For centuries this rural outpost 'behind the mountains' *(trás-os-montes)* was largely isolated, and it retains a tantalisingly lost-in-time quality, with a culture all its own. In places such as Rio de Onor and Miranda do Douro, ancient Latin-derived dialects have survived alongside Portugal's official tongue. Throughout the region residents dressed as devils and horned beasts throng the streets each December, celebrating solstice with revels dating back to pagan times.

Geographically, Trás-os-Montes ranges from the steep vineyard-clad hillsides around Vila Real, to the olive groves, almond orchards and canyonlands of the sun-baked eastern *terra quente* (hot land), to the chestnut-shaded highlands of the *terra fria* (cold land), where villagers must endure chilly, sometimes snowy, winters.

The region's uncommon beauty has led to the establishment of three natural parks: Parque Natural do Douro Internacional, renowned for its raptors and dramatic river gorge; Alvão, home to waterfalls, idyllic swimming holes and alpine vistas; and Montesinho, whose heather-clad hills are threaded with trails and speckled with lovely old stone villages.

Still one of Europe's most economically challenged regions, Trás-os-Montes has witnessed an exodus as young people abandon traditional rural life. With EU support, the region's cities have seen 21st-century development in the form of museums, parks and modern highways. Yet in the hinterlands much remains unchanged, including the robust *transmontano* hospitality, expressed in the phrase *'entre quem é'*, meaning 'come in, whoever you may be'.

HIGHLIGHTS

- Strolling the formal gardens and tasting fine wines available only in Portugal at the stately 18th-century **Palácio de Mateus** (p469)
- Cruising between the steep granite walls of the Rio Douro gorge in the **Parque Natural do Douro Internacional** (p490)
- Delighting in the devilish grins of winter carnival masks at the new Museu Ibérico da Máscara e do Traje in **Bragança** (p479)
- Diving, swimming and sliding into natural pools below the dramatic Fisgas de Ermelo waterfall in **Parque Natural do Alvão** (p473)
- Watching the sheep return home at sundown in **Rio de Onor** (p483), a town built squarely on the Portugal–Spain border

- POPULATION: 281,900
- AREA: 11,772 SQ KM

TRÁS-OS-MONTES

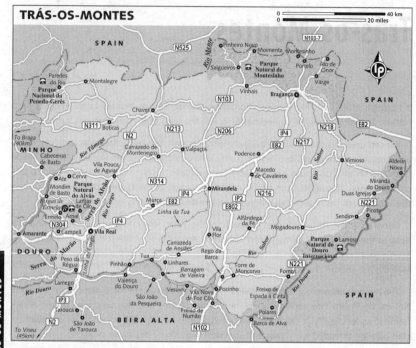

WESTERN TRÁS-OS-MONTES

VILA REAL

pop 24,500 / elev 445m

Clinging to steep hillsides above the confluence of the Rios Corgo and Cabril, the university town of Vila Real is short on charm, although its historic centre, dotted with picturesque old churches, is pleasant enough. Its key attractions lie just beyond the city limits: the dramatically rugged highlands of the Parque Natural do Alvão; and the resplendent Palácio de Mateus, one of Europe's most elegant country houses, surrounded by lovely vineyard country east of town.

Orientation

Accommodation and food options cluster around the axis of Avenida Carvalho Araújo. The train station is about 1km across the Rio Corgo from the *turismo* (tourist office); the Rodonorte bus station

is 300m northwest on Rua Dom Pedro de Castro. The bus stand for AV Tâmega, Rede Expressos and Santos buses is about a further 100m northwest.

Information

Espaço Internet (Av 1 de Maio; ⏲ 10am-2pm & 4-7pm Mon-Fri) Free internet near Hotel Miracorgo.

Hospital de São Pedro (☎ 259 300 500; Lordelo)

Parque Natural do Alvão office (☎ 259 302 830; pnal@icnb.pt; Largo dos Freitas; ⏲ 9am-12.30pm & 2-5.30pm Mon-Fri)

Police station (☎ 259 330 240; Largo Conde de Amarante)

Post office (Av Carvalho Araújo; ⏲ 8.30am-6pm Mon-Fri, 9am-12.30pm Sat)

Regional Turismo (☎ 259 322 819; rtsmarao@gmail .com; Av Carvalho Araújo 94; ⏲ 9.30am-12.30pm & 2-6pm Mon-Sat Oct-May, 9.30am-7pm Mon-Fri, 9.30am-12.30pm & 2-6pm Sat & Sun Jun-Sep) Located in a Manueline house in the town centre.

Sights

AROUND THE CENTRE

Once part of a Dominican monastery, the Gothic **sé** (cathedral; Igreja de São Domingos; Travessa de

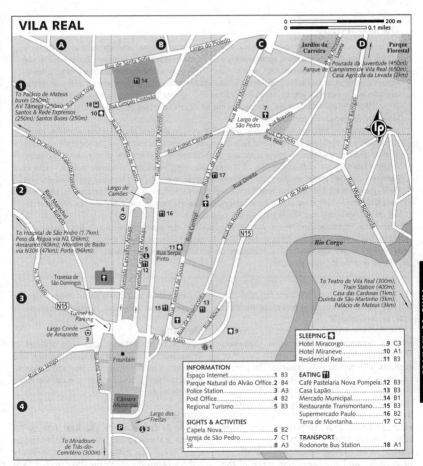

VILA REAL

0 ——— 200 m
0 ——— 0.1 miles

INFORMATION
Espaço Internet...................1	B3
Parque Natural do Alvão Office.2	B4
Police Station....................3	A3
Post Office.......................4	B2
Regional Turismo.................5	B3

SIGHTS & ACTIVITIES
Capela Nova......................6	B2
Igreja de São Pedro.............7	C1
Sé................................8	A3

SLEEPING 🛏
Hotel Miracorgo..................9	C3
Hotel Miraneve...................10	A1
Residencial Real.................11	B3

EATING 🍽
Café Pastelaria Nova Pompeia.12	B3
Casa Lapão.......................13	B3
Mercado Municipal...............14	B1
Restaurante Transmontano...15	B3
Supermercado Paulo............16	B2
Terra de Montanha..............17	C2

TRANSPORT
Rodonorte Bus Station.........18	A1

São Domingos) has been given a lengthy facelift that has restored the 15th-century grandeur of its rather spare interior.

Northeast of the cathedral is the magnificently over-the-top baroque façade of the 17th-century **Capela Nova** (Igreja dos Clérigos; varies). Inside are fine, 18th-century *azulejos* (hand-painted tiles) and large-headed cherubs with teddy-boy coifs.

More baroque, and more *azulejos,* are on view at the **Igreja de São Pedro** (Largo de São Pedro; admission free), one block north of Capela Nova.

For a fine view across the gorge of the Rio Corgo and Rio Cabril, walk south to the **Miradouro de Trás-do-Cemitério**, just beyond a small cemetery and chapel.

PALÁCIO DE MATEUS
Famously depicted on bottles of Mateus rosé, the 18th-century **Palácio de Mateus** (Solar de Mateus; ☎ 259 323 121; admission palace & gardens/gardens only €7.50/4.50; 9am-7pm Jun-Sep, 9am-1pm & 2-6pm Mar-May & Oct, 9am-1pm & 2-5pm Nov-Feb) is one of Portugal's great baroque masterpieces – probably the work of Italian-born architect Nicolau Nasoni.

Its granite wings ('advancing lobster-like towards you,' wrote English critic Sir Sacheverell Sitwell) shelter a lichen-encrusted forecourt dominated by an ornate stairway and guarded by rooftop statues. Surrounding the palace is a fantasy of a garden, with tiny boxwood hedges, prim statues and a fragrant cypress tunnel that's blissfully cool on even

TRÁS-OS-MONTES

THE NEW MATEUS

If 'Mateus' conjures up images of sickly sweet pink 'starter wine' and ubiquitous 1970s wine bottles-as-candleholders, think again and try a sip of Alvarelhão. This distinctive Portuguese grape is the original base for Mateus rosé, which in the 1950s was retooled for mass marketing in North America, where palates were considerably less sophisticated. Now the growers and vintners of Lavradores de Feitoria, whose numbers include the current Count of Vila Real and heir to the famous Palácio de Mateus itself, are producing an Alvarelhão rosé that more fully honours the legacy of this uniquely Iberian varietal.

Some growers describe Alvarelhão as a grape that is impractical and near-impossible to grow. It matures late, well into October, and falls easy prey to mildews and other pathogens – so much so that growers traditionally grew it closest to their homes and estates so they could be more easily alerted to possible outbreaks of disease. As one Lavradores producer puts it, 'Here in Portugal, we love tradition. We grow something because our fathers and our grandfathers and their grandfathers did. It's said that because of this we still have here in Portugal hundreds of varietals, which have died out in other places. But we are not efficient. We are not practical. So we are still growing this Alvarelhão because we love it.'

Because of its temperamental nature, Alvarelhão – like many of Portugal's best wines – is bottled in small quantities, mostly for use in Portugal. So until these delicious and deserving wines get wider international distribution, do yourself a favour while touring the Palácio de Mateus and sip it while you can!

the hottest days. (Don't miss the fanciful 5m-tall curved ladders used to prune the tunnel's exterior branches!)

Guided tours of the mansion (in English, French, Spanish and German) take you through the main quarters, which combine rusticity with restrained grandeur. The library contains one of the first editions of Luís Vaz de Camões' Os Lusíadas (p49), Portugal's most important epic poem, and one room houses an unintentionally droll collection of religious bric-a-brac, including 50 macabre relics bought from the Vatican in the 18th century: a bit of holy fingernail, a saintly set of eyeballs, and the inevitable piece of the true cross – each with the Vatican's proof of authentication.

Near the guided tour starting point, a wine shop offers tastings of three locally produced wines for €1 (waived with the purchase of a bottle). Especially interesting is the Alvarelhão, which is essentially the same fine rosé originally bottled by Mateus in the 1940s (see above).

The palace is 3.8km east of the town centre. Take local Corgobus bus 1 (€1, 20 minutes) towards the university (UTAD). It leaves from Rua Gonçalo Cristóvão in front of the *mercado municipal* (municipal market) roughly half-hourly between 7.30am and 8pm, with fewer buses on weekends; inquire at the *turismo* for the current timetable. Ask for 'Mateus' and the

driver will set you down about 250m from the palace (if you don't ask, he may not stop).

Sleeping

Appealing budget and midrange options in downtown Vila Real are in short supply. The best accommodations, including some charming semirural guest houses, are on the city's outer fringes.

BUDGET

Parque de Campismo de Vila Real (☎ 259 324 724; Rua Dr Manuel Cardona; sites per adult/child/tent/car €3.75/1.88/2.30/2.65; ☼ Mar-Nov) This simple, shady hillside camp site above the Rio Corgo, 1.2km northeast of the centre, has a small restaurant and pool nearby.

Pousada da Juventude (☎ 259 373 193; vilareal@ movijovem.pt; Rua Dr Manuel Cardona; dm €9, d with/without bathroom €22/18) Situated on the top floor of Vila Real's youth centre, in a dreary high-rise residential neighbourhood about 20 minutes on foot from the town centre, this hostel is rather basic, but the clean rooms all come with balconies and the staff is friendly and helpful. No meals are available, but you can use the kitchen, and there are a few cafes nearby.

Residencial Real (☎ 259 325 879; hotelreal@sapo .pt; Rua Central 5; s/d/tr €30/40/50) Most appealing of the limited budget options downtown, this family-run place is nicely positioned in the middle of a pedestrian zone, above a popular *pastelaria* (pastry shop). Some of the bright, neatly kept rooms have high ceilings and French windows.

MIDRANGE

Hotel Miraneve (☎ 259 323 153; hotel.miraneve@clix.pt; Rua Dom Pedro de Castro 17; s/d €35/55; P ✖) Directly above the bus station, this blandly modern affair has nothing to recommend it other than its central location. If you do stay, opt for one of the upstairs rooms with balcony and mountain views. Lower, front-facing rooms can be noisy.

Casa das Cardosas (☎ /fax 259 331 487; Rua Central, Folhadela; s/d €50/65; P ✖) This 18th-century farmhouse in a semirural setting has traditionally kitted-out rooms, fine gardens and views. It's 600m south of the train station.

Hotel Miracorgo (☎ 259 325 001; www.hotelmiracorgo.com; Av 1 de Maio 78; s/d/ste €49/71/98; P ✖ ⬛ ✖) Boasting fine views of the Rio Corgo canyon, this central, modern, midrise business hotel has well-appointed, if unexciting rooms, all with large verandas.

our pick **Casa Agrícola da Levada** (☎ 259 322 190; www.casadalevada.com; Timpeira; d/4-person apt with breakfast from €75/100 per night, 2-/3-/5-person self-catering house €350/380/700 per week; P ✖ ⬛ ✖) At the end of a long, shady drive lies this little gem of an inn. The friendly, multilingual owners have deep roots in the region and are generous in sharing their knowledge of the area's natural beauty and viticulture. A collection of tastefully renovated old houses surrounds grounds that include rose gardens, a large grassy lawn and swimming pool. Weekly rates on the self-catering apartments start as low as €50 per night for two people, including fresh bread delivered daily.

Quinta de São Martinho (☎ 259 323 986; www.quintasaomartinho.com; Lugar de São Martinho, Mateus; s/d €60/75, 2-/4-person apt €95/140; P ✖) Only 400m from the Palácio de Mateus, this rambling granite farmhouse-turned-inn is surrounded by pretty gardens. Rooms aren't fancy but have wood-beamed ceilings and are traditionally furnished. The adjacent restaurant (three-course meals around €15; reservations essential) is also well regarded.

Eating

Café Pastelaria Nova Pompeia (☎ 259 338 080; Av Carvalho Araújo 82; mains €4.50-8.50; ⏰ 8am-8pm Oct-May, to 11pm Jun-Sep) A few doors down from the tourist office, this large, bright cafe and bakery serves omelettes and light meals at reasonable prices. Free wi-fi is icing on the cake.

Restaurante Transmontano (☎ 259 323 540; Rua Teixeira de Sousa; mains €6.50-10; ⏰ lunch & dinner) Popular with locals, this plain-faced, family-run place in the central pedestrian zone serves delicious, belly-filling regional dishes.

our pick **Terra de Montanha** (☎ 259 372 075; Rua 31 de Janeiro 16-18; mains €10-14.50; ⏰ lunch & dinner Mon-Sat; ✖) From the black crockery to the halved wine casks that serve as booths, everything

TRÁS-OS-MONTES

GHOST TOWNS: THE TRANSMONTANA EXODUS

Portugal is one of the few European countries to experience mass emigration well into the 20th century. In the 1970s alone, it's estimated that 775,000 people left the country – nearly 10% of the total population.

With difficult agricultural conditions and little industry, it's little surprise that Trás-os-Montes (along with the neighbouring Minho) contributed more than its share to the exodus. The region's population shrank by nearly 29% between 1960 and 1991. To get an idea of the kinds of conditions they were fleeing, consider this: 60% of the region's workforce was engaged in agriculture into the 1990s – a figure higher than in many developing nations.

At the turn of the 20th century, the lion's share of emigrants headed to Brazil, which was undergoing a coffee boom. Later, many left for Portugal's African possessions, which received increased investment and interest during Salazar's regime. Then as Europe's postwar economy heated up in the 1960s and '70s, *transmontanas* began to stick closer to home, finding work as labourers in Germany, Belgium and especially France.

The effect of this exodus is still visible, especially in rural areas. Many villages have been abandoned wholesale, left to a few widows and a clutch of chickens. Around others you will find a ring of modern construction, almost always paid for not by the fruit of the land but by money earned abroad. And don't be surprised to meet a villager, scythe in hand and oxen in tow, who speaks to you in perfect Parisian argot.

here is rigorously *transmontana*. The hearty local cuisine includes specialities such as *posta barrosã* (grilled veal steak) and *cabrito assado no forno* (oven-roasted goat – served only on weekends). Weekday lunch specials are a great deal at €6.50, including bread, main dish, fruit and coffee.

Casa Lapão (Rua de Misericórdia 54; ☾ breakfast, lunch & dinner) This spruce tearoom specialises in traditional local sweets, including *cristas de galo* (almond and egg paste in a buttery pastry dough).

Self-caterers can stock up on rural produce at the **mercado municipal** (Rua de Santa Sofia; ☾ Mon-Sat), and pick up other goods at **Supermercado Paulo** (☎ 259 378 780; Rua António de Azevedo 84; ☾ 9am-8pm Mon-Sat).

Drinking & Entertainment

The slick, modern **Teatro de Vila Real** (☎ 259 320 000; www.teatrodevilareal.com, in Portuguese; Alameda de Grasse), in a parklike area across the Corgo from the city centre, stages high-quality dance and theatre performances, as well as classical, jazz and world music. It also screens biweekly films and serves as a venue for the Douro Jazz Festival (www.dourojazz.com) during wine harvest season. At the back of the building, the theatre's bright cafe overlooking the Corgo is popular with Vila Real's beau monde.

Getting There & Around

Parking along Avenida Carvalho Araújo is generally not difficult. Alternatively, there is a fee-charging lot behind the *câmara municipal* (town hall).

BUS

There are several bus lines serving Vila Real. **AV Tâmega** (☎ 259 322 928; www.avtamega.pt, in Portuguese) and **Rede Expressos** (☎ 962060655; www.rede-expressos.pt, in Portuguese) leave from a lot at the corner of Rua Dr António Valente Fonseca and Avenida Cidade de Ourense. **Rodonorte** (☎ 259 340 710; www.rodonorte.pt, in Portuguese) buses leave from the station below Hotel Miraneve on Rua Dom Pedro de Castro.

Within Trás-os-Montes, all three serve Chaves (€6.90 to €7.20, 70 minutes) and Bragança (€9.10 to €9.40, two hours).

Rodonorte and Rede Expressos have frequent services to Porto (€7.30 to €7.50, 1½ hours), as well as to Lamego (€5.50 to €5.70, 45 minutes) and Lisbon (€17.50 to €18, five to 5½ hours).

Rodonorte also serves Miranda do Douro (€10.60, three to 3½ hours).

TRAIN

Vila Real is linked to Peso da Régua (€1.70, 55 minutes) by the narrow-gauge Linha do Corgo, a pretty route snaking along the Rio Corgo. For service to Porto (€9.65, 2¾ to four hours), change trains in Peso da Régua. A taxi between Vila Real's train station and the town centre costs €4.

PARQUE NATURAL DO ALVÃO

With its rock-strewn highlands, schist villages, waterfalls and verdant pockets where cows graze in stone-walled pastures, the pristine Parque Natural do Alvão comes as a delightful revelation to travellers climbing from the hotter, drier country below. A drive of less than half an hour brings you from Vila Real to this extraordinary park straddling the central ridgeline of the Serra de Alvão, whose highest peaks reach more than 1300m. The small (72 sq km) protected area remains one of northern Portugal's best-kept secrets and shelters a remarkable variety of flora and fauna thanks to its position in a transition zone between the humid coast and the dry interior.

The Rio Ôlo, a tributary of the Rio Tâmega, rises in the park's broad granite basin. A 300m drop above Ermelo gives rise to the spectacular Fisgas de Ermelo falls, the park's major tourist attraction.

Exploring the park on your own is not simple, as maps, accommodation and public transport are limited. Whether you plan to walk or drive in the park, it's worth visiting one of the park offices beforehand for bus schedules and hiking maps.

Information

There are park offices in Vila Real (p468) and Mondim de Basto (p474). Both sell leaflets, with English-language inserts, on local products (including linen cloth and smoked sausages), land use and wildlife.

Sights

ERMELO

The 800-year-old town of Ermelo is famous for its schist cottages capped with fairy-tale slate roofs that seem to have been constructed from broken blackboards. Once the main village of the region, it boasts traditional *espigueiros* (stone granaries; see p460), an ancient chapel, a sturdy granite *pelourinho* (pillory), a workshop that still practises the ancient local art of linen-making, and **Ponte de Várzea** – a Roman bridge rebuilt in medieval times.

The Ermelo turn-off is about 16km south of Mondim de Basto on the N304. The heart of town is about 1km uphill. Ask at the Mondim de Basto or Vila Real *turismo* (p474) about bus services via Rodonorte/Mondinense.

FISGAS DE ERMELO
About 1.3km closer to Mondim de Basto on the N304 is a turn-off to the dramatic Fisgas de Ermelo waterfalls. From this junction, it's a shadeless 4km climb to the falls; take water and snacks. Near the falls you'll find a natural waterslide and a series of pools perfect for cooling off on a hot day. To get here by bus, check current schedules at Mondim de Basto's *turismo* (p474).

LAMAS DE ÔLO
Set in a wide, verdant valley some 1000m above sea level, somnolent Lamas de Ôlo is the park's highest village, best known for its photogenic thatched roofs, as well as a nearby mill that was long driven by water from a crude aqueduct.

Activities
There are a number of fine hikes in the park. For a three-hour jaunt around the southern village of **Arnal**, get hold of *Guia do Percurso Pedestre*, a park leaflet with an English-language insert. The signposted hike delivers views east beyond Vila Real to the Serra do Marão. While you're in Arnal, track down the slate-roofed centre for traditional handicraft techniques.

Another popular route is the 13km, five-hour loop through the high country starting just north of the Cimeira dam along the Vila Real–Lamas de Ôlo road. The trail, marked with red and yellow blazes, traverses the rock-strewn *planalto* (high plateau) for 8km to the village of Barreiro. From here, you can return 5km by road to your starting point, passing through Lamas de Ôlo en route.

Some other walks, ranging from 2.5km to 11.5km, are outlined in the Portuguese-language booklet *Percurso Pedestre: Mondim de Basto/Parque Natural do Alvão*, with a rough, 1:50,000 trail map.

Fernando Gomes runs local company **Basto Radical** (☎ 963056673; bastoradical@portugal

mail.pt), which arranges hiking, rock climbing, mountain biking, canyoning, canoeing and rafting excursions with English- or French-speaking guides. Prices range from €5 to €7.50 per person per hour.

Local **Clube de Parapente Asas da Senhora da Graça** (☎ 965375354; parapentebasto@sapo.pt) organises weekend paragliding in the Mondim de Basto area.

Sleeping & Eating
Camping is prohibited in the natural park, and other food and lodging options are scarce. In Ermelo, **Dona Benedita** (☎ 255 381 221; r €25) rents out simple rooms with bathroom. At the time of writing, the Mondim de Basto *turismo* was also able to arrange bookings of private houses in Lamas de Ôlo. Aside from these, your best bet is to use Vila Real or Mondim de Basto as your base, or ask at the *turismo* in either town to see if new accommodation has opened up inside the park.

A few steps from the town bus stop, Café Albina de Ôlo is Lamas de Ôlo's only in-town eating option, with limited food and high prices.

In Bobal, halfway between Lamas de Ôlo and Mondim de Basto, **A Tasca da Alicia** (☎ 255 381 381; ☉ Oct-Aug) serves snacks all day and can also arrange full meals for groups of six or more with advance notice.

Getting There & Away
From Vila Real, **Rodonorte** (☎ 259 340 710) operates one midday and one evening bus to Lamas de Ôlo (€2.10, 30 minutes, weekdays only). Rodonorte also offers connecting services with Auto Mondinense from Vila Real to Ermelo, with a change of buses in Aveção do Cabo (€2.30, 40 minutes).

From Mondim de Basto at the north edge of the park, **Auto Mondinense** (☎ 255381296) runs local buses to Lamas de Ôlo (€2.60, one hour) and Ermelo (€2.15, one hour).

It's worth checking at park offices for other school-year services.

MONDIM DE BASTO
pop 3500 / elev 200m
Sitting in the Tâmega valley at the intersection of the Douro, Minho and Trás-os-Montes regions, low-lying Mondim de Basto has no compelling sights beyond a few flowery squares, but it makes an attractive base from which to explore the heights of the Parque

Natural do Alvão. The vineyards surrounding town cultivate grapes used in the fine local *vinho verde* (young wine).

Orientation & Information

Buses stop behind the *mercado municipal*, 150m west of the **turismo** (☎ 255 389 370; turismo@cm-mondimdebasto.pt; Praça 9 de Abril; ☼ 9am-1pm & 2-5pm Mon-Sat Jul–mid-Sep, 9am-1pm & 2-5pm Mon-Fri mid-Sep–Jun) and what remains of the old town.

About 700m west of the *turismo* is the **Parque Natural do Alvão office** (☎ /fax 255 381 209; pnal@icnb.pt; Lugar do Barrio; ☼ 9am-12.30pm & 2-5.30pm Mon-Fri).

There is street parking along Avenida Augusto Brito.

Activities

HIKING

Hikers wanting to feel a little burn in their thighs should consider the long haul up to the 18th-century Capela da Senhora da Graça on the summit of pine-clad **Monte Farinha** (996m). It takes two to three hours to reach the top. The path starts east of town on the N312 (the *turismo* has a rough map). By car, turn off the N312 3.5km from Mondim towards Cerva; from there it's a twisting 9.5km to the top.

SWIMMING

At Senhora da Ponte, 2km south of town on the N304, there's a rocky swimming spot by a disused watermill on the Rio Cabril. Follow signs to the Parque de Campismo de Mondim de Basto and then take the track to the right.

WINE-TASTING

The refreshing local 'Basto' *vinho verde* is produced nearby at Quinta do Fundo (right). The *turismo* has details of further-flung wineries.

Sleeping

Parque de Campismo de Mondim de Basto (☎ /fax 255 381 650; mondim.basto@fcmportugal.com; sites per adult/car €4/2.65, per tent €2.65-4.35; ☼ Jan-Nov) This shady, well-run facility is about 1km south of town on hard ground beside the Rio Cabril. The river offers a cool plunge on hot summer days and there's a snack bar (but no restaurant).

Residencial Carvalho (☎ 255 381 057; Av Dr Augusto Brito; s/d €20/30; P ☒) For affordable indoor accommodation, your best bet is this graceless, modern *residencial* (guest housewest of the *turismo*, next to the GALP petrol station.

Quinta do Fundo (☎ 255 381 291; www.quintado fundo.com; Vilar de Viando; d/ste €50/75; P ☒ ☒) This idyllic spot, set amid a sea of vineyards 2km south on the N304, has decent rooms, fine mountain vistas, a tennis court and a swimming pool. The *quinta* (estate) also produces its own *vinho verde*. Ask about discounts for multinight stays.

Casa das Mourôas (☎ 255 381 394; Rua José Carvalho Camões; r €55; P) Occupying an old stone house on the same flower-filled square as the *turismo*, this little place has three humble but neat rooms ranged around a delightful, vine-covered terrace. English is spoken. Reservations are recommended on weekends and in summer.

Casa do Campo (☎ 255 361 231; www.casadocampo .pt; Molares, Celorico de Basto; d/ste €80/100; P ☒ ☒) If you have wheels and funds, consider this antique-packed, whitewashed 17th-century manor house with its own crenellated stone tower, chapel and extravagant (if weedy) topiary gardens. Rooms are modest but pleasant, with wood floors and plain country furnishings. Suites include a small living room with TV and frigobar. It's 5km west of Mondim.

Eating

Adega Sete Condes (☎ 255 382 342; Rua Velha; half-portions €5-7, mains €6-10; ☼ lunch & dinner Tue-Sun, lunch Mon) Tucked into a tiny corner behind the *turismo*, this rustic, granite-walled spot has a small menu of well-prepared traditional dishes, including *bacalhau* (dried salt-cod) and a very tasty *feijoada* (pork and bean stew).

Adega São Tiago (☎ 255 386 957; Rua Velha; mains €7-10; ☼ lunch & dinner Fri-Wed, lunch Thu) Very similar to Adega Sete Condes, this restaurant is just up the street.

Getting There & Away

Auto Mondinense (☎ 255 381 296) has eight weekday and three to four weekend buses to Porto (€6.05, 2½ hours) via Guimarães (€4, 1½ hours), as well as twice-daily services to Lisbon (€17.50, 6½ hours).

CHAVES

pop 17,500 / elev 340m

A spa town with a long and fascinating history, Chaves (*shahv*-sh) is a pretty and engaging place, straddling the mountain-fringed banks of the Rio Tâmega only a few kilometres south of the Spanish border. Its well-preserved historic centre is anchored at the edges by a 16-arched Roman bridge dating back to

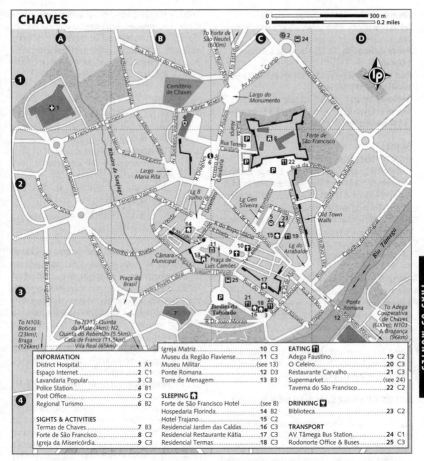

CHAVES

INFORMATION	
District Hospital	**1** A1
Espaço Internet	**2** C1
Lavandaria Popular	**3** C3
Police Station	**4** B1
Post Office	**5** C2
Regional Turismo	**6** B2

SIGHTS & ACTIVITIES	
Termas de Chaves	**7** B3
Forte de São Francisco	**8** C3
Igreja da Misericórdia	**9** C3
Igreja Matriz	**10** C3
Museu da Região Flaviense	**11** C3
Museu Militar	(see 13)
Ponte Romana	**12** D3
Torre de Menagem	**13** B3

SLEEPING	
Forte de São Francisco Hotel	(see 8)
Hospedaria Florinda	**14** B2
Hotel Trajano	**15** C2
Residencial Jardim das Caldas	**16** C3
Residencial Restaurante Kátia	**17** C3
Residencial Termas	**18** C3

EATING	
Adega Faustino	**19** C2
O Celeiro	**20** C3
Restaurante Carvalho	**21** C3
Supermarket	(see 24)
Taverna do São Francisco	**22** C2

DRINKING	
Biblioteca	**23** C2

TRANSPORT	
AV Tâmega Bus Station	**24** C1
Rodonorte Office & Buses	**25** C3

TRÁS-OS-MONTES

Trajan's reign, a beautiful medieval tower (the Torre da Menagem) and the rock-solid Forte de São Francisco.

All of these remnants testify to Chaves' earlier strategic importance in controlling the small but fertile plain that surrounds it. Romans built a key garrison here, and it was subsequently contested by the Visigoths, Moors, French and Spanish alike. It saw particularly fierce fighting during the Napoleonic invasion, when it was at the forefront of resistance against French domination.

Nowadays Chaves is a placid backwater – where the Portuguese come not to defend the national honour but to pamper themselves in the natural hot springs that bubble up in the city's heart.

Orientation

Chaves' town centre is a 700m walk southwest of the AV Tâmega bus station, and it's a few blocks northeast of the Rodonorte bus stop on Rua Joaquim J Delgado. The backbone of the old town is formed by Rua de Santo António, which eventually leads to the Roman bridge. The spa is near the river, just south of the centre.

There is fee-charging public parking near the river in and around Jardim do Tabolado.

Information

District hospital (☎ 276 300 900; Av Francisco Sá Carneiro) Northwest of the centre.

Espaço Internet (⏰ 9am-7pm Mon-Fri) Free internet near the bus station.

Lavandaria Popular (☎ 276 332 621; Rua do Tabolado; wash, dry & iron service per kg €2.80; ☼ 9am-1pm & 3-7pm Mon-Fri, to 1pm Sat)

Police station (☎ 276 323 125; Av Bombeiros Voluntários)

Post office (Largo General Silveira; ☼ 8.30am-6pm Mon-Fri, 9am-12.30pm Sat)

Regional turismo (☎ 276 340 660; www.rt-atb.pt; Terreiro de Cavalaria; ☼ 9am-12.30pm & 2-5.30pm Mon-Sat) Helpful multilingual tourist office.

Sights

PONTE ROMANA

Cars and trucks still rumble across Chaves' handsome, 140m-long, Roman-era bridge, completed in AD 104 by order of Emperor Trajan (hence its other name, Ponte Trajano). It likely served as a key link on the important road between Braga and Astorga (Spain), as two engraved Roman milestones on the centre of the bridge indicate.

MUSEU DA REGIÃO FLAVIENSE

This regional archaeological-ethnographic **museum** (☎ 276 340 500; Praça de Luís Camões; incl Museu Militar adult/under 18 yr & senior €1/0.50; ☼ 9am-12.30pm & 2-5.30pm daily except holidays) has (naturally) lots of Roman artefacts, but the most interesting items are stone menhirs and carvings, some dating back over 2500 years. There are also temporary art displays.

TORRE DE MENAGEM & MUSEU MILITAR

The lovely Torre de Menagem (castle keep) stands alone on a grassy embankment behind the town's main square, the only major remnant of a 14th-century castle built by Dom Dinis. Around the tower are attractive manicured flowerbeds and a stretch of old defensive walls, with views over the town and countryside.

The *torre* now houses a motley collection of military gear in the **Museu Militar** (incl Museu da Região Flaviense adult/under 18 yr & senior €1/0.50; ☼ 9am-12.30pm & 2-5.30pm daily except holidays). A series of creaky stairs leads up to the roof.

FORTE DE SÃO FRANCISCO & FORTE DE SÃO NEUTEL

Reached by a drawbridge and bordered by a park with floral designs, hedges and grand old oaks, the 17th-century Forte de São Francisco is the centrepiece of Chaves' old town. The fort, with its thick walls, was completed in 1658 around a 16th-century Franciscan convent. These days it's a top-end hotel, though

nobody minds if you snoop around inside the walls. The smaller, 17th-century Forte de São Neutel, 1.2km northeast of the centre, is open only for occasional summertime concerts. Both forts were inspired by the work of the French military architect Vauban.

CHURCHES

The 17th-century **Igreja da Misericórdia** (Praça de Luís Camões) has an eye-catching facade with distinctive, twisting columns, plus some huge 18th-century *azulejos* inside.

Also on the square is the **igreja matriz** (parish church), which is Romanesque in form. It was thoroughly remodelled in the 16th century, though the doorway and belfry retain some original features.

Activities

The warm waters of the **Termas de Chaves** (☎ 276 332 445; www.termasdechaves.com; Largo das Caldas), which emerge from the ground at 73°C, are said to relieve everything from rheumatism to obesity. After shelling out an initial €65 for a medical consultation and sign-up fee, you have access to a plethora of reasonably priced treatments (€5 to €23), ranging from steam baths to massage. You can also drink the bicarbonate-heavy waters, though they taste pretty awful.

The **Adega Cooperativa de Chaves** (☎ 276 322 183; coopagrichaves.no.sapo.pt, in Portuguese; Rua de São Bento; ☼ 9am-6pm Mon-Fri), 1km southeast of the centre, is open weekdays for tours and wine-tastings. Check out the São Neutel (reds and sparkling whites), Flavius (sturdy reds and whites) and Vespasiano (reds) wines. You may even risk the rough red *vinho dos mortos* (wine of the dead), which is aged at least one year underground – a technique that likely began when locals buried the stuff to safeguard it from invading Napoleonic troops.

Sleeping

Try to book ahead in summer, when the spa is in full swing. Most places offer big discounts from September to May.

BUDGET

Quinta do Rebentão (☎ /fax 276 322 733; Vila Nova de Veiga; sites per adult/child/car/tent €3/1.80/3/3; ☼ Jan-Nov) Just off the N2 6km southwest of Chaves is this grassy, partly shaded, suburban camping facility with free hot showers, pool access and basic supplies. Bike rentals are also available.

Hospedaria Florinda (☎ 276 333 392; fax 276 326 577; Rua dos Açougues; s/d €20/30; ⊠) In an older building on a narrow street near the Torre de Menagem, Florinda offers small, spotless, refurbished rooms with floral prints, and a tiny dining room that serves top-notch regional meals. The lady of the house is a paragon of *transmontana* hospitality.

Hotel Trajano (☎ 276 301 640; www.hoteltrajano.com; Travessa Cândido dos Reis; s/d/ste from €25/35/55; ⊠) One of the best deals in town, thanks to recently reduced rates, this '70s-style hotel (with decor to match) offers solid comforts and good views from the higher rooms.

Residencial Termas (☎ 276 333 280; fax 276 333 190; Rua do Tabolado; s/d €30/35; ⊠) This place has small-ish, workaday rooms with linoleum floors, but decent beds and private bathrooms make it a reasonable budget option. Bedraggled travellers will also appreciate the laundry just next door.

Residencial Restaurante Kátia (☎ 276 324 446; Rua do Sol 28; s/d €30/35) The service may be a bit lackadaisical, but this family-run guest house offers small, prim, spotless rooms – some with verandas.

Residencial Jardim das Caldas (☎ 276 331 189; www.residencialjardimdascaldas.com; Alameda do Tabolado 5; s/d €30/40) In a modern building facing Chaves' riverside park, this guest house has tidy and well-kept, if rather institutional, rooms. If there's nobody at reception, ask at the restaurant on the ground floor.

MIDRANGE & TOP END

Casa de France (☎ 276 965 453; www.geocities.com /casadefrance; N314, France; s/d €37.50/50; P ⊠) In the village of France, 12km south of Chaves, this lovely stone-and-timber *transmontana* country house has been converted into an attractive inn. Amenities include a billiard room with fireplace and a poolside garden commanding sweeping vistas of the surrounding plains and mountains.

Quinta da Mata (☎ 276 340 030; www.quintadamata .net; Nantes; d €80; P ⊠ ⊠) This isolated and family-friendly country haven, just 4.5km southeast of Chaves off the N213, centres on a lovingly restored and elegantly appointed 17th-century manor house with terracotta tile floors and stone walls. The grounds include tennis courts, a sauna and beautiful, flower-filled gardens on the lush hills overlooking the city.

Forte de São Francisco Hotel (☎ 276 333 700; www.forte-s-francisco-hoteis.pt; s/d/ste from €135/150/180; P ⊠ ⊠) For stylish digs in downtown Chaves, look no further than this remarkable historic inn. Housed inside a 16th-century convent that lies within the walls of the city's 17th-century fort, this extraordinary blend of four-star hotel and national monument has flawless rooms, tennis courts and a sauna, not to mention a rare-bird aviary, a centuries-old private chapel with piped-in Gregorian chants and an upscale restaurant and bar.

Eating

O Celeiro (☎ 276 321 971; Alameda do Tabolado 7; 🕙 9.15am-1pm & 2.30-8pm Mon-Sat, 9.15am-1pm & 2.30-6pm Sun) This store is packed to the rafters with the delicious smoked *presunto* (ham) and sausages for which Chaves is famous. It's also a great place to sample other regional delicacies such as *pastéis de Chaves*, meat pastries that are especially tasty when accompanied by local white wine.

Adega Faustino (☎ 276 322 142; Travessa Cândido dos Reis; dishes €3-7.50; 🕙 lunch & dinner Mon-Sat) Resembling a fire station from the outside, this atmospheric ex-winery manages to feel intimate despite its cavernous interior. The menu features a long list of carefully prepared regional snacks, from *salpicão* (small rounds of smoked ham) to pig's ear in vinaigrette sauce, plus an excellent selection of quaffable local wines.

Restaurante Carvalho (☎ 276 321 727; Jardim do Tabolado; dishes around €8-13; ☺ lunch & dinner Fri-Wed) Carvalho's top-notch regional dishes have earned recognition as some of Portugal's best. It's hidden away amidst the cluster of parkside cafes opposite the Jardim do Tabolado.

Taverna do São Francisco (Forte de São Francisco; mains €9-16; ☺ lunch & dinner Tue-Sat) Set in the guard's quarters, right inside the fort's thick walls, this atmospheric joint with checked tablecloths and exposed stonework specialises in regional fare, including the dozens of hams and cheeses hanging from the ceiling.

For self-caterers, there's a supermarket upstairs from the AV Tâmega bus station.

Drinking

Biblioteca (Travessa Cândido dos Reis) This bar-cum-disco with a name meaning 'library' attracts a raucous and decidedly nonliterary younger crowd. Weekly events include a Thursday ladies' night and Friday karaoke night.

More upmarket is the bar and disco at Forte de São Francisco Hotel (p477).

Getting There & Away

AV Tâmega (☎ 276 332 384) has services to Porto (€11.20, 2¼ hours) six times daily; and to Vila Real (€6.90, 1¼ hours), Coimbra (€13.50, 3¾ hours) and Lisbon (€19.10, six to seven hours) three times daily. These services drop off at weekends, especially Saturday. Tâmega also has one daily service to Bragança (€10, three hours), plus Friday and Sunday services to Braga (€11.10, three hours).

Rodonorte (☎ 276 333 491; Rua Joaquim J Delgado) runs via Vila Real (€6.90, 1¼ hours) and Amarante (€9.50, two hours) to Porto (€11.20, 2¾ hours) several times per weekday, less often at the weekend.

EASTERN TRÁS-OS-MONTES

BRAGANÇA
pop 20,300 / elev 650m

The historical capital of Trás-os-Montes, Bragança is at once a modern city of grimy streets and suburban high-rises, and an overgrown medieval village where from al-most any vantage point one can still look out over the surrounding countryside and see small farms, fields, and oak-chestnut forest. While many streets – especially some in the older *centro* (centre) – give the appearance of a town down on its luck, new construction and civic projects express Bragança's enduring pride and dynamism. Recent additions to the city's cultural life include a new municipal theatre; museums dedicated to contemporary art, science and regional folk traditions; and fine public sculptures such as the bronze postman outside the *correio* (post office) or the massive fighting bulls in the Rotunda do Lavrador Transmontano north of town.

For the visitor, the main attraction remains the ancient walled Cidadela (citadel), high atop the hill at Bragança's eastern edge. Walk through the arched gates into this extraordinarily well-preserved medieval village, with its tangle of narrow streets, multistorey keep and towering pig pillory, and it's easy to imagine life in the Middle Ages unfolding around you. The view from the topmost tower – for those brave enough to climb a steep, ancient wooden ladder – is truly astounding.

History

Known as Bragantia to the Celts and Juliobriga to the Romans, Bragança is an ancient city. Its location mere kilometres from the Spanish border made it an important post in the centuries-long battles between Spain and Portugal. The walled citadel was built in 1130 by Portugal's first king, Afonso Henriques I. His son and successor, Sancho I, improved the fortifications by building Bragança's castle, with its watchtowers, dungeons and keep, in 1187, after reclaiming the city from the king of León.

In 1442 Afonso V created the Duchy of Bragança for his uncle, an illegitimate son of the first Avis king João I, thus launching one of Portugal's wealthiest and most powerful noble families. The Braganças assumed the Portuguese throne in 1640, ending Spain's 60-year domination of Portugal, and reigned until the dissolution of the monarchy in 1910.

During the Napoleonic Wars, Bragança again served as an important strategic point against foreign invaders: it was from here that Sepúlveda launched his call to resistance against French forces.

Orientation

The town centre is Praça da Sé, the square in front of the old cathedral: from here one road runs to the citadel, one to Spain and one to the rest of Portugal.

The main axis is Avenida João da Cruz, Rua Almirante Reis and Rua Combatentes da Grande Guerra (commonly called Rua Direita).

The defunct train station at the top of Avenida João da Cruz now serves as the central bus station.

Parking is generally not difficult. There are lots of spots in the square just south of the *sé*.

Information

Biblioteca Municipal (☎ 273 300 854; Praça Camões; ⏰ 9am-12.30pm & 2-5.30pm Mon-Fri) Free internet at the public library.

Cyber Centro Bragança (☎ 273 331 932; 1st fl, mercado municipal; per hr €1; ⏰ 10am-11pm Mon-Fri, 10am-7pm Sat, 2-7pm Sun) Internet access.

District Hospital (☎ 273 310 800; Av Abade de Baçal) West of the centre.

Lavandaria Brasiliera (☎ 273 322 425; Rua do Paço 22; per kg €2.50; ⏰ 9am-noon & 2-7pm Mon-Fri, 9am-1pm Sat) Next-day laundry service.

Parque Natural de Montesinho office (☎ 273 300 400; pnm@icnb.pt; Rua Cónego Albano Falcão 5; ⏰ 9am-12.30pm & 2-5.30pm Mon-Fri) Northeast of the central *turismo*.

Police station (☎ 273 303 400; Rua Dr Manuel Bento) Just north of the *câmara municipal*.

Post & telephone office (⏰ 8.30am-5.30pm Mon-Fri, 9am-12.30pm Sat)

Turismo Centre (☎ 273 381 273; turismo@cm-braganca.pt; Av Cidade de Zamora; ⏰ 9am-12.30pm & 2-5pm Mon-Fri, 10am-12.30pm Sat); Cidadela (☎ 273 381 067; Rua Dom Fernão o Bravo; ⏰ 10am-12.30pm & 2-6pm Tue-Sat) The extremely helpful centre office is open year-round; at the time of writing, opening hours were in flux because of the newly opened branch inside the Cidadela.

Sights

MUSEU DO ABADE DE BAÇAL

Set in a restored 18th-century bishop's palace, the **Museu do Abade de Baçal** (☎ 273 331 595; www.ipmuseus.pt; Rua Abílio Beça 27; adult/under 14 yr/student €2/free/1, 10am-2pm Sun free; ⏰ 10am-5pm Tue-Fri, to 6pm Sat & Sun) is one of Portugal's best regional museums. Its diverse collections include local artefacts from the Celtic and Roman eras, along with objects, paintings and photographs depicting daily life in Trás-os-Montes to the present. Of particular interest are the handful of Iron Age stone pigs called *berrões* (see the boxed text, p477). The museum also features works by Portuguese naturalist painter Aurelia de Sousa and her contemporaries. Not to be missed from the episcopal collection are pieces of Christian art from India, which depict Jesus in a style highly influenced by Hindu and Buddhist art.

MUSEU IBÉRICO DA MÁSCARA E DO TRAJE

The **Museu Ibérico da Máscara e do Traje** (Iberian Mask & Costume Museum; ☎ 273 381 008; www.cm-braganca.pt; Rua Dom Fernão o Bravo 24/26; admission €1; ⏰ 10am-12.30pm & 2-6pm Tue-Sun), which opened in 2007, displays a colourful and fascinating collection of masks and costumes from the ancient pagan-based solstice and Carnaval festivities celebrated in Trás-os-Montes and neighbouring Zamora (Spain). Costumes are displayed across three floors, with the upper exhibits dedicated to the work of local artisans.

CENTRO DE ARTE CONTEMPORÂNEA GRAÇA MORAIS

The **Centro de Arte Contemporânea Graça Morais** (☎ 273 302 410; www.cm-braganca.pt; Rua Abílio Beça 150; admission €2; ⏰ 10am-12.30pm & 2-6.30pm Tue-Sun), which opened in 2008, is another cross-border collaboration between Portugal and Spain. Its permanent collection features the work of local painter Graça Morais, including haunting portraits of Trás-os-Montes residents alongside more abstract work; the modern annexe showcases rotating special exhibitions.

CENTRO CIÊNCIA VIVA

Inaugurated in 2007, the **Centro Ciência Viva** (www.braganca.cienciaviva.pt, in Portuguese; adult/child €2.50/1; ⏰ 10am-6pm Tue-Fri, 11am-7pm Sat & Sun) Edifício Principal (☎ 273 313 169; Rua do Beato Nicolão Dinis); Casa da Seda (☎ 273 382 207; Rua dos Batoques 25) offers permanent exhibits on silk (a key element of Bragança's economy from the 15th to the 19th century), recycling, the environment and the natural history of the Parque Natural de Montesinho. The museum's pleasant cafe has free internet and a terrace overlooking the Rio Fervença.

BRAGANÇA

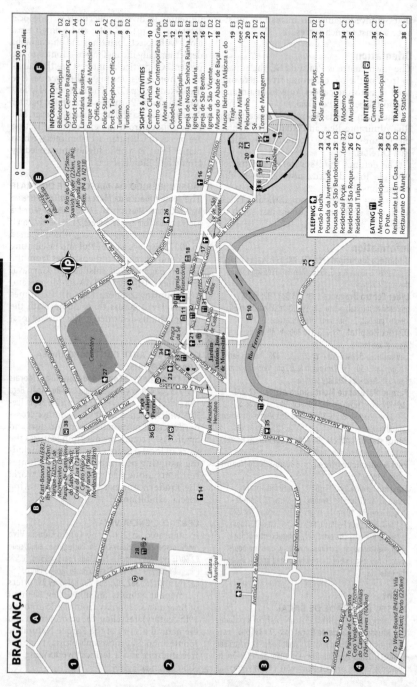

INFORMATION	
Biblioteca Municipal...................	1 D2
Cyber Centro Bragança..............	2 B2
District Hospital........................	3 A4
Lavandaria Brasileira..................	4 D2
Parque Natural de Montesinho	
Office.....................................	5 E1
Police Station............................	6 A2
Post & Telephone Office............	7 C2
Turismo.....................................	8 E3
Turismo.....................................	9 D2

SIGHTS & ACTIVITIES	
Centro Ciência Viva...................	10 D3
Centro de Arte Contemporânea Graça	
Morais....................................	11 D2
Cidadela...................................	12 E3
Domus Municipalis.....................	13 E3
Igreja de Nossa Senhora Rainha.	14 B2
Igreja de Santa Maria................	15 E3
Igreja de São Bento...................	16 E2
Igreja de São Vicente.................	17 D2
Museu do Abade de Baçal..........	18 D2
Museu Ibérico da Máscara e do	
Traje.......................................	19 E3
Museu Militar.......................	(see 22)
Pelourinho................................	20 E3
Sé..	21 D2
Torre de Menagem.....................	22 E3

SLEEPING	
Pensão Rucha............................	23 C2
Pousada da Juventude................	24 A3
Pousada de São Bartolomeu.......	25 D3
Residencial Poças...................	(see 32)
Residencial São Roque...............	26 E2
Residencial Tulipa......................	27 C1

EATING	
Mercado Municipal....................	28 B2
O Pote.......................................	29 C3
Restaurante Lá Em Casa.............	30 C2
Restaurante O Manel..................	31 D2
Restaurante Poças......................	32 D2
Solar Bragançano......................	33 C2

DRINKING	
Moderno....................................	34 C2
Musicália...................................	35 C3

ENTERTAINMENT	
Cinema......................................	36 C2
Teatro Municipal........................	37 C2

TRANSPORT	
Bus Station................................	38 C1

TRÁS-OS-MONTES

SÉ

Bragança's modest old **cathedral** (☎ 273 300 360; admission free; ⊙ varies) started out in 1545 as the Igreja de São João Baptista, but moved up the rankings to become a cathedral in 1770 when the bishopric moved here from Miranda do Douro. It was then downgraded again when Bragança's contemporary cathedral, the **Igreja de Nossa Senhora Rainha**, opened just west of the centre.

OTHER CHURCHES

Bragança's most attractive church is **Igreja de São Bento** (☎ 273 300 360; Rua São Francisco), with a Renaissance stone portal, a wonderful trompe l'œil ceiling over the nave and an Arabic-style inlaid ceiling above the chancel.

Facing little Largo de São Vicente a block westwards is the **Igreja de São Vicente**, Romanesque in origin but rebuilt in the 17th century. A chapter in Portugal's favourite – and grisliest – love story may have been played out here, where tradition has it that the future Dom Pedro secretly married Inês de Castro around 1354 (see p303 for the whole tragic tale).

CIDADELA

Keep climbing uphill from Largo de São Vicente and you'll soon set foot inside the astonishingly well-preserved 12th-century citadel. People still live in its narrow, atmospheric lanes, unspoilt by the few, low-key handicrafts shops and cafes that have crept in.

Within the ruggedly ramparted walls is the original castle – built by Sancho I in 1187 and beefed up in the 15th century by João I, then heavily restored in the 1930s. The stout **Torre de Menagem** was garrisoned up until the early 20th century. It now houses a lacklustre **Museu Militar** (Military Museum; ☎ 273 322 378; adult/child under 10 yr €1.50/free, 9-11.45am Sun free; ⊙ 9-11.45am & 2-4.45pm Fri-Wed), but the price of admission is well worth the chance to climb storey after storey and take in its rooms and halls. The military artefacts themselves bring home the impact of the first Republic's choice to join Allied forces in WWI and the cost of the Salazar dictatorship's colonial exploits. In front of the *torre* is an extraordinary, primitive **pelourinho** (stone pillory) atop a granite boar similar to the *berrões* (see the boxed text, p477) found around the province.

Squatting at the rear of the citadel is an odd pentagonal building known as the **Domus Municipalis** (Town House; admission free; ⊙ 9am-4.45pm Fri-Wed), the oldest town hall in Portugal – although its precise age is a matter of scholarly disagreement – and one of the few examples of civil Romanesque architecture on the Iberian Peninsula. Bragança's medieval town council once met upstairs in an arcaded room studded with weathered faces of man and beast and scratched with symbols of the stonemasons.

Beside the Domus Municipalis is the early-16th-century **Igreja de Santa Maria**. Of particular interest are its brick Mudéjar columns, vividly painted ceiling, and a dramatic 17th-century Santa Maria Madalena at the high altar, with her traditional long hair and ragged garb.

Festivals & Events

Bragança's biggest annual market, **Feira das Cantarinhas**, takes place from 2 to 4 May. It's a huge street fair of traditional handicrafts (a *cantarinha* is a small terracotta pitcher) held in and around the Cidadela.

Sleeping

Bragança's central hotels are largely dreary low-budget affairs whose glory days seem to have peaked sometime in the early 1970s.

BUDGET

Pensão Rucha (☎ 273 331 672; Rua Almirante Reis 42; s/d with shared bathroom €15/25) The kind proprietress at this simple *pensão* (guest house) offers spotless but lacklustre rooms with shared bathroom at a good price. No breakfast.

Pousada da Juventude (☎ 273 304 600; braganca@movijovem.pt; Av 22 de Maio; dm €11, d with/without bathroom €32/26, apt with kitchenette €60; ℗ ▣) Given a four-star rating by HI, this modern hostel includes amenities such as self-service laundry, pay-for-service wi-fi, comfy common areas, and an on-site restaurant. The two-bedroom apartment with its own kitchen and washer-dryer is one of the best deals in town. It's located in nondescript suburbs west of the centre, about a 30-minute walk from the Cidadela.

Residencial Poças (☎ 273 331 428; Rua Combatentes de Grande Guerra 200; s/d/tr/q €15/25/30/40) The high-ceilinged rooms here are cheap and spacious, even if the mismatched and battered furniture looks like it was salvaged off a truck. Check out the hundreds of swallows' nests under the eaves as you enter; the building is reputed to be the second-biggest urban nesting site in Europe.

Residencial São Roque (☎ 273 381 481; fax 273 326 937; Rua Miguel Torga; s/d €25/35) This otherwise graceless blocky high-rise near the *turismo* distinguishes itself with great views of the Cidadela from upper-floor rooms with balconies. The decor is ageing 1970s institutional and the atmosphere is generally dreary.

There are also two camping grounds in the nearby Parque Natural de Montesinho – the Parque de Campismo Municipal do Sabor (p485) and the Parque de Campismo Cepo Verde (p486).

MIDRANGE

Residencial Tulipa (☎ 273 331 675; tulipaturismo@iol.pt; Rua Dr Francisco Felgueiras 8-10; s/d/tr €38/45/58; P 🞵) With uniformly clean but uninspiring modern rooms, the Tulipa's main attraction is its central location between the bus station and downtown. One room has been adapted for visitors with disabilities.

Ibis Bragança (☎ 273 302 520; www.ibishotel.com; Rotunda do Lavrador Transmontano; r without breakfast €53; 🞵) Despite its bland chain-hotel predictability, the Ibis is far nicer than comparably priced hotels in the centre. The recently constructed rooms are small but bright and cheery. In-room wi-fi (€3 per hour) is available; and there's a convenient restaurant on-site. Located across from the monumental bull statues in the high-rise suburbs just off the IP4, it's a 30-minute walk to the Cidadela. Outside peak summer season, rates for up to three people drop to €37 (without breakfast).

TOP END

Pousada de São Bartolomeu (☎ 273 331 493; recepcao .sbartolomeu@pousadas.pt; Estrada do Turismo; d high season €198, low season €144; P 🞵 🞵) This whitewashed modern affair may not, in itself, be the most arresting *pousada* (upmarket inn) in Portugal, but its views over the Cidadela and countryside are way up there. It sits proudly alone, on a hilltop 1.5km southeast of the centre, and boasts lots of creature comforts, including a great breakfast buffet and bright contemporary rooms with balconies overlooking the pool and the castle.

Eating

Restaurante Poças (☎ 273 331 428; Rua Combatentes da Grande Guerra 200; dishes €5-8; 🕑 lunch & dinner) Despite the touristy, multilingual menus, Restaurante Poças serves very good *transmontano* food at nontouristy prices. Especially tasty is the *lombo de porco com castanhas* (roast pork with chestnuts).

O Pote (☎ 273 333 710; Rua Alexandre Herculano 186; dishes €7.50-12; 🕑 lunch & dinner Mon-Sat) This friendly eatery is divided into a formal upstairs dining room and a more relaxed downstairs cafe, both serving excellent regional specialities. For dessert, try the *peras bêbadas* ('drunk' pears soaked in wine).

Restaurante O Manel (☎ 273 322 480; Rua Oróbio de Castro 27-29; dishes €8.50-14; 🕑 lunch & dinner Mon-Sat) O Manel offers excellent food in a bright, simple dining room. Specialities include *ossinhos de porco á transmontana* (marinated pork chops served with fried egg).

our pick **Solar Bragançano** (☎ 273 323 875; Praça da Sé 34; mains €8.50-14; 🕑 lunch & dinner) Upstairs in a manor house opposite the cathedral square, this elegant eatery boasts oak-panelled rooms, chandeliers, wide plank floors, a leafy and sun-dappled outdoor terrace and a seasonal menu weighted towards local game, with specialities including wild boar, partridge with grapes and pheasant with chestnuts.

Restaurante Lá Em Casa (☎ 273 322 111; Rua Marquês de Pombal; mains €9-14; 🕑 lunch & dinner) This place serves platters heaped with excellent, wood-grilled local meats in a stone-walled, pine-panelled dining room with fireplace. The veal and lamb are especially savoury.

Pousada de São Bartolomeu (left) This inn has a very good upmarket restaurant, with less atmosphere but better views than Solar Bragançano; cuisine and prices are similar.

Self-caterers will find numerous *minimercados* (grocery shops) in the backstreets. It's a longish walk to the new, rather antiseptic **mercado municipal** (🕑 8am-7pm Mon-Sat), behind the *câmara municipal*.

Drinking

Moderno (☎ 273 327 766; Rua Almirante Reis; 🕑 midnight-4am) This is the city's principal disco, with DJs spinning everything from electronica to *tuna* (a Portuguese brand of alternative rock).

Musicália (Av Sá Carneiro 121; 🕑 5pm-2am Mon-Sat, 8pm-2am Sun) The stylish Musicália serves up varied live music, from rock to jazz to fado, plus Guinness on tap.

There are also atmospheric bars in the Cidadela where you can down shots of *ginja* (cherry liqueur) with Bragança's version of good ole boys.

Entertainment

The boxy new **Teatro Municipal** (☎ 273 302 744; Praça Cavaleiro Ferreira) has given the city's cultural life a great boost, by hosting high-quality music, theatre and dance performances most nights, plus afternoon performances for children.

There's also a multiscreen **cinema** (☎ 707 220 220; Forum Theatrum), featuring mostly standard Hollywood fare, in the shopping centre next door.

Getting There & Away

Bragança's centrally located bus station is served by **Rede Expressos** (☎ 966482215; www.rede-expressos.pt, in Portuguese), **Rodonorte** (☎ 273 326 552; www.rodonorte.pt, in Portuguese) and **Eurolines** (☎ 273 327 122; www.eurolinesportugal.com). Station offices tend to be open only at departure times.

Rodonorte offers daily services to Mirandela (€6.10, one hour), Vila Real (€9.10, two hours), Porto (€11.40, three hours), Guimarães (€13.60, 3½ hours) and Braga (€13.80, four hours).

Rede Expressos goes daily to Porto (€12, three hours), Vila Nova de Foz Côa (€7.50, 1¾ hours), Trancoso (€9.80, 2¼ hours), Viseu (€13, 3½ hours) and points south all the way to Lisbon (€18.50, seven hours).

Eurolines operates buses daily (except Sunday) to Paris (€76, 19 hours), and also goes three times a week to Nice (€107, 23 hours), Geneva (€116, 21 hours) and Zurich (€116, 21 hours).

Remember that service drops off significantly at weekends, especially on Saturdays.

PARQUE NATURAL DE MONTESINHO

The peaceful highlands along Portugal's northeastern border with Spain constitute one of Trás-os-Montes' most appealing natural and cultural landscapes – it's a patchwork of rolling grasslands, giant chestnut trees, oak forests and deep canyons, and it's sprinkled with ancient stone villages where an ageing population still ekes out a hardscrabble existence.

The 750-sq-km Parque Natural de Montesinho was established to protect the area's 88 lean villages as much as their natural setting. This harsh, remote *terra fria* inspired early Portuguese rulers to establish a system of collective land tenure and then leave the villagers to their own devices, allowing for a remarkably democratic, communal culture, which persists today.

Unfortunately, remote villages continue to be deserted by their young, and many have not a single resident under the age of 60. However, these settlements – mostly just small clusters of granite houses roofed in slate and sheltering in deep valleys – retain an irresistible charm, especially in late April, when cherry and chestnut trees are in flower. In some towns, the government has helped preserve traditional slate-roofed stone houses as well as churches, forges, mills and the characteristic, charming *pombais* (dovecotes).

Villages that retain lashings of character include Pinheiro Novo, Sernande, Edroso, Santalha, Moimenta and Dine in the west, and Montesinho, Donai, Varge, Rio de Onor and Guadramil in the east.

The natural base from which to explore the park is Bragança. Smaller villages within the park also offer accommodation, but public transport is patchy.

Information

There are park offices at Bragança (p479) and **Vinhais** (☎ 273 771 416; Casa do Povo, Rua Dr Álvaro Leite; ⊗ 9am-12.30pm & 2-5.30pm Mon-Fri). A free schematic park map is available from both offices. Brochures on flora, archaeology, handicrafts and park walks are in Portuguese, although English-speaking staff at Bragança are more than willing to answer questions.

Sights

The most famous inhabitant of the eastern Serra de Montesinho is the rust-coloured Iberian wolf (p77). Indeed, this natural park and the adjoining Spanish park together form the last major refuge for this seriously endangered animal. Other threatened species include the royal eagle and the black stork.

In vast forests of Iberian oak and chestnut, and among riverside alders, willows, poplars and hazel, there are also roe deer, otters and wild boar; in the grasslands are partridges, kites and kestrels. Above 900m the otherwise barren ground is carpeted in heather and broom in spring.

RIO DE ONOR

This lovely little town of 70 souls situated in the eastern half of the park is entirely unfazed by the Spanish-Portuguese border splicing it down the middle. It's interesting not just for its rustic stone buildings, whose ground floors still house straw-filled stables for goats,

sheep and donkeys, but also for its staunch maintenance of the communal lifestyle once typical of the region. Spend an afternoon here and you'll see elderly locals trundling wheelbarrows from the well-tended community gardens surrounding town, stopping in at the local cafe whose communally shared proceeds are used to fund town festivals, or trading jobs with each other – one cousin staying to mind the store while the other goes to bring in the sheep. The twinned village also has one other claim to fame – a hybrid Portuguese-Spanish dialect known as Rionorês.

The border runs east–west through the middle of the village, while the Rio de Onor trickles along perpendicular to it. The road from Bragança continues north through town into Spain, branching right just before the border to cross an old stone bridge to the prettiest part of the village, where you'll find the community cafe.

STUB bus 5 (€1.15, one hour) heads to Rio de Onor via Varge twice daily. A taxi from Bragança costs around €20/40 one way/return, with an hour's wait.

MONTESINHO

Hidden literally at the end of the road in a narrow valley wedged between forbidding granite heights, this tiny village is one of the park's best-preserved, thanks to a program to restore old dwellings and stop construction of new ones. The village is also the jumping-off point for a hiking trail through the rugged

hills to a nearby dam. There is no bus service to Montesinho. A taxi from Bragança will cost under €20.

DINE & MOIMENTA

A new road has finally connected Dine and Moimenta, two of the loveliest villages in the western half of park – both a stone's throw from the Spanish border. In well-preserved Dine, you can visit a tiny **archaeological museum**, which documents the 1984 find by a Danish diplomat of Iron Age remains in a nearby cave. The museum is usually locked, but just ask around and someone will rustle up the French-speaking caretaker, who may also lead you around to the cave itself – pointing out wild-growing medicinal herbs on the way.

The beautiful drive between Dine and Moimenta takes you past a remarkably well-preserved **medieval bridge** with a single impressive arch. Moimenta has a lovely core of granite houses roofed in terracotta, plus a small baroque church – a rare dose of luxury in this austere corner of Portugal. However, a ring of modern construction keeps Moimenta from being as pristine as Dine.

Activities

There are plenty of opportunities for biking and hiking. Park offices offer free brochures detailing several **hiking trails** around the park.

The **Centro Hípico de França** (☎ 273 919 141) is a park-run stable north of Bragança offering

KINDNESS OF STRANGERS Robert Landon

The people of Portugal are, in my book, the least ego-driven in Europe. That is not to say they're saints immune to concerns of status or always perfectly patient or generous. However, they value amiability above all things, and since 'attitude' is an impediment to this, it's considered not a show of power but very poor form. Travels in Portugal's former colonies have only confirmed this impression. Brazil vs Argentina, Guinea-Bissau vs Senegal, Macau vs Hong Kong – every time, the former Portuguese colony comes out on top, at least in terms of easy sociability.

In the hills of the Parque Natural de Montesinho, I encountered the logical extension of my theory. As I stepped out of my car in a town whose main road had only recently been paved, an old man greeted me and asked what I was doing in his town. 'What business is it of his?' I thought. 'Why is he trying to make me feel unwelcome?' Within half an hour I was, happily, proven so very wrong as he poured me glasses of port, then homemade cherry hooch (it was April and the hills all around us were in high bloom with next year's batch). His wife arrived, scythe in hand, and encouraged me to take pictures of her goats. 'They're so beautiful,' she said. At one point, she pointed at her wrist, where there was no watch. 'We don't have to worry about that here.'

As we stood there together, it dawned on me that this man had asked what I was doing not to mark his territory (as would have been the case in my country) but merely so he could help me find whatever it was that I'd been seeking. I'd had no idea that what I wanted above all was simply to spend this moment with him and his wife and then his neighbours who, as the shadows lengthened, were returning from their fields and soon joining us with their hoes and staffs, pleased to have a stranger among them.

horse riding, including guides and lessons (per hour/day from €10/40).

If you come in summer, you can always cool off in the park's plentiful (if chilly) rivers and streams.

For other adventure activities, including climbing, kayaking and archery, contact **Montesinho Aventura** (☎ 964082619; www.montesinho aventura.com, in Portuguese; Rua do Meio, Montesinho).

Sleeping & Eating

For a more complete list of sleeping options in the area, pick up a free *Turismo no Espaço Rural* booklet from Bragança's tourist office.

EASTERN PARK

There are a number of self-catering studios in stone cottages in the village of Montesinho. Note that rooms book up in July and August.

Camping ground (☼ Apr-Sep) Rio de Onor has set up this bare-bones camp ground off the main road just as you arrive in town. Inquire at the town's cafe (across the Rio de Onor) for the town 'presidente' to negotiate your stay. From Bragança take STUB bus 5 (€1.15, one hour, two daily).

Parque de Campismo Municipal do Sabor (☎ 273 322 633; N103-7, km 6; sites per adult/car/tent €1.15/2/5.25; ☼ Apr-Sep) This flat, featureless but shady and quiet municipal camping ground is 6km

north of Bragança by the Rio Sabor. Facilities include bikes for hire, a cafe and a *minimer-cado*. From Bragança take STUB bus 7 (€1.15, 20 minutes).

Casa das Pedras (☎ 919860500, 273 919 248; www .casadaspedras.com, in Portuguese; Montesinho; d with/with-out kitchen from €50/35) Senhor Antero Pires rents out four rustic stone and wood cottages ranging from a basic studio to multiroom units with kitchenettes.

Dona Maria Rita (☎ 273 919 229; Montesinho; d/q €35/50; P) This place has a few cosy rooms and a kitchen complete with an old stone oven, plus a tiny but charming cottage at the edge of the village.

Café Montesinho (☎ 273 919 219, 936272876; Montesinho; 2-bedroom apt €50) A cosy spot at the hub of the village, Café Montesinho serves snacks and drinks, and also rents an upstairs two-bedroom apartment that sleeps up to four people, complete with kitchen and a pleasant veranda. The cafe's stone walls are hung with baskets, as well as letters and photos from appreciative customers. The kind owners chat affably with people passing through, and will sometimes serve more substantial meals for an extra fee.

our pick **A Lagosta Perdida** (☎ 273 919 031; www .lagostaperdida.com; Montesinho; d incl breakfast & dinner €120; P 🖳 🐖) Montesinho's most luxuri-ous lodging is this refurbished stone-walled house, run by a friendly Anglo-Dutch couple. It retains numerous period features, including high, beamed ceilings and a wonderful old stone water trough downstairs. The comfortable rooms come equipped with internet connections, tea-making facilities, flat-screen TVs, DVD players and beautifully tiled modern bathrooms with tubs. Other amenities include a heated swimming pool, mountain bikes and six hiking trails right out back. Two meals a day from the vegetarian-friendly kitchen are included in the price. Kids will love the playroom, not to mention the big sheepherding dog, cats, bunnies, horse and donkey.

In Rio de Onor, there is a little cafe where you can get snacks and drinks. You can also ask here about the possibility of renting rooms in town.

WESTERN PARK

Parque de Campismo Cepo Verde (☎ 273 999 371, 933224503; sites per adult/child/car/tent €3.25/1.60/2/2; ☯ Apr-Sep; ☒) This medium-sized rural facility is 12km west of Bragança near the tiny village of Gondesende on the park's southern border. It comes equipped with a cafe, shade and pool. STUB bus 4 between Bragança and Gondesende passes within 1km of the site (€1.15, 35 minutes).

Gondesende itself has two self-catering, converted schist cottage options: **Casa da Bica** (☎ 273 999 454, 273 323 577; www.bragancanet.pt/casad-abica; s/d €35/40) and the more charming **Casa do Passal** (☎ 273 323 506; www.casadopassal.no.sapo.pt; cottage €100). The latter requires a minimum two-night stay and sleeps up to four adults and two children. From Bragança, take STUB bus 4 to Gondesende (€1.15, 35 minutes).

Just north in Espinhosela, **Casa d'Ó Poço** (☎ 273 325 135; d/q €60/70) offers similar digs. STUB bus 6 (€1.15, 30 minutes) runs twice daily between Bragança and Espinhosela.

Abrigo de Montanha da Senhora da Hera (☎ 273 999 414; Cova da Lua; s/d €30/50; ☯ Feb-Dec; ℗ ☒) In Cova da Lua, this modern, simple inn serves breakfast and has a pool to cool off in. There's also a little restaurant where, with advance notice, you can get simple meals.

Casa dos Marrões (☎ 273 999 550; www.casa dosmarroes.com; Vilarinho; s/d €47.50/50; ℗ ☒ ☒) In Vilarinho, 17km northwest of Bragança, this 18th-century home built of oak, chestnut and schist has lovely beamed ceilings and

exposed-stone walls. An outdoor pool, plus nearby hiking trails and riverside beaches, enhance its appeal.

Moinho do Caniço (☎ 273 323 577; www.bra gancanet.pt/moinho; Castrelos; house for 4/5/6 people €100/110/120; ℗) This tastefully refurbished watermill – complete with centuries-old kitchen and open fireplace – is 12km west of Bragança on the N103. The rustically furnished stone-floored cottages sleep up to six people, with trout fishing in the Rio Baceiro just outside the door. STUB bus 2 (€1.15, 55 minutes) stops nearby.

Moimenta has a cafe–snack bar where you can ask about accommodation.

Note that at the time of writing there was no bus service to Cova da Lua, Vilarinho or Moimenta.

Getting Around

Exploring the park is difficult without a car, a bike or sturdy feet. The park's new map clearly indicates which roads are paved – unpaved roads can be dicey both during and after rains.

Only parts of the park are served by bus. For up-to-date schedules, check with local tourist offices or contact Bragança's municipal bus company, **STUB** (☎ 273 304 211, 800 207 609; www.stub.com.pt, in Portuguese). Trips to towns within the park cost €1.15 and generally take an hour or less.

MIRANDELA

pop 10,800 / elev 270m

Built along the Rio Tua in the centre of Trás-os-Montes' agricultural heartland, Mirandela makes a pleasant way-station for travellers looking to break the journey between Vila Real and Bragança, or those coming up from the Alto Douro via Tua. While primarily a down-to-business market town, Mirandela offers a couple of delightful places to stroll: a picturesque, flower-bedecked medieval bridge, and a newly established downtown pedestrian zone, where shop windows are hung with the region's renowned sausages and smoked hams.

Orientation

Rua Dom Afonso III runs in front of the newly combined train and bus stations. Take it to the right, then right again (north) along the river, to the town's medieval bridge and an adjacent new one. By the old bridge you can either carry on along pedestrianised Rua da República to the *turismo* and market (about 800m from the train station), or turn right and uphill on Rua Dom Manuel I to the *câmara municipal* and the old town.

Information

District hospital (☎ 278 260 500; Av Nossa Senhora do Amparo) Just across the old bridge.

Espaço Internet (☎ 278 261 924; mercado municipal, 1st fl; ☯ 9am-12.30pm & 3-7pm Mon-Fri, to noon Sat) Free internet; bring a photocopy of your ID.

Police station (☎ 278 265 814; Praça 5 de Outubro) Four blocks north of the post office.

Post office (☎ 278 200 450; Rua Dom Manuel I; ☯ 8.30am-12.30pm & 1.30-6pm Mon-Fri) Just below the *câmara municipal*.

Turismo (☎ 278 203 143; postodeturismo@cm-mirandela.pt; Praça de Cocheira; ☯ 9am-7pm Jun-Aug, 9.30am-12.30pm & 2-6pm Mon-Fri, 9.30am-1pm Sat Sep-May) On a grassy square one block north of Rua da República and the *mercado municipal*; scheduled to move to Avenida Afonso III along the riverfront as early as 2009.

Sights

The star attraction in Mirandela is the 15th-century **Ponte Românica** (Romanesque bridge) across the Rio Tua. Featuring 20 uniquely proportioned arches and lined with flower boxes, it's a leading candidate for Portugal's most elegant and photogenic footbridge.

Old Mirandela is centred on the *câmara municipal*, in the splendiferous **Palácio dos Távoras** (Praça do Município), built in the 17th century for António Luiz de Távora, patron of one of northeast Portugal's powerful aristocratic families. The adjacent Praça de Outubro has a church and several palaces from the same period.

Sleeping

Parque de Campismo dos Três Rios (☎ 278 263 177; www.parquedecampismodemirandela.com; Maravilha; sites per adult/child/car/tent €3.50/2.50/3/3, 2-/4-person bungalows €50/65; ☒) This flat, shady camping ground at the confluence of three rivers is 3km north of the centre on the N15. It has a restaurant and *minimercado*.

Hotel Mira-Tua (☎ 278 200 140; fax 278 200 143; Rua da República 42; s/d/ste €30/55/70; ☒) Pleasantly situated in the heart of Mirandela's pedestrian

zone, this modern '70s hotel has seen some wear but is kept in good trim. Some of the smallish but comfortable midrange rooms have verandas.

Hotel Dom Dinis (☎ 278 260 100; www.hoteis-arco.com, in Portuguese; Av Nossa Senhora do Amparo; s/d/tr €72/88/115; P ☒ ☐ ☒) Despite its run-down and charmless exterior, this oversized business hotel at the far end of the medieval bridge has comfortable rooms, many with balconies offering fine views of the bridge and river.

Eating

Lots of photogenic delicatessens sell the local speciality, *alheira de Mirandela*, a smoky, garlicky sausage of poultry or game. Also keep an eye out for fresh fish dishes from the Rio Tua.

Restaurante O Pinheiro (☎ 278 263 806; Calçada de São Cosme; mains €6-8.50; ☯ lunch & dinner) Up a little alley just off pedestrianised Rua da República, this immensely popular local eatery serves an extensive range of Portuguese fare. The daily handwritten specials go for €6.

Flor de Sal (☎ 278 203 063; Parque Dr José Gama; mains €15-19; ☯ lunch & dinner Tue-Sun) With a breezy riverside terrace, fancy white tablecloths, elegant red-and-black-clad waiters and jazzy ambient music, this upmarket restaurant is pleasantly situated in a park across the new bridge. It's won high praise for creative, beautifully presented regional dishes such as stewed partridge with truffles, Mirandela-style veal with creamy sheep-milk cheese and corn, or fresh tuna grilled with melon and julienned vegetables in a port and balsamic vinegar reduction.

The *mercado municipal* hums along every morning except Sunday, trailing off into the afternoon.

Getting There & Away

BUS

Rede Expressos (☎ 278 265 805) and **Rodonorte** (☎ 278 262 541) buses go to Bragança (€6.30, one hour) and Porto (€10.10, 2½ hours). Rodonorte also serves Vila Real (€6.10, one hour) and Miranda do Douro (€8.50, 2¼ hours, Sunday to Friday only).

TRAIN

At the time of writing, service was suspended on the scenic narrow-gauge Linha da Tua route from Mirandela to Tua in the Douro

---

SPEAKING MIRANDÊS

France has Provençal, Britain has Welsh and Gaelic, and Italy has dozens of distinct regional dialects. Portugal, by contrast, is one of Europe's most linguistically monolithic countries, thanks both to its long-stable borders (unchanged since the 13th century) and to the fact that it was conquered and consolidated within a very short period of time (less than 200 years).

The region around Miranda do Douro is a significant exception. Because of its proximity to Spain and long isolation from the rest of Portugal, residents of the towns and villages around Miranda still speak what linguists have now recognised as an entirely distinct language. Closely related to Astur-Leonese – the regional language of the adjacent Spanish province – Mirandês is in fact closer to Iberian Latin, the language spoken during the Roman period, than it is to either Portuguese or Spanish.

While Mirandês has largely died out in the city of Miranda do Douro itself, it's still the first language of some 10,000 people in the surrounding villages. The Portuguese government officially recognised it as a second language in 1998, and increasingly the region's road signs are bilingual.

In 1882 Portuguese linguist José Leite de Vasconcelos described Mirandês as 'the language of the farms, of work, of home and love'. The same is true today.

Resurgent local pride in the language is evident in the window display of Miranda do Douro's Papelaria Andrade, whose collection of Mirandês-language titles includes translations of Asterix comic books.

---

valley. The closure was prompted by four accidents in an 18-month period, including fatal derailments in February 2007 and August 2008. Pending further developments, taxi service was being offered as an alternative to the train. Check at the *turismo* or www.cp.pt for current schedules and to see if train service has been reinstated.

MIRANDA DO DOURO
pop 2000 / elev 560m

A fortified frontier town hunkering on the precipice of the gorgeous Rio Douro canyon, Miranda do Douro was long a bulwark of Portugal's 'wild east'. With its crumbling castle still lending an air of medieval charm, modern-day Miranda has now taken on a decidedly different role – receiving weekending Spanish tourists, as opposed to repelling Castilian attacks.

The town's beautifully hulking, 16th-century church may seem all out of proportion to the rest of the town, but it once served as cathedral for the entire region. Visitors shouldn't miss Miranda's ethnographic museum, which sheds light on the region's border culture, including ancient rites such as the 'stick dancing' of the *pauliteiros* (see boxed text, p491).

Street signs around town are written in Mirandês, an ancient language that developed during Miranda's long centuries of isolation from the rest of Portugal (above).

Romance-language buffs will enjoy names like 'Rue de la Santa Cruç', which read like a fantastical blend of French, Spanish and Portuguese.

History

Miranda was a vital stronghold during Portugal's first centuries of independence, and the Castilians had to be chucked out at least twice: in the early days by Dom João I, and again in 1710, during the War of the Spanish Succession. In 1545, perhaps as a snub to the increasingly powerful House of Bragança, a diocese was created here – hence the oversized cathedral.

During a siege by French and Spanish troops in 1762, the castle's powder magazine exploded, pulverising most of the castle and killing some 400 people. Twenty years later, shattered Miranda lost its diocese to Bragança. No-one paid much attention to Miranda again until the nearby dam was built on the Douro in the 1950s.

Orientation

Largo do Menino Jesus da Cartolina, a roundabout perched at the edge of the river gorge, roughly divides the old and new town. The *turismo* sits on the north edge of the roundabout in a glass kiosk. The bus station lies just downhill, on the road descending towards the bridge to Spain.

Uphill (southwest) from the roundabout, past the old walls and castle ruins, are the old town and what was once the citadel. The main axis is Rua da Alfândega (also called Rua Mouzinho da Albuquerque), which runs into central Praça de Dom João III and, a little further on, Largo da Sé and the cathedral.

The new town's commercial hub is Rua do Mercado, running northeast from the roundabout and parallel to the Rio Douro gorge.

Information

Centro de Saúde (☎ 273 430 040; Rua Dom Dinis) Health centre with 24-hour emergency service.

Espaço Internet (☎ 273 417 077; Central de Camionagem; ☿ 9am-1pm, 2-7pm & 8-10pm Mon-Sat) Free internet in the bus station.

Parque Natural do Douro Internacional office (☎ /fax 273 431 457; Palácio da Justiça, Rua do Convento; ☿ 9am-12.30pm & 2-5.30pm Mon-Fri) Around the block from the cathedral and across from a baroque church that has been converted into a public library.

Police (☎ 273 430 010; Largo de São José)

Post office (Largo da Sé; ☿ 9am-12.30pm & 2-5.30pm Mon-Fri)

Turismo (☎ 273 430 025; turismo@cm-mdouro.pt; Largo do Menino Jesus da Cartolina; ☿ 9am-12.30pm & 2-5.30pm Mon-Sat, to 7pm Jul & Aug)

Sights & Activities

It's possible to see everything in a couple of hours, but the vagaries of public transport make it almost essential for nondrivers to stay longer.

MUSEU DA TERRA DE MIRANDA

In a handsome, 17th-century building and former city hall, this modest **museum** (☎ 273 431 164; mtmiranda@ipmuseus.pt; Praça de Dom João III; adult/youth 14-25 yr/senior €1.50/0.75/0.75, to 2pm Sun free; ☿ 9.30am-12.30pm & 2-6pm Wed-Sun, 2-6pm Tue Apr-Oct, 9am-12.30pm & 2-5.30pm Wed-Sun, 2-5.30pm Tue Nov-Mar) houses a fascinating collection of local artefacts: ceramics, textiles, clothing, furniture, musical instruments and tribal-looking masks. It may be laid out like a school project, but the museum sheds light on a unique culture that has preserved millennial traditions into the 21st century.

OLD TOWN

The backstreets in the old town hide some dignified **15th-century facades** on Rua da Costanilha (which runs west off Praça de Dom João III) and a **Gothic gate** at the end of it.

Inside the right transept of the handsomely severe 16th-century **sé** (cathedral; admission free), look for the doll-like Menino Jesus da Cartolinha, a Christ child in a becoming top hat whose wardrobe rivals Imelda Marcos', thanks to deft local devotees. It's open the same hours as the Museu da Terra de Miranda.

BARRAGEM DE MIRANDA & RIVER CRUISES

A road crawls across this 80m-high dam about 1km east of town, and on to Zamora, 55km away in Spain. Even dammed, the gorge is dramatic.

You can take a one-hour boat trip through the gorge with **Europarques** (☎ 273 432 396; www .europarques.com; adult/child under 10 yr €14/7; ☿ trips 4pm Mon-Fri, 11am & 4pm Sat & Sun). Boats leave from beside the dam on the Portuguese side. Outside August, call in advance to check that there are enough passengers (minimum 20). In August there are also trips at 11am during the week.

Sleeping

Parque de Campismo de Santa Luzia (☎ 273 431 273; Rua do Parque de Campismo; sites per adult/child/car/tent €1.50/0.75/2/2; ☿ Jun-Sep) This modest municipal camp site is at the end of a residential street, 1.8km west of Largo da Moagem across the Rio Fresno.

Residencial Vista Bela (☎ /fax 273 431 054; Rua do Mercado 63; s/d/q from €20/30/47.50) On the main street of the new town, this modern place is spotless if unspectacular. Rooms tend to be gloomy but some have terrific views over the gorge.

Residencial a Morgadinha (☎ 273 438 050; fax 273 438 051; Rua do Mercado 57/59; s/d €20/35; 🅿) Next door to the Vista Bela, this simple place with tiled hallways features spacious rooms with parquet wood floors and bathtubs. There are nice river views from the upstairs breakfast area and from many of the rooms.

Residencial Santa Cruz (☎ 273 431 374; Rua Abade Baçal 61; s/d €25/35; 🅿) This family-run spot in Miranda's old town is just off the *largo* (small square) by the castle ruins. Rooms are clean, if a bit prim and uninspiring.

Hotel Turismo (☎ 273 438 030; fax 273 438 031; Rua 1 de Maio 5; r €60; 🅿) With common areas that glisten with black granite, this newer place opposite the *turismo* offers large, spotless rooms with cable TV and great marble bathrooms. Front rooms have large windows with views across to the castle ruins.

Estalagem Santa Catarina (☎ 273 431 005; www
.estalagemsantacatarina.pt; Largo da Pousada; s/d/ste
from €82.50/92/122; P ⊠ ⊡) Every guest gets
a private veranda with spectacular views of
the gorge at this luxurious, modern hotel
perched on the canyon's edge. Rooms are a
handsome mix of traditional and contemporary, with hardwood floors and large marble
bathrooms. The attached restaurant is the
most upmarket in town.

Eating

Restaurante-Pizzeria O Moinho (☎ 273 431 116; Rua do
Mercado 47D; individual pizza from €3.50, mains €4.50-10.50;
☉ lunch & dinner) Despite lacklustre service and
cryptic menu translations like 'sausage to the
hell' and 'codfish of the bras', this new-town
spot serves up glorious Douro views along
with a wide-ranging menu featuring pizza,
pasta, salads and Portuguese standards.

Restaurante São Pedro (☎ 273 431 321; Rua Mouzinho
de Albuquerque; mains €6-10; ☉ lunch & dinner; ⊠) This
spacious restaurant, just in from the main old-
town gate, serves up a fine *posta á São Pedro* –
delicious grilled veal steak dressed with garlic
and olive oil. The €12.50 tourist menu comes
with soup, main, dessert and wine.

Capa d'Honras (☎ 273 432 699; Travessa do Castelo
1; mains €10-11.50; ☉ lunch & dinner) Named after
the sinister-looking cape that is traditional
to the region, this more upmarket place just
inside the old town gates serves local specialities like *posta* (veal steak) as well as very
good *bacalhau*.

Drinking

Atalaia Bar (☎ 965 447 802; Largo do Castelo; ☉ mid-
night-4am) Miranda's neon-lit, old-school disco
serves up pop and dance standards.

Getting There & Around

Rodonorte (☎ 273 432 667) offers service daily except Saturday to Mogadouro (€6.30, 50 minutes), with onward connections to Vila Nova
de Foz Côa (€8.50, 2½ hours), Mirandela
(€8.50, 2½ hours), Vila Real (€10.60, 3½
hours) and Porto (€12.40, five hours).

By car, the quickest road from Bragança
is the N218 and N218-2, a winding 80km
trip. The 80km route (N216/N221) from
Macedo de Cavaleiros via Mogadouro is one
of the loveliest – and curviest – in Portugal. It
crosses a *planalto* dotted with olive, almond
and chestnut groves, with a dramatic descent
into the Rio Sabor valley.

Look for parking around Largo do Menino
Jesus da Cartolina.

PARQUE NATURAL DO DOURO INTERNACIONAL

Tucked into Portugal's far northeast corner,
this 852-sq-km, Chile-shaped park runs for
120km along the Rio Douro and the monumental canyon it has carved along the border
with Spain. The canyon's towering, granite
cliffs are the habitat for several threatened
bird species, including black storks, Egyptian
vultures, griffon vultures, peregrine falcons,
golden eagles and Bonelli's eagles.

The human habitat is equally fragile. In the
plains that run up to the canyon lip, there are
some 35 villages, many inhabited by descendants of banished medieval convicts, as well as
Jews who fled the Inquisition. The region's isolation has enabled its people to preserve even
more ancient roots, such as the Celtic *dança
dos paulitos* (opposite). Many villagers still
speak Mirandês, a language distinct from both
Spanish and Portuguese that linguists believe
descends directly from Iberian Latin (p488);
you'll see town names written in Portuguese
and Mirandês throughout the park.

As you move south along the river, the terrain gains a distinctly Mediterranean air, with
rolling orchards of olives and chestnuts and,
in the southernmost reaches, land demarcated
for port-wine grapes.

Orientation & Information

The park's headquarters are in **Mogadouro**
(☎ 279 340 030; pndi@icnb.pt; Rua Santa Marinha 4; ☉ 9am-
12.30pm & 2-5.30pm Mon-Fri) with smaller park offices in **Miranda do Douro** (☎ /fax 273 431 457; Palácio
da Justiça, Rua do Convento), **Figueira de Castelo Rodrigo**
(☎ 271 313 382; Rua Artur Costa 1) and **Freixo de Espada
à Cinta** (☎ 279 658 130; Av Guerra Junqueiro).

Park maps, as elsewhere in Portugal, are
in short supply; at the time of writing, the
existing map was out of print, and park offices
had only reference copies on hand. English-
speaking staff at the Mogadouro headquarters can answer general questions, but leaflets
about the park are in Portuguese only.

Miranda do Douro and Mogadouro are the
best places from which to explore the park.

Sights & Activities

There are three marked **trails** in the park. One
of the most convenient – and most beautiful –
is the 18km loop from Miranda do Douro to

THE HILLS ARE ALIVE: STRANGE WAYS IN TRÁS-OS-MONTES

For centuries, the remoteness of Trás-os-Montes has insulated it from central authority, helping its people preserve nonconformist ways that sometimes still raise eyebrows in other parts of Portugal.

A number of licentious – and blatantly pagan – traditions still survive in the countryside. Witness the antics of the Caretos of Podence (near Macedo de Cavaleiros) – where gangs of young men in *caretos* (leering masks) and vividly striped costumes invade the town centre, bent on cheerfully humiliating everyone in sight. Prime targets are young women, at whom they thrust their hips and wave the cowbells hanging from their belts. Similar figures are to be seen in Varge, in the Parque Natural de Montesinho.

Colourful festivals derived from ancient Celtic solstice rituals take place in many villages in the two weeks between Christmas Eve and Dia dos Reis (Epiphany). During the so-called Festa dos Rapazes (Festival of the Lads), unmarried men over 16 light all-night bonfires and rampage around in robes of rags and masks of brass or wood. Un-Christian indeed!

Then there are the *puliteiros* (stick dancers) of the Miranda do Douro region, who look and dance very much like England's Morris dancers. Local men deck themselves out in kilts and smocks, black waistcoats, bright flapping shawls, and black hats covered in flowers and ribbons, and do a rhythmic dance to the complex clacking of *paulitos* (short wooden sticks) – a practice that likely survives from Celtic times. The best time to see *puliteiros* in Miranda is during the Festas de Santa Bárbara (also called Festas da Cidade, or City Festival) on the third weekend in August.

Finally, there are the region's so-called crypto-Jews. During the Inquisition, Jews from Spain and Portugal found that they could evade ecclesiastical authorities here. Many families secretly observed Jewish practices – often without realising that they were in fact Jewish – well into the 20th century (see boxed text p377).

São João das Arribas, starting and ending at Miranda's cathedral. The trail – open to hikers, cyclists and horses – passes through mixed oak woodlands and small villages, and includes striking vistas of the river at São João.

For fabulous, near-aerial views of the gorge and its birdlife, you can also visit five sturdy **viewing platforms** throughout the park. North to south, with the nearest village in parentheses, these are São João das Arribas (Aldeia Nova), Fraga do Puio (Picote), Carrascalinho (Fornos), Penedo Durão (Poiares) and Santo André (Almofala).

The easiest way to see the Douro gorge is on Europarques' hour-long cruise from Miranda do Douro (see p489).

Based in Torre de Moncorvo, **Sabor Douro e Aventura** (☎ 279 258 270; www.sabordouro.com, in Portuguese; Rua Abade Tavares) offers guided hikes, as well as canoeing and rafting.

Sleeping & Eating

With its impressive views of the river gorge, Miranda do Douro is the most attractive base for exploring the park. Mogadouro also offers tourist services, but at nearly 15km from the Douro, it's a far less scenic option.

Restaurante-Residencial A Lareira (☎ 279 342 363; Av Nossa Senhora do Caminho 58, Mogadouro; s/d €25/30) This place has small, spotless, well-equipped rooms that are excellent value. The downstairs restaurant (mains €8 to €15) offers outstanding local beef and veal grilled on an open fireplace by the French-trained proprietor. Warmly recommended.

Solar dos Marcos (☎ 279 570 010; www.solar -dos-marcos.com; Rua Santa Cruz, Mogadouro; s/d/ste €70/90/130; P ⊠ ℞) About 12km northeast of Mogadouro in the ramshackle village of Bemposta, this place is the most upmarket option in the region. The reception is in an 18th-century manor house, while the comfortable rooms are in a modern annexe at the back.

Getting There & Around

Rodonorte (www.rodonorte.pt) offers regular bus services to Miranda do Douro and Mogadouro. However, public transport to smaller villages within the park is extremely limited, and mostly designed to serve schoolchildren. Schedules change, so it's best to check with the park offices or the *turismo* in Miranda do Douro for current schedule information.

DIRECTORY

Directory

CONTENTS

ACCOMMODATION

There's an excellent range of good-value, inviting accommodation in Portugal. Budget places provide some of Western Europe's cheapest rooms, while you'll find atmospheric, charming, peaceful accommodation in farms, palaces, castles, mansions and rustic town houses – usually giving good mileage for your euro.

In tourist resorts, prices rise and fall with the seasons. Mid-June to mid-September are firmly high season (book ahead); May to mid-June and mid-September to October are midseason; and other times are low season, when you can get some really good deals. Outside the resorts, prices don't vary much between seasons.

> **BOOK YOUR STAY ONLINE**
>
> For more accommodation reviews and recommendations by Lonely Planet authors, check out the online booking service at www.lonelyplanet.com/hotels. You'll find the true, insider lowdown on the best places to stay. Reviews are thorough and independent. Best of all, you can book online.

In the big Algarve resorts, you'll pay the highest premium for rooms from mid-July to the end of August, with slightly lower prices from June to mid-July and all of September, and substantially less (as much as 50%) if you travel between November and April. For example, a room that's listed as €120 in July may cost €160 in August, €100 in June and September, €85 in May and October, and €70 the rest of the year. Note that a handful of places close in winter.

We list July prices throughout this book. Listings are in order from least to most expensive (budget to top end), starting with barebones camping grounds and ending with glam *pousadas* (upmarket inns). Unless otherwise indicated, rooms have en suite bathroom.

In general, we categorise hotels or guest houses costing less than €40 for a double room as budget accommodation, and include camping grounds and hostels in this category. In some budget places, you might have to share a bathroom.

In the middle range, a double room runs from €40 to €80. For this you'll almost always get an en suite bathroom, TV (sometimes satellite), often air-conditioning and telephone.

In the top end of the lodging category you'll pay anywhere from €80 to €300, with the odd stratospheric place where you can chill by the pool with visiting royals or football stars.

We list rack rates for midrange and topend places in this book, but often you won't be charged the full whack – ask about special deals and packages. The websites on p20 also sometimes feature special offers. Most *pousadas* are cheaper during the week; they have lots of discount deals and prices.

Your bargaining power depends on what season it is and how much choice you have. If

---

PRACTICALITIES

■ Portugal uses the metric system for weights and measures. (See the inside front cover for a metric conversions chart.) Decimals are indicated by commas, thousands by points.

■ The electrical current is 220V, 50Hz. Plugs are rounded with two prongs (sometimes with a third middle prong), as used elsewhere in Continental Europe.

■ Portugal uses the PAL video system, incompatible with both the French SECAM system and the North American NTSC system.

■ Main newspapers include *Diário de Notícias, Público, Jornal de Notícias* and the tabloid best seller *Correio da Manhã*.

■ English-language media mostly comprises Algarve offerings: the *APN,* the *Portugal News* (www.the-news.net) and the *Algarve Resident* (www.portugalresident.com).

■ TV channels include Rádio Televisão Portuguesa (RTP-1 and RTP-2), Sociedade Independente (SIC) and TV Independente (TV1), with RTP-2 providing the best selection of foreign films and world-news coverage. Other stations fill the airwaves with a mix of Portuguese and Brazilian soaps, game shows and dubbed or subtitled foreign movies.

■ Portugal's national radio stations consist of state-owned Rádiodifusão Portuguesa (RDP), which runs Antena 1, 2 and 3 and plays Portuguese broadcasts and evening music (Lisbon frequencies 95.7, 94.4 and 100.3). For English-language radio there's the BBC World Service (Lisbon 90.2) and Voice of America (VOA), or a few Algarve-based stations, such as Kiss (95.8 and 101.2).

---

it's low season or echoingly empty, people will usually drop prices without you even needing to ask. If you plan to stay more than a few days, it's always worth inquiring whether lower rates are available for longer stays. If you're looking for somewhere cheaper than the room you have been shown, just say so; frequently the management will show you the cheaper rooms they previously forgot to mention.

Turismos (tourist offices) hold lists of accommodation and *quartos* (private rooms), but they overlook anywhere not registered with them – sometimes the cheapest options. The government grades accommodation with a star system that's bewildering and best ignored. Good websites for browsing include www.manorhouses.com and www.innsofportugal.com.

Camping & Caravan Parks

Camping is massive in Portugal, with countless excellent camping grounds, often in good locations and near beaches. Prices for camp sites usually range from about €3 to €4.50 per adult, around €4.50 per tent and €3 to €4 per car.

The swishest places are run by **Orbitur** (www .orbitur.pt) but there are lots of other good companies, such as **Inatel** (www.inatel.pt). Most towns have municipal camp sites, which vary in quality.

To be a really happy camper, or at least a well-informed one, pick up the **Roteiro Campista**

(www.roteiro-campista.pt; €6.50), updated annually and sold at *turismos* and bookshops. It has details of most Portuguese camping grounds, with maps and directions.

The Camping Card International (CCI) can be presented instead of your passport at camping grounds affiliated with the Federation Internationale de Camping et de Caravanning (FICC). It guarantees third-party insurance for any damage you may cause and can be good for discounts. Sometimes certain camp sites run by local camping clubs may be used by foreigners *only* if they have a CCI, so don't forget to pick one up before you travel. The CCI is available to members of most national automobile clubs, except those in the USA; the RAC in the UK charges members £6.50 for a card. It is also issued by FICC affiliates such as the UK's **Camping & Caravanning Club** (www.campingandcaravanningclub.co.uk) and the **Federação de Campismo e Montanhismo de Portugal** (Map pp102-3; ☎ 218 126 890; www.fcmportugal .com, in Portuguese; Av Coronel Eduardo Galhardo 24D, Lisbon).

Guest Houses

Government-graded guest houses are small-scale budget or midrange accommodation, with the personal feel that can be lacking in larger hotels. The best ones are often better than the cheapest hotels. High-season *pensão* (guest house) rates are roughly €35 to €65 for a double.

DIRECTORY

Residenciais (guest houses) may be more expensive, and usually include breakfast. The title *residencial* means it hasn't received the official approval that a *pensão* has, but this doesn't mean that it's a bad place to stay. *Hospedarias* and *casas de hóspedes* (boarding houses) are usually cheaper, with shared bathrooms.

Hostels

Portugal's 36 or so *pousadas da juventude* (youth hostels) are all affiliated with Hostelling International (HI). Although the accommodation is basic, hostels offer excellent value and are often in lovely settings or historic buildings.

High-season beds cost €11 to €16. Most also offer bare doubles and some have small apartments. Bed linen and breakfast are included in the price. Many have kitchens, cafes and internet access, and some have swimming pools, such as those in Alcoutim and Portimão.

In summer you'll need to reserve, especially for doubles. Contact **Movijovem** (Map p109; ☎ 707 203 030; www.pousadasjuventude.pt; Rua Lúcio de Azevedo 27, Lisbon).

If you don't have a HI card, you can get a guest card, which requires six stamps (€2 per time) – one from each hostel you stay at – after which you have paid for your membership.

Most hostels open 8am to midnight. Some (Almada, Braga, Bragança, Foz Côa, Foz do Cávado, Lagos, Lisbon, Porto and Viana do Castelo) are open 24 hours. Staff will usually let you stash your bags and return at check-in time (usually 8am to noon and 6pm to midnight).

Portugal has a small number of private hostels as well, which offer similar services at similar prices.

Pousadas

In 1942 the government started the **pousadas network** (☎ 218 442 001; www.pousadas.pt), turning castles, monasteries and palaces into luxurious hotels, roughly divided into rural and historic options. July prices range from €130 to €250; prices in August are €10 to €20 more. You can pick up a comprehensive list at any of the group. You may be able to take advantage of frequent special offers, such as reduced prices for those aged over 60, or 18 to 30 years.

Private Rooms

In coastal resorts, mostly in summer, you can often rent a *quarto* in a private house. These usually have a shared bathroom, are cheap and

clean, and might remind you of a stay with an elderly aunt. If you're not approached by an owner or don't spot a sign *(se aluga quarto)*, try the local *turismo* for a list. Prices are generally from €25 to €35 per double.

Rental Accommodation

Plenty of villas and cottages are available for rent. The site www.chooseportugal.com lists hundreds of private houses and apartments for rent, with the majority found in the Algarve. You'll find characterful houses in the north on www.casasnocampo.net.

Turihab Properties

These charming properties are part of a government scheme, either Turismo de Habitação, Turismo Rural or Agroturismo, through which you can stay in a farmhouse, manor house, country estate or rustic cottage as the owner's guest.

Divided into historic, heritage and rustic categories, these properties provide some of the best bargains in Portugal. Though they are more expensive than some other options, you'll usually be staying in splendid surroundings. A high-season double ranges from €60 to €100. Many have swimming pools and usually include breakfast (often with fresh local produce).

Turismos keep detailed information of Turihab properties in the area. You can also look them up online at www.turihab.pt or www.solaresdeportugal.pt.

ACTIVITIES

In Portugal there are many ways to spend a sun-drenched afternoon. Surfing, biking, hiking, birdwatching and horse riding are among the best ways to enjoy the country's fine climate and geography. See p82 for details.

BUSINESS HOURS

Most shops open 9.30am to noon and 2pm to 7pm Monday to Friday. Many close Saturday afternoon (except at Christmas) and Sunday. Malls open around 10am to 10pm daily. Banks open 8.30am to 3pm and government offices 9am to noon and 2pm to 5pm or 5.30pm Monday to Friday. Post offices keep similar hours, though some stay open at lunch. Museums usually close Monday, and open around 10am to 12.30pm and 2pm to 5pm or 6pm Tuesday to Sunday. If Monday is a holiday, they often close Tuesday too. Most eating places open noon to 3pm and 7pm to 10pm.

CHILDREN

The great thing about Portugal for children is its manageable size and the range of sights and activities on offer. There's so much to explore and to catch the imagination, even for those with very short attention spans.

The Algarve has to be the best kid-pleasing destination in Portugal, with endless beaches, zoos, water parks, horse riding and boat trips. Kids will also be happy in Lisbon and its outlying provinces. There are trams, puppet shows, a huge aquarium, a toy museum, horse-drawn carriages, castles, parks and playgrounds.

As for fairy-tale places, Portugal has these in spades. Some children enjoy visiting churches if they can light a candle. They'll enjoy the make-believe of the Knights Templar buildings at Almourol (see boxed text, p317) and Tomar (p319), and can explore castles in Sintra (p152), Castelo de Vide (p265) and Elvas (p258).

Near Fátima, north of Lisbon, thrill the kids with the sight of dinosaur footprints: visit the extraordinary Monumento Natural das Pegadas dos Dinossáurios (see boxed text, p313), with huge dinosaur dents. Special kid-pitched tours are available.

In towns, hop-on, hop-off tours are good for saving small legs, and miniature resort trains often cause more excitement than you would have thought possible.

Kids will like Portugal almost as much as they like sweets, and they are welcome just about everywhere. They can even get literary: Nobel Prize–winner José Saramago, the great Portuguese novelist, has written a charming children's fable, *The Tale of the Unknown Island*, available in English. For an entertaining guide packed with information and tips, turn to Lonely Planet's *Travel with Children*.

Turismos can often recommend local childcare, and branches of the youth-network **Instituto Português da Juventude** (IPJ; Map p109; ☎ 707 203 030; Av da Liberdade 194, Lisbon) sometimes advertise babysitting.

CLIMATE CHARTS

Portugal has a warm, sunny climate, with mild winters. Summer temperatures in the Algarve can top 30°C, and the mercury climbs in the Alentejo and Alto Douro too, with temperatures as high as 47°C recorded in the Alentejo. In the northwest, weather is milder and damper, so bring an umbrella. Up to 2000mm of rain can fall annually (the national average is 1100mm). See p17 for more information.

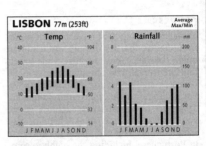

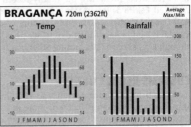

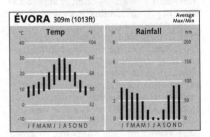

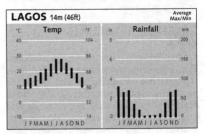

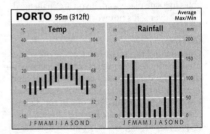

COURSES

Travellers hoping to come back with something besides bottles of port and a suntan might consider taking a course while travelling in Portugal. You can spend all day in the waves by signing up for surf classes (p87). For a different type of adventure, there are a number of equestrian academies, where you can learn to ride (p86). There are also schools where you can take a crash course in Portuguese, including the highly recommended **Centro de Informação e Documentação Anti-Colonial** (CIDAC; www.cidac.pt) in Lisbon. The capital is a good base for studying (see p124), though Lagos (see p220), among other places, also offers language study.

CUSTOMS REGULATIONS

You can bring as much currency as you like into Portugal, though €10,000 or more must be declared. Customs regulations say anyone who needs a visa must bring in at least €50 plus €10 per day, but this isn't enforced.

The duty-free allowance for travellers more than 17 years old from non-EU countries is 200 cigarettes or the equivalent in tobacco, and 1L of alcohol that's more than 22% alcohol, or 2L of wine or beer. Nationals of EU countries can bring in 800 cigarettes or the equivalent, plus either 10L of spirits, 20L of fortified wine, 60L of sparkling wine or a mind-boggling 90L of still wine or 110L of beer! There's no longer duty-free shopping in Portugal's airports.

DANGERS & ANNOYANCES
Crime

Compared with other European countries, Portugal's crime rate remains low, but some types of crime – including car theft – are on the rise. Crime against foreigners is of the usual rush-hour-pickpocketing, bag-snatching and theft-from-rental-cars variety. Take the usual precautions: don't flash your cash; keep valuables in a safe place; and, if you are challenged, hand it over – it's not worth taking the risk.

Driving

Once behind the wheel of a car, the otherwise mild-mannered Portuguese change personality. Macho driving, such as tailgating at high speeds and overtaking on blind corners, is all too common. Portugal has one of the highest road accident rates in Europe. Police have responded by aggressively patrolling certain dangerous routes, such as on the cheerfully named 'highway of death' from Salamanca in Spain.

DISCOUNT CARDS

Portugal's network of *pousadas da juventude* (p494) is part of the HI network. An HI card from your hostelling association at home entitles you to the standard cheap rates.

A student card will get you reduced admission to almost all sights. Likewise, those aged over 65 with proof of age will save cash.

If you plan to do a lot of sightseeing in Portugal's main cities, the Lisboa Card (p113) and Porto Card (p390) are sensible investments. Sold at tourist offices, these cards allows discounts or free admission to many attractions and free travel on public transport.

EMBASSIES & CONSULATES

Your embassy or consulate is the best first stop in any emergency. Most can provide lists of reliable local doctors, lawyers and interpreters. If your money or documents have been stolen, your embassy might help you get a new passport or advise you on how to have funds transferred, but a free ticket home or a loan for onward travel is highly unlikely. Most embassies no longer have mail-holding services or reading rooms with home newspapers. Foreign embassies and consulates in Portugal include the following:

Australia (Map p109; ☎ 213 101 500; www.portugal .embassy.gov.au; 2nd fl, Av da Liberdade 200, 1250-147 Lisbon)

Canada Lisbon (Map p109; ☎ 213 164 600; http://geo .international.gc.ca/canada-europa/portugal; 3rd fl, Av da Liberdade 196, 1269-121 Lisbon); Faro (☎ 289 803 757; Rua Frei Lourenço de Santa Maria 1, 8000-352 Faro)

France Lisbon (Map p108; ☎ 213 939 100; www.amba france-pt.org; Rua de Santos-o-Velho 5, 1249-079 Lisbon); Porto (☎ 226 078 220; Av da Boavista 1681, 4100-132 Porto)

Germany Lisbon (Map p109; ☎ 218 810 210; www .lissabon.diplo.de; Campo dos Mártires da Pátria 38, 1169-043 Lisbon); Porto (Map p385; ☎ 226 052 810; 6th fl, Av de França 20, 4050-275 Porto) Also in Faro.

Ireland (Map p108; ☎ 213 929 440; www.embassyof ireland.pt; Rua da Imprensa, Estrela, 1200-684 Lisbon)

Morocco (Map pp102-3; ☎ 213 020 842; www.emb-marrocos.pt, in Portuguese; Rua Alto do Duque 21, 1400-099 Lisbon)

Netherlands Lisbon (Map p108; ☎ 213 914 900; www .emb-paisesbaixos.pt; Av Infante Santo 43, 1399-011

Lisbon); Porto (☎ /fax 222 080 061; Rua da Reboleira 7, 4050-492 Porto) Also in Faro.

New Zealand (☎ 213 705 779) There's no New Zealand embassy in Portugal. In emergencies, New Zealand citizens can call the honorary consul at this Lisbon number. The nearest New Zealand embassy is in Madrid (☎ 34 915 230 226; www.nzembassy.com).

Spain Lisbon (Map p109; ☎ 213 472 381; embesppt@correo.mae.es; Rua do Salitre 1, 1269-052 Lisbon); Porto (☎ 225 363 915; cgespporto@correo.mae.es; Rua de Dom João IV 341, 4000-302 Porto) Also in Valença do Minho and Vila Real de Santo António.

UK Lisbon (Map p108; ☎ 213 924 000; www.british embassy.gov.uk/portugal; Rua de São Bernardo 33, 1249-082 Lisbon); Porto (☎ 226 184 789; Travessa Barão de Forrester 86, Vila Nova de Gaia, Porto) Also in Portimão.

USA Lisbon (Map p109; ☎ 217 273 300; http://portugal .usembassy.gov; Av das Forças Armadas, 1600-081 Lisbon); Porto (☎ 226 172 384; Rua Marechal Saldanha 454, 4150-652 Porto)

FOOD

In this book, budget-designated places are generally those with snacks or mains costing less than €6, midrange costs around €6 to €12, and top end is about €12 and up. For more tasty nuggets, see p66.

GAY & LESBIAN TRAVELLERS

How out you can be depends on where you are in Portugal. In Lisbon, Porto and the Algarve, acceptance has increased, whereas in most other areas, same-sex couples would be met with incomprehension. In this conservative Catholic country, homosexuality is still outside the norm. And while homophobic violence is pretty much unknown, discrimination has been reported in schools and workplaces.

Lisbon has the country's best gay and lesbian network and nightlife (see boxed text, p140). Lisbon, Porto (see boxed text, p402) and Leiria hold Gay Pride marches, but outside these events the gay community keeps a discreet profile. When you go to a gay bar or club, you'll usually have to ring a doorbell for admission.

HOLIDAYS

Banks, offices, department stores and some shops close on the public holidays listed here. On New Year's Day, Easter Sunday, Labour Day and Christmas Day, even *turismos* close. For details of festivals and events see p21.

New Year's Day 1 January
Carnaval Tuesday February/March – the day before Ash Wednesday
Good Friday March/April
Liberty Day 25 April – celebrating the 1974 revolution
Labour Day 1 May
Corpus Christi May/June – 9th Thursday after Easter
Portugal Day 10 June – also known as Camões and Communities Day
Feast of the Assumption 15 August
Republic Day 5 October – commemorating the 1910 declaration of the Portuguese Republic
All Saints' Day 1 November
Independence Day 1 December – commemorating the 1640 restoration of independence from Spain
Feast of the Immaculate Conception 8 December
Christmas Day 25 December

INSURANCE

Don't leave home without a travel-insurance policy to cover theft, loss and medical problems (see p516). You should get insurance for the worst-case scenario; for example, an accident or illness requiring hospitalisation and a flight home.

If you can't afford insurance, you certainly can't afford to deal with a medical emergency abroad. There are loads of policies available; the international policies handled by youth and student travel agencies are good value.

Check the small print, as some policies specifically exclude 'dangerous activities' such as scuba diving, motorcycling or even trekking. If these activities are in your sights, either find another policy or ask about an amendment (usually available for an extra premium) that includes them.

Make sure you keep all documentation for any claims later on. Some policies ask you to call back (reverse charges) to a centre in your home country, where an immediate assessment of your problem is made.

Citizens of the EU are eligible for free emergency medical treatment if they have a European Health Insurance Card (EHIC), which replaces the no-longer-valid E111 certificate. In the UK, you can apply for this card online (www.ehic.org.uk) or pick up an application at a post office.

Worldwide travel insurance is available at www.lonelyplanet.com/bookings. You can buy, extend and claim online anytime – even if you're already on the road.

See also p507 for information about motor-vehicle insurance.

INTERNET ACCESS

Free internet access is more and more prevalent in Portugal. Try local branches of the Instituto Português da Juventude (IPJ), some of which are attached to IPJ hostels; at the nearest *biblioteca municipal* (municipal library); or at a growing number of municipal **Espaços Internet** (www.espacosinternet .pt, in Portuguese). Usually you have to show some ID and then get 30 minutes free time (unless there's no-one waiting). Cybercafes, common in cities and towns, charge from around €2 per hour. Some post offices have terminals for NetPost, an internet facility payable with a special card, but these are often out of order.

If you have your own laptop, a small number of hotels offer wireless access. There are also a few locations – mostly in Lisbon – where you can find wi-fi. For a complete list, visit www.wi-fihotspotlist.com.

LEGAL MATTERS

Fines for illegal parking are common. If you're parked illegally you'll be towed and will have to pay around €100 to get your car back. Be aware of local road rules, as fines for other transgressions will also be enforced.

Narcotic drugs were decriminalised in 2001 in an attempt to clear up the public-health problems among drug users, and to address the issue as a social rather than a criminal one. You may be brought before a commission and subject to fines or treatment if you are caught with up to 10 doses of a drug. Drug dealing is still a serious offence and suspects may be held for up to 18 months before coming to trial. Bail is at the court's discretion.

LEGAL AGES

- Drinking: no minimum age
- Driving: 17
- Sex (hetero-/homosexual): 14/16
- Voting: 18

Smoking

In 2008 Portugal passed a law that bans smoking in public indoor areas. Most restaurants and bars are now smoke-free. Places that do allow smoking are required to have a separate section for smokers with adequate ventilation.

MAPS

Most current, though not indexed, is the 1:350,000 *Mapa das Estradas*, updated every June by the Automóvel Club de Portugal (p510). More or less equivalent is Michelin's 1:400,000 *Portugal, Madeira*, No 940.

Two government-mapping agencies exist: the military **Instituto Geográfico do Exército** (IGeoE; Army Geographic Institute; Map pp102-3; ☎ 218 505 368; www.igeoe.pt, in Portuguese; Av Dr Alfredo Bensaúde, Lisbon), which is located in the middle of nowhere, 2km northwest of Gare do Oriente station; and the civilian **Instituto Geográfico Português** (IGP; Portuguese Geographic Institute; Map p109; ☎ 213 819 600; www.igeo.pt; Rua Artilharia Um 107, Lisbon). IGeoE publishes 1:25,000 topographic sheets covering the entire country, plus less-useful 1:50,000 and 1:250,000 series, including *Portugal Continental Mapa de Estradas*, which is precise, but not always up to date. IGP's 1:50,000 maps tend to be more current, but lack the precision of the military publications. Both agencies sell maps from their Lisbon headquarters.

National and natural park offices usually have simple park maps, though these are of little use for trekking or cycling. Other local sources for topographic maps are noted in the text. The following offer a good range of maps:

Maps Worldwide (☎ 012-2570 7004; www.mapsworld wide.co.uk; Datum House, Lancaster Rd, Melksham, UK)
Omni Resources (☎ 336-227 8300; www.omnimap .com; 1004 South Mebane St, Burlington, NC, USA)
Stanfords (☎ 020-7836 1321; www.stanfords.co.uk; 12-14 Long Acre, Covent Garden, London, UK)

MONEY

Since 1 January 2002 Portugal has used the euro, along with 14 other European nations.

Banks and *bureaux de change* are free to set their own rates and commissions, so a low commission might mean a skewed exchange rate.

ATMs & Credit Cards

The most convenient way to get your money is from an ATM. Most banks have a Multibanco ATM, complete with annoying animated graphics, accepting Visa, Access, MasterCard, Cirrus and so on. You just need your card and PIN. Your home bank will usually charge around 1.5% per transaction. But it's wise to have a back-up source of money; sometimes ATMs temporarily stop accepting a certain type of card, usually a hiatus lasting a day or so. You'll be asked for a six-digit PIN, but it still works fine if yours is only four digits.

Credit cards are accepted at smarter hotels and restaurants and in larger towns, but won't be any use to pay for things in the budget arena or in rural outposts.

Tipping

If you're satisfied with the service, tip 5% to 10%. Bills at pricier restaurants may already include *serviço* (service charge). After a snack at a bar or cafe, some shrapnel is enough. Taxi drivers are not generally tipped, but 10% for good service would be appreciated.

Travellers Cheques

These are a safe way to carry money, as they will be replaced if lost or stolen, but are less convenient than the card-in-machine method. Amex, Thomas Cook and Visa are most widely recognised. It's best to get cheques in euros, and keep a record of the ones you've cashed in case you do mislay them. However, although travellers cheques are easily exchanged, with better rates than for cash, they are poor value because commission is so high.

POST

Post offices are called **CTT** (www.ctt.pt). *Correio normal* (ordinary mail) goes in the red letterboxes, *correio azul* (airmail) goes in the blue boxes. Postcards and letters up to 20g cost €0.75/0.60/0.30 outside Europe/within Europe/locally. International *correio azul* costs €1.85 for a 20g letter. Post to Europe takes up to five working days, and the rest of the world up to seven. Economy mail (or surface airlift) is about a third cheaper, but takes a week or so longer.

You can send mail to poste restante in main post offices of cities and large towns.

Many post offices have NetPost for internet access, but the machines are frequently out of order. If they do work, it costs €2.50 per hour, with cards costing €5.50.

SHOPPING

Home of ceramics, port, wine, lace and crazy cockerel mascots, Portugal is a splendid place to shop, not least because it moves at a relaxed pace that's ideal for browsing and window-shopping. Its low prices also mean more gain for less pain.

TOP FIVE BIZARRE SOUVENIRS

- Umbrellas, baseball caps and aprons made of cork
- Barcelos Cockerel (p434)
- Port bottles shaped like shoes, swords or ships
- Beautifully wrapped canned fish (p147)
- Glow-in-the-dark Virgin Marys (p310)

Port, Wine & Food

Port is Portugal's best-known export, and is easy to find. To hunt it to its source, visit port-wine lodges at Vila Nova de Gaia (p393), across the river from Porto, or pop into a supermarket, where you'll find a good range. Lisbon, Porto and other cities have specialist shops. In Lisbon or Porto you can visit port-tasting places, then note down your favourite to buy later.

Buying wine is also popular, with some excellent drops at affordable prices. You can follow a route through vineyards in the Douro (see boxed text, p420), the Alentejo (p247) and other regions, visiting wineries, tasting and buying. Other areas to try are Estremadura and near Setúbal; Dão also has some excellent lodges where you can tour and taste.

Olive oil and honey are also good buys all over the country. Try Mértola and Serpa in Alentejo, or Parque Nacional da Peneda-Gerês in the Minho.

Linen, Cotton & Lace

Hand-embroidered linen and cotton, traditional costumes, and lacework (a speciality of coastal fishing towns) are sold at modest prices all over the country, but especially in seaside resorts such as Nazaré and Viana do Castelo. Guimarães has been famous for its linen since medieval times, so it must be doing something right. Castelo Branco is a hot spot for embroidered bed covers. Bobbin lace comes from Vila do Conde, Peniche and the eastern Algarve. There are also several speciality shops in Lisbon selling lacework and linen.

Music

Take home a tragic, stoic soundtrack for those dramatic moments. Try the good speciality music shops, *turismos* and the fado museum (p115) in Lisbon. Most towns have a selection of small music shops, all of which will have some fado. To help you choose, see p54.

Ceramics

Portugal produces beautiful ceramics, from refined tiling to rustic bowls, all bursting with brilliant colours. See p144 for where to buy the best ceramics in the capital. Caldas da Rainha (p297) is a ceramics centre, with museums devoted to its masters, and many artisan workshops and shops. Also try São Pedro do Corval (p248), with around 30 businesses producing brightly coloured, rustic ceramics.

Estremoz (p252) in the Alentejo produces unique, charming figurines – mainly saints with flowing robes that look like they've been caught in a wind machine. The town has several small shops and a wonderful workshop selling these (and other crafts), as well as a fantastically thriving Saturday market where you can combine your figurine-shopping with purchasing a goat.

Rugs, Jewellery & Leather

Portugal's finest carpets are produced in Arraiolos in the Alentejo; they are hand-stitched and prices reflect this. More rustic *mantas* (woollen rugs and blankets) are a speciality of Reguengos de Monsaraz and Mértola in the Alentejo.

The exquisite gold and silver filigree jewellery of the Porto area is expensive, but good value. Leather goods, especially shoes and bags, are also good buys.

Other Handicrafts

Rush, palm and wicker basketwork pieces are appealing and cheap. They're best found in municipal markets all over the country. Trás-os-Montes is good for woven handicrafts and tapestries and, with Beira Alta and Beira Baixa, for wrought-iron work.

In the Alentejo you can buy lovely traditional hand-painted wooden furniture, such as you will see in many local hotel rooms. Monchique sells unique small wooden scissor stools.

In the Algarve, Loulé's Saturday market (p204) is a great place to buy all sorts of crafts, from brass to basketware to leather goods and every sort of souvenir.

Lisbon and Porto are also good places to buy traditional crafts from all over the country; see p144 and p404 for details.

Bargaining

Bargaining is only really done at markets, although you may sometimes be able to bargain down accommodation prices when things are quiet.

SOLO TRAVELLERS

The Portuguese tend to be friendly and welcoming, and with lots of other travellers on the road you're unlikely to feel lonely if you're on your own. In rural areas it's odd to see a woman travelling alone, but this is likely to be put down to foreign weirdness, and unlikely to provoke anything more than a little curiosity.

Single rooms usually cost about two-thirds of the double-room price, so it's more expensive to travel alone. Youth hostels are a good bet if you're on a budget; not only are they cheap, but they are also good places to meet other travellers.

TELEPHONE

To call Portugal from abroad, dial the international access code (☎ 00), then Portugal's country code (☎ 351), then the number. All domestic numbers have nine digits, and there are no area codes. On a public phone, it's easiest to call from a card-operated phone, as coin-operated telephones have an annoying habit of munching your money. You can also make calls from booths in Portugal Telecom offices and some post offices – pay when your call is finished.

Calls from public card-operated phones are charged per number of *impulsos* (beeps or time units) used. The price per beep is fixed (€0.09) with a phonecard, but the length of time between beeps depends on destination, time of day and type of call. Coin telephones cost €0.10 per beep; phones in hotels and cafes rack up three to six times the charges. It costs two/three beeps extra to make a domestic/international connection.

All but local calls are from cheaper 9pm to 9am weekdays, all weekend and on holidays.

Directory Inquiries & Reverse-Charge Calls

Portugal's directory inquiries number is ☎ 118; operators will search by address as well as by name. The international directory inquiries number is ☎ 177.

To make a *pagar no destino* (reverse-charge call) with the help of a multilingual operator, dial ☎ 120. For international reverse-charge calls, you'll have to access an international operator for the country you're dialling. A few access numbers:

Australia ☎ 800 800 610
Canada ☎ 800 800 122
UK ☎ 800 800 440
USA ☎ 800 800 128 (AT&T), 800 800 123 (MCI), 800 800 187 (Sprint)

International Calls & Cards

From Portugal Telecom, you can get a Hello CardPT or PT Card Europe, both costing €5. You call an access number then key in the code on the back of the card. This is a cheaper way of making international calls. There are lots of competing cards offering much the same service. Note that peak and off-peak periods vary from company to company.

Local, Regional & National Calls

The cheapest way to call within Portugal is with a Portugal Telecom *cartão telefónico* (phonecard). These are available for €3/5/10 from post and telephone offices and many newsagents. A youth or student card should get you a 10% discount.

Local calls cost around €0.09 per minute to land lines and €0.30 to mobile phones. Numbers starting with 800 (*linha verde*; green line) are toll free. Those starting with 808 (*linha azul*; blue line) are charged at local rates from anywhere in the country.

Mobile Phones

Mobile-phone usage is widespread in Portugal, with extensive coverage provided in all but the most rural areas. The main domestic operators are Vodafone (www.vodafone.pt), Optimus and TMN. All of them sell prepaid SIM cards that you can insert inside a GSM mobile phone and use as long as the phone is not locked by the company providing you service. If you need a phone, you can often buy one at the airport and shops throughout the country with a package of minutes for under €100. This deal is generally cheaper than renting a phone. Note that mobile-phone numbers usually begin with a 9.

It's illegal in Portugal to drive while talking on a mobile phone.

TIME

Portugal, like Britain, is on GMT/UTC in winter and GMT/UTC plus one hour in summer. This puts it an hour earlier than Spain year-round (which is a strange thought when you are crossing the border). Clocks are set forward by an hour on the last Sunday in March and back on the last Sunday in October.

TOURIST INFORMATION

Portugal's umbrella tourism organisation is **Investimentos, Comércio e Turismo de Portugal** (ICEP). The **head office** (☎ 217 909 500; www.visitportugal.com; Av 5 de Outubro 101) is in Lisbon, and there are branches in **Porto** (Map p387; ☎ 222 057 514; Praça Dom João I 43) and at **Porto airport** (☎ 229 412 534, 229 432 400).

Locally managed *postos de turismo* (tourist offices, usually signposted '*turismo*') are everywhere, offering brochures and varying degrees of help with sights and accommodation. ICEP maintains a *regiões de turismo* (regional office) in the main town of each of its regions, and information desks at Lisbon, Porto and Faro airports. Lisbon, Porto, Coimbra and a few other towns have municipal and ICEP *turismos*.

Multilingual staff at the toll-free tourist helpline **Linha Verde do Turista** (☎ 800 296 296; ⏱ 9am-9pm) can provide basic – though not uniformly accurate – information on accommodation, sightseeing and so on.

There are various regional tourist offices:
Alentejo Serra de São Mamede (☎ 245 300 770; www.rtsm.pt; Região de Turismo de São Mamede, Estrada de Santana 25, Portalegre); Planície Dourada (☎ 284 310 150; www.rt-planiciedourada.pt; Praça da República, Beja)
Beiras Coimbra (☎ 239 488 120; rtc-coimbra@turismo-centro.pt; Largo da Portagem); Aveiro (☎ 234 423 680; aveiro.rotadaluz@inovanet.pt; Rua João Mendonça 8); Covilhã (☎ 275 319 560; turismo.estrela@mail.telepac.pt; Av Frei Heitor Pinto); Viseu (☎ 232 420 950; turismo@rt-dao-lafoes.com; Av Calouste Gulbenkian)
Douro Lamego (☎ 254 612 005; douro.turismo@mail.telepac.pt; Av Visconde Guedes Teixeira, Lamego)
Minho Viana do Castelo (☎ 258 822 620; fax 258 827 873; Rua Hospital Velho); Bairros (Adere-Soajo; ☎ /fax 258 576 427; turismo.adere-soajo@sapo.pt; Turismo de Aldeia, Largo da Cardeira)
Trás-os-Montes Vila Real (☎ 259 322 819; turismarao@mail.telepac.pt; Av Carvalho Araújo 94); Chaves (☎ 276 340 660; rturismoatb@mail.telepac.pt; Terreiro de Cavalaria)

TRAVELLERS WITH DISABILITIES

The term *deficientes* (Portuguese for disabled) gives some indication of the limited awareness of disabled needs. Although public offices and agencies are required to provide access and facilities for people with disabilities, private businesses are not.

Lisbon airport is wheelchair-accessible, while Porto and Faro airports have accessible toilets. The useful website www.allgohere.com has information on facilities offered by all airlines.

Parking spaces are allotted in many places but are frequently occupied. The EU parking card entitles visitors to the same street parking concessions given to disabled residents. If you're in the UK, contact the **Department for Transport** (☎ 020-7944 8300; www .dft.gov.uk/transportforyou/access).

Most camping grounds have accessible toilets (noted in the text) and many hostels have facilities for people with disabilities. Newer and larger hotels tend to have some adapted rooms, though the facilities may not be up to scratch; ask at the local *turismo*.

Lisbon, with its cobbled streets and hills, may be difficult for some travellers with disabilities, but not impossible. The Baixa's flat grid and Belém are fine, and all the sights at Parque das Nações are accessible.

For more details, contact the following:

Accessible Portugal (☎ 217 203 130; www.accessible portugal.com; Rua João Freitas Branco 21D, Lisbon) This Lisbon-based tour agency offers a wide range of itineraries and can arrange accommodation, transfers, overnight trips and outdoor activities such as tandem skydiving and hot-air balloon trips.

Cooperativa Nacional de Apoio Deficientes (CNAD; Map pp102-3; ☎ 218 595 332; cnad-sede@clix.pt; Praça Dr Fernando Amado, Lote 566-E, 1900 Lisbon) This is a private organisation that can help with travel needs.

Dial-a-ride Disabled Bus Service Lisbon (☎ 217 585 676); Porto (☎ 226 006 353)

Secretariado Nacional de Reabilitação (Map p109; ☎ 217 929 500; snripd@seg-social.pt; Av Conde de Valbom, 63-1069-178 Lisbon) The national governmental organisation representing the disabled supplies information, provides links to useful operations and publishes guides (in Portuguese) that advise on barrier-free accommodation, transport, shops, restaurants and sights.

Taxi Services for Disabled Persons Braga (☎ 253 684 081); Coimbra (☎ 239 484 522)

Wheeling Around the Algarve (☎ 289 393 636; www.player.pt; Rua Casa do Povo, 1, Almancil) Another private set-up, with great advice on accommodation, transport, care hire, sport and leisure facilities, and equipment.

VISAS

Nationals of EU countries don't need a visa for any length of stay in Portugal. Those from Canada, New Zealand, the USA and (by temporary agreement) Australia can stay for up to 90 days in any half-year without a visa. Others, including nationals of South Africa, need a visa unless they're the spouse or child of an EU citizen.

The general requirements for entry into Portugal also apply to citizens of other signatories of the 1990 Schengen Convention (Austria, Belgium, Denmark, Finland, France, Germany, Greece, Iceland, Italy, Luxembourg, the Netherlands, Norway, Spain and Sweden). A visa issued by one Schengen country is generally valid for travel in all the others, but unless you're a citizen of the UK, Ireland or a Schengen country, you should check visa regulations with the consulate of each Schengen country you plan to visit. You must apply for any Schengen visa while you are still in your country of residence.

To extend a visa or 90-day period of stay after arriving in Portugal, contact the **Foreigners' Registration Service** (Serviço de Estrangeiros e Fronteiras; Map p109; ☎ 213 585 545; Rua São Sebastião da Pedreira 15, Lisbon; ☺ 9am-3pm Mon-Fri); major tourist towns also have branches. As entry regulations are already liberal, you'll need convincing proof of employment or financial independence, or a pretty good story, if you want to stay longer.

VOLUNTEERING

In the Algarve, volunteers are welcome to help the reforestation project **Monchique Verde** (☎ 282 418 881). Launched after the big forest fires of 2003–04, the group meets on Saturday mornings at 9.30am in Monchique's Café O Lanche to clear, plant and water.

WOMEN TRAVELLERS

Women travelling alone in Portugal report few serious problems. As when travelling anywhere, women should take care – be cautious about where you walk after dark and don't hitch.

If you're travelling with a male partner, people will expect him to do all the talking and ordering, and pay the bill. In some conservative pockets of the north, unmarried couples will save hassle by saying they're married.

If you're a victim of rape or violence while you're in Portugal, you can contact the following organisations:

Associação Portuguesa de Apoio à Vítima (APAV; Portuguese Association for Victim Support; ☎ 218 884 732; www.apav.pt) Can offer assistance for rape victims.

Comissão para a Igualdade e para os Direitos das Mulheres (Commission for the Equality & Rights of Women; Map p109; ☎ 217 983 000; www.cidm.madbug .com, in Portuguese; Av da República 32, Lisbon) There's no specific rape-crisis hotline, but the commission operates the number for victims of violence.

WORK

The most likely kind of work you will be able to find is teaching English, if you have Teaching English as a Foreign Language (TEFL) certification. If you're in the UK, contact the British Council, or get in touch with language schools in the area where you want to teach as possible avenues of work.

Bar work is a possibility in the Algarve, particularly in Lagos; ask around. You can also try looking in the local English press for job ads (see boxed text, p493).

Transport

TRANSPORT

GETTING THERE & AWAY

ENTERING THE COUNTRY

Coming from within Europe, you'll have no problems entering Portugal by land, sea or air. However, if you're arriving from further afield, check p502 to see if you'll need to secure a visa before arrival.

Flights, tours and rail tickets can be booked online at www.lonelyplanet.com/bookings.

AIR
Airports & Airlines

Portugal has international airports at **Lisbon** (airport code LIS; Map pp102-3; ☎ 218 413 500), **Porto** (airport code OPO; ☎ 229 432 400) and **Faro** (airport code FAO; ☎ 289 800 800). For more information, see www.ana-aeroportos.pt. Portugal's flagship international airline is TAP Air Portugal, which is also its main domestic airline.

AIRLINES FLYING TO/FROM PORTUGAL

Aer Lingus (airline code EI; ☎ 218 925 831 in Portugal; www.aerlingus.com)
Air Berlin (airline code AB; ☎ 808 202 737 in Portugal; www.airberlin.com)
Air France (airline code AF; ☎ 707 202 800 in Portugal; www.airfrance.fr)

Alitalia (airline code AZ; ☎ 800 307 300 in Portugal; www.alitalia.com)
British Airways (airline code BA; ☎ 808 200 125 in Portugal; www.britishairways.com)
British Midland/BMIbaby (airline code WW; ☎ 44 870 126 6726; www.bmibaby.com)
Continental Airlines (airline code CO; ☎ 808 200 079 in Portugal; www.continental.com)
Delta (airline code DL; ☎ 213 139 860 in Portugal; www.delta.com)
EasyJet (airline code U2; ☎ 218 445 278 in Portugal; www.easyjet.com)
Finnair (airline code AY; ☎ 213 522 689 in Portugal; www.finnair.com)
Grupo SATA (airline code S4; ☎ 707 227 282 in Portugal; www.sata.pt)
Iberia (airline code IB; ☎ 707 200 000 in Portugal; www.iberia.com)
KLM (airline code KL; ☎ 707 222 747 in Portugal; www.klm.nl)
Lufthansa (airline code LH; ☎ 707 782 782 in Portugal; www.lufthansa.com)
Monarch Airlines (airline code ZB; ☎ 800 860 270 in Portugal; www.flymonarch.com)
Regional Air Lines (airline code FN; ☎ 218 416 802 in Portugal; www.regional.com)
Ryanair (airline code FR; ☎ 353 1249 7791; www.ryanair.com)
Swiss International Air Lines (airline code LX; ☎ 808 200 487 in Portugal; www.swiss.com)
TAP Air Portugal (airline code TP; ☎ 707 205 700 in Portugal; www.tap.pt)
Transavia Airlines (airline code HV; ☎ 707 780 009 in Portugal; www.transavia.com)
Tunisair (airline code TU; ☎ 218 496 350 in Portugal; www.tunisair.com.tn)

THINGS CHANGE...

The information in this chapter is particularly vulnerable to change. Check directly with the airline or a travel agent to make sure you understand how a fare (and ticket you may buy) works and be aware of the security requirements for international travel. Shop carefully. The details given in this chapter should be regarded as pointers and are not a substitute for your own careful, up-to-date research.

Australia & New Zealand

There are no direct flights from the Antipodes to Portugal, though airlines offer tickets through Asian and European hubs. Plan on 26 hours of travel time with good connections. Major carriers such as Air France, KLM, British Airways and Cathay Pacific offer the best deals.

Continental Europe

FRANCE

Carriers with multiple daily Paris–Lisbon and Paris–Porto connections include Air France and TAP. Direct connections to Lisbon from elsewhere in France include those from Bordeaux, Nice, Lyon and Toulouse. More-expensive flights to Porto go daily from Bordeaux, and weekly from Nice. Flights to Faro are less easy to come by.

Agencies with branches around Portugal:

Nouvelles Frontières (☎ 08 250 00 747; www .nouvelles-frontieres.fr)

Voyages Wasteels (☎ 08 92051155; www.wasteels.fr)

Voyageurs du Monde (☎ 08 92235656; www.vdm .com)

SPAIN

Carriers with daily Madrid–Lisbon connections include Iberia and TAP, both of which also fly between Barcelona and Lisbon. TAP also has direct flights to Lisbon from Bilbao, La Coruña, Málaga and Valencia.

For Porto, TAP has daily direct flights from Madrid and Barcelona.

Reliable Madrid-based airfare specialists with offices throughout Spain include **Barceló Viajes** (www.barceloviajes.es).

ELSEWHERE IN CONTINENTAL EUROPE

An airfare specialist with branches around Germany is **STA Travel** (☎ 069 743 032 92; www.sta travel.de). In Belgium go to **Usit Connections** (☎ 070 233 313; www.connections.be). In the Netherlands, try Amsterdam-based **Air Fair** (☎ 090 077 177 17; www.airfair.nl).

The major links from Germany are Frankfurt, Berlin and Munich to Lisbon; and Frankfurt to Porto. Other direct connections to Lisbon are from Cologne, Hamburg and Stuttgart; and to Faro from Frankfurt. Germany also has busy charter traffic to Portugal.

From Amsterdam, there are daily flights to Lisbon and Porto, and several weekly to Faro. Charter specialist **Transavia** (☎ 0900 0737; www.transavia.nl) also offers scheduled flights from Amsterdam to Porto, and Rotterdam to Faro.

For a similar fare, there are multiple daily flights from Brussels to Lisbon and weekend connections to Faro.

UK & Ireland

Thanks to the UK's long love affair with Portugal and its 'bucket-shop' tradition, bargains are plentiful. The UK's best-known bargain agencies and internet-based dealers:

Expedia (www.expedia.co.uk)

Flight Centre (www.flightcentre.co.uk)

Lastminute (www.lastminute.com)

STA Travel (☎ 0871 2300 040; www.statravel.co.uk)

Trailfinders (☎ 0845 0585 858; www.trailfinders.co.uk)

Reliable sources in Ireland:

Trailfinders (☎ 01 677 7888; www.trailfinders.ie)

Usit (☎ 01 602 1906; www.usit.ie)

Scheduled direct flights go daily to Lisbon from London Heathrow, Gatwick and Manchester. Porto flights also leave daily from Heathrow and Manchester, and less frequently from Gatwick. There's also a veritable bandwagon of flights to Faro. Cheap, 'no-frills' carriers to Portugal include EasyJet (London, Bristol and East Midlands to Faro), BMIbaby (East Midlands to Faro), Monarch (London to Lisbon and Faro; Manchester to Faro) and Ryanair (Dublin and Shannon to Faro; Dublin, Liverpool and London Stansted to Porto).

Charters operate from all over the UK, mostly to Faro. A reliable charter-flight clearing house is **Destination Portugal** (www.destination -portugal.co.uk).

USA & Canada

To Lisbon, there are daily flights from New York JFK, Newark and Los Angeles, and less frequent departures from Boston. There's also a daily flight from Newark to Porto. There are no direct flights between Canada and Portugal.

Circle the Planet (☎ 800 799 8888; www.circlethe planet.com) is a leading consolidator, and you can always try your luck with **Orbitz** (www.orbitz .com), **Expedia** (www.expedia.com) or **Hotwire** (www .hotwire.com). A big airfare specialist in the USA is **STA Travel** (☎ 800 781 4040; www.statravel.com). Canada's best bargain-ticket agency is **Travel CUTS** (☎ 866 246 9762; www.travelcuts.com).

CLIMATE CHANGE & TRAVEL

Climate change is a serious threat to the ecosystems that humans rely upon, and air travel is the fastest-growing contributor to the problem. Lonely Planet regards travel, overall, as a global benefit, but believes we all have a responsibility to limit our personal impact on global warming.

Flying & Climate Change

Pretty much every form of motor travel generates CO_2 (the main cause of human-induced climate change) but planes are far and away the worst offenders, not just because of the sheer distances they allow us to travel, but because they release greenhouse gases high into the atmosphere. The statistics are frightening: two people taking a return flight between Europe and the USA will contribute as much to climate change as an average household's gas and electricity consumption over a whole year.

Carbon Offset Schemes

Climatecare.org and other websites use 'carbon calculators' that allow jetsetters to offset the greenhouse gases they are responsible for with contributions to energy-saving projects and other climate-friendly initiatives in the developing world – including projects in India, Honduras, Kazakhstan and Uganda.

Lonely Planet, together with Rough Guides and other concerned partners in the travel industry, supports the carbon offset scheme run by climatecare.org. Lonely Planet offsets all of its staff and author travel.

For more information check out our website: lonelyplanet.com.

LAND
Bicycle

Bicycles can be taken on aeroplanes, but check this with the airline well in advance. Let some of the air out of the tyres to prevent them from bursting in the low-pressure baggage hold. Bikes are not allowed as baggage on Eurolines buses. For information on cycling in Portugal, see p509.

Bus

Buses are slower and less comfortable than trains, but they're cheaper, especially if you qualify for an under-26, student or senior discount. The major long-distance carriers that serve European destinations are Eurolines and Busabout, neither of which have services in Portugal (you'll have to go to Spain first). Eurohop services Spain and two Portugal destinations.

EUROLINES

Eurolines (www.eurolines.com, www.eurolinesportugal.com) is a consortium of coach operators forming Europe's largest network. A Eurolines Pass gives you unlimited travel among 35 European cities, although Madrid is currently the closest city to Portugal covered by the pass.

Eurolines' main Portugal offices are in **Lisbon** (Map pp102-3; ☎ 218 957 398; Loja 203, Gare

do Oriente), **Porto** (Map p385; ☎ 225 189 303; Centro Comercial Central Shopping, Campo 24 de Agosto 215) and **Bragança** (Map p480; ☎ 273 327 122; bus station, Av João da Cruz). For some European routes, Eurolines is affiliated with the big Portuguese operators **Intercentro** (Map p109; ☎ 213 301 500; www.intercentro .pt, in Portuguese; Rua Actor Taborda 55, Lisbon), **Internorte** (☎ 226 052 420; www.internorte.pt, in Portuguese; Praça da Galiza 96, Porto) and **Eva Transportes** (☎ 289 899 700; www.eva-bus.com).

BUSABOUT

Busabout (www.busabout.com) is a hop-on, hop-off network linking 36 cities in Europe. Buses run from May to October, and travellers can move freely around one of three networks. The bus picks up and drops off near select hostels and campsites.

Passes range from UK£330 to UK£650, giving you from two weeks to up to six months to complete your journey. Youth (under 26 years) and student-card holders pay about 10% less. The nearest stops to Portugal are in Spain (Madrid, Barcelona and San Sebastián).

CONTINENTAL EUROPE
France

Eurolines offers regular connections from Paris to all over Portugal, including Porto (25 hours), Lisbon (26 hours) and (less often) Faro (29 hours). Expect to pay €80 to €110. Hefty surcharges apply to one-way or return tickets for most departures from July to mid-August and also on Saturday year-round.

Spain

UK–Portugal and France–Portugal Eurolines services cross to Portugal via northwest Spain. Sample fares to Lisbon include €40 from Salamanca.

From Madrid, Eurolines/Internorte runs daily via Guarda to Porto (€46 one way, 8½ hours) and also via Badajoz and Évora to Lisbon (€41, eight hours); twice weekly, the Lisbon service departs from Barcelona (€92, 18 hours). The Spanish lines **Avanza** (☎ 902 020 052; www.avanzabus.com) and **Alsa** (☎ 902 422 242; www.alsa.es) each have regular Madrid–Lisbon services (€46).

From Seville, Alsa/Eurolines goes five to six times weekly via Badajoz and Évora to Lisbon (€44, seven hours).

The Portuguese carrier **Eva** (☎ 289 899 700; www.eva-bus.com) and the Spanish line **Damas** (☎ 959 256 900; www.damas-sa.es) operate a joint service three times weekly from Seville to Lisbon (€33 to €42, 4½ hours); with connecting buses to other cities at Ficalho.

Eurolines affiliate **Intersul** (☎ 213 301 500; www.internorte.pt/intersul) runs from Seville to Lagos regularly in summer, and Eva/Damas runs a twice-daily service from Seville to Faro (€16, four to five hours), Albufeira and Lagos (€22, 4½ hours) via Huelva.

Elsewhere in Continental Europe

Eurolines has services to Portugal from destinations all across Europe, typically running about twice a week. One-way fares running from Hamburg to Porto/Lisbon/Faro are around €165/174/196. Fares from Amsterdam or Brussels are around €145 to Lisbon or Faro.

UK

Eurolines runs several services to Portugal from Victoria coach station in London, with a stopover and change of bus in France and sometimes Spain. These include two buses a week to Viana do Castelo (34 hours), five to Porto (33 hours), five via Coimbra to Lisbon (35 hours) and two via Faro to Lagos (38 hours). These services cost around UK£169 return.

Car & Motorcycle

Of more than 30 roads that cross the Portugal–Spain border, the best and biggest do so near Valença do Minho (E01/A3), Chaves (N532), Bragança (E82/IP4), Guarda/Vilar Formoso (E80/IP5), Elvas (E90/A6/IP7), Serpa (N260) and Vila Real de Santo António (E1/IP1). There are no longer any border controls.

INSURANCE & DOCUMENTS

Nationals of EU countries need only their home driving licences to operate a car or motorcycle in Portugal, although holders of the UK's old, pre-EU green licences should also carry an International Driving Permit (IDP). Portugal also accepts licences issued in Brazil and the USA. Others should get an IDP through an automobile licensing department or automobile club in their home country (or at some post offices in the UK).

If you're driving your own car or motor-cycle into Portugal, you'll also need vehicle registration (proof of ownership) and insur-ance documents. If these are in order you should be able to keep the vehicle in Portugal for up to six months.

Motor vehicle insurance with at least third-party cover is compulsory throughout the EU. Your home policy may or may not be extendable to Portugal, and the coverage of some comprehensive policies automatically drops to third-party only outside your home country unless the insurer is notified. Though it's not a legal requirement, it's wise to carry written confirmation from your home insurer that you have the correct coverage.

If you hire a car, the rental firm will provide you with registration and insurance papers, plus a rental contract.

UK

The quickest driving route from the UK to Portugal is by car ferry to northern Spain. Take **P&O Portsmouth** (☎ 0871 6645 645; www.poferries.com) from Portsmouth to Bilbao (35 hours, twice weekly mid-March to mid-December), or **Brittany Ferries** (☎ 0870 3665 333; www.brittany-ferries.com) from Plymouth to Santander (18 hours, twice weekly from March to November). From Bilbao or Santander it's roughly 1000km to Lisbon, 800km to Porto and 1300km to Faro. Fares are wildly seasonal. A standard weekday, high-season, return ticket for a car/motorcycle with driver and one passenger (with cabin accommodation) starts at about

UK£855/598, but you can usually beat this with special offers.

An alternative is to catch a ferry across the Channel (or the Eurotunnel vehicle train beneath it) to France and motor down the coast. The fastest sea crossings travel between Dover and Calais, and are operated by P&O Portsmouth. For travel through the Channel Tunnel, visit **Eurotunnel** (www.eurotunnel.com).

Train

Trains are a popular way to get around Europe – comfortable, frequent and generally on time. But unless you have a rail pass the cost can be higher than flying.

There are two standard long-distance rail journeys into Portugal. Both take the *TGV Atlantique* from Paris to Irún (in Spain), where you must change trains. From there the *Sud-Expresso* crosses into Portugal at Vilar Formoso (Fuentes de Oñoro in Spain), continuing to Coimbra and Lisbon; change at Pampilhosa for Porto. The other journey runs from Irún to Madrid, with a change to the *Talgo Lusitânia,* crossing into Portugal at Marvão-Beirã and on to Lisbon. For trips to the south of Portugal, change at Lisbon.

Two other important Spain–Portugal crossings are at Valença do Minho and at Caia (Caya in Spain), near Elvas.

You will have few problems buying long-distance tickets as little as a day or two ahead, even in the summer. For those intending to do a lot of European rail travel, the exhaustive *Thomas Cook European Timetable* is updated monthly and is available from **Thomas Cook Publishing** (☎ 01733-416417; www .thomascooktimetables.com) for UK£13.50 online, plus postage.

TRAIN PASSES

Many of the passes listed here are available through **Rail Europe** (www.raileurope.co.uk); most travel agencies also sell them, though you'll save a little by buying directly from the issuing authority. Note that even with a pass you must still pay for seat and couchette reservations and express-train supplements.

The **Inter-Rail Pass** (www.interrailnet.com) allows a certain number of travel days within a set time frame. The network includes 30 countries. A pass for five days of travel over 10 days costs €329, while a month of unlimited travel runs at €809. The Inter-Rail Pass is available to anyone residing in Europe for six months

before starting their travels. You cannot use it in your home country.

The **Eurail Global Pass** and the **Eurail Selectpass** (www.eurail.com), both for non-European residents, are meant to be purchased while you are still in your home country but are available at a higher price from some European locations. The Eurail Global pass is valid for unlimited travel (1st/2nd class) in 20 European countries, including Portugal. It's valid for 15 days (€503/327) up to three months (€1413/920); various 'flexi' versions allow a chosen number of travel days over a longer period. The Eurail Selectpass allows you to travel between three, four or five of your chosen Eurail countries (they must be directly connected by Eurail transport). You can choose from five to 10 travelling days (or up to 15 for five countries), which can be taken at any point within a two-month period. Three countries cost €319/207 for five days, and up to €483/313 for 10 days, while five countries cost €393/255 for five days up to an increased total of 15 days for €706/459. For both these passes, there is also a 'saver' option available for those travelling in groups (two people qualify as a group).

The **Iberic Rail Pass** (www.europeanrailguide.com), available only to non-European residents, is also valid for a specified period of 1st-class travel in Spain and Portugal during a two-month period, from three days (adult/youth US$271/217) to 10 days (US$471/280).

CONTINENTAL EUROPE
France

The daily train journey from Paris (Gare d'Austerlitz) to Lisbon takes 20 hours. An adult, 2nd-class (Apex), under-26 ticket costs around €250 return for a couchette on the overnight Irún–Lisbon section. You can book directly with French railway **SNCF** (www.voyages-sncf.com).

Spain

The daily Paris–Lisbon train goes via Vitória, Burgos, Valladolid and Salamanca, entering Portugal at Vila Formoso. A 2nd-class, one-way, reserved seat from Salamanca to Lisbon costs €62.

The main Spain–Portugal rail route is from Madrid to Lisbon via Cáceres and the border station of Marvão-Beirã. The nightly journey on the *Talgo Lusitânia* takes 10½ hours. A 2nd-class, one-way, reserved seat costs €120; add on €88 for a berth in a four-person compartment or €102 in a two-person compartment.

The Badajoz–Caia–Elvas–Lisbon route (€22, five hours), with two regional trains a day and a change at Entroncamento, is tedious, though the scenery through the Serra de Marvão is grand. Onward Seville–Badajoz connections are by bus.

In the south, trains run west from Seville only as far as Huelva, followed by bus connections. You're better off on a bus.

UK

The fastest and most convenient route to Portugal is with **Eurostar** (www.eurostar.com) from London Waterloo to Paris via the Channel Tunnel, and then onward by TGV.

SEA

There are no scheduled seagoing ferries to Portugal, but many to Spain. For details on those from the UK to Spain, see p507.

The closest North African ferry connections are from Morocco to Spain; contact **Trasmediterranea** (www.trasmediterranea.es), **Euro Ferrys** (www.euroferrys.com) and **FerriMaroc** (www.ferrimaroc.com) for details. Car ferries also run from Tangier to Gibraltar.

Car ferries cross the Rio Guadiana border from Ayamonte in Spain to Vila Real de Santo António in the Algarve every 20 minutes from 8.30am to 7pm Monday to Saturday, and from 9.15am to 5.40pm on Sunday; buy tickets from the waterfront office (€1.45/4.50/0.80 per person/car/bike).

GETTING AROUND

A helpful website for schedules and prices to assist with your trip planning is www.transpor.pt.

AIR

Flights within mainland Portugal are expensive, and for the short distances involved, not really worth considering. Nonetheless, **TAP Air Portugal** (☎ 707 205 700; www.tap.pt) has multiple daily Lisbon–Porto and Lisbon–Faro flights (taking less than one hour) year-round. For Porto to Faro, change in Lisbon.

BICYCLE

Mountain biking is hugely popular in Portugal, even though there are few dedicated bicycle paths. Possible itineraries are numerous in the mountainous national/natural parks of the north (especially Parque Nacional da Peneda-Gerês), along the coast or across the Alentejo plains. Coastal trips are easiest from north to south, with the prevailing winds. More demanding is the Serra da Estrela (which serves as the Tour de Portugal's 'mountain run'). You could also try the Serra do Marão between Amarante and Vila Real.

Local bike clubs organise regular Passeio BTT trips; check their flyers at rental agencies, bike shops and *turismos* (tourist offices). Guided trips are often available in popular tourist destinations. For jaunts arranged from abroad, see p84.

Cobbled roads in some old-town centres may jar your teeth loose if your tyres aren't fat enough; they should be at least 38mm in diameter.

Documents

If you're cycling around Portugal on your own bike, proof of ownership and a written description and photograph of it will help police in case it's stolen.

Hire

There are numerous places to rent bikes, especially in the Algarve and other touristy areas. Prices range from €8 to €20 per day. Rental outfits are noted in the text.

Information

For listings of events and bike shops, buy the bimonthly Portuguese-language *Bike Magazine,* available from larger newsagents.

For its members, the UK-based **Cyclists' Touring Club** (CTC; ☎ 0844 7368 450; www.ctc.org.uk) publishes useful and free information on cycling in Portugal, plus notes for half a dozen routes around the country. It also offers tips, maps, topography guides and other publications by mail order.

Transporting Your Bicycle

Boxed-up or bagged-up bicycles can be taken free on all *regional* and *interregional* trains as accompanied baggage. They can also go, unboxed, on a few suburban services on weekends or for a small charge outside the rush hour. Most domestic bus lines won't accept bikes.

BOAT

Other than river cruises along the Rio Douro from Porto (p418) and the Rio Tejo from Lisbon (p124), Portugal's only remaining waterborne transport is cross-river ferries. Commuter ferries include those across the Rio Tejo to/from Lisbon (p148), and across the mouth of the Rio Sado (p174).

BUS

A host of small private bus operators, most amalgamated into regional companies, run a dense network of services across the country. Among the largest companies are **Rede Expressos** (☎ 707 223 344; www.rede-expressos .pt), **Rodonorte** (☎ 259 340 710; www.rodonorte .pt) and the Algarve line **Eva** (☎ 289 899 700; www.eva-bus.com).

Bus services are of three general types: *expressos* are comfortable, fast buses between major cities, *rápidas* are quick regional buses, and *carreiras,* marked CR, stop at every crossroad (never mind that *carreiras* means something like 'in a hurry' in Portuguese). Some companies also offer a fast deluxe category called *alta qualidade.*

Even in summer you'll have little problem booking an *expresso* ticket for the same or next day. A Lisbon–Faro express bus takes four hours and costs €15; Lisbon–Porto takes 3½ hours for around €18. By contrast, local services can thin out to almost nothing on weekends, especially in summer when school is out.

Seniors and students get a small discount of 5%; children aged under 12 years usually ride for half price.

Don't rely on *turismos* for accurate timetable information. Most bus-station ticket desks will give you a little computer printout of fares and all services.

CAR & MOTORCYCLE

Portugal's modest network of *estradas* (highways) is gradually spreading across the country. Main roads are sealed and generally in good condition. And if you choose to travel around on lesser routes you'll find most of the roads empty.

The downside is your fellow drivers. A leading Swedish road-safety investigator

was quoted as saying that the Portuguese 'drive like car thieves' and the prime minister described what happens on Portugal's major highways as 'civil war'. The country's per-capita death rate from road accidents has long been one of Europe's highest, and drinking, driving and dying are hot political potatoes.

The good news is that recent years have seen a steady decline in road-death rates, thanks to a zero-tolerance police crackdown on accident-prone routes and alcohol limits. The legal blood-alcohol level of 0.5g/L is pretty stringent, plus there are fines of up to €2500.

Along those lines, it's also illegal in Portugal to drive while talking on a mobile phone.

Driving can be tricky in Portugal's small walled towns, where roads may taper down to donkey-cart size before you know it, and fiendish one-way systems can force you out of your way.

A common sight in larger towns is the down-and-outers who lurk around squares and car parks, wave you into the parking space you've just found for yourself, and ask for payment for this service. Of course it's a racket and of course there's no need to give them anything, but the Portuguese often do, and €0.50 might keep your car out of trouble.

For information on what to bring in the way of documents, see p507.

Accidents

If you are involved in a minor 'fender bender' with no injuries, the easiest way for drivers to sort things out with their insurance companies is to fill out a *Constat Aimable* (the English version is called a European Accident Statement). There's no risk in signing this: it's just a way to exchange the relevant information and there's usually one included in rental-car documents. Make sure it includes any details that may help you prove that the accident was not your fault. To alert the police, dial ☎ 112.

Assistance

Automóvel Club de Portugal (ACP; Map p109; ☎ 808 502 502; www.acp.pt, in Portuguese; Rua Rosa Araújo 24, Lisbon; ⏱ 8am-8pm Mon-Fri), Portugal's national auto club, provides medical, legal and breakdown assistance for its members. Road information and maps are available to anyone at ACP offices, including the head office

ROAD DISTANCES (KM)

	Aveiro	Beja	Braga	Bragança	Castelo Branco	Coimbra	Évora	Faro	Guarda	Leiria	Lisbon	Portalegre	Porto	Santarém	Setúbal	Viana do Castelo	Vila Real	Viseu
Aveiro	---																	
Beja	383	---																
Braga	129	504	---															
Bragança	287	566	185	---														
Castelo Branco	239	271	366	299	---													
Coimbra	60	329	178	314	191	---												
Évora	305	78	426	488	191	251	---											
Faro	522	166	643	732	437	468	244	---										
Guarda	163	369	260	197	102	161	291	535	---									
Leiria	126	273	244	402	179	72	195	412	233	---								
Lisbon	256	183	372	530	264	202	138	296	402	146	---							
Portalegre	276	178	403	390	93	222	100	344	193	172	219	---						
Porto	71	446	58	216	308	123	368	585	202	189	317	339	---					
Santarém	188	195	309	464	181	134	117	346	295	78	80	147	251	---				
Setúbal	299	143	420	575	316	246	105	256	406	189	47	186	362	123	---			
Viana do Castelo	144	519	56	241	382	191	441	658	275	262	387	412	73	324	435	---		
Vila Real	169	528	94	120	261	199	450	683	159	282	412	352	98	349	460	150	---	
Viseu	86	415	185	228	177	86	366	554	75	158	288	268	127	220	331	241	113	---

TRANSPORT

in Lisbon and branches in Aveiro, Braga, Bragança, Coimbra, Évora, Faro, Porto and elsewhere.

If your national auto club belongs to the Fédération Internationale de l'Automobile or the Alliance Internationale de Tourisme, you can also use ACP's emergency services and get discounts on maps and other products. Among clubs that qualify are the AA and RAC in the UK, and the Australian, New Zealand, Canadian and American automobile associations.

The 24-hour emergency help number is ☎ 707 509 510.

Fuel

Fuel is expensive – about €1.46 (and rising) for a litre of *sem chumbo* (unleaded petrol) at the time of writing. There are plenty of self-service stations, and credit cards are accepted at most.

Highways & Toll Roads

Top of the range are *auto-estradas* (motorways), all of them *portagens* (toll roads); the longest of these are Lisbon–Porto and Lisbon–Algarve. Toll roads charge cars and motorcycles a little over €0.06 per kilometre (eg a total of €19.10 for Lisbon–Porto and €18.30 for Lisbon to the Algarve).

Nomenclature can be baffling. Motorway numbers prefixed with an E are Europewide designations. Portugal's toll roads are prefixed with an A. Highways in the country's main network are prefixed IP *(itinerário principal)* and subsidiary ones IC *(itinerário complementar)*. Some highways have several designations, and numbers that change midflow.

PARKING

Parking is often metered within city centres, but is free Saturday evening and Sunday. Central Lisbon has car parks, and these cost around €10 per day. For more details on driving and parking in Lisbon see p149. In towns where parking is difficult we've included parking information in the Orientation, Getting There & Away or Getting Around sections.

TRANSPORT

Numbers for the main two-lane *estradas nacionais* (national roads) have no prefix letter on some road maps, whereas on other maps they're prefixed by N. If you want to get off the big roads, consider going for the really small ones, which tend to be prettier and more peaceful.

Hire

To rent a car in Portugal you must be at least 25 years old and have held your driving licence for more than a year (some companies allow younger drivers at higher rates). The widest choice of car-hire companies is at Lisbon, Porto and Faro airports. Competition has driven Algarve rates lower than elsewhere.

Some of the best advance-booking rates are offered by internet-based brokers such as **Holiday Autos** (www.holidayautos.com). Other bargains come as part of 'fly/drive' packages. The worst deals tend to be those done with international firms on arrival, though their prepaid promotional rates are competitive. Book at least a few days ahead in high season. For on-the-spot rental, domestic firms such as **Auto Jardim** (www.auto-jardim.com) have some of the best rates.

Renting the smallest and cheapest available car for a week in high season costs as little as €135 (with tax, insurance and unlimited mileage) if booked from abroad, and a similar amount through a Portuguese firm. It can cost up to €400 if you book through Portuguese branches of international firms such as Hertz, Europcar and Avis.

For an additional fee you can get personal insurance through the rental company, unless you're covered by your home policy (see p507). A minimum of third-party coverage is compulsory in the EU.

Rental cars are especially at risk of break-ins or petty theft in larger towns, so don't leave anything of value visible in the car. The ultracautious unscrew the radio antenna and leave it inside the car at night; they might also put the wheel covers (hubcaps) in the boot (trunk) for the duration of the trip.

Motorcycles and scooters can be rented in larger cities, and all over coastal Algarve. Expect to pay from €30/60 per day for a scooter/motorcycle.

Road Rules

Despite the sometimes chaotic relations between drivers, there are rules. To begin with, driving is on the right, overtaking is on the left and most signs use international symbols. An important rule to remember is that traffic from the right usually has priority. Portugal has lots of ambiguously marked intersections, so this is more important than you might think.

Except when marked otherwise, speed limits for cars (without a trailer) and motorcycles (without a sidecar) are 50km/h in towns and villages, 90km/h outside built-up areas and 120km/h on motorways. By law, car safety belts must be worn in the front and back seats, and children under 12 years may not ride in the front. Motorcyclists and their passengers must wear helmets, and motorcycles must have their headlights on day and night.

The police can impose steep on-the-spot fines for speeding and parking offences, so save yourself a big hassle and remember to toe the line.

HITCHING

Hitching is never entirely safe anywhere, and we don't recommend it. In any case it isn't an easy option in Portugal. Almost nobody stops on major highways, and on smaller roads drivers tend to be going short distances so you may only advance from one field to the next.

LOCAL TRANSPORT
Bus

Except in Lisbon or Porto, there's little reason to take municipal buses, as most attractions are within walking distance. Most areas have regional bus services, for better or worse (see p510).

Metro

Both Lisbon and Porto have ambitious underground systems that are still growing; see p150 and p406.

Taxi

Taxis offer fair value over short distances, and are plentiful in large towns and cities. Ordinary taxis are usually marked with an A (which stands for *aluguer*, for hire) on the door, number plate or elsewhere. They use meters and are available on the street and at taxi ranks, or by telephone for a surcharge of €0.75.

The fare on weekdays during daylight hours is about €2.50 *bandeirada* (flag fall) plus around €0.80 per kilometre, and a bit more for periods spent idling in traffic. A fare of €6 will usually get you across bigger towns. It's best to insist on the meter, although it's possible to negotiate a flat fare. If you have a sizeable load of luggage you'll pay a further €1.50.

Rates are about 20% higher at night (9pm to 6am), and on weekends and holidays. Once a taxi leaves the city limits you also pay a surcharge or higher rate.

In larger cities, including Lisbon and Porto, meterless taxis marked with a T (for *turismo*) can be hired from private companies for excursions. Rates for these are higher, but standardised; drivers are honest and polite, and speak foreign languages.

Tram

Tram lovers shouldn't miss the charming relics rattling through the narrow streets of Lisbon (p149) and Porto (p407).

TOURS

Lisbon-based **Cityrama** (☎ 213 191 090; www.cityrama.pt), Viana do Castelo's **AVIC** (☎ 258 820 360; www.avic.pt), Porto's **Diana Tours** (☎ 227 160 624; www.dianatours.pt) and the Algarve's **Megatur** (☎ 289 807 485; www.megatur.pt) all run bus tours.

Caminhos de Ferro Portugueses (CP; ☎ 808 208 208; www.cp.pt; ☉ 7am-11pm), the state railway company, organises Saturday day trips up the Douro valley on an old steam engine during the summer months. See p418 for more details.

If you prefer to assemble your own holiday, Portugal specialist **Destination Portugal** (www.destination-portugal.co.uk) will tell you all you need to know and can help with flights, car hire and accommodation, separately or together.

Locally run adventure tours are noted in individual town listings; activity-based tours are listed in Portugal Outdoors (p82). Try the following for special-interest tours:

Arblaster & Clarke (☎ 01730-263111 in the UK; www.arblasterandclarke.com) Offers wine tours in the Douro.

Martin Randall Travel (☎ 020-8742 3355 in the UK; www.martinrandall.com) Cultural specialist that arranges first-rate escorted tours, including a historical tour covering Wellington's Iberian campaign.

Naturetrek (☎ 01962-733051 in the UK; www.naturetrek.co.uk) Specialist in birdwatching and botanical tours; runs an eight-day excursion around southern Portugal.

TRAIN

If you can match your itinerary to a regional service, travelling with **Caminhos de Ferro Portugueses** (CP; ☎ 808 208 208; www.cp.pt), the state railway company, is cheaper than by bus. Trains tend to be slower than long-distance buses, however.

Since the completion of main-line tracks to Pinhal Novo, there is now a direct rail link from Lisbon to the south of Portugal.

Three of the most appealing old railway lines, on narrow-gauge tracks climbing out of the Douro valley, survive in truncated form: the Linha da Tâmega from Livração to Amarante (p413); the Linha da Corgo from Peso da Régua to Vila Real (p472); and the beautiful Linha da Tua from Tua to Mirandela (p487).

Discounts

Children aged under four years travel free; those aged four to 12 go for half-price. A youth card issued by Euro26 member countries gets you a 30% discount on *urbano*, *regional* and *interregional* services on any day. For distances above 90km, you can also get a 20% discount on *intercidade* (express) services and a 10% discount on Alfa Pendular (AP) trains – though the latter applies only from Tuesday to Thursday. Travellers aged 65 and over can get 50% off any service by showing some ID.

Information & Reservations

You can get hold of timetable and fare information at all stations and from **CP** (www.cp.pt). You can book *intercidade* and Alfa Pendular tickets up to 30 days ahead, though you'll have little trouble booking for the next or even the same day. Other services can only be booked 24 hours in advance. A seat reservation is mandatory on most *intercidade* and Alfa trains; the booking fee is included in the price.

Types & Classes of Service

There are three main types of long-distance service: *regional* trains (marked R on timetables), which stop everywhere; reasonably fast *interregional* (IR) trains; and express trains, called *rápido* or *intercidade* (IC). Alfa Pendular is a deluxe, marginally faster and pricier IC service on the Lisbon–Coimbra–Porto main line. International services are marked IN on timetables.

TRANSPORT

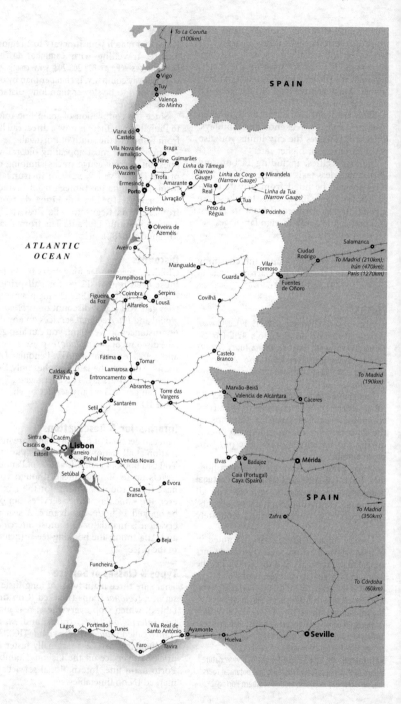

Lisbon and Porto have their own *urbano* (suburban) train networks. Lisbon's network extends predictably to Sintra, Cascais and Setúbal, and up the lower Tejo valley. Porto's network takes the definition of 'suburban' to new lengths, running all the way to Braga, Guimarães and Aveiro. *Urbano* services also travel between Coimbra and Figueira da Foz. The distinction matters where long-distance services parallel the more convenient, plentiful, and considerably cheaper, *urbanos*.

Only the Faro–Porto *Comboio Azul* and international trains like *Sud-Expresso* and *Talgo Lusitânia* have restaurant cars, though all IC and Alfa trains have aisle service and most have bars.

Train Passes

The Portuguese Railpass gives you unlimited 1st-class travel on any three, four or six days over a month period. The price for three/four/six days is US$155/197/264, which doesn't make for great value unless you plan to crisscross the country a few times. It's only available to travellers from outside Europe, and must be purchased before you arrive; contact **Rail Europe** (www.raileurope.com).

Special CP *bilhetes turísticos* (tourist tickets), valid for unlimited travel during seven/14/21 consecutive days, cost €118/196/288 (half-price for those aged under 12 or over 65), and are on sale at major stations. For other rail passes, see p508.

TRANSPORT

Health Dr Caroline Evans

CONTENTS

BEFORE YOU GO

Prevention is the key to staying healthy while abroad. A little planning before departure, particularly for pre-existing illnesses, will save trouble later. See your dentist before a long trip, carry a spare pair of contact lenses and glasses, and take your optical prescription with you. Bring medications in their original, clearly labelled, containers. A signed and dated letter from your physician describing your medical conditions and medications, including generic names, is also a good idea. If carrying syringes or needles, be sure to have a physician's letter documenting their medical necessity.

INSURANCE

If you're an EU citizen, be sure to get the European Health Insurance Card (EHIC), which is available online at www.ehic.org.uk, or you can pick up an application at any British post office. It will not cover you for nonemergencies or emergency repatriation. Citizens from other countries should find out if there is a reciprocal arrangement for free medical care between their country and Portugal. If you do need health insurance, strongly consider a policy that covers you for the worst possible scenario, such as an accident requiring an emergency flight home. Find out in advance if your insurance plan will make payments directly to providers or reimburse you later for overseas health expenditures. The former option is generally preferable, as it doesn't require you to pay out of pocket in a foreign country.

RECOMMENDED VACCINATIONS

The WHO recommends that all travellers should be covered for diphtheria, tetanus, measles, mumps, rubella and polio, regardless of their destination. Since most vaccines don't produce immunity until at least two weeks after they're given, visit a physician at least six weeks before departure.

INTERNET RESOURCES

The WHO publication *International Travel and Health* is revised annually and available online at www.who.int/ith. Other useful websites include www.mdtravelhealth.com (travel health recommendations for every country; updated daily), www.fitfortravel.scot.nhs.uk (general travel advice), www.ageconcern.org.uk (advice on travel for the elderly) and www.mariestopes.org.uk (information on women's health and contraception).

TRAVEL HEALTH WEBSITES

It's usually a good idea to consult your government's travel health website before departure, if one is available:
Australia (www.smartraveller.gov.au)
Canada (www.hc-sc.gc.ca)
UK (www.doh.gov.uk)
USA (www.cdc.gov/travel)

IN PORTUGAL

AVAILABILITY & COST OF HEALTH CARE

Good health care is readily available and for minor illnesses pharmacists can give valuable advice and sell over-the-counter medication. Most pharmacists speak some English. They can also advise when more specialised help is required and point you in the right direction. The standard of dental care is usually good, but it is sensible to have a dental check-up before a long trip.

TRAVELLER'S DIARRHOEA

If you develop diarrhoea, be sure to drink plenty of fluids, preferably an oral rehydration solution (eg Dioralyte). A few loose stools don't require treatment, but if you start having more than four or five stools a day, you should start taking an antibiotic (usually a quinolone drug) and an antidiarrhoeal agent (such as loperamide). If diarrhoea is bloody, persists for more than 72 hours or is accompanied by fever, shaking, chills or severe abdominal pain you should seek medical attention.

ENVIRONMENTAL HAZARDS
Heat Exhaustion & Heat Stroke

Heat exhaustion occurs following excessive fluid loss with inadequate replacement of fluids and salt. Symptoms include headache, dizziness and tiredness. Dehydration is already happening by the time you feel thirsty – aim to drink sufficient water to produce pale, diluted urine. To treat heat exhaustion, replace lost fluids by drinking water and/or fruit juice or an oral rehydration solution, such as Dioralyte, and cool the body with cold water and fans. Treat salt loss with salty fluids such as soup or Bovril, or add a little more table salt to foods than usual.

Heat stroke is much more serious, resulting in irrational and hyperactive behaviour and eventually loss of consciousness and death. Rapid cooling by spraying the body with water and fanning is ideal. Emergency fluid and electrolyte replacement by intravenous drip is recommended.

Insect Bites & Stings

Mosquitoes are found in most parts of Europe. They may not carry malaria but can cause irritation and infected bites. Use a DEET-based insect repellent.

Bees and wasps cause real problems only to those with a severe allergy (anaphylaxis). If you do have a severe allergy to bee or wasp stings, carry an EpiPen or similar adrenaline injection.

Sand flies are found around Mediterranean beaches. They usually cause only a nasty itchy bite but can carry a rare skin disorder called cutaneous leishmaniasis.

Bed bugs lead to very itchy, lumpy bites. Spraying the mattress with crawling-insect killer then changing the bedding will get rid of them.

Scabies are tiny mites that live in the skin, particularly between the fingers. They cause an intensely itchy rash. Scabies is easily treated with lotion from a pharmacy; other members of the household also need treating to avoid spreading scabies between asymptomatic carriers.

Snakes & Scorpions

Avoid getting bitten by snakes – don't walk barefoot or stick your hand into holes or cracks. Half of those bitten by venomous snakes are not injected with poison (envenomed). If bitten by a snake, don't panic. Immobilise the bitten limb with a splint (eg a stick) and apply a bandage over the site firmly, similar to a bandage over a sprain. Do not apply a tourniquet, or cut or suck the bite. Get medical help as soon as possible so that antivenene can be administered if necessary.

Scorpions are found in Portugal and their sting can be extremely painful but is not considered fatal.

Jellyfish, Sea Urchins & Weever Fish

Stings from jellyfish are painful but not dangerous. Douse the wound in vinegar to deactivate any stingers that haven't 'fired'. Applying calamine lotion, antihistamines or analgesics may reduce the reaction and relieve the pain.

Watch for sea urchins around rocky beaches. If you get their needles embedded in your skin, immerse the limb in hot water to relieve the pain. But to avoid infection visit a doctor and have the needles removed.

Thankfully, it is very rare to find the dangerous weever fish that inhabit shallow tidal zones along the Atlantic coast. They bury themselves in the sand with only their spines protruding and inject a powerful toxin if trodden upon. Soaking your foot in very hot water breaks down the poison, but you should seek medical advice in any event, since in rare cases this can cause permanent local paralysis.

Rabies

Rabies, though rare in Portugal, is a risk, and transmissible via the bite of an infected animal. It can also be transmitted if the animal's saliva comes in contact with an open wound. If you've been bitten by a wild animal, a treatment of shots must begin at once.

TRAVELLING WITH CHILDREN

All travellers with small children should know how to treat minor ailments and when to seek medical treatment. Make sure the children are

HEALTH

up to date with routine vaccinations, and discuss possible travel vaccines with your doctor well before departure as some vaccines are not suitable for children less than a year in age.

In hot moist climates any wound or break in the skin is likely to let in infection. The area should be cleaned and kept dry.

Remember to avoid potentially contaminated food and water. If your child has vomiting or diarrhoea, lost fluid and salts must be replaced. It may be helpful to take rehydration powders for reconstituting with boiled water.

Children should be encouraged to avoid and mistrust any dogs or other mammals because of the risk of rabies and other diseases. Any bite, scratch or lick from a warm-blooded, furry animal should immediately be thoroughly cleaned. If there is any possibility that the animal is infected with rabies, immediate medical assistance should be sought.

WOMEN'S HEALTH

Travelling during pregnancy is usually possible, but always consult your doctor before planning your trip. The most risky times for travel are during the first 12 weeks of pregnancy and after 30 weeks.

SEXUAL HEALTH

Emergency contraception is most effective if taken within 24 hours after unprotected sex. The **International Planned Parent Federation** (www.ippf.org) can advise about the availability of contraception in different countries.

When buying condoms, look for a European CE mark, which means they have been rigorously tested, and then store them in a cool and dry place or they may crack and perish.

Abortion is legal in Portugal until the 10th week of pregnancy.

Language

CONTENTS

Portuguese is the language spoken by 10 million Portuguese and 180 million Brazilians, and is the official language of the African nations of Angola, Mozambique, Cape Verde, Guinea-Bissau, and São Tomé e Príncipe. In Asia you'll hear it in the former Portuguese territories of Macau and East Timor, and in enclaves around Malaka, Goa, Damão and Diu.

As you travel through Portugal, the use of a few Portuguese words and phrases (such as greetings, the essentials of getting a room, ordering a meal, catching a bus or train, timetable basics, 'please', 'thank you', 'yes' and 'no') can transform people's willingness to welcome and help you. For useful culinary language, see p73, and for information on institutes that offer language courses in Lisbon, see p124, and Lagos, see p220.

Nearly all *turismo* (tourist office) staff in Portugal speak some English. In Lisbon, Porto, most of the Algarve and other big tourist destinations it's fairly easy to find English speakers, especially among younger people. Some in the service industry, like waiters and baristas, may insist on showing off their English skills, despite your attempts to stick to Portuguese. Among older folk and in the countryside, English speakers are rare. In the Minho and other areas where local emigrant workers have spent time abroad, you may find people able to speak French or German.

If you'd like a more detailed guide to Portuguese in a compact and easy-to-use form, get yourself a copy of Lonely Planet's *Portuguese Phrasebook*.

LANGUAGE HISTORY

Like French, Italian, Romanian and Spanish, Portuguese is a Romance language derived from Latin. Its pronunciation is quite different from that of other Romance languages, but the similarities are clear when you see it in the written form.

The pre-Roman inhabitants of the Iberian Peninsula were responsible for Portuguese's most striking traits, but the influence of the vulgar Latin of Roman merchants and soldiers gradually took over from indigenous languages and caused a strong neo-Latin character to evolve.

After the Arab invasion in AD 711, Arabic became the prestige cultural language in the Peninsula and exerted a strong influence on the Portuguese language. This connection was significantly weakened when the Moors were expelled in 1249.

Portuguese underwent several changes during the Middle Ages, mostly influenced by French and Provençal (another Romance language). In the 16th and 17th centuries, Italian and Spanish were responsible for innovations in vocabulary.

PRONUNCIATION

Most sounds in Portuguese are also found in English, with the most difficult ones being nasal vowels and diphthongs (explained on p520). The letter ç is pronounced like an English 's' and the letter x sounds like the 'sh' in 'ship' – *criança* is said 'kree-*an*-sa' and *Baixe Alentejo* 'baysh a-leng-*te*-zho'. The letter h is silent, but when combined to form lh it's pronounced like the 'lli' in 'million' and in nh it's like the 'ny' in 'canyon'.

Word Stress

Stress generally falls on the second last syllable of a word, though there are quite a few exceptions. When a word ends in i, im, l, r, u, um or z, or it is pronounced with a nasal-ized vowel, the stress falls on the last sylla-ble. If a vowel is marked with a circumflex (eg ê), an acute (eg é) or a grave (eg è) ac-cent, the stress falls on that syllable.

To make things nice and simple, our transliteration system shows the stressed syllable in italics.

Vowels

In this pronunciation guide, we've used the following symbols for vowel sounds.

a	as the 'u' in 'run'
ai	as in 'aisle'
aw	as in 'saw'
ay	as in 'day'
e	as in 'bet'
ee	as in 'bee'
o	as in 'lot'
oh	as in 'Oh!'
oo	as in 'moon'
ow	as in 'how'
oy	as in 'boy'

Nasal Sounds

A characteristic feature of Portuguese is the use of nasal vowels and diphthongs (vowel combinations). Pronounce them as if you're trying to make the sound through your nose rather than your mouth. English also has nasal vowels to some extent – when you say 'sing' in English, the 'i' is nasalized by the 'ng'. In Portuguese, written vowels that have a nasal consonant after them (m or n), or a tilde over them (eg ã), will be nasal. In our pronunciation guide, we've used 'ng' to indicate a nasal sound.

Consonants

These symbols represent the trickier con-sonant sounds in Portuguese.

ly	as the 'lli' in 'million'
ng	see 'Nasal Sounds' above
ny	as in 'canyon'
r	as in 'run'
rr	as in 'run' but stronger and rolled
zh	as the 's' in 'pleasure'

GENDER

Portuguese has masculine and feminine forms of nouns and adjectives. Alternative endings appear separated by a slash with the masculine form first. Generally, a word ending in o is masculine and one ending in a is feminine.

ACCOMMODATION

I'm looking for a ...
Procuro ...   proo·koo·roo·...
Where's ...?
Onde é que há ...?   ong·de e ke aa...
  a bed and breakfast
  um turismo de   oong too·reezh·moo de
    habitação   a·bee·ta·sowng
  a camping ground
  um parque de campismo   oong par·ke de kang·peezh·moo
  a guesthouse
  uma casa de hóspedes   oo·ma ka·za de osh·pe·desh
  a hotel
  um hotel   oong oo·tel
  an inn
  uma pousada   oo·ma poh·za·da
  a room
  um quarto   oong kwar·too
  a youth hostel
  uma pousada da   oo·ma poh·za·da da
    juventude   zhoo·veng·too·de

I'd like a ... room.
Queria um quarto de ...   ke·ree·a oong kwar·too de ...
Do you have a ... room?
Tem um quarto ...?   teng oong kwar·too de ...
  double
  de casal   ka·zal
  single
  de solteiro   de sol·tay·roo
  twin
  duplo   doo·ploo

How much is it per ...?	Quanto custa por ...?	kwang·too koosh·ta por ...
night	noite	noy·te
person	pessoa	pe·so·a
week	semana	se·ma·na

For (three) nights.
Para (três) noites.   pa·ra (tresh) noy·tesh
Does it include breakfast?
Inclui o pequeno   eeng·kloo·ee oo pee·ke·noo
  almoço?   al·mo·soo
May I see it?
Posso ver?   po·soo ver
I'll take the it.
Fico com ele.   fee·koo kong e·le
I don't like it.
Não gosto.   nowng goosh·too
I'm leaving now.
Vou sair agora.   voh sa·eer a·go·ra

MAKING A RESERVATION

(for phone or written requests)

To ...	*Para ...*
From ...	*De ...*
Date	*Data*
I'd like to book ...	*Queria fazer uma reserva ...* (see the list under 'Accommodation' for bed/room options)
in the name of ...	*no nome de ...*
for the nights of ...	*para os dias ...*
from ... to ...	*de ... até ...*
credit card ...	*cartão de credito ...*
number	*número*
expiry date	*data de vencimento*

Please confirm availability/price.
Por favor confirme a disponibilidade/o preço.

CONVERSATION & ESSENTIALS

Hello.	*Bom dia.*	bong *dee*·a
Hi.	*Olá.*	o·*la*
Good day.	*Bom dia.*	bong *dee*·a
Good evening.	*Boa noite.*	bo·a *noy*·te
See you later.	*Até logo.*	a·te lo·goo
Goodbye.	*Adeus.*	a·de·*oosh*
How are you?	*Como está?*	ko·moo shta
Fine, and you?	*Tudo bem, e docê?*	to·doo beng e vo·*se*
Yes.	*Sim.*	seeng
No.	*Não.*	nowng

Please.
Por favor.   poor fa·*vor*
Thank you (very much).
(Muito) Obrigado. (m)   (*mweeng*·too) o·bree·*ga*·doo
(Muito) Obrigada. (f)   (*mweeng*·too) o·bree·*ga*·da
You're welcome.
De nada.   de *na*·da
Excuse me. (to get past)
Com licença.   kong lee·*seng*·sa
Excuse me. (before asking a question/making a request)
Faz favor.   fash fa·*voor*
Sorry.
Desculpe.   des·*kool*·pe
What's your name?
Como se chama?   ko·moo se *sha*·ma
My name is ...
Chamo-me ...   *sha*·moo·me ...
I'm pleased to meet you.
Prazer em   pra·*zer* eng
  conhecê-lo/-la. (m/f)   ko·nye·se·loo/la
Where are you from?
De onde é?   de *ong*·de e

I'm from ...
Sou (da/do/de) ...   soh (da/do/de) ...
May I take a photo of you?
Posso tirar-lhe   po·soo tee·*rar*·lye
  uma foto?   oo·ma *fo*·too

DIRECTIONS

Where's ...?
Onde fica ...?   ong·de *fee*·ka ...
Can you show me (on the map)?
Pode-me mostrar   po·de·me moosh·*trar*
  (no mapa)?   (noo *ma*·pa)
What's the address?
Qual é o endereço?   kwal e o eng·de·*re*·soo
How far is it?
A que distância fica?   a ke deesh·*tang*·sya *fee*·ka
How do I get there?
Como é que eu chego lá?   ko·moo e ke e·oo *she*·goo la

Turn ...	*Vire ...*	veer ...
at the corner	*na esquina*	na *shkee*·na
at the traffic lights	*nos semáforos*	noosh se·*ma*·foo·roosh
left	*à esquerda*	a *shker*·da
right	*à direita*	a dee·*ray*·ta

here	*aqui*	a·*kee*
there	*lá*	la
near ...	*perto ...*	*per*·too ...
straight ahead	*em frente*	eng *freng*·te
north	*norte*	*nor*·te
south	*sul*	sool
east	*leste*	*lesh*·te
west	*oeste*	o·*esh*·te

SIGNS

Posto de Polícia	Police Station
Pronto Socorro	Emergency Department
Aberto	Open
Encerrado	Closed
Fechado	Closed
Entrada	Entrance
Saída	Exit
Não Fumadores	No Smoking
Lavabos/WC	Toilet
Homens (H)	Men
Senhoras (S)	Women

HEALTH

I'm ill.
Estou doente.   shtoh doo·*eng*·te
I need a doctor (who speaks English).
Preciso de um médico   pre·*see*·zoo de oong *me*·dee·koo
  (que fale inglês).   (ke *fa*·le eeng·*glesh*)

EMERGENCIES

Help!
Socorro! — soo·ko·rroo
It's an emergency.
É uma emergência. — e oo·ma ee·mer·zheng·sya
I'm lost.
Estou perdido/a. (m/f) — shtoh per·dee·doo/da
Where are the toilets?
Onde é casa de banho? — ong·de e ka·za de ba·nyoo
Go away!
Vá-se embora! — va·se eng·bo·ra

Call ...!
Chame ...! — sha·me ...
　a doctor
　um médico — oong me·dee·koo
　an ambulance
　uma ambulância — oo·ma ang·boo·lang·sya
　the police
　a polícia — a poo·lee·sya

It hurts here.
Dói-me aqui. — doy·me a·kee
I've been vomiting.
Tenho estado a vomitar. — ta·nyoo shta·doo a voo·mee·tar
(I think) I'm pregnant.
(Acho que) Estou grávida. — (a·shoo ke) shtoh gra·vee·da

Where's the nearest ...?	Qual é ... mais perto?	kwal e ... maish per·to
dentist	o dentista	oo deng·teesh·ta
doctor	o médico	oo me·dee·koo
hospital	o hospital	oo ash·pee·tal
medical centre	o centro de saúde	oo seng·troo de sa·oo·de
(night) pharmacist	a farmácia (de serviço)	a far·ma·sya (der ser·vee·soo)

I feel ...	Sinto-me ...	seeng·too·me ...
dizzy	tonto/a (m/f)	tong·too/ta
nauseous	enjoado/a (m/f)	eng·zhoo·a·doo/a

asthma	asma	ash·ma
diarrhoea	diarréia	dee·a·rray·a
fever	febre	fe·bre
pain	dor	dor

I'm allergic to ...
Sou alérgico/a à ... — soh a·ler·zhee·koo/ka a ...
　antibiotics
　antibióticos — ang·tee·bee·o·tee·koosh
　aspirin
　aspirina — ash·pee·ree·na
　bees
　abelhas — a·be·lyash
　peanuts
　amendoins — a·meng·doo·engsh
　penicillin
　penicilina — pe·nee·see·lee·na

antiseptic
antiséptico — ang·tee·se·tee·koo
contraceptives
contraceptivos — kong·tra·se·tee·voosh
painkillers
analgésicos — a·nal·zhe·zee·koohs

LANGUAGE DIFFICULTIES

Do you speak English?
Fala inglês? — fa·la eeng·glesh
Does anyone here speak English?
Alguém aqui fala inglês? — al·geng a·kee fa·la eeng·glesh
Do you understand (me)?
Entende(-me)? — eng·teng·de(·me)
I (don't) understand.
(Não) Entendo. — (nowng) eng·teng·doo

Could you please ...?
Podia ... por favor? — po·dee·a ... poor fa·vor
　repeat that
　repetir isto — rre·pe·teer eesh·too
　speak more slowly
　falar mais devagar — fa·lar maish de·va·gar
　write it down
　escrever isso — shkre·ver ee·soo

NUMBERS

0	zero	ze·roo
1	um/uma (m/f)	oong/oo·ma
2	dois/duas (m/f)	doysh/doo·ash
3	três	tresh
4	quatro	kwa·troo
5	cinco	seeng·koo
6	seis	saysh
7	sete	se·te
8	oito	oy·too
9	nove	no·ve
10	dez	desh
11	onze	ong·ze
12	doze	do·ze
13	treze	tre·ze
14	quatorze	ka·tor·ze
15	quinze	keeng·ze
16	dezasseis	de·za·saysh
17	dezassete	de·ze·se·te
18	dezoito	de·zoy·too
19	dezenove	de·za·no·ve
20	vinte	veeng·te

21	vinte e um	veeng·te e oong
22	vinte e dois	veeng·te e doysh
30	trinta	treeng·ta
40	quarenta	kwa·reng·ta
50	cinquenta	seeng·kweng·ta
60	sessenta	se·seng·ta
70	setenta	se·teng·ta
80	oitenta	oy·teng·ta
90	noventa	no·veng·ta
100	cem	seng
200	duzentos	doo·zeng·toosh
1000	mil	meel

QUESTION WORDS

Who?	Quem?	keng
What?	Quê?	ke
When?	Quando?	kwang·doo
Where?	Onde?	ong·de
Why?	Porquê?	poor·ke
Which? (What?)	Qual (sg)/	kwal/
	Quais? (pl)	kwaish

SHOPPING & SERVICES

What time does ... open/close?
A que horas abre/ fecha ...?   a ke o·rash a·bre/ fe·sha ...
I'd like to buy ...
Queria comprar ...   ke·ree·a kong·prar ...
I'm just looking.
Estou só a ver.   shtoh so a ver
May I look at it?
Posso ver?   po·soo ver
How much is it?
Quanto custa?   kwang·too koosh·ta
That's too expensive.
Está muito caro.   shta mweeng·too ka·roo
Can you lower the price?
Pode baixar o preço?   po·de bai·shar oo pre·soo
Do you have something cheaper?
Tem algo mais barato?   teng al·goo maish ba·ra·too
I'll give you (five euros).
Dou-lhe (cinco euros).   doh·lye (seeng·koo e·oo·roosh)
I don't like it.
Não gosto.   nowng gosh·too
I'll take it.
Vou levar isso.   voh le·var ee·soo

Where is ...?
Onde fica ...?   ong·de fee·ka ...
  an ATM
  um caixa automático   oong kai·sha ow·too·ma·tee·koo
  a bank
  o banco   oo bang·koo
  a bookstore
  uma livraria   oo·ma lee·vra·ree·a

  the ... embassy
  a embaixada do/da ...   a eng·bai·sha·da doo/da ...
  a foreign-exchange office
  um câmbio   oong kang·byoo
  a laundrette
  uma lavandaria   oo·ma la·vang·de·ree·a
  the market
  o mercado   oo mer·ka·doo
  a pharmacy/chemist
  uma farmácia   oo·ma far·ma·sya
  the police station
  a esquadra da polícia   a shkwa·dra da poo·lee·sya
  the post office
  o correio   oo koo·rray·oo
  a supermarket
  o supermercado   oo soo·per·mer·ka·doo

Can I pay ...?
Posso pagar com ...?   po·soo pa·gar kong ...
  by credit card
  cartão de crédito   kar·towng de kre·dee·too
  by travellers cheque
  traveller cheques   tra·ve·ler she·kesh

less	menos	me·noosh
more	mais	maish
large	grande	grang·de
small	pequeno/a (m/f)	pe·ke·noo/na

I want to buy ...
Quero comprar ...   ke·roo kom·prar ...
  a phone card
  um cartão telefónico   oong kar·towng te·le·fo·nee·koo
  stamps
  selos   se·loosh

Where can I ...?
Onde é que posso ...?   ong·de e ke po·soo ...
  change a travellers cheque
  trocar travellers cheques   troo·kar tra·ve·ler she·kes
  change money
  trocar dinheiro   troo·kar dee·nyay·roo
  check my email
  ler o meu email   ler oo me·oo e·mayl
  get internet access
  ter accesso à internet   ter a·se·soo a eeng·ter·net

TIME & DATES

What time is it?
Que horas são?   ke o·rash sowng
It's (ten) o'clock.
São (dez) horas.   sowng (desh) o·ras

| now | agora | a·go·ra |
| this morning | esta manhã | esh·ta ma·nyang |

LANGUAGE

this afternoon	esta tarde	esh·ta tard
today	hoje	o·zhe
tonight	hoje a noite	o·zhe a noyt·e
tomorrow	amanhã	a·ma·nyang
yesterday	ontem	ong·teng

Monday	segunda-feira	se·goong·da·fay·ra
Tuesday	terça-feira	ter·sa·fay·ra
Wednesday	quarta-feira	kwar·ta·fay·ra
Thursday	quinta-feira	keeng·ta·fay·ra
Friday	sexta-feira	saysh·ta·fay·ra
Saturday	sábado	sa·ba·doo
Sunday	domingo	doo·meeng·goo

January	Janeiro	zha·nay·roo
February	Fevereiro	fe·vray·roo
March	Março	mar·soo
April	Abril	a·breel
May	Maio	ma·yoo
June	Junho	zhoo·nyoo
July	Julho	zhoo·lyoo
August	Agosto	a·gosh·too
September	Setembro	se·teng·broo
October	Outubro	oh·too·bro
November	Novembro	noo·veng·broo
December	Dezembro	de·zeng·broo

TRANSPORT
Public Transport

Which ... goes	Qual é ... que	kwal e ... ke
to (Lisbon)?	vai para (Lisboa)?	vai pa·ra (leezh·bo·a)
boat	o barco	oo bar·koo
intercity coach	a camioneta	a kam·yoo·ne·ta
local bus	o autocarro	oo ow·too·ka·rroo
ferry	o ferry	oo fe·ree
plane	o avião	oo a·vee·owng
train	o comboio	oo kong·boy·oo

When's the ...	Quando é que sai	kwang·doo e ke sai
(bus)?	o ... (autocarro)?	oo ... (ow·too·ka·rroo)
first	primeiro	pree·may·roo
next	próximo	pro·see·moo
last	último	ool·tee·moo

Is this the (bus) to ...?
Este (autocarro) vai   esh·te (ow·to·ka·rroo) vai
  para ...?   pa·ra ...?

What time does it leave?
A que horas sai?   a ke o·ras sai

What time does it get to ...?
A que horas chega a ...?   a ke o·rash she·ga a ...

Do I need to change train?
Preciso de mudar   pre·see·soo de moo·dar
  de comboio?   de kong·boy·oo

A ... ticket	Um bilhete	oong bee·lye·te
to (...)	de ... para (...)	de ... pa·ra (...)
1st-class	primeira classe	pree·may·ra kla·se
2nd-class	segunda classe	se·goong·da kla·se
one-way	ida	ee·da
return	ida e volta	ee·da ee vol·ta

the luggage check room
o balcão de guarda   oo bal·kowng de gwar·da
  bagagens   ba·ga·zhengsh

a luggage locker
um depósito de   oong de·po·zee·to de
  bagagens   ba·ga·zhengsh

Is this taxi available?
Este táxi está livre?
esh·te tak·see shta leev·re

How much is it (to Silves)?
Quanto custa (até ao Silves)?
kwang·too koosh·ta (a·te ow seel·vesh)

Please put the meter on.
Por favor ligue o taxímetro.
poor fa·vor lee·ge oo tak·see·me·troo

Please take me to (this address).
Leve-me para (este endereço), por favor.
le·ve·me pa·ra (esh·te en·de·re·soo) poor fa·vor

Private Transport
I'd like to hire ...

Queria alugar ...		ke·rya a·loo·gar ...
a bicycle		
uma bicicleta		oo·ma bee·see·kle·ta
a car		
um carro		oong ka·rroo
a 4WD		
um quatro por quatro		oom kwa·troo por kwa·troo
a motorbike		
uma moto		oo·ma mo·too

Is this the road to ...?
Esta é a estrada para ...?
esh·ta e a shtra·da pa·ra ...

(How long) Can I park here?
(Quanto tempo) Posso estacionar aqui?
(kwang·too teng·poo) po·soo shta·see·oo·nar a·kee

The (car/motorbike) has broken down at ...
(O carro/A moto) avariou-se em ...
(oo ka·rroo/a mo·too) a·va·ree·oh·se eng ...

The car won't start.
(O carro) não pega.
(oo ka·rroo) nowng pe·ga

I need a mechanic.
Preciso de um mecânico.
pre·see·soo de oong me·ka·nee·koo

ROAD SIGNS

Ceda a Vez	Give Way
Entrada	Entrance
Portagem	Toll
Proibido Entrar	No Entry
Rua Sem Saída	Dead End
Saída	Freeway Exit
Sentido Único	One-way

I've had an accident.
Tive um acidente.
tee·ve oong a·see·*deng*·te

I've run out of petrol/gas.
Estou sem gasolina.
shtoh seng ga·zoo·*lee*·na

Where's a petrol/gas station?
Onde fica um posto de gasolina?
ong·de *fee*·ka oong *posh*·too de ga·zoo·*lee*·na

Please fill it up.
Encha o tanque, por favor.
en·sha oo *tang*·ke poor fa·*vor*

I'd like ... litres.
Ponha ... litros.
po·nya ... *lee*·troosh

diesel	*diesel*	dee·zel
LPG	*gás*	gash
petrol/gas	*gasolina*	ga·zoo·*lee*·na

TRAVEL WITH CHILDREN

I need (a/an) ...
Preciso de ...
pre·*see*·zoo de ...

Do you have (a/an) ...?
Aqui tem ...?
a·*kee* teng ...

  baby change room
  uma sala para mudar o bebé
  oo·ma *sa*·la *pa*·ra moo·*dar* o be·*be*

  baby seat
  um assento de criança
  oong a·*seng*·too de kree·*ang*·sa

  child-minding service
  um serviço de ama
  oong ser·*vee*·soo de *a*·ma

  children's menu
  um menu das crianças
  oong me·*noo* das kree·*ang*·sash

  (disposable) nappies/diapers
  fraldas (descartáveis)
  fral·dash (desh·kar·*ta*·vaysh)

  (English-speaking) baby-sitter
  uma ama (que fale ingles)
  oo·ma *a*·ma (ke *fa*·le eeng·*glesh*)

  formula (milk)
  leite em pó (para bebés)
  lay·te eng po (*pa*·ra be·*besh*)

  highchair
  uma cadeira para crianças
  oo·ma ka·*day*·ra *pa*·ra kree·*ang*·sash

Do you mind if I breastfeed here?
Importa-se que eu amamente aqui?
eeng·*por*·ta·se ke eu a·ma·*meng*·te a·*kee*

Are children allowed?
É permitida a entrada a crianças?
e per·mee·*tee*·da a eng·*tra*·da a kree·*ang*·sash

LANGUAGE

Glossary

adegas – wineries
Age of Discoveries – the period during the 15th and 16th centuries when Portuguese sailors explored the coast of Africa and finally charted a sea route to India
albergaria – upmarket inn
albufeira – reservoir, lagoon
aldeia – village
alta – upper
anta – see *dolmen*
arco – arch
armillary sphere – celestial sphere used by early astronomers and navigators to chart the stars; a decorative motif in Manueline architecture and atop *pelourinhos*
arraial, arraiais (pl) – street party
artesanato – handicrafts shop
avenida – avenue
azulejo – hand-painted tile, typically blue and white, used to decorate buildings

bairro – town district
baixa – lower
balneário – health resort, spa
barcos rabelos – colourful boats once used to transport port wine from vineyards
barragem – dam
beco – cul de sac
biblioteca – library
bilhete diário/turístico – day pass/tourist ticket

caderneta – booklet of tickets (train)
câmara municipal – city or town hall
caldas – hot springs
Carnaval – Carnival; festival that takes place just before Lent
casa de hóspedes – boarding house, usually with shared showers and toilets
casais – huts
castelo – castle
castro – fortified hill town
cavaleiro – horseman
CCI – Camping Card International
Celtiberians – descendants of Celts who arrived in the Iberian Peninsula around 600 BC
centro de saúde – state-administered medical centre
cidade – town or city
citânia – Celtic fortified village
claustro – cloisters
concelho – municipality, council
cortes – Portugal's early parliament

couvert – cover charge added to restaurant bills to pay for sundries
CP – Caminhos de Ferro Portugueses (the Portuguese state railway company)
cromeleque – circle of prehistoric standing stones
cruz – cross

direita – right; abbreviated as D, dir or Dta
dolmen – Neolithic stone tomb (*anta* in Portuguese)
Dom, Dona – honorific titles (like Sir, Madam) given to royalty, nobility and landowners; now used more generally as a very polite form of address

elevador – lift (elevator), funicular
entrada – entrée/starter or entrance
espigueiros – stone granaries
esplanada – terrace, seafront promenade
estação – station (usually train station)
estalagem – inn; more expensive than an *albergaria*
estradas – highways
expressos – comfortable, fast buses between major cities

fadista – singer of *fado*
fado – traditional, melancholic Portuguese style of singing
feira – fair
festa – festival
FICC – Fédération Internationale de Camping et de Caravanning (International Camping & Caravanning Federation)
fortaleza – fortress

GNR – Guarda Nacional Republicana; the national guard (the acting police force in rural towns without *PSP* police)
gruta – cave
guitarra – guitar

hipermercado – hypermarket
horários – timetables
hospedaria – see *casa de hóspedes*

IC (intercidade) – express intercity train
ICEP – Investimentos, Comércio e Turismo de Portugal; the government's umbrella organisation for tourism
IDD – International Direct Dial
igreja – church
igreja matriz – parish church
ilha – island
IR (interregional) – fairly fast train that doesn't make too many stops

jardim – garden
jardim municipal – town garden
jardim público – public garden
judiaria – quarter in a town where Jews were once segregated

largo – small square
latifúndios – Roman system of large farming estates
lavandaria – laundry
Lisboêta – Lisbon dweller
litoral – coastal
livraria – bookshop
loggia – covered area or porch on the side of a building
lugar – neighbourhood, place

mantas alentejanas – handwoven woollen blankets
Manueline – elaborate late Gothic/Renaissance style of art and architecture that emerged during the reign of Dom Manuel I in the 16th century
marranos – 'New Christians', ie Jews who converted during the Inquisition
menir – menhir; a standing stone monument typical of the late Neolithic Age
mercado municipal – municipal market
mesa – table
MFA – Movimento das Forças Armadas; the military group that led the Revolution of the Carnations in 1974
minimercado – grocery shop or small supermarket
miradouro – viewpoint
Misericórdia – derived from Santa Casa da Misericórdia (Holy House of Mercy), a charitable institution founded in the 15th century to care for the poor and the sick; it usually designates an old building that was founded by this organisation
moliceiro – high-prowed, shallow-draft boat traditionally used for harvesting seaweed in the estuaries of Beira Litoral
mosteiro – monastery
mouraria – the quarter where Moors were segregated during and after the Christian *Reconquista*
museu – museum

paço – palace
parque de campismo – camping ground
parque nacional – national park
parque natural – natural park
pelourinho – stone pillory, often ornately carved; erected in the 13th to 18th centuries as symbols of justice and sometimes as places where criminals were punished
pensão, pensões (pl) – guest house; the Portuguese equivalent of a bed and breakfast (B&B), though breakfast is not always served

planalto – high plain
pombal – dovecote, a structure for housing pigeons
ponte – bridge
portagem – toll road
pousada, Pousada de Portugal – government-run scheme of upmarket inns, often in converted castles, convents or palaces
pousada da juventude – youth hostel; usually with kitchen, common rooms and sometimes rooms with private bathroom
praça – square
praça de touros – bullring
praia – beach
PSP – Polícia de Segurança Pública; the local police force

quinta – country estate or villa; in the Douro wine-growing region it often refers to a wine lodge's property

R (regional) – slow train
Reconquista – Christian reconquest of Portugal (718–1249)
reservas naturais – nature reserves
residencial, residenciais (pl) – guest house; slightly more expensive than a *pensão* and usually serving breakfast
retornados – refugees
ribeiro – stream
rio – river
romaria – religious pilgrimage
rua – street

saudade – melancholic longing for better times
sé – cathedral
sem chumbo – unleaded (petrol)
senhor – man
senhora – woman
serra – mountain, mountain range
solar – manor house
supermercado – supermarket

tabacaria – tobacconist-cum-newsagent
tasca – tavern
termas – spas, hot springs
terra quente – hot country
torre de menagem – castle tower, keep
tourada – bullfight
Turihab – short for Turismo Habitação, a scheme for marketing private accommodation (particularly in northern Portugal) in cottages, historic buildings and manor houses
turismo – tourist office

vila – town

The Authors

REGIS ST LOUIS   Coordinating Author, The Douro, The Minho

Regis' long-time admiration for wine, rugged coastlines and melancholic music made him easy prey for Portugal. His earliest love affair (sadly unrequited) began with the Alfama some years back, and in subsequent trips he has fallen for huge swaths of the Alentejo, the Minho and the magnificent Douro valley. On his most recent journey, he drank mead with armour-wearing warriors at a medieval fair, clambered around countless old castles and celebrated with hammer-wielding Braga folk at the Festa de São João. Regis has written more than a dozen guidebooks for Lonely Planet, and his travel essays have appeared in the *Los Angeles Times* and the *Chicago Tribune* among other publications. He lives in New York City.

KATE ARMSTRONG   Food & Drink, The Algarve, The Alentejo

Kate first backpacked around Portugal 20 years ago with four former East Berliners. She shared with them the freedom and space of the Alentejan countryside, the joys of Algarvian seafood and Portuguese hospitality. Years later, lured by the language of fado, she returned to study Portuguese. For this edition she chomped her way through the country, acquiring a taste for tripe (plus an ample *barriga* – tummy). At her final site, serendipity struck. The remarkable owners of Convento de São Francisco offered her a stint as a writer-in-residence. Surrounded by kinetic sculptures, former spirits and creative souls, she wrote her chapters with Portuguese passion. Kate also contributes to Lonely Planet's Africa, Greece and South America titles.

GREGOR CLARK   Portugal Outdoors, Estremadura & Ribatejo,
The Beiras, Trás-os-Montes

Gregor's first trip to Portugal in 1986 started badly – an overnight train ride from Paris with a drunken compartment-mate, followed by the discovery that Fátima's station was nowhere near Fátima and his college training in Brazilian Portuguese was virtually useless in deciphering Continental idiom. Despite these setbacks, Gregor became an instant fan. Two decades later, he still loves Portugal's end-of-the-world feeling, its kind-hearted people, its *azulejos* (hand-painted tiles) and its simple meals of fish, salad and wine. Favourite experiences researching this book include crossing Portugal's highest summit by moonlight and exploring the cliffs of Berlenga Grande on his birthday.

LONELY PLANET AUTHORS

Why is our travel information the best in the world? It's simple: our authors are passionate, dedicated travellers. They don't take freebies in exchange for positive coverage so you can be sure the advice you're given is impartial. They travel widely to all the popular spots, and off the beaten track. They don't research using just the internet or phone. They discover new places not included in any other guidebook. They personally visit thousands of hotels, restaurants, palaces, trails, galleries, temples and more. They speak with dozens of locals every day to make sure you get the kind of insider knowledge only a local could tell you. They take pride in getting all the details right, and in telling it how it is. Think you can do it? Find out how at **lonelyplanet.com**.

KERRY WALKER
Lisbon & Around

Kerry's love affair with Portugal began when she was an 11-year-old who wanted to climb the cliffs of the Algarve alone. She soon fell for Lisbon – its addictive *pastéis de nata* (custard tarts), dazzling Atlantic light and party-mad locals dragging her (yeah, right!) on Bairro Alto bar crawls. She studied Portuguese translation as part of her MA at the University of Westminster. Born in Essex and based in Germany's Black Forest, she lives up to her name as an avid walker. Her itchy feet have taken her to 40ish countries, inspiring numerous articles and around 15 travel books, including Lonely Planet's *Lisbon Encounter*.

CONTRIBUTING AUTHOR

Dr Caroline Evans wrote the Health chapter. Having studied medicine at the University of London, Caroline completed general-practice training in Cambridge. She is the medical adviser to Nomad Travel Clinic, a private travel-health clinic in London, and is also a GP specialising in travel medicine. Caroline has acted as expedition doctor for Raleigh International and Coral Cay expeditions.

Behind the Scenes

THIS BOOK

The 7th edition of *Portugal* was coordinated by Regis St Louis. Regis headed up a team of expert authors including Kerry Walker, Gregor Clark and Kate Armstrong. The 6th edition was written by Regis and Robert Landon, while the following authors made significant contributions to previous editions: Abigail Hole, Charlotte Amelines (nee Beech), Richard Sterling, John King and Julia Wilkinson. The Health chapter was written by Dr Caroline Evans. This guidebook was commissioned in Lonely Planet's London office and produced by the following:

Commissioning Editors Fiona Buchan, Michala Green, Korina Miller, Lucy Monie, Clifton Wilkinson
Coordinating Editors Laura Gibb, Kate Whitfield
Coordinating Cartographer Tadhgh Knaggs
Coordinating Layout Designer Jessica Rose
Managing Editor Brigitte Ellemor
Managing Cartographer Mark Griffiths
Managing Layout Designer Celia Wood
Assisting Editors Kim Hutchins, Sally O'Brien, John Mapps, Laura Stansfeld, Diana Saad, Stephanie Pearson
Assisting Cartographers Alissa Baker, Mick Garrett, Karen Grant, Andy Rojas
Cover Designer Pepi Bluck
Project Manager Fabrice Rocher
Language Content Coordinator Quentin Frayne

Thanks to Shahara Ahmed, Imogen Bannister, Jessica Boland, Csanad Csutoros, Sally Darmody, Ryan Evans, Martin Heng, Laura Jane, Valentina Kremenchutskaya, Lisa Knights, Charity Mackinnon, Trent Paton, Lyahna Spencer, Gerard Walker

THANKS
REGIS ST LOUIS

I'd like to thank Korina Miller for inviting me on board. A big thanks to all the lovely LP people who worked on this book. *Beijos* to Cassandra and Magdalena for joining on this wondrous journey. I'd also like to thank the many travellers, tourist offices and kind-hearted locals for their helpful tips along the way.

KATE ARMSTRONG

Muito obrigada to Korina Miller and fellow authors, and the hospitable, generous Portuguese people. Thanks to TAP Airlines for allowing the extra kilos, plus, in Lisbon: Guida, Paula and Familha Gomes. In the Algarve: Jon & Pauline, Stefan and Saskia, Jill and Uwe, Carl Hawker and Emanuel Ribeiro. In the tourist industry: Isabel Almeida; Monika Gruner; Carine Batista; Miguel in Vila Nova Milfontes; Eduardo in Lagos; Patrice in Portalegre; Jones Fernandes in Evora; Rosa in Mertola. For sharing their passion of viticulture and Portugal:

THE LONELY PLANET STORY

Fresh from an epic journey across Europe, Asia and Australia in 1972, Tony and Maureen Wheeler sat at their kitchen table stapling together notes. The first Lonely Planet guidebook, *Across Asia on the Cheap*, was born.

Travellers snapped up the guides. Inspired by their success, the Wheelers began publishing books to Southeast Asia, India and beyond. Demand was prodigious, and the Wheelers expanded the business rapidly to keep up. Over the years, Lonely Planet extended its coverage to every country and into the virtual world via lonelyplanet.com and the Thorn Tree message board.

As Lonely Planet became a globally loved brand, Tony and Maureen received several offers for the company. But it wasn't until 2007 that they found a partner whom they trusted to remain true to the company's principles of travelling widely, treading lightly and giving sustainably. In October of that year, BBC Worldwide acquired a 75% share in the company, pledging to uphold Lonely Planet's commitment to independent travel, trustworthy advice and editorial independence.

Today, Lonely Planet has offices in Melbourne, London and Oakland, with over 500 staff members and 300 authors. Tony and Maureen are still actively involved with Lonely Planet. They're travelling more often than ever, and they're devoting their spare time to charitable projects. And the company is still driven by the philosophy of *Across Asia on the Cheap*: 'All you've got to do is decide to go and the hardest part is over. So go!'

David Baverstock, Andrew Birks and Luke Williams. In the Alentejo: Lino and Fernanda. Special thanks to Geraldine, Christiaan and Louis Zwanikken and to *minha familha Portuguesa*: Antonio Pedro, Mina, Katy, Pedro and David.

GREGOR CLARK

Gregor Clark would like to thank the numerous kind-hearted people who helped him navigate Portugal's shorelines and mountain tops, especially José Conde at CISE, Kate and Jacques at the Paintshop Hostel, Else and Anja at Casa Pombal, the Oliveira family in Viseu, Vitor in Batalha, Silvia Guimarães and Margarida Pereira-Mueller. Heartfelt thanks also to my commissioning editor Korina Miller and coordinating author Regis St Louis for their steadfast support throughout this project. Finally, big hugs and kisses for my loving family and sometime travelling companions Gaen, Meigan and Chloe, for helping me stay sane and reminding me to eat more *gelado*.

KERRY WALKER

Heartfelt thanks to my fiancé, soul mate and travel companion, Andy Christiani. I'm *muito obrigada* to Rafael Vieira for feeding me invaluable tips, especially on Lisbon nightlife. Sincere thanks also to Carmo Botelho at Turismo de Lisboa, and to Jorge Moita for providing a fascinating insight into life as a designer in Lisbon. A big thank you also to all the locals I met on the road who shared their stories, including Olivier da Costa, Joana Amendoeira, Carlos Martins, Ana Salazar and Alberto Bruno. Finally, a big thank you to Korina Miller for entrusting me with this gig, and thanks to the entire Lonely Planet production team.

OUR READERS

Many thanks to the travellers who used the last edition and wrote to us with helpful hints, useful advice and interesting anecdotes:

Joe Bazinet, David Blood, Fred Boley, Michelle Bottazzi, Renato Braz, Lawson Bronson, Alexander Buchanan, Len Buurman, Iris Candirisk, Ana Carvalho, Colin Cho, Vicki Christini, Bjørn Clasen, Isabella Coelho, Sandra Contente, Luis Da Silva, Lisa Davis, Carla De Beer, Maurice De Heus, Vitor De Souza, Monique Dehaese, Helen Dodd, Jay Espejo, Bastian Etzold, Sérgio Ferreira, Fabio Fiorini, John Gallagher, Teresa Maria Barreiros Garcia, Leigh Gates, Jay Geller, Sepi Gilani, Maggie Gore, Steve Gorton, Molly Hamilton, Rhia Heusel, Craig Hill, Gary Hill, Anna Holmberg, Louise Hora, Navid Imani, Femke Janssen, Anders Jeppsson, Camilla

Johannessen, Kate Karpf, Edward Keefe, Kai Chuen Law, Colin Little, Marcus Lloyd, Anabel Loyd, Robert Lynch, Zoe Marcham, Albert Mcmurdie, Michael Melhuish, Matthew Metcalfe, Richard Mieli, Emma Neill, Keith Newitt, Catherine Noack, Maria João Arriscado Nunes, Karin Nygaard, Katherine Ohlsen, RF Parsons, Adelino Pereira, Hans Pettersson, Thibault Philibert, Cynthia Phipps, Joao Prudencio, Beth Pullman, Albert Rapp, Mike Robinson, Sandra Robinson, Francesco Russo, Aaron Sagers, Sahba Sanai, Carlos Seixas, Jacinta Shaw, Terry Shubkin, Hugo Silvestre, Katrin Sippel, Darius Sunawala, Nanda Talsma, Filipe Teles, Jim Toth, Raef, Lise Trap, Steven Tung, Julie Anne Van Eijk, Martijn & Esther Van Geelen & De Waal, Ernst Van Nieuwburg, Wim Vandenbussche, Esther Veen, Paula Verlinden, Marc Feyaerts, Charles Wardell, Stefanie Weber, Vivienne Wild, Bev Wilson

ACKNOWLEDGEMENTS

Many thanks to the following for the use of their content:

Globe on title page ©Mountain High Maps 1993 Digital Wisdom, Inc.

Internal photographs by Kerry Armstrong p94 (top) & p95; Vasco Célio/F32 p98; Andy Christiani p95 (portrait); Uwe Heitkamp p98 (portrait); Isabel Pinto p92 (top). All other photographs by Lonely

BEHIND THE SCENES

Planet Images and by Paul Bernhardt p5 (bottom), p6 (#1), p8 (#4), p10 (#3), p11, p91; Pascale Beroujon p93 (top); Anders Blomqvist p6 (#2), p7 (#4, #5), p8 (#2), p12 (#1), p97 (bottom); David Borland p5 (top), p12 (#4); Mark Daffey p8 (#1); Greg Elms p92, p93 (bottom), Alain Evrard p10 (#1); Richard l'Anson p9; Gareth McCormack p96, p97 (top); Brent Winebrenner p94 (bottom).

All images are the copyright of the photographers unless otherwise indicated. Many of the images in this guide are available for licensing from Lonely Planet Images: www.lonelyplanetimages.com.

Index

INDEX

INDEX

000 Map pages
000 Photograph pages

GreenDex

GOING GREEN

Sustainability is increasingly important in the travel industry. But how can you know which businesses are actually eco-friendly and which are simply jumping on the environmental bandwagon?

The following sights, accommodation, eating/entertainment/drinking options have been selected by Lonely Planet authors because they demonstrate a commitment to sustainability. We've selected oceanariums and wetlands playing host to numerous species of birds and swimming critters, concept stores with recycled luxury design goods, free bike hire, even an environmentally friendly festival. In addition, we've covered hotels that we deem to be environmentally friendly, for example for their commitment to recycling or energy conservation. Attractions are listed because they're involved in conservation or environmental education. For more tips about travelling sustainably in Portugal, turn to the Getting Started chapter (p18).

We want to keep developing our sustainable-travel content. If you think we've omitted somewhere that should be listed here, or if you disagree with our choices, contact us at www.lonelyplanet.com/contact and set us straight for next time. For more information about sustainable tourism and Lonely Planet, see www.lonelyplanet.com/responsibletravel.

548

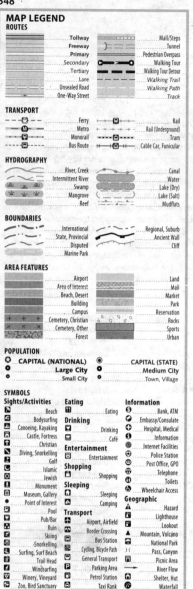

MAP LEGEND

ROUTES
..............Tollway
..............Freeway
..............Primary
..............Secondary
..............Tertiary
..............Lane
..............Unsealed Road
..............One-Way Street
..............Mall/Steps
..............Tunnel
..............Pedestrian Overpass
..............Walking Tour
..............Walking Tour Detour
..............Walking Trail
..............Walking Path
..............Track

TRANSPORT
..............Ferry
..............Metro
..............Monorail
..............Bus Route
..............Rail
..............Rail (Underground)
..............Tram
..............Cable Car, Funicular

HYDROGRAPHY
..............River, Creek
..............Intermittent River
..............Swamp
..............Mangrove
..............Reef
..............Canal
..............Water
..............Lake (Dry)
..............Lake (Salt)
..............Mudflats

BOUNDARIES
..............International
..............State, Provincial
..............Disputed
..............Marine Park
..............Regional, Suburb
..............Ancient Wall
..............Cliff

AREA FEATURES
..............Airport
..............Area of Interest
..............Beach, Desert
..............Building
..............Campus
..............Cemetery, Christian
..............Cemetery, Other
..............Forest
..............Land
..............Mall
..............Market
..............Park
..............Reservation
..............Rocks
..............Sports
..............Urban

POPULATION
○ **CAPITAL (NATIONAL)**
● **Large City**
● Small City
◉ **CAPITAL (STATE)**
○ **Medium City**
○ Town, Village

SYMBOLS

Sights/Activities
..............Beach
..............Bodysurfing
..............Canoeing, Kayaking
..............Castle, Fortress
..............Christian
..............Diving, Snorkelling
..............Golf
..............Islamic
..............Jewish
..............Monument
..............Museum, Gallery
..............Point of Interest
..............Pool
..............Pub/Bar
..............Ruin
..............Skiing
..............Snorkelling
..............Surfing, Surf Beach
..............Trail Head
..............Windsurfing
..............Winery, Vineyard
..............Zoo, Bird Sanctuary

Eating
..............Eating

Drinking
..............Drinking
..............Café

Entertainment
..............Entertainment

Shopping
..............Shopping

Sleeping
..............Sleeping
..............Camping

Transport
..............Airport, Airfield
..............Border Crossing
..............Bus Station
..............Cycling, Bicycle Path
..............General Transport
..............Parking Area
..............Petrol Station
..............Taxi Rank

Information
..............Bank, ATM
..............Embassy/Consulate
..............Hospital, Medical
..............Information
..............Internet Facilities
..............Police Station
..............Post Office, GPO
..............Telephone
..............Toilets
..............Wheelchair Access

Geographic
..............Hazard
..............Lighthouse
..............Lookout
..............Mountain, Volcano
..............National Park
..............Pass, Canyon
..............Picnic Area
..............River Flow
..............Shelter, Hut
..............Waterfall

LONELY PLANET OFFICES

Australia
Head Office
Locked Bag 1, Footscray, Victoria 3011
☎ 03 8379 8000, fax 03 8379 8111
talk2us@lonelyplanet.com.au

USA
150 Linden St, Oakland, CA 94607
☎ 510 250 6400, toll free 800 275 8555
fax 510 893 8572
info@lonelyplanet.com

UK
2nd fl, 186 City Rd,
London EC1V 2NT
☎ 020 7106 2100, fax 020 7106 2101
go@lonelyplanet.co.uk

Published by Lonely Planet Publications Pty Ltd
ABN 36 005 607 983

© Lonely Planet Publications Pty Ltd 2009

© photographers as indicated 2009

Cover photograph: Fishing boat and village near Portimão, the Algarve, Portugal, Tom Egan/Getty Images. Many of the images in this guide are available for licensing from Lonely Planet Images: www.lonelyplanetimages.com.

Mixed Sources
Product group from well-managed forests and other controlled sources
www.fsc.org Cert no. SGS-COC-005002
© 1996 Forest Stewardship Council
FSC